CONTEMPORARY MANAGEMENT IN CANADA

SECOND EDITION

Frederick A. Starke
The University of Manitoba

Robert W. Sexty
Memorial University of Newfoundland

PRENTICE HALL CANADA INC., SCARBOROUGH, ONTARIO

Canadian Cataloguing in Publication Data
Starke, Frederick A., 1942–
Contemporary management in Canada

2nd ed.
Includes index.
ISBN 0-13-292160-X

1. Management – Canada. 2. Management – Canada – Problems, exercises, etc. I. Sexty, Robert W. (Robert William), 1942 . II. Title.

HD70.C2S73 1995 658'.00971 C94-931647-4

Prentice-Hall, Inc., Englewood Cliffs, New Jersey
Prentice-Hall International (UK) Limited, London
Prentice-Hall of Australia, Pty. Limited, Sydney
Prentice-Hall Hispanoamericana, S.A., Mexico City
Prentice-Hall of India Private Limited, New Delhi
Prentice-Hall of Japan, Inc., Tokyo
Simon & Schuster Asia Private Limited, Singapore
Editora Prentice-Hall do Brasil, Ltda., Rio de Janeiro

ISBN 0-13-292160-X

Acquisitions Editor: Jacqueline Wood
Developmental Editor: Maurice Esses
Copy Editor: Shirley Corriveau
Production Editor: Valerie Adams
Production Coordinator: Deborah Starks
Permissions/Photo Research: Angelika Baur
Cover and Interior Design: Alex Li
Cover Image: Robert George Young/Masterfile (Clock parts); Phototone by Letraset (Wood Background)
Page Layout: Zena Denchik

1 2 3 4 5 VH 99 98 97 96 95

Printed and bound in the United States of America

This book is printed on recycled paper.

BRIEF TABLE OF CONTENTS

TABLE OF CONTENTS

CHAPTER 3
MANAGING IN THE CANADIAN ENVIRONMENT

PART TWO
PLANNING AND DECISION MAKING

CHAPTER 4
THE PLANNING PROCESS

CHAPTER 5
STRATEGIC MANAGEMENT

CHAPTER 6
MANAGERIAL DECISION MAKING

PART THREE ORGANIZING

CHAPTER 7 ORGANIZATIONAL STRUCTURES

CHAPTER 8
AUTHORITY, RESPONSIBILITY, AND ORGANIZATIONAL DESIGN

CHAPTER 9
WORK GROUPS, TEAMS, AND THE INFORMAL ORGANIZATION

CHAPTER 10
POWER AND POLITICS

CHAPTER 11 PLANNING FOR AND DEVELOPING HUMAN RESOURCES

PART FOUR LEADING

CHAPTER 12 MOTIVATION

CHAPTER 13 LEADERSHIP

CHAPTER 16 ORGANIZATIONAL CULTURE AND DEVELOPMENT

PART FIVE CONTROLLING

CHAPTER 17 THE CONTROLLING PROCESS

CHAPTER 18
CONTROL TECHNIQUES

CHAPTER 19
INFORMATION MANAGEMENT

PART SIX SPECIAL ISSUES IN CONTEMPORARY MANAGEMENT

CHAPTER 20 MANAGING SMALL BUSINESS

CHAPTER 21
MANAGING INTERNATIONALLY

CHAPTER 22
SOCIAL RESPONSIBILITY AND ETHICS

PREFACE

This is the second edition of *Contemporary Management in Canada*. Three goals were set for the first edition: (1) to convey the nature and importance of management, (2) to balance theory with practical applications, and (3) to profile the practice of management in Canada. These goals continue to guide the development of this second edition.

After reading this text, students will have an understanding of what managers actually do, what the day-to-day dynamics of managerial work are, what issues Canadian managers face, and what it's like to be a manager in Canada in the 1990s.

How management in Canada differs from management in other countries, especially the U.S., has been a topic of debate. In this text, the nature of management in the Canadian context is examined in depth, while examples of managerial practice in other countries are also presented. Conclusions are drawn about how Canadian management is similar to, and different from, management elsewhere. Understanding these similarities and differences will allow readers to make an informed choice about what practices are most effective.

Throughout the text, theory and practice are linked. Whenever a theoretical point is made, a real-life example from a Canadian organization is presented to demonstrate how the theory is put into practice. Examples are drawn from all types of public and private sector organizations.

Because management involves people, it is not simply a rational process following prescribed steps. Rather, it is a process involving a blend of rational issues and emotional considerations as it deals with both "things" and people. In dealing effectively with both these areas, a manager, this text assumes, has a direct impact on organizational productivity.

To be successful, a manager must use more than one approach. An underlying idea in *Contemporary Management in Canada* is that both the systems approach and the contingency approach are necessary in management. The systems and contingency concepts are introduced in the second chapter and referred to frequently thereafter. Since every manager operates within a larger system, actions taken by an individual manager will have an impact on other areas. Considering how managerial decisions will affect the total organization is a major responsibility of managers. As well, because of the complexities of management, no single approach works in every circumstance. Rather, what works in each situation is contingent upon the key factors operating in that situation.

CHANGES TO THE SECOND EDITION

This edition incorporates many changes that were suggested by professors and students who used the first edition. It also reflects many changes that were suggested by reviewers. Three new chapters have been written, and existing chapters have been extensively revised. All chapters have been updated with the latest information about the practice of management in Canada. The changes are described briefly below.

New Chapters

Chapter 2 (The Development of Management Knowledge) is new to this edition. Some of this material was contained in Chapter 1 of the previous edition of the text. The chapter introduces students to the research on the practice of management that was conducted during the first half of the twentieth century, and how that research has given us important insights into the practice of management.

Chapter 11 (Managing Human Resources) is an entirely rewritten chapter focussing on the importance of recruiting, training, compensating, and motivating the human element in organizations.

Chapter 19 (Information Management) is a new chapter which illustrates the importance of management information systems in organizational success. Some of this material was included in the decision making chapter in the first edition of the text.

Chapters Containing Major Revisions

Several chapters have been significantly revised to present a more comprehensive treatment of certain subjects, and to highlight recent developments in the field of management.

- Chapter 1: New material has been added under the headings "Management and Organizations" and "Becoming a Manager." These two additions explain why management is important for organizations, and some common career paths to management.
- Chapter 6: There is a completely new section describing the "escalation of commitment" phenomenon (i.e., how some managers get so committed to a certain course of action that they are reluctant to give it up, even if there is evidence that it is not working). This discussion should be very interesting to students. A discussion on electronic brainstorming, which describes how computer technology improves the quality of managerial decisions, has also been added to this chapter.
- Chapter 7: A major new section has been added on "downsizing." Many examples from Canadian organizations are presented.
- Chapter 9: A new section has been added on integrated work teams and self-managed teams. As well, new material has been added on the process of group development.
- Chapter 12: A new section has been added on the compressed workweek. The description of expectancy theory has been completely rewritten and simplified. New material has also been written on job satisfaction.
- Chapter 16: A new section has been added which describes the differences between "clan" cultures and "market" cultures.
- Chapter 18: A major new section has been added which focusses on Total Quality Management. Included in this material is a new boxed insert explaining how TQM works at one Canadian business.

ORGANIZATION OF TEXT

The text is organized into six sections as follows:

Part I: Management and Organizations

This section introduces the concept of management and outlines why it is important in all types of organizations. Chapter 1 introduces the four functions of management and describes other skills that managers need to be effective. Chapter 2 (a new chapter) describes how knowledge about management has developed over the last 100 years or so. Chapter 3 describes the external environment which managers must cope with, and how that environment affects the way they carry out the management functions.

Part II: Planning and Decision Making

In Chapter 4, the basic planning process is described. Chapter 5 focusses on the strategic planning process and describes strategic plans that organizations develop. In Chapter 6 managerial decision making is analyzed, including the rational decision-making process and several techniques that help managers make decisions.

Part III: Organizing

The key elements in the organizing function are examined in this section. In Chapters 7 and 8, elements of the formal organization are investigated, while Chapter 9 looks at the informal organization. Chapter 10 introduces the issue of organizational politics, and Chapter 11 (a new chapter) discusses the activities involved in organizing a firm's human resources.

Part IV: Leading

This part stresses the people aspect of the manager's job. Chapter 12 probes the managerial responsibility for motivating employees, while Chapter 13 assesses what is necessary to lead subordinates. Chapter 14 shows how managerial effectiveness can be improved through the clear and appropriate communication of ideas to individuals and groups. Chapter 15 covers three topics—conflict, change, and stress—and demonstrates how they are interrelated. Chapter 16 introduces the concepts of corporate culture and organization development.

Part V: Controlling

The controlling function ensures that plans become reality. Chapter 17 describes the basic control process, while Chapter 18 describes several financial and nonfinancial control techniques. Chapter 19 (a new chapter) addresses the important issue of information management by noting the importance of management information systems and how they help managers make better decisions.

Part VI: Special Issues in Contemporary Management

The concluding part of the text focusses on particular management concerns. Chapter 20 analyzes small business management, noting differences between small and large businesses. Chapter 21 discusses the considerations involved in operating internationally, and Chapter 22 addresses the complex issue of social responsibility and business ethics.

Chapter Features

Each chapter in this text contains the following features to stimulate student interest in, and understanding of, the field of management:

Learning Objectives

A list of learning objectives is found at the beginning of each chapter, and each objective is repeated in the margins of the chapter opposite the material relevant to it.

Management Challenge

Each chapter begins with an incident based on an actual occurrence (company names are sometimes disguised). The incident introduces the subject of the chapter by presenting a problem managers actually faced. Students are encouraged to think about the problem and propose a solution before they read the chapter.

There are many new "Management Challenges" leading off various chapters. In the first edition, these "Management Challenges" were hypothetical (but realistic) situations. The new additions are all based on real companies that have recently been in the news.

Meeting the Challenge

At the end of each chapter, the Management Challenge is reviewed and analyzed using material presented in the chapter. Students can compare their solution with the one presented here and see how the ideas in the chapter can be applied and what their value is.

Real-World Management Inserts

Each chapter contains 4-6 boxed inserts describing how ideas introduced in the text are applied in real Canadian organizations. These boxed inserts are organized into three series which run throughout the text: (1) Management at Work (descriptions of current management practices in Canadian organizations), (2) Global Management (management practices in organizations in other countries), and (3) Ethics in Management (discussions of ethical issues faced by managers).

Examples

Each chapter also contains numerous brief examples of current Canadian business practice embedded in the text. This feature further assists students in seeing how managerial ideas are put into practice. The text contains over 200 such examples.

Summary

The material in each chapter is concisely summarized to help students understand the main points and the logic of their presentation.

Key Terms

In each chapter, the key terms that students should know are highlighted and defined in the text, repeated in the margin, and listed at the end of the chapter with page references.

Review Questions

These end-of-chapter questions determine how well students can recall the information presented in the chapter.

Discussion Questions

These questions require students to go beyond the simple recall of information and do some integrative or creative thinking about management issues.

Exercises

Several exercises are presented at the end of each chapter. These encourage students to get involved in a variety of activities, including interviewing managers, having class debates on controversial issues, or summarizing articles on some aspect of management.

"Management on Location" Cases

Each chapter concludes with two or more short case studies based on actual situations. These cases allow students to analyze an actual management situation using the material presented in the chapter. At the end of each case, several questions are presented to guide students in their analysis. There are over 60 short cases in the text.

Comprehensive Cases

Two or three comprehensive case studies are found at the end of each major section of the text. Based on actual events, these cases are longer than the end-of-chapter cases, and they raise several issues that are important in the practice of management. These cases further build students' analytical skills and help them understand the complexities of management. Specific questions appear at the end of each case for instructors who wish to direct student attention to certain problems. Other instructors may wish to ask students to use the scientific method in analyzing the case (define the problem; develop alternatives; analyze the alternatives; pick the best one).

SUPPLEMENTARY MATERIAL

The following items are available to supplement the text:

- Test Bank
- Computerized Test Bank
- Instructor's Manual
- Study Guide/Workbook
- Colour Transparencies
- Videos

A separate 1600 item Test Bank is available for adopters. For each chapter in the text, there are 50 multiple choice questions, 20 true-false questions, 5 short essay questions, and 5 long essay questions. A computerized version of the Test Bank in IBM PC format is also available.

The Instructor's Manual contains suggestions on how to use the text effectively. It contains many features, including transparency masters, suggested lecture outlines, and solutions for end-of-chapter and comprehensive cases.

A Study Guide/Workbook is available which will enable students to review management concepts and gain insight into their application.

Generic Colour Transparencies are also available. These transparencies complement the transparency masters contained in the Instructor's Manual.

A series of Canadian videos depicting Canadian workplace and management issues, and the *ABC News/PH Video Library of Management* are available.

ACKNOWLEDGEMENTS

We owe special thanks to the acquisitions editor, Jacqueline Wood, to the developmental editor, Maurice Esses, and to the production editor, Valerie Adams.

The following individuals helped by reviewing the manuscript:

Linda Ament	Robert Ankli
Lowell Epp	Mia Gladstone
Brian Harrocks	Susan Quinn
J.I. Rubinstein	Marilyn Sorensen
R.W. Verity	

Their comments were carefully considered and implemented wherever possible.

Frederick A. Starke *Robert W. Sexty*
1995

PART 1

MANAGEMENT AND ORGANIZATIONS

CHAPTER

1

THE NATURE OF MANAGEMENT

LEARNING OBJECTIVES

After reading this chapter, you will be able to:

1. Explain what management is and why it is important for all types of organizations.
2. Explain the difference between profit-oriented business firms and not-for-profit organizations.
3. Describe the main features of sole proprietorships, partnerships, and corporations.
4. Describe what is involved in each of the four major functions of management—planning, organizing, leading, and controlling.
5. Understand and outline the activities involved in the three major managerial roles—interpersonal, informational, and decisional.
6. Identify three important skills of management and what they involve.

MANAGEMENT CHALLENGE

BUT I DIDN'T KNOW WHAT WAS INVOLVED IN MANAGEMENT!

In May, 1993 James Kenner graduated from high school. Kenner had the reputation among his friends of being a first-rate mechanic. During the summer after graduation, he worked as an automobile mechanic at a local garage, but somehow that didn't satisfy him. In September he was hired as a maintenance mechanic at Blair Systems Ltd.

The maintenance department at Blair employed eight people, and was responsible for routine maintenance and repair of machinery and other equipment at Blair's manufacturing facility. Kenner liked his job and got along well with the other maintenance mechanics. Within a couple of months he was very comfortable with all aspects of his new job. His six-month job evaluation was very positive.

About one year later, Kenner was called into the office of Arthur Bendel, the plant superintendent. After some small talk, Bendel informed Kenner that the head of the maintenance department was leaving. He then asked whether Kenner was interested in a promotion to head of the maintenance department. Kenner accepted on the spot.

Kenner wanted very badly to succeed, so he threw himself into his new job with great energy. He came to work early, stayed late, and was the dominant force in the maintenance department. His interest in repairing machinery remained high, and he often did repair work himself. Kenner discovered that he disliked paperwork, so he spent most of his time in the plant. He continually referred to "problems on the firing line" that needed his attention.

...

After six months on the job, Kenner was called into Bendel's office for his performance evaluation. Bendel began by recognizing Kenner's enthusiasm and long hours on the job, but he also noted that there were three emerging problems in Kenner's area: (1) incomplete or late maintenance reports, (2) decreasing productivity in the maintenance area, and (3) complaints by maintenance mechanics that Kenner was continually interfering in their work. Bendel indicated that Kenner simply had to start showing some leadership in his department. He reminded Kenner that he was now a manager, and that Kenner was responsible for both the performance and satisfaction of the maintenance mechanics reporting to him. Bendel concluded the interview by noting that unless the situation improved, he would have to consider replacing Kenner.

Kenner returned to his office feeling very low. He knew that on occasion he hadn't felt "right" about some of the things that had happened in his area during the last few months, but Bendel's comments had come as a complete surprise. ▲

The Canadian economy is made up of many kinds of organizations. Canadians regularly come into contact with organizations such as hospitals, schools, religious organizations, charities, business firms, colleges, universities, daycare centres, government agencies, and labour unions. The Management Challenge shows that one of the most significant factors affecting the performance of these organizations is the quality of management. In this book, we will examine the field of management and the activities of managers. Our focus is on all kinds of organizations, including profit-seeking business firms and the numerous not-for-profit organizations in Canada.

We begin this chapter by defining management and describing the functions and roles that all managers carry out regardless of the organization they work for. Second, we describe the characteristics of profit-seeking businesses and not-for-profit organizations. Third, we examine management activity at different levels, and how different skills are needed at these various levels.

WHAT IS MANAGEMENT?

management

manager

LEARNING OBJECTIVE 1

Explain what management is and why it is important for all types of organizations.

Management is the process of planning, organizing, leading, and controlling other people so that organizational objectives are reached. Thus, management is the art of getting things done through people.[1] A **manager** is a person who works through others to accomplish organizational objectives. A manager carries out the functions of planning, organizing, leading, and controlling. Managers are found in all kinds of for-profit and not-for-profit organizations.

Managers are judged on the basis of how well the people who work for them do their jobs. If the manager's subordinates do not perform adequately, the manager will be called to task for that failure. Good managers realize that they cannot do all of the tasks that are necessary to reach organizational goals. Rather, they must direct the work of others so that organizational resources are mobilized to achieve the goals that have been set. The Management Challenge shows that this is a difficult lesson for some aspiring managers to learn. People with specific technical skills (for example, engineers, salespersons, accountants, computer operators) who are promoted into management are sometimes unable to resist the urge to continue with the technical work they did before being promoted. If this happens, they spend most of their time actually doing the technical work instead of mobilizing and organizing others to do the work. While they may feel comfortable continuing to do the technical work at which they excel, they are not doing the job of a manager.

EFFICIENCY AND EFFECTIVENESS IN MANAGEMENT

When carrying out the functions of management, managers must make sure that they are doing so in an effective manner. This is done by focussing on two important elements of work: (1) the tasks that subordinates do, and (2) the satisfaction of subordinates as they do these tasks. Effective managers are those who have subordinates who are both productive and satisfied.

Managers are more likely to be effective if they understand the difference between "efficiency" and "effectiveness." **Efficiency** means achieving the greatest possible output with a given amount of input. An organization that is efficient is able to achieve a given level of output with fewer inputs than an inefficient organization.

efficiency

Improving efficiency has become a key goal for many Canadian firms. Imperial Oil's refinery at Dartmouth, Nova Scotia, used to be one of the least efficient in North America. In 1992, management decided to close the plant unless there was a dramatic turnaround. Within nine months, the refinery had reduced the human effort previously used in operations by 46 percent.[2] North American car manufacturers continue to improve their efficiency. Ford Motor Co., for example, now sells nearly as many vehicles as it used to, but with half the number of production workers. But while Ford has reduced labour time to produce stampings for the typical automobile from 15 hours to about 7 hours, that is still double what the Japanese need.[3]

Efficiency alone is not enough. A manager must also be effective. **Effectiveness** means achieving the organizational goals that have been set. An effective manager is one who pursues goals that are consistent with overall organizational objectives; thus he or she would make sure that the goods or services that are produced are what customers or clients want. A manager who efficiently manages the production of goods or services that are not demanded by the firm's customers is not effective. In short, effectiveness means "doing the right things" while efficiency means "doing things right."[4]

effectiveness

MANAGEMENT AND ORGANIZATIONS

The study of management immediately implies the study of organizations. An **organization** exists when two or more people decide to cooperatively work toward the achievement of some goal. The fans attending a Toronto Blue Jays baseball game do not constitute an organization, but the players and managers of the Blue Jays do. Likewise, a crowd of people at the beach is not an organization, but the nearby concession stand is.

organization

Organizations exist because people can accomplish more working together than they can working alone. This means that organizations can achieve *synergy* (the whole is greater than the sum of its parts). In a well-managed organization, the outcome of combined effort is more than just the sum of individuals' work.

All organizations have a *purpose* (providing a product or service), a *structure* (which defines a hierarchy of authority), and a *division of labour* (the work that is to be done is broken down into specialized jobs that can be performed by individuals with specific training). Every organization also has both formal and informal features. The formal organization is defined by the organization chart, rules, objectives, procedures, standard operating procedures, etc., while the informal organization is the network of social relationships that spontaneously arises. In this book, we focus largely on the management of formal organizations, but as we shall see in Chapters 9 and 10, managers must deal with the informal aspects of organization if they hope to be effective.

WHY STUDY MANAGEMENT?

The Izaak Walton Killam Hospital in Halifax, Nova Scotia, is a not-for-profit organization dedicated to the medical treatment of children. The hospital does not pursue a profit, but stresses service. However, like a profit-oriented business firm, the hospital does set objectives, and managers are needed to lead and motivate employees to pursue these objectives.

Several arguments can be made in support of studying the field of management. First, the success of an organization depends to a considerable degree on the quality of its management. Did you know that almost half of all new Canadian businesses fail in the first six years of operation?[5] In the majority of these cases, managerial incompetence and inexperience are the causes of the failure. As the Management Challenge suggests, the costs of poor management can be great—to individuals, to organizations, and to Canada's economic stability. Not only are financial and physical resources wasted when businesses fail, but individuals may suffer psychological damage.

Second, organizations have a profound influence on Canadians. As noted above, Canadians routinely come into contact with a wide variety of different organizations in their day-to-day activities. The level of satisfaction obtained from these organizations is determined by how well they are managed.[6]

Third, most Canadians will work for an organization as either a manager or as a person who is managed.[7] In either position, it is useful to understand what management involves, and how it contributes to organizational goal achievement and to individual satisfaction with work.

BECOMING A MANAGER

Formal education is increasingly important as a background for management. A frequently used path to management is a degree in management from a university or a diploma in business administration from a college. One survey showed that chief executive officers (CEOs) were most likely to have a degree in business, followed in frequency by engineering and then arts.[8] After finishing their schooling most people spend some time working in a first-line supervisory position. After a few years, they may return to school for a Master of Business Administration (M.B.A.) degree, and then back into the work force for more managerial experience at a somewhat higher level.

During their careers, managers frequently take one- to two-day management development seminars as part of their firm's career development program. These courses present managers with new ideas in areas such as leadership, decision making, motivation, and conflict resolution. Some managers also become involved in more in-depth courses that take them away from their jobs for extended periods. At the Banff School of Advanced Management (BSAM), for example, managers live in residence for four weeks and take a variety of intensive courses that are designed to broaden their knowledge base and increase their promotability to upper management. Decision Dynamics is a two-week executive development course offered at a resort hotel on Lake Winnipeg; it focusses on improving executives' decision-making skills.

WHAT IS "CANADIAN" ABOUT MANAGEMENT?

Is there something unique about the practice of management in private and public sector organizations in Canada? In one sense, Canadian managers are much like their counterparts around the world because their key function is to accomplish organizational goals through the work of other people. They do this by performing the managerial functions of planning, organizing, leading, and controlling, which are described in the next section.

However, if we look at the specific practice of management in various countries around the world, we will see that there are many differences (see the Global Management insert describing management in the People's Republic of China). A manager who has been successful in one country will find that many new things

GLOBAL MANAGEMENT

Management in the People's Republic of China

With increasing globalization of the world's economy, interest in international management is increasing. One country with considerable potential is the People's Republic of China. What is it like to be a manager in that country?

To understand the practice of management in China, we must consider the important forces that shape the behaviour of managers.

1. *Economic reform* The government has attempted to stimulate both factory and agricultural production. Communes, for example, were abolished in 1978; the government rents the land to tenants and requires them to produce a certain quota. The tenants are free to keep or sell any excess.
2. *The Communist party* The Party shares power with managers in organizations. It prevents workers from being fired and transferred, assigns workers to jobs, and forces managers to employ all workers that are assigned to them.
3. *Socialism* Two Marxist views prevail: First, workers (not management) create wealth, and second, the managers work for the workers (dictatorship of the proletariat).
4. *Feudalistic values* A paternalistic view of management is evident, and business organizations are expected to provide for the welfare of the workers and their families.
5. *Guanxi (influence peddling)* Although officially condemned, *guanxi* serves as a "second currency" in China, and fills a void created by social and economic conditions.
6. *The economy* China has an excess supply of labour, and many people who are working are underemployed. Factory technology generally is unsophisticated, and the communications, transportation, and utilities sectors have significant problems.

What does all this mean for the individual manager in China? Interviews with 50 Chinese workers and 120 managers in Jiangsu province revealed that managers were expected to increase productivity, but were given very little power to do so. As a result, their management style was influenced by their desire to increase their power. Managers exhibited the following tactics while managing workers:

1. *Loosening the rules* Workers are allowed to be late, take unauthorized days off, sleep on the job, and work on their own personal projects with company tools.
2. *Creating warm relationships with workers* Managers work hard to establish harmonious interpersonal relationships with workers. This helps managers get worker conformity and also increases worker satisfaction.
3. *Granting favours and making promises* Managers will do favours for workers, both at work and away from the job. For example, when a worker's father died, his manager helped him find wood for a coffin.
4. *Shaming* Managers may tell workers how they should think or behave, or they may criticize workers in front of their peers.
5. *Involving the family* If a worker is a poor performer, the manager may visit the worker's family. The pressure brought to bear by the family usually resolves the problem. The worker's family is also involved if the worker is promoted.
6. *Pushing reform* Most managers claim they use a "reformed" management style, but they actually pick and choose which government reforms they implement. Most managers seem to believe in the bonus system, but bonuses are so small (about $5 per month), and their implementation so inconsistent that the system probably doesn't work.
7. *Back-dooring* Chinese managers cope with *guanxi* by paying off inspectors who will certify that the output of their factory or restaurant meets government standards, even if it doesn't. ▲

must be learned about the managerial environment in another country before he or she can be successful. But skilled managers can definitely make the transition. In fact, many Canadian managers have been going abroad to work (see the Global Management insert describing the managerial brain drain).

The practice of management in Canada is not exactly like that of any other country because there are a unique set of factors that define Canadian management. These factors, and the way they affect management in Canada, are summarized in Table 1-1.

GLOBAL MANAGEMENT

THE MANAGERIAL BRAIN DRAIN

When David Preston was the president of Gillette Canada, he thought he had a lot of power and influence. He was responsible for the work of 600 employees, and dealt with all aspects of Gillette's diverse product line in Canada. But when he moved to the U.S. parent's safety razor division in Boston, he discovered that one division produced 4 times the sales and 10 times the profits of the entire Canadian operation. He also found far greater levels of new product innovation, as well as greater opportunities for personal advancement. He left Canada in 1983, and probably will not return.

Preston's story is not unusual. Canadians are much in demand in other countries, but Canadian firms often find it difficult to recruit managers to work here. Some examples of the trend:

1. There has been a 30 percent increase in U.S. work visa applications by Canadian managers since 1988.
2. Canadian managers are very successful in job competitions in the U.S.
3. Nearly all Canadian executives who obtain a work visa later apply for landed immigrant status in the U.S.

Canadian firms recognize the value of sending managers abroad to get international experience, and with the advent of the Free Trade Agreement, there has been an increase in intracompany transfers of Canadian executives to U.S. postings. Under the agreement, Canadian managers transferring within a company can get a temporary work visa almost immediately, while managers from other countries must wait weeks or months for such approval.

Here is where the catch-22 arises. Once a Canadian executive has gone abroad, he or she may decide to stay permanently. Jacques Boisvert, former president of Sterling-Winthrop Inc., is now the president of a pharmaceutical firm in New York. He will not return to Canada because he cannot find an executive position here that would give him adequate scope (he now manages 3000 people instead of the 400 he managed in Canada).

The problem exists even with new graduates. Stephane Gosselin graduated from Sherbrooke in 1988 and now works in Toulouse, France. He says he has more responsibility than he would have in Canada, and he is also making 40 percent more than he would here. He is therefore reluctant to return.

Problems are also evident when Canadian firms try to recruit candidates from the U.S. While gross compensation levels may not be too different, the take-home pay is much less in Canada due to higher taxes, no mortgage deductibility, and the high cost of housing. Most candidates demand that the employer top up their pay package so they can maintain the lifestyle they had in the U.S. This can be very costly.

Perhaps even more significant than the financial problem is the job challenge problem. Canada's "branch-plant economy" has historically been viewed as a stepping-stone to bigger and better jobs in other countries. In Canada, managers could get good training by managing subsidiary units that had considerable autonomy. With the advent of globalization, however, many U.S. subsidiaries in Canada have seen their autonomy reduced as the parent firm centralizes decision making in the areas of production, finance, and marketing. ▲

MANAGEMENT IN THE CANADIAN SETTING

A wide variety of organizations operate in Canada. The list in Table 1-2 constitutes only a tiny fraction of the ones that you might come into contact with in your personal and professional life. Some of the organizations—Falconbridge Nickel, Mad Max's Carpet Cleaning, and the Royal Bank of Canada—are profit-oriented, private-sector business firms. Some private-sector firms—Imperial Oil, Cashway Lumber, and Mind Computer Products—produce a physical product, while others—CompuScan Protection, Minaki Lodge, the Toronto Blue Jays, and Stevenson Real Estate—provide an intangible service. Still others—Underground Gourmet, Shell Canada, and Bristol Aerospace—provide both physical goods and intangible services.

TABLE 1-1 FACTORS INFLUENCING THE PRACTICE OF MANAGEMENT IN CANADA.

Factor	Description	Implications for Management
1. Geographical uniqueness	Canada is the world's second largest country in terms of area, but the vast majority of our population is found in a long east-west band near the U.S. border. The Rocky mountains separate B.C. psychologically from the rest of the country, and economic development of the far north has proved difficult.	It is difficult to cover a national market given Canada's geography. Transportation costs are major considerations in management decisions. The size of the country makes business travel time-consuming; it also means that significant events that occur in one part of the country are reacted to very belatedly in other parts of the country (there is, for example, a four-and-one-half-hour time difference between St. John's, Newfoundland and Vancouver).
2. Significant government involvement in the economy	The Canadian government has played a large role in industries such as transportation, petrochemicals, fishing, steel making, textiles, and building materials. The largest Crown corporations have revenues which make them as large as the major business firms. Government controls business and competes with it.	Many managerial jobs are found in government; critics argue that with no profit motive to guide them, government managers fail to stress performance, excellence, and output. Government regulations also influence the decision-making processes of private-sector managers. Senior bureaucrats often have extensive business experience, and senior business managers often have government experience.
3. Proximity to the U.S.	The U.S., with a population 10 times that of Canada's, presents both problems and opportunities. Many of the largest firms operating in Canada are foreign-owned. The long-term impact of the Canada-U.S. Free Trade Agreement and the North American Free Trade Agreement (NAFTA) has yet to be determined.	In foreign-controlled corporations, Canadian managers must serve two masters: one in Canada, and one in the foreign country where the company is headquartered. There may be conflicts between how the parent company wants things done, and how the local managers think they should be done. But there can be advantages to being a subsidiary; small size and greater flexibility have been observed in several Canadian subsidiaries.
4. Importance of international trade	There is increasing emphasis on global competition. Canada has historically exported more goods than it has imported, but our trade surplus with the U.S. has masked our trade deficit with many other countries. Productivity increases in countries like Korea are far greater than those in Canada.	Canadian managers face the challenge of having to compete in the global market. To do so, we must increase our productivity, but Canada's productivity record during the last decade is second-worst among the 13 industrialized countries for which statistics are gathered.
5. Importance of French Canada	Quebec accounts for approximately 25 percent of the Canadian market for goods and services. In the last decade, there has been a surge of entreprenuerial activity in the province, and several Quebec businesspeople were listed on the first annual *Canadian Business* Power List.	Official bilingualism is expensive. Translation costs, language training, and administration of official languages programs costs millions of dollars each year. If managers want to operate nationally, they must be able to speak both English and French.
6. Small population	At 26 million people, Canada's population is among the smallest of the major industrial nations. This small domestic market influences many business decisions that hinge on volume production.	Flexibility, agility, sensitivity to needed changes, and proper assessment of risks are crucial for Canadian managers. Trends often begin elsewhere (for example, clothing styles), but nimble Canadian companies can capitalize on them.

Some of the organizations in Table 1-2—the Canadian Mint, the University of Calgary, and the Government of the Northwest Territories—are public-sector or government organizations and do not pursue a profit. Eldorado Nuclear Ltd. and the Canadian Mint are examples of public-sector firms that produce a physical product, but most public-sector firms, such as Canada Post, the British Columbia Institute of Technology, and the Canadian Forces concentrate on intangible services. Other nonprofit organizations—the Salvation Army, the United Way, Elim Chapel, and the Canadian Wildlife Federation—are not government organizations. All of the private-sector business firms are profit-oriented, but most public-sector firms are not.

What do all these organizations have in common? In spite of their apparent diversity, they all need effective management if they are to reach their respective goals. Let's consider the differences between profit and not-for-profit organizations, and how the managerial job is important to each kind of organization.

TABLE 1-2 WHAT DO THESE ORGANIZATIONS HAVE IN COMMON?

Air Canada	Cooperative federee de Quebec	Human Resources Development Canada	Ron's Hairstyling
Alcan Aluminum	Corydon Family Practice Clinic	IBM	Royal Bank of Canada
Algonquin College	Creditel	Imperial Oil	Rural Municipality of Springfield
Atlas Van Lines	D'Eschambault Insurance Service	Interocean Steamship Corporation	Safeway
Atomic Energy of Canada	Eaton's	Inuit Tapirisat	Salvation Army
Auto Rescue Towing Services	Eldorado Nuclear Ltd.	Jim's Taxi	Saskatchewan Telephones
B.C. Plumbing and Heating	Elim Chapel	Keystone Office Services Ltd.	Scott Mission
Blackwoods Beverages	Erv's Taxidermy	Korban Funeral Chapel	Shell Canada
Bristol Aerospace	European Health Spa	Lotto Canada	Shoppers Drug Mart
B.C.I.T.	Falconbridge Nickel	Lual Import Corp.	Shopsy's
Bumper-to Bumper	Farm Credit Corp. of Canada	Mad Max's Carpet Cleaning	Stevens Real Estate
Burger King	Ferguson Lake Lodge	Manitoba Liquor Commission	Swat Professional Exterminators
Canada Post	First City Trust	Mienke and Mienke Meat Market	Sweeping Beauties
C.A.U.T.	Gemini Dental Care	Minaki Lodge	Toronto Blue Jays
CBC	General Motors of Canada	Mind Computer	Toronto Stock Exchange
Canadian Forces	George Weston	Ontario Hydro	Underground Gourmet
C.I.B.C.	Gree-C-Spoon	Parvaneh's Facials	United Cooperative of Ontario
Canadian Kidney Foundation	Greyhound Lines	Pearson International Airport	United Way
Canadian Mint	Government of the N.W.T.	Perth's Cleaners	University of Calgary
Canadian National Railways	Great Canadian Travel Company	Petro Canada	Winnipeg Transit
Canadian Tire	Holiday Inn	Pitblado & Hoskin	Women's College Hospital
Canadian Wildlife Federation		Public Service Alliance	YMCA/YWCA
Cashway Lumber		Revenue Canada	Yuk Yuk's
Chrysler Canada			
Coiffure Caprice			
Compu-Scan Protection			

THE PROFIT-ORIENTED BUSINESS FIRM

business firm

LEARNING OBJECTIVE 2

Explain the difference between profit-oriented business firms and not-for-profit organizations.

Business firms play an important role in the Canadian economic system. A **business firm** is an entity that seeks to make a profit providing products or services that satisfy consumer demand. Although business firms are mainly found in the private sector, some government organizations (for example, Canada Post) also pursue a profit. In the past, when the term "business firm" was used, most people immediately thought of factories with smokestacks, assembly lines, and workers with lunch pails. While the manufacturing of products is still important in Canada, two-thirds of the jobs in Canada are now provided by firms emphasizing services instead of physical products. Banking, insurance, transportation, consulting, real estate, sports, and home cleaning are just a few examples of profit-oriented businesses that emphasize services.

Most manufacturing firms also provide services in addition to the products they make. IBM, for example, manufactures computers, but its after-the-sale service and its advice to customers on how best to use the computer are clearly service activities. Fast food organizations like Burger King produce an array of physical products, but they also stress services such as convenience, cleanliness, and birthday parties for children.

Whether it provides a product or a service, the business firm is the basic building block of the economy in Canada. The business firm is an input-output system. The inputs are the resources it buys in the marketplace and the outputs are the goods and services it produces and sells in the marketplace. In business firms, resources are organized for production, and land, labour, and capital are assembled and converted into products and services that can be sold. This activity is directed and guided by managers (see Figure 1-1). This issue will be discussed in more detail later in the chapter.

The reason people start business firms is the hope of making a profit. **Profit** is the difference between the cost of inputs and the revenue from output. If revenues are greater than costs, a profit is earned. Profit will only be realized if the firm is managed effectively and if it provides goods and services that consumers want. Any after-tax profit earned by a firm is either reinvested in the firm or distributed to owners. For many firms, reinvested profits are the principal source of funds to finance their growth. The owners, in effect, are willing to reinvest their profit in the firm instead of taking it out and spending it.

profit

While all business firms seek to make a profit, there is a debate about whether profit should be their only goal. Governments, for example, have profits in mind when they form business firms, but they also take other goals into account, such as providing employment.

Forms of Business Ownership

LEARNING OBJECTIVE 3

Describe the main features of sole proprietorships, partnerships, and corporations.

Business firms vary in size from single-owner firms to giant corporations owned by thousands of people. A business firm may be a sole proprietorship, a partnership, or a corporation.

The sole proprietorship is the oldest and still the most common form of legal ownership in Canada. A **sole proprietorship** is a business owned and managed by one person. That person, however, may have help from others in operating the business. Only a sole proprietor can say "I am the company." Ron's Hairstyling and Jim's Taxi are sole proprietorships.

sole proprietorship

A **partnership** exists when two or more individuals combine their financial, managerial, and technical abilities for the purpose of operating a company for profit. Mienke and Mienke Meat Market is a partnership. Many accounting and law firms also operate as partnerships.

partnership

People who invest in sole proprietorships or partnerships have *unlimited liability*. This means that if the firm gets into financial difficulty, creditors can seize the proprietor's or partners' personal assets like a home or car and sell them in order to pay the bills. Actually, the law does protect some personal assets, but many can be claimed. A practical illustration of unlimited liability concerns people who invested in Lloyd's of London (see the Global Management insert on Lloyd's of London).

FIGURE 1-1 BASIC BUSINESS ACTIVITY.

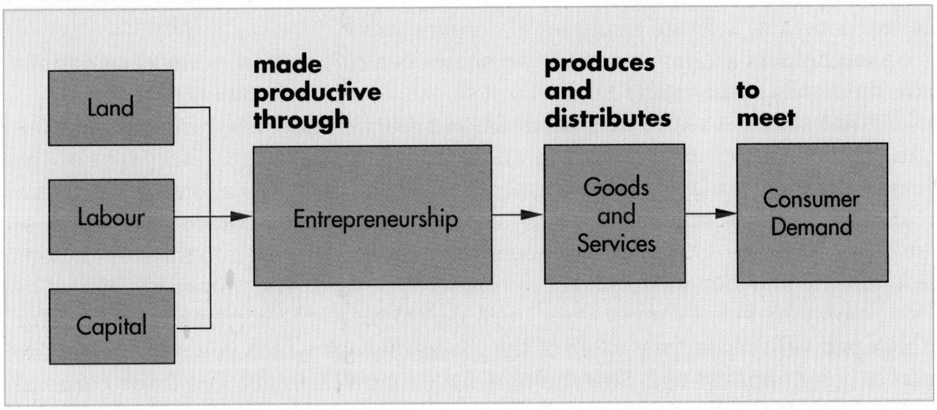

GLOBAL MANAGEMENT

Unlimited Liability at Lloyd's of London

Lloyd's of London is one of the most famous insurance companies in the world. It began operations several centuries ago by insuring British merchant ships. The individuals who invest in Lloyd's are called "names." These names have unlimited liability, i.e., they are liable for any losses incurred by the company. Their liability for losses is not limited to their original investment, but rather to the amount of money they have. Thus, their personal property can be seized to pay off their liabilities.

Why would a person invest in a company like Lloyd's when they know they will have unlimited liability? The reason is that historically such investments have yielded good returns. Traditionally, names have been wealthy people who could afford to take the occasional loss. But during the go-go 1980s, many new names were recruited who were not wealthy (but had dreams of wealth). When their involvement brought losses instead of profits, many of the new names lost everything they owned. The British press plays up cases of names being forced to move out of expensive homes that have been in a family for generations, but many poorer people have also lost their homes.

Why has Lloyd's run into financial difficulty? The answer is that changing times are threatening the company. It is clear that an insurance system designed in the year 1600 cannot cope with certain twentieth century realities—natural disasters, terrorism, pollution, industrial accidents, and a trend toward increasing litigation.

All of these factors have sent insurance claims sky-high. During the last three years, for example, Lloyd's has lost a total of $12 billion. In that same period, the number of names has fallen from 27 000 to 19 000. Several members who were part of a group of names that lost $800 million committed suicide. Another group of names from Canada have sued the company, alleging fraud to prevent Lloyd's from seizing their assets to make good on claims. In April 1993 Lloyd's CEO David Rowland introduced a plan that would end the company's tradition of unlimited liability and allow corporations to become new members with limited liability. But existing names will continue to have unlimited liability. ▲

corporation

A **corporation** has been defined as "an artificial being, invisible, intangible, and existing only in contemplation of law." Unlike a sole proprietorship or a partnership, the corporation has a legal existence apart from its owners. It can buy, hold, and sell property in its own name, and it can sue and be sued. Originally, the corporation was used for charitable, educational, and public purposes. In order to incorporate, a charter was required from the government, which is why the corporation is legally separate from its owners. It is a creation of government authority. Eaton's, Imperial Oil, Shopsy's, Safeway, Falconbridge Nickel, and Shoppers Drug Mart (as well as many others listed in Table 1-2) are examples of corporations.

shareholders

Shareholders are persons who own shares in a corporation. Some corporations have thousands of shares and hundreds of shareholders, while others have few shareholders and shares. A shareholder need not, and generally does not, participate in managing the corporation. Ownership and management are separate. Most of the shareholders in Canada do not participate in managing the corporations in which they hold shares. A shareholder owns only a partial interest in a corporation. Suppose you own 100 shares of Imperial Oil. You are not entitled to walk into the corporation's headquarters and demand to see the "property" you own. The property is owned by the corporation. What you own is a small part of the entire corporation. The value of that part varies, since the value of the shares of stock which you own changes as market conditions change. Shareholders have limited liability, i.e., if the corporation has financial difficulties, shareholders can lose only that money which they invested in the shares of stock.

The two basic types of stock are common and preferred stock. **Common stock** confers ownership and voting rights in a corporation. The number of votes a shareholder has depends on the number of shares of stock she or he owns. Common shareholders have the right to decide which individuals will sit on the board of directors. They also have the right to the residual earnings that remain after the corporation has met the prior claims of bondholders (people who have loaned the corporation money) and preferred shareholders. The actual payment of a common stock dividend (money for each share held) does not occur until the board of directors declares a dividend. If the corporation goes bankrupt, the common shareholders are the last to receive any proceeds from the sale of the corporation's property.

common stock

Preferred stock also shows ownership in a corporation, but preferred shareholders usually do not have voting rights. They do, however, enjoy certain preferences with respect to dividends and assets. They have a right to receive the dividend indicated on their share certificates before common shareholders receive any dividends. This dividend is also not owed to the shareholder until it is declared by the board of directors. If the corporation goes out of business and pays off its debts, preferred shareholders have the right to receive their share of any remaining assets before the common shareholders receive anything.

preferred stock

A corporation's board of directors is elected by its shareholders (see Figure 1-2). The **board of directors** is a group of people who are given the power to govern the corporation's affairs and to make general policy. The board of directors is accountable for guiding the overall activity of the business. The board holds periodic meetings at which

board of directors

FIGURE 1-2 CORPORATE STRUCTURE.

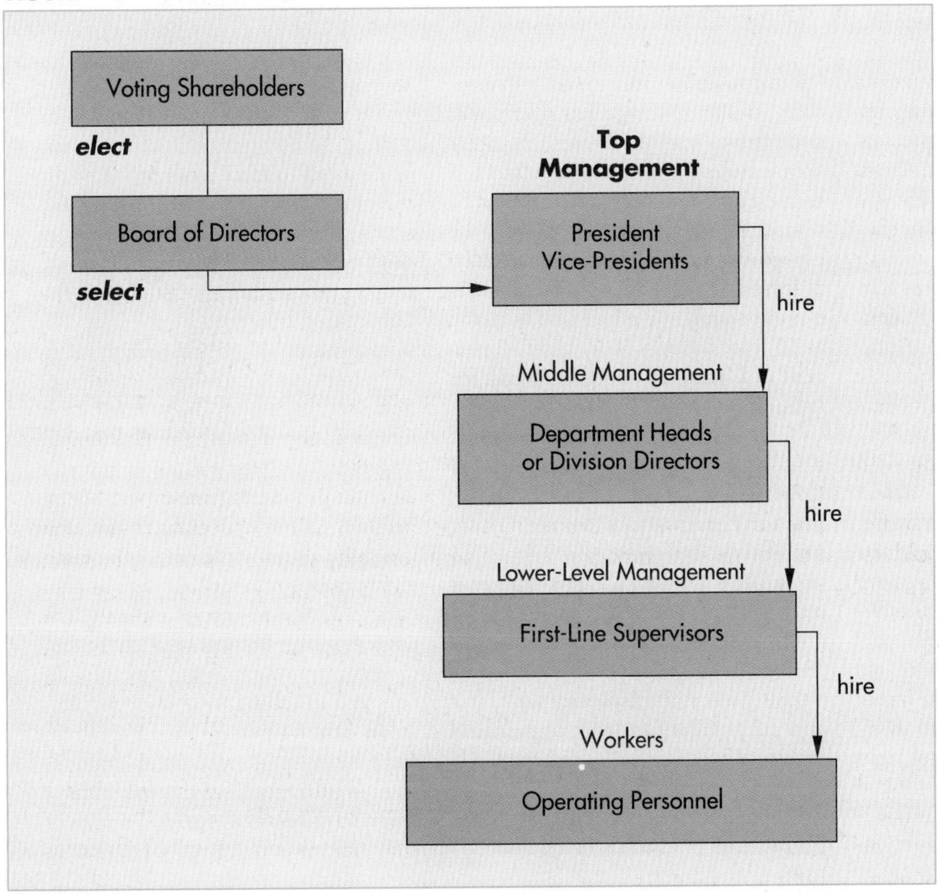

Safeway tries to make a profit by providing consumers with goods and services they want. Managers direct activities like gathering resources, and organizing land, labour, and capital.

corporation bylaws

it makes major policy decisions. It selects the corporation's top managers, including the president, vice-presidents, secretary, and treasurer. These top managers, in turn, hire middle- and lower-level managers to help run the corporation. In many firms, the board selects only the president, who then selects the other corporate officers.

The board is accountable to the shareholders for the actions of the corporate officers. It must act in the best interest of the shareholders and be reasonable and prudent when making decisions concerning the corporation. Board members must be as careful in managing the corporation as they are in managing their own personal business activity (see the Management at Work insert "Changes in the Boardroom"). In some corporations, it plays a very active role in managing the corporation, while in others it operates in a very "hands-off" fashion. The distinction between "board member" and "corporate officer" is often blurred in practice. In some corporations, the chairperson of the board is also the company president. The corporation's other top managers may also be on the board.

The board of directors usually drafts the bylaws for the organization. **Corporation bylaws** are the rules by which the corporation operates. They stipulate such matters as the time and date of the corporation's annual meeting, procedures for calling management meetings, directors' duties and salaries, regulations for new stock offerings, and procedures for changing the bylaws. Shareholders must approve such bylaws.

MANAGEMENT AT WORK

CHANGES IN THE BOARDROOM

Recruiting members for a company's board of directors is becoming increasingly difficult. There are two reasons for this situation. First, directors' responsibilities and workloads are much more significant now than they used to be. The days are gone when a person could sit on the boards of 8 or 10 major companies and attend a couple of meetings a year. Now, most directors sit on only 2 or 3 boards because each one requires considerable work.

The second reason has to do with increased expectations about directors' liability for their decisions. Federal and provincial regulations have made directors substantially more responsible to shareholders, employees, and customers than in the past. Shareholders have grown more sophisticated and are now more likely to sue board members for bad decisions. Directors are also being held personally liable if an ex-employee wins a suit for wrongful dismissal. Liability insurance is also a problem. Premiums have increased substantially, dollar coverage has decreased, deductibles are higher, and insurers are excluding more types of claims. A survey by the Conference Board of Canada revealed that 16 percent of the companies surveyed had experienced at least one legal action against their directors, and some had had as many as 15 legal actions. More than 70 percent of Canadian companies pay for liability insurance for their directors.

Changes in board composition are also evident. A survey by the Conference Board of Canada shows that the percentage of women sitting on boards has more than doubled since 1984. However, it still stands at only 5.8 percent. Most women who are board members are "outside" directors, not employees of the company. This is consistent with the general trend away from appointing top-level executives to the board.

Shareholders have shown increased willingness to vote out board members if they feel a poor job is being done. At Sherritt Gordon Ltd., one shareholder group accumulated more than 5 percent of the company's stock and then made a bid to elect a new slate of directors. The group claimed that the board of directors had failed to take proper steps to deal with potential problems regarding oversupply in the Canadian fertilizer industry. The dissident shareholders sent an appeal to all shareholders explaining their position and requesting support for their plan at a special shareholders' meeting. The company sent out its own letter defending its management of the firm. President Charles Heinrich said that the people who were doing the criticizing didn't understand how the firm operated. At the special meeting, the dissident shareholders were successful in voting out the existing board members and installing their own people.

In other firms, board members have been sued, with shareholders claiming that the board members have failed to fulfill their duties. For example, 10 ex-directors of Peoples

• • •

Jewellers Ltd. are involved in a $35 million lawsuit which alleges that the directors failed to disclose risks associated with a bond issue that was sold to the public in 1990. The directors could be forced to pay out of their own pocket if the judgment exceeds the $10 million in liability insurance that covers them. Liability fears such as this have caused directors to leave financially troubled companies like PWA and Westar Mining Ltd.

Many investors feel that board members are not independent enough to make objective decisions because, traditionally, directors have usually seen themselves as being chosen by management (usually the CEO) and, therefore, have felt a responsibility only to management, and not to the shareholders. If problems arose, board members often gave managers only a "slap on the wrist." They also seemed reluctant to reduce management salaries when the firm was doing poorly. And when takeover bids came along, board members often rejected them, even if the takeover would benefit the shareholders. Board members rejected these bids so they could maintain their power and position. These are problems investors have been fighting to change.

These challenges come at a time when the role of the board of directors is more important than ever. In an era of intense global competition, strategic leadership is absolutely essential. This will mean that big changes will have to occur in the way that boards operate. The "old code" of keeping the board in the background and letting management set strategy and operate the company will have to be replaced with a "new code" that requires board members to be actively involved in confronting problems the firm is facing. ▲

Not-for-profit Organizations

Many organizations in Canada do not have profit as an objective. In fact, business firms are the only organizations in Canada that do pursue a profit. All other kinds of organizations—labor unions, religious organizations, charities, universities, community colleges, the military, environmental groups, consumer advocate organizations, municipal, provincial and federal governments, community clubs, and professional organizations—do not pursue a profit. **Not-for-profit organizations** stress service objectives instead of profit. The Public Service Alliance of Canada, for example, provides expert service for its members regarding grievance arbitration and wage negotiations. The United Way provides a wide variety of community activities by acting as a central collection agency for contributed funds. The Scott Mission provides food and shelter for needy individuals.

not-for-profit organizations

Comparing Profit-oriented and Not-for-profit Organizations

In spite of the apparent differences between profit-oriented and not-for-profit organizations, two crucial similarities make management important to both. First, both kinds of organizations have objectives that must be reached if the organization is to remain in existence. Second, in both types of organizations, people must be directed and motivated to pursue the organization's goals. Since managers play a central role in these activities, they are needed in both profit-oriented and not-for-profit organizations.

This common need becomes clear when we compare the activities of two organizations that appear to be quite different: the Canadian Wildlife Federation (CWF) and Imperial Oil. The CWF needs managers to ensure that it reaches its objective of protecting and managing wildlife in Canada. To reach these objectives, individuals in the CWF must be motivated to make the public aware of its goals and to act in ways that are consistent with preserving wildlife. Imperial Oil also needs managers to reach its goals of providing energy products to Canadian consumers so that it can make a profit. Managers at Imperial Oil must also motivate their employees so that these goals can be reached. Thus, even though these two organizations have markedly different (and perhaps conflicting) goals, they both need managers to be effective.

THE FUNCTIONS OF MANAGEMENT

LEARNING OBJECTIVE 4
Describe what is involved in each of the four major functions of management—planning, organizing, leading, and controlling.

Managers perform four basic functions: planning, organizing, leading, and controlling. These functions are necessary regardless of the specific setting in which the manager operates.

PLANNING

planning

Planning is the process of deciding what objectives to pursue and choosing strategies that will help the organization reach those objectives. Planning is essential for organizations as diverse as Eaton's, the Vancouver Stock Exchange, Elim Chapel, and Lotto Canada. Planning is carried out by managers at all levels of an organization. Top-level managers are primarily concerned about long-range plans, while lower-level managers focus on short-range plans.

When planning, managers must ensure that the objectives set are specific and measurable. A profit-oriented firm like Molson's might decide that it wants to achieve a 30 percent share of the Canadian beer market and a 15 percent return on investment. The company must then develop step-by-step plans for producing and marketing its products so that it can achieve these goals. A not-for-profit firm like the United Way also sets specific goals, in this case dealing with the amount of money it wants to raise each year. It then develops a detailed strategy for reaching its objectives. The planning function—including decision making—is discussed in detail in Chapters 4, 5, and 6.

ORGANIZING

organizing

Once the overall objectives and strategies have been established, managers must translate these into reality. **Organizing** is the process of creating a structure of authority that helps the organization reach its objectives. It involves activities such as describing the tasks that must be accomplished, assigning individual workers to these specific tasks, grouping related tasks into departments, and allocating resources to these departments.

Many types of organizational structures result from this process. Some are very rigid (i.e., employees are strictly controlled in their work), while others are quite flexible (i.e., employees enjoy greater flexibility in how to achieve work goals). The nature of an organization's activity obviously has a strong influence on its structure. Tellers at the Royal Bank of Canada, for example, follow prescribed routines more than fishing guides at Ferguson Lake Lodge do. Employees in both these organizations are subject to managerial authority, but the way in which it is exercised is different.

Firms in the same industry may have similar looking organizational structures (for example, the Steel Company of Canada and Algoma Steel), but no two structures are exactly the same. Firms that provide different products or services may have very different organizational structures (for example, Bristol Aerospace and the Toronto Blue Jays). We discuss the organizing process in detail in Chapters 7 to 11.

LEADING

leading

Once the organization's objectives have been established, and the structure for achieving those objectives has been put in place, attention must be focussed on leading the people in the organization. **Leading** is the process of motivating and communicating with the organization's human resources to ensure that they pursue the organization's objectives. The leading function has also been called "directing," "influencing," and "actuating." In a recent survey, business managers said that motivating and leading subordinates was management's most important responsibility.[9]

Two important observations must be made about the leading function. First, this definition does not mean that leading is unimportant until planning and organizing have been accomplished. In fact, leading is a crucial element in both planning and organizing. Second, while the planning and organizing functions deal mainly with rational ideas like objectives and structure, the leading function deals mainly with people. Successful managers must be able to deal with both rational ideas and the emotional needs of its subordinates. We discuss the leading function in Chapters 12 to 16.

CONTROLLING

controlling

It is necessary for all organizations to determine if what was supposed to happen actually happened. **Controlling** is the process of ensuring that organizational performance matches what was planned. It involves establishing standards of performance, comparing actual performance to those standards, and taking any corrective action that is necessary. For example, when a salesperson sets a goal to sell a certain number of units (planning), the manager must later check to see whether the goal has been reached (controlling). If it hasn't, certain actions must be taken to see that the salesperson reaches the goal during the next period.

The controlling function is just as vital for managers at Atlas Van Lines as it is for managers at the Public Service Alliance of Canada. All organizations must pay attention to information indicating whether they are, or are not, achieving the objectives they have set. The controlling function is discussed in Chapters 17 and 18.

MANAGERIAL ROLES

LEARNING OBJECTIVE 5
Understand and briefly outline the activities involved in the three managerial roles—interpersonal, informational, and decisional.

Identifying the four basic functions that managers perform gives us a good overall idea of what management is all about. But there are two shortcomings in this "functions" approach. First, it often does not give us a detailed understanding of what managers actually do on a day-to-day basis. Second, it may be difficult to determine what function a manager is performing at a particular time. For example, when a manager presides at a ground-breaking ceremony for a new factory, or resolves a conflict between two subordinates, or testifies at a price-fixing hearing, what functions is she or he performing?

Henry Mintzberg of McGill University addressed this important problem by interviewing and observing five chief executive officers from different companies over a two-week period.[10] Overall, Mintzberg found that top executives were extremely busy (working at least 50 hours per week); they also worked at an unrelenting pace each day. They did not spend a lot of time on any one project, and even that work was often interrupted as they dealt with crises that arose. Managers generally worked with other people (not alone), and they carried on much face-to-face verbal communication during both formal and informal meetings.

role

Mintzberg also identified 10 specific roles that managers performed. A **role** is the pattern of behaviour that is expected of a person in a certain job. Mintzberg organized the 10 roles he observed into three main categories—interpersonal, informational, and decisional (see Table 1-3). Subsequent research has supported Mintzberg's view of the manager's job.[11]

TABLE 1-3 TEN MANAGERIAL ROLES.

Main Category	Specific Role	Activity
Interpersonal	Figurehead	Acts as a representative of the organization in a ceremonial or symbolic capacity
	Leader	Motivates, communicates, and coordinates the activities of subordinates
	Liaison	Develops relationships with members of the organization outside his or her area of authority
Informational	Monitor	Gathers information about the unit's external environment
	Disseminator	Transmits information to subordinates
	Spokesperson	Transmits information to people outside his or her area of authority
Decisional	Entrepreneur	Develops and implements new ideas
	Disturbance Handler	Takes action to resolve crises or conflicts
	Resource Allocator	Decides how the unit's limited resources will be allocated
	Negotiator	Formally bargains with other individuals in the organization over issues affecting his or her unit

INTERPERSONAL ROLES

interpersonal roles

Interpersonal roles involve the manager in relationships with other individuals both inside and outside the firm. Because a manager has formal authority in the management hierarchy, he or she must interact with people in certain ways. In the *figurehead role,* the manager acts as a representative of the organization in a ceremonial or symbolic manner. For instance, the dean of a business school may hand out diplomas at graduation, the president of a manufacturing firm may preside at a sod-turning ceremony, and the mayor of a large city may host a luncheon for a visiting Canadian astronaut.

In the *leader role,* the manager motivates, communicates, and coordinates the activity of subordinates. Examples include a personnel manager conducting a performance appraisal meeting with a subordinate, a sales manager developing an incentive scheme to increase the motivation of the company's salespeople, and a government department head deciding which training programs are appropriate for which subordinates.

In the *liaison role,* the manager develops relationships with members of the organization outside the manager's area of authority. Examples include a plant manager clarifying budget issues with the corporate controller, a college dean resolving a conflict with another dean about whose faculty should teach a certain course, and a vice-president meeting with a consumer advocate group regarding the safety of one of the company's products.

INFORMATIONAL ROLES

informational roles

Informational roles put the manager in a central position for sending and receiving information. As managers carry out the interpersonal roles described above, they gain access to a great deal of information which helps them carry out the three informational roles.

In the *monitor role,* the manager seeks to gain information about the unit's environment. This information may come from inside or outside the firm. Examples include a marketing manager gathering information about a competitor's new products, a college dean reading a provincial government funding document, and a church administrator examining a report on church attendance and financial support.

In the *disseminator role,* the focus is reversed. Here, the manager transmits important information to subordinates. The manager may, of course, transmit information selectively, perhaps toning down information that makes the unit look bad, and playing up information that makes the unit look good. Thus, a personnel manager may pass along confidential information to a trusted subordinate, a supervisor may tell travel agents not to book clients with a certain hotel because of poor service, and a Revenue Canada supervisor may inform subordinates of the latest interpretation of a tax law dealing with the deductibility of certain expenses.

When assuming the *spokesperson role,* the manager transmits information to other people, this time to those outside his or her area of authority. This information may go to individuals inside or outside the organization. For instance, a marketing manager at General Motors of Canada might write a report on new product development to the board of directors, a camp manager at Ferguson Lake Lodge might verbally report to the president on the progress of construction at a new outcamp, and the president of Falconbridge Nickel might supply information on the firm's pollution abatement activity to a government commission.

DECISIONAL ROLES

decisional roles

Much of what goes on in the roles described so far involves information. In the **decisional roles**, the manager uses information to make important decisions about the unit's direction and how resources should be committed to reach the unit's objectives. The decisional roles may be the most important of all the roles the manager plays.

In the *entrepreneur role,* the manager develops and implements new ideas that will improve the functioning of the unit. The head of a college or university department may propose a review of the courses the department offers, a public relations manager at a provincial telephone utility may develop a survey to see how satisfied business customers are, and a marketing manager in a manufacturing firm may work with the engineering department to develop a new product.

A manager assumes the *disturbance handler role* when she or he is called on to deal with problems that are beyond their immediate control, often during a crisis. A plant manager reacting to a wildcat (unauthorized) strike, a company president informing the purchasing manager to stop buying from a supplier that is almost bankrupt, and a restaurant manager trying to resolve a conflict between a waitress and a cook are all examples of this role.

The manager takes on the *resource allocator role* when he or she decides how the unit's limited resources (equipment, time, personnel, and money) will be allocated. The chair of a university or college department fulfills this role when deciding whether or not to offer a certain course; members of Parliament occupy this role when deciding how much money to allocate to military spending or social programs; and a marketing manager assumes this role when deciding how much of the marketing budget will be allocated for advertising and how much will be allocated for training salespeople.

In the *negotiator role,* a manager formally bargains with others in the organization over issues that influence the functioning of the manager's unit. A marketing manager could negotiate with the production manager about the production of a custom item for a major customer; a school department head might negotiate with a principal about obtaining a new microcomputer for an advanced class; and a personnel manager might negotiate with a union representative over a grievance filed by a worker.

Characteristics of Managerial Roles

Three general points should be kept in mind about mangerial roles:

1. As is true with managerial functions, managerial roles are interrelated. Managers continually move among the 10 roles as they carry out the functions of management.
2. Generally speaking, the various roles receive a different emphasis at different managerial levels. Top managers, for example, spend more time in the figurehead role than lower-level managers do, while lower-level managers spend more time in the leader role. Managers at all levels spend considerable time in the disturbance handler role.
3. Specific roles may have different meanings at different levels of the organization. For example, assuming the monitor role for top managers means scanning the organization's external environment for changes that will affect the organization. For lower-level managers, on the other hand, it means scanning the organization's internal environment for developments which will have an impact on their own unit.

THE LEVELS OF MANAGEMENT

first-line managers

The management hierarchy of any organization has three general levels. Each of these levels has its own type of manager. **First-line managers** supervise operative workers and are directly responsible for the production of goods and services. In the Management Challenge at the beginning of the chapter, James Kenner was a first-line manager. A foreman on an assembly line at Ford of Canada, a technical supervisor in a research lab at Procter & Gamble, a clerical supervisor at Revenue Canada, and a department head at Seneca College are all first-line managers. These managers are responsible for seeing that the actual production of goods and services takes place. They do this by making sure that workers are at their work stations, by giving instructions on the tasks that are to be performed, and by regularly checking the output of workers to see that it is acceptable. They are the only managers in the organization who supervise nonmanagerial personnel. All other managers supervise other managers.

middle managers

Middle managers work in the middle of the management hierarchy; they supervise first-line managers and have a wider area of responsibility than first-line managers. The director of the research lab at Canadian Industries Ltd., the dean of the Faculty of Administration at the University of Regina, and the head of the industrial products division at Beltone Manufacturing are all middle managers. These managers are responsible for ensuring that work is completed through the first-line supervisors. They do this by coordinating the work of the first-line supervisors who report to them. Middle managers must also ensure that the overall plans of top management are translated into specific activities at the lower levels of the organization.

top managers

Top managers are responsible for the overall operation of the organization. Examples of top managers include the chief executive officer (CEO) of Federal Industries, the president of the University of Calgary, the executive director of the Winnipeg Foundation, and the executive vice-president of the Bank of Montreal. Top managers decide on the overall direction of the firm, providing a "vision" of where it should be going and conveying this vision to the middle managers.

Increasing rates of technological change, a growing reliance on databased information systems, and organizational downsizing, or streamlining, have contributed to serious problems in middle management at some firms. These problems include the ineffective delegation of decision making, poor communication and coordination among departments, excessive concern about functional specialties like marketing, finance, and production, lack of understanding of the organization's overall strategy, and a reluctance to take risks.

Moving individuals through the different levels of management therefore requires careful planning. Peter Stephenson, manager of RHR International's Canadian practice, says that middle managers who focus on functional matters like marketing, finance, or production may lack the skills to move up to senior management positions. To ensure an effective transition, organizations must focus on developing middle managers with a broader conceptual outlook.[12]

MANAGEMENT FUNCTIONS AT DIFFERENT ORGANIZATIONAL LEVELS

As we have seen, all managers perform the basic functions of management. But not all managers put equal emphasis on each function. In fact, there are wide variations in how managers at the various levels divide their time among planning, organizing, leading, and controlling.

Generally speaking, top managers attach more importance to planning, organizing, and controlling than middle managers do. Middle managers, in turn, place more emphasis on these three functions than first-line supervisors do. The reverse is true for the directing function: first-line supervisors place more emphasis on it than middle managers, and middle managers place more importance on directing than top managers do. These general relationships are shown in Figure 1-3.

In one study demonstrating these relationships, the importance of planning (on a 100-point scale) was rated at 84 by top managers, 45 by middle managers, and only 25 by first-line supervisors.[13] The importance of directing, on the other hand, was rated at 65 by first-line supervisors, 50 by middle managers, and only 33 by top managers. These relationships are shown in Figure 1-4.

In another study of 1412 managers, first-line supervisors said they placed the greatest emphasis on managing individual performance and instructing subordinates. Middle-level managers said that managing group performance, planning, and

FIGURE 1-3 MANAGEMENT FUNCTIONS AT VARIOUS MANAGEMENT LEVELS.

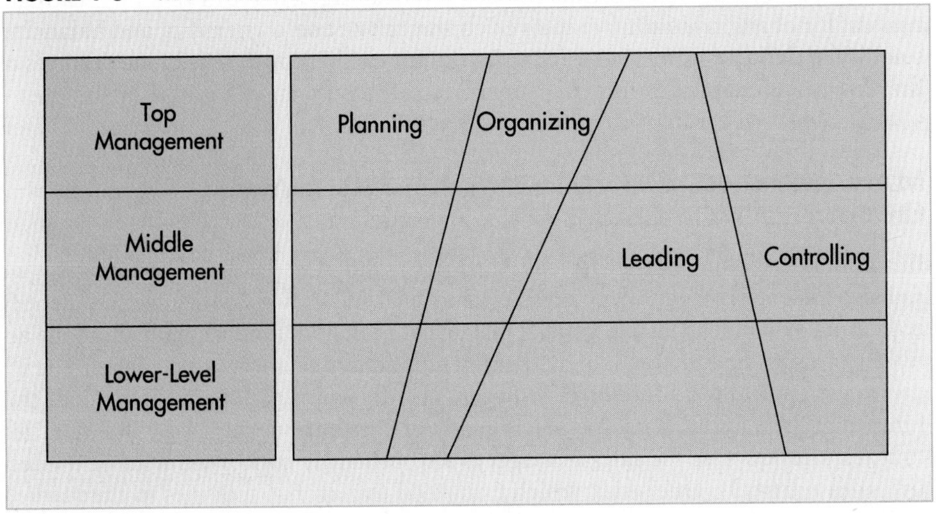

FIGURE 1-4 MANAGEMENT FUNCTIONS AT VARIOUS ORGANIZATIONAL LEVELS.

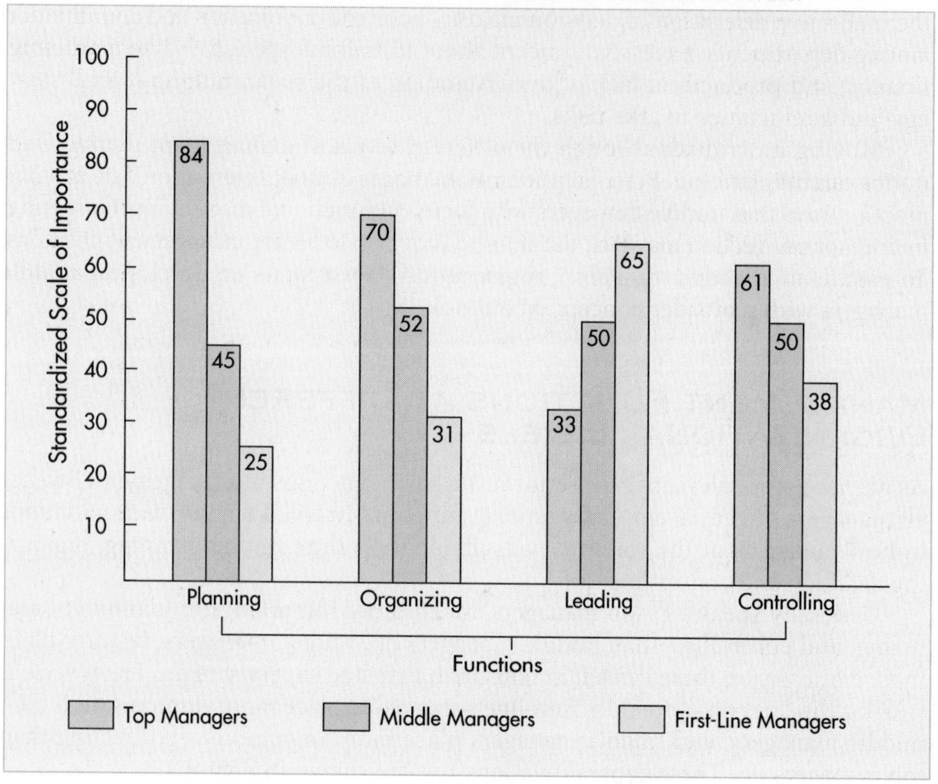

resource allocation were most critical, while top-level managers emphasized monitoring the external environment.[14] Representing one's staff was rated as important by managers at all levels.

Asking managers to rate the importance of the traditional management functions leads to some useful insights, but it may overlook others. In a study of 24 chief executive officers, most accepted the importance of planning, organizing, leading, and controlling.[15] However, these CEOs saw their role as "making sense of the world" for themselves and for the individuals they were leading. They did this by creating a context for change, building employee commitment and ownership, and balancing stability and innovation. These activities do not easily fit into the four categories of the "functions" approach to management.

Management Functions at the Same Organizational Level

functional managers

In addition to looking at the work of managers at different levels in the hierarchy, we can also look at managerial work at the same level. When we do this, we can identify both functional managers and general managers. **Functional managers** oversee the activities of a specific function like marketing, production, finance, or personnel. The individuals reporting to functional managers also focus on the specific details of this function. For example, a salesperson is concerned with the specific activities required to reach sales quotas; the sales manager is also primarily concerned with how effective sales activity is. One study which examined managerial activities in the marketing and production functions found both similarities and differences.[16] Both types of managers felt it was necessary to manage individuals and to plan for and allocate resources, but production managers put more emphasis on instructing subordinates, while marketing managers put more stress on monitoring the external environment.

general managers

General managers oversee the activities of an entire division or organization. The general manager supervises the work of several functional managers, exercising a broader outlook than the functional managers. For example, the general manager of a firm manufacturing paint would be concerned not only about how well the paint was selling, but also about unit costs in the production area, the financial implications of starting a new production line, and the implications of hiring new people to increase output. The larger the firm, the more general managers it will have. A large conglomerate, for example, might have 8 or 10 general managers, each in charge of a major division in the firm. A small firm would likely have only one general manager.

THE SKILLS OF MANAGEMENT

technical skills

LEARNING OBJECTIVE 6

Identify three important skills of management and what they involve.

To manage effectively, managers need technical, people, and conceptual skills. These skills can be learned if the manager has the motivation to learn them. **Technical skills** allow a person to apply certain procedures or techniques that are relevant to a specific field of work. Such skill can be used in the production of both goods and services. Computer technicians, plumbers, accountants, musicians, doctors, lawyers, market researchers and many others possess technical skills. While managers usually possess some technical skills, their job is primarily to manage those who possess a high level of technical skills.

Individuals with technical skills are often promoted to managerial jobs. But technical skills, by themselves, are no guarantee that managerial work will be done well. The Management at Work insert "Is Experience Necessary for Success?" illustrates this problem.

people skills

People skills include the ability to lead, motivate, and communicate with both groups and individuals. Because managing involves getting work done through others, this skill is crucial for managers at all levels.

conceptual skills

Conceptual skills are those which help a manager see the organization as a complete unit, and to integrate and give direction to its diverse activities so that organizational objectives are achieved. Conceptual skills are necessary for all managers, but they are critical for top managers.

MANAGEMENT AT WORK

Is Experience Necessary for Management Success?

One of the great debates in management is whether a person needs specific experience in a certain line of work or a certain company in order to be effective as a manager of people doing that work. For example, can a person be a successful sales manager without ever having been a salesperson? Can a person be a successful engineering manager without ever having been an engineer? Most managers seem to think not, but several interesting exceptions are evident.

The Toronto law firm of Borden & Elliot hired John Herrick as its chief operating officer. Herrick spent over 30 years producing and marketing products such as Cheerios; he had no no experience in the legal business. He was hired because the law firm wanted someone who had a lot

• • •

of experience in managing people. Borden & Elliot is believed to be the first law firm in Canada to have hired a nonlawyer for such a crucial position. This idea has already been implemented in several U.S. law firms.

The idea in hiring Herrick is that the lawyers will practise law and Herrick will manage the business. Borden & Elliot is really saying that they are a business firm and need to be managed like one. One of Herrick's first jobs was to draw up a strategic plan for the firm. He therefore helped the partners decide on the growth rate of the firm, and the specific areas the firm should get involved in.

Paul Tellier became president and CEO of Canadian National Railways in 1993. He has been a deputy minister, clerk of the Privy Council, and secretary to the federal Cabinet, but he does not have any experience in the railroad business. This is a time of crisis for CN, which is $2 billion in debt, and has a payroll that will have to be ruthlessly cut. Tellier's critics argue that his lack of experience in the business will reduce his chances of success.

Tellier says his inexperience is not a problem. He feels that CN does not need an experienced railroader at the top during its time of crisis; rather, what it needs is someone who will provide leadership to make the tough decisions which will be necessary to get the firm back on the right track. One of Tellier's first acts was to inform the union that 10 000 jobs would have to be cut in the next five years if CN is to survive. He also cut some top-level managerial jobs to show the union that CN's problems are company-wide. It might be argued that an outsider is just what CN needs. Such a person will not be bound by the kind of thinking that got CN into its current mess.

These two individuals are not the only examples that can be cited. In fact, increasing numbers of Canadian business firms are selecting CEOs with little or no direct knowledge of the industry. Consider the following examples:

- David Clark, former CEO of Campbell Soup Ltd. became the publisher of *The Globe and Mail*
- Stanley Hartt, formerly a senior partner at the law firm of Stikeman Elliott, became the CEO of Camdev Inc.
- John Cassaday, formerly president of Campbell Foods PLC, became CEO of CTV Television Network
- Donald Lander, formerly president of Chrysler Canada Ltd., became CEO of Canada Post
- Paul Godfrey, formerly chair of the Municipality of Metropolitan Toronto, became president of the Toronto Sun Publishing Group

The trend to hiring top executives from outside the firm is not really surprising. During the 1980s, companies cut many middle-management positions as part of their downsizing efforts. But that drained their internal pool of talent, so now they are more likely to look outside for a CEO. ▲

Management Skills at Different Levels

The mix of the three skills listed above varies from level to level in the management hierarchy (see Figure 1-5). At the lowest level of management, technical skills and people skills are the most important. Thus, a production line supervisor at General Motors of Canada will likely have considerable knowledge of the technical tasks that workers are doing. That supervisor will also find that many instances arise that require people skills, since he or she will be called upon to resolve conflicts, motivate workers, and communicate management directives. In the Management Challenge, James Kenner exhibited a lack of people skills.

Middle managers have a greater need for conceptual skills and less need for technical skills than first-line managers. But like first-line managers, they must have good people skills. Middle managers also need some conceptual skills because they are required to translate top management's overall objectives into specific, practical plans.

Top managers must possess excellent conceptual skills because they must oversee the entire organization. The ability to look downward through the hierarchy and see how the entire operation fits together is critical for these executives to be effective. But people skills are also vital. Failure to motivate, lead, and communicate with middle managers will cause a lack of enthusiasm necessary to carry out the plans of top management.

FIGURE 1-5 SKILLS OF MANAGEMENT AT VARIOUS LEVELS.

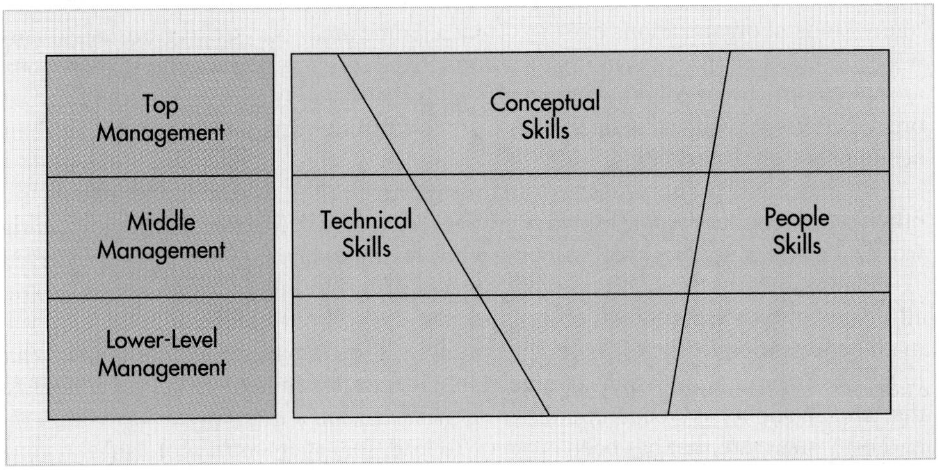

THE RELATIONSHIP OF MANAGEMENT SKILLS AND MANAGEMENT FUNCTIONS

The relationship between management skills and functions is quite simple—the *skills* of management are needed to perform the *functions* of management. For example, communication and people skills are necessary to perform the leading function; technical skills are needed to perform the controlling function; and conceptual skills are needed to perform the planning function.

MEETING THE CHALLENGE

But I Didn't Know What Was Involved in Management!

James Kenner had a rather unpleasant introduction to the practice of management because he did not understand what management was all about. In this chapter, we defined management as the accomplishment of organizational objectives through the efforts of other people. Kenner's experience suggests that he was ignoring this very fundamental aspect of management. He was trying to do most of the work himself, and he was acting as if he was still a maintenance mechanic. Kenner's situation changed dramatically when he was promoted, but he didn't realize it.

People who occupy managerial positions must understand that their responsibility is to accomplish organizational goals through the direction of others. This responsibility is fulfilled by performing the functions of management (planning, organizing, leading, and controlling).

In his new position, Kenner became a lower-level manager. As such, he should have been making certain decisions about how to spend his time. Figure 1-4 indicates that managers at the lower levels in an organization must allocate varying amounts of time to all the basic functions of management, but most of their time should be spent on leading others. Kenner spent very little time on any of the management functions and was particularly remiss with respect to leading. As a result, he had little impact on his subordinates. Their performance declined when Kenner took over the maintenance area, and his interpersonal relationships with his subordinates suffered (the workers asked the plant manager to talk to Kenner about his "meddling" in their work, rather than talking directly to Kenner). Overall, Kenner did not understand the difference between managing the work of others and actually doing the work himself. Until he understands this distinction, he will continue to have trouble in a managerial position. ▲

SUMMARY

Many kinds of organizations exist in Canada. Some are profit-seeking business firms, while others are not-for-profit organizations that stress service instead of profit. Some are sole proprietorships, others are partnerships, and still others are corporations. All organizations, regardless of their goals or their form of ownership, need quality management if they are to be effective.

Management is the process of planning, organizing, leading, and controlling other people so that organizational objectives are reached. Managers cannot do all the work themselves, so they coordinate the work of others so that objectives are achieved.

Planning involves deciding what objectives to pursue and then choosing specific strategies to reach those objectives. It is carried out by managers at all levels in all organizations. Organizing is the process of creating an authority structure that helps the organization reach its objectives. It requires outlining the specific tasks that must be done, as well as coordinating these tasks in a meaningful way within the authority structure that has been created. To lead, managers must motivate and communicate with the organization's human resources to ensure that they know what the organization's goals are and what their part is in achieving them. The leading function deals with the important issue of people in organizations. The controlling function requires managers to ensure that organizational performance matches what was previously planned. In order to carry out this function, managers must establish standards of performance, compare actual performance to the standard, and then take corrective action if necessary.

Looking at managerial functions may not give enough detailed insight into what managers actually do. To understand what managers do in their day-to-day work, we need to look at the roles they play. Three such roles can be identified: (1) interpersonal roles—figurehead, leader, and liaison—involve the manager with other individuals inside and outside the organization; (2) informational roles—monitor, disseminator, and spokesperson—put the manager in a central position for sending and receiving nonroutine information; and (3) decisional roles—entrepreneur, disturbance handler, resource allocator, and negotiator—require the manager to use information to make decisions about how resources should be allocated to reach the organization's goals.

A different kind of manager is found at each of the three basic levels of management in organizations. First-level managers supervise workers who actually perform manual tasks, while middle- and top-level managers supervise other managers. Top-level managers spend more time on the planning, organizing, and controlling functions than middle-level managers, who in turn spend more time on these functions than lower-level managers do. Lower-level managers spend more time on leading than either middle- or top-level managers.

In order to perform the functions of management, managers must possess three basic skills: technical skills (knowledge of work techniques), people skills (the ability to get along with others), and conceptual skills (the capacity to see the organization as a complete unit). The emphasis placed on these skills varies according to organizational level, with lower-level managers placing a great deal of emphasis on technical and human skills, and top managers stressing conceptual skills.

KEY TERMS

management (p. 4)
manager (p. 4)
efficiency (p. 5)
effectiveness (p. 5)
organization (p. 5)
business firm (p. 10)
profit (p. 11)
sole proprietorship (p. 11)
partnership (p. 11)
corporation (p. 12)
shareholders (p. 12)
common stock (p. 13)
preferred stock (p. 13)
board of directors (p. 13)
corporation bylaws (p. 14)
not-for-profit organizations (p. 15)
planning (p. 16)
organizing (p. 16)
leading (p. 16)
controlling (p. 17)
role (p. 17)
interpersonal roles (p. 18)
informational roles (p. 18)
decisional roles (p. 19)
first-line managers (p. 20)
middle managers (p. 20)
top managers (p. 20)
functional managers (p. 22)
general managers (p. 23)
technical skills (p. 23)
people skills (p. 23)
conceptual skills (p. 23)

REVIEW QUESTIONS

1. How are profit-seeking business firms and not-for-profit organizations different? How are they similar?
2. What is management? What are the functions that all managers perform?
3. Briefly describe the 10 managerial roles identified by Mintzberg. What is the difference between management "roles" and "functions?"
4. How are first-level, middle-level, and top-level management jobs different? What is the relative emphasis on the functions of management in each of these jobs?
5. List and briefly describe the three skills of management that are necessary to perform the management functions. How does emphasis on these three skills change as one moves from first-level to middle-level to top-level management?

DISCUSSION QUESTIONS

1. Why is the study of management important?
2. Explain the similarities and differences in the following managerial jobs: police chief, hospital administrator, YMCA director, and plant manager.
3. Choose one of the jobs in question 2 and describe how Mintzberg's managerial roles would be carried out for that job.
4. Is a person who has been successful at managing in a private-sector organization likely to be successful at managing in a public-sector organization? Why or why not?
5. Do students in universities and colleges learn simply what management is about, or do they learn things that will help them to be good managers?

EXERCISES

1. Find an article in *Canadian Business* in which a manager is interviewed or profiled. Try to develop answers to the following questions:
   a. What is the person's view of what management is all about?
   b. What major functions does the person perform as a manager?
   c. What skills are necessary for effective management?
2. Obtain a recent copy of either *The Globe and Mail* or your local newspaper. Look at the classified ads for management positions. What kind of educational training is needed to become a manager? How important is experience?
3. Think back to a full- or part-time job you have had. What functions did your boss perform? Was your boss a good manager? Why or why not?
4. Consider five profit-oriented businesses and five not-for-profit organizations of your choosing. Compare them, using whatever dimensions you feel are important. What are the similarities in the organizations? What are the differences?

MANAGEMENT ON LOCATION

CASE 1-1
Leading the League

Paul Beeston is the CEO of the Toronto Blue Jays. His associates think that, like Tom Hanks in the movie *Big*, he walks a fine line between crazy kid and top-notch executive. Beeston, who is legendary for his commitment to the organization, started as the team's first full-time accountant and rose through the ranks to become president in 1989. He arrives at work between 7 a.m. and 7:30 a.m. each day, and hasn't taken a vacation in four years. With the team's 1992 and 1993 World Series victories and its profitable condition, Beeston has much to be proud of.

Beeston works closely with executive vice-president Pat Gillick. Beeston handles the administration and balances the books, while Gillick monitors the team's on-the-field performance. Beeston has signed players like Dave Winfield, Roberto Alomar, and George Bell to big-time deals and has a reputation as a tough but fair negotiator. He responds to fan outrage at high player salaries by saying that baseball players need a good environment to work in. The Blue Jays' salary budget for 1992 was over $40 million.

Beeston is under constant pressure to win games and pennants. This is not a simple matter, since the club has 25 often temperamental ballplayers. It is necessary to continually find new players through the scouting system and to keep those players coming through the system. ▲

QUESTIONS

1. What skills of management does Paul Beeston need to be effective? How have these changed over the years as he has moved from accountant to CEO?
2. Briefly describe how each of the functions of management are carried out by Paul Beeston.
3. Is being CEO of a baseball team much different than being CEO of a manufacturing firm? Explain.

CASE 1-2
From Professor to Manager

Gerhard Bruckner was born and raised in the U.S., but moved to Canada after he received his M.B.A. in 1968. He took a job at a Canadian university in the Faculty of Management, and taught introduction to business, and principles of management. In 1971, the school offered to pay part of his expenses if he returned to school for his Ph.D. He accepted the offer, and completed his degree in 1974.

By the late 1970s, Bruckner was a fairly well-established academic. He had several articles published in refereed journals, had written one book, and was working on another. He taught a variety of management courses, and his teaching ratings were good. He was involved in faculty committees, and was active in conducting executive development seminars for public- and private-sector managers.

In 1981, the head of the Management Department decided to step down and a search committee was formed to look for a replacement. The former head asked Bruckner if he was interested in applying, and after considering the idea for a few weeks, Bruckner submitted his name for consideration. One month later, he was informed that he had been chosen by the selection committee as the new head of the Department of Management. He later discovered that he had been the only candidate.

The first few months on the job were quite hectic, but the former head was very helpful in explaining how to handle the wide variety of issues that demanded decisions. There were some major changes in Bruckner's work schedule, the most notable being that he now taught fewer courses (two instead of five). This allowed him to give the appropriate level of attention to his administrative duties.

Initially, Bruckner felt pretty comfortable with his new duties as department head. But as time passed, he began to feel some ambivalence about

• • •

the job because it seemed to prevent him from pursuing some of the activities that he had formerly enjoyed as a full-time academic. Eventually he came to the conclusion that he was feeling "harassed" by his job.

After further thought, he identified three problem areas. First, he felt that his administrative duties were pressuring him to the point where he could not devote as much time as he wanted to writing books and articles. Second, he was beginning to view student consultations with annoyance because they also took time away from his writing. He felt somewhat guilty about this, reasoning that, after all, a professor's job is to teach. He knew that his students could sense his impatience with them because his most recent teaching evaluations had been the lowest of his career. Finally, he had been told by two members of his department that he was not available enough for consultation with faculty members, and that when he did talk to them he conveyed the impression that he had better things to do.

As he sat in his office late one afternoon, Bruckner realized that he was not very happy. ▲

QUESTIONS

1. What is the basic problem that Bruckner is facing? What are the causes?
2. How does being a professor differ from being a department head?
3. Did the selection committee make a mistake in promoting Bruckner to department head?
4. What skills are important for Bruckner as a department head in a university?
5. Does being a good professor guarantee success as a department head? Why or why not?

CASE 1-3
BOARD RESPONSIBILITIES AT ROYAL TRUSTCO

Royal Trustco Ltd. had faded into history, but debate continues about the role the members of the board of directors played in the company's bankruptcy. Royal Trustco's chairperson Hartland MacDougall told a meeting of shareholders that the board had worked very hard in pursuing shareholder interests, and that they had done a good job. But Jack Hickman, a U.S. banker, said the failure at Royal Trustco is a failure of the board. Donald Thain, a business professor at The University of Western Ontario, says that board members have the responsibility to stop management from taking risks which will bankrupt the company.

The board at Royal Trustco (which included hockey legend Jean Beliveau) apparently came to grips with the company's problems in time to save depositors, but not shareholders. The board was apparently captive of management right to the end. This is not unusual in Canada, where power is concentrated in the hands of a few people, and the same names come up again and again on different boards. Institutional investors do not make waves like they do in the U.S., and the balance of power rests with the CEO.

What actually happened around the boardroom table is not known, but in retrospect, the mistakes are easy to see. The board went along with former CEO Michael Cornelissen's fast-track growth strategy and watched as the company made high-risk investments in commercial real estate in Canada, the U.S., and Britain. At least one director feels that the company did not have enough concern for its depositors.

The chairperson of the board, on the other hand, feels that the company's troubles started when nervous depositors started moving their savings elsewhere when they heard rumours that the company was in trouble. Some other directors argue vigorously that they challenged management on many occasions regarding the company's strategy. Each time, top managers were able to convince board members that the company was on the right track. When disastrous financial results eventually were presented to the board, they were in shock, and couldn't believe things were that bad. ▲

MANAGEMENT ON LOCATION

QUESTIONS

1. What are the responsibilities of members of the board of directors? Were those responsibilities fulfilled by members of Royal Trustco's board of directors? Defend your answer.
2. Can board members reasonably be expected to comment on the rightness of specific actions or strategies that managers are pursuing?
3. Is it reasonable to expect Royal Trustco's directors to be able to predict external environment changes like a recession and the accompanying decline in the commercial real estate market? Explain.
4. What recourse do shareholders and depositors have when board members do not perform adequately?

CHAPTER 2

THE DEVELOPMENT OF MANAGEMENT KNOWLEDGE

LEARNING OBJECTIVES

After reading this chapter, you will be able to:

1. Explain how thinking about management developed during the last 100 years.
2. Understand the three main streams of the classical approach to management: scientific management, bureaucracy, and administrative management.
3. Explain why the Hawthorne studies were so important in the development of thinking about management.
4. Describe the essential features of the systems approach and the fundamental idea on which it is based.
5. Understand the difference between universalist and contingency approaches to management.
6. Describe the contingency approach to management and give an example of how it works.

MANAGEMENT CHALLENGE

UNITED PARCEL SERVICE

Each day, more than 122,000 boxy, brown delivery trucks from United Parcel Service hit the streets in Canada, the U.S., Puerto Rico, the German Republic, and many other countries. The company, which was started in 1907, delivers 11.5 million packages (750,000 by air) for 2 million different business customers each day. The company has 162 airplanes working out of more than 500 airports. The managers at UPS own most of the company's stock, and many who began as clerks and drivers have retired on very comfortable incomes.

Perhaps the most distinguishing feature of the company is the rigid control that it maintains over every aspect of its operations. Time-and-motion studies have been conducted on virtually every task that workers do. For example, delivery people are supposed to walk three feet per second, hold their key rings with their middle finger, and fold their money face up, sequentially ordered. Drivers are instructed to climb aboard their trucks with their left foot first to avoid wasted steps. Packages are arranged in a precise fashion in the trucks (which have overhead lights so the drivers can read the addresses better). Workers at sorting centres are carefully timed according to strict standards for each task. Drivers are closely timed also; each delivery is timed with a stopwatch. All trucks are washed every day, and they are kept on a strict maintenance schedule.

All these activities have resulted in a very efficient operation, and these efficiencies enabled UPS to achieve market success for more than 50 years. Because of the efficiencies it was able to achieve,

• • •

UPS historically emphasized competing on price. Then, in 1973 a new company called Federal Express began competing on "quick service" rather than price. UPS didn't respond quickly to this challenge; it did not even begin offering overnight delivery until 1982. By the late 1980s, UPS was playing an expensive game of catch-up by expanding overseas, spending massively on package sorting equipment, and enlarging its overnight delivery service. It has also spent considerable time learning about its new overseas markets, and integrating its new employees into its legendary corporate culture. That culture—described by some as "half-Marine, half-Quaker meeting"—emphasizes teamwork rather than individual achievement.

Until very recently, UPS has been legendary for its inward focus. The combination of employee ownership and tight controls on work activity meant that little had changed in the company over the years. Many operating systems had been in place for decades because the corporate culture was skeptical of automation. Because procedures were so finely tuned, most people in the company thought it was impossible to achieve greater efficiency with automation than they were already achieving. When competitors began moving toward high-speed sorting equipment, UPS kept doing things the old way because they were so good at it.

Partly because of its emphasis on internal efficiency, UPS was reluctant to give discounts. Instead, it prided itself on charging the same rates to residential customers as it did for business customers. This policy alienated several large clients. Competitors who were willing to give discounts jumped in to fill the void. Roadway Package System Inc. began offering widespread discounts on large-volume shipments and now offers a package-tracking service to customers. Its market share is expected to double from 5 percent to 10 percent by 1995.

UPS's most formidable competitor is Federal Express, which gives volume discounts and tracks packages for customers. Federal controlled about 45 percent of the air cargo market in 1992, while UPS held about 25 percent. In 1989, Federal acquired Tiger International so that it could increase its market share in the Far East. This will increase the competitive pressures on UPS.

The company is also being challenged by the way that people communicate. UPS believes that electronic data transfer is the wave of the future, and it is determined to be a major player when that time comes. ▲

THE DEVELOPMENT OF MANAGEMENT KNOWLEDGE

LEARNING OBJECTIVE 1

Explain how thinking about management developed during the last 100 years.

Management has been an essential activity since human beings first began to group together. Writings that have come down to us from ancient civilizations clearly show the value of management. The Sumerian civilization gives us the first written indication of management practices in commercial activities and in the development of a postal system. In the Babylonian empire, the Code of Hammurabi deals explicitly with the regulation of trade, business profits, hiring practices, and bad debts. The management activities of the ancient Egyptians are well known. Much has been written about the management skills needed to construct the pyramids, and about the management techniques used to administer the Egyptian empire, particularly those dealing with the centralization and decentralization of authority in government.

Closer to the present time, the Middle Ages in Europe saw developments in the management of business firms, charities, government, and religious organizations. Machiavelli's book entitled *The Prince* was a much-criticized statement about how to manage others to get one's own way.[1]

LEARNING OBJECTIVE 2

Understand the three main streams of the classical approach to management: scientific management, bureaucracy, and administrative management.

In spite of the fact that we can observe management activity throughout human history, it is generally agreed that the serious, systematic study of management did not begin until the late 1800s. In retrospect, it is clear that the development of management thought since the turn of the century has proceeded along five basic lines. These are generally called the classical management approach, the behavioural approach, the management science approach, the systems approach, and the contingency approach. Each is discussed in the following sections.

THE CLASSICAL MANAGEMENT APPROACH

The **classical management approach** tried to provide a rational and scientific basis for the practice of management. Writers from three different countries—Frederick Taylor in the U.S., Max Weber in Germany, and Henri Fayol in France—began developing theories which were to have a great impact on the practice of management. These three writers developed the notions of scientific management, bureaucracy, and administrative management.

classical management approach

Scientific Management

Scientific management attempts to discover the one best way to do a job, and to scientifically select and train workers to do that job. Although many individuals were involved in the scientific management movement, Frederick Taylor (1856–1915) is generally called the "father of scientific management." Taylor was an American mechanical engineer who thought that the best way to improve industrial production was to get people to work more *efficiently*.[2] In his early years as a foreman at the Midvale Steel Company in Philadelphia, Taylor observed different workers doing the same job in different ways. Logically, this meant that each man could not possibly be doing his job in the most efficient way. Using time and motion studies, Taylor set out to find the "one best way" for doing each job. **Time and motion studies** involve using a movie camera and a stopwatch to do a detailed analysis of how a worker is doing a job. The worker's motions are analyzed to determine the most efficient way to do the job. For example, the work of bricklayers was observed and timed to determine which movements would be the most efficient for laying bricks.

scientific management

time and motion studies

Through scientific analysis of jobs, and through the use of incentive payment schemes, Taylor achieved productivity increases of up to 400 percent in worker output. In the loading of iron on rail cars, for example, this meant that each worker could increase his output from 12 tonnes per day to 36 tonnes per day. Under Taylor's scheme, workers were also paid substantially higher wages than their counterparts who were not part of the system.

In his attempt to increase worker productivity, Taylor followed four basic principles:

1. A science of management must be developed to replace rules of thumb, guesswork, and intuition.
2. Workers must be scientifically selected and trained in the one best way to do a job.
3. Workers are motivated largely by money and should therefore be paid on a piece rate basis with an incentive included. Workers who exceed the standard should be paid a bonus on all pieces they produce, not just those above the standard.
4. Labour and management should cooperate because each will benefit by the increased efficiency caused by scientific management.

Taylor has been criticized for putting too much emphasis on the job and not enough on the worker, for dehumanizing the workplace, and for making the overly simplistic assumption that workers are motivated solely by money. Workers often resisted Taylor's attempts to increase output because they feared they would work themselves out of a job if they produced too much. Because of worker suspicion, and because Taylor failed to deal with the emotional and social aspects of work, the cooperation between labour and management that Taylor envisioned never materialized. The developing union movement also worked against Taylor's attempts to deal with workers on an individual basis. Taylor was also accused of falsifying some of his experiments, and of using ideas from others who were researching industrial management.[3]

On balance, however, evaluations of Taylor's work are very positive. Much of our current emphasis on efficient mass production methods can be traced to Taylor's concern for systematically analyzing jobs. Peter Drucker, a management writer, believes that Taylor's work has had the same impact on management as the work of Karl Marx on politics and Sigmund Freud on psychology.[4] Another writer notes that Taylor's ideas on time study, the standardization of work practices, goal setting, money as a motivator, and scientific selection of workers are all successful management techniques that are still useful today.[5]

In addition to Taylor, other individuals also made contributions to scientific management. Henry Gantt, who at one time worked with Taylor, revised Taylor's incentive schemes to increase its motivational impact. He also developed a production scheduling chart—the Gantt chart—which is still widely used today as a production scheduling device.[6] The husband-and-wife team of Frank and Lillian Gilbreth pioneered the use of time and motion studies to increase industrial efficiency. Their work with groups such as bricklayers and surgeons showed how scientific management could improve efficiency.[7] When her husband died at age 46, Lillian Gilbreth continued her work, outlining ways to develop the full potential of workers, rather than simply trying to find the one best way to do a job.

Bureaucracy

Max Weber (1864–1920) was a German sociologist who introduced the notion of bureaucracy.[8] He observed that in the late 1800s, as organizations were increasing in size, many of them were having difficulty making the transition from small to large. Decisions were often influenced by personal and family ties, which caused inconsistency and inefficiency in operations. Individuals often felt more loyalty to other individuals than they did toward the firm.

bureaucracy

Weber felt that organizations could overcome these problems if they were managed on a rational, impersonal basis. A **bureaucracy** emphasizes rules and regulations, clearly defined authority and responsibility, and rational, impersonal decision making to increase organizational effectiveness. The specific characteristics of a bureaucracy are shown in Table 2-1. Overall, the bureaucracy was designed to maintain equal treatment for customers and employees, process customers efficiently, and increase the rationality of decisions.

In spite of these good intentions, bureaucracy is now often viewed as synonymous with inefficiency and bungling. This negative connotation is ironic because Weber saw the bureaucracy as an efficient form of organization. While problems can arise in bureaucracies (see Table 2-2), overall, they are an effective form of organization, so long as the following criteria are met.[9]

1. The organization needs to process large amounts of information (e.g., Revenue Canada, Bank of Montreal, Canada Post, or Great-West Life Assurance).

2. Customer needs are known and do not change rapidly (e.g., registering students at the University of Saskatchewan, or selling auto parts at Bumper-to-Bumper).

3. Employees can be quickly trained to operate the technology to deliver a standardized service to customers (e.g., Wendy's, Mr. Submarine, or Super Lube).

Weber did not prescribe the bureaucratic form as "best." He believed that social scientists should be as neutral as possible in their work and that prescriptions should be left to politicians and management practitioners. He was also concerned

TABLE 2-1 CHARACTERISTICS OF BUREAUCRATIC ORGANIZATIONS.

Characteristics	Description
1. Specialization of labour.	1. Organizational goals are divided into functional specialities, and individuals become experts in their own functional area.
2. Hierarchy of authority.	2. Managerial positions are arranged in strict hierarchial order, with each level being controlled by the next level above it.
3. Clearly defined authority and responsibility.	3. Duties of each manager are clearly spelled out, and lines of authority and accountability are clear.
4. Rules and procedures.	4. Managers are guided by specific rules and procedures to ensure consistency in decision making.
5. Impersonality.	5. Logic, rather than emotions, dictates managerial actions and protects subordinates from managerial whims.
6. Promotion based on technical qualifications.	6. Technical competence and merit are the basis for promotion, instead of some subjective basis.
7. Centralization of authority.	7. To ensure coordination of organizational activities, authority is concentrated at the upper levels of management.
8. Written records.	8. To ensure consistent decisions, files of previous decisions are kept.

TABLE 2-2 POTENTIAL PROBLEMS WITH THE BUREAUCRATIC FORMS OF ORGANZIATION.

Potential Problems	Explanation
1. Rigidity of behaviour.	1. Managers may become more interested in following bureaucratic rules than in effective management.
2. Impersonal treatment of workers, customers, and clients.	2. Although impersonal treatment creates a fairer system, it may also cause employees and customers to feel resentment because they are treated simply "as a number."
3. Overemphasis on functional area goals.	3. Managers within each functional area of the organization may become overly concerned with their area and ignore the overall goals of the organization.
4. Minimum acceptable behaviour.	4. Managers may do only the minimum required by the rules and procedures and not exhibit any initiative or creativity.
5. Resistance to change.	5. The rigidity of the system makes the introduction of change difficult.
6. Red tape and slow decision making.	6. The mass of rules and regulations slows down decision making and reduces the likelihood of timely decisions.

about the impact of bureaucracy on people. He feared that an overemphasis on rationality would lead to a culture which was cold, depersonalized, and lacking in moral purpose; individuals in this kind of culture would feel trapped in an **iron cage of bureaucracy**, both in their work and in their life in general.[10]

iron cage of bureaucracy

Administrative Management

Whereas scientific management focussed on improving performance on the factory floor, the administrative management school of thought focussed on managing the total organization. Henri Fayol (1841–1925), a French industrialist, is one of the major contributors to administrative management thought. Based on his many years of experience in top management, Fayol developed the view that management could be systematically analyzed.[11] He also felt that management skill was not something that a person was born with, but rather, was something that could be developed.

According to Fayol, managers would be most effective if they followed his 14 "principles of management" (see Table 2-3). Fayol stressed that these principles were not absolutes and should not be rigidly applied. A manager should temper these principles with experience and judgment, and take into account relevant situational factors.

Fayol also proposed that the practice of management could be described by refering to four functions: planning, organizing, commanding (leading), and controlling. These functions are still used as the basis for many management textbooks, including this one.

Summary of the Classical Approach

The classical approach identified management as a fundamental activity in society. It also developed many specific techniques to help practising managers (e.g., time and motion studies, wage incentive systems, and scheduling charts). Its notions about the functions of management, and its insights into efficiency and effectiveness in the workplace have provided a foundation for the practice of management.

The classical approach does, however, have some shortcomings. The greatest deficiency derives from the fact that it evolved when organizations operated in relatively stable and predictable environments. The increasing uncertainty in organizational environments caused by globalization of the world's economy makes some of the classical ideas now seem simple-minded. Another criticism is that the classical principles are vague. As we shall see, management is a complex phenomenon, and trying to explain all of its variations by reference to a few general principles is impossible.

TABLE 2-3 FAYOL'S 14 PRINCIPLES OF MANAGEMENT.

Principle	Explanation
1. Division of labour.	1. The greater the specialization of work, the greater the efficiency that will be achieved (e.g., the mass production assembly line).
2. Authority.	2. Authority allows managers to carry out their basic function of achieving goals through others.
3. Discipline.	3. Employees must adhere to the rules and regulations that govern the organization.
4. Unity of command.	4. Each person should report to only one boss, otherwise confusion could develop as a result of conflicting orders.
5. Unity of direction.	5. Each area of the organization should be headed by one person so that plans will be focussed.
6. Subordination of the individual to the common good.	6. The interests of the organization as a whole take precedence over the interests of individual employees.
7. Remuneration.	7. Employees should be paid on a fair basis for the work they do.
8. Centralization.	8. Managers should retain final responsibility for decisions, but should give subordinates enough authority to do their jobs properly.
9. Hierarchy.	9. The chain of authority runs clearly from top management to the lowest employee in the organization.
10. Order.	10. Material resources should be in the right place at the right time. People should be put in jobs that are appropriate for them.
11. Equity.	11. Subordinates should be treated fairly by bosses.
12. Stability.	12. Employee turnover should be kept as low as possible.
13. Initiative.	13. Subordinates must have freedom to do their job, even if this occasionally results in errors.
14. Esprit de corps.	14. Team spirit should be promoted in the organization so that everyone feels part of a unified team.

THE BEHAVIOURAL APPROACH

The ideas of the classical school led to increased efficiency in the production of products. However, managers continued to be frustrated by the unpredictability of people's behaviour, and therefore they were receptive to new approaches which would address the "people problem." The **behavioural approach** stresses the importance of people in attaining organizational productivity. This school of thought includes the human relations movement, the writings of Mary Parker Follett and Chester Barnard, and modern behavioural science.

behavioural approach

The Human Relations Movement

In a general sense, human relations refers to the ways that people interact. The **human relations movement** examines how managers and subordinates interact and advocates that management make the gratification of workers' social and psychological needs a primary concern. Thus, managers should get to know their subordinates as people, not simply as workers who are filling a position. If managers do this, so the argument goes, they will get important insights into what motivates their workers, and, with these insights, managers can more effectively manage people.

human relations movement

The Hawthorne studies are perhaps the most well known studies in the human relations tradition. The **Hawthorne studies** found that social factors in the workplace were at least as important as physical factors in determining employee productivity. These studies were conducted over a nine-year time span, and dealt with issues such as the effect of rest periods, the impact of lighting intensity, and the influence of work groups on individual behaviour (see Figure 2-1).[12]

Hawthorne studies

LEARNING OBJECTIVE 3

Explain why the Hawthorne studies were so important in the development of thinking about management.

One early study in the series was designed to explore the relationship between lighting and productivity. If this relationship could be determined, management could set levels of illumination that would maximize productivity. The researchers were unable to find a systematic relationship between illumination and productivity, so they were forced to look for other explanations of variations in employee output. After conducting several additional studies, the researchers concluded that social factors had a greater effect on employee behaviour than physical working conditions. The manager's style of supervision, interpersonal relationships on the job, freedom to choose work methods, and group norms all were found to affect work output.

One of the noteworthy and unanticipated outcomes of the Hawthorne studies was the identification of the so-called Hawthorne effect. The **Hawthorne effect** refers to the tendency of work groups to show improved productivity if management pays special attention to them. In the various studies in the Hawthorne series, special groups had been formed so that the impact of different working conditions (e.g., rest periods) could be measured. But workers interpreted this to mean that management was concerned about them and had therefore singled them out for special attention. Hence, they worked harder because they felt valued.

Hawthorne effect

Another significant finding was that work groups had an impact on the behaviour of individuals. In an interviewing program, the researchers found that workers felt that factory life was dull and rather meaningless; interpersonal relations within work groups, however, gave meaning to workers' lives. Because the group was more highly valued than work, it had a stronger influence on employee productivity than management activity.[13]

Mary Parker Follett and Chester Barnard

After observing practising managers in action, Mary Parker Follett (1868–1933) reached several conclusions about effective management.[14] In spite of the fact that Follett was writing during the heydey of scientific management, her ideas stress the importance of the human element in organizations. Among her proposals were the following:

FIGURE 2-1 THE FLOW, CONTENT, AND CONCLUSIONS OF THE HAWTHORNE STUDIES.

Flowchart	Physical work environment	Physical work requirements	Management and supervision	Social relations of workers	Description and Conclusion
(1) ILLU-MINATION	X				Three exploratory studies that suggested human factors, rather than physical working conditions, determined work satisfaction and performance.
(2) FIRST RELAY	X	X	X	X	The major Hawthorne experiment, testing effects on performance of rest pauses, shorter work periods, increased worker autonomy, and small-group incentive pay. This study concluded that benefits to worker performance resulted from improved human relations, and to a lesser extent from rest pauses.
(3) SECOND RELAY			X		Derivative experiment suggesting only moderate effects of small-group incentive pay upon worker performance.
(4) MICA SPLITTING		X			Derivative experiment suggesting only moderate effects of rest and shorter work periods upon worker performance.
(5) INTER-VIEWING			X	X	Derivative survey reinforcing prior conclusions regarding importance of social interactions (worker-worker and worker-supervisor) in the satisfaction of workers. First indications, during intensive inter-views early in 1931, of problems resulting from employee inter-relations, especially in restriction of output.
(6) BANK WIRING				X	Derivative observation noting the effectiveness of social interactions in a large group of workers in standardizing the pace of work (restricting output during period of economic depression).

1. Decentralization of authority (individuals closest to "the action" should make the decision).
2. Two-way communication between managers and workers (this would allow managers to make better decisions).
3. Participative management (involve workers in decisions).
4. Partnership between labour and management (establish a good working relationship so that organizational goals can be accomplished).

As president of New Jersey Bell Telephone, Chester Barnard (1886–1961) expressed a number of views that are still popular today.[15] He regarded organizations as places where individuals and resources came together to achieve certain goals. But he reasoned that people would not work for an organization unless they could satisfy some of their own needs at the same time. An organization would be most effective if organizational and individual goals were kept in balance.

Barnard also looked at the role and limits of authority. The **zone of acceptance** demarcates what workers are willing to do without questioning a manager's authority. For example, if a manager asks a worker to make a parts pickup at a local supplier, the worker would likely do it because it falls within the worker's normal activities. But if the manager asked the worker to drive 150 kilometres to a parts supplier, the worker might feel that this was outside the zone of acceptance.

zone of acceptance

Barnard felt that management should strive to move as many activities as possible into the zone of acceptance because this would lead to a smooth functioning organization. The zone could be widened by increasing the rewards given to workers for complying with management requests. Barnard also recognized the existence of the informal organization (see Chapter 9), and stressed that management had to support it if it hoped to utilize groups in the pursuit of organizational goals.

Modern Behavioural Science

The human relations movement pioneered the use of systematic analysis to study human behaviour in organizations. By the 1950s, researchers who had been trained in fields like anthropology, psychology, and sociology were beginning to examine people at work in earnest. These researchers gradually became known as behavioural scientists. Chris Argyris, Abraham Maslow, Frederick Herzberg, and Douglas McGregor became famous for their investigations into the role of people in organizations. We discuss these and other behavioural scientists in later chapters.

Behavioural scientists believe people in organizations are much more complex than either the "economic being" of scientific management or the "social being" of the human relations approach. They are also interested in finding ways to motivate and lead employees, and in matching individuals and jobs through a systematic assessment of both people and the work environment.

THE MANAGEMENT SCIENCE APPROACH

The **management science approach** emphasizes the use of mathematics and statistics to solve management problems in the areas of production, marketing, and finance. This approach originated during World War II when the Allies gathered together teams of experts to develop systems for helping shipping convoys avoid German submarines. These systems were based on mathematical techniques that were designed to show the optimum solution to complicated problems. After the war, many of the management science techniques that had been developed were applied to business problems.

management science approach

Recently, the computer has become a powerful tool in management science because it can do the massive calculations that are needed to solve many management science problems. Management science focusses much more on technical problems facing organizations than it does on social and psychological problems. In that sense, management science is a modern version of scientific management.

Management science has made a contribution to management through the development of mathematical formulas and modelling to resolve complex problems. In spite of these contributions, management science has not yet reached the point where it can make a noticeable contribution to the management of people.[16] Perhaps this is not so much a criticism of management science as it is of our general lack of understanding about people. Until this understanding develops, management scientists will not be able to formulate mathematical models and equations that will tell managers how to deal with the human side of organizations.

The Systems Approach

systems approach

The **systems approach** views an organization as a complex set of interrelated factors that must be integrated in order for the organization to reach its goals. This approach also views all parts of the system as both consequences and determinants of each other, i.e., all parts of the system are closely related and influence each other. Thus, changing one part of the system will have some effect (large or small) on other parts of the system.[17]

LEARNING OBJECTIVE 4

Describe the essential features of the systems approach and the fundamental idea on which it was based.

Suppose a firm that wants to improve the accuracy of its sales forecasts introduces an incentive scheme which gives salespeople a bonus if their sales forecast is within 2 percent of their actual sales. Such a system will obviously have consequences for salespeople, but it may also have consequences for the production area. If sales forecasts are more accurate, the production area will be able to schedule its output more accurately so that shortages or excesses do not develop. Thus, a change in one part of the system benefits another part of the system.

Failure to think in systems terms causes disruptions in organizations. Consider the company that was confronted with lower-than-expected output in its start-up production of a new product. It called in a consultant to make recommendations on how to get output up to standard. The consultant's suggestions worked and output increased. But this increased output—which was the input for one department—caused problems because another department could not cope with increased input without making changes in its own operation.

open system

The systems approach also emphasizes the integration of the organization with its external environment. Organizations are **open systems** which take inputs from their external environment, transform them into outputs (physical goods or services), and then direct these outputs out to the external environment (see Figure 2-2). All organizations are open systems, but some are more open than others. Procter & Gamble, for example, is more open to its external environment than Stony Mountain Penitentiary. The effect of the external environment on organizations is discussed in Chapter 3.

The external environment of each organization affects how it operates. A union's decision to go on strike closes down the processor which turns inputs into output. If a supplier goes on strike, some companies will be unable to get the raw materials (inputs) that are necessary to operate the processor. Government legislation may place certain restrictions on a firm that inhibit its activities (e.g., the banning of tobacco advertising in 1989). Or competitors may develop a new product that makes one of the firm's current products obsolete. The impact of the external environment on organizations is the subject of Chapter 3.

FIGURE 2-2 A SYSTEMS MODEL OF ORGANIZATIONS.

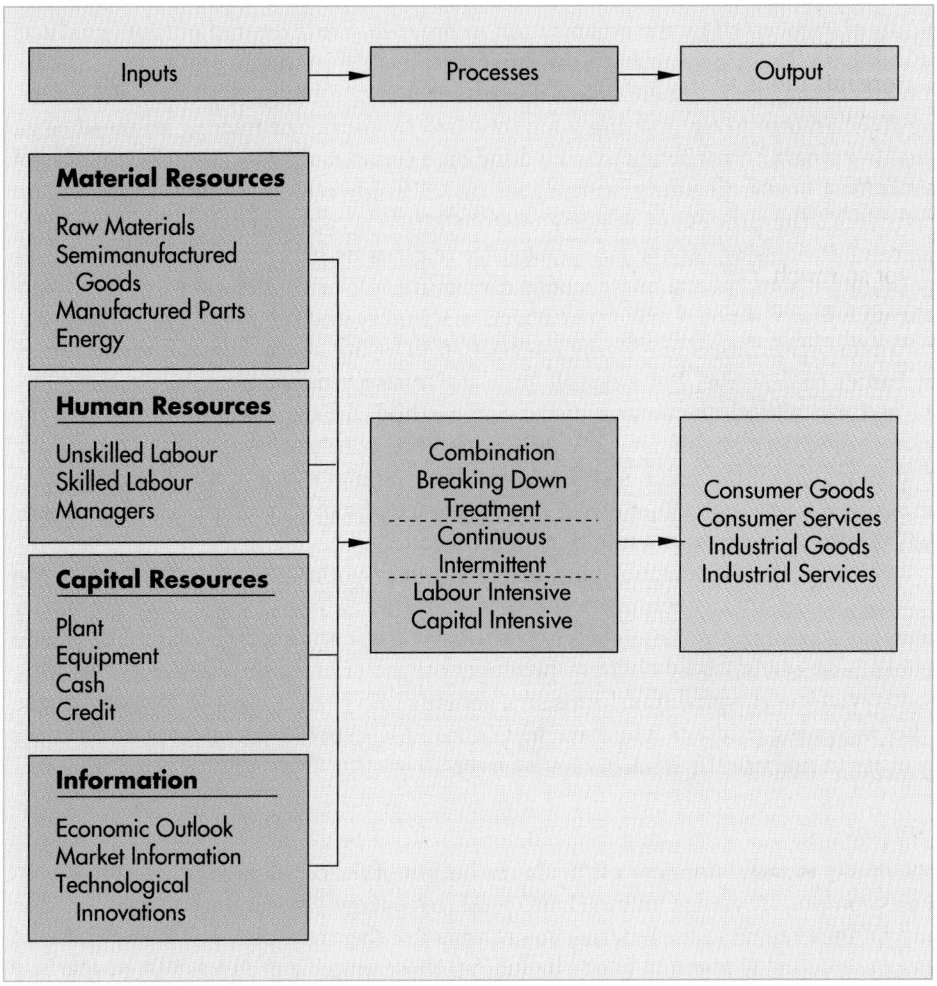

Inputs

Just as people cannot live without food and water, organizations cannot survive without inputs. These inputs may be (1) materials (energy, raw materials, semi-manufactured products, or manufactured parts), (2) human resources (unskilled labour, skilled labour, and managers), (3) capital resources (cash, credit, plant, and equipment), and (4) information (data about the market). The inputs needed by the system vary according to the objectives or goals of the organization. A manufacturer of high-quality jewellery requires hard-to-find precious metals, gems, and skilled workers. In contrast, the operator of a fast food outlet requires easy-to-obtain food, packaging supplies, and a supply of unskilled employees willing to work for the minimum wage.

A profit-seeking business firm like Mad Max's Carpet Cleaning uses inputs like cleaning supplies, cleaning equipment, and human skill to produce a service (carpet cleaning). A not-for-profit organization like Humber College uses instructors, buildings, and teaching materials to produce educated graduates. As we shall see in the next chapter, every organization is dependent on its external environment for the specific inputs it needs.

SmithBooks focusses largely on physical products (books) for the consumer market by providing educational, self-help, and entertainment-oriented books to individual consumers.

Processing

Inputs are processed by the organization in order to create desired output (products or services). In an organization producing a physical product, processing may involve *combining* two or more material inputs (e.g., assembling an automobile), *breaking down* an input (e.g., cutting a log into two-by-fours), or *treating* an input (e.g., smoking a ham). Processing may be done on a *continuous* basis (e.g., the process of converting crude oil into gasoline goes on 24 hours a day), or on an *intermittent* basis (e.g., the process of making custom kitchen cabinets starts and stops frequently). Processing may be *labour intensive* (e.g., using many workers to pick apples by hand without the use of specialized machinery), or *capital intensive* (e.g., harvesting wheat with expensive specialized machinery and relatively few workers).

In an organization producing a service, processing also occurs, although it may be harder to describe. For example, in a university, students may be processed by the lecture method, the lecture-discussion method, the experiential method, or the case method. In a health care situation, patients may be processed within a hospital, or they may treat themselves at home and have regular visits by a qualified visiting nurse. In a food service operation, customers may be processed by waiters, or they may go through a cafeteria line to get their food.

Whether the organization produces a physical good or a service, a conversion process occurs that is central to the organization's activity. Ford Motor Company takes steel, aluminum, and glass and converts these inputs into automobiles and trucks. Canada Safeway changes products on the shelves into desired consumer goods. Victoria Hospital transforms sick patients into healthy people. Seneca College takes incoming students who have had certain life experiences and builds on these in order to prepare the students for a career.

Output

consumer goods

consumer services

industrial goods

industrial services

The products and services of a firm are the output of the conversion process. IBM produces computers, while Ontario Hydro produces energy. Once inputs are converted to output, they return to the external environment of the organization. This output is of four basic types. **Consumer goods** include all those tangible products that people buy for their own consumption. Pencils, toothpaste, VCRs, breakfast cereal, and automobiles are examples. **Consumer services** include all those intangible items that people buy for their own enjoyment. Hairstyling, insurance, sporting events, education, dry cleaning, and bowling are consumer services. **Industrial goods** are tangible products purchased by businesses and other institutions to use in producing other goods or services. Among such goods are construction equipment, diesel locomotives, electric motors, office supplies, truck tires, and office buildings. **Industrial services** are intangible items purchased by businesses and other institutions to use in producing other goods or services. These include security services, market research reports, and legal advice. Examples of the input and output of a variety of organizations are shown in Table 2-4.

THE CONTINGENCY APPROACH

LEARNING OBJECTIVE 5

Understand the difference between universalist and contingency approaches to management.

universalist theories

As we shall see later in this book, two fundamental types of theories have developed in the field of management. **Universalist theories** propose that there is "one best way" to manage organizations and people. These theories hold that management can be reduced to certain principles that are universally applicable. They neither consider individual differences in people, nor do they consider how different situations might influence the kind of management that should be used. They take the view that a given managerial practice will always be effective.

TABLE 2-4 EXAMPLES OF INPUTS AND OUTPUTS.

Organization	Input	Output
Jewellery store	Merchandise	Customer sales
	Store building	
	Salesclerks	
	Registers	
	Jeweller	
	Customer	
Post office	Sorting machines	Delivered mail
	Trucks	
	Postal clerks and carriers	
	Postmaster	
	Mail	
Hospital	Doctors and nurses	Recovered patient
	Staff	
	Buildings	
	Beds and equipment	
	Power	
	Supplies	
	Patients	
Manufacturing plant	Machines	Consumer goods
	Plant	Materials for purchase
	Raw Materials	by other firms
	Workers	
	Managers	
University	Faculty and staff	Graduates
	Classrooms	Research
	Library	Public service
	Supplies	
	Students	

Contingency (situational) theories assume that different individuals and situations require different managerial practices.[18] Gordon Allan, president of Gordon Allan Consultants of Toronto, noted that managers must be flexible and adapt to the characteristics of specific situations if they hope to be effective.[19] Contingency theories developed because managers and researchers observed that techniques or ideas that worked well in one situation often failed to work when applied in other situations. Thus, it would be inappropriate to try to manage the University of Toronto in the same way as Canada Cement Lafarge. Though the management functions are the same in all types of organizations, the way they are carried out varies with the type of organization. Figure 2-3 illustrates the basic difference between the universalist and contingency approaches.

contingency (situational) theories

LEARNING OBJECTIVE 6

Describe the contingency approach to management and give an example of how it works.

FIGURE 2-3 A COMPARISON OF THE UNIVERSALIST AND CONTINGENCY APPROACHES TO MANAGEMENT.

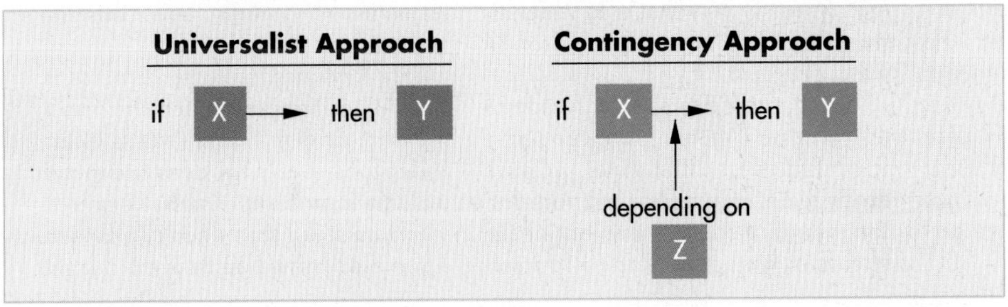

Contingency theories try to specify the variables that determine which managerial practices should be used in which situation. As might be expected, contingency theories are more complicated than universalist theories. Table 2-5 contrasts universalist and contingency theories in several areas of management. The Management at Work insert entitled "A Real-Life Contingency Analysis" illustrates how contingency theory works to solve an everyday problem.

TABLE 2-5 EXAMPLES OF UNIVERSALIST AND CONTINGENCY THEORIES.

Universalist Theories	Contingency Theories
1. Democratic leadership is always more effective than autocratic leadership.	1. The type of leadership which is most effective depends on the characteristics of the leader, the followers, and the situation.
2. All workers desire more challenge and responsibility in their work.	2. Whether a given worker wants more challenge and responsibility in his or her work depends on individual characteristics of the worker.
3. Employees at all levels in the organization are motivated by money.	3. Whether employees are motivated by money depends on several factors, including the nature of the job, the characteristics of the employee, and the intrinsic interest the employee has in doing the job.
4. Low morale causes lower productivity.	4. Low morale may lead to low productivity in certain situations (e.g., unstructured jobs), but not to lower productivity in other situations (e.g. assembly line operations).
5. There is an ideal structure for all organizations.	5. The best structure for an organization depends on a variety of factors, including size, the technology that is used to produce the product or service, the environment in which the organization operates, and so forth.

MANAGEMENT AT WORK

A Real-Life Contingency Analysis

Imagine that you have just arrived home after a hard day at work. You decide that a hot shower is just what you need to unwind. You hop in the shower, adjust the water to just the right temperature, and proceed to enjoy yourself. Suddenly, the water pressure drops noticeably. Seconds later, the water temperature also drops. You leap out of the way of the now-cold water and flatten yourself against the wall of the shower, muttering not-so-pleasant thoughts under your breath. Seconds later, both water pressure and temperature return to normal.

At this point, you may be tempted to develop a universalist theory of taking showers. You say to yourself, "Whenever the pressure drops, I will leap out of the way to avoid the cold water that is sure to come." This theory obviously says that cold water always (universally) follows a drop in water pressure.

You continue to shower, ready to test your new theory. Sure enough, a few minutes later the water pressure drops again. Having learned your lesson, you immediately leap out of the stream of water and flatten yourself against the wall. However, this time as you reach out your hand to test the water temperature, you notice that the water is still nice and hot. Your universalist theory has just failed, so you must begin to think in contingency terms if you intend to solve this annoying problem.

The key question to be answered is this: What happens when the water pressure drops? The answer is clear: It depends. But what does it depend on? An important insight is gained when we recall that when two taps in a home are turned on, you will not get ...

as much pressure out of either tap as you would if only one were on. Most people also know that if one tap is running a mixture of hot and cold water, and another hot water tap is turned on, the temperature of the first tap will decline. Combining these two pieces of information allows us to construct a contingency theory of taking showers.

In the first instance (where the drop in water pressure also resulted in a drop in water temperature) we can hypothesize that one of the other hot water taps in the house was turned on. This extra demand for hot water diverted some hot water from your shower and hence the temperature dropped shortly after the pressure dropped. In the second instance (when the temperature did not drop following a drop in pressure) we can hypothesize that someone turned on both the hot and cold water at another tap at the same time. This caused a drop in pressure, but not a drop in temperature.

This contingency perspective can be applied in your work as a manager. In all likelihood, if you have a contingency approach to management, you will be more effective because you will not make simplistic assumptions about cause-and-effect relationships in the workplace. ▲

MEETING THE CHALLENGE

UNITED PARCEL SERVICE

After losing business to aggressive competitors like Federal Express and Roadway Package System, UPS has dramatically changed the way it does business. In 1990, CEO Kent Nelson ordered a sweeping examination of the company's business methods. The company's flaws were identified and fixed so that UPS could more effectively respond to competitive rivals.

The "we know what's best for the customer" attitude was one of the first casualties. Previously, UPS had the view that they knew what was best for their corporate customers. But in 1990, with Eastman Kodak thinking about dropping UPS because of its "bad attitude," things began to change. Now, UPS emphasizes customer satisfaction, offers flexible pickup and delivery times, customized shipment plans, and discount prices to volume shippers.

The head office marketing staff has been increased from 7 to 175, and face-to-face interviews have been conducted with 25,000 customers to find out what services they want. UPS has increased its advertising budget from $75,000 in 1981 to $18 million in 1990. It is also trying to improve its image with the public. It launched a $35 million television advertising campaign (its first ever) focussing on the now well-known slogan "We run the tightest ship in the shipping business."

UPS has added to its air fleet and is matching technically advanced rivals with such devices as electronic scanners in its sorting centres and on-board computer in its delivery trucks. Between 1986 and 1991, UPS increased its spending on information technology almost tenfold, spending an average of $300 million per year. By 1996, the company will have spent an additional $3.2 billion on information technology. The company is in good shape financially, with only $114 million in debt, compared with $2.5 billion in employee equity.

In addition to its spending on advertising and equipment, UPS has also purchased a number of small foreign companies to get a foothold in the overseas package delivery market. It has also spent $1.4 billion on a system to efficiently track packages from door-to-door. A key part of the system is an in-house invention called a "dense code" which holds twice the information in a normal bar code. Scanners in the field and at sorting centres can read information on package origin, destination, and contents. The system is designed to leapfrog Federal Express's system. A system called GroundTrac has also been introduced; it allows shippers to get status reports on their ground packages 24 hours a day just by calling a toll-free number.

But with all these changes, UPS is still committed to its emphasis on worker efficiency and commitment. That's the way the company achieved its success, and it will continue to bring new workers into a corporate culture where efficiency is a key word. ▲

SUMMARY

The serious, systematic study of management began about 100 years ago. The classical approach tried to make a rational and scientific study of management. It had three major streams: (1) scientific management (which focussed on improving the efficiency of operative work); (2) bureaucracy (which developed rules and regulations and clearly defined structures for organizations); and (3) administrative management (which developed management principles which could be used to manage all aspects of the enterprise). The behavioural approach, which emerged later, examined the social and psychological factors that influenced organizational effectiveness. The human relations stream of the behavioural approach advocated treating employees well so that they would work enthusiastically for the organization, while behavioural scientists stressed systematic analysis of organizations and the people in them to determine how to effectively manage. The management science approach emphasizes the use of mathematics and statistics to solve management problems, typically in the areas of production, finance, and marketing.

The systems approach views each organization as a complex set of interrelated factors that must be integrated in order for the organization to reach its goals. The contingency approach holds the position that different managerial practices are required in different situations. It tries to identify the variables in each situation that determine exactly how management should be carried out.

KEY TERMS

classical management approach (p. 33)
scientific management (p. 33)
time and motion studies (p. 33)
bureaucracy (p. 34)
iron cage of bureaucracy (p. 35)
behavioural approach (p. 37)
human relations movement (p. 37)
Hawthorne studies (p. 37)
Hawthorne effect (p. 37)
zone of acceptance (p. 39)
management science approach (p. 39)
systems approach (p. 40)
open system (p. 40)
consumer goods (p. 42)
consumer services (p. 42)
industrial goods (p. 42)
industrial services (p. 42)
universalist theories (p. 42)
contingency (situational) theories (p. 43)

REVIEW QUESTIONS

1. What was the main goal of the classical approach to management?
2. List and briefly describe the three main streams of thought within the classical approach to management.
4. Why did the behavioural science approach gain momentum in the 1920s?
5. What are the essential features of the management science approach? Why does this approach have difficulties in dealing with the human element in organizations?
6. Describe the key ideas in the systems approach to management. How are these ideas relevant to the management of organizations? Give an example.
7. What is involved in the universalist and contingency approaches to management? How are they different?
8. What are the advantages and disadvantages of division of labour?

DISCUSSION QUESTIONS

1. Frederick Taylor believed that management and labour should work toward a common cause. Was Taylor's idea sound? Why or why not?
2. Explain the similarities and differences in the scientific management and administrative management approaches to management. Compare and contrast each of these with Weber's bureaucracy approach.
3. How is behavioural science different from human relations?
4. Explain how knowledge of the history of management thought is useful to an aspiring manager in the 1990s.
5. The notion of "one best way to do a job" is key in scientific management. Do you agree that there is one best way to do each job? Defend your answer.
6. Henry Fayol's 14 principles of management were developed as a result of his many years of experience in the industrial sector. To what extent do these principles hold in other sectors (e.g.,

non-profit organizations, service organizations, government organizations)?

7. Consider the following statement: "In the early twentieth century, managers had very specific guidelines to follow in managing workers, but with the emergence of the contingency approach, managers are given only vague guidelines about how to deal with workers. Management theory has made little progress in the twentieth century." Do you agree or disagree? Defend your answer.

EXERCISES

1. Visit a local manufacturing firm and a local fast food operation. In each of them, observe the way production work is carried out. Compare the two organizations in terms of the extent to which scientific management principles are being used.
2. Interview a manager in a large government bureaucracy and determine the following:
   a. the extent to which the organization exhibits the characteristics of a classic bureaucracy.
   b. whether the manager feels that the organization is indeed efficient.
   c. the shortcomings the manager sees in the bureaucratic approach to management.
   d. whether the manager feels that the bureaucratic approach to management is likely to continue into the future, or other forms of organization will take its place.
3. Read an article about a specific company in *The Globe and Mail* or *Canadian Business*. Indicate ways in which the firm has been influenced by the ideas in scientific management, administrative management, and bureaucracy.
4. Use the systems approach to analyze the workings of your university or college. To what extent does the systems approach give you helpful insights about your school?

MANAGEMENT ON LOCATION

CASE 2-1
THE WHITE COLLAR FACTORY

In the head office of a large insurance company, there is an area known as the "white collar factory." This area consists of 60 workstations, each equipped with a computer terminal placed on a specially designed desk, a small bookshelf for computer software manuals, a two-drawer filing cabinet, and a specially designed chair for computer operators. The workstations are separated from each other by two-metre movable partitions. The room has the most modern heating, air conditioning, and lighting equipment available.

At the beginning of each work day, the supervisor of the department analyzes the types and amount of work that have come in from the various other departments in the company. She then decides how this work should be distributed to the various operators. Each workstation is monitored by a computer program which records the type and number of documents processed, errors made, and downtime. At the end of each working day, the program produces a printout of each operator which compares actual output to established standards, total output to standards, and downtime. If the output is below the norm, the first thing the following day the supervisor speaks with the employee about his or her performance level in relation to the standards. She then distributes the new work assignments for the day.

By means of her computer terminal, the supervisor is able to determine from her office the document each employee is processing and how efficiently the worker is processing the document. About once an hour, the supervisor walks through the work area to ensure that the employees are concentrating on their work.

The employees are paid a fixed salary on a monthly basis. The salary is approximately 10 percent above the average for similar jobs in other companies in the area. Every six months, employees who have maintained their performance at or above the standard receive a bonus equivalent to 2 percent of their salary for that period. Those employees who fail to reach the standard by the sixth month of their employment (about 20 percent of those hired) are terminated. Employees who have been in the department for more than six months and fall below the standard are first given a written warning, then placed on probation for three ...

months, and finally terminated if their performance does not improve.

About half the employees in the department are single, and most are between the ages of 18 and 23. For many, this is their first job since graduating from a technical course in keyboarding. During the last year, several of the employees have applied for transfer to other departments which require people with their particular skills. ▲

QUESTIONS

1. What management theories are being applied in this department and what assumptions are being made about the workers?
2. What are some outcomes which might be caused by the practices followed in this department?
3. What advice would you give to senior management about managing in this department? Defend your answer, citing theories and empirical evidence.

CASE 2-2
SCIENTIFIC MANAGEMENT AT UNITED PARCEL SERVICE

As Joseph Polise leaves his United Parcel Service delivery truck, he is closely followed by Marjorie Cusack, an industrial engineer who is timing his every move with a digital timer. She counts the number of steps he takes, how much time he spends with the customer, and numerous other details of his job, including how much time he spends on bathroom breaks.

The way work is carried out at UPS demonstrates that scientific management principles are alive and well. The company was founded in 1907 by James Casey, who relied on Frank Gilbreth and other time and motion pioneers in the 1920s to determine the one best way for drivers to carry out their duties. This emphasis on worker efficiency has continued into the 1990s. While some management consultants see time and motion studies as a throwback to the dark ages, UPS executives have no intention of changing their highly successful operating methods.

Most workers appear to be motivated by the fast pace of work. Some workers have nicknames like Slick, Ace, Hammer, and Rocket Shoes. UPS drivers earn a higher hourly wage than any other workers in the industry. There is a joke in the company that a good driver can deliver a package and get back to the truck before his seat belt stops swaying. But not all drivers enjoy the fast pace of the job. And some supervisors feel that there is a fine line between worker motivation and harassment.

Although UPS has no intention of changing its work methods, its competitors may have something to say about that. Roadway Package System is a competitive package delivery system that is based on an entirely different set of assumptions about how to best manage workers. At Roadway, drivers (nonunionized) are owner-operators; they are motivated by the challenge of running their own business. They don't just drive trucks, they own them. And Roadway is cutting labour expense by 20-30 percent by using nonunion drivers.

Recently, Roadway tried to gain a productivity edge by introducing electronic scanners, bar codes, and mechanical package sorters. UPS executives dismissed these high-tech gadgets as unreliable. Roadway argued that UPS's emphasis on manual sorting was also unreliable. ▲

QUESTIONS

1. Explain how scientific management principles are being put into practice at UPS.
2. Contrast the underlying assumptions that are being made about human beings at UPS and Roadway.
3. What are some of the behavioural outcomes that are likely at these two companies, given their management practices?
4. Are scientific management principles outdated, or will they continue to be useful to business managers?

CHAPTER 3

MANAGING IN THE CANADIAN ENVIRONMENT

LEARNING OBJECTIVES

After reading this chapter, you will be able to:

1. List and describe the seven major environmental factors that affect an organization and its managers as they manage in a Canadian setting.
2. Identify four principal structural features of the Canadian economy.
3. Describe the influences different types of owners have on managers.
4. Outline the challenges imposed on business organizations by competition from within Canada and from outside Canada.
5. Identify the types of government involvement in the Canadian economic system.
6. Describe the changes occurring in the Canadian work force and the expectations of employees.
7. Explain the importance that technological research and development has in ensuring that innovation occurs.
8. Understand the implications of societal trends on managers of organizations.
9. Explain why a manager must continually monitor the environment in which the organization operates.

MANAGEMENT CHALLENGE

BELL CANADA'S ENVIRONMENT: BEFORE AND AFTER 1992

Not even Canada's largest and oldest companies can escape the challenges of the changing Canadian economic, social, and political environment. Bell Canada, incorporated by a Special Dominion Charter in 1880, is Canada's largest supplier of telecommunications services. It owns and operates a public switched network for voice, data, and image communications in Ontario, Quebec, and parts of the Northwest Territories.

Bell Canada grew by expanding its operating area, and merging and acquiring dozens of small telephone companies that operated at one time. It is by far the largest of the 12 telephone companies operating in Canada today. The company provides network access to 2.5 million businesses and 6.5 residential customers. It's revenues are derived from three activities, provision of local access services (33.3 percent), toll and network services (48.4 percent), and terminal, directory, advertising, and other (18.3 percent).

In 1991, local access services generated $2.6 billion in revenue and involved providing basic services to customer, private branch exchange trunks, and Centrix Systems. Toll and network services totalled $3.7 billion and included long distance message toll, WATTS and 800,

...

private voice, and business data services. Terminal, directory, advertising, and other services including the rental, sale and maintenance of equipment totalled $1.4 billion. The $7.7 in revenues generated $986 million in net income, the company made about $2.3 billion in gross capital expenditures, and had 52 661 employees, of which 38 375 were nonmanagement and mostly unionized.

As the company provides a monopoly service, it is a regulated company, in recent years by the Canadian Radio-Television and Telecommunications Commission (CRTC). The CRTC regulates profits and services, and in the 1980s allowed Bell to earn between 12 and 13 percent average rate of return on common equity.

The company was considered to have provided the best telecommunication network in the world. The company, its shareholders, management, and employees were very satisfied in providing a monopoly service while earning very good, and consistent, profits. But things started to change in the 1980s. In 1982 the CRTC allowed customers to purchase their own equipment. Corporate customers claimed that the company was slow in offering state-of-the-art services, and competition appeared in 1990 when resellers started providing selected telecommunications services to large customers.

A major challenge arose when Unitel Communications Inc. applied in the late 1980s to enter the long-distance market. The CRTC made its decision regarding long distance competition in June 1992 and allowed Unitel to enter the market. Bell Canada's environment changed drastically.[1] ▲

In Chapter 1, we introduced the concept of management and talked about what managers do in business and other organizations. We looked at the problems and considerations managers face within an organization. As Bell Canada's circumstances indicate, managers must also be concerned about challenges that arise from circumstances outside of the organization they manage. Changes in the environment of an organization can have a major impact on it. In this chapter we describe some of the principal environmental factors that managers must deal with if they are to be successful. Since there are hundreds of situations a manager might encounter, it is not feasible to identify them all. We will focus on the major factors that are critical to managers in the 1990s.

ENVIRONMENTAL FACTORS IN THE CANADIAN SETTING

LEARNING OBJECTIVE 1

List and describe the seven major environmental factors that affect an organization and its managers as they manage in a Canadian setting.

What happens if the external environment influences the performance of managers and the organization they manage? Managers must be aware of developments outside the firm and take them into account when making decisions. Figure 3-1 shows the major external environmental factors business organizations must consider in Canada: (1) the structural features of the economy; (2) the nature of ownership; (3) the degree of competition; (4) the role of government; (5) the work force; (6) technology and innovation; and (7) societal trends. The circle representing the organization in Figure 3-1 is broken to indicate that the organization does not operate as a closed system isolated from the environment. Note also that the environment does not have boundaries to indicate that the organization does not operate in a closed system. The environment is continually changing depending upon the range and scope of any organization's activities as determined by managers.

Several general observations about the seven factors can be made. First, managers at different levels in the management hierarchy have differing degrees of involvement with the external environment. Generally speaking, the higher in the organizational hierarchy managers are, the more their work is affected directly by the external environment. First-line supervisors have less managerial concern for activities outside the organization. For example, these managers are unlikely to contact politicians or senior civil servants regarding a government regulation. Top-level managers, such as vice-presidents, on the other hand, may spend a great deal of their

FIGURE 3-1 ENVIRONMENTAL FACTORS IN THE CANADIAN SETTING.

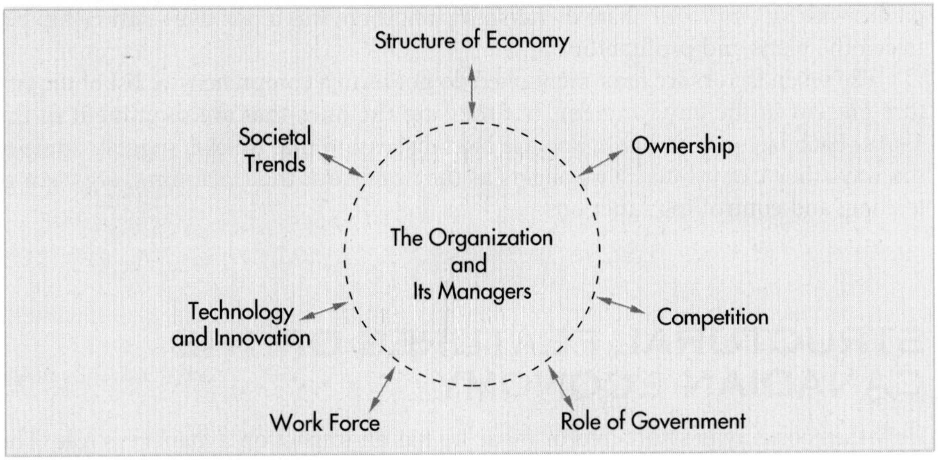

work time dealing with labour unions, government agencies, and special interest groups. For example, if a proposed environmental regulation affected the firm, top management would make representations to government and might even lobby environmental groups.

Second, these external environment factors may be in conflict with one another as well as with the organization. Employees may seek higher wages when increasing competition in the marketplace is forcing prices down and reducing profitability. This situation was faced by the North American automobile manufacturers in the 1980s when they were experiencing intense competition from foreign producers. In 1990, the Canadian Automobile Workers union was seeking increased wages and other benefits. Another example is exemplified where shareholders, or owners, demand higher dividends on their investments. This is also illustrated by the automobile industry when General Motors had to respond to large groups of shareholders who were displeased with the company's performance. When faced with such conflicts, managers seek compromises that satisfy some of the demands of each group. However, since each group may insist that all its needs be met, this approach may not work very well.

The $5. billion government-supported Hibernia mega-project began in September 1990 and will be operational in 1998. Oil will be produced by this Gravity Base Structure rig. The rig will be operated by the Hibernia Management and Development Company, a joint venture of Chevron Canada Resources, Mobil Oil Canada, Murphy Atlantic Offshore Oil, Petro-Canada, and the Government of Canada.

Third, the importance of a given external environmental factor to a manager depends to some extent on that manager's specific responsibilities in the firm. The vice-president of human resources in a unionized manufacturing company may serve as the head of the firm's bargaining team when the labour contract is due for review. At that time, the most important element of the external environment the vice-president has to contend with is the union; at other times, that same vice-president may be more concerned with general labour market conditions. A superintendent of a pulp and paper mill may be concerned mainly with ensuring a steady flow of raw materials from suppliers. But if townspeople living downstream from the mill report suddenly increased amounts of a pollutant in the river, that same manager's responsibilities will expand. The plant superintendent will then find that responding to environmental groups becomes the most significant aspect of his or her job at that point.

Fourth, while we have presented these environmental factors individually, they tend to work in combination with one another, and this makes their impact difficult to predict. Technological developments may improve the firm's competitiveness, but may also cause unemployment. Traditionally, an employer-employee relationship has existed, while today increasing numbers of employees are also owners through employee stock ownership plans. According to a Toronto Stock Exchange study, 63 percent of listed companies offered at least one form of employer share ownership plan to their employees. The study also found that in a majority of companies with an employee share ownership plan, there was a positive relationship between the plans and profitability.[2]

The seven factors we have mentioned do not form a comprehensive list of the factors present in the environment, but they are the ones that are prominent in the 1990s. Each factor is complex, and the brief discussion that follows suggests some of the ways they can influence managers as they carry out their planning, organizing, leading, and controlling functions.

STRUCTURAL FEATURES OF THE CANADIAN ECONOMY

LEARNING OBJECTIVE 2
Identify four principal structural features of the Canadian economy.

How the economy is structured or made up has an impact on a manager's role. The four principal structural features of the Canadian economy are that it is resource-based, contains one-industry communities, sometimes uses megaprojects for economic development, and has shifted from an economy that produces goods, to one that provides services.

RESOURCE-BASED ECONOMY

Canada's economy has historically been resource-based. This has meant that our main exports have been commodities (for example, forest products, minerals, and grains). Managing resource-based industries presents a special challenge to planning. The output of these industries are commodities whose price is determined on a world market. There is nothing managers can do to influence this market setting of prices. Thus, if prices fall, managers have to reduce costs, often requiring the laying off of employees.

Sometimes the supply of the resource raw materials is affected by events or circumstances beyond the control of managers. For example, the nonavailability of fish off the east coast in 1990 leaves managers in companies such as FPI Inc. and National Sea Products with little choice but to lay off employees and/or close plants. In resource based industries, managers must learn to plan despite having no control over such events.

SINGLE-INDUSTRY COMMUNITIES

single-industry communities

Although there is no agreed upon definition of **single-industry communities**, two are commonly used: (1) a community of between 25 000-35 000 where at least 75 percent of the working population is employed by a single industry and its supporting institutional services; and (2) a community that has a single dominant economic activity, that is, a single employer or group of employers in a single industry, and is not in commuting distance of another area offering alternative employment opportunities.

Single-industry communities also present unique problems for managers, requiring them to become involved in providing community infrastructure such as roads, schools, and hospitals. Actions a business takes can have a direct influence on the local community. This places an additional burden of responsibility on the company and its managers to provide the amenities of community life for employees and their families often in remote locations. The Ethics in Management insert "Closing a Town" illustrates an ethical issue for managers in a single-industry community.

MEGAPROJECTS

Large-scale construction and development undertakings such as hydro generation sites (like those in Northern Manitoba and Quebec), pipeline construction (like the proposed MacKenzie Valley Pipeline) and petroleum development (such as that off the East Coast) are referred to as **megaprojects.** Such projects pose challenges for managers as it is difficult to attract and retain employees in remote and hostile areas. **Project management** is the process of planning, organizing, leading, and controlling the work of employees, and all available resources, to complete the undertaking of such a project, on schedule and within budget. Techniques used in project management are discussed in other chapters of this book.[3]

megaprojects

project management

A variation on project management is used to plan for and carry out large sporting events such as the Commonwealth Games held in Victoria, B.C., in 1994. The Hibernia project in Newfoundland and the Prince Edward Island Link also utilize project management techniques. It is important to note that a megaproject would only have a life cycle including, for example, negotiating the contract or agreement, budgeting, making procurement decisions, supervising operations, and assuring quality control. Once the project is complete, a normal management approach would be used to operate the undertaking.

THE SHIFT TO SERVICES

Figure 3-2 illustrates the shift in employment from goods-producing to service-providing industries. Further evidence of the increasing importance of the service sector is the fact that it equals almost 70 percent of Canada's GNP and makes up about 40 percent of exports. Managing service companies that produce intangible goods presents different challenges including the inability to inventory services and the increased difficulty of quality control.

Since services cannot be inventoried, managers cope with matching demand and supply in other ways, such as providing price incentives to use facilities at off-peak times, using part-time help at peak business times, or allowing the waiting period by consumers to increase. Matching demand and supply require planning and organizing skills different than those needed for producing manufactured goods.

FIGURE 3-2 EMPLOYMENT SHIFT TO SERVICE SECTOR.

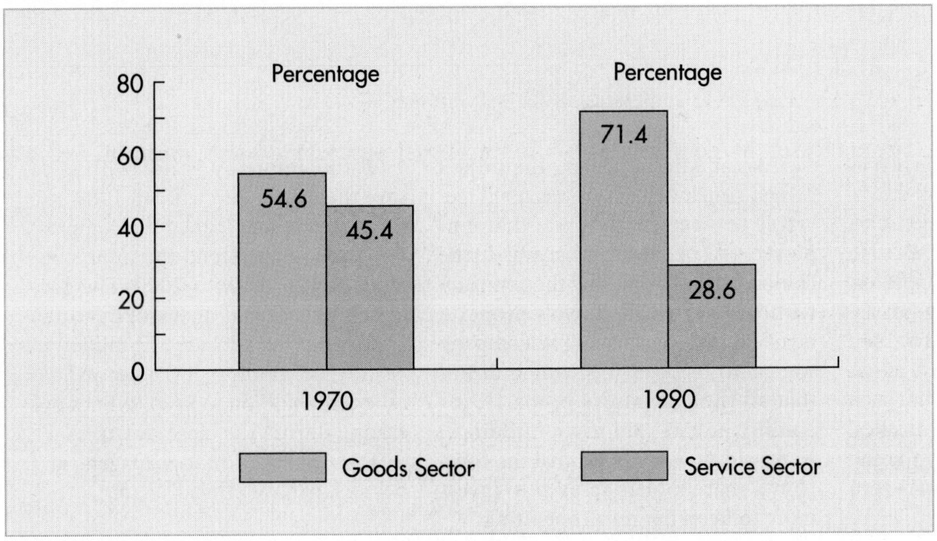

For example, the Ford Motor Company can have an inventory of automobiles to meet demand thus levelling production over time. Wendy's, on the other hand, has to plan and organize so that they can meet high demands at peak meal times.

Quality control is difficult in service industries because of the intangible nature of the product. For example, the Four Seasons Hotels has a reputation for excellent service. The quality of their service in large part involves the pleasantness and efficiency of their employees. The manager must use her or his "leadership" and human resource skills to inspire the employees to maintain that high level of service.

THE OWNERSHIP OF BUSINESS CORPORATIONS

LEARNING OBJECTIVE 3

Describe the influences different types of owners have on managers.

Who owns the business corporation influences the behaviour of managers. Although the principles upon which planning, organizing, leading, and controlling are much the same regardless of ownership, the objectives of the owners and their methods of operation vary requiring managers to use different management practices. Figure 3-3 categorizes the principal owners of Canadian business. This section will outline the principal owners of Canadian business, and discuss three topics that relate to ownership: joint venture, foreign ownership, and family ownership.

INDIVIDUAL DIRECT OWNERS

direct owner

Direct owners are Canadians who own shares in corporations as investors, but also as entrepreneurs, managers, employees, customers, and producers. Investors own shares in corporations whose stock is traded on a stock exchange. About 16 percent of Canadians over 18 years of age own shares in this manner.[4] For example, Canadian Pacific Limited, which operates in transportation and waste services, natural resource development, real estate, hotel operations, and telecommunications, had approximately 67 000 shareholders in 1990. BCE Inc., the owner of Bell Canada Telephones, has over 280 000 shareholders. These investors seldom interfere with the

ETHICS IN MANAGEMENT

CLOSING A TOWN

Who is responsible for a town when its only industry closes? Is there an ethical issue involved? These are questions that can be asked about Cassiar, British Columbia, a town that has disappeared.

The town's sole industry, an asbestos mine, closed in February 1992 after operating for 40 years. Cassiar was a town of 1200 with facilities such as roads, school, hospital, churches, and commercial businesses. By the end of 1992, everything was gone—not even a ghost town remained.

Cassiar Mining Corp., the mine's owner, concluded that it was no longer viable to operate the mine that employed 400 people. Cassiar was a true company town—built by the company with most of all the town's property owned by the company. The company went into receivership, which meant that all the company's property, including houses and town buildings, were sold. It was alleged that the company's shareholders refused to invest more to keep the mine operating.

If the company is not willing to save the town, who will? In 1988, the B.C. government loaned the company $25 million to extend the mine's operation until the year 2000. The government refused any more money although it did allocate $12 million to pay for the wind-up of Cassiar and another $3.4 million to keep utilities operating during the close-down.

Did Cassiar Mining managers, and owners, behave ethically? ▲

management of the corporations as the investors are dispersed throughout Canada and abroad. Managers are independent of the owners unless dividends are not paid. If this happens, owners may sell their shares.

Entrepreneurs or the operators of small businesses are also owners. In this case, the owner and the manager are the same person and has control over all management functions. This type of ownership is discussed in Chapter 20.

Managers can become owners, usually by purchasing the corporation, or a part of it, from previous owners. In 1987, the Hudson's Bay Co. sold its northern stores division to a group of managers which operated them as the North West Co.[5] In cases where owners are also managers, they are free to operate the corporation as they wish.

Employees can own corporations outright or through employee share purchase plans. Some examples of employee owned corporations are: Great Western Brewery, Saskatoon, Saskatchewan, a producer of seven brands of Canadian beer; Britex Ltd., Bridgetown, Nova Scotia, a manufacturer of elasticized fibres; Lar Machinerie Inc., Metabethchouan, Quebec, a manufacturer of metal equipment; and Sooke Forest Products Ltd., a lumber mill in New Westminister, B.C. Former employees may become managers, or they may hire professional managers. In either case, there is greater consultation on decisions when employees are also owners.

Finally, the most common method through which customers and producers become owners is via cooperatives. Retail consumer cooperatives such as the Calgary Co-operative Association Ltd. is owned by customers and has about a one-third share of the city's grocery market. Similarly, the grain producers own the Alberta Wheat Pool. Managers of cooperatives are very aware of members' (owners') wishes and their actions are guided by the principles of the cooperative movement.

Alcan Aluminum Limited, one of the largest Canadian industrial corporations, is a publicly traded company. It sells shares to the general public through stock exchanges. About 40 000 individual owners, direct investors and indirect investors hold shares in the company.

INDIVIDUAL INDIRECT OWNERS

Canadians also become **indirect owners** by contributing to mutual and pension funds which in turn make investments in business. These funds are pools of money contributed by individual Canadians and managed by a financial institution such as a trust company, insurance company, or a company exclusively set up for this purpose. In the case of mutual funds, investors own units of the funds and receive dividends and may receive capital gains when the units are sold. Eleven percent of Canadians over 18 years of age have purchased mutual funds that have invested in shares of businesses.[6] Many Canadians contribute to pension plans that are similarly managed on their behalf.

indirect owners

FIGURE 3-3 OWNERS OF CANADIAN BUSINESS FIRMS.

Individual Owners	
Direct	Indirect
Investors Entrepreneurs Managers Employees Customers Producers	Mutual Funds Pension Funds

Corporate Owners
Corporations Venture Capitalists

Government Owners
Federal Provincial Municipal

An important point for managers of business enterprises to take into account is that the individuals who operate the mutual and pension funds may begin to make demands if there is insufficient return on their investment. If this is the case, they might sell their investment, or they may intervene more directly. An example of the influence of mutual and pension funds as owners in businesses is Sherritt Gordon Ltd. where the board of directors was replaced and senior management ousted.[7]

Intercorporate Ownership

Corporations own each other. Large conglomerates exist that own dozens of other businesses—for example, Empire Co. Ltd., Canadian Pacific Ltd., Brascan Ltd., Jim Pattison Group, Power Corp. of Canada, and Federal Industries Ltd. BCE Inc. (formerly Bell Canada), owns a variety of businesses, including BCE Mobile Communications Inc., Montreal Trustco Inc., Northern Telecom Limited, and Tele-Direct (Publications) Inc., in addition to whole or part ownership of eight telephone companies in Canada.

Instead of being accountable to thousands of investors or owners, managers of owned corporations are responsible to the managers of the corporation. For example, the managers of Shoppers Drug Marts are accountable to the managers of Imasco Inc. The managers of the owned corporations might be closely supervised with their discretionary powers reduced or may be given some freedom, depending upon the management policies of the owner corporation. The parent corporation usually has objectives the managers must meet and failure to achieve them may lead to dismissal.

venture capital

venture capitalist

Another situation where managers are constrained by another owner occurs when venture capitalists have part ownership of the business. The Association of Canadian Venture Capital companies defines **venture capital** financing as the provision of equity (common stock) or equity-related funds to any business entity where there is risk of loss of capital and when such financing cannot be obtained from conventional sources upon reasonable terms. A **venture capitalist** is an individual or company that provides such financing. Although only a minority equity position is held, the venture capitalist can influence management action by demanding certain people be on the board of directors, approving major decisions, granting or withholding financing, and assuming more control if the enterprise does not perform well.

Government Ownership

Lastly, governments own hundreds of business enterprises in Canada either wholly or in part. These enterprises are often referred to as Crown corporations, and are owned by federal, provincial, and municipal governments. The challenges confronting managers in these corporations differ somewhat from those in business corporations. For example, the objectives of government-owned business are not as clear as those of privately owned business. In private business, profit is often the main objective while governments might be more concerned with preserving jobs and providing a needed service. Management in these corporations is complicated by the political environment that requires greater disclosure and by the influence of political parties and other interest groups on the activities of the enterprise. Therefore, much of the planning in such an enterprise might be done by the government, who may even interfere in some of the day-to-day operations.

There are three other matters related to ownership that influence the actions of managers: the increasing use of joint ventures, the degree of foreign ownership, and the presence of family ownership.

JOINT VENTURES

In recent years, managers have been required to participate in a variety of alliances with other firms. The term often used to describe such businesses is "joint ventures." Several other terms are also used including alliances, consortium, networks, and partnerships. The word "strategic" is often used in conjunction with these terms, for example, strategic alliances, cooperative strategies, and strategic partnerships.

joint ventures

Joint ventures, also known as strategic partnerships or alliances, are firms created by two or more sponsoring firms which combine resources and skills for a new venture. Ownership is shared in proportion to the contributions made by each firm. There are several reasons firms form joint ventures. Cooperation through a joint undertaking can reduce costs and achieve economies of scale (long-run average costs decrease as output increases), and each partner can provide some resource, skill, or information the other lacks. Access to certain supplies or markets might also be obtained. Sometimes joint ventures are entered into for economic survival, usually in the face of increasing global competition.

Managers must carefully plan for these joint ventures. Selecting a "partner" is not easy, and skill and cooperation are necessary to maintain a good working relationship. As in any partnership, choosing the wrong partner may be fatal to the agreement. Negotiating the agreement is usually complicated and maintaining control over the venture may be difficult to do.

MANAGEMENT AT WORK

MANAGING THE JOINT VENTURES LIFE CYCLE

The joint venture form of business operation is being used increasingly in Canada. The following are some examples and a description of the joint venture life cycle.

Canadian biotechnology companies are entering into joint ventures, or strategic partnerships, in order to obtain the financial resources to develop and commercialize biotech breakthroughs. It is not uncommon for some companies to enter into several joint ventures. Novopham Ltd. of Toronto, a generic drug maker, entered into joint ventures with the Canadian branches of Marion Merrell (Don) Canada of Laval, Quebec, and Merck Frosst Inc. of Kirkland, Quebec. The agreements allow Novapham to make and market generic versions of drugs to treat ulcers and diabetes.

During the 1980s, joint ventures were common in the automobile industry. For example, General Motors of Canada Ltd. and Suzuki Canada Inc. have invested $550 million in Cami Automotive Inc. of Ingersoll, Ontario, which produces Chevrolet, Pontiac, and Suzuki vehicles.

Companies often enter foreign markets by joining forces with local enterprises. Delta Hotels Ltd. of Toronto enters into joint venture partnerships in the development and operation of hotels. For example, in December 1993, it invested between $50 and $75 million in five properties: a resort in Port Dixon and Kuala Lumpur, Malaysia; and hotels in Bangkok, Thailand, Ho Chi Minh City, Vietnam, and Manila, the Philippines. Local investors usually hold majority stakes in such joint ventures.

Even cooperatives enter into joint ventures. The three prairie wheat pools, the Alberta Wheat Pool, the Saskatchewan Wheat Pool, and the Manitoba Pool Elevators, jointly own Western Co-operatives Fertilizers, XCAN Grain Ltd. (a grain-trading company), and grain terminals (in Vancouver, Prince Rupert, and Thunder Bay).

However, not all joint ventures are successful:

- Cascades Inc., the Quebec paper company, disassociated itself from a partnership with Groupe Pinault SA of France to operate a French newsprint company. The reason given for the break-up was "conflicting philosophies."
- Noranda Forest Inc. planned to build a $1 billion pulp mill in Tasmania in partnership with the Australian company North Broken-Hill. The project was shelved in 1988 when the Australian government imposed tougher pollution regulations. Noranda Forest Inc. management felt that North Broken-Hill had handled the environmental issue poorly because of its inexperience in the area.

• • •

As the examples suggest, joint ventures are being used across a wide spectrum of businesses. They have a relatively high rate of failure, estimated at 70 percent. Joint ventures are viewed as having a life cycle from "start-up" to "operational" to "termination" with different demands upon managers at each phase.

"Start-up" requires careful planning and the careful development of working relationships between the partners. Venture start-up usually requires substantial financial and other resources including management time and effort.

The "operational" phase requires the partners to make compromises and to adapt to changing environments including the tightening or lessening of the degree of control or ownership structure depending upon circumstances. Lastly, the "termination" phase occurs when the joint venture fails or has achieved the partners' objectives, for example, the completion of a construction project or promotion of a new technology development. ▲

FOREIGN OWNERSHIP

indirect investment
direct investment

In Canada, a substantial portion of enterprises are owned to some extent by foreign interests. Foreign investment is categorized as indirect and direct. **Indirect investment** involves the purchase of corporate stocks and bonds, while **direct investment** involves the commitment of capital to take over an existing Canadian corporation, or to establish a wholly owned corporation in Canada. Both types of investment have implications for Canada and Canadian managers. Although we are more concerned about the influence of foreign ownership upon managers, the following data outlines the extent of foreign ownership in Canada. Recent statistics indicate that from 1987 to 1991 there was an increase of $34.4 billion in foreign control of Canadian corporations. It is estimated that about 20 percent of Canadian corporate assets are now controlled by foreign interests dominated by U.S. corporations followed by British and French companies.[8] Thirty-eight of Canada's largest corporations are controlled by foreigners.[9]

MANAGEMENT AT WORK

MANAGING A BRANCH PLANT

Many Canadians are employed as managers of branch plants or offices of companies owned by foreigners, most frequently by Americans. This arrangement gives rise to some interesting predicaments for the Canadian manager:

1. Although Canadian managers appear to have authority over the Canadian operations, in reality they have little or no authority. Most decisions are made at head offices, often, with little or no consultation with the Canadian manager. For example, Canadian subsidiaries might be arbitrarily assigned product lines by the foreign owner.
2. Canadian managers often build their operations only to find they become "cash cows" for the parent company to "milk" and are not left enough money for reinvestment. Even though Canadian managers may want to reinvest profits in Canada, the parent companies remove profits to be invested elsewhere. This means that the Canadian operations cannot expand as they might wish.
3. Profit expectations of the foreign-owned corporation must be met by any method, including the use of transfer pricing (the practice of charging a price for goods and services "sold" between divisions or subsidiaries of a company). Parent companies often set high profit objectives for the Canadian operation which managers are under considerable pressure to meet. One method is through manipulation of the prices at which goods and services are sold to, or purchased from, other units of the parent company.
4. Canadian executives sometimes become "passive" followers, seldom rocking the boat. They develop an emotional and intellectual dependency that destroys creativity and self-esteem. Managing in such a manner is not very effective and may not be in the best interests of Canadian business. ▲

Canadians who manage foreign-owned enterprises in this country are confronted with a different management situation, which is described in the Management at Work insert, "Managing a Branch Plant." Controls are imposed from the foreign head offices that must be complied with by the Canadian managers. Even the organizing and leading management functions are affected. An example is the Japanese management approaches adopted by their operations in Canada. At the Toyota Motor Manufacturing Canada Inc. plant in Cambridge, Ontario, workers have redesigned their jobs themselves, a philosophy known as *Kaizen,* and work in teams.[10]

FAMILY OWNERSHIP

A substantial portion of Canadian businesses is owned and controlled by families, most of whom operate private corporations. Family businesses control about one third of the 100 largest companies in Canada. Some familiar family names are Bronfman (Seagram and other businesses), Eaton (department stores), Ghermezian (real estate including the West Edmonton Mall), Irving (petroleum and other businesses in N.B.), McCain (food processing), Reichmann (real estate), Sobey (supermarkets and real estate in Atlantic Canada), and Weston (food manufacturing and retailing).

Nonfamily managers face additional challenges in such corporations. They may be caught in family squabbles and asked to "choose sides." Owners often procrastinate about major expansion possibilities and succession plans.

COMPETITION

Both domestic and international competition influence Canadian managers, and is reflected in the focus on productivity and quality.

COMPETITION IN CANADA

concentration

LEARNING OBJECTIVE 4

Outline the challenges imposed on business organizations by competition from within Canada and from outside Canada.

The nature of competition between business firms in Canada is reflected in the degree of industrial concentration in the economy. **Concentration** refers to the degree to which the economy is dominated by a few large firms. Table 3-1 illustrates the magnitude of this concentration showing that a relatively small number of firms control a large portion of business activity. This concentration is especially evident in a few specific industries; for example, over 90 percent of the market for tobacco products is controlled by Imperial, MacDonald, and Rothmans Benson & Hedges while two companies, Molson and Labatt, dominate the Canadian brewery industry. By contrast, less than 10 percent of the market in the furniture, clothing, and construction industries is controlled by the four largest businesses.

TABLE 3-1 CONCENTRATION IN CANADIAN BUSINESS.

Shares of Total Assets, Revenue and Profits of Largest Enterprises, All Industries 1988

		Percentage of	
	Assets	Revenue	Profits
Largest 25	41.2	20.8	26.6
Largest 100	55.9	34.6	45.4
Largest 500	68.7	49.7	64.0
Largest 1000	73.2	55.2	70.0

Managers in more highly concentrated industries must plan quite differently than managers in industries where there are many competitors. In highly concentrated industries, firms behave in a similar fashion. For example, packaging changes and prices are copied. In less concentrated industries, it is much more difficult to keep track of all competitors and to predict their behaviour. But competition is not restricted to the Canadian environment. Managers also face competitive pressures from foreign markets.

International Competition

While competition may be reduced in some industries by concentration within Canada, business firms are facing increasing competition from imports. This is due to the lowering of tariff and nontariff barriers through the renegotiated General Agreement on Trade and Tariffs (GATT) completed in 1993, the North American Free Trade Agreement (NAFTA) with the U.S. and Mexico, which is now in effect, and the Free Trade Agreement with the U.S. in effect since 1988. While having to compete with additional imports at home, Canadian managers are also finding it more difficult to sell Canadian products in foreign markets. As business becomes increasingly global in nature many Canadian businesses have become multi- or transnational. Managers have had to improve their skills at marketing in foreign markets by, for instance, learning foreign languages and studying foreign cultures.

There is another dimension of foreign competition that must be considered: how competitive Canadian business is in relation to industry in other nations.

National Competitiveness

The competitive nature of business within Canada is one dimension, and the competitiveness of Canadian business outside of the country is another. The success of Canada's business enterprises is very important to trade and thus, to the country's economic well-being. Obviously, managers can influence the competitiveness of Canadian corporations.

One measure of national competitiveness in industrialized countries is completed annually by the World Economic Forum and the International Institute for Management Development. Overall, Canada's rank was fifth out of 24 industrialized countries in 1990. The *World Competitiveness Report 1990* defines **business competitiveness** as: the ability to design, produce and market goods and services, the price and nonprice qualities of which form a more attractive package of benefits than those of competitors. The assessment of national competitiveness is based upon responses to questionnaires to executives in all the countries in the report.[11] Table 3-2 describes the eight factors of competitiveness and lists Canada's ranking on each factor in the 1992 report. Overall, Canada's ranking dropped to 11 out of 22 in the recent report.

business competitiveness

Of particular concern is Canadian business' low ranking in the "management" factor. The reasons identified for this low ranking included: implementation of strategies falls short of set goals, managerial rewards encourage short-term orientation, senior management is rarely experienced in international business, the price/quality ratio of domestic products is seen to be inferior to foreign competitors, time to innovate or to market a new product is longer, total quality control is neglected, and corporate profits are expected to be low. The report indicates that Canadian managers must not only plan for domestic competition but must also be prepared to manage their businesses in such a way as to be competitive internationally.

TABLE 3-2 CANADA'S RANKING ON THE EIGHT FACTORS OF NATIONAL COMPETITIVENESS. (RANKING BY FACTOR OUT OF 22 DEVELOPED COUNTRIES)

Factor	Ranking
• Domestic economic strength—The size of the economy, investment, inflation, and economic growth are evaluated.	15
• Internationalization—The measures involved include: extent of participation in international trade, investment flows, protectionism, international links, and export diversity.	17
• Government—This is a measure of the type of government interventions that are detrimental to the international competitiveness of business. Included are consideration of debt and reserves, tax rates and revenues, and the legislative and regulatory environment.	11
• Finance—The size of banks, capitalization of stock markets, availability of venture capital, interest rates and financial alternatives are used to assess the performance of capital markets and financial services.	7
• Infrastructure—The presence of the necessary resources and systems needed by business is assessed by examining: oil imports, resource self-sufficiency and adequacy of communications and transportation systems.	3
• Management—This factor considers the extent to which enterprises are managed in an innovative, profitable and responsible manner. This is measured by looking at product quality and pricing, productivity, compensation, use of technology, employee turnover, corporate financial performance, and managerial behaviour.	15
• Science and Technology—The success in basic and applied research is assessed by considering business expenditures in R&D, the number of scientists in industry and patents and protection of intellectual property.	17
• People—This is a measure of the workers in the economy including age distribution, unemployment rates, educational levels, and motivation and skills.	8

PRODUCTIVITY AND QUALITY

productivity

Increased competition on world markets has also meant that Canadian businesses have had to emphasize productivity and quality. **Productivity** refers to the ratio of physical output to physical input. Improving productivity means getting more output from the same input or the same output with less input. In the past, productivity has usually been measured as output per employee. If Canadian business is to be competitive, it must improve its productivity. As Figure 3-4 illustrates, Canadian productivity is being surpassed by some G-7 countries, and the productivity of others, Japan and the United Kingdom, is catching up.

But measuring productivity is not that simple, and traditional measures have not assisted in understanding what can be done to improve productivity. The traditional measure is labour productivity, and any contributions to increased output from using more plant and equipment, energy consumption, and use of materials and services has been ignored. In order to find a solution to Canada's lagging productivity, Statistics Canada has developed a better way to measure it.

Statistics Canada has developed two "multifactor" productivity measures for the Canadian business sector as a whole and for 100 industries. The first measure takes

FIGURE 3-4 PRODUCTIVITY LEVELS IN MANUFACTURING, G-7 COUNTRIES, 1950, 1980, AND 1990.

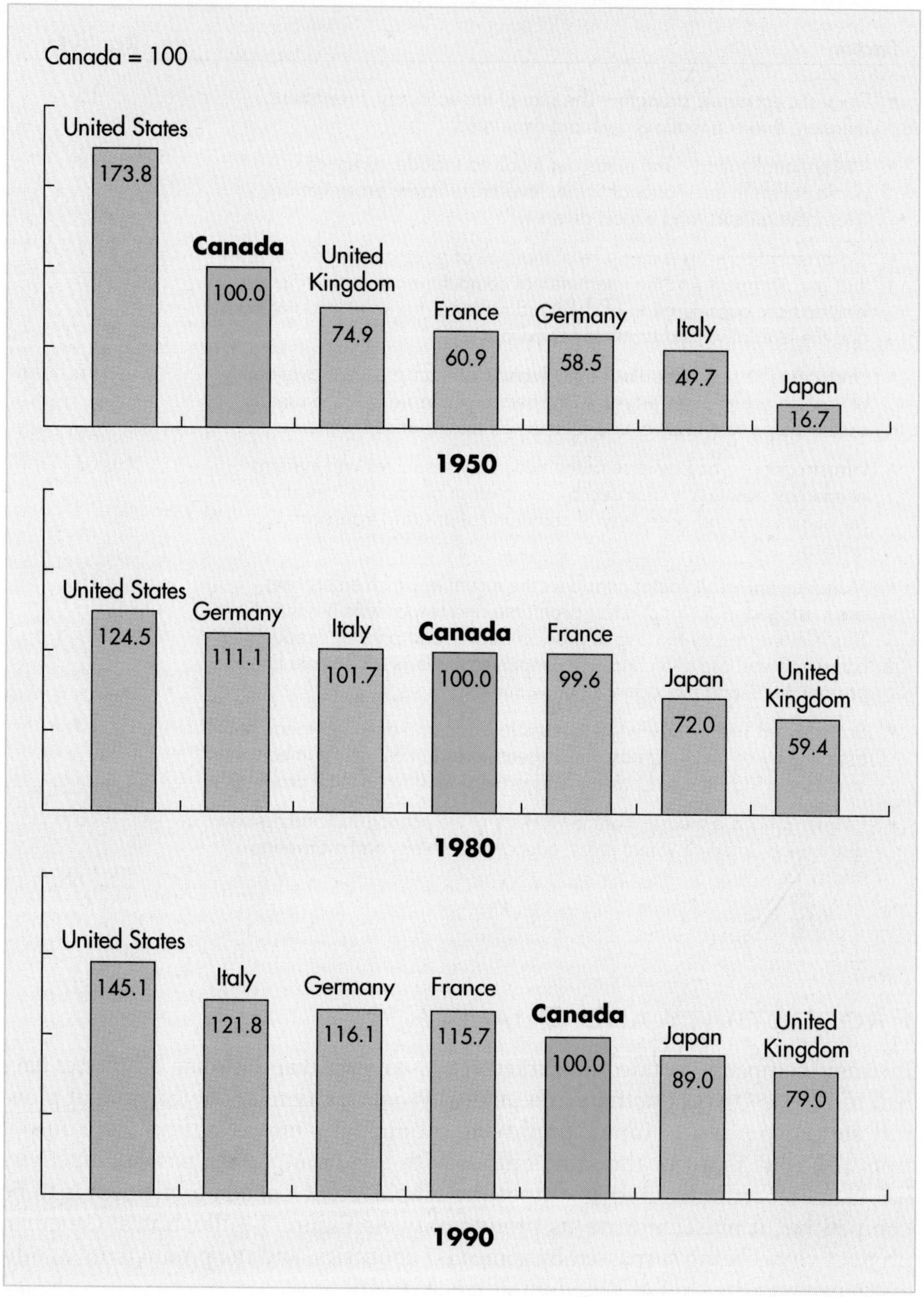

into account the change in all the factors of production. This measure usually indicates lower productivity than the labour productivity measure. The second measure includes not just the productivity gains in a particular industry itself but also in all the industries' supplying energy, materials, and services to it. As these productivity measures take into account more inputs, they will assist managers in deciding upon what changes are necessary to improve productivity and increase their capability to compete on world markets.[12] Not all the news on Canadian productivity is bad. Statistics

Canada reports that manufacturers increased output by 4.2 percent in 1992 while all businesses increased productivity by 2.2 percent.[13]

Not only do managers have to improve productivity in their firms but they must also increase the quality of the goods produced. **Quality** is defined as all of the features and characteristics of a product or service that bears on its ability to satisfy stated or implied needs. Customers expect better quality goods and services from Canadian business when quality imported goods are available. An example of how managers have influenced quality is shown in the Management at Work insert that describes the quality improvement program at the Ford Motor Co. of Canada.

quality

Programs such as the one at Ford are referred to as **total quality management** (TQM). TQM is a set of principles, tools, and procedures providing guidance to the creation of an environment that will enable employees to do a good job and allow good ideas to work. It involves suppliers and focusses on the satisfaction of the customer or consumer. The process involves everyone in an organization in controlling and continously improving how work is done in order to meet customer expectations of quality. It is also referred to as "service quality" and "continuous improvement" and can be applied to government and non-profit organizations as well as business. Many governments are implementing some form of service quality approach. For example, the British Columbia government has a service quality agency to promote the approach, and the Quebec Department of Recreation, Fish and Game has implemented a continuous improvement process.

total quality management

A quality assurance standards group known as the International Standards Organization (ISO) 9000 has been established. The ISO is a nongovernmental body formed in 1947 to develop worldwide standards to ensure product quality, compatibility,

MANAGEMENT AT WORK

"Quality is Job 1"—Management at Ford Motor Co.

The Ford Motor Co. of Canada Ltd. became very concerned in the early 1980s about the quality of its product. The company decided to focus on managing quality in all aspects of the production and marketing process. This approach involved creating an environment that would make employees more productive, involve suppliers, and focus on the satisfaction of the customer or consumer.

The following is a brief description of the approach taken with Ford's major stakeholders.

For the employees, two processes were initiated: participative management and employee involvement. Teamwork became "a way of life" and employees were "empowered." Managers were trained to be better supervisors, and training programs institutionalized "quality" with all employees.

Suppliers were encouraged to improve quality and were publically recognized by Ford for doing so.

The concept of total quality was extended to Ford's dealers. Ford worked with the dealers to improve the quality of predelivery prepping and the consumers' delivery experience.

Finally, consumers were surveyed to ascertain the levels of satisfaction and dissatisfaction and their reasons for both.

Ford has been recognized for its efforts to improve quality by winning a 1993 Canada Award for Business Excellence, sponsored by the National Quality Institute, a non-profit organization formed to promote the principles and practices of total quality in the Canadian workplace. The award, in the Total Quality category, was won by the Ford Electronics Manufacturing Corporation, Markham plant, which produces electronic automotive components such as air-bag modules and temperature controls. In addition to outside competitors, it must compete with eight other Ford Electronics plants throughout the world. By focussing on customer satisfaction and the consistent application of its quality-improvement program, the Markham Plant has achieved many outstanding business results and positive performance trends. ▲

safety, and reliability. It is comprised of standards organizations from several industrialized nations and includes the Standards Council of Canada. The ISO 9000 was designed to meet several objectives: to ensure that customers receive the product or service that they expect, to prevent errors in all operations, to prevent delivery delays, to reduce costs of operation, to increase productivity, to increase the reliability of the product or service, and to meet all quality assurance requirements specified by customers.

In Canada, a registration process is performed by the Quality Management Institute, a division of the Canadian Standards Organization. An example of a business so registered is Byrne Architects of Halifax who are the first architectural firm in North America to receive one of the ISO 9000 standards. As the standard is recognized in more than 50 countries, many Canadian businesses are complying with the requirements in order to improve their competitiveness within Canada but especially to increase their capability to sell goods and services around the world.

Managers respond to competition by planning, organizing, leading, and controlling more effectively. This is reflected in the way in which managers focus on improvements in productivity and quality of products and services.

THE ROLE OF GOVERNMENT

LEARNING OBJECTIVE 5
Identify the types of government involvement in the Canadian economic system.

Canadian managers must deal with government at three levels—federal, provincial and municipal. Table 3-3 lists the various types of government involvement and provides examples. Almost every aspect of managing an organization is touched by government in some ways. Government policies influence the planning process, determine staffing practices, place constraints on how employees can be treated, and stipulate what information must be disclosed when selling shares to the public. The introduction of the Goods and Sales Tax (GST) by the federal government in January 1991 is another example of government involvement in management. The GST requires managers to keep track of the collection and forwarding of the taxes. For some firms, additional staff had to be hired, and detailed information on the taxes collected, and any rebates requested, had to be forwarded to the government. Managers, particularly those in top management, must keep well informed about government policies and actions.

Table 3-3 and the paragraph above provide some appreciation for the scope of government's role in the economy. Two topics of particular importance to managers recently have been constitutional issues and the trend to less government involvement.

CONSTITUTIONAL ISSUES

Canada is a federation of provinces, a political arrangement that has an impact on managers by restricting their actions. The following are examples of those restrictions:

1. *Local hiring restrictions* Some provinces require that local workers be hired on construction and development projects.
2. *Capital movement restrictions* Some provinces have prevented a corporate takeover of a business enterprise within their borders.
3. *Product standards* There is a lack of uniformity in standards among governments which may impede the free flow of goods across provincial borders.
4. *Marketing boards* These boards regulate the supply of some agricultural products and sometimes restrict the movement of goods across provincial borders.
5. *Purchasing policies* Most federal, provincial, and municipal governments have preferential purchasing policies for business enterprises located within their jurisdictions.

TABLE 3-3 GOVERNMENT INVOLVEMENT IN THE CANADIAN ECONOMY.

Type of Involvement	Examples
Government Purchasing The federal government purchases over $10 billion of goods and services each year.	Acquisition of military equipment for the armed forces. Purchase of stationery supplies for offices.
Funding for Business Governments supply debt capital to business through loans and loan guarantees.	In 1989, Alberta wanted to develop its forests. It made loans and provided loan guarantees to several pulp and paper companies.
Taxation Governments require business to collect taxes and profits are taxed.	Collection of retail sales taxes. Income deduction from payrolls.
Incentives/Tax Relief Payments are made to pay the cost of some activities. Taxes are reduced if business performs certain tasks.	A federal government program pays up to half the cost of a company's participation in activities such as trade missions, market research trips, and the cost of project bidding in order to encourage exports. Small businesses are taxed at a lower rate than larger businesses.
Regulation The controlling of various business activities.	Competition Act controls business trade practices and mergers/takeovers. Canada Labour Code and provincial labour legislation controls how employees are treated, for example, how overtime is calculated, statutory holidays, and hours and conditions of work. Canadian Radio-Television and Telecommunications Commission Act regulates the services offered and rates charged for telephone and other telecommunications services, e.g. Bell Canada. Most businesses and professions are licensed to operate by government, e.g., hair dressers, funeral homes, engineers, and social workers.
Bailouts Governments assisting business through grants or loans to prevent the firms from going bankrupt. The purpose of such involvement is usually to save jobs.	In the early 1980s, Massey-Ferguson, a manufacturer of farm and industrial equipment, was provided assistance by the federal and Ontario governments that prevented it from going bankrupt and enabled the company to reorganize in Varity Corp. About the same time, Maislin Industries, a Quebec trucking firm, was assisted by the federal government but went bankrupt anyway. In January 1991, the Ontario government was studying the possibility of assisting Algoma Steel Corp. of Sault Ste. Marie, which was experiencing financial difficulties.
Ownership of Business Enterprises The government operates businesses that it wholly or partly owns. Wholly owned enterprises are often referred to as Crown corporations.	Ontario Hydro Corp.; Saskatchewan Telephones; Petro Canada; Marystown Shipyard (Newfoundland); Keltic Lodge (Hotel in Nova Scotia)

In 1992, the federal and the provincial governments formed a task force to find ways to reduce the barriers to trade among provinces at a time when trade among nations was becoming freer. Late in 1993, Quebec and Ontario engaged in a "trade war" after Quebec refused to reduce restrictions on the awarding of construction contracts. The two provinces agreed to reduce barriers as have the Atlantic provinces with regard to government purchasing policies. For businesses and their managers, trade barriers within Canada create additional work and make operations less efficient.

Deregulation and Privatization

deregulation

In recent years government involvement has decreased through deregulation and privatization. **Deregulation** entails a reduction in the number of laws affecting business activity and of the powers of government enforcement agencies as well as other forms of governmental control or intervention. In most cases, deregulation frees the corporation to do what it wants without government interference, thereby simplifying the task of management. For example, deregulation of the financial services industry has allowed banks to enter the brokerage business and may allow them to sell insurance.

privatization

Privatization refers to the transfer of functions or activities from the government to the private sector. This includes the selling off of government-owned businesses but also such things as private companies operating hospitals or collecting garbage. The federal government has sold several corporations, including Air Canada, Teleglobe Canada, and Canadair Ltd. Provincial governments are also selling off businesses, for example, the Ontario Transportation Development Corp., Manitoba Oil and Gas Corp, and Pacific Western Airlines which was sold by the Alberta government. Privatization does not only involve the selling of businesses. In some provinces, private business firms contract to manage hospitals and other health care institutions previously operated by government employees. Terminal 3 at Lester B. Pearson International Airport in Toronto, which opened in February 1991, was built and is operated by a private firm. Privatization changes the environment in which managers have to make decisions and might also provide opportunities to expand the business or even purchase it themselves.

THE WORK FORCE

LEARNING OBJECTIVE 6
Describe the changes occurring in the Canadian work force and the expectations of employees.

Managers must hire employees from a pool of individuals referred to as the Canadian work force. In 1990, this work force was comprised of approximately 13 million people, about double the figure for 1964 (see Figure 3-5). Unemployment rates were high in the 1980s reflecting problems in providing employment for the growing

FIGURE 3-5 CANADIAN EMPLOYED WORK FORCE 1964-1990.

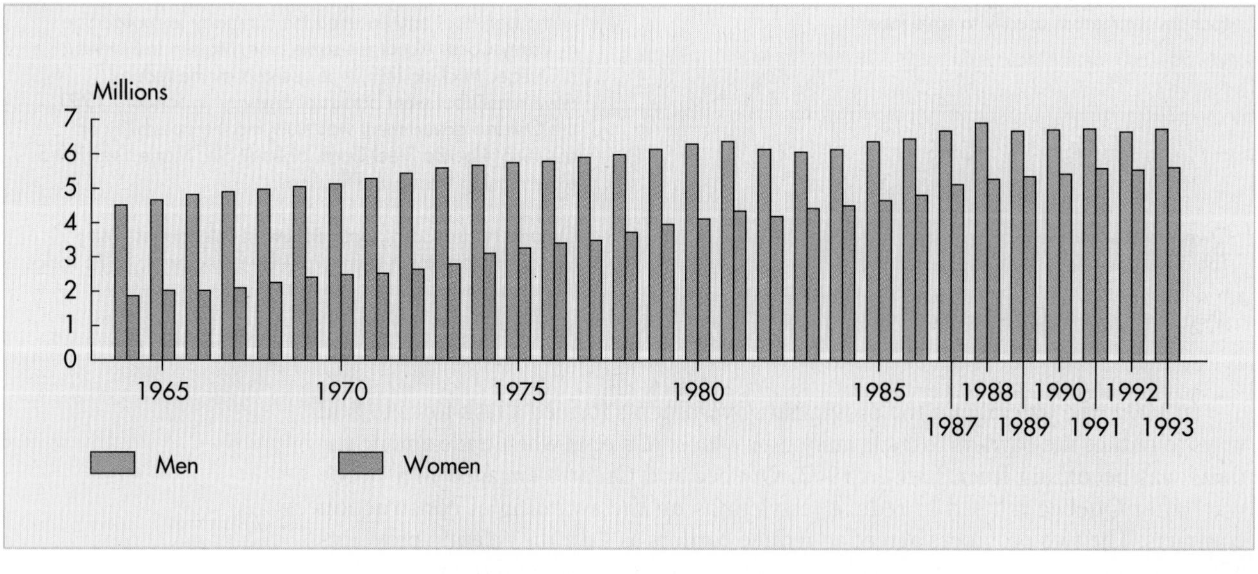

work force. It was also argued that there would be a shortage of skilled workers in the 1990s particularly in the trades because neither governments nor businesses were doing enough to train workers.

The industries that will employ the majority of workers will be different from those that dominated past employment in Canada. As mentioned, employment in goods-producing industries such as mining, forestry, and manufacturing, is either stable or declining. Unemployment has been created by failures of many large corporations such as Woodwards Stores, Central Guaranty Trust, and Olympia and York Developments, and by downsizing in many companies that resulted in layoffs; for example, in September 1993, Bell Canada announced that it would reduce its work force by 5000 within a year. Job opportunities are expected to increase in health care, personal and household servies, professional business services, education, accommodation, printing and publishing, and entertainment, amusement and recreation activities.

The composition of the labour force is changing as illustrated in Figure 3-5. Increasing numbers of women are entering the work force and are being employed in occupations that have traditionally been closed to them, for example, computer sales, public accounting, and management. A challenge for managers is the implementation and monitoring of pay equity and affirmative action programs often required by governments.

Unionization of the Work Force

A portion of the work force belongs to unions that influence the actions of managers. About 30 percent of Canadian workers are unionized. The reduction of employment in traditionally highly unionized industries such as transportation (57 percent) and forestry (51 percent) and increasing employment in less unionized service industries (34 percent) may reduce union influence in the future.[14] But managers can also expect increasing efforts to recruit members from workers in service industries. Unions are also objecting to use of new managerial approaches to motivating workers. Managers who use quality of life, quality circles, and other modern techniques can expect to be challenged by labour unions.

The relationship between management and unions has changed in many situations as changes in work rules and reduced wages are sought by companies because of difficult economic times. In 1993, unionized workers at Domtar Inc., a pulp and paper company operating mainly in Quebec, agreed to workplace changes, such as more flexible hours, and to performing a greater variety of tasks. Workers at Canada Safeway in Alberta agreed to work longer hours for less money. Concessions of this type are not without some *quid pro quo* from management, for example, bonus payments or assurances of job security.

Challenges in the Workplace

Other trends are also occurring to make management of employees more complex and demanding. The numbers of part-time employees is increasing, acquiring different management practices. On site child care facilities are being requested by employees. Women are seeking flexibility in their career plans to accommodate the raising of families, and employee wellness programs are gaining in popularity as the importance of healthy employees becomes more evident to employers. More examples of these challenges are discussed in the Management at Work insert "Supervising Employees Who Work at Home" and in Table 3-4.

TABLE 3-4 CHALLENGES IN THE WORKPLACE.

Issue	Challenge for Management
Work Force Reduction	Permanent shut-downs and large layoffs create serious personal and social problems for workers and communities and must be handled with care.
Managing Part-Time Employees	Increasing use of part-time employees means that managers must learn how to motivate this type of employee.
Occupational Health and Safety	Workplace accidents and illness still occur even in modern offices.
Political Correctness	Managers must accommodate differing religious observances, maternity leaves, differences among employees of various nationalities, and use correct language.
Employee Privacy	Managers must be sensitive to the privacy of employees in such matters as drug and polygraph testing, employee surveillance, and confidentiality of employee records.
Work and Family Commitments	Managers must consider the impact of children or elderly parents on employees.
Approaches to Pay	Pay based upon performance is more common and pay equity is important.
Harassment	Sexual and personal harassment is not tolerated in the workplace.
Accessibility	The workplace must to accessible to the disabled.
Substance Abuse	The abuse of drugs and alcohol is a growing problem.
Expectations for Promotions	Managers must learn to motivate employees in an environment where promotions are less likely.
Whistle-blowing	The treatment of persons who disclose undesirable practices of their employers is a problem.
Appointment/Promotion of Women	Relatively few women are appointed to boards of directors and glass ceilings exist to promotions.

MANAGEMENT AT WORK

Supervising Employees Who Work at Home

The use of computers combined with telecommunications technologies has resulted in the phenomenon known as *telecommuting*.

An increasing number of employees are working at home on computers instead of at the office, and "commuting" to the office through the telephone system. The types of tasks that can be performed at home include: inputing data, designing computer systems and programs, word processing, and data analysis. People in research occupations like consulting engineers or financial analysts can obtain access to the databases they use in their work from their homes.

For example, a researcher employed by a stockbroker only requires a microcomputer with modem, a hard disk with business-applications software, accounts in various databases, and a desktop publishing capability. The telephone can be used to transmit the researcher's output to the office and to communicate with other microcomputers in the employer's network all over the country.

Some Canadians are working at home. For example, Philip Creighton, an accountant, and Martin Geffen, a computer consultant, both of Toronto, work at home. The federal government is also exploring the possibilities of telecommuting. Luc Fourneer, a Department of Communications employee was asked to work at home and "telecommute" for a year. The effectiveness of the experiment is being studied.

According to organizations and employees that have been involved in telecommuting, employees experience fewer work interruptions, increased productivity, more flexible hours, a greater sense of control over work scheduling, savings in food, clothing, and transportation, and no need to cope with congested roads.

The most frequently mentioned benefits of telecommuting to employ-

• • •

ers are improved recruitment and retention of employees attracted by the work style, greater staffing flexibility, less office space needed, and greater computer literacy.

There are several areas where these "invisible" employees require special attention from a manager. It is sometimes difficult to measure and evaluate the performance of such employees effectively so control becomes troublesome. A lack of personal contact makes influencing the employee's behaviour awkward. Employees who work at home are not plugged into the informal organization and grapevine at the office and are therefore less aware of events and changes in policies. Training is necessary as some technical aspects can be problematic, and the possibility of computer fraud exists.

Other challenges exist for management from telecommuting. There is a need for planning the selection of people and the identification of the type of work that can be done. Managers must be trained for the new supervisory situation and better definitions of the job expectations are necessary along with increased skills in giving performance feedback.

Although telecommuting was originally defined as working at home, it has been broadened to include working at a satellite office or a customer's office. Telecommuting is also referred to as "teleworking" "location-independent work," "the electronic cottage," the "flexiplace," and "worksteading." ▲

TECHNOLOGY AND INNOVATION

LEARNING OBJECTIVE 7

Explain the importance that technological research and development has in ensuring that innovation occurs.

Canada has a history of technological advance and innovation. In a series of stamps issued by Canada Post from 1986 to 1988, innovations were recognized in transportation (the rotary snowplough, and the Canadarm), in communications (newsprint pulp, and the transatlantic cable), in energy (the development of kerosene), in food (the development of marquis wheat), and in medicine (the development of cobalt cancer therapy).

For technological innovation to occur, research and development (R&D) must take place. R&D is defined as the "systematic investigation carried out in the natural and engineering sciences by means of experimental analysis to achieve a scientific or commercial advance." **Research** is original investigation undertaken on a systematic basis to gain new knowledge; **development** is the application of research findings, or other scientific knowledge, for the creation of new or significantly improved products or processes.[15]

research
development

Managers must see to it that R&D occurs in business. The survival of the enterprise often depends upon discoveries leading to the development of new products. The production and marketing of these new products improves international trade opportunities, increases the standard of living, and provides employment for Canadians. Both government and business has been criticized for not spending enough money on research and development, despite the obvious advantages it will bring to business and the improvements it will make to the Canadian economy.

Managers must not only encourage R&D but must adapt new technologies to improve productivity and quality. This involves the planning, organizing, leading and controlling management functions. Managing the changes involved, in itself will be challenging. For example, managers will have to cope with displaced workers and will have to be involved in the retraining or relocation of employees. Consumers will be affected as new products are introduced making existing products obsolete, such as the replacement of vinyl long-play records with compact discs.

Wascana Energy Inc. of Regina uses new and developing technology in all aspects of its business so that it can become a low-cost producer of oil and gas in its Western Canada and international operations.

Research and development activities in Canada are not restricted to large corporations such as Northern Telecom, Alcan Aluminum, Kodak Canada, Pratt & Whiney, IBM Canada, and CAE Industries. Hundreds of inventions and innovations are developed by small businesses throughout Canada, for example:

- GWN Systems Inc. of Edmonton develops civil engineering software for planning construction projects.
- Andronic Devices of Richmond, B.C., uses robotics to help enhance the safety and quality of modern medical procedures.

- Softimage Inc. of Montreal developed 3-D computer graphics software that helped create the dinosaurs in *Jurassic Park*.
- Cinram Ltd. of Toronto is a world leader in the production of low-cost CDs.
- Instrumar Limited of St. John's, Newfoundland, has developed a clean-wing detection system to ascertain whether or not deicing is necessary on aircrafts.

Two inserts illustrate the importance of technology and innovation. The Global Management insert describes how Husky Injection Moldings Systems Ltd. successfully exports its technology-intensive product around the world. Following shortly after that, the Management at Work insert identifies the importance of technology in the footwear industry. Managers will require increasing skills to manage the changes and opportunities resulting from technology and innovation.

SOCIETAL TRENDS

LEARNING OBJECTIVE 8
Understand the implications of societal trends on managers of organizations.

Canadian society as a whole also exerts pressure on managers. The general public is not always willing to accept the actions of business without question. Pressure has been brought to bear on business by issues such as safeguarding the environment, women's involvement in business, and misleading advertising. The general public can affect managers through government, if a sufficiently large segment of society elects representatives who will support legislation to control the business activities of a corporation. But the attitudes of the public can affect companies in other ways, too. In the

GLOBAL MANAGEMENT

Husky Injection Moldings Systems Ltd.

From its humble beginnings in 1953 as a small machine shop, Husky Injection Molding Systems Ltd. has grown into one of the world's leading suppliers of injection molding equipment for the plastics industry.

With its equipment producing everything from bottle caps and plastic cutlery to compact disc cases and headlight lenses for cars, Husky has established its presence in 61 countries around the world.

The Bolton, Ontario, company's molding systems are made up of three main components—a machine that melts and injects the plastic resin; a mold that forms the plastic part; and a robot and product-handling equipment used to sort, stack, and package the parts. While Husky sells its molds, machines and components separately, it also provides complete turnkey systems to its customers.

Husky's injection molding systems are used in a wide variety of applications, including polyethylene teraphthalate (PET), a recyclable resin used for soft drink bottles, and for making automotive products such as wheel covers. They are also used in the manufacture of such plastic products as vending machine cups, yogurt containers, and 3.5" computer floppy disc shells, to name only a few items.

Over 730 people work in the Bolton plants and the corporate headquarters. An additional 430 work in Husky's sales offices in 12 countries and manufacturing facilities in Massachusetts, Luxembourg, and Germany.

In the past three years, the 40-year-old company has stacked up an impressive exporting record. Export sales from its Bolton manufacturing facilities topped $200 million in 1992, an increase of 51.1 percent from 1991, and nearly double its 1989 total. Bolton exports have risen to 88.5 percent of total sales over the same period.

Husky has cracked 11 new foreign markets since 1990—the Czech Republic, Poland, Slovania, Romania, Hungary, Iceland, Jordan, Malaysia, Saudi Arabia, the Philippines, and Thailand.

Its largest export markets are the United States, with over $116 million in sales, and Europe, with over $33 million. Latin American and Asia-Pacific countries are also key customers, with over $31 million and $19 million in sales. ▲

1970s and 1980s, public concerns about pollutants were expressed so widely that business firms became much more conscious of how their activities would affect air and water quality. For example, FibreCo Pulp Inc. of Taylor, B.C., was fined $200 000 for leaking toxic materials into the Peach River.[16] It has become more socially acceptable for women to be involved in business, yet their advancement to the ranks of senior management and corporate directors has been slow.[17] It will be interesting to monitor this issue during the 1990s. In a different area, public pressure lead to the banning of most forms of tobacco advertising in 1989 despite strong lobbying by the firms in the industry.

Consumer preferences are another expression of society's wishes. Such preferences must be monitored by managers, as these trends can directly affect business. An example of the importance of consumer preferences is the "yuppie" era of the 1980s. The yuppie, or young urban professional, was concerned with "getting ahead" and making (and spending) a lot of money. They bought expensive cars, homes, clothing, entertainment units, and appliances and were therefore a strong influence on business. Consumers preferences continue to influence manager decision making as illustrated by the Management at Work insert "Managing to Take Advantage of Fashion Fads."

LEARNING OBJECTIVE 9

Explain why a manager must continually monitor the environment in which the organization operates.

By 1990, there was evidence that the yuppie era was over: fewer Saabs and BMWs were being sold, retailers of high-priced clothing were failing (in fact, Creeds, a well-established, expensive high-fashion store in Toronto went out of business), and dining in expensive restaurants declined. The impact of reduced consumer expenditures was felt by business as was the shift of consumer spending to other items. More money was being spent on old cars instead of new ones and more practical, better made products were being sought. This new trend has been labelled "living lightly" and might be associated with the emphasis being placed on protecting the environment as fewer resources are being used in unnecessary or frivolous products.

Societal trends affect organizations in many ways in addition to those mentioned above. The important point is that managers must monitor the environment for these trends and plan responses.

MANAGEMENT AT WORK

MANAGING TO TAKE ADVANTAGE OF FASHION FADS

Managers must be aware of societal trends, an expression of which is fads in fashions. One example is footwear and the popularity of Dr. Martens' shoes, and other heavy-duty, combat- or work-type boot and shoe styles.

Dr. Martens were first popular with British "skinheads" in the 1960s and later spread to North America. The shoes became popular with junior and senior high school students and are now fashionable with well-heeled older customers. They have become a status symbol in mainstream consumer culture.

While Dr. Martens are the original heavy-duty shoe, other manufacturers are benefiting from the trend to such rugged, military-style footwear—for example, Terra Footwear Ltd. of Harbour Grace, Nfld., and Markdale, Ontario. It's products are Terra, Terra Lites, and Wild Sider work boots. About 35 percent of its sales are private label boots for Mark's Work Wearhouse, Sears, and Kmart. Twelve percent of sales are exported to the United States and Europe. According to an article in *The Globe and Mail*, "the company's workboots have become a fashion statement among trend-setters in Paris and London."

Terra Footwear also provides an example of a company taking advantage of high technology to improve its production and marketing functions. The Newfoundland plant operates with state-of-the-art injection molding equipment, electronic data interchanges (EDI) which are to be extended to customers' operations, computer-assisted production systems and a computer-assisted design/computer-assisted manufacturing (CAD/CAM) systems. ▲

MEETING THE CHALLENGE

BELL CANADA'S ENVIRONMENT: BEFORE AND AFTER 1992

Bell Canada was influenced by major changes in several environmental factors. In June 1992, the CRTC decided that competition would be allowed in the long-distance business. Unitel Communications Inc. and other companies would be allowed to offer long-distance services to Canadian customers. Government, through the CRTC, had decided that the time had come to change the environment in which Bell Canada operated.

In addition to the changes being brought in by competition and the government, other changes related to technology and the work force are occurring at a rapid rate. Companies will be able to offer an array of services such as caller identification and call trace, call forwarding, voice messaging, video on demand, and personal 1-800 numbers. Technological advances will enable cable television companies to provide customers interactive communications for shopping and banking services in the near future. An American company even considers it will be feasible to offer a competing residential phone service. The forces of competition did not end with the 1992 introduction of long-distance competition.

Pressures also came from shareholders and adjustments that were necessary for the work force. Bell Canada is owned by BCE Inc., which also had investments in other businesses. Shareholders were unhappy with BCE's performance and put pressure not only on BCE's management but also on Bell Canada's.

Bell Canada's work force was downsized through attrition, early retirements, and layoffs. The company even considered a four-day work week for its employees in order to prevent further reductions. The job security evident at the company prior to 1992 disappeared as the company had to reduce costs and change work practices to meet the challenges.

For 100 years, Bell Canada operated in a protected, secure environment, but a turning point occurred in 1992 when it had to change from a monopoly to a customer-oriented, market-driven organization. ▲

SUMMARY

The environment which is outside or external to the organization must be considered in the management process. In this chapter, the environment was described by seven factors: the structural features of the economy; the nature of business enterprise ownership; the degree of competition within Canada and from outside the country; the role of government; the characteristics of the work force from which organizations must select their employees; the extent of technological innovation; and the impact of societal trends. Whenever a manager is involved in the management functions, planning, organizing, leading and controlling, there is likely to be some impact from one or more of these factors.

Attention to the environment is necessary for all managers, from the chief executive officer to the first-line supervisor. These factors often impact the organization in contradictory ways, for example, when the introduction of new technology leads to reductions in employees. Different managers will be influenced by one factor more than others, such as a manager responsible for human resources who would be most interested in the work force. Finally, the environmental factors often work in combination with one another making their impact difficult to predict.

The Canadian economy is largely comprised of resource-based industries instead of being dominated by manufacturing industries such as in Japan or Germany. The resource industries have lead to the establishment of hundreds of single-industry communities throughout the country and are sometimes in the form of megaprojects. However, in the past 20 years, there has been a shift from goods-producing to service-providing industries which is reducing the country's dependence on resource-based industries.

Canadian businesses are owned by several different types of investors who have different degrees of influence over managers. Effective managers are aware of owner influence and adjust management practices accordingly. Joint venture ownership is popular now and requires special management skills in negotiation and coordination. Finally, large portions of Canadian business are either owned by foreigners or are owned by families.

Most managers must consider other organizations that are providing the same goods or services, that is, their competition. This rivalry for business not only comes from other businesses in Canada, but also from the international business community. The performance of business organizations is a major component of Canada's national competitiveness and is accomplished through the levels of productivity and quality that are achieved by Canadian managers.

Governments play an important role in the operation of most organizations in Canada by purchasing the products of Canadian business, lending or giving money, taxing profits and property, regulating most aspects of operations, and even owning enterprises. Managers must take into account the political events in the country including the discussion of Canada's constitution and the trend towards deregulation and privatization.

Organizations require employees to produce goods or to provide services. These employees are obtained from a pool of individuals called the Canadian work force. Employees have certain expectations that managers must respond to, and may also be represented by unions that look out for their interests.

Research and development into new technologies is important to many businesses as their future performance depends upon new products. Other businesses must respond to, or adapt to, new technologies if they are to remain competitive. Innovation is a critical element that managers must somehow encourage in the organizations they operate.

No society stands still. In fact, the opposite occurs. Managers must recognize societal trends and respond or adapt to them. Change in society's preferences never stops making the task of a manager challenging.

KEY TERMS

single-industry communities (p. 52)
megaprojects (p. 53)
project management (p. 53)
direct owners (p. 54)
indirect owners (p. 55)
venture capital (p. 56)
venture capitalist (p. 56)
joint ventures (p. 57)
indirect (foreign) investment (p. 58)
direct (foreign) investment (p. 58)
concentration (p. 59)
business competitiveness (p. 60)
productivity (p. 61)
quality (p. 63)
total quality management (p. 63)
deregulation (p. 66)
privatization (p. 66)
research (p. 69)
development (p. 69)

REVIEW QUESTIONS

1. From the perspective of the management of a business organization, what approach should be taken towards the influence of the seven environmental factors?
2. What is meant by a resource-based industry?
3. Why are there so many single-industry communities in Canada?
4. Who are the main owners of Canadian business?
5. What generalizations can be made about the influences of ownership on managers?
6. Which two sources of competition should be of concern to managers?
7. List the ways in which governments are involved in business.
8. What is the difference between deregulation and privatization?

9. Define a joint venture and give an example.
10. What are the challenges for managers provided by the Canadian work force?
11. What is the difference between research and development?
12. What are the implications of the trend away from "yuppie" consumer preferences?

DISCUSSION QUESTIONS

1. What are the implications for managers of the trend from goods-producing to service-providing industries?
2. Which of the following owners of Canadian business is likely to have the most influence on managers? Why?
   Individual investors
   Mutual funds
   Corporate
3. Why would one corporation want to own another?
4. Why has the membership in Canadian unions plateaued as a percentage of the work force?
5. Why should the owners and managers of Canadian businesses be interested in national competitiveness?
6. What are the challenges for managers of being involved in a joint venture with another company?
7. What are the implications for managers of telecommuting?

EXERCISES

1. Review an issue of *The Globe and Mail*, *The Financial Post*, or *The Financial Times of Canada* and identify examples of the seven environmental factors.
2. Interview the manager of a local business and ask what are the main environmental factors impacting upon their business.
3. Identify a single-industry community in your province. Describe the industry upon which it is based and the name(s) of the business corporation(s) involved. Determine when the community was established and whether or not its future is threatened.
4. Select a large corporation or family business and look up the intercorporate holdings using the *Intercorporate Ownership*. Ottawa: Supply and Services Canada. Cat. No. 61-517. It should be in your college or university library.
5. Technology and innovation were discussed as a factor in the environment. Prepare a list of technological innovations developed by Canadians and identify high-technology Canadian business enterprises.
6. List what you consider to be the main trends in society that are affecting business. Indicate the nature of the effect.

MANAGEMENT ON LOCATION

CASE 3-1
GREAT WESTERN BREWERY COMPANY

In January 1990, 15 employees purchased a Saskatoon, Saskatchewan, brewery from Molson Cos. Ltd. for $3 million. Molsons had acquired the brewery when it took over Carling O'Keefe but did not need the production capacity. Each employee invested between $50 000 and $100 000 for a 25 percent equity with the rest of the purchase financed by a loan from the Saskatchewan Economic Development Corporation. Even though Molsons had offered to transfer the workers to other operations, they decided to go into business for themselves.

The new owners knew that they would have to improve the efficiency of the plant and lower costs. In order to get costs down, they even agreed to a 15 percent reduction in wages. Also, they knew they would have to learn about being managers and become knowledgeable of marketing practices.

Operating a small brewery would not be easy given the conditions in the industry. Two breweries, Molsons and John Labatt Ltd., dominated the market with 90 to 95 percent of sales. These large breweries had the advantages of large-scale production, elaborate and ...

extensive advertising, and the capability of introducing new brands. The consumption of beer was levelling off as Canadians drank less or consumed substitute products like wine. Beer drinkers were no longer as loyal to particular brands and shifted from one brand to another. The owners knew that sales could be drastically affected by a summer of cool weather.

Governments controlled everything about the distribution and marketing of beer including where it would be produced and sold, and the pricing. In addition, there was the possibility of competition from U.S. breweries as trade barriers were lowered between Canada and the United States and between Canadian provinces. Such competition was a serious threat as U.S. production costs were less, and therefore the prices were lower. There was also speculation that a supermarket chain would introduce its own private label no-alcohol draft beer.

Despite these obstacles, over a dozen small breweries (referred to as microbreweries) have opened up across the country and are now considered by the large breweries to be serious competition. Managers, and in the case of Great Western, owners, realized that operating an efficient brewery and convincing drinkers to purchase their beer would be a challenge. ▲

QUESTIONS

1. Given what you know about managing in the Canadian environment and with your knowledge of the beer industry, what are the implications for Great Western Brewery of the following environmental factors:
   (i) structure of the economy
   (ii) ownership
   (iii) competition
   (iv) role of government
   (v) work force
   (vi) technology
   (vii) societal trends
2. If you had been an employee at the Saskatoon brewery, would you have invested your life savings in Great Western Brewery and taken a cut in pay? Why or why not?

CASE 3-2
AAA PERFECTION CLEANERS

Alberto Capone opened his first dry cleaning plant/store in a Southern Ontario city of 150 000 in 1958. He borrowed the money to purchase a small plant, and he and other family members worked hard to provide a good quality service at reasonable prices. The business expanded every year by opening more stores, each with a small dry cleaning plant. In 1970 Capone centralized the cleaning operations into a large, modern plant and converted the stores to depots. Over the next few years he installed coin operated laundromats at each depot. The attendant at the depot could monitor the laundromats, give out change, and sell soaps and related products in addition to receiving and returning dry cleaning.

The centralized plant was equipped with commercial laundry equipment and Capone bid on and won several laundry contracts from nursing homes, motels, restaurants, and some government institutions. During the 1980s, AAA Perfection Cleaners started buying out other dry cleaners. The recession in the first half of the decade lead to many business failures and Capone was able to "pick up" several enterprises at bargain prices. By 1990, AAA Perfection Cleaners had over 90 percent of the dry cleaning business and operated all but two of the laundromats in the city and surrounding area. In addition, the firm controlled about 75 percent of the commercial laundry business in the area.

Capone's success was amazing considering that it was relatively easy for others to enter the dry cleaning business. The technology involved was well known and several franchise operations were available. A local community college instructor attributed Capone's success to several factors. AAA Perfection Cleaners' advertising and promotions were very effective and constantly changing, the depots and laundromats were clean and attractively decorated, and service was prompt. The laundromats became "meeting" places as people did their laundry, watched televisions in lounge areas or played billiards. Capone was active in the Dry Cleaners Association of Canada and regularly attended trade shows to learn of new technology which he immediately introduced in his operations.

AAA Perfection Cleaners was incorporated but operated as a private business and profit levels were not publicly known. Alberto admitted that he was "reasonably" well off even though he still lived in the same small house as he did in 1958. Other members of the Capone family were involved with the business, but Alberto Jr., in particular, had demonstrated that he had his father's sense for business. In February 1991, Alberto Sr. was 65 years old and planned to let his son take over running the business and he would at least "semiretire."

Two days before the celebration of his birthday and the official handing over of the business, Capone was informed that AAA Perfection Cleaners was under investigation by the Director of Investigation and Research, Competition Act, Consumer and Corporate Affairs Canada, for "abuse of dominant position." This meant that AAA Perfection Cleaners had been engaging in anticompetitive behaviour as the dominant dry cleaning firm in the city, that is, obtaining and maintaining too large a market share. Alberto couldn't understand why the government was concerned. He believed that through hard work and progressive management he had built a successful business which he hoped his family would continue to operate. ▲

QUESTIONS

1. What did Capone do wrong?
2. Why should the government be concerned with a very successful businessperson?
3. What should Capone do?

CASE 3-3
THE TOY INDUSTRY ENVIRONMENT

Carson Toys Ltd. produced a line of children's toys for the Canadian market. The toy industry was very competitive and volatile and close monitoring of market and social trends was critical for survival. In Canada, the industry had $1.2 billion in sales and included Canadian companies such as Irwin Toy Ltd. of Toronto and foreign firms such as Fisher-Price, Mattel, and Hasbro. Success was based on a firm having a market hit, for example the Cabbage Patch Kids, Oopsie Daisy doll, or Teenage Mutant Ninja Turtles. In addition, most firms had stable products such as Lego building blocks or board games such as Scrabble.

Carson Toys had been quite prosperous but recent reports showed that sales of two of Carson's most successful nonseasonal toys were down substantially. If allowed to continue, this would have a negative effect on profits, so Jonathan Carson, president of Carson Toys, called in Martha Bucyk, the vice-president of marketing, for an explanation. She gave several possible reasons for the decline.

First, Bucyk said that she had been told by several Carson salespersons that some customers were placing trial orders with a toy manufacturer in Taiwan. This manufacturer produced two high-quality toys which were very similar to two of Carson's toys. The major difference was the price. In Canada the imported toys sold at retail for 75 percent of the retail price of Carson's two toys. Bucyk suggested that retail toy buyers were growing more price conscious, because the uncertain economy in Canada was causing customers to demand more for their money.

Bucyk also suggested that the recent increase in the cost of plastic had led to a reduction in the thickness of the plastic used to make several Carson products, including the two problem products. She thought that this had hurt the company's reputation for making quality toys. In fact, Carson had received 150 letters from retail customers complaining about "shoddy" toys, and three customers said they were reporting the problem to Consumer and Corporate Affairs Canada. They claimed that their children had received cuts on their hands from jagged pieces of plastic, which became exposed when the toys broke during normal play. Bucyk and Carson worried about this. They knew that ...

three competitors had removed several unsafe toys from the market. Bucyk suggested, however, that this was a production problem and not directly her concern.

Bucyk's third suggestion for decreased sales was the declining birth rate in Canada. The two problem toys appeal to children between the ages of two and four, she pointed out, and so, with the number of potential users declining, Carson Toys cannot be surprised if sales also decline.

She suggested, too, that many parents were complaining about the tremendous volume of advertising aimed at children and that the constant bombardment of television commercials was "bad" for them. Carson had concentrated its advertising on Saturday morning children's television shows and several parents had written to Carson and accused the company of "taking advantage" of children. Bucyk also knew that the government was investigating these complaints from parents and that restrictive legislation was possible. As a result, the company had decided several months ago to reduce its advertising. However, they may have been too late and these complaints may have caused the decline in sales.

Finally, Martha Bucyk reminded Carson that more and more toys were now being sold through fewer large retail stores. One of the retailers, Toys "R" Us, dominated the market. This retailer had tremendous purchasing power and if it did not place orders for a new toy product, that item was most certain to fail on the market. ▲

QUESTIONS

1. List and describe briefly the environment factors affecting Carson Toys Ltd.
2. How are these environment factors causing problems for Carson Toys Ltd.?
3. Develop a plan of action for dealing with each one of these environment factors.

COMPREHENSIVE CASES
PART I

HOW TO ANALYZE COMPREHENSIVE CASES

There are two comprehensive cases at the end of each major section of this text. These cases are longer than those at the end of each chapter, and they require attention to a wider range of problems. In these comprehensive cases, you are given a great deal of information about a real company that has certain management problems. Your task is to analyze the information and then make suggestions that will resolve the management problems facing the company.

There are two basic approaches that can be used with cases studies. Your instructor may ask you to answer the questions found at the end of each case. These questions focus on specific topics that have been covered in the text, such as leadership, communication, conflict, or change. To answer the questions, reread the relevant section in the text and then decide how it can be applied to the practical problems that are evident in the case. Using the text material to answer the case questions will help you bridge the gap from management theory to management practice.

The second approach to case analysis is a more general one and involves using a four-step problem solving process. Your instructor may suggest that you ignore the questions provided for you. Instead, you will be required to:

1. *Define the problem or opportunity*: In each case you will be able to observe either a problem that needs to be solved or an opportunity that can be exploited. When defining problems, don't be sidetracked by symptoms of the problem. For example, if a company's employees have low productivity, this is not the problem but a symptom of the problem. What you must do is discover specifically what is causing low employee productivity. Be careful about the assumptions you make. For example, don't automatically assume that something is wrong with the employees just because their productivity is low; management may not have designed the work system properly, and employees therefore might not be able to be productive even if they are highly motivated.
2. *Develop plausible alternative solutions*: Once you have defined the problem or opportunity, you must develop several plausible alternatives that might solve the problem or help management exploit the opportunity. Make sure that your alternatives will actually improve the situation; a "do nothing" suggestion is generally not worthwhile. Creative thinking is also important when you are developing alternatives. Try to think of unconventional ways to solve the problem or exploit the opportunity. Some of the most successful managers are those who are able to see alternatives that other, more traditional, managers cannot see.
3. *Evaluate the alternatives*: Each alternative that you develop must be evaluated. This is probably the most difficult part of case analysis. Do not start this step with an opinion about which alternative is best and then try to find information to support that opinion. Rather, develop a list of pros and cons for each alternative through a systematic assessment of the material in the case. This takes time, but when you have completed this step you will be able to decide which alternative(s) should be chosen.
4. *Choose the best alternative(s)*: Select the alternative which, considering all the pros and cons, promises to do the best job of resolving the problem or exploiting the opportunity you have defined. More specifically, pick the alternative which best satisfies the specific criterion you think is important to the company—for example, profit, employee satisfaction, or product quality. In some situations, there will be multiple and conflicting criteria that should be satisfied. In these situations, the decision will be much tougher. Be aware that, no matter which alternative you choose, some individuals or groups in the case are going to be unhappy. From a management perspective, your job is to decide what will benefit the organization as a whole. ▲

COMPREHENSIVE CASES
PART I

CASE I-1
VALLEY DRUG MART: THE LAWTON'S ENTRY

As 1984 drew to a close, George Fairn wondered what the new year would bring for the Valley Drug Mart, the business he had started and built in Middleton, Nova Scotia, over the last fifteen years. He had recently learned that a major chain, Lawton's Drugs, was moving into Middleton in the new year. Could he hope to survive?

BACKGROUND

George was born in 1930 in Albany, a small satellite community of Middleton, a town of 2000 people nestled in the Annapolis Valley halfway between Halifax and Yarmouth. He grew up and went to school in the Middleton area, graduating from the old MacDonald School before going on to study pharmacy at Dalhousie University. After completing his training, he took a job in Saint John, New Brunswick.

In 1964, George had the opportunity to return to the Annapolis Valley, "the best place to live in North America." He also had a family now and did not want to raise his children in the city. So, he moved back to Middleton to work in the Eaton Drug Store. At the time, two retail drug stores operated in Middleton, Eaton and Mumford's, both independently owned. Both of these drug stores were fairly small establishments (about 1200 square feet each) located near the intersection of the two main streets of Middleton (see Exhibit 1). Neither had an extensive front store, the section that displayed the sundry (nonprescription) items available at the store.

EXHIBIT 1 MIDDLETON, NOVA SCOTIA.

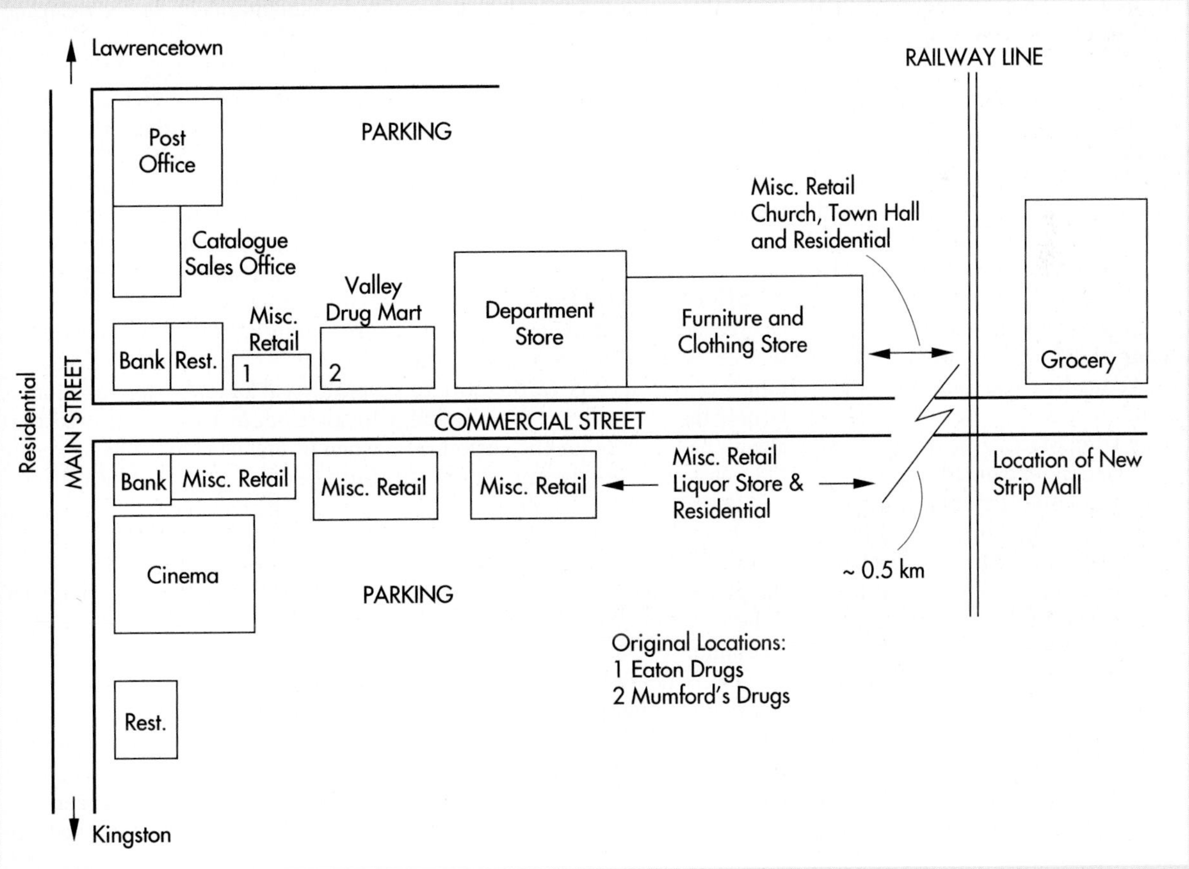

After a few years, George took the opportunity to purchase the Eaton drug store and, on January 1, 1969, took over the business. Over the next few years, George worked many long hours. Not only was he the owner, but he was also the only pharmacist. He had a staff of four clerks who worked the front store.

George preferred to focus on prescription service and did not particularly favour a large front store, especially since 95 percent of profits came from prescriptions. Most front stores in Canada operated at a loss. However, he realized that by not providing one, he was only inviting competition. If he did not provide the services the public demanded, someone else would. In 1973, in order to expand to provide these services, he bought a neighbouring building that leased space to several small retail outlets, including his competition, Mumford's Drug Store.

On November 3, 1975, he moved into the new building and the Valley Drug Mart was born. The new name reflected the change in services and philosophy of the business. Shortly afterwards, he purchased Mumford's Drug Store and expanded the Valley Drug Mart even further. The former owner of Mumford's worked with George for five years and then continued to serve on the board of the Valley Drug Mart. Over the next few years, George expanded into spaces vacated by other tenants, using the space for storage, office, and front store. Finally, in 1983, the Valley Drug Mart occupied the entire building, comprising over 7000 square feet.

To provide a full range of front store services, George investigated a number of buying groups for pharmaceutical goods. Affiliation with any one of these groups would allow the Valley Drug Mart to carry a line of "house" products. Through these associations, independents could jointly purchase many of their products with the same volume discounts enjoyed by larger chains. Carrying the branded goods from any of these associations involved somewhat higher advertising costs for radio advertising and flyers, but George felt, once again, that it was expected by the public.

At first, the Valley Drug Mart was affiliated with the Associated Retail Pharmacies (ARP) buying group. However, George had recently switched to Guardian Drugs as the merchandising arm of his store due to its superiority in several factors, including cost. George had since been appointed a director of the Guardian plan.

George saw the Valley Drug Mart as a full-service store. Not only did it have prescription service and an extensive front store, but it also offered a host of other services, such as ortho and breast prostheses.

With the growth of the store, George increased not only his front store staff, but also had added a front store manager and three additional full-time pharmacists.

BUSINESS PHILOSOPHY

George had very strong feelings about service, both in the store and in the community. It was important to George that the staff was friendly and always had a smile for the customer. "The customers are the ones doing *us* a favour by coming into the store. It's not the other way around."

In a town the size of Middleton, the pharmacist was almost expected to be active in civic affairs and to be a community leader. These expectations were possibly enhanced by the fact that the pharmacist was the only retailer *required* to have a university education. Whatever the expectations, most Middletonians felt that George far exceeded them, having served on the town council, as chair of the merchants' committee, in church activities and in the Rotary Club. He had recently been recognized for his community involvement with a reward from AH Robbins, a pharmaceutical company. George felt that his involvement with the community was further enhanced by the fact that he lived in the town itself.

On several occasions, when the local hospital had needed key equipment for its intensive care unit or for its veterans' wing, the Valley Drug Mart had purchased this equipment for them. George felt that it was part of his responsibility to contribute to the community which provided his living.

Advertising for the Valley Drug Mart was strongly service-oriented. It included the sponsorship of fire and birth announcements on the radio and community bulletin boards. Each month, the Valley Drug Mart brought in a nurse from the Victorian Order of Nurses (VON) to run a blood pressure clinic for the public.

Most recently, George had been investigating the possibility of sponsoring a van to chauffeur local residents who needed special medical tests in Halifax into the city, which was approximately 160 kilometres away (Exhibit 2). This idea arose from conversation at a Lion's Club function. A local resident had mentioned that when he had been in Halifax recently for a test at the Victoria General Hospital, he had encountered several other people from Middleton at the hospital. Some had travelled by car, some by train, and some by bus. This conversation had sparked the idea of running a van into Halifax two or three days a week to transport these people more efficiently.

Further investigation had shown that this commuter service could be used to transport blood, frozen sections, and other crucial items between

• • •

EXHIBIT 2 NOVA SCOTIA.

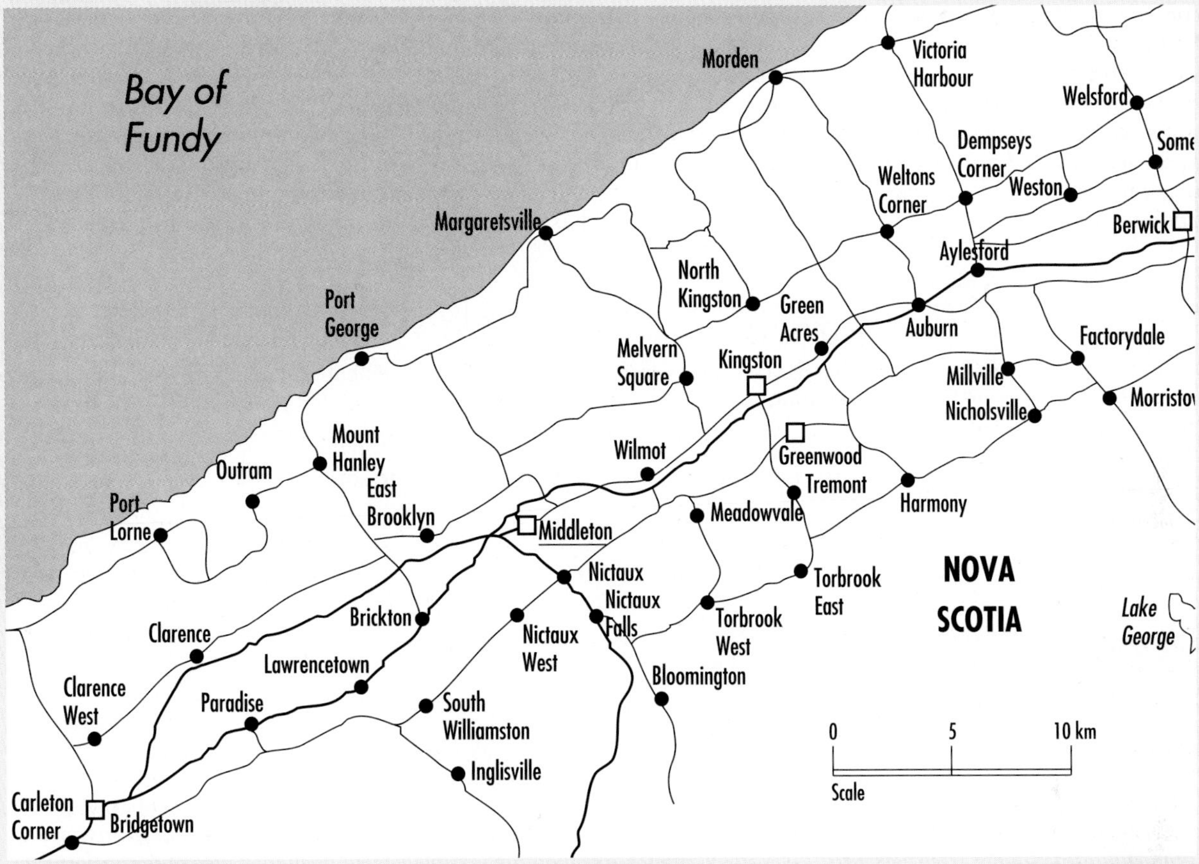

the local hospital and the city. The cost of a van would be $17 000 and the cost of each round trip, including gas, maintenance, and a driver's salary, would be approximately $100. George was seriously considering the implementation of this service, but he still had to consider several issues, such as its frequency and what he should charge for its use. Should he sponsor part or all of the service?

THE LAWTON'S ENTRY

At the end of 1984, after a fairly comfortable period of continued growth, the Valley Drug Mart was facing a major competitive challenge. As George was preparing to welcome in the new year and the 16th anniversary of his business, he learned that a new strip mall was to be built approximately one kilometre from his business (Exhibit 1) and that one of the stores that would be in this mall would be a Lawton's Drug Store. The anchor store for this mall would be a department store.

By 1984, the greater Middleton area had a population of approximately 4000 people, approximately half of whom lived in the town, with the remainder living in surrounding communities. The closest pharmacies were in Kingston and Lawrencetown, two slightly smaller towns located 12 kilometres on either side of Middleton (Exhibit 2). Adjoining Kingston was Greenwood, a community centred about a Canadian Forces Base. Greenwood had a population of about 5000 and housed a major regional mall. Another drug store was located in this mall. None of these pharmacies were part of any major chains. Given the local market, George felt that Middleton could not support another major pharmacy.

Lawton's Drugs was a major chain that was owned by Sobey's, a powerful and wealthy organization that had grown from a regional grocery chain. Its resources were on a scale far removed from those of the Valley Drug Mart, and George felt he had no hope

• • •

of surviving a price war, should it come to that. He did not know what he could do that Lawton's, with its vastly superior resources, could not only match, but exceed.

George loved his work. He arrived at his store by 7:45 a.m. each morning, even though the store did not open until 8:30 a.m., and he often came in at odd hours to fill urgent prescriptions. He had no intentions of giving up, even though he had planned to retire in four or five years anyway. Some friends had privately asked him if the fight was worth the effort. He had often received offers from major chains, such as Shopper's Drug Mart, to purchase the Valley Drug Mart, but he strongly opposed turning his business over to these corporations, having invested so much of himself into both the Valley Drug Mart and the town of Middleton. Yet Lawton's would be opening its doors within six months. How could he hope to compete, let alone survive against this threat? ▲

QUESTIONS

1. What has George Fairn done right in the management of Valley Drug Mart and in the community?
2. How has the environment changed for Valley Drug Mart?
3. What can businesses like Valley Drug Mart do to survive against large corporations?

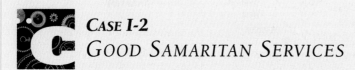

CASE I-2
GOOD SAMARITAN SERVICES

Good Samaritan Services (GSS) is a national voluntary agency founded in Canada approximately 100 years ago to direct geriatric health care services and training to the public. The Good Samaritans deliver first aid training to thousands of Canadians each year; they also provide a program of health care courses. Some of the organization's activities are financed by contributions from the United Way, and some revenue is derived from the training courses provided.

ORGANIZATION STRUCTURE

GSS is divided into two basic structural units—the branch and the unit. The branch is the administrative arm of the organization and exercises control through the guidance of the board of directors. Branches are located across Canada; the larger ones usually have a full-time paid secretary and one full-time paid training coordinator. Generally, branch members are volunteers from the community with some background in business or finance.

The unit provides at-home visits and first-aid services for shut-ins and the elderly. Unit members are well trained in first aid and cardiopulmonary resuscitation (CPR). They conduct the courses that the organization offers to the public. The first aid course instructors receive a nominal fee for teaching the courses.

THE SUDBURY, ONTARIO, BRANCH

The structure of the Sudbury branch of the Good Samaritans is shown in Exhibit 1. Jim Stanley (a volunteer) is the chair of the board of directors. The board of directors which is comprised of representation from both the branch and the unit, meets monthly and is open to all members of the Samaritans. The management committee is composed of selected members of the board of directors and functions as an executive committee of the board. The management committee was set up to address management issues that continually arose as the branch grew. Its membership is restricted so that it can handle issues quickly as they arise. At the present time, the Sudbury branch has no general manager. (This position is found only in the larger branches.) If the Sudbury branch grows, it could require such a position.

The Sudbury branch has operated out of several different older buildings during the past 20 years. In 1980, the building that housed the branch burned down, so the branch moved • • •

to the former residence of a local hospital. During this time pubic interest in the first-aid classes declined, as did the morale of Samaritan volunteers. It became obvious that the organization's effectiveness was slipping.

Dan Foster, the head of the unit, therefore spearheaded a campaign to raise funds for a new building to be called the Samaritan Centre. The project was successful, and, in January 1985, the Sudbury Good Samaritans moved into the new premises. Everyone was pleased with the new building and morale improved. The unit members were particularly elated with their new quarters.

EXHIBIT 1 ORGANIZATIONAL STRUCTURE OF SUDBURY, ONT., GOOD SAMARITANS BRANCH.

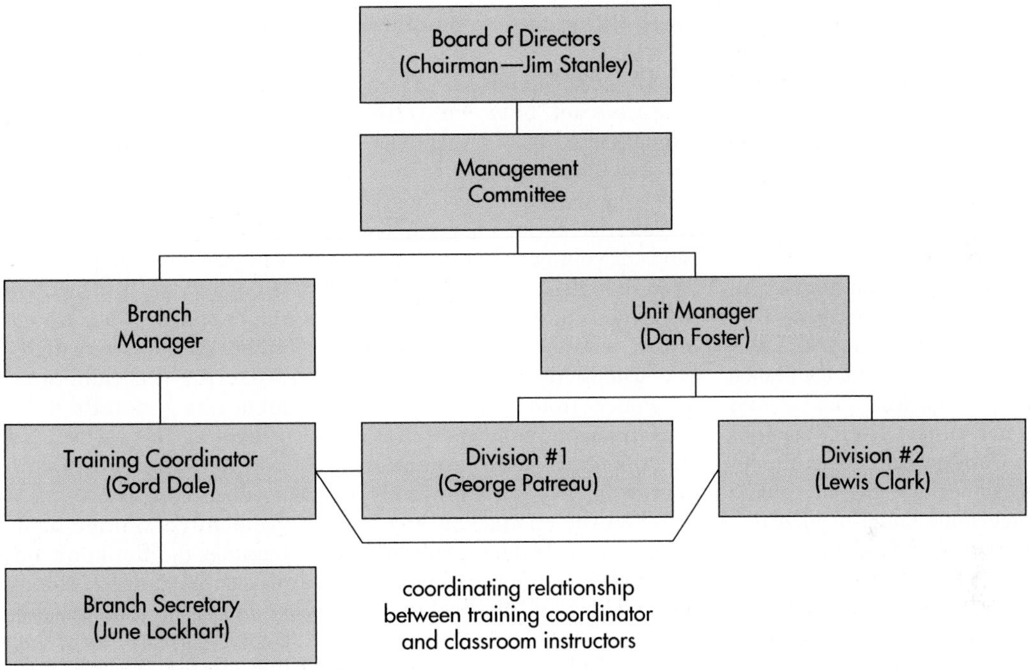

THE PROBLEM BEGINS

When the vice-chair returned to Sudbury in January 1985 after the Christmas vacation, he was summoned to the Samaritan Centre for a special meeting. Dan Foster wanted the board to enlist the services of Tom Jennings, a consultant, to act for the branch to raise money.

The branch, in its move to the new site, quickly realized it did not have the kind of operating money it needed. It also required substantially more time commitment and managerial skill than had been available in the past. Foster had known Jennings for many years and believed that he had the management skills that were necessary to put GSS on its feet. These were much needed skills, as the majority of people in the organization were there on a voluntary basis, only one or two nights a month. Restructuring and organizing were necessary if the organization was to meet its potential and become a more useful non-profit enterprise. Foster believed the organization needed to improve its marketing of courses to the general public. Therefore, he proposed to the board that Jennings be hired as a full-time consultant for $30 000 a year.

Jennings was asked questions about his plans and his ideas for GSS. He responded in a capable and professional manner and presented pro forma statements that made the financial picture look very promising. He believed that the Samaritans should increase course offerings by 60 percent and that doing so would put the operation in the black within six months. Jennings

high utilization rates for the classrooms, including a program of evening and weekend rentals. These figures were projected over a three-year period to show GSS on an exceedingly firm financial footing. He also made clear that he would cover his consulting fee with the money he generated from donations and fund raising.

The board was concerned about Jenning's fee but, after considerable discussion, decided to hire him. Several board members considered that $30 000 was too much money for a non-profit organization to spend in the face of financial stress. These concerns turned out to be well founded.

OPEN CONFLICT

Almost immediately on beginning his work, Jennings had disagreements with Gord Dale, the branch training coordinator. Jennings, Dale and the branch secretary, June Lockhart, had moved into the new office. They were supposed to work together to set up operations and begin selling the courses to produce some much-needed revenue. Dale was older than Jennings and resented the fact that Jennings was being paid more than he was. Jenning's manner was brusque and tactless. He had no knack for diplomatically persuading Dale to change his job. The arguments between Jennings and Dale were heated, and Dale began to think about resigning.

The disagreements between Dale and Jennings were to some extent aggravated by the volunteer nature of the organization. According to the formal structure of the branch, Dale reported to Jim Stanley, the chair of the board of directors. (See Exhibit 1.) However, because Stanley was a volunteer, he was in the office only once a week or so. Dale made it clear to Jennings that Jennings was not his boss and that Dale would not take orders from him. However, Dale did need some direction because the whole complexion of his job was changing. A much more aggressive style of selling the courses and marketing the organization was needed; he had to go to the public and sell, not wait for the public to come to him. Despite these realities, Dale sat behind his desk waiting for business to come in. This refusal of Dale to alter irked Jennings. Lockhart had to work tirelessly to keep peace in the office.

UNIT VERSUS BRANCH

The conflict between Dale and Jennings also caused a split to develop between the unit and the branch. The unit comprised the grass roots of the organization. Its members put in thousands of volunteer hours every year. Even though Dale was branch training coordinator (see Exhibit 1), he felt aligned with the unit. The unit members usually received their teaching assignment from Dale.

Dale made his negative feelings about Jennings known to unit members, who listened attentively and watched the changes taking place around them. As the verbal battles between Dale and Jennings continued, both Stanley and Foster became increasingly concerned. At the monthly meetings of the Sudbury branch, this conflict was discussed frequently. It was always a strained affair. Foster had taken a dislike to Dale because Dale constantly complained about Jenning's behaviour and insensitivity. The management committee tended to side with Jennings, who it considered was getting the office organized. Jennings, now signing himself as "Director of Good Samaritan Services," had the support of the volunteer branch members. Dale sensed this support and felt that his efforts to perform well and get ahead in the organization were in vain. Dale began drinking heavily to escape these stressful developments.

Dale wanted to earn more money and decided to investigate the possibility of becoming branch manager. Foster, who had the most informal influence with the management committee, would not hear of it. Foster was a popular man, both in GSS and in the community. He had lived in Sudbury all his life and had recently retired from Ontario Hydro.

By now, the conflict between Dan and Jennings was full-blown. Dale was taking time off from work on doctor's orders and Jennings was taking time off to pursue other interests. As a consequence, the financial affairs of the organization were suffering and courses were not being solicited as planned. The official opening of the Samaritan Centre was drawing closer and plans were in place for a gala affair, which the lieutenant-governor of the province would attend. Tension in the office was very high.

During this time of crisis, unit members generally defended the struggling Dale, who tried to avoid having to deal with Jennings. Unit members complained to branch management committee members that Jennings did not know how to handle people and that communication in the organization was deteriorating. George Patreau, one of the officers of the unit, became very annoyed one evening when his division was left without a place to prepare for the opening ceremonies. It seems that Jennings had booked the hall for a meeting of an outside group. Patreau, a senior man in the organization and a well-respected leader, was beside himself when Jennings flippantly told him that he should have read the notice board in advance.

As another example of poor communication, Dale returned the wine glasses for the formal opening dinner to the caterer because there was no invoice with the delivery. This occurred while Jennings was out of the office, and earned Dale a sharp rebuke from Foster after Jennings complained.

• • •

At the monthly meetings of the board of directors, unit members became tight-lipped and sullen about the situation. They complained about the need for more money and new equipment. They claimed they could not run good quality classes with audio-visual equipment that broke down frequently. At the same time, they were asked to vote on motions for money to go to the branch office for the "big party" (the formal opening) that was coming up. The unit became increasingly defensive and upset. They participated at tag day with limited enthusiasm, which showed in the final tally of money.

The unit held private meetings to discuss their concerns. Dale participated actively in these discussions and pleaded that something be done about Jennings. The members of the unit, who normally follow Foster's direction on most matters, elected to ignore him and proceed with a letter signed by all unit members asking to have the problems in the branch office attended to immediately. The letter of complaint was addressed to Stanley and read at a management committee meeting. The committee was upset by this gesture and the conflict deepened. Many members of the unit also approached Foster independently to mention the struggle and the lack of cooperation.

Foster sadly had to admit that Jennings had not raised one cent since he had been hired as a consultant. Course offerings and a few rentals were up, but produced insufficient revenue to resolve the financial problems facing the branch. Nevertheless, Jennings was perceived as a good business manager, and the plans were in place for the formal opening of the new centre.

However, behind the scenes business at Good Samaritan Services was changing. Foster was forced to spend more time on administrative duties than with his normal unit duties. Disenchantment among unit members grew as new office furniture arrived including a rather expensive microcomputer for Jenning's exclusive use. The unit was extremely envious. Members wondered why they were wearing old uniforms and why fund raising was meeting only branch needs, while the unit went without. Dale made it known that Jennings was spending more time pursuing outside interests. There was also a rumour that Jennings was negotiating with a company to purchase a small gas station and diner near the edge of town.

The conflict reached its peak when Dale refused delivery on the printed programs for the opening day events. The printing company required payment in full and there was no money available. Jennings was off on another jaunt to assess his latest business operation. Word was out that he was planning to run both Good Samaritans and the diner at the same time. Jennings claimed that he could make both operations successful.

The president of the Ontario council for Good Samaritan Services called the Tuesday before the grand opening and was told that everything was in readiness for Saturday's activities. But the office was in turmoil. To make matters worse, on Wednesday morning, the Royal Bank manager called Foster and Stanley to his office to have a discussion about the branch's financial status. He told them that their line of credit had reached its limit of $10 000 and that no further money would be forthcoming until the branch developed a realistic financial plan. Then, on Wednesday afternoon, Lockhart called Foster to tell him that Dale had been admitted to hospital suffering from chest pains and shortness of breath. She had driven him there after he had collapsed at the branch. The doctors said that Dale was near exhaustion and needed a rest.

Foster called Stanley and told him to convene an emergency meeting of the board of directors as soon as possible. Swift action was needed if a complete breakdown of the organization was to be averted. ▲

QUESTIONS

1. What kind of structural problems are evident at GSS?
2. Construct a new organization chart for the Sudbury branch that will solve the structural problems you've noted.
3. What kind of people problems are evident at Sudbury's branch of GSS?
4. Suggest ways to solve the people problems you've noted.

PART 2

PLANNING AND DECISION MAKING

CHAPTER

4

THE PLANNING PROCESS

LEARNING OBJECTIVES

After reading this chapter, you will be able to:

1. State ten important facts about planning.
2. List five benefits of and seven potential problems with planning.
3. Describe the steps in the formal planning process.
4. Write a good goal statement.
5. Describe how plans, policies, and procedures differ.
6. Explain seven forecasting techniques.
7. Describe the concept of contingency planning and state why it is important to managers.
8. Explain what management by objectives is, and identify the six principal steps in the process.
9. Describe the benefits of and potential problems with management by objectives.

MANAGEMENT CHALLENGE

PLANNING IN AN UNCERTAIN ENVIRONMENT

The airline industry has recently experienced numerous problems, and Canadian Airlines International (CAI) is no exception. In a video made for employees, company president Kevin Jenkins and senior vice-president of finance David Murphy explained how external factors have affected the company's fortunes. The firm incurred significant losses in the early 1990s, partially due to factors over which the company had no control.

The Gulf War in 1991, for example, caused a dramatic increase in fuel prices for several months, and this increased operating expenses. The recession of 1990-1992 was longer and more severe than anyone expected, and this reduced demand for air travel. Because of higher prices and lower demand, there was less cash from operations than expected, so the company had to borrow money. But this increased interest costs. All these things worked together to cause significant problems.

To make matters worse, CAI was dealt another setback when Japan Air Lines decided to bow out of an agreement to share the costs of Toronto-Tokyo flights. This was just part of a bigger decision by JAL to cut joint service operations with other airlines because it was losing so much money. The change meant that CAI's costs on the Tokyo run would double. The change also suggests that demand for the Toronto-Tokyo run has declined.

Vice-president Murphy noted that CAI has to make enough money to cover four items: (1) the cost of employee salaries, fuel, parts, rent, and other day-to-day expenses; (2) interest payments on money the company has borrowed; (3) capital purchases such as new airplanes; and (4) profits. Sales revenue is not sufficient to cover these factors.

There are several possible solutions to CAI's difficulties. One is purchase by another airline. In 1992, American

• • •

Airlines offered to invest $246 million in CAI, with the understanding that CAI would join American's Sabre reservation system. But there was an immediate problem with this alternative: when Gemini (the reservation system that CAI and Air Canada jointly operate) heard about American's offer, it sued CAI for $1 billion, claiming that if CAI withdrew, Gemini would no longer be a viable company and that Gemini employees would lose their jobs.

Another possibility was a merger with archrival Air Canada. But as merger talks began, the federal Bureau of Competition stepped in and required CAI to demonstrate that Air Canada was the only serious buyer. The Bureau of Competition took this action because it was concerned that once the two firms merged, the new firm would have a monopoly on air travel in Canada.

When this new uncertainty arose, CAI asked the four western provinces and the federal government for a $190 million bailout so it could continue to operate on its own. The request came at about the same time that the federal government received a report from its transportation commission saying there should be no airline bailouts. The government finally agreed to a $50 million bailout plan which required CAI to cut a number of its flights, lay off several thousand workers, and eliminate many discount fares.

In spite of this bailout, CAI remains in a precarious position. In a free market economy, there is simply no guarantee that a company will survive. It is indeed tough to plan! ▲

The Management Challenge shows the importance of planning to business firms. But all managers need to be effective planners, whether they work in a business firm, a government agency, a religious institution, a military establishment, a union, a school, or a volunteer organization. Nor does it matter whether the organization is a profit-oriented business or a not-for-profit enterprise. Planning is one of the four basic functions of management. In the three chapters in this section, we analyze this critical management function.

In this chapter, we first present some introductory observations about planning and how managers conduct it. Second, we discuss the planning process, with special emphasis on the many types of plans organizations develop. The chapter concludes with an examination of management by objectives (MBO).

PLANNING, MANAGERS, AND ORGANIZATIONS

LEARNING OBJECTIVE 1
State ten important facts about planning.

We noted in Chapter 1 that planning is the process of deciding what objectives to pursue and choosing strategies that will help the organization reach those objectives. Keeping this definition in mind, we can make the following observations about the management function of planning:

1. *Planning is a prerequisite for the successful performance of the other managerial functions* While the functions of management are interrelated, the fact that planning must be done first gives it a certain fundamental significance that the other functions do not have.

2. *Planning occurs in the present, but is oriented toward the future* Thus, planning always entails some uncertainty.

3. *Planning focusses on the means used to achieve an organization's ends* In order to reach objectives (the ends), every organization must develop plans (means) to achieve them.

4. *Planning may be formal or informal* In large enterprises, planning tends to be very visible and formalized, but in small organizations planning may be quite informal.

5. *Planning is an ongoing process, not a one-time event* Plans for major projects may receive so much attention that observers may think that plans are developed only intermittently, that is, when large projects are involved. But planning is a continual process.

6. *Planning does not imply inflexibility* Some managers feel that plans lock them into a rigid course of action. But good plans are flexible, and allow managers to adjust their activity in response to feedback from the environment.

7. *Planning is an analytical process* Careful thought is required to devise appropriate plans, and once plans are made, judgments must be made on how best to put them into practice. Bridging the gap between thinking and action is crucial.

8. *Planning involves scanning both the internal and external organizational environments* When developing plans, managers must take into account any inhibiting or facilitating factors, whether these factors are found within the organization or in the organization's external environment.

9. *Planning helps an organization cope with environmental change and uncertainty* Some people argue that uncertainty makes planning fruitless. However, systematic study of the constraints and opportunities in the external environment may lead to strategies that help the organization cope with uncertainty. Bovar Inc., an oil drilling operation, decided to transform itself into an environmental and waste management company because it had financial problems in its former business, and because it saw great market opportunities in waste management.[1]

10. *Planning does not guarantee organizational success* While planning is necessary for success, it is insufficient by itself. Managers must also focus on the functions of organizing, leading, and controlling to reach organizational objectives. These functions are described in detail in later chapters in this text.

MANAGERS AND PLANNING

Do managers actually spend time doing systematic and formal planning? Henry Mintzberg's research showed that the typical manager's day was characterized by different activities, frequent interruptions, and a need to cope with unexpected problems that demanded immediate solutions.[2] In this kind of environment, it is easy to see how formal planning might take a back seat to other activities. Mintzberg concluded that managers plan implicitly, rather than explicitly. In other words, managers do not allocate specific time to carry out the planning function, nor do they engage in formal, reflective planning because the hectic pace of their job discourages it.[3] The Management at Work insert, "Planning and Restructuring," addresses this interesting question.

At Wascana Energy, identifying the resources which will best generate future growth is a critical first step in the planning process. Systematic assessment of potential gas and oil sites is necessary in order for other steps in the planning process to be carried out effectively.

Managers do, however, spend a considerable amount of their time planning. Some of it occurs in formal planning sessions, where a group of managers will come together for the explicit purpose of developing, say, an overall strategy for the organization. But much planning also occurs in short bursts as the manager responds to various problems that arise in the course of a normal day's work. This informal, hard-to-observe planning is crucial for managerial success.

Some managers dislike spending time on planning. They see themselves as active, energetic individuals, who are accustomed to making rapid decisions and achieving goals. Because much of their work has a day-to-day perspective, they may have difficulty thinking about the future. But in order to continue achieving goals, managers must be prepared for the future. To be prepared, they must plan.

MANAGEMENT AT WORK

PLANNING AND RESTRUCTURING

In the 1980s, companies faced with difficulties usually resorted to "cost-cutting" and "downsizing." Although these approaches usually worked in the short term, they didn't prepare companies for business once the tough times were over. Most firms simply returned to doing things the way they used to, and restored the 10-15 percent of the company that had been cut or downsized. Thus, the procedures didn't alter the fundamental way the business was conducted; nor did they improve corporate efficiency or productivity.

In the 1990s, more and more managers are recognizing that dramatic changes in the external environment must be dealt with. Restructuring emphasizes doing things differently instead of just trying to do the same old thing more cheaply.

There seem to be two approaches to restructuring. The first is the desperate manoeuvres of companies like Campeau Corp., which failed to recognize danger signals and plan accordingly. The other kind of restructuring is characterized by deliberate planning by managers that involves rethinking markets, considering corporate strengths and weaknesses, what business the firm should be in, and how it should compete. Companies taking this approach restructure when the time is right, not when they are forced to.

Canada Malting, a division of Canada Malting Company Ltd., recently completed a restructuring effort. John Bramberger, vice-president of finance, recognized that earnings were declining on flattening sales, and that the balance sheet indicated assets that were underutilized. After convincing company presidents of the need to rethink the way they were doing business, the firm embarked on a three-month planning exercise where senior managers analyzed corporate strengths and weaknesses and looked at the company's standing in its markets.

The managers concluded that there was overcapacity in the world malting industry. They decided to close their three least productive plants, and to stop dealing with Central and South American markets because of increasing risk in those areas. The company targeted brewing companies as its main customers and expanded its production in improved facilities in order to supply them. Revenues and earnings have increased significantly as a result of the planning exercise. ▲

PLANNING AT DIFFERENT ORGANIZATIONAL LEVELS

Plans must be developed for all levels of management, although their focus will differ at different levels of management. The planning activities of top managers and lower-level managers reveal four principal differences (see Table 4-1). The situation in the Management Challenge is one that requires planning by top-level managers because the survival of the firm is at stake.

THE BENEFITS OF PLANNING

LEARNING OBJECTIVE 2

List five benefits of and seven potential problems with planning.

Planning has several benefits:

1. *It helps identify opportunities for the organization* Planning requires an organization to look for opportunities to earn profits or provide a service that otherwise may be overlooked. If opportunities are identified, steps can be taken to capitalize on them. Essentially, this means that planning helps an organization to cope with change.
2. *It helps identify possible problems* The analysis involved in planning can reveal situations that could threaten the organization. If such potential hazards are noticed or anticipated, steps can be taken to minimize their impact.
3. *It forces managers to set objectives* As we shall see shortly, the planning process demands that managers make decisions about which objectives to pursue. Once these objectives are set, employees have a clearer idea of how their work helps achieve the organization's goals. When these goals are met, both managers and workers share a feeling of accomplishment.

TABLE 4-1 PLANNING AT DIFFERENT MANAGEMENT LEVELS

Top Managers	Lower-Level Managers
1. Develop organizational objectives and the overall plans to achieve them.	1. Develop plans that will fit the overall objectives that have been developed by top management.
2. Spend a large proportion of their time on the planning function.	2. Spend a much smaller proportion of their time on the planning function.
3. The time frame for planning activities is very long (more than one year).	3. The time frame for planning activities is very short (often week-to-week).
4. Focus on both internal and external organizational factors when planning.	4. Focus largely on internal organizational factors when planning.

4. *It forces managers to set standards* As part of the planning process, managers must decide what standards of performance are necessary to reach the objectives. These standards convey to employees what they must do; they also help managers fulfill the controlling function.
5. *It coordinates organizational activity* Well-developed plans for the whole organization and for each of its major components assist individuals in seeing how their particular work fits in with the work of others. This understanding can reduce wasted actions and increase organizational efficiency.

PROBLEMS IN PLANNING

Although the benefits of planning are substantial, effective planning can be impeded in firms (see the Management at Work insert "Poor Planning at Leigh Instruments"). Some of the barriers to planning are as follows:

1. *Lack of support from top management* If top management is nonchalant about planning, lower-level managers will conclude that planning is unimportant.
2. *Poor information* Information is a key element in planning. If poor-quality information is used as the basis for plans, good plans cannot be developed.
3. *Resistance to change* Planning may result in decisions to change organizational practices. These changes can cause resistance in people who have become accustomed to certain ways of behaving.
4. *Over- or undercommitment to plans* If managers spend a lot of time and energy implementing plans, they may become emotionally attached to them. Once that happens, they may be unable to objectively assess the plan, and will reject any comments that are critical of the plan. Conversely, managers like quick feedback after they make a decision, and if this feedback is not forthcoming, they may be tempted to drop the plan and draft a new one.
5. *Managers are not involved in the planning process* If objectives are simply imposed from above, lower-level managers will lack the motivation to achieve them.
6. *Managers are too busy to plan* Many managers are so busy in their day-to-day responsibilities that they lack the time for planning. A failure to plan, in turn, means they will continue to have no time to plan.
7. *Lack of competence in planning* Some managers lack the experience, motivation, or aptitude for systematic planning. Deficiencies in experience and motivation can be overcome, but an inability to plan cannot; someone who lacks planning skills cannot be an effective manager.

MANAGEMENT AT WORK

Poor Planning at Leigh Instruments

A fascinating case of poor planning is illustrated by the story of Leigh Instruments Ltd. Founded in 1961, the firm made money in all but five years of its existence. John Shepherd, the president and founder, believed that a small, innovative company like Leigh, backed by the ideas of technical entrepreneurs, should be able to reach great heights with the right financial support.

This support came from the federal government. Leigh had the opportunity to develop multibillion dollar international markets for its products, which included advanced systems and electronic parts for aircraft and ships. Leigh followed the pattern of planning that most companies with defence contracts seem to use. They took on the long-term development of products and estimated their profitability each year. If estimates were incorrect, the company simply had to absorb the losses and proceed. The trouble was that Leigh was usually very wrong in its estimates and they repeated their mistakes year after year. The firm lacked effective planning and vigilant monitoring of its overall corporate picture.

In 1982, a $6.3 million contract was awarded from the Department of National Defence (DND) to do the preliminary work on integrated communications systems. Although Leigh had some expertise in this area, the contract meant a substantial shift in emphasis. The company estimated that it would cost $8 million to complete the project, but that the export potential would help them recoup the loss. The federal government even agreed to cover half the $1.7 million difference. Leigh concluded that it could do the project simply by revamping equipment that had already been developed at Northern Telecom.

But they discovered that the system would actually have to be built from scratch. That was the beginning of the downfall of Leigh. Problems began to snowball, and were caused by the company moving too quickly from manufacturing electronic products into the realm of integrated systems. In the process, company management was stretched beyond its capabilities. The firm also bid too low for contracts, most of which were never completed, and therefore got itself into financial difficulties.

The prototype of the first integrated system was delivered a year late, full of flaws that Leigh promised to fix. The company then accepted a $2.8 million contract, feeling that they could make delivery schedules and redesign along the way. In 1986, a $24.2 million contract was awarded from the DND on the understanding that all the bugs were out of the system (this was not so).

This pattern continued for the next several years. Contracts were awarded and cost overruns were absorbed with management always planning to tidy up previous problems at the next stage and "piggybacking" new contracts on top of old ones. The firm continually planned to make good on the next contract until, in April of 1990, after losing $72 million on revenues of $53 million, Leigh was forced to close its doors. Ironically, the company's slogan was "strength through growth." ▲

Planning and Organizational Performance

It seems logical that organizations that plan will perform better than those that do not. Many studies have been conducted to test this idea. Using traditional financial measures of success like profits, sales, and return on investment, the majority of these studies show that companies with formal planning procedures do perform better than those without formal procedures.[4] In addition, when organizations introduce formal planning programs, they typically find that they improve on their own past performance.[5] However, the existence of formal planning procedures is no guarantee of success.[6]

When organizations with formal planning systems experience poor performance, it is often because some unexpected event in the external environment negated the benefits of planning. For example, Canadian firms in the trucking industry have encountered increased competition from giant U.S. firms as a result of the Canada-U.S. Free Trade Agreement. No matter how well these firms planned their activities, some of them simply could not compete. Similarly, the Iraqi invasion of Kuwait in August 1990 disrupted the plans of both government and business organizations.

These groups made plans based on the assumption that oil prices would remain at about $20 a barrel. But after the invasion, oil prices rose to $40 per barrel, and plans had to be revised. The federal government found that its deficit was higher than anticipated, and business firms found the cost of oil-based raw materials had increased substantially. By 1991, oil prices had again dropped to around $20 a barrel, but the war in the Middle East created great uncertainty about oil prices. By 1993, oil prices had dropped even further, and analysts were predicting that prices would stay low for some time.

Since unexpected short-run events can lead to lowered performance, organizations should have a longer-term perspective on performance. Too many corporations make heroes out of executives who produce big profits immediately, but fail to build the business for the future. Instead of looking only to the next quarter, businesses should look to the next quarter century.[7]

THE PLANNING PROCESS

LEARNING OBJECTIVE 3
Describe the steps in the formal planning process.

The steps in the planning process are shown in Figure 4-1. There are four points to remember about this process:

1. Managers at all levels proceed through these steps when they carry out the planning function.
2. The planning process takes place within an organization, but it is influenced by factors outside the organization.
3. The planning process is not as neat and orderly as the model implies; some steps may be repeated several times.
4. Contingency planning is necessary to take into account unexpected events.

SET ORGANIZATIONAL OBJECTIVES

objectives

Managers have a responsibility to set objectives that will help fulfill the corporate mission. **Objectives** are the results that the organization wants to achieve. (We use the terms "objectives" and "goals" synonymously.) The highly respected management consultant, Peter Drucker, argues that organizations should set objectives in eight key result areas. These are shown in Table 4-2.[8]

Objectives focus employee attention on tasks that are consistent with the organization's mission. Unitel Communications Inc. set a goal to capture 5 percent of the residential and business long-distance phone market within three years of its startup, and 16 percent by its tenth year of operation.[9] Xerox Corp. set an objective to begin

FIGURE 4-1 THE PLANNING PROCESS.

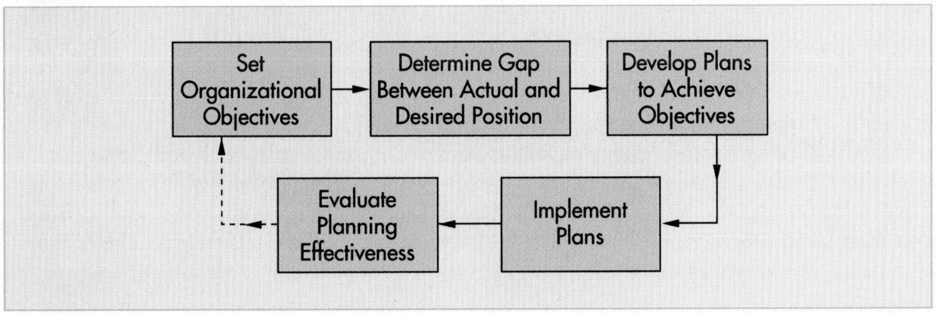

TABLE 4-2 OBJECTIVES FOR KEY RESULT AREAS.

Key Result Area	Explanation
1. Market Share	The proportion of the total market for a product or service that the company controls.
2. Innovation	The development of new products or services.
3. Productivity	Maximizing the amount of goods or services produced while minimizing the resources necessary to produce them.
4. Physical Resources	Physical facilities and their most effective use.
5. Financial Resources	Sources of funds and how these funds will be used.
6. Profitability	Monetary gain resulting from organizational activity.
7. Human Resource Development	Attract and develop high-quality managers and employees.
8. Social Responsibility	Concern for issues like ethical behaviour and good corporate citizenship.

competing in the rapidly expanding field of document processing because it promises higher profit margins than traditional photocopying.[10] Shell Canada Ltd. adopted the objective of changing its fossil fuel companies to energy companies that will put as much effort into solar and wind power as they will into oil and gas exploration.[11]

Goal setting focusses employee activity on goals that are critical for organizational survival. In February of 1992, the managers at Imperial Oil's Dartmouth, Nova Scotia, plant were given until the end of the year to improve their refinery's status from one of the worst to one of the best. The refinery manager says the workers got real clarity that day about what goals would have to be achieved to keep the plant open. Nine months later, management and workers at the refinery had achieved their goal.[12] The Management at Work insert "Planning for Prevention at Northern Telecom and Dupont" illustrates how planning and goal setting work together.

MANAGEMENT AT WORK

PLANNING FOR PREVENTION AT NORTHERN TELECOM AND DUPONT

Planning can be oriented toward a variety of important organizational activities, including employee health and safety. When Northern Telecom experienced a disturbing increase in repetitive strain injuries to employees, and an accompanying increase in the amount of lost time, they developed a well-planned and thoroughly executed program to reverse the trend.

The company began by giving existing injuries the best treatment available through a multidisciplinary team of professionals. Then they proceeded to educate their work force on how to identify and promptly report repetitive strain injuries. Workers were also shown how to avoid certain movements which would cause or aggravate such injuries.

Interestingly, the initial result was a further increase in the reporting of strain injuries, probably caused by increased awareness. But within a few months, the number of serious new cases was virtually eliminated. Since repetitive strain injuries were still apparent, the company tried another approach. They formed an ergonomics committee composed of managers and employees, all of whom were trained to identify and resolve problems, and to develop a cost justification for correcting the situation. Several teams were formed, each of which had the skills and awareness to develop systems for predicting problems and developing ways of preventing them. One team developed a comprehensive ergonomics manual for a new manufacturing process.

Another approach is used at DuPont Inc. They have devised a health and safety plan aimed at having no occupational injuries or illnesses. Although this is a lofty ambition, the goal is perceived as inspiring, believable, and meaningful to company employees. By building the company culture around this goal, DuPont has planned for a situation where the corporate philosophy, principles, and beliefs embrace the notion of a safe work environment. ▲

Goals perform a variety of functions. They serve as guidelines for action (by describing future desired results and clarifying expectations), as constraints (by stating what should and should not be done), as a source of legitimacy (by justifying an organization's activities), as a facilitator of the controlling function (by stating specific output expectations), and as a source of motivation (by presenting a challenge to employees).[13]

Goals are normally set at three levels in organizations. *Strategic goals,* which are set by top management, support the organization's overall mission. Because these goals deal with the performance of the organization as a whole, they are usually stated in fairly general terms (e.g., to be the market leader in semiconductors). *Tactical goals* are more specific than strategic goals and are set by middle managers (e.g., to introduce a new management information system within two years). *Operational goals* are the most specific, and are set by first-line managers (e.g., to reduce employee absenteeism to 1 percent within three months). These three levels of goals form a **hierarchy of objectives**, with operational and tactical goals feeding into, and being consistent with, strategic goals. This ensures that employees working at various levels in the organization avoid working at cross-purposes. Figure 4-2 demonstrates the hierarchy of objectives concept.

hierarchy of objectives

Goals or objectives should be stated in such a way that people will be motivated to achieve them. A good goal statement takes the following form:

LEARNING OBJECTIVE 4
Write a good goal statement.

TO *(action verb)* TO *(single result)* BY *(a realistic date)*

Examples of good goal statements are as follows:

1. To reduce my blood pressure to 120/80 by the end of this year.
2. To reduce the absenteeism rate of subordinates to 1 percent within six months.
3. To reduce unit costs on product 436-A by 10 percent within one month.
4. To write a new procedures manual to be used by all mechanics by June 30.

FIGURE 4-2 THE HIERARCHY OF OBJECTIVES.

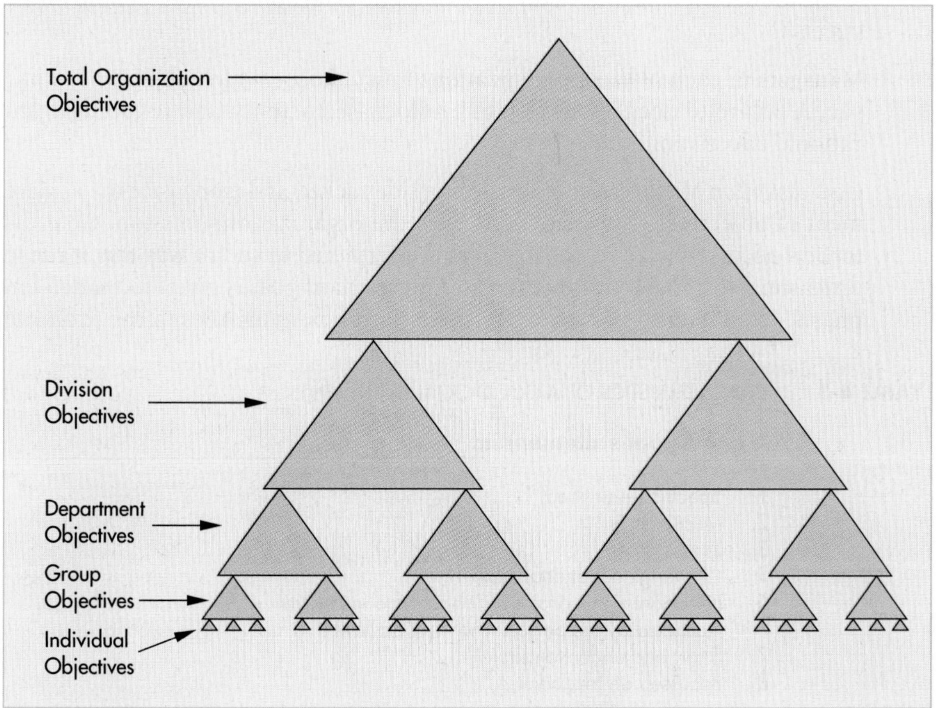

The general characteristics of a good goal statement are shown in Table 4-3. Studies of goal setting clearly demonstrate that people who set goals with these characteristics consistently perform better than individuals who do not set such goals.[14] Virtually all of the studies supporting the benefits of goal setting focus on its effect on individual performance. It seems plausible that goal setting should improve the performance of the organization as well, but only preliminary evidence is available on this issue. One study of 16 simulated organizations showed that setting specific organizational goals led to high-quality organizational planning and to better organizational peformance.[15]

As powerful as objectives are in motivating employee behaviour, managers must be wary of the following hazards when establishing goals:

1. *Different real and stated objectives* The goals that an organization publicly professes may be inconsistent with the goals it actually pursues. For example, a company might claim that it is committed to environmental protection, yet budget virtually nothing for pollution control equipment. Some managers may claim that their objective is to make decisions that will benefit the company, while actually making decisions that benefit their own careers.

2. *Conflicting objectives* Employees are sometimes put in the position of trying to achieve contradictory objectives. This predicament severely reduces the effectiveness of objectives in motivating employees. For example, is the objective of a prison to punish prisoners or to rehabilitate them? It is difficult for prison officials to work toward both these objectives. Numerous other organizations face the same problem. What is the main objective of the organizations listed below?[16]

   - A business firm (pursuing profit or providing employment)?
   - A religious organization (spiritual guidance or a place to socialize)?
   - A medical school (medical research or training students)?
   - A psychiatric hospital (therapy or confinement)?
   - A vocational high school (skill development or keeping young people off the streets)?

   Managers in each of these organizations must choose which objectives to pursue. A failure to decide will result in unfocussed activity, and reduced organizational effectiveness.

goal distortion

3. *Goal distortion* Managers occasionally get sidetracked and emphasize the achievement of objectives that are at odds with the organization's mission. **Goal distortion** occurs when a reasonable goal is interpreted in such a way that it causes unreasonable behaviour, or when an unimportant goal is given too much emphasis. In a business, for example, if marketing pursues sales to the exclusion

TABLE 4-3 CHARACTERISTICS OF A GOOD GOAL STATEMENT.

A good goal statement is:
1. Specific (quantified)
2. Measurable
3. Time-framed
4. Challenging, yet attainable
5. Important to the organization and the individual
6. Accepted by the person who must achieve it
7. Short and understandable
8. Focussed on feedback

of other important organizational objectives such as marketing research, the organization will suffer. The departmentalizing of activities in organizations always presents the risk of goal distortion, as we shall see in Chapter 7.

Goal distortion often occurs when one goal is easy to quantify, while another goal is difficult to quantify. For example, in universities the goal of "excellence in education" is difficult to quantify. It obviously has something to do with good teaching and good research, but there are great ambiguities in how to measure excellence in education. Administrators may therefore overstress what can be measured—for instance, the number of books and articles published by faculty members. As another example, Health and Welfare Canada can measure how many dollars it distributes through its funding programs. There may be a tendency to conclude that it is effective because it has distributed ever-increasing amounts of money. Unfortunately, an agency may not really be achieving its goals of helping people simply because it is spending more money.

Accurate information is a critical factor in the planning process. For example, construction and road building companies need the sand and gravel information supplied by the Alberta Geological Survey. This information is provided by the Alberta Research Council, a Crown corporation offering research and testing capabilities in areas like biotechnology, electronics, geology, and forestry.

Identify the Gap between Actual and Desired Positions

In this step of the planning process, managers need to determine how well organizational objectives are being achieved. In the Management Challenge, Canadian Airlines experienced a gap between actual and desired positions because its sales revenues were not high enough to cover expenses like employee salaries, interest payments on borrowed money, and money spent to buy new airplanes. The focus may be on the entire company, a department within the company, or an individual within a department. Consider the following examples:

1. A year-end financial analysis of the company will determine whether the company reached its profitability objectives.
2. At the end of a recruiting period, a department can assess whether it reached its hiring objectives of four new people.
3. An annual performance appraisal of an individual will tell the boss and subordinate whether the subordinate reached his or her goals for the year.

These and other activities will tell the manager if a gap exists between actual and desired results, and how significant the gap is. The manager must then decide exactly how the gap will be closed. As described in the next section, this involves developing various types of plans.

Develop Plans to Achieve Objectives

While objectives indicate what results are desired, *plans* indicate how these objectives are to be achieved. **Plans** indicate the activities that are required, the person or group who will carry them out, and the deadline for their completion. There are many types of plans, including strategic plans, tactical plans, operational plans, single-use plans, and standing plans.

plans

LEARNING OBJECTIVE 5

Describe how plans, policies, and procedures differ.

Strategic Plans

strategic plans

Strategic plans deal with the activities needed to achieve an organization's overall objectives over a two- to five-year period. As noted earlier, Xerox Corp. set a goal to enter the document-processing business. To achieve this goal, it developed a strategic plan which included the introduction of a family of products called the DocuTech

Publishing Series. One of the products in that series—the Production Publisher—can digitally reproduce high-quality copies. It also serves as fax and computer printer.[17] (Strategic planning is examined in detail in the next chapter.)

Tactical Plans

tactical plans

Tactical plans specify the activities that departments within an organization must carry out if overall strategic objectives are to be reached. They are more specific than strategic plans, and their time frame is usually one to two years. These plans are made by middle managers (perhaps in consultation with lower-level managers) and involve activities such as developing annual budgets for departments and making decisions about how to improve departmental operations.

Operational Plans

operational plans

Operational plans identify the activities in each functional area that will make the strategic plan a success. Operational plans in the Xerox Corp. for example would be drafted for the marketing, production, finance, and personnel departments that would facilitate the strategic plan. In the production area, for instance, low-cost production techniques might be introduced in order to get the price of the product down to a point where it will be more attractive to consumers. Operational plans have a shorter time frame than either strategic or tactical plans, usually less than one year.

Single-use Plans

single-use plans

Single-use plans are those which are developed for a specific purpose and which will not be used again. Single-use plans are developed to achieve one-time objectives the organization pursues. For example, the plan developed by the Canadian Forces to deal with the Mohawk blockade at Oka, Quebec, in 1990 was a single-use plan.

Standing Plans

standing plans

Standing plans deal with issues that continually arise in organizations, and they state how these issues are to be dealt with. Company policies, procedures, and rules are all examples of standing plans.

policy

A **policy** is a guide to action; it suggests in general terms what managers should do in various decision situations. Policies do not tell the manager exactly what to do. For example, a company might have a policy that says "purchasing agents will not accept gifts from suppliers that are sufficient to cause undue influence on the decisions of the purchasing agent." This policy does not tell the purchasing agent how large a gift he or she can accept from a supplier, but it does convey the principle that accepting gifts can lead to problems. The purchasing agent must make purchasing decisions keeping the spirit of this policy in mind.

Policies help managers make consistent decisions over time. They also help the organization to coordinate the activities of various departments or divisions. Well-developed policies increase organizational effectiveness. Table 4-4 lists the principles that should be followed when developing policies.

procedure

Once an organization's broad policies have been established, more detailed plans may be needed to ensure compliance with them. A **procedure** is a step-by-step description of how certain activities should be carried out. Procedures leave employees little discretion in performing their jobs. If the procedure is carried out improperly, problems usually arise.

standard operating procedures

Standard operating procedures are those which are performed over and over in the normal course of organizational activity. Examples of standard operating procedures are: aircraft maintenance procedures for commercial jet aircraft, expense account procedures for reimbursing salespeople for travelling expenses, safety procedures

TABLE 4-4 PRINCIPLES FOR DEVELOPING EFFECTIVE POLICIES.

Principle	**Rationale for Principle**
1. Policies should be consistent with overall organizational objectives.	1. Policies must be consistent with organizational objectives so that employee behaviour is directed toward objectives. For example, a company policy stressing quality products is consistent with the firm's objective to stay in business and make a profit.
2. Policies should be clear and understandable.	2. If policies are not understood by those they govern, the policies will have little effect on employee behaviour.
3. Policies should be communicated in writing.	3. If employees are unaware of corporate policies, they cannot be held accountable for actions which violate them. Communicating policies in writing shows management's concern that they be followed.
4. Policies should be flexible, yet stable.	4. Policies must not be changed so frequently that they create confusion for employees, but they must be flexible enough to accomodate the inevitable changes that occur over time in organizations.

for operating machinery in a manufacturing plant, constitutional procedures for introducing new bylaws in a volunteer organization, and preflight procedures for launching an interstellar rocket.

rule

The most detailed type of plan is the rule. A **rule** requires employees to behave in a specific way. Rules allow employees no discretion in their behaviour. Examples of rules are: "No smoking within 3 metres of the gas pumps," "No running in the pool area," "Hardhats are required on the construction site," "All military personnel must be on the base by midnight," and "Emergency stop buttons must be depressed during maintenance checks."

policy manual

In many organizations, policies, procedures, and rules are kept together in a **policy manual.** Policy manuals may also contain other items such as the organization's code of ethics and its views about corporate social responsibility.

Forecasting

forecasting

To be effective, a plan must include forecasting, but forecasting is not synonymous with planning. **Forecasting** means predicting future events which will have a positive or negative effect on the organization. A forecast can be based on simple intuition, or on systematic studies that cost thousands of dollars. An organization may or may not have control over the events that are forecast. Once the forecast has been made, managers can develop plans to capitalize on positive aspects of the forecast, or to cope with negative aspects. We saw in the Management Challenge that Canadian Airlines ran into difficulty because they were unable to forecast events like the 1990-1992 recession (which lasted longer than people thought it would), and the Gulf War (which caused dramatic short-run increases in the price of oil).

Errors in forecasting can cause major problems. Central Capital Corp., for example, acquired many firms which it never intended to actually operate, but instead planned to sell at a profit. All this was premised on the notion that commercial real estate would continue rising in value. When the real estate market collapsed, the company was caught with a huge debt.[18] In 1989, the Ontario Workers Compensation Board forecast that its unfunded liability (the difference between its assets and the future costs of worker compensation claims already on the books) would be reduced to zero by the year 2007. In 1993, the board made a new prediction: the unfunded liability would be $50 billion by the year 2014![19] Ontario Hydro has made some wildly inaccurate forecasts. In the 1960s, it predicted that it would need 80 000 megawatts of capacity by the year 2000; the actual number will be closer to 30 000 megawatts.

Making accurate forecasts about start-up costs of new manufacturing plants is particularly difficult. The actual costs of Ontario Hydro's Darlington nuclear generating station are more than triple the original forecast.[20] Domtar's new high-tech fine paper mill at Windsor, Quebec, has been a problem for most of its existence. The mill began producing paper in 1987, but by 1990 it was still 20 percent below capacity. The mill is now producing above capacity, but this comes at precisely the time that demand for the mill's products is stagnant.[21]

qualitative forecasting

Forecasting can be divided into two types. **Qualitative forecasting** makes predictions based on subjective managerial judgments and intuition. It is used when "hard" data are unavailable. This type of forecasting is often used when a company is trying to make decisions about activities with which they have no prior experience.

quantitative forecasting

Quantitative forecasting makes predictions based on trends and patterns found in statistical data. A company that has been selling a certain product for a long time will have much statistical data that can be used to help forecast future sales of the product.

LEARNING OBJECTIVE 6
Explain seven forecasting techniques.

Numerous forecasting techniques are employed by managers.[22] Some frequently used qualitative techniques are intuition, scenarios, and informed judgment; commonly used quantitative techniques include extrapolation/time series analysis, correlation, simulation, and content analysis.

intuition

Intuition is a judgment by an individual or a group based on limited information. If a manager says that she or he has a "gut feeling" that a certain event is going to occur, the manager is making a forecast based on intuition.

scenarios

Scenarios are written descriptions of how future events might unfold. Statistical techniques are sometimes used in scenario building, but usually scenarios mean developing a qualitative picture of how a system or organization will look at some time in the future. For example, one scenario about the weather states that within 20 years, the average annual temperature in Canada will rise by three degrees. A scenario about work is that typing skills will become obsolete with the development of a voice synthesizer. Scenarios can be developed for almost any topic of interest to managers.

informed judgment

Informed judgment refers to a forecast based on the opinion of experts in a field. While this approach often does yield accurate forecasts, it is easy to find examples of experts who were completely wrong in their predictions. One of the most famous expert predictions was made by U.S. Admiral William Leahy in 1945 regarding the atomic bomb: "This is the biggest fool thing we have ever done. The bomb will never go off, and I speak as an expert in explosives."[23] Other expert forecasts that were off the mark are shown in Table 4-5.

One widely used type of informed judgment is the Delphi approach which uses a panel of experts to make predictions on issues that are of interest to management. The Delphi approach is discussed in Chapter 6.

extrapolation

Extrapolation is the projection of past and present circumstances into the future. Environmentalists have used this approach to predict that pollution is going to overwhelm the earth in the future. Sophisticated extrapolation involves the use of a technique called regression analysis to extend past trends into the future.

correlation

Correlation involves making a prediction about one outcome based on knowledge of other outcomes. For example, if a company observes a close relationship between sales volume of its products and consumer disposable income, it might attempt to predict future sales of its products based on government forecasts of future consumer disposable income.

simulation

Simulation involves developing a model of an actual situation and working through the simulation to see what kind of outcome results. The model may be a computer model, an algebraic formula, or a miniature physical model. A computer simulation is used by the Canadian Forces to train fighter pilots at Cold Lake, Alberta.

TABLE 4-5 EXPERT PREDICTIONS THAT WENT AMISS.

1. "*Gone With The Wind* is going to be the biggest flop in Hollywood history. I'm just glad it'll be Clark Gable who's falling flat on his face and not Gary Cooper." (Gary Cooper, 1938, commenting on Clark Gable's acceptance of the role of Rhett Butler after Cooper had turned it down)
2. "Babe Ruth made a great mistake when he gave up pitching. Working once a week, he might have lasted a long time and become a great star." (Tris Speaker, 1922, manager of the Cleveland Indians, commenting on Babe Ruth's decision to switch from pitching to the outfield)
3. "Well-informed people know it is impossible to transmit the voice over wires and that were it possible to do so, the thing would be of no practical value." (Editorial in the *Boston Globe,* 1865, commenting on the arrest of Joshua Coopersmith for fraud as he attempted to raise funds for work on a telephone)
4. "The radio craze will die out in time." (Thomas Edison, 1922)
5. "There is no reason for any individual to have a computer in their home." (Ken Olson, 1977, president of Digital Equipment Corporation, speaking at the convention of the World Future Society)
6. "The horseless carriage is at present a luxury for the wealthy, and although its price will probably fall in the future, it will never, of course, come into as common use as the bicycle." (*Literary Digest,* October 14, 1899)
7. "Man will not fly for fifty years." (Wilbur Wright, to his brother Orville, in 1901)
8. "Man will never reach the moon, regardless of all future scientific advances." (Dr. Lee DeForest, inventor of the auditron tube, quoted in the *New York Times,* February 25, 1957; early in his career, DeForest had been told that the auditron tube was a scientific impossibility)
9. "I cannot imagine any condition which would cause a ship to founder. Modern ship-building has gone beyond that." (Captain Edward J. Smith, 1906, future commander of the *Titanic*)

The system simulates high-speed chases, gunfire, tracer shells, and changes in gravity as the pilot's "airplane" manoeuvres. The pilots must shoot down an aggressor aircraft before it fires upon them.[24] Simulations of management problems are not as well developed as aircraft simulations because not as much is known about the dynamics of managerial situations.

content analysis

Content analysis involves examination of the contents of publications for reference to specific items of interest. For example, analyzing scientific journals to see how frequently they make reference to a technological advance like cold fusion could be used by management to predict breakthroughs in the development of new energy sources.

Contingency Planning

contingency planning

Managers have no guarantee that future outcomes will be favourable, but they can at least develop plans for what to do if they are unfavourable. **Contingency planning** involves identifying possible future outcomes and then developing a plan for coping with them. It can be used for both small- and large-scale problems. Marlin Fast Freight might have a contingency plan to rent a delivery truck if one of its own trucks breaks down unexpectedly. Imperial Tobacco might have a much more elaborate contingency plan for dealing with possible government legislation that is detrimental to cigarette sales. Manitoba Telephone System (MTS) realized that deregulation of their industry meant the eventual loss of their monopoly. So they developed a contingency plan that involved getting customers to sign long-term leasing agreements. This strategy will make it difficult for new competitors to compete with MTS.[25]

LEARNING OBJECTIVE 7

Describe the concept of contingency planning and state why it is important to managers.

As noted in the Management Challenge, Canadian Airlines has tried to develop contingency plans for some of their unexpected problems. For example, they tried to get funds from both the Canadian government and from American Airlines. They also considered a merger with Air Canada. When they tried to develop contingency plans, they found that many of these plans would not work.

Forecasting in the oil industry has been very difficult during the last 20 years because of unstable prices. Political upheavals in oil-producing countries, the 1991 war with Iraq, and attempts at price controls by OPEC have all caused significant fluctuations in the price of oil.

Managers should concentrate on developing contingency plans for outcomes which have a reasonable probability of occurring; otherwise they will waste time on the planning function. Ontario Hydro, for example, is beginning to experience staff shortages in some areas; the director of the planning and integration division believes the problem will worsen by the year 2000, when the first baby boomers begin to retire.[26] Training of some individuals like nuclear station operators takes up to four years, so Hydro must plan a long way ahead for staff. The contingency plan involves hiring more part-time workers, an approach that Hydro has not traditionally used.

Implement Plans

The steps that we have discussed so far—setting objectives, determining the gap between the desired and actual, and developing plans to achieve objectives—all require managers to think about what is to be accomplished. At some point, however, this thinking must be converted into action. This is the point at which many managers encounter problems because the implementation of plans involves the introduction of change. We discuss the issue of organizational change in Chapter 15. For now, we simply point out that introducing any change, including new plans, is likely to meet with resistance from employees. This opposition must be addressed before the plans begin taking effect if managers are to be successful in carrying out the planning function.

Evaluate Planning Effectiveness

In Chapter 1, we noted that efficiency means doing things right and effectiveness means doing the right things. A plan is effective if it helps an organization reach its objectives. (See the Global Management insert "Planning and Polar Exploration.") Consider the issue of corporate policies. Suppose a firm has a policy that purchasing agents may not accept gifts from suppliers if those gifts will unduly influence their purchasing behaviour. Such a policy is effective if it motivates purchasing agents to buy supplies that are best for the company. The plan is ineffective if it causes purchasing agents to spend time trying to figure out how to get around the policy. Gauging the effectiveness of plans can be frustrating, especially if plans (1) deal with the entire firm, or (2) have a long-term impact. It is easy to judge a plan intended to make the company the industry leader in sales, but it is much harder to measure the effectiveness of a plan to develop the most creative work force in the industry.

Regardless of these obstacles, the final step in the planning process must be an assessment of the effectiveness of plans. Without such an assessment, little will be learned about how the plans helped the organization to reach its objectives.

Management by Objectives

In the early 1950s, Peter Drucker started a revolution in management when he proposed management by objectives (MBO).[27] Drucker felt that the specialization of labour in large organizations isolated workers from the direction and purpose of the organization. As a result, they failed to identify with the goals of the enterprise. He proposed MBO as a remedy for this predicament.

management by objectives (MBO)

MBO is a system in which managers and subordinates set mutually agreed upon goals; these goals motivate subordinates and encourage them to exercise self-control over their performance. MBO is a philosophy that emphasizes the achievement of results. It is based on the assumption that encouraging employee participation in goal setting will improve employee motivation and performance.

GLOBAL MANAGEMENT

Planning and Polar Exploration

The management functions of planning, organizing, leading, and controlling are obviously important in business organizations. But these functions are also important in many other kinds of organizations. Consider the race between the British and Norwegians in 1911–1912 to see who could reach the South Pole first.

To achieve the goal, it was first necessary to secure financial support to pay for such a major expedition. The appropriate sailing ships had to be acquired, and tonnes of supplies and animals had to be taken to the jumping off point on the continent of Antarctica. Once there, a base camp had to be set up and men and equipment readied for the trek to the pole. The trip to the pole was made in conditions that are hard to imagine. On foot or on skis, the explorers made their way over 1200 kilometres of ice, snow, –40°C temperatures, and mountains nearly 3000 metres high. Once at the Pole, they had to turn around and fight their way back to the coast through the same conditions.

The Norwegians, led by Roald Amundsen, won the race primarily because they were better managed. Amundsen, who realized that meticulous planning was absolutely essential for a successful expedition to the South Pole, had spent years familiarizing himself with conditions at both the North and South Poles. In the crucial area of food and fuel, Amundsen developed a system for laying out supply depots so that they could be found even in a raging blizzard. This ensured that the Norwegians had enough supplies to make it safely back to their base camp after they reached the Pole. By studying polar conditions, he knew that sled dogs were the best animals to haul supplies. He also knew that going to the Pole on skis was far superior to walking.

A good leader, Amundsen carefully selected the four men who would accompany him and live in very close quarters during the 3-month trek to the Pole and back. Amundsen's men had complete confidence in his ability. He, in turn, allowed his men to participate in many of the important decisions that had to be made during the expedition.

By contrast, the British expedition led by Robert Scott, was poorly managed. The planning of important details of the expedition was left to the last minute. Major mistakes were also made in decisions about animals and equipment. For example, Scott decided to rely on ponies for hauling supplies. This decision ignored the obvious fact that ponies were inferior to dogs for hauling supplies in bitter cold weather. He also favoured the "man-hauling" system, whereby the explorers would haul their own supplies on foot after the ponies had died. Scott took skis, but few in his party knew how to use them properly. They therefore wasted precious energy and covered fewer kilometres each day than they might have.

The planning of supply depots was also haphazard, and insufficient care was taken in the storage of precious fuel. In the extreme cold of the Antarctic, much of the fuel that Scott had stored in supply depots evaporated. On his return trip, therefore, he consistently ran short of fuel. Amundsen had no such problems because he had designed an airtight seal for his fuel.

Scott's leadership ability was also limited: there was dissension in the ranks because of poor communication, conflicting orders, and interpersonal conflict. Scott did not inspire confidence in his men and did not allow them to participate in important decisions.

Although Scott also reached the South Pole (one month after Amundsen), he and his group of five paid dearly for his lack of management competence—they all died of starvation and exposure while attempting to get back to their base camp. ▲

LEARNING OBJECTIVE 8

Explain what management by objectives is, and identify the six principal steps in the process.

According to Drucker, the MBO system should:[28]

1. *Provide a basis for more effective planning* The objectives for all the levels of management in an organization must be coordinated.
2. *Improve communication between managers and subordinates* Goal-setting discussions between bosses and subordinates provide the vehicle for improving superior-subordinate communication.
3. *Encourage acceptance of participative management* The negotiations between bosses and subordinates about goals should facilitate participative management.

THE MBO PROCESS

The steps in the typical MBO process are shown in Figure 4-3. The various arrows in the diagram indicate that there is continual interaction among the steps. For this process to succeed, it must be strongly supported by top management.

Set Strategic Objectives

The first step in the MBO process requires management to set the organization's overall objectives. These goals must be consistent with the organization's mission—its reason for existence. Consider a company whose mission is to produce and market agricultural implements. The following strategic objectives might be developed in keeping with this mission:

1. To achieve a 15 percent rate of return on shareholder investment.
2. To have the largest market share of any agricultural implements firm in the Canadian market.
3. To achieve the lowest per unit production cost in the industry.

By stipulating these strategic objectives, top management conveys to managers and employees the overall aims of the firm.

Set Departmental Objectives

Once these corporate objectives have been set, each of the departments must set more specific goals that will help achieve the overall goals. In the example above, various departments might set the following targets:

1. To increase the sale of self-propelled combines by 10 percent over last year (marketing).
2. To reduce production costs by 5 percent within one year (production).
3. To reduce borrowing costs by 10 percent within one year (finance).
4. To hire 35 new workers by year-end (personnel).

Each of these departmental goals must contribute to company goals.

Set Individual Objectives

In this phase of the MBO process, managers and workers negotiate specific goals for each subordinate to attain within a definite period, usually six months or one year. If the negotiations are conducted properly, the goals that each subordinate sets

FIGURE 4-3 THE MBO PROCESS.

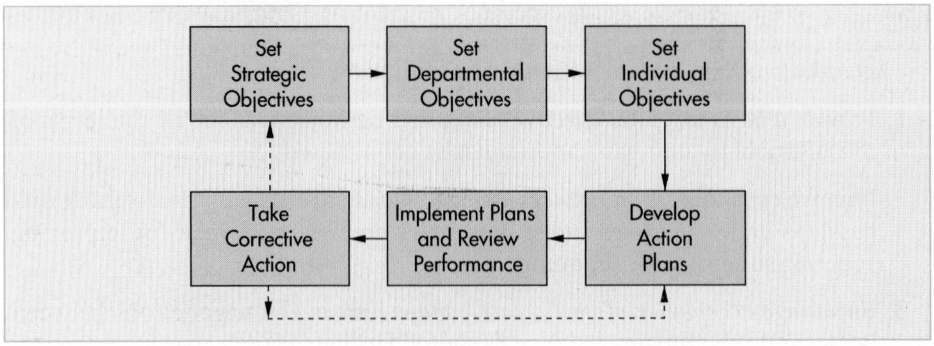

will boost her or his performance. In the agricultural implements company, for example, a salesperson in the central region and the sales manager for that region might jointly agree on the following objectives:

1. To increase sales of self-propelled combines in the north Saskatchewan region by 10 percent by June 30.
2. To reduce travel expenses by 5 percent by June 30.
3. To increase "cold calls" on new prospects by 15 percent by June 30.

Develop Action Plans

action plans

Critical to the setting of objectives is the establishment of action plans. **Action plans** detail the specific tasks that must be done in order to fulfill the objectives that have been set. Action plans identify the activities that must be carried out to reach a goal, the cost of these activities, and an estimate of how long these activities will take. The agricultural implements salesperson, for example, might decide that to increase combine sales, he or she will have to become more knowledgeable about product characteristics and sales techniques. This awareness can be achieved by attending a series of sales seminars; these will cost $250, which will be paid by the company. The seminars will require 14 hours of class time, plus 40 hours of practice time to master the new skills.

Implement Plans and Review Performance

Once individual and department objectives have been agreed upon and action plans devised, the scheme is put into practice. After the stipulated time has passed, the manager and the subordinate meet to review the subordinate's performance. Because definite goals have been set, employee performance can be easily assessed.[29] The review concentrates on whether or not negotiated goals have been attained, rather than on the subordinate's personal characteristics.[30] It emphasizes employee self-control, instead of control by the manager. For example, the agricultural implements salesperson and the sales manager will determine if the salesperson has carried out the action plan, and what effect the implementation of the plan is having on the progress toward the goal. This interaction between the superior and subordinate has a significant effect on employee behaviour. The focus is upon the development of employees and the relationship of that development to the achievement of corporate objectives.

Take Corrective Action

If the subordinate's performance meets expectations, goals for the next period are negotiated. If performance is below expectations, action must be taken to rectify the problem. For instance, if the agricultural implements salesperson attended the agreed upon sales seminars, yet sales goals were not reached, some other action plan would have to be negotiated to help the salesperson fulfill her or his objectives. If some uncontrollable event has made the goal unattainable, the goal itself may have to be changed.

Two widely used approaches to taking corrective action are incentive programs and training programs. The most effective incentive programs are those which determine exactly what motivates each employee (e.g., money, flexible work schedule, etc.). These things are then given to the employee when desired goals are achieved. Training employees in the specific techniques needed to perform the job is also effective, particularly for jobs in which work activity can be clearly specified.

The Management at Work insert "MBO at Investors Group Financial Services" describes how MBO works at a large Canadian company.

MANAGEMENT AT WORK

MBO AT INVESTORS GROUP FINANCIAL SERVICES INC.

Sales representatives at Investors Group Financial Services sell a wide range of financial services including mutual funds, investment certificates, insurance programs, pension plans, annuities, and tax-sheltered plans. The company has financial planning centres in every major metropolitan area of Canada, and employs over 3000 salespeople. It has the largest direct sales force of any company in the financial services sector.

Investors has used MBO since 1974 to motivate its sales force in selling financial services. The MBO process begins when the vice-president of sales develops general goals for the entire sales force. These goals may be based on last year's performance, or on desired growth over last year's performance. This sets the stage for Planning Week, which is held annually in 73 regional centres across Canada during the first week of December. The purpose of Planning Week is to give salespeople a chance to (1) review their personal, career, and financial accomplishments, (2) relate their individual results to the goals of the whole company, and (3) think through personal, career, and financial goals for the coming year.

During Planning Week, sales reps meet with their division managers and set specific sales objectives for the next year. This process involves five steps:

1. *Determine franchise operating costs.* Since each sales rep in essence owns a franchise, the first step is to calculate what it will cost to operate the franchise during the upcoming year.
2. *Determine personal requirements.* Each salesperson decides how much money he or she needs to meet living expenses in the upcoming year.
3. *Determine total financial requirements.* The costs from steps 1 and 2, plus a profit requirement, determine the sales rep's total financial requirements for the year.
4. *Develop an activity plan.* The sales rep prepares a plan of action to reach the goals set in steps 1-3. This involves setting goals for the number of contacts and presentations the sales rep will have to make in order to reach the dollar sales goal.
5. *Measure productivity.* This involves completion of a detailed MBO summary sheet showing the sales rep's monthly production in the year just ended, as well as goals for each month's production in the upcoming year.

Once these five steps are completed, division managers meet with the salesperson and come to a consensus about what the sales rep's goals will be. Each division manager then forwards the proposed objectives for his or her division to the appropriate regional manager. This process continues all the way up to the vice-president of sales, who gives final approval to the overall sales objectives of the company for the coming year.

On occasion, a saleperson will set a goal that a manager considers either too low or too high. When this happens, negotiation between the salesperson and the manager takes place to find a goal that is satisfactory to both. The company has found that resolving problems through negotiation early in the process helps to prevent serious disagreements later on.

Recognition and rewards are an important part of the MBO process. For example, sales production of $2 million per year qualifies the salesperson for the "Millionaire" plaque; sales of $8 million qualifies the person for a diamond ring. Most salespeople earn an award of some type, and they are publicly recognized for their achievement. Each salesperson feels that he or she is making a positive contribution to the company.

About 75 percent of Investors' salespeople conscientiously fill out the MBO forms, and it has made a noticeable difference in their sales performance. A few salespeople, however, view MBO as a game of paper shuffling, and for them, it is probably not very helpful. In such cases, managers try to "sell" MBO to their staff, rather than trying to force it on them.

Investors has found that MBO is well suited to its sales function. The goals of salespeople can be stated in quantitative terms, and the sales reps can easily tell whether they have reached their goals. The company has also found that salespeople often set much more challenging goals for themselves than they would have in the absence of MBO. All of this impacts favourably on the bottom line—Investors profitability continued uninterrupted right through the recession of 1991-1993. ▲

AN EVALUATION OF MBO

LEARNING OBJECTIVE 9
Describe the benefits of and potential problems with management by objectives.

How well does MBO work in practice? A review of 185 MBO studies (see Table 4-6) showed that MBO seemed to have a positive impact in 153 of the 185 organizations.[31] However, a closer examination of the data reveals that research based on case studies and surveys led to favourable conclusions much more frequently than quasi-experiments and true experiments. Since these last two research methodologies are much more rigorous than case studies and surveys, it is possible that the effects of MBO are less positive than they first appear to be.

Another way to answer this question is to look at the perceptions of managers who have actually used MBO. A survey of 135 companies found that managers' expectations about MBO were usually not met (see Table 4-7).[32]

The strengths and weaknesses of MBO are summarized in Table 4-8. Overall, MBO will probably have a positive effect on an organization if it focusses on individual goal setting, participation, and communication between bosses and subordinates.[33] However, if it is used as a top-down "club" to control employees, it will not have a positive effect.[34] As the Management at Work insert demonstrates, MBO can work very well in sales-related jobs like those at Investors Group. For other types of occupations, it may be less effective.

TABLE 4-6 MBO EFFECTIVENESS AS APPLIED IN 185 ORGANIZATIONS.

Research Approach	Positive	Mixed	Not Positive	Ratio Positive: Not Positive
Case studies	123	8	10	12:1
Surveys	9	2	1	9:1
Quasi-experiments	20	3	4	5:1
True experiments	1	2	2	1:2
Totals/average	153	15	17	9:1

TABLE 4-7 EXPECTED AND REALIZED MBO BENEFITS.

	Benefits Expected* (Percent)	Benefits Realized* (Percent)
Improved communication between subordinates and managers on individual job objectives and responsibilities	88.9	41.9
Improved objective criteria for more effective manager appraisal	80.1	44.0
Improved planning for individual jobs	76.7	34.0
Improved overall planning	75.2	24.0
Improved employee performance	64.1	16.0
Increased participation in decision making by subordinates	63.2	27.0
Increased employee motivation	56.4	14.0
Increased coordination between the various departments of the organization caused by clearer descriptions of departmental functions and responsibilities	54.7	18.0
Increased control over employee efforts	54.3	26.0
Improved time management	52.6	12.0

*Five-point scale ranging from "none" to "extensive." Includes categories "considerable" and "extensive."

TABLE 4-8 STRENGTHS AND WEAKNESSES OF MBO.

Strengths	Weaknesses
1. Employee behaviour is directed toward the achievement of important organizational goals.	1. Lack of commitment by top management conveys to employees that MBO is not genuinely important to the organization.
2. The goals of each department in the organization are consistent with overall organizational objectives.	2. Paperwork becomes routine and does not increase employee motivation; as well, it distracts people from their work.
3. Managers are required to do systematic planning and to set standards of performance.	3. Managers may be unwilling or unable to effectively participate in the setting of goals with subordinates.
4. Employees participate in the setting of goals.	4. There may be an overemphasis on the short run at the expense of the long run.
5. Once goals are set, employees know exactly what is expected of them.	
6. The process of monitoring goal achievement helps managers carry out the controlling function and gives subordinates feedback on their performance.	
7. Communication between managers and subordinates is improved.	

MEETING THE CHALLENGE

PLANNING IN AN UNCERTAIN ENVIRONMENT

Meeting the management challenge at CAI has been a frustrating experience not only for managers at the company, but also for government bureaucrats and managers at other business firms like Gemini, Air Canada, and American Airlines.

In April 1993 a federal competition tribunal ruled that CAI could not leave the Gemini reservation system. CAI chairman Rhys Eaton vowed to appeal the decision, and to continue operating CAI in the meantime, noting that the summer season is good for airline profitability. He also said that American Airlines still wanted to invest $246 million in CAI as long as CAI joined American's Sabre reservation system. The tribunal ruling means increased job security for employees of Gemini, but serious problems for CAI. After the ruling, Air Canada again expressed the opinion that CAI and Air Canada should merge.

The situation was further complicated in May 1993 when the National Transporation Board (NTB) approved CAI's partnership with American Airlines, saying that it would not result in undue control of CAI by American Airlines. The decision increases the threat of job losses for employees of Air Canada. The NTB ruling did not address the Gemini issue, so CAI was still left with the problem of extricating itself from that arrangement.

The ill-will generated by the dispute about the Gemini system became apparent during hearings before the Competition Tribunal. At those hearings, an internal Air Canada plan to frustrate CAI's efforts to walk away from Gemini came to light. The document suggested that Air Canada work with Gemini in order to frustrate CAI's attempts to leave the system. During the hearings, CAI argued that if it were not allowed to leave Gemini it would fail because American Airlines would not invest its $246 million. If CAI failed, then Air Canada would have a domestic monopoly on air travel.

In an unrelated case, but one with ironic timing, early in 1993 an Ontario court ruled that Air Canada must pay lost profits, punitive damages, and interest charges of about $18 million to rival AMR Corp. (the parent company of American Airlines) for breach of contract. Air Canada had previously attempted to get into the entertainment ticketing business and had agreed to develop software for Ticketnet Corp.,

• • •

a small firm which was developing a box office automation system which would allow customers to go to a local Ticknet outlet and buy tickets to entertainment events anywhere in Canada. Because of Air Canada's slow progress in getting the system to market, Ticketnet decided to sell out to AMR. The court ruled that Air Canada's breach of contract made the company fail, and this failure cost AMR dearly. AMR expressed satisfaction that Air Canada had been found guilty of breach of contract.

In November 1993 a federal tribunal ruled that CAI *could* leave the Gemini reservation system. Gemini's president immediately said that if the order stood, Gemini would be dissolved in November 1994 and 700 people would lose their jobs.

The final resolution of the CAI case is still uncertain. But if the events are any indication, there are more surprises in store for CAI as it tries to extricate itself from its financial predicament. ▲

SUMMARY

Planning is one of the basic functions of management. All managers need to be effective planners, regardless of what type of organization they are employed by, and regardless of their level in the organizational hierarchy. Planning may be done on either a formal or informal basis.

Planning helps the manager to identify opportunities and potential problems, set objectives and standards, and coordinate organizational activity in general. Planning may be done poorly or may not be effective if top management fails to support it, if it is based on poor information, if managers are over- or undercommitted to plans, or if managers lack competence in planning.

Organizations that plan generally perform better than those that don't. But the existence of formal plans is no guarantee of organizational success because unexpected occurrences in the external environment may upset the best plans.

The planning process involves five distinct steps: (1) set organizational objectives, (2) determine the gap between the organization's actual and desired position, (3) develop plans to achieve the objectives, (4) implement the plans, and (5) evaluate the effectiveness of planning.

Objectives (goals) are the desired results that the organization wants to achieve. A good goal is specific (quantified), measurable, time-framed, and challenging; allows feedback; and is accepted by the individual that must achieve it. Individuals who set goals with these characteristics consistently and significantly perform better than those who do not.

Plans focus on the activities that are necessary to achieve objectives. Strategic plans deal with the activities that are necessary to achieve an organization's overall objectives, while operational plans state the specific activities that are necessary to implement the strategic plans. Single-use plans are developed for a specific occasion and are not used again, while standing plans are used over and over again. Policies, procedures, and rules are examples of standing plans. Policies are guides to action and suggest in general terms what managers should do in various decision situations. Procedures are step-by-step descriptions of how certain activities must be carried out. Rules are the most specific type of plan and require employees to behave in a certain way.

Forecasting means predicting events which will have a positive or negative effect on an organization. Qualitative forecasting techniques include intuition, scenarios, and informed judgment. Quantitative forecasting techniques include extrapolation, correlation, simulation, and content analysis. Contingency planning means indentifying possible outcomes that might occur, and then developing a plan for coping with them. Contingency planning can deal with very detailed matters, or with large-scale organizational issues.

Management by objectives is a system in which managers and subordinates set mutually agreeable goals. These goals motivate subordinates and encourage them to exercise self-control over their performance. The MBO process involves: (1) setting strategic objectives, (2) setting departmental objectives, (3) setting individual objectives, (4) developing action plans, (5) implementing plans and reviewing performance, and (6) taking corrective action.

MBO directs employee behaviour toward the achievement of organizational goals, coordinates the goals of different departments, forces managers to do systematic planning, and facilitates employee participation in goal setting. MBO may not work as planned if there is insufficient support from top management, if MBO paperwork becomes routine, and if managers are unable or unwilling to negotiate goals with subordinates.

KEY TERMS

objectives (p. 95)
hierarchy of objectives (p. 97)
goal distortion (p. 98)
plan (p. 99)
strategic plans (p. 99)
tactical plans (p. 100)
operational plans (p. 100)
single-use plans (p. 100)
standing plans (p. 100)
policy (p. 100)
procedure (p. 100)
standard operating procedures (p. 100)
rule (p. 101)
policy manual (p. 101)
forecasting (p. 101)
qualitative forecasting (p. 102)
quantitative forecasting (p. 102)
intuition (p. 102)
scenarios (p. 102)
informed judgment (p. 102)
extrapolation (p. 102)
correlation (p. 102)
simulation (p. 102)
content analysis (p. 103)
contingency planning (p. 103)
management by objectives (MBO) (p. 104)
action plans (p. 107)

REVIEW QUESTIONS

1. What does the management function of planning involve?
2. Do managers actually spend time doing systematic and formal planning? What other kind of planning might managers do?
3. How is the planning behaviour of top managers and lower-level managers different?
4. How does planning benefit an organization? What potential problems exist in planning?
5. What is the relationship between planning and organizational performance?
6. What are the steps in the planning process?
7. What is the format of a good goal statement? Write an actual personal goal using this format.
8. What are the characteristics of a good goal? What does research say about people who set goals vs. those who don't?
9. What is goal distortion? Give an example of goal distortion from your own personal experience in an organization.
10. Explain the difference between the following pairs of terms:
    Standing plans and single-use plans
    Strategic plans and operational plans
    Policies and procedures
11. Explain how the simulation technique is used as a forecasting device.
12. What is MBO? Why does it increase employee motivation?
13. Summarize the results of the two major surveys dealing with the effectiveness of MBO.

DISCUSSION QUESTIONS

1. Consider one of the forecasting techniques described in the chapter and find a real-world example of it. Explain how the technique was used. How well did the technique work? What shortcomings were evident?
2. What are the implications of the planning function for the other managerial functions?
3. "Planning does not imply inflexibility." Do you agree or disagree? Why?
4. If planning deals with the future, and if the future is difficult to predict, how can planning benefit an organization?
5. What is the relationship between contingency planning and the increasingly rapid pace of change in our society?
6. How closely does MBO at Investors parallel the general MBO model in Figure 4-3? Explain any differences that exist.
7. What practical problems arise when an organization attempts to assess how effective its planning efforts have been?

EXERCISES

1. Have an in-class debate on the following claim: Planning deals with an uncertain future where many unexpected and unpredictable events will occur. As a result, planning is not very helpful to an organization.
2. Read a journal article that addresses the question of whether planning increases organizational success. Give a 15-minute presentation to the class summarizing the article. Give special attention to the author's way of measuring planning and organizational success, and what specific conclusions the author reached.
3. Visit a business firm in your area and ask a manager in the company about his or her reaction to MBO. What are the strengths and weaknesses of MBO from the manager's perspective? How well do they match up with the strengths and weaknesses mentioned in the chapter?

MANAGEMENT ON LOCATION

CASE 4-1
HIGH SPIRITS

Karl Kaiser is the co-owner and wine maker at Inniskillin Wines Inc. at Niagara-on-the-Lake. As he looks out over the vineyards, he notes that last summer was not a good one, with unseasonably cool weather, too much rain, and two hailstorms that devastated about 60 percent of the grapes. Kaiser says it's difficult to watch one hailstorm wipe out all your hard work. But, he notes that the weather the year before was great, and the company had its best harvest ever.

The weather is difficult to control, but there are other things the company can do something about. Donald Ziraldo, the firm's president, recently announced a merger with Cartier Wines & Beverages, Canada's second largest wine producer. The merger will give Inniskillin access to Cartier's network of 47 retail stores. And Karl Kaiser has just purchased two additional grape presses and three fermenters in Europe in order to increase production of the firm's well-known ice wine. It was an ice wine from Inniskillin that won one of the 19 Grands Prix d'Honneur at the 1989 VinExpo in Bordeaux, France, and put Canadian ice wine on the map. Inniskillin's president said it was like winning an Academy Award.

Positive news like this is something of a surprise. Just a few years ago, there was much doom and gloom in the industry because of the Canada-U.S. Free Trade Agreement. When the FTA first took effect in 1989, the price differentials between Canadian and foreign wines were eliminated. It was thought that this might destroy the Canadian industry. Indeed, the market share of Canadian firms did decline, vineyard hectarage was reduced, and some vintners closed their doors. But, the increased competition forced the remaining firms to increase product quality, and in so doing, find new markets for Canadian wine.

The quality improvement has occurred because *vitis labrusca*, the native North American grapevine, has been banned from table wines. It has been replaced with *vitis vinifera*, a higher-quality and more delicate stock. While Canadian wineries can get up

...

to $1200 per tonne for *vinifera*, and only $200 per tonne for *labrusca*, replanting all the vineyards is an expensive and time-consuming process. It takes five years to get a new *vinifera* crop into production, and five to seven more years to recover initial investment costs. Bad weather along the way can extend the time even further.

Other uncertainties continue to create problems for the Canadian wine industry. For one thing, the 42 percent market share now held by Canadian companies is a far cry from the 75 percent share they held in their heydey in the 1960s. For another, the quota program in B.C. that ensures that wineries will purchase the entire grape crop from provincial growers will be phased out in 1995. Buyers will then be able to purchase wine juice from foreign producers if they wish. And consumers are still not convinced that Canadian wine has the quality that French or California wines do. ▲

QUESTIONS

1. How is the planning process in the wine industry similar to that in an industrial firm? How is it different?
2. What kinds of contingency plans are necessary in the wine business?
3. In what areas of the wine business should plans be made, and over what time frames should the plans extend?

CASE 4-2
MBO at York Investments

York Investments provides a wide range of financial services to consumers and business firms. The company introduced a management by objectives (MBO) program two years ago. Top management of the firm was convinced that MBO would significantly improve the company's overall effectiveness in planning and would provide a system for a more accurate evaluation of personnel. Prior to the implementation of MBO, the company had no formal planning system and had used a performance appraisal system that primarily evaluated such factors as quantity of work, quality of work, judgment, and adaptability. The performance factors were rated from 1 (very poor) to 5 (exceptional). All personnel, including managerial employees, were evaluated using this system. The considerable dissatisfaction with this rating system was the primary reason why the company decided to implement MBO.

At the beginning of each year, overall company objectives as well as departmental goals are formulated and communicated to managers throughout the firm. The following is a description of the company's MBO program as it is applied in the Accounting Services department.

Jean Stelmach, the Accounting Services manager, had four supervisors reporting to her. These supervisors are responsible for accounts payable, accounts receivable, payroll, and customer services. At the beginning of each year, Stelmach discussed the company and departmental objectives with each of her four supervisors.

The payroll supervisor is Romain Grodecki, a CMA who has been with York for nine years. He had four years experience in payroll operations at another company before coming to York. He is considered to be a competent supervisor, and has eight clerks reporting to him. The department processes the payroll for almost 1000 employees. Grodecki and Stelmach had agreed on the following goals for the payroll department during Grodecki's first year as a supervisor:

1. Establishment of a consistent account reconciliation program for the 160 payroll-related accounts in the general ledger by June 1.
2. Establishment of a cross-training program for the payroll clerks by June 1.
3. Creation of written documention for all payroll department procedures by September 1 (in accordance with the company's broader statements on policy and procedures).
4. Reduction of employee turnover to 15 percent during the year.

During the year, the company experienced rapid growth, adding an average of 10 employees per month. Turnover of clerical personnel in the payroll department began in February. By April, payroll lost three experienced employees. These personnel changes required considerable on-the- • • •

job training of new employees. Near the end of the year, Stelmach reviewed the progress of the payroll section with Grodecki, and found that although some progress had been made on each objective, none of the objectives were accomplished.

Stelmach expressed extreme disappointment with the overall performance of the payroll department. She asked Grodecki why payroll had experienced these problems. He agreed the goals were not achieved, but said that employee turnover had greatly affected his ability to achieve the goals. "Of the three people I hired," he said, "only one was as effective as those who quit." ▲

QUESTIONS

1. Evaluate the MBO program as it is used by York Investments. Does it meet the criteria for a successful program as discussed in the chapter?
2. If you were Jean Stelmach, what would you do now?

CASE 4-3
PROBLEMS WITH A PLANNING SYSTEM

On a dreary November afternoon, Marie Beliveau sat in her office staring out the window at the mix of rain and snow that was falling. Far below, the afternoon rush-hour traffic was building up. It had been a long day, and Beliveau was physically and mentally tired. Her thoughts were interrupted by Gurmail Singh, head of accounting, who asked her if she wanted to go for coffee.

"That sounds like a good idea," said Marie. "I need to get my mind off this latest memo from our president. You know, I just can't figure this guy out. Today I received a memo which basically dictates what our division's goals are for next year. Oh, it is couched in nice sounding terms and all that, but it really dictates what we must do. Nobody in my area had anything to say about whether these goals are feasible or even desirable. When I tell my people about this, there are going to be some real problems. They're not going to be the least bit committed to the president's precious goals."

"I understand your frustration," said Gurmail. "My department is being treated the same way."

Marie continued, "Why doesn't the president ask us which goals our division should be pursuing, and what level of accomplishment we think is reasonable? I'm not saying he has to accept everything we say, but we are supposed to be the experts in this area. Don't you ask the experts what they think? I thought that this new management by objectives program was supposed to ensure that there were discussions between the boss and the subordinates about what the goals should be. Why did I fill out all those forms regarding next year's goals if the president is going to completely ignore them?"

Gurmail smiled sympathetically. "Come on, Marie, let's get that cup of coffee and think about more pleasant things. There's more to life than trying to meet the president's goals."

"That's true," said Marie. "But if you don't meet the president's goals, you can start looking for a new job." ▲

QUESTIONS

1. Comment on the way that MBO has been implemented in this organization. What mistakes have been made?
2. How committed is top management to MBO?
3. What improvements can you suggest?

CHAPTER 5

STRATEGIC MANAGEMENT

LEARNING OBJECTIVES

After reading this chapter, you will be able to:

1. Identify the eight components of strategic management.
2. Define strategic management and strategy.
3. Identify factors that distinguish strategic from operational decisions.
4. Understand the application of strategic management at different levels in an organization.
5. Identify strategists and understand their role.
6. Describe the influence of organizational values on strategic decision making.
7. Outline the methodologies managers follow when applying the components of strategic management.
8. Identify the strategic options available to an organization.
9. List the challenges of applying strategic management.

MANAGEMENT CHALLENGE

STRATEGIC MANAGEMENT AT SCHNEIDER CORP.

Schneider Corp. was started in 1890 by John Metz Schneider who made sausage in the basement of his Kitchener, Ontario, home and sold it door to door. During the first century of its operation, the company had grown to a mid-sized meat processor with a very good reputation for quality products. The company has grown to six production plants, the main one still in Kitchener, and employs about 3250 people. Despite its size, reputation, and age, by the late 1980s Schneiders was floundering for various reasons.

Consumers had lost their taste for red meat and pork products as dietary trends favoured poultry and pasta. The economic downturn made consumers resistant to price increases and many who were still purchasing red meat sought cheaper cuts. Prices were under pressure and fluctuated as there was a concentration of market power in the retail food industry, Schneider's main customers.

Overcapacity existed in the industry, and a rationalization of firms had occurred as some failed or were merged with or taken over by stronger competitors. The Alberta Government complicated the situation by becoming involved with the failing Gainers plants in Western Canada instead of allowing them to fail.

In the early 1980s, the company had restructured into separate units under the name, The Heritage Group Inc., and diversified into bakery products and poultry mainly through joint ventures. The restructuring complicated operations and resulted in high overheads, and the company's culture resisted the changes. The limitations on the availability of chickens caused by the supply management system restricted the growth in the poultry business.

In 1986, another restructuring refocussed the company back to its basic

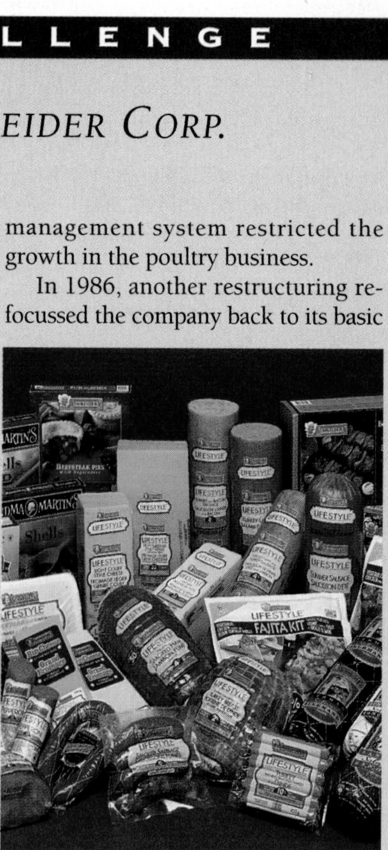

• • •

food products and included a major cost-cutting program with 300 employees laid off. Built in the 1930s, the main Kitchener plant was old fashioned and organized on a functional basis making it inefficient. In 1988, the union at the plant struck, the first strike in the company's history. Although the strike was settled, the morale of employees was poor and productivity was low. Costs were high with costly raw materials and high hourly wages. Infighting occurred among the workers, forepeople, middle managers, and executives. Finally, the company had mediocre financial performance which was reflected in the stock market price of its shares.

Douglas Dodds, president since 1986, knew that changes had to be made if the company was to survive given the competitive nature of the industry with overcapacity, the changing environment, and the internal problems existing in the company. The course of action undertaken by Dodds illustrates the nature of strategic management. ▲

LEARNING OBJECTIVE 1
Identify the eight components of strategic management.

In Chapter 4, the planning process in organizations was discussed in general terms. In this chapter, a particular type of planning that is playing an increasingly important role in modern organizations is described—strategic management. Strategic management is fundamental to the planning process in any organization. It does not take the place of the various planning processes described in Chapter 4, but forms an umbrella, or overall structure for all planning processes.

The description of the strategic management challenge at Schneider Corp. is the first to be presented in this chapter. Strategic management practices at a variety of Canadian businesses are presented throughout the chapter to illustrate the variations of approaches used. There is no one approach and enterprises adopt approaches that are meaningful and work for them. However, there are some common, underlying "Components" to any approach which are listed in the centre column of Figure 5-1.

The contents of this chapter follow the framework in Figure 5-1. After defining strategic management, the "Influences" from the left column, level of organization, strategic values, strategic leadership, and stakeholders' expectations, are discussed. Next, the eight "Components" are described along with some of the "Methodologies" from the right column. There are more "Methodologies" listed than discussed, and they can be used by more than one component. "Methodologies" have been selected from the right column and described with the component where they are most commonly used. Finally, the remaining "Influences" from the left column are discussed at the end of the chapter.

STRATEGIC MANAGEMENT AND STRATEGY DEFINED

strategic management

Strategic management establishes an organization's mission and objectives, analyzes the environment and resource capabilities in order to formulate a strategy, creates the organizational systems and processes needed to implement the strategy, and devises mechanisms for monitoring and reviewing the organization's performance that results from the strategy chosen. The centre column in Figure 5-1 identifies the components of this process.

strategy

A **strategy** is the unified, comprehensive, and integrated plan that applies the resources of the firm to the challenges of the environment and ensures that the mission and objectives of the organization are achieved through the systems and processes of implementation.[1] A strategy is the plan that ties together the components of strategic management.

LEARNING OBJECTIVE 2
Define strategic management and strategy.

An important distinction must be made between strategic management and strategy. Strategic management is the process that an organization goes through to formulate, implement, and evaluate what the organization is and where it wants to be. A strategy is the plan, or scheme, that guides the organization to where it wants to be, that is, to accomplish its objectives.

FIGURE 5-1 STRATEGIC MANAGEMENT FRAMEWORK.

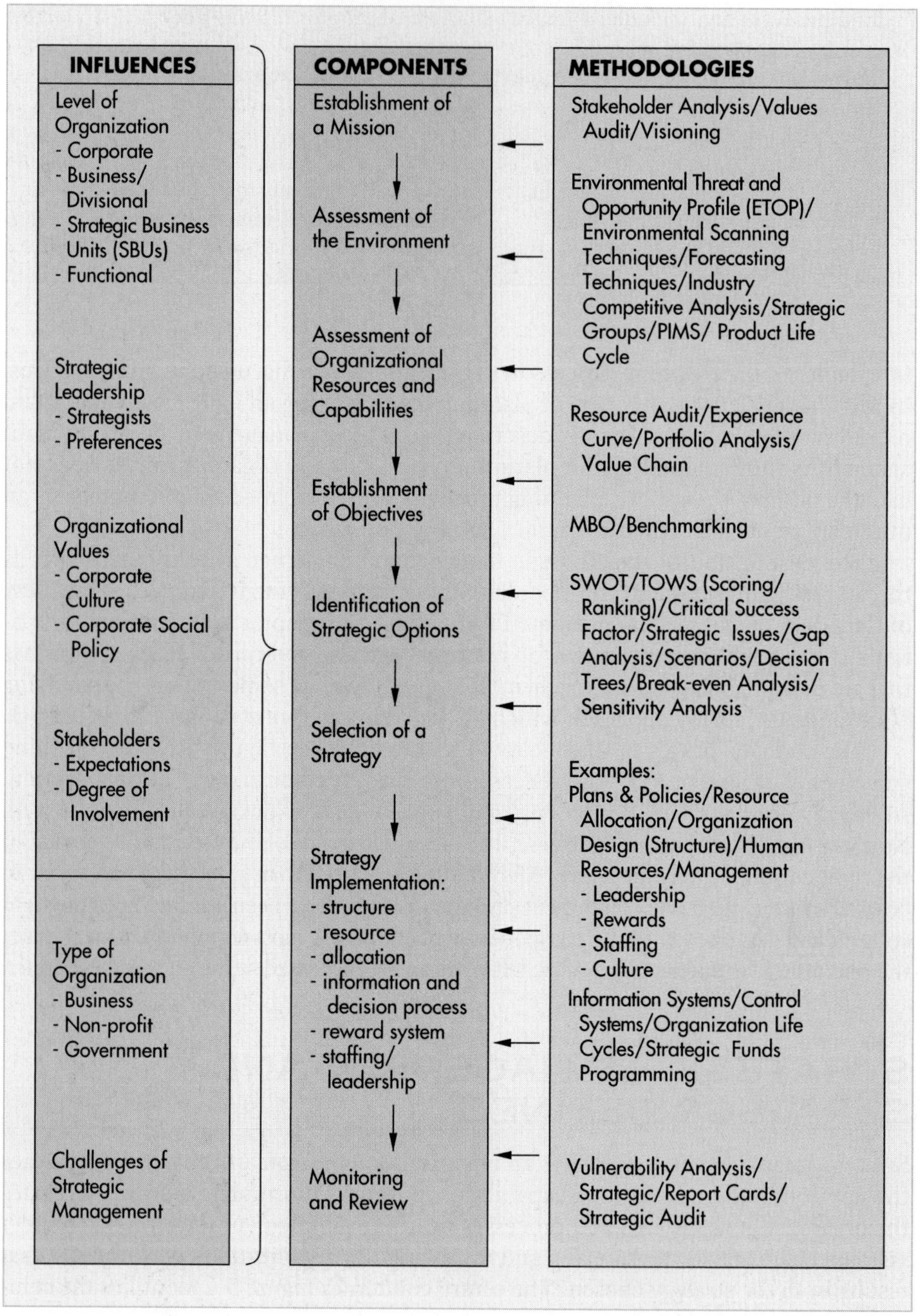

long-range plans

Strategic management is a concept that changes continually. This concept should not be confused with long-range planning and strategic planning. Long-range planning was the predecessor of the recent strategic approach to management. **Long-range plans** were forecasts based upon current and past performance. Usually the plans were for five-year intervals with a five-year plan being the most common. While managers were at least attempting to think ahead, the planning was rather static in nature. Past performance and experience were heavily relied upon for the projections made by managers.

Strategic planning advanced the planning process across another threshold. Planning became more externally oriented than previously with environmental analysis including increased focus on markets and competition. Resource audits or assessments were conducted more realistically with resources being allocated to areas where present and future opportunities to succeed were found rather than by traditional approaches based on past practice. Finally, there were more rigorous evaluations of strategic alternatives. According to Figure 5-1, strategic planning is represented by the "Assessment of Environment," "Assessment of Organizational Resources and Capabilities," "Establishment of Objectives," "Identification of Options," and "Selection of Strategy" components in the centre column. However, many managers found that their organizations were not responding to the "plans." A key aspect of planning was still missing, and it involved the capability of an organization to implement the strategic plan.

strategic planning

Wayne Gretzky is often quoted in strategy textbooks as having said, "I skate to where the puck is going to be, not where it's been." All managers should think about where their organizations will be in the future.

Strategic management involves not only aspects of long-term and strategic planning but also strategy implementation. The scope of an organization's activities is determined, and these activities are matched to the environment in which the organization operates and to resource capability. Strategy implementation takes place after the strategy is decided upon and objectives established. The strategic management process is carried through to completion by such things as the action plans needed, the organizational structure to be put in place, the reward or incentive systems for managers, and so on. This further step that makes sure implementation occurs is what results in strategic management.[2]

The Management at Work insert illustrates the use of strategic management at the well-known Canadian retailer, Mark's Work Warehouse.

MANAGEMENT AT WORK

Strategic Management at Mark's Work Warehouse Ltd.

Mark's Work Wearhouse operates 105 owned and 30 franchise stores across Canada that sell quality name brand, private label, and captive label (that is, labels owned by Mark's but not associated with the name of the store, for example, Wind River and Denver Hayes), work wear, casual wear and related apparel. In order to focus their activities in the very competitive retail industry, the company developed a strategic plan which provides direction and goals for management.

The following section, "Strategic Direction," from their *Annual Report* summarizes management's efforts at strategic management.

> In fiscal 1992, the Company developed a Strategic Plan called Thrive in '95. It is a three-year plan that targets a 4 percent after-tax profit on sales in fiscal 1995.
>
> We've established the practice of holding an annual think tank just after our busy Christmas season to incorporate the lessons we've just learned into both our Strategic Direction and our Strategic Plan. A one-year Strategic Direction is developed to confirm our focus. As an outgrowth of this work, the three-year plan is updated and extended one year. Our planning requires that the annual direction is drafted and buy-in completed between December and February. In February, we embed the direction into the performance contracts of senior management. Between March and June, we update the three-year plan for presentation at our June board meeting.
>
> The strategic direction for fiscal 1994 includes the following general components:
>
> 1) We caution ourselves to live in the present and to be aware of opportunities and changes, not foreseen in the plans.
> 2) We will implement the management system referred to as individual performance contracting which commits managers to the plan.

...

3) We will establish greater consistency within our advertising and marketing activities while redefining the marketplace perception of workwear to include a broader merchandise content.

4) While aggressively pursuing the development of our own private label programs, we are committed to being a leading retailer of brand-name merchandise.

5) We have identified retailers of similar merchandise in markets in the United States, and we are challenging ourselves to price our products competitively with such retailers in equivalent currency.

6) We have adopted a gross margin dollar focus on some commodities and a gross margin rate focus on other commodities within our strategic direction and strategic plan.

The primary activities of management focus in the fiscal 1994 strategic direction are as follows:

1) National Events—the execution of a number of promotional events intended to increase traffic.

2) Custom Uniform Sales—a strategic alliance to establish a stronger presence in this segment of our business.

3) System Roll Out—completion or enhancement of the computer systems, including our franchise network.

4) MAG's—Merchandise Assortment Guides—the installation by August 1 of standardized merchandise presentations of key commodities.

5) Service Quality—the establishment of service quality standards, monthly reports, collection of WOW's (Unsolicited Letters of Commendation).

We've identified thirty-six key success factors for our merchandise directions, some examples of which are:

— purchase and timely delivery of 300,000 units of a key merchandise program.

— Electronic Data Interchange (EDI) replenishment process with a key supplier on an important program in place by August 1.

— end-of-season inventory target in particular seasonal businesses.

— sales target in a specific category, concurrent with one of our national events, which challenges that particular category to outperform its operating budget.

In addition, Mark's has established corporate and financial objectives to accompany the strategic plan. Commitment of management to the plan is obtained through a management system centred on individual performance contracting where each manager participates in a process by agreeing to three or four key results or objectives.

Mark's has not yet achieved its objective of 4 percent after-tax profit on sales but is still aiming for it despite the competitive market and difficult economy for retailers. ▲

THE NATURE OF STRATEGIC DECISIONS

LEARNING OBJECTIVE 3
Identify factors that distinguish strategic from operational decisions.

Decisions of a strategic nature involve high degrees of uncertainty and complexity. Some of the factors[3] that make strategic management decisions difficult follow:

1. *Multiple objectives* Most organizations have more than one objective. Despite claims that business enterprises only seek profits, most businesses are also concerned with the social, environmental, and human impacts of their activities. Government and non-profit organizations also have several objectives. Seldom does one alternative satisfy all objectives and a strategic decision must be evaluated in terms of the extent to which it meets the many objectives.

2. *Long time horizons* Strategic decisions are concerned with the future. They involve the scope of business activity decisions and the type and magnitude of resource commitments having implications for the long term. For example, in the airplane industry, decisions to purchase new aircraft must be made years in advance and involve large amounts of capital. A decision regarding aircraft also affects the size and type of markets that will be served. Many of these types of decisions are irreversible in the short term and thus pose some risk to organizations.

3. *Difficulty of identifying good options* It takes considerable innovation and creativity on the part of managers to generate good strategic options or alternatives since few options are desirable in all respects. For example, when tariffs were lowered, Canadian shoe manufacturers were confronted with undesirable options: close down, move to a low-cost country, or go into a different business. Another option was to cut costs and specialize but this one was not easy either because strong international competition existed.
4. *Intangibles* Not all ingredients of a successful operation can be assessed, measured, or even identified, since they are not tangible. For example, the value of a corporation's name is difficult to assess, as Coleman Co. found out. Coleman is a well-known name in camping equipment but it did not help in selling sailboats and windsurfers. Also, most organizations are unable to identify all future government regulation or deregulation since governments can be unpredictable.
5. *Multiple stakeholders* Strategic decisions require consultation and often the approval of several stakeholders, that is, those individuals or groups who can influence the organization. These stakeholders frequently have different expectations of what they want from the organization. The influence of stakeholders will be discussed in later sections.
6. *Risk and uncertainty* Risk and uncertainty increase as predictions for the future are made. The primary reasons for such uncertainties include (1) a lack of sufficient financial, economic, and social data; (2) the expense and time associated with data retrieval and analyses; (3) natural but unpredictable phenomena, such as earthquakes and droughts; (4) shifts in population; (5) changes in priorities; and (6) the unpredictability of other influential stakeholders (e.g., governments, competitors).[4]
7. *The consequences of many functions on businesses* As strategic decisions have implications for the whole organization and require coordination, many, if not all, divisions, departments, or units of an organization are involved. For example, decisions often demand cooperation from, or coordination among, functional departments such as marketing, production, finance, and human resources. In the case of a conglomerate, coordination among the enterprises owned may be needed.
8. *Value trade-offs* Seldom do strategic issues have clear-cut answers. Some form of trade-off is usually inevitable. One of the trade-offs may be an effect on the environment. Assuring complete protection of the environment may increase costs and make a plant uneconomic. Today managers are sensitive to such trade-offs. Another example involves the use of animals in the testing of lifesaving drugs. If forced to use other means of testing, the availability of the drug may be delayed and more people may die before its development.
9. *The allocation of large amounts of resources* Strategic decisions usually concern large amounts of resources, including money, people, physical assets, or managerial time and energy. Securing the required resources, such as by hiring persons with particular skills, or reallocating present resources from the production of one product to another, can be costly, hurt morale, and require a lot of time.
10. *The sequential nature of strategic decisions* Usually a particular strategic decision is in some way connected with other decisions. One strategic decision might affect the availability of certain options in the future and the desirability of those options. Moreover, any strategic decision affects day-to-day operational decisions and has ramifications for the entire organization. For example, when General Motors decided to introduce new technology into the manufacturing process, it did not fully anticipate the difficulties of compatibility with other technological equipment or the reaction of employees.

STRATEGIC MANAGEMENT WITHIN ORGANIZATIONS

LEARNING OBJECTIVE 4
Understand the application of strategic management at different levels in an organization.

strategist

LEARNING OBJECTIVE 5
Identify strategists and understand their role.

Strategic management takes place at different levels within the organization. The four levels usually identified within an organization are corporate, business/divisional, business unit, and functional. Figure 5-2 illustrates these levels. In addition, different types of strategists can be found in any organization. A **strategist** is someone responsible for the success or failure of an organization through the initiation, formulation, implementation and review of a strategic management process (see Table 5-1).

Strategists include members of the board of directors; top managers referred to as CEOs, presidents, and vice-presidents; middle managers identified as divisional, departmental, subsidiary or plant managers; managers in charge of functional areas such as marketing, finance, and production; planning staffs; consultants; entrepreneurs; and strategic business unit (SBU) executives.

Strategic decisions are not restricted to top managers. Although the role of strategists varies from one organization to another, the following discussion relates the organizational levels with the role of strategists.

CORPORATE LEVEL STRATEGY

The strategic management process at the corporate level is involved in establishing the strategy for the whole organization. In a small organization, the corporate strategy is the only one, but in larger organizations it serves as the umbrella or comprehensive strategy for the whole organization. The corporate strategy for Renaissance Energy Ltd. involves limiting exploration activities to a particular geographic region, adding more petroleum reserves at a reasonable cost, and expanding and diversifying markets.[5]

The corporate strategy is usually established by the board of directors, and top managers and sets objectives for and approves strategic decisions made at lower levels. Strategic decisions at this level are usually long-term, affect the overall direction of the organization, and involve large commitments of resources, especially

FIGURE 5-2 LEVELS OF STRATEGIC MANAGEMENT.

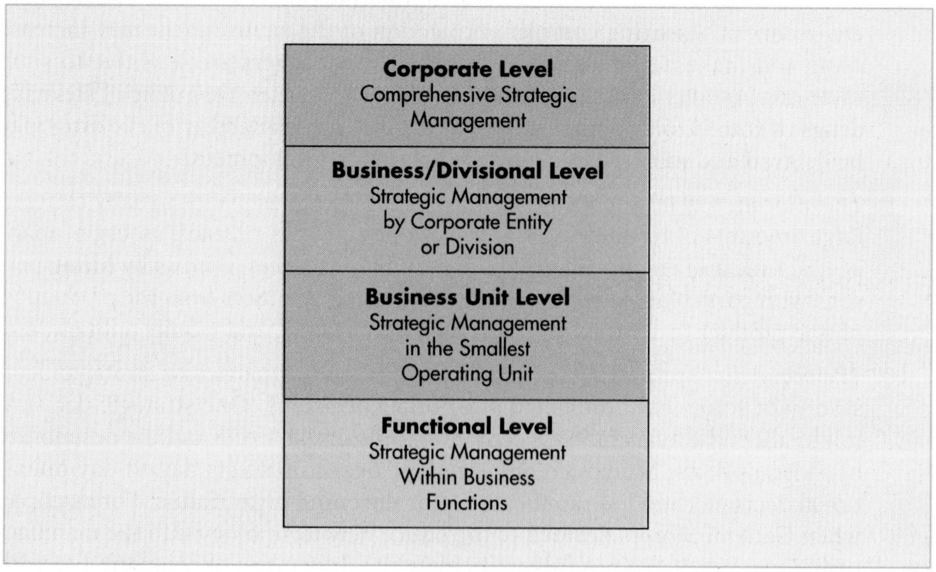

TABLE 5-1 EXAMPLES OF CEO STRATEGISTS IN CANADIAN BUSINESS ENTERPRISES.

Gerald J. Maier
President & Chief Executive Officer
TransCanada PipeLines Ltd. Calgary, AB
Gerald J. Maier, a petroleum engineer, is Prairie born and raised and has worked in the petroleum and mining industries on several continents. TransCanada's core business is gas transmission via pipelines but it also owns a leading Canadian gas marketer and an international producer and marketer of thermal carbon black.

William A. Etherington
President and Chief Executive Officer IBM Canada Ltd., Toronto
William Etherington began his career with IBM in 1964 in London after graduating from the University of Western Ontario with a B.Sc. degree in Electrical Engineering. He has held numerous positions in the company and has worked in Latin America for IBM. His greatest career achievement? "Making Latin America the fastest-growing part of IBM."

Lynn Poslums
President, Fairweather, Division of Dylex Limited, Toronto, ON
Fairweather is a coast-to-coast chain of 135 women's fashion stores and a division of Dylex Limited. Lynn Poslums joined the Dylex organization at Tip Top in 1983 after obtaining her B. Comm. and M.B.A. degrees from the University of Toronto. She moved to Fairweather in 1987 and was appointed President in 1989. Retailing has experienced tough times, but Lynn's stated mission is for Fairweather to be the recognized leader in women's wear retailing.

Anthony Thomas Leon
Chairman of the Board and CEO, Leon's Furniture Limited, Weston, ON
Leon's Furniture was founded in 1909 by Ablan Leon, Tom Leon's father. From one store in Welland, Ontario, the company has grown to 28 corporate stores and 21 franchise outlets. Tom Leon was born and raised in Welland and occupied every position in the company before becoming Chairman and CEO. He is active in community, church and business organizations, and is a director of several other corporations.

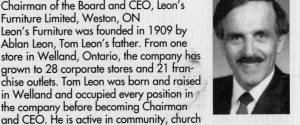

Jim Pattison
President and Chief Executive Officer, Jim Pattison Group Inc., Vancouver, BC
Jim Pattison founded the Jim Pattison Group in 1961 with the purchase of a General Motors automobile dealership. Today the company has 13 000 employees, annual sales of over $2.5 billion, and operates in five industries: transportation, communications, food products, packaging, and financial services. Pattison serves on several Boards of Directors, was the volunteer Chairman and CEO of Expo '86 held in Vancouver, and has received the Orders of Canada and BC.

Sheelagh Dillon Whittaker
President of Information Technology of EDS Canada, a subsidiary of Electronic Data Systems Corp., Dallas, Texas, which is owned by General Motors Corp. EDS supplies information technology services to financial and insurance companies, manufacturing operations, and government and is headquartered in Toronto. From 1989 to 1993 she was President and Chief Executive Officer of Cancom Inc., Canada's leading satellite network service. She was educated at the University of Alberta (B.Sc. 1967), University of Toronto (B.A. 1970), and York University (M.B.A. 1975).

financial ones. Strategic management at this level is concerned with coordinating the activities of many divisions and units, and often includes managing a portfolio of businesses. Strategic management must begin at this level if an organization is to develop a sense of direction and overall strategy.

Business/Divisional Level Strategy

Organizations are broken down into divisions. In the case of conglomerates, these divisions comprise separate business enterprises, which operate at a tier below the corporate one, while other enterprises are departmentalized in the same manner. The strategic directions established at the corporate level are translated into concrete objectives and strategies at the divisional level by middle managers. The separate businesses or divisions are involved in the components of the strategic management process listed in Figure 5-1, but they focus on their particular business or division and must coordinate with the corporate strategy.

BUSINESS UNIT LEVEL STRATEGY

strategic business unit (SBU)

A **strategic business unit** (SBU) is the smallest operating division of an enterprise that is given authority to make its own strategic decisions within corporate guidelines. A SBU is usually established after meeting certain requirements. Although these requirements vary among enterprises, they often include the following:

1. The SBU has a distinct business concept and mission.
2. The SBU has its own identifiable set of competitors.
3. The SBU is a competitor in its market and is not dependent on internal corporate business to survive.
4. SBU managers can make and implement a strategic decision relatively independent of other SBUs.
5. The SBU has the resources to conduct the business and is able to make crucial operating decisions.[6]

An example of a SBU at C-I-L Inc. is the operation for lawn fertilizer bagged for the home market. Large chemical companies such as C-I-L Inc. produce several chemical products. One division produces fertilizer and within this division the producers of bagged lawn fertilizer would be a SBU.

The use of SBUs allows strategic management to be implemented at the lowest strata of the enterprise by SBU executives. Each SBU sets business strategies to suit its environment and resources. The divisional level will help the SBU define its scope of operations and limits or enhance the SBU's operations by deciding what resources the SBU should have. The use of SBUs allows for a high degree of decentralization and encourages entrepreneurship within larger business enterprises. This activity is often referred to as **intrapreneurship** or internal corporate venturing. An intrapreneur is an individual operating as an entrepreneur within an organization and is supplied with the resources and given the responsibility necessary to develop an innovation or venture. In other words, the individual manager operates in much the same way as a small business owner. A well-known example of intrapreneurship is the creation of "Post-it Notes" at 3M. The researcher who developed the product became the executive responsible for all decisions relating to the development, production, and marketing of "Post-it Notes."[7]

intrapreneurship

FUNCTIONAL LEVEL STRATEGY

A functional level strategy refers to the strategic management process within the "functions" of an organization; for example, in a business enterprise these functions would be marketing, production, finance, research and development, and human resources. This level focusses on the efficiency and effectiveness of operational areas such as purchasing, maintenance, and cost accounting; the results usually are quantifiable. Objectives and strategies are established for each function and the time allowed for implementing the strategies and fulfilling the objectives is the shortest of any level.

In addition to managers, strategy is determined by planning staffs and consultants. Both assist by familiarizing managers with the strategic management process and acting as facilitators in the process.

STRATEGIC LEADERSHIP

strategic leadership

Strategic leadership concerns the people who have overall responsibility for an organization—their characteristics, what they do, and how they do it. Hambrick makes a useful distinction between the strategic leadership task and other management tasks:

1. The strategic leader has to consider the external and internal environments and to align them with the strategic thrust of the organization.
2. The task confronting the strategic leader is ambiguous, complex, and is overloaded with information.
3. The task is multifunctional, that is, it cuts across marketing, finance, production, and human resources. The task is therefore complex and integrative, and involves dealing with subordinate managers who have more expertise in particular areas than the strategy leader.
4. The strategic leadership task involves managing others. Strategic management cannot be handled alone; others must be enticed to participate.[8]

THE INFLUENCE OF A STRATEGIST'S PREFERENCES

The previous section focussed on the role of strategists, or the importance of strategic leadership. Strategists engineer the strategic management process in an organization. However, strategists can be influenced by personal preferences. A manager's biases will affect whether or not the organization will even practise strategic management, and if it will, the form it will take. A strategist's outlook shapes all the components in the process, including the business activity of the enterprise and the selection of a strategy. The factors listed below mold a strategist's preferences, including the values they hold, their beliefs about society, the personal needs that motivate them, the circumstances of their workplace or industry, and the influence of peer groups. These factors shape the attitudes of strategists regarding risk, ethics, social issues, profits, and short- versus long-term planning either positively or negatively. They can create the force that drives the initiation and maintenance of the strategic management process, or they may act as filters that prevent the identification of all viable strategic options, or even result in strategic decisions biassed by self-interest.

ORGANIZATIONAL VALUES

LEARNING OBJECTIVE 6
Describe the influence of organizational values on strategic decision making.

Organizations are also influenced by values or preferences, and they often publicly state the values they hold. For example, Bell Canada's values are customer satisfaction, profit orientation, excellence, innovative and action-oriented behaviour, market leadership, and team spirit. Organizational values can be expressed in a variety of ways. Two expressions of organizational values are corporate culture and corporate social policy.[9]

corporate culture

Corporate culture is discussed in Chapter 16 and will only be dealt with briefly here in its relation to strategic management. **Corporate culture** is the complex set of values, beliefs, assumptions, and symbols that define the way in which an organization conducts its business.[10] Often this culture is not stated explicitly and instead is reflected in structures, behaviours, processes, rites and rituals, myths, traditions, symbols, language system and metaphors (terminology), and value systems (the values generally held by the employees of the organization). Well-run organizations have a distinctive culture that promotes the creation, implementation, and maintenance of successful strategies. Culture is often the reason an organization experiences difficulties when it attempts to shift its strategic direction, as described below.

> Not only has the"right" corporate culture become the essence and foundation of corporate excellence, but success or failure of needed reforms hinges on management's sagacity and ability to change the firm's driving culture in time and in tune with required changes in strategies.[11]

As discussed in Chapter 16, changing corporate culture is challenging and time-consuming, but, on occasion, strategists find they have no choice but to do just that.[12]

Organizational values are also influenced by societal expectations or social concerns. As we discuss in detail in Chapter 20 enterprises must respond to these issues to some degree and establish corporate social policies. An example of how one company expresses its organizational values is presented in the Ethics in Management insert.

THE INFLUENCE OF STAKEHOLDERS

stakeholder

A **stakeholder** is an individual or group who can influence, or is influenced by, the operations or activities of an organization.[13] Stakeholders may also be referred to as claimants, influencers, publics, or constituencies. The most common stakeholders are shareholders, employees, customers, suppliers, creditors, competitors, society at large, and government. But there are numerous other stakeholders, including interest groups, educational institutions, charities, the media, and business organizations.

Stakeholders have control over the resources the organization needs; they have expectations of what the organization should do for them, or not do to them; and they are a reflection of much of what is happening in the environment in which the organization must operate, so it is important for managers to identify the complete array of stakeholders.

Not all stakeholders influence the organization's strategy all the time. But the key, or influential, stakeholders must be accommodated if the strategy is to be successful. For example, Ford Canada recognized the key role of its parts suppliers and ran newspaper advertisements thanking them for the quality of the parts. NCR Canada identified five stakeholders that were critical to the success of its business: customers, employees, shareholders, suppliers, and communities.

ETHICS IN MANAGEMENT

WASCANA ENERGY INC.'S CORPORATE VALUES

Corporations express their organizational values in different ways, by using different words and formats. Wascana Energy has prepared the following expression of its values:

> The history of Wascana Energy has been characterized by change and progress. The values shared by the Company's employees have enabled them to perform their daily tasks with a sense of trust and confidence. Respect, high ethical standards, teamwork and innovation has helped Wascana Energy achieve its corporate objectives. In 1992, a formal statement of values was adopted to serve as a guideline for positive change and to provide employees with a consistent framework to define relationships with fellow employees, partners, customers and the communities in which Wascana Energy is active.
>
> Profitability—We conduct our business to ensure that Wascana Energy has the profits to continue to meet its obligations to its employees, investors, host communities, customers, suppliers and other stakeholders.
>
> Integrity—We conduct our activities with integrity, displaying the highest ethical standards.
>
> Teamwork—We encourage and place a high value on teamwork.
>
> Confidence—We approach our work with confidence in our abilities, individually and collectively.
>
> High Standards—We strive for high standards in technology, business and our personal lives.
>
> Respect—We exercise care, attention, consideration and respect for our stakeholders and strive to earn the same in return.
>
> Innovation—We promote creative and entrepreneurial skills to foster innovation in concepts, methods, opportunities and solutions.
>
> Job Satisfaction—We approach work with enthusiasm, dedication and good humour and take enjoyment from our daily activities. ▲

THE COMPONENTS OF STRATEGIC MANAGEMENT

The eight components of the strategic management process as outlined in Figure 5.1 will be explained in the following sections. For each component, some appropriate methodologies will be briefly described.

ESTABLISHMENT OF A MISSION

mission

The development of a **mission** statement is the first step in a strategic management process. It is an enduring statement that specifies in very broad, even philosophical terms, the organization's "reason for being" and what distinguishes it from similar organizations. Considerable diversity exists among organizations in the composition and uses of mission statements, variously called creed statements, statements of purpose, statements of beliefs, statements of business principles, or statements defining our business.[14] Examples of mission statements are provided in Table 5-2. Note the differences in content.

The following list illustrates the reasons King and Cleland believe an organization should develop a written mission statement. Note how these reasons relate to the components of strategic management.

1. To ensure unanimity of purpose within the organization.
2. To provide a basis, or standard, for allocating organizational resources.
3. To establish a general tone or organizational climate.
4. To serve as a focal point for individuals to identify with the organization's purpose and direction; and to deter those who cannot from participating further in the organization's activities.

TABLE 5-2 EXAMPLES OF MISSION STATEMENTS.

Examples of Mission Statements

Bell Canada's mission is to be a world leader in helping communicate and manage information.

Transit Windsor is a Company which provides Public Transportation for the City of Windsor and adjacent areas. Our mission is to continually improve public transportation services for the people of Windsor at a reasonable cost to both the customer and the taxpayer.

The Canadian Red Cross Society is a volunteer-based organization which provides emergency relief and humanitarian service to the public

- in time of disaster or conflict in Canada and around the world,
- through the operation of a national blood service,
- through community-based health and social service initiatives,
- in accordance with the fundamental principles of the Red Cross.

The business mission of Atco Ltd. is to achieve an international reputation for excellence by providing products and services to the energy and resource industries and to invest principally in energy-related assets in North America.

Noverco is a Quebec public company with a North American vocation. It was formed with the purpose of acquiring, financing, and managing large-scale companies, which will afford its shareholders solid guarantees for the future and excellent rates-of-return, in various activities principally related to the energy field.

The business mission of Investors Group is to satisfy clients in need of general and comprehensive financial planning. Through product development and a well-trained sales distribution organization, Investors will assist in implementing financial plans and providing effective ongoing service.

5. To facilitate the translation of objectives into a work structure involving the assignment of tasks to responsible elements within the organization.

6. To specify organizational purposes and the translation of these purposes into objectives in such a way that cost, time, and performance parameters can be assessed and controlled.[15]

A survey by Fred R. David identified the following as the main items included in the mission statements of business enterprises:

1. *Customers* Who are the enterprise's customers?

2. *Products or services* What are the firm's major products or services?

3. *Location* Where does the firm compete?

4. *Technology* What is the firm's basic technology?

5. *Concern for survival* What is the firm's commitment to economic objectives?

6. *Philosophy* What are the basic beliefs, values, aspirations and philosophical priorities of the firm?

7. *Self-concept* What are the firm's strengths and competitive advantages?

8. *Concern for public image* What are the firm's public responsibilities and what image is desired.

9. *Concern for employees* What is the firm's attitude towards its employees?[16]

The development of a mission statement is the first step in a strategic management process. The definition and the list of reasons for such statements clearly indicate the fundamental sense of purpose, direction, and priority given to the organization. The strategists most involved in mission development are the board of directors and top management. The mission statement becomes a critical document in communicating and influencing other strategists and the firm's employees.

Methodologies for Developing Mission Statements

Mission statements are usually developed through group processes involving the board of directors and top management strategists. Some of the methodologies that may be used are stakeholder analysis, a values audit, and visioning.

stakeholder analysis

Stakeholder analysis Performing a stakeholder analysis at the beginning of the strategic management process is important since all strategies must satisfy key stakeholders. A **stakeholder analysis** identifies the criteria by which the organization will be judged by stakeholders and how well the organization is performing against these criteria.[17] Freeman claims that an organization must manage its relationships with influential stakeholders in a way that ensures that their influence is recognized. He suggested three levels where an organization has to manage these relationships:

LEARNING OBJECTIVE 7

Outline the methodologies managers follow when applying the components of strategic management.

1. At a rational level where stakeholders and their "stakes" are identified.

2. At the process level which formulates the approach or procedure to be used by the organization to manage the relationships.

3. At the transactional level involving actual interactions with the stakeholders.

These three levels result in what Freeman referred to as a "stakeholder management capability"[18] that is, an organization's ability to recognize, understand, and respond to stakeholders.

Values audit A **values audit** is a systematic effort to discover the beliefs or attitudes held by all members in an organization. Sometimes organizations will conduct surveys to identify the values held so that they can be taken into account when formulating and implementing a strategy. Similar surveys are also referred to as social or ethics audits.[19]

values audit

Visioning **Visioning** is the process of establishing a vision for an organization, that is "a framework which guides those choices that determine the nature and direction of an organization."[20] Visions provide an indication of the future direction of the organization and become the foundation for the mission statement and objectives.

visioning

Visions usually emerge from a consensus of top management strategists and become a force in improving employee communications, participation, and commitment. In other words, a vision helps to translate a strategy into action by providing focus for what needs to be done. These are examples of vision statements:

1. *Scintrex, Concord, Ontario* To be Canada's top instrumentation company in selected world markets.
2. *Canadian National Sportman's Shows, Toronto* "The leader in event management in North America that channels its profits into making a better outdoor environment."
3. *Carrier Canada, Mississauga* "Being the biggest and the best."
4. *Liptons International Ltd., Etobicoke, Ontario* Belief in "fashion, quality service, value, store excellence and you."[21]

Overall, the mission component initiates the strategic management process and is critical to identifying a direction and persuading others to support the organizational objectives and efforts.

Assessment of the Environment

The following headlines illustrate challenges confronting business enterprises: "Store Sales Down by 1.4% in May: Second Dismal Month in a Row"; "U.S. Currency Moves Higher"; "Canada Threatened With Ice Cream War: U.S. Wants Import Restrictions Removed"; and "Shareholder activism brewing: pay disclosure rules to create intense scrutiny, observers say." Dozens of similar headlines concerning businesses appear in newspapers everyday. A downturn in sales is bad news to enterprises in retailing or to manufacturers of the goods retailers sell. Firms that export or import goods from or to the U.S. will be affected by currency changes. Dairy processors might face increased competition if U.S. companies can sell their ice cream more easily in Canada. Managers may be held more accountable as one stakeholder, shareholders, become more demanding. To survive such events, an organization must somehow develop the capability of assessing the external environment in which it operates and to understand when and how this environment influences them.

Carrier Canada is a leading supplier of residential and commercial heating and cooling equipment that is committed to a vision, "Being the biggest and the best." The vision is realized by constantly reminding all stakeholders, especially employees, of Carrier's objectives and the need to perform better.

Environmental Variables

The forces and trends influencing an organization can arise from many factors in the environment, such as those discussed in Chapter 3. Other factors include the general economic conditions as reflected in the Gross National Product (GNP), price levels, interest rate and income per capita statistics, and the capital markets that provide financing for the enterprise.

The organization's strategists must continuously scan the environment, gathering and synthesizing relevant information. As special attention must be given to information about the particular industry and geographical area in which the organization operates, not every organization performs its scan in the same way or monitors the same variables.

opportunity

From the analysis of the environment variables, opportunities for and threats to the organization are identified. An **opportunity** is a favourable circumstance or condition that represents a good chance or prospect for the organization. For example, the increasing popularity of designer name clothing was an opportunity that John Forsyth Company, a clothing manufacturer, took advantage of as the Canadian supplier of such names as Pierre Cardin, Hubert de Givenchy, Nino Cerutti, and Oscar de la Renta.

threats

Environmental **threats** arise from the possibility of an adverse or harmful trend or event. For example, the North American Free Trade Agreement poses a threat to Canadian food processors. U.S. food processors will be able to export their products to Canada as tariffs are removed. At the same time, Canadian food processors are faced with higher prices for raw material than their U.S. counterparts, due to restrictions imposed by marketing boards for chicken, eggs, milk, and other agricultural products. Dominion Textiles Inc. encountered threats from global trade and had to formulate a new strategy to reflect this environment (refer to the Global Management insert below).

GLOBAL MANAGEMENT

Domtex Rebuilds Abroad

Dominion Textile Inc. (Domtex), based in Montreal, was a full-range Canadian textile producer which included such products as sheets and towels. It had operated successfully in Canada behind tariff protection until the Canada–U.S. Free Trade Agreement. During the 1980s, the company grew through acquisition of a wide variety of textile businesses around the world. The company experienced large losses in the late 1980s and early 1990s due to free trade making the industry more competitive, a worldwide slump in the textile business, and the cost of financing the debt acquired during expansion.

A turnabout strategy was necessary and lead to the shifting of Domtex operations abroad. In 1989, the company had 41 factories and 14 000 employees, and by 1993 had 35 plants with 8800 employees. Six Canadian plants were shut and most employees were now outside of Canada. Some of the company's operations were integrated with U.S. plants acquired during the 1980s. Caldwell towels and Wabasso and Texmade bed sheets were put into a joint venture with a larger U.S. manufacturer of bathroom accessories. With the acquisition of a large denim plant in the U.S. in 1988, Domtex became the world's leading producer of denim used in jeans. Domtex's Canadian denim plant was able to survive due to productivity improvements, a lower Canadian dollar, and lower cotton prices.

The focus on denim production was one elment in Domtex's turnabout strategy. The company decided to move away from commodity-type products of low margin, to specialize in value-added products and provide customers with quality service, and to focus on products with a global client base. In addition to denim, the company concentrated on a few international businesses: yarn, workwear, and nonwoven fabrics used as interlinings and in disposable diapers. As an example of its global operations, Domtex produces woven and nonwoven linings and related products in Brazil, Columbia, Britain, France, Germany, Hong Kong, Italy, Morocco, Northern Ireland, Portugal, and Spain. It is considering building a new denim plant in Southeast Asia to serve that market. In order to survive in the very competitive textile industry and to return to profitability, it was necessary for Domtex to move most of its operations abroad. ▲

It is often difficult to distinguish between opportunities and threats, since what is a threat to one organization may be an opportunity to another. The trend to an aged population is a threat to the manufacturer of baby food such as Gerber, since it means the number of infants is declining, but it is an opportunity for Extendicare, the operator of nursing homes for the elderly.

Environmental Assessment Methodologies

Environmental threat and opportunity profile (ETOP) This profile consists of a systematic assessment of all the circumstances that exist in the environment. Items under the various environmental variables are listed with a "+" to indicate an opportunity, a "–" to signify a threat, or a "0" standing for a neutral impact. The advantage of such a profile is that it captures in a concise format the environmental circumstances in which the organization is to operate.[22]

Environmental spanning techniques These are processes for continuously monitoring external factors, events, trends, and projections. Many techniques can be used for such monitoring. SPIRE (Systematic Procedure for Identification of Relevant Environments) is a computer-assisted, matrix-generating tool for systematically anticipating environment changes that can have an impact on operations;[23] and QUEST (Quick Environmental Scanning Techniques) is designed to scan the environment quickly and spot events or trends that are critical for the organization's strategy.[24]

Forecasting techniques Many techniques exist for forecasting environmental factors.[25] Techniques that are often utilized for anticipating changes in the strategic environment are:

1. *The Delphi Technique* Panels of experts are asked to assign importance to and probability for various future developments.
2. *Cross-Impact Analysis* The effects of different events or trends are identified and the results are used to develop a "domino theory" to show how one event might trigger others.
3. *Barometric Forecasts* Past trends are used in an attempt to predict the future.
4. *Trend-Impact Analysis* Various data times series are examined to identify whether or not a trend will occur and what impact an event will have on future trends.
5. *Multiple Scenarios* This is a method of developing alternative futures[26] (discussed in "The selection of a strategy" section).

Industry/competitive analysis Another approach to assessing the environment is to examine the firms in the industry in which the enterprise operates. An industry profile is developed that differentiates the competitors in an industry. For example, industries dominated by a few large enterprises, such as brewing, differ significantly from the fragmented industries in which no enterprise has a large share such as exists in the clothing, metal fabricating, and leather products industries.

The reasons for conducting an industry analysis are twofold: to ascertain the nature of competition, and to identify those factors that are key to success in the industry. One model of competitive analysis was developed by Porter.[27] The nature of competition, or competitive rivalry, is influenced by potential entrants, suppliers, substitutes, and buyers who have some "power" or represent a "threat." A strategy can only be formulated after the nature of competition is understood using models of this type. By examining the industry and the nature of competition, strategists attempt to identify those aspects or characteristics that are key to success in a particular industry. For example, a key to success in the toy manufacturing industry is to anticipate and develop products that will be this year's fad because most sales are generated from such products. Strategic groups is a methodology related to industry/competitive analysis.

strategic group

Strategic groups Competitors in an industry can be positioned according to how they compete with one another; for example, what geographic areas they cover, the market segments they represent, and how well they use their plants. A **strategic group** consists of those enterprises with similar competitive approaches and positions in the industry. Strategic groups are identified to observe the actions of competitors and to learn how the competition can be confronted or avoided.

Profit impact of marketing strategy (PIMS) The Strategic Planning Institute of Cambridge, Massachusetts, collects data on the performance of about 1000 diverse businesses. The data are pooled into a database that is used for research activities, the development of models, and reports to individual businesses. The PIMS project attempts to ascertain what factors influence the profitability of an enterprise, and how return on investment (ROI) changes in response to changes in strategy and market conditions. Among the many findings this project has made are the following:

1. Business enterprises with relatively large market shares tend to have above-average profits.
2. Business enterprises which are capital intensive tend to have lower ROIs.
3. Market growth is positively related to ROI.
4. High inventory levels damage profitability, particularly in businesses with few fixed assets such as service industries.[28]

PIMS is a widely discussed methodology and far more complex than has been presented here.

Product life cycle The idea of the product life cycle is a common basis for understanding the ways in which forces in the environment affect an organization. Figure 5-3 depicts the five stages of a product life cycle. The environment of an enterprise alters as the product advances through the cycle. For example, fitness clubs mushroomed during the health and fitness craze of the 1980s (growth stage in cycle).

FIGURE 5-3 THE PRODUCT LIFE CYCLE.

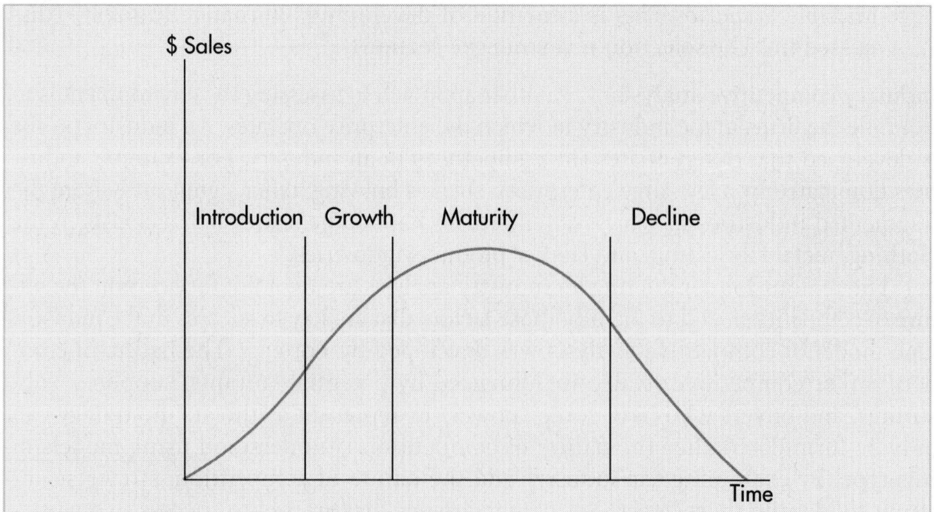

Recently, several fitness clubs have failed, including some Gold's Gyms in Toronto. It appears that fitness clubs are at the maturity, or possibly the decline stages of their product cycle.

Assessment of Organizational Resources and Capabilities

After the assessment of the organization's external environment and the identification of opportunities and threats, the next stage in the strategic management process is to assess the internal resources. This evaluation is needed to ascertain the ability of an organization to take advantage of the opportunities in the environment and to overcome the threats.

organizational strength

organizational weakness

Internal resources can be identified as either strengths or weaknesses. An **organizational strength** is a resource or capability that assists the organization in carrying out its activities. An **organizational weakness**, by contrast, is an inadequacy that prevents the organization from doing what it wants. The strategist must be able to distinguish one from the other as strategies should be built on strengths while minimizing the influence of weaknesses. In effect, the availability or shortage of resources determines the "capabilities" of an organization to perform.

Strategists must systematically assess resources to understand the capability of the organization to undertake a particular strategy. Usually the functional areas of the organization are examined, that is, functions such as marketing, finance, production, and human resource management. This assessment leads to an understanding of where resources are used and an identification of core strengths. Avon Cosmetics had a resource strength in its thousands of neighbourhood distributors; however, as fewer women began staying at home, the distribution system became less effective, and a strategic decision was considered to sell through retailers.

distinctive competence

By examining resources, a strategist looks for a distinctive ability around which a strategy can be formulated. This resource is often referred to as a **distinctive competence**; it is a function that the organization performs particularly well and generally better than its competitors. This ability is also referred to as a competitive advantage[29] or a key success factor.[30] Table 5-3 lists the key success factors found from a survey of U.S. manufacturing firms. The resource competences of organizations vary, and organizations can base strategies on different capabilities. Resources and capabilities also vary among industries and over time.

Some of the methodologies available to strategists to assess organizational resources and capabilities are outlined in the next section.

TABLE 5-3 KEY SUCCESS FACTORS.

1. Image, including goodwill, prestige and reputation.
2. Technical knowledge of the sales force.
3. Marketing knowledge of the sales force.
4. Advertising and sales promotion.
5. Applied product research and development.
6. Service, including quality and availability to customers.
7. Process research, that is, research at improving the way the products are manufactured.
8. Firm size to exploit economies of scale.
9. The availability of financial agreements to assist customers.
10. The distribution system.
11. The location of the manufacturing facilities.
12. Technical skills of the work force.
13. Quality control system.
14. Production management, that is, the planning and organization of operations.
15. The effectiveness of the purchasing department in obtaining supplies.
16. Labour relations that lead to fewer accidents, less absenteeism, and low number of strikes.
17. The technical sophistication of equipment used.

Resource and Capability Assessment Methodologies

resource audit

A **resource audit** is a systematic examination and verification of the capabilities available to the organization. Such audits can take various forms. Simple checklists for each function assist strategists in identifying strengths and weaknesses, for example, are facilities located effectively? Are the advertising media well chosen? Has profitability been increasing? Are working conditions clean and safe? Another approach is to identify strengths and weaknesses by functional areas in a strategic advantage profile in which "+" indicates a strength, "–" indicates a weakness, and "0" indicates a neutral situation.[31] The internal factor evaluation (IFE) matrix goes a step further and assigns weights and ranking to an organization's key strengths and weaknesses.[32]

experience curve

An **experience curve** is an organized framework for analyzing the production cost and selling price of a product over a period. According to this concept, unit cost in many manufacturing and some service industries declines as experience is gained. Thus, economies of scale improve and employees learn to perform better as production increases; management discovers more efficient ways to perform tasks, and capital is substituted for labour.[33] By utilizing what is known about the effects of the experience curve, strategists can anticipate the resources and capabilities required as production increases, thereby ascertaining costs and appropriate pricing. A good example is provided by the consumer electronics industry. The price of products such as VCRs or camcorders fell soon after they were introduced and started selling in volume.

portfolio analysis

The PIMS and product life cycle methodologies discussed in the previous section along with the experience curve are among the bases for portfolio analysis. **Portfolio analysis** is a classification of the present and future positions of businesses, products, or SBUs according to the attractiveness of the market and the ability to compete within the market. The classification is usually presented in a visual display like that in Figure 5-4. Several classification systems are used; the one shown in Figure 5-4 was developed by the Boston Consulting Group.

In the matrix in Figure 5-4, the classification is based on the market growth rate and market share. A star is a product (or business) which has a high market share in a growing market. The company may be spending heavily to gain that share, but the experience curve effect will mean that costs decline over time. A company hopes

FIGURE 5-4 PORTFOLIO ANALYSIS MATRIX.

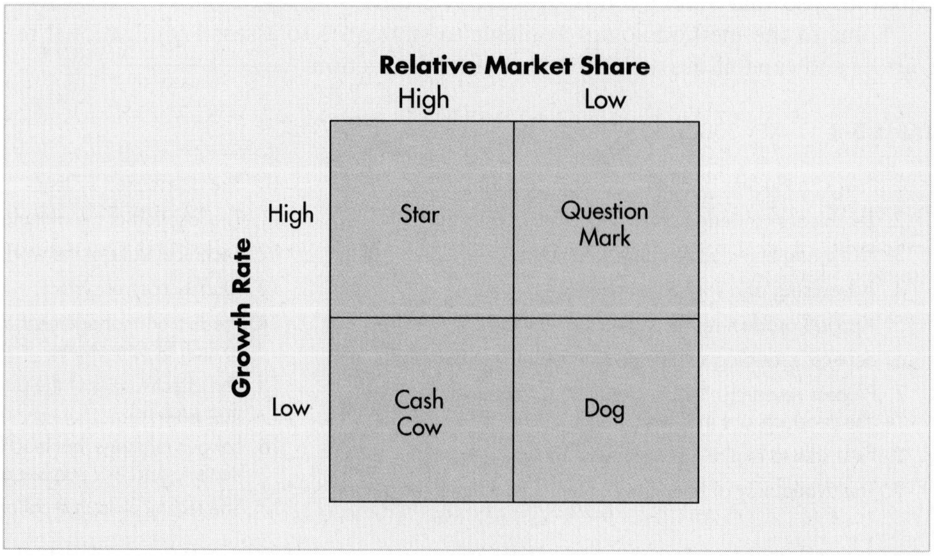

their costs fall at a faster rate than those of the competition. The product (or business) could then be self-financing. This is a very dynamic environment in which to operate, and strong strategic management skills are necessary for success.

The question mark (or problem child) is also in a growing market but does not have a high market share. There are good growth prospects but capital will be required along with marketing and product development skills.

The cash cow is a product (or business) with high market share in a mature market. Because growth is low and market conditions more stable, the need for investment in marketing is less. The cash cow is a provider of capital to products (or businesses) that are in the question mark category. Strategists need skills in production and marketing.

Dogs have a low market share in static or declining markets and are thus in the worst situation. They are often a cash drain and use up a disproportionate amount of company time and resources. Strategists need financial and legal backgrounds to manage this type of business.

Note that for each category, the management skills needed were specified. This is a principal reason for using this methodology especially in multiproduct or multibusiness enterprises. Portfolio analysis could also be used in industry/competitive environmental analysis where the positions of the products of various enterprises could be plotted. The strategist would then know where her or his enterprise's product was situated in relation to its competitors.[34]

Imasco Ltd. of Montreal could use portfolio analysis in managing the companies it owns. It owns Imperial Tobacco Ltd. and the Shoppers Drug Mart Ltd./Pharmaprix drug store chain both of which would be considered cash cows. Canada Trust, Genstar Development Corp. (residential real estate firm) and United Cigar Stores would be question marks, although Canada Trust may be close to a star. Recently, the performance of Hardee's fast food chain has improved, making it a question mark, but part of the Roy Rogers restaurant chain acquired in 1990 was a dog and has been sold.

value chain

The **value chain** is a diagnostic process for pinpointing and analyzing the activities of an enterprise that add value to a product or service. Activities can fall into two categories: primary, which are resource input supplies, marketing and sales, and service; and support, which are firm infrastructure, human resource management, technology development, and procurement.[35]

Not only are the resources (value activities) identified, but they are also examined in relation to one another. The relationships between resources can often form the basis for a strategic competitive advantage. Also, the value chain concept can be applied outside the enterprise to suppliers and customers, allowing the strategist to obtain a complete assessment of the organization's resources and capabilities. Canadian Tire Corporation is an excellent example of the concept's application. Merchandise is assembled from hundreds of suppliers and distributed to hundreds of retailed outlets by primary activities. Numerous activities support this process, including automated warehousing, electronic inventory systems, the franchised dealer network, and profit-sharing plans to name a few.

Establishment of Objectives

Objectives are discussed in Chapter 4. The setting of objectives is critical to strategic management from the outset, since the mission statement is an objective stated in general terms. However, not all objectives can be established at the beginning of the strategic management process. After assessing the environment and organizational resources, strategists are in a position to set specific objectives and priorities, as they now have a better understanding of what the organization is likely able to achieve. Without objectives (the end) strategists cannot know what the strategy (the means) is needed to accomplish it. An example of an enterprise's strategic objectives is provided in Table 5-4.

Two basic methodologies are used to establish objectives:

1. *Management by objectives (MBO)* MBO is an approach that allows the objectives set at lower levels to be congruent with corporate or organizational objectives (see Chapter 4). Progress toward the fulfillment of the agreed upon objectives is monitored and feedback is given to the managers accountable for their achievement.[36]

benchmarking

2. *Benchmarking* **Benchmarking** is a comparative analysis of competitors' strategies and objectives to establish reference points, or benchmarks, that assist in the formulation of organizational objectives.[37]

IDENTIFICATION OF STRATEGIC OPTIONS

The components of strategic management discussed so far provide a basis for outlining the strategic options available to the organization. There are many terms used to identify strategic options and several ways of classifying them. Table 5-5 lists the most commonly referred to options and classifies them into eight groups. These options are not mutually exclusive. Each classification will be briefly described in the following section.

TABLE 5-4 CAMECO CORPORATION'S CORPORATE OBJECTIVES.

- To operate profitably and reduce debt
- To maintain Cameco's position as a leading supplier of uranium concentrates and fuel services
- To acquire an inventory of promising exploration properties
- To enhance the corporation's diversification opportunities
- To conduct all operations in a manner which safeguards the environment
- To provide a workplace that protects and promotes the health and safety of all employees
- To implement research and development activities which improve Cameco's operations

Cameco Corporation is one of the world's largest, lower-cost, integrated uranium producers. It operates uranium mines in Saskatchewan with processing facilities in Blind River and Port Hope, Ontario. Cameco employs about 1100 people and its head office is located in Saskatoon, Saskatchewan.

TABLE 5-5 STRATEGIC OPTIONS.

1. Generic
   - Cost Leadership
   - Differentiation
   - Focus (Niche)
2. Internal Growth
   - Market Penetration
   - Market Development
   - Product Development
3. Integration
   - Vertical
     - Backward
     - Forward
   - Horizontal
4. Diversification
   - Concentric
   - Conglomerate
5. Cooperative
   - Joint Ventures
6. Retrenchment and Rejuvenation
   - Stabilization
   - Retrenchment
   - Turnaround
   - Divestiture
   - Liquidation
7. Combination
8. "Do Nothing"

Generic Strategic Options

Generic strategies were outlined by Porter[38] and fall into one of three broad categories: cost leadership, differentiation, and focus. Cost leadership occurs when an enterprise strives to have the lowest costs in the industry through the use of a range of functional policies relating to marketing, production, research and development, and finance. Most enterprises in the resource industry base their strategies on cost leadership since the prices of the products are often established in markets over which they have no control. Thus, Canadian newsprint producers must control costs and seek supplies of raw materials that will enable them to be a cost leader.

When pursuing a strategy of differentiation, an organization strives to provide goods or services that are distinctive from those of its competitors. Many firms dealing in consumer products attempt to differentiate, or distinguish, their products from others through distinctive advertising or packaging. Calvin Klein clothing is an example of a differentiated product.

LEARNING OBJECTIVE 8
Identify the strategic options available to an organization.

The third of Porter's generic strategies is a focus, or niche, strategy. In this case an enterprise concentrates on serving a particular market segment, or providing particular products, often referred to as a market niche. An enterprise choosing the focus strategy may be able to achieve it on the basis of either cost leadership or differentiation. Refer to the Management at Work insert entitled "Bible Paper—A Niche in Paper Manufacturing" for an example of a focussed strategy.

Internal Growth Strategic Options

Market penetration occurs when an enterprise seeks to increase the market share of its existing products or services in their present markets through greater efforts, usually concentrated on marketing. This option is not an easy one especially if the market is not growing, since sales must be taken from competitors.

MANAGEMENT AT WORK

BIBLE PAPER—A NICHE IN PAPER MANUFACTURING

The Bible is a constant best seller. It is not known how many Bibles and New Testaments are sold or given away in Canada each year but it is estimated to be over one million copies. Demand for the Bible and New Testament is increasing with the liberalization of Eastern Europe, and even in poor economic times, sales tend to increase rather than decrease.

The producers of paper for magazines and newspapers face a very competitive market. Two Canadian paper manufacturers, E.B. Eddy Forest Products Ltd. of Ottawa, and Fraser Inc. of Edmundston, N.B., are seeking market niches that require a higher-value, more specialized product; they would like to produce paper for Bibles.

The paper used for Bibles is special: it must be thin and lightweight as the book is quite large; it must be of high quality and durable as Bibles are used very often; and it must be of a constant quality. Producers who can provide such paper may follow a focus strategy to secure a niche in the market.

The strategy is not an easy one. Large investments are required in specialty machinery to produce the high-quality paper. The companies must also have expertise in the management of the production process.

There are some positive features of such a strategy. If quality Bible paper can be produced and the companies become reliable suppliers, the publishers of Bibles will pay a premium price for the paper. For example, in 1989, newsprint sold for thirty-five cents per pound, magazine-quality paper for fifty-seven cents, and lightweight Bible paper for eighty-nine to ninety-five cents. Also, once a company is established in Bible paper production, it is less likely that other manufacturers will enter the market because of the high investments and the questionable benefits of sharing the market.

Establishing a niche in the Bible paper business could be a "good news" strategy! ▲

By contrast, market development involves introducing existing products into new geographic areas. Kodak has increased sales in foreign markets, including Japan, in an effort to develop new markets.

Product development takes place when enterprises attempt to increase sales by improving or modifying their existing products or services for either existing or new customers.

Integration Strategic Options

vertical integration

horizontal integration

There are two basic integration options, vertical or horizontal. With **vertical integration** the corporation can seek ownership or control of a supplier, or it can seek ownership or control over a firm's distribution or retailers. **Horizontal integration** occurs when a company purchases, or increases control over, another enterprise in the same business (i.e., a competitor).

Diversification Strategic Options

concentric diversification

conglomerate diversification

Concentric diversification involves adding new, but related, products or services to the existing business. Both CP Rail and Canadian National diversified into trucking, an activity clearly related to railway operations.

The addition of unrelated products or services is referred to as **conglomerate diversification.** In 1983, Bell Canada decided to diversify by forming BCE Inc., which acquired interests in such unrelated businesses as trust companies, pipelines, and real estate.

Cooperative Strategic Options

cooperative strategies

Cooperative strategies, which may take the form of joint ventures, alliances, networks, strategic partnering, and strategic networks have become more popular in the past decade. In each form, enterprises establish a collaborative arrangement for sharing or splitting managerial control in a particular undertaking. The arrangements can be very formal, as is the case with joint ventures, and can be in the domestic or international markets. An example of a joint venture is the joining of Stelco Inc., a large steel maker, with Jannock Ltd. to go into the metal-fabricating business. Not all cooperative strategies are successful. Cascades Inc., a Quebec paper company, ended a partnership to operate a French newsprint company when they concluded that their operating philosophy was in conflict with that of their French partner.

Retrenchment and Rejuvenation Strategic Options

Strategic options do not always entail growth. They can also involve a withdrawal or a concerted effort to revive an enterprise. Such strategic options are:

1. *Stabilization* This option is designed to maintain revenues and profits. Growth may occur but strategic decisions are only made on a gradual basis.
2. *Retrenchment* Reduction in sales with declining or no profits leads to efforts to increase efficiency through asset reduction or cost cutting.
3. *Turnaround* A turnaround strategy often follows a retrenchment when sales and profits are improved. A recent book described the turnaround strategies of several Canadian companies, including: Niagara Helicopters, Canadian Pizza Crust, Manufacturers Life Insurance, Royal Trust, and Turbo Resources.
4. *Divestiture* As a form of retrenchment, parts or units of an enterprise may be sold.
5. *Liquidation* This option involves selling all the enterprise's assets and terminating the business.

Combined Strategic Options

In many enterprises, two or more of the above strategies may be followed at the same time. This is often the case in larger organizations.

"Do Nothing" Strategic Option

It is possible for an enterprise to initiate no strategic actions, but this rarely occurs as environments and strategists are constantly changing.

SELECTION OF A STRATEGY

The next task in the strategic management process is to select one of the options listed above, as the organization's strategy. The strategist must evaluate each option to ascertain which is the most appropriate. One factor that must be considered in this evaluation is how well the option fits the situation identified in the assessment of the environment and organizational resources. For example, does the strategic option capitalize on the company's strengths, overcome or avoid weaknesses, and counter environmental threats? Strategists assess whether or not the strategic option can be implemented. For instance, they must determine whether the organization has the resources to carry out the strategy. Lastly, strategists attempt to determine the acceptability of the option to all stakeholders of the organization. Will it generate the growth and profits expected by senior management and shareholders? Will the enterprise's relationship with outside stakeholders, such as governments or public interest groups, have to change?[39]

Alcan Aluminum's strategy is to focus its activities on aluminum products and their application to a variety of uses. The company has restructured to concentrate on the aluminum industry in which it has resources, knowledge and experience. Alcan managers believe that they have an advantage over their competitors as a result.

Once an option has been selected, organizations prepare a formal statement of strategy that describes the primary strategic management components. The format and content of such a statement can vary, but often includes descriptions of the types of products and services it sells and the markets it serves; the organization's objectives; the competition the organization faces; the opportunities and threats it might encounter in the environment; the organization's capabilities expressed, for example, in terms of marketing, finance, and production; its managerial capability (the organization's distinctive competencies are also noted); and how the organization will organize its resources in order to carry out its strategy.

Enterprises in competitive industries seldom disclose their strategy in detail, but statements are helpful for strategists to conceptualize and understand the strategy selected and to assist them in communicating it to various stakeholders such as employees and shareholders.

There is a vast array of methodologies for selecting a strategy, some of which are described in the next section.

Strategic Option Selection Methodologies

A common technique is a scoring and ranking methodology called the SWOT, TOWS or WOTS-UP analysis (strengths, weaknesses, opportunities, and threats, rearranged). It provides a mechanism for understanding the firm's resource capabilities and the extent to which the organization can cope with its environment. It produces a matrix that combines the ETOP (a profile of the threats and opportunities in the environment) and a resource audit to summarize the circumstances in which the organization finds itself.[40]

critical success factors (CSF)

The **critical success factors** (CSF) methodology identifies a limited number of variables in which high performance is crucial to the success of a strategy. These variables must be given special and continual attention by strategists. Discussions between a CSF analyst and the key strategist of an organization is one way in which these factors can be isolated.[41] For example, a critical success factor for Alcan Aluminum is a cheap source of electricity as aluminum refining requires huge amounts of energy.

strategic issues

The strategic issues approach identifies **strategic issues** that must be addressed if the organization is to succeed. An issue is a trend, threat or opportunity that has a potentially large (positive or negative) impact on the future performance of the organization. A strategic issue concerns a fundamental policy about the organization's mandates or constitution; mission; values; product or service level and mix; clients, payers, or users; costs; financing; organizational design; or management. Strategic issues emerge from the way the organization chooses to, or is forced to, relate to its external and internal environments. The issues define what sort of "fit" with its environment the organization can choose.[42] This approach is particularly useful in non-profit and government organizations.

gap analysis

After strategists have identified alternative strategic options, they determine the performance potential (usually expressed as sales) of each strategic option. They then perform a **gap analysis**; the "gap" is the difference between the performance possible with the existing strategy and the performance result, or objective, desired by the strategists (see Figure 5-5). The strategic option selected will be the one strategists ascertain to be capable of filling in the "gap" (i.e., meeting the objectives established). An early description of this methodology was given by Ansoff.[43]

scenario

A **scenario** is the description of a consistent set of conditions or circumstances that defines the environment within which business will be conducted in the future. Scenarios are qualitative instead of quantitative forecasts, and several are usually formulated based upon different assumptions about future events or trends. Scenario analysis, or forecasting, is not based upon past data or information; it provides a means of encouraging managers to think more freely and creatively about the future. Each strategic option could be considered a "scenario" or could be evaluated in the context of various scenarios.[44]

decision trees

Decision trees are explained in Chapter 6, and can be applied to the selection of strategic options. Each option is plotted as a decision on the decision tree with subsequent events or decisions being identified.

break-even analysis

Break-even analysis is illustrated in Chapter 18. Strategic options could be evaluated relative to break-even points, and an option could be selected that matches the organization's capabilities.

sensitivity analysis

Sensitivity analysis is a useful technique for incorporating the assessment of risk into the selection of a strategy. The methodology allows each of the important assumptions underlying a particular option to be questioned and changed. The purpose

FIGURE 5-5 STRATEGIC GAP ANALYSIS.

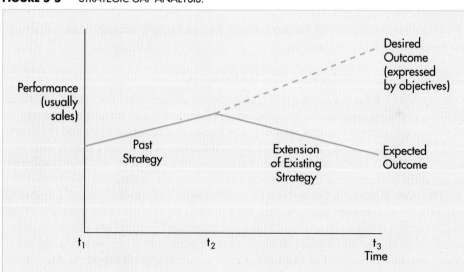

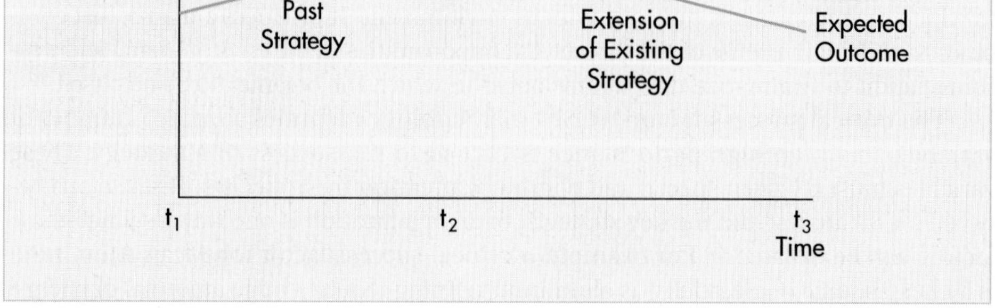

is to test how sensitive the predicted performance or outcome of each option is to each of these assumptions. For example, the key assumption underlying a strategy might be that the market will grow by 5 percent per annum. Sensitivity analysis asks what would be the effect on performance if, for example, the market grew at only 1 percent or by as much as 10 percent. Strategists would have to decide if either of these estimates would alter the decision to pursue a particular strategy. This methodology assists strategists in identifying the risks involved with various options.[45]

cost/benefit analysis

Cost/benefit analysis attempts to put a monetary value on all the costs and benefits of a strategic option. Strategists can then select a strategy with all factors identified and quantified, even intangibles.[46]

The selection of a strategy completes an important phase in the strategic management process, but it also represents the beginning of another, the implementation of the strategy.

STRATEGY IMPLEMENTATION

This component in the strategic management process will not be examined at length in this chapter as topics discussed in other chapters are aspects of implementation. However this brief treatment should not diminish the importance of the component (see Figure 5-1). Strategy implementation includes designing the organization's structure, allocating resources, developing information and decision processes, and managing human resources, including such areas as the reward system, approaches to leadership, and staffing. These activities are facets of the management functions of planning, organizing, leading and controlling examined in this book. After studying these functions, you will understand more about what goes into the implementation of strategic management.

It is only recently that significant attention has been given to strategy implementation. In the past, strategists focussed on formulating strategy and failed to implement the selected strategy in a successful manner. Now much more attention is devoted to implementation by strategists and academics.[47] Two views of how strategy implementation is approached are outlined in the next section. See the Management at Work insert "Strategic Management at Interprovincial Pipe Line Systems Inc." for an example of strategy implementation.

LEARNING OBJECTIVE 9

List the challenges of applying strategic management.

Hambrick and Cannella claim that strategists have numerous concepts and techniques (methodologies) to assist them in formulating strategies, but implementing the strategy poses difficulties. They described five steps for effective strategy implementation:

1. Input from a wide range of sources is required in the strategy formulation stage (i.e., the mission, environment, resources, and strategic options component).
2. The obstacles to implementation, both those internal and external to the organization, should be carefully assessed.
3. Strategists should use implementation levers or management tasks to initiate this component of the strategic management process. Such levers may come from the way resources are committed, the approach used to structure the organization, the selection of managers, and the method of rewarding employees.
4. The next step is to sell the implementation. Selling upward entails convincing boards of directors and senior management of the merits and viability of the strategy. Selling downward involves convincing lower-level management and employees of the appropriateness of the strategy. Selling across involves coordinating implementation across the various units of an organization, while selling outward entails communicating the strategy to external stakeholders.
5. The process is ongoing and a continuous fine tuning, adjusting, and responding is needed as circumstances change.[48]

MANAGEMENT AT WORK

Strategic Management at Interprovincial Pipe Line System Inc.

Interprovincial Pipe Lines operates the world's largest petroleum pipeline system in Canada and the United States. Its corporate office is in Edmonton, Alberta. The description below of Interprovincial's strategy is from its *1992 Annual Report*. Note how the company is using "continuous improvement" methodology as one way to make sure that their strategy is implemented.

Strategic Direction

Interprovincial is more than an extensive pipeline infrastructure. Our continued success requires a clear future direction which recognizes our people and the pipeline system as key assets. On this basis, we have adopted the following long-term goals:

- Continue to be recognized as a significant participant in pipeline transportation and related facilities;
- Expand our business beyond the transportation of liquid hydrocarbons;
- Be an industry leader, through a proactive approach, in safety and environmental protection; and
- Achieve above average growth as a widely held public corporation.

To achieve these long-term goals, the Corporation has developed a number of strategies. These include: identifying and developing key growth areas; increasing efficiency and effectiveness through Continuous Improvement; improving relations with shippers; working with regulators to create a more positive regulatory climate; and ensuring that the Corporation's human resources are appropriately trained to achieve our objectives.

We have identified and are currently exploring several opportunities to expand our business, including:

- feeder pipeline systems in North America;
- acquisition of linefill;
- refined products pipelines;
- natural gas pipelines;
- tankage and terminalling facilities; and
- pipelines and associated facilities outside of North America.

Continuous Improvement

The North American petroleum industry has undergone a major restructuring and downsizing due to increasing competition in world oil markets. To enable the industry to remain competitive, we must focus our efforts on controlling costs while enhancing shipper service.

A Continuous Improvement initiative was introduced in 1992 to clarify customer needs and empower employees to continuously improve the level of service provided, while maximizing efficiency. Continuous Improvement is not a short-term program; it is an ongoing effort involving the participation, contribution and commitment of every employee. By stressing the importance of service and efficiency, we will continue to meet the industry's need for a safe, reliable and cost effective pipeline transportation system. ▲

The integration of the implementation component with other strategy components is important as is the coordination of an organization's activities toward the implementation of the strategy.

While Hambrick and Cannella's steps stress the importance of coordinating managerial tasks or functions in an organization's activities in the implementation of a strategy, the McKinsey 7-S Framework highlights the integration of implementation with other strategic management components. There are seven elements that must be integrated, or "fit" together if a strategy is to be implemented successfully. The framework is shown in Figure 5-6 and the seven elements are: strategy (the coherent set of actions selected as a course of action); structure (the division of tasks as shown on the organization chart); systems (the processes and flows that show how an organization gets things done); style (how management behaves); staff (the people in the organization); shared values (values shared by all in the organization); and skills (capabilities possessed by the organization).[49]

Strategists must check on the "fit" among these elements. If all of the elements are not organized to work in coordination with each other, the strategy is unlikely to be implemented successfully.

Strategy Implementation Methodologies

Two strategy implementation methodologies will be discussed in detail in this section: organization life cycles and strategic funds programming.

Organizational life cycles The stages in a product's life cycle are often expressed as embryonic, growth, maturity, and decline. Industries also have a life cycle, consisting of fledgling, growth, maturity, and decline stages. Organizations have a cycle identified as entrepreneurial, growth, maturity, and decline. Strategists must be sensitive to these changes and use implementation processes to match the strategies to each stage. For example, in the growth stage, resources may be committed to increasing plant size, while at the maturity stage, cost cutting and increased productivity with existing resources is stressed.

Strategic funds programming **Strategic funds programming** is a "budget and control system that provides management [strategists] with the decision-making information needed to implement strategy. It is designed to balance the financial requirements of maintaining current business with the financial risks of a new strategy."[50] Funds to support the organization's current business are referred to as baseline funds. Strategic funds are those invested in the new programs required to meet the organization's strategic objectives. This type of programming helps strategists focus on the longer-term strategy while at the same time ensuring that present business operations are not neglected.[51]

strategic funds programming

MONITORING AND REVIEW

The final component in the strategic management process is "monitoring and review." Any planning process needs to be monitored and reviewed to see whether or not it is accomplishing what was intended. Various control systems are available to provide the monitoring and reviewing necessary for effective planning and are outlined in Chapters 17 and 18. In this chapter, we will only discuss control briefly from a strategic perspective. There are three reasons for establishing a strategic control system:

FIGURE 5-6 MCKINSEY 7-S FRAMEWORK.

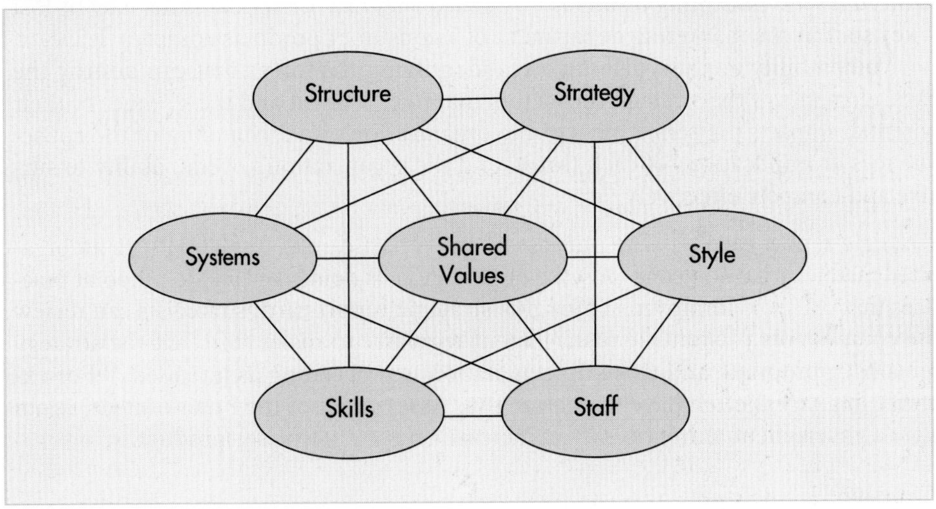

1. In order to coordinate the efforts of all managers and units, agreement should be reached on the objectives of a strategy. Without objectives, a strategy cannot be effectively evaluated. Therefore, the establishment of "control" objectives is an essential step in the strategic management process.

2. Personal incentives must be provided to align individual and corporate objectives and to motivate managers to devote their best efforts to achieving them.

3. Even the best-laid plans sometimes fail, and strategists have to decide when and how to intervene. This intervention may take the form of changing objectives, changing the strategy, or changing how the strategy is implemented. A control system is needed to prompt the necessary action.[52]

A control system consists of monitoring mechanisms that provide feedback on performance. Budgetary control is needed, but it is not enough to ensure the implementation of strategic plans. For example, budgetary control fails to measure performance relative to competitors, nonfinancial considerations, and social concerns.

A new approach to strategic control proposes a feedforward process rather than the traditional feedback framework. A feedback-control approach is inappropriate, since information about strategic actions may come too late to make corrections; it also takes the standards of performance for granted. Strategically relevant circumstances in the environment or the organization's resources may have altered long before the results of a particular action can be measured.

Control in strategic management is a challenging task requiring strategists to continually question plans. Not all organizations have the ability to think of control in these terms, but it is a logical aspect of strategic management.[53]

Monitoring and Review Methodologies

Vulnerability analysis, strategic "report cards," and strategic audits are some examples of monitoring and reviewing methodologies relevant to the strategic management process.

vulnerability analysis

Vulnerability analysis Strategists tend to emphasize opportunities and strengths upon which the organization's strategy is based and neglect threats and weaknesses. **Vulnerability analysis** is a process that forces strategists to question the strategy or plan. A vulnerability analysis begins by identifying the "supporting elements or underpinnings" which, if taken away, might seriously endanger or even destroy the organization. For example, customer goodwill may be destroyed and demand greatly reduced if food poisoning results from canned shellfish, or special skills may be lost if key staff in the marketing department of a consumer products company leave.

Vulnerability analysis also involves identifying the forces that can destroy the basic elements of the strategy, the factors that pose a threat and the strength of their potential impact, the seriousness of the organization's understanding of the consequences or implications of each threat, and the organization's overall ability to survive and compete effectively.[54]

strategic report card

Strategic report cards The purpose of any report card is to highlight in an organized manner what someone, or some organization, is doing well and to pinpoint practices that could be improved. Through a **strategic report card**, strategists can review the components of strategic management regularly to make sure that the strategy remains appropriate and that implementation is proceeding as intended.[55] For example, managers often have to analyze the "Assessment of the Environment" again after a government announces a tax increase on the enterprise's product.

Strategic audit All components in the strategic management process are systematically examined in a **strategic audit** to ascertain or verify whether or not appropriate strategic decisions have been made. It provides an integrated view of strategic management in action and enables the strategist to understand the ways in which all components, functional areas, and organizational units are interrelated and interdependent. In effect, a strategic audit is an evaluation of the overall performance of the organization and its management from a strategic perspective.

strategic audit

THE USES AND SHORTCOMINGS OF STRATEGIC MANAGEMENT

The discussion of the strategic management process in this book has focussed on its application in business enterprises. The process is important for both large enterprises and small business, where it is just as effective without the use of complicated methodology. Strategic management has been applied successfully to non-profit and government organizations, too, including health care and educational institutions, religious organizations, arts and theatre organizations, government departments and agencies, unions, charities, volunteer organizations, and interest groups. Some examples of the application of strategic management to these organizations are given in the Management at Work insert called "Application of Strategic Management in Non-profit and Government Organizations."

The application of strategic management in an organization is challenging, and the process has been criticized. Most managers understand the concept of strategic management, but fail to properly implement the process. Table 5-6 is a list of ten barriers to effective strategic management and is representative of the complaints made against the process. Note that the barriers range from lack of management commitment to inadequate data to the excessive use of written materials. Strategic management is a process that is evolving and imperfect. The business environment cannot be predicted with accuracy; strategists are humans and misapply strategic concepts and methodologies; and implementation can be very difficult. Some managers claim to use strategic management but in reality make only a token effort at developing a comprehensive process. To be successful, the strategic management process should become a way of thinking for strategists throughout the organization.

TABLE 5-6 TEN BARRIERS TO EFFECTIVE STRATEGIC MANAGEMENT.

1. Lack of commitment by senior management.
2. Conflict between short- and long-term planning.
3. Lack of management time to devote to planning.
4. Organizational conflict between line management and staff planners.
5. Lack of quality data.
6. Environmental uncertainties.
7. Lack of understanding and skill in strategic planning.
8. Too much paper.
9. Lack of commitment by middle management.
10. Difficulty in achieving implementation of plans.

MANAGEMENT AT WORK

Application of Strategic Management in Non-profit and Government Organizations

TAFELMUSIK BAROQUE ORCHESTRA

The Tafelmusik (German for "table music") Baroque Orchestra, the Toronto chamber group, is one of the world's finest interpretors of baroque and classical music. It is made up of 16 musicians and is based at Trinity-St. Pauls United Church in downtown Toronto. The orchestra is widely known for its musical accomplishments, but is not as well known for its management accomplishments.

The orchestra uses strategic management and establishes long-term objectives. One such objective was to obtain an international recording contract which it did with Sony Classical. As a result of this contract, fifteen compact discs have been released in two years. Plans are made two to four years in advance for tours and recordings. These plans are implemented through more detailed 18-month financial and marketing plans. Strategic management is made workable through a system of committees with membership from musicians and administrators, extensive consultation on all aspects of operations, and a very flat organizational structure.

THE ANGLICAN DIOCESE OF CENTRAL NEWFOUNDLAND

The Anglican Church in Central Newfoundland undertook a strategic management process that resulted in the following statement of "Our Shared Vision": The Anglican Church of Central Newfoundland in response to the Love of God is called to proclaim the Gospel of Jesus Christ by worship and sacrament, by word and action, under the guidance and power of the Holy Spirit. Following Jesus we are led to be a Servant Community which ministers and witnesses in the world to the transforming power of God's Love.

Eight goals were identified in areas such as evangelism, resources, outreach, leadership, worship, caring community and communications. Several objectives were formulated for each goal as were the strategies necessary to achieve the objectives.

THE CANADIAN MUSEUM OF CIVILIZATION CORPORATION (CMCC)

The CMCC prepared a Strategic Plan for 1993-1998 entitled *A Vision for the 21st Century*. The planning process involved questioning past practices and rethinking how the CMCC serves the Canadian public. Its main facilities are the Canadian Museum of Civilization and the Canadian War Museum in Ottawa/Hull.

The board of trustees and senior management participated in the process which included the formulation of a vision statement, environmental and activities analyses, and an identification of major strategic issues. From this analysis, the key features of a strategic direction were formulated, scope of activities and publics listed, and priorities and key capabilities identified.

One conclusion in the planning document was that the process would ensure that CMCC (trustees and staff) is properly oriented towards the future and that the plan would inspire and guide them in the years to come. ▲

MEETING THE CHALLENGE

Strategic Management at Schneider Corporation

Douglas Dodds initiated a series of strategic changes necessary to create highly efficient plants despite the high wages paid employees. The beef slaughter and boning operations were shut in 1989 and the company purchased its raw material as dressed carcasses on the open market while hog killings were reduced by 30 percent.

New products were developed including low-fat, low-salt meat products, luncheon meats, and snacks. The company also sought long-term strength in diversification through acquisitions. A Quebec sausage and meat pie operation was purchased and later Fleetwood Sausage Ltd. in B.C. was acquired. A joint venture with Horizon Poultry Products Inc. built a modern poultry-processing plant, and the 50 percent acquisition of Saville Food Products increased the supply of fresh chicken. A 72 percent share of Mother Jackson's Open Kitchens Ltd., a bakery which makes baked goods and meat filled pastries was acquired. Another joint venture with competitor Maple Leaf Foods Inc. established National Meats Inc., which manufactures generic meat patties (burgers and steaks for grocery chains).

The Kitchener plant was redesigned as several miniplants instead of a large one with functional departments. In effect, miniplants were established for the company's various products, for example, bacon, weiners, and sausages. Employees were allowed a role in decision making and the authority of foremen was reduced. Employees were formed into committees accountable for their performance. The new approach was introduced across the plant, but failed to produce the results expected.

Dodds examined other approaches to involving employees in decision making and decided upon the continuous-improvement approach. This approach involved employee teams and relied upon their suggestions to cut production costs. However, this time the change was introduced as a pilot in one section of the plant and then gradually introduced throughout the remainder of the plant as employees could see the results achieved. Costs have been reduced, absenteeism is lower, antagonism among employees and managers is fading, and accident claims are down. Management claims that a cultural change has been achieved as employees and managers have a new attitude towards work and the company.

The company's sales are stable but profit increased by 24 percent in 1992 despite an industry downturn. Douglas Dodds is sold on the concepts of worker decision making and continuous improvement and plans to introduce self-managed work teams as the next stage in the strategic turnaround of Schneiders. The changes in strategy and its implementation have positioned Schneiders to enter other joint ventures and to move back into the U.S. market in the future. ▲

SUMMARY

Managers need a systematic approach to identify the purpose of an organization, assess the circumstances or environment in which it operates, examine the resource capability of the organization, and establish objectives. Strategic management is a process that enables managers to accomplish such an analysis and to identify the alternative feasible strategic options. From these alternatives one is selected as the organization's strategy (i.e., a unified, comprehensive and integrated plan). Strategic management is not merely long-term planning but also the determination of what the organization wants to be and what it wants to accomplish. The process also incorporates how the strategy is implemented, an aspect neglected in the past.

Strategic management has eight components: the establishment of a mission, assessment of the environment, assessment of organizational resources and capabilities, setting of objectives, identification of strategic options, selection of a strategy, strategy implementation, and monitoring and review. Managers can utilize dozens of methodologies in the strategic management process and these are discussed with the component where they are likely to be used. Not all the methodologies are used by every organization, but managers should be aware of the array of methodologies available and select the ones suitable for the circumstances in which the organization operates.

Strategic management is used at various levels in the organization: corporate, divisional, unit, and functional. Although the components are the same, their application at the different levels will vary. The strategists who provide leadership at these levels also influence the strategic management process as do the values held by the organization which are often referred to as corporate culture. The stakeholders of the organization also have expectations that influence strategy selection, and some stakeholders are directly involved in the process.

Strategic management is applicable not only to business enterprises but also to non-profit and government organizations. The use of strategic management in providing a comprehensive assessment mechanism for an organization poses some challenges. Most successful and progressive organizations are involved in some form or aspect of strategic management.

KEY TERMS

strategic management (p. 117)
strategy (p. 117)
long-range plans (p. 118)
strategic planning (p. 119)
strategist (p. 122)
strategic business unit (p. 124)
intrapreneurship (p. 124)
strategic leadership (p. 124)
corporate culture (p. 125)
stakeholder (p. 126)
mission (p. 127)
stakeholder analysis (p. 128)
values audit (p. 129)
visioning (p. 129)
opportunity (p. 130)
threats (p. 130)
strategic group (p. 132)
organizational strength (p. 133)
organizational weakness (p. 133)
distinctive competence (p. 133)
resource audit (p. 134)
experience curve (p. 134)
portfolio analysis (p. 134)
value chain (p. 135)
benchmarking (p. 136)
vertical integration (p. 138)
horizontal integration (p. 138)
concentric diversification (p. 138)
conglomerate diversification (p. 138)
cooperative strategies (p. 138)
critical success factors (CSF) (p. 139)
strategic issues (p. 140)
gap analysis (p. 140)
scenario (p. 140)
decision trees (p. 140)
break-even analysis (p. 140)
sensitivity analysis (p. 140)
cost/benefit analysis (p. 141)
strategic funds programming (p. 143)
vulnerability analysis (p. 144)
strategic report card (p. 144)
strategic audit (p. 145)

REVIEW QUESTIONS

1. What is the difference between long-range planning, strategic planning, strategic management, and strategy.
2. Why is the implementation of the strategic management process so challenging for managers?
3. How is strategic management applied throughout an organization?
4. Who are the strategists in a business organization and what influences their application of the strategic management process?
5. What is strategic leadership?
6. How do the preferences of the strategists influence strategic management?
7. What influence do organizational values have on the strategic management process?
8. Why should stakeholders be considered in the strategic management process?
9. List the eight components of strategic management and describe each briefly.
10. Why is it necessary to monitor and review the strategic management process?
11. Can strategic management be applied to organizations other than business organizations?
12. What are the challenges associated in the strategic management approach?

DISCUSSION QUESTIONS

1. Does an organization give up long-range planning if it uses strategic planning?
2. Why would a "mission" be the first component in a strategic management process?
3. Why are the organization's objectives established after the assessment of the environment and resources capabilities?
4. How do employees contribute to the strategic management process?
5. How does the strategist get the organization to think in strategic terms?
6. Why doesn't the application of strategic management ensure an organization's success?
7. Why is strategic management considered to be a unified, comprehensive and integrated plan?

EXERCISES

1. Interview the manager of a local business about whether or not the enterprise uses a strategic management approach.

2. Mission statements are available at many businesses. Examine statements you obtain to determine how many of the items listed in this chapter are included.
3. Write a mission statement for your school.
4. Prepare an Environmental Threat and Opportunity Profile (ETOP) for a business enterprise in your community.
5. Identify the stakeholders that might influence the strategy of a particular business in your community. List their expectations of the business. You could also select a non-profit or government organization.
6. Read articles on the activities of business enterprises and try to determine what strategic option they are following.

MANAGEMENT ON LOCATION

CASE 5-1
HARLEQUIN ROMANCE'S MOVE INTO TV, VIDEOS

Harlequin Enterprises Ltd. is the world's most successful publisher of paperback romance novels. Based in Toronto, Harlequin is a very successful operation producing 13 romance and other series for markets around the world. The following statistics tell a lot about Harlequin's successful story:

- In 1992, the company had revenues of $418 million and profits of $62 million.
- Seventy-two titles are released each month and about 210 million books sell each year.
- Romance novels account for 44 percent of the mass market paperback business and Harlequin has 80 percent of the series romance fiction market.
- The Company sells its books in 100 markets, including Eastern Europe, Russia, and China, and has translations into 24 languages. Fifty-five percent of the company's sales are outside North America.

The books are written to a formula including an established plot, standard characters, and a set length. The formula varies by series but the output is a highly formatted romance novel. Harlequin contracts with hundreds of writers who usually write under a pseudonym. An editorial staff insures that all novels adhere to the formula that has proven so successful.

Romance fiction publishing differs from other publishing. The products are standardized, and at Harlequin returns, which are problematic for most publishers, are very low. In effect, every title is a bestseller unlike other publishing. Regular purchasers, some belonging to mail order clubs, insure each title's success.

The keys to Harlequin's strategy are its ability to maintain a consistently high editorial quality, its distribution system, and its marketing capabilities. Even with expansion around the world, Harlequin is seeking out other growth possibilities.

Harlequin has attempted to grow by publishing science fiction, romance novels based upon doctors and nurses, historical romances, and romantic suspense series. The science fiction project was a failure, and the other efforts met with modest success. Presently the company is marketing a male adventure and a mystery reprint series.

In April 1993, Harlequin announced that it had made a deal with Alliance Communications Corp., a large Canadian independent production company, to produce romantic fiction movies for television and home videos from Harlequin's inventory of more than 16 000 novels. Previous attempts at movies in the late 1970s and 1980s were not successful. However, Harlequin and Alliance are convinced that this new direction in Harlequin's strategy will be successful. ▲

QUESTIONS

1. Prepare a statement describing Harlequin's strategy.
2. Which strategic options has Harlequin implemented prior to the agreement to produce television and video movies?
3. What type of strategic option is the agreement to enter the romantic fiction television and video movies business? Will the strategy be successful? Why or why not?

CASE 5-2
FOREST CITY COUNCIL'S PLANNING EFFORTS

Forest City, a community of 40 000 residents, just held a municipal election and Maureen Brown was elected mayor. Brown was taking over at a time when the city appeared to be in decline as population had fallen from 45 000 five years ago, and several large plants had closed, reducing employment opportunities.

The city had 227 employees and an annual budget of $35.1 million. The staff was directed by a city manager who was supported by a nine-person senior management team. The council was also comprised of nine persons, all of whom represented wards or constituencies. The council met weekly, except in the summer, and the mayor spent the equivalent of two days a week at City Hall.

The city faced numerous challenges. The city centre was declining as more retailers moved to the shopping centres being built just outside Forest City's boundaries. The city's roads and sidewalks were in need of repair, and the urban transit system had to have new equipment to be efficient and operated with a massive deficit. The water and sewage system required constant maintenance, a new source of water had to be found within the next five years, and the sewage treatment plant had to be upgraded to meet government regulations. City parks were rundown and the city recreational facilities were deteriorating. The fire and police departments were understaffed and inadequately funded.

The city's staff were unmotivated and were the brunt of various jokes about their lack of enthusiasm and efficiency. Taxation revenue was falling even though tax rates were increasing. Overall, the image of the city was deteriorating and Forest City was not a place a person would choose to live and work. Brown was aware of these challenges and had campaigned on the platform that "she would do something to turn Forest City around!" The majority of the newly elected councillors also felt something had to be done to rescue the city.

The mayor had suggested a strategic planning session for the council and senior management. The city manger's response was "we've done that before and it didn't work." Some members of management were not as negative but were looking for some leadership in addressing the challenges facing the city.

The mayor admitted that she did not know where or how to begin to improve the condition of Forest City. She still felt that things had to be sorted out with some kind of planning process and strategic planning seemed to be a sensible approach to her. But, the question remained "how to get things started?" ▲

QUESTIONS

1. Is it appropriate to use a strategic management approach in government?
2. Who should be the strategist in Forest City?
3. What types of values, attitudes or beliefs might be included in a mission statement for Forest City?
4. What should the strategist do to formulate and implement a strategy for Forest City?

CASE 5-3
ROUSSEAU FURNITURE INC.

Rousseau Furniture Inc. was a medium-sized manufacturer among the approximately 2000 firms in the Canadian furniture industry. The company had been operating for 138 years in the eastern townships of Quebec and had been moderately successful in supplying mid-price-range bedroom, living room, and dining room furniture to Quebec households. André Rousseau was the president of the company which was 60 percent owned by members of the Rousseau family. The other 40 percent of the shares had been sold to numerous individuals in Quebec under the Quebec Stock Savings Plan, a government sponsored program to encourage residents to invest in local companies.

Despite having paid a dividend every year and having invested in new •••

MANAGEMENT ON LOCATION

plant and equipment, the company was able to accumulate a cash surplus of over $1 million. Rousseau decided that it was time for the company to do something with the money. There were numerous possibilities for expansion of the business. Rousseau Furniture had specialized in medium-priced household furniture sold through independent furniture retailers in Quebec and could attempt to increase its share of this market. The company could increase its product line to include lower-priced and/or higher-priced household furniture. There was also the possibility of manufacturing furniture designed for family or recreation rooms including IKEA-type furniture which the customer assembled at home. Office furniture could be manufactured in their plant as could furniture designed for institutions such as schools, hospitals, and homes for the elderly. One approach to doing this would be to enter into a joint venture with another manufacturer.

Rousseau and his managers also considered the possibility of marketing Rousseau Furniture outside of Quebec, in particular to Atlantic Canada and Ontario. With the Free Trade Agreement, there was even the possibility of selling their products in the New England region of the U.S. Rousseau had also given some thought to the idea of purchasing the sawmills that supplied the lumber for their furniture and had even considered the idea of opening furniture stores in cities such as Quebec, Montreal, and Sherbrooke. Rousseau also considered purchasing another furniture manufacturer as there were always several for sale in Quebec or Ontario.

Rousseau could also sell to the large furniture chains such as The Brick or Leon's or sell to the large department store chains. It could produce private brand furniture for Sears or Woolco, or sub-contract production from IKEA or Sears.

Possibilities outside of the furniture business were not ignored. Rousseau could invest in unrelated businesses such as a fast food outlet or trust company. Lastly, Rousseau could sell out to another company and distribute the proceeds to shareholders.

No shortage of possibilities existed and Rousseau and his managers started the process of investigating each in detail. ▲

QUESTIONS

1. Identify the strategic options available to Rousseau.
2. Which option should Rousseau accept and why?
3. What implementation challenges is Rousseau likely to encounter?

CHAPTER 6

MANAGERIAL DECISION MAKING

LEARNING OBJECTIVES

After reading this chapter, you will be able to:

1. Define decision making.
2. Distinguish between decision making and problem solving.
3. Explain the difference between crisis decisions, problem decisions, and opportunity decisions.
4. Understand the concepts of certainty, risk, and uncertainty.
5. Compare four managerial decision-making models: rational, bounded rationality, political, and garbage can.
6. Describe five decision-making techniques for helping managers make good decisions.
7. Explain the advantages and disadvantages of group and individual decision making.

MANAGEMENT CHALLENGE

MAKE A DECISION NOW!

"Rama, you've got a problem, and you've got to make a decision immediately about how to straighten it out," said Pat McGlothin, manager of distribution for the *Daily Harold*. McGlothin was speaking to Rama Chakalas, the supervisor of the truck drivers who delivered the newspapers to the carrier drop-off stations and to newsstands in the surrounding towns. There are 25 drivers who put hundreds of kilometres per day on the trucks.

The conversation between McGlothin and Chakalas continued:

McGlothin: I've been watching the maintenance costs on the trucks and right now our costs are up 20 percent over last year. That's a big jump.

Chakalas: Well, maybe a different maintenance program is being carried out on the trucks and that has increased the expense.

McGlothin: No, that can't be it. I've already talked to the maintenance supervisor and he says that they're doing what they've always done. That means that your drivers are responsible for the increased costs. What are you going to do about it?

Chakalas: I'm not sure.

McGlothin: What do you mean, you're not sure? The facts speak for themselves. You certainly can't argue with the facts, can you?

Chakalas: I'm not trying to argue with the facts. I'd like to do some additional checking to see what might be causing the problem before I make any hasty decisions.

McGlothin: I can't see what additional checking there is to do. We've got to get this thing resolved quickly or the V.P. is going to have us on the carpet. I'll bet he's already seen the cost figures, so it won't be long before I'm called in to explain them. I want you to do something now!

Chakalas: That's putting a lot of pressure on me. I think it would be better to look into this more carefully instead of making a snap decision.

McGlothin: I want a decision by tomorrow at noon!

Chakalas: I'll do my best. ▲

The situation described in the Management Challenge shows that decision making is a key activity of all managers at all levels in organizations. When planning, for example, managers must decide what the organization's mission and objectives will be, how the objectives will be achieved, and what changes will be introduced so the objectives can be achieved. When organizing, the manager must decide how many subordinates should report to each manager, how to departmentalize the firm, how to design jobs, and when to introduce a new structure. When leading, managers must decide how to motivate subordinates, what leadership style to use, how to communicate change to employees, and how to manage conflict. When controlling, managers must make decisions about the key activities that need to be controlled, techniques which are most appropriate to facilitate control, and the measures of performance that are critical. In the Management Challenge, Chakalas and McGlothin were trying to make a decision which would help them perform the controlling function effectively.

LEARNING OBJECTIVE 1
Define decision making.

LEARNING OBJECTIVE 2
Distinguish between decision making and problem solving.

decision making

problem solving

Decision making is the process of choosing between alternative courses of action to cope with a crisis, solve a problem, or take advantage of an opportunity. The substance and focus of managerial decisions differs across levels and across organizations, but the underlying process of decision making remains the same. **Problem solving** refers to only those managerial actions that are necessary to determine what the problem is and why it occurred. Thus, decision making refers to an entire process, while problem solving is one part of the process.

Three general observations can be made about decision making:

1. *Decision making is the essence of management* It is the central activity of managers as they carry out the functions of management. Regardless of whether the manager is planning, organizing, leading, or controlling, decisions must be made.
2. *Decision making is both a process and an event* The point at which the actual decision is made is an event. While this point is obviously important, often too much attention is paid to the event and not enough to the process which led to the event.
3. *Managerial effectiveness in decision making should be judged over time* A manager may make a very good or very bad decision at a given point in time, but managerial effectiveness should be judged on the basis of multiple decisions. In practice, however, careers may turn on a single decision.

In this chapter, we address the critical issue of managerial decision making. First, we make some general observations about the environment in which decision making is carried out in organizations. Second, we describe four major models of managerial decision making—the rational model, the bounded rationality model, the political model, and the garbage can model. Third, several decision-making techniques are described. Fourth, we assess group and individual decision making, pointing out the strong and weak points of each. Fifth, the issue of creativity in decision making is briefly examined.

DECISION MAKING IN ORGANIZATIONS

As we examine decision making in organizations, it becomes apparent that certain distinguishing characteristics are common. In this section we deal with several of these fundamental matters, including: (1) the nature of crises, problems, and opportunities, (2) the difference between programmed and nonprogrammed decisions and (3) the degree of risk in the decision-making environment.

LEARNING OBJECTIVE 3

Explain the difference between crisis decisions, problem decisions, and opportunity decisions.

Crises, Problems, and Opportunities

If we look at the thousands of public and private sector organizations operating in Canada, and consider the myriad of decisions that managers in them make every day, it may seem like an impossible task to briefly describe the kinds of decisions that managers make. But all these decisions can be placed in one of three general categories.[1] **Crisis decisions** are necessary when a major disruptive event occurs that requires immediate action. Examples of crises in private-sector firms include a catastrophic fire at the company's head office, a new law that dramatically affects the company's method of operation, the death of the chief executive officer, or negative publicity about the safety of a company's product. In the Management Challenge, Chakalas was under pressure from his boss to make a crisis decision because McGlothin wanted an answer immediately. Examples of crises in non-profit organizations include a wartime defeat for a military unit, a college or university experiencing a large drop in its provincial grant money, or a labour union being decertified as the bargaining agent for employees.

crisis decisions

Problem decisions are necessary when results are different from those that were expected, but time is still available to plan a response. An example is the dramatic loss by the Progressive Conservative party in the 1993 federal election. This was certainly a "crisis" in the generic sense of the term, but since the party has several years to rejuvenate, the decisions the party would be called upon to make in the meantime are considered to be problem decisions.

problem decisions

Managers become aware of problems in various ways—when a deviation from historical experience occurs, when an expectation is not met, or when bosses, subordinates or individuals outside the organization tell the manager there is a problem.[2] Whatever the source of the problem, it is necessary to develop a consensus that there *is* a problem before any action will be taken. If the manager is not motivated to solve the problem, or if there is no consensus that the problem is serious, or if resources are not available to solve the problem, no action is likely to be taken.

Opportunity decisions involve taking new initiatives or doing a current activity more effectively even if no problem exists. Such decisions are often not made because many managers take the view that "if it ain't broke, don't fix it." An organization made up of managers with this view will rarely ever get involved in innovative activity. Yet innovative activity is a source of organizational growth, increased profitability, and employee motivation. A humorous—but realistic—view of the "do-nothing" tendency is shown in Figure 6-1.

opportunity decisions

programmed decisions

nonprogrammed decisions

Drilling for oil is an example of an opportunity decision. Objectives must first be set, various alternatives (well sites) considered, and the most promising alternatives chosen. Geologic and seismic information is a crucial component in the decision-making process.

Programmed and Nonprogrammed Decisions

Programmed decisions are recurring decisions on routine matters which are made using established procedures. Examples of programmed decisions include the personnel at the University of Calgary deciding how to register students each fall, Revenue Canada deciding on an auditing procedure for income tax returns, and Ferguson Lake Lodge deciding how to schedule float plane flights to bring tourists to the lodge each Saturday. **Nonprogrammed decisions** are one-time decisions for which no routines or standard procedures have been established. The Toronto Stock Exchange made a nonprogrammed decision when it decided to install state-of-the-art equipment for tracking stock transactions, as did IBM when it decided to enter the home computer market. Algonquin College made a new program of studies available to students, and the province of Manitoba introduced border duties on liquor purchases

FIGURE 6-1 THE DECISION-MAKING PROCESS.

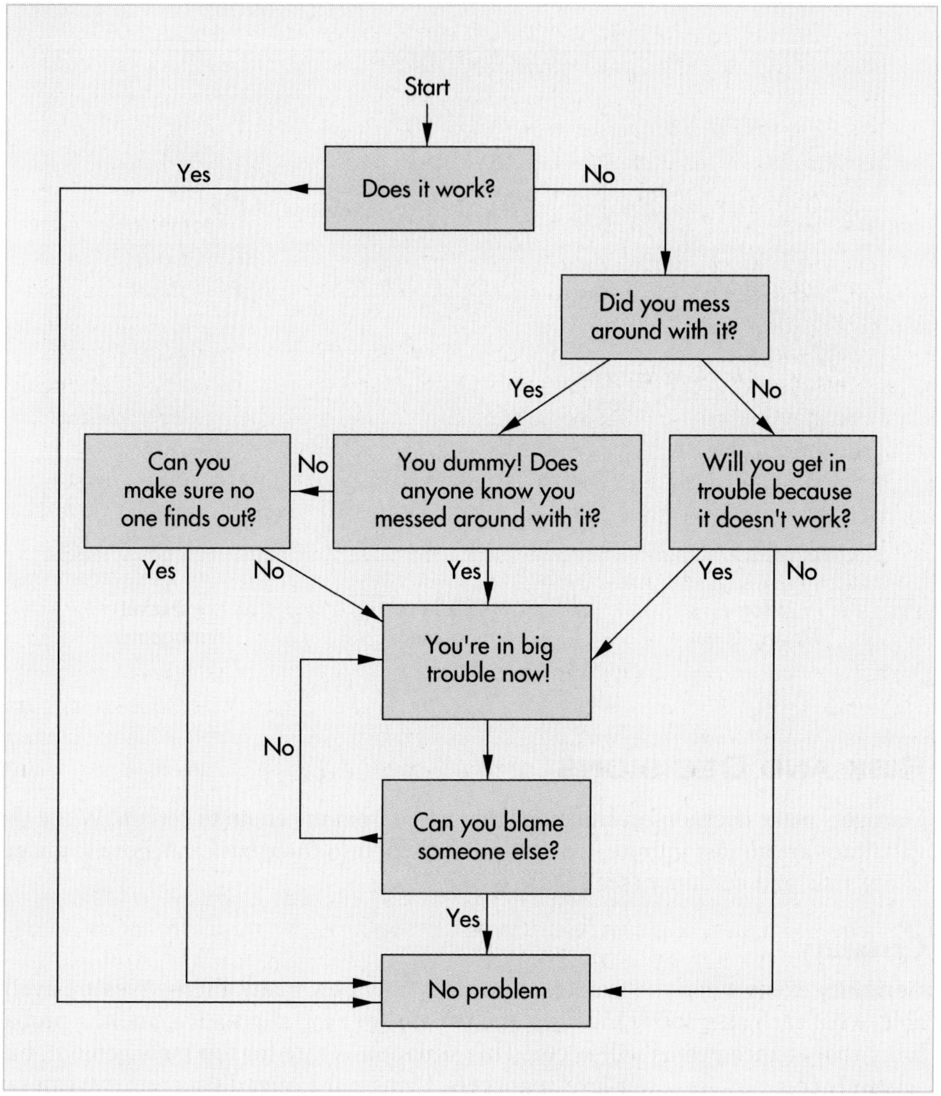

in the U.S. In the Management Challenge, Chakalas had to make a nonprogrammed decision about truck maintenance costs, because he had never faced that particular situation before. All organizations need to make both programmed and nonprogrammed decisions. Nonprogrammed decisions are more common at the top levels of the management hierarchy, and programmed decisions are more common at lower levels in the hierarchy (see Figure 6-2).

The balance of programmed and nonprogrammed decisions is upset when top management becomes too involved in making programmed decisions. When this happens, lower-level employees may become demotivated because top management is making decisions that should be within the employees' area of responsibility. If top management becomes too heavily involved in programmed decisions, it is also likely that too little attention will be given to the important nonprogrammed decisions (such as corporate strategy) that every organization needs to make.

Sobey's, of Stellarton, N.S., must decide where to open a new food retail outlet—an example of decision-making under risk.

FIGURE 6-2 TYPE OF DECISIONS AT DIFFERENT MANAGEMENT LEVELS.

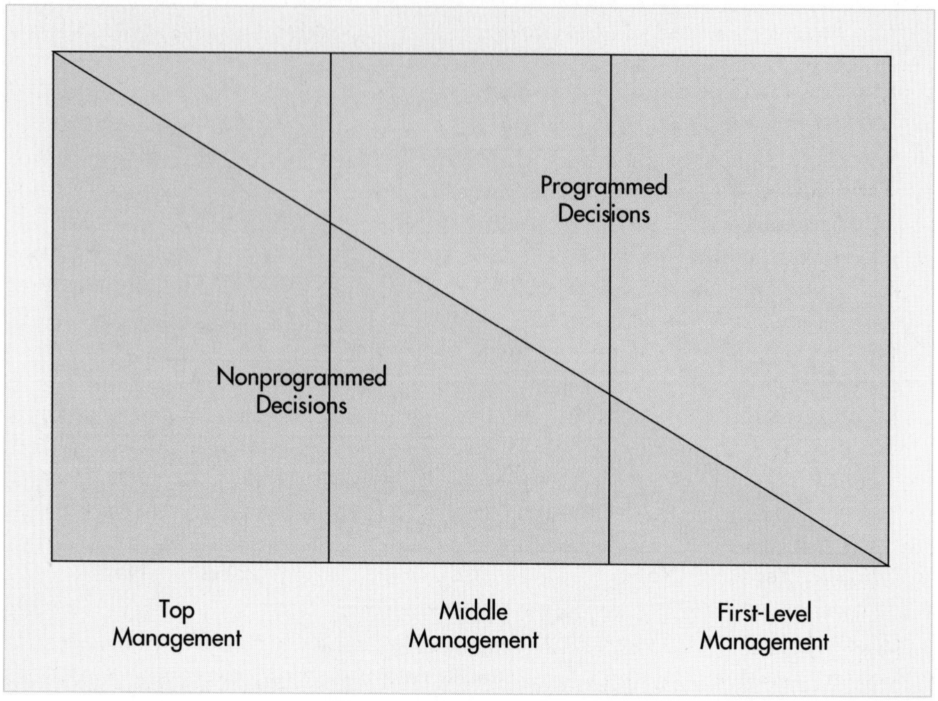

RISK AND DECISIONS

Managers make decisions in situations that range from uncertain to certain. While the variations are almost infinite, we can group them into three basic categories: uncertainty, risk, and certainty (see Figure 6-3).

Certainty

certainty

LEARNING OBJECTIVE 4

Understand the concepts of certainty, risk, and uncertainty.

Certainty exists when the manager knows exactly how many alternatives are available, what each alternative involves, the payoffs for each alternative, and the probability that chance events will occur. This situation is rare for top management, but relatively common for lower-level managers. Using our earlier distinction, we can say that programmed decisions are made in relatively certain circumstances, while nonprogrammed decisions are made in relatively uncertain circumstances.

Risk

risk

The state of **risk** exists when the manager is able to define the problem clearly, can list many (but not all) alternatives, and can estimate the probability of the payoffs for each

FIGURE 6-3 UNCERTAINTY, RISK, AND CERTAINTY.

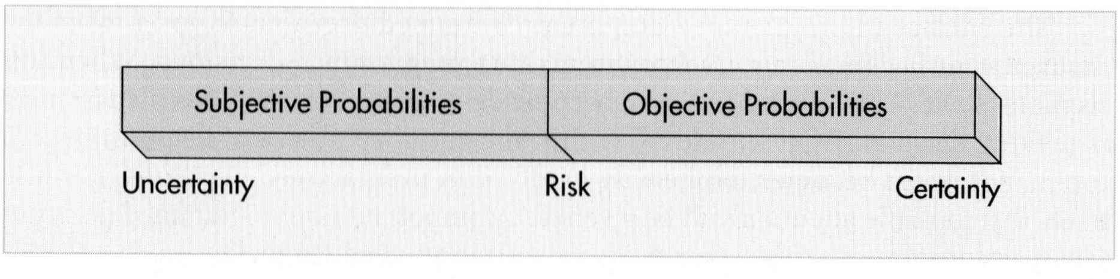

alternative. In this situation, there is no way to guarantee that a particular alternative will lead to a particular payoff. For example, when Shoppers Drug Mart opens a new outlet, it cannot predict precisely what the sales or profits of the new store will be.

Probability theory is often used by managers to cope with risk. Shoppers Drug Mart might, for example, analyze data that has been generated by existing outlets in its chain and use this data to predict the probability of success of the new store.

objective probabilities

Objective probabilities are based on quantifiable facts. The simplest example is flipping a coin; the probability of heads is 50 percent because there are only two sides to a coin. But even objective probabilities are not foolproof, since circumstances change over time and data developed in one time period may not be useful in another. When Iran and Iraq began attacking oil tankers in the Persian Gulf in the 1980s, insurance for tankers heading into the Persian Gulf increased 800 percent in a very short period of time.[3]

subjective probabilities

Subjective probabilities are those based on management intuition, values, preferences, and experience with similar situations. If a personnel manager is hiring someone for the position of director of marketing research, and the firm has never had such a position before, the personnel director can only make a subjective estimate of the probability of success of a given candidate (probably based on interviews with the candidate prior to hiring).

Uncertainty

uncertainty

Uncertainty exists when managers cannot assign even subjective probabilities to the possible outcomes of each of the alternatives they are considering. In extreme situations, the manager may not even be able to define clearly what the problem is, what alternatives exist, or what the payoffs of each alternative might be. For example, the former Soviet Union faced great uncertainty as it tried to make dramatic changes in its economic system. The many years of absolute communist control and the lack of a free market system meant that no one had any significant experience with the free market system or its likely outcomes.

MODELS OF DECISION MAKING

The process that managers use to make decisions has been the subject of much research. Several competing models of managerial decision-making behaviour have been identified, including the rational model, the bounded rationality model, the political model, and the garbage can model.

THE RATIONAL MODEL

rational model

LEARNING OBJECTIVE 5

Compare four managerial decision-making models: rational, bounded rationality, political, and garbage can.

The **rational model** of decision making (see Figure 6-4) assumes that decision makers proceed through a series of well-defined steps before making a decision.[4] If the decision maker is dealing with a problem or crisis, the process starts at step 1; for opportunity decisions, the process starts at step 5. In the discussion that follows, we describe the ideal, rational process; however, since the ideal is rarely achieved, some of the things that can go wrong in each step of the process are also noted.

The Problem Analysis Phase

problem analysis phase

In the **problem analysis phase**, the decision maker's goal is to come to a clear understanding of what the problem is. Four steps are involved in this phase.

FIGURE 6-4 THE RATIONAL MODEL OF THE DECISION-MAKING PROCESS.

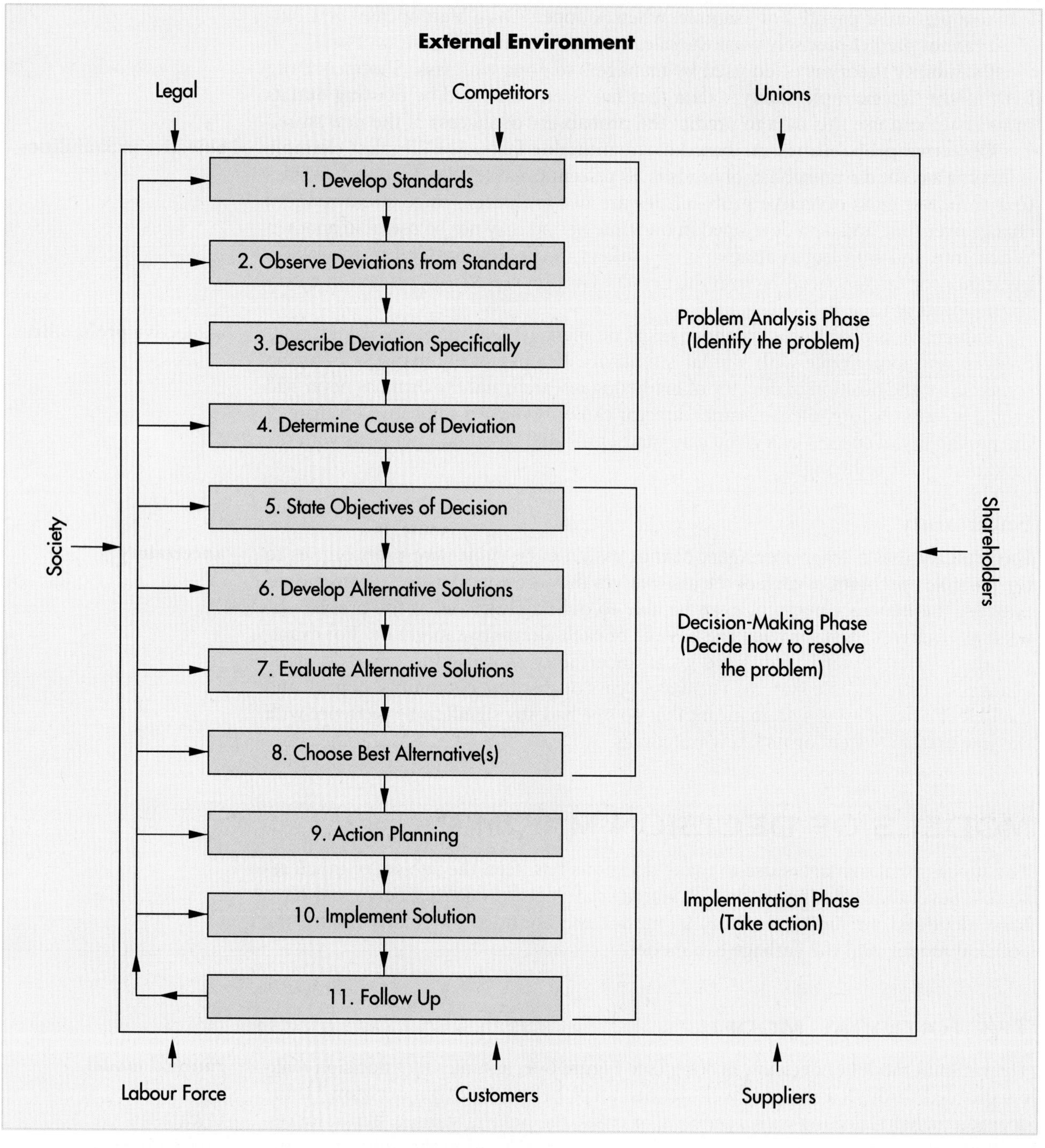

Step 1. Develop standards. Standards indicate the level of performance that should be achieved under normal conditions. Standards can be stated qualitatively or quantitatively, but because quantitative measurement is easier to achieve and subject to less interpretation, it is preferred. A manufacturing firm like Dofasco will have a standard relating to the amount of steel produced in a certain time period; Victoria Hospital may set a standard for occupancy rates; Canadian Airlines stipulates the

proportion of seats that should be filled on any flight; and Revenue Canada may set a standard governing the number of clients served each day.

Unfortunately, the development of standards often causes much controversy and conflict. Individuals who will be governed by the standard may feel that they have too little input when the standard is first set. Even if workers are involved in setting the standard, they may feel that the way in which output is measured is inappropriate. Employees may also feel that management will use performance standards against them, or that their job cannot be quantified (see the Management at Work insert "But You Can't Quantify That").

Step 2. Observe deviations from the standard. The performance of either a machine or a person is observed in order to determine if there is a deviation from the standard. Such deviation may be either above or below the standard, but getting agreement on whether or not a deviation exists may be difficult, even if everyone agrees on a standard. Consider the church that built an enclosed balcony over part of its sanctuary. At one board of directors meeting, a debate erupted about the amount of noise that children in Sunday School classes were making in the enclosed balcony during church services. Some directors said there was a problem with noise, while others said they saw no problem at all. Each board member agreed that it should be "quiet" in the sanctuary during church services, but the standard was loose enough that each person could interpret it his or her own way.

Just what constitutes a "serious deviation" may also be in dispute. Is a 1 percent shortfall significant? How about 5 percent? 10 percent? Think of the last time you were within one mark of the next highest grade in a course. Should the instructor have raised your grade because you were just one point away from an A? Should the professor have lowered your grade because you were just one point above a D?

Step 3. Describe the deviation specifically. The old saying that "a well-defined problem is a half-solved problem" is an oversimplification, but its point is well taken—we cannot solve the problem until it is clear what the problem is. This step

MANAGEMENT AT WORK

BUT YOU CAN'T QUANTIFY THAT!

Quantifying significant variables when making decisions is useful because many decision-making techniques require numerical values before they can be used. However, difficulties arise when decision makers attempt to quantify matters like the value of a park to community residents, the value of a vanishing species of animal, or the value of a human life. Can such variables be quantified? Should they be quantified?

Suppose an automobile manufacturer is alerted to a design flaw that is dangerous to human life. Should the manufacturer correct the flaw? Suppose that, after doing some research on the problem, the company estimates that (1) the flaw will cost $20 million to fix; (2) 23 people will likely die if it is not fixed; and (3) class-action damage suits against the company by close relatives of those killed will amount to $10 million.

In purely quantitative terms, executives of the firm might decide not to fix the flaw because at most it will cost them $10 million in damage claims. This is clearly less than the cost of fixing the flaw. However, if this decision is made, it implies that the manufacturer has computed that a human life is worth $434 782 (i.e., $10 million divided by 23 people). Because this sounds terribly mercenary and heartless, the company would certainly not be willing to admit that it made the decision on this basis.

So, a decision maker can quantify the value of a human life in a given situation. But few do. Most people (including managers) prefer to talk in generalities about such issues as human life and say, "You can't quantify that!" ▲

requires that the observed deviation be described in detail. This involves stating the location, magnitude and timing of the deviation, as well as any additional information that gives the decision maker a better understanding of the deviation.[5]

People may overlook this step altogether. Typically, an individual observes a deviation from standard, and then immediately leaps to a conclusion about what caused the deviation. This was the behaviour exhibited by Pat McGlothin in the Management Challenge. Failure to describe the deviation specifically often results in failure to find the root cause of the problem.

Step 4. Determine the cause of the deviation. Step 4 requires the use of information that has been gathered in the previous three steps. If clear standards are set, if the deviation from standard is observed, and if this deviation is described in detail, the decision maker will be successful in determining the cause of the problem.

The Decision-Making Phase

decision-making phase

Once the cause of a problem is known, the decision maker must decide how to resolve it. In the **decision-making phase**, the decision maker develops a solution to the problem or capitalizes on an opportunity that has arisen. The following steps are required:

Step 5. State the objectives of the decision. For problem decisions, the objective is to solve the problem that has been defined in Step 4. For opportunity decisions, the objectives must first be stated. These objectives deal with issues such as the level of profit or service desired, employee productivity, rejection rates, absentee rates, or any other area where management would like to improve.

Here again, human idiosyncracies can make the step troublesome. For example, it may be difficult to arrive at a consensus about the objectives that the organization should pursue. Even with agreement on general objectives, different parts of an organization may find themselves in conflict over specific issues. The classic example of this is the dispute that occurs between production and marketing people. The production people want long production runs and standardized products, while the marketing people want speedy delivery and a wide variety of products.

Step 6. Develop alternative solutions. In this step, the decision maker develops as many possible solutions to the problem (or opportunity) as can be generated. Creativity is important in this step, since innovative solutions often resolve problems that traditional measures will not.

When people attempt to develop alternative solutions, they tend to suggest those that have worked in similar circumstances in the past. The conservative nature of most decision makers means that innovative alternatives are dismissed because "we've never done it that way."

Step 7. Evaluate alternative solutions. Once a list of potential courses of action has been created, it must be analyzed and the alternatives ranked. To do this, some sort of criterion must be used so that the alternatives can be compared to each other. Some of the techniques for selecting the option to pursue are discussed later in this chapter.

In practice, individuals neglect evaluating the alternatives because they lack the necessary motivation to do the evaluation, because they don't want to take the time, because they feel that the analysis required is beyond their ability, or because there is disagreement about which method to use to make the evaluation.

Step 8. Choose the best alternative. Once Steps 1-7 (for problem decisions) or Steps 5-7 (for opportunity and problem decisions) have been completed, the decision maker can choose the best alternative according to the criterion established. Once a particular option has been selected, the decision-making phase is complete.

The Implementation Phase

implementation phase

In the **implementation phase**, the goal is to put into practice the solution that has been chosen. In this phase, thoughts must be converted into actions, and the key skill required is the ability to introduce change. Three specific steps are required in this phase.

Step 9. Action planning. When a detailed plan of action is being developed, certain questions must be answered: Should employees participate in planning the implementation of a change, or should they simply be required to implement the change? What kind of coordination is required between the decision maker and those who will implement the decision? Who will monitor the implementation to see if it is working properly? What criteria will be used to determine if the proposed course of action actually solves the problem or achieves the desired objective?

Problems in this step arise when people fail to plan their actions adequately, thereby rendering the actions ineffective or counterproductive.

Step 10. Implement the solution. The most effective decisions are those which are of high quality, and which are accepted by those they affect, as indicated in the following important formula:[6]

$$\text{Decision Effectiveness} = \text{Quality} \times \text{Acceptance}$$

A high-quality decision that is not accepted by those who must live with it is useless. Likewise, a low-quality solution that is implemented strictly because the employees will accept it, will not be very effective either.

Step 10 can be extremely frustrating for decision makers. Many managers who attempt to introduce change find that those affected have vigorous objections and therefore sabotage the change. Such problems can be avoided by allowing those who will be affected to participate in the decision-making phase, but this process is often resisted by managers because they feel it takes too much time and energy.

Step 11. Follow up. Once a solution has been implemented, management must monitor the extent to which it achieves what it is supposed to achieve. Often a solution that appears perfect on paper runs into considerable technical or human difficulties once it is put into practice. A control system must therefore be put in place to measure the success of the solution.

The greatest practical difficulty with Steps 9-11 is bridging the gap between thinking and action. Steps 1-8 require mainly mental action, while steps 9-11 require both mental and practical action. Many individuals are proficient in Steps 1-8, but they lack the interest, inclination, or ability to make the transition from thinking to action. The decision-making process is long and complicated, and much can (and does) go wrong. Knowledge of both the task and human elements in the process is important if the decision maker is to be successful at making and implementing decisions. The ethical aspects of the decision must also be considered (see the Ethics in Management insert "Ethical Dilemmas in Decision Making").

Managers will often say that they follow rational procedures when making decisions. But when asked to analyze a successful decision, they may attach more significance to the process than is warranted. In one study, managers read one of four versions of a case study in decision making in a military setting. All four cases were identical except for (a) feedback on how successful the decision was, and (b) whether the person in the case obeyed orders. In those cases where a successful decision outcome occurred, the managers felt that superior decision-making processes had been used, even though that was not true.[7]

ETHICS IN MANAGEMENT

ETHICAL DILEMMAS IN DECISION MAKING

As a manager, you will regularly encounter ethical dilemmas—that is, you will wonder, when faced with decisions, about which decision is "right." Because management is not an occupation where decisions are cut-and-dried, you must develop the ability to deal with the rational, emotional, and ethical dimensions of each decision. Consider the following realistic situation that you might someday find yourself in:

You are 51 years old, and the executive vice-president of the toy division of a large and very successful consumer products company. Your division has been very profitable under your leadership. Last year your base salary was $156,000; you also earned $48,000 in bonuses.

You have been with the company for 24 years. You began as a salesperson and worked your way up through the ranks to your current position. As you think back on your career, you recall many long (but gratifying) days where you poured your heart and soul into your work.

Your career goal is to be the CEO of a large firm just like the one for which you are now working. In your current position, you are just one step away. Last week the current president announced that he will retire in eight months. You know from very reliable sources that you are one of two internal candidates being seriously considered by the board of directors to be the new CEO. Naturally, the competition for this position is fierce. You also know that your chances for the presidency will be very much affected by your division's financial performance during the next year. If it is good, you have a good chance to be chosen; if it is not, your chances are much reduced.

You know that your division's financial performance is going to be heavily influenced by one particular hot-selling toy which your division recently put on the market. This one product accounted for 43 percent of your division's profits last year. You would like to see a more balanced profit contribution from the various toys your division sells, but you also realize that toys are very faddish, and that it is difficult to know in advance which products will be winners.

There is only one piece of bad news—a consumer group has recently claimed that your high-performing product may not be safe for children. While there is no hard evidence that this is true, you do recall seeing some test reports a couple of years ago that were a bit worrisome.

Here is your ethical dilemma: Should you push ahead with an aggressive marketing strategy for this toy, recognizing that it will probably sell very well (and perhaps get you the position as CEO), or should you institute the time-consuming safety studies needed to determine if the consumer group's claims have any merit? Taking the latter course of action will almost certainly mean that sales of the toy will be far less. To put it more bluntly, if you conduct the safety studies your chance of becoming CEO will be sharply reduced. *What decision would you make in this situation?* ▲

THE BOUNDED RATIONALITY MODEL OF DECISION MAKING

bounded rationality model

Unlike the rational model of decision making which prescribes how managers *should* make decisions, the bounded rationality model tries to explain how managers *actually* make decisions. The **bounded rationality model** makes the assumption that managers do not have perfect information about problems, and that they do not use rational decision processes when they make decisions. This model is an attempt to take into account the fact that human beings cannot possibly deal with all aspects of all problems that confront them.

satisficing

An important concept in this model is the idea of satisficing.[8] **Satisficing** means choosing an alternative which is acceptable, but which is not ideal. For example, suppose you are going fishing in northern Canada. An hour before the float plane is scheduled to take off to fly you to the fishing lodge, you discover that you have forgotten your fishing rods. You rush into town and quickly buy replacements at The Bay, thankful that they even have fishing rods in stock. This decision is not optimal (in terms of money spent or in terms of the equipment you purchased), but it does allow you to reach your fundamental goal of fishing.

Or, consider the sales manager who decides to buy a microcomputer to keep track of the activity of the company's salespeople. The manager knows what information the computer must generate, but does not know very much about computers in general. A business contact who has given the manager good advice in the past has an opinion on which of the top brands would be most appropriate, and the sales manager accepts the opinion. In making the decision in this way, the sales manager has probably not purchased the ideal computer, but has gotten a computer that will do the job that is required.

Overcommitment to Decisions

escalation of commitment

The idea of bounded rationality helps to explain why managers sometimes stick with a course of action long after it has become unwise or unprofitable. **Escalation of commitment** refers to the situation in which a manager becomes increasingly committed to a previously chosen course of action even though it has been shown to be ineffective.[9] Basic economic theory argues that costs which have already been incurred on a project (sunk costs) should not be considered when decisions are made about whether to invest additional money. Yet these costs do appear to be taken into account by managers, particularly if the manager made the original decision to invest money in the project.[10] Recent research also suggests that such additional investment is more likely when a project is close to completion.[11]

A good example of overcommitment is Expo '86, the world's fair held in British Columbia in 1986. When the project was first conceived, the deficit was projected at about \$6 million. Over the next few years, the projected deficit kept rising, until it was over \$300 million. In spite of this, the project went forward.[12]

But at least Expo '86 took place. The Shoreham Nuclear Power Plant project in New York was started in 1966; at that time its cost was projected at \$75 million. By 1989, that figure had risen to \$5 billion. The project was finally abandoned without the plant ever having produced any power.[13] Cost overrun problems have also been evident at the Darlington and Pickering nuclear plants in Ontario.

Why would supposedly rational managers get into difficulties like these? Managers may become overcommitted to a project for one or more of the following reasons:

- They are hard-driving, self-focussed, and success-oriented, and are motivated to defend their initial decisions.[14]
- They are reluctant to admit they made a mistake.
- They fear that their career will be harmed if "their" project fails.
- People and resources have been committed to the project, and it may seem too costly to withdraw.
- The manager believes that current project difficulties can be overcome if everyone will simply work harder.
- "Image" considerations dictate that the project be a success, so everyone involved feels they must continue working on the project.[15]

How can managers avoid overcommitment? The most obvious way is for managers to set specific goals ahead of time that deal with how much time and money they are willing to expend. Once the limit is reached, the project should be abandoned even if some individuals make emotional appeals to continue it. The existence of specific time and money goals makes it harder for the manager to interpret unfavourable news in a positive light.

In a laboratory experiment designed to test the value of various deescalation strategies, students made investment decisions after reading a case study. Those who set minimum performance goals experienced significantly less problems with overcommitment than those who did not set performance goals.[16]

Managers can also reduce the likelihood of overcommitment by asking themselves the following tough questions:[17]

- If the project fails, will I revise my opinion of myself?
- Is it hard to define what constitutes failure on the project?
- If I took charge of this project today, would I think it is a bad project?

If the answers to these questions are "Yes," the manager is in danger of becoming overcommitted to the project.

Before you conclude that you would never make similar managerial mistakes as the ones described, consider a personal decision. You have a used car which is costing you increasing amounts of money to repair. At what point should you withdraw from this "project" and buy a different car? While each individual repair costs far less than a new car, if the repairs get frequent enough, you will end up with an expensive old car instead of a new one. In that event, your friends will not be impressed with *your* decision making!

The Political Model of Decision Making

political model

The **political model** of decision making assumes that organizational decisions are made on the basis of whether or not they will increase the status, power, or economic well-being of the decision maker. Like the bounded rationality model, this model tries to describe how managers actually make decisions. Unlike either the rational or bounded rationality model, the political model assumes that individuals will pursue their own self-interest, even if doing so hurts other individuals or the organization.

As an example of political decision making, consider a manager of a department in a government agency or a business firm who makes a proposal to absorb another department. The proposal will probably be made on the very rational-sounding criterion of administrative efficiency, but what the manager may really want is the increased power and status that go with having more subordinates and a bigger budget. (The political model is described in detail in Chapter 10.)

The Garbage Can Model of Decision Making

The most pessimistic (or perhaps realistic) view of organizational decision making is the garbage can model.[18] The premise of this model is that the decision-making process in organizations is so complex that it is virtually impossible to describe how managers make decisions. Problems, solutions, decision makers, and decision-making techniques all exist in a state of flux. According to the **garbage can model**, decisions are made only when several factors happen to come together at the right time. These factors are (1) a solution to a problem is discovered, (2) the solution does not require excessive amounts of organizational resources, and (3) the problem and its solution are known to a decision maker who happens to have the time and interest in making the decision. Thus, in two situations which look very similar, two different decisions may be made.

garbage can model

Decision-Making Techniques

LEARNING OBJECTIVE 6
Describe five decision-making techniques for helping managers make good decisions.

A large number of techniques have been developed to help managers make better decisions. In this section, we discuss six of the most popular decision-making techniques: (1) the decision matrix, (2) decision trees, (3) brainstorming, (4) the Delphi technique, (5) nominal grouping, and (6) dialectical inquiry. The first two can be used by either groups or individuals, while the last four require a group setting.

THE DECISION MATRIX

Managers are often faced with problems in which multiple criteria must be considered before a decision can be made. To make matters worse, the relative weights of these criteria may be in dispute. In these situations, a decision matrix can be useful. A **decision matrix** helps the decision maker to systematically develop and weight the criteria that are to be used in making a decision. The Management at Work insert "Using the Decision Matrix at SAIT" describes the steps that are involved in the decision matrix, using a real problem that a manager actually solved.

decision matrix

MANAGEMENT AT WORK

USING THE DECISION MATRIX AT SAIT

Weights	**120**	**150**	**20**	**75**	
Criteria					
Alternatives	Discount	Assurance of Supply	Credit Terms	Equipment Loans	**Totals**
Company A	10	8	3.33	3.33	2716.35
Company B	9	10	3.33	0	2646.60
Company C	6	9	10	10	3020.00

Some time ago, the Southern Alberta Institute of Technology (SAIT) wanted to choose a supplier of petroleum products. Three companies were interested in handling such a contract. The SAIT purchasing department decided to use a decision matrix to determine which supplier to use. The following steps were carried out:

1. *Listing alternatives* In this case, there were three alternatives—suppliers A, B, and C.
2. *Establishing criteria* The criteria decided upon were discounts, assurance of supply, credit terms, and equipment loans that suppliers were willing to make.
3. *Weighting the criteria* The purchasing department concluded that an assurance of supply was the most important criterion; it was given a weight of 150. Discount was second at 120, equipment loans was third at 75, and credit terms were considered the least important and weighted at 20.
4. *Rating each alternative on each criterion* Assurance of supply was judged on the basis of a firm's reputation, location, management, and financial condition. Firm A was given 8 points, B received 10, and C received 9 points. Ratings on the discount criterion were calculated using ratios. Firm A received 10 points because its discount was best (20 percent). B's discount was 18 percent so it received 9 points (18/20 × 10 = 9). C's discount was 12 percent, so it received 6 points (12/20 × 10 = 6). The score for equipment loans was determined by the value of the equipment offered by each company. Firm C offered $21 000 worth of equipment and was given 10 points. Firm A offered $7000 worth of equipment and was given 3.33 points (7/21 × 10 = 3.33). Firm B offered no equipment and received 0 points. For credit terms, Firm C offered 30 days and received 10 points. Firms A and B both offered 10-day credit and received 3.33 points (10/30 × 10 = 3.33).
5. *Calculating the score for each alternative* For each alternative, the weight for each criterion was multiplied by the value for each criterion. Then the weighted ratings for each alternative were added together. The scores for the three companies were as follows:

   Company A – 8(150) + 10(120) + 3.3(75) + 3.3(20) = 2716.35

   Company B – 10(150) + 9(120) + 0(75) + 3.3(20) = 2646.60

   Company C – 9(150) + 6(120) + 10.0(75) + 10.0(20) = 3020.00
6. *Choosing the alternative with the highest score* Company C was chosen because it had the highest score. The decision matrix above summarizes the main points in this case. ▲

The decision matrix may be used in either individual or group decision making. In the former, the manager simply decides on the criteria that will be used to assess the problem, and the weights that should be attached to each criterion. In a group setting, debates may occur about the criteria and the weights, and lengthy group discussions may take place before a consensus is achieved.

DECISION TREES

decision trees

In situations where a manager (1) is able to quantify payoffs, (2) must deal with a series of future events, and (3) can reasonably estimate the likelihood of future events, decision trees can be very helpful. **Decision trees** are pictorial representations of problems or opportunities, showing the alternatives, chance events, and payoffs in a way that allows management to compare the desirability of each alternative.[19]

To demonstrate how decision tree analysis works, consider the following simplified problem: A company has developed two products that have market potential; however, only one product can be developed because of resource limitations. The company conducts market tests and concludes that two levels of sales are possible for each product—high (probability = 0.6) or low (probability = 0.4). The predicted profits (in millions) for the two products under high and low demand are as follows:

Product	High Demand	Low Demand
1	25	−5
2	10	3

Which product should the company market? To answer this question, two basic steps are necessary. First, the problem must be conceptualized, that is, the decision tree must be drawn. Second, a mathematical analysis must be performed. The outcome of these steps is shown in Figure 6-5.

Conceptualizing the Problem

The goal of this step is to pictorially represent the decision problem and the sequence of events that can occur. The decision maker works from left to right. To draw the tree, we first determine how many alternatives there are. In this simplified case, there are two. Once these alternatives are shown, the implications of each must be represented and the probabilities indicated. The payoffs for each outcome are then shown at the extreme right of the tree.

FIGURE 6-5 SOLUTION TO THE TWO-PRODUCT PROBLEM.

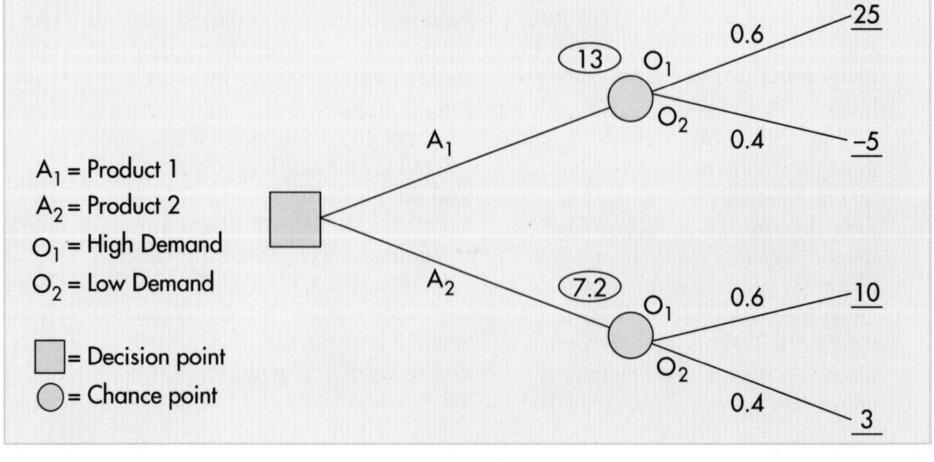

Mathematical Analysis

The goal of this step is to discover which alternative is superior. For this step, we work from right to left. Assume the manager has decided to use the criterion of expected value to make the choice. This criterion is based on the idea that because we cannot predict the future, we should take a weighted average of possible future occurrences. **Expected value** is calculated by multiplying the probability of an outcome by the dollar return that would result from that outcome. The expected value for the two alternatives is:

expected value

$$\text{Expected value (alternative \#1)} = [0.6(25) + 0.4(-5)] = 13.0$$
$$\text{Expected value (alternative \#2)} = [0.6(10) + 0.4(3)] = 7.2$$

In this case, the manager should pick alternative #1 because it promises (but does not guarantee) the best return.

Managers can employ decision trees individually or collectively. The advantage of using it in group decisions is that any idiosyncrasies or biases affecting subjective probabilities can be caught and corrected. Group discussions are also likely to bring out additional information and reveal other areas of the problem that must be clarified before a good decision can be made.

BRAINSTORMING

This technique was developed by Alex Osborn, a partner in an advertising agency.[20] **Brainstorming** is a technique which is designed to encourage creativity by having group members present freewheeling solutions to problems in a nonjudgmental setting.

brainstorming

Brainstorming usually involves getting 8 to 12 people together for about an hour to develop creative solutions to problems. The idea in brainstorming is to create an atmosphere of enthusiasm and spontaneity so that suggestions flow without fear of judgment. The following guidelines are used in brainstorming sessions:

1. Criticism of ideas is not allowed.
2. No idea is considered too ridiculous. People are encouraged to express any ideas that come to mind.
3. Participants are encouraged to build on the suggestions of other group members. The emphasis is on group, not individual, development and ownership of ideas.
4. As many ideas as possible are encouraged. The greater the number of ideas, the greater the chance that one will be found that is useful.

The brainstorming technique has been used by many firms in both the public and private sector. Some managers use it because it helps achieve broad goals like building team spirit, making work more enjoyable, and improving communication among employees and management.[21]

Interestingly, the shortcomings of brainstorming have not received much publicity. During the 1960s and 1970s, studies were conducted which consistently showed that brainstorming actually produced fewer and lower-quality ideas than those produced by individuals working alone.[22]

Apparently brainstorming is not as effective because people don't work as hard in groups as they do individually (social loafing), because people are reluctant to express their ideas for fear of ridicule (evaluation apprehension), and because everyone in a group cannot talk at once (production blocking).[23]

Advances in computer technology show promise for enhancing the performance of both *nominal groups* (where individuals first work alone and then combine their ideas) and those working in *brainstorming groups* (where individuals interact during

electronic brainstorming

discussion of the problem). In **electronic brainstorming**, group members type ideas into a computer; these ideas then show up simultaneously on the computer screens of other group members. Studies of electronic brainstorming indicate that performance increases as group size increases. As well, the problems of production blocking and evaluation apprehension are reduced.

In one study which compared the performance of electronic and nonelectronic brainstorming groups with electronic and nonelectronic nominal groups, it was found that electronic nominal groups had the highest performance, followed by electronic brainstorming groups and then nonelectronic nominal groups. Nonelectronic brainstorming groups had the lowest performance.[24] In another study, 12-person electronic brainstorming groups outperformed 12-person nonelectronic nominal groups.[25]

Executives from Metropolitan Life who gathered at Queen's University spent their time seated side-by-side in front of microcomputers. They typed in ideas for how their firm could improve its operations. The company's vice-president estimates that the managers accomplished in one day what would normally take five days. Many other Canadian firms are also using electronic brainstorming. In fact, IBM Canada, Royal Trust, and Sears Canada have set up their own electronic meeting rooms.[26]

THE DELPHI TECHNIQUE

Delphi technique

This technique was developed at the Rand Corporation, a "think tank" in the U.S. and is mainly used for forecasting future events or assessing current needs.[27] The **Delphi technique** is a procedure for getting consensus among experts through the use of questionnaires and feedback of results. The procedure usually works as follows:

1. The organization identifies 15 to 20 experts on the topic they are interested in, and then prompts each expert to give an individual opinion. The experts are not brought together to form a group, nor do they talk to each other.

2. A questionnaire is sent to the experts asking them to give numerical estimates of the likelihood that particular future events will occur. These questions can deal with virtually any issue, including electrical consumption, women in top management positions, energy prices, interest rates, or pollution levels.

3. The responses of the experts are tabulated and a summary of the results is given to each one. The summary typically shows the average and median response, as well as the range of answers on each question. The experts are asked to consider the information in the summary and then fill out the same questionnaire again.

4. The second round of questionnaires is summarized to give the same type of information as the first round. This summary may draw some conclusions about what the emerging consensus is on the issue under examination. Experts who have given responses that are not close to the emerging consensus may be asked to justify their opinions.

5. The experts are then asked to make a third estimate. A final summary is developed from these answers and is presented to the management of the organization doing the study.

The Delphi technique has one major advantage over other group decision-making techniques—it is free of any face-to-face interaction among participants. Consequently, it is impossible for particular strong-willed individuals to dominate the group. Experts simply give their responses on the questionnaires and consider the summaries they receive. They know that the other respondents are also experts in the field and so take the other views that are expressed seriously. If experts want to change their estimates after considering the summary, they will do so only because they became intellectually convinced that their answer should be changed, not because a domineering person is putting pressure on them to do so.

Nominal Grouping

Nominal grouping is a decision-making technique emphasizing the equal contribution of group members through the mechanism of voting.[28] Five to ten individuals are assembled in a room and asked to write solutions to a problem that has been given to them by the group moderator. The group might be asked how to improve communication between functional groups in their organization, how to train employees so they will be more productive, how to reduce conflict between the company and some external group, or how to attack a variety of other problems and opportunities.

nominal grouping

The procedure for using nominal grouping involves four phases:

1. *Listing* Individuals write down their solutions to the problem without discussing them with other members of the group.
2. *Recording* After approximately 20 minutes, the individuals are asked to give the solutions they have written down to the group recorder. The recorder writes each person's solutions on a flip chart. No discussion of any solutions is permitted until all solutions have been written on the flip chart.
3. *Clarification* After all solutions are listed on the flip chart, a general discussion takes place. The purpose of this discussion is to clarify what each solution involves; critiquing solutions is not allowed.
4. *Voting* Ballots are distributed to members of the group and they are asked to rank the solutions that are listed on the flip chart. The ballots are then tabulated and the alternative with the highest score is designated as the choice of the group.

Group decision making provides knowledge from more than one person, encourages different perspectives on problem solving, and gives employees the opportunity to participate in decision making. Here, managers at Prentice Hall Canada consider the implications of marketing research data during the process of making a decision about whether to produce a textbook for a certain market.

Like the Delphi technique, nominal grouping is premised on the idea that group discussion inhibits creativity by making people fear that their ideas will be ridiculed. Note that none of the four phases allow a critique of the solutions. However, the participants are encouraged to present their solution to the group.

How well does nominal grouping work? A review of studies comparing nominal grouping with other techniques revealed that nominal grouping was superior to, or as good as, other techniques with respect to decision quality and participant satisfaction.[29] The technique also appears to motivate people to implement decisions that have been made using nominal grouping. In one study, nurses in a problem-solving workshop made decisions using one of three techniques: nominal grouping, structured discussion (groups used the rational decision-making process), and open discussion (groups discussed one alternative at a time). Problems were categorized as simple, moderately complex, and complex. After the nurses returned to their home organization, an assessment was made of how many attempts they made to implement the changes that had been developed in the workshop. For all levels of problem complexity, nurses in the nominal groups made more implementation attempts than nurses in the open discussion groups. For simple problems, they also made more implementation attempts than nurses in the structured discussion groups.[30]

Dialectical Inquiry

Dialectical inquiry is an approach to group decision making that deliberately introduces conflict into decision-making deliberations so that conflicting assumptions and solutions will be seriously considered.[31] Dialectical inquiry has most frequently

dialectical inquiry

been used in strategic management decision making where a group of 15 or more people make decisions that will affect the entire organization.

The process has four basic phases: (1) clarifying managers' assumptions about the problem and the ways in which they feel it should be solved; (2) identifying assumptions that are the opposite of those identified in the first phase; (3) integrating the opposing assumptions; and (4) deciding what course of action to take.[32]

Because the purpose of dialectical inquiry is to develop and clarify opposing points of view, we should not be surprised if conflicts develop in groups using this method. Because numerous points of view are considered, this method can lead to superior decisions. However, introducing conflict into group deliberations may also reduce participant commitment because negative interpersonal feelings may develop during the discussion process. In two different studies, groups using dialectical inquiry developed higher-quality decisions than groups using consensus decision making, but the consensus groups were more willing to work together on future tasks, and were more accepting of their group's decision than were the members of the dialectical inquiry groups.[33]

As a group decision-making technique, dialectical inquiry appears most promising in situations where the participants are in agreement on fundamental issues (e.g., the organization's reason for existence), and they wish to develop some specific strategies to fulfill the organization's mission. If participants are hostile to each other at the beginning of a dialectical inquiry session, it is unlikely that very much will be accomplished.[34]

GROUP VERSUS INDIVIDUAL DECISION MAKING

In organizations, decisions can be made by one person or by a group of people working together. Robert Campeau made many decisions affecting Campeau Corporation on his own.[35] Laurent Beaudoin, CEO of Bombardier, is an autocrat who does not share power, so there is little group decision making at that firm.[36] At CP Rail, by contrast, an executive committee makes major decisions affecting the firm.[37] At General Electric's Bromont, Quebec, plant, where employees are involved in a wide range of decision making, productivity has increased by over 300 percent since the plant opened in 1983.[38]

Whether made by an individual or group, good decisions are those that are made efficiently, demonstrate high quality, and are accepted by people who have to implement them. Research suggests that (1) the quality of group decisions is higher than the quality of the decisions of the average individual in the group, but lower than the best individual, (2) individual satisfaction and acceptance is enhanced when decision-making authority is delegated to groups, and (3) groups require more time to make decisions than individuals.[39]

ADVANTAGES OF GROUP DECISION MAKING

LEARNING OBJECTIVE 7
Explain the advantages and disadvantages of group and individual decision making.

Group decision making has several advantages. First, groups possess the knowledge of more than one individual, all of which can be brought to bear on the problem that needs to be solved or the opportunity that might be exploited.

Second, because each person may view a situation from a different perspective, a group can consider various approaches to a problem or opportunity. An individual making decisions without ideas from others may become stuck in a pattern of thinking that is unsuitable for solving the problem at hand. In a committee, a variety of approaches are generally offered, so that the chances of finding an effective response are increased.

Third, group decision making means increased participation by the individuals in the group. Although the participation of many people does not guarantee a high-quality decision, it does increase member satisfaction.[40] Employees who have been involved in making a decision are more likely to support and accept it than those who have simply had the decision imposed upon them.

Fourth, collective decision making tends to improve the participants' understanding of the issues in the decision. Through group discussions on a specific issue, a person gains insight into the need for a decision, the factors that influence the decision, and peoples' feelings about the issue.

Disadvantages of Group Decision Making

The most obvious disadvantage of group decision making is the time required to make decisions. In most organizations, the need for action is urgent, but groups or committees have a reputation for being slow. Decisive individuals can become frustrated waiting for a group to make up its mind.

A second problem is that certain individuals invariably dominate group discussions. As a result, the dominant person's preferences and ideas may be accepted, while other equally worthy ideas may be ignored.[41]

A third problem is the compromises that may occur as groups try to work through controversial issues. The compromise may mean low commitment to the decision, since neither side got what it wanted.

social loafing

A fourth problem is **social loafing**, which is the tendency of individuals to put forth less effort in a group than they do when they work individually.[42] Social loafing is most likely when the nature of the task makes it difficult to tell how hard a person is working, and when the person's interest in the task is low.[43]

Finally, group members may be so concerned about maintaining group solidarity that they fail to come to grips with the problem facing them. The term "groupthink" has been coined to describe this problem[44] (see Chapter 9 for a discussion of this important issue).

stepladder technique

The **stepladder technique** reduces the likelihood of some of these problems by structuring the entry of group members into a core group. In a four-person group, for example, two members (the core) first work on a problem together. A third member then joins the core and presents his or her solution, after which a three-person discussion follows. A fourth person then presents his or her solution and a four-person discussion ensues.

One study showed that stepladder groups produced significantly higher-quality decisions than conventional groups.[45] The quality of the group's decision exceeded the quality of the *best* individual's decision 56 percent of the time; in the conventional groups, this happened only 13 percent of the time. Members of stepladder groups also reported working harder than members of conventional groups, and they felt more organized in their work.

CREATIVITY AND DECISION MAKING

creativity

innovation

Creativity is the discovery of new and useful ideas. A creative decision is one that solves a problem or exploits an opportunity by coming up with new and useful ideas. From an organization's point of view, creativity alone is not sufficient; new ideas must also be put into practice. **Innovation** involves taking a creative idea and actually putting it into use.[46] It is important that there be some coordination between these two activities. The invention of the internal combustion engine is an example of creativity; using the engine to power cars, airplanes, lawn mowers, chain saws, and boats is an example of innovation.

The Creative Process

The creative process is difficult to describe because we do not yet understand precisely what goes on in the human mind. Nevertheless, four basic phases have been identified.[47]

1. *Preparation* The preparation stage involves hard work and a high level of motivation in order to assemble relevant information on the problem to be solved. The commonly held view that creativity is something that "just happens" is not supported by research.
2. *Incubation* In this stage, the decision maker stops thinking intensively about the problem and simply allows it to exist in the back of her or his mind. During this phase, the person may appear to be doing little or no work on the problem.
3. *Inspiration* This may be either a flash of insight (the "Eureka!" phenomenon) or a gradual awareness that the problem has a solution. This is the most satisfying and publicized stage in the creative process, but without the work that was done in the preparation and incubation stages, the inspiration stage would not occur.
4. *Validation* Here, the creative solution is tested to see if it actually works. This may take a considerable amount of time. If the idea does not work, the decision maker returns to the preparation stage.

Characteristics of Creative Individuals

Various research studies have looked into the question of whether creative individuals are somehow different from the average person. These studies reveal that creative people have certain characteristics:[48]

1. *They are nonconformists* Creative individuals are not overly concerned about conventions; they have their own view of the world and pursue it.
2. *They value thinking* Creative people get much satisfaction from using their mental faculties to solve knotty problems.
3. *They resist leaping to conclusions* Creative people rarely say, "It can't be done." Rather, they are motivated to find out how it can be done.
4. *They are relatively young* By far the most creative time for people is between 30 and 40 years of age.
5. *They are not productive in authoritarian environments* Because many organizations have just such an environment, managers often see creative people as difficult to work with.

Improving Creativity in Organizations

If organizations hope to gain the benefits of creative decision making, they must work toward developing an environment that will encourage creativity. Research in this area suggests the following strategies:[49]

1. *Positive reinforcement* Rewarding desirable behaviour increases the probability that behaviour will recur. Applying this logic to the issue of creativity means that management should reward new ideas and creative decisions.
2. *Appropriate resource support* If organizations expect creative decisions, employees must have the resources to facilitate creative decision making (e.g., a well-equipped research lab for scientific research).

3. *Set deadlines* While many people feel that this idea goes against the notion of free-wheeling creativity, the establishment of realistic deadlines actually facilitates creativity.
4. *Encourage interdepartmental communication* When employees from different functional areas interact with each other, the flow of information increases, and new perspectives on issues may develop, leading to new ideas and fresh ways of meeting challenges.

Sometimes creativity develops even if the organization does not encourage it. Such a situation can occur when individuals or groups get so interested in a new idea that they pursue it even though the company may not be formally willing to commit resources at that time. **Skunkworks** are informal groups of people that develop innovations that are outside the formal structure of the organization.[50] These groups may have little or no funds to work with, and are usually made up of people from different parts of the organization. The participants may be willing to work evenings and weekends without reward because they believe so strongly in the product idea they are working on. Skunkworks have been responsible for some notable new products, including IBM's first personal computer and 3M's Post-it notes.[51] As skunkworks become more formalized and recognized within organizations, they are typically renamed *new venture units*. But their goal remains the same—to develop new product or service ideas.

skunkworks

MEETING THE CHALLENGE

MAKE A DECISION NOW!

The Management Challenge illustrates the belief that "a quick decision is better than a slow decision." This notion is evident in many organizations. McGlothin is trying to force Chakalas to come up with a solution to a problem whose cause is not understood. If you refer to Figure 6-4, it is evident that McGlothin is completely bypassing the problem analysis phase of the decision-making process. In particular, he has totally ignored step 3—"describe deviation specifically." He has noticed a deviation from standard (i.e., maintenance costs are up by 20 percent), but with no additional information he has concluded that the drivers are at fault.

The pressure that McGlothin is putting on Chakalas may result in a solution to a problem that doesn't exist. It is quite possible, for example, that the standard is no longer reasonable and attainable. If the standard is changed, the deviation will disappear and no problem will exist. But McGlothin's conviction that Chakalas must "do something" may lead to a failure to examine the standard.

Why might the standard no longer be reasonable? For one, maintenance costs may have risen simply because the trucks are delivering to more locations and are therefore covering more kilometres than before. If the company wants to sell more newspapers, they must set a higher standard for maintenance costs. Another reason may be that the truck fleet is simply getting old and increased maintenance expenditures are unavoidable. In either case, concluding that the drivers are responsible for rising costs is indefensible.

Chakalas needs to be given time to gather additional information before he can decide what is causing the problem. Of course, a major obstacle to this neat, rational solution exists—McGlothin wants a decision by tomorrow. How can Chakalas overcome this practical problem? He might consider by-passing McGlothin and take his concerns directly to the vice-president. However, since this strategy has risks—such as alienating McGlothin or getting no sympathy from the vice-president—it should only be tried if McGlothin remains rigid in his request for an immediate decision. To make a good decision in this case is going to require some creative thinking on Chakalas' part. One promising strategy is for Chakalas to appeal to McGlothin's concern for his image with the vice-president. Chakalas could point out that a hasty decision will make both Chakalas and McGlothin look bad. He could also ask for a couple of days in which to discover the real cause of the problem. Once the cause is determined, they could both go to the vice-president with a well-reasoned proposal for solving the problem. McGlothin could then take credit for effectively solving the maintenance cost problem. If the vice-president is a good manager, he will be more impressed with a thorough analysis of the problem than he will with a quick solution to the wrong problem. The implementation phase could then begin. ▲

SUMMARY

Decision making is the process of selecting from among various alternatives a course of action that will deal with a crisis, solve a problem, or take advantage of an opportunity. Crisis decisions are made when a major disruptive event occurs that demands management's immediate attention. Problem decisions are made when actual performance does not match what was planned. Opportunity decisions are made when managers decide to improve existing work, or when they take on new initiatives, even when no problem exists.

Programmed decisions are those for which a standard procedure exists for making the decision; no standard procedure exists for nonprogrammed decisions. When making decisions, managers encounter three basic situations—certainty, risk, and uncertainty. Each of these situations requires a different approach to decision making.

The rational model shows managers how they should make decisions; it breaks the decision-making process into three phases: (1) the problem analysis phase—determining exactly what the problem is; (2) the decision-making phase—deciding how to resolve the problem; and (3) the implementation phase—putting the chosen solution into practice. The bounded rationality model assumes that managers cope with complex problems by satisficing (choosing the first acceptable alternative that comes along) rather than searching for the ideal solution. The political model assumes that decisions are made in an organizational setting where individuals are influenced by power, status, and economic considerations when they make decisions. The garbage can model views organizations as extremely complicated places where decision makers, problems, and solutions are all in flux. Decisions are made when these three factors come together in a fortuitous way.

Some managers have no problem making a decision to get involved in a certain project, but they may stick to the chosen course of action long after it has become unprofitable or ineffective. Managers may become overcommitted to a decision because they are reluctant to admit they made a mistake, because they fear their career will be harmed if the project fails, or because they believe that the current difficulties with the project can be overcome. The most obvious way of avoiding overcommitment is to set specific goals ahead of time that deal with how much time and money will be spent on a project. When the limit is reached, the project should be dropped.

Many decision-making techniques are available to help managers make decisions. Decision matrices are useful whenever a choice is to be made between alternatives that have multiple characteristics which must be weighted and valued. Decision trees can be used when payoffs can be quantified and probabilities can be stated with some confidence. Brainstorming is an idea-generating technique in which people suggest alternatives without regard to their feasibility in a nonevaluative environment. The Delphi technique uses a series of questionnaires to get a consensus from experts on a specific research question. Nominal grouping is a technique designed to get equal contribution from group members in solving a problem. It involves listing all potential solutions and having the group vote on those it prefers. Dialectical inquiry deliberately introduces conflict into group decision making so that opposing views are seriously considered.

In organizations, both individuals and groups make decisions. Group decisions are generally of higher quality than those made by the average group member, but lower than those of the best member. Members of an organization are more satisfied with decisions they participated in than with those imposed on them, but group decisions take more time than those made by individuals working alone.

Creativity means developing new and useful ideas, while innovation focuses on putting the new ideas into practice. Creative individuals tend to be nonconformists, suspicious of authority, and very persistent in search of solutions to problems. Organizations can encourage creative decision making by giving employees incentives to make creative decisions, setting realistic deadlines for creative projects, and encouraging interaction among functional departments within the organization.

KEY TERMS

decision making (p. 153)
problem solving (p. 153)
crisis decisions (p. 154)
problem decisions (p. 154)
opportunity decisions (p. 154)
programmed decisions (p. 154)
nonprogrammed decisions (p. 154)
certainty (p. 156)
risk (p. 156)
objective probabilities (p. 157)
subjective probabilities (p. 157)
uncertainty (p. 157)
rational model (p. 157)
problem analysis phase (p. 157)
decision-making phase (p. 160)
implementation phase (p. 161)
bounded rationality model (p. 162)
satisficing (p. 162)
escalation of commitment (p. 163)
political model (p. 164)
garbage can model (p. 164)
decision matrix (p. 165)
decision trees (p. 166)
expected value (p. 167)
brainstorming (p. 167)
electronic brainstorming (p. 168)
Delphi technique (p. 168)
nominal grouping (p. 169)
dialectical inquiry (p. 169)
social loafing (p. 171)
stepladder technique (p. 171)
creativity (p. 171)
innovation (p. 171)
skunkworks (p. 173)

REVIEW QUESTIONS

1. Define decision making and differentiate it from problem solving.
2. What factors must be present before a decision to a problem can be made?
3. How do crises, problems, and opportunities differ? Give an example of each.
4. What is the distinction between programmed and nonprogrammed decisions?
5. How are certainty, risk, and uncertainty different?
6. What are the major phases in the rational model of decision making? What is the main goal in each phase?
7. How are the decision matrix and decision tree techniques different? Under what conditions should each be used?
8. What is brainstorming? What are its strong and weak points?
9. Describe the similarities and differences between brainstorming, nominal grouping, and the Delphi technique.
10. What are the advantages of group decision making? What are the disadvantages?

DISCUSSION QUESTIONS

1. "Decision making is the essence of the manager's job." Do you agree? Why or why not?
2. "Since groups make better decisions than individuals, organizations should require decision making to be done on a group basis." Do you agree or disagree with this statement? Explain your reasoning.
3. Pick one of the decision-making techniques described in the chapter and explain how it could improve your own decision making.
4. Under what conditions might a manager decide not to resolve a problem that he or she is facing? Can this type of behaviour be rational?
5. What problem in group decision making is nominal grouping designed to overcome?
6. How are the bounded rationality model and the political model similar? How are they different?
7. What is creativity? Why is it important to organizations?

EXERCISES

1. From your own experience describe three decisions you recently made—one under a condition of certainty, one under risk, and one under uncertainty.
2. Describe three programmed and three nonprogrammed decisions you made during the last week. What basis did you use to classify the decisions as programmed or nonprogrammed?
3. List five decisions that you made today. Did you consciously use some sort of procedure for making them, or did you just make them? Why did you use the approach you used?
4. Consider a decision you made recently. Is the process you used consistent with the model of decision making presented in Figure 6-4? Identify specific points of agreement and disagreement. In those cases where the process was not followed, speculate on *why* it wasn't followed.
5. Write out the facts that exist in an important decision that you are currently facing (e.g., which job to take, which car to buy, which courses to take, etc.). Review the decision-making techniques presented in the chapter, and decide which one is appropriate for your problem. Use the technique to solve your problem. What strengths and weaknesses did the technique have?

MANAGEMENT ON LOCATION

CASE 6-1
A TEXTBOOK CASE OF DECISION MAKING

During the last two decades major changes have been evident in the Canadian market for university textbooks. In the late 1960s, when Canadian business schools began their rapid expansion, U.S. texts were used in almost all courses. By the mid-1970s, strong pressures were beginning to emerge for texts with more Canadian content. Publishers therefore began to contract with Canadian professors to "Canadianize" U.S. texts. This involved rewriting sections of the U.S. text which did not accurately reflect the Canadian business environment, adding new material which described how Canadian business operated, and developing Canadian examples and case studies. By the mid-1980s, these "Canadianizations" dominated the market for business school textbooks.

By the late 1980s, however, new competitive pressures were evident. Most texts were now two colour (i.e., one colour in addition to black-and-white). As well, accompanying materials, like computerized test banks, instructor's manuals, and colour transparencies were available. In 1989, a full-colour marketing book hit the market, and achieved a substantial market share.

These facts were all very relevant for John Adams, a professor of management at a major Canadian business school. Besides teaching, research, and university service work, he is actively involved in "Canadianizing" textbooks. The time has come to revise one of the books Adams has written (the normal revision cycle is three years). In discussions with his editor, Julie Mears, Adams discovered that she wanted him to think about doing a completely new Canadian book from scratch instead of simply revising the Canadianization. She felt that the next step in the evolution of the Canadian market was the development of texts that were completely Canadian, not just Canadianizations. She noted that there was some dissatisfaction with Canadianizations, and she felt that a new Canadian book would be more competitive.

As an inducement, she offered to do a first-rate production job on the book, including making it a full-colour text. She also indicated that Adams would get three times the royalty rate on a new Canadian book than he was currently getting on his Canadianization.

Like most people, Adams was intrigued by the prospect of making more money, but he also knew that writing a book was a monumental undertaking. He would have to do considerable background research before starting to write, and then actually get the material down on paper in such a way that it made sense to students. He knew that the finished manuscript would be about 1200 pages long, and even when that was completed, much work remained. After submitting the manuscript, he would have to proofread galleys, write permission letters for material he wanted to include in the book, and work on the instructor's manual and the test bank. All of this would take at least 500 hours for a Canadianization and roughly triple that time for a new Canadian book. Given all this, Adams was concerned about how well a new Canadian book would sell. He expressed these concerns to Mears in the following conversation:

Adams: I'm really interested in this idea, but the time involvement concerns me. I think I'd like to get a co-author to do

• • •

MANAGEMENT ON LOCATION

one-third of the work and I'll do two-thirds. I just don't have time to do the whole thing.

Mears: That's fine with me.

Adams: I'm also concerned about your assumption that a new book will do well. What level of sales do you project for a new Canadian book?

Mears: Our marketing research people estimate that a new Canadian book would sell 8000 units each year. There are $6 in royalties on each copy, so if you do two-thirds of the work, you'll get two-thirds of $6.00, or $4.00. If the book sells 8000 units, that means $32 000 per year for you in royalties.

Adams: Well, that sounds good, but there is no guarantee that the book will sell 8000 units per year. And, as you know, in the last two years there have been two new Canadian books in this field and both of them flopped.

Mears: I know, but there are good reasons for both of those failures. We won't have those problems.

Adams: Let's explore some other alternatives. I assume that I could simply revise the two-colour Canadianization that I'm currently involved in. That was, after all, the basis on which our conversation started.

Mears: Yes, you can do that. But I'm concerned that a revised Canadianization won't compete as effectively with other publishers in this market. If the revised Canadianization doesn't sell at least 5500 copies per year, then we won't revise it again. If it sells at least 5500 copies per year, then we will put out another edition in three years.

Adams: If I don't do the new Canadian book, will you sign a contract with someone else to do it?

Mears: Well, as publishers we have to think of our long-term strategic position in the market. If you aren't interested in writing a Canadian book, we will have to deal with someone else because we simply must have a purely Canadian book to compete. But look at this positively. I'm approaching you first because I think you can do a good job on a new Canadian book. It's like a manager being offered a promotion. You either "move up or move out."

Adams: How about letting me do a revision of the Canadianization and you make it a full-colour book instead of just two-colour so it sells better?

Mears: Well, that's a possibility. When you're thinking about that, keep in mind that a full-colour book—whether its a new Canadian book or a Canadianization—must sell very well in order for us to revise it after its first three years. If it doesn't sell 8000 units per year, we can't afford to revise it. I think a new Canadian full-colour book is more likely to sell 8000 units per year than a full-colour Canadianization.

Adams: But whether I do a new full-colour Canadian book or a full-colour Canadianization, it will have to sell very well to make it to another edition. That's taking a big risk, isn't it? Wouldn't I be better off going with a revised two-colour Canadianization because it only needs to sell 5500 to go into another edition?

Mears: Well, not really. If you remain with your two-colour Canadianization, you're taking a risk that we will have to drop the book within three years because it can't compete.

Later, Adams reflected on his rather complicated conversation with Mears and decided he had to systematically analyze his options. Before doing so, he made the following assumptions that were important for his decision:

1. A full-colour text is likely to sell more than a black-and-white or two-colour text, other things being equal. This is because the visual appearance is more attractive to those who make the decision to adopt the text (i.e., the professors).
2. There are three basic levels of annual demand that are possible: high (8000 units), moderate (5500 units), and low (3000 units).
3. The publisher must sell 8000 units per year of a full-colour book (Canadianization or new book) or it will not go into a second edition. A two-colour book will go into a subsequent edition if it sells at least 5500 copies per year.
4. The new Canadian full-colour book would have a 10 percent chance of selling 8000 units, but it also might sell only moderately well (0.6), and it could even do poorly (0.3).
5. A full-colour Canadianization would have a slightly better chance of high volume (0.2) because the book already has a track record of good sales in the marketplace. It would have a 70 percent chance of moderate volume, and a 10 percent chance of poor sales.
6. A two-colour Canadianization would have no chance of selling 8000 units, a 60 percent chance of selling 5500 units, and a 40 percent chance of selling only 3000 units.
7. Adams has decided that his time is worth $50 per hour, and that his time frame for considering revenues is six years into the future (i.e., two revision cycles of three years each).

As he thought about all these numbers, John Adams wondered what he should do. ▲

QUESTIONS

1. How many alternatives are open to John Adams?
2. Draw a decision tree which reflects the information that is available in this problem.
3. What should John Adams do (assuming that expected value is his decision criterion)?

MANAGEMENT ON LOCATION

CASE 6-2
WHO SHOULD GET THE JOB?

El-Tech Ltd. is involved in the manufacture and sale of four main lines of industrial and consumer products: (1) heavy equipment, (2) consumer appliances, (3) electronics, and (4) chemical products. Sales in these four divisions are roughly equal, but profits vary widely. The most profitable division is chemical products, followed (in order) by heavy equipment, consumer appliances, and electronics. Overall, the firm is doing well. Last year, sales were the fourth largest in the company's history, and its net profits were the third largest.

Recently, the president announced that he will retire in six months. The Board of Directors of El-Tech has decided to replace the retiring president with one of the four internal candidates who currently head the major divisions. The board sees no pressing problems or crises in the company at this time, but it would like to see more attention paid to corporate strategy so that the firm will not be surprised by rapid developments in the fields in which they are now competing.

The four candidates are as follows:

Paul Cloutier (Chemical Products Division)—Paul's division is one big happy family. Turnover, spoilage, absenteeism, and grievances are the lowest in the company. Various groups of managers in Paul's division meet on Friday afternoons for a social time, and Paul feels that this is important in building a good team spirit among his people. Other executives accuse Paul of being unduly extravagent with his workers. To support their argument, they point to the fact that his division regularly runs up the largest employee relations bills in the company. As well, there is concern that Paul really doesn't have a long-range plan for his division, but rather is simply following the path of least resistance. The argument continues that Paul is very paternalistic in the treatment of his subordinates, and that they could not replace him if he moved up. Paul responds to these criticisms by saying that the "acid test" of good management is profitability. He notes that his division has contributed more profit to the overall firm in the last five years than any other division.

Mario Tuzi (Electronics Division)—Mario has the reputation of being El-Tech's greatest creative thinker. His ideas have resulted in some lucrative patents for the firm, and this has, on occasion, resulted in some spectacular profits in his division. But Mario is also stubborn. It's difficult to talk him out of a project once he has his mind set on it. In the past, several large losses have been incurred by Mario's division as he doggedly pursued projects that never quite panned out. Mario says that creative genius must not be stifled because a company will reap tremendous benefits from it. Mario argues that without the proper emphasis on creativity—and the new products and patents that result from it—El-Tech cannot hope to survive in an increasingly competitive environment. He argues that a top executive's main job is to "light a fire" under subordinates so that they will enthusiastically pursue those things which will ensure a steady stream of new products emerges. This will contribute to the firm's overall profitability and long-run survival.

Marilyn Byars (Consumer Appliances)—Marilyn brings out the best in her subordinates. An unusually large proportion of them have been promoted to other jobs in the organization. But there are concerns that Marilyn leans too heavily on the opinions of her subordinates and does not have enough ideas of her own. On several occasions, crucial deadlines weren't met because Marilyn was unable to get her subordinates to reach a consensus on a controversial question in the time allotted. Marilyn is of the view that disagreements among subordinates must be ironed out before major decisions are made. She notes that the Japanese management system works this way, and she points out that it has been extremely successful. She feels that if Canadian firms do not start moving in this direction, they will be unable to compete in the international market. Marilyn feels that a top executive does not need to know much about the technical details of her subordinates jobs. Rather, she argues, she should spend most of her time helping her subordinates develop a consensus on important issues. She also feels that she is responsible for ensuring that subordinates in her division see the "big picture" of where the division is going.

Serge Lapointe (Industrial Heavy Equipment)—Serge is extremely competent and hard working, and the people in his division seem to have a clearer conception of their mission and strategy than people in the other divisions. Serge continually pursues the most advanced technology available, and his division has the lowest capital cost per unit of output of any division in the firm. He stresses the importance of systematic thinking in every aspect of his division's work. Some people feel that he is too rigid in his thinking, and is too much like an old-fashioned scientific manager in the Frederick Taylor vein. They also say he is too eager to use formulas in decision making (e.g., he refuses to hire prospective managers who fail a test he devised, even if they make a favourable impression on everyone who interviews them). Serge also has difficulty with subordinates who are

• • •

less capable than he is. The result is chronic turnover among his immediate staff. Some people also question Serge's motives. On several occasions, he has stepped on people's toes in order to improve his own status in the company. Serge says that anyone who wants to be a top manager has to be willing to make tough decisions, and these decisions will sometimes hurt other people's feelings. He points to his division's high profitability (second overall) as proof that his management ideas are sound. ▲

QUESTION

1. Indicate which individual you would recommend for promotion to the presidency. Defend your answer. Include in your defence a description of the process you used to make the decision.

CASE 6-3
WHAT'S THE PROBLEM?

Laidlaw Furniture began operations in 1971 as a custom manufacturer of furniture for the mass consumer market. The company has grown steadily, and in 1993 had sales revenue of $80 million and net profits of $4.6 million. This Calgary-based company now manufactures wood, plastic, and steel furniture in a factory that runs three separate production lines. Recently, due to the company's strong growth, a fairly large number of new production employees have been added.

Like most companies, as Laidlaw has grown, it has added a variety of departments which allow it to specialize its activities and therefore perform at a higher level of efficiency. One of the departments that was added in 1993 was an Information Systems Department. The goal of this department is to provide management with better, faster, and more accurate information about the market and company operations so that top management can make more timely and effective decisions. One of the key activities of this department was the development of a computerized order system including the ordering forms which form an integral part of it.

The company's products are sold through retailers across Canada such as department stores (like The Bay), specialty stores (like Furniture Mart) and warehouse clubs (like Costco). Laidlaw classifies retailers as "Class 1" (high sales volume), "Class 2" (moderate sales volume), or "Class 3" (low sales volume). The company's marketing strategy involves selective distribution, i.e., only a small number of retailers in a given geographical area are licensed to sell Laidlaw's products.

As part of this selective distribution deal, the retailers have agreed to allow Laidlaw to ship them up to 12-weeks supply of furniture products. This is often done just before the company embarks on a promotional program, or just before it intends to raise prices. Such a shipment was made to many retailers in March 1993 just prior to the start of a promotional program.

For Class 1 and 2 retailers, Laidlaw makes twice-a-month deliveries to its retailers from one of its three warehouses. For Class 3 retailers, the company uses an independent wholesaler who takes orders and delivers furniture once every two months. Recently, in an attempt to be more responsive to Class 1 retailers, Laidlaw started delivering products once a week. (All retailers, of course, want reliable deliveries from the company, irrespective of how often deliveries are made.)

In September, 1993 the company began receiving complaints from some retailers that the specific pieces of furniture they ordered were out of stock at Laidlaw's warehouses. By the middle of October, the number of complaints had increased dramatically. Some individuals in the distribution department recalled that a similar problem happened about eight years ago when Laidlaw had only one warehouse. ▲

QUESTIONS

1. Refer back to Figure 6-4 on p. 158. Indicate how each of the four steps in the "problem analysis" phase of the decision-making model relate to this problem.
2. Assume for a moment that you have been given the responsibility for determining the cause of this problem. Develop a list of questions that you would ask in order to demonstrate to your boss that you have done a good job on step 3 of the problem analysis phase (describing the deviation specifically).

COMPREHENSIVE CASES

PART II

CASE II-1
THE HEAD SHOPPE

Peter Mahoney had become director of operations of The Head Shoppe Limited in 1984. By early 1990, The Head Shoppe was the largest chain of hairstyling salons in the Canadian Maritime provinces, with salons in six major urban centres in Nova Scotia and New Brunswick and annual sales approaching $6 million. The industry had matured, but unlike most of its competitors, The Head Shoppe was enjoying unprecedented sales and profits. The company had implemented a state-of-the-art computerized accounting system in 1989, with a terminal in each salon, making it a leader of the industry nationally. The terms of the contract with the computer software designer included an option to acquire exclusive Canadian distribution rights for this system and for others to be developed for other types of retail operations. The decision on whether the option would be exercised had to be made by March 31, 1990, six weeks hence. Mahoney knew that the software package was the best available in the hairstyling field, and preliminary research indicated that the designer's packages in other fields were also superior. He was convinced that, if properly marketed, distribution of these products could be very profitable. He also knew that the decision would have major strategic implications for The Head Shoppe.

THE COMPANY

Wayne Drew opened the first Head Shoppe in 1968. The son of a barber, he had grown up in a small Nova Scotia town and entered his father's trade at 18. He relocated to Halifax in 1967, and started a shop in partnership with another barber. Differences between the partners led to a split within two years and left Drew as sole owner of the Head Shoppe.[1] By 1984, the chain had eight salons and a hairstyling school. However, Drew's entrepreneurial success had resulted in an operation too large for him to manage or control.

Drew hired Peter Mahoney to be director of operations in 1984. An M.B.A. graduate of Dalhousie University, Mahoney brought his energy and organizational skills to the Head Shoppe. His first task was to examine the structure of operations, with a view to improving efficiency and effectiveness and to expanding the chain. He conducted a comprehensive internal study to determine the strengths and weaknesses of the corporate structure and to examine employee attitudes (see Exhibit 1 for Executive Summary and Recommendations sections of the study's report). The findings of this study formed the basis of the Head Shoppe's organizational strategy for the following years.

The most significant outcome of the 1984 study was the development of a formalized corporate structure with input from the managers of the individual salons, and Drew and Mahoney of central office. They prepared a policy and procedures manual which defined the roles of central office and salon managers and the relationships between them. Central office retained control over all matters of overall corporate policy, including standard personnel and accounting procedures, staff and management training, advertising, and site leasing arrangements. Individual salon managers were given authority over all matters associated with day-to-day management of their salons. In addition, employee satisfaction was given a high priority: a generous employee benefits package and attractive incentives for top performers were introduced, and the basis of remuneration for virtually all hairstylists was changed from chair rental to salary plus commission.[2] As a result, the Head Shoppe's hairstylist turnover rate became the lowest in the industry.

Franchising as a mechanism for expansion was introduced in 1985. By 1990, the chain included 19 salons, 7 of which were owned by franchisee-operators, and two hairdressing schools.

STRATEGIES

From the outset, The Head Shoppe had established a reputation for being aggressive and innovative. It had led a battle with civic authorities in the late 1960s to eliminate by-laws prohibiting barber shops from operating on Saturdays. In 1972 The Head Shoppe became the first salon operator to open a hairstyling school to train men's hairstylists. However, the techniques taught were equally applicable to men's and women's hairstyling. This led to the establishment of the first "unisex" beauty salons in the Maritimes, which integrated hair and beauty services for men and women, and broadened the range of hair care services provided to men beyond the traditional "haircutting only" services of a barber shop. This, too, involved the Head Shoppe in legal battles which were fought and won.

[1] The partnership's first shop, the Golden Clipper, was opened in 1967. When the partnership ended, the other partner retained the original Golden Clipper. Within a short time, however, Drew had become owner of both names. The name "Golden Clipper" had been retained for two of the early shops, but these were treated as part of The Head Shoppe chain.

[2] These two systems of hairstylist remuneration are discussed further in the Industry section.

• • •

EXHIBIT 1 EXTRACTS FROM HEAD SHOPPE MANAGEMENT REPORT OCTOBER 30, 1984.

Executive Summary

Purpose: To collect and analyze internal data in order to measure the opinions of employees, improve the work environment, and increase the long-term productivity and profitability of the Head Shoppe and Golden Clipper Organizations.

Method: Employee Survey

Results: From our analysis of survey data for The Head Shoppe and Golden Clipper Organizations we have determined the following:

- Stylists are aware of the importance and relatedness of education to their personal growth and development as well as that of the organization.
- Stylists in general realize retail selling is an important aspect of total client service; however, they feel their present effort is not totally satisfactory and could be improved through product education.
- Staff meetings are felt to be beneficial and are presently held more frequently in wage and commission shops than in rental salons.
- Sixty-three percent of staff operate on a chair rental basis, 31 percent on wage plus commission and 6 percent on other methods of compensation such as salary.
- Money is not perceived as the most important characteristic of a hairstylist's job and diminishes rapidly in importance as income level increases.
- The importance of fringe benefits relative to one another is related to the demographic profile of the hairdressing population.
- The most important aspect of a hairstylist's occupation is job security, regardless of income level.
- Hairstylists recognize the need for more frequent encouragement and feedback from their managers on a day-to-day basis and by way of periodic performance reviews.
- Both rental and nonrental hairstylists are, with few exceptions, satisfied with their jobs despite a significant difference in average income between the two groups.
- Sixty-three percent of rental stylists would consider equal compensation on another basis.

Recommendations:

- Continue to provide top-quality education in all aspects of the hairstyling business on an ongoing basis.
- Maintain accurate salon records of names, dates, and nature of all educational shows and seminars attended by staff members for assessment purposes.
- Monitor and record, at the salon level, the retail effort being extended by individuals as well as the salon in terms of retail sales/client for the purpose of measuring and improving productivity.
- Ensure that mandatory classes in permanent waving and product knowledge are being attended, when necessary, and skills are being appropriately applied in the salon.
- Review present retail incentive plan and investigate the potential of funding educational shows and seminars through this medium.
- Conduct salon meetings between management and staff on a regular monthly basis in all locations. A brief agenda should be used accompanied with regular changes in format, and points of interest to help stimulate discussion and prevent boredom.
- As managers, recognize the importance employees place on characteristics of their jobs other than money and help to enrich their position and improve their sense of job security and motivation by being an encouraging manager.

• • •

- Try to improve job security for employees by increasing benefits when justified.
- Formulate and implement a formal performance appraisal technique to be administered on a semiannual basis for use in evaluating employee performance and determining increases in compensation, benefits and promotion to senior status.
- Evaluate and negotiate, upon request, alternate compensation with all rental stylists who request so.

Source: Report of study conducted by Peter Mahoney, 1984.

Although it served the entire market, The Head Shoppe targeted the 18 to 45 age group. This group represented the largest and most profitable segment in the geographic markets served. In targeting this segment, The Head Shoppe created and jealously guarded an image of quality, with the primary focus on hairdresser skill and customer satisfaction.

Given its target market, Head Shoppe management arbitrarily established a minimum urban population of 15 000 for centres in which it would locate a salon. By 1990, there was at least one Head Shoppe in most of the urban centres of this size in Nova Scotia and New Brunswick (see Exhibit 2 for population figures for major urban centres in Atlantic Canada). Exhibit 3 presents location and activity levels for the salons in The Head Shoppe chain as of 1989.

The Head Shoppe's innovations in the industry also included attempts to broaden the range of services offered to its clientele, by what Mahoney referred to as "fashion merchandising." However, it quickly found that related services such as manicuring and beautician services could not be provided profitably, and The Head Shoppe returned to focussing on the basic hairstyling business. The exception to this rule was the retailing of a broad range of hair care products, which represented 16 percent of total sales by 1989.

The financial management of the Head Shoppe was conservative, largely because its management anticipated that the hairdressing industry would quickly reach maturity. Use of long-term debt had been minimal, and expansion in recent years had been primarily through franchising. This, combined with a net income in excess of $200 000 in each year from 1985 to 1989, provided the solid financial base necessary for future growth (see Exhibits 4 and 5 for Financial Statements). ▲

EXHIBIT 2 POPULATIONS OF MAJOR URBAN CENTRES IN ATLANTIC CANADA.

Newfoundland	
Corner Brook	22 718
Mount Pearl	20 293
St. John's	96 215
New Brunswick	
Bathurst	14 683
Fredericton	44 722
Moncton/Riverview (combined)	71 106
Saint John (metropolitan area)	121 265
Nova Scotia	
Glace Bay	20 467
Halifax (metropolitan area)	295 990
New Glasgow/Stellarton (combined)	15 281
Sydney	28 115
Truro	12 124
Prince Edward Island	
Charlottetown	15 572

Source: 1986 Census data, Statistics Canada

• • •

EXHIBIT 3

Head Shoppe

Sales by Urban Centre
1989

Urban centre	Number of shops	Number of hairstyles done per month
Halifax, NS (metro area)	14[1]	20 100
Saint John, NB	1	950
Moncton, NB	1	1 000
New Minas, NS	1	950
New Glasgow, NS	1	1 000
Sydney, NS	2[1]	2 000

[1] Including hairstyling schools, which provided service to customers at reduced rates

Source: As reported by Peter Mahoney

EXHIBIT 4

Head Shoppe Company Limited

Statement of Income
For the period 1985 to 1989[1]
(000s)

	1985	1986	1987	1988	1989
Revenue	$3423	$3657	$3905	$4196	$4194
Direct Costs	2592	2857	3040	3364	3329
Income (Shop Operations)	831	800	865	832	865
Selling, General & Admin. Expenses	531	521	542	509	504
Income Before Tax	300	279	323	323	361
Income Taxes	80	70	81	81	90
Net Income	$220	$209	$242	$242	$271

[1] Revenue figures include franchise fees received from franchisees. Franchisees' revenues and direct costs are not included. In 1989, franchisees' revenues were $1.5 million and franchise fees received from franchisees were $75 000.
The figures presented have been disguised; relationships between items and from year to year have been preserved.

Source: Company Records

THE INDUSTRY[3]

The size of the market for hairstyling services was directly related to the size of the population. In Maritime urban centres, traditional men's barber shops and women's beauty salons had been almost totally replaced by three types of salons, virtually all of which catered to both sexes as clientele: discount salons which targeted price-conscious consumers; full-line salons which targeted the mainstream of consumers; and up-

[3] Information in this section was collected from Mahoney's 1984 comprehensive internal study, a market study conducted by the Head Shoppe Ltd. by Corporate Research Associates, Inc. in 1988, and interviews of other industry members in 1989 and 1990.

...

EXHIBIT 5

Head Shoppe Company Limited

Balance Sheet
December 31, 1989

Assets		
Current Assets		
Cash	$92 000	
Short-term Investments	94 000	
Accounts Receivable	50 000	
Inventory	149 000	
Prepaid Expenses	6 000	
Total Current Assets		$391 000
Long-term Assets		
Advance to Director	$126 000	
Real Estate Holdings	283 000	
Total Long-term Assets		409 000
Fixed Assets at Cost		
Equipment and Furnishings	$794 000	
Less Accumulated Depreciation	558 000	
Total Fixed Assets at Cost		236 000
Other Assets		
Leasehold Improvements (Net)		$134 000
Total Assets		$1 170 000
Liabilities and Shareholders' Equity		
Current Liabilities		
Accounts Payable — Trade	$101 000	
Other Payables & Actuals	81 000	
Current Portion — LTD	80 000	
Total Current Liabilities		$262 000
Long-term Debt		145 000
Shareholders' Equity		
Capital Stock	144	
Retained Earnings	762 856	
Total Shareholders' Equity		763 000
Total Liabilities and Shareholders' Equity		$1 170 000

Source: Company Records

• • •

scale salons which targeted the small minority of consumers who were extremely conscious of personal image and concerned about being on the leading edge with changes in fashion and style.[4]

The establishment of customer loyalty was the single most important key to success in all segments. The fact that location was an important factor in attracting clients had stimulated a move by hairdressing salons into urban shopping centres and suburban strip malls. All Head Shoppe salons were located in shopping centres and malls. The 1980s had begun with 95 percent of the industry being comprised of single-salon independent operations, but there had been a strong move toward consolidation into chains which brought with it economies of scale and professional management. It was anticipated that by 1995, 85 percent of hairstyling salons in the region would be chain members.

The most profitable segment of The Head Shoppe's target market, the 18 to 45 years age group, representing 60 percent of the total population, tended to be conscious of style and fashion, and had the shortest cycle for repeat business.[5] Three-quarters of the population in this age bracket were regular users of salon service in the full-line salon category. Competition was strong in this segment and was expected to intensify even further over the next five years. As a result, a shake-out was expected to occur, leaving only the well-managed salons that provided high-quality service to the client. Criteria used by clientele in selecting a hairstyling salon are presented in Exhibit 6.

One problem area faced by the industry was an ongoing shortage of qualified hairstylists. This was largely due to the low prestige associated with the profession and a relatively low average income level compared to other professions. Although a top hairstylist could gross as much as $70 000 per year, many earned little more than the minimum wage. Most had a high school education or less, plus training in a hairstyling school. Historically, barbers and hairdressers who did not own their own shop paid a fixed amount to the shop owner for rental of a chair and were paid directly by their clientele. In the years after 1985, though, a trend toward regular employee status, with payment on a salary plus commission basis, had begun.[6] No significant change in the attractiveness of the profession was anticipated for the foreseeable future, and the supply of qualified hairstylists was expected to continue to lag behind demand.

STRATEGIC OPTIONS

Strategic options for the future under consideration at The Head Shoppe included further geographic expansion, backward integration and diversification out of the industry.

1. Geographic Expansion

Geographic expansion had a strong appeal for Peter Mahoney. The Head Shoppe had been very successful in

EXHIBIT 6 FACTORS CONSIDERED IN SELECTION OF A HAIRSTYLING SALON.

Rank		Importance[1]
1	Skill/Experience of Hairstylist	96
2	Convenience of Location	45
3	Specific Hairstylist	44
4	Price	35
5	Overall Quality of Service	20
6	Cut	18
7	Friendliness of Staff	14

[1] — 100 point scale

Source: Adapted from a market study of the target market in the Halifax metro area, conducted for the Head Shoppe Ltd. by Corporate Research Associates, Inc., in 1988.

[4] A second chain, TopCuts, based in Newfoundland, rivalled The Head Shoppe's size in the Maritimes, but it targeted the price-conscious segment. The Head Shoppe had established one upscale salon, called the Estetica Hair and Beauty Clinic, in the new upscale Spring Garden Place mall in Halifax.

[5] The averge cycle in this segment was slightly less than six weeks. In other segments it ranged as high as three months. The average client in the 18 to 45 category spent from $20 to $30 per month on hair care, including retail products. Three quarters had their hair shampooed and professionally dried when having it cut.

[6] The Head Shoppe had established this trend for the industry. It benefited junior stylists by ensuring a fixed minimum control over operations. It also reduced the likelihood of Head Shoppe hairstylists moving to a competing shop, and taking their clients with them. Senior hairstylists with the Head Shoppe were given the option of operating on a chair rental basis, though few did so.

• • •

developing the existing chain of shops. Management had proven capable, key success factors in the industry had been identified, and distinctive competencies had been developed. However, Mahoney felt that further geographic expansion would necessitate going outside the Maritimes. The market in large urban centres in the region appeared to be saturated and shops in smaller centres could not be expected to produce the level of return necessary to make them attractive. In addition, qualified hairstylists in the region were already in short supply in spite of the fact that The Head Shoppe operated two schools. Although Mahoney was confident about the Head Shoppe's ability to compete in markets outside the region, this would entail competing head-on with chains targeting the same market segment. Further, qualified hairstylists elsewhere were in even shorter supply than in the Maritimes.[7]

2. Backward Integration

Backward integration, (i.e., becoming one's own supplier), appeared to be worthy of serious consideration. The Head Shoppe had already done this with regard to the training of hairstylists, through its establishment of two hairstyling schools. Retail sales of hair care products had increased from 7 percent of total sales in 1984 to 16 percent in 1989 (the industry average was 10 percent of total sales). Average markup was one third of retail price. As Mahoney jokingly pointed out, from a management perspective hair care products had three advantages over hairstylists: "the margin is better, there isn't a supply problem, and they don't talk back!" Retail product sales had become a major new emphasis in the industry and dramatic growth was anticipated for the future. Product lines were distributed through very few supply companies, and each line was exclusively available through only one supplier. Given that product loyalty among consumers was high, having the popular lines would be the key to success. Suppliers worked on a markup of 40 percent of their selling price, making the distribution business even more attractive. Maritime Beauty Products, a privately owned company, was the biggest supplier of hair care products in the region, with 35 percent of the market. It carried most of the lines that The Head Shoppe retailed to its clients, and Mahoney estimated that The Head Shoppe represented about 18 percent of Maritime Beauty Products' sales. The Head Shoppe had always used, and retailed, Maritime Beauty Products' lines and had encouraged its clients to use them. Maritime Beauty Products had exclusive distribution rights for these product lines, which would make it very difficult for The Head Shoppe to secure distribution rights. Also, relations between The Head Shoppe and Maritime Beauty Products had always been extremely good. In fact, Wayne Drew and the owner of Maritime Beauty Products were close friends.

3. Diversification

The third strategic option for The Head Shoppe was diversification out of the hairstyling industry. The most attractive possibility on this front, in Mahoney's view, lay in the introduction of retail operating systems for computers.

THE SOFTWARE PROPOSAL

The Head Shoppe had successfully introduced a computerized accounting system early in 1989, with a terminal in each salon. By the end of 1989, the system had already begun to return benefits in terms of improved record-keeping, reduced staff time required for accounting, employee satisfaction, and indications that the tracking of clients it allowed was improving repeat business (see Exhibit 7 for a summary of highlights from the system designer's promotional materials). The contract between The Head Shoppe and the designer of the system included an option for The Head Shoppe to become the exclusive Canadian distributor for the system and for similar systems to be designed for other segments of the retailing industry. Less than 1 percent of hairstyling salons in Canada had computerized accounting systems and Mahoney suspected the same was true of other types of retailing operations. Preliminary research showed that arrangements could be made with computer equipment suppliers to provide discounts to system purchasers who lacked the hardware necessary to implement the system, and that the net return to The Head Shoppe would be approximately $2500 per system sold, even when allowance was made for the provision of training and trouble-shooting services.

Mahoney was convinced that The Head Shoppe could enter the software systems distribution business profitably. It had successfully implemented the software system in its own operations, but its experience, expertise and success was limited to the hairdressing industry.

The one thing that was clear to Mahoney was that maintaining the status quo was out of the question: The Head Shoppe was a growth company, and must continue to be. A strategy had to be developed for the future, and a decision on whether to take up the computer system option had to be made. ▲

[7] The characteristics of the industry in the Maritimes were representative of those in the rest of Canada, except other regions had large established chains targeting the full-line segment (although none were significantly larger than the Head Shoppe), a greater shortage of qualified hairstylists, and a larger overall market size.

EXHIBIT 7 SUMMARIZED HIGHLIGHTS FROM SOFTWARE SYSTEM DESIGNER'S PROMOTION MATERIALS.

Industry experts consider the system to be 5 years ahead of competing systems, citing six dimensions on which it is the industry leader.

Minimum staff time required to make inputs and secure reports
- Fast "checkout screens," re client checkout after service
- One or more letters of client's name is enough to display entire client record
- Immediate availability of reports

User friendliness; Ease of learning and operation
- Any operator can learn one-finger operation
- Simple error reports (e.g., "printer out of paper")
- Consistency of function key utilization
- Pop-up "help" windows present codes re entries to be made

Flexibility
- Can run on MS-DOS, Xenis, and Unix operating systems
- Software alone, or software and hardware available
- Customized, on-site fitting of programs for applications desired, with reprogramming
- Storage of dates and data to allow compilation of reports whenever desired for whatever period desired
- Reporting available on a wide variety of items (e.g., payroll, sales, trends, client address, client birthdate)

Error Prevention
- Prevention of double entry of single transaction
- "Are you sure?" query before final entry
- Checks for "reasonability" of entries (e.g., length, alpha-numeric)

Marketing Applications
- Listing of clients in 25 different categories (e.g., service used, sex)
- Listing of clients soon due for repeat service (with phone number/address) and/or automatic preparation of letters and address labels
- Detail of client likes and dislikes, allergies, etc.

Quality and Reliability
- Highly qualified programming/development team (Ph.D's): state-of-the-art system design and updating
- Utilities to assist users with unforeseen problems
- Toll Free "800" support lines, available 7 days a week
- Simple, easy to read User Manuals.

Source: Software System Designer's Promotional Materials

QUESTIONS

1. Analyze the industry and competitive conditions for The Head Shoppe in terms of:
   (a) rivalry among competing sellers
   (b) availability of substitutes
   (c) availability of suppliers
   (d) characteristics of buyers
   (e) possibility of new entrants.
2. What is your assessment of The Head Shoppe's competitive position?
3. What are the strategic options available to The Head Shoppe?

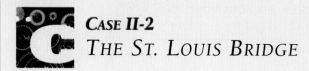

CASE II-2
THE ST. LOUIS BRIDGE

PART A
AN INCIDENT AT THE ST. LOUIS BRIDGE

John Black, president of the St. Lawrence Seaway Authority (SLSA), replaced the phone in its cradle and reflected that if he did not have enough on his plate before the call from his Eastern Region, he certainly had enough now.

The *Seawise Jewel*, a 13 000 ton cargo ship out of Bombay, India, had rammed the southern end of the St. Louis Bridge near Montreal.[1] The bridge, jointly operated by SLSA and Canadian National Railways (CN), was extensively damaged. Among other things, the huge moveable centre span of the bridge was jammed in the up position, blocking one of only three east-west rail links to southern Quebec. Luckily, no one was injured when an oil tanker on the southern approach to the bridge was toppled into the water but oil was now leaking out of the sunken truck and moving downstream. An eastbound train was stalled on the north end of the bridge and the *Seawise Jewel* blocked movement through the Seaway.

The accident could not have occurred at a worse time. It was late November and ships like the *Seawise Jewel* were racing for the open sea before freezeup. If that was not enough, Seaway pilots were about to go on strike to back demands for wage parity with U.S. pilots. But Black took satisfaction from the fact that his experienced organization had so far responded well to the crisis. Seaway Beauharnois, a control centre, quickly

ANNEX A DIAGRAM OF THE ACCIDENT SITE.

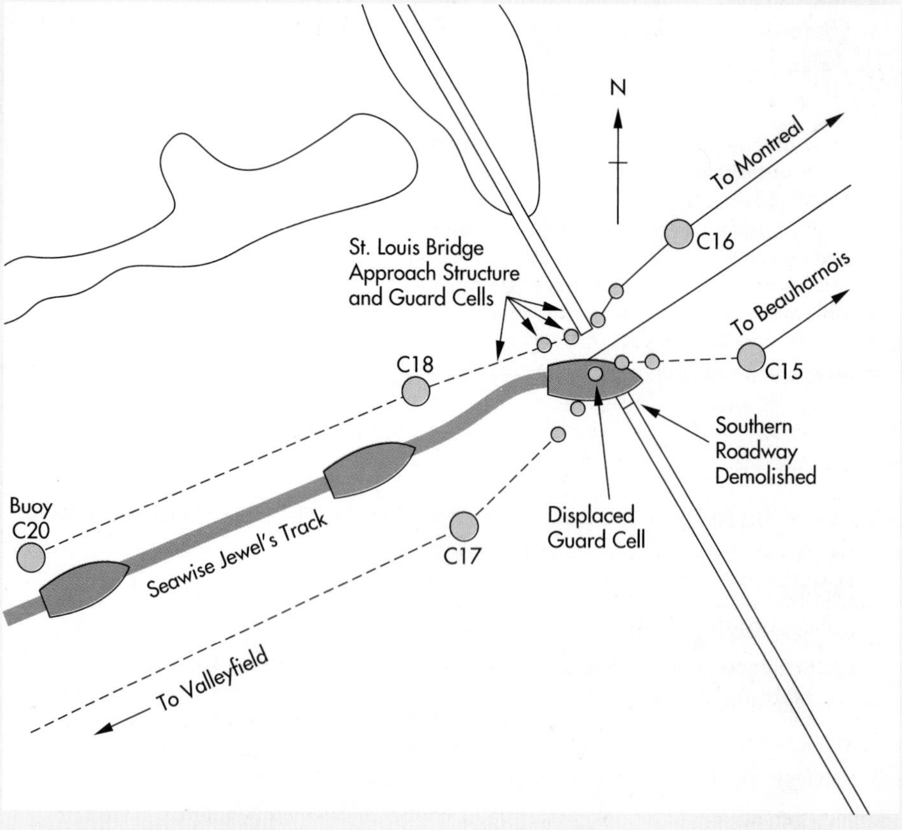

[1] Annex A is a map of the site.

suspended all traffic in the waterway, instructing ships to seek emergency anchorages. CN authorities had been notified to reroute train traffic away from the bridge and the Coast Guard had been warned to initiate and manage pollution countermeasures. At the same time, SLSA experts were dispatched to assess the situation at the bridge.

There was the usual pressure from the shipping community to keep the Seaway open to the last possible minute. In the past, the Dominion Marine Association had appealed to the Minister and had frequently been able to keep the waterway open until Christmas, even though it really should have been shut down several weeks before that.

Black was a 54-year-old civil engineer whose 33-year career had been spent in the Seaway. He had run the old Beauharnois lock system before the Seaway had been developed and had watched in fascination as the huge system was put in place. In the years since 1970 he had run both the Seaway's Western Region and the Welland Canal, and the Eastern Region with its series of locks from Kingston to Montreal.

A natural leader, Black had managed many crises in the past and often felt he was most comfortable when in coveralls at the scene of an incident. Black had been president for two years and felt he was only now getting the feel of the Ottawa environment. It was far removed from the operational world that he knew so well. Nothing in his previous jobs could have prepared him for the subtleties of serving the Minister, or coping with the central agencies and the new parliamentary committee system.[2] He felt fortunate that the Seaway, a Crown corporation, was relatively isolated from political pressures.

Annex B

Department of Transport and The St. Lawrence Seaway Authority

Legal Context

Federal responsibility for marine transportation is derived from the Canadian Act. It includes coordination and regulation to ensure the safety and efficiency of navigation, shipping, ferries, railways and canals. This responsibility is exercised through the Department of Transport.

The St. Lawrence Seaway Authority is found within the vote structure of DOT's Marine Transportation Program. This program is headed by an Assistant Deputy Minister. The Seaway president liaises with this officer for operational purposes but maintains an "arm's length" relationship.

The Seaway has its own enabling legislation, The St. Lawrence Seaway Authority Act, under which the president reports to the Minister of Transport.

Black envied his vice-president of the Eastern Region in St. Lambert, who would be in charge of the operational response to the crisis. At least he would be able to assess the physical evidence and establish a plan of action to solve a problem. By contrast, Black sometimes felt he was trying to swim upstream through quicksand.[3,4]

Annex C

The St. Lawrence Seaway Authority Organizational Structure and Key Issues

The formal organizational responsibilities and authority of the position of president of the Seaway are considerable. The position is an order-in-council appointment. In his capacity as the chief executive officer of the SLSA, the president is charged with the general direction and control of the corporation. In 1984, the president controlled an operating budget of $62.71 million, and a staff of about 1200.

The Seaway delivers one large program; moving ships between Montreal and Lake Erie. The SLSA's strategic goals are financial and operational: to operate the system to ensure financial self-sufficiency, and to maximize operational capacity.

The functions include the administration of a toll structure, regulation of marine traffic, and development of by-laws and policies. The president is also involved in the management of the Seaway International Bridge Corporation, and is a director of the Jacques Cartier, Champlain, and Thousand Island Bridge Authorities.

The decision-making system within the Seaway works through a classic hierarchy on two levels. On the first, the Seaway Executive Committee consists of branch heads. This committee provides policy. On the higher level, all key corporate and operational decisions are taken by the "Authority" consisting of the president, a vice-president, and a member.

There are six main areas where key decisions are taken:

1. to open or close the Seaway system;
2. to increase or decrease the toll structure;
3. to reduce the workforce;
4. labour relations;
5. productivity, and;
6. stakeholder relationships.

Black was scheduled to have lunch today with Archer MacLean, a nationally syndicated columnist with a Toronto daily. By coincidence, MacLean was researching a document entitled "Vulnerability of Bridges in Canadian Waters" for a series of articles he was writing on Canada's aging

[2] Annex B describes the legal context of the SLSA.

[3] Annex C describes the SLSA's organizational structure and identifies several key issues.

[4] Annex D provides an organizational chart.

transportation system. Black suspected MacLean would try to show the negative effects of planned government cutbacks on safety. The study, published in 1982, gave the St. Louis Bridge a vulnerability rate of seven out of a possible ten.

Despite the crisis, Black was hesitant about cancelling the lunch engagement. He planned to give MacLean information about the pilots' strike and the need to settle it quickly. As well, cancelling could hurt Black's effort to build relationships with senior members of the media. Would an exclusive on the incident ensure positive coverage?

In the afternoon, Black was scheduled to meet with the Minister of Transport and his staff to review the strike situation. The Deputy Minister and Associate DM would likely be there, as would the Assistant DM (Marine) and the chairperson of the Great Lakes Pilotage Authority.

Across North America, the tide seemed to be running against the union movement and several large ones had recently been forced to make concessions in bargaining. Most public sector employers were resisting wage demands.

Inflationary wage pressures were being resisted by the Bank of Canada, the Minister of Finance and the Minister of Transport. Granting the pilots' demands could send an inappropriate signal to the private sector, something that would incur the wrath of the Prime Minister's Office.

The president hoped that the meeting would be short so that he could raise the bridge situation and get some advice on his forthcoming appearance before the Commons Standing Committee on Transportation. Several transport groups had received a rough ride when they presented their spending estimates. Black would be no exception since the chairperson's riding included the St. Louis Bridge.

Black planned to discuss his support for the government's deficit control and cost-recovery policies. He would also deal with the downsizing and privatization recommendations contained in the just-released Ministerial Task Force Report on Program Review (the Neilsen Task Force). He hoped to explain why traffic had dropped by more than 20 percent from the previous year to the lowest levels recorded in 15 years. The 1984-85 loss of $25.2 million was the largest since the Seaway had been refinanced in 1977. As well, the Seaway's reputation had already suffered. There was a serious accident at the Valleyfield Bridge in 1984 and there had been a blow-out this year of the canal wall at Lock 7 on the Welland Canal.

In light of these events, the committee would want to know why nothing had been done to protect the St. Louis Bridge, given the 1982 study, and an incident in July 1980. The *Lawrencecliff Hall* had hit the bridge and put it out of action until the spring of 1981. Black was confident that, with the Minister's support, he could demonstrate the importance of the Seaway to Canada's economy.

Right now, he needed information to develop options. How were they going to get the ship dislodged? Was it safe to move it? Black put out a call to the Seaway's legal counsel and called St. Lambert for a situation report. Told the vice-president was in Montreal on private business for the day, Black instructed St. Lambert to find him. Then he dialed the bridge, hoping to speak to the bridgemaster.

PART B
MORE INFORMATION

At the St. Louis Bridge, the *Seawise Jewel* still lay wedged in the wreckage of the southern roadway. A containment boom had been deployed and skimming operations were under way. A TV camera crew was filming the devastation and interviewing bystanders.

Ninety minutes after the incident, ships had begun calling for permission to move to safe anchorages to ride out an impending storm. The Seaway's heavy lift barge *Hercules* was en route.

The inspection team found the bridge structure was damaged and the lifting gear for the centre span was wrecked. Several sheaves of the hauling gear had cracked and the axle of one of the main drive motors had sheared off. The *Seawise Jewel* had electrical power and her main engines were available for use.

The team's view was that the bridge was going to be out of action for up to six weeks.

In bridgemaster Plante's opinion, the key questions were: how was the ship to be moved and how was the bridge going to be placed out of service while repairs were made? Centre span up or down? Even though the lifting mechanism was useless, the *Hercules* could help ease the structure down.

With the span up, marine traffic could get under way, providing the pilots' strike was settled. All outbound traffic could likely clear the Seaway by mid-December. However, all rail and road traffic would be suspended for the duration of repairs. This would be serious since the bridge was a major rail link between Ontario and the western provinces, and Quebec and Atlantic Canada, with several trains crossing each day. As well, the bridge was a road link between Montreal and communities to the southwest. Local road traffic would have to detour, adding 120 km to a round trip to Montreal.

With the span down, rail and road traffic could proceed but all Seaway traffic would be forced to wait. All the ships would probably have to winter over. Aside from the legal ramifications, financial losses would be staggering. Claims against SLSA and CN alone could run into the hundreds of millions of dollars.

• • •

Before calling Black, Plante answered some questions from two people he did not immediately recognize. Only when one of them shut off a pocket recorder did Plante realize he was talking to the media.

PART C
CHOICES FOR THE PRESIDENT

Black checked with the Seaway's legal counsel to confirm they had the power to seize the *Seawise Jewel* if necessary. While there was still no response from his vice-president, Black had been called by a Montreal newspaper, the Minister's chief of staff, and the president of CN.

Speaking with the CN president, Black recalled the earlier accident at the St. Louis Bridge. In 1980, the major problem had been to find a company to manufacture the huge sheaves, gearing and drive shafts for the hauling gear. To Black's knowledge, there were only three firms in Canada with the engineering capability of casting replacement parts. Would they be able to speed up or set aside the normal tendering process?

In addition to the blockage, major issues included: the real probability of a walkout by all Canadian Seaway pilots in about twelve hours' time; a halt of marine traffic in the waterway; the loss of one-third of the rail links joining eastern Canada with Ontario and the western provinces, a continued decline in public confidence in the transportation system, and a potentially messy contract situation with the repair or replacement of the bridge's lifting gear.

Black faced a potentially hostile Commons Committee and a rapidly deteriorating media environment. A Montreal newspaper already had first-hand knowledge of the incident in greater detail than he did. In addition, Black was going to have lunch with a reporter who probably knew as much about the background to the story as he did. ▲

ANNEX D ORGANIZATION CHART.

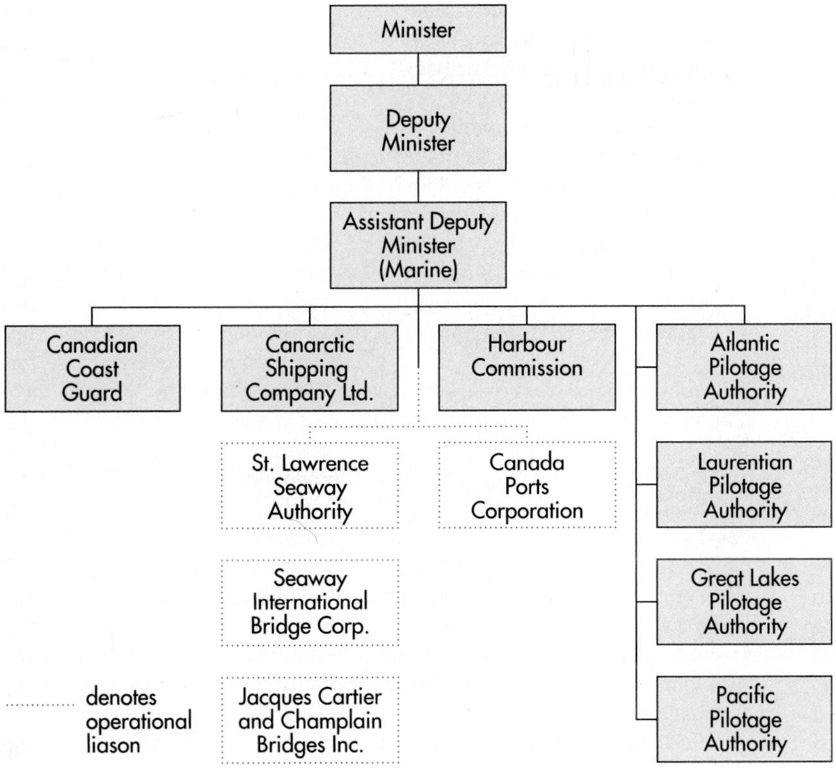

...

COMPREHENSIVE CASES PART II

QUESTIONS

1. What is the core issue in this case, i.e., what major decision must be made?
2. What are the secondary issues?
3. What issues are of least importance?
4. How deeply involved should John Black get in the operational details of making this decision?
5. Should priority be given to rail traffic or marine traffic? Why?

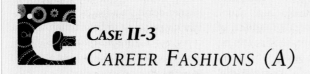

CASE II-3
CAREER FASHIONS (A)

In late February 1987, Cheryl Roche suddenly faced a situation that threatened the very survival of her business. After fourteen months of operating Career Fashions, Cheryl's business partner, Carolyn Knox, had decided to leave the company and pursue other interests. Cheryl wondered how she could deal with losing the only expertise the business had in design and production, which were crucial to the success of Career Fashions.

COMPANY BACKGROUND

In late 1985, Cheryl Roche had been managing her own used furniture and antique store in Montague, Prince Edward Island. Prior to that she had studied business at Holland College in Charlottetown. Because the used furniture and antique business is seasonal, Cheryl found herself with a great deal of time on her hands.

> *As she puts it:*
>
> I really had too much free time and found it boring to wait in my store for customers during the off-season. I looked around and decided to study the market for clothing, so I constructed a little survey and administered it myself. When I look at that survey now, I'm amazed at how simplistic it seems to me, but it identifies uniforms as a market and I went with the results.
>
> That wasn't the only reason I decided to start the new business. I wanted to use my skills and knew the opportunities would be limited if I worked for someone else. Also, I wouldn't have the opportunity to make as much money if I worked for another company, and let's face it, the number of jobs in Montague are limited. But don't get the wrong idea; personal satisfaction was my driving force.

The questionnaire was constructed by Cheryl using information from one of her business courses; it was quite short and very basic. The questionnaire identified the respondents' age and income groups and whether or not they were employed. It then asked about the type of clothing respondents bought and where they purchased it. One question asked if there were any problems with clothing available on the market. Cheryl administered the questionnaire by telephone to women who worked in nursing homes and hospitals. An interesting piece of information Cheryl obtained was that many women who wore uniforms on the job were dissatisfied with the design, comfort, and availability. The same point was made by nurses, waitresses and nursing home workers. Based on that data, Cheryl decided to manufacture and market uniforms for women in the service industries.

Cheryl asked her sister, Carolyn to join her in the new company. Carolyn had a background in fashion technique design and therefore, would be a valuable person who could design the clothing and run the production line. Carolyn agreed to join, and the two women, who were very close, formed Career Fashions in December of 1986.

The start up of Career Fashions had proven to be surprisingly easy. The production area was obtained by moving the used furniture and antique business to an upper floor in its former building and using the cleared lower floor for the new company. Sturdy and serviceable second-hand equipment was found with little difficulty. Three women were hired from the local area. Since they required training, Career Fashions was eligible for aid from a government program. This program was administered through the Canadian Employment and Immigration Commission (CECI) and helped keep costs down for Career Fashions by paying part of the new employees' wages for the first year of operation. Career Fashions, which was formed as a partnership, was financed by a combination of personal capital, bank loans and assistance from government programs. By December of 1986, Career Fashions produced its first uniforms.

Right from the start, Cheryl and Carolyn specialized in different areas. Cheryl was the marketer who pushed the product on the road and took orders in the factory. She spent at least one day of every week on the road visiting nursing homes, hotels and other places on Prince Edward Island where uniforms were used. Cheryl would show the Career Fashions lines and take orders. As she said later, "It was the personal touch that paid off; the other companies weren't on the Island and didn't use the approach we did." A retail outlet was opened at the factory and proved to be a success. Demand for uniforms increased to such an extent that the sewers couldn't keep up with the demand even though Cheryl had visited fewer than half of the institutions on Prince Edward Island. Based on her experience, Cheryl estimated yearly uniform demand to be slightly higher than 2600 uniforms in the province.

Career Fashions was located in Montague, a picturesque town of approximately 2000 people located on the extreme easterly part of Prince Edward Island. Montague was a 20 minute drive from a ferry which ran to Pictou, Nova Scotia, between May and November. Near Pictou was the largest manufacturer of uniforms in the Maritime Provinces. Montague was also approximately 90 minutes by car from a second ferry which ran between Cape Tormentine, New Brunswick and Prince Edward Island. This ferry operated year round. Major population centres were close to both mainland ferry terminals.

Because of Carolyn's training and background, she was in charge of production and design. Most of the designs the company produced were developed by her. Her designs were similar to street wear clothing and were very comfortable. The uniforms were easy to care for and less formal than the more traditional "stiff" uniforms. Carolyn's designs proved to be very popular and were very versatile. With minor modifications, one pattern could produce several designs. The small production facility also proved to be a plus because large runs of one style were not required due to the small size of the average order. Because individual orders could rapidly be accommodated, the small production facility and small order size actually helped Career Fashions be more responsive to their customers. With Carolyn working in production and thus able to supervise the seamstresses, potential problems were kept to a minimum. Quality control was also assured because if a problem arose, Carolyn was on the spot and made the necessary modifications.

PRODUCTION

When fabric came to the shop it went to the fabric roller where it was cut into the proper shapes and sizes for a particular pattern. The pieces then went to the thread serger for a finished edge. This process is called serging. The next steps involved sewing pockets onto the main pieces, then sewing the side seams, the skirt bottoms and tops together. Collars were then sewn onto the uniforms, and any other required touches added to the garments. Next the Career Fashions label was placed on the garment, and finally the button holes were made and buttons put on.

The completed uniforms were ironed and then placed in inventory. Cheryl and Carolyn tried to keep uniforms of each size and style in stock as they felt this would allow a short lead time when orders arrived. This proved difficult because the demand for uniforms was so great that production had difficulty keeping up with the orders. Because of the high demand to expand production to other clothing lines, although that was the original plan.

In April of 1987, the grand opening of the store was held and this was reported in a local paper (Exhibit 1). The partners felt that both the opening and the resultant publicity were a help in establishing Career Fashions. Sales grew as did the number of lines and styles Cheryl and Carolyn offered. This was possible because of the adaptability of the patterns; small changes in design created a different garment and the original pattern easily evolved into several styles. Additional original designs had also been created by Carolyn over the course of the year. The number of designs proved to be a strength as did the small production facility which enabled Career Fashions to have small, individualized production lines.

Both partners worked long hours to make the business a success. That's not to say there weren't problems, however. Cheryl and Carolyn had several minor arguments over production but these were cleared up quickly. As Cheryl later said, "It almost seems that sales and production sometimes work against one another no matter what the intention of the people involved." In December, financial statements were drawn up by a local chartered accountant and showed that Career Fashions had made a profit (Exhibit 2 and 3). In February, Carolyn decided to leave Career Fashions to pursue some of her other interests.

• • •

EXHIBIT 1 YOUNG FASHION BUSINESS GROWS QUICKLY.

After only four months in business, Career Fashions of Montague is diversifying.

The company owned and run by Cheryl Roche and Carolyn Knox, which made only uniforms at first, will show off some of their new easy care fashions at a grand opening at the store April 3.

"We've had some unbelievable changes in a short space of time," Cheryl said. "Restaurants, supermarkets, and nursing homes have shown a lot of interest in our uniforms, and we're retailing more casual wear than we expected to for a year at least."

The women's most successful idea for promoting their wares is visiting places where uniforms are worn. They display the different styles available and take orders.

"I was surprised at how cooperative everyone has been in allowing us to come and set up our displays."

"With the wider variety of easy care clothes Career Fashions now have available," Carolyn added, "they look forward to supplying the staff with whatever type workwear they prefer."

"As we developed our retail sales, our variety of street and casual wear kind of went along with it. Many of our uniforms look more like street wear, they don't have that stiff, washed out look," said Carolyn.

Cheryl noted that the company is still mainly into uniforms, selling three to each street wear outfit. Street clothes cost more to make because the designs are more complicated, different materials are preferred and fewer of each kind are made.

Despite the overhead, they agree their prices are competitive with those of larger manufacturers.

"We can offer a wider variety than you can get out of a catalogue," Carolyn stressed, "because we make almost everything individually. We mainly have each seamstress make one outfit at a time, rather than production line style. It gives us a more relaxed atmosphere and better quality control."

The manufacturing end of the business provides jobs for three seamstresses, Janet MacKinnon, Debby Ryan and Gladys Hancock. The company received a subsidy while training them but now carries all of their wages.

The sisters will wing to Montreal April 8 to check cost and availability of fabrics they hope to bring into their street wear operation.

At the opening April 3, the two intend to display more career and casual fashions than ever, award handcrafts to the first customers, provide refreshments and hold a draw in which the winner will receive her choice of a workwear outfit.

Carolyn is the operations' main creative person, bringing the training she received in UPEI's Home Economics program and a course in fashion technology and design at Holland College, Summerside Centre, to bear in designing the company's outfits.

Cheryl's main responsibility is the business end, putting the skills she developed in Holland College's Business Course and running Cheryl's Used Furniture and Country Collectibles to good use.

The furniture business is still in operation, having been moved upstairs in the same building to accommodate Career Fashions. Cheryl said the building is big enough to hold both businesses with no difficulty.

"They seem to complement each other well," she said. "People often come in to buy furniture and end up buying clothes, or vice versa. This place is a good size, and we'd have to expand our staff a lot before we needed to move to a larger building."

They agreed that the company has had a lot of support, not only from the area where they are located, but the rest of the Island as well.

"There are no other uniform manufacturing operations like ours on the Island," Carolyn said. "We've gotten a lot of inquiries and sales from Charlottetown, like the Queen Elizabeth Hospital," she added.

"It seems a lot of people on the Island would rather buy from us than from a mainland factory. People have been very supportive," Cheryl said.

Source: "Markets Expand," *Eastern Graphic*, April 7, 1987; Progress '87, p. 3, Montague, Prince Edward Island.

Personal factors may have played a role in Carolyn's decision to leave. While Cheryl was married and lived in the area, Carolyn was single. Cheryl still maintained the furniture and antique store, although it had become less important as Career Fashions developed. As time went on, Cheryl became more committed to the new business on a personal and professional level, while it appeared that Carolyn became less committed.

Cheryl now had to make some important decisions. As she put it, "Should I continue Career Fashions or should I close and go back to antiques? If I do continue, what lines of clothing do I handle? What markets do I serve—only Prince Edward Island, or the mainland also? How do I handle production and sales by myself? After all, I have no training or background in production. Should I hire a sales person? Or a product manager? How do I develop new clothing styles?" ▲

EXHIBIT 2 CAREER FASHIONS STATEMENT OF INCOME FOR THE YEAR ENDED DECEMBER 31, 1987.

Sales		$74 950
Cost of Goods Sold		
Cost of Goods Manufactured[1]	$54 020	
Finished Goods Inventory, ending	$14 180	
		39 840
Gross Profit		$35 110
Selling Expenses		
Advertising	2460	
Automobiles	2870	
Bank Charges	1810	
Office	2670	
Telephone	1830	
Travel	670	
		12 310
Operating Income		22 800
Extraordinary Expense[2]		6 560
NET INCOME		$16 240

[1] Includes seamstresses' salaries; provision made for Cheryl and Carolyn.
[2] Draws by Cheryl included.

EXHIBIT 3 CAREER FASHIONS BALANCE SHEET AS OF DECEMBER 31, 1987.

Assets	
Accounts Receivable	$4 850
Inventory	27 050
	31 900
Equipment	4 090
	35 990
Liabilities	
Bank Loans (Current)	$16 940
Accounts Payable	2 810
	19 750
Owner's Equity	
Capital	16 240
	$35 990

QUESTIONS

1. What are the strengths and weaknesses in the internal operations of Career Fashions?
2. What risks and opportunities exist in the external environment of Career Fashions?
3. Outline Cheryl's choices. Summarize the advantages and disadvantages of each.
4. What personal factors will affect Cheryl's decision?
5. What should Cheryl do now? Why?

PART 3

ORGANIZING

CHAPTER 7

ORGANIZATIONAL STRUCTURES

LEARNING OBJECTIVES

After reading this chapter, you will be able to:

1. Understand the concept of organizational structure and the dimensions of structure.
2. Explain what an organization chart does and does not indicate.
3. State four classical organizing principles.
4. Understand the span of control concept and the factors that influence the span of control.
5. Describe the major bases of departmentation that are used by organizations.
6. Explain the difference between the functional structure and the divisional structure.
7. Explain the concepts of differentiation and integration.
8. Describe seven strategies for achieving coordination in organizations.

MANAGEMENT CHALLENGE

RICHTER'S HARDWARE STORE

Karl Richter grew up in Winnipeg's North End. He exhibited an interest in entrepreneurialism and after high school went on to study marketing. By the time he graduated from the marketing program, he had already been involved in several small-scale business deals. Richter returned home after graduation in 1970 to take over his father's hardware store and to refine his entrepreneurial skills. He thought this would give him an opportunity to put into practice some of the ideas he had learned at school.

After carefully analyzing the Winnipeg market, he added some completely new product lines, expanded others, and discontinued some altogether. He streamlined record-keeping by instituting a mechanized data processing system (microcomputers had not yet been invented). Within three years, profits and sales had increased dramatically. Encouraged by this success, Richter opened two new stores in Winnipeg in 1973. These were also successful and by 1975, the company employed 51 people (see Figure 7-1).

Richter decided to expand farther west in the next few years, since he felt that the Winnipeg market was getting saturated. He branched out regionally to include such cities as Brandon, Portage la Prairie, Dauphin, and Regina. By 1985, the company employed 103 people at 16 different locations. Richter observed that these regionally dispersed stores were reasonably successful, but they were not as profitable as the additional stores he had originally opened in Winnipeg.

Over the next several years the company expanded into Saskatoon, Calgary, and Edmonton. By 1993, the company had 29 stores and employed 203 people. At this point, difficulties began to crop up. The financial statements for 1993 showed that the company was still making a profit, but that profit margins had fallen significantly. Richter therefore called a meeting of the three vice-presidents to get their views on what the problem might be.

The meeting was not pleasant. All three complained that in the last several years their jobs had become almost impossible. The marketing vice-president explained that she was forced to spend promotion money in new markets that she didn't know much about. She noted that her travel expenses were up considerably. The merchandising vice-president complained that he was unsure what product lines should be offered in the different regions. He implied that the marketing vice-president didn't seem interested in cooperating with merchandising. He noted that several advertisements had recently appeared in local newspapers for products the company didn't even have in stock. The marketing vice-president retorted angrily that it wasn't her job to coordinate the marketing and merchandising functions.

The operations vice-president wasn't happy either. He claimed that regional store managers paid little attention to his suggestions for store operations. He indicated that the regional store managers held the view that the operations vice-president didn't know much about their local markets and that he shouldn't try to impose unreasonable ideas on them. He admitted some sympathy for their argument.

Richter listened to these and other complaints for three hours. He heard of discord among members of top management and apathy among employees at the retail outlet level. Head office employees in the marketing, operations, and merchandising functions seemed reasonably content, but some couldn't see how their particular job fit into the total scheme of things.

Richter knew the company could not survive financially if it had another couple of years like the last one. ▲

FIGURE 7-1 RICHTER'S HARDWARE STORES.

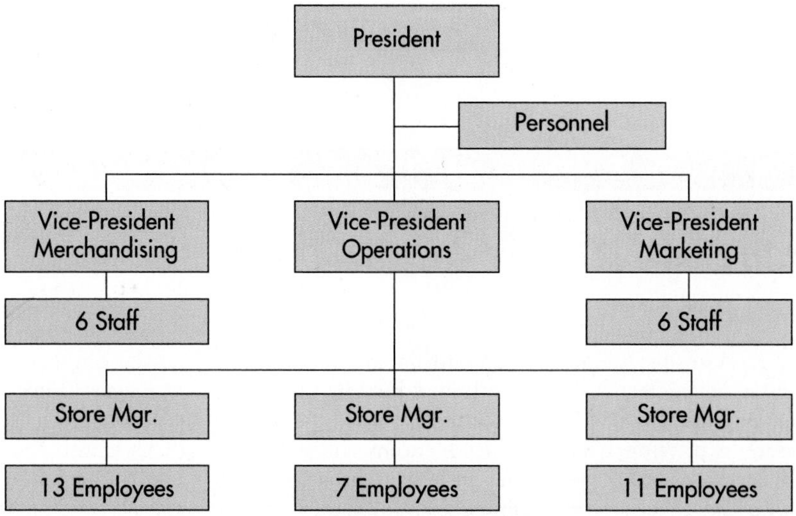

organizing

In Chapters 4, 5, and 6, we observed that an important part of the planning function is the setting of goals. Once goals have been developed, managers must decide how to organize activities so these goals can be reached. Simply stated, planning is deciding what to do, while organizing is deciding how to do it.[1] **Organizing** is the process of deciding which specific functions must be performed, and how these functions should be coordinated so that organizational goals are reached. The Management Challenge shows that Richter Hardware is now having some difficulty coordinating its various activities so that organizational goals are reached. The organizing function is important for all types of organizations—business firms, universities and colleges, the military, religious organizations, labour unions, hospitals, and government agencies.

Like most other activities in organizations, organizing is not a completely rational process. The structure of an organization reflects both rational considerations (for example, the kind of tasks that need to be done) and political considerations (for example, the ways in which powerful managers want their departments organized). Approximately 50-60 percent of the variation in organizational structure can be explained by rational factors; the remainder is due to emotional or subjective factors.[2] Structure must therefore facilitate organizational performance *and* satisfy the needs of those working in it.

In this chapter, we first describe the concept of organizational structure and indicate the steps in the organizing process. Next, we outline some principles that have helped managers carry out this function. We then discuss the various bases of departmentation that can be used to create departments, and describe the two basic organizational structures that result from the departmentation process. The chapter concludes with a discussion of how the various departments in an organization are coordinated.

ORGANIZATIONAL STRUCTURE

LEARNING OBJECTIVE 1
Understand the concept of organizational structure and the dimensions of structure.

organizational structure

Organizational structure is the pattern of formal relationships that exists among groups and individuals in an organization. Every organization, regardless of size or function, has a structure. The larger the firm, the greater the likelihood that the structure will be documented and circulated to organizational members.

restructuring

In the past few years, much has been written in the business press about **restructuring**, the changing of an organization's structure so that it can more effectively cope with changes in its customers, markets, and products. The Global Management insert entitled "A Structural Change at Pharmex" describes such a restructuring.

DIMENSIONS OF ORGANIZATIONAL STRUCTURE

Organizational structure can be analyzed along several dimensions: formalization, centralization, complexity, and specialization.[3] We briefly introduce these concepts here, and discuss them in more detail later in this chapter and in Chapter 8.

Formalization

formalization

Formalization refers to the amount of written job descriptions, rules, policies, and procedures that guide employee behaviour. In small firms, the degree of formalization is low, and most of the direction that employees receive is oral. The reverse is often true in large organizations, particularly those that are highly bureaucratic (see Chapter 2). An organization with a high degree of formalization is a firm that requires all potential employees to go through a standardized set of interviews and tests, or a university which requires faculty members to submit documentation of their teaching and research activities in order to get tenure. Organizations formalize activities in an attempt to ensure that they are done correctly, but on occasion, formalization may be nothing more than "red tape." The mere existence of written rules is no guarantee that employees will pay any attention to them.[4]

GLOBAL MANAGEMENT

A Structural Change at Pharmex

The international division of a multinational pharmaceutical company (Pharmex) discovered that a patent on one of its important products had expired. Because of this and other negative economic factors, division profitability was declining. The division began analyzing its structure to determine if changes could be made in such a way that staff reductions were possible; these reductions would obviously contribute to increased profitability.

There were approximately 250 employees at division headquarters. Reporting to the divisional headquarters were three regions: Europe, Latin America, and Asia and in each region there were several subsidiary firms. Total employment at the three levels (headquarters, region, and subsidiaries) was about 200 people. The company wanted the answers to two questions: (1) could it reduce employment in either the division or the regions without reducing efficiency, and (2) should regional operations be controlled from division headquarters, or should division headquarters be abolished and the regions upgraded to divisional status?

Not surprisingly, each group thought that its role was the most important. After interviewing many executives, a consultant identified the following alternatives:

1. *Make no change* This would be a good alternative if the difficulties that were being experienced were only temporary.
2. *Eliminate unnecessary positions, but maintain the overall structure* It was apparent that some jobs could be cut, but there was concern about what this would do to morale, and whether this approach would really address the problems that Pharmex was experiencing.
3. *Abolish the regional level and control the subsidiaries in each region directly from division headquarters* This approach had already been adopted by some of Pharmex's competitors. It would allow for a greater reduction of personnel, and would improve communications between the division and the subsidiaries. However, it meant that the division would have to become knowledgeable about the vast cultural differences in all the countries where the subsidiaries conducted business.
4. *Strengthen the regions and downgrade divisional headquarters* The advantages and disadvantages of this alternative are the mirror-image of alternative 3.
5. *Change the mission of the regional offices from one of control to one of support* This would mean increased authority to subsidiary managers and would allow for staff reductions in the regions. It would capitalize on local knowledge in the various regions, which would mean more responsiveness to consumers. It would also encourage the development of managerial competence in the subsidiaries because those managers would be making more decisions.

Pharmex decided to adopt alternative 5. It abolished the three geographic regions, and created two new regions—one for developing countries and the other for developed countries. Pharmex felt that its previous mission had become a self-fulfilling prophecy (that is, divisional headquarters controlled the subsidiary staffs because they were weak, but they were weak because they were never allowed any discretion). The company also felt that alternative 5 was more responsive to the problems facing the firm. ▲

Centralization

centralization

Centralization deals with the issue of how much authority is held at the various management levels in the organizational hierarchy. In a centralized organization, top management makes decisions for most areas of operations; workers at lower levels are allowed to make decisions and initiate actions only in limited areas. The Management Challenge suggests that authority at Richter Hardware is highly centralized. In a decentralized operation, on the other hand, authority is dispersed throughout the organization, and lower-level employees are given the authority to make many decisions without consulting top management.

Complexity

Complexity concerns the number of distinctly different job titles and departments in an organization. Organizations with many different departments and job titles are more complex than organizations with only a few job titles and departments.

complexity

Specialization

Specialization means breaking a complex task into simple parts so that the individual or group performing the task can focus on specific parts of it. In his classic book *The Wealth of Nations,* Adam Smith dramatically demonstrated how 10 men doing non-specialized work might produce only 20 pins a day apiece.[5] But once those same 10 men divided the work so that one person cut the wire, one person sharpened the wire, and so forth, they could produce thousands of pins each day. Specialization is widely used in modern organizations for both managerial and operative jobs. A shelf stocker at Loblaws, for example, does not normally operate a cash register. A sales manager at Vita Health does not generally do production planning.

specialization

Specialization has disadvantages as well as advantages (see Table 7-1). Recently, concern has been expressed that specialization has been carried so far that workers who only do "narrow tasks" are unhappy and unmotivated. The motivational implications of overspecialization are examined in Chapter 12.

TABLE 7-1 ADVANTAGES AND DISADVANTAGES OF SPECIALIZATION OF LABOUR.

Advantages	**Disadvantages**
1. Workers become very efficient when doing the same small portion of a complex task over and over again.	1. Workers fail to develop any sense of pride for the product or service that they are producing.
2. One manager can supervise large numbers of workers doing identical tasks.	2. Motivation among workers erodes, and a sense of alienation from work may develop.
3. Workers can learn specialized jobs much faster than jobs requiring many different skills.	3. Workers may feel that they are not using valued skills to do their work.
4. Quality may improve because workers know their jobs exceedingly well.	4. Boredom, absenteeism, and turnover among workers may cause quality to decline.
5. The coordination of many specific tasks may be the only way for the organization to achieve its complex overall goals.	5. Workers may be unaware of how their area of specialization fits into the overall goals of the organization.

Specialization of labour is clearly evident in a pit crew in professional car racing. The overall task of winning a race is broken into simple tasks, such as changing tires and adding fuel, thereby enhancing group performance. Properly coordinated, these specialized tasks lead to high performance.

THE ORGANIZING PROCESS

The organizing process includes four steps:[6]

1. Determining the totality of work that must be done in order for the organization to reach its goals.
2. Dividing the total work into functions that can be performed by groups or individuals.
3. Grouping together those individuals whose work is closely related.
4. Coordinating the work of the different groups and individuals.

These four steps take place within both the internal environment of the organization and the external environment in which the organization operates (see Figure 7-2). The Management at Work insert "The Organizing Process at CSL" describes how this process was carried out in one organization.

FIGURE 7-2 THE ORGANIZING PROCESS.

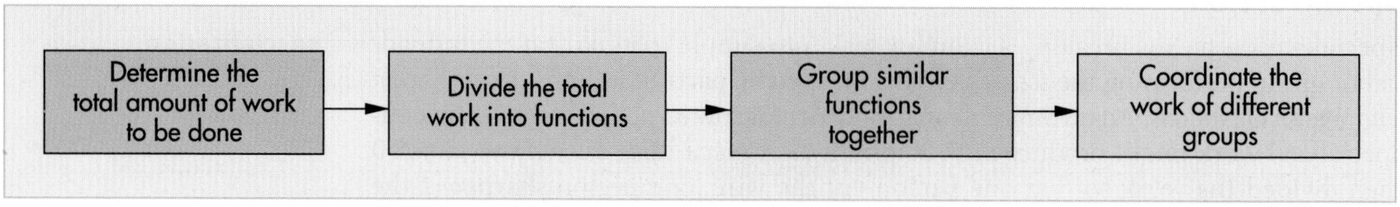

The Organization Chart

organization chart

Organizational structure reduces the uncertainty and confusion that results when people are unaware of how their work fits into the overall activity of the organization. An **organization chart** is a pictorial representation of formal authority relationships in an organization at one point in time. It shows where each person is placed in the formal structure. Figure 7-3 shows a typical organization chart.

MANAGEMENT AT WORK

The Organizing Process at CSL

Bruce Lougheed was a systems engineering manager for 10 years at a major computer company. He resigned his position to form his own computer services company, which he named Computer Systems Ltd. (CSL). Lougheed and two partners, Gerry Zakus and Marion Spence, made plans to develop a computer services firm specializing in the development, installation, and maintenance of computer software systems for life insurance companies.

CSL's goal was to provide high-quality, specialized computer services to life insurance companies. After establishing the objectives for their new company, the three partners determined that the functions CSL had to accomplish included systems engineering and design, programming development, and the installation and maintenance of computer systems. Based on these functions, CSL would require, highly trained systems analysts, computer programmers, and marketing personnel, as well as clerical support staff. In addition to the personnel required, physical resources such as capital, computer equipment, office space, and office furnishings were needed. The partners had to determine not only the type of personnel needed, but also the number of specialists needed for each major function. Zakus was in charge of recruiting prospective employees. In addition, the company had to secure sufficient capital from banks, shareholders or other sources to begin and continue operations. Spence was responsible for finding the funds to lease office space, purchase or lease equipment, compensate personnel, and pay for supplies.

Lougheed realized that he needed to coordinate the functions and the physical and human resources into a workable organization structure. He decided that three departments were needed: (1) systems design and programming, (2) installation and maintenance, and (3) marketing. In this newly formed company, the personnel would perform a variety of tasks, but as CSL grew, they would begin to perform more limited, specialized functions. Once each function had been grouped into a coordinated organizational structure, Lougheed would assign appropriate levels of responsibility, authority, and accountability to all employees. The final phase of the organizing process was the assignment of specific work activities. For instance, the marketing manager had to call on potential customers, design promotion and advertising, and recruit and train sales personnel. ▲

FIGURE 7-3 AN ORGANIZATION CHART.

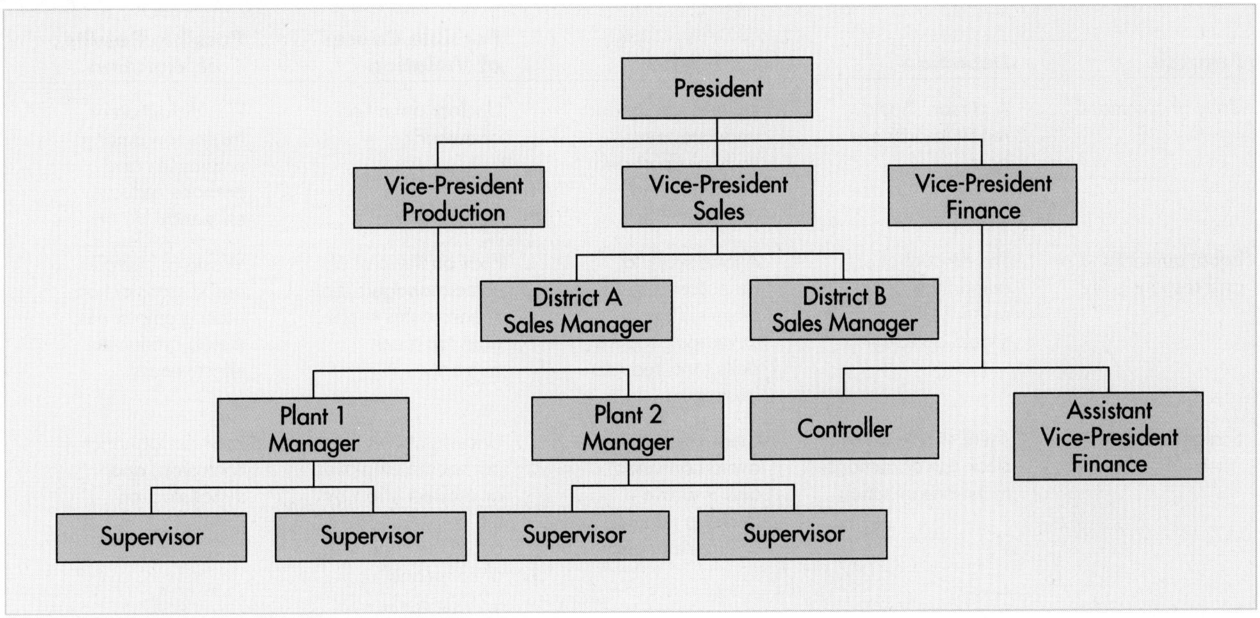

Such charts convey several characteristics of an organization:

LEARNING OBJECTIVE 2
Explain what an organization chart does and does not indicate.

1. The vertical authority relationships that exist between bosses and subordinates.
2. The general type of work performed.
3. The different departments that do the work.
4. The formal communication channels.
5. The various levels of management.

The organization chart of a manufacturing firm would contain such departments as marketing, production, and finance, while an organization chart for a church might show departments such as music, adult education, and Sunday school. The various managerial positions in an organization are represented in chart form because the authority structure can be more effectively conveyed by a drawing than by a written description.

Organization charts do not show all details of an organization.[7] They do not indicate how much authority each of the positions on the chart possesses, what the organization's objectives are, what the significant factors in the organization's external environment are, what technology is used, what the comparative importance of the jobs in various departments is, how much horizontal interaction occurs between departments, or what informal relationships have arisen spontaneously among workers.

CLASSICAL ORGANIZING PRINCIPLES

LEARNING OBJECTIVE 3
State four classical organizing principles.

During the twentieth century, a large number of organizing principles have been developed by research scholars and practising managers. These principles are generally helpful for managers but there are exceptions to the principles, so they must be applied in a flexible way. The most widely known of these principles are summarized in Table 7-2 and discussed below.

TABLE 7-2 ORGANIZING PRINCIPLES.

Principle	Definition	Rationale	Possible Causes of Violation	Possible Results of Violation
Unity of command	A person should report to only one boss	Ensures clarity and understanding, unity of effort and direction, and avoids conflicts	Unclear definition of authority	Dissatisfaction or frustration among employees and perhaps reduced efficiency
Equal authority and responsibility	The amount of authority and responsibility should be equal	Allows work to be accomplished more efficiently, develops people's skills, and reduces frustration	Fear on the part of some managers that subordinates might gain too much authority	Waste of energies and dissatisfaction among employees, thereby reducing effectiveness
Scalar principle	There should be a clear line of authority in the organization	Clear relationships avoid confusion and improve decision making and performance	Uncertainty on the part of the employee or a direct effort by the employee to avoid the chain of command	Poor performance, confusion, and dissatisfaction
Span of control	The number of employees a manager supervises should be limited	Increases a manager's effectiveness in providing direction and control	Overloading a manager due to growth in number of personnel	Lack of efficiency and control, resulting in poor performance

Unity of Command

unity of command principle

The **unity of command principle** states that each person in an organization should report to only one boss. If this principle is followed, subordinates will not be faced with conflicting orders from different bosses. As we shall see in the next chapter, this principle may be purposely violated in some large organizations where both technical experts and managers give directions to employees.

Equal Authority and Responsibility

The essence of this principle is that each person who is responsible for doing a certain task must be given sufficient authority to do it. Managers who fail to delegate sufficient authority to subordinates to enable them to do a job properly frustrate their employees. Suppose that a sales manager is responsible for achieving certain sales goals, but lacks the authority to discipline or reward salespeople. The sales manager cannot do what is necessary to motivate the salespeople to achieve the organization's sales goals. Many organizations inadvertently create situations where authority and responsibility are not equal.

The Scalar Principle

scalar principle

According to the **scalar principle**, a clear, unbroken line of authority should run from the top to the bottom of an organization. In an organization following this principle, all members will communicate with each other by "going through the proper channels." Such a system is orderly, but it may be inadequate for meeting the many communication needs of an organization. As a result, much informal communication develops that by-passes the formal channels.

THE SPAN OF CONTROL

span of control

The **span of control** refers to the number of subordinates that report directly to a manager. Managers who have relatively few subordinates have a narrow span of control, while managers with a large number of subordinates have a wide span of control.

LEARNING OBJECTIVE 4

Understand the span of control concept and the factors that influence the span of control.

There is a direct relationship between the span of control and the "shape" of an organization. In a *tall structure,* there are many levels of management, but each manager has a narrow span of control. In a *flat structure,* there are fewer levels of management, but each manager has a wider span of control. In Figure 7-4, there are 29 employees in both organizations, yet one organization is tall (7 levels), while the other is flat (only 3 levels of management). The taller the organization, the more managers are required.

A variety of factors affect the span of control (see Table 7-3), but it is not possible to state the optimum span of management.[8] Narrow spans permit close supervision of employees, but they create vertical communication problems because information must be filtered through many management levels. Wide spans give more discretion to employees, but they also create the possibility for bad decisions on the part of inexperienced people. Overall, wide spans are more *efficient,* but at some point they become less *effective.*

Downsizing and the Span of Control

downsizing

Increasing international competition has caused many firms to downsize. **Downsizing** refers to the planned reduction in the scope of an organization's operations. It usually means cutting large numbers of employees and reducing the number and variety of products a company produces. It has meant the loss of thousands of jobs in many companies, including Air Canada, General Motors, IBM, and General Electric. Consider the following:[9]

- The Royal Bank is cutting 4100 jobs.
- Coca-Cola is cutting staff and shutting plants in order to streamline its business.

FIGURE 7-4 FLAT AND TALL ORGANIZATIONAL STRUCTURES.

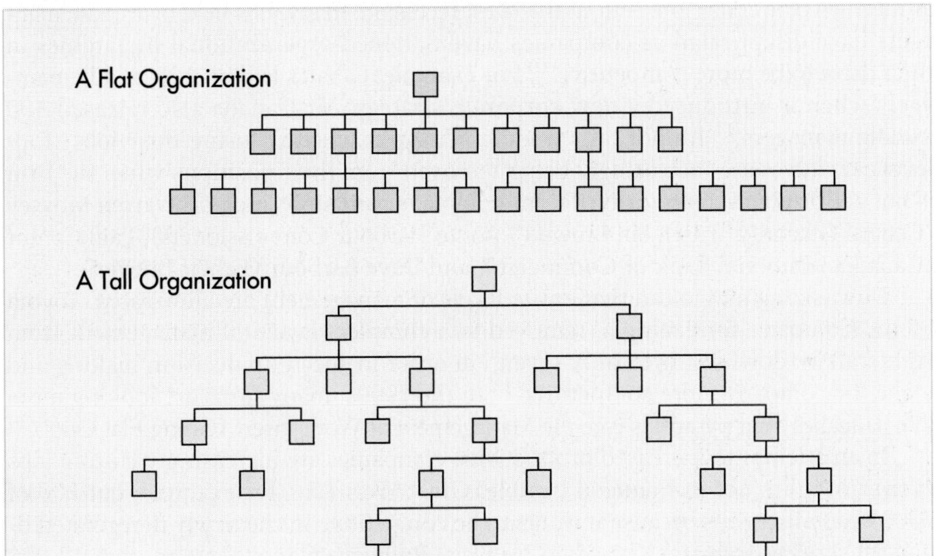

TABLE 7-3 FACTORS AFFECTING THE SPAN OF CONTROL.

Factor	Guideline
1. The competence of the manager and the subordinates.	1. The greater the competence, the wider the span of control may be.
2. The degree of interaction between subordinates.	2. The greater the required interaction, the narrower the span should be.
3. The amount of nonmanagerial work the manager must do.	3. The greater the amount of nonmanagerial work, the narrower the span should be.
4. The similarity of subordinate tasks.	4. The greater the similarity of subordinate tasks, the greater the span may be.
5. The existence of standardized procedures.	5. The greater the standardization of work, the greater the span may be.
6. The physical closeness of subordinates.	6. The closer together the subordinates are, the greater the span may be.

- The province of Alberta announced that if government employees do not take a 5 percent salary cut, there will be layoffs.
- Northern Telecom Ltd. is closing 2 of its 19 Canadian plants and cutting 782 jobs.
- Bell Canada is slashing 5000 jobs and reducing its capital budget by $300 million after being denied approval to raise telephone rates.
- Abitibi Price Inc. is scaling back its operations and downsizing its administration; it is not known how many jobs will be lost.
- The Canadian Imperial Bank of Commerce wants to cut 2500 jobs.

In previous recessions, employment levels in white collar jobs did not decline nearly as much as blue collar jobs. But in the latest recession, many jobs held by middle managers have disappeared as companies have flattened organizational hierarchies in their drive to be more competitive.[10] For example, Labatt's laid off 120 middle managers when it introduced a new corporate strategy. Air Canada also released 400 middle managers.[11] It's not only middle managers who are losing their jobs. Top-level executives are increasingly being removed from their positions when the firm is not performing satisfactorily. Recent notable terminations include Warren Moysey (Central Guaranty Trust), Ian Brown (Toronto Harbour Commissioners), Paul Cantor (Canadian Imperial Bank of Commerce), and Dave Barbour (Labatt Breweries).[12]

Downsizing may mean that entire levels of management are eliminated. Toyota Motor Company, for example, removed two complete layers of management from its hierarchy, downsizing to only seven, in order to speed up decision making and make the company more competitive.[13] In the 1990s, many firms are looking more like pancakes than pyramids (see the Management at Work insert "Going Flat Out").[14]

In an attempt to increased productivity, companies are increasingly cutting jobs even if they are not in financial trouble. Great West Life, for example, cut 200 of 2000 head office jobs because it wants to be competitive in the newly deregulated financial services industry. Canadian National Railways plans to cut another 10 000 workers in addition to the 15 000 it has already eliminated. Imperial Oil cut 5000 employees between 1990 and 1993. Even IBM, once a company renowned for its lifetime employment practices, has begun reducing its work force.[15]

MANAGEMENT AT WORK

GOING FLAT OUT

Most businesses have traditionally been organized in the shape of a pyramid. The largest number of workers formed the base and gradual movement upward created layers of management until the apex of the pyramid was reached.

But intense competition in the global marketplace has forced business to find new ways to stay competitive and to improve profits. In an attempt to streamline their bureaucracies and operate more efficiently, many businesses have decided to reshape their organizational structure along the Japanese lines. These new organizations, flat and shaped more like a pancake than a pyramid, are geared toward improving response time, getting new products to market more quickly, speeding up decision making, and increasing profits.

What is the pancake company like? First, there are far fewer middle managers. Second, and perhaps more important, the role played by middle managers has been fundamentally redefined. No longer charged with the responsibility of controlling and making decisions, middle managers are now expected to delegate down and encourage their staff to make decisions.

For some, this change has meant new-found freedom and increased autonomy. Working in a "participatory" structure, these managers now have easy access to top executives, can get decisions made more quickly, and can focus on more aspects of the business. Those who thrive on change seem particularly well suited to the flattened organizational structure.

On the negative side, however, these changes have required tremendous sacrifices. Many people have lost their jobs. And managers who have survived the cuts experience the stress of working with a new set of rules. The most common complaint by middle managers is extreme overwork.

Stresses and pressures increase when the streamlining processes are not well planned. Eliminating layers of management does not by itself ensure increased profits. Careful study of which jobs can be eliminated and a clear definition of a company's goals are critical ingredients to successful reorganization.

In spite of the difficulties involved, many companies that have flattened their management structure say the rewards have been worth the effort. Management teams, in which managers work with colleagues from other sections of the company, have proven very effective. The team approach gives managers first-hand knowledge of how and where the company is most efficient and profitable.

Moving managers around an organization to broaden their understanding of the company's business has also proven successful. Their value to the company increases and managers benefit personally by finding new opportunities to use their talents. The continued challenge of doing something new builds enthusiasm and creativity.

Is the thinning of middle management only a trend? Probably not. Most experts agree that the pressures of global competition and improved bottom lines will only intensify in the coming years. This means that streamlined organizations are here to stay. ▲

Downsizing often results in increased spans of control for those individuals who remain with the company. At General Electric and Reynolds Aluminum, for example, spans of control are now twice as large as they were fifteen years ago.[16] Because spans of control are wider, corporate structures are flatter after downsizing. This means improved communication and increased speed in decision making. Michael Cowpland (one of the co-founders of Mitel Corp.) is now the CEO of a computer software firm named Corel Systems Corp. The firm has a very flat structure with only three layers of management. Cowpland's office is right in the middle of the action and his door is open to anyone at any time.[17]

Some companies have tried to avoid downsizing by having each employee work fewer total hours. While this does save jobs, the jobs that remain are not full-time, and this causes employee morale to drop. The hard reality is that globalization of business and the intense competition that goes with it have driven companies to become more efficient. To date, most companies have decided that downsizing is the way to achieve this. But downsizing can also cause problems:[18]

- When headquarters staff are let go, line managers find that they have an increased workload.
- Anticipated cost savings often do not materialize.
- Employee productivity often stays the same or declines.
- Employee morale and motivation usually drops.

If downsizing is done as a quick-fix, cost cutting tactic, it is not likely to result in any long-term gains for an organization. On the other hand, if it is part of a carefully thought-out strategy to become more focussed and more competitive, it may well mean improved performance for the organization.

DEPARTMENTATION

departmentation

Departmentation means grouping functions or major work activities into coherent units. Two primary questions must be answered when departmentation is considered: (1) what functions are similar enough to be grouped together, and (2) what basis to use for departmentation.

Department stores like Zellers carry a wide range of goods that are departmentalized along product lines. Higher in the organization, departmentation by territory is common, with stores grouped by region and each region reporting to a separate regional manager. At the top levels of the organization, departmentation is usually by function.

GROUPING SIMILAR FUNCTIONS

Ideally, each department in an organization would be made up of jobs that are almost identical. The manager of such a department would then know exactly what each worker was doing. In practice, this is generally not possible, so organizations have to be content with grouping jobs that are merely similar. Even with this solution, there are several factors that complicate matters:

1. *Volume of work* If there is insufficient volume of work to allow specialization, then dissimilar functions may be grouped together.
2. *Formal work rules or traditions* Tasks may be similar, but work rules or tradition may prevent them from being assigned to one department. For example, installing electrical conduit is similar to installing water pipes, but electricians install conduit and plumbers install water pipes.
3. *Functional duplication across several departments* Inventory control, for example, is relevant to both purchasing and production departments. Where should the inventory control function be placed?
4. *Conflict of interest* Combining functions may create a conflict of interest. For example, the quality control function is important to production, but the quality control inspector should be independent from the production manager to ensure that objective decisions are made about quality.
5. *Need for coordination* Dissimilar functions may have to be combined to coordinate activities. For example, buying and selling in a department store are so interdependent that one person may be responsible for both.

BASES OF DEPARTMENTATION

LEARNING OBJECTIVE 5
Describe the major bases of departmentation that are used by organizations.

Once the issue of grouping similar functions has been settled, the organization must decide which criterion it will use to form departments. The most widely used bases of departmentation are (1) functions, (2) products, (3) customers, (4) territories, and (5) projects.

FIGURE 7-5 DEPARTMENTATION BY FUNCTION.

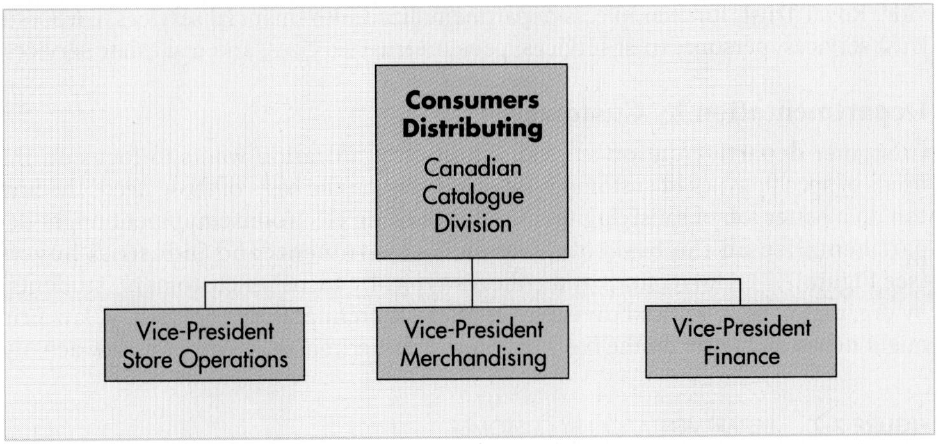

Departmentation by Function

This is the most traditional and probably the most common way to group functions. In **functional departmentation**, units are formed on the basis of the functions that must be carried out to reach organizational goals. Consumers Distributing Canadian Catalogue Division is organized along functional lines. Their key functions are store operations, merchandising, and finance (see Figure 7-5).

functional departmentation

Functional departmentation has the advantage of focussing organizational activity on the key functions that must be performed. It may, however, cause managers and employees to become so involved in their own functional area that they forget how it fits into the total activity of the organization.

Departmentation by Product

Product departmentation is used when it is important to focus on the products or services the organization sells. Each product (or group of similar products) is placed under the authority of one individual who specializes in this product and who is responsible for the product's success. This type of departmentation is used when an organization is providing either a wide range of products or technologically complex products. Product departmentation allows management of Noranda Inc. to give the proper attention to each product (see Figure 7-6). For many years, General Motors had five product divisions: Chevrolet, Pontiac, Oldsmobile, Buick, and Cadillac. Recently, the company reorganized into two product divisions: (1) Chevrolet, Pontiac, and GM Canada, and (2) Buick, Oldsmobile, and Cadillac. The former manufactures small cars, and the latter large cars.[19] Canadian Pacific is also organized around products—oil, mines, pulp and paper, transportation, and communication.[20] Service organizations

product departmentation

FIGURE 7-6 DEPARTMENTATION BY PRODUCT.

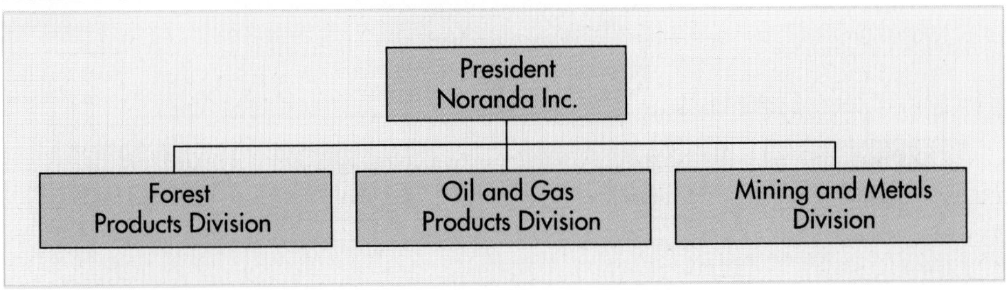

that use this basis of departmentation are organized around the services they provide. Royal Trust, for example, is departmentalized into financial services, corporate trust services, personal trust services, pension trust services, and real estate services.

Departmentation by Customer

customer departmentation

Customer departmentation is used when an organization wants to focus on the needs of specific types of customers. By organizing on the basis of those needs the firm can do a better job of satisfying them. A firm selling electronic equipment might departmentalize on the basis of consumer, government, and industrial buyers (see Figure 7-7). Universities and colleges typically focus on customers (students) by organizing faculties and divisions to offer different patterns of study. A law firm might departmentalize on the basis of commercial, criminal, or corporate law activity.

FIGURE 7-7 DEPARTMENTATION BY CUSTOMER.

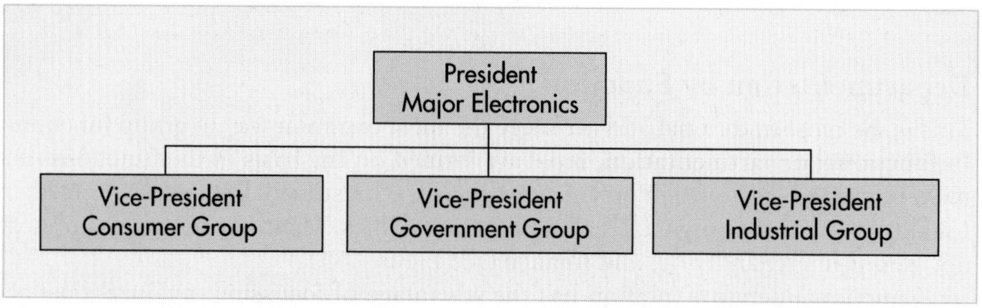

Departmentation by Territory

territorial departmentation

Territorial departmentation is used when an organization carries on its activities over large geographic areas. The Personal Services Division of Montreal Trust, for example, is organized around four regions—Atlantic, Quebec, Central, and B.C./Western regions (see Figure 7-8). Regional vice-presidents in the marketing function at Air Canada are organized into western, central, eastern, Atlantic Canada, U.S., and European regions. McCain Foods is organized along geographic lines, with Wallace McCain responsible for North and South America, Asia, Austraila, and New Zealand, and his brother Harrison McCain responsible for Britain, Europe, the Middle East, and Africa. Bata Ltd. is also organized on a territorial basis (see the Global Management insert entitled "Corporate Structure at Bata Ltd."). Territorial departmentation encourages better service to customers because local personnel know the special needs and problems of their local market.

FIGURE 7-8 DEPARTMENTATION BY TERRITORY.

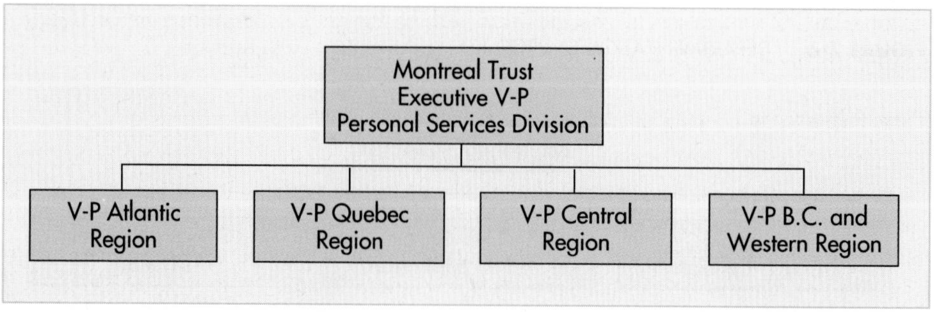

GLOBAL MANAGEMENT

Corporate Structure at Bata Ltd.

Bata Ltd. is headquartered in Toronto. It has 66 000 employees, 6300 shoe stores, and operates in 68 countries. Bata sells more than 1 million pairs of shoes each day. In an industry where footwear trends have to be quickly sensed and acted upon, the enormous size of Bata means that it must work hard to be responsive to changes demanded by the market.

The company is departmentalized on a territorial basis with divisions operating in Europe, Africa, the Far East, and South America. Each of these regions is headed by a regional executive. In spite of its international operations, Bata has not been considered a global corporation in the usual sense of the word. It is not a vertically integrated production and marketing company. In fact, the company's products vary from region to region in accordance with the local population's wants and needs. The result is that the company is a "multidomestic" operation, with each of the subsidiaries operating more or less autonomously.

The economics of the footwear industry have changed in recent years, and Bata has been running to keep up with companies like Reebok International Ltd. and Nike. Reebok and Nike manufacture shoes in low-cost areas like Korea, Taiwan, and China and then use a central office to market and distribute them. Bata, by contrast, operates factories around the world, gearing its production to the local population. This arrangement has led to poor integration of its operations.

Recognizing the need to change, the company has embarked on a major streamlining of its operations. Even though Bata has been highly decentralized, it still had excess layers of management at head office. The first step in revamping the operation was to flatten the organizational pyramid so that changes in the market could be quickly responded to. The restructuring has meant great improvements, according to Tom Bata, Jr. He noted that having a series of executives in Toronto resulted in duplication and power struggles. The restructuring means that there is now just one layer of managers between top management and the managers in the various countries where Bata operates.

The shift has meant an increase in power and responsibility for managers remaining in the hierarchy, and a decrease in the amount of time key figures spend politicking and selling their ideas to the entrenched hierarchy. Now, the four men who make up the international head office are out of the country 60-70 percent of the time.

The company has evolved into a "horizontal corporation," a term used by Harvard Business School professor Michael Porter to describe corporations that must resolve both global interests and local interests. The horizontal corporation is based on the premise that the old-style multinational company is too rigid, too hierarchical, and too attuned to the interests of the "home country." Horizontal corporations stress lateral decision making and a common set of shared ideas, not the vertical chain of command. ▲

Departmentation by Project

project departmentation

Project departmentation is typically used when the work of an organization consists of a series of projects with a specific beginning and ending. Project departmentation is often used in the construction and aerospace industries (see Figure 7-9). When a project starts (e.g., a hydroelectric generating station or a rocket guidance system), it is added to the organization chart, and when it is completed, it is taken off the organization chart. Organization charts for firms with many projects are therefore revised frequently. Project departmentation is discussed in detail in Chapter 8.

Combination Departmentation

In practice, most organizations use multiple bases of departmentation. No one form of departmentation meets the needs of firms such as Bell Canada, Bristol Aerospace, Revenue Canada, Eaton's, Saskatchewan Telephones, or First City Trust. The organization of Montreal Trust illustrates how multiple bases of departmentation can be used within one organization (see Figure 7-10). At the top (divisional)

FIGURE 7-9 DEPARTMENTATION BY PROJECT.

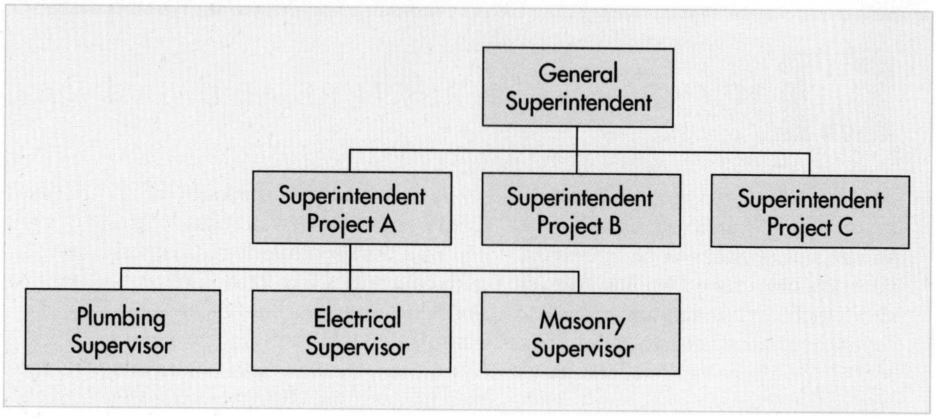

level, departments are organized mainly on the basis of the customers the firm sells to. Within the personal services division, functional departmentation is used, while the branch offices in the personal services division are departmentalized on a territorial basis. Figure 7-11 shows some of the complexities in determining how Canadian business firms are departmentalized.

In practice, the basis of departmentation a company is using is not always clear. In the Metals Group division at Federal Industries, the basis of departmentation is obviously functional, with vice-presidents of corporate development, planning, human resources, and a controller (Figure 7-11a).

At Falconbridge Ltd., on the other hand, the organization is not as clear-cut. Functional departmentation dominates, with senior vice presidents in charge of human resource management, finance, business development and planning, public affairs, and environmental services. But there are also two product vice-presidents, one for nickel and one for gold (Figure 7-11b).

FIGURE 7-10 COMBINATION DEPARTMENTATION.

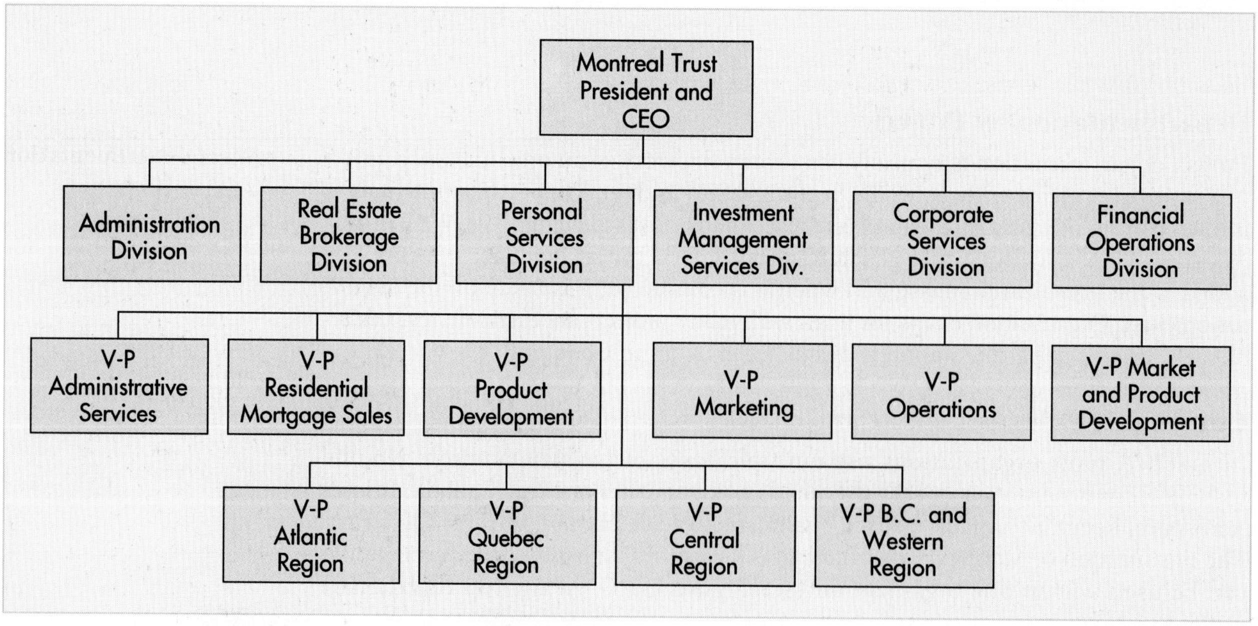

FIGURE 7-11 DEPARTMENTATION IN CANADIAN BUSINESS FIRMS.

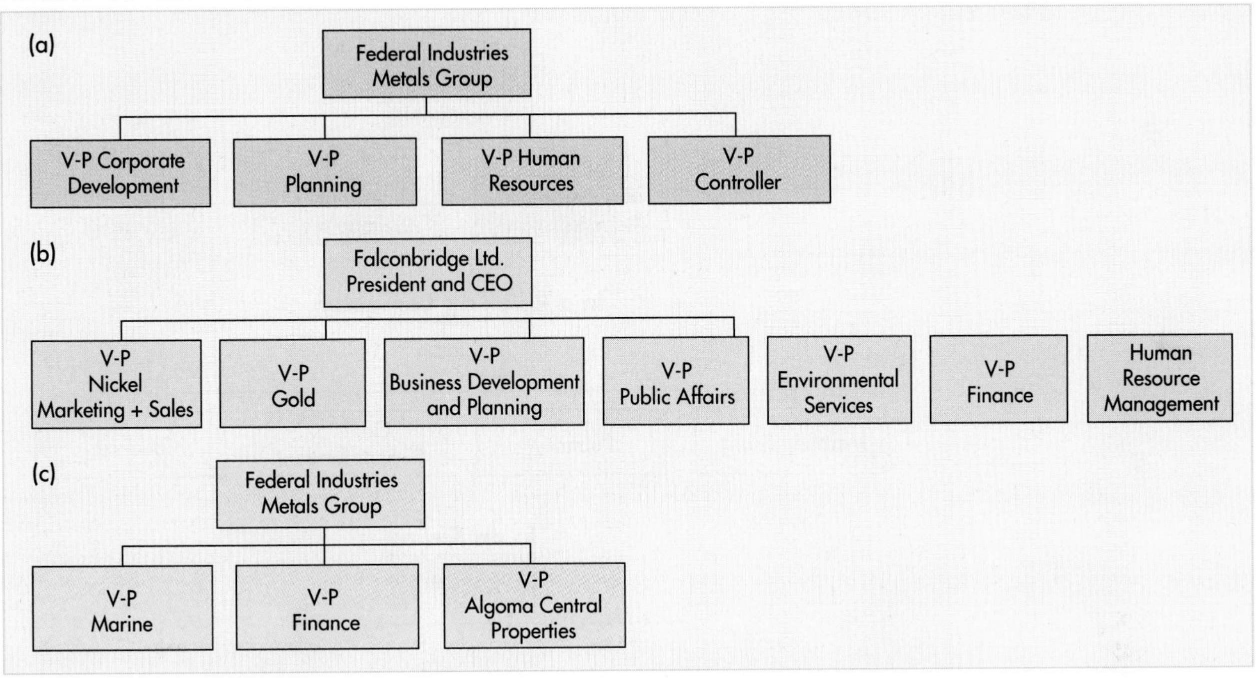

Algoma Central Railway is also departmentalized on multiple bases at the same organizational level, with both functional departmentation (finance) and product departmentation (marine division, Algoma Central Properties) being represented (Figure 7-11c).

Multiple bases of departmentation, even at the same level, are common in Canadian business firms.

TWO BASIC ORGANIZATIONAL STRUCTURES

LEARNING OBJECTIVE 6
Explain the difference between the functional structure and the divisional structure.

So far we have looked at what an organizational structure is, some classical organizing principles, and some specific ways that the total work of the organization can be divided. An important question still remains: what basic organizational structures exist? A glance at the organization charts of many organizations will reveal what appears to be an infinite variety of structures. However, a close examination shows that most of them fit into one of two basic categories: functional or divisional.

THE FUNCTIONAL STRUCTURE

functional structure

The functional structure is the oldest and most commonly used structure. In the **functional structure**, the various units in the organization are formed on the basis of the functions that must be carried out to reach organizational goals. The functional structure makes use of departmentation by function. Examples of functional structures are shown in Figure 7-12. In each example, the activities of the various functional areas must be coordinated by the highest level of management so that they fit together in a coherent way. If this coordination is not achieved, the organization will not reach its goals. The ways in which this coordination might be achieved are discussed later in this chapter.

FIGURE 7-12 EXAMPLES OF FUNCTIONAL STRUCTURES.

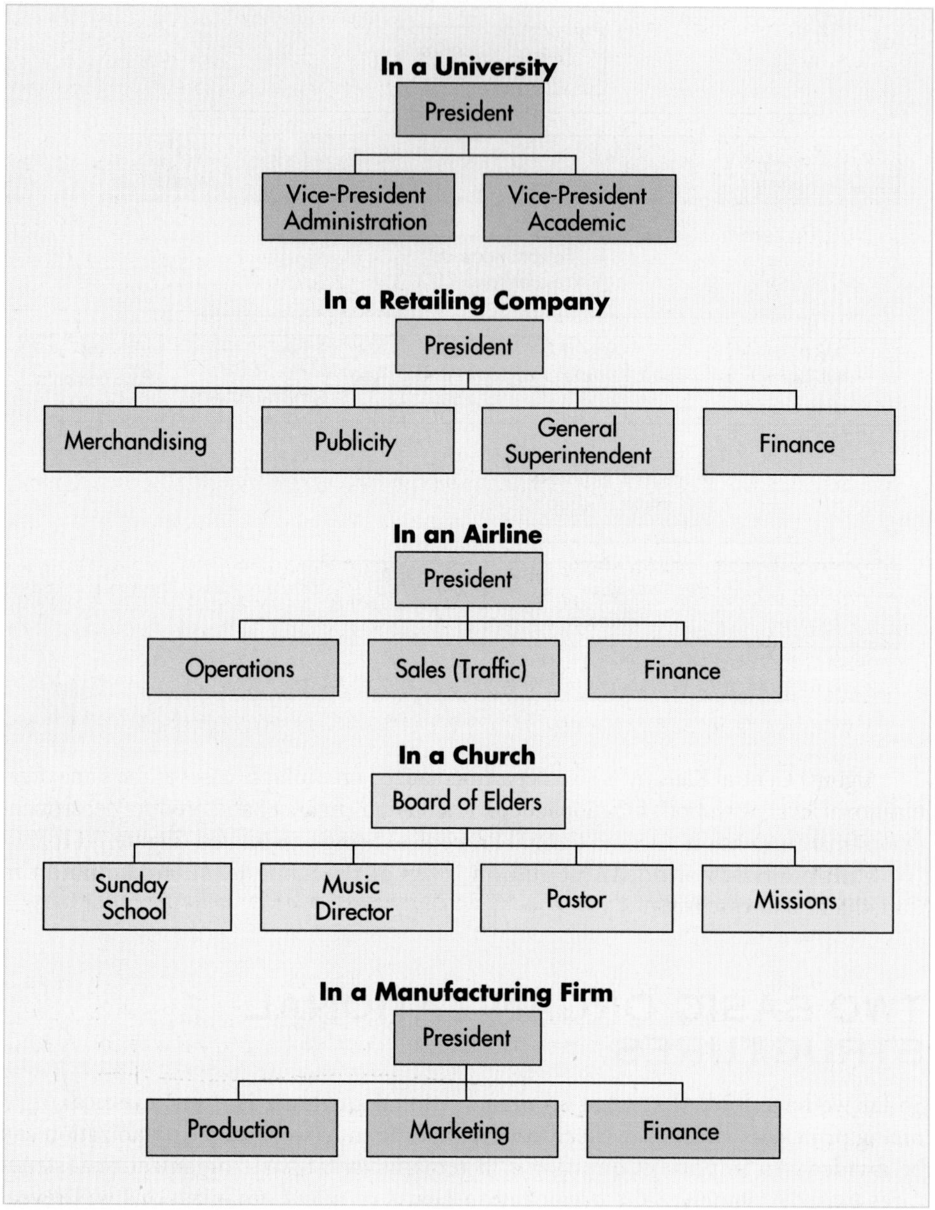

Advantages of a Functional Structure

The functional structure has several advantages.

1. *It focusses attention on the key functions that must be performed* Setting up a structure that stresses specific functions conveys to employees the tasks the organization must perform to be successful.
2. *It encourages the specialization of labour* Specialization normally leads to efficiency in the performance of tasks. A person who is a specialist in marketing, for example, will likely do a better marketing job than a person who knows only a little bit about marketing.

3. *It provides a career path for people with specialized skills* Individuals can begin work in a certain functional area and spend their career developing expertise in that area. As well, employees in each of the functional areas work with people who have training similar to theirs. Tasks are easily accomplished because employees are pursuing the same goals as their co-workers.

4. *It is easy for employees to understand the structure* The identification of specific functional areas conveys to employees what the major functions of the organization are.

5. *It eliminates the duplication of activities* In this structure, there is only one marketing department, one production department, one finance department, and so on. With only one department for each of the key functions, it is unlikely that duplication of activities will occur.

Disadvantages of a Functional Structure

In spite of its advantages, the functional structure does have some disadvantages.

1. *Employees may become overly concerned with their own specialized area* When employees become excessively concerned with their particular function and ignore its relation to the rest of the organization, overall organizational performance may decline. This problem often arises between marketing and production. Marketing wants a diverse product line and quick delivery times in order to maximize sales, but production wants a limited product line and long production runs in order to minimize costs. If these departments are allowed to pursue their own goals, the total organization will suffer.

2. *No single function is accountable for overall organizational results* Since no single function can achieve organizational goals by itself, each one can argue that it is blameless if the organization as a whole doesn't perform well. If a company fails to make a profit, which functional area is to blame? Marketing? Production? Finance?

3. *Top management may lack the proper training* Since each manager works in a specialized area, he or she may not be getting suitable training for a position in top management (e.g., president). The top executive must be able to see how all aspects of the organization fit together, but someone who has risen through the ranks of one specialized area may have difficulty seeing the contribution of other functional areas. Thus, a person who is promoted to president after a career in finance might stress finance to the detriment of marketing and production. Likewise, if a marketing executive is given the job of president, he or she might stress marketing at the expense of finance and production.

4. *Coordinating the activity of specialized functions may be difficult* The employees in each functional area will naturally focus their attention on the work of their function. Coordinating the activity of the functional areas may be difficult because people are preoccupied with their specific functional work. In the Management Challenge, Richter Hardware used a functional structure. The merchandising and marketing vice-presidents got into an argument because no one was coordinating their activities, and the marketing vice-president argued that it wasn't her job to coordinate the marketing and merchandising functions. Overcoming this deficiency may mean shifting from a functional structure to a more integrated one which emphasizes interdepartmental coordination.[21]

TABLE 7-4 ADVANTAGES AND DISADVANTAGES OF A FUNCTIONAL STRUCTURE.

Advantages	Disadvantages
1. Focusses attention on the key activities that must be performed.	1. Conflicts may arise among the functional areas.
2. Expertise develops within each function.	2. No single function is responsible for overall organizational performance.
3. Employees have clearly defined career paths.	3. Employees in each functional area have a narrow view of the organization.
4. The structure is simple and easy to understand.	4. Decision making is slowed because functional areas must get approval from top management for a variety of decisions.
5. Eliminates duplication of activities.	5. Coordinating highly specialized functions may be difficult.

5. *Conflict may arise among the various functional areas* Each area may have strong views about how it can best contribute to the organization as a whole. Purchasing agents may want to be involved in more than just placing orders, while managers in the marketing, finance, and production areas may want to restrict purchasing agents to the order-taking function. A conflict between purchasing agents and functional managers in this situation is likely.

The advantages and disadvantages of the functional structure are summarized in Table 7-4.

THE DIVISIONAL STRUCTURE

divisional structure

The **divisional structure** divides the organization into several divisions, each of which operates as a semiautonomous unit and profit centre. For example, Ontario Hydro is divided into three semiautonomous businesses, each of which is responsible for its own bottom line. Even partial privatization has been mentioned.[22] Another instance occurred in 1990, Alberta's Conservative government unveiled a new divisional structure and a new name for Alberta Government Telephones (AGT).[23] The organization is called Telus Corporation, and is patterned after Montreal-based BCE. It will oversee the telecommunications activity of seven operating companies, including AGT.

Divisions in organizations are most commonly set up on the basis of products, customers, or geography (refer back to Figures 7-6, 7-7, and 7-8 for examples). Whatever basis is used, divisional performance can be assessed each year because the division operates as a separate company. Firms with this structure are often called *conglomerates.*

Advantages of a Divisional Structure

This type of structure has several advantages.

1. *It accommodates change or expansion* If a company wishes to expand into additional product lines, it can simply add another division to focus on these new products or markets. If it wishes to expand into another geographic region, it can simply add another division to handle the new region. If it wishes to sell to new customers, it can set up a division to identify and deal with these new customers.

2. *It increases accountability* Each of the divisions is responsible for reaching its own profit targets. Regardless of whether the division is based on products, customers,

or geography, managers within each division think in terms of actions that will generate profits for the division.

3. *Expertise is developed in each division* If a division is organized by the products it sells, the managers within that division will have detailed knowledge about those products. If a division is organized by geographic location, managers in that division will have detailed knowledge about the markets they serve. If a division is organized by the customers it serves, managers will have detailed knowledge about those customers. In each case, such understanding helps the organization deliver a desired product or service to the market.

4. *It encourages training for top management* Since the head of a division must coordinate the various areas in the division, the divisional structure is a good training ground for top managers. A person who has successfully headed a single division in a company could likely take over as chief executive officer of the entire firm because of his or her previous experience as a division chief. Since a firm that is divisionally organized typically has several divisions—each with its own top management—the organization will have a pool of experienced managers who can be promoted to the job of CEO when the need arises.

Disadvantages of a Divisional Structure

Divisional structures also have some definite problems.

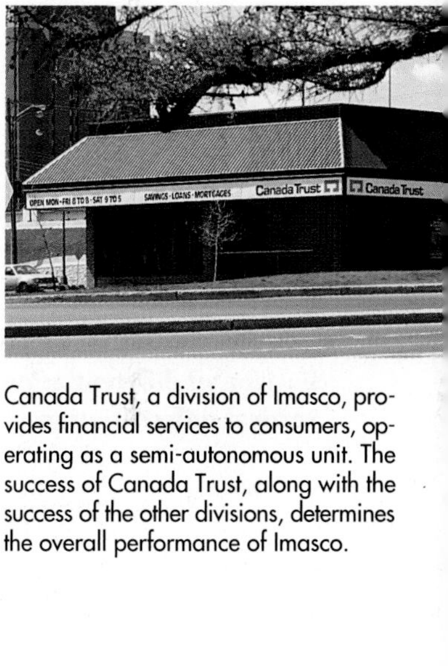

Canada Trust, a division of Imasco, provides financial services to consumers, operating as a semi-autonomous unit. The success of Canada Trust, along with the success of the other divisions, determines the overall performance of Imasco.

1. *Lack of communication among the divisions* Each division in a conglomerate will have specialists (e.g., chemists, geologists, engineers, etc.) that carry out the work of their division. The communication between, say, engineers working in the consumer products division and engineers working in the military products division may be infrequent. If specialists do not have face-to-face discussions about problems they are working on, the overall firm will not benefit as it would if each specialist knew what all other specialists were doing.

2. *Activities may be duplicated* Consider a large conglomerate with 2000 employees and seven divisions. It is quite possible that two divisions could work on the same problem and be unaware that they were doing so. For example, two divisions may each develop a new rust-inhibiting paint for their particular market and know nothing of each other's work. As a result of the duplication of tasks, less work may be accomplished than if their work had been coordinated. The costs of duplication can easily run into millions of dollars.

3. *Adding diverse divisions may cause the firm to become unfocussed* Such a diverse set of activities may be taken on that the mission of the organization becomes blurred. Many conglomerates have aggressively acquired new businesses, only to be forced to divest themselves of their acquisitions because they didn't have the product or market knowledge to make them succeed. Federal Industries, for example, sold off several divisions which had not performed as well as the company had hoped.

4. *Divisional politics may influence the allocation of resources to different divisions* Since each division is responsible for its own profit or loss, there may be some manoeuvring for resources which can be used to achieve profits. In addition, divisions may try to enhance short-run profitability at the expense of long-term division viability as they try to reach profit goals imposed by the parent company.

The advantages and disadvantages of the divisional structure are summarized in Table 7-5.

TABLE 7-5 ADVANTAGES AND DISADVANTAGES OF A DIVISIONAL STRUCTURE.

Advantages	Disadvantages
1. Accommodates change and expansion.	1. Activities may be duplicated across divisions.
2. Increases accountability.	2. A lack of communication among divisions may occur.
3. Develops expertise in the various divisions.	3. Adding diverse divisions may not be helpful to the organization.
4. Encourages training for top management.	4. Politics may affect the allocation of resources.

COORDINATION

We saw earlier in this chapter that each organization must decide on the degree of specialization of labour that it will use to reach its goals. While specialization of labour is necessary for the achievement of objectives, it can also create problems. The major pitfall is that members of different departments often come to believe that their way is the only way of looking at a certain situation. This may lead to competition or conflict among departments.

DIFFERENTIATION

LEARNING OBJECTIVE 7
Explain the concepts of differentiation and integration.

differentiation
horizontal differentiation
vertical differentiation

Departments develop their own distinct characteristics because each one is engaged in specialized work. **Differentiation** refers to the differences that exist across departments in an organization. **Horizontal differentiation** refers to differences among departments at the same level in the hierarchy. **Vertical differentiation** refers to differences among departments at different levels in the hierarchy. Differentiation can be measured by looking at four specific factors:[24]

1. *Differences in goals* Separate departments set separate goals. For example, production people may strive for low unit cost, which they feel can be achieved by producing only a few standard products. Marketing people may set a goal of high sales, which they feel can be achieved by having a variety of products that cater to many consumer preferences.
2. *Differences in structure* Different departments use different structures to achieve their goals. In some departments, all work is rigidly controlled and done "by the book." In others, a less rigid structure may exist.
3. *Differences in time orientation* Different departments have different time horizons in their work. For example, in the production area, a sense of urgency may be felt about what will be produced in the next hour, while in the research and development department, the concern may be that the current research project be completed within six months.
4. *Differences in interpersonal relations* The nature of interpersonal relations varies across departments. Where a hierarchy of authority is strictly followed, there is likely to be very little sharing of ideas among personnel, but where the input of all members is encouraged, there is likely to be a great deal of discussion and sharing of ideas.

In combination, these four factors can lead to marked differences among departments. In a research lab there may be a very loose structure, a long time horizon, extensive sharing of ideas, and goals which are stated in very general terms. In a production department, on the other hand, there may be a rigid hierarchical structure, a short time horizon, little sharing of ideas, and goals which are stated in very specific terms.

While differentiation allows each department to develop the atmosphere which is necessary to attain its own goals, the dissimilarities may lead to conflict among departments. In a school of business, for instance, marketing and organizational behaviour instructors may feel that the curriculum contains too many "technical" courses like accounting, finance, and quantitative methods. The accounting, finance, and management science faculty, by contrast, may feel that marketing and organizational behaviour are "soft" areas where students are not given definitive answers to management problems. Such discrepant views can cause intense friction.

INTEGRATION

While an organization must divide its overall goals into specific ones for each department, it also has to make sure that the various differentiated departments are coordinated (integrated) so that their work contributes to the overall organizational goals. **Integration** is the state of collaboration that exists among the various departments in an organization. Integration must be achieved if an organization is to be successful. Vertical and lateral strategies can be used to achieve coordination in organizations.

integration

Vertical Strategies for Achieving Integration

LEARNING OBJECTIVE 8

Describe seven strategies for achieving coordination in organizations.

Vertical coordination strategies rely on traditional management techniques and vertical information systems to coordinate the activities of the various departments in the organization.

Traditional management techniques Some organizations try to coordinate their activities by relying solely on traditional management techniques like the chain of command, rules, procedures, policies, goals, and plans. These systems may work well if the organization does not have to cope with rapid changes in its external environment or in the technology it uses to produce goods and services. In the Management Challenge, Richter Hardware was using traditional management techniques to try to coordinate the activity of the various functional areas. With the changes that have occurred in the firm, these traditional techniques are not working very well anymore.

Vertical information systems A **vertical information system** sends information up and down the hierarchy so that more informed decisions can be made. Vertical information systems include written reports, teleconferences, computer networks, electronic mail, and so forth. These systems allow management to access large amounts of data that are needed to make decisions. They also tend to centralize decision making because the data needed to make decisions can be easily generated for top management.

vertical information systems

Many retail organizations make extensive use of vertical information systems. Canada Safeway, for example, uses optical scanners at its checkout counters. These scanners "read" data from the Uniform Product Code and store it in computer memory. Safeway can use this data to compare the effectiveness of a coupon program at one outlet, to compare sales volume at different outlets, or to compare sales volume in the various departments in each store.

Lateral Strategies for Achieving Integration

lateral relationships

Lateral relationships are those which develop between organizational members who do not interact through formal lines of authority on the organization chart. Lateral relationships help break down the barriers that develop between departments because of the division of labour. These relationships may either complement formal authority relationships or conflict with them. Because communication is so vital in lateral relationships, some writers view integration as mainly a problem of information processing.[25]

Although lateral relationships are not formally recognized on organization charts, it is imperative that they take place. Some of the important lateral relationships happen spontaneously when individuals take it upon themselves to coordinate their department's work with that of another department. But on many occasions, organizations find that they must set up systems that are specifically designed to improve lateral coordination. Commonly used lateral coordination systems include direct contact, boundary spanning roles, task forces, standing committees, and integrator roles.

Direct contact One of the simplest ways to resolve coordination problems is to have the relevant individuals get together to see if they can develop a solution to the problem. This contact often results in fast, high-quality decisions. Suppose that the production area is having problems fitting a stainless steel case on a water cooler. This problem can be solved if someone from engineering meets with the people who are actually trying to fit the case on the water cooler, even though the formal organization chart does not recognize this possibility (see Figure 7-13). Trying to resolve this problem by working upward through the chain of command would take much longer than using direct contact.

boundary spanners

Boundary spanning roles When contact between two departments is necessary on a regular basis, a boundary spanning role may be created. **Boundary spanners** facilitate coordination between two departments that have an ongoing need to coordinate their work. A boundary spanner works in one department but has regular contact with another department. Thus, a person in the systems and procedures department may be assigned to answer questions from individuals who use computing services. This person must have technical knowledge about the computer, but must also be able to understand the needs of the various users of the computer. Other examples of boundary spanners are project managers and expediters. Because of the nature of their work, boundary spanners often do not follow the formal lines of communication in the organization.

FIGURE 7-13 RESOLVING PROBLEMS THROUGH DIRECT CONTACT.

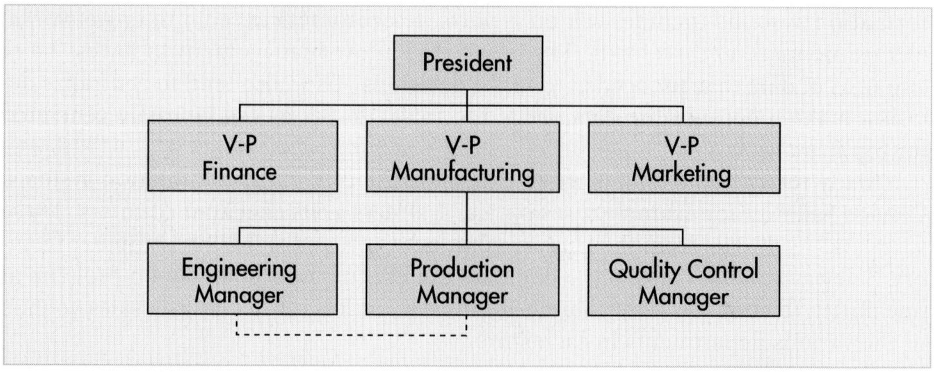

task force

Task forces A **task force** is a temporary team of specialists who are organized to solve a problem involving two or more departments.[26] Each member of the task force is expected to represent his or her area and make well-reasoned, unbiassed suggestions about how to solve the problem for the good of the organization. The task force is disbanded once it has developed a solution to the problem.

Consider how a task force worked at one of the major Canadian broadcasting organizations. In this organization, a dispute had developed between the announcers and producers. The announcers felt that they had the expertise to do a variety of on-air jobs, but several of the producers wanted to hire free-lance announcers to do these jobs. A task force—composed of announcers, producers, management, and two outside consultants—was formed to address this problem. The task force met numerous times to define problems and analyze possible solutions. After agreement had been reached on how to resolve the problem, the task force presented its recommendations to top management. Once the recommendations were implemented, the task force was disbanded.

standing committees

Standing committees **Standing committees** meet on a regular basis and are a relatively permanent feature of the organization's structure. Like task forces, they are usually composed of individuals from various departments in the organization. Unlike task forces, however, standing committees work on problems that recur with some regularity.

MEETING THE CHALLENGE

RICHTER'S HARDWARE STORE

Karl Richter has made numerous improvements to his hardware chain, but the success of his company has declined as of late. The basic problem here is that Richter has concentrated on expansion without giving much thought to the structural implications of doing so. Richter has added product lines and expanded regionally without adequately preparing existing managers, and without altering his head office's perspective of the organization.

Some of the specific manifestations of this problem emerged in the dispute between the marketing and merchandise vice-presidents. The lack of coordination between them is probably caused by the company's unstructured growth. This was probably not a problem when the company was small because these two managers would have been operating in only the Winnipeg market, and coordinating their product lines and inventory would have been quite easy through direct contact. The expanded structure has contributed to the lack of coordination by forcing managers into specialized jobs without allowing them to develop an organization-wide perspective. Therefore, they have difficulty making suggestions about how to head off these problems.

Richter needs to introduce some techniques for achieving the necessary level of coordination. Improvements in traditional management techniques and the vertical information system are clearly needed. Boundary spanning roles may have to be created to ensure that ongoing coordination needs are met in areas like merchandising and promotion.

Richter is also running into problems with the new outlets outside of Winnipeg because they are so far away from head office. For example, the vice-president of marketing in Winnipeg really didn't understand some of the these distant markets, yet her job was to advertise in them. The company's functional structure has contributed to the company's problems. In a functional structure, coordination must come from the very top of the hierarchy. Apparently this coordination has not been evident because the company is having increasing difficulty coordinating the diverse regions where Richter has stores. One obvious alternative is to use another basis of departmentation. Perhaps the most reasonable is departmentation by geographic territory. Richter could appoint two vice-presidents, one for the Winnipeg area, and one for the outlying areas. Each of these vice-presidents would be in charge of marketing, merchandising, and operations managers. If growth continues, additional vice-presidents could be added by subdividing the outlying regions even further. ▲

In manufacturing firms, for example, new product committees are normally standing committees. They are composed of members from various departments in the organization, and they consider new product proposals that come forward, either from inside or outside the organization. In churches, the missions committee is normally a standing committee. It decides which missionaries will be supported, and how much financial support they will receive.

integrator

Integrators An **integrator** is a person who is assigned responsibility for coordinating the ongoing work of several departments whose work is highly interdependent. Unlike any of the coordinating positions described above, the integrator may have considerable authority over the various areas that he or she is coordinating. Project managers (discussed in Chapter 8) are integrators.

SUMMARY

Organizing is the process of deciding which specific functions should be performed, and how these functions should be coordinated so that organizational goals are reached. Organizational structure is the pattern of formal relationships among groups and individuals in an organization. Organizational structures exhibit varying degrees of formalization, centralization, complexity, and specialization.

The organizing process involves (1) determining the specific tasks that must be accomplished, (2) dividing the total work into functions, (3) grouping those individuals whose work is closely related, and (4) coordinating the work of different groups and individuals.

The organization chart is a pictorial representation of formal authority relationships in an organization. It shows vertical authority relationships, the types of work performed, the different departments that do the work, the formal communication channels, and the various levels of management. It does not show how much authority each manager possesses, what the organization's objectives are, the significant factors in the external environment of the organization, the comparative importance of jobs in different departments, or the informal relationships that exist in the organization.

Several organizing principles guide the behaviour of managers. These principles include the unity of command (each subordinate should have only one boss), equal authority and responsibility (a person must have enough authority to do a job properly), the scalar principle (a clear unbroken line of authority should run from the top of the organization to the bottom), and the span of control (there is a limit to the number of subordinates a manager can control). In recent years, spans of control have increased in many companies as entire layers of management have disappeared because of downsizing.

Departmentation is the grouping of functions or major work activities into coherent units. Organizations commonly use departmentation by function (units are formed on the basis of the organization's key functions), by products (units are formed on the basis of the products sold), by customer (units are formed on the basis of who the customers are), by territories (units are formed on the basis of where the product is sold), and by project (units are formed for temporary, time-framed projects).

Two basic types of organizational structures exist—functional and divisional. In a functional structure, departments are set up on the basis of the key functions the organization must perform in order to be effective. The functional structure encourages specialization of labour, provides a career path for people with specialized skills, is easy for the employees to understand, and eliminates duplication of activities. However, a functional organization may also encourage employees to become overly concerned with their own specialized area, it may fail to provide training for a position in top management, and have no single function accountable for overall organizational results.

In a divisional structure, semiautonomous divisions are created to operate as profit centres. A divisional structure readily accommodates expansion, increases accountability, and encourages training for top management. However, a divisional structure may cause a duplication of activities, create poor communication between divisions, and encourage the acquisition of businesses that fit poorly together.

Differentiation refers to the differences that exist across departments as a result of the different work they do. Different departments have differences in goals, structure, time orientation, and interpersonal relations. These differences require coordination if the organization is to reach its goals. Integration (coordination) is the state of collaboration that exists among the various departments of an organization. The two main strategies used to achieve coordination are vertical and lateral coordination. Vertical strategies include traditional management techniques (rules, policies, procedures, etc.), and vertical information systems (written reports, teleconferences, computer networks, etc.). Lateral strategies include direct contact (getting individuals from different departments together informally to solve a problem), boundary spanning (formally assigning an individual to coordinate the work of two departments), task forces (temporary interdepartmental teams who work on problems), standing committees (permanent interdepartmental teams who work on problems), and integrators (individuals who are assigned responsibility for coordinating the ongoing work of two or more departments whose work is highly interdependent).

KEY TERMS

organizing (p. 200)
organizational structure (p. 201)
restructuring (p. 201)
formalization (p. 201)
centralization (p. 202)
complexity (p. 203)
specialization (p. 203)
organization chart (p. 204)
unity of command principle (p. 206)
scalar principle (p. 206)
span of control (p. 207)
downsizing (p. 207)
departmentation (p. 210)
functional departmentation (p. 211)
product departmentation (p. 211)
customer departmentation (p. 212)
territorial departmentation (p. 212)
project departmentation (p. 213)
functional structure (p. 215)
divisional structure (p. 218)
differentiation (p. 220)
horizontal differentiation (p. 220)
vertical differentiation (p. 220)
integration (p. 221)
vertical information systems (p. 221)
lateral relationships (p. 222)
boundary spanners (p. 222)
task force (p. 223)
standing committees (p. 223)
integrator (p. 224)

REVIEW QUESTIONS

1. What are the primary dimensions of an organization's structure? Use these dimensions to contrast two different organizations that you are familiar with.
2. What is specialization of labour? What are its advantages? Its disadvantages?
3. What are the major steps in the organizing process?
4. What criterion is normally used to decide which functions should be grouped together? Why might it be difficult to use this criterion?
5. What does the organization chart show? What is not shown on an organization chart?
6. State four principles of organizing.
7. What factors influence the span of control?
8. List the various bases of departmentation that can be used to subdivide tasks in an organization. What is the rationale for each basis of departmentation?
9. What are the advantages and disadvantages of each basis of departmentation?
10. What are the two fundamental organization structures that organizations use? Describe the strengths and weaknesses of each. Which type is best?
11. What is differentiation? What factors are used to measure the amount of differentiation that exists in an organization?
12. What is integration? What strategies are available for achieving integration in organizations?

DISCUSSION QUESTIONS

1. What is the relationship between specialization and departmentation?
2. What would you say to a manager who wanted to reduce the number of organizational levels to improve vertical communication, and also wanted to have narrow spans of management so that subordinates could be closely controlled?
3. What are some of the factors which should be considered when management is trying to decide whether to use a functional or a divisional structure?
4. What is the relationship between the span of control and the shape of an organization? How has downsizing affected the span of control?
5. How can a person tell whether a company is organized functionally or divisionally?
6. What is the relationship between differentiation and integration?

EXERCISES

1. Obtain the annual reports of two corporations of your choice. Answer the following questions:
   a. Which of the two basic structures (functional or divisional) does each firm have?
   b. What bases of departmentation are used within the basic structure of the firm?
   c. Do the structures used in the two firms seem to be consistent with the structure that should be used?
2. Find an article in *The Globe and Mail* or *Canadian Business* which describes a corporate reorganization. Prepare a five-minute talk on the subject which covers the following points:
   a. the organization's structure before the reorganization
   b. the problems which motivated the reorganization
   c. the organization's structure after the reorganization
   d. the benefits that should be evident as a result of the reorganization
3. Interview a manager on the subject of differentiation and integration. Obtain the manager's responses to the following questions:
   a. What do differentiation and integration mean in your firm?
   b. What kind of coordination problems exist?
   c. What coordinating mechanisms are used to solve these problems?

MANAGEMENT ON LOCATION

CASE 7-1
CONDUCTING BUSINESS

The market for classical music, like the market for many products and services, has been difficult for the past few years. The Toronto Symphony Orchestra, for example, has been losing approximately 5 percent of its subscriber base each year. In addition, government grants have been steadily declining. On top of this are the usual problems of personnel squabbles, rigid hierarchies, and labour strife.

But there is one organization that has been able to avoid all of these problems. The Tafelmusik (German for "table music") Baroque Orchestra is a Toronto chamber group with a worldwide reputation for interpreting baroque and classical music. Harmony in the organization extends from the concert stage to the management offices. The orchestra has a flat organization structure, and its musicians are more concerned with performance than with promotion. In fact, the orchestra doesn't even have an organization chart; rather, it fits structure around people.

In spite of the economic downturn of the past few years, the orchestra has managed to increase its Toronto box office revenue from $170 000 to $528 000. The number of season subscribers has more than doubled to 3200. Its record company—Sony Classical—has released 15 compact discs in two years, and its recordings promote the orchestra around the world.

The conductor-CEO is Jeanne Lamon, a virtuoso violinist and concertmaster; she coaxes award-winning performances out of the gifted musicians around her. She also chooses the pieces the orchestra will perform, but she welcomes suggestions from musicians and critiques from her colleagues in senior management. The other members of the management team are Ottie Lockey (a soprano before she developed her administration talents) and Heather Clark (a music graduate of McGill). These three women bring to Tafelmusik a combination of strategic planning, creative marketing, and modern management and financial controls, a combination which is rare in arts organizations.

A case study by Douglas Buck, an arts management professor at York University, describes Tafelmusik as a horizontal management structure in which decisions are made in a consensus-building environment. The 16 core members of the orchestra are consulted on issues as diverse as the orchestra's repertoire and its box office computer system. Musicians also sit on committees dealing with costumes, fund raising, and photography. They even rotate simple jobs like setting up chairs when necessary and sometimes play for free at fund-raisers. ▲

QUESTIONS

1. How have the four dimensions of organizational structure manifested themselves in this organization?
2. How is Tafelmusik able to operate without an organization structure?
3. Is authority centralized or decentralized? (Consult Chapter 8 before answering this question.)
4. Does Tafelmusik have a functional or divisional structure? Explain.

CASE 7-2
CARLTON'S VARIETY STORES

John Carlton is the owner of Carlton's Variety Stores, a chain of small, but well-known stores in Ontario. The stores carry a diverse line of products including magazines, tobacco products, greeting cards, toiletries, school supplies, vitamins, and paper products. The depth of each product line is limited.

Carlton's has been successful since its beginning 24 years ago. At present, there are 16 stores in the chain and Carlton is continually adding more. John Carlton is a hard-driving, take-charge type of person, and has always felt that he must be knowledgeable about every aspect of store operation. He closely supervises his subordinates and has instituted several management systems including management by objectives (MBO), which is designed to

• • •

ensure high efficiency and motivation among his employees.

Carlton believes that his company has been successful because he has kept a tight rein on operations. Four vice-presidents and the 16 store managers report directly to him (see Figure 7-14).

During the last year or so, the firm has experienced declining profitability and a rate of sales increase that is below the company's normal standards. Carlton senses that something is wrong with the business, but he's not sure what is causing the problem or what to do to solve it. All he knows is that each year he is busier and more harried than ever.

At a recent meeting of the executive committee (comprised of Carlton and the four vice-presidents), several comments were made which indicated that the firm was having difficulty adjusting to changes in consumer preferences. Complaints have increasingly been heard at the store level that the lines of merchandise that are carried are not what customers want. It was also pointed out that the motivation levels of retail salesclerks left much to be desired. ▲

FIGURE 7-14 ORGANIZATION CHART OF CARLTON'S VARIETY STORES.

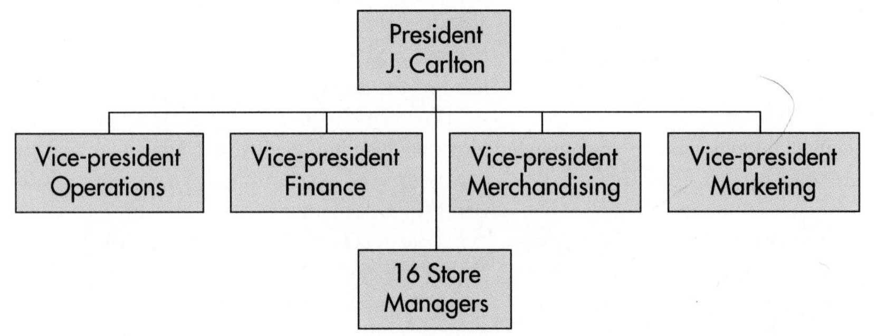

QUESTIONS

1. Identify the sources of the problems that Carlton's is experiencing.
2. Redesign the organization chart to make it more effective.

CASE 7-3
ACQUISITION VS. INDEPENDENCE

On September 15, 1991, June Gaboury, president of Central Energy, had an in-depth discussion with Albert Fournier, the chief executive officer of Dynamics, Ltd. about the possibility of being acquired by Dynamics in a friendly takeover. For some time, Gaboury had been frustrated with her inability to move Central Energy into the big time. She thought that being acquired by a large conglomerate might be useful because Central Energy would then have a much larger resource base from which to work.

Gaboury realized that this strategy was not without risks. She feared that Central might slowly (or perhaps quickly) lose its small company atmosphere if it became part of Dynamics. She was also concerned that her firm would have to adhere to certain guidelines that would be imposed by the head office of Dynamics. Given these concerns, Gaboury wanted to hear Fournier's views about an acquisition and how it might affect her firm. The conversation during the meeting ran as follows:

Gaboury: Will this merger affect the way my company is managed?

Fournier: You'll hardly notice it. You are running a successful business and we want it to continue that way. The best way to achieve this is to let you make operating decisions in the same way you have always made them.

• • •

MANAGEMENT ON LOCATION

Gaboury: Could you be more specific?

Fournier: Well, Dynamics will act as a sort of resource centre, providing you with financial resources and specialized expertise to enable you to be even more successful than you have been in the past. For example, when you need something, you put in a request and it will be considered along with the requests we receive from our nine other divisons. Of course, you will need to follow certain procedures in submitting your requests, and we will require an accounting of how your resources were expended.

Gaboury: Will Central Energy have to fit into some sort of rigid mold that is decided by Dynamics Ltd.?

Fournier: I wouldn't characterize it as rigid, but you would have to use the same accounting system and compensation program as the other divisions so that we can ensure that all divisions are treating employees equally.

Gaboury: What other requirements are there?

Fournier: You will have to submit one-year and five-year sales forecasts and an annual profit objective. But I think you'll find this to be helpful to you in clarifying what you want Central to achieve each year.

Gaboury: What if we don't meet our targets?

Fournier: If you run into problems, our experts in production, marketing, and cost control will help you determine the causes and recommend solutions. You will continue to run your business as you did before, only now it will be within the context of a large organization which will provide direction and support when it is needed.

After the meeting with Fournier, Gaboury found herself deep in thought about the acquisition. She realized than many questions remained unanswered. She felt that Central Energy could substantially improve its performance if it was backed by a powerful conglomerate like Dynamics, but she worried about a lot of potential problems, including the possibility that she would be let go at some future date if Central did not meet Dynamics' standards. ▲

QUESTIONS

1. What kind of organizational arrangement will exist between Central Energy and Dynamics Ltd. if the takeover occurs?
2. What issues need to be clarified before June Gaboury agrees to let Central Energy be acquired by Dynamics Ltd.?

CHAPTER

8

AUTHORITY, RESPONSIBILITY, AND ORGANIZATIONAL DESIGN

LEARNING OBJECTIVES

After reading this chapter, you will be able to:

1. Define the terms authority, delegation, responsibility, and accountability.
2. Describe five advantages of delegating authority.
3. Understand the concepts of centralization and decentralization, and identify the factors that determine the level of each in an organization.
4. Describe the main features of the line organization and the line-staff organization.
5. Explain what functional authority is and why it is used.
6. Draw a chart showing how a project organization would look.
7. Explain how organizational structure is influenced by the external environment, by technology, and by organizational size.
8. Distinguish between mechanistic and organic organizations.

MANAGEMENT CHALLENGE

RESTRUCTURING IN THE OIL INDUSTRY

The petroleum industry has been having its share of problems during the last 10 years. In 1991, the Canadian Petroleum Association (representing "big oil") and the Independent Petroleum Association of Canada (representing smaller firms) commissioned a study of the long-term prospects for the industry. The report noted the unprofitability of the oil business in the last half of the 1980s, and projected that it would continue well into the 1990s. It predicted that losses and layoffs would continue to occur, reserves will continue to decline, and operating costs would continue to go up. All of this has already been reflected in the price of oil stocks, which have declined more than 20 percent.

Oil production in western Canada has been declining since the mid-1970s. Canada still produces about as much oil as it did in the mid-1980s, but it takes twice as many wells to produce it. Esso's Redwater oil field, for example, produced 100 000 barrels per day in the early 1970s, but now produces only about 5000 in the same time. Also, other expenses, such as pumping water back into the ground to keep the field going, are now higher.

In the early days of the oil boom in Alberta in the 1940s, it appeared that the price of oil was going to rise forever. With oil costing less than $1.50 per barrel to extract, and selling for more than $3 per barrel, it made sense for oil companies to get a piece of as many potential oil-producing properties as they could. The

...

result was that major companies like Esso Resources Canada, Shell Canada Ltd., and Amoco ended up owning thousands of investments representing 7 percent of this, 4 percent of that, and 1 percent of something else. One fifth of the properties produced 80 percent of the revenues, while the other four fifths produced the other 20 percent (and a large bureaucracy).

The amount of overhead required to keep track of all these properties was enormous; for example, hundreds of land specialists were employed to track properties under lease. Company printing shops, legal departments, data processing departments, and accountants were also part of the large bureaucracy that was evident.

By the mid-1980s, it was becoming clear that the oil fields weren't pumping enough oil to pay for this bureaucracy. Oil companies now realize that they are going to have to respond to tough economic times. And many oil executives are starting to take a hard look at their strategies and operating methods. What is disappearing are some relics of the past such as diverse investments, large bureaucracies, multilayered organizational structures, and tendencies toward departmental empire building. They are being replaced with a team-oriented culture that focusses on the company's core assets. ▲

In Chapter 7, we looked at the organizing process and how organizations are structured. In this chapter, we examine several concepts that have an impact on how well the formal organizational structure works. First, we define four important terms: authority, delegation, responsibility, and accountability. Second, we discuss centralization and decentralization of authority, and the factors that determine the extent to which authority will be decentralized. Third, we make the distinction between line and staff managers, and describe the authority that each possess. Fourth, the concept of project management is introduced, and the authority relations in this structure are analyzed. The chapter concludes with an analysis of the impact of four factors on organizational structure—the external environment, the production technology, organizational size, and the stage of the organizational life cycle.

AUTHORITY, DELEGATION, RESPONSIBILITY, AND ACCOUNTABILITY

LEARNING OBJECTIVE 1
Define the terms authority, delegation, responsibility, and accountability.

We have seen that managers work through others to accomplish organizational goals. In order to effectively work through others, managers must have the right to assign jobs to subordinates, and to require that these subordinates carry out the jobs they have been assigned. Consequently, the concepts of authority, delegation of authority, responsibility, and accountability become central to managers in their day-to-day work.

AUTHORITY

authority

Authority is the right given to managers to take certain actions themselves or to require their subordinates to take certain actions. All managers have a certain amount of authority. Managers near the top of the organizational hierarchy have a wide scope of authority, while those near the bottom have a narrower scope (see Figure 8-1). A vice-president of marketing at Imperial Oil, for example, has more authority to take action than a first-line supervisor at an Imperial refinery.

In some organizations, who has what authority may be a matter of debate. The *Harvard Business Review* is the journal that managers turn to when they want to know how to do something right. But in 1993, the journal announced the hiring of a new executive editor, Joel Kurtzman, without even mentioning T. George Harris, current editor who had been hired only four months before. It seems that Harris had

FIGURE 8-1 THE SCOPE OF AUTHORITY AT DIFFERENT MANAGEMENT LEVELS.

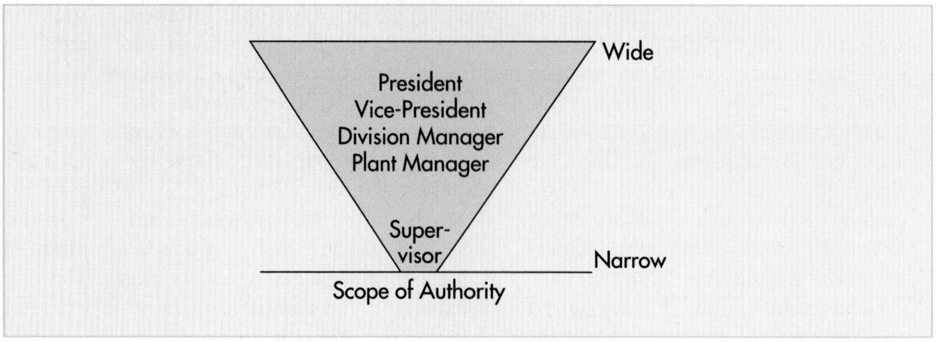

helped recruit Kurtzman for the No. 2 spot at the publication without knowing that Kurtzman was slated to be the top person, and that he himself was on his way out.[1]

Several observations can be made about managerial authority. First, authority is a right. When a manager is put into a position in the organizational hierarchy, that manager is given certain rights to command subordinates. Generally speaking, subordinates recognize this fact because the formal authority of the organization backs the manager. The right to command is available to whomever occupies the managerial position. As we shall see in the next chapter, this does not automatically mean that each manager is effective in using authority.

Second, authority must be used to accomplish the legitimate goals of the organization. Managers who use authority to "order people about" just to please their own whims will be ineffective. Managers are given authority to help achieve organizational goals rather than their own personal goals. A rather radical view of how to best use authority is described in the Management at Work insert entitled "The Circular Organization."

Third, the exercise of authority should cause managers to consider how their jobs interrelate with those of their subordinates. If managers understand this relation, the interaction of managers and subordinates will result in positive outcomes for the organization.

Finally, the amount of authority given to managers varies across departments at the same level in one organization, and across similar departments in different organizations. For example, in the matter of acquiring new personnel, a middle manager in one organization may have the right to recruit, screen, interview, and make the final hiring decision on all new personnel. A middle manager in another organization may only have the right to recruit and hire subject to approval from top management. In still another organization, a manager may have virtually no authority in this area; instead, he or she may be forced to accept whomever the personnel department has chosen.

Delegation of Authority

delegation

Managers cannot do all the work that is required of their unit. They must delegate some of their authority to subordinates. **Delegation** is the assignment of specific tasks to subordinates along with the authority to carry out those assignments.

One of the classic faults of managers is the failure to delegate authority (see the Management Challenge in Chapter 1). A failure to delegate means that (1) the manager will have to make all the decisions for the unit, (2) subordinates will be unhappy because they are given no discretion when doing their jobs, and (3) the manager will not give adequate attention to the functions of planning, organizing, leading, and controlling. Managers who do not delegate authority usually rationalize their behaviour on

MANAGEMENT AT WORK

The Circular Organization

The concept of the "circular organization" was originally developed to achieve three organizational goals: (1) to implement organizational democracy, (2) to increase the ability of organizations to change, and (3) to improve the quality of working life for employees. The basic idea of the circular organization is that every manager must answer to a board. Thus, there are boards at every level of the organization, not just the top. The board includes the manager, the manager's immediate boss, and the manager's immediate subordinates. Any manager who has three or more subordinates will find that subordinates constitute a majority of the board. Their views must therefore be taken seriously. Participation on the board is mandatory for managers, but voluntary for subordinates.

Boards have the following responsibilities:

1. *Planning and policy making for the unit* The board establishes the policy, but the manager makes the decisions that are necessary to carry out the policy. Managers consult their boards regarding decisions that need to be made, but responsibility for those decisions belongs with the manager.
2. *Coordinating and integrating plans and policies of units above and below the board's level* Since managers at the next lowest level are, by definition, members of the board at the next level up, coordination and integration happen naturally. Likewise, since the manager of a board at one level is also a member of a board at the next highest level, managers have an extended vertical view of the organization. Boards are not permitted to develop plans or policies that affect other units at the same level or a higher level, unless that unit agrees.
3. *Decision making about quality of working life issues of those on the board* As in traditional hierarchies, managers retain responsibility for the quantity and quality of work done. However, when employees are given control over the quality of their working life, the quantity and quality of work output usually increases.
4. *Evaluating the performance of the manager on the board* Because subordinates are a majority on the board, the manager must satisfy them in order to maintain his or her position. Subordinates meet with their boss once a year and indicate what the boss can do to help the subordinates (who are also managers) to manage more effectively. Bosses can respond to suggestions by accepting them outright, rejecting them outright, or taking them under advisement and reporting back after a specified period of time. About half the firms that use the circular organization allow subordinates to evaluate their managers. In those that do, managers have been removed in only a few cases. Subordinates were usually able to get what they wanted through constructive criticism of their manager.

The introduction of the circular organization idea means converting an organization from an autocratic one to a democratic one. This is a profound change. Under the new system, managers are required to be leaders, educators, and facilitators, and therefore time must be allowed to make these substantial changes. ▲

the grounds that subordinates may make mistakes if they are given additional authority. Of course this might happen, but subordinates must be allowed to make some mistakes if they are going to develop as employees. Subordinates who are never given any authority will lack the training needed for managerial positions.

Advantages of Delegation

LEARNING OBJECTIVE 2
Describe five advantages of delegating authority.

The primary advantages of delegation of authority are shown in Figure 8-2. An obvious advantage is that it increases the speed of decision making. Since subordinates do not need to get their boss's permission every time a decision is made, the decision-making process is accelerated. Allowing subordinates the latitude to make certain decisions also enhances their development, and prepares them to be managers. Giving subordinates some discretion is also likely to increase their morale and their motivation to do their jobs well. Over time, as subordinates become more confident

FIGURE 8-2 FIVE ADVANTAGES OF DELEGATING AUTHORITY.

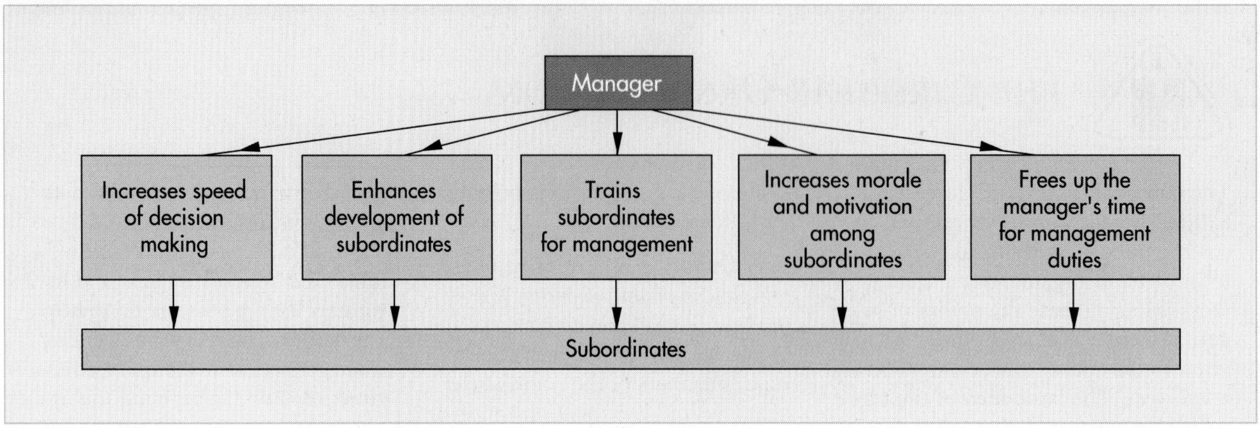

and experienced in making decisions, they are likely to make better—more well informed—decisions. Delegation also helps the manager. If subordinates are involved in making most of the decisions about the day-to-day work of the unit, the manager has more time to devote to the planning, organizing, leading, and controlling functions of management. Attention to these areas will improve the functioning of the unit.

To reduce the chance that subordinates will make costly mistakes when authority is delegated, certain guidelines should be followed:

1. Subordinates must keep the manager posted on what they are doing; otherwise the manager may lose control over what is happening.
2. The limits of authority given to subordinates must be clearly defined; if not, subordinates may try to make decisions outside their authority.
3. Authority should be delegated only to individuals who are trained to exercise it.
4. Subordinates must be given sufficient authority to allow them to do the job properly.

The delegation of authority in no way relieves managers of the ultimate responsibility for decisions made in their area. Delegation simply means assigning some part of the manager's work to someone else for completion.

Responsibility

When authority is delegated, subordinates are given certain rights to make decisions on their own without checking with their boss first. But once subordinates are given authority, they are also responsible for keeping their boss posted, and for completing the work. This fact explains why some individuals have no interest in being managers. As workers, they have very little authority, but they also have very little responsibility.

responsibility

Responsibility is the obligation of a subordinate to carry out a job in a timely fashion. When managers delegate authority, they must also tell subordinates what their responsibilities are. A failure to make the duties clear can lead to frustration for both the boss and worker.

Consider the following situation where a subordinate (Joan Diering) is trying to clarify her responsibility for certain activities with her boss (Harry Dorish):

Diering: Is my unit responsible for handling the new commercial fire insurance policies, or should Max Lanier's section handle them?

Dorish: I don't think it really matters which unit handles these new policies as long as the work is done correctly and thoroughly.

Diering: But who is ultimately responsible for seeing that these insurance policies are applied correctly?

Dorish: I'm very busy and don't have time to make a decision on this at the moment. Why don't you and Lanier get together and work it out?[2]

By refusing to clearly state what Diering's responsibilities are, Dorish is creating the possibility that (1) Diering will not know what to do, and (2) if the policies are not applied correctly there will be a dispute later on about who is at fault. For her part, Diering wants clarification so she can do her work properly. She is also concerned that if anything goes wrong, or if certain work is not done on time, that she will be blamed. Dorish must make a clear decision about who is responsible in order to avoid unsatisfactory work, confusion, and resentment.

Accountability

Every organization must have a system in place to ensure that people are accountable for completing their work in a satisfactory manner. **Accountability** involves making people answerable for the results of the work assigned to them. It means giving credit when good work is done, and attaching blame if work is not done well. If an accountability system is not in place, organizations will find that when performance is below standard, it may be impossible to determine how to fix the problem.

accountability

There are three conditions that must exist before a manager or subordinate can be held accountable for their actions.[3]

1. *Responsibilities must be clearly understood* A person who is not made aware of what tasks they are responsible for cannot easily be held accountable for those tasks. People cannot be expected to do a job they did not know they were supposed to do.

2. *The person doing the job must be capable of fulfilling the obligation* A person with no training in accounting, for example, can hardly be expected to do an accounting job properly.

3. *Sufficient authority must be delegated to the person doing the job* Making a manager responsible for the profitability of a division without giving the manager the right to hire and fire people is an example of insufficient authority. A manager without such authority cannot take the actions that are necessary to influence divisional profits.

Employees can be made accountable in several ways. The simplest and most direct way is for the manager to check on the work of subordinates. Another alternative is to have the subordinate report to the manager—either verbally or in written reports—on how the work assigned has been executed. A third option is to have someone from outside the work unit check on the progress of the work. For example, a quality control inspector could make an assessment of product quality, or surveys could be conducted to determine if customers are satisfied with the company's products or services.

CENTRALIZATION AND DECENTRALIZATION OF AUTHORITY

centralization

LEARNING OBJECTIVE 3
Understand the concepts of centralization and decentralization, and identify the factors that determine the level of each in an organization.

In every organization, management must decide how authority will be distributed throughout the hierarchy. **Centralization** occurs when top management retains the right to make most of the decisions that need to be made. Top management makes all decisions regarding the hiring and firing of personnel, the purchasing of equipment and supplies, and other key decisions. Lower-level managers and workers do what is required to ensure that top-level decisions are followed. For example, Cedric Ritchie, the CEO of the Bank of Nova Scotia, knew all the details of the bank's operations and made many decisions that CEOs of other banks delegated to subordinates.[4] Most Japanese business firms are very centralized, and their overseas managers do not have much discretion. In practice, complete centralization never happens because there are simply too many decisions to be made, even in relatively small organizations.

decentralization

Decentralization occurs when the right to make decisions is pushed down to the middle and lower levels of the management hierarchy. When Paul Tellier became president and CEO of Canadian National Railways in 1993, he introduced many changes in an attempt to return the railroad to profitability. One of these changes involved decentralizing the organization because it was too head-office-oriented. Decentralizing will mean putting responsibility for running trains at the regional level.[5]

At General Electric's Bromont, Quebec, plant every effort has been made to get employees involved in a wide range of decision making.[6] Traditional jobs like supervisor and foreman don't exist at the plant, and all hiring is done by committees made up of workers. Some workers spend only 65 percent of their time on production work; the other 35 percent is spent on training, planning, and in meetings. At Hymac Ltee., a Laval, Quebec, producer of pulp-processing machinery, managers encourage employees to meet with customers to determine how Hymac can more effectively serve them.[7] Even Japanese business firms are starting to move toward decentralization. Managers at Honda's U.S. subsidiary, for example, are allowed considerable discretion when making marketing and production decisions.[8]

Complete decentralization would mean that every person in the organization would do exactly as he or she wanted. In practice, complete decentralization virtually never happens because total chaos would result. In most decentralized organizations, managers and workers at lower levels are given considerable discretion to make decisions on their own. Middle- and lower-level managers, for example, are allowed to make decisions about who will be hired and fired, how the budget for equipment and supplies will be spent, and other substantial decisions.

Keep in mind that centralization and decentralization are *authority* concepts. The terms do not refer to the physical dispersion of the organization's facilities. Thus, an organization may have only one operating site, yet be decentralized. Conversely, it may have many operating sites and be centralized. Other combinations are possible as well (see Figure 8-3).

In Figure 8-3, centralization and decentralization are treated as either-or situations. However, in practice, the two extremes are rare, and companies generally fall somewhere between them. The real issue is not whether an organization should decentralize, but rather how much (see the Management at Work insert "Are Hierarchies Good or Bad?"). Recent trends in Canadian business seem to favour decentralization on the grounds that it will increase employee involvement, participation, empowerment, and motivation. However, this may be an oversimplification. Top managers often report that lower-level managers either don't want more authority, or that they don't know what to do with it when they get it. Subordinates, on the other hand,

FIGURE 8-3 THE RELATIONSHIP BETWEEN AUTHORITY, DECENTRALIZATION, AND PHYSICAL DECENTRALIZATION.

Number of Outlets	Degree of Centralization: High	Degree of Centralization: Low
Many	Franchise Operations (e.g., Midas Muffler, McDonald's) Banks (e.g., Bank of Montreal, Bank of Nova Scotia)	Conglomerates (e.g., Canadian Pacific, Procter & Gamble)
Few	Most small firms	Some small firms and some large, one-location firms

report that decentralization schemes really haven't given them any additional authority, and that top management is just paying lip service to the idea.[9]

Decentralization has advantages and disadvantages. Centralization generally fosters consistent employee behaviour, reduces the risk of costly mistakes, and allows for tight control of the organization's operations. Decentralization generally enables faster decision making, decisions that are adapted to local conditions, higher motivation and professionalism on the part of managers, and more time for top management to do strategic planning.

MANAGEMENT AT WORK

ARE HIERARCHIES GOOD OR BAD?

We live in an era in which decentralization, team building, quality circles, and participative management are viewed as solutions to many of management's problems. One person who disagrees with this assessment is Elliott Jaques, a psychoanalyst who argues that the most effective managers are those that set up clearly demarcated levels of authority and responsibility and make sure that employees at each level of the organization are mentally equipped to do their jobs.

Jaques' ideas are called Stratified Systems Theory (SST), which he has developed over the last 40 years. A key idea in SST is that the various levels of work in an organization are defined by how much time it takes to perform the longest task. So, while it may take a secretary only 20 minutes to type a letter, it may take a CEO five years to turn a company around. The longer the time frame, the more money and responsibility the person gets, and the greater the cognitive complexity required to do the job. Jaques argues that his research has shown that there is universal agreement about the time spans associated with different levels in organizations: three months for level 1, one year for level 2, two years for level 3, five years for level 4, ten years for level 5, and twenty years for level 6.

The controversial aspect of Jaques' work is his argument that there are people who are meant to occupy each of the levels in an organization. People who can't see beyond their next paycheque usually end up at level 1, while individuals who can see the long term operate at level 5 or 6.

SST contradicts much of current management wisdom, which stresses participative management, total quality management, teams, and the reduction of management layers. Jaques argues that as long as North American firms continue pursuing these ideas, the Japanese will continue to outperform us. He argues that we should not

• • •

abolish hierarchies, but make them work more effectively.

Much of the resistance to Jaques' ideas comes from his basic premise that each person has some inherent potential for cognitive development and is therefore equipped to rise only so high in an organization. Thus, only some people can rise to the level of CEO. In a culture obsessed with self-development, this is considered heresy.

Some admirers believe that SST represents a body of insights that explains organizational behaviour in the same way that Adam Smith described economic systems and Sigmund Freud explained the mysteries of the human psyche. Critics dismiss his work as a form of "managerial fascism", which arbitrarily slots people into positions.

The few companies that have actually applied Jaques' ideas have reported dramatic success. Canadian Tire Acceptance Ltd. (CTA) introduced SST in 1988. Several departments were merged so that the person running them would be accountable for overall results. Four vice-presidents who weren't equipped to occupy the positions they held were let go. But staff reductions were not the goal of the analysis (in fact, the company now employs more people than it did before). Instead, the goal was to identify the calibre of person that should be in each job. Profits at CTA have increased every year since 1988, right through the recession. Salary costs as a percent of revenue have dropped sharply, and revenues have increased 73 percent since 1988.

Elliott Jaques is not the only person reflecting on the value of hierarchies. Some managers have come to the conclusion that they cannot afford the costs of maintaining an extensive hierarchy, but they are not quite sure how to go about reducing it. One approach to resolving this problem is to first note what activities managers are expected to carry out and then introduce programs that will transfer some of these activities to workers. Once this is done, the need for an extensive hierarchy is reduced.

Managers are responsible for activities like motivating subordinates, record-keeping, coordinating, making work assignments, making personnel decisions, acting as a source of expertise, setting goals, planning, communicating, leading, training, coaching, and controlling. How can some of these activities be done by workers? Some of the organizational design features and practices that can be adopted as a substitute for a formal hierarchy are as follows:

1. *Work design* In many organizations, tasks have become so specialized that an extensive hierarchy is needed to control workers; when workers are made responsible for producing the whole product or service, the problems of worker coordination and motivation often disappear, and the hierarchy becomes less necessary.
2. *Information systems technology* Computers allow workers to use self-management to carry out the record-keeping function traditionally reserved for the supervisor.
3. *Financial data* Giving individuals and groups cost, sales, and profitability data enhances their awareness of economic performance. Motivation, coordination, and goal setting are facilitated when this type of information is made available to workers.
4. *Reward system practices* Profit sharing plans and skill-based training have a positive impact on motivation, coordination, and communication.
5. *Supplier/customer contact* Control of inputs (from suppliers) and output (to customers) gives workers feedback on how well they are performing.
6. *Training* The reliance on hierarchy can be reduced by encouraging extensive on-the-job peer training, providing skill-based pay, and making work teams responsible for their own training.
7. *Vision/values* If employees are given a clear sense of overall direction, they will focus on those activities that are consistent with the organization's overall values. If people know what to do, less hierarchy is needed.
8. *Emergent leadership* The emergence of informal group leaders reduces the need for hierarchy.

These substitutes require a substantial alteration in the way most organizations view hierarchy. Adopting them means moving from a hierarchy based on control to one based on commitment. ▲

Factors Influencing the Degree of Decentralization

To what extent should authority be decentralized in an organization? Before making this decision, top management must consider the following factors:

1. *Competence of employees* If subordinates have become accustomed to simply following orders from above, giving them decision-making authority may be disastrous. On the other hand, if subordinates are well-trained and motivated, decentralization is likely to be very effective.

2. *Size of the organization* The larger the organization, the greater the likelihood that decentralization will be needed to achieve organizational goals. With increasing size comes an increasing number of decisions, and top managers simply do not have the time to make all these decisions.

3. *Nature of the organization* If the organization is involved in diverse activities, decentralization will be necessary because each major division in the firm must cope with different markets, customers, and products.

4. *Physical dispersion of the organization* Organizations that have widely scattered locations are generally more decentralized than organizations that have only a few locations. This is because it is more difficult for head office to control operations that are physically dispersed. There are some notable exceptions, however. Organizations like the Bank of Montreal operate hundreds of widely dispersed locations, yet they are relatively centralized due to the nature of the banking business. Convenience stores like 7-Eleven are also widely dispersed, yet authority tends to be highly centralized. This is possible because top management has implemented procedures and rules that require each store to operate in exactly the same way.

5. *Consistency of action required* Managers in some organizations feel that employees should behave in a consistent fashion with respect to internal procedures and with respect to customers. In these cases, centralization will be imposed. If top management does not feel that consistency is crucial, then decentralization is more likely.

6. *Cost of errors* When authority is decentralized, employees may make errors in judgment. If the cost of these errors is small, decentralization will likely be pursued. However, if the cost of the errors is large, top management will likely not allow lower level managers to make many decisions. For example, a supervisor at General Motors of Canada might be given authority to spend up to a certain amount of money on machine maintenance, but that same supervisor would not be given the authority to buy a new computer-controlled robot welding machine for the production line.

7. *Information processing capabilities* The greater top management's ability to keep informed about the organization's operations, the greater the potential for centralization. The advent of the computer has meant that top management can keep close track of inventory, sales, and a host of other items. The availability of computer-generated information enables top management to centralize control if so desired.

8. *History of the organization* The way in which an organization has grown over the years also influences the degree of decentralization. If an organization has "grown by acquisition" (i.e., by buying up other firms), it will tend to be decentralized. Since the addition of new products or services could involve top management in areas where it lacks expertise, the managers of the acquired companies tend to be allowed considerable freedom in making important decisions about operations. By contrast, if a company has "grown from within" (i.e., by doing a greater volume of business with the same products or services), it may remain centralized. In this case, the top executives of the company know a great deal about its products and services.

9. *Environmental demands* As we saw in Chapter 3, there are many external influences on organizations. Federal and provincial government regulations, equal employment laws, tax regulations, and many other factors mean that some top-level control is needed to ensure that the organization is meeting the requirements of good corporate citizenship. The greater the number of environmental influences that impact the total organization, the more centralized it will be. Strict pollution laws, for example, may force top management to centralize pollution policy so that the firm does not violate the law.

The simple listing of advantages and disadvantages, and of factors affecting the amount of centralization and decentralization leaves out a significant factor in organizational success: teamwork. When structuring organizations, managers must balance the concepts of cooperation (teamwork), control (centralization), and autonomy (decentralization).[10] Each organization is unique and will therefore have a slightly different blend of the three.

LINE AND STAFF AUTHORITY

staff experts

line managers

Whether an organization adopts a functional or a divisional structure, it must make a decision about whether or not to use staff experts. **Staff experts** are people who have specialized training in technical areas like law, market research, industrial safety, and accounting. Staff experts are not in the chain of command, and generally have no authority. Instead, they give advice to line managers based on their technical knowledge. **Line managers** are in the regular chain of command of the organization. They receive advice from staff experts and have the authority to decide whether or not they will implement the advice. Organizations with no staff experts have a simple line structure; those that do use staff experts have a line-staff structure. These structures are described below.

THE LINE ORGANIZATION

line organization

Suppose Shel Greenberg starts a company and, over a period of several years, the firm grows and becomes quite successful. Shel (now president) heads an organization that looks like the one shown in Figure 8-4. In a **line organization**, all the positions are line positions and there is a direct line of authority from the top of the firm to the bottom. Each level in the organization is subordinate to the one above it, and there are no advisory specialists. Each department is involved in activities that are geared toward the primary goal of the firm. In the manufacturing firm shown in Figure 8-4, production, marketing, and finance are the primary functions. Note that this line organization is structured on a functional basis.

LEARNING OBJECTIVE 4

Describe the main features of the line organization and the line-staff organization.

In the line organization, authority and responsibility are clear, and each subordinate has only one boss. The line structure works well as long as an organization is small. But as a firm grows, functional managers acquire more subordinates. These subordinates may be doing very diverse tasks, and managers may find that it is difficult to keep up with the latest technical developments in all these areas *and* perform their day-to-day administrative duties. When the firm reaches this point, it may have no alternative but to move to a line-staff structure.

FIGURE 8-4 A LINE ORGANIZATION IN A PRODUCTION-ORIENTED BUSINESS.

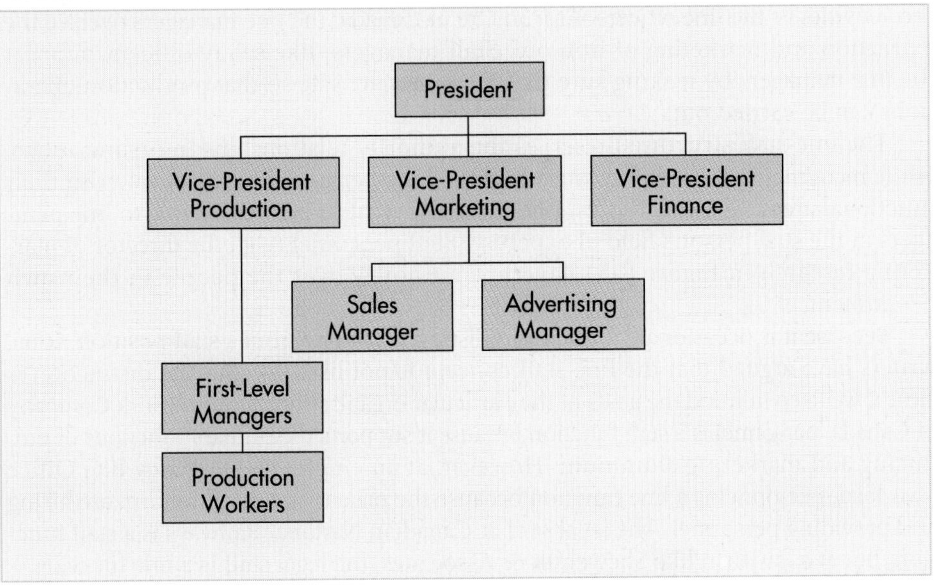

THE LINE-STAFF ORGANIZATION

When staff experts are added in areas like marketing research, legal, workplace health and safety, industrial engineering, the organization becomes a line-staff organization (see Figure 8-5). A **line-staff organization** is one which has both line managers and staff experts. The line-staff structure recognizes that certain functions in an organization (the line functions) are directly related to the organization's reason for existence, while other functions (staff functions) support the line functions. In the Canadian Forces, for example, the line officers are the ones who actually engage in

line-staff organization

FIGURE 8-5 TYPICAL LINE-STAFF STRUCTURE IN A PRODUCTION-ORIENTED ORGANIZATION.

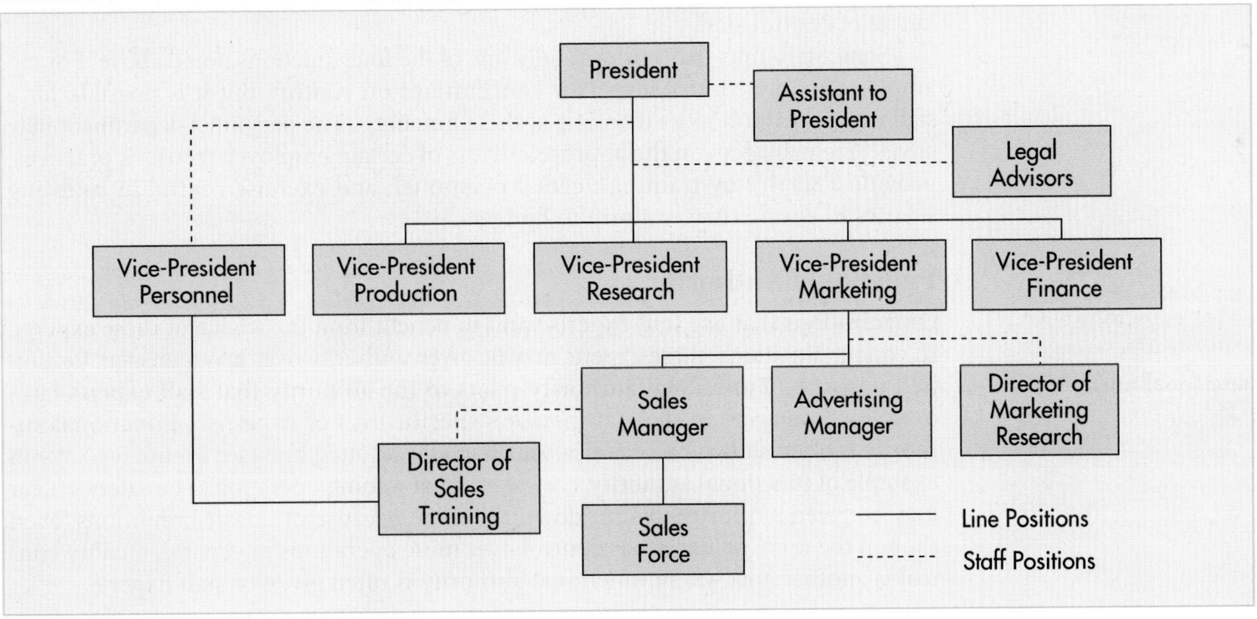

battle. The staff officers perform functions like military intelligence, which support the activities of the line officers. At Iron Ore of Canada, the line managers oversee the extraction and marketing of iron ore. Staff managers, like safety officers, support the line managers by making sure that the mines are safe so that production operations can be carried out.

The line-staff structure preserves the authority relationships in organizations, while recognizing the need for staff experts. Line personnel have authority in their functional areas, while staff personnel have the right to provide advice to line managers in the staff person's field of expertise. Staff personnel (e.g., the director of marketing research in Figure 8-5) have line authority over the people in their own department.

Because it is occasionally difficult to distinguish a line from a staff position, some writers have argued that the line-staff concept is not useful.[11] But the distinction is clear if we keep in mind the goals of the particular organization. At Aluminum Company of Canada, personnel is a staff function because it supports the primary functions of producing and marketing aluminum. However, at an employment agency like Office Overload, personnel is a line function because the primary goals of the firm are hiring and providing personnel. The legal staff at Canadian National Railways is a staff function, but at a law firm like Shewchuk & Associates, the legal staff is a line function.

Types of Staff

personal staff

advisory staff

service staff

control staff

Four distinct types of staff experts are found in organizations. **Personal staff** assist specific line managers, but generally lack the authority to act for them in their absence. For example, the "assistant to the president" carries out a wide variety of jobs as directed by the president, but does not have authority over the vice-presidents. **Advisory staff** advise line managers in areas where the staff has particular expertise. For example, the legal department may provide advice on the likelihood of success of prosecuting a competitor who is thought to be infringing on the company's patent, but the legal staff does not decide whether the firm will go ahead and prosecute the competition. **Service staff** provide specific services to line managers. For example, the personnel department interviews and tests prospective employees for various line departments. **Control staff** are responsible for controlling some aspect of the organization. A quality control inspector at Chrysler's Windsor plant is an example of control staff.

Some staff units may perform only one of the four functions noted above. For example, a quality control inspector concentrates on control. But it is possible for a staff unit to perform more than one of these functions. The personnel department may *advise* line managers on the appropriateness of certain employee relations practices, provide a *service* by training needed personnel, and exercise *control* by auditing salaries to ensure they conform to budgets.

Functional Authority

functional authority

Organizations that use staff experts want to benefit from the advice of these experts. In various situations, these experts may be given authority over line managers for limited purposes. **Functional authority** refers to the authority that staff experts have over line managers in the staff person's specific area of expertise. Functional authority is often shown on organization charts by a dotted line (see Figure 8-6). As an example of functional authority, consider a coal mining operation. The safety officer may be given authority to shut down the mine because of unsafe conditions, even though the mine manager has control over mine operations in general. Quality control is another area where functional authority is often given to staff experts.

FIGURE 8-6 FUNCTIONAL AUTHORITY.

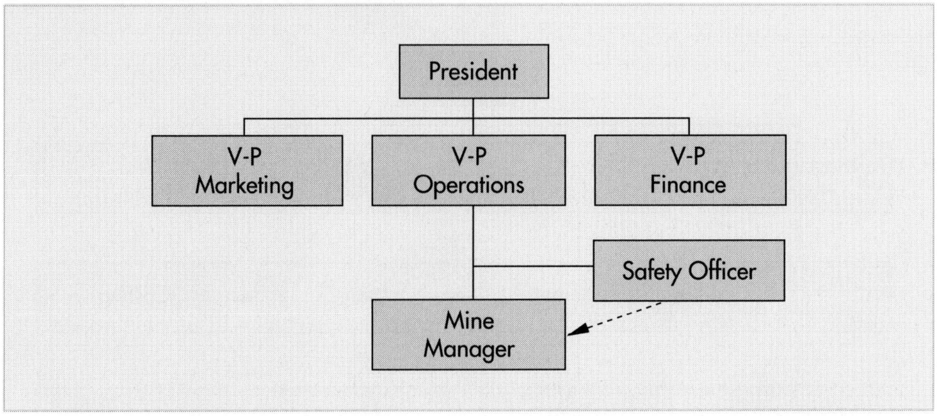

The construction of oil and gas pipelines is typically organized on a project basis. These projects are complex, requiring the coordination of many tasks, and time-framed, with a definite start and end.

Functional authority can cause conflict between the line manager and the staff person. For example, the safety officer may want to shut down the coal mine because of bad air conditions, while the mine manager may argue that conditions aren't that bad. Company policies are usually developed to deal with anticipated conflicts, but there are always gray areas, which will allow conflicts to develop.

LEARNING OBJECTIVE 5
Explain what functional authority is and why it is used.

In many firms, line-staff conflicts are caused by factors other than functional authority. Line managers may claim, for example, that staff ideas are not workable; staff people, on the other hand, may argue that line managers are unwilling to try new ideas that will benefit the firm. Or, staff people may feel that line managers do not give them enough credit for their technical expertise when making decisions; line managers may counter by citing the lack of weight given by the staff to the manager's many years of experience.

PROJECT ORGANIZATION

LEARNING OBJECTIVE 6
Draw a chart showing how a project organization would look.

A typical line or line-staff organization is characterized by unchanging vertical authority relationships. It has such a set-up because the organization produces a product or service in a repetitive and predictable way. Procter & Gamble, for example, produces millions of tubes of Crest Toothpaste each year using standardized production methods. The company has done this for years and intends to do so indefinitely.

But some organizations find themselves faced with new product opportunities, or with projects that have a definite starting and ending point. These organizations often use a project structure to deal with the uncertainty encountered in new situations. **Project organization** involves forming a team of specialists from different functional areas of the organization to work on a specific project.[12] A project structure is usually temporary; the project team is disbanded once the project is completed and team members return to their regular functional area or are assigned to a new project. Figure 8-7 shows the general structure of project management.

project organization

A project organization is appropriate when the task to be accomplished is:

1. *Temporary* It has a distinct starting and ending point.
2. *Unique* It has not been done by the organization before.
3. *Complex* It has many interrelated elements that must be coordinated.
4. *Critical* It is important for the survival of the organization.

FIGURE 8-7 THE GENERAL STRUCTURE OF PROJECT MANAGEMENT.

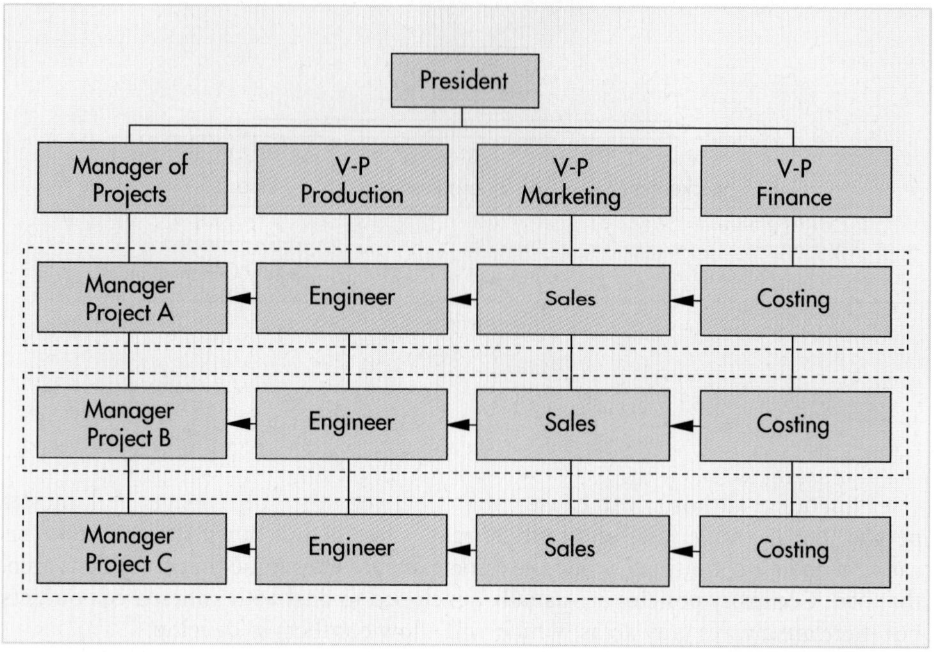

The project organization is used extensively by Canadian firms, although it is much less common than the functional structure. It is very likely to be used in the construction of hydroelectric generating stations like those developed by Hydro Quebec on the La Grande River, and those developed on the Nelson River by Manitoba Hydro. When the generating station is complete, it becomes part of the traditional structure of the provincial hydroelectric utility. Project organization has also proven useful for coordinating the many elements needed to extract oil from the tar sands.

Project management is also used in other kinds of tasks, including shipbuilding, construction, military weapons, aerospace, and health care delivery.[13] The Management at Work insert entitled "Project Management at Genstar Shipyards Ltd." describes how project management works at the Vancouver firm.

THE PROJECT MANAGER

project manager

Each project has a project manager. The **project manager** (PM) is the person who is responsible for completing the project on time and within budget. The amount of authority given to the PM varies widely (see Figure 8-8). At one extreme, the PM may have complete authority over all members of the project team, while the functional manager may have none. This is known as the *aggregate* form of project management. A good example of this was the Manhattan Project—the building of the atomic bomb by the U.S. during World War II. In that project, nuclear physicists, chemists, and other relevant personnel were physically moved from their normal place of work (e.g., a university or research and development laboratory) to an isolated place in the New Mexico desert where they worked on the development of the atomic bomb under tight security. The PM had complete control over the workers, and their former line bosses (e.g., university department heads) could not even communicate with them.

MANAGEMENT AT WORK

PROJECT MANAGEMENT AT GENSTAR SHIPYARDS LTD.

Genstar Shipyards Ltd. is a Vancouver firm that specializes in the custom building and repair of icebreakers, research vessels, ferries, tugs, and barges. In peak periods, it delivers a new ship every two months. The value of ships varies from a low of about $2 million for a small tugboat to a high of nearly $60 million for a state-of-the-art icebreaker. Construction periods for ships vary from four months to two years. Project management is really the only structure that makes sense for shipbuilding. Since time is of the essence in every construction contract, and since costs must be closely monitored, the project structure is necessary.

The shipyard has an operations manager who is responsible for the overall shipbuilding activity. Two project managers (PMs) report to the operations manager. Each ship the company builds is treated as a project, and the two PMs are responsible for seeing that projects are finished on schedule, to specification, and within budget. Some projects employ up to 400 people, so the PM's job may have a major administrative component.

The PM is responsible for the development of a master schedule for each vessel's design and construction. The PM identifies personnel and equipment that are necessary to complete the job, and interacts with all departments involved in the project. Once the master schedule has been set, the PM is responsible for seeing that the schedule and budget are met. After the ship is built and launched, the PM oversees the trial run and delivery to the owner.

The PM has authority to decide the construction sequence on the project as well as the number of workers that will be assigned to each phase of the project. These decisions are made after consulting the project plans. Workers on the project report to a supervisor. If the PM and the supervisor disagree about who should be assigned to a project, the PM can appeal to the superintendent (the supervisor's boss). The PM usually gets his way on staffing issues.

Other areas of potential disagreement also exist. For example, a supervisor might think work on some aspect of a ship's construction ought to be done in a particular way, while the PM thinks it should be done in some other way. If the disagreement is a question of sequencing of the work, the PM will usually prevail; but if the disagreement is about specific trade practices, the supervisor will generally get his way. As another example, a supervisor may try to assign more tradespeople to a project than the PM thinks are necessary. The supervisor may do this to give himself a cushion in meeting the construction schedule. In these cases, the PM usually wins out because he has the total project schedule and budget in mind, whereas the supervisor may be thinking only of the work that his particular crew is doing.

The PM does not have the authority to hire, lay off, or fire workers; this is the responsibility of the supervisor. The PM works with the supervisor to determine when the work force should be increased or decreased. The PM also has the authority to approve payment to outside sources from which the company has purchased materials.

To be effective, the PM requires interpersonal skills (the ability to instill enthusiasm in workers), administrative skills (the ability to keep the project on schedule and within budget), and technical skills (the ability to communicate with the technically skilled people who are working on the project). ▲

FIGURE 8-8 THREE TYPES OF PROJECT MANAGEMENT AUTHORITY.

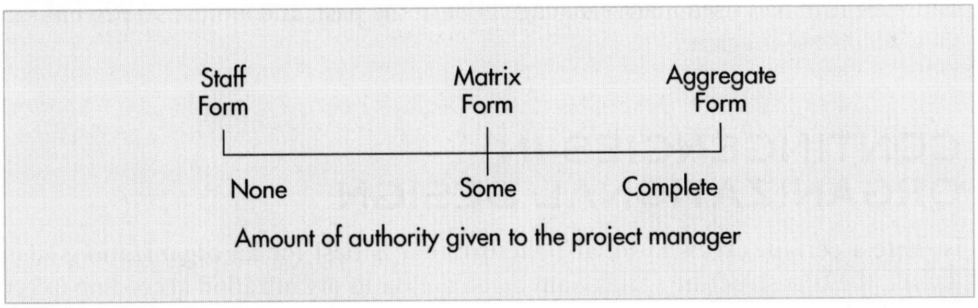

At the other extreme, the PM may have virtually no formal authority over members of the project team. This is known as the *staff* form of project management. When the PM has little or no authority, influence must be used to get the job done. For example, if a retailing firm wanted to develop a new "customer satisfaction" survey, a project team might be formed to develop the survey. Individuals from various area of the firm might be assigned to the project. The PM of such a project might not be given formal authority over team members. In such a case, the PM would have to use influence to get the team members to do the necessary work. This requires considerable interpersonal and leadership skills.

In the *matrix* form of project management, the project manager has some authority, but it may not be clear how much. Looking back at Figure 8-7, we can see that while the PM has some authority over the people on the project, the traditional functional managers also retain some authority over the workers. In the matrix form of project management, workers have two bosses. This situation creates the potential for conflict between the project manager and the functional line boss. DuPont Canada has a matrix form of organization. Research and development, manufacturing, and accounting usually don't report to the general manager; rather, the emphasis is on creating effective teams led by the general manager.[14]

ADVANTAGES AND DISADVANTAGES OF THE PROJECT ORGANIZATION

The principal benefit of project management is its ability to bring together and coordinate the different specialized skills that are necessary to complete a project. Project management also stimulates interdepartmental cooperation. When people with different skills work together on a project, they can see how the various parts of the organization work together. In addition, project management gives the organization flexibility since the expertise needed on particular projects can be moved as required.

The primary shortcoming of the project structure is the ambiguous authority relationships it creates. The project structure violates the unity of command principle, and this means that individuals may be unclear about who reports to whom. Such ambiguity may result in power struggles between functional and project managers. Another disadvantage is that uncertainty may arise as projects near completion. Workers who are assigned to a certain project may wonder what project they will be assigned to next, or if there will even be another project for them to work on.[15] The advantages and disadvantages of the project structure are summarized in Table 8-1.[16]

While the aggregate and staff forms of project management remain common, the matrix form of project management has been increasingly criticized, and its popularity may be declining.[17] The exceptions to this trend are pharmaceutical, aerospace, computer, and telecommunications companies, where a survey of 500 managers showed that project management is still popular.[18] Over 75 percent of the respondents said their firm had used matrix management in the past, and almost 90 percent said they would use it again.

CONTINGENCIES IN ORGANIZATIONAL DESIGN

Is there a certain organizational structure that is best for all organizations? No. Rather, the best structure varies from organization to organization according to certain variables, or contingencies—the external environment of the organization, the

TABLE 8-1 ADVANTAGES AND DISADVANTAGES OF PROJECT MANAGEMENT.

Advantages	Disadvantages
1. Increases flexibility for the organization.	1. Creates ambiguity in authority relationships (may violate the unity of command principle).
2. Results in more efficient use of resources.	2. Encourages power struggles between functional and project managers.
3. Helps individuals see the benefits of interdepartmental cooperation.	3. May cause concerns over job security as the project nears completion.
4. Coordinates the activities of diverse technical experts.	4. Is costly to implement.
5. Focusses employee attention on the project.	5. May lead to more discussion than action.
6. Helps employees develop their technical and interpersonal skills.	6. Assumes that managers have good interpersonal skills.

technology the organization uses, and its size. These contingency variables must be taken into account when managers are trying to decide how to design an organization. **Organizational design** is the process of structuring or restructuring an organization in the most appropriate way, given the organization's external environment, technology, size, and stage in the organizational life cycle.

LEARNING OBJECTIVE 7
Explain how organizational structure is influenced by the external environment, by technology, and by organizational size.

organizational design

THE ENVIRONMENT AND ORGANIZATIONAL STRUCTURE

In Chapter 3, we noted that each organization operating in Canada has an external environment that influences it (refer back to Figure 3-1). The external environment can have a significant effect on the organization's internal structure. One aspect of the environment—the rate of change—is particularly important in its influence on an organization's structure. If we focus on the rate of change in the external environment, we see two types of environments—stable and changing.

Stable Environments

stable environment

A **stable environment** is one in which there are only minor changes in the type of customers the firm deals with, in the products customers demand, and in the technology used to convert inputs into output. In stable environments, the products manufactured or the services provided change little over time. McDonald's hamburgers, Labatt's beer, Sherwin-Williams paint, and Revenue Canada's tax collecting have remained basically the same over the years. When the products or services do not change much, there is little impetus for technological innovation or for changes in the organization's production technology. The changes that do occur in the production area have more to do with the quantity of products or services than they do with quality. In stable environments, the type of customer remains basically the same over time; demand for the product or service is therefore predictable. Thus, while there may be great competition between McDonald's and Wendy's, the total dollars that will be spent on that type of fast food can be quite accurately forecasted.

Changing Environments

changing environment

A **changing environment** is one where major shifts occur in products, in customers, and in the technology used by the organization. In such an environment, the products manufactured or the services provided can change quite dramatically in a short time due to demographic shifts, technological advancements, or to changes in government regulations. IBM, Apple, Mind, and many other computer companies operate in rapidly changing environments because of continual innovations in the computer products they produce. Kingsway Trucking, Air Canada, and First City Trust find their environments changing due to government deregulation of their respective industries. We saw in the Management Challenge at the beginning of the chapter that oil firms are also experiencing difficulties because the price of oil has not continued to rise, and because new technologies have to be employed to keep oil production up in old oil fields.

When one company introduces a new product or service, other companies may have to change their products and production technologies, too. The introduction of digital watches strengthened the competitive position of North American firms like Timex, but weakened the competitive position of Swiss firms producing traditional mechanical watches. The major features of stable and changing environments are summarized in Table 8-2.

TABLE 8-2 CHARACTERISTICS OF ORGANIZATIONAL ENVIRONMENTS.

Stable Environment	Changing Environment
1. Products or services remain basically the same over time.	1. Products or services change rapidly over time.
2. The type and number of customers are relatively constant.	2. The type and number of customers are constantly changing.
3. The rate of technological innovation is slow.	3. The rate of technological innovation is fast.
4. Demand for the product or service is predictable.	4. Demand for the product or service is unpredictable.

Matching the Environment and Structure

LEARNING OBJECTIVE 8

Distinguish between mechanistic and organic organizations.

mechanistic organizations

organic organizations

Burns and Stalker identified two types of organizational systems: mechanistic and organic.[19] **Mechanistic organizations** are those that stress highly structured work, clearly stated authority relations, centralized authority, and vertical communication. Mechanistic organizations are represented by the bureaucratic form of organization discussed in Chapter 21. **Organic organizations** are those that put little emphasis on hierarchical authority and that encourage managers and subordinates to work together as a team to solve problems. Organic structures emphasize lateral communication and encourage employees to develop a wide variety of task skills. At Strong Equipment Corp., for example, CEO Jordan Sullivan tries to break down the formal hierarchy and encourages managers to get involved in planning the company's future.[20] In the Management Challenge, the major oil companies are starting to get rid of past practices like bureaucracy and multilayered organization structures, and are replacing them with a team-oriented culture that focusses on the company's core business.

The mechanistic-organic contrast is important because it captures a fundamental property of organizations.[21] The characteristics of these two types of structures are summarized in Table 8-3.

TABLE 8-3 CHARACTERISTICS OF MECHANISTIC AND ORGANIC STRUCTURES.

Mechanistic	Organic
1. Highly specialized tasks.	1. Interdependent tasks.
2. Task definition remains the same over time.	2. Task definition changes over time.
3. Roles tightly defined for employees.	3. Emphasis on generalized roles.
4. Precise authority structure with centralized authority.	4. Ambiguous authority structure with decentralized authority.
5. Emphasis on vertical communication.	5. Vertical and horizontal communication emphasized.
6. Emphasis on communicating orders to subordinates.	6. Emphasis on communicating information to subordinates.
7. Coordination achieved through formal means.	7. Coordination achieved through informal means.

Firms operating in changing environments are most effective if they have an organic structure, while firms operating in stable environments are most effective if they adopt a mechanistic structure (see Figure 8-9). This general conclusion has been supported by several research studies. Lawrence and Lorsch measured the degree of differentiation and integration in three different functional areas (production, marketing, and R&D) of companies in the plastics, food, and container businesses.[22] They found that departments facing unstable environments (e.g., marketing departments in the plastics firms) were more differentiated than departments operating in stable environments (e.g., production departments in the container firms). They concluded that the degree of differentiation was dependent on the type of external environment the firm faced. Thus, in one firm a marketing department might be differentiated to cope with a rapidly changing environment, while in another firm the marketing department might exhibit very little differentiation because the external environment is very stable. The researchers also found that integration was always important, and that the most successful firms had a higher level of integration than the less successful firms, regardless of the type of environment the firms faced.

FIGURE 8-9 RELATING INTERNAL STRUCTURE TO THE EXTERNAL ENVIRONMENT.

Type of Structure	Type of Environment: Changing	Type of Environment: Stable
Organic	Effective Organization (Structure is consistent with organization's external environment.)	Ineffective Organization (Structure is too "loose" to cope effectively with the stable environment facing the organization.)
Mechanistic	Ineffective Organization (Structure too rigid to cope with rapid changes in external environment.)	Effective Organization (Structure is consistent with the organization's external environment.)

To provide high-quality service to their customers, resort hotels organize work exactly. Individual jobs are highly specialized, and performance expectations are clearly stated, resulting in a mechanistic organizational structure.

A study by Morse and Lorsch compared the effectiveness of two manufacturing departments and two R & D departments in one firm.[23] The manufacturing departments operated in a more stable environment than the R & D departments. Using effectiveness measures such as growth in profits and in new products, they found that the most effective manufacturing department had a mechanistic structure, while the most effective R & D department had an organic structure. The least effective manufacturing department had an organic structure, while the least effective R & D department had a mechanistic structure. Thus, the most effective departments adopted a structure that was best able to cope with the external environment they faced.

Various writers have taken the position that organic structures are the wave of the future, and that mechanistic structures simply cannot cope with the new organizational realities. Tom Peters, for example, argues that the traditional organization—hierarchical, inflexible, rule-bound, functionally oriented, and out of touch with its environment—is going to be less and less effective. He proposes an organization structure that encourages flexibility, adaptation, and quick action.[24] Other writers say that managers of the future will have to operate without the "crutch" of structure, and that position, title, and authority will no longer be adequate for effectiveness in managerial jobs.[25] Still others talk of the coming death of bureaucracy. In spite of all these predictions, mechanistic structures continue to be evident in both public and private sector organizations.

Technology and Structure

technology

Technology is the application of knowledge about how to use work methods, labour (people), and materials to convert inputs to output. Technology therefore has an impact on every organization and its structure. There are several different technologies that are available to goods- and services-producing organizations.

Goods-Producing Technologies

Thousands of different products are produced in Canada. In spite of this diversity, it is possible to put manufactured products into one of three basic categories based on the technology that is used to produce them. Any organization that produces a physical product uses one of these three technologies. **Unit production** involves the manufacture of small quantities of custom products for specific customers. Kitchen cabinets, tailor-made suits, ships, homes, and aircraft are examples of products that are often custom-made. The manufacturer begins production of such products only after the customer's order and specifications are received.

unit production

mass production

Mass production involves the manufacture of large volumes of identical products for sale to the mass market. These items are produced before any customer orders are received, and are stored in inventory in anticipation of customer demand. This type of production is used in the manufacture of products like toothpaste, VCRs, automobiles, toys, and hamburgers.

process production

Process production involves the manufacture of standardized products that are sold by weight or volume. This type of production process goes on continuously (i.e., 24 hours a day) and is characterized by very large investment in the plant and the equipment in it. Products manufactured using this process include gasoline, paint, and drugs. In the refining part of their business, the oil companies described in the Management Challenge use process production.

Service-Producing Technologies

Approximately two out of every three people employed in Canada work in service-producing organizations. Services are quite different from physical products in two important areas.[26] First, services are intangible. The hairstyling provided by Coiffure Caprice, the seat on a Canadian International Airlines flight, and the advice provided by H & R Block Income Tax Services are intangible and cannot be stored in inventory. Physical products, by contrast, can be stored in inventory and later sold.

Second, employees in service-producing organizations interact face to face with customers or clients, i.e., production and consumption are simultaneous. In service organizations like the Gemini Dental Centre, Holiday Inn, Mad Max's Carpet Cleaning, and the Salvation Army, employees have direct contact with customers. In goods-producing firms like automobile companies, technical employees may never see customers.

At Dofasco, computer technology assists an operator in controlling quality variables in steel production.

mediating technology

There are two major types of service-producing technologies. The **mediating technology** brings buyers and sellers together. The Bank of Nova Scotia, for example, provides an exchange point for those who want to loan money and those who want to borrow it. Stockbrokers at Burns Fry provide a system for bringing together people who want to buy stock and people who want to sell stock. Canada Safeway provides a place where buyers of food and sellers of food can interact. Other organizations using mediating technologies include First City Trust, Century 21, Canada Post, and Eaton's.

intensive technology

The **intensive technology** is used to create a change in a specific object. The object may be animate or inanimate. Primary, secondary, and postsecondary schools in Canada are intensive technologies because they incorporate students and intensively "work them over" to educate them. Hospitals are intensive technologies because they take in patients and convert them from sick people to healthy people. Other examples of intensive technologies include Kingston Penitentiary, the Benedictine Monastary, and the Hydro Quebec construction sites on the La Grande River.

Technological Interdependence

Different technologies have different effects on a firm's structure because they require differing amounts of interdependence between individuals and departments.

technological interdependence

Technological interdependence refers to the amount of coordination that is necessary to successfully complete tasks.

pooled interdependence

Three types of technological interdependence have been identified: pooled, sequential, and reciprocal.[27] **Pooled interdependence** exists when the various departments in an organization can each work independently to make their contribution to overall organizational effectiveness. For example, the various divisions in a conglomerate can make their contribution to the overall organization by doing as well as they can in their own area of expertise. In a franchising operation like Midas Muffler or 7-Eleven, each store makes an independent contribution to the profit of the total corporation. With pooled interdependence, overall organizational goals can be achieved with only a low level of cooperation among the various divisions or outlets. This coordination can be achieved by corporate policies, rules, and procedures.

sequential interdependence

Sequential interdependence exists when work must be completed in a specific way, and when the output of one individual or department becomes the input for another individual or department. At Ford Motor of Canada, for example, the output of the radiator subassembly line becomes the input for the main production line. At McDonald's, the output of the hamburger production line becomes the input for the person at the counter who is filling customer orders. During the construction of a hydroelectric dam by Ontario Hydro, a cofferdam to divert water must be completed before work can start on the main dam. Sequential interdependence requires a higher level of coordination than pooled interdependence. It can be achieved by developing detailed plans and schedules to ensure that all work is done in the proper sequence.

reciprocal interdependence

Reciprocal interdependence exists when individuals and departments must deal with work continually flowing back and forth until the job is completed. For example, at Victoria Hospital, surgeons, anesthetists, x-ray technicians, nurses, and other specialists work together as a team to complete a complicated surgery. At an advertising agency like Baker Lovick, creative individuals develop an advertising program only after much intense give-and-take in meetings and brainstorming sessions. Reciprocal interdependence requires the most sophisticated level of coordination. It can be achieved by group meetings and by mutual adjustment of individuals and departments. Figure 8-10 illustrates these three basic types of technological interdependence.

FIGURE 8-10 POOLED, SEQUENTIAL, AND RECIPROCAL INTERDEPENDENCE.

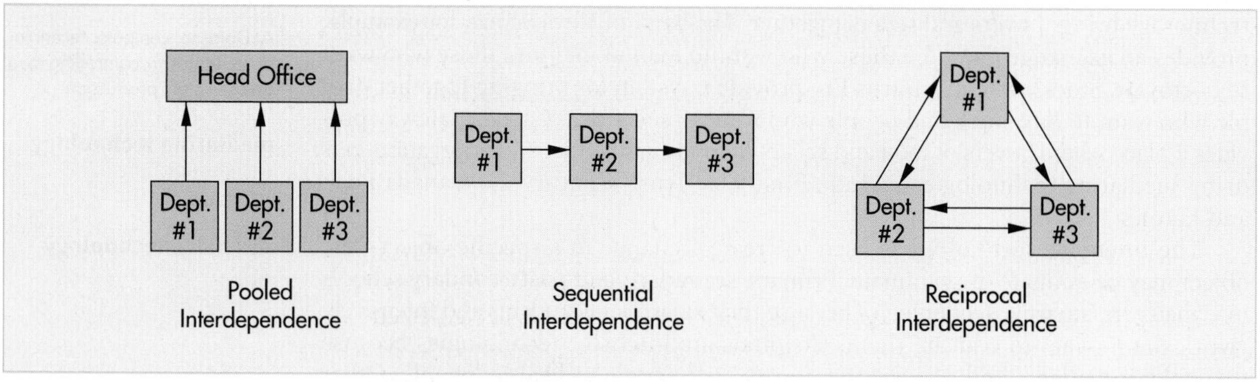

Research on the Impact of Technology on Structure

The first systematic studies examining the effect of technology on organizational structure were done in England during the 1960s. Joan Woodward analyzed 100 English manufacturing firms and found that technology had an impact on both organizational effectiveness and organizational structure.[28] Firms using either the unit or process technology were most effective if they adopted an organic structure, while firms with a mass production technology were most successful if they adopted a mechanistic structure.

Woodward also found that the most successful firms in each category—unit, mass, or process—tended to have similar structural characteristics. For example, successful firms using a mass production technology tended to have spans of management that were close to the median for mass production firms. Less successful mass production firms had spans of management that were higher or lower than the median. The same finding was evident for other structural measures like the number of management levels in the organization, the ratio of production to nonproduction labour, and the ratio of top administrators to all other administrators. Firms using a unit technology, for example, had a median of three management levels, mass production technologies four, and process technologies six.

Other research done since Woodward's study generally supports the idea that the technology a firm uses influences the kind of structure it must have to be effective. The one qualification is that the organization's size may have an influence. In large firms, technology seems to have its greatest impact at the lowest levels of the firm, but in small firms, the effect of technology pervades the entire firm.[29] But the main point remains: in goods-producing firms, technology influences organizational structure to the point that if the structure is not appropriate for the technology, the firm is likely to be less successful than if its structure is appropriate for its technology. For service firms, little research exists that allows conclusions to be made.

The Impact of Computers on Organization Structure

During the 1980s, there was a dramatic increase in the use of computer-based management information systems, microcomputers and end-user computing. These have caused several structural changes, including the creation of new managerial positions, new departments, and new organization structures.

Some firms, like Northern Telecom, have created a position called chief information officer. The **chief information officer** (CIO) is responsible for determining the organization's overall information needs, and for controlling the information that is contained in the organization's databases. The CIO typically reports to one of the senior executives in the firm. However, information experts who want to rid themselves of the "computer-nerd" image feel the time has come to give the CIO direct access to the corporate boardroom, rather than reporting to other senior executives.[30]

chief information officer (CIO)

Because some managers are not knowledgeable about all aspects of the information system in their organization, some firms have also created entirely new departments called information centres. **Information centres** help users deal effectively with computer departments.[31] The individuals working in the information centre have expertise about computer hardware and software, and they can help managers develop their own end-user skills.

information centres

Computer technology may allow an organization to create an entirely new structure that is based on electronic information transfer. In the **network corporation structure**, the organization is a small central processing unit connected electronically to other organizations that perform functions like production, sales, and engineering. Schwinn Bicycle, for example, imports bicycles from the Far East and then sells them through electronically coordinated independent dealers. Other business firms use this basic type of structure, but do not rely totally on electronic information transfer. Instead, they simply contract out much of the work that needs to be done. Firms using this structure include Nike, Liz Claiborne, Ocean Pacific Sunwear, and many book publishers.

network corporation structure

Because the new information technology allows managers to monitor subordinates more effectively, there is a tendency for managers to have larger numbers of subordinates reporting to them. Wider spans of control, in turn, lead to fewer levels of management and a flatter organizational structure. Improved communication through the reduced number of vertical levels in the organization may result in greater employee motivation to perform at a higher level.

Computer and information technology have also altered the structure of organzations in more subtle ways. Employees are able to communicate with others outside their own department who have the information they need. This development has caused some organizations to think in terms of systems rather than separate units, because it increases coordination while blurring departmental boundaries.

Size and Structure

Owners and managers in many organizations often have an irresistible desire for their firm to grow. Owners enjoy the monetary benefits and prestige that accompany being the owner of a successful large organization, and managers like the power and status that go along with managing many subordinates.

Organizational size—as measured by the number of employees in the organization—is one of the major determinants of organizational structure.[32]

In Chapter 7, we noted that there are four dimensions of structure: formalization, centralization, complexity, and specialization. As an organization increases in size, these four dimensions are affected as follows.[33]

1. *Formalization increases* Written job descriptions, rules, policies, and procedures are the norm in large organizations, but these are often absent in small organizations.
2. *Centralization decreases* As an organization increases in size, top management finds it increasingly difficult to make decisions for all aspects of the organization. As a result, authority tends to be decentralized to those who are very familiar with what needs to be done. In a conglomerate, for example, each division typically has a great deal of leeway about how it will conduct its activities.
3. *Complexity increases* As an organization grows, job titles and departments increase as do both vertical and horizontal differentiation.
4. *Specialization increases* As an organization grows in size, jobs tend to be defined in ever-narrower terms. This specialization is caused by the organization's need to achieve efficiency in the production of goods and services. Each of these four trends is noticeable in the oil companies described in the Management Challenge.

Research on the impact of size on structure suggests that increasing size does not uniformly affect an organization's structure. While formalization, complexity, and specialization increase with the increasing size of a company, they do so at a decreasing rate.[34] Thus, an organization that increases in size from 50 to 1000 employees will show a greater *relative change* in formalization, complexity, and specialization than a firm that grows from 25 000 to 30 000 employees. But the firm with 30 000 employees will have more formalization, complexity, and specialization than the firm with 1000 employees.

THE ORGANIZATIONAL LIFE CYCLE AND STRUCTURE

organizational life cycle

Like people, organizations are born, mature from youth into old age, and finally die. The **organizational life cycle** is the series of events that takes place from the time an organization is formed until the time it ceases to exist. The four stages in the life cycle are birth, youth, midlife, and maturity.[35] During each of these phases, variations in structure will be evident. In the first stage of an organization's existence, for example, the number of employees is small, the founders do a variety of tasks, departments are not formally recognized, rules and procedures are informal, and the organization is very organic. At maturity, however, the number of employees has increased, each employee carries out a narrowly defined task, departments are formally recognized, rules and procedures are highly formalized, and the organization is much more bureaucratic.

SUMMARY

Authority is the right to take certain actions or to require subordinates to take certain actions. All managers have authority. Since managers cannot possibly do all the work themselves, they must delegate authority. Delegation involves assigning specific tasks to subordinates and giving them the authority to carry out those assignments. Delegation increases the speed of decision making, enhances the training of subordinates, improves subordinate morale and motivation, and helps the manager focus on how to improve the functioning of the unit.

Responsibility is the obligation of a subordinate to do a job he or she has been assigned. Accountability involves making people answerable (giving credit or blame)

MEETING THE CHALLENGE

Restructuring in the Oil Industry

Why did it take so long for the oil industry to identify its problems? The answer might be found in the "herd psychology" concept. When one oil company thought something was a good idea and acted on it, most of the others followed suit. The discovery of oil in the Arctic led to a stampede there, but oil companies discovered that the oil was often uneconomical to extract.

This follow-the-leader pattern is still evident, although now it is part of a strategy to solve the industry's problems. For example, when Esso bought Texaco Canada in 1989, Investment Canada required it to sell $350 million of its oil and gas assets to Canadian buyers. Once it started selling its many holdings, other companies began to follow suit. Now, every large oil firm is doing it. The pattern continues as Esso has disposed of an additional $370 million in assets since it acquired Texaco and Petro-Canada's property holdings have dropped from 500 to 300. Shell plans to reduce its current portfolio of properties from 650 to 50.

The big oil firms are also making do with fewer employees, and are redesigning their structures around interdisciplinary teams rather than departments. This strategy has helped Esso to reduce overhead by 30 percent and to eliminate 1400 jobs. Similar actions at Amoco have resulted in the loss of 1100 jobs.

On the human side, a new buzzword has emerged: "empowerment." More influence and power is being given to employees in an attempt to enlist their trust. For example, in the past a supervisor didn't have the authority to hire a contract welder unless the welder was on the approved supplier list. Now, welders can be checked and hired without getting approval from above.

Perhaps the most dramatic restructuring has taken place at Petro-Canada, where the decentralization philosophy has led to the creation of "value centres." These act like small petroleum companies operating inside Petro-Canada. The centres hold geographically defined pieces of land and are staffed by a cross-section of operations specialists. They are designed to prevent departmental empire building by focussing everyone's attention on the total operation. Early evidence shows that Petro-Canada is now taking less time to find and develop new properties; conflict between departments has also been reduced. ▲

for the results of the work assigned to them. In order for a subordinate to be held accountable, responsibilities must be clearly understood, the person doing the job must be capable, and sufficient authority must be delegated.

Centralization of authority occurs when top management retains the right to make most of the decisions that are made in the organization. Decentralization occurs when the right to make decisions is pushed down the management hierarchy to middle and lower management.

Many factors influence the degree of centralization or decentralization in an organization. These include the competence of employees (the greater the competence, the greater the decentralization), the size of the organization (the larger the size, usually the greater the decentralization), the nature of the organization (the greater the diversity of activities, the greater the decentralization), the physical dispersion of the organization (the greater the dispersion, usually the greater the decentralization), the consistency of action required (the lower the uniformity required, the greater the decentralization), the cost of errors (the lower the cost of errors, the greater the decentralization), information processing capabilities (the lower the capability, the greater the decentralization), the history of the organization (the greater the growth by acquisition, the greater the decentralization), and environmental demands (the greater the impact of the external environment, the greater the centralization).

In a line organization, all positions in the organization are in a direct line of authority from the top of the firm to the bottom. In a line-staff organization, both line managers and staff experts may have authority. Staff have expertise in certain technical areas (e.g., marketing research, accounting, law). Staff generally advise line managers on what actions to take in areas of the staff's expertise, but they may also be given functional authority over line managers in some situations.

Personal staff (e.g., the assistant to the president) assist specific line managers, but lack authority to act in the manager's absence. Advisory staff (e.g., company lawyers) advise line managers in areas where the staff has particular expertise. Service staff provide a specific service to line managers (e.g., the personnel department conducts employee testing). Control staff are responsible for controlling some aspect of operations (e.g., quality control).

The project form of organization consists of teams of specialists assembled from different functional areas of the firm to work on specific projects. This form of organization is appropriate if the task is temporary, unique, complex, and very important. Each project is headed by a project manager. Project managers may have complete authority over team members (the "aggregate" form of project management), moderate authority (the "matrix" form of project management), or no authority (the "staff" form of project management).

No one structure is ideal for all organizations. Several important variables, such as an organization's external environment, its technology, and its size, determine what the optimal structure is for that organization. Organization design is the process of structuring or restructuring an organization in the most appropriate way to take into account these variables.

The external environment of an organization may be stable or changing. A stable environment is one in which only minor changes occur in the products the organization sells, the customers it sells to, and the technology it uses to convert inputs into output. A changing environment has the opposite characteristics. Firms operating in stable environments are most effective if they adopt mechanistic structures, while firms operating in changing environments are most effective if they adopt organic structures. Mechanistic organization structures stress highly structured work, clearly stated authority relations, centralized authority, and vertical communications. Organic structures have the opposite characteristics.

Technology is the application of knowledge about how to use work methods, labour (people), and materials to convert inputs into output. There are three types of goods-producing technologies: unit production (the manufacture of small quantities of custom products for specific customers), mass production (the manufacture of large volumes of identical products for the mass market), and process production (the manufacture of standardized products that are sold by weight or volume). Service-producing technologies can be grouped into two basic types: the mediating technology (which brings buyers and sellers together), and the intensive technology (which is used to create a change in an object or person).

Firms that use either unit or process technology are most effective if they adopt an organic structure, while firms that use a mass production technology are most effective if they use a mechanistic structure. In large firms, technology has its greatest impact at the lowest level of the firm, but in small firms the impact of technology is felt throughout the structure. The dramatic increase in the use of computers during the last 15 years has caused noticeable structural changes, including the creation of new managerial positions and new departments.

Organizational size—as measured by the number of employees—has a strong influence on organizational structure. With increasing size comes an increase in formalization, complexity, and specialization, and a decrease in centralization. The stage in the organization's life cycle also affects its structure.

KEY TERMS

authority (p. 231)
delegation (p. 232)
responsibility (p. 234)
accountability (p. 235)
centralization (p. 236)
decentralization (p. 236)
staff experts (p. 240)
line managers (p. 240)
line organization (p. 240)
line-staff organization (p. 241)
personal staff (p. 242)
advisory staff (p. 242)
service staff (p. 242)
control staff (p. 242)
functional authority (p. 242)
project organization (p. 243)
project manager (p. 244)
organizational design (p. 247)
stable environment (p. 247)
changing environment (p. 248)
mechanistic organization (p. 248)
organic organization (p. 248)
technology (p. 250)
unit production (p. 250)
mass production (p. 250)
process production (p. 250)
mediating technology (p. 251)
intensive technology (p. 251)
technological interdependence (p. 251)
pooled interdependence (p. 251)
sequential interdependence (p. 251)
reciprocal interdependence (p. 252)
chief information officer (p. 253)
information centre (p. 253)
network corporation structure (p. 253)
organizational life cycle (p. 254)

REVIEW QUESTIONS

1. Define the following terms:
   a. authority
   b. delegation of authority
   c. responsibility
   d. accountability
2. Describe four advantages of delegation of authority.
3. Describe the concepts of centralization and decentralization. What factors determine the extent to which an organization should be decentralized?
4. How are the "line" and "line-staff" organizations different? What are the advantages and disadvantages of each?
5. What is functional authority? Why is it used? What is the potential problem with functional authority?
6. How much authority does the project manager have in the "aggregate," "staff," and "matrix" forms of project management?
7. What is the principal disadvantage of the project structure?
8. How does the rate of change in the external environment affect an organization's structure?
9. How do "mechanistic" and "organic" organizations differ? How does the external environment influence the kind of structure that should be used?
10. What role does the environment play in influencing the level of differentiation and integration in an organization?
11. Summarize Woodward's research regarding the impact of technology on organization structure.

DISCUSSION QUESTIONS

1. How can managers reduce the possibility that subordinates will make a major mistake if the manager delegates authority to them?
2. What are the advantages and disadvantages of working in a centralized organization structure? In a decentralized organization structure?
3. Why do problems sometimes arise when staff personnel are given functional authority?
4. What is the fundamental idea of the project structure? Under what conditions is it appropriate to use a project structure?
5. In terms of organizational effectiveness, how important is the structure of an organization? If people are highly motivated, does it really matter what kind of structure an organization has?
6. If you were asked the question, "What is the best organization structure?" what would you say?

EXERCISES

1. Find an article in *The Globe and Mail* or *Canadian Business* that describes a company's attempt to decentralize authority. Write a one-page report that answers the following questions:
   a. Why did the firm move toward decentralization?
   b. What benefits does it hope to get from decentralization?
   c. How will decentralization affect the average manager in the firm?
2. Write a short report on the benefits and potential problems with delegation of authority. From your own experience, describe an incident where delegation caused problems, and what might have been done to avoid the problems.
3. Interview a manager on the topic of line-staff conflict. Ask the manager to give you examples of typical conflicts that arise between line and staff in the organization. Are the conflicts caused largely by a lack of clarity in authority relationships, or do they have another cause?

MANAGEMENT ON LOCATION

CASE 8-1
THE FACULTY OF ADMINISTRATION

Noorani Salam was the head of the management department in the Faculty of Administration at Micmac College. John Gebhart was an associate dean in the same faculty. Salam and Gebhart had attended college together and both had come to Micmac about 15 years ago. They remained good friends, often lunching together and talking over faculty business. Two years ago, Gebhart had given up the position of head of the marketing department to become an associate dean for the faculty. Salam was chosen to replace Gebhart as department head (see Figure 8-11 for the current organizational structure of the Faculty of Administration).

One function Salam performed as department head was assigning classes to the members of his department. Recently he had completed this activity and sent the members of his department their schedules for next year. Soon after the schedules were distributed, Gebhart approached Salam about his schedule, noting that he had been assigned two sections of the marketing course. Gebhart asked Salam if the two sections could be combined so that both full- and part-time students could be handled in one class. Salam said that he was reluctant to do so because he had heard various faculty members complaining that administrators (associate deans and department heads) only taught two classes per year, while regular faculty members were required to teach five classes. He was afraid that, if he let Gebhart teach only one class, the criticism would grow and he would be accused of "playing favourites." (It was well-known that Salam and Gebhart were friends.)

When Salam expressed this concern, Gebhart responded that he really wasn't interested in faculty members' views about the teaching loads of administrators. Gebhart said that he was working hard at his job and that members of Salam's department shouldn't question how many classes administrators taught. Salam again raised the concern that members of his department might accuse him of favouritism if he assigned only one course to Gebhart. Salam said he would like to leave Gebhart's schedule as it was, with Gebhart teaching two sections of marketing.

At this point, the two were interrupted and the matter was left unresolved. Since it was Friday afternoon, Salam had the weekend to mull over his problem. He didn't want this incident to affect his friendship with Gebhart, but he also didn't want to be accused of favouritism by members of his department. Either one would reduce his ability to lead the marketing department effectively. ▲

MANAGEMENT ON LOCATION

FIGURE 8-11 ORGANIZATIONAL STRUCTURE OF THE FACULTY OF ADMINISTRATION.

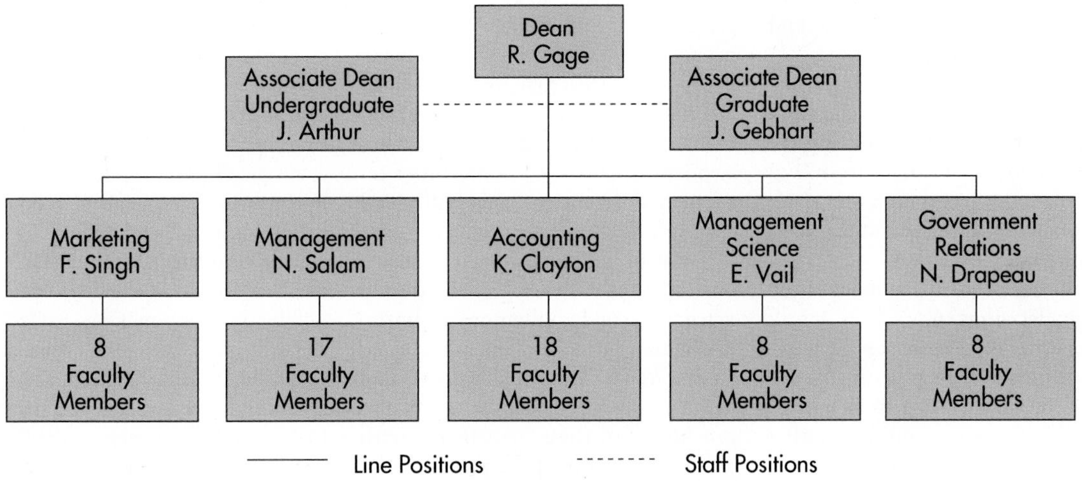

QUESTIONS

1. What is the basic structural problem here?
2. How should this problem be resolved? Be specific. Indicate how your solution solves not only this specific problem, but will also prevent problems like this from occurring in the future.

CASE 8-2
JERSAK HOLDINGS LTD.

Vaclav Jersak was born in Prague, Czechoslovakia, in 1930. His family had long been active in the retail trade in that city. Vaclav's family was very close, but the 1930s and 1940s were a time of great turbulence in central Europe. In 1938, Hitler's troops invaded Czechoslovakia and five years of war followed. After the war, Czechoslovakia came under the influence of the Soviet Union, and capitalistic ventures that had been such an integral part of the Jersak family were severely restricted. By the early 1960s, there were some hints of a return to a more capitalist economy. To Jersak's dismay, these were snuffed out by the Soviet Union's invasion of Czechoslovakia in 1968.

The invasion was the last straw for Jersak, who had felt for some years that the environment for private business activity was very poor. At age 38, he decided to leave Czechoslovakia for a better life in Canada. He arrived in Toronto in December, 1968 determined to apply his entrepreneurial talents in a more promising business environment.

Jersak quickly discovered the freedom that entrepreneurs had in Canada. He started a small gas station, and over the next three years, he opened several more. In 1971, he purchased a franchise of a major fast food outlet, and by 1977 he owned four fast food restaurants. His entrepreneurial instincts led him into a wide variety of business operations after that. From 1977 to 1991, he expanded his activity into the manufacture of auto parts, microcomputers, textiles, and office furniture. He purchased five franchises of a retail auto parts store, two automobile dealerships, and a carpet business that sells to both residential and commercial users. A mining company, a soft drink bottling plant, and a five-store chain of shoe stores are also part of Jersak Holdings Ltd.

As each new business venture was ...

added, Jersak hired a person to manage the operating company. He also added individuals with expertise in accounting, finance, marketing, and production in his head office. Currently, Jersak Holdings Ltd. contains 17 operating companies, each headed by a manager (see Figure 8-12). Employment ranges from 5 to 60 people in each company. In 1991, sales totalled $37 million and profits $4.7 million.

Head office staff make most of the strategic decisions in the firm. Jersak and the other top executives have frequent informal meetings to discuss matters of importance to the firm. Discussions usually continue until a consensus is reached on a course of action. The operating managers are expected to put into practice the strategic plans that are made at head office.

As Vaclav Jersak looks back on the last 25 years, he feels a great sense of satisfaction that he has accomplished so much. He has been thinking of retiring, but he is not sure how well the company will perform once he is gone. He recognizes that the top management group operates smoothly because the people have worked together for many years. But he feels that areas of authority should be more clearly defined so that when changes occur in top management because of his and other retirements, the new people will know exactly what they are responsible for.

Some of Jersak's business acquaintances are of the view that he should delegate considerably more authority to the managers of the operating companies. In effect, they recommend that he turn these operating managers into presidents of their own firms, with each of them being responsible for making a profit in their particular enterprise. His acquaintances point out that giving the managers of the operating companies this level of responsibility will motivate them to achieve much more than they are now doing. Also, it should motivate the employees in these firms because they will have more discretion as well. Jersak sees some real benefits in this approach, but worries that the current managers of the operating companies haven't had much experience in making important decisions. He also fears that head office will lose control of the operating companies. Jersak feels that it is important for head office staff to know some of the details of each operating company. Without this knowledge, he feels that the head office staff will be unable to make good decisions regarding the operating companies.

Other friends of Jersak argue that the time has come to centralize control at head office because the firm has gotten so large and is so diverse. Only in this way, they argue, will top management be able to effectively control all the activities of Jersak Holdings Ltd.

Jersak is uncertain about what to do, but he feels he must do something to ensure that his life's work will not disappear when he retires. ▲

FIGURE 8-12 ORGANIZATION OF JERSAK HOLDINGS LTD.

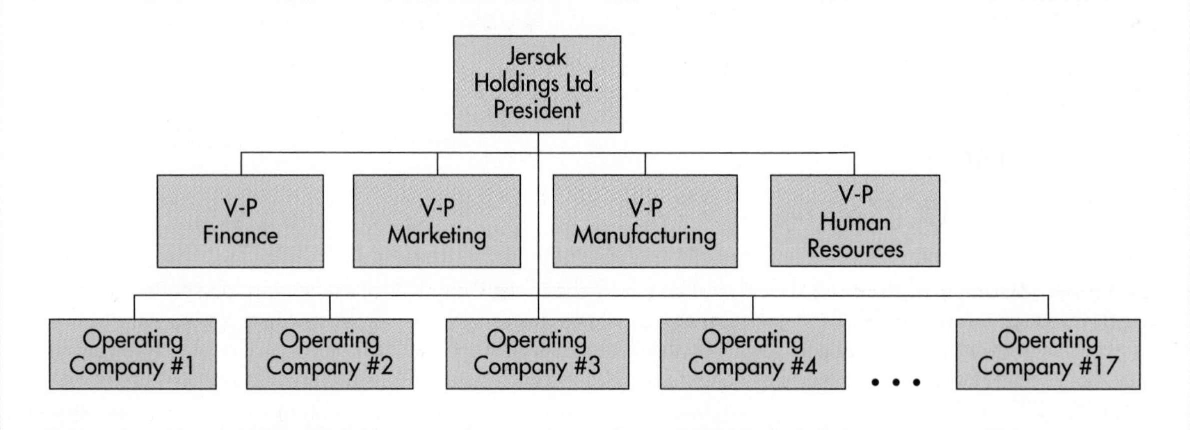

QUESTIONS

1. Discuss the advantages and disadvantages of centralization and decentralization as they relate to Jersak Holdings Ltd.
2. Which basic approach—centralization or decentralization—should Jersak Holdings Ltd. adopt? Defend your answer.
3. What problems are evident in the current organization structure of Jersak Holdings Ltd.? Design a new organization chart for the company that will solve these problems. (Refer to Chapter 7 when developing your answer for this question.)

MANAGEMENT ON LOCATION

CASE 8-3
HUTTON SOLVENTS

Hutton Solvents manufactures paint thinner, liquid cleaners, and automobile windshield de-icer. The company owns a large plant in Ontario where these products are manufactured on a mass-production basis. Most of the production line supervisors have been with the company for many years and do not have a lot of formal schooling.

During the last few years, the company has been having problems with quality control and machine breakdowns. In an attempt to resolve these problems, a quality control/engineering (QC/E) department was formed six months ago to monitor the manufacturing processes. The QC/E department has two main functions: (1) to run quality control checks on finished products, and (2) to keep abreast of the latest developments in specialized, high-speed machinery for the manufacture and packaging of solvents. The department makes recommendations to line managers about changes that should be adopted, but it has no authority to implement changes. The new department is staffed with individuals with experience in both quality control and industrial engineering, but most of the people are industrial engineers by training. They have considerable formal education.

Within a short while of the new department's formation, problems became evident. Brendan MacDuff, the head of the QC/E department, indicated to the vice-president of production that his department was being largely ignored, and that the supervisors of the various production lines in the plant hadn't changed their work patterns one bit. He argued that this was not what was intended when the QC/E department was set up. He claimed that the quality control and engineering expertise in the QC/E department was being wasted because production line supervisors were ignoring advice from his department.

MacDuff supported his arguments by noting that quality control and machine breakdown problems were still very much in evidence. He concluded by saying that the only way to resolve these problems was to give the QC/E department functional authority over the supervisors with respect to quality control and new machinery decisions.

The vice-president said he would have to think that over very carefully. He agreed that the quality control problems had to be solved, but he wasn't sure that the machinery question was as clear-cut. He noted that the production line supervisors were very valuable to the company because they "got the product out the door." He was therefore reluctant to institute changes that would make them unhappy. He promised to get back to MacDuff after speaking with the production supervisors. ▲

QUESTIONS

1. Why are the production supervisors reluctant to accept the ideas proposed by the QC/E department?
2. What are the advantages and disadvantages of giving functional authority to the QC/E department? Should such authority be given to them? Defend your answer.
3. What alternatives to functional authority exist to help resolve this conflict between the line managers and the QC/E department?

CHAPTER

9

Work Groups, Teams, and the Informal Organization

LEARNING OBJECTIVES

After reading this chapter, you will be able to:

1. Identify the different kinds of groups that exist in organizations.
2. Understand the recent emphasis on work teams, and explain the difference between integrated and self-managed work teams.
3. Explain how group norms influence individual behaviour in organizations.
4. Outline the social structure of small groups.
5. Describe the relationship between group cohesiveness and productivity.
6. Explain what the informal organization is and why it exists within every formal structure.
7. Compare and contrast the formal and informal organizations.
8. Explain the concept of status and the function it serves in organizations.
9. List several common status symbols and indicate why they are important.

MANAGEMENT CHALLENGE

Work Teams at Black Diamond

The Black Diamond Cheese factory in Ontario processes and packages cheese slices and blocks for households and for commercial operations such as trains and airplanes. The factory turns out about 400 combinations of brands and products.

Many problems were evident at this plant, and the company did not turn a profit for quite a few years because of them. A succession of different owners (four in six years) were unsuccessful in any attempt to turn the company around. One of these owners, Canada Packers, introduced a quality management program into the plant. The problem was, however, that the program provided plenty of measurements about what was wrong, but few suggestions about how to fix the problems.

Not surprisingly, the 250 unionized workers at the plant suffered from low morale. Even though they had very little knowledge about the financial condition of the company, they were fearful and uncertain about the future of their jobs.

But then Ault Foods (a division of John Labatt Ltd.) purchased Black Diamond. The operations manager was replaced, and an employee satisfaction survey was taken. When Black Diamond got the lowest rating in the Ault system, Tim Adlington, the new operations manager, decided that a major overhaul was needed.

He decided to run every department with employee teams that would be organized to address problems such as waste reduction, productivity, excessive rework, lost time from accidents, and customer returns. Progress is reviewed on a weekly basis. Under this system, managers are "facilitators" rather than order-givers. ▲

To this point, we have talked about managers in positions within the formal structure of organizations. Chapters 7 and 8 outlined the major elements of formal organizational structures, and focussed on how managers carry out the organizing function. Throughout that discussion, we made little reference to the human element that is so important to organizations, nor did we distinguish between individual and group behaviour.

In this chapter, we begin to examine the relationship between the human and structural aspects of organizations. We first introduce several concepts that are important in understanding group behaviour in organizations. Next, we describe the informal organization—what it is, how it differs from the formal organization, how it benefits the formal organization, and the problems it may create for the formal organization. The chapter concludes with a discussion of the function of status within organizations, the different types of status that exist, and the importance of status symbols.

CENTRAL CONCEPTS IN GROUP DYNAMICS

The Management Challenge suggests that managers must be sensitive to the importance of groups in organizations. This requires knowledge of (a) what a group is, (b) why people join groups, (c) the types of groups that exist in organizations, (d) the process of group development, (e) the nature and impact of group norms, (f) the social structure of groups, and (g) the nature and impact of group cohesiveness. Each of these issues is addressed below.

WHAT IS A GROUP?

group
formal group
informal group

A **group** is a collection of two or more interdependent individuals who must coordinate their activity in order to achieve goals. **Formal groups**—for example, departments, task forces, quality circles, and project teams—are established to achieve certain organization goals, and are part of the formal structure of the organization. **Informal groups**—for example, a coffee-break group or a company bowling team—are set up to meet people's social needs, and are not part of the formal structure of the organization. The leaders of informal groups can have a big impact on the formal organization because of the influence they have over the members of their informal group.

A group may consist of people who are in close physical proximity, or be made up of those who have only a psychological attachment. The Canadian Wildlife Federation, for example, has some of the same characteristics as a section gang that maintains railroad tracks for Canadian National Railways (e.g., each group is pursuing certain goals). It is usually easier to observe group behaviour in small, face-to-face groups than it is in groups with just a psychological attachment.

WHY DO PEOPLE JOIN GROUPS?

Most people belong to several formal and informal groups. People join groups for a variety of reasons:[1]

- security (there is strength in numbers)
- status (group members get recognition when the group achieves something notable)
- self-esteem (belonging to an effective group raises an individual's feelings of self-worth)

- affiliation (satisfies the basic human need to interact with others)
- power (group members can influence others to take actions desired by the group)
- goal achievement (goals can be achieved that could not be achieved by each person working individually)

Types of Groups

LEARNING OBJECTIVE 1
Identify the different kinds of groups that exist in organizations.

interacting groups

coacting groups

counteracting groups

Three types of formal groups can be found in organizations: interacting, coacting, and counteracting.[2] In **interacting groups**, the work of each group member is dependent upon that of the others. At Chrysler's Windsor, Ontario, assembly facility, for example, workers near the end of the production line cannot perform their functions unless the people at the beginning of the line have properly done theirs. In order for the Montreal Canadiens to win hockey games, members of the team must each do their part in a coordinated fashion. In **coacting groups**, the work of individual group members is independent. At Federal Industries, the activities of the aerospace, industrial distribution, and transport divisions are basically independent. Each division contributes to the overall effectiveness of Federal Industries, but each division focusses on its own activities. **Counteracting groups** are those who interact to reconcile differences between them. Included in this category are groups such as the Ontario Secondary School Teachers Federation and provincial school boards, which come together to settle labour disputes, or the United Food and Commercial Workers and Safeway as they negotiate a collective agreement. The Management at Work insert "An Alliance between Union and Management" describes how counteracting groups can work together to make members of both groups better off.

Work Teams

work teams

LEARNING OBJECTIVE 2
Understand the recent emphasis on work teams and explain the difference between integrated and self-managed work teams.

integrated work teams

self-managed teams

Work teams are formal work groups established by the organization to achieve a specific goal. Defining teams this way means that all teams are groups, but not all groups are teams. Top managers in many firms are beginning to see the use of teams as the way to increase worker morale, to capitalize on the potential benefits of an increasingly diverse work force, and to increase productivity. This is precisely what the plant manager at Black Diamond Cheese did in an attempt to resolve some long-standing problems.

There are two basic types of work teams. **Integrated work teams** are assigned certain tasks by management; team members then decide how they will divide up the work. The foreperson of a janitorial crew may, for example, identify the tasks that must be done to keep the building clean, but allow the workers to decide among themselves who will do which tasks.

Self-managed teams are groups that have greater discretion in how they do their work; they usually decide which tasks they are going to do, order the supplies necessary to do their work, hire new team members, and set their own quality standards. At Johnsonville Food Products, for example, workers are organized into teams of 5-20 workers. These work groups have almost complete control over how they work. Productivity and profits have increased substantially since the work teams were formed.[3]

Self-managing teams are also used at Volvo's Uddevalla plant in Sweden. The plant has no traditional assembly lines; rather, teams of 7-10 workers assemble entire automobiles. Team members are cross-trained in all the assembly jobs, and the work teams are responsible for most aspects of the job, including production scheduling, product quality, and hiring new members.

MANAGEMENT AT WORK

An Alliance between Union and Management

On June 30, 1992, Chrysler's new LH cars were launched at the Bramalea, Ontario, plant. On the podium that day were Lee Iacocca and union leaders who together took turns declaring their commitment to quality. Outside the plant, union and company flags were flying side by side.

This symbolic gesture is part of the new reality of union-management relations that is developing in some companies. In the automobile business, the recession of 1990-92 and tough Japanese competition have worked together to motivate union and management to reconsider their confrontational thinking. As North American car manufacturers have steadily lost market share to the Japanese, the conviction has grown that something must be changed in order to turn this situation around and regain the market.

Chrysler's Bramalea plant, which was constructed in the mid-1980s, has undergone a $400 million modernization program. It now contains over 300 robots, computerized quality-control systems, and state-of-the-art assembly equipment. But its most dramatic feature may be the new relationship between workers and management. Management has given workers a voice in designing both the assembly plant and the cars it will produce. Employees also have much greater authority than they had previously; any employee can, for example, shut down the production line if he or she notices a problem.

Traditionally, car manufacturing plants have been designed by engineers who never actually worked on the production line. At the Bramalea plant, by contrast, Chrysler has incorporated ideas from workers about plant organization. Issues like the placement of hoses, lighting, noise levels, and the distances that workers have to walk were all considered.

The social hierarchy has been changed too. Rigid divisions between managers and assembly line workers are gone. All people wear shop coats, and neckties are discouraged. The plant also has an ergonomist who ensures that physical stress on workers is minimized. The absenteeims rate of 1.9 percent is the lowest of any Chrysler assembly plant, and well below the average of 4-5 percent. The company is also spending a lot of money on training. In fact, during 1992 the plant's 3000 employees participated in 900 000 hours of it! The union and management worked together to develop the training modules. A committee that took input from employees included eight plant workers. The committee talked to workers and managers to determine what topics the training should cover, and then went to management for approval and financial support.

The new system encourages continuous suggestions from workers, who fill out special forms describing problems they've noticed. Solutions to problems are also encouraged. The engineering staff (which is responsible for acting on these suggestions), acknowledges each request within a day, and responds with some type of action within 72 hours. When an employee's idea is adopted, a reward is given, ranging from a free lunch to the use of an LH car for the weekend.

A quality awareness workshop group, including the plant manager meets each Friday to discuss issues related to quality. In these meetings, workers are able to discuss issues that the plant manager may not be aware of and have reported that the support they receive from the manager in response to this is very strong. ▲

Work teams composed of 40-50 workers per team have also been introduced at Imperial Oil's Dartmouth, Nova Scotia, refinery. Each team is responsible for an entire segment of the refinery's operations. For example, the team responsible for first stage conversion of crude oil into more useful forms is now headed by a single leader. Formerly, the work had been done by a variety of workers representing various trades and skills, each one reporting to a different manager. Under the new team approach, employees have taken on new responsibilities and a layer of supervision has disappeared. Other work teams focus on oil movement and storage, product upgrades, and maintenance support.[4]

Levi Strauss has used employee teams since the early 1980s. Teams are involved in making decisions from overall corporate strategy down to the hiring of a new factory worker. Collective effort on the production line has meant increased quality, safety, and employee satisfaction.[5]

Simply setting up a work team does not guarantee success. For work teams to be effective, they should possess the following characteristics:[6]

- clear goals
- skilled members
- mutual trust among team members
- member commitment to the team
- good communication within the team
- negotiating skills
- appropriate leadership
- a supportive organizational climate for the team

A dramatic example of how "doing the right things" may not always lead to positive outcomes is described in the Global Management insert "Not Always a Happy Ending."

GLOBAL MANAGEMENT

NOT ALWAYS A HAPPY ENDING

In Canada, Milliken & Co. used to manufacture modular carpet tiles, a floor covering that is easier to maintain and install than traditional carpet. But in late 1992, owners trimmed back the operation and limited its role to printing patterns on carpet made in the U.S. The final blow to the company came when the polyvinyl chloride backing that was used on the carpet was discovered to be environmentally unfriendly. The owners decided that to change to a substitute backing would be too costly for the small Canadian plant. In 1993, the company shut down its Canadian manufacturing operation altogether, putting 22 workers out of work.

It wasn't supposed to end this way, because Milliken had done all of the things that modern managers believe are crucial for success:

- Workers were "empowered" and were called "associates."
- Self-managed teams ran every process and machine.
- Supervisors were available for consultation, but they were rarely seen on the production floor.
- There was no union at the plant, and workers felt they had lots of discretion in decision making.
- When production problems arose, workers would thrash out a solution in meetings.
- Workers interviewed prospective team members and could veto them if they didn't think they would fit into the team.
- Rewards were given for regular attendance and for creative ideas.
- Milliken actually won the Baldridge Award for quality in the U.S. and had set its sights on winning the Canadian equivalent (the Canada Award for Business Excellence). It came in a respectable third place in the 1990 competition.

Workers routinely say that they will have trouble finding a better job than the one they had at Milliken. What went wrong? Why did a firm that was doing all the right things have to close?

The answer lies to a large extent outside the company. Two factors were key: (a) the recession of the early 1990s cut back demand for office carpet, and (b) the Free Trade Agreement caused a huge increase in foreign imports. The company eventually decided that it made more sense to ship products into Canada from its lower-cost U.S. production facilities than to make them in Canada. This decision confirmed the worst fears of free trade opponents.

An important lesson can be learned from this experience: Although much has been written about the importance of teamwork, worker involvement, and total quality management, by themselves these are not enough for success in the 1990s. There must also be strong demand for a firm's products and market share growth based on competitive costs and prices. Worker involvement can take a company only so far. ▲

THE PROCESS OF GROUP DEVELOPMENT

Groups do not form overnight. The process of developing a group of strangers into a well-coordinated team requires much time and interaction between group members. Consider your own experience in a student group that is given the responsibility of achieving some goal that is relevant to the course. At the beginning, there is considerable uncertainty about both social and task aspects of the group. But within a few weeks time, these issues have been sorted out and the group is working toward its goal.

Research on groups reveals that there are five basic stages in the process of group development.[7] As you consider these, compare them with your own experience in student work groups. Are they similar?

Forming

In the **forming** stage, group members get acquainted with each other and with the roles they are expected to carry out. There is usually considerable uncertainty about the group's goals, structure, and leadership patterns. When group members begin to think of themselves as a group, the forming stage is complete.

forming

Storming

In the **storming** stage, conflict appears within the group. The conflict may be caused by interpersonal disagreements, by task demands, or by conflicts about who will have control over the group. When a clear hierarchy of leadership has emerged, this stage is complete.

storming

Norming

The **norming** stage is characterized by cooperation, not conflict. The group has now resolved the issues that caused conflict, and it has developed to the point where it is a cohesive unit with a strong sense of group identity. Most importantly, the group has established norms indicating what is acceptable behaviour of group members.

norming

Performing

In the **performing** stage, the group has reached a productive maturity where members spend most of their time working on the central task for which the group is responsible. For permanent organizational groups, this is the final stage of development, but for temporary teams, one stage remains.

performing

Adjourning

In the **adjourning** stage, the group is terminated. The devastating loss experienced by the Conservative party in the 1993 election meant that almost all of the members of that group would no longer be interacting with each other. Even if termination is planned, as in the case of an organizational task force that has successfully completed its work, the group must spend some time dealing with the end of some interpersonal relationships. If the group has been successful, this is a time for positive reflection on group accomplishments, but if the team has been unsuccessful, or if it has been forced to disband, it may be a time of depression for group members.

adjourning

GROUP NORMS

Norms are standards of behaviour resulting from the interaction of individuals in a group. Norms control group members by defining desirable and undesirable behaviour. Behaviour must have certain characteristics before it will be enforced as a group norm. Norms are likely to be enforced if they:

norms

LEARNING OBJECTIVE 3

Explain how group norms influence individual behaviour in organizations.

1. Facilitate group survival (e.g., eating only your share of the food on a wilderness expedition).
2. Simplify or make predictable the behaviour that is expected of group members (e.g., being on time for meetings of the group).
3. Help the group avoid embarrassing interpersonal problems (e.g., don't talk about the group's problems to people outside the group).
4. Express the central values of the group and clarify what is distinctive about the group (e.g., do timely, high-quality work to maintain the group's reputation as the most productive group in the plant).[8]

The specific norms that groups adopt vary. For example, in one group a particular dress code will be enforced, while in another, eating lunch at a particular place in the company cafeteria will be the norm.

Norms generally change little in the short run. However, if the group is affected by a strong force from the outside, norms may change very quickly. For example, when management at Imperial Oil announced that the Dartmouth refinery would be closed unless productivity increased, many work-related group norms changed very quickly.[9]

production norm

The **production norm** is the range of "acceptable" production behaviour among group members. A production norm may exist in work groups because of fear that management will reduce the amount paid for each unit of output produced (if production gets too high), or because of fear of reprisal against workers (if production drops too low). Figure 9-1 illustrates the types of production behaviour observed in the Hawthorne studies (see Chapter 2) and the terms workers used to identify those who did not adhere to the group's production norms.

Lower-level blue and white collar employees such as production workers, clerks, and secretaries, often adopt restrictive production norms. The production norms of other white collar employees, however, vary widely. Some groups seem to have no detectable norm, but most white collar groups (e.g., managers) do not restrict production. In fact, since many white collar workers are looking for promotions, a norm of high production usually develops.

Individuals violating norms are physically or psychologically isolated from the group. Blue-collar work groups may have easier-to-observe norms because they do more structured work.

FIGURE 9-1 THE PRODUCTION NORM.

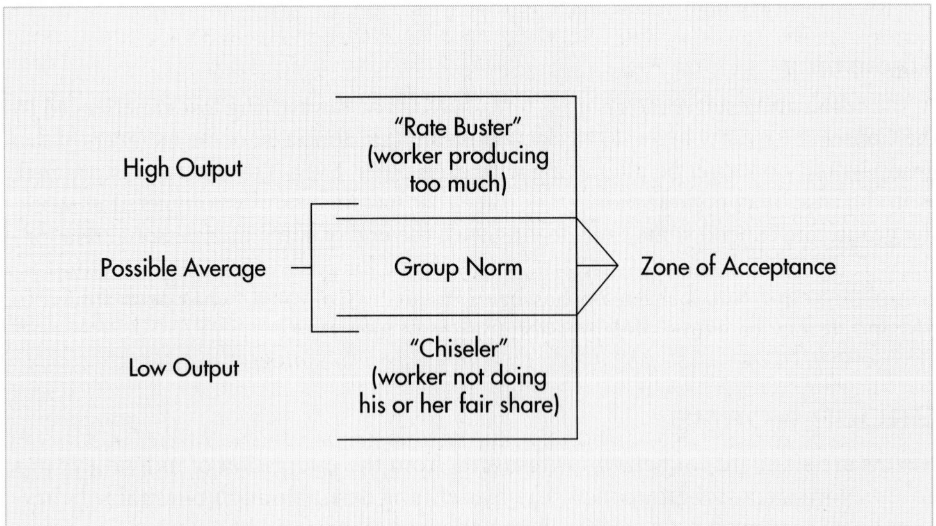

THE SOCIAL STRUCTURE OF GROUPS

LEARNING OBJECTIVE 4
Outline the social structure of small groups.

One of the major outcomes of the group development process is the establishment of group roles. The process of developing roles in the small group is similar to the process in the large, formal organization, except that it is behavioural rather than technical. The result of the interaction of group members is a social stratification in which each member occupies a role that carries certain expectations. Within this general social structure are four specific roles.

informal group leader

The **informal group leader** is that person who best satisfies the needs of the group. If a primary need of the group is security, for example, the individual who can best serve this function will likely be the most influential. However, should a need arise for a particular type of technical expertise, the individual who is technically skilled will adopt the role of group leader until that function is no longer needed.

Groups generally have two types of leaders: a *task leader* who exercises influence relating to task accomplishment, and a *social leader* who occupies the role of the human relations specialist and promotes the social processes that increase group harmony and satisfaction.[10] Since the skills necessary to perform these two functions are very different, they are seldom found in a single person.

regular members

Individuals whose behaviour remains in the zone of acceptance of group norms are called **regular members.** Some variation occurs within this category, since not all members will be accepted to the same degree. Regular members exert less influence on the group than group leaders.

deviates

Group members who violate group norms are called **deviates** and are excluded from normal group functions. Deviates pose a threat to the group's security since their unusual behaviour may attract the attention of management. A group of salespeople, for example, may resent someone who accomplishes more than the others, since the sales manager may then pressure the rest of the group to increase its productivity.

isolate

If the group fails to induce a deviate to conform to group norms, the deviate becomes an isolate. An **isolate** is a group member who is psychologically, socially, and possibly physically isolated from the group. This exclusion—in some ways similar to solitary confinement in a prison—is a further attempt to protect the group from the individual's unacceptable behaviour.

GROUP COHESIVENESS

group cohesiveness

Group cohesiveness is the degree of attraction a group has for its members. The more desirable group membership is seen to be, the more cohesive the group may become. Other factors being equal, smaller groups are more likely to be cohesive than larger groups. The principal research findings on group cohesiveness follow.[11]

1. *The greater the similarity of the status of group members, the greater the cohesiveness of the group* Individuals with similar status are more likely to be attracted to one another.

2. *Cohesiveness of a group is greater if membership changes are infrequent or do not occur at all* Time is required for groups to sort out acceptable and unacceptable behaviours. New group members disrupt this process because they must learn what is acceptable.

3. *The more cohesive the group, the more communication will be directed at deviates* The stronger the perceived need for conformity, the more effort will be directed at those who do not conform. Cohesive groups exert great influence on both regular members and deviates.

4. *Cohesive groups have higher levels of intermember communication than noncohesive groups* Persons of similar status have more in common than those with dissimilar status; this similarity facilitates communication among members.

5. *Competition within a group has a negative influence on cohesiveness* Competition for scarce resources within a group can diminish cohesiveness.

6. *Competition between groups increases the cohesiveness within the groups* When an outside threat arises, a group reacts to it by becoming more cohesive.

Group Cohesiveness and Productivity

LEARNING OBJECTIVE 5
Describe the relationship between group cohesiveness and productivity.

The practical importance of group cohesiveness is its effect on group productivity. Research into the relationship between group cohesiveness and group productivity is summarized below.[12]

1. *People in highly cohesive groups generally experience fewer work-related anxieties* In cohesive groups, friction and interpersonal conflicts have been sorted out, so anxieties are minimized. Since work-related anxieties can reduce productivity, a cohesive group can facilitate productivity.

2. *Highly cohesive work groups tend to have low absenteeism and turnover* Since a prerequisite for productivity is that employees be at work, cohesive work groups can create the conditions necessary for high productivity.

3. *The effect of cohesiveness upon productivity varies with the source of the cohesiveness* If a group is cohesive simply because of its members' strong interpersonal attractions for each other, or because they all dislike the boss, there may be very little effect on productivity. If the group is cohesive because they are all well trained and want to achieve challenging goals, cohesiveness will lead to high productivity.

4. *The effect of cohesiveness upon productivity varies with the type of leadership received* If supportive leadership is given to a highly cohesive group, it is likely that productivity will be high. However, if the leadership is not supportive, productivity may be low.

The impact of cohesiveness on productivity depends on the match between organization and group goals (see Figure 9-2 for a summary of these relationships). The most dysfunctional type of group (from management's point of view) is the one that is highly cohesive but does not identify with the goals of the organization. The most functional type is the highly cohesive group that identifies with the goals of the formal organization and encounters no technical obstacles in meeting those goals.

Some firms make formal attempts to develop cohesive work groups because of the increased "energy" that is evident in such groups. For example, at Campbell Soup Canada, the president and six vice-presidents went on an Outward Bound program near Lake Superior. The trip included four days of canoeing, spending one day alone in the wilderness, and scaling a sheer granite cliff. After the group returned, they spent time discussing what they had learned and how it could be applied to business management. The president felt that the trip resulted in "team bonding."[13] Other firms are also trying to develop cohesive work groups (see the Management at Work insert "Work Teams at Shell Canada").

FIGURE 9-2 INTERACTION EFFECTS BETWEEN GROUP COHESIVENESS AND GOAL IDENTIFICATION.

Group Cohesiveness	Group Goal Identification: With Company	Group Goal Identification: Against Company
High	High Performance	Very Low Performance
Low	Moderate Performance	Low Performance

MANAGEMENT AT WORK

WORK TEAMS AT SHELL CANADA LTD.

Shell Canada's lubricants factory at Brockville, Ontario, was built at a cost of $75 million. Starting operations in 1992, it replaces older plants in Montreal and Toronto. The plant takes tankloads of base oils and mixes in various additives to make oil for automobiles, boats, and industrial applications. The heart of the blending process is an operations control centre where a bank of computers stores the "recipes" for 240 different oil blends. The computer also gives operators step-by-step directions on how to do the mixing.

The plant's 75 factory floor workers are grouped into three teams called "job families." Each team manages one of the plant's three basic activities—blending of lubricants, packaging, and warehousing. Each worker must be able to perform all the jobs allocated to her or his team. Operators are also expected to be knowledgeable about where raw materials come from and where final products are sold.

Teams are given the information and authority they need (including the right to talk to suppliers or customers) to make the plant perform up to standard. Missing from the plant are the traditional foreperson and superintendent who tell people what to do and how to do it. In their place is a system that turns all employees into supervisors by allowing them to tap into the information they need to manage themselves. Teams are responsible for cost control, developing vacation and training schedules, and disciplining nonperforming workers. In essence, the old "command and control" hierarchy has been abandoned and has been replaced by a dynamic organization structure that runs on worker commitment, enthusiasm, and group cohesion.

It is difficult to predict the effect of these far-reaching changes, but the outlook is promising. The Brockville plant produces about the same level of output as the Toronto and Montreal plants formerly did, but with half as many workers. It has also found customers in 44 different countries, whereas export sales were formerly a rarity. Absenteeism is running at about one-third the normal rate in manufacturing.

The philosophy at the Brockville plant is that a company's strategy must be built around people. Shell has therefore tried to create an environment where people can better contribute to the business. To achieve this environment, systematic testing of applicants was necessary. Of the 46 people from the Toronto and Montreal plants who applied to move to Brockville, only 20 passed the screening tests. Shell received an additional 1200 applications from workers in the Brockville area; applicants went through a rigorous series of tests before 40 more operators were selected. ▲

Groupthink

groupthink

One of the hazards of a cohesive work group is the phenomenon known as "groupthink."[14] **Groupthink** occurs when members of a group voluntarily suspend their critical thinking abilities and repress any conflict and disagreement that could challenge group solidarity. Groupthink is a problem because it suppresses minority opinions and unpopular views, both of which can help the group to critically examine its decision-making processes.

Eight symptoms of groupthink have been identified (see Table 9-1). When these symptoms are evident in a group, the likely outcome is poor development and analysis of alternatives, a poor choice of decision, a failure to consider the difficulties in implementing the decision, and a failure to reexamine the assumptions that were used to make the decision.

Perhaps the most dramatic example of groupthink was the Challenger disaster. The management group ignored warnings from engineers about "O-ring" problems because they were under pressure to maintain their launch schedule.

Groupthink can occur in any highly cohesive group. It has been observed in business firms that made poor competitive decisions, and in non-profit organizations that adopted inappropriate strategies. Groupthink is probably best known from some spectacular examples of poor decision making in U.S. government circles, most notably Pearl Harbor, the Bay of Pigs invasion, Watergate, and the Challenger disaster. In the case of the space shuttle Challenger, for example, warnings were raised by engineers that the air temperature on the morning of the rocket launch was low enough to cause hardening of "O-rings" which kept hot gases from escaping the fuel tank and causing an explosion. But these warnings were ignored by NASA management who felt pressure to stay on schedule with the launch of the space shuttle. So, the shuttle was launched and seven astronauts died when the O-rings failed.

In each case of groupthink, certain members of the group are not really in agreement with the decision that is being contemplated, but they fail to speak up for fear of being considered a nuisance or being ostracized by the group. They are more motivated to agree with the group than to critically analyze the decision.

The likelihood that groupthink will develop can be reduced if certain strategies are adopted (see Table 9-2). These strategies require that group members accept the view that conflict and disagreement—while time-consuming and perhaps uncomfortable—must be encouraged if bad decisions are to be avoided. Legitimizing dissent is the underlying theme of the strategies listed in Table 9-2.

TABLE 9-1 SYMPTOMS OF GROUPTHINK.

Symptom	Explanation
1. Illusion of invulnerability	1. Members of the group believe that they are invulnerable to any actions that opponents or competitors might take.
2. Rationale	2. Group members develop rationalizations to reassure themselves that the decision they made was the right one.
3. Morality	3. Group members believe that their chosen course of action is "right" and is therefore justified.
4. Stereotyping	4. Viewing the enemy or competition as evil, incompetent, weak, or ineffective.
5. Pressure	5. Applying pressure to anyone in the group who expresses doubts about the group's illusions.
6. Self-censorship	6. Group members say nothing about their misgivings and minimize the importance of their own doubts.
7. Illusion of unanimity	7. Group members have the feeling that they alone have doubts about the wisdom of the decision, and that every one else in the group is in favour of it.
8. Mindguards	8. Some group members take it upon themselves to protect other group members from negative information that might jolt the group out of its complacency.

TABLE 9-2 REMEDIES FOR GROUPTHINK.

Remedies	Explanation
1. Legitimize dissent.	1. The group leader should assign the role of critical evaluator to every member of the group.
2. Stress impartiality.	2. The leader should adopt an impartial stance on major issues instead of stating preferences at the outset.
3. Divide group into subgroups.	3. The group should be divided into subgroups who meet separately and then come together to work out their differences.
4. Consult constituents.	4. Each member should be required to discuss the group's tentative consensus with members of the unit he or she represents.
5. Consult outside experts.	5. Outside experts should be invited to meetings to give their views and to challenge the views of group members.
6. Assign devil's advocate role.	6. The devil's advocate role should be assigned on a rotating basis to group members.
7. Assess warning signals.	7. One or more sessions should be devoted to assessing the warning signals from enemies or competitors.
8. Give "last chance" opportunity.	8. After a tentative consensus has been reached, a "last-chance" meeting should be held to allow group members to express any doubts they may have.

THE INFORMAL ORGANIZATION

In Chapters 7 and 8, we examined several types of formal organization structures and discussed their potential impact on employee behaviour. In addition to the formal structure, another "structure"—the informal organization—shapes employee behaviour. The **informal organization** is the pattern of social behaviour and influence that arises spontaneously whenever people work together within the formal structure. It blurs the clear, logically designed official structure that so appeals to some managers. These managers are proud of the formal structure they have created, precisely because it is logical and orderly (see Figure 9-3). Everyone knows exactly who he or she reports to and the task each person is expected to do.

informal organization

LEARNING OBJECTIVE 6
Explain what the informal organization is and why it exists within every formal structure.

FIGURE 9-3 THE FORMAL ORGANIZATION.

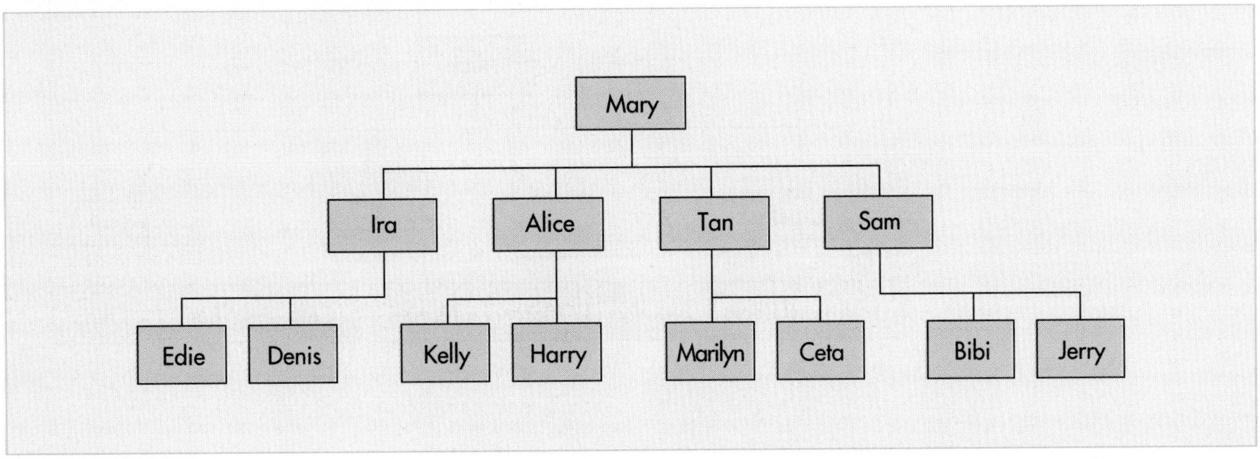

Some managers believe that they have fulfilled their organizing responsibilities once they have developed an orderly formal structure. This is not so. The orderly structure devised by managers is often drastically altered to conform to people's wants and needs. An illustration of the way the informal group operates within the formal organization is shown in Figure 9-4. Mary, the president by title, actually has little influence. Alice is recognized as the most influential decision maker, even by Mary herself. Ira, Tan, and Sam defer to Alice rather than Mary. All three compete with one another for Alice's attention, hoping for a promotion if Mary steps aside. Alice is so busy she hasn't noticed that Kelly and Harry, who report to her, dislike each other and try constantly to undermine one another's efforts. Denis, taking advantage of the hostility between Kelly and Harry, deals more often with Alice than with his own supervisor, Ira. Edie, who also reports to Ira, wonders who's really in charge and who should be doing Denis's neglected work. Marilyn and Ceta, although they report to Tan, are more interested in him as a possible romantic interest. Bibi, Ceta's friend, is more interested in the romance in the adjacent area than in working for her supervisor, Sam. Jerry, who also reports to Sam, spends much of his time trying to influence Mary because he is sure that one day she will take back her rightful authority.

Figure 9-4 shows that employee behaviour often does not conform to the formal structure that has been prescribed. Rather, spontaneous friendships and relationships develop that are based on criteria that are not recognized by the formal structure. The informal organization emerges because the formal structure does not satisfy all employee and organizational needs. Remember, managers do not have a choice as to whether or not the informal organization will develop. Informal relationships will *always* develop within any formal structure. Managers should understand, rather than suppress, the informal organization, and channel its energies toward organizational goals.

COMPARING FORMAL AND INFORMAL ORGANIZATIONS

LEARNING OBJECTIVE 7

Compare and contrast the formal and informal organization.

Informal organizations represent the human side of organizations, and are influenced by the nature of individuals in the organization. Formal organizations are highly structured and give less emphasis to human considerations. The formal organization is "how it should be" and the informal organization is "how it actually is." Table 9-3 summarizes the key differences between formal and informal structures.

FIGURE 9-4 THE INFORMAL ORGANIZATION.

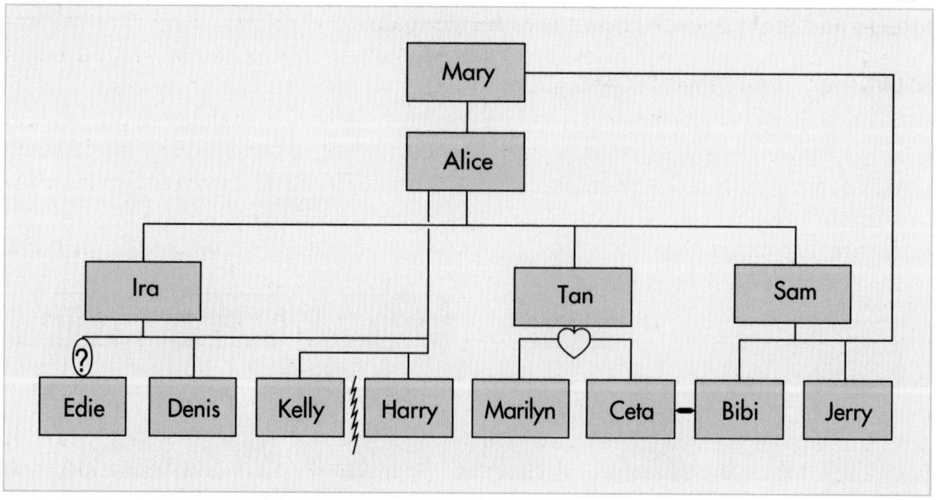

TABLE 9-3 A COMPARISON OF FORMAL AND INFORMAL ORGANIZATIONAL CHARACTERISTICS.

Characteristic	Informal Organization	Formal Organization
Structure		
Origin	Spontaneous	Planned
Rationale	Emotional	Rational
Characteristics	Dynamic	Stable
Representation	Contact Chart	Organization Chart
Position terminology	Role	Job
Goals	Member satisfaction	Profitability or service to society
Influence		
Base	Personality	Position
Type	Power	Authority
Flow	Bottom up	Top down
Control mechanisms	Norms	Threat of discipline, firing, demotion
Communication		
Channels	Grapevine	Formal channels
Networks	Poorly defined, cut across regular channels	Well defined, follow formal lines
Speed	Fast	Slow
Accuracy	Moderate	High
Membership		
Individuals included	Only those "acceptable"	All individuals in work group
Interpersonal relations	Arise spontaneously	Prescribed by job description
Leadership role	Result of membership agreement	Assigned by organization
Basis for interaction	Personal characteristics, ethnic background, status	Functional duties or position
Basis for attachment	Cohesiveness	Loyalty

Structure

Formal structures are the result of conscious thought, and are intended to facilitate the rational pursuit of organizational goals. Changes in the formal structure can be made by administrative decree. By contrast, the informal organization develops spontaneously. It is the result of emotion rather than logic. When changes occur in the informal structure, they are the result of consensus among the members, not the result of a decision imposed by management.

The structure of the formal organization is shown on an organization chart. If a job description changes, or if the company is reorganized, the boxes and lines on the chart are simply redrawn to reflect the design of the new structure. The informal organization has its own structure, and it must be charted differently than the formal structure. A **contact chart** identifies the informal connections that an individual has with other members of the organization (see Figure 9-5). Levels of management are often by-passed, and contact between one chain of command and another occurs. For example, the number of workers who contact individual "J" indicate that he or she is very popular and is probably the informal leader.

contact chart

A contact chart does not show the reasons relationships develop. These causes could be important, since they can reveal whether the relationships work for or against the formal organization. Individual "J" could be assisting other employees in doing their work, or could be stirring up trouble and promoting disharmony.

FIGURE 9-5 A CONTACT CHART.

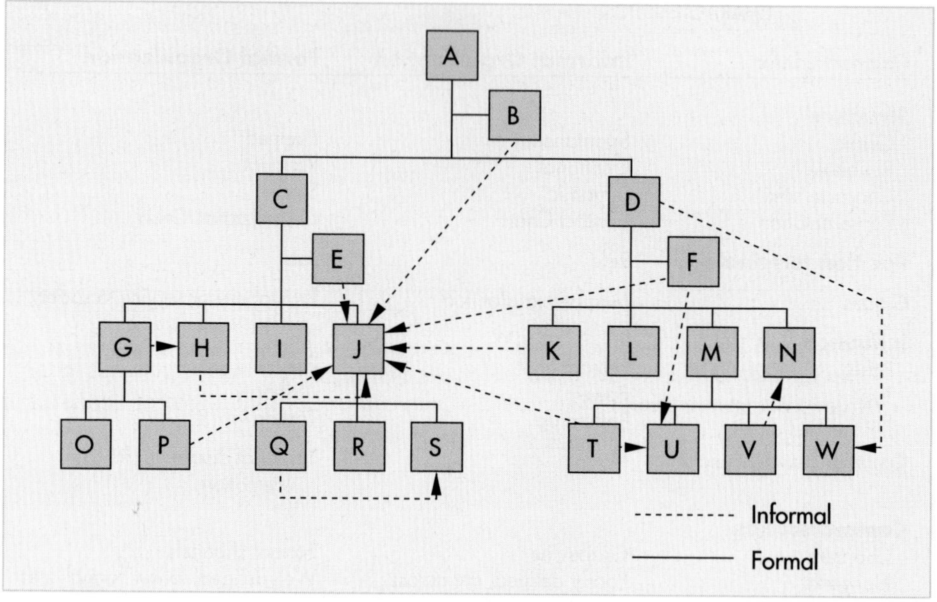

A contact chart is used to chart informal relationships throughout the organization. A technique that can be used to chart informal relationships within a specific work group is that of sociometric analysis. The outcome of this type of analysis is a sociogram, an example of which is shown in Figure 9-6. A **sociogram** illustrates how the members of a work group interact with each other; it is developed by observing the actual behaviour of group members. Through such observation it is possible for the manager to answer such questions as which group member has the most influence, which group members do not adhere to group norms, and which individuals are excluded from the group.

sociogram

FIGURE 9-6 A SOCIOGRAM.

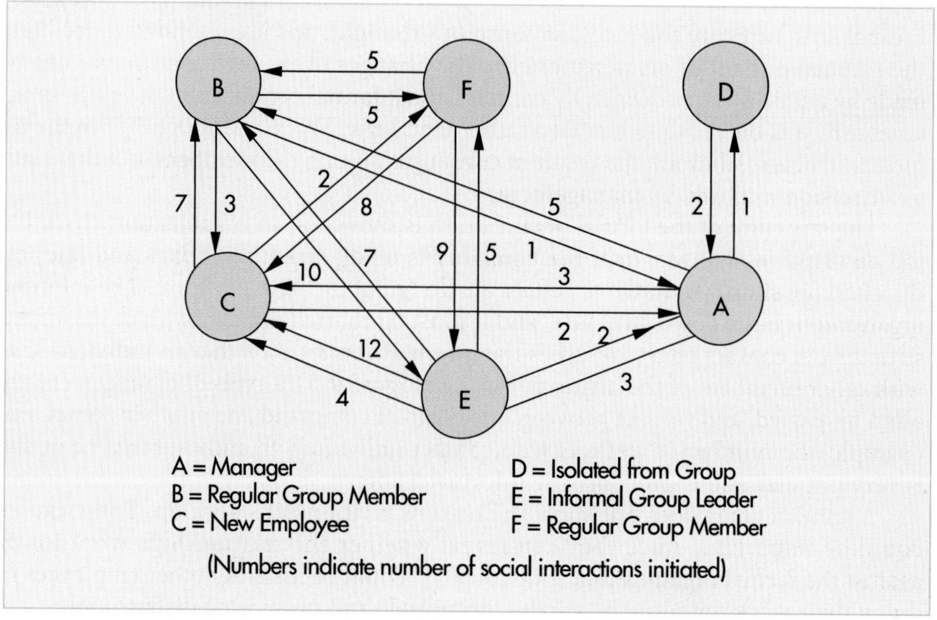

Position Terminology

In the formal organization, the relationship between the individual and the organization tends to be mechanical and impersonal. The responsibilities and behaviours required of individuals are specified in job descriptions, which are designed without regard for who will be performing the job. The informal organization's equivalent of the "job" is the "role." A **role** consists of the total pattern of behaviour expected of a person. The concept of organizational role is more complex than that of a job since it includes not only the individual's formal responsibilities and expectations, but also other people's expectations of the role occupant (see Figure 9-7).

role

It is not unusual to find that the formal job description's requirements and the role expectations of an individual's colleagues are in conflict. For example, the formal organization may require a certain level of productivity, but the informal organization may place pressure on its members not to exceed a certain level of production.

Role expectations come from many sources, and they make greater demands on workers than do formal job demands. Job descriptions prescribe behaviour only within the organization, but role expectations can come not only from the person's job but also from family, friends, colleagues, and so on. Because an individual occupies many roles, each having a different set of obligations, he or she is frequently confronted with conflicting expectations. A worker may have to choose between an evening with the family or bowling with the company team. This situation is likely to present considerable role conflict as the person attempts to sort out the priorities of each activity (more about this in Chapter 15).

FIGURE 9-7 THE ORGANIZATIONAL ROLE.

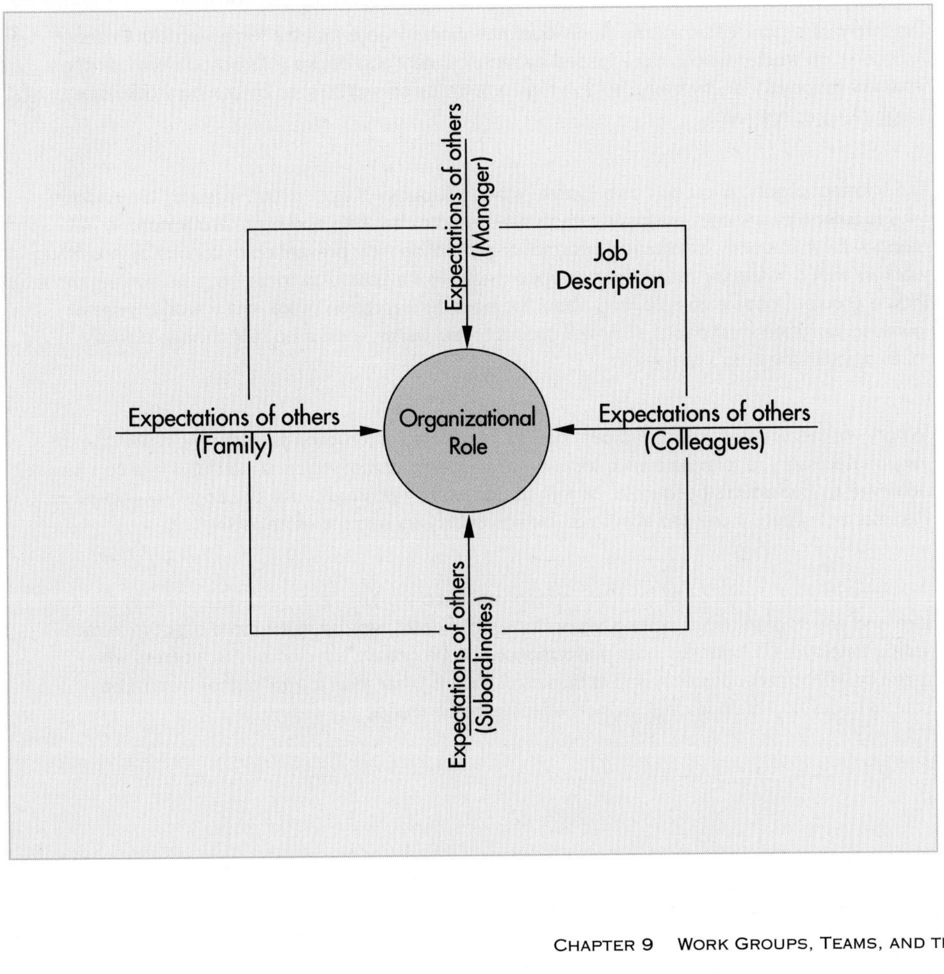

TABLE 9-4 POTENTIAL BENEFITS AND COSTS OF THE INFORMAL ORGANIZATION.

BENEFITS	EXPLANATION
1. SECURITY	People like to know where they stand in a social structure, and the informal organization conveys this. Deviant or abnormal behaviour is not tolerated, and this assures members a degree of stability in their interpersonal relationships. The informal organization also increases member security by protecting members from outside influences such as management or other work groups.
2. SATISFACTION OF SOCIAL NEEDS	People have social needs that they attempt to satisfy while at work, and the informal organization satisfies these needs. Activities such as coffee and lunch breaks, idle conversation, hockey and football pools, and going-away parties illustrate some of the more common forms of informal activities. These activities may actually benefit the formal organization because important needs of the workers are being satisfied in the workplace.
3. COMMUNICATION	The informal organization provides an additional channel of communication in the form of the grapevine. Information that is deemed important by the informal organization is sought and communicated to interested group members. Because the information is seen as important, it is transmitted quickly. Regardless of the accuracy of the information, the mere act of communicating it tends to fulfill the needs of the informal organization.
4. BALANCING DEVICE	The informal organization overcomes deficiencies in the formal structure. Consider a person who is promoted to a position that exceeds his or her present capabilities. This condition is not unusual for a newly promoted manager. While the new manager is learning how to do the job, the informal organization may compensate for his or her lack of knowledge and experience. Experienced employees may show the new manager how certain tasks are done and why they are done that way.
5. EGO SATISFACTION	The informal organization satisfies individual members in ways that the formal structure cannot. A production worker who is disregarded by management can derive satisfaction from being an informal group leader, by being held in high esteem by co-workers, or by having workmates laugh at his or her jokes.
6. SAFETY VALVE	The informal organization acts as a "safety valve." Suppose a work group is led by a manager who is authoritarian, acts arbitrarily, treats subordinates harshly, and is generally hard to get along with. A smoothly functioning informal organization may prevent open conflict by providing workers with a forum for airing their complaints about the boss. This forum may be nothing more than a group of people complaining about the boss during coffee break, but if workers are allowed to vent their frustrations, they will probably feel better, even if no real change actually takes place in the boss's behaviour.
7. MOTIVATION	When workers are involved in tedious, boring jobs, social interaction provides them with the diversion necessary to tolerate such a task. Another source of motivation is the status that can be achieved by individuals because of certain attributes they possess or the position they occupy in the informal group. Increased status can be ego-satisfying and therefore motivating.
8. MANAGEMENT IMPROVEMENT	A manager who enjoys good informal relations with co-workers, and who is sensitive to the nature and effects of relations among his or her subordinates, will be much more effective in motivating employees. Organizational performance can be greatly affected by the workers who grant or withhold cooperation and enthusiasm. Means other than formal authority must be sought to develop attitudes that support effective performance.

• • •

COSTS	EXPLANATION
1. EXCESSIVE SOCIALIZING	Activities such as horseplay, betting pools, or idle conversation may divert people from their work. Many managers find such conduct extremely frustrating, and conclude that time is being wasted and productivity is suffering. However, employees have social needs that must be satisfied, and if the satisfaction of these needs is prevented, lowered motivation and productivity may develop. In order to increase productivity, managers may have to allow or even encourage some apparently nonproductive behaviours.
2. OBSTRUCTION OF WORK	On occasion, informal groups engage in tactics like work restriction, pressuring co-workers into disregarding company requirements, disloyalty, insubordination, or unauthorized actions that harm the organization.
3. RESISTANCE TO CHANGE	The norms of behaviour that develop increase the chances that there will be resistance to change.
4. STAFFING INFLEXIBILITY	From the formal organization's perspective, technical qualifications such as education or training are necessary requirements for good job performance. But the informal organization may see these as only partly relevant and may add other factors such as personality, or an applicant's ability to get along with established group members.
5. RUMOURS	The grapevine is the communication tool of the informal organization. It can be very gratifying to members of the informal organization, but the need for information can be so great that the grapevine creates its own information (rumours). Depending on the nature of the relationship between management and employees, even hard facts about the situation may not squelch the rumour. Because of the rumours, employees may become concerned about their job security, job duties, pay, and other important work-related factors. This concern—and the resulting discussions among workers about the rumour—can reduce employee morale and productivity.
6. REDUCED MANAGERIAL	Some managers feel uncomfortable with the informal organization because it reduces their control over their subordinates, and some subordinates have much more informal influence than their position on the formal organization chart suggests.

Goals

The goals of the formal organization are set by the owners and managers. They are usually described in terms of profitability, efficiency, or service. In contrast, the informal organization's major goal is satisfaction of the social needs of its members. But, the informal organization can make a significant contribution to the fulfillment of the formal organization's goals by motivating workers to do tasks they are not technically required to do by their formal job description.

Informal activities at the workplace give employees the opportunity to satisfy important social needs. Although this type of activity does not directly cause increased productivity, it generally benefits the formal organization because it means increased satisfaction levels for employees.

Influence

Influence within the formal structure comes from the formal position a person occupies. Job descriptions indicate the extent of the authority in the position, so the formal organization equates authority with influence. In contrast, a person *acquires* influence in the informal organization by gaining approval from the relevant group. Influence in the informal organization is attached to the *person*, whereas in the formal organization it is attached to the *position*.

Control Mechanisms

Controls such as rules, policies, and procedures are used in the formal organization. In the informal organization, norms are communicated to members through social processes. The primary function of norms in the informal organization is to increase the predictability of desirable behaviour as defined by the group.

Communication

Hierarchical lines of authority in formal structures identify the correct channels of communication. Therefore, lines of authority can also be viewed as lines of communication. The informal organization devises its own channel of communication; it is called the **grapevine**. The grapevine is much faster than formal channels of communication, but it often passes along distorted information and rumours. **Rumours** are unsubstantiated statements about what is happening in an organization. If employees are expecting to be laid off because of a downturn in demand for the company's products, rumours will probably begin to circulate before an official statement is released. Rumours may, of course, turn out to be true, but they are often false.

grapevine
rumours

BENEFITS AND COSTS OF THE INFORMAL ORGANIZATION

The informal organization provides both benefits and costs for the formal organization. If a manager accepts the informal organization and makes use of it, employee satisfaction and productivity will be enhanced. However, if a manager is hostile toward informal work groups or tries to suppress their activities, the informal organization will become uncooperative. Table 9-4 summarizes the potential benefits and costs of the informal organization.

STATUS IN ORGANIZATIONS

LEARNING OBJECTIVE 8
Explain the concept of status and the function it serves in organizations.

In Chapter 7, we noted that the formal organization attempts to organize jobs rationally so that organizational goals will be achieved. In this chapter, we have observed that the informal organization can either facilitate or inhibit the achievement of organizational goals. Now consider the following example of the *interaction* of the formal and informal organizations. A manufacturing firm has three vice-presidents: finance, marketing, and production. From a strictly structural perspective, each of these vice-presidents is equal to the others. But everyone in the organization knows that one of the vice-presidents really has much more influence than the other two and is next in line for the presidency. Situations like this are common in organizations because of differences in status.

status

Status is the relative position of an individual in a group. This position is determined by status attributes, that is, those factors that are used to rank individuals. Characteristics such as age, sex, ethnic origin, occupation, job title, education, and religious beliefs are some of the common attributes employed to place individuals in a status hierarchy. Even though it is illegal to use some of these characteristics to discriminate between people, they do play a role in the development of status hierarchies in organizations.

Certain jobs are given more status than others. In the most general sense, white collar jobs have higher status than blue collar jobs. But within this broad classification, additional distinctions are made. For example, electricians have more status than cleaners, even though both are blue collar jobs. Computer programmers have more status than office clerks, even though both are white collar jobs. Even finer distinctions can be made. Long-distance telephone operators have more status than local operators; cafeteria personnel who serve beef have higher status than those who serve fish; pilots and airline attendants on international flights have more status than their peers on domestic flights; and graduate students have more status than undergraduates.

A status attribute is valued if two conditions are met: the attribute is *scarce* and it is *desirable*. Individuals with large incomes have high status because money is perceived as both scarce and desirable by most people. Any attribute may have value if the relevant group perceives that the attribute is both scarce and desirable. Thus, what is high status to one group may be totally meaningless to another. In a group where education is a desired attribute, an individual with a Ph.D. would have high status, but in a group where education is not relevant, a person with a Ph.D. might have very low status.

Types of Status

ascribed status

achieved status

There are two types of status: ascribed and achieved. **Ascribed status** is that which a person possesses because of certain unchangeable characteristics such as age, sex, and ethnic background. **Achieved status** is that which a person attains through personal choice, such as education, job skills, or marital status. In both the formal and informal organization, the status of a person can be the result of ascribed status, achieved status, or a combination of the two. Thus, in certain business firms, individuals who belong to the Kiwanis Club may have high status; on a basketball team the tallest player may have the highest status (no pun intended).

scalar status

functional status

Within formal organizations, two additional types of status can be identified: scalar and functional. **Scalar status** refers to a person's level in the hierarchy. A vice-president of marketing, for example, possesses higher scalar status than a salesperson. **Functional status** derives from an individual's function within the organization. It recognizes that some jobs are more desirable or attractive than others. For example, even though a janitor and a clerk may have the same scalar status (i.e., they are both on the same organizational level), the clerk will have a higher functional status if the work of the janitor is considered less desirable.

Generally a strong relationship exists between functional and scalar status, but this is not always the case. A well-known exception is the position of secretary to the president. This position has relatively low scalar status, since the job lacks any formal authority. But the job is often seen as having high functional status because the secretary reports to a position with high functional and scalar status. The opposite condition exists when a manager is "kicked upstairs," meaning the manager is given a high-sounding job title but nothing to do.

Status Symbols

status symbol

Since status dictates how we should behave with each other, it is important to be able to identify another individual's status quickly and efficiently. Status symbols have been devised to facilitate this identification. A **status symbol** is a tangible sign of a person's social position. Perhaps the best example of this is found in military organizations where the status hierarchy is quite visible. Each formal position has officially designated symbols, such as the number of stripes or type of insignia worn on one's uniform. Symbols of this type make it possible for members to identify formal positions immediately, so that little interaction is required to determine the other's organizational status. Generally speaking, however, status symbols are useful for making preliminary judgments. Precise judgments are possible only after prolonged social interaction has taken place.

LEARNING OBJECTIVE 9
List several common status symbols and indicate why they are important.

Status symbols can take many forms. A person's position in the formal hierarchy can usually be judged by such indicators as the size of one's office, its type of decor, or the size of one's desk (see the following Management at Work insert "Status Symbols"). The informal organization also creates status symbols. For example, a production worker may have high informal status because he can regularly hit home runs for the company softball team. In Japanese companies where everyone wears the same uniform, supervisors put 4-5 pens in their shirt pocket as a status symbol. Workers can't do this because the pens would fall out as they bend over to do their work.[15] In this way, supervisors clearly distinguish themselves from workers.

Status symbols can cause unhappiness and envy in organizations. Executives have been observed on their hands and knees, measuring the size of their offices in order to compare it with others. Windows are counted, carpet thickness measured, steps from the president's office paced off, parking space fought for, and company cars wangled. Because these activities are considered petty and unproductive, some companies have tried to abolish all status symbols by equalizing privileges, offices, and furnishings. Other companies have eliminated executive dining rooms, and some use open-area offices. In others, windowless buildings have been constructed, office sizes are standardized, and only one type of company car is made available. Top executives may start driving Caravans and Cherokees instead of Mercedes to show that they are more "down to earth."

To some people, the end of the "Yuppie era" meant a minimization of status symbols, and a rejection of the status symbol as being superficial and plastic. Generally speaking, however, attempts to do away with status symbols are not very successful. People want to distinguish their position in the organization from the position occupied by other people, and status symbols allow them to fulfill this desire. If certain status symbols are not formally allowed, others will informally emerge. If no one's office has a window, then some other criterion of status will develop (desk size, thickness of carpet, size of plants, etc.).

MANAGEMENT AT WORK

STATUS SYMBOLS

Most large companies spell out status symbols quite clearly, and Ontario Hydro is no exception. It has very detailed specifications regulating office size and furnishings for its managers. For example, the office sizes are as follows:

Chairperson 56 square metres
Executive vice-president 46 square metres
Vice-president 37 square metres
Director 32 square metres

Office furnishings are also specified in detail. Directors get no extras except two plants and a couch; vice-presidents are allowed three plants and several pieces of furniture; the executive vice-president gets even more plants and furniture; and the chairperson gets two glass walls, a television and videotape machine, even more furniture, and custom-made white carpet.

Even small firms seem concerned about spelling out what managers at various levels are allowed to possess in the way of status symbols. Crows Nest Resources is a Calgary-based coal mining company with 600 employees. Its office area specifications are as follows:

President 30 square metres
Vice-presidents 28 square metres
Managers 21 square metres
Others 14 square metres

As far as furnishings are concerned, the president gets two plants and expensive Chippendale furniture; the vice-presidents get one plant and walnut furniture; managers get no plants and even cheaper furniture; and others get nothing beyond a desk and chair.

One Canadian university specifies that a dean shall have one desk (180 × 90 × 72.5 cm), one 3-seater couch, one occasional table, and two plants; department heads get one desk (165 × 90 × 72.5 cm) and one plant; faculty members get one desk (150 × 90 × 72.5 cm) and no plants. ▲

MEETING THE CHALLENGE

Work Teams at Black Diamond Cheese

How well have the changes at Black Diamond worked? On the financial side, sales are up by 15 percent, rejects of finished goods are down 33 percent, and inventories have been cut by a third since the plant was acquired by Ault Foods. The division made a small profit for the fiscal year ending May 1, 1993 (this is a $6 million turnaround in earnings from fiscal 1992).

Interestingly, the impact on the human side has been mixed. One manager estimates that one-quarter of the workers are strongly committed to the new system, another one-fifth don't care one way or another, and the remainder are in the wait-and-see category. On the positive side, morale in the plant has improved dramatically since Ault Foods took over. Many workers are excited about their new autonomy, and one team is working on a brand new product. The company sent one worker to Europe to check out a new production technology. Repetitive strain injury rates have also declined because workers rotate through many different jobs

On the negative side, some workers have found it difficult to adapt to the new system, which requires them to make many of the decisions that were formerly made by management and then imposed on workers. Some managers have also had problems. Adlington had to replace 5 of the 10 production supervisors because they couldn't adapt to the new system. One manager who successfully adapted says that he used to spend all his time watching workers. Now he spends less than half his time doing that; the majority of his time is spent on facilitating, organizing, and chairing meetings. ▲

SUMMARY

A group is a collection of two or more interdependent individuals who must coordinate their activity in order to achieve goals. There are three basic kinds of groups: (1) interacting (the work of one group member is dependent on that of the other group members); (2) coacting (the work of individual group members is independent of that of other members); and (3) counteracting (groups that interact as they try to resolve mutual conflicts). Work teams are formal work groups established by an organization to achieve a specific goal. Integrated work teams are assigned their tasks by management, whereas self-directed work teams have greater discretion to decide how they will do their work.

Groups develop over time and go through a number of stages: forming (members get acquainted with one another), storming (resolving conflicts about the leadership hierarchy in the group), norming (acceptable behaviour is defined), performing (productive maturity), and adjourning (group activity is terminated). High turnover in a group slows this process, while low turnover speeds it up.

Group norms are standards of behaviour that emerge from the interaction that occurs among individuals in a group. Norms exist for many different activities in groups, but the production norm is particularly important. Various roles develop in groups, including that of informal group leader, regular member, deviate, and isolate. Deviates and isolates are ostracized because of their failure to adhere to group norms.

Group cohesiveness is the degree of attraction a group has for its members. Smaller groups are typically more cohesive than larger groups. Group cohesiveness can affect productivity either positively or negatively. In very cohesive groups, groupthink may cause group members to suspend their critical thinking abilities and suppress conflict to maintain group solidarity.

The informal organization is the pattern of social relationships that arises spontaneously within the formal structure of organizations. The formal and informal organizations differ significantly on the dimensions of structure, position terminology, influence, control mechanisms, communication, and membership (see Table 9-3). The informal organization serves several functions. It provides security, satisfies social needs, serves as a communication channel, acts as a balancing device to overcome deficiencies in the formal structure, provides motivation for its members, and encourages good management. The potential problems with the informal organization include excessive socializing, obstruction of work, resistance to change, staffing inflexibility, rumours, and a reduction of managerial control.

Status is the relative position of a person in a group. A person's status is determined by status attributes. An attribute will be valued if it is both scarce and desirable. There are two types of status: ascribed (unchangeable personal characteristics) and achieved (attained through personal choice). Within formal organizations, two additional types of status can be identified: scalar status (a person's place in the formal hierarchy) and functional status (the job the person does).

Status symbols are tangible signs of a person's social position. All organizations have status symbols, and although they may cause some unhappiness, attempts to do away with them generally fail.

KEY TERMS

group (p. 263)
formal group (p. 263)
informal groups (p. 263)
interacting groups (p. 264)
coacting groups (p. 264)
counteracting groups (p. 264)
work teams (p. 264)
integrated work teams (p. 264)
self-managed teams (p. 264)
forming (p. 267)
storming (p. 267)
norming (p. 267)
performing (p. 267)
adjourning (p. 267)
norms (p. 267)
production norm (p. 268)
informal group leader (p. 269)
regular members (p. 269)
deviates (p. 269)
isolate (p. 269)
group cohesiveness (p. 269)
groupthink (p. 272)
informal organization (p. 273)
contact chart (p. 275)
sociogram (p. 276)
role (p. 277)
grapevine (p. 280)
rumours (p. 280)
status (p. 280)
ascribed status (p. 281)
achieved status (p. 281)
scalar status (p. 281)
functional status (p. 281)
status symbol (p. 281)

REVIEW QUESTIONS

1. Distinguish each of the following: interacting, counteracting, and coacting groups.
2. What are the primary functions of group norms?
3. What are the major functions of the informal group leader?
4. How do deviates and isolates differ from regular group members?
5. How can group cohesiveness affect productivity?
6. In what ways can a cohesive group be detrimental to the organization?
7. What is groupthink? How can a group tell if it might be a victim of groupthink? What can the group do to reduce the likelihood of groupthink developing?
8. What is the informal organization? What functions does it perform?
9. Compare and contrast the formal and informal organizations.
10. In what ways does the informal organization benefit the formal organization? In what ways might it act as a detriment to the formal organization?
11. How does the informal organization motivate those in it?
12. Describe the function of communication in the informal organization.
13. Describe the costs and benefits of the informal organization.
14. What is status? Why is it important in organizations?
15. Define the terms scalar status and functional status. Give examples of each from your own experience. How are these two types of status related?
16. What are status symbols? What function do they perform?

DISCUSSION QUESTIONS

1. If you were the manager of a group that was restricting output, what would you do to increase performance?
2. Compare and contrast your experience in a group that you were part of as a result of paid employment and with a group you were part of in a volunteer organization. What were the similarities and differences in the ways the two groups influenced your behaviour?
3. Why do informal groups inevitably emerge in organizations?
4. "Most people think organizations force workers to conform, but informal groups actually put more pressure on people to conform." Do you agree or disagree with this statement? Give reasons for your answers.
5. Think back to the last group project you were involved in. What informal group norms emerged? How were they enforced?
6. What is the relationship between group cohesiveness and group productivity?

EXERCISES

1. Think of an organization that you currently belong to and that you know fairly well (for example, a business firm, a hockey team, a student club, or a church). Draw a contact chart for the organization and interpret the results.
2. Consult three people who can tell you what status symbols are important in a group they belong to. Describe several status symbols that are important in each group. Do the status symbols differ? If so, why?
3. Interview a person that has been a manager in a private or public sector organization for at least five years. Have the person give you examples of how the informal organization works in his or her organization. How consistent is the person's description with that given in the chapter?
4. Write an essay analyzing the pros and cons of removing all official status symbols in organizations so that they are more democratic.

MANAGEMENT ON LOCATION

CASE 9-1
MARK BERQUIST'S DISCOVERY

The summer after he graduated from high school, Mark Berquist landed a job at Canada Post. Mark's job was to take over various mail routes when the regular carriers were on holidays. Just before a carrier was scheduled to go on holidays, Mark would walk the route with him or her to get acquainted with it. Each route had about 350 stops, so the one-day familiarization was important. During the training, the regular carrier would normally comment on the interesting people and things to see along the route. The carrier would also indicate the times at which Mark should reach various spots on the route. The mail carriers began work at 6:15 A.M., sorted their mail until 8:15, and then went out on their routes. They returned about 2:45 P.M. and punched out at 3 P.M.

Early in his training, Mark was walking a route with Ray Narleski, a veteran of 27 years with Canada Post. Narleski had a reputation for having a bad temper, and Mark tried his hardest to be agreeable. Narleski was actually quite reserved throughout the day, and offered only intermittent comments about the route. Before he left for holidays he told Mark to "make sure you don't louse up my route while I'm away." Mark assured him that he would do his best.

The next week Mark carried Narleski's route and all seemed to go very well. In fact, Mark found this route to be particularly easy, and on his first day he was able to finish by about 2 P.M. As he entered the substation, he noticed surprised looks on the faces of some of the inside workers but he didn't think too much about it at the time. He sorted some mail until 3 P.M. and then left. He continued this pattern for two weeks until Narleski returned from holidays.

On the first day of Narleski's return, Mark was just leaving the office on the way to his new route when he was confronted by an angry Narleski at the back of the substation.

Narleski: What in the world were you doing on my route the last two weeks?

Berquist: What do you mean? I thought everything went very well. I got to know the route very quickly and I think I did a good job. I was able to get back to the substation by 2 P.M. every day. The people on the route were happy because they got their mail earlier than usual.

Narleski: Now there's the problem. How do you think it makes me look when a greenhorn like you comes in here and during his first week on the job is able to carry the route quicker than a guy whose been on it for 27 years? You're making me look bad, Berquist! You've got a lot to learn about the way we do things around here. If I ever hear that you've come in before 2:45 again, I'm going to cause you some pain.

At this point, Narleski stomped off. Mark felt his knees shaking. ▲

QUESTIONS

1. Using concepts that you learned in this chapter, comment on the significance of the 2:45 return time at this post office. Why is Mark not very sensitive to the importance of the 2:45 return time?
2. In terms of the different types of group members discussed in the chapter, how is Mark categorized by Narleski? What possible future classifications could occur? How?
3. What alternatives are open to Mark? What should he do?
4. What would you do in Mark's situation? Why?

CASE 9-2
A View of the River

The professors in the Faculty of Administration at a major Canadian university were scheduled to move into a new building in May, 1991. The building was the culmination of much hard work and fund raising by the dean, the student body, and the business community.

The new building was extremely attractive and all faculty members were looking forward to occupying their new offices. All offices in the new building were larger (and much nicer) than the current offices that faculty members occupied. All faculty offices in the new building also had a window (this was not true in their present quarters). Some offices overlooked the river that flowed by the campus and others overlooked the parking lot. The offices overlooking the river were considered to be the most desirable, and had been picked first when faculty members were given the opportunity to choose their new office.

One of the items on the agenda of the October, 1990, faculty meeting was a report by the Building Committee regarding building security. During the discussion of the security issue, one professor raised the question of what procedures had been used to allow faculty members to pick their new office. The response was that a special committee had been set up to determine criteria for the assignment of offices in the new building. That committee had reported at a previous faculty meeting, and had proposed that the criteria be rank and seniority (in that order). Thus, full professors would get to pick before associate professors, and associate professors would get to choose before assistant professors. The proposal also meant that a full professor who had been with the faculty for, say, two years would get to pick before an associate professor who had been with the faculty for 20 years. This proposal had been approved by majority vote at a previous faculty meeting.

The administrative assistant for the faculty had then implemented the system, and all professors picked from the offices that were still available when their position on the priority list was reached.

As this issue was reviewed, several people expressed dissatisfaction with the criteria that had been used to establish the priority list. Most of those who complained were professors who had been forced to pick offices overlooking the parking lot because all the offices overlooking the river had already been taken. A major discussion then took place regarding whether or not the process should be done over again, this time using different criteria. At the end of the discussion it was agreed that the process would not be repeated, but for any new office allocations it might be reconsidered. ▲

QUESTIONS

1. Using concepts presented in this chapter, explain why certain professors were unhappy with their new offices, even though they got better offices than they formerly had.
2. Can you develop a procedure for making this allocation that will make everyone happy?

MANAGEMENT ON LOCATION

CASE 9-3
MARY CHAN'S LESSON

Mary Chan was excited. She had just received a phone call from the personnel manager at Jay-Mar Garments informing her that she had been hired to work in its garment factory. She was told that she would be paid on a piece-rate basis, i.e., she would receive a certain amount of money for each garment she produced. In addition, she would receive a bonus for every garment she produced above a certain level.

She was looking forward to working under this system because she was a fast worker. At her previous job, she had been paid on an hourly basis and she didn't like it because both productive and unproductive workers received the same wages. Mary felt very strongly that it was unfair to pay both kinds of workers the same wages. Mary viewed her new job as an opportunity to show off her production skills. She also wanted to make enough money to send a monthly cheque to her mother living in Hong Kong.

Mary was friendly, enthusiastic, and helpful on the job. She had no trouble fitting in with her co-workers, at least not at first. Because of her positive attitude, she rapidly learned the production system, and before long she was exceeding the production quota. Two weeks into her new job, Mary received her first paycheque (which included a large bonus for production above the standard). As she was leaving work, Mary ran into Alice Poholsky, one of the other women she worked with.

Mary: I am really happy with my first paycheque. A person can make a pretty good wage here if she works hard.

Alice: Well, I'm glad you're happy with your cheque. But you should keep in mind that what you're doing may not be a good idea in the long run.

Mary: What do you mean?

Alice: Smarten up, Mary. If you keep producing like you are, management will probably reduce the piece rate or raise the level of production you need to achieve in order to get a bonus. Then you'll be working twice as hard for the same pay. You don't want that to happen, do you?

Mary: Do you really think management would do that?

Alice: You really are naïve, aren't you? This industry has a long history of doing exactly that. I think you should bring your output into line with the rest of us. That way we can all make a reasonable bonus and everybody will be happy.

Despite Alice's disapproval, Mary continued to work hard and earn big bonuses. Before long, she noticed that virtually all of her co-workers were avoiding her. As well, several of them spoke to her privately and gave her the same message that Alice had earlier given her. One of them told her in no uncertain terms to reduce her output—or else! ▲

QUESTIONS

1. Using concepts introduced in this chapter, explain why Mary Chan is having difficulties in her job.
2. What alternatives are open to Mary? What are the consequences of each alternative?
3. What should Mary Chan do?

CHAPTER 10

POWER AND POLITICS

LEARNING OBJECTIVES

After reading this chapter, you will be able to:

1. Explain what power is and how it differs from authority.
2. Describe five types of power.
3. Identify the key assumptions in the rational and political models of organization.
4. Explain how politics affects decision making in the areas of careers and budgets.
5. Understand the arguments for and against organizational politics.

MANAGEMENT CHALLENGE

THE PUBLISHING DEPARTMENT

Ginny DeVor is one of 46 employees in the publishing department of a large federal government agency in Ottawa. She has been on the job for three years. While having coffee with several colleagues one afternoon, she learns that the head of her department has been promoted to a new job in another agency. Not surprisingly, much discussion follows and many rumours about who the new head will be are exchanged.

The department is presently composed of two distinct groups of people: the younger "climbers" and the older, more established workers. There is some animosity between the two groups on several issues, including the criteria for promotion. The young workers feel that performance should be the criterion, while the older workers generally feel that seniority should be used. DeVor, who has been with the department for four years, is a member of the younger group and would like to become the new department head. She also knows Carl Ryan, the informal leader of the older group, assumes he will get the job because he has been in the department for 11 years.

Several years ago, the department adopted the practice of using a four-person selection committee to recommend to the agency director who the new department head should be. Members are elected to this selection committee at a meeting of the entire department. The director is not required to accept the committee's choice, but the present director is reluctant to ignore it because he firmly believes in participative management.

In the month before the election of members to the selection committee, DeVor makes a point of refining friendships that she has developed during her time in the department. In one-on-one meetings with various members of the department, she determines their

...

likes, dislikes, fears, hopes, and preferences. She makes a point of going to lunch with various groups in the department and participates discreetly in ongoing discussions about the qualities the new head should possess. Before long, she finds that all the members in the younger group—and even some of the older workers—are urging her to apply for the job.

Given this support, DeVor becomes more open in her strategy. In the week before the meeting when the selection committee is to be elected, she consults many members of the younger group. They agree to nominate four members from their group and then concentrate all their votes on those four candidates. They also agree to nominate seven or eight members from the older group in order to split that group's votes over a large number of nominees.

At the meeting, all four candidates favourable to DeVor are elected. Various supporters come by her office after the meeting to congratulate her and to say that the important activity of choosing a new head is now complete. All that remains is the formality of the selection committee going through the motions of selecting the new head.

One month later, the agency director announces that Ginny DeVor is the new head of the publishing department. ▲

In Chapter 9, we introduced the idea of the informal organization. The basic point in that discussion was that management cannot formally structure everything that goes on in the organization. In this chapter, we continue with this theme by focussing on the importance of power and politics in organizations, and how these ideas and behaviours are also difficult to formally structure. These informal, political behaviours are clearly evident in the Management Challenge.

We begin by introducing the concept of power and the various types of power available to managers. Next, we analyze two conflicting views of how organizations operate. Third, we define the term organizational politics and explain why political behaviour is evident in all organizations. Fourth, we look at the dynamics of organizational politics at the individual and group level, as well as the effect politics has on budget allocations and promotions in organizations. The chapter concludes with a discussion about whether organizational politics is good or bad.

THE CONCEPT OF POWER

power

LEARNING OBJECTIVE 1

Explain what power is and how it differs from authority.

Power is the ability to get another person to do what you want them to do, even if they do not want to do it. We use the terms "power" and "influence" interchangeably. Managers in organizations have little trouble understanding the role and importance of power. In one study, 10 department managers were each asked to rank themselves and 20 other department managers, based on how much influence each had.[1] Only one manager asked what was meant by "influence." The overall results showed that there were virtually no disagreements in the ranking of the top five and bottom five managers on the list, even though ranking 21 people is not an easy task.

Until recently, there had not been a great deal of systematic research on the use of power in organizations. This area may have been neglected because everyone—students, managers, and the general public—wants to believe that human behaviour in organizations is rational.[2] Management students, for example, would like to believe that they are entering a career in which they will rationally allocate resources for the good of society, rather than one where they will be involved in power struggles with other people (see the Management at Work insert "Power Struggle at Kruger and McCain's"). Practising managers want to believe that their career progress is based on rational considerations and merit, not on power. The general public would like to believe that businesses allocate the resources of society in an efficient and rational way.

MANAGEMENT AT WORK

POWER STRUGGLES AT KRUGER AND MCCAIN'S

Some business firms have two or more family members in important management positions. This creates the potential for bitter power struggles between the family members. Recently, such struggles have created problems for two of Canada's old-line companies.

Kruger Inc. Kruger Inc. is an international paper and packaging firm based in Montreal with annual revenues currently estimated at around $1 billion. It is Canada's fourth largest newsprint producer, and the world's tenth largest. It suffered along with other firms in the newsprint industry during the recent recession, and has lost as much as $130 million since the newsprint market peaked in the late 1980s. Because it is one of the few privately held corporations in the industry, it has not been able to tap equity markets for funds.

In the early twentieth century, Joseph Kruger founded the company and it still bears his name. When he died in 1927, his two sons, Gene (then 25) and Bernard (then 15) became actively involved in the business. Although Gene tended to dominate Bernard, the two brothers got along quite well for many years, although Gene's insistence on controlling sometimes caused tension between them.

Both men had sons who were appointed to the Board of Directors in the 1960s. At this point, the real troubles began. Joseph (Gene's son) took an active role in the company, and by the late 1970s was making many major decisions. Bernard discovered that his position was being eroded by his nephew. Joseph was acting more and more like his father; he even began to overrule decisions made by Bernard. Bernard was willing to tolerate this kind of behaviour from his brother, but not from his brother's son. In 1979, Bernard retired to reduce the friction that had developed.

After his retirement, Bernard realized that he was in an awkward position, because his brother and nephew controlled his sources of income. So he began asking about finances. However, he was unable to find out from Gene and Joseph how much he was owed. In a face-to-face meeting with his brother, he was told to get a lawyer if he didn't like the way things were being handled.

In 1982, Bernard sued his brother, alleging that Kruger Inc. had cut off his $40 000 annual pension, fired his secretary, cancelled his company credit cards, and stopped his dividend payments (which were Bernard's major source of income) even though the company had net earnings of over $12 million.

The squabbling was apparently resolved in a 1989 out-of-court settlement, with the company agreeing to buy out Bernard's minority stake for $99 million, payable over 5 years. But in 1993, the family of Bernard Kruger filed a $40 million lawsuit, alleging that the company had reneged on the 1989 deal. The company responded by saying that it did not have enough money to continue paying on the deal. The renewal of the dispute is a sad ending to a long-standing feud that saw two embittered brothers refusing to speak to each other in their final years.

Bernard, who is now in his eighties, is the only surviving original member of the company which is now headed by Gene's son Joseph (Gene died in 1988). Joseph is renowned in the industry for his unorthodox management style, which is characterized by paying his subordinates well, but giving them very little authority—if they don't do what he wants, they are out of the company.

McCain Foods. McCain foods was started in 1956 by four brothers—Wallace, Harrison, Andrew, and Robert McCain (Andrew and Robert are now deceased). Each person put up $25 000 to build a french-fry plant in Florenceville, New Brunswick. They worked closely, and over the years expanded the firm and made it prosper. It is now a $3-billion multinational corporation with operations in 50 countries.

In 1991, the two remaining brothers set up a holding company to get the heirs involved in the business. The board of directors was composed of six sons—two of Wallace's, two of Harrison's, one of Robert's, and one of Andrew's. Fighting began over discussions about who would succeed the two brothers when they reached 75 and then worsened when Wallace unilaterally appointed his son Michael as the head of U.S. operations. The two brothers have been in a serious power struggle ever since.

In August, 1993, the board formally voted to oust Wallace. The four sons of Harrison, Robert, and Andrew voted for the motion, and the two sons of Wallace voted against it. Wallace took the company's board to court to get an injunction to stop them from ousting him as co-CEO (he is co-chair with his brother). His suit also included a proposal to divide up the company or sell it. Wallace said that the motion to get rid of him was part of a secret family deal that was set up by Harrison. After he discovered the company wanted him out, Wallace offered to buy out Harrison. Harrison made a counter-offer to buy out Wallace. Both deals were rejected. Now there is concern that management of the firm is paralyzed because of the dispute.

In September, 1993, the two brothers agreed to try to patch up their relationship in private. As part of the deal, Wallace dropped his lawsuit and was allowed to stay on as co-CEO of the company. The brothers tried to work out a solution to the problem of who will succeed them, but they were unable to. As a solution, they have appointed a private arbitrator, whose decision will be binding on both brothers. ▲

LEARNING OBJECTIVE 2
Describe five types of power.

To understand how power operates in organizations, it is necessary to understand the sources of power. What is it that allows one person to influence another, even though no formal right to do so exists? Table 10-1 lists seven sources of power, defines these sources, and gives an example demonstrating each source.[3]

One study of subordinates and peers who interacted with 49 managers found that legitimate, expert, and persuasive power were the most important sources of influence, and coercive and reward power were the least important. Referent and information power were intermediate in importance.[4] The study also identifies two fundamental sources of power in organizations: *position power* (deriving from the formal position the manager occupies) and *personal power* (deriving from the personal characteristics of the manager).

The concept of power is much broader than the concept of authority. Note that some of the examples in Table 10-1 deal with situations that are not found in organizations. An individual's total power can be represented by the following formula.[5]

$$\begin{aligned}\text{Total power} = {} & \text{legitimate power} \pm \text{reward power} \pm \text{coercive power} \pm \\ & \text{referent power} \pm \text{expert power} \pm \text{information power} \pm \\ & \text{persuasive power}\end{aligned}$$

There are two major organizational implications of this formula. First, the only power that is given by the formal organization is legitimate power. The other forms of power—which enhance or inhibit a manager's total power—are given by the informal organization. Second, a manager with little legitimate power may be quite powerful, while a manager with a great deal of legitimate power may be quite weak.

TABLE 10-1 SOURCES OF POWER.

Type of Power	Definition	Example
1. Reward power	Person A has the ability to control the rewards that Person B receives.	Dindar Singh, who needs money, agrees to do a job for Vijay Prasad, who promises to "make it worth Singh's while."
2. Punishment power	Person A has the ability to determine punishments that Person B receives.	Julie Parish gives her purse to a man who threatens to harm her if she does not comply.
3. Referent power	Person B does what Person A wants because Person B admires Person A.	Menno Friesen takes the advice of his pastor on a personal matter because he admires the pastor.
4. Expert power	Person A possesses some expert knowledge that Person B needs.	June Bielaczka, a manager in one department of a firm, follows the advice of John Kordic, an engineer in another department, because Kordic is the acknowledged expert on the problem facing Bielaczka.
5. Information power	Person A has information that convinces Person B to pursue a course of action desired by Person A.	Jonah Etah pays money to a blackmailer in return for that person not revealing embarrassing information about Jonah.
6. Persuasive power	Person A is able to convince Person B to take a certain course of action by making logical arguments.	Jonathan Etheridge convinces Henry Hill to support a warehouse expansion decision because of increased demand for the company's product.
7. Legitimate power	Person B believes that Person A has the "right" to give orders.	Alex Osig picks up a visitor from head office because his manager, Marion Hill, told him to do so.

reward power

punishment power

referent power

expert power

information power

persuasive power

legitimate power

The Significance of Power to the Manager

Managers who want to be effective have to develop and use power. The most successful managers possess the following characteristics:[6]

1. *High need for power* This refers to the desire to be strong and influential. They want this power not for personal gain, but to influence employees to achieve organizational goals.
2. *Low need for affiliation* Successful managers are not overly concerned about how well they are liked.
3. *High inhibition in exercising power* The power managers have is exercised in a controlled way. The successful manager does not threaten subordinates.
4. *High level of maturity* The manager is willing to seek advice on problems.
5. *A coaching style* Rather than trying to force people to act in a certain way, the manager tries to help them discover better ways of doing their job.

Increasing Managerial Power

law of reciprocity

Managers with a lot of power are able to accomplish more than managers with little power. It is therefore important for managers to understand how to increase their power. The first step in doing so is to recognize the "**law of reciprocity**": the belief that people should be compensated for what they do. When a manager does a favour for someone, that manager expects to be paid back sometime in the future. This expectation makes influence possible. Managers can, for example, do the following things in order to gain allies who will be responsive when the manager makes a request in the future:[7]

1. Give budget increases, personnel, or space to targets of influence.
2. Take responsibility for undesirable tasks.
3. Provide quick response time to requests from other executives.
4. Give a person a task that will help that person get promoted.
5. Enhance the way another person is seen in the organization.
6. Give emotional backing to a person.
7. Express appreciation for work that has been done.
8. Express confidence in a person to significant people in the organization.

The manager who wants to be successful when influencing others needs to do the following:[8]

1. *Clarify precisely what is wanted from the target of influence* Decide which aspects of the request are critical, and which are less important.
2. *View the target of influence as an ally, not as an adversary* The goal here is to find areas of mutual interest so that a sustainable relationship that is beneficial to both parties can develop.
3. *Understand the goals and needs of the influence target* Without such knowledge, influence attempts will be unsuccessful and a mutually beneficial relationship will not develop.

TWO VIEWS OF ORGANIZATIONS

LEARNING OBJECTIVE 3

Identify the key assumptions in the rational and political models of organization.

If we look back on the study of organizations during the twentieth century, we find two fundamentally different views, or models, of how organizations operate. The **rational model** sees organizations as places where resources are rationally and efficiently used to pursue the objectives of the organization. According to this model, managers make decisions on the basis of hard data and avoid individual idiosyncracies or biases, while groups and individuals cooperate to reach organizational goals.

rational model

The political model takes a much different view of organizations. The **political model** sees organizations as places where much competition occurs for resources, and where people with different values and biases are often in conflict with each other. In this environment, managers make decisions on the basis of what is good for their department, individual idiosyncracies routinely influence decisions, and groups and individuals are in conflict with each other over what the organization's goals should be. Several of these elements existed in the Management Challenge as Ginny DeVor worked behind the scenes to get promoted to department head.

political model

Table 10-2 summarizes the assumptions inherent in the rational and political models of organization.[9] These assumptions are discussed in the following paragraphs.

MEASURING ORGANIZATIONAL EFFECTIVENESS

The rational model assumes that organizations measure how effective they are in reaching their goals, and that the various parts of the organization are able to agree on the criteria to use to determine whether or not the organization is effective.

In contrast, the political model assumes that it is very difficult to get consensus on criteria for measuring organizational effectiveness. It recognizes that people have certain goals they wish to pursue and that they will attempt to get criteria stated in such a way that they will look good. For example, a salesperson who is good at sales, but lacks interest in follow-up service will try to get sales established as the criterion of effectiveness. Because organizations are full of people with diverse interests and skills, in practice it is usually difficult to get agreement on organizational effectiveness criteria.

TABLE 10-2 RATIONAL AND POLITICAL MODEL ASSUMPTIONS.

Rational Model	Political Model
1. Organizational effectiveness criteria can be clearly defined and measured.	1. Debate and conflict occur over organizational effectiveness criteria and how to measure them.
2. Information is available about contingencies that are important to the organization.	2. Information on contingencies may be available, but it is routinely distorted to suit the needs of certain powerful people.
3. Rational structural planning takes place in organizations.	3. Structure is usually not planned, and often emerges in response to pressure from various powerful people in the organization.
4. Organizations are tightly linked to their environments.	4. Organizations are only loosely linked to their environments; if an error occurs, no one may notice, but even if they do it will be difficult to determine who was at fault.
5. Individuals and groups will work together to reach organizational goals.	5. Individuals and groups will frequently find themselves in conflict over what goals to pursue.

The Availability of Information

Much of the literature on organizations deals with questions about how contingencies such as organizational size, technology, and environment affect managers and the structure of an organization. The rational model assumes that managers first gather information about how these various contingencies will affect the organization and then act in a rational way to deal with them.

The political model contends that information about contingencies is indeed available, but that it is distorted to suit particular needs. Thus, for any piece of supposedly "objective" information, there will be numerous subjective interpretations about what the information means. For example, if sales have declined for the past three months, a production manager might interpret this information to mean that marketing is doing a poor job of sensing the environment. Marketing, on the other hand, might argue that production is causing the problem because quality control has not been up to par. Arguments like these are difficult to resolve.

Structural Planning

In the rational model, the assumption made is that before managers decide on a structure for the organization, they do some sort of formal planning and decision making. This preparation takes into account the kind of work the organization does, the products or services it provides, the environment it operates in, and so forth. A structure is established only after these issues have been considered.

The political model, on the other hand, sees structure emerging as a response to certain pressures, rather than the result of planning. If a powerful executive wants to introduce a matrix structure, that structure may well be adopted without first examining the value of other alternatives. Structural variations can also be imposed by powerful external groups such as consumers, government, and labour unions. For example, many organizations have established departments with consumer hotlines to deal with consumer complaints and questions.

Relationships with the External Environment

The rational model assumes that a close relationship exists between an organization and its environment. Thus, if the organization does a poor job of corporate planning, violates pollution or ethics laws, or makes a shoddy product, a decline in performance will immediately be evident because significant groups in the firm's environment (e.g., customers) will stop dealing with the firm.

The political model assumes that organizations are only loosely linked to their external environment; bad decisions, therefore, may or may not be detected by groups or individuals outside the organization. Since it may be difficult for external groups to determine if a decision is actually bad, organizational performance may or may not suffer. The dispute in British Columbia between environmentalists and companies that want to cut old-growth forests is a case in point; the debate pits jobs against environmental concerns, and which decision is "right" is difficult to determine.

Working Together

One of the outcomes of the human relations school of management that was discussed in Chapter 2 is the widespread belief that if people are treated properly by management they will work together to reach organizational goals. According to the rational model, people are cooperative, rather than competitive.

The political model asserts that people pursue their own self-interest. As a result, people in organizations will frequently find themselves in conflict over what goals should be pursued. Conflict between superiors and subordinates, between line and staff, and between management and labour are therefore inevitable.

CONCLUSION

Which of these two views most accurately describes organizations? For many years, students and managers accepted the notion that people behaved rationally in the pursuit of *organizational* goals. Recently, a number of researchers have argued that people actually spend their time and energy pursuing their own *individual* goals, occasionally at the expense of the organization. As we shall see, powerful forces are at work in organizations which motivate people to behave in a political fashion.

ORGANIZATIONAL POLITICS

organizational politics

Organizational politics refers to the activities individuals pursue in organizations to develop and exercise power to achieve their own desired outcomes. Ginny DeVor engaged in political behaviour just before she was promoted to department head. Organizational politics is a pervasive, yet elusive phenomenon. It influences managers' careers, strategic decision making, and organizational structure. An understanding of organizational politics is crucial for anyone with career aspirations in management. In today's complex organizations, individuals do not move rapidly up the hierarchy unless they have a good grasp of the political aspects of their work environment.

Consider the results of a study that analyzed 149 managers in a manufacturing firm over a five-year interval.[10] During the period, 47 percent of the managers were promoted, 14 percent were transferred laterally, 22 percent stayed in their job, and 17 percent were demoted. The individuals who were promoted exhibited the following characteristics:

1. They understood the complex nature of the organization and the overlapping responsibilities in it.
2. They recognized that it was more important to get along with their peers than with their subordinates if they wanted to get ahead in the company.
3. They realized that good performance was not automatically rewarded.
4. They recognized that it was more important to seize the opportunity to become known than to simply do a good job and hope for the best.

These comments by practising managers are not unusual. To demonstrate the diverse situations in which political activity occurs, consider the examples (from actual organizations) that are described in the Ethics in Management insert "What's the Right Thing to Do?"

THE UNIVERSALITY OF ORGANIZATIONAL POLITICS

Political behaviour in organizations is both universal and inevitable. It can be observed in all kinds of organizations—manufacturing firms, government agencies, service organizations, religious organizations, military forces, charities, and schools. Any attempt to suppress political behaviour is certain to fail because the forces that encourage it are so powerful.

ETHICS IN MANAGEMENT

What's the Right Thing to Do?

Consider the following incidents:

1. Suresh reports to the vice-president of marketing of a provincial hydroelectric utility. He is aggressive and considers himself top management material. By ingratiating himself with the vice-president's secretary, he is able to gather considerable evidence that the vice-president is frequently out of the office on activities unrelated to his work. Suresh informally presents this evidence to certain key members of the board of directors who belong to the same country club that Suresh's father does. Two months later, the vice-president is fired and Suresh is chosen as his replacement.

2. Joanna and Kirk are management trainees for a major food marketing company. They dislike each other. Both are in line for a promotion, and both are members of the new product committee. At one meeting, Kirk makes what appears to be an impressive presentation on a new product idea. During the discussion following the presentation, Joanna notes a critical logical flaw in Kirk's reasoning. Kirk's proposal is quietly dropped from the agenda for the committee's next meeting. When the next promotion is announced, Joanna gets it.

3. Marsha is a sales representative with a major computer manufacturer. One Thursday afternoon her boss informs her that one of the vice-presidents from head office is arriving at the airport and that she is to pick him up. Marsha feels complimented that her boss has chosen her for the job. Moments later, however, Marsha's boss says: "By the way, don't take your car. It isn't good enough for the boss. I think it's time you bought a new one." Marsha feels threatened by this comment, since she can't afford a new car.

4. Ron is one of the top regional sales managers in his firm. He is also an excellent golfer. Last week he was invited to join a foursome composed of his boss (the national sales manager), the vice-president of marketing (his boss's boss), and the president of the firm. Ron knows that these people are crucial to his career plans, so he wants to make a good impression. He played his best, and shot a 71; two strokes better than the president, and far lower than the scores of the other members of the foursome. Ron left the golf course in high spirits. When he arrived at his office the next day, he was immediately approached by his boss who demanded: "Ron, what in the world were you doing yesterday? *Nobody* beats the president at golf!" Ron felt depressed the rest of the day.

5. Manfred is the pastor of a large church. He is energetic, creative, and innovative, and spends much time thinking up new ideas to make the church more effective in meeting people's needs. At a recent meeting of the board of directors, he proposed a new idea that was a substantial departure from established ways of doing things at the church (he had not discussed this idea with any of the board members before the meeting). He was surprised at the open hostility expressed toward the idea by the board members. Manfred knew his idea was a good one, so he was surprised and disappointed when the board rejected it.

Incidents like these happen every day in organizations. They demonstrate that some individuals (e.g., Suresh and Joanna) are able to assess the realities of organizational life and then act in a way that is beneficial to their careers. However, others (e.g., Kirk, Marsha, Ron, and Manfred) are less attuned, and they experience difficulties. The incidents also show that people in organizations are positively or negatively affected by organizational politics.

One of the primary problems with political behaviour is deciding what conduct is ethical and what is unethical. It is often difficult to know where to draw the line between reasonable and unreasonable political behaviour. Would it have been acceptable for Ron to let the president beat him at golf, even though Ron was a better golfer? Was it reasonable for Suresh to extract valuable information from the vice-president's secretary and then use that information to get the vice-president fired? Was it reasonable for Marsha's boss to express the view that she should get a new car? Was it reasonable for Ginny DeVor to do what she did in the Management Challenge? These are difficult questions, and you should keep them in mind as you consider the issue of organizational politics. Remember that in your career, you will be faced with decisions like these, and you will have to make some hard choices about how to behave. An understanding of what political behaviour is all about will help you make informed choices. ▲

What are these forces? The most fundamental is self-interest—people's desire to improve their own financial situation, status, or ego. Since organizations are made up of many people, different self-interests are likely to be evident. When people observe that the goals they are pursuing could be thwarted by someone else, political behaviour may arise.

A second reason political behaviour is so widespread is that organizations have limited resources. They must therefore decide which of many possible goals they will pursue. Various groups and individuals in the organization will normally be in conflict with one another over which goals are going to be pursued and, in the process of trying to get their way, these groups are likely to indulge in political behaviour. Such tactics are particularly likely if no objective evidence exists about which goals are the "best" ones to pursue.

Self-interest and limited resources guarantee that political behaviour will be evident in all organizations. Even charitable organizations, which pursue goals that society values, exhibit political behaviour because employees pursue their own self-interest in an environment of limited organizational resources. Individuals who overlook these two realities may be surprised and dismayed at the behaviour of others. Conversely, those who take these realities into account will find that they are better prepared to deal with politics in the workplace.

The Dynamics of Political Behaviour

Consider a situation where an industrial engineering department has developed a new work procedure for production employees, and the head of the engineering department wants the line manager in production to approve it. If the formal lines of authority are followed, the chief engineer would simply submit the recommendation to the production manager for approval. But what if the manager rejects the proposal? The chief engineer might just give up on the idea, but it is more likely that he or she would turn to informal, or political means to obtain the approval.

The chief engineer might try any one (or all) of the following:

1. Get to know the production manager on a personal basis and pretend to be the manager's friend.
2. Take the manager out to lunch and have low-key, casual conversations about the proposed work procedures.
3. Offer to exchange favours within the regular operating rules and procedures (e.g., offer to do an immediate restudy of a job rate that has been causing the manager trouble).
4. Agree to bend formal rules and procedures slightly (e.g., delay the introduction of a new system for keeping track of inventory until the manager feels more comfortable with it).
5. Agree to a more significant bending of the rules (e.g., get an engineering study team to say that a work speed-up on the assembly line is perfectly reasonable when, in fact, the line is already operating at capacity).
6. Agree to "cover" for the line executive (e.g., let the executive blame the engineering department for causing the production area to miss a deadline when, in fact, it was not the engineering department's fault).
7. Agree to transfer some funds from engineering to the manager's department to help the manager on a project that she or he wants to pursue but cannot get funds for until the next budget year.

TABLE 10-3 COMMONLY USED POLITICAL TACTICS.

Image building Engaging in activities designed to create and maintain a good image. Includes dressing appropriately, drawing attention to one's successes, being enthusiastic about the organization, adhering to group norms, and having an air of confidence about work activities.

Selective use of information Using information selectively to further one's career. Includes withholding unfavourable information from superiors, keeping useful information from competitors, interpreting information in a way that is favourable to oneself, and overwhelming people with technical information they don't understand.

Scapegoating Ensuring that someone else is blamed for a failure. Individuals who are skillful organizational politicians make sure that they will not be blamed when something goes wrong and that they will get credit when something goes right.

Forming alliances Agreeing with several key people that a certain course of action will be taken. If a conflict develops, the people in the coalition will get their way because they are strong enough as a group to impose their will on others.

Networking Ensuring that one has many friends in positions of influence.

Compromise Giving in on an unimportant issue in order to gain an ally who will be on your side when an issue of importance to you arises at a later date.

Rule manipulation Refusing an opponent's request on the grounds that it is against company policy, but granting an identical request from an ally on the grounds that it is a "special circumstance."

These and many other activities are possible as the chief engineer tries to convince the production manager to implement the new work procedures. Sometimes these tactics will succeed, and sometimes they will fail. In either case, they give us some understanding of the dynamics of political behaviour. (See Table 10-3 for a list of political tactics that are generally used in organizations.)

We can further demonstrate the dynamics of political behaviour in organizations by looking at politics at the individual and subunit (departmental) level.

Individual Political Behaviour

One early study analyzed the tactics used by 142 purchasing agents to expand their influence in their respective organizations.[11] The formal task of purchasing agents was to negotiate prices and expedite orders. Politically, however, many agents viewed these functions as a bare minimum; they felt that they should also be keeping management informed about market developments, new sources of supply, price trends, ways to save money in purchasing, and so forth. In most of the firms studied, purchasing agents had disagreements about the scope of their jobs with engineering (which was the ordering department); their influence attempts were therefore directed at engineering. The tactics used by the purchasing agents are summarized in Table 10-4.

TABLE 10-4 TACTICS USED BY PURCHASING AGENTS TO INFLUENCE ENGINEERS.

1. **Rule-oriented tactics** Using the formal rules of the organization to increase one's influence (e.g., applying company rules forbidding engineering to order on short notice).
2. **Rule-evading tactics** Evading the formal rules of the organization (e.g., a purchasing agent might appear to comply with a rule but do so only half-heartedly so that engineering would experience delays).
3. **Personal-political tactics** Using interpersonal connections to either facilitate or inhibit an order (e.g., expediting a close friend's order in spite of the fact that it is late).
4. **Educational tactics** Trying to persuade engineering to think in purchasing terms (e.g., presenting the facts in such a way that engineering did what purchasing wanted).
5. **Organizational-interactional tactics** Attempting to change the formal or informal interaction patterns between purchasing and engineering (e.g., trying to get engineering to ask purchasing for help rather than having engineering decide who to order from and then getting into an argument if purchasing suggested someone else).

With the possible exception of rule-oriented tactics, all these behaviours are political, i.e., they involved purchasing agents using their influence to get their own way. Interestingly, in many situations the interests of the purchasing agents and the engineers actually converged, so political behaviour resulted in better decisions from an organizational perspective.

A case study of how a person in a newly created position increased his influence gives further insight into the dynamics of organizational politics at the individual level.[12] Figure 10-1 notes the key players in this situation. The new person (Moss) was formally appointed to head a department, but encountered two problems: (1) his boss (Katz) delegated very little authority, and (2) his foreperson (Tom) was seen by the other employees to be the informal leader of the department. Moss decided the situation would have to change if he were going to be effective, so he began using the following tactics to expand his influence:

Power and authority interact in the corporate boardroom to determine what course the organization will take. Individuals who are outside members of the board have no line authority within the firm, but are likely to have knowledge or expertise that give them power. Inside members of the board—who are also managers in the company—have both line authority and power.

1. *Neutralizing his boss's supporters* Moss was able to convey to Tom that he (Moss) was going to be a force to be reckoned with. Tom was reluctant to continue relying completely on his old boss (Katz) because Tom thought that Moss might eventually succeed in acquiring additional authority. If that happened, Tom would be in an untenable position. As a result, Tom became more amenable to attempts at influence from Moss.
2. *Replacing Katz's supporters* Moss felt that a quality-control inspector (Queenie) who was not well liked by her peers (but who was highly valued by Katz) should be removed because she continually held up production at a time when top management wanted increased output. Approaching Katz, Moss questioned whether Queenie's high-quality standards were functional and implied that she was a liability to the company. Since Katz was under pressure to increase production, he eventually agreed to remove her. Moss then installed a quality-control inspector who was loyal to him.

FIGURE 10-1 FORMAL REPORTING RELATIONSHIPS.

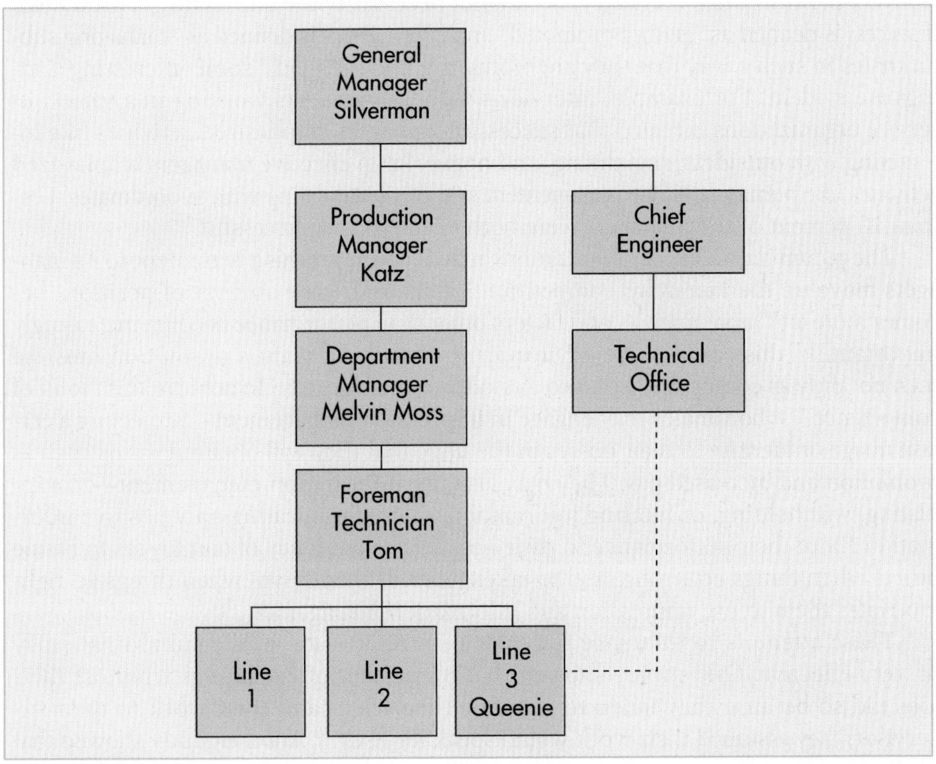

3. *Getting commitment from those not committed to Katz* By using various tactics, Moss was able to mobilize the support of (1) new career workers that Katz had not yet influenced, (2) older workers who felt that they had been treated badly in the past, and (3) young workers who didn't intend to make factory work their career.
4. *Mobilizing support from Katz's superiors* Moss was able to convince Katz's boss (Silverman) that Katz should be less involved in the day-to-day operations of the department than he had been. Katz agreed because he was concerned about falling out of favour with Silverman.

Notice in this case that Moss had formal authority because of his position as department head, but he knew that he could achieve little without developing some informal power. Moss skillfully used various tactics to get the power he needed to run his department the way he saw fit. Had he simply tried to give orders to subordinates based on his formal authority, he probably would not have gotten very far.

LEARNING OBJECTIVE 4

Explain how politics affects decision making in the area of careers and budgets.

The Politics of Careers Individuals exhibit political behaviour because they believe it will have a positive impact on their career. In the Management Challenge, Ginny DeVor clearly believed that politics would be helpful to her in getting the department head's job. How politics affects careers can be assessed from two vantage points—how it influences who gets a job in the first place, and how it influences who gets favourable evaluations or who gets promoted once they are in a job.

Various studies have demonstrated the value of personal contacts in getting a job. One study investigated whether formal applications or personal contacts were more important in finding a job in three occupations—technical, professional, and managerial.[13] Personal contacts were found to be more important than formal applications for professional and managerial jobs, but not for technical jobs. Since technical jobs can usually be evaluated objectively, these findings are consistent with the idea that political behaviour is more likely to be found in areas where procedures or criteria are not explicitly stated.

Politics is often a deciding factor in managerial promotions. Managers who effectively perform their assigned tasks are not necessarily the ones who get promoted. If *success* is defined as "getting promoted" and *effectiveness* is defined as "managing subordinates in such a way that they are productive and satisfied," some interesting findings are evident. For example, interviews with 44 managers working in a variety of service organizations revealed that successful managers emphasized activities like interacting with outsiders, socializing, and networking; effective managers emphasized activities like human resource management and communicating with subordinates. Less than 10 percent of the managers were both effective and successful.[14]

The pyramidal shape of organizations may account for this phenomenon. As managers move up the hierarchy, competition for the restricted number of positions becomes more and more intense, and factors other than performance become increasingly important. In this competitive environment, those who want a promotion must be seen not only as competent, but also as skilled in many areas. To achieve this "look of competence," subordinates may engage in **impression management**—projecting a certain image or identity to their bosses in the hope that they will obtain rewards such as promotion and increased pay. They may also use **information management**—manipulating, withholding, or filtering information, or communicating only positive information about their performance to their boss.[15] The tendency of employees to blame others when things go wrong, and to take credit for themselves when things go right motivates them to use impression and information management.[16]

impression management

information management

These attempts to influence the manager's impression of the subordinate may be very effective. One survey showed that 83 percent of executives who lost their jobs did so because they failed to promote themselves and their work to their supervisor; they assumed their work would speak for itself.[17] Another study showed that subordinates who flattered the boss or did favours for the boss were more liked and received more positive performance appraisals than subordinates who did not.[18]

Given these facts, what can be said about the characteristics that are necessary to get promoted? The most critical characteristic may be the ill-defined one of "fitting in." As one author notes,

> ... job performance is not a sufficient condition for career advancement in many organizational contexts and may not even be necessary. Social similarities, social background, and social contacts *are* necessary and in many instances sufficient (emphasis added).[19]

One way to help aspiring managers learn how to fit in is to pair them with an experienced executive who "knows the ropes" in the organization. This is called **mentoring**. The experienced manager helps the aspiring manager by giving advice, conveying important informal rules of behaviour, and generally acting as a sounding board for the aspiring manager's ideas and behaviour. Canadian Pacific Hotels Corp. has instituted a mentoring program in order to attract new middle managers.[20] By matching senior executives with trainees in entry-level positions, the company hopes to have well-prepared staff ready to step into higher-level jobs when required. The mentoring program has also increased vertical coordination by motivating senior managers to stay in touch with what is happening in the company's hotels across Canada.

mentoring

One approach to measuring the effectiveness of mentoring is to have the performance appraisal of the mentoring executive include an assessment of how well he or she is carrying out the mentor's responsibilities. A recent task force report at Southam Newspaper Group recommended that the work environment be made more conducive to female managers by having mentors' performance reviews influenced by the amount of recruiting and promoting of women that was evident.[21] Performance appraisal can itself be an extremely political exercise (see the Management at Work insert "The Politics of Employee Appraisal").

Subunit Political Behaviour

Individuals are not the only entities in organizations that behave in a political fashion. Organizational subunits, or departments, also exhibit political behaviour. Of course, the "department" is not a thinking entity, so it cannot make decisions. But the collective behaviour of people in a given department may very well result in political behaviour.

In one factory, a group of maintenance engineers had an unusual amount of power.[22] An analysis showed that the engineers were the only people in the organization who were able to cope with a crucial problem in the factory—machine breakdowns. The plant manager was able to deal with absenteeism and turnover of production workers, production scheduling, changes in demand, and raw material difficulties, but he was unable to cope with random machine breakdowns. As a result, the maintenance engineers became a strategic subunit, because the problem they were able to cope with was crucial to the organization. They were therefore consulted on a wide variety of plant decisions, some of which had little to do with machine breakdowns.

Another study was conducted by researchers who developed a strategic contingencies model.[23] Using questionnaires and interviewing, they analyzed the power relationships among the engineering, marketing, production, and accounting departments in seven manufacturing firms. They found that three variables—coping with uncertainty, absence of substitutability, and centrality—were important in determining how much power a department had. The most powerful departments were those that scored high on all three variables. Departments that scored high on only two variables had less power. Two other studies—using university administrators and oil company executives—tested whether the original results could be repeated.[24] The researchers found that in universities, the absence of substitutability was an important determinant of subunit power, but it was not as clear a predictor in the oil companies.

Because politics is so evident during the performance appraisal process, success in management is influenced by performance, and other factors—for example, the ability to "fit in." Research shows that factors like being able to work with others in a group situation, being helpful to those whose work is interconnected with yours, and taking part in social activities in the workplace are important facilitators of career progress.

MANAGEMENT AT WORK

THE POLITICS OF EMPLOYEE APPRAISAL

Sixty executives were interviewed to determine their views about performance appraisal, and their behaviour during the process. There were five principal findings in the study:

1. *Politics was almost always evident in performance appraisal* Those interviewed said politics was important because managers had to "live with" subordinates after giving performance ratings, because written documents were seen by people in other departments, and because performance ratings have an impact on the rated employee's career.
2. *Accuracy was not the main criterion in performance appraisal* The executives who were interviewed said they rated subordinates in such a way that the rating would motivate the subordinate to keep performance up to par. Some said they would consciously misstate a subordinate's rating if they felt it would improve the subordinate's performance.
3. *Executives often inflated subordinate ratings* They did this for a variety of reasons: to avoid hurting the subordinate's feelings, because they felt sorry for the subordinate, because they wanted to avoid a confrontation, because the subordinate put out good effort but not performance, or to get a problem employee promoted out of the department.
4. *Executives deflated subordinate ratings on occasion* They did this for several reasons: to shock an employee into performing better, to build a case for dismissal later on, to make a subordinate so unhappy that he or she would quit, or to teach a rebellious subordinate a lesson.
5. *The overall performance evaluation was decided first and then individual items were completed to make them consistent with the overall evaluation* Executives first developed a global opinion of a subordinate and then rated him or her on specific categories to make their global opinion look as if it had evolved from the particular items.

Overall, the executives indicated that the main goal of performance appraisal was not accuracy; rather, the goal of the process was to motivate and reward (or punish) subordinates. This was, of course, never admitted publicly. The executives also felt that inflating or deflating performance ratings was not wrong, but was simply a recognition of certain organizational realities. Apparently, political necessity superseded accuracy on many occasions. ▲

Factors like values and beliefs about what an organization should be are also likely to influence the amount of power a department has. Research in a fast food chain and a robotics company, for example, found that top managers ascribed significantly more power to those departments that had the same values as the top managers. Departments that did not subscribe to those values had significantly less power.[25]

The Politics of Budgets The decision about which departments of an organization will get what proportion of the total funds available is obviously an area for political manoeuvring by subunits. Although many organizations set up formal procedures for allocating funds, the fact is that nonrational elements frequently enter into these decisions.

One study of budget allocations at a major university over a 13-year period showed that both rational measures (credit hours taught) and political measures (committee representation) affected budget allocations.[26] One interesting finding was the -0.60 correlation in one department between the proportion of the budget it received and the proportion of credit hours it taught. It was found that in this powerful department—which was well represented on university committees—as the number of credit hours taught declined, the department's proportion of the general budget increased! By contrast, less powerful departments showed a positive correlation between the number of credit hours taught and their representation on university committees. Two other studies focussing on universities came to similar conclusions.[27]

A study of budget allocations in 66 United Way campaigns over a 10-year period further demonstrates how politics affects the budgeting process.[28] The researchers hypothesized that the power of groups in the United Way would be determined by two factors: the proportion of the group's budget that was received from the United Way (the greater the proportion, the less power the group had); and the proportion of the United Way's total budget that went to the group (the greater the proportion, the greater the group's power). Support was found for both these hypotheses. There was rarely any significant relationship between important demographic variables and actual budget allocations to social service agencies. For example, no relationship was found between the funds provided to agencies serving young people and the age distribution of young people in the area. Another study, which analyzed a single United Way organization, showed the same kind of results.[29] Both these studies support the view that political behaviour plays an important role in budget allocations.

How Managers View Political Behaviour

In the last 20 years or so, researchers have begun to systematically study how managers regard organizational politics. Most of these studies have involved interviewing managers or having them fill out questionnaires on the issue of politics.

In one study, 428 Canadian managers in the public and private sector were given a series of statements and asked to agree or disagree with them.[30] Several interesting findings emerged. First, 60 percent of the managers felt that most casual talk at work was political in nature; 70 percent agreed that politics was common in their organizations.

Second, a majority of the managers felt that political behaviour was self-serving and detrimental to the organization in which it occurred. Overall, political behaviour was viewed as bad, unfair, unnecessary, and conflict-causing. When managers were asked to write a brief story demonstrating political behaviour in action, 84 percent of the stories portrayed it as being irrational.

Third, managers at lower levels in organizations perceived more politics than did people at higher levels. Apparently, they saw themselves as "victims" of political behaviour. We can speculate that people in upper levels saw less politics because they felt that they had achieved their position through meritorious service rather than political behaviour.

Fourth, there was no difference in the perceived level of political behaviour between public- and private-sector organizations. If we recall our earlier notion that individuals pursue their own self-interest regardless of the organizational setting, we should not be surprised at this finding.

Fifth, over 70 percent of the managers agreed that successful and powerful executives act in a political fashion. They also felt that a manager had to be a good politician to get ahead in their organization.

Finally, political behaviour was most frequently perceived in areas where explicit policies or procedures were lacking. Political behaviour was commonly seen in the areas of promotions and transfers, delegation of authority, and interdepartmental coordination. Although it may appear that objective criteria exist for such areas as promotions, most of the incidents described by the managers mentioned people who were promoted by "pull" rather than merit.

Is Organizational Politics Good or Bad?

Until recently, the majority of people who analyzed organizations or worked in them assumed that political behaviour was bad because it hurt both the organization and the people who work in the organization. However, some researchers and managers are now accepting the idea that political behaviour has positive aspects.

In one study, managers were asked to identify good and bad outcomes of organizational politics on both an individual and organization level.[31] The responses of the executives illustrate the divided opinion on the effect of politics. A majority of the respondents felt that politics was helpful for an individual's career. However, politics was also mentioned as a factor that hurt peoples' careers by reducing their credibility and their power.

Politics was also seen by some managers as helpful in achieving organizational goals, getting work done, facilitating organizational survival, and coordinating activities. However, it was seen by more managers as distracting people from organizational goals, causing the misuse of resources, creating divisiveness and tensions in the workplace, and causing the advancement of incompetent people.

LEARNING OBJECTIVE 5

Understand the arguments for and against organizational politics.

At a minimum, this study shows that political behaviour is a fact of organizational life that managers cannot ignore. Politics can lead to better results for both organizations and individuals, but it can also cause serious problems. Table 10-5 summarizes the arguments for and against political behaviour that are presented in more detail in the following paragraphs.

Are People Treated Unfairly?

Argument Saying that people are treated "unfairly" means a variety of things. For example, it could mean that women and minorities are discriminated against when employment decisions are made. This practice is, of course, illegal but that doesn't prevent it from happening. It could also mean, as opponents of political behaviour argue, that politics causes decisions to be based on mysterious criteria known only by an "in-group" that answers to no one. The existence of this group, traditionally called the *old-boy network*, is considered unreasonable in a democratic society where everyone is supposed to have some say in what happens. Overall, politics means that people do not have equal opportunities in organizations.

Counterargument Supporters of politics argue that the old-boy network benefits organizations because it generates good information and because it is efficient. They argue that decisions can be made quickly and accurately on the basis of personal contacts, and that the organization benefits because the decision maker feels confident about the results. Since information is crucial in making good decisions, political decision making gives better results than decision making where politics plays no role.

TABLE 10-5 ARGUMENTS FOR AND AGAINST POLITICAL BEHAVIOUR.

Arguments Against	Arguments in Favour
1. People are treated unfairly when political decisions are made.	1. Determining what is "fair" is a subjective process and is a vague argument.
2. Political behaviour distorts the decision-making process in organizations and results in decisions that are bad for the organization.	2. In a free society people must be allowed to pursue their own interests, as long as their behaviour is not illegal.
3. The use of power allows an organization to ignore internal and external groups that may be unhappy with the organization.	3. Political behaviour forces an organization to behave in a way that is consistent with important internal and external groups.
4. Politics is time consuming and inefficient.	4. Political processes are very fast because decision makers can get the "real story" on an issue through their own personal network of contacts.
5. Political processes give certain people too much power.	5. Those who get power are those who have demonstrated an ability to solve the organization's key problems.

Does Political Behaviour Distort Decision Making?

Argument Opponents of political behaviour feel that political manoeuvring causes bad decisions because decisions are made by individuals pursuing their own selfish interests. Consider the example of the executive who is brought in to "shape up" a weak division or department. Typically, some drastic actions are taken in the short run, and performance often does improve noticeably. After a couple of years, the executive is promoted to another position on the basis of his or her success at "turning the division around." However, increased profits may have been achieved by reducing employee training, equipment maintenance, or other necessary long-term expenditures. In an attempt to look good and further his or her own career, the executive may have made decisions that were ultimately bad for the organization.

Counterargument Supporters of political behaviour agree that some managers behave unreasonably. They also note, however, that in a free society, individuals must be allowed to pursue their own self-interest as long as they keep within the law. They point out that it is usually impossible to determine when an individual has shown too much interest in his or her own success, and not enough interest in the organization's success. But when disagreements do arise, they must be resolved in some way, and the most effective resolution mechanism is the use of power.

Do Powerful People Ignore Others?

Argument Critics of politics claim that powerful people (and organizations) are so concerned about increasing their own power that they ignore the needs and rights of others (see the Ethics in Management insert entitled "A Fight for Canadian Tire"). In the process, they ignore their own social responsibilities. Examples include corporations refusing to voluntarily do what consumer groups believe they should do, such as controlling pollution, behaving ethically, avoiding the manufacture of military weapons, and hiring more minorities.

Counterargument Supporters of political behaviour reject this argument and say that just the opposite actually happens. Politics, they say, forces organizations to be responsive to their employees and to groups in their external environment. They note that if an organization does not respond to pressure for change, it will eventually find itself in trouble. The overthrow of numerous communist governments in Eastern Europe in 1989 is overwhelming evidence of this. In 1990, a consumer group threatened to boycott Burger King because it sponsored television programs the group felt placed too much emphasis on sex and violence; as a result, the company dropped its sponsorship of those programs.

Is Politics Time-Consuming and Inefficient?

Argument According to this argument, political decision making is very slow because people in organizations spend excessive time engaging in political behaviour. They therefore have little time or energy left to do their own work. For example, during 1990, there was constant speculation at the Bank of Nova Scotia about who would head the bank after chairman Cedric Ritchie stepped down. The bank atmosphere became very political, and executives spent much time and energy worrying about their turf and who would win the race for the top spot.[32] Critics of political behaviour argue that if people stopped wasting time on political behaviour, organizational performance would improve.

Counterargument Supporters of political behaviour point out that rational decision-making processes are time-consuming because information must be gathered and its meaning openly debated. Political decisions are actually made more quickly because they are private and informal.

ETHICS IN MANAGEMENT

A Fight for Canadian Tire

In March, 1986, Fred Billes, son of the founder of Canadian Tire (CT), received a phone call from a representative of Carling O'Keefe Ltd. The person informed Fred that he had found a way to pay Fred, his sister Martha, and his brother David triple the market value of their stocks if they were interested in selling their combined 60 percent voting-share interest in CT (the company also had many nonvoting shares called A-shares). Fred was interested because he was ready to get out of his involvement with the company.

But there was a problem. As Fred's lawyer reviewed CT's articles of incorporation, he discovered a "coattail," a clause which said that if any party was to buy a majority of CT's common shares, they must also purchase the nonvoting A-shares (which constituted 96 percent of the firm's equity). Failure to make this additional purchase would result in the A-shares being converted to voting shares, and the buyer of the common shares then risked having the deal voted down.

Carling O'Keefe wanted to buy all the shares—common and Class A—so the coattail wasn't a problem. However, one of the lawyers looking at the case saw a way around the coattail, observing that if less than 49 percent of the common stock was purchased, then a buyout of A-shares was not required. Using such an interpretation, one could pay a premium price (say, four times market value) for up to 49 percent of Fred, Martha, and David's voting shares and gain control of CT for only $105 million. By not purchasing the majority of the voting shares and not triggering the coattail, the buyer could save approximately $1.2 billion by not being required to buy the nonvoting A-shares.

It seemed simple enough, but there was a nagging feeling that since 96 percent of the shareholders wouldn't have anything to say about the deal, that the Ontario Securities Commission (OSC) would disallow it. Still, the parties thought it was a risk worth taking and, when Carling O'Keefe withdrew its offer, other prospective buyers were sought.

The news that CT was up for sale sent shock tremors throughout CT's dealers across Canada because they feared that the sale of CT would threaten their livelihoods. There seemed to be only one solution: unite the dealers in an attempt to purchase the voting shares from Fred, Martha, and David. By the middle of November, 1986, dealer representatives had collected $290 million in promissory notes that could be used to secure a bank loan. In December, the dealers group successfully purchased 49 percent of CT voting stock and gained control of the Canadian Tire Corporation.

The celebration was brief. One day after the deal was signed, the OSC informed all parties that it had some serious reservations about what had happened. The hearing was scheduled for the following week. At issue was the abuse of the nonvoting A-shareholders who would receive nothing from the deal. Still, the lawyers felt that the dealers' offer was within the literal wording of the coattail clause and that there had been no violation of the articles of incorporation. They therefore felt that the deal would go through.

But there was a violation in the eyes of the OSC. It took over 1500 pages of testimony, but in the end the OSC decided that the deal was unfair. Tommy Keirans, an independent representative of the financial community, testified that the issue went beyond what the contract said. The deciding consideration was that it violated what he called the "de facto agreement," and the broader understanding of the coattail, which was intended to provide takeover protection. To allow the deal to go through, the OSC decided, would be to deny the basic tenets of "fairness and equity." ▲

Does Politics Give Some People Too Much Power?

Argument Central to the thinking of those who answer yes to this question is the belief that power corrupts people and that differences in power should therefore be minimized. Opponents of political behaviour argue that the best way to diminish these power differences is to eliminate political behaviour.

Counterargument Supporters of political behaviour argue that it is simply impossible to eliminate power differences in organizations because those differences are intimately tied to the existence of politics itself. The pyramidal shape of organizations, limited organizational resources, and individual self-interest all ensure that both power differences and political behaviour will arise in organizations.

A Final Thought on Corporate Politics

Managed properly, political behaviour can be helpful in organizations (see the Management at Work insert "Politics and Your Career"). Unfortunately, our current level of understanding of corporate politics prevents us from stating simple rules for managing it. Any attempt to regulate political behaviour may therefore be doomed to failure. Somehow, people always find ways to get around the rules. Perhaps the following quotation will help put the conflicting views about politics into perspective:

> Power—because of the way it develops and the way it is used—will always result in the organization suboptimizing its performance. However, to this grim absolute, we add a comforting caveat: If any criterion other than power were the basis for determining an organization's decisions, the results would be even worse.[33]

MANAGEMENT AT WORK

Politics and Your Career

During your formal studies, you will take many different courses that are designed to give you a better understanding of complex organizations. Courses in quantitative methods, marketing, accounting, capital budgeting, and production all emphasize systematic and rational approaches to organizational decision making. Many students never question the accuracy or utility of this view of organizational life.

Now that you have been exposed to another point of view—the political one—you have several questions to answer:

1. Do you think that the political view of organizations is a realistic one?
2. Are you disappointed that organizations are not places where strictly rational criteria are used to make decisions?
3. What does this imply about the rational and systematic management techniques you will learn about during your school years?
4. Will what you learn in school be helpful in furthering your career in the organization where you work?
5. How do you feel about engaging in some of the political tactics mentioned in this chapter?

These are interesting and difficult questions, but you will benefit by asking them now, and then carefully considering how and why you answered the way you did. ▲

MEETING THE CHALLENGE

The Publishing Department

Recall in the Management Challenge that Ginny DeVor wanted to be promoted ahead of an older, more experienced person who was an informal group leader of an important group. DeVor's success was, in part, a result of her sensitivity to organizational politics.

DeVor's tactics included refining friendships just prior to the time when these friendships could be used to secure crucial votes. In order to get the job, DeVor knew that the selection committee's decision must be in her favour; the most direct approach was to influence the nomination and election of committee members. With four sympathetic members on the selection committee, DeVor was virtually certain of being chosen. DeVor's behaviour is quite consistent with the definition of politics presented in this chapter. Carl Ryan was undoubtedly unhappy with the outcome since he wanted the job. If Ryan was insensitive to, or aloof from, office politics, he would certainly have disapproved of the tactics used by DeVor. He would probably also say that DeVor's actions were unfair, and that she deprived him of a position that he deserved.

Whether the political activities behind DeVor's appointment as department head are in themselves positive or negative is difficult to say. At the individual level, some people are hurt and some are helped by political behaviour.

• • •

At the organizational level, if political behaviour results in a more capable individual being promoted, the organization benefits and the net effect is positive. Of course, the definition of "capable" is subject to debate. In this case, we might argue that DeVor was more capable than Ryan because she saw what was necessary to get the job, and she was more sensitive to interpersonal relations in the department. Individuals who aspire to positions of authority must be sensitive to important organizational characteristics, and DeVor certainly was sensitive.

On the negative side, we might argue that DeVor was less capable than Ryan because she appeared quite willing to do whatever was necessary to get her preferred outcomes. In this case, nothing very bad happened, but in future cases, she might make questionable decisions as she pursues her own interests. This could possibly cause negative outcomes for her staff, for the publishing department, and ultimately for the agency as a whole.

All individuals must make their own decisions about how much they should get involved in organizational politics. But it may often appear that a given manager has little choice, since so many other managers in the organization are prepared to become heavily involved in politics if that is what is necessary to further their career. ▲

SUMMARY

Power is the ability to influence the behaviour of another person. The concept of power is important since managers cannot accomplish all their work simply by relying on their formal authority. There are several types of power: legitimate power (which results from a person's place in the formal hierarchy), reward power (derived from a person's ability to reward others), punishment power (derived from a person's ability to punish others), referent power (based on a liking for a person or a desire to be like that person), information power (based on a person's ability to get information that others need), persuasive power (the ability to convince others using logical arguments), and expert power (resulting from possession of special knowledge about a particular area).

There are two basic models of how organizations operate. The rational model sees organizations as places where managers make rational decisions about how resources should be allocated. The rational model assumes that (1) organizational effectiveness can be clearly defined and measured, (2) information is available about important contingencies affecting the organization, (3) structural planning takes place, (4) organizations are tightly linked to their environments, and (5) individuals and groups will cooperate to achieve organizational goals.

The political model sees organizations as places where individuals pursue their own self-interest, irrespective of whether or not this helps the organization. The assumptions of the political model are the opposite of those of the rational model.

Organizational politics refers to the activities individuals pursue in organizations to develop and exercise power to achieve their own desired outcomes. Such behaviour is found in all types of organizations because resources are scarce and because each person is interested in improving his or her own situation. Some tactics that are used when people behave politically are image building (creating a good image for oneself), using information selectively, scapegoating (blaming others for one's own shortcomings), forming alliances, networking, compromising, and rule manipulation (selectively applying rules to gain advantage over others).

One study of Canadian managers found that while they viewed political behaviour as harmful, they also felt that it was widespread in organizations. Lower-level participants perceived more political behaviour than upper-level managers, but no difference was evident in the amount of politics perceived in public- and private-sector firms. Managers believed that political behaviour was necessary if a person wanted to get ahead in an organization.

Five major arguments have been made against the use of political behaviour: (1) it results in unfair treatment of people, (2) it distorts the decision-making process, (3) it allows powerful people to ignore those who are less powerful, (4) it is inefficient and time consuming, and (5) it gives certain people too much power. Supporters of political behaviour reject these arguments and say that political behaviour can be good for an organization. They argue that political decision making is effective and that it recognizes the various contributions that different individuals and groups make to the organization. Organizational politics makes an organization very sensitive to its internal and external environment.

KEY TERMS

power (p. 289)
reward power (p. 291)
punishment power (p. 291)
referent power (p. 291)
expert power (p. 291)
information power (p. 291)
persuasive power (p. 291)
legitimate power (p. 291)
law of reciprocity (p. 292)
rational model (p. 293)
political model (p. 293)
organizational politics (p. 295)
impression management (p. 300)
information management (p. 300)
mentoring (p. 301)

REVIEW QUESTIONS

1. Define the term "power." Discuss the five types of power, giving an example of each.
2. Describe the characteristics of managers who use power effectively in organizations.
3. What strategies might managers use to increase their power?
4. Outline the differences between the rational and political models of organization.
5. Define the term "organizational politics."
6. Why is political behaviour evident in all organizations?
7. Describe five tactics that are commonly used by corporate politicians.
8. What factors influence the degree of "clout" an organizational subunit possesses?
9. Why is politics so common in budget allocation decisions? In promotion decisions?
10. How do practising managers view corporate politics? Why do they feel as they do?
11. Summarize the principal arguments for and against political behaviour in organizations.

DISCUSSION QUESTIONS

1. "When power differences between individuals are minimized, organizational performance will improve." Do you agree or disagree with this statement? Give reasons for your answer.
2. You have just been promoted to a new position. What would you do to increase your power base?
3. Can formal organizational rules and regulations ever be used in a political way? Explain.
4. "Technical competence is a necessary but not sufficient condition for advancement in an organization." Is this statement true or false? Why?
5. Is it possible for a person with no real managerial skills to move up the hierarchy using only his or her political abilities? Explain.

EXERCISES

1. Consider the formula for calculating total power presented in the chapter. State the specific type of power, and how much total power each of the following individuals is likely to have:
   a. President of Canadian National Railways
   b. A computer repair technician
   c. A community college student
2. Interview a manager on the subject of organizational politics. Ask the manager to provide information on the following issues:
   a. The role of politics in the manager's organization
   b. An example of political behaviour
   c. The manager's view on whether politics is good or bad
3. Consider an organization that you are part of. What kinds of political behaviour are evident in the organization? Give an example.
4. Collect three articles from your local newspaper or from a national business newspaper that deal with the use of power. Describe how power was used to achieve results (or, how it failed to achieve results).

CASE 10-1
THE PROMOTION

March 17 was a great day for James McKechnie, and not just because it was St. Patrick's day. On that day, James was promoted to product manager for one of the major lines of the company. He joined three other product managers who all reported to the vice-president of marketing. The product managers were very interdependent, and cooperated with each other so that they could effectively carry out their responsibilities and reach their sales goals.

The first six months were exciting for James as he familiarized himself with his new job. There was promising sales growth in several of the products he was responsible for, and this gave him a genuine sense of achievement. But before too long, several dimensions of his job began to emerge that made him feel uncomfortable.

One day last week, he experienced several stressful moments. Early in the day, Sig Parnitzky of the accounting department dropped by with the budget preparation sheets. This was the first time James had been involved in developing a complete budget, and he was anxious to do it properly. Sig offered to help James, and noted in a hushed tone that it was important to "pad" budget requests by at least 10 percent. Sig continued, "It's the way things work in this company. Top management wants to feel that they are in control, so they always cut budget requests back from what product managers write down."

Sig also reminded James that the product managers' meeting was in two days, and asked James to support a proposal to delay the expansion of the warehouse. He justified this request by saying that the information systems area had much more pressing needs, and that the money should be spent upgrading the firm's computers. He asked James to indicate at the managers' meeting that warehousing was not a problem for the products James was responsible for. This, in fact, was true—James had never experienced any problems with the warehouse.

Shortly after Sig Parnitzky left, Helen Hrynkiw (the vice-president of marketing and James' boss) came by and told James that his six-month performance review was scheduled for next week. She asked him to put together a statement of how the job was working out and (among other matters) what he would like in the way of management development training. She specifically mentioned the opportunity to attend a four-week seminar sponsored by a prestigious Canadian business school. James knew that most of the managers who were on the "fast promotion track" had attended this seminar, so he was very pleased with this offer.

Just before leaving, Helen commented on the importance of the product managers' supporting the expansion of the warehouse. She said, "If we don't allocate funds for warehouse expansion now, I just don't know when it will happen. It's in this year's capital budget, but it has come up for review again. We really need the extra space, and it would certainly improve relations with production and shipping if the warehouse was expanded. We need your support, James."

Later in the day, James had lunch with Raymond Novotny and Jennifer Nawrocki, two other product managers. The conversation eventually turned to the recent quarterly sales report. James had come out on top and ahead of target. The others were below target, although not by much. James got the distinct impression that they both felt that he had been too aggressive in promoting his product line this past quarter. While they commended him for his new advertising campaign, they felt that his actions had made them look bad. Raymond said, "It is important that we work together and share our ideas so that we all do well. If you come up with ideas that you don't share with us, we aren't working as a team like we should be."

James was surprised at Raymond's comment. He knew that the company had established the position of product manager in order to create some internal competition to stimulate higher sales. To reinforce this expectation, a bonus of 25 percent of annual salary was paid to those who surpassed their sales targets. James thought to himself, "It's unreasonable to expect too much cooperation under a system like this."

As he sat in his office after lunch, James began to wonder what was expected of him as a middle manager. He felt that managers should be honest and truthful and perform their duties in accordance with the policies and procedures set out by the company. Now he was hearing that his job was dependent on cooperating with the "right" people, even if cooperating meant less money for him and lower sales for the company. But he also realized that cooperating might mean a promotion sometime in the near future.

He also worried about what he was going to say at the product managers' meeting in two days. He felt that he had to come down on one side or the other of the warehouse expansion issue, but he knew that taking either position would make him some enemies. James thought back to when he had first read his job description, and how doing so had given him a feeling of security. In the first few months of his new job, it had served him well, but lately he had gotten involved in numerous situations where his job description was absolutely no help. He was rapidly coming to the conclusion that his job description didn't mean much. ▲

QUESTIONS

1. What role is organizational politics playing in this situation? Describe the impact of politics on James' job description.
2. Should James support the warehouse expansion? Why or why not? Defend your answer.
3. Assume that James comes to you for some advice on how to be effective in his current position. What would you tell him?

CASE 10-2
POWER PLAY

Gilles Henri grew up on a farm near Bedford, Quebec. His parents were firm disciplinarians, conservative in their views, and over the years helped him develop a strong sense of right and wrong. Gilles had a happy childhood because his parents stressed the value of hard work, doing what was right, and harmony in the family.

After he graduated with an engineering degree from Laval University, he went to work for Latimer Hydraulics, a firm that specialized in the custom manufacture of liquid-pumping systems for agriculture and industry. Customers would approach the firm with a specific problem, and its hydraulic engineers would design a system to meet the customer's needs. Since the systems were custom-made, testing them was important.

Gilles was a first-rate engineer, and his boss, Armand Mikolash, soon recognized him as a valuable addition to the firm. Gilles was given increased responsibility in a variety of areas, and he performed well in all of them. Four years after he joined the firm, a large contract was landed by Latimer. The contract involved building a state-of-the-art system for Creighton Manufacturing, and Gilles was named chief engineer on the project. In that role, he had the responsibility of overseeing all aspects of the contract, including the final testing of the system.

Design and production went well for the first four months. The work was proceeding on time, and preliminary test results were positive. However, two months before the new system was due, Gilles received the results of a test on a critical component of the system, indicating that it did not work. The tests were repeated, but the results were the same. Gilles therefore began redesign work in order to remedy the defect. He also informed Armand that additional time would be needed to complete the project.

When Armand received the memo, he called Gilles into his office for a chat, and the following conversation took place:

Mikolash: I'm sorry, but I can't give you additional time to complete the project. The customer needs it in two months. Just sign the test report saying that the system works, and we'll get the system working before we deliver it. We've done that before when we had problems like this.

Henri: I can't do that. The system doesn't work. It wouldn't be right.

Mikolash: As the chief engineer, you've got to sign the test report.

Henri: I'll be happy to sign it, but not until the system is working.

Mikolash: Now, Gilles, listen to reason. This contract is going to put Latimer on the map. You want to be part of that, don't you? This will give a big boost to your career. Now sign the report.

Henri: You can sign it if you want. I won't be part of a deception like that. It's unethical.

Mikolash: Well, I'll have to sign it in your place. I'm sorry to say this, but I'm going to have to remove you from the project, effective immediately.

Disappointed and shocked, Gilles continued to argue his point, but to no avail. Mikolash seemed completely unable to understand his concerns. The next day, Gilles resigned.

Several months later, Gilles read a story in the Montreal paper describing a problem that had developed between Latimer Hydraulics and Creighton Manufacturing involving a hydraulic pumping system that didn't work. The paper noted that, after some negotiations between Latimer and Creighton, a satisfactory arrangement had been worked out. It also noted that Armand Mikolash had been promoted to executive vice-president of Latimer Hydraulics. ▲

QUESTIONS

1. What factors contributed to Gilles Henri's resignation?
2. What could he have done to avoid the situation that led up to it?
3. Evaluate Mikolash's decision to sign the report even though the system did not work.
4. What would you have done in the situation?

MANAGEMENT ON LOCATION

CASE 10-3
THE RETURN OF THOMAS PALATUK

In 1987, Thomas Palatuk entered the University of Toronto and began working toward his B. Comm. degree. In the summer of 1990, he got a temporary job in the Systems and Procedures Department at Burrows Ltd.

One of the responsibilities of the Systems and Procedures Department was to monitor the budgeting process at Burrows to ensure that expenditures were orderly and that budgets were not exceeded. Thomas found that he was required to follow rigid work procedures, but he didn't mind too much since he was just learning the job and the procedures gave him clear guidance about what to do. The emphasis of his job was on checking computer printouts containing budget data for various departments. If a deviation was found, he informed his supervisor, Dominique Mangotti, and she followed up on it with the head of the department in question.

At the end of the summer, Dominique called Thomas in and complimented him on the work he had done. She indicated that he should apply at Burrows for a career position when he graduated the next spring. Thomas thanked her and said he would consider it.

Thomas graduated with his B. Comm. in 1991, right on schedule. After interviewing several companies, he decided to go to work full-time for Burrows. Since he was familiar with the company, and had worked well there on a temporary basis, he felt good about his choice. He was told that he would again be working for Dominique, but this time in a position of considerably increased authority and discretion. On his first day with the company, he was greeted enthusiastically by Dominique, and after some small talk, the following conversation took place:

Mangotti: I'm glad you chose to go with us full-time. I have just the job for you.

Palatuk: What have you got in mind?

Mangotti: Well, last summer you worked in an area that really didn't let you exercise all your skills. You were limited to checking computer printouts for budget deviations.

Palatuk: Oh, I didn't mind too much. You've got to start somewhere.

Mangotti: Well, that's true, but I've got a much more important project for you to work on. Top management has decided to implement a management audit that will complement our financial auditing system. The purpose of the management audit is to assess the quality of our management team.

Palatuk: That's an important area in any company. In one of my personnel courses, we did a major term project on the issue of management audits. I think that should be helpful.

Mangotti: That's great! I wasn't aware that you already had some relevant experience in this area. I'm putting you in charge of a three-person task force. You will have the authority to gather data on each of the company's managers and to write a report to top management indicating the current expertise Burrows possesses in its management ranks.

Palatuk: What kind of authority do I have to gather information?

Mangotti: You have the full authority of the Systems and Procedures Department behind you. As well, each of the managers knows that the top management group in the company supports this management audit.

Palatuk: What kinds of data am I supposed to gather?

Mangotti: We've already got a questionnaire worked out. You and your team simply administer it and analyze the data that the managers provide. If you wish, you can develop additional questions to ask the managers and include those as well.

Palatuk: When do I start?

Mangotti: Right away. I'll show you your office and introduce you to the other members of the audit team. You know, this project will allow you to really make a name for yourself around here. By the time you're finished, all the top managers will know who you are. Most people don't get an opportunity like this.

Thomas returned to his office and began developing his strategy for doing the management audit. ▲

QUESTIONS

1. What problems might Thomas encounter as he conducts the management audit? Explain why each of these problems might develop.
2. What can Thomas do to reduce the chance that problems will develop during the audit procedure?

CHAPTER

11

PLANNING FOR AND DEVELOPING HUMAN RESOURCES

LEARNING OBJECTIVES

After reading this chapter, you will be able to:

1. Define human resource management and explain why businesses must consider job-relatedness criteria when managing human resources.
2. Discuss how managers plan for human resources.
3. Identify the steps involved in staffing a company.
4. Describe ways in which managers can develop workers' skills and deal with workers who do not perform well.
5. Explain the importance of wages and salaries, incentives, and benefits programs in attracting and keeping skilled workers.
6. Describe how laws regarding employment equity, pay equity, and worker safety affect human resource management.

MANAGEMENT CHALLENGE

ACHIEVING EMPLOYMENT EQUITY IN CANADA

The Employment Equity Act of 1986 is designed to improve the representation in federally regulated industries and businesses of four population groups who are designated as "employment disadvantaged"—women, visible minorities, Aboriginal people, and people with disabilities. Since the act came into force, progress toward reaching its goals has been slow but steady. Two large Canadian firms—Ontario Hydro and Canadian National Railways—illustrate the effect the act is having.

ONTARIO HYDRO

Ontario Hydro is Canada's largest public utility, employing 28 000 people. It will need 15 000 new employees in the 1990s alone. With the decline in numbers in the under-25 age group, Ontario Hydro needs to look beyond its traditional base (white men under 25) to fill its human resource requirements. Affirmative action is therefore not just a moral imperative but a practical necessity.

The company began to address the issue of employment equity in 1984 by establishing an affirmative action department. Since that time, the percentage of women in managerial positions has risen from under 1.5 percent to just over 7 percent. There are also many more women in professional jobs in the company.

But Hydro has a long way to go.

• • •

The percentage of women and Aboriginal people employed by Hydro is far lower than their numbers in the general population. For members of visible minorities and people with disabilities, their representation at Hydro is about equal to their numbers in the overall population. The company's goal is to have women occupying one-third of all jobs at Hydro by 2000. Hydro's goal for members of the other target groups is representation equal to that in the general population. Employees will continue to be hired and promoted on merit, but when two candidates are equal and one is a member of a designated group, that person will get the job.

To help achieve its goals, Hydro has organized seminars for women engineers and scientists, has provided space for daycare centres, and has supported alternative working arrangements. No sexual harassment is tolerated, and the new office complex in North York is a barrier-free facility to accommodate people with disabilities. In northern Ontario, Hydro is making special efforts to recruit Native workers and is providing scholarships for Aboriginal students.

CANADIAN NATIONAL RAILWAYS

Canadian National Railways established its employment equity department in 1984 and by 1990 had appointed its first woman vice-president. Like Ontario Hydro, CN has set goals to have the four designated groups represented in the firm at the same levels they are represented in the general population. The current levels are as follows: women, 8.1 percent; visible minorities, 3.7 percent: Aboriginal people, 1.3 percent; and people with disabilities, 2.4 percent.

All vice-presidents must submit plans for increasing the representation of the four target groups. Managers attend training seminars to learn how to manage an increasingly diverse work force. Forty-three women are now part of senior management. In 1991, the company was awarded first prize by *Les femmes regroupées pour l'accessibilité aux pouvoirs politique et économique* (FRAPPE), a Quebec group that promotes the economic and political advancement of women.

CN recognizes that it still has a long way to go. It has designed several plans to achieve employment equity goals, including scholarships to encourage women to study in transportation and nontraditional work, paid leave for women employees to complete their university degrees, and apprenticeship and work-experience programs to help employees acquire nontraditional work skills. ▲

In this chapter, we will explore the major aspects of hiring, training, and maintaining an efficient work force, as well as some of the special issues facing companies in their relations with employees. But first we need to consider the general principles that govern good employer-employee relations.

FOUNDATIONS OF HUMAN RESOURCE MANAGEMENT

human resource management

LEARNING OBJECTIVE 1

Define human resource management and explain why businesses must consider job-relatedness criteria when managing human resources.

Human resource management involves developing, administering, and evaluating programs to acquire and enhance the quality and performance of people in a business. Human resource specialists—sometimes called personnel managers—are employed by all but the smallest firms. They help plan for future personnel needs. They recruit, train, and develop employees. And they set up employee evaluation, compensation, and benefits programs.

But in fact all managers are personnel managers. Managers of production, accounting, finance, and marketing departments choose prospective employees, train new workers, and evaluate employee performance. As you will see in this section, all managers must be aware of the basis of good human resource management—job-relatedness and employee-job matching.

JOB-RELATEDNESS AND EMPLOYEE-JOB MATCHING

job-relatedness

According to the principle of **job-relatedness**, all personnel decisions, policies, and programs should be based on the requirements of a position. That is, all criteria used to hire, evaluate, promote, and reward people must be tied directly to the job they perform. For example, a policy that all secretaries be young women would not be job-related since neither youth nor femaleness is essential in performing secretarial work. Such a policy represents poor human resource management because the company loses the chance to hire more experienced help and to consider skilled men for the position. On the other hand, a policy of hiring only young women to model teenage girls' clothing would be job-related and would thus reflect sound human resource management.

Fundamental to the concept of job-relatedness—and to human resource management in general—is the idea of matching the right person to the right job. The direct result of good human resource management is the close match of people, skills, interests, and temperaments with the requirements of their jobs. When people are well matched to their jobs, the company benefits from high rates of employee performance and satisfaction, high retention of effective people, and low absenteeism. All personnel activities relate in some fashion to the employee-job match. Job matching may not be easy to achieve, as shown in the Management at Work insert "Problems in Matching Jobs and Skills."

MANAGEMENT AT WORK

PROBLEMS IN MATCHING JOBS AND SKILLS

There is a "mismatch" problem in Canada—people have skills the market no longer wants, and companies have needs that unemployed people cannot satisfy. The Canadian Labour Market and Productivity Centre estimates that 22 percent of the unemployed have skills that didn't match their former employers' needs. Interestingly, this figure is down from the 64 percent estimate in 1989. However, during the 1990s, the matching problem is likely to worsen again as companies become ever-more demanding in what they want in employees.

The mismatch problem is obvious in a field like information technology. In an industry that relies almost solely on human brainpower and creativity, companies are in desperate need of computer programmers, software developers, and computer scientists. Yet Canadian universities graduated one-third *fewer* computer scientists in 1990 than they did in 1986. During this same period, university enrollment increased 12 percent, with the number of students studying history increasing 59 percent, and sociology 31 percent. Neither of these areas are promising in terms of available jobs.

Why have students not become interested in information technology? Attitudes and perceptions probably play a negative role. Computer experts are often portrayed as socially inept individuals who are nerds or geeks. There is still something in Canadians that allows them to dismiss careers in technology as uninteresting.

But this is only part of the reason that a mismatch problem exists. There is also a growing recognition that we must change the way people are trained. Education should be a lifetime experience, not merely something that ends when a person graduates from school. Pressure to change and adapt comes from the workplace as companies adopt new technologies to deliver new services. Employees who were hired in the 1960s or 1970s may not want to adapt to the new realities.

Honeywell Ltd. is just one firm that has had to come to grips with some unpleasant new realities. Its Toronto plant, which makes instrumentation for heating and cooling equipment, found that customers were demanding that the firm be certified under the ISO 9000 international quality program. This meant that Honeywell would have to introduce just-in-time inventory, total quality management, and self-directed work teams. But when the company looked at its work force, it found that only half had English as their first language, and that many had not finished high school.

Before the workers could cope with the new demands being imposed on the company, they needed to be trained. This gradually evolved into a "learning for life" program, which involved English, math, and computer courses. Employees were also trained in production and inventory management, total quality, and communication skills. Part of the training was provided at Humber College in Toronto. Each year, Humber sells about $30 million worth of education to private sector firms like Kodak Canada and John Labatt Ltd.

The mismatch problem will be solved when people on the job market have a total mix of characteristics—both skills and attitudes—that companies are looking for. A recent Conference Board of Canada study asked employers what they were looking for in employees. Some of the things—teamwork, ability to think, ability to communicate—can be taught in school. But others—positive attitudes, responsibility, and adaptability—are more difficult to develop in educational programs. ▲

Effective managers analyze their personnel needs carefully. They then select employees who have the necessary abilities and skills. They develop the skills of their employees so that their workers meet job demands. They provide feedback on performance to help employees adjust their behaviour to meet job requirements when necessary. And they provide compensation sufficient to retain valued employees. In the rest of this chapter, we will consider how each of these activities contributes to a good employee-job match.[1]

PLANNING FOR HUMAN RESOURCES

LEARNING OBJECTIVE 2
Discuss how managers plan for human resources.

Just as planning for financial, plant, and equipment needs is important, so too is planning for personnel needs. As Figure 11-1 shows, such planning involves two types of activities by managers—job analysis and forecasting.

JOB ANALYSIS

job analysis

To accurately forecast for human resources, managers must first identify the nature of the various jobs within the organization. **Job analysis** is the detailed study of the specific duties required for a particular job and the human qualities required to perform that job. For simple, repetitive jobs, managers might ask workers to create a checklist of all the duties they perform and the importance of each of those duties for the job. In analyzing more complex jobs, managers might combine checklists with interviews of job holders to determine their exact duties. Managers might also observe workers to record the duties they perform.

job description

job specification

Using the job analysis, human resource managers can develop **job descriptions.** A job description outlines the objectives, responsibilities, and key tasks in a job. It also describes the conditions under which the job will be done, the relationship of the job to other positions, and the skills needed to do the job. The skills, education, and experience necessary to fill a position make up the **job specification.** Figure 11-2 shows a job advertisement that includes element of a job description and a job specification.

FIGURE 11-1 PLANNING FOR HUMAN RESOURCES.

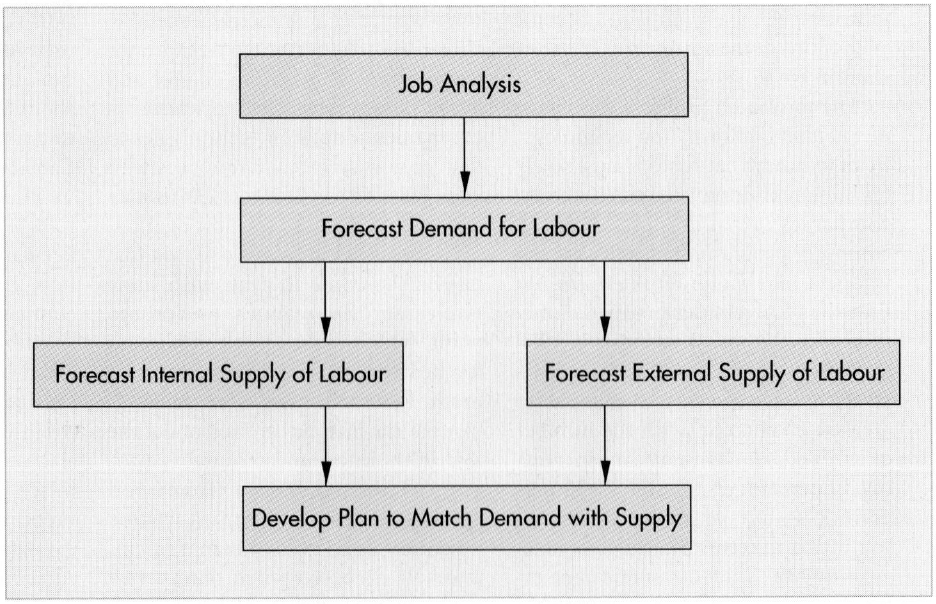

FIGURE 11-2 PRENTICE HALL CANADA INC. USES A VARIETY OF ADVERTISEMENTS IN ITS RECRUITING EFFORTS. THIS ADVERTISEMENT IS DESIGNED TO ATTRACT INDIVIDUALS WHO ARE INTERESTED IN MEETING CHALLENGES AND WHO HAVE CERTAIN EDUCATIONAL AND EXPERIENCE CHARACTERISTICS.

DIRECTOR

FINANCIAL PLANNING

PRENTICE HALL CANADA INC., a successful leader in the publishing industry, offers a career opportunity for a self-motivated professional to lead our Financial Planning team successfully in achieving their budgeting and forecasting requirements.

In this key role, your primary accountabilities lie in the participation and preparation of our annual budget, quarterly budget update, monthly forecasts and asset management reporting. To meet these challenges, you must possess an accounting designation, university degree and five years' related experience. Excellent communication skills and the ability to succeed in a deadline-oriented environment are essential.

To explore this opportunity, please forward your résumé, in confidence, to:

Gillian McCarthy
Human Resources Coordinator
Prentice Hall Canada Inc.
1870 Birchmount Road
Scarborough, Ontario M1P 2J7

PRENTICE HALL

Job analysis and the resulting job descriptions and specifications are the foundations of effective human resource management. They serve as tools in hiring personnel for specific positions, as guides in establishing training programs, and as sources of comparison in setting wages. But most important, by defining job requirements objectively, they allow managers to make personnel decisions in keeping with the principles of job-relatedness.

FORECASTING

Once they have analyzed the nature of their needs, managers must forecast their needs. Managers need to forecast both their demand for employees of different types and the likely supply of such employees in the short term (less than one year), intermediate term (one to five years), and long term (over five years). Only then can they formulate specific strategies for responding to any potential employee surplus or shortage. As in any forecast, however, the manager's true purpose is to minimize major surprises, not to predict future needs exactly.

In forecasting demand, managers must take into account their businesses' plans for growth (if any). They must also figure in the normal rate of turnover and the number of older employees nearing retirement, among other factors. In forecasting supply, managers must consider the complexity of the job and which current employees could be promoted to fill higher positions. But they must also predict whether the labour market for a particular job will be in a state of surplus or shortage. As they develop strategies, managers must balance this combination of circumstances.

For example, a maker of credit cards planning to add another plant will need more employees. Managers for the firm may decide that the new plant manager must be hired from outside the company. Accordingly, they may embark on a thorough search for the right candidate. At the same time, the firm's managers may feel that three current employees could be promoted to printing supervisors in the new plant. They may begin training these workers months before the new facility opens. But the managers will probably delay hiring workers to box and ship the cards until the plant is ready, because unskilled labour is generally easy to hire.

Managing a forecasted need for fewer employees also requires careful consideration. Although some firms simply lay off employees during slow periods, the corporate culture of other companies prohibits or limits such behaviour. For example, when IBM needed to reduce its work force in 1986-1987, the firm used early retirement incentives and retraining programs instead of layoffs. Some of its more recent cutbacks in the 1990s, however, have involved layoffs and outright terminations.

STAFFING THE ORGANIZATION

LEARNING OBJECTIVE 3
Identify the steps involved in staffing a company.

Once managers have decided what positions they need to fill, they must find and hire individuals who meet the job requirements. Staffing of the corporation is one of the most complex and important aspects of good human resource management. In this section, we will consider how businesses fill positions from both outside and inside the organization. Sometimes personnel must be recruited and chosen from the outside. As well, decisions must be made about employee promotions to fill vacancies within the organization.

EXTERNAL STAFFING

A new firm has little choice but to acquire staff from outside itself. Established firms may also turn to the outside to fill positions for which there are no good internal candidates, to accommodate growth, or as a way to bring in fresh ideas. Such external staffing can be divided into two stages: recruitment and selection.

Recruitment

recruitment

In the first step, the company needs to develop a pool of applicants who are both interested in and qualified for the open positions. The purpose of **recruitment** is to generate a large number of potential employees. Thus, successful recruitment focusses only on the most basic qualifications of a job.

An in-depth interview with a prospective employee is often part of the recruiting process, particularly for managerial jobs.

For example, recruitment ads for a financial analyst might require applicants to hold an M.B.A. degree with an emphasis on finance. But requiring a degree from a particular school will unnecessarily restrict the number of applicants. Recruitment specifications should always be clearly job-related.

Companies have many options in recruiting employees, depending in part on the nature of the job. As we will discuss in more detail later in this chapter, current employees may be recruited to fill openings within the firm. In seeking outside applicants, businesses may visit high schools, vocational schools, colleges, and universities. In some cases, labour agreements may specify that new employees be found using the labour union's membership rolls. Of course, many companies advertise in newspapers or trade publications or seek the help of public and private employment agencies. Word of mouth and personal recommendations are often factors in the hiring of top management personnel. Even unsolicited letters and résumés from job seekers can produce the right person for a job.

When recruiting, firms must be careful to avoid violating antidiscrimination laws. The key federal antidiscrimination legislation is the Canadian Human Rights Act of 1977. The goal of this act is to ensure that any individual who wishes to obtain a job has an equal opportunity to compete for it. The act applies to all federal agencies, federal Crown corporations, any employee of the federal government, and business firms that do business interprovincially. Thus, it applies to such firms as the Bank of Montreal, Air Canada, Telecom Canada, Canadian National Railways, and many other public- and private-sector organizations that operate across Canada. Even with such wide application, the act affects only about 10 percent of Canadian workers; the rest are covered under provincial human rights acts.

Canadian Human Rights Act

The Canadian Human Rights Act prohibits a wide variety of practices in recruiting, selecting, promoting, and dismissing personnel. The act specifically prohibits discrimination on the basis of age, race and colour, national and ethnic origin, physical handicap, religion, gender, marital status, or prison record (if pardoned). Some exceptions to these blanket prohibitions are permitted. Discrimination cannot be charged if a blind person is refused a position as a train engineer, bus driver, or crane operator. Likewise, a firm cannot be charged with discrimination if it does not hire a deaf person as a telephone operator or as an audio engineer.

These situations are clear-cut, but many others are not. For example, is it discriminatory to refuse women employment in a job that routinely requires carrying objects with a mass of more than 50 kilograms? Ambiguities in determining whether discrimination has occurred are sometimes circumvented by using the concept of **bona fide occupational requirement**. An employer may choose one person over another based on overriding characteristics of the job in question. If a fitness centre wants to hire only women to supervise its women's locker room and sauna, it can do so without being discriminatory because it established a bona fide occupational requirement.

bona fide occupational requirement

Even after referring to bona fide occupational requirements, other uncertainties remain. Consider three cases: Would an advertising agency be discriminating if it advertised for a male model about 60 years old for an advertisement that is to appeal to older men? Would a business firm be discriminating if it refused to hire someone as a receptionist because the applicant was overweight? Would a bank be discriminating because it refused to hire an applicant whom the human resources manager considered would not fit in because of his appearance?

We might speculate that the advertising agency is not discriminating, the business firm might or might not be discriminating, and the bank could probably be accused of discrimination, but we can't be sure. The human rights legislation cannot specify all possible situations; many uncertainties remain over what the law considers discriminatory and what it considers acceptable. Nevertheless, the spirit of the legislation is clear, and managers must try to abide by it.

Enforcement of the federal act is carried out by the Canadian Human Rights Commission. The commission can either respond to complaints from individuals who believe they have been discriminated against, or launch an investigation on its own if it has reason to believe that discrimination has occurred. During an investigation, data are gathered about the alleged discriminatory behaviour and, if the claim of discrimination is substantiated, the offending organization or individual may be ordered to compensate the victim.

Each province has also enacted human rights legislation to regulate organizations and businesses operating in that province. These provincial regulations are similar in spirit to the federal legislation, with many minor variations from province to province. All provinces prohibit discrimination on the basis of race, national or ethnic origin, colour, religion, sex, and marital status, but some do not address such issues as physical handicaps, criminal record, or age. Provincial human rights commissions enforce provincial legislation.

Employment Equity Act of 1986

As we saw in the Management challenge, the **Employment Equity Act of 1986** also addresses the issue of discrimination in employment by designating four groups as employment disadvantaged—women, visible minorities, Aboriginal people, and people with disabilities. Companies covered by the act are required to publish statistics on their employment of people in these four groups.

In various foreign countries, employment practices are permitted that would not be allowed in Canada. The Global Management "No More Tea and Sympathy" describes the work situation for women in Japan.

GLOBAL MANAGEMENT

No More Tea and Sympathy

A society steeped in tradition, Japan has long had clearly defined roles for its citizens. Until World War II, a woman's place was only in the home: first her father's home, then her husband's. Since the 1950s, however, that world has broadened slightly as Japanese women have been welcomed into the business world. Welcomed to pour the tea. Welcomed to clean the ashtrays. Welcomed to answer phones and greet visitors. And welcomed only while young and unmarried. Indeed, many a Japanese boss saw it as his duty to help his young female workers find suitable husbands and leave. (Only 2 percent of Japanese women never marry—the lowest such rate in the world.) Once married, a woman was expected to stay home and raise her children, largely without the help of her husband, who traditionally worked late and then socialized with colleagues until even later.

But Japan, which once shut itself off from the world for centuries to avoid being tainted by outside influences, is finding itself unable to resist change from the outside now. Slowly but surely, Japanese women are asserting their right to remain single, to work after marriage—even when they have children—and to hold meaningful jobs. Under pressure from other nations, in 1986 the Japanese Diet passed a law banning discrimination on the basis of gender.

Another imported change in Japan is a decline in corporate loyalty by workers to companies and by companies to workers. To lower costs and remain competitive, some Japanese corporations have reduced or eliminated traditional pledges of lifelong employment, which were limited to men. With men moving from one company to another, a male no longer has a strong edge over a woman who may have taken off a year or two to have children.

In addition to outside pressure, two powerful internal forces—economics and demographics—have aided the rise of women in the Japanese workplace. Japan is a very costly place to live. Land and housing are scarce and expensive. Many products must be purchased from other nations, raising prices. Today, a Japanese couple who want to buy a home and provide their children with the private tutoring necessary to get into college often need a second income. Moreover, as Japan's economy has grown, it has been faced with a labour shortage, particularly in the service industries. This shortage is expected to accelerate as Japan's rapidly aging population continues to retire. In 1977, 45 percent of married women in Japan worked outside the home.

In 1987, 51 percent did. In 1977, only 239 000 women held any type of management position in Japan. By 1987 that number had more than doubled to 486 000. The Bank of Tokyo has 150 women with titles, including 12 section chiefs. In 1989, nearly 25 percent of the new engineers joining NEC, a large Japanese computer company, were female. Perhaps because some Japanese corporations still refuse to give women real authority, five out of six new businesses in Japan are started by women.

But serious problems remain. Japanese women still make only 52 percent as much as Japanese men. None of Japan's major industries has even one woman on its board of directors. About 20 percent of Japanese corporations still pay new female college graduates less than comparably trained new male graduates. Laws restricting the hours women may work still keep many factory workers from rising to first line supervisory positions. Sexual harassment appears to be widespread. A magazine columnist protested a recent rise in sexual harassment suits in Japan, arguing that "an executive ought to be able to innocently ask his secretary about the colour of her underwear that day."

After the antidiscrimination law was passed, initially it appeared to be having a positive effect as the number of women hired rose dramatically (to 40 percent of the work force). But the majority of the hiring took place in clerical jobs (those traditionally held by women). Many who were hired

• • •

were middle-aged women who had reentered the work force after their children reached school age. Most were also classified as part-time workers, even though they often worked more than 40 hours each week. When the economic boom came to an end in the early 1990s, many of these women were let go. For example, when JVC, a consumer electronics company, terminated 300 workers almost all of them were women.

Problems are also evident in the middle- and upper-management ranks. Japanese companies are reluctant to give women authority over other employees, particularly men. At the largest and most prestigious firms, the number of women in top management positions can be counted on the fingers of one hand. At the entry level, the situation is the same: in 1992, Mitsubishi hired 4 women and 213 men; Itohchu hired 4 women and 198 men, and Nissho Iwai hired 3 women and 127 men. Recruit Research Company reported that there are 2.2 job openings for every male seeking a position, but less than one opening for each woman seeking a position. Women who already hold managerial jobs express concerns about the same things their Canadian counterparts do: a "glass ceiling" that bars promotion to top jobs, lack of suitable daycare, and an all-male power structure.

Executives in the human resource areas of firms offer the view that the equal opportunity laws have given women many opportunities, but that women simply have not taken advantage of them. But women tell another story. They say that companies have no intention of giving them serious work, and that they are treated very differently from men. Critics contend that equal opportunity laws have no teeth. Companies are encouraged to reach certain hiring goals, but face no penalty if they fail.

Some observers of the Japanese scene feel that the problem is partly the result of a conservative view of the world on the part of Japanese women. Many Japanese women profess interest in a career, but they also feel compelled to raise their children in the traditional Japanese way—with extraordinary motherly attention to education. They are also hesitant to step out of gender roles that are ingrained in them from birth, and that are reinforced in the media. Yoko Ohara, a senior executive at Asahi Chemical Industry Company, and one of the few women to climb to the top of Japan's managerial ladder, notes that the conflict Japanese women feel about these fundamental issues makes it hard for them to pursue a career with the vigour that is necessary. ▲

Selection

selection

Once a pool of applicants has been identified, managers must sort through those individuals and select the best candidate for the job. **Selection** is by no means an exact science, since it is difficult to predict any given individual's behaviours and attitudes. Nevertheless, it is an important process. Hiring the wrong employee is costly to the firm and is unfair to that individual.

To reduce the element of uncertainty, personnel experts and other managers use a variety of selection techniques. The most common of these methods, as shown in Figure 11-3, are applications and résumés, screening interviews, ability and aptitude tests, reference checks, on-site interviews, and medical, drug, and polygraph tests. Each organization develops its own mix of selection techniques and may use them in any order.

The application form, used for almost all lower-level jobs, asks for information about the applicant such as background, experience, and education. A résumé is a prepared statement of the applicant's qualifications and career goals, and is commonly used by people seeking managerial or professional positions.

In many cases, companies receive several applications or résumés for a job opening. Human resource personnel must narrow the field, first on the basis of the applications and then by holding screening interviews. In these ways, clearly unqualified individuals are weeded out, especially walk-in applicants for low-level jobs who simply do not have the required job skills. Line managers (those with hiring authority) then interview qualified applicants at greater depth. Other people in the hiring manager's department may also interview job candidates. In some companies, potential subordinates of the prospective employee are included in the interview process.

FIGURE 11-3 GENERAL STEPS IN THE SELECTION PROCESS.

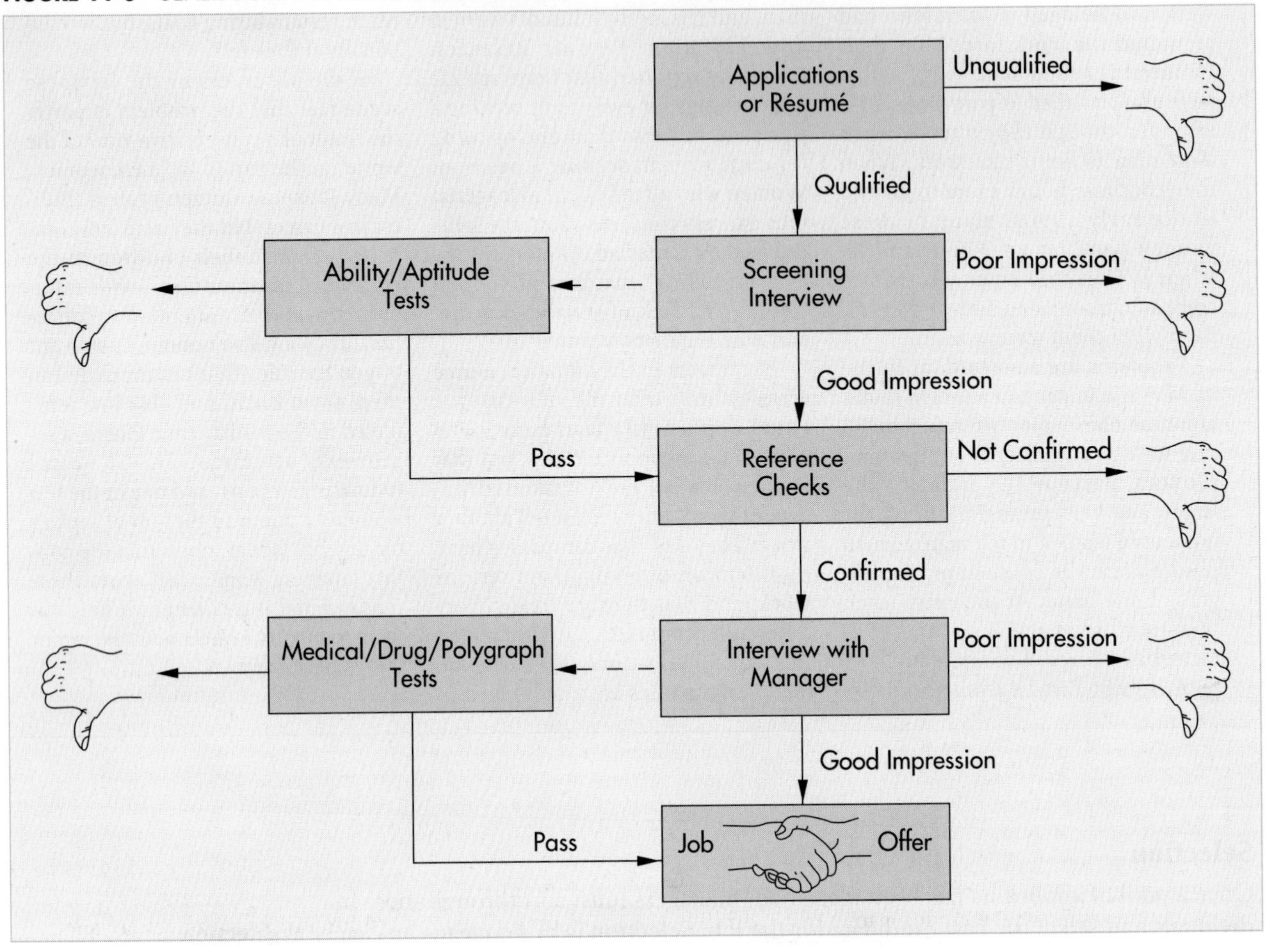

During both types of interviews, the interviewer asks questions about the applicant's background and qualifications. The interviewer must be careful to address only job-related issues. For example, he or she cannot ask a female applicant whether she plans to marry or have a family. Such questions can further sex discrimination. In addition to asking questions, interviewers also provide information about the company and answer any questions applicants may have.

It is important that managers not overstate the opportunities in a job when hiring for it. If they do, turnover will probably increase. Getting suggestions for new employees from current employees is a good strategy since studies show that people hired on the recommendation of someone in the company tend to stay with the company longer.[2]

For some positions, ability or aptitude tests may be part of the initial screening process.[3] When Toyota hired workers for its Cambridge, Ontario, plant applicants were put through a series of tests to determine their math, verbal, and communication skills and their ability to work on a team. Even though most of the workers hired had never worked for an automobile firm before, they are now producing the highest-rated car in North America.[4]

Regardless of the type of test used, it must meet two conditions. First, the test must be job-related. A company cannot, for example, ask an applicant for a secretarial job to take a test on operating a forklift. It is clearly appropriate, however, to ask the person to take a typing test. The second requirement of an employment test is that it must be a valid predictor of performance. That is, there must be evidence that people who score well on the test are more likely to perform well in the job than are people who score poorly on the test. A test used for selection must not serve as a basis for discrimination against anyone for reasons unrelated to the job. A new kind of selection test using video technology is described in the Management at Work insert "Using Video to Screen Job Applicants."

Another step used in employee selection is to check references. Reference checks often provide little useful information about an applicant's personality because applicants usually list as references only people likely to say good things about them. Even former employers may be reluctant to say negative things, fearing a lawsuit. But crosschecks can confirm information about an applicant's experience or education. For example, if you tell an interviewer that you graduated with a B. Comm. (Honours), a quick call to the student records office of your university can verify the truth of your statement.

MANAGEMENT AT WORK

Using Video to Screen Job Applicants

Finding, screening, and hiring new employees can be a big expense for companies. It can cost $5000-$10 000 to hire a clerical person, and much more to hire a top manager. In this cost-conscious era, companies are always ready to consider alternatives to the traditional hiring techniques.

One such promising new technique is video assessment. Potential new hires view videos that show a series of realistic work situations (portrayed by actors). For example, one scenario shows an assistant to a department manager who is trying to convince the supervisor of the word processing pool to give his job top priority because the boss wants some last-minute changes made in a report. The supervisor refuses and the assistant goes back to the boss asking him to intercede. At the end of each situation the viewers choose one of four courses of action to resolve the problem shown in the video. The test administrator then uses the computer to score candidate choices (much like a university or college instructor would grade student exams).

Video assessment is fast, reliable, cheap, and versatile. It also lets managers screen more extensively for jobs at the lower levels in the organization. Improving selection at entry level jobs should mean better customer service and greater chances for promotion from within.

Video assessment can also give management greater insight into employee strengths and weaknesses before they are hired, and this can help the company solve long-standing problems. For example, in the banking industry, turnover among tellers has always been a problem. When Confederation Trust used video assessment to hire tellers, it found that turnover dropped sharply.

Video assessment evolved from assessment centres, which have been in use for more than 30 years (see the description later in this chapter). While assessment centres do get results, they are high-cost operations (up to $5000 for each person who is assessed). Videos are cheap by comparison. They take about an hour to complete and cost between $25 and $100. Canadian firms using video assessment include Weyerhaeuser, Reebok, Northern Telecom, Eaton's, and B.C. Hydro.

But care must be taken when using video assessment. If a company simply buys a ready-made video from a consulting firm it may get lax about doing its homework—stating the specific knowledge, skills, and motivation needed to do various jobs. Mindlessly using video assessment could, for example, cause a company to hire a salesperson who is good at "cold calls" when what they really needs is a salesperson who is good at maintaining existing accounts.

Another potential problem is that managers don't have a stake in selection criteria the way they do when they interview people. Some companies overcome these limitations by using multiple methods. Weyerhaeuser used both video assessment and an assessment centre to hire a supervisor for a sawmill. Some companies also use video assessment for ongoing training purposes. At Reebok, employees view the videos on a regular basis in training and development sessions. ▲

Once a number of applicants have been interviewed and checked out, the manager will make a hiring decision. Before a job offer is actually made, however, some companies require an extra step—a physical exam, a polygraph test, and/or, increasingly, a drug test.[5] These tests are designed to protect the employer. For example, a manufacturer afraid of injuries from workers hurt on the job might require new employees to have a physical examination. The company gains some information about whether the employees are physically fit to do the work and what (if any) preexisting injuries they have. Polygraph (lie detector) tests are largely illegal now, and drug tests are also coming under fire. However, some companies still use one or both as insurance against theft or drug abuse by employees.

Only when all the required interviewing and testing is done can a manager finally make an applicant a job offer. For many jobs, the terms of the offer (including salary, benefits, and working hours) are dictated by the firm's current policies. But for a managerial position, the terms may be more flexible and negotiations may extend over weeks or even months.

INTERNAL STAFFING: PROMOTIONS

No matter how careful it is, the selection process of new applicants cannot compare with a company's knowledge of its current employees. It is not surprising that many firms prefer to "hire from within"—to promote or transfer existing staff members—whenever possible. However, some firms that have historically practised promotion from within are rethinking that strategy. IBM, for example, has had only six CEOs in its history, all of whom were appointed after they had spent many years working their way up the hierarchy at IBM. But with the replacement of CEO John Akers with an outsider, the company will have an easier time breaking with old traditions as it works on solving its massive problems.[6]

closed promotion system

Handling of promotions and job changes varies from company to company. Some firms use **closed promotion systems** in which managers decide which workers will even be considered for a promotion. In such companies, promotion decisions tend to be made informally and subjectively and to rely heavily on the recommendations of an employee's supervisor. Closed systems remain popular, especially in small firms, because they minimize the time, energy, and cost of making promotion decisions.

open promotion system

Other firms maintain **open promotion systems** in which available jobs and their requirements are posted. Employees who feel they possess the qualifications fill out applications, take tests, and interview with managers, much as if they were outside applicants. Open systems allow individual employees to have more say in their career paths. The democratic nature of such systems may also contribute to higher employee morale. But an open system can be somewhat time-consuming and expensive. Resources must be spent processing, interviewing, and screening internal applicants.

In addition to open and closed systems, some promotions are determined in part by seniority. Employees with more years of service in the company receive the promotions. This pattern—a standard feature of many union contracts—assures that those promoted have experience. It does not guarantee promotion of the most competent candidate, however.

DEVELOPING THE WORK FORCE

LEARNING OBJECTIVE 4

Describe ways in which managers can develop workers' skills and deal with workers who do not perform well.

Following the principles of job-relatedness in hiring and promoting employees, a firm can fill positions with people whose skills closely match the jobs' requirements. One of the first things that newcomers participate in is their orientation to the organization. It then falls to personnel experts and other managers to maintain and enhance the employee-job match and employees' performance on the job. Toward this end, some companies have instituted training and development programs on many levels. In addition, every firm has some system for performance appraisal and feedback that helps managers and employees assess the need for more training.

ORIENTATION

Most organizations have all their new employees go through an orientation process. The purpose of the **orientation** is to help employees learn about and fit into the company. At one level, the orientation can focus on work hours, parking priorities, and/or pay schedules. People may simply watch films, read manuals, and be introduced to new co-workers. At another level, orientation can indoctrinate the worker into the corporate culture and provide valuable insights into how to succeed.

orientation

EMPLOYEE TRAINING AND DEVELOPMENT

After orientation, the new employee starts to work. However, both old and new employees may receive training or be enrolled in a development program. Such training generally occurs for one of two reasons: to make up for some deficiency or to give the employee a chance to acquire skills needed for promotion. GM Canada, for example, recently spent $24 million on employee training as part of a program to increase quality levels at its Canadian production plants.[7]

Statistics Canada reports that 16 percent of Canadian adults cannot read the majority of written material they encounter in everyday life, and that 22 percent do not have the reading skills to deal with complex instructions. Companies like Northern Telecom and CCL Custom Manufacturing are finding that they have to train workers because the equipment they must use is increasingly complex.[8] A study by the Conference Board of Canada found that large companies spend an average of $475 per year on training employees. This amount is only half as much as American firms spend, and American companies, in turn, spend only a fraction of the amounts that Japanese firms spend.[9]

The reasons for training and development differ, as do the methods used. The most common methods are on-the-job training, off-the-job training, and management development programs.[10]

On-the-job Training

As the term suggests, **on-the-job training** is training that occurs while the employee is actually at work. In 1991, Ford Motor trained 140 workers for a year to work in a new aluminum casting plant in Windsor, Ontario. Because workers will need to know many jobs (e.g., melting aluminum and molding and cleaning engines), they need a lot of training.[11] Much on-the-job training is unplanned and informal, as when one employee shows another how to use the new photocopier. Someone needs some help, so it is provided.

on-the-job-training

In other cases, on-the-job training is quite formal. For example, secretaries may learn to operate a new word processing system at their desks. The advantages of on-the-job training are that it occurs in the real job setting and can be done over an extended period of time. The biggest disadvantage is that distractions on the job site may make training difficult.

Off-the-job Training

In contrast, **off-the-job training** is performed at a location away from the work site. It may be at a classroom within the same facility or at a different location altogether.

off-the-job-training

For example, refresher courses are offered for managers of McDonald's 600 Canadian restaurants at the Canadian Institute of Hamburgerology; training videotapes are also shown to restaurant workers.[12]

Coffee College is a two-week cram course run by Second Cup Ltd., Canada's largest retailer of specialty coffee. During their stay at Coffee College, franchisees and managers learn a lot of details about coffee; as well they learn how to hire workers, keep the books, detect employee theft, and boost Christmas sales.[13]

The advantage of this method is that the instructor can focus intensely on the subject without interruption and in a controlled environment. On the other hand, many off-the-job locations seem artificial and lack the realism necessary to really learn more about a job. Many companies provide a combination of on-the-job and off-the-job training. The Management at Work insert "Training at Burger King Canada" describes that company's approach to training.

Many companies are reluctant to retrain older workers, fearing that workers are uninterested in training, or that the company will not recoup its training investment because the workers have only a few years left in their career. But Kenworth, the heavy truck manufacturer, found that after it trained a group of older workers, productivity rose nearly 20 percent, and the time spent correcting manufacturing defects dropped from about 40 hours per truck to less than 10.[14]

Management Development Programs

management development programs

These programs are targeted specifically at current or future managers. In contrast to regular training, which focusses on technical skills, **management development programs** try to enhance conceptual, analytical, and problem-solving skills. Most large organizations have management development programs. Some programs are run in-house by managers or training specialists. Others take place at management development centres on university campuses. Still others require managers to get completely away from the work place and study certain subjects intensively. For example, Decision Dynamics is a two-week management development program conducted at a resort hotel on Lake Winnipeg. A well-conceived strategy for developing managerial talent is almost mandatory if an organization is to prosper.

Management development programs are built around a variety of techniques. The *lecture method* is useful for presenting facts. It is therefore a good way to inform managers about things like the meaning of new laws that regulate business activity. In the case method, participants are given a problem situation to analyze and solve. Simulation techniques require trainees to act out realistic business situations to give them practice in decision making. In a management game, for example, several teams compete against each other. Each team is a separate "company." In *role playing,* each trainee is given a specific role to read and act out. The aim here is to create a realistic situation and then have the trainees assume the roles of specific persons in that situation.

Because of the globalization of business, managers will increasingly have to work with customers, other managers, and owners from different cultures. The International School of Management Development takes high-potential managers and trains them to understand and work with people from other cultures. The training session takes several weeks, and the 40-50 participants engage in a variety of exercises as part of 6- or 7-person work groups.[15]

Assessment Centres

assessment centre

An **assessment centre** is a series of exercises in which management candidates perform realistic management tasks under the watchful eyes of expert appraisers. Each candidate's potential for management is assessed or appraised.

MANAGEMENT AT WORK

TRAINING AT BURGER KING CANADA

Training is a crucial job in any well-run company. People cannot do their jobs well if they are not properly trained, so in a sense all good performance starts with effective training.

Training is also a basic step in a company's human resource management process. Remember that employees must be recruited, hired, and then trained before their work can be evaluated and a reward system developed for them.

While you might enter Burger King management as a crew member, the most likely starting point according to Burger King University would be as an assistant manager (AM) in a restaurant. This job generally requires a high school degree and some college or equivalent experience. What kind of training can you expect as a new AM?

You will start with BMT-Restaurant (Basic Management Training), which involves seven weeks of in-restaurant training. The purpose here is to turn you into an AM trainee who is familiar with, and who can execute with some proficiency, all the crew level production, service, and cleanliness-related duties in the restaurant. To do this, you will need a basic working knowledge of restaurant equipment. Once you have learned those jobs "from the bottom up" you will need to learn the basic duties of the shift coordinator (who is an hourly employee with some supervisory responsibility during his or her shift). During this BMT-Restaurant phase you will also complete the training that enables you to do the daily opening and closing paperwork.

Here is a run down of the RMT program (Restaurant Management Training), which is actually conducted over about a two-year period:

BMT Classroom:
This is a one-week classroom training program in which you will learn things like Crew Training, Time Management, Customer Service, Product Quality & Food Safety, Safety/Security, and Production Control Systems.

BMT Shift Certification:
Here you will return for two weeks of in-restaurant training. The purpose is for your manager to rate your execution of actual shift management duties and certify you as a "shift-ready" manager. In other words, the restaurant manager will have to decide whether you have what it takes to run a restaurant.

BMT Execution:
This part of the program usually takes six months and is conducted in a Burger King restaurant. This is where you will practise and perfect everything that you have learned so far. You will be given specific things to achieve in crew training, administrative control, safety/security, equipment maintenance, and restaurant operations. You will be expected to manage them all effectively. At the end of six months, you will be rated by your supervisor.

IMT Classroom (Intermediate Management Training):
During one week of classroom training, you will begin moving into more "managerial" training. You will learn more about employee interviewing, crew motivation, and scheduling employees.

IMT Execution:
During another six months of in-restaurant training, your responsibilities will be expanded a bit. You will be expected to apply the skills of interviewing, motivation, crew development, performance appraisal, and managing restaurant finance. Notice that you are gradually taking on more and more managerial responsibilities. You will be evaluated again at the end of your six-month period.

AMT Classroom (Advanced Management Training):
You will return for a one week classroom session where you will improve your skills in delegation, problem solving/decision making, training for results, delegating responsibility, STP (Supervisory Training Program) reinforcement, and full equipment seminars. The AMT is for Senior Assistant Managers.

AMT Execution:
This is the last of the required RMT program. During another six months in a restaurant, you will be expected to accomplish specific performance objectives in delegation, problem solving, and personal planning under the guidance of your restaurant manager. If you have done a good job, you might well be on your way to a promotion to restaurant manager. ▲

A typical assessment centre might be set up in a large conference room and go on for two or three days. During this time, managers and potential managers might take selection tests, engage in management games, make individual presentations, and conduct group discussions. In a program like this the assessors look to see how each participant reacts to stress or to criticism by colleagues. They also watch to see which candidates emerge as leaders of the group discussions.

Evaluating Training and Development Programs

The goals of any training or development program are to improve employees' skills and performances, and thus the performance of the company as a whole. Any program that does not meet these goals wastes company resources. Accordingly, human resource specialists are often called upon to assess the effectiveness of training and development programs. Generally, assessment evaluates how well people perform before and after they go through the training.

For example, consider a clerical staff member who types 50 words per minute. If a training program raises that individual's typing speed to 70 words per minute, the manager will probably be satisfied that the training was effective. On the other hand, if accident rates remain unchanged following a training program in accident prevention, the manager will probably conclude that the training was not effective.

PERFORMANCE APPRAISAL

performance appraisal

Performance appraisals are a formal evaluation of how well workers are doing their jobs. Every company assesses the performance of its employees in some way, even if it is only the owner telling the only employee, a receptionist, "Good job. You're getting a raise." In larger firms, the process is more extensive. A formal performance evaluation system generally involves a regularly scheduled written assessment. The written evaluation, however, is only one part of a multistep process.

The appraisal process begins when a manager makes job performance expectations clear to an employee. The manager must then observe the employee's performance. If the standards are clearly defined, a manager should have little difficulty with the next step—comparing expectations with actual performance. For some jobs, a rating scale like that illustrated in Figure 11-4 is useful. This comparison forms the basis for a written appraisal and for decisions about any raise, promotion, demotion, or firing of the employee. The final step in the appraisal process is for the manager to meet with the employee to discuss the appraisal and reach an agreement about the employee's general level of performance.

When job performance expectations are based on the actual requirements of the job, formal appraisals benefit both the company and workers. The company is protected from lawsuits charging unfair treatment. It also has a reasonably objective basis on which to compare individuals for promotions. Workers benefit from clear goals to work toward and knowledge of how well they are doing. They often feel that such systems are fairer than subjective evaluations.

Formal appraisal systems do have drawbacks, however. Most problems revolve around difficulties in measuring employees' actual performance. For a few jobs, measuring actual performance is easy and straightforward. But for most employees, it is much harder to assess their performance.

COMPENSATING THE WORK FORCE

compensation system

Employees who do not meet managers' expectations are a fact of business life. But in a company that follows the principles of good human resource management, such individuals should be few in number. Workers who perform well—who show a good employee-job match—are a real asset to a firm. Therefore, it is in every business's self-interest to retain effective employees. A major factor in retaining skilled workers is a company's **compensation system**—what it offers employees in return for their labour.

FIGURE 11-4 GRAPHIC RATING SCALES.

VM Variety Manufacturing

Employee's Name ______________________________

Supervisor's Name ______________________________

Part 1. Circle the most descriptive point on each scale.

INITIATIVE

1	2	3	4	5
Never Does Anything Without Being Told		Handles Simple Matters Alone		Handles All Functions Without Help

PUNCTUALITY

1	2	3	4	5
Is Almost Always Late		Is Seldom Late		Is Never Late

CLEANLINESS

1	2	3	4	5
Work Area Is Always Dirty and Messy		Work Area Is Generally Clean and Orderly		Work Area Is Always Clean and Orderly

Please complete the separate evaluation form on page two.

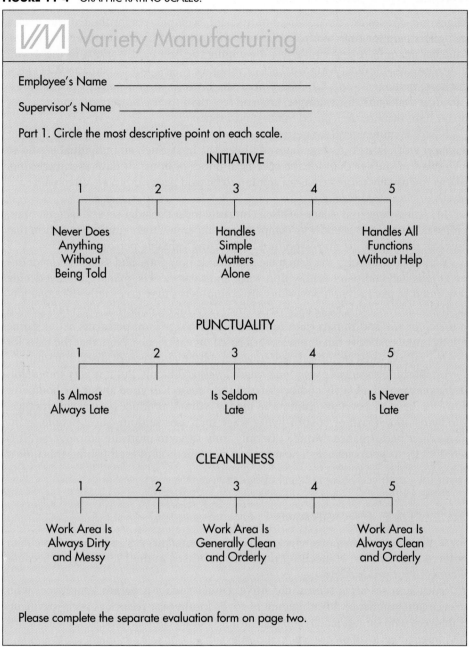

Wages and salaries are a key part of any compensation system, but most systems also include features such as incentives and employee benefits programs. We will explore each of these elements in this section. Bear in mind, however, that finding the right combination of elements is complicated by the need to make employees feel valued while simultaneously keeping company costs to a minimum. Thus, compensation systems are highly individualized, depending on the nature of the industry, the company, and the types of workers involved.

WAGES AND SALARIES

wages

LEARNING OBJECTIVE 5

Explain the importance of wages and salaries, incentives, and benefits programs in attracting and keeping skilled workers.

Wages and salaries are the dollar amounts paid to employees for their work. **Wages** are dollars paid for time worked. Workers who are paid by the hour receive wages. Canadian manufacturing employees are among the best paid workers in the world. Only German manufacturing workers earn higher wages. But Canadian white collar workers, managers, and CEOs are near the bottom in compensation rankings. Canadian managers, for example, are paid less than their counterparts in Germany, Japan, Italy, Britain, the United States, and France.[16]

salary

Salary is money paid for getting a job done. An executive earning $100 000 per year may work five hours one day and fifteen the next. Such an individual is paid to get a job done rather than for the specific number of hours or days spent working. Salaries are usually expressed as an amount to be paid per year but are often paid each month or every two weeks.

In setting wage and salary levels, a company must consider several factors. First, it must take into account how its competitors compensate their employees. A firm that pays less than its rivals may soon find itself losing valuable personnel.

Within the company, the firm must also decide how wage and salary levels for different jobs will compare. And within wage and salary levels, managers must decide how much to pay individual workers. Two employees may do exactly the same job, but the employee with more experience may earn more, in part to keep that person in the company and in part because the experienced person performs better. Some union contracts specify differential wages based on experience. Note that the basis for differential pay must be job-related, however, not favouritism or discrimination.

Establishing acceptable wage and salary levels is difficult. But it is very important. Employees must feel fairly compensated if they are to feel good about the company. However, beyond a certain point more money will not produce better performance. And across-the-board or cost-of-living wage increases seldom cause people to increase their performance. Money can only truly serve to motivate employees if it is tied directly to performance. The most common method of establishing this link is to use incentive programs.[17]

INCENTIVE PROGRAMS

incentive program

The term **incentive programs** refers to special pay programs designed to motivate high performance. The use of incentive programs increased in the 1980s, largely because of concern for productivity.

Sales bonuses are a typical incentive. Under such a program, employees who sell a certain number or dollar amount of goods for the year receive a special payment. Employees who do not reach this goal earn no bonus. Similarly, *merit salary systems* link raises to performance levels in nonsales jobs. For example, many baseball players have clauses in their contracts that pay them bonuses for hitting over .300, making the All-Star game, or being named Most Valuable Player. Executives commonly receive stock options and bonuses as an incentive.

gain-sharing plan

profit-sharing plan

Some incentive programs apply to all employees in a firm. **Gain-sharing plans** distribute bonuses to all employees in a company based upon reduced costs from working more efficiently. **Profit-sharing plans** are based on profit levels in the firm. Profits earned above a certain level are distributed to employees.[18] Stock ownership by employees serves as an incentive to lower costs, increase productivity and profits and thus increase the value of the employees' stock. The Ethics in management insert "Are Top Executives Paid Too Much?" addresses the controversial issue of compensation levels of top managers.

ETHICS IN MANAGEMENT

Are Top Executives Paid Too Much?

Top executives in Canada can earn well over $500 000 per year. Some earn over $1 million, and a few earn even more. Illustrative salaries for top Canadian managers in 1992 are as follows:

Robert Smith (American Barrick)	$4.5 million
Edgar Bronfman (Seagram)	3.7 million
Anthony Petrina (Placer Dome)	2.6 million
Desmond Hudson (Northern Telecom)	2.3 million
William Holland (United Dominion)	1.0 million

In addition to getting high compensation when they are working for a company, executives may also receive large compensation when they leave. When Paul Stern resigned as president and CEO of Northern Telecom, for example, the company came up with a severance package that totalled approximately $3 million. This included two years' salary and benefits, 10 years of credited service to his pension plan, and the purchase of his home.

Some business firms will end up paying large sums of money to executives after they retire. An executive who earned a large salary during his or her time with the company may represent a liability to the company of more than $5 million dollars (assuming that the executive lives for 15 years after he or she retires).

In spite of this, the compensation of top Canadian managers does not appear to be out of line in comparison with what executives in other countries are paid. A 1991 compensation study by Towers Perrin showed that the average compensation for CEOs heading up companies with sales of about $250 million was as follows:

Country	CEO Compensation
United States	$747 500
France	448 500
Italy	421 300
Canada	407 600
United Kingdom	399 600
Japan	371 800
Germany	364 500

While Canadian salaries are higher than those of top executives in Japan and Germany, they are much lower than those in the U.S. The chair of UAL Corp., for example, was paid over $18 million in 1990. In 1990, the top twenty U.S. executives each earned more than $5.8 million.

Besides the question of absolute salaries paid to top executives, there is the issue of whether their salaries should move up and down in relation to their company's performance. Does this happen? Sometimes, but it is not hard to find cases where executive salaries go up while company profit goes down. For example, Imperial Oil Ltd. where, in a year when profit fell 37 percent, Chairman Arden Haynes' total compensation package went up 12 percent. Similar situations were evident in other companies, including Bell Canada Enterprises, Canadian Occidental Petroleum, Canadian Pacific, and Westcoast Transmission Co. Ltd.

Recent Statistics Canada data show that the average hourly paid worker in Canada earns slightly more than $20 000 per year. Are the large differences in compensation between hourly workers and CEOs warranted? How do we determine what a top executive is worth? Those who defend large executive salaries suggest an instructive comparison with professional sports, where one superstar can make a team. A similar argument might be made that a certain CEO could make a company. As in professional sports, a business firm may have little alternative but to pay a seemingly large salary to a top manager.

A key issue in this debate is the determination of executive performance. Unlike a professional superstar—whose performance stats are objective and easily measured, a top executive operates in an environment of considerable uncertainty. How should executive performance be measured? Ideally, the board of directors should clearly indicate the goals they want the company to achieve (for example, a certain level of competitiveness or quality), and then reward the CEO for achieving those goals. Unfortunately, many boards do not have the confidence or insight to set such goals. They may also be reluctant to deal firmly with CEOs on the issue of salary.

But shareholders have no such reluctance, and they are increasingly demanding a say in executive compensation decisions. For example, there has recently been much lobbying for laws that force companies to disclose the salaries and benefit schemes of their executives. The Ontario Securities Commission has put a proposal before the Ontario government to require companies to describe the internal process that is used to determine executive compensation.

The recession of the early 1990s has put the brakes on executive compensation to some extent. A survey conducted by Hay Group management consultants showed that 40 percent of CEOs received no increase at all in 1993.

Still, to many critics, it is simply not "right" that top executives receive 20, 50, or even 100 times more than their workers receive. They argue that it is unethical to pay top executives $1 million or $5 million a year for what they do.

Is it unethical for top executives to receive such high salaries? What are the alternatives? ▲

Comparable Worth

LEARNING OBJECTIVE 6
Describe how laws regarding employment equity, pay equity, and worker safety affect human resource management.

In spite of recent advances, women still earn less than men. Women who work full-time earn about 65 percent as much as men who work full-time ($21 012 vs. $31 865).[19] The ratio is only four percentage points higher than it was in the late 1970s. Single women earn 93.5 percent of what single men earn, while married women earn only 60.8 percent of what married men earn. Most top jobs in the federal civil service are held by men, while women continue to be concentrated in the lower paying clerical positions.

comparable worth

Comparable worth is a legal concept that aims at paying equal wages for jobs that are of comparable value to the employer. This might mean comparing dissimilar jobs, such as those of nurses and truck mechanics or secretaries and electricians. Proponents of comparable worth say that all the jobs in a company must be evaluated and then rated in terms of basic dimensions such as the level of skill they require. All jobs could then be compared based on a common index. People in different jobs that rate the same on this index would be paid the same. Experts hope that this will help to reduce the gap between men's and women's pay.

Critics of comparable worth object on the grounds that it ignores the supply and demand aspects of labour. They say, for example, that legislation forcing a company to pay people more than the open market price for their labour (which may happen in jobs where there is a surplus of workers) is another example of unreasonable government interference in business activities. They also argue that implementing comparable worth will cost business firms too much money. A study prepared for the Ontario Ministry of Labour estimated that it would cost approximately $10 billion for the public and private sectors in Ontario to establish equitable payment for jobs of equal value. Yet the cost defence cannot be easily used. In one case, the Quebec Human Rights Commission ruled that 24 female office employees of the Quebec North Shore Paper Company were performing work of equal value to that done by male production workers. The company was required to increase the secretaries' salaries by $701 annually and give them over $1000 in back pay.[20]

PROVIDING HUMAN RESOURCE SERVICES

As well as the major functions already noted, human resource departments are involved in other activities important to the firm's personnel. These include benefits programs, employee health and safety, retirement, and miscellaneous other services.

Benefits Programs

benefits

A growing part of nearly every firm's compensation system is **benefits** programs. Benefits now often comprise over half a firm's total compensation budget. Most companies are required by law to provide workers' compensation, holiday pay, and Canada Pension Plan and unemployment insurance contributions. Most businesses also voluntarily provide extended health, life, and disability insurance. Many also allow employees to buy stock through payroll deductions at a slightly discounted price. In the 1980s, many firms began to provide vision care and dental benefits to employees. Some even provide free legal services to employees.

As the range of benefits has grown, so has concern about containing their cost. Businesses are experimenting with a variety of procedures to cut benefits costs, while maintaining the ability to attract, retain, and maintain the morale of employees.[21] One new approach is the use of **cafeteria benefits.** These plans provide a set dollar amount in benefits and allow employees to pick among alternatives. Employees at Toyota's Cambridge, Ontario, plant are given the opportunity once each year to structure their benefits packages. For example, they can give more weight to dental coverage if they have young children, or to life insurance or disability coverage, depending on their circumstances.[22] More and more firms are using "temporary" workers on a long-term basis. Since they are not covered by most companies' benefits, temporary workers allow businesses to keep staff levels high and benefits costs low.

cafeteria benefits

Benefits are an important part of most compensation programs. Some are provided by the employer while others are mandated by the government. A new parental leave provision allows either parent to take up to ten weeks of paid leave after the birth or adoption of a child.

Rising benefits costs have also made managers more aware of the need for businesses to communicate with their employees about benefits. Often, employees do not fully understand—and thus appreciate—their benefits. Personnel specialists can increase employees' awareness about their benefits by providing clearly written handbooks and by holding meetings in which workers can get answers to their questions about benefits.

EMPLOYEE SAFETY AND HEALTH

Employee safety and health programs help to reduce absenteeism and labour turnover, raise productivity, and boost morale by making jobs safer and more healthful.

Government regulations about employee safety are getting stricter. Ontario, which loses more than 7 million working days yearly because of on-the-job injuries, has passed amendments to the Ontario Occupational Health and Safety Act. Officers and directors of companies will be held personally responsible for workplace health and safety and will be punishable by jail terms and fines for permitting unsafe working conditions.[23]

Some industrial work—logging, construction, and mining—can put workers at risk of injury in obvious ways. But other work, such as typing or lifting, can also cause painful injuries. Repetitive strain injury is becoming much more common. At Cuddy Food Products (the sole supplier of poultry products to McDonald's), as many as 44 workers per month became disabled from repetitive strain injury. The company instituted a plan to redesign how workers performed their jobs and trained people to avoid injuries. During one nine-month period after the training, not a single repetitive strain injury was reported. At CP Rail, injuries were reduced 50 percent when employees did ten minutes of warm-up exercises before beginning work.[24]

In Canada, each province has developed its own workplace health and safety regulations. The purpose of these laws is to ensure that employees do not have to work in dangerous conditions. These laws are the direct result of undesirable conditions that existed in many Canadian businesses at the close of the nineteenth century. While much improvement is evident, Canada still has some problems with workplace health and safety. In one study of six western industrialized nations, Canada had the worst safety record in mining and construction and the second worst record in manufacturing and railways.

The Ontario Occupational Health and Safety Act illustrates current legislation in Canada. It requires that all employers ensure that equipment and safety devices are used properly. Employers must also show workers the proper way to operate machinery. At the job site, supervisors are charged with the responsibility of seeing that workers use equipment properly. The act also requires workers to behave appropriately on the job. Employees have the right to refuse to work on a job if they believe it is unsafe; a legal procedure exists for resolving any disputes in this area.

In most provinces, the Ministry of Labour appoints inspectors to enforce health and safety regulations. If the inspector finds a sufficient hazard, he or she has the authority to clear the work place. Inspectors can usually come to a firm unannounced to conduct an inspection.

Increasing numbers of companies are providing pre-retirement counselling services to employees. This counselling provides both financial and lifestyle information to those employees who are nearing retirement.

Retirement

Some employees are ready for retirement much earlier than others. But because most retirement plans are based on an employee's age, some workers who should retire earlier stay on the job while others, who are still useful workers, leave before they would like to. This policy is short-sighted. A compromise is to grant year-to-year extensions to productive employees who want to continue working but who have reached retirement age. Recently several workers in different locations across Canada have successfully challenged mandatory retirement rules. Their employers must allow them to work even though they are past the traditional retirement age.

More and more executives will be staying on past the age of 65, partly because the company needs their expertise and partly because the idea of mandatory retirement at age 65 has become outdated. Arthur Childs (CEO of Burns Foods) is 80; Sol Kanee (Soo Line Mills Ltd.) is 81; Vernon Aanenson (Old Dutch Foods Ltd.) is 74; and Jack Diamond (Western Coast Reduction Ltd.) is 81. All these people are active managers.[25]

Many personnel departments provide preretirement counselling. Special educational programs inform people who are about to retire about important retirement-related matters like Social Insurance benefits, Canada Pension Plan provisions, investments, and second careers inside or outside the firm. In a sense, such preretirement counselling is the final step in the human resource department's overall employee career management program.

Miscellaneous Services

Human resource departments also provide many other services, which vary widely among firms. These range from setting policies to deal with allegations of sexual harassment on the job to helping employees arrange car pools.

At Levac Supply Ltd. of Kingston, Ontario, one employee harassed another with derogatory remarks over a 14-year period. In spite of the fact that the Ontario Human Rights Code excludes companies from liability in the case of sexual harassment (as long as they make a reasonable effort to stop the harassment), a board of inquiry ruled that the company was jointly responsible with the employee who had actually done the harassing. The woman who was harassed was awarded $48 273 in a settlement.[26]

Time and circumstances greatly affect the nature of human resource work. For example, a firm may experience a big decrease in one department's workload and a big increase in another department's workload. The human resource department might help the two department managers to shift workers between departments, help arrange retraining if that is needed, or help to develop a plan for sharing the available work among employees—shorter work weeks for all workers or layoffs in order of seniority.

Human resource departments in many firms help to develop flexible work schedules. Flextime, as opposed to fixed working hours, makes it easier for many workers, especially working mothers, to enter the labour force. The concept of flextime is discussed in more detail in Chapter 12. Although it may present some scheduling problems, flextime also makes it possible for some employees to work full-time instead of having to settle for part-time work.

Companies are increasingly making provisions for disabled employees. At Rogers Cable TV Ltd., for example, a large workplace area was completely redesigned to accommodate workers who were either visually disabled or in wheelchairs. Special equipment was also installed—a large-print computer for workers with partial sight, and a device that allows blind workers to read printed materials.[27]

TERMINATING AND DEMOTING WORKERS

Written appraisals are especially important when a business must fire or demote employees either because of poor worker performance or because the firm is reorganizing or is in economic trouble. Whether the worker or the company is the problem, demoting or firing employees is one of the duties a manager least wants to perform. The task may be made easier by writing a glowing recommendation or securing a good severance arrangement for an employee let go because of company changes. And when the employee is causing a problem, a systematic process can help the manager—and the employee.

Most companies with formal systems have a step-by-step process of warnings and punishments leading up to dismissal. For the first warning, the manager might well talk informally to the employee, expressing disappointment over the problem—poor job performance or attendance, for example. To protect itself from lawsuits, many companies require managers to give the offending employee a written warning. An employee causing a problem can also expect to hear about it during a formal appraisal. At that time, the manager will specify certain changes that the employee must make or lose the job. This system not only protects the company, it also lets employees know that their jobs are in jeopardy and offers them a chance to do better.

Companies must be careful when dismissing employees. For example, a general manager at Jumbo Video Inc. who was fired when he refused to take a large pay cut, was awarded more than $226 000 in damages from his employer. The manager had earlier signed a contract containing certain stipulations that the company later tried to void because of financial problems. The manager was told that if he did not take the reduction in pay, he would be let go. The judge ruled that the company had reneged on the contract.[28] The Management at Work insert "The World of 'Unjust Dismissal' " gives further information on the issue of employee dismissal.

MANAGEMENT AT WORK

THE WORLD OF "UNJUST DISMISSAL"

Legislation on unjust dismissal was added to the Canada Labour Code in 1978. It covers nonunionized, nonmanagement employees in federally regulated industries such as banking, transportation, and telecommunications and is designed to provide a cheap, fast, and effective route for employees to appeal an unfair firing without having to go to court.

An employee who thinks he or she has been unjustly fired files a complaint with Labour Canada. If the complaint is judged worthwhile, the employer is contacted and asked to give the reason why the employee was fired. A Labour Canada inspector then reviews the case and tries to persuade the two parties to agree. If the parties cannot agree, the case is sent to an adjudicator who either upholds the dismissal or orders the employee reinstated. If either side disputes the judgment, it can request a judicial review.

The legislation requires that the employee be given the benefit of the doubt whenever possible. The company must prove it had "just cause" in firing the person. Since adjudicators do not have to base their decisions on precedent, it is difficult for a company to predict the outcome of a complaint.

Critics of the legislation point to cases in which they feel poor decisions were made. Consider the case of a Canadian Imperial Bank of Commerce employee who was fired because of her off-hours associations. Police burst into her apartment at precisely the time five men were dividing the loot from a robbery at a nearby CIBC branch. The Labour Canada adjudicator who reviewed the case ruled that the bank did not have "just cause" for firing her because she had not done anything wrong herself. CIBC was ordered to give her back pay. A bank supervisor from another bank got her job back even after she admitted that she had planned to steal customers' money. A consumer credit officer in

• • •

another firm was reinstated despite his conviction on weapons charges.

Because of the time and risk involved, many employers settle before the adjudication stage. Nearly 75 percent of the 600 complaints that are brought annually are resolved before they get to adjudication and another 10 percent are resolved before the adjudicator's report. Critics of the legislation argue that the cost of the procedure and the potential for reinstatement give "daring" employees an incentive to complain. They would like to see more training of adjudicators, transcriptions of proceedings, and adjudicators given the right to award costs against a frivolous complaint.

Even prominent managers may go to court over wrongful dismissal. Robert Campeau, who took Campeau Corp. to the edge of bankruptcy, is asking for damages of $10 million from the company. He claims his employment was improperly terminated when he was fired as CEO of Campeau. Recently, Joel Bell, who was fired as head of Canada Development Investment Corp., received $3.3 million in a wrongful dismissal suit. ▲

If a problem persists, a manager may have little choice but to discipline, demote, or dismiss the employee. Disciplinary actions—such as suspending a worker from the job without pay for several days—are usually taken only when the employee's behaviour is dangerous or disruptive. For example, someone who strikes a fellow worker might be sent home to "cool off."

Demotions may be used when managerial personnel fail to meet expectations. Because demoted managers are humiliated by this downgrading they may seek jobs elsewhere. Companies sometimes demote managers they want to get rid of—actually hoping the person will quit.

Finally, in extreme cases, outright termination of the employee may be the only recourse. For example, a salesperson who continually falls far short of the established quota may be a drag on corporate profitability. Although firing is never pleasant, managers of companies with sound human resource policies can take some solace in knowing that, by the time such a dismissal takes place, the employee should be expecting it.

MEETING THE CHALLENGE

Achieving Employment Equity in Canada

In 1990, to determine what progress has been made on employment equity, the Conference Board of Canada sent a questionnaire to 365 federally regulated organizations covered under the Employment Equity Act. The following results were reported:

- More than 80 percent of the responding firms had developed an employment equity program.
- Forty-six percent had established an employment equity office to coordinate initiatives.
- Seventy-five percent of respondents said they were in the process of reviewing their recruitment, hiring, and development practices.
- Ninety-six percent reported that a senior person was responsible for the program—nearly half report directly to the CEO and half to the head of human resources.
- Seventy percent of firms' employment equity budgets go to administration, staffing and reporting requirements. This leaves 10 percent for developing actual programs, 10 percent for management and supervisory training, and 10 percent for employee communications.

Organizations were asked to rate the effectiveness of equity programs in raising the employment levels of the four designated groups. Advertising and outreach programs were rated only moderately successful whereas interviewer training was seen as much more effective. Women were judged as benefiting most, with visible minorities following closely. Employment equity programs were noticeably less effective in raising the employment levels of Aboriginal people and people with disabilities.

The Conference Board survey also identified some barriers to employment equity. Some firms said that factors beyond their control were inhibiting their ability to meet their employment equity goals. For example, several airline and shipping firms noted that government licensing requirements often screen out members of the four designated groups. They also noted that candidates were simply not available in some occupations. ▲

SUMMARY

Human resource management involves developing, administering, and evaluating programs to acquire and enhance the quality and performance of people in a business. Good managers always bear in mind the principle of job-relatedness—that human resource decisions and policies should be based on the requirements of a job. Managers who apply this principle and match the right employee to the right job produce satisfied, effective workers.

Planning for future human resource needs entails several steps. Conducting a job analysis enables managers to create detailed, job-related job descriptions and specifications. Managers must then forecast supply and demand for the types of workers they will need. Only then can managers devise strategies to match supply with demand.

Staffing a business may involve hiring from outside the company. Such external staffing requires the company first to recruit applicants and then to select from among the applicants. Companies must ensure that they do not discriminate against candidates during this phase of the process. The selection phase typically includes interviewing, testing, and checking the references of applicants. Whenever possible, however, many companies prefer to fill positions internally, by promoting existing personnel.

If a company is to get the most out of its workers; it must develop those workers. Nearly all employees undergo some initial orientation process. Many also acquire new skills through on-the-job training, off-the-job training, and/or management development programs. Performance appraisals help managers decide who needs training and who should be promoted. Appraisals also tell employees how well they are doing at meeting expectations. Employees who continually fail to meet performance or behaviour expectations may be disciplined, demoted, or terminated.

Compensation programs include wages and salaries, incentives, and benefits for workers. By paying its workers as well as or better than competitors do, a business can attract and keep qualified personnel. Incentive programs such as sales bonuses, gain-sharing, and profit-sharing can also motivate existing personnel to work more effectively. Benefits programs may increase employee satisfaction but are a major expense to businesses today.

In hiring, training, compensating and/or firing workers, managers must obey many laws. Equal employment opportunity and equal pay laws forbid discrimination other than that based on legitimate job requirements. Controversy over what constitutes discrimination in paying men and women who hold different jobs is a current issue. Managers are also required to provide employees with a safe working environment.

KEY TERMS

human resource management (p. 314)
job-relatedness (p. 314)
job analysis (p. 316)
job description (p. 316)
job specification (p. 316)
recruitment (p. 318)
Canadian Human Rights Act (p. 319)
bona fide occupational requirement (p. 319)
Employment Equity Act of 1986 (p. 320)
selection (p. 321)
closed promotion system (p. 324)
open promotion system (p. 324)
orientation (p. 325)
on-the-job training (p. 325)
off-the-job training (p. 325)
management development programs (p. 326)
assessment centre (p. 326)
performance appraisal (p. 328)
compensation system (p. 328)
wages (p. 330)
salary (p. 330)
incentive program (p. 330)
gain-sharing plan (p. 330)
profit-sharing plan (p. 330)
comparable worth (p. 332)
benefits (p. 332)
cafeteria benefits (p. 333)

REVIEW QUESTIONS

1. Explain how the job description, job analysis, and job specification differ.
2. What is the purpose of the Canadian Human Rights Act? What are its specific provisions?
3. Explain how an assessment centre operates.
4. What are the two bases that are used to pay employees?
5. What is "comparable worth?" Give examples of pay adjustments that have been made as a result of this concept.
6. What actions have the federal and provincial governments taken to ensure employee safety on the job?
7. Why is a good employee-job match important? Who benefits more, the organization or the employee? Why?
8. Identify as many advantages and disadvantages as you can for internal and external staffing. Under what circumstances is each more appropriate?
9. Why is formal training so important? Why not just let people learn about their jobs as they do them?

DISCUSSION QUESTIONS

1. What problems exist in Canada regarding matching jobs with people?
2. "Government legislation in the human resources area reduces a firm's flexibility, and hence its effectiveness, in its use of human resources." Comment.
3. Under what circumstances would on-the-job training be most appropriate? When would off-the-job training be most appropriate?
4. How might an assessment centre be an example of a self-fulfilling prophecy?
5. What practical problems might arise as the concept of comparable worth is implemented?
6. Is the human resource management function valuable to business organizations? Defend your answer.
7. How has government legislation affected the human resource management process?
8. "The process of hiring people is really an art; since you cannot know in advance whether a person will work out, selection and testing activities are really not worthwhile." Comment.
9. "Since the concept of comparable worth ignores the market in determining what wages should be paid to people, it is inconsistent with our capitalist economy and should not be used." Comment.
10. How are overtime wages different from and similar to incentive program payments?
11. Select a job currently held by you or a close friend or relative. Draw up a job description and job specification for this position.
12. Did you have to take a test to be admitted to school? How valid do you think your score was as a predictor of academic success? Why?
13. What benefits do you consider most and least important in attracting workers? In keeping workers? In motivating workers?
14. Have you or anyone you know been discriminated against in a hiring decision? Was anything done about it?

EXERCISES

1. Read an article in a Canadian business publication on the topic of comparable worth. What arguments are made for and against the concept? What is the prevailing view of the appropriateness of comparable worth?
2. Have a debate on the following issue: "Employees whose skills are obsolete should be replaced with new employees whose skills are up-to-date because this is cheaper than retraining the existing employees."
3. For the following jobs, which phase of the human resource management process (recruiting, selecting, training, appraising, compensating, and promoting) would require special attention?
   a. an assembly line worker
   b. an instructor in a community college
   c. a secretary
   d. a sales representative for a computer manufacturer

4. Look in the "Employment Opportunities" section of *The Globe and Mail* for advertisements for salespeople and computer technicians. Do these jobs require a clear pattern of experience and training?
5. Interview a human resource manager at a local company. Select a position for which the firm is currently recruiting applicants and identify the steps in the selection process.
6. Obtain a copy of an employment application. Examine it carefully and determine how useful it might be in making a hiring decision.

MANAGEMENT ON LOCATION

CASE 11-1
BEING FAIR TO EMPLOYEES

The Employment Equity Act of 1986 requires federally regulated companies to hire more members of four designated groups: visible minorities, women, Native people, and people with disabilities. Companies must file annual reports stating their progress and if they do not, they face penalties. Canada Messenger Transportation Systems Inc. is one company that has learned this lesson. During a period of rapid expansion in 1990, the firm was so busy hiring 200 new workers that it did not file its report on time. The controller at Canadian Messenger estimated it would take two to three weeks to complete the report satisfactorily for Employment and Immigration. The government laid a failure-to-comply charge, and the firm was fined $1500; Employment and Immigration's 1990 annual report also named it for its failure to report.

Many firms are concerned that the regulations will become even stricter. In 1988, an advocacy group for the disabled filed nine complaints with the Canadian Human Rights Commission, charging that not enough workers with disabilities were being hired. In 1990, the Assembly of Manitoba Chiefs filed 49 comparable complaints dealing with Native rights. And now, municipal governments are introducing tighter regulations. Companies doing business with the City of Toronto must file a report that details their hiring practices for each of the four groups. Other cities, including Calgary, Montreal, and Halifax, have also set equity policies.

Obtaining the information needed to file reports with Employment and Immigration can be time-consuming and costly. Most of the implementation costs are incurred through surveying employees, tracking their career paths, and reporting the results to government. Bell Canada's Associate Director of Human Rights and Employment Equity explains that Bell began planning for employment equity in 1986 by sending a questionnaire to the firm's 60 000 employees in Ontario and Quebec. It then developed a system to track an employee's job history and to generate the required government report. Because the response rate to the questionnaire was 80 percent, there was some concern that some of the 20 percent of nonrespondents may have been members of one of the designated groups. ▲

QUESTIONS

1. Assume that you are the owner of a small but rapidly expanding business. How might the Employment Equity Act of 1986 affect your day-to-day operations?
2. Suppose that in trying to comply with the act you send out a questionnaire to your employees asking them to state whether they are members of any of the four groups identified in the legislation. What would you do if some employees refused to respond to the questionnaire and you knew that many of the nonrespondents were members of a minority group well represented among your employees?
3. To what extent is government legislation going to help solve the problem of discrimination against groups like Native people, women, disabled people, and visible minorities?

MANAGEMENT ON LOCATION

CASE 11-2
WORKING FOR TWO

For decades, business had one simple rule for dealing with pregnant employees—get rid of them. At worst, a pregnant woman might be handed her walking papers and told to have a nice life. At best she would be told to go home until her "delicate condition" had passed. But as increasing numbers of young women have streamed into the workplace armed with antidiscrimination laws, businesses have been forced to rethink their attitudes and rework their policies.

The Canadian Human Rights Act prohibits discrimination against women because of pregnancy as does all provincial human rights legislation. Under the Manitoba Human Rights Act, for example, women cannot be "unreasonably discriminated against in any aspect of employment because of pregnancy, the possibility of pregnancy, or circumstances related to pregnancy." Refusing employment, firing, biassed treatment, or reduced benefits are all against the law.

While the United States has a similar sounding law, it (along with South Africa) is the only industrialized nation that has no policy guaranteeing maternity leave and pay. Even Japan, noted for its discrimination against working women, requires that women receive 12 weeks of leave at 60 percent of their normal pay. Canadian law permits a woman up to 17 weeks of paid maternity leave at 60 percent of her salary. Either parent can take an additional ten weeks of paid parental leave.

Women employed by more enlightened firms may still face special problems during pregnancy. Of perhaps greatest concern is the risk to the developing fetus posed by hazards in the work environment. For example, studies have shown much higher miscarriage rates among women working in the "clean" rooms of microchip manufacturers. Experts believe that the acids and gases used to etch these vital silicon computer components may be at the root of a 39 percent miscarriage rate (versus 20 percent in the general population) among women who work there.

It appears that not all environmental hazards are confined to the factory floor, though. In fact, if preliminary studies are borne out, one of the greatest threats to the pregnant woman may come in the form of VDT radiation. VDTs—video display terminals for computers—have been shown to double the miscarriage rate among women who use them more than 20 hours a week. So far, neither government nor labour seems inclined to investigate this finding. But the day may come when companies face a need to shuffle office work away from machines that are anything but user friendly for pregnant employees. ▲

QUESTIONS

1. Identify three types of jobs, other than those given in this case, in which employers could legally refuse to hire a pregnant woman. Name three types of jobs in which such a refusal would be illegal.
2. Do you believe pregnant women should be given at least partial pay while on leave? Why or why not?
3. Assume you own a small company. What do you believe is the greatest advantage in holding open a position for a pregnant worker who wishes to return to her job? What do you see as the greatest drawback?
4. How might a manager of a department with many young women employees assure that work gets done despite the absence of some on maternity leave?

CASE 11-3
UP AND OUT

Donovan Retzlaffe, chairman and chief executive officer (CEO) of Lanark Products Ltd. announced on July 1, 1989, that he had reluctantly accepted the resignation of the firm's vice-chair, Lorenzo Valli. In his announcement, Retzlaffe indicated that Valli had served the firm well and had been a "rock of Gibraltar" during the 49 years he had worked there.

The rise of Valli from mailroom clerk to vice-chair is the stuff that legends are made of. Valli constantly said that there was nothing more important than loyalty to the firm. He joined Lanark in 1940 at the age of 19. He began working in the mailroom, and over the next 43 years gradually worked his way up the corporate ladder until he became vice-chair in 1983. Valli fondly remembers the time that the company loaned him $4500 in 1958 to pay some legal bills that he had incurred. Valli was a no-nonsense, simple man. When he stepped down, he still lived in the same modest home that he had purchased in 1961.

Although the public announcement indicated that Valli had resigned, insiders at Lanark knew that he had actually been asked to leave because his management style was just too "abrasive" for the new image Lanark Products Ltd. was cultivating. It was also widely believed that there was a basic personality conflict between the CEO and Valli, even though the two had been working closely together for about 10 years. Some senior managers expressed the view that the company should never have given Valli the position of vice-chair if they thought his style was too abrasive.

The "resignation" of Valli had some industry observers worried because of other events at Lanark. Employment statistics in early 1989 showed that nearly half of Lanark's upper management personnel had been with the firm for less than two years. This was partially the result of rapid expansion of the firm's activities. There had also been a rather large number of middle-level managers leaving the firm. Although the reasons weren't completely clear, there were indications that they were not happy with the new direction of the firm. ▲

QUESTIONS

1. Do you think that Lanark Ltd. treated Valli fairly in asking him to resign after 45 years of service?
2. Was his dismissal handled properly? How would you have handled the situation?
3. If you were the CEO of Lanark Ltd., would you be concerned that nearly half the top managers had been with the firm for less than two years? If you were concerned, what would you do about it? How would you go about determining if there is a problem with the middle-level managers?

CASE 11-4
THE HARRIED DEPARTMENT HEAD

Ron Colindale was the head of the department of management at a large university. Total university enrollment for the past year had been approximately 20 000 and was increasing slowly each year, despite earlier predictions that it would decline in the 1980s. Demand for spaces in the business school was even higher than that for the university as a whole. For example, the previous year 1345 students applied for admission to the business school; only 485 were admitted because of limited teaching staff.

Unlike many other faculties on campus, the business school was actively recruiting teachers in an attempt to satisfy the demand for management education. As a department head, Colindale was responsible for recruiting, but he was rapidly becoming frustrated by the rigid rules and regulations he had to follow. Two factors were at the root of his frustration: (1) very few ...

people who had a Ph.D. in business could be attracted to teaching, and (2) recruiting rules were very strict. For example, Colindale had discovered that if he wanted to hire an American, he had to prove that no equally qualified Canadian applicants were available. Colindale didn't have any particular preference for American faculty but, since many more candidates with Ph.D.s were produced in the United States than in Canada, he would have more candidates to choose from.

Explicit directions had been provided for the wording and publication timing of advertisements Colindale wanted to place in various university journals. The wording directions concerned both the Canadian-American issue and the gender bias issue. Although no laws demanded that a certain number of women be hired, the university required that equal opportunity be heavily emphasized in the ads. Colindale considered himself personally supportive of equal opportunity, but he found himself starting to worry about satisfying the restrictions confronting him. For the timing deadlines, Colindale's ad had to appear in at least two consecutive issues, at least 60 days before the closing date for applications.

The rules and regulations did not stop there. Once Colindale had received curriculum vitae from various candidates, he had to meet with a committee of faculty members from his department. This committee—one member of which had to be a woman—would choose the three most promising applicants and invite them for an interview. Several lengthy meetings occurred, during which Colindale and one committee member disagreed persistently about the qualifications of several applicants.

Colindale finally had the following discussion with the Dean of the Faculty of Business, Gene Moeller:

Colindale: You know, Gene, this recruiting is starting to get me down.

Moeller: What's the problem?

Colindale: Well, all these rules and regulations make it difficult to do an efficient job of staffing my department. Every time I turn around there's another restriction. Making sure I'm adhering to all these rules sure takes a lot of time.

Moeller: But these rules are designed to ensure equal treatment for all applicants.

Colindale: I know, but I have to get special permission to make decisions that managers in other organizations could do in the normal course of their work.

Moeller: Like what?

Colindale: Well, take the initial screening of applicants: surely I should be able to do that on my own. I could then present my short list of candidates to the recruiting committee and we could decide which candidates to have in for an interview. I have spent hours involved in detailed discussions of every applicant with all the committee members. I don't have the time to do that and keep up my teaching, administrative work, and research.

Moeller: I'd like to help, but I'm afraid you don't have any alternative in this area. The recruiting rules are quite specific. But you've done a good job so far; keep up the good work and don't let it get you down. Well, it's time for the dean's council meeting, Ron. Nice talking to you. ▲

QUESTIONS

1. What circumstances have motivated the university to state recruiting regulations so specifically?
2. What federal laws are relevant for this case?
3. What should Ron Colindale do? Why?

COMPREHENSIVE CASES

PART III

CASE III-1
ELECTRONICS UNLIMITED

Mike Craig, an economics major from Laurentian University, was employed by Agriculture Canada for three years and worked at the government offices for this department in the downtown area of Hamilton, Ontario. His work was assessed as above average and his ability to organize and present work efficiently as noteworthy. His job involved preparing reports and statistics based on current trends and developments in farm management. Mike had a number of colleagues with whom he worked on a cooperative basis, each supplying the others with pertinent data for their studies. The organizational hierarchy under which he worked was a traditional bureaucratic structure; supervisors tended to be formal and impersonal and there was strict adherence to procedure. It was within this atmosphere that Mike performed his research and administrative activity.

Mike's role was very clearly defined: he was assigned a supervisor to whom he reported directly. His research work was submitted at various intervals, but current progress was frequently examined. While there was cooperative effort among the workers, there was very little enthusiasm for the work. The challenge seemed to be missing from the required task, for seldom were the results of his research implemented into a strategy for action. Instead, much of the work was collated with other material for government reports sent to Ottawa.

Mike had been dissatisfied with his job for about six months. He felt he had nowhere to go in this government position and, since he was still single and without family responsibility, he thought it was time to look for a more challenging job. He watched the newspapers for an interesting position and consulted a Toronto placement agency for opportunities. His interests, as he described them to an interviewer, were in joining a growing and dynamic company, possibly a young company looking for people to train as managers in an expanding operation.

Eventually the placement agency in Toronto uncovered an opportunity for Mike in a Montreal firm with a new subsidiary company in northern Toronto, called Electronics Unlimited. The company was new and growing in the field of electronic equipment for the home and office. It had a growing sales and distribution network with production to follow in the near future. The product line the company distributes is broad and serves both the industrial and commercial markets. There are many new and innovative developments in this field and in this organization. For example, the Toronto plant is organizing for a more sophisticated warehousing and distribution operation, and plans are forthcoming for a fully integrated Marketing Department.

Frank Wilson, the personnel manger, interviewed Mike Craig for an opening at Electronics Unlimited. Mike was immediately impressed not only with the organization but with the personal style of Frank Wilson who, as a manager, appeared innovative and progressive. He was quite empathetic to Mike's predicament and understood the value of growth opportunities in any company; also, the discussion of money and potential advancement in the organization seemed very promising. Wilson further discussed the young company's need for energetic managers with ambitious goals for achievement. As he suggested: "We have outlets to develop, contacts to be made, people to recruit, and many more activities that will challenge a young college graduate."

Mike was very excited about his meeting with Frank Wilson and his application to the company. He felt sure that Wilson liked him and would offer him a job with the company. The situation, too, he thought would be a complete change from his current position and a welcome relief from the routine. For the first time in three years Mike was enthusiastic about his life and the prospects it held for him. The job offer came through three weeks later, and he accepted the position with a substantial increase in salary. He was due to begin in early September, and he proceeded to resign from his government position and to find an apartment in Toronto.

The first two months on his new job were a real learning experience as Mike Craig made himself acquainted with the people and the situation. Three other recent college graduates were hired from the area at about the same time. One of these was John Corrigon, a marketing major from the University of Western Ontario, a very aggressive, outgoing individual. The other two co-workers had degrees from McMaster in engineering and were studying for the M.B.A. degree in the evening. The four new employees to the company all seemed to hit it off well at the start.

For the first six months the four young men were expected to get acquainted with the firm's operation and make themselves available to do reports and other tasks as required by the managers. (See the firm's organizational chart in Exhibit 1.) Mike Craig and John Corrigon became involved in the distribution and sales ...

EXHIBIT 1 ORGANIZATION CHART OF ELECTRONICS UNLIMITED.

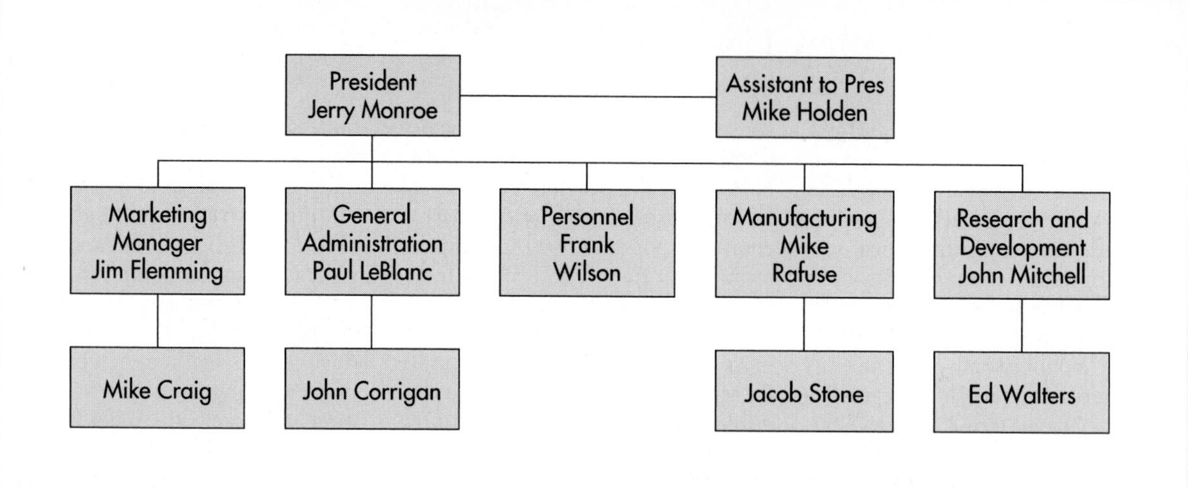

side of the organization. Their first task was to generate a report on potential users of electronic equipment in the area on a commercial basis. Their guidelines were to examine demographic trends, store openings, potential volumes, and customer needs. The existing group had made some contacts in this area but a thorough report and strategy were required. The managers of various departments indicated they would be available for consultation and inquiries. Craig felt very confident about this new assignment. His economics background provided him with all the knowledge to complete a thorough analysis of the area. Though he and Corrigon kept each other informed about their activities, they worked independently in different areas. Their plan was to meet before the date of submission and review their efforts.

Mike followed a steady pattern of work in the next week, confining much of his efforts to written material and research. Statistics Canada, *Financial Post* surveys of markets, and other books were among his sources of information. He gained confidence as the time passed. Corrigon, to avoid duplication, spent much of his time out of the office and in the field. He visited people and talked to them of their needs and requirements.

When Corrigon was in the office, he frequently visited the executive offices to gather information and to learn about the operation. Mike, for his part, conversed with the managers only at lunch. He would also take work home with him at night and on weekends. Many of the avenues he was pursuing were of great interest to him, and he wanted to follow them through in what was now becoming a lengthy report.

Craig and Corrigon met at the end of the month just prior to their submission to management. It was a brief meeting, with Corrigon flipping through Craig's typed pages of report material. Then, behind closed doors on a Friday afternoon, two of the managers, Flemming and LeBlanc, discussed the research and activities with the two new employees. The meeting was expected to take most of the afternoon, a rather formal atmosphere prevailing throughout the early part of the encounter. Later, over coffee, the meeting became more relaxed. Jerry Munroe, the president, came in for a moment and exchanged casual comments with the group. It seemed as though Corrigon had got to know Munroe, since they were on a first-name basis. Much of the discussion centred around Corrigon's ideas. He quoted names of people in key locations and presented an understanding of the needs and requirements of the area. Corrigon did not hesitate to initiate discussion and when necessary to focus the direction of the meeting. Craig, on the other hand, spoke infrequently and made vague references to his written report, his confidence dwindling as the time passed. Mike was continually forced to confirm by figures much of what Corrigon was expressing in his ideas and proposals. At the conclusion of the meeting, a short summary was sketched out by Flemming and LeBlanc on a flip chart summarizing much of what Corrigon had suggested.

Mike Craig left the office that afternoon somewhat dismayed by the results of the meeting. He felt Corrigon had dominated the discussion and not contributed Mike's ideas as he had expressed them in their premeeting discussion. He thought over Corrigon's

• • •

ease with managers and the way they responded to him. Ideas and action were clearly the bywords of this company.

In the next few weeks many of the major ideas of the meeting were broken down into smaller areas of focus; both Craig and Corrigon were left alone on their jobs without too much direction. The managers continued to hurry through one task, then address another. Potential customers were given full details of the company aspirations and frequently Corrigon was asked to entertain customers and show them the operations. His aggressive and outgoing style seemed most suited to this task. Craig was given small reports to make and was generally left to muddle in the details. He would ask Corrigon for support from time to time on some of the matters, but seldom could he sit Corrigon down long enough for a meaningful exchange of ideas or plans. At the bimonthly meetings, Corrigon was never short of a comment or an idea for a particular project.

The manufacturing side of Electronics Unlimited was now coming online for full production. The two engineers who had been hired were working well under Rafuse and Mitchell in their departments. They had settled in their own offices and were very productive in their field, developing changes and ideas for the product line. Both Rafuse and Mitchell were satisfied with the new employees, particularly since they provided current ideas for their work. They had already been invited to Montreal to visit the main plant and production operation.

Flemming and LeBlanc continued to make good use of Corrigon and Craig, who were busy on the marketing side of the operation. However, nothing was clearly defined in this company. John Mitchell for example, frequently provided data and reports for Paul LeBlanc on distribution networks for the area. The organization was run on a flexible pattern of interactions and responsibilities. Corrigon continued his aggressive style and developed an excellent rapport with Jim Flemming. They were in the process of hiring salespeople for the field and Corrigon was given an opportunity to conduct the interviewing and initial screening. Craig, on the other hand seemed always to be preparing more reports and analyzing data, largely because he had not been asked to take other responsibility.

Mitchell and Rafuse had also begun to take advantage of Craig's report writing. By now, however, Craig had had enough and had become quite discouraged at these frequent requests. He began to wonder just what he was expected to do on this "dynamic job." This uncertainty bothered him. At the same time, Corrigon was now beginning to annoy him with his abrasive style. He would ask for information and request of Craig routine jobs a secretary could do. Craig resented these requests but, in the interest of the company, would complete the tasks. Despite Craig's increased efforts at establishing rapport with the Marketing Manager, Flemming, he couldn't seem to produce results.

After six months on the job Craig had still not found it a satisfying experience. He was determined not to give up, however, and proceeded to present lengthy and detailed studies of market trends and other reports that would help the company. All the managers took advantage of his services to the point where Craig was frequently working on weekends.

Corrigon, well on his way to organizing a sales staff, also requested a lengthy analysis of sales potential for the company. Craig had worked himself in to complete frustration. He refused Corrigon's request. He didn't feel he was there just to write reports but rather to become more involved with managing the company. He felt he was receiving little recognition for his contribution, while Corrigon and the two engineers were progressing much more rapidly. However, his refusal to write the report for Corrigon earned him a sharp rebuke from Flemming. This upset Craig and he felt he had to redeem himself.

Electronics Unlimited had been growing and stabilizing in the months that had passed. The retail outlets had been contacted and connections organized to complete the network of distribution. New products had been developed by the company and were marketed in an effective manner. The administrative staff had been growing to meet the requirements of the production and sales force. An incentive system for the sales force had been designed in the Toronto office and had received wide recognition from the Montreal company. Corrigon was instrumental in this effort and was appropriately rewarded for his contribution. A small achievement award was presented to Corrigon for his part in the design of the plan that had been implemented. The award was presented to him at an office get-together.

The event further deflated Craig's self-image in the growing company. What little spirit of camaraderie that had existed among the four employees who had arrived almost together had been lost by this time. Mike Craig had retreated into a gloomy silence, anticipating a difficult time in an upcoming evaluation that had been announced. The notice had come to the desks of the respective employees that they would be evaluated in the next month by the managers. It would be a formal evaluation, one that would take place in their offices over coffee. It would be verbal and based on discussion rather than a written document channelled through personnel.

Craig looked glum as he peered up from his desk after reading the memo, the first of its kind. Corrigon, with his usual cockiness, suggested that he

• • •

would have to get the boss a bottle of good Scotch but that he really didn't have much to worry about.

Craig had less secure feelings about the whole procedure. He had this terrible feeling that he would handle himself poorly. In a brief discussion with Flemming one afternoon, he made inquiries about the method of evaluation, pointing out the traditional function of personnel administration. Flemming laughed at this idea, responding that around there they worked to get things done and did not worry too much about who did the evaluations.

The evaluation day arrived and Craig was assigned to Rafuse, the person he felt was least involved with his work. The interview and discussion went smoothly and very cordially. There were many silent moments during the course of the interview, and he went away feeling that his work was regarded as less than satisfactory. Rafuse had hinted that the company's interest lay in more outgoing individuals. Craig was left with mixed feelings about the company and his future.

Indeed, Craig felt the time had come for a confrontation with the management of the company and he proceeded to make an appointment with the personnel office for a lengthy discussion about his future. He felt he might be able to get some straight answers from Frank Wilson, but he knew that he was taking a chance of finding out the worst. Some hard discussions would follow. ▲

QUESTIONS

1. What kinds of problems is Mike Craig having at Electronics Unlimited? Discuss in detail why you think Craig is having these problems.
2. What can Craig do to increase his job satisfaction? What can he do to make his performance look better to management?
3. What factors might limit Craig's ability to improve his situation?

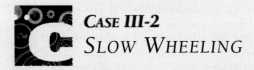

CASE III-2
SLOW WHEELING

Fred Mills paced the floor in his office wondering why operations in the railyard were so backlogged. This was March, the time of highest demand for rail services, and the company could ill afford delays. Fred had been supervisor of the yard operations at C & R Rail's Thunder Bay location for 12 years and had never seen the yard so disorganized. Worse, the yard crew workers were very displeased with working conditions. Fred recalled that the new computers that were recently installed at the various terminals in the yard were supposed to make operations more efficient and decrease the cost of operations. To his dismay, the reverse had occurred. Conflict between workers and complaints from customers were rampant. The dreariness and chill of winter added to the problems as Fred slumped behind his desk trying to fight his gloomy feelings.

THE THUNDER BAY TERMINAL

Thunder Bay is an active railway centre and a crucial link in the Canadian rail transportation system. The operations at the terminal commence with the arrival of freight trains from the east (Toronto) or from the west (Winnipeg). Trains from the west stop at the Westform terminal. These trains include grain cars destined for the various grain elevators in Thunder Bay, wood cars for Great Lake Paper, and miscellaneous cars containing merchandise for the various businesses in Thunder Bay.

Trains from the east terminate at the East End terminal. These contain cars with merchandise for businesses in Thunder Bay, as well as empty grain cars that are to continue further on to western Canada. Approximately one-quarter of the arrivals are run-through trains; i.e., they simply stop at the main station where new road crews take over for the continuation of the trip. Trains that enter Thunder Bay have an average of 175 cars per train.

•••

OPERATIONS PRIOR TO COMPUTERIZATION

Before computers were installed, the yard supervisor (who was located in the central office) obtained a master car list for each arriving train (a car list indicates the contents of each rail car as well as its destination). This list was then given to the yard master (who was located within the yard limits). Using this list, the yard master then wrote out by hand four separate lists—one for each of the four yard crews that were responsible for a specific territory in the yard (see Exhibit 1).

Each yard crew was made up of one engineer and two switchpersons. After receiving their lists, the yard crews switched out the various cars from the main train and delivered them (via spur lines) to designated customers in Thunder Bay. The cars that were left either contained special goods or were designated for depots outside Thunder Bay. Train cars were checked by car-checkers and the list given to the supervisor for verification and distribution of work assignments.

OPERATIONS AFTER COMPUTERIZATION

With the introduction of computers, programs now format the various trains and their cars on computer printouts. These printouts have all the necessary information that the yard masters require to allocate work assignments to the yard crews. The system provides the yard master with a detailed switch list and increases the speed of distribution of the work assignments. The yard master no longer has to write out the switch lists by hand (which requires writing the car numbers, contents, weights, track numbers, and destination). Instead, the computer prints all this information on a list and the yard master simply distributes the list to the appropriate crews. This system is designed for greater accuracy, speed, and control and should mean better service for customers. Unfortunately, the system doesn't always work.

PROBLEMS BEGIN

Before installation of the computers, the yard crews finished their required work list in six or seven hours. Upon completion of their switch list, they were allowed to leave the premises and were not required to return to work until their next scheduled shift. The full eight-hour work day was seldom needed to complete the work list. This was a well-established and understood work norm among the railway workers. At present, even with the new computers, the switch crews are not completing their required work in the eight-hour shifts. Delays of all kinds have developed, even with the best crews. Under these circumstances, the yard master either has to instruct the crews to work overtime or call in a spare crew. Since yards crews consist of an engineer and two switchpersons, the overtime and spare crew creates substantial extra cost for the company. Also, the various businesses in Thunder Bay are beginning to complain about late arrivals and missing shipments.

There is a rumour among the office staff that the yard crews are "slow wheeling" (working slower than normal) because they are no longer able

EXHIBIT 1 WORKFLOW AT THE C&R TERMINAL.

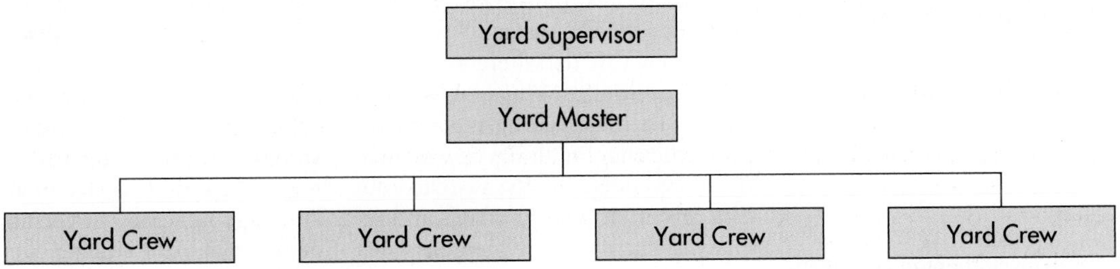

to achieve the hour to an hour-and-a-half "quits" (yard jargon for leaving early). There is also a rumour that the yard crews are deliberately placing cars on the wrong tracks after switching them out. This creates an error in the computer list that the yard master uses to assign work. Because certain cars are not on the appropriate switch crews list, the customer in Thunder Bay receives the wrong merchandise. There is a chance that a rail car can be placed at Great Lakes Forest products, for example, and really be designated for Fitzsimmons Food Company. On occasion, rail cars examined by the computer car-checkers have also been found emptied of their contents.

A lost car incident creates extra paper work for the office staff and also requires investigation by company police and insurance personnel. The yard crews seem to enjoy these incidents. They feel good about getting even with management for disrupting their previously enjoyable work schedule. Unfortunately, these incidents disrupt the delivery process and customers must seek out other alternatives for their delivery and distribution needs. The end result is that company relations with the business community are frequently strained.

Company management is presently addressing the issue of slow wheeling, but they are not sure what to do about it. The United Transportation Union of Railroad Workers handbook contains the following references:

> The speed at which all switching movements are to be performed is to be left entirely to the discretion of the switch crew members.

The company and union agreement stipulates that

> the speed of switching movement is not to exceed that of restricted speed.

Restricted speed is defined as the speed that allows stopping an engine within half the vision of the line of sight and to have complete control of all movement and able to stop movement within a safe distance in regard to public transportation.

SWITCHING OPERATIONS

In the past, car-checkers monitored every track within the yard limits at various times during the day to determine an accurate listing of the car numbers, contents, and destination in the order that they were positioned on the correct track. The introduction of the computer relieved the car-checker of this duty, a fact that the union has watched very carefully because it does not want to see a reduction of jobs in the rail yards.

The computer controls the various cars using an elimination process. If a car is assigned to a crew on one of its computer listings, then that specific car is simply removed from the computer terminal listing. The sequence of the cars on that track is assumed to be in the same order minus the car that is switched out. Over a three-or four-day period, the cars on a track may not match the updated computer printout because the crews have not properly carried out their switching moves.

With the involvement of car-checkers under the old system, switchpersons knew exactly where a required car was positioned. This enabled them to plan their switching moves with great efficiency. With the new system, the trains containing the switched-out cars are often disorganized, and on many of them, a crew member must go searching for a specific car that is needed by a particular business in Thunder Bay. Consequently, the switchpersons are beginning to feel as if they are glorified car-checkers. This does not appeal to them, and their lack of job satisfaction is evident from their increased absenteeism.

THE ROAD CREW SITUATION—MORE PROBLEMS

The Brotherhood of Rail Transportation Union requires that the company give road crews (an engineer and three brake-persons) a two-hour notice before they go on duty. It is the responsibility of switch crews to have the road crews' trains made up and ready for the road crews to depart Thunder bay. The slow wheeling of the yard crews makes it difficult for the company to plan the departure time. As a result, road crews are waiting at the station while on duty.

This costs the company money. For every twenty minutes a road crew is delayed at a station while on duty, the company is required to compensate the crew for twenty-five miles. All workers are paid on a per mile basis. The older workers like the extra money they get when they have to wait. The younger, single members, who are not as concerned about the extra money, are unhappy with the delayed departures because it makes it difficult for them to know exactly when they will be back in Thunder Bay after completing a trip. This, in turn, creates havoc with their social lives. Their frustrations are evident in the radio conversations between them and the switch crews. The messages are mostly verbal hassling, but on occasion there has been pushing and shoving in the locker room on this issue. The hostile behaviour and crude language in some conversations are detrimental to the company image and reflect poorly on the management of the company.

An observer would be surprised to learn that yard crews and road crews both belong to the same union. The

• • •

comradeship is deteriorating, the cooperation between the two units is decreasing, and the overall morale of the switchpersons is diminishing. The high cohesiveness of each group is a contributing factor in the conflict as each group attempts to protect its own interests.

The disruptions at the workplace are affecting the workers, management, and customers. The problem is compounded by the fact that the economic situation in Thunder Bay is not good at the moment, and the transportation business has many new entries. Trucking companies have become very aggressive in the region, particularly since highways have been improved and the trucking industry has been deregulated.

Since Fred Mills was a switchperson prior to moving up to management, he knows the impact that yard crews have on operations. He also knows that it is his responsibility to analyze the situation and restore operations to an efficient and controlled level. Top management from the operations area is scheduled to arrive in Thunder Bay at the end of the month for inspections. They will also do a performance evaluation of the supervisors. Fred is feeling stress and frustration in his job for the first time. It is a complex situation and the latest correspondence from the union expressing concern about the unrest among the workers has compounded the difficulties facing him. ▲

QUESTIONS

1. List and briefly discuss the factors that are causing the conflict between the yard crews and the road crews.
2. Assuming that the yard crews are "slow wheeling," why are they doing so?
3. What actions might Fred Mills take in an attempt to resolve the "slow wheeling" of the yard crews?

CASE III-3
ATHLETE'S WAREHOUSE (B)

Late in February 1993, Colin Power, majority owner of Athlete's Warehouse and a number of other companies in Grand Falls-Windsor, and a human resource consultant from the Small Business Centre were seated in Colin's office in the back of Athlete's Warehouse. Colin was speaking to his brother Ed on the phone. "Sorry I can't run with you today, I'm all tied up. How about tomorrow morning at 7:00?" Hanging up the phone Colin exclaimed to the Small Business Centre consultant "for the last year I haven't had time to turn around. Every day it is just a rush from one store to another, phone calls all day long and never enough time to do the things that need to be done. I need someone else to help run things, but I don't know whether to promote someone from within the businesses or to hire from outside. Not only that, I'm not sure what the job should be."

BACKGROUND

Colin Power started in business full-time when he opened Athlete's Warehouse, a sporting goods store, in the Exploit's Valley mall in 1985. For the first two years that the business was in operation, Colin supplemented his personal income by teaching computer courses at a local private school. With the initial success of Athlete's Warehouse, and with the support of his wife who was employed full-time as a teacher, Colin had the financial resources to take on additional challenges. Starting in 1987 he began to extend business undertakings in many directions and opened a printing store (Print Plus), a computer store (EduComp), and acquired a Tim Horton's franchise.

To help him in his analysis of the situation Colin prepared a review of the factors influencing the expansion of his business interests and he drew up a list of the job duties for three of his businesses (Athlete's Warehouse, Print Plus, and EduComp) included as Exhibit 1. He did not include job duties for the Tim Horton's store because these were part of the franchise package and there was no overlap of duties with the employees of the other businesses.

• • •

EXHIBIT 1 JOB DUTIES.

	ATHLETE'S	EDUCOMP	PRINT PLUS
Buying, Ordering	C M	C P	C T
Receiving, Pricing	D M	P	T
Operating cash	D M	P	T
Serving customers	D M T	C P	C T
Preparing displays	D M T		T
Answering telephone	D M	P	T
Cleaning store	D M		
Receiving customer returns	D M	C P	C
Investigating customer complaints	M	C P	C T
Maintaining premises	M		
Operating heat press	M T		C T
Stringing raquets	M T		
Sharpening skates	M T		
Installing ski equipment	T		
Opening & closing store	D M	P	T
Selling door to door		P	
Tendering & preparing quotes	M	P	C
Preparing computer artwork			C T
Administering payables/receivables	D T	P	
Installing networks			
Recording and making deposits	C	C	C
Printing using silk screen			C T
Making signs			T
Assembling and making trophies			C T
Preparing payroll	C	C	C
Preparing advertising	C	C	C
Granting credit	C M	C	C
Printing			T
Training employees	C	C	C
Bookkeeping	OUTSIDE	P	OUTSIDE

Colin Power C
Darlene Little D
Mike Wade M
Pamela Horwood P
Troy Piercey T

(shaded) not applicable

Source: Company Records

ATHLETE'S WAREHOUSE

Athlete's Warehouse opened in 1985 in a 81-square-metre location at the Exploit's Valley Mall with Colin and his brother-in-law, Mike Wade, as the only full-time staff. The store carried sporting good products centred around Colin's interest in running and included shoes and sporting outfits. First year sales exceeded the forecast level of $135 000 and amounted to approximately $180 000. Colin attributed this success to the changing fashions and the acceptability of using sporting clothes as daily wear. Basketball shoes now became street shoes, and jerseys with team names on them became the fashion for school wear.

With the growth of sales, Athlete's Warehouse required additional space. In 1988, the business moved to another location in the mall. The only spot with adequate square footage consisted of two floors. Although not ideal, because there was now a need to always have two employees working, Colin relocated. Business continued to grow and in addition to hiring a second full-time person, Darlene Little, Colin hired two part-time employees.

The business expanded to include many different product lines and services. Included in these were skate sharpening, ski binding installation, and racquet stringing. In addition, Athlete's Warehouse offered printing services, which initially consisted of putting transfers on T-shirts and printing team logos or numbers on clothing purchased from Athlete's Warehouse. Training in all these areas was provided to Mike and Troy Piercey (a part-time employee who became full-time in 1988).

As his other business interests grew, Colin was not able to spend much time at the Athlete's Warehouse store; therefore in 1991 he appointed Mike Wade as manager. Darlene was the only other full-time employee at the store as Troy was shared between Athlete's Warehouse and Print Plus.

PRINT PLUS

One of the first offshoots of the athletic wear business was a growing demand for custom-printed or numbered sportswear. This led Colin to invest in transfer and screen printing equipment in 1987.

After operating in the same location as Athlete's Warehouse for five years, the printing end of the business required too much space and a new location was sought. In 1990, space was rented on Southcott Avenue (about one-half kilometre away from the Exploit's Valley Mall) and Troy began to work most of his time at the new location periodically returning to the mall to provide lunch-time relief, when Athlete's Warehouse was very busy or when there was no printing to do.

The printing business was closely related to Athlete's Warehouse sales, especially to the sale of the sports uniforms and school clothes. As a former high school physical education teacher, Colin had a lot of contacts at the schools throughout central Newfoundland. These contacts were the source of approximately 25 percent of the sales of Athlete's Warehouse and at least 50 percent of the printing business. Because of his commitments to other businesses, Colin no longer spent as much time visiting schools to sell his line of clothes and starting in 1989 that part of Athlete's Warehouse and Print Plus business began to decline.

EDUCOMP

At the same time that he moved the printing operation, Colin had decided that there was room for a computer company in Grand Falls. His experience at Athlete's Warehouse in setting up a computer system to control inventory, his knowledge of computers from his teaching, and his general interest convinced him that there was an opportunity here. He began selling computers and in the spring of 1991 hired Pam Horwood, a graduate of the local community college computer programming course to run the store. Initially, this job involved computer sales and customer service.

It was soon apparent that there was not much profit in just selling computers, so Colin undertook to train Pam and himself in the installation and service of Novell™ computer networks. This broadened the base of the business considerably. In order to further use his resources, Colin became a local Xerox distributor and EduComp became a sales agent.

Things got busier and busier. One of the requirements of offering network services was the fact that if a customer's network goes down, it must be fixed. This task fell to Colin for a couple of reasons. Pam's strengths were not in technical aspects of computer systems, and he did not have to pay himself overtime.

TIM HORTON'S

Just as Colin was starting to get a handle on his businesses, he was successful in a bid to obtain a Tim Horton's franchise for Grand Falls-Windsor. While this appeared to add considerably to his workload, Colin stated that the existing businesses were not big enough to provide the level of income that he wanted to support his desired lifestyle. In December 1991, the Grand Falls-Windsor Tim Horton's store opened.

In order to minimize his involvement, Colin made sure his two brothers (Eric and Ed who owned 49 percent between them) were trained in the baking end of the business. Because the business was open 24 hours a day there could be no interruption of the supply of product. If an employee did not report to work, the owner had to fill in at a moment's notice.

To further lighten his load, Colin was in the process of training a manager for the Tim Horton's store. This would hopefully reduce his daily involvement with the store, which during start-up and up to this point had been well over four hours a day.

Colin's days were now packed going from store to store dealing with the day-to-day problems of the four businesses. There were lots of things that he wanted to do with the businesses but did not have time to implement nor did he have the confidence to delegate.

One step that Colin did take was to construct a building next to his Tim Horton's store (see Exhibit 2) and by the end of March 1993 he planned to relocate all his other businesses under one roof. This would certainly cut down on travel between the businesses and improve communications between

• • •

Colin and the staff. Exhibit 3 shows the organizational structure of the businesses.

THE PROBLEMS

Sitting in his cluttered office in the back of Athlete's Warehouse, Colin outlined his concerns for the business to the Small Business Centre consultant.

1. "I haven't been able to visit the local high schools for a couple of years and although we are still getting a few phone-in orders, we are losing business in this area. I really need someone to go visit these schools, but it is not a full-time job."
2. "I've tried letting Mike or my brother Ed do the ordering for Athlete's Warehouse, but this hasn't worked out. They don't seem to have the same feel for what will

EXHIBIT 2 TIM HORTON'S LOCATION MAP.

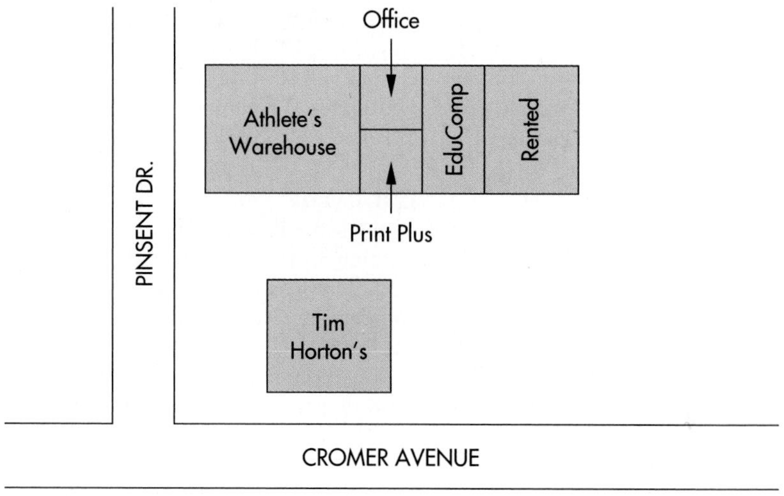

Source: Company records

EXHIBIT 3 ORGANIZATIONAL STRUCTURE.

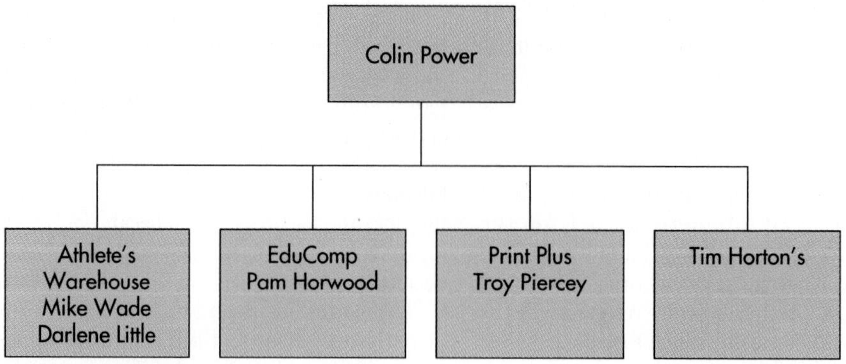

Source: Company Records

sell as I do and I have ended up with a lot of slow-moving merchandise. I am in full agreement with the saying that 'goods well bought are half sold.' For the last year when I was unable to go to the athletic goods show, I ordered from a catalogue. This hasn't given me the chance to see the products and I don't have the same feel for good sellers."

3. "Because of my lack of involvement and also this recession, sales at Athlete's Warehouse peaked in 1990 and have been dropping ever since."
4. "The computer side of the business is doing well, however there are avenues I wish to pursue but can't because I don't have enough time. Pam has been getting out on the road and has been doing reasonably well selling the computers, networks and Xerox, but we need more coverage for our territory, which covers from Bay D'Espoir to Baie Verte (about 350 km)."
5. "To try to respond to this problem I hired a sales person on a three-month trial basis through a Canada Employment Centre program to sell half-time for Athlete's Warehouse and the other half for Xerox. This hasn't worked out mainly because of personality problems and I am not going to keep this person."
6. "I still have a problem because I am the only one who can fix most of the technical problems for our computer network customers and this certainly wrecks any sort of schedule I try to run. I must admit that this is the part of the businesses that I enjoy the most."
7. "I am no longer getting called to Tim Horton's as much as I used to be and I am now trying to get around to managing the other businesses, but things keep happening."
8. "As far as Print Plus is concerned the business is working well. Troy is a good worker and fairly well trained although he still calls on me to do the difficult printing jobs. Maybe he doesn't want to ruin some products, but he has to realize that at some time he must take responsibility and I am sure that he will do a good job. Troy is also valuable because he started out with Athlete's Warehouse and can fill in there when needed giving lunch breaks to the staff."
9. "I realize that I need help, but I really don't know what type of person to hire even if I could get what I wanted. I need help with the network service because it is now the one aspect of the business that I have to attend to regardless of what else is happening. But for the business to grow I need someone to get out and sell."

Sitting back in his chair he answered the phone again. Putting down the receiver he said to the consultant, "Troy just quit." ▲

QUESTIONS

1. Prepare job descriptions for all the employees.
2. With the relocation of the business under one roof, is there an opportunity to combine or realign any of the job descriptions that would provide some benefits or efficiencies to Colin?
3. What suggestions would you give Colin to solve his problem?
4. Draw an organization chart reflecting the suggestions you made in Question 3.
5. What human resource planning procedures should Colin put in place for the future?

PART 4

LEADING

CHAPTER 12

MOTIVATION

LEARNING OBJECTIVES

After reading this chapter, you will be able to:

1. Define the term "motivation" and explain why it is important in all types of organizations.
2. Describe the difference between intrinsic and extrinsic motivation.
3. Discuss the relationship between employee satisfaction and employee productivity.
4. Write a simple formula showing how motivation and ability interact to affect employee performance.
5. Outline the two basic philosophies of human nature.
6. Explain the difference between content and process theories of motivation.
7. Identify the essential features of four content motivation theories.
8. Identify the essential features of three process motivation theories.
9. Show how reinforcement theory can be used to motivate employees.
10. Explain the role that money plays in motivation.
11. Outline the main features of job enrichment, quality circles, and flextime.

MANAGEMENT CHALLENGE

BAYLOR'S DEPARTMENT STORE

For the past 20 years, Baylor's Department Store had annually surveyed its customers about their feelings toward the store. Recent surveys had shown a disturbing trend—customers felt that the salesclerks in the store were unfriendly and not very helpful. These feelings had been reflected in sales. George Homenchuk, vice-president of operations, noted that the data revealed that both absolute sales volume and profit margins had declined for the past three years.

Homenchuk believed the problem was very serious, so he called a meeting of Baylor's executive committee to deal with it. In attendance were the vice-presidents of marketing, finance, personnel, and merchandising. After a lengthy discussion with considerable input from the personnel vice-president, the executive committee decided that the real problem was low motivation levels among the salesclerks. These low motivation levels apparently had resulted in indifferent attitudes toward customers. Several executives commented that rumours had filtered up to them that clerks on the floor were not happy

• • •

because they felt they were being ignored by management.

The vice-president of personnel, Lise Daniels, pointed out that attitude surveys of employees revealed that: (1) salesclerks did not find their jobs interesting; (2) they received little feedback on how well they were doing; and (3) they felt that there were inequities across departments in terms of workload. A discussion then ensued about how these problems could be resolved. Daniels pointed out that, since the salesclerks were on straight salary, they were all paid the same amount of money regardless of their sales. She suggested that the clerks be put on commission. If this were done, Daniels argued, salesclerks would show much more interest in customers and would therefore sell more. She cited evidence from a number of organizations showing that the introduction of an incentive system had resulted in increased output by employees and increased profit for the organization.

Some of the members of the executive committee thought that this step was rather drastic and that employee turnover would surely increase if the system was implemented. They cited evidence from other companies where this had happened. Other members thought than an incentive scheme really wouldn't solve the problem of poorly motivated employees because money wasn't effective in motivating people.

In view of these disagreements, Homenchuk scheduled a second executive committee meeting for one week later. This would give members time to mull over the problem and come up with a workable solution. ▲

Throughout human history, managers in all kinds of organizations have made assumptions about what motivates workers, and these assumptions have influenced managerial behaviour. When slave labour was used, threats and abuse were common. Even in firms using paid labour, managers were often paternalistic and condescending toward employees. Managers typically assumed that employees worked out of necessity, not out of love for work. This assumption naturally led to the conclusion that money was a powerful motivator of work effort. This view was supported by Frederick Taylor and the scientific management movement early in the twentieth century. As we saw in Chapter 2, Taylor's concern for productivity led him to introduce payment schemes based on the idea that money is a powerful motivator of behaviour. Although this view is now recognized as an oversimplification, money is still important to people.

In the 1930s a new view of motivation emerged. The Hawthorne studies showed that factors other than economics, such as group norms and management concern for workers, could influence employee motivation and productivity. Many managers eagerly accepted these findings because they felt that if they could substitute "being nice" to employees for paying them a lot of money, the organization would benefit. This view has also proven an oversimplification. By the 1960s and 1970s, managers were encountering a "new breed" of worker who was suspicious of management, apparently unimpressed by money, and unconcerned about productivity. Motivating workers with these views was a challenge. By the 1980s, however, worker concern for money began to grow again, and there was an increased emphasis on the acquisition of material goods among the so-called "yuppies." In the 1990s, understanding worker motivation has become even more important as competitive pressures have forced companies to downsize. With fewer workers to do the same amount of work, the motivation of those who remain must be high. Managers must therefore have a good understanding of employee motivation (see the Management at Work insert "Downsizing and Employee Motivation").

Recently, attention has also been given to managerial motivation as well. A "new breed" of managers is more likely to reject the motivators and incentives traditionally offered by organizations. These managers are more concerned with self-fulfillment, entrepreneurial activities, and independence.[1] Executives, for example, are sometimes refusing transfers and promotions in the interest of pursuing leisure-time and family-oriented activities. One executive wouldn't accept a new job until the company would provide special education classes for his handicapped child. Another executive turned down a transfer to Europe in order to complete a charitable project.[2]

MANAGEMENT AT WORK

DOWNSIZING AND EMPLOYEE MOTIVATION

When large numbers of employees are let go because of downsizing, companies generally focus on compensation and counselling packages for the workers who lose their jobs. But what about the workers who are lucky enough to keep their jobs? Do they think it will be just a matter of time before the same thing happens to them? Will they be less motivated in an uncertain work environment?

In order to avoid the downside of downsizing, companies must develop strategies to deal with the resultant anxiety, guilt, and bitterness that remaining employees often feel. Without a strategy, the company will face slumping motivation and productivity. This, in turn, will undercut the purpose of the downsizing.

The key is communicating with workers before and after job cuts are made. Because the remaining employees are watching management very closely, it is important that management communicate openly with them. This means telling employees how layoff decisions were made, who made them, alternatives that were considered, and outlining how work will change in the newly downsized organization.

Labatt Breweries has gone through three major reorganizations and has laid off 25 percent of its work force since 1989. To help the remaining employees cope with uncertainty, the company instituted workshops, established sales teams, set new sales objectives, and instituted a financial reward program. Even with this, however, worker morale is not what it used to be.

Workers are not the only employees to be affected by downsizing. Managers are also losing their jobs as companies struggle to deal with intense competition in the marketplace. In the 1980s, the drive to be "lean and mean" led many Canadian companies to downsize their operations. But as organizational pyramids got flatter, managers found themselves stranded on occupational plateaus. Since many of those who were stranded are ambitious people with high aspirations, companies are concerned about whether downsizing has reduced managerial motivation.

Firms are trying to keep valuable individuals using numerous tactics, including lateral moves, special training, awards, improved working conditions, and increased job flexibility. They are also trying to downplay the importance of promotions. At Abitibi-Price Inc., a company which has done some serious downsizing, lateral rotation of employees is done on a case-by-case basis. For example, a communication specialist might move temporarily into marketing, or a human resources staff member might move into administration. Jobs are now more loosely defined so the job occupant has more responsibility and challenge. Staff can also design their own weekly work schedules. The company is even prepared to let some employees work at home through the use of workstations and fax machines.

But other companies may find it more difficult to motivate plateaued managers. At Ford Motor of Canada, for example, the company cannot be creative with bonuses and incentives because they are trying to be very competitive. At the Royal Bank of Canada, a high-growth period is just ending, so the company will face the plateau problem before long.

Still other firms are actively looking ahead to see what might be in store for their managers. At Imperial Oil, employees were asked to view the merger with Texaco Canada Inc. as an advantage because the new organization would have more opportunities for promotion. Employees filled out a questionnaire which asked them to indicate what positions they wanted in the new organization. Seventy-nine percent got their first choice, and 93 percent got one of their top three choices.

At IBM Canada, an elaborate horizontal career path has been developed that complements the traditional upward route through the hierarchy. A systems engineer, for example, can move through the technical ranks and end up being paid more than some managers. IBM also conveys to employees that plateauing may be caused by factors beyond the employee's control, and that reaching a plateau should not be viewed as a failure. ▲

In this chapter we analyze what is known about human motivation and how these findings can be applied in the workplace. We first define the term "motivation," note its importance, and describe the two types of motivation that exist. Included in this discussion is an analysis of how concepts like motivation, ability, and performance are related. Second, we outline two basic philosophies of human nature and show how these philosophies influence managerial behaviour and subordinate motivation. Third, we briefly describe the most popular motivation theories. Fourth, the role of money in motivation is examined using the motivation theories described in the chapter. The final section investigates the issue of job design and how the nature of the job influences employee motivation.

THE FUNDAMENTALS OF MOTIVATION

motivation

Motivation is the result of factors that initially cause behaviour, channel it in certain directions, and maintain it over time. The factors which cause motivation may be found within a person (needs) or outside the person (the external environment). The salesclerks at Baylor's Department Store are exhibiting low motivation levels.

THE IMPORTANCE OF MOTIVATION

LEARNING OBJECTIVE 1

Define the term "motivation" and explain why it is important in all types of organizations.

Most managers intuitively believe that the organization benefits if workers are enthusiastic and persistent. On balance, this belief is correct.[3] Motivated employees make an organization more effective for several reasons. First, motivated employees always look for better ways to do a job. This fact applies to top managers who are developing innovative corporate strategies, to middle managers who are looking for better ways to help implement those strategies, and to production workers who are looking for better ways to do certain production procedures. When people look for improved ways to do a job, they often find them.

Second, motivated employees are generally more concerned about quality than unmotivated workers. A motivated sales manager at Willson's Stationers will spend extra time analyzing market research; a salesclerk at Eaton's will take extra care when dealing with customers; and a technical worker at duPont Canada will carefully check to see that a product is put together properly. Organizations benefit when employees, clients, and customers are treated with care because it increases the chance that they will want to interact with the organization in the future.

Third, highly motivated workers are more productive than apathetic workers. Much has been written about the high productivity of workers in Japan, where fewer people, for instance, are needed to produce an automobile than in North America.[4] The high productivity of Japanese workers makes Japanese organizations very competitive in world markets. The World Competitiveness Report published by the World Economic Forum ranked Canada 13th in industrial efficiency among 24 developed countries, and last among large industrial nations.[5] If Canadian business firms are to effectively compete in international markets, they must have highly motivated employees in order to get the benefits of higher productivity.

Fourth, highly motivated workers are less likely to be absent from work. In the Canadian automobile industry, absenteeism has been a long-standing problem, and it regularly arises in labour negotiations at General Motors, Ford, and Chrysler. Absenteeism reduces efficiency and costs the organization money. While some of the daily absenteeism at Canadian companies is for legitimate reasons like illness, a portion of it stems from poor motivation.[6] Creating a motivated work force reduces costs and increases efficiency.

FACTORS AFFECTING MOTIVATION

individual characteristics

job characteristics

organizational characteristics

The factors contributing to employee motivation fall into three categories: individual characteristics, job characteristics, and organizational characteristics.[7] **Individual characteristics** include the needs of people, their attitudes about work, their value system (what they think is important), and their feelings about different kinds of jobs. Each individual has different characteristics, and is therefore motivated differently in the work place. **Job characteristics** are the attributes evident in the job the employee is performing. Included in this category are the variety of skills needed to do a job, the amount of autonomy the job provides, the conceptual completeness of the job, the type of feedback the person gets, and so forth. **Organizational characteristics** include the reward system, rules, policies, procedures, and managerial practices evident in the organization. If employees see little connection between their performance and the rewards they receive, motivation will likely be low. Or, if rules, policies, and procedures stifle individual initiative, motivation may be low. In this chapter, these three factors will appear again and again as we examine the topic of motivation.

Intrinsic and Extrinsic Motivation

An important reason people work is that they receive "rewards." We can break these rewards down into two general classes. **Extrinsic rewards** are separate from the task performed and are controlled by other people. Pay, promotions, compliments, and recognition are examples of extrinsic rewards. For example, at AMP Canada Ltd., a producer of electrical connection systems, customers can nominate employees who have helped them in some way. Any employee who is nominated receives a button that says "I delighted a customer." The award is presented by the general manager in the presence of all the employees.[8]

extrinsic rewards

Intrinsic rewards are an integral part of the task and are administered by the individual doing the task. Examples of intrinsic rewards include a student who pats himself or herself on the back after scoring well on a test, and a worker who gets a feeling of accomplishment after completing a task that was challenging and interesting.

intrinsic rewards

LEARNING OBJECTIVE 2

Describe the difference between intrinsic and extrinsic motivation.

These two types of rewards lead to two distinct types of motivation. **Extrinsic motivation** exists when a person works hard at a task because of the promise that some obvious reward will be given if the job is done well. **Intrinsic motivation**, on the other hand, exists if the person performs a task in the absence of any obvious reward for doing so. Consider two examples. Suppose that you feel that the work of the United Way is important, and you therefore volunteer to work on the annual fundraising team. When the drive is complete, you will probably feel a great sense of satisfaction for having done what you feel is socially useful. You rewarded yourself for doing well and were not dependent on someone else to give you rewards. You were intrinsically motivated.

extrinsic motivation
intrinsic motivation

Now suppose that you are a salesperson working on commission. You know that if you close a big sale, you will receive a bonus. So you work hard and make the sale. In this case, you have been extrinsically motivated by the promise of a reward for making a sale. There might, of course, at the same time be an element of intrinsic motivation here if you get some pleasure out of doing a good job.

Both intrinsic and extrinsic rewards can motivate people. Intrinsic rewards are particularly powerful because they involve people's beliefs about what is right or wrong. If an organization's employees believe that they are selling a product or service that is helping others, the workers will feel an enthusiasm about their tasks and the organization will benefit. To boost employee performance, managers should try to let employees work in such a way that intrinsic motivation is maximized. For a number of reasons, creating such a situation is usually impossible, so most organizations rely on extrinsic rewards (primarily money) to motivate workers.

Both intrinsic and extrinsic motivation are usually present in the workplace. Although it may seem that this combination would give managers more opportunities to motivate workers, some evidence exists that intrinsic and extrinsic rewards work against each other. In one experiment, students worked on several interesting puzzles.[9] One half of the subjects were paid for working on the puzzles and the other half were not. Subjects were given free time during the experiment when they could do whatever they wished. The activity they engaged in during their free time was an indication of their intrinsic motivation. Students who were not paid for working on the puzzles spent significantly more free time working on the puzzles than did subjects who were paid. Thus, it appeared that extrinsic rewards reduced intrinsic motivation. This likely happened because the external rewards caused the subjects to attribute their behaviour to external rather than internal sources.

Extrinsic rewards commonly motivate people. Stephen Mooney, a Century 21 agent, uses a cellular telephone and a Cadillac to conduct his business. These extrinsic rewards convey to Mr. Mooney that he is valued.

The possibility that intrinsic motivation is reduced when extrinsic rewards are given has interesting practical implications. In the extreme, it suggests that if the pay of workers is tied completely to performance, only extrinsic motivation will be evident and none of the benefits of intrinsic motivation will remain. More realistically, it is probably the case that several other factors also affect the relationship between extrinsic and intrinsic motivation. For example, the nature of the task may be an intervening variable. If the reward the employee receives is an integral part of the task (for instance in commission selling), giving extrinsic rewards may not reduce intrinsic motivation. The most recent research on this issue suggests that extrinsic rewards do not consistently reduce intrinsic motivation.[10]

JOB SATISFACTION, MOTIVATION, AND JOB PERFORMANCE

job satisfaction

Job satisfaction refers to employees' overall attitudes about their jobs. If that attitude is favourable, they are satisfied; if it is unfavourable, they are dissatisfied. Job satisfaction surveys conducted in Canadian business firms show the following mixed results:

- A survey of 2300 workers found that 75 percent are satisfied with the content of their jobs, but less than 50 percent felt that management showed genuine interest in them. Less than one-third felt that promotions were based on merit.[11]
- Another survey of employees in 94 companies across the U.S. and Canada found that while workers were optimistic and committed to their work, they also felt frustrated because they did not have enough control over what happened in their jobs, and because their skills were not used to the fullest extent.[12]
- Because of downsizing, all employees felt less secure than they did just a few years ago.[13]
- Many workers were dissatisfied with their salaries, and felt that pay was not tied to performance.

Many managers assume that providing good working conditions for employees and showing personal concern for them will cause them to be satisfied. They further assume that satisfied workers will respond with higher productivity. Unfortunately, research studies have shown that the relationship between employee satisfaction and productivity is rather weak, at least at the individual level.[14] At the organizational level, the relationship may be a bit stronger. One study based on data from 13 808 teachers in 298 different schools showed that the highest performing schools also had the highest levels of individual employee satisfaction.[15]

LEARNING OBJECTIVE 3

Discuss the relationship between employee satisfaction and employee productivity.

When we look at the relationship between employee satisfaction and employee productivity, it is important to ask the right questions. Before asking, "Is a *satisfied* worker a *productive* worker?" we should ask "Is a *satisfied* worker a *motivated* worker?" Need satisfaction may cause some people to work hard (to get even more need satisfaction), but it may cause others to put forth less effort once some basic level of it is achieved (see the "assumptions" box in Figure 12-1).

Once this question is answered, we can ask, "Is a *motivated* worker a *productive* worker?" Once again, the answer varies depending on the situation and the people involved (see Figure 12-1). If tasks are poorly designed, for example, productivity will be low regardless of worker motivation levels. A well-designed task system, on the other hand, can enhance productivity even if employee motivation is relatively low. Individual abilities, attitudes, and aptitudes also modify the motivation-performance

FIGURE 12-1 THE SATISFACTION-MOTIVATION-PRODUCTIVITY MODEL.

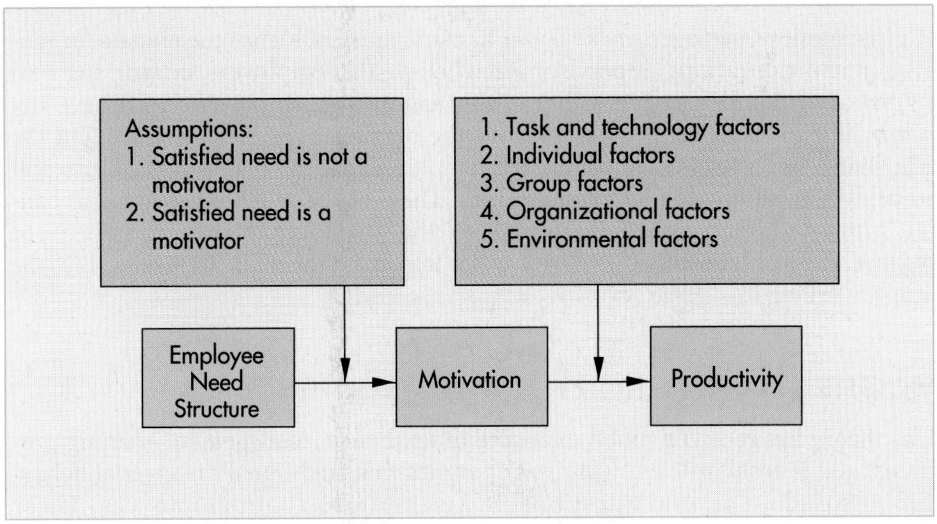

relationship. If an individual's abilities are low, high motivation cannot lead to high productivity. If the individual's role perception (his or her view of what is appropriate job behaviour) is inaccurate, there may not be a clear connection between motivation and performance. Group norms can also have a positive or negative influence on individual productivity.

LEARNING OBJECTIVE 4
Write a simple formula showing how motivation and ability interact to affect employee performance.

Employee performance is the result of many factors, some of which are unknown to the manager, and some may not even be consciously understood by workers. But much of the variation in employee performance can be explained by two variables: employee motivation and employee ability. These variables are related as follows:

$$\text{Performance} = \text{Motivation} \times \text{Ability}$$

ability

Ability refers to a person's competence at a certain task. It is different from motivation, which refers to a person's desire to do a task. The distinction between ability and motivation is important in many situations. For example, if two defensive linemen are vying for a starting position on a football team, they may do so with equal enthusiasm. However, if the first player averages five tackles per game and the second averages only one, the coach will pick the first player. In business, two salespeople may pursue customers with equal vigour, but one may sell much more than the other. Although they have the same level of motivation, their aptitude for the job is at different levels.

A low score on either motivation or ability results in low performance, but the formula also implies that a high score on one variable can overcome a moderate score on the other variable. The 1990 Montreal Expos, for example, had many players on their roster who were cast-offs from other baseball teams, yet they were pennant contenders for much of the season. One player, Dennis (Oil Can) Boyd, said that the team members were motivated to prove that their previous teams made a mistake when they got rid of them.[16]

In the Management Challenge, the managers at Baylor's concluded that their salespeople had low motivation (and perhaps they did), but they might also have low ability. Either one of these factors could explain the poor performance results. Management has a responsibility to influence both motivation and ability so that workers can be high performers.

PHILOSOPHIES OF HUMAN NATURE

LEARNING OBJECTIVE 5
Outline the two basic philosophies of human nature.

The assumptions managers make about human nature influence the climate for motivation in organizations. Supervisors who believe that employees are working simply out of economic necessity will probably assume that employees won't have any worthwhile ideas about how to improve the organization's performance. On the other hand, supervisors who believe that employees are interested in their jobs will probably make quite different assumptions. They will be much more likely to consult with employees about how to improve the workplace. Managers' positive or negative views of human nature have a major impact on the motivational levels of the people working for them.

McGregor's Theory X and Theory Y

This theory has received much exposure in textbooks, management training programs, and journal articles.[17] McGregor argues that traditional managerial behaviour is based on several questionable assumptions about employees. These assumptions, which he labelled Theory X, are shown on the left-hand side of Table 12-1. **Theory X** managers assume that it is necessary to coerce, control, or threaten employees in order to motivate them.

Theory X

McGregor claims that conventional management practices are based on Theory X assumptions, pointing, for instance, to the use of hierarchical models of organization where one person controls another, and to the existence of quality-control inspectors, who check on the behaviour of others.

Theory X assumptions, according to McGregor, are outdated; employees, he says, would contribute far more to an organization if a completely different set of assumptions, which he labelled **Theory Y**, were the guiding force behind managerial behaviour (see Table 12-1). Theory Y managers assume that employees are mature and responsible, and do not require coercion or excessive control in order to perform effectively. McGregor believes that Theory Y represents a realistic assessment of people in the workplace, and that Theory Y managers will create an environment where employees can fulfill their potential.

Theory Y

TABLE 12-1 A COMPARISON OF MCGREGOR'S THEORY X AND THEORY Y ASSUMPTIONS ABOUT HUMAN NATURE.

Theory X	Theory Y
The average person inherently dislikes work and will avoid it if possible.	The expenditure of physical and mental effort in work is as natural as play or rest.
Because of the dislike of work, most people must be coerced, controlled, directed, and threatened with punishment to get them to perform effectively.	People will exercise self-direction and self-control in the pursuit of objectives to which they are committed.
The average person lacks ambition, avoids responsibility, and seeks security and economic rewards above all else.	Commitment to objectives is a function of the rewards associated with achievement.
Most people lack creative ability and are resistant to change.	The average person learns, under proper conditions, not only to accept but to seek responsibility.
Since most people are self-centred, they are not concerned with the goals of the organization.	The capacity to exercise a relatively high degree of imagination, ingenuity, and creativity in the solution of organizational problems is widely, not narrowly, distributed in the population.

Argyris' Maturity Theory

A theory put forward by Chris Argyris suggests that a conflict exists between the demands of the mature personality and the demands of the typical organization. In many organizations, subordinates are expected to be submissive and passive, and to carry out orders without questioning them. Employees are:

1. Allowed minimal control over their work.
2. Expected to have a short time perspective.
3. Induced to use a few limited abilities.
4. Expected to produce under conditions which lead to psychological failure.[18]

When mature employees encounter these conditions, they can: (1) escape (e.g., quit the job, be absent from work, get promoted to a position where the structure is less rigid); (2) fight (e.g., put pressure on the organization by means of informal groups, formally organized labour unions, or ombudsmen); or (3) adapt (e.g., be apathetic or indifferent). Many employees adopt the latter strategy. When managers fail to recognize subordinate maturity, they create a counterproductive work environment.

The Self-Fulfilling Prophecy in Motivation

self-fulfilling prophecy

Some managers expect employees to act in an immature manner, and as a result, they do. A **self-fulfilling prophecy** is a prediction which comes true because people do things to make it come true. Numerous studies have demonstrated that self-fulfilling prophecies occur. In one classic study, elementary school teachers were told that about 20 percent of their students were intellectual "bloomers."[19] The teachers were told that these youngsters would achieve remarkable progress during the school year. In fact, the 20 percent sample was chosen at random and did not differ in intelligence or ability from the rest of the class. The only variable was the teachers' expectations. During the school year, the students actually did achieve significantly greater progress. The teachers' expectations became a self-fulfilling prophecy.

The work of McGregor and Argyris suggests a way of using self-fulfilling prophecy to advantage. A manager should have high expectations of subordinates rather than low expectations; high productivity will then result. Because many managers have low expectations of employees, many organizations fall victim to self-fulfilling prophecies. Therefore they fail to develop their most valuable resource—their employees. Managers who fail to communicate high expectations may significantly damage the attitudes and career aspirations of employees.[20] Theory Y managers—who assume that employees are enthusiastic about work and want responsibility—are much more likely to develop the organization's human resources than Theory X managers are.

Theories of Work Motivation

LEARNING OBJECTIVE 6
Explain the difference between content and process theories of motivation.

content theories
process theories

Research on motivation has resulted in the development of many motivation theories. Three basic types of theories exist: content theories, process theories, and reinforcement theory. **Content theories** try to identify the needs that motivate people. They are based on the assumption that people's behaviour can be explained and predicted by discovering the basic needs that people are trying to satisfy. **Process theories** focus not on individual needs, but on the processes that motivate people. In process theories, needs are just one element in motivation. For example, a person may have a need for money, but other factors such as working conditions, the nature of the compensation scheme, or the job the person must do to get the money, will determine how motivated the person will be. Reinforcement theory views internal needs as unimportant, and says that a person's motivation can be explained through knowledge of a person's past experience. If a person has had a pleasant (unpleasant) experience doing a task, the theory argues that the person is more (less) likely to do the task again in the future.

CONTENT THEORIES OF MOTIVATION

Although each person has a unique set of needs, similarities exist in the way these needs motivate people. Figure 12-2 shows the basic content model of motivation. The person's needs create tensions (drives) to fulfill those needs. These tensions cause specific behaviours which are aimed at relieving the tension. Once the behaviour has taken place, the drive is reduced and the need is no longer felt (at least until the need arises again). Consider someone who is hungry (the person has a need for food). This person experiences tension (hunger pangs), which causes the person to get some food to eat (the behaviour). Once the food is eaten, the tension is reduced and the need is satisfied (until the individual gets hungry again).

This model explains some human activities, but it fails to account for complex situations like people's jobs. It neglects the following facts: (1) each person has a different set of needs and these needs change over time; (2) needs are translated into action in different ways by different people; (3) people may be inconsistent in translating their needs into actions; and (4) people react differently to need fulfillment or lack of need fulfillment.[21]

LEARNING OBJECTIVE 7
Identity the essential features of three content motivation theories.

In spite of these shortcomings, some of the most popular motivation theories—Maslow's hierarchy of needs, Alderfer's ERG theory, Herzberg's two-factor theory, and McClelland's acquired needs theory—are need-based.

MASLOW'S HIERARCHY OF NEEDS

Maslow's hierarchy of needs

Abraham Maslow proposed a hierarchy of needs based on the idea that unsatisfied needs motivate behaviour. In **Maslow's hierarchy of needs**, those needs which are lower in the hierarchy must be largely satisfied before needs further up the hierarchy will emerge to motivate behaviour.[22] In Maslow's view (see Figure 12-3), there are five needs in the hierarchy:

1. *Physiological needs* Those needs concerned with the basic biological functions, such as eating and sleeping.
2. *Safety needs* Those needs concerned with protecting the person from physical and psychological harm, such as clothing, shelter, and safety.

FIGURE 12-2 THE CONTENT MODEL OF MOTIVATION.

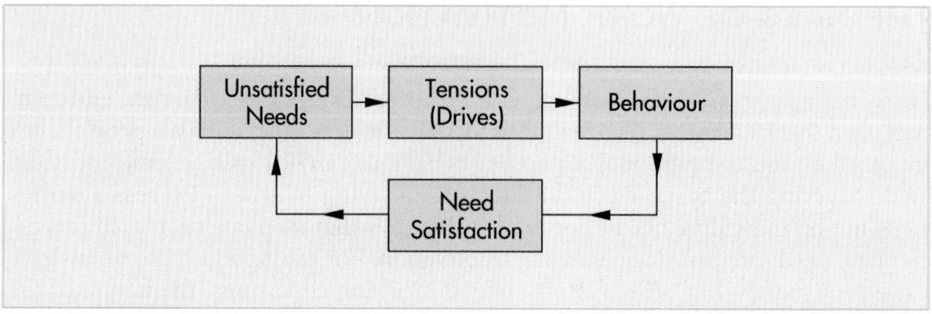

FIGURE 12-3 MASLOW'S NEED HIERARCHY AND HOW NEEDS ARE SATISFIED BY THE ORGANIZATION.

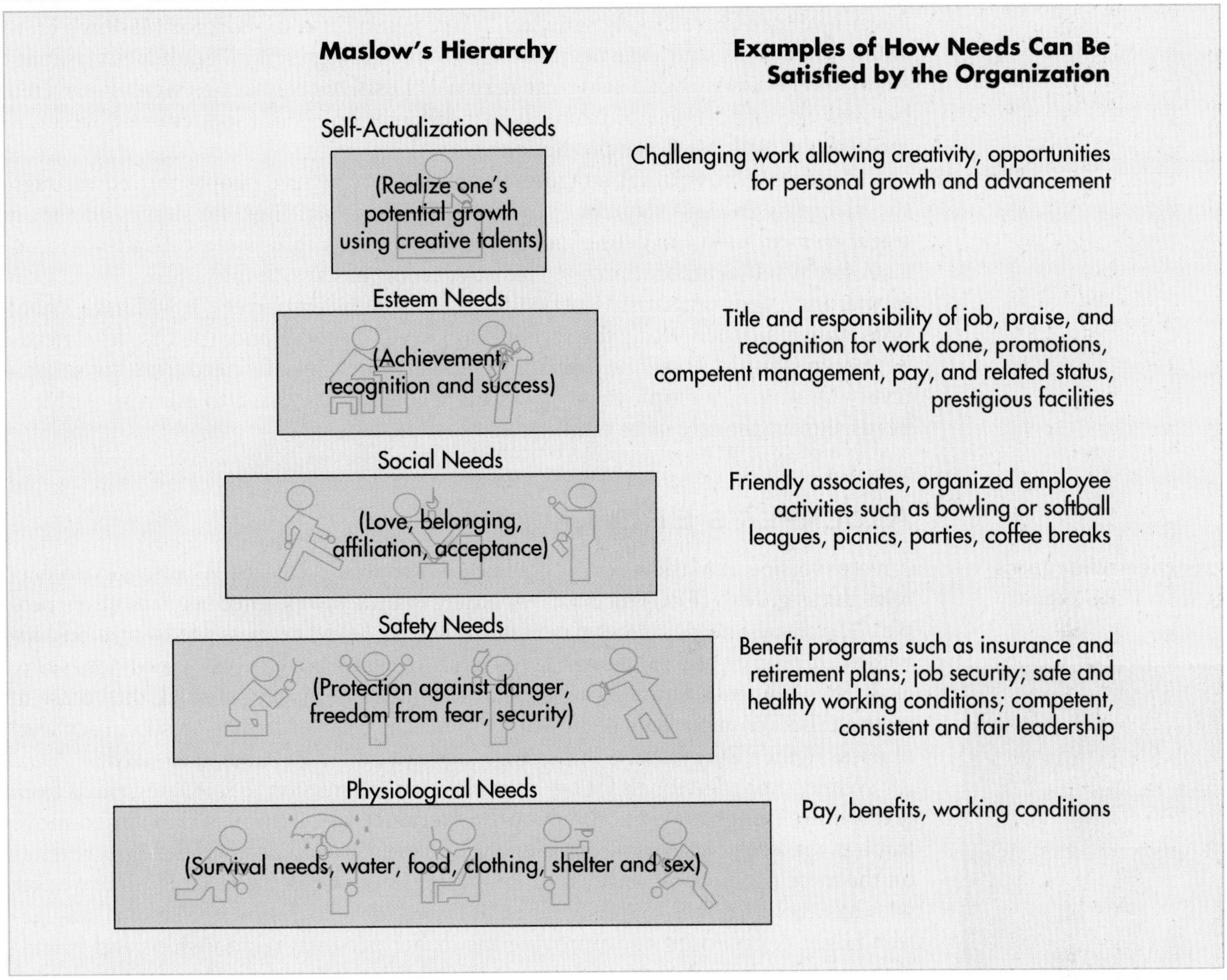

3. *Belonging needs* The need to associate with one's own kind; social interaction, love, acceptance, and group membership.
4. *Esteem (status)* The need to feel important; feelings of self-worth.
5. *Self-actualization* The need to reach one's ultimate potential, or to fulfill one's destiny.

Once a particular need becomes largely satisfied, it declines in importance as a motivator of behaviour, and the next level of need increases in importance as a motivator.

For most people, higher-order needs are less satisfied than lower-order needs. A typical person might be 95 percent satisfied with physiological needs, 90 percent with safety needs, 60 percent with love needs, 40 percent with esteem needs, and 10 percent with self-actualization needs. Differences in satisfaction levels are likely to appear across cultures. In developing countries, lower-order needs are often poorly satisfied, while in Canada they are generally satisfied for most of the population.

Although it is a popular and widely accepted theory of motivation, Maslow's hierarchy has not been strongly supported by data gathered in organizations. A study of managers in one organization over a five-year period tested the extent to which changes in needs correlated with need strengths. Little support was found for the hierarchy.[23] Another study tested the idea that upper-level needs emerge only when lower-level needs are largely satisfied. It too found little support for Maslow's hierarchy.[24] In a third study, the need strength of recent high school graduates was measured several times over a two-year period.[25] Positive correlations were discovered between the importance of needs at two different levels in the hierarchy, which is inconsistent with Maslow's predictions.

Maslow's own writings suggest that he did not believe people moved through the hierarchy in rigid sequence. In one of his later writings, he suggested that it might be most useful to define just two levels of needs (physiological/safety and social/esteem/self-actualization).[26] This suggestion has two implications: First, if an organization does not satisfy the first-level needs of its employees, it will have a hard time motivating them using the second-level needs. Second, once the first-level needs have been satisfied, it will be difficult to predict which specific need from the second level will motivate employees. Thus, management will have to address multiple needs simultaneously in its employees.[27]

Alderfer's ERG Theory

existence-relatedness-growth (ERG) theory

A recent version of Maslow's concept of needs hierarchy is Clayton Alderfer's **existence-relatedness-growth (ERG) theory.**[28] According to ERG theory, three needs motivate people: (1) existence needs (physical or material needs); (2) relatedness needs (relationships with other people); and (3) growth needs (creative efforts used to satisfy needs for esteem and self-fulfillment). Once existence and relatedness needs are satisfied, they cease to motivate. But the importance of growth needs may increase as they are satisfied. Each level of needs in the ERG system is increasingly abstract and more difficult to satisfy.

According to Maslow, once people have satisfied their physiological, safety, and social needs, they begin to be motivated by higher-level needs like self-actualization (the need to become all that a person is capable of becoming). Gaining increased knowledge about a specific subject area is just one example of fulfilling self-actualization needs.

While some individuals follow a step-by-step progression in satisfying needs from levels one through three, some people experience frustration as they try to move through the levels. A person may be unable to satisfy growth needs and so concentrates on the more concrete relatedness or existence needs. Thus, an assembly-line worker who has a job that fails to satisfy his or her need for recognition or personal satisfaction might concentrate on improving his or her personal relationships and friendships with other employees and on gaining additional pay and job security.

Herzberg's Two-Factor Theory

A departure from much of the thinking about work motivation is the two-factor theory proposed by Frederick Herzberg.[29] Until Herzberg, researchers had usually assumed that job satisfaction and job dissatisfaction were at opposite ends of the same continuum. This meant that what caused job satisfaction would cause job dissatisfaction if it were removed.

Based upon unstructured interviews with 200 engineers and accountants, Herzberg concluded that this view of job satisfaction was incorrect and that satisfaction and dissatisfaction were actually distinct outcomes caused by different phenomena in the work environment. In the study, he asked the engineers and accountants to think of a time when they felt especially good or bad about their jobs, and to describe the circumstances leading to those feelings. After analyzing their responses, Herzberg concluded that one group of factors was causing job satisfaction and another group of factors was causing job dissatisfaction. **Motivators** are factors that are concerned with the work itself; they alone can cause a worker to be satisfied. **Hygienes** are factors that are concerned with the environment in which work is performed; their absence causes workers to be dissatisfied (see Table 12-2). Thus, in Herzberg's view, it is possible to increase job satisfaction without reducing job dissatisfaction and vice versa.

motivators
hygienes

TABLE 12-2 MOTIVATORS AND HYGIENES IN HERZBERG'S THEORY.

Motivators	Hygienes
Achievement	Company policy, administration
Recognition	Technical supervision
Advancement	Interpersonal relations
Work itself	Salary
Possibility of growth	Job security
Responsibility	Personal life
	Working conditions
	Fringe benefits
	Status

Herzberg's ideas have been criticized on the following grounds:

1. his results can't be repeated unless his unstructured methodology is used (i.e., his theory is method-bound)
2. the two categories of motivators and hygienes are not as distinct as Herzberg claimed (e.g., blue collar workers often see pay as a motivator)[30]
3. human nature explains Herzberg's findings (i.e., people take credit for their achievements and blame others for their failings.)[31]

Maslow, Alderfer, and Herzberg Compared

The ideas of Maslow, Alderfer, and Herzberg are widely accepted by students, academics, and managers. Several similarities can be found among the theories; the most basic one is that they all assume that needs motivate behaviour. There is also much similarity in the needs that are identified. Figure 12-4 shows how the needs in the three proposals are related. Herzberg's "motivators" are equivalent to Maslow's "higher-order needs" and to Alderfer's "growth needs." Herzberg's "hygienes" correspond to Maslow's physiological, safety, and social needs, and to Alderfer's "existence" and "relatedness" needs.

FIGURE 12-4 A COMPARISON OF MASLOW, ALDERFER, AND HERZBERG.

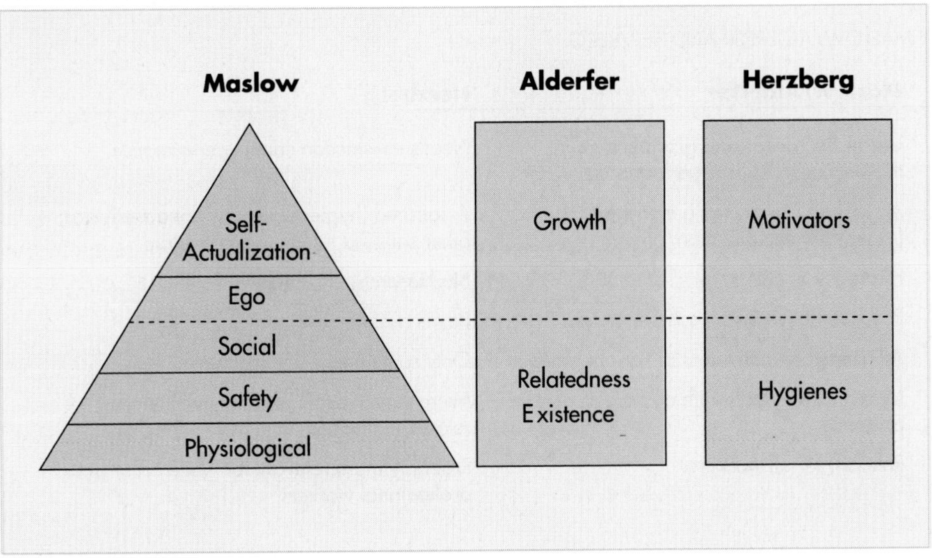

The theories do, however, display some important differences (see Table 12-3). The table reveals obvious differences in underlying assumptions. Herzberg, for example, assumes money is not a motivator, while Maslow assumes that money is a motivator if it satisfies needs. In spite of differences like this, many people seem to accept both theories.

McClelland's Acquired Needs Theory

need for achievement (nAch)

need for power (nPow)

need for affiliation (nAff)

The research of David McClelland emphasizes that needs are learned as individuals interact with their environment.[32] He has identified three basic human motives: achievement, affiliation, and power. Individuals with a high **need for achievement (nAch)** get satisfaction from reaching goals. People high in nAch want immediate feedback on their work, and they prefer tasks of moderate difficulty. Tasks that are too easy or too difficult do not provide satisfaction to people with high nAch. They also like to work independently so that successful task performance (or failure) can be traced to their own efforts rather than the efforts of someone else. Individuals high in nAch are often wealthy, but they are not motivated by money per se. Rather, they use money as a method of "keeping score" of their achievements. People high in nAch often own their own businesses or work in sales-related occupations.

People with a high **need for power (nPow)** get satisfaction from controlling others, and from being in positions of influence. The actual achievement of goals is of secondary importance to the high nPow person; instead, the means by which goals are achieved (that is, the exercise of power) are of primary importance. Organizations that encourage the exercise of power tend to attract high nPow individuals—for example, military and political organizations.

Individuals with a high **need for affiliation (nAff)** get their satisfaction from social and interpersonal activities. They form strong interpersonal ties and try to "get close" to people emotionally. If asked to choose between working at a task with those who are technically competent or with those who are their friends, high nAff people will choose working with their friends.

McClelland believes that each person possesses all three needs (as well as others), but that one need dominates a person's behaviour. The Thematic Apperception Test (TAT) is used to determine which need dominates. In this test, people are shown several pictures and are asked to write a short story about what is "going on" in each

TABLE 12-3 A COMPARISON OF MASLOW/ALDERFER AND HERZBERG.

Issue	Maslow/Alderfer	Herzberg
1. The satisfaction-performance relationship	Unsatisfied needs energize behaviour; this behaviour causes performance	Needs satisfaction causes performance
2. Effect of need satisfaction	A satisfied need is not a motivator (except self-actualization/growth)	A satisfied (hygiene) need is not a motivator; other satisfied needs are motivators
3. Need order	Hierarchy of needs	No hierarchy
4. Effect of pay	Pay is a motivator if it satisfies needs	Pay is not a motivator
5. Effect of needs	All needs are motivators at various times	Only some needs are motivators
6. View of motivation	Macro view—deals with all aspects of existence	Micro view—deals primarily with work-related motivation
7. Worker level	Relevant for all workers	Probably more relevant for white collar and professional workers

one. What is "going on" is, of course, determined by the person's subjective perceptions. The written comments are converted to an objective measure of the strength of each of the three needs using a scoring technique developed by McClelland.

McClelland says that the need for achievement can be learned or unlearned. He has reported numerous instances in which individuals with a low initial need to achieve were subjected to a series of classroom experiences that resulted in an increased need to achieve. He believes that cultures that are economically backward can be changed by inducing and stimulating the need to achieve.

Much of McClelland's recent research has concentrated on the impact of the three needs on managerial success. It was once believed that high achievers did not make good managers since many of the conditions facing managers—for example, dependence on others and lack of concrete feedback—did not satisfy the needs of high achievers. More recently, however, successful managers have been found to have a high need for achievement as well as a high need for power.[33]

McClelland's work has been criticized in three areas. First, the use of a technique like the TAT requires the interpretation of subjective comments, and this is an art which critics say is as likely to show the bias of the researcher as it is the motives of the person writing the story. Second, the argument that need for achievement can be taught to adults conflicts with much of the psychological literature showing that the acquisition of motives normally occurs in childhood and is difficult to change once established. Third, even if the need to achieve can be taught, its effects may be only temporary.

PROCESS THEORIES OF WORK MOTIVATION

LEARNING OBJECTIVE 8
Identify the essential features of the three process motivation theories.

As we have seen, content theories emphasize the needs that motivate people. Process theories do not ignore needs, but they focus more on the goals or outcomes that people desire, and how those goals and desired outcomes motivate people. There are three process theories that are currently popular: equity theory, expectancy theory, and goal setting.

Equity Theory

equity theory

This motivation theory is based on the notion that people are motivated by their desire to be treated equitably. In organizations, employees exchange their services (inputs) for pay and other benefits (outcomes). **Equity theory** proposes that individuals compare their input-outcome ratio to the input-outcome ratio of others doing similar work.[34] If a person feels inequitably treated after making this comparison, he or she will be motivated to reduce the inequity. This problem of inequity was mentioned by salesclerks at Baylor's in the Management Challenge.

A number of inequity-reducing strategies might be tried, including:

1. Increasing or decreasing inputs or outcomes relative to those of the comparison person (e.g., producing more output and therefore earning more money).
2. Distorting one's perceptions of one's own inputs or outcomes, or those of the other person (e.g., convincing yourself that your job outcomes are better than they actually are, or that the comparison person isn't really as well off as you originally thought).
3. Changing to a different comparison person (e.g., deciding that your comparison person is no longer appropriate to compare yourself to).
4. Leaving the situation (e.g., quitting the job).

Two factors are important in determining the amount of inequity employees feel: (1) whether they are paid on the basis of how much they produce or on the hours they spend at work, and (2) whether they feel underpaid or overpaid. A large number of studies have tested equity theory under the four conditions possible by combining these two factors. The predictions for each situation are indicated in Figure 12-5. The strongest support for equity theory predictions is evident when people are paid on a piece-rate basis.[35]

In one study, 198 employees in the underwriting department of an insurance company had their offices renovated. While the work was being done, these employees were randomly assigned to an office of either higher, equal, or lower status than the one they previously occupied. The performance of employees assigned to higher status offices increased, and the performance of employees assigned to lower status offices decreased during the renovation period.[36] These effects are consistent with equity theory predictions.

Most tests of equity theory focus on the behaviour of employees. However, equity theory also predicts that employees may change their attitudes in an attempt to reestablish equity. In one study, 114 clerical workers in a nonunion manufacturing firm received a pay cut. During this time, workers reestablished equity by increasing their subjective perception of the positive aspects of their work environment.[37]

Equity theory may help management make decisions about pay reductions. When the amount of employee theft in a manufacturing plant was measured after pay rates had been reduced by 15 percent, groups whose pay was reduced stole twice as much as they did when they felt equitably paid.[38]

While equity theory looks intuitively promising, some important questions remain unanswered. How does a person choose a comparison person? Can a given factor—for example, responsibility—be an input for one person and an outcome for another person? What alternatives will employees use as they try to reduce their feelings of inequity—complaining, reducing output, quitting?

EXPECTANCY THEORY

expectancy theory

Expectancy theory assumes that people think about how much effort they will put into a task before they start to work on it, and that a person's motivation to do a job is determined by three things: outcomes the person sees as desirable (valence), the probability that effort will lead to good performance (the effort-performance (E→P) expectancy), and the probability that good performance will lead to the desired outcomes (the performance-outcome (P→O) expectancy).[39] These three components are combined as follows:

$$\text{Motivation} = (E \rightarrow P) \times (P \rightarrow O) \times \text{Valence}$$

FIGURE 12-5 EQUITY THEORY PREDICTIONS.

	Underpayment		Overpayment	
	Quality	Quantity	Quality	Quantity
Piece Rate	Decrease	Increase	Increase	Decrease
Hourly	Decrease	Decrease	Increase	Increase

Valence is the desirability of outcomes as subjectively perceived. The valence of an outcome is positive when one desires it and negative when one wants to avoid it.

valence

The **effort-performance expectancy** reflects one's belief that effort expenditure will lead to good performance. It is a probability estimate ranging from 0 (no chance) to 1 (certainty). Thus, if a person has a great deal of training or experience in the job she is being asked to do, she would probably rate the E→P expectancy very high. If she is inexperienced, she would probably rate it as low.

effort-performance expectancy

The **performance-outcome expectancy** reflects a belief about the connection between performance and rewards. It is also a probability estimate ranging from 0 (no connection) to 1 (certain connection). Thus, if someone knows that in the job in question people who have high performance get big rewards, he would probably assign a high rating to the P→O expectancy. On the other hand, if he thinks there is very little connection between performance and rewards, he might assign a much lower number.

performance-outcome expectancy

If all three elements are high, a person will be very highly motivated. If any one of the three elements is close to zero, however, the person's motivation level will be very low. This is because the three variables are multiplied by each other, and any number multiplied by zero equals zero.

Consider, for example, what might happen in a course you are not interested in, but you are forced to take as part of your curriculum. There may not be many desired outcomes for you in such a course (valence is low or negative). In addition, assume that you have heard that former students could not see any relationship between the amount of time they spent studying for exams in the course and the grade they got on exams (E→P expectancy is low). This leads them to conclude that there is no connection between performance and rewards (P→O expectancy is low). In this situation, it is very likely that you will not be motivated to work hard in the course.

As we saw earlier in the chapter, many Canadian workers do not see much connection between their performance and the rewards they receive from their job. Expectancy theory tells us that we should not be surprised to find that these workers are not very motivated.

A great deal of research has been conducted in testing expectancy theory.[40] The typical study involves gathering data from managers on valence, expectancy, and effort. To determine how well expectancy theory predicts behaviour, correlation analysis is used. Changes in the independent variables (valence, E→P, and P→O) are correlated with changes in the dependent variable (effort). Generally, expectancy theory accounts for only about one-quarter of the variance in behaviour; this leaves the cause of a lot of behaviour unexplained. For an interesting application of expectancy theory and equity theory, see the Global Management insert "Expectancy, Equity, and Major League Baseball."

Kurt Browning has the motivation to practice the long hours necessary to win the gold medal in the World Figure Skating Championship—a goal he has achieved several times. Effective managers motivate others to perform the tasks needed for organizational success.

GOAL SETTING

The concept of goal setting was introduced in Chapter 4, where we noted that people who set goals that satisfy the criteria listed in Table 4-3 usually outperform those who do not. Goal setting has recently received a lot of attention as a motivational technique.[41] Many laboratory and field studies have examined the effect of goal setting on performance.[42] Two field studies in the lumber business are typical of the results. In the first study, the productivity of 292 independent pulpwood producers was analyzed.[43] The highest productivity was found in logging crews where the supervisor set specific production goals for the workers and stayed with them in the field while they did their work. Productivity was high even in groups that had little mechanized equipment to help in their work.

GLOBAL MANAGEMENT

EXPECTANCY, EQUITY, AND MAJOR LEAGUE BASEBALL

Expectancy and equity theory may seem like very abstract ideas. But these theories have extremely practical applications. Consider the case of major league baseball. This is a "business" in which (1) players are well paid for high performance, and (2) there is widespread agreement about what constitutes high performance. Since volumes of statistics are gathered annually about players' performances, when a contract dispute arises about how much one player should be paid, it is relatively easy to compare that player's performance with others and adjust his salary accordingly.

Expectancy and equity theory make predictions about what kind of performance a player will exhibit, given that we have some knowledge of how satisfied he is with his pay. As it happens, there is a way to estimate player satisfaction because of something called "free agency." Beginning in 1976, major league baseball's collective bargaining agreement allowed players who had spent six years in the major leagues to "play out their option," i.e., to play out the year without a contract. After that, the player was allowed to become a "free agent" and see if any other team wanted to bid for his services.

As part of the agreement, individuals who were playing out their option received only 80 percent of their contract. Because the players had not signed a contract, and because they were getting only 80 percent of their normal pay, it seems reasonable to assume that they were dissatisfied with their pay in an option year. In the jargon of equity theory, these players were experiencing "inequitable underreward," and therefore their performance in an option year should decline. (Note that expectancy theory makes a contradictory prediction: it says that if the player sees a strong connection between high performance and high rewards, the player will be motivated to increase performance in his option year.)

Several research studies have been conducted to determine how well player performance can be predicted by these two theories. A study conducted after the first year of free agency confirmed equity predictions. Compared with the average of their previous three seasons, option players had lower batting averages, a lower home run ratio (home runs divided by the number of times at bat), and fewer runs batted in. When the players joined their new teams, their performance returned to normal. These results are what is predicted by equity theory.

A second study which analyzed the performance of free agents over a three-year period found no declines in performance. This seemed to contradict equity theory. However, when first-year and then second- and third-year free agents were analyzed separately, the results for the first-year free agents were found to be consistent with the first study. The performance of second- and third-year free agents did not decline, probably because they saw how much money first-year free agents had been able to get. They knew that if they played well in their option year, they would receive high bids for their services. In expectancy theory jargon, the P→O relationship was higher for second- and third-year free agents than it was for those in their first-year.

A third study looked at the performance of all nonpitching free agents for the years 1977–1980. It found that performance on those variables that were strongly linked to future salaries (e.g., home run ratio) did not decrease during the option year. Thus, the "expectancy effect" appeared to override the "equity effect." But player performance on those variables that were not strongly related to future salaries (e.g., batting average) did decline in the option year. This study suggests that equity theory will predict performance if the P→O link is weak (which it is in many occupations).

A fourth study compared pitchers who lost when they went to arbitration with those who won. It found that the performance of losing pitchers declined after arbitration; they had fewer strike outs, allowed more batters to get on base, and allowed more earned runs than did pitchers who won in arbitration. This is consistent with equity predictions.

A final study of nonpitching players who went to arbitration during the period 1974-1987 found that performance increased in the option year, and then declined to the player's average performance in the years following (whether the player won or lost the arbitration). Losers were also more likely to change teams and to leave major league baseball. The finding that player performance increased during the option year is consistent with expectancy theory; the finding that performance decreased after losing arbitration is consistent with equity theory. The performance of players who won in arbitration also decreased simply because a player is not likely to be able to continue playing at a level higher than his long-term average. ▲

The organization that sponsored the study felt that increased mechanization was the way to improve productivity, so they were somewhat skeptical of these findings; they had difficulty believing that performance would go up simply because goals were set. A second study was therefore conducted. In that study, 892 logging crews were analyzed. The results were similar to those in the first study.[44]

Many other goal-setting studies have yielded similar results.[45] At Campbell Soup's Toronto plant, for example, 120 000 cases of defective soup were sitting in the warehouse. Employees set a goal to cut that number in half within three months. The inventory was reduced to only 20 000 cases by the target date.[46] The company also organized middle- and upper-level managers into "power teams" of highly committed individuals. Each team set difficult goals, such as generating $100 000 for the bottom line in three months. Another goal was to reduce costs to those of the best Campbell's plant in the U.S. In 1990, it cost $3.87 more to produce a case of soup in the Toronto plant than it did in Campbell's Maxton, North Carolina, plant. By early 1991, that difference was only $.32.

The empirical evidence strongly supports the claim that goal setting improves performance. The setting of a goal focusses worker attention on that goal, encourages them to come up with innovative ways to achieve the goal, and generally increases their motivation.[47]

REINFORCEMENT THEORY

The motivational theories we have examined so far all view the human being as a complex, thinking organism. **Reinforcement theory** departs from that kind of thinking and says that human behaviour is shaped by the previous positive or negative outcomes that a person has experienced. Simply put, it claims that people tend to repeat behaviours that have produced pleasant outcomes and avoid behaviours that have produced unpleasant outcomes. According to this theory, people are motivated to behave in certain ways not because of their attitudes, but because of their past experiences. In contrast to the other motivation theories, reinforcement theory views people as largely unthinking organisms that simply respond to environmental stimuli.

reinforcement theory

The concept of reinforcement is a key element in this theory. A **reinforcement** is any event that increases or decreases the likelihood of a future response. If a student studies hard for an exam (a response) and then receives a high grade (the reinforcement), there is a greater chance that the student will study hard for the next exam.

reinforcement

TYPES OF REINFORCEMENT

Environmental stimuli can be (1) pleasant or unpleasant, and (2) present or absent. Combining these stimuli yields four possible situations, each of which has a different effect on behaviour (see Figure 12-6). **Positive reinforcement** occurs when a pleasant stimulus is presented to a person. It increases the likelihood that a behaviour will be repeated. For example, if an employee does a job well and is complimented on it by the boss, the probability that the employee will repeat the behaviour is increased.

positive reinforcement

Negative reinforcement occurs when an unpleasant stimulus is withheld from a person. Negative reinforcement also increases the likelihood that a behaviour will be repeated, but here the individual exhibits the desired behaviour in order to avoid something unpleasant. Suppose an employee knows that arriving late at work will cause a reprimand from the boss. The employee arrives on time in order to avoid the reprimand.

negative reinforcement

FIGURE 12-6 THE EFFECT OF PRESENTING AND REMOVING PLEASANT AND UNPLEASANT STIMULI.

	Stimulus Presented	Stimulus Removed
Pleasant Stimulus	Positive Reinforcement	Omission
Unpleasant Stimulus	Punishment	Negative Reinforcement

omission

Omission occurs when a pleasant stimulus is withheld from the person. Omission decreases the likelihood that behaviour will occur in the future. When a manager ignores an employee who spends a lot of time playing practical jokes, omission is occurring. Although this approach involves doing nothing, it does have an effect on behaviour. Since reinforced behaviour has a greater chance of recurring, it follows that not reinforcing behaviour reduces the chance that it will happen again.

punishment

Punishment occurs when an unpleasant stimulus is presented to a person. Punishment also decreases the likelihood of the behaviour occurring again. For example, when an employee arrives late to work, the boss may berate the employee. This decreases the chance the behaviour will recur in the future. Note that in punishment, an unpleasant stimulus is presented, while in negative reinforcement an unpleasant stimulus is withheld. Punishment discourages certain behaviours, while negative reinforcement encourages certain behaviours.

Schedules of Reinforcement

continuous reinforcement schedule

In the previous paragraphs, we discussed the *types* of reinforcers an employee could experience. In this section, we look at the *timing* of these reinforcements. Two basic schedules can be used: continuous and intermittent. In a **continuous reinforcement schedule**, a reward or a punishment follows each time the behaviour of interest occurs. Thus, a parent may praise a child each time a puzzle is done correctly, or a boss may punish a worker each time an error is made. This type of schedule increases the desired response, but if the schedule is not maintained, the response decreases rapidly.

intermittent reinforcement schedule

In partial, or **intermittent reinforcement schedules**, the behaviour of interest is rewarded or punished only some of the time. The general result of such schedules is that learning is more enduring than learning in continuous schedules. Partial schedules of reinforcement are relatively slow in stimulating the desired behaviour, but once established, the behaviour tends to last. They are therefore useful for managers.

fixed interval schedule

variable interval schedule

In a **fixed interval schedule**, a reinforcement is applied after a certain time period has passed, regardless of the number of responses that have occurred. A manager may visit a certain department once every fifth day, or workers may be paid once every two weeks. In a **variable interval schedule**, a reinforcement is applied after a varying amount of time has passed, regardless of the number of desired responses that have occurred. A manager may visit a certain department once a week, but subordinates don't know which day the visit will take place. Or, a manager may praise (or punish) a subordinate only some of the time the person does a good (or poor) job.

In a **fixed ratio schedule**, a reinforcement is applied after a fixed number of desired behavioural responses have occurred, regardless of the time that has passed. For example, the department manager may come to the department and congratulate the members every fourth time they achieve their production quota, or employees may be paid on a piece-rate or commission basis. In a **variable ratio schedule**, behaviours are reinforced after a varying number of responses have occurred; sometimes a reinforcement occurs after three responses, sometimes after ten, sometimes after fifty, and so on. A manager following this schedule may come through a department irregularly, without the workers knowing why or when. All they know is that at apparently random times their boss visits and reinforces their behaviour (positively or negatively).

fixed ratio schedule

variable ratio schedule

The schedules of reinforcement listed above and their effects are summarized in Table 12-4.

TABLE 12-4 SCHEDULES OF REINFORCEMENT AND THEIR EFFECTS.

Schedule	Description	Effects on Responding
Continuous (CRF)	Reinforcer follows every response.	(1) Steady high rate of performance as long as reinforcement continues to follow every response. (2) High frequency of reinforcement may lead to early satiation. (3) Behaviour weakens rapidly (undergoes extinction) when reinforcers are withheld. (4) Appropriate for newly emitted, unstable, or low-frequency responses.
Intermittent	Reinforcer does not follow every response.	(1) Capable of producing high frequencies of responding. (2) Low frequency of reinforcement precludes early satiation. (3) Appropriate for stable or high-frequency responses.
Fixed ratio (FR)	A fixed number of responses must be emitted before reinforcement occurs.	(1) A fixed ratio of 1:1 (reinforcement occurs after every response) is the same as a continuous schedule. (2) Tends to produce a high rate of response which is vigorous and steady.
Variable ratio (VR)	A varying or random number of responses must be emitted before reinforcement occurs.	(1) Capable of producing a high rate of response which is vigorous, steady, and resistant to extinction.
Fixed interval (FI)	The first response after a specific period of time has elapsed is reinforced.	(1) Produces an uneven response pattern varying from a very slow, unenergetic response immediately following reinforcement to a very fast, vigorous response immediately preceding reinforcement.
Variable interval (VI)	The first response after varying or random periods of time have elapsed is reinforced.	(1) Tends to produce a high rate of response which is vigorous, steady, and resistant to extinction.

ORGANIZATIONAL BEHAVIOUR MODIFICATION

LEARNING OBJECTIVE 9
Show how reinforcement theory can be used to motivate employees.

organizational behaviour modification (OBM)

Reinforcement theory has been shaped by the work of B.F. Skinner, who believes that people's behaviour can be controlled and shaped by rewarding desired behaviour and ignoring undesirable behaviour.[48] **Organizational behaviour modification (OBM)** is the application of Skinner's reinforcement theory to the behaviour of people in organizations. OBM rests on two fundamental assumptions: (1) people act in ways they find personally rewarding, and (2) behaviour can be shaped and determined by controlling the rewards. Which reinforcers actually work in motivating people is determined by trial and error. What is successful with one employee may not work with another because needs and wants differ. Praise is used most frequently because it is the most readily available reinforcer. However, its effectiveness decreases whenever it becomes predictable or is continuously applied. Money is also used, as are letters of commendation, time off, and promotions. The top management at Baylor's might try introducing an OBM program for their salesclerks.

Studies Using OBM

A properly administered incentive system increases employee motivation and performance. The Alberta Research Council holds an annual awards dinner to recognize outstanding achievements made by its staff. Sheila Binda, secretary for the Alberta Geological Survey, receives the Past President's Award of Excellence from president Clem Bowman.

OBM has been used to improve employee performance in many organizations. In one company, it was used to reduce absenteeism.[49] Each day that an employee came to work on time, he or she received a playing card. At the end of the week, the highest poker hand received \$20. Over a three-month period, the absenteeism rate of the experimental group decreased 18 percent, while the rate of the control group actually increased.

A telephone company identified several desirable behaviours among its operators and embarked on an OBM program to increase these behaviours.[50] Praise and recognition were the main reinforcers that were used. Attendance improved 50 percent and productivity and efficiency levels rose above past standards. The Emery Air Freight OBM program was a similar success story.[51] It used reinforcers such as information feedback and praise to dramatically improve employee responses to customer inquiries about service and schedules. As a result of the application of OBM, the company estimated it saved about \$650 000 per year.

In a study involving a city transit company, behaviour modification methods were applied to improve the safety record of bus drivers.[52] The system reduced accident rates by nearly 25 percent. At SAS Airlines, agents were trained in specific sales techniques, the key one being the "offer." An offer was the attempt by the agent to sell a seat to a customer who had called in for information. Sales supervisors were also trained in positive reinforcement techniques designed to improve the skills of the agents. By the end of the program, agents had capitalized on 84 percent of the potential-offer opportunities, as compared to only 34 percent at the beginning of the program.[53] (See the Management at Work insert "Behaviour Modification at Burroughs Memorex" for a detailed example of OBM.)

These studies show that OBM has great promise in motivating desired behaviour among employees. Table 12-5 shows the steps that are necessary to design a workable OBM system.

Through OBM, employees are conditioned to change their behaviour in the direction desired by management. Consequently, OBM has been criticized as a manipulative and autocratic approach to motivation. All of the other motivation theories we have described assume that people are motivated by their own internal needs and are capable of self-control. OBM, by contrast, assumes that the causes of behaviour are outside the individual.

MANAGEMENT AT WORK

BEHAVIOUR MODIFICATION AT BURROUGHS MEMOREX

Burroughs Memorex, a producer of computer products, was experiencing several problems at its Winnipeg plant—poor quality, failure to meet schedules, high scrap costs, and less-than-ideal labour relations. In an attempt to resolve these problems, the company introduced a behaviour modification program called Performance Management.

The first step was to train 75 managers and supervisors how to use behaviour modification properly. Once the training had been completed, supervisors identified their "key result areas." They then began applying behaviour modification principles in order to improve performance in these key result areas. Both verbal and written positive reinforcement were given to employees who had achieved the standards which had been set. Output graphs were also posted in the factory so that all workers could see the extent to which they were achieving quality and output goals. An incentive system for rewarding good suggestions was also implemented.

Prior to the introduction of the behaviour modification program, the "arrival quality" of the plant's shipments was only 59 percent (that is, only 59 percent of the customers were happy with the product when it arrived at their plant). Burroughs workers set a goal of 80 percent arrival quality for the next year; they actually achieved 83 percent. They then set a goal of 90 percent for the next year and achieved 91 percent.

Another example: Scrap costs on a certain part were running at $6500 per week. One employee discovered that these costs were incurred by improper handling of the product so he wrote a 20-minute training program that explained the proper way to handle that particular part. His program is now used to train all people who handle the part. After being made aware of the cause of the problem, the employees set a goal to reduce scrap costs to $2500 per week. Feedback graphs were posted in all departments who handled the part and appropriate reinforcement was applied for improved performance. Scrap costs were reduced to $400 per week. ▲

TABLE 12-5 STEPS IN DESIGNING AN ORGANIZATIONAL BEHAVIOUR MODIFICATION PROGRAM.

Step	Activity
1. Identify the problem to be solved.	1. Decide what specific behaviour is to be encouraged (or eliminated).
2. Specify the behaviour in observable, measurable terms.	2. Define what is to be changed and how it is to be changed.
3. Identify the reinforcements.	3. Examine those reinforcers that appear to be common to most people, as well as those that are unique to certain individuals.
4. Design the contingencies.	4. Develop a system that allows the desired reinforcers to be contingent upon the desired behaviour.
5. Ensure that there is a method for applying the contingency relationship.	5. Reward desired behaviour when it occurs. This may require the physical presence of the manager in the early stages of the process.
6. Give the employee feedback about how the system operates and what it takes to "win."	6. Outline specifically what the employee is doing right and wrong, what the rewards are, how they will be applied, and the nature of the contingency relationship.
7. Apply the system fairly and consistently.	7. Once the system is established, maintain it in a consistent manner. Do not change the contingencies in the middle of the game.

Social Learning Theory

social learning theory

self-efficacy

vicarious learning

self-control

The debate about whether human beings are motivated by internal attitudes or the external environment is a long-standing one. But both of these extreme views are moderating. **Social learning theory** takes a middle-ground position and says that human motivation results from the interaction of both internal and external factors.[54] This theory recognizes the fact that the environment influences individuals, but that individuals also influence their environment. It also takes into account the fact that people learn by imitating others.

There are three basic interacting elements in social learning theory. **Self-efficacy** refers to people's beliefs about their ability to perform certain tasks. A person with high self-efficacy is more likely to be motivated and productive than a person with low self-efficacy. One study of life insurance agents, for example, showed that those agents who felt competent about selling tended to sell more; this, in turn, increased their self-confidence and increased the likelihood that they would be highly productive in the future.[55] **Vicarious learning** refers to learning that occurs as a person observes others. This allows someone to learn about the consequences of various behaviours without actually having to do them. **Self-control** occurs when one sets goals and then rewards herself or himself for achieving them. For example, you might set a goal to get 85 percent on an exam; if you achieve that mark, you may reward yourself by taking three days off from studying for that course.

WHAT DO THE MOTIVATION THEORIES SAY ABOUT MONEY?

LEARNING OBJECTIVE 10

Explain the role that money plays in motivation.

The role of money in motivation has been debated vigorously for many years.[56] One of the difficulties in measuring the impact of money on motivation is that financial rewards have various meanings to people. In addition to providing the means to satisfy basic needs, pay can indicate social status, social value, and competence. Therefore, workers and managers can also satisfy higher-order needs such as self-esteem and self-actualization with their paycheques. To complicate the situation further, people's perceptions of the degree to which their lower-order needs are satisfied may change as their income rises.

Managers want to know how to use money effectively to motivate employees to perform well. This is what the executive committee at Baylor's is trying to come to grips with. Each of the motivation theories we have looked at in this chapter has something to say about the role of money as a motivator. From Maslow's perspective, money helps employees increase their need satisfaction or to satisfy needs that are not currently satisfied. Money is therefore a motivator because it facilitates need satisfaction. Herzberg says that pay is not a motivator, but a hygiene, i.e., it simply keeps workers from being dissatisfied. Robert Glegg, president of Glegg Water Conditioning Inc., agrees with Herzberg. He says that paying someone a lot of money is never enough by itself; it simply removes a possible negative.[57] In McClelland's theory, the person high in nAch is not motivated by money at all. Rather, money is simply a way of keeping track of how well the person's goals have been achieved. Equity theory predicts that payment either above or below expectations will motivate a person to reduce the dissonance associated with the felt inequity. Expectancy theory says that if money is valent to the individual, and if the individual sees that it is possible to do the things necessary to get it, then money will be a motivating force. The Management at Work insert entitled "Incentives and Motivation" describes how incentives are used in several Canadian companies.

MANAGEMENT AT WORK

INCENTIVES AND MOTIVATION

Canadian companies are realizing that offering incentives beyond the normal benefits can result in creative ideas as well as large increases in employee productivity. These incentives may be monetary or nonmonetary. Consider the following:

1. At BC Tel, a suggestion system was implemented that gives cash rewards to employees for ideas that generate revenue or save the company money. The employee receives 10 percent of the money the company saved or the revenue generated (employees have received up to $20 000 for ideas).
2. Drexis Inc. recently flew 12 employees and their families to Disney World as a reward for increasing sales by over 100 percent in one year.
3. Proctor & Redfern Ltd., a consulting engineering firm, lets high achievers serve on committees with senior executives, represent the firm at outside functions, or enroll in development courses where the company pays the bill.
4. Avatar Communications Inc. sent employees on a weeklong Outward Bound expedition into the wilderness. The trip had both reward and motivational components.
5. Pitney Bowes Canada Ltd. sent 60 of its top salespeople and their spouses to Hong Kong after they achieved 135 percent of their sales quota (salespeople who achieved 112 percent received a trip to San Diego).
6. At Cloverdale Paint, employees who come up with innovative ideas to improve customer service receive a personal letter from the president and a coffee mug or T-shirt bearing the company logo. The best idea submitted each quarter earns the originator a restaurant gift certificate worth $50. The employee who makes the best suggestion of the year receives $200 and an engraved plaque which is presented at a workplace ceremony.
7. Manitoba Telephone System instituted a suggestion system called IDEA$PLUS, which gives employees cash awards up to $10 000 for good ideas.
8. At the Toronto Skydome, employees are given coupons for exceptional service, such as finding a lost child or repairing a broken seat. The coupons can be used to accumulate points which can be redeemed for prizes.
9. Emery Apparel Canada Inc. conducts an annual "Oscar" awards ceremony. With great hoopla, the CEO asks for the envelope with the name of the winner of the top award. Last year, a 12-year employee won the award for figuring out (on her own time) how to satisfy a customer's difficult request.
10. At Ford Motor Company, workers are rewarded for suggestions which save the company money. For example, when a metal press operator found a way to save on the amount of sheet metal used in floor panels, the company gave $14 000 of the $70 000 first year savings of the idea back to the worker. A recent study shows that activity like this has an effect—it takes workers at Ford one-third less time to build a car than workers at GM.

Incentives are important for top managers as well. The higher a manager is placed in a firm, the more likely it is that a good chunk of the manager's pay will be performance-based. A Conference Board of Canada study of executive compensation in Canada showed that up to 40 percent of top executives' total compensation comes in the form of incentives. For lower-level managers, the figure was 20 percent, and for other employees it was 10 percent. Top managers in the U.S. often receive up to 60 percent of their total compensation in the form of incentives. Most Canadian companies have set up some type of incentive plan for their senior executives.

Incentives systems must be carefully developed, or they will not motivate employee behaviour in the right direction. In addition to the usual sales and profit goals, firms are beginning to look at incentive systems that reward managers for achieving goals like effective downsizing, increasing environmental consciousness, and improving the corporate culture. A decision must also be made about whether the incentive system will be directed at individual employees or groups. Historically, incentives have been directed at individuals, but with the new emphasis on teamwork in organizations, this is changing. Now, a group may get an incentive if it gets a new product launched on time.

Incentive systems must be used with care because they may unintentionally motivate employees to engage in undesirable behaviour. In the sale of mutual funds, for example, brokers are often given bonuses for making sales. Super salespeople may be given trips to exotic locations in return for making their sales goals. This may motivate the salesperson to push a product or service that really doesn't meet the customers' needs. ▲

Reinforcement theory principles are very useful for analyzing the role of money in motivation. OBM ideas usually open people's eyes to the fact that most organizations do not use money effectively to motivate employees. The awarding of money is frequently not contingent upon employees demonstrating behaviour that is desired by management, so money often has little impact on employee behaviour. Generally, managers respond to the behaviour of employees only when it becomes extreme: someone who is extremely bad is fired and someone who is extremely good is given a raise or promotion. This is consistent with the exception principle of management. However, for the majority of employees who are somewhere in between these extremes, this means that on-the-job behaviour tends to go unrecognized.

For money to motivate behaviour, the following reinforcement principles must be adhered to:

1. Pay must be reinforcing to the employee.
2. Pay must be made contingent upon previously agreed upon behaviours.
3. The interval between the desired behaviour and the receipt of pay must be as short as possible.
4. The payment must be large enough to overcome the effect of competing reinforcements.

Different payment schemes influence how much money will be a motivator (see Table 12-6). Determining the importance of money to employees requires knowledge of each individual's current need level. If employees have a need for higher pay and expect to receive it if they perform more effectively, then pay can motivate performance.

TABLE 12-6 THE MOTIVATIONAL POWER OF VARIOUS PAY SYSTEMS.

Pay System	Effectiveness
1. *Wages and salaries*	These are widely used, but are generally ineffective since they pay people for the time they spend at work, not for how much they produce. They can be partially reinforcing, depending on how they are administered.
2. *Commission*	Compared to wages and salaries, these are usually highly effective, provided that employees have a reasonable chance of accomplishing what is necessary, and the amount of the commission is sufficiently large to be reinforcing.
3. *Salary plus bonus*	These can be reasonably effective since the salary reinforces the workers' need for a predictable standard of living and the bonus (if contingent upon behaviour) provides the opportunity to increase the standard of living.
4. *Profit-sharing*	These can be effective in small firms, but are generally ineffective in large firms since too many variables beyond the employees' control affect the company's profit.
5. *Retirement plans*	These are usually ineffective because the time period when rewards will be received is too far in the future to motivate current behaviour.

JOB DESIGN AND MOTIVATION

With industrialization comes the specialization of labour. This specialization can result in tremendous productivity and an abundance of goods for consumers. However, the extreme simplification and standardization of jobs may also cause reduced motivation. This raises the question of whether jobs can be designed in such a way that employee motivation, satisfaction, and productivity are all high. This question can be answered by considering some research from the field of study known as job design.

job design

Job design is the process of altering the nature and structure of jobs for the purpose of increasing productivity.[58] It is concerned with outlining not only the specific tasks to be performed, but also the methods to be used in performing them and how the job is integrated with other work in the organization. Job design is important in developing a motivated work force.

Several constraints must be recognized before a particular job design program is implemented. These constraints include:

1. *Technological* The type of equipment and tools needed as well as the particular work layout and methods used in producing the product or service.
2. *Economic* Sufficient resources must be available to the organization if it wishes to redesign some or all of its jobs.
3. *Governmental* Requirements and regulations covering a wide variety of organizational activities.
4. *Union* The contract specifies types of jobs, duties and responsibilities of workers.
5. *Personnel* Abilities, attitudes, and motivation of employees.
6. *Managerial* Management's philosophies, objectives, strategies, and commitment to job redesign.

On occasion, these constraints present serious problems, but if management is committed to the process and works with employees, jobs can usually be redesigned.

LEARNING OBJECTIVE 11
Outline the main features of job enrichment, quality circles, and flextime.

Many job design strategies have emerged during the last two or three decades. We have already described work teams (Chapter 9) and telecommuting (Chapter 19). Other popular job design strategies are job enrichment, quality circles, flextime, the compressed workweek, job sharing, and free-lancing. Each of these is discussed below.

JOB ENRICHMENT

job rotation

job enlargement

One possible way to increase worker motivation is to increase the variety in jobs. This can be done through job rotation, job enlargement, or job enrichment. In **job rotation**, a worker is rotated through a series of similar jobs. At Domtar, for example, production workers rotate between two or three jobs each day.[59] **Job enlargement** requires the worker to learn several different jobs involving somewhat different skill levels. Assemblers at National Cash Register perform four to five different jobs as a normal part of their work.[60] Neither job rotation nor job enlargement involves changing the level of responsibility in a worker's job.

job enrichment

Job enrichment is quite different from the previous two techniques. **Job enrichment** increases the level of responsibility in a job. This means adding tasks that require the worker to make higher-level decisions. Three features must be evident in an enriched job:

1. *Workers must feel that the job is meaningful* A meaningful job requires workers to use skills that are possessed by a relatively small segment of the general population or of the worker's reference group. Thus, the jobs of professionals (e.g., doctors, lawyers, architects) are very motivating because the skills that are used are valued and are uncommon. A job is also meaningful if the employee works on a product from start to finish. In a typical mass production factory, workers see only a small portion of the total product and have little sense of completeness in their work.

2. *Workers must receive feedback on how well they are performing* If workers can clearly see how their work is helping or hindering the organization, they may want to improve their performance. One of the best ways to give workers feedback is to let them inspect their own work.

3. *The worker should be allowed discretion in deciding how to complete the job* If workers are told what criteria the finished product or service must satisfy, and are then allowed to set up their own procedures to reach these goals, they may experience increased motivation to perform the task. Workers can be given increased responsibility over the (a) pace of work (workers decide how fast a job is to be done and in what sequence the tasks are to be completed); (b) quality of work (they judge the quality of completed work and balance quality with pace); and (c) selection of resources (they decide which resources are necessary to perform the required tasks and how these resources should be allocated among the tasks).

Job enrichment is used by many organizations that want to cut costs, improve employee morale, and reduce turnover and absenteeism. Low-level, white or blue collar jobs are usually selected for enrichment. Consider the changes in job design that occurred at the General Foods pet food plant in Cobourg, Ontario.[61] Before job enrichment was implemented, job classifications were very strict; each classification included only a limited number of tasks. These classifications were changed so that several related tasks were combined and one person was given a complete job. Quality control and janitorial duties were added to most classifications (the latter because the plant had a sanitation problem). Workers received general instructions from supervisors on a blackboard, and were given the right to decide how to handle any problems which arose. Although there were some conflicts with the union over the idea of job enrichment, implementation of the plan led to increased productivity, improved sanitation, and increased worker satisfaction.

This example demonstrates the principles of an enriched job noted above. First, by combining tasks, the workers experienced increased job demands and a "whole" job. Second, because the quality control function was given to the workers, they received feedback on how well the job had been performed. Third, workers were given increased freedom to decide how best to do their jobs.

QUALITY CIRCLES

quality circles (QCs)

Quality circles (QCs) consist of periodic meetings of groups of 5 to 15 employees who discuss ways to improve the quality and quantity of work.[62] Quality circles are part of the "Japanese management system" that gained popularity in Canada in the 1980s.

Great-West Life Assurance Company has an active productivity improvement program, which involves employee participation in decision making and the use of quality circles.

The quality circles are designed to:

1. Build an attitude of continuous improvement and problem prevention through creative thinking, open communication, and teamwork.

2. Provide all employees with the opportunity to contribute ideas for change and to participate in decisions affecting their work.

3. Achieve an enchanced quality of working life for employees, a higher level of productivity, and a superior quality of service to customers.

Each QC is comprised of volunteer members who meet once a week on company time to consider ways to do higher-quality, more effective work. There are no monetary rewards for participation. Each group has a leader who has received formal training in leading a QC. The leader is usually the group's supervisor, but the leader position often rotates after the group has been meeting for a while. Group leaders also train their group members. An agenda is prepared for each meeting; it may include discussion of several minor items, or the entire meeting may be devoted to one issue. When a group has completed a given project—large projects may take six months or more—a presentation is made to management. All team members are encouraged to take part in these presentations.

Quality circle programs at three other Canadian firms are illustrated in the Management at Work insert "Quality Circles at B.C. Tel, Camco Inc., and Burroughs."

Despite the popularity of quality circles, there is little research on their effects. Most of the evidence is either in case study form or in stories describing how well quality circles worked. Two field studies confirmed that quality circles improved employees' perceptions of their influence in the organization, and their communications with supervisors, but there were only minor effects on perceptions of job design.[63] Other studies suggest that when quality circles are supported by top management, they do cause increased quality and productivity.[64]

MANAGEMENT AT WORK

QUALITY CIRCLES AT B.C. TEL, CAMCO INC., AND BURROUGHS

Camco Inc., a Montreal manufacturer of household appliances, had a serious quality-control problem. At the peak of the problem, 42 percent of the output of one line was rejected because of substandard quality. In spite of warnings to employees and the addition of quality-control inspectors, the problem remained. Since the plant's survival depended on its ability to produce high-quality output, something had to be done.

The problem was solved when quality circles pinpointed the problem: a management system that motivated first-line supervisors to stress production quantity at the expense of quality. The quality circles caused a plant-wide reorganization to occur to deal with the problem. The results have been dramatic. The rejection rate has dropped to 10 percent, and this has been achieved with a sharp reduction in the number of staff involved with quality control (from 55 to 10). Productivity per employee has also increased 30 percent.

B.C. Tel introduced a voluntary quality circle program so that employees would have the opportunity to identify and solve problems in their own work area. More than 90 quality circles are now in operation, and several have won national and international awards for excellence. Each circle consists of 6-10 members and meetings are held during regular working hours. Employees develop skills in problem solving and analysis, and the company benefits from more efficient operations. The quality circles are supplemented by Quality Councils (which focus on better ways of doing work) and Quality Action Teams (which deal with specific quality projects within a department).

Burroughs Memorex introduced a voluntary quality circles program to improve its operations. Each quality team is made up of 8 to 10 people who meet once a week (on company time) for one hour. All quality team members receive formal training in quality control. Each team identifies "levels" for the ideas it comes up with. Level 1 solutions can be implemented without managerial approval; Level 2 solutions must be submitted for managerial approval; and Level 3 solutions are taken to management at the idea stage so that information can be gathered regarding their feasibility. ▲

FLEXTIME

flextime

Organizations have recently started to allow employees some freedom in setting their working hours in the hope that job satisfaction and productivity will increase. **Flextime** is a system which allows workers increased discretion in deciding when they will be at their place of work. Technically speaking, flextime does not involve job redesign, but it does have an impact on how employees see their job.

Flextime generally works as follows: Management decides which hours of the day are "core hours." These are the hours when it is absolutely essential that all workers be at the workplace. In many firms the core hours are 10 A.M. to 2 P.M. The individual is left to decide when to spend the remaining number of required working hours. An early riser might start work at 7 A.M. and finish at 3 P.M., while a person who likes to sleep late might not come in until 10 A.M. and then stay until 6 P.M. Start and finish times for each worker must satisfy two constraints: all employees must be present for the core hours, and they must work a fixed number of hours in total each day. While this is the normal flextime system, other variations are possible.

At National Cash Register, employees can begin their workday anytime between 7:30 A.M. and 9:00 A.M., and end their workday anytime between 4:30 P.M. and 6:00 P.M. Employees must work eight hours per day. There are no time clocks. At Steelcase Canada, employees are allowed up to two hours for lunch and may work anytime between 7 A.M. and 6 P.M. They may work four-day weeks if it does not interfere with operations. Employees must arrange their schedules with their supervisors.[65] Edwards, a unit of General Signal Ltd., designs and manufactures alarm systems. It has instituted flexible work hours for female employees in an attempt to improve their utilization of this resource.[66]

In a survey of 1600 Canadian companies, the Conference Board of Canada found that almost half of the employers had instituted flextime programs.[67] Generally speaking, the introduction of flextime is associated with an increase in morale, a decline in employee absences and turnover, and an increase in productivity.[68] In two well-controlled studies, flextime led to a significant reduction in employee absences and small increases in productivity.[69]

Flextime does have some potential drawbacks. The main one is that management continues to resist the idea. A survey of human resources professionals showed that over 40 percent of them felt that middle-management resistance was the main obstacle to the introduction of flextime in their firm.[70] Another problem is that communicating with and coordinating the work of subordinates with staggered working hours can be troublesome for managers. Overall, however, flextime appears to be a system which can be implemented with little cost and which generally yields benefits in employee satisfaction and productivity.

THE COMPRESSED WORKWEEK

compressed workweek

There are other variations besides flextime. In the **compressed workweek**, the number of days that employees work is reduced, but the number of hours worked per day is increased. The most popular compressed workweek is four days, 10 hours per day, but some companies have also experimented with three days, 12 hours per day. The "weekend worker" program at 3M Canada in London, Ontario, offers members of the Canadian Auto Workers 12 hour shifts on Saturday and Sunday only, and pays them the same wage as if they had worked Monday through Friday. Absenteeism has declined, productivity has increased, and costs have been lowered by the introduction of the program.[71] There is a long waiting list to transfer to weekend work. One city introduced a 12-hour workday for its police officers, who now work four days on, four days off. The police officers report lowered levels of fatigue and stress, and an improvement in life satisfaction and leisure time.[72]

The compressed workweek has some obvious advantages: for example, lowered commuting costs, more leisure time for employees, reduced employee demands for time off for personal matters, and easier recruiting for the company. But it also has some disadvantages: worker fatigue and reduced productivity near the end of long shifts, unwillingness to work overtime when unexpected deadlines must be met, and poorer quality service to clients and customers.[73]

JOB SHARING

job sharing

Job sharing means that two or more workers collectively take responsibility for doing a traditional full-time job. For example, if two people share a job, one of them might work only mornings, while the other works afternoons. This might be seen as desirable by the two workers, particularly if neither one wants to work full-time, or if they each have responsibilities outside the workplace that must be regularly attended to.

FREE-LANCING

free-lancers

Many workers who want to work full-time are simply not able to find such work. Increasingly, organizations are relying on **free-lancers**—individuals with special skills who supplement the organization's core group of full-time employees. The Ethics in Management insert "Free-lancing" describes the increasing importance of free-lancing, and also raises some ethical questions about it.

ETHICS IN MANAGEMENT

FREE-LANCING

When people think about careers, they usually think of going to work full-time for a company and, if they like it, staying at that company for many years. In fact, until recently the notion of "lifetime employment" was touted as the wave of the future. Even if a person didn't stay at one firm, the idea was that the person would work full-time for a company for at least a few years.

But times are changing. Statistics Canada estimates that 30 percent of working adults now fall into the category of non-standard work—self-employment, part-time work, or anything else outside the tradition of full-time employment.

Why is this happening? Perhaps the main reason is competitive pressures that are forcing firms to reduce their costs and increase their productivity. The current buzzword is "flexibility" and this can often be achieved by outsourcing (hiring independent free-lancers to deal with specific company problems). This allows a firm to maintain a minimum number of full-time workers and then supplement them with free-lancers—individuals who work on time-framed projects, and who move on to another firm when the project is finished. Companies are increasingly using contract workers to do specific jobs—it's like a baseball team trading for a niche player to help them win the pennant. Contact Management Resources is a company that is meeting the increasing demand for contract managers. It provides executives to various companies that want someone only for a specified period of time.

Management experts predict that free-lancing will increase in importance. With the massive layoffs that have been evident in recent years, workers are beginning to realize that job security is not provided by large firms; rather, security comes from having confidence in your own knowledge and skills, and marketing yourself in innovative ways. Also, free-lancing has been facilitated by the recent advances in information technology, since workers do not necessarily have to be at the workplace in order to do their work.

There are both positive and negative

• • •

aspects to the idea of nonstandard work. From the worker's perspective, those with marketable skills will will receive high pay for satisfying work. For those without marketable skills, the shift will likely mean part-time work in low-paying service jobs. Individuals who lack either the ability or interest to capitalize on nonstandard work will find much uncertainty in their career.

From the organization's perspective, the value of nonstandard work and the benefits of the increased flexibility that is possible with part-time free-lancers must be weighed against the value of long-term employee loyalty and commitment.

People who feel that the use of free-lancers is ethically questionable point to two problems. First, the organization is using the free-lancer's skills, but it is not providing that person with a full-time job in return. Thus, the organization is achieving the benefits of flexibility at the worker's expense. Second, free-lancers are often paid less than full-time workers, and they may also not be eligible for certain benefits like dental care plans and retirement plans. In the view of some, this amounts to exploiting workers. ▲

MEETING THE CHALLENGE

BAYLOR'S DEPARTMENT STORE

If you were a member of the executive committee and attended the second meeting called by the vice-president of operations, what useful comments could you make about the problem facing Baylor's Department Store? First of all, you could challenge the assumption that employees are poorly motivated. We saw in Chapter 6 that one of the classic problems in management is leaping to conclusions about causes because of insufficient data about the problem. Although surveys showed that customers thought the salespeople were not helpful or friendly, that does not necessarily mean that the salesclerks were not motivated. Employee attitude surveys suggested three other possible areas where further study should be done. These data must therefore be analyzed more carefully.

At the executive committee meeting, management seemed to place more emphasis on rumours than they did on the attitude survey data. Several members of the executive committee apparently thought that introducing an incentive scheme would solve the problems. But how this would make employee jobs more interesting or give them more feedback about their work is unclear. It seems more likely that the introduction of job enrichment would satisfy the customers' complaints from the survey. Regarding the inequity complaint of the employees, management must develop more information on exactly what this means; equity theory can be a useful guide here.

Further analysis might lead management to the conclusion that low performance is caused not by a lack of motivation, but by a lack of employee confidence about how to do their jobs, or by low ability. If this is the problem, retraining is probably the best solution. Only after gathering more data on the problem can management determine if low motivation is actually the cause. If they determine that it is, they can take the actions which are necessary to increase it.

As far as the debate about money as a motivator is concerned, several insights are provided by the motivation theories which were discussed in the chapter. If you accept Herzberg's view of motivation, you would disagree with Lise Daniel's incentive scheme as a solution to the motivation problem. Herzberg does not see money as a motivator. Instead, he would propose a restructuring of the job so that it would be psychologically rewarding to employees and would motivate them to sell enthusiastically.

If you accept Maslow's arguments, the role of money as a motivator is less clear. Money could be a motivator for any needs, but it is particularly important for physiological and safety needs. For some needs, however, money is only one of the ways to achieve satisfaction. The need for status, for example, may be satisfied by having a certain job title even though the job does not pay very well. Thus, the role of money in motivation according to Maslow's theory is dependent on the level of the need hierarchy at which the individual finds him- or herself. It also depends on the individual's general view of money.

Equity theory says that money may be a motivator if people are underpaid or overpaid. If the person perceives an inequity involving pay, he or she will be motivated to resolve it. This motivation may, of course, be positive or negative, as the person may produce more or less. Baylor's must determine if salary schedules for salesclerks are perceived to be equitable before implementing the incentive scheme.

Expectancy theory argues that money is a motivator if it is positively valued, and no organizational factors inhibit the performance of the task. At Baylor's, management would have to ensure that these two criteria are satisfied before an incentive scheme could be successfully implemented. ▲

SUMMARY

Motivation is the result of processes—internal or external to the individual—that create enthusiasm and persistence to pursue a certain course of action. Organizations benefit from having motivated employees because such employees look for better ways to do their jobs, they are more quality-oriented, and they are more productive than unmotivated workers.

Extrinsic motivation exists when a person works hard at a task because he or she has been promised a reward for doing a good job. Intrinsic motivation exists when a person works hard at a job even though no obvious reward will be given. The giving of extrinsic rewards may reduce a person's intrinsic motivation.

The two main determinants of an employee's performance are motivation and ability (performance = motivation × ability). If either variable is low, performance will be low. Managers can increase subordinate performance by focussing on the variable where the subordinate is weak.

There are two basic philosophies of human nature: that people are lazy and dislike work (Theory X), or that people find work to be a natural activity and will approach work with enthusiasm (Theory Y). Managerial assumptions about workers may become a self-fulfilling prophecy (one which comes true because people behave in ways to make it come true).

Many motivational theories have been developed during the twentieth century. Need (content) theories assume that all people have certain needs which they are trying to satisfy. If these can be satisfied in the workplace, the worker will be motivated. Maslow proposed that people work through a hierarchy of needs, including physiological, safety, social, esteem, and self-actualization needs. Needs at higher levels emerge to motivate behaviour only after lower-level needs have been largely satisfied. Alderfer proposed a simpler, three-step hierarchy of existence, relatedness, and growth needs that is parallel to Maslow's idea. McClelland identified three needs in a nonhierarchical arrangement: the need for achievement, affiliation, and power.

Several process motivation theories have also been developed. Equity theory says that people compare their input/outcome ratio with the input/outcome ratio of others doing similar work. If a person feels inequitably treated, the person will be motivated to resolve the inequity. Expectancy theory proposes that a person's motivational level is determined by the outcomes the person sees as desirable, the probability that the expenditure of effort will lead to performance, and the probability that performance will lead to rewards ($\text{Motivation} = \text{valence} \times [E \rightarrow P] \times [P \rightarrow O]$). Goal setting is an effective motivational technique. Studies consistently show that people who set specific, difficult goals achieve significantly more than people who set "do your best" goals.

Reinforcement theory is a departure from most thinking about motivation. It says that human behaviour can be explained on the basis of previous positive or negative outcomes that a person has experienced. In reinforcement theory, the attitudes of the person are not considered; rather, the impact of environmental stimuli is all-important. Social learning theory takes a middle-ground postion in the debate about how much internal or external factors motivate individuals. It recognizes that the environment influences individuals, but that individuals also influence their environment.

The role of money in motivation has been debated for many years. Since money can be used to satisfy a variety of needs, it may be difficult to determine its place in motivation. Most motivation theories allow for the possibility that money will be a motivator (an exception is Herzberg's theory). Money is most likely to motivate if it is desired by the employee, is contingent upon certain work behaviours, and is strong enough to overcome the effect of competing reinforcements.

Job design is the process of altering the nature and structure of jobs for the purpose of increasing employee productivity. Several job design strategies are popular at present. Job enrichment increases the level of responsibility in a work role. Quality circles involve employees in group discussions about how to improve the quality of their work. Flextime gives workers flexibility in choosing when they will work. The compressed workweek allows workers to work longer hours at a time, and spend fewer days at work (e.g., four days, 10 hours per day). Job sharing allows people who do not want to work full-time to share a full-time job between them.

KEY TERMS

motivation (p. 360)
individual characteristics (p. 360)
job characteristics (p. 360)
organizational characteristics (p. 360)
extrinsic rewards (p. 361)
intrinsic rewards (p. 361)
extrinsic motivation (p. 361)
intrinsic motivation (p. 361)
job satisfaction (p. 362)
ability (p. 363)
Theory X (p. 364)
Theory Y (p. 364)
self-fulfilling prophecy (p. 365)
content theories (p. 365)
process theories (p. 365)
Maslow's hierarchy of needs (p. 366)
existence-relatedness-growth (ERG) theory (p. 368)
motivators (p. 368)
hygienes (p. 368)
need for achievement (p. 370)
need for power (p. 370)
need for affiliation (p. 370)
equity theory (p. 371)
expectancy theory (p. 372)
valence (p. 373)
effort-performance expectancy (p. 373)
performance-outcome expectancy (p. 373)
reinforcement theory (p. 375)
reinforcement (p. 375)
positive reinforcement (p. 375)
negative reinforcement (p. 375)
omission (p. 376)
punishment (p. 376)
continuous reinforcement schedule (p. 376)
intermittent reinforcement schedule (p. 376)
fixed interval schedule (p. 376)
variable interval schedule (p. 376)
fixed ratio schedule (p. 377)
variable ratio schedule (p. 377)
organizational behaviour modification (OBM) (p. 378)
social learning theory (p. 380)
self-efficacy (p. 380)
vicarious learning (p. 380)
self-control (p. 380)
job design (p. 383)
job rotation (p. 383)
job enlargement (p. 383)
job enrichment (p. 383)
quality circles (p. 384)
flextime (p. 386)
compressed workweek (p. 386)
job sharing (p. 387)
free-lancers (p. 387)

REVIEW QUESTIONS

1. What is the definition of motivation?
2. What is the difference between intrinsic and extrinsic motivation?
3. What is the relationship between motivation, employee ability, and performance?
4. What is the relationship between job satisfaction and job performance?
5. What are the main points of Argyris' maturation theory? How does the theory apply to motivation?
6. Compare and contrast Herzberg's theory of motivation with the theories developed by Maslow and Alderfer.
7. Describe McClelland's theory of human motives. What are the basic characteristics of high nAch individuals?
8. What is expectancy theory, and how can managers use it in the motivation process? Provide two examples.
9. Describe the basic idea in equity theory.
10. What is organizational behaviour modification? How can it be used in motivating people? Give two examples.
11. What is the role of money in motivation? How important is the issue of pay equity in terms of motivation? Discuss.
12. How does job enrichment differ from job enlargement? How would you apply job enrichment? Give an example.
13. What are quality circles and how successful have they been in improving the quality and quantity of work?
14. How is the compressed workweek different from flextime?

DISCUSSION QUESTIONS

1. Describe the main points of McGregor's Theory X and Theory Y. What are some examples of managerial practices that are consistent with a Theory Y philosophy of human nature?
2. What is a self-fulfilling prophecy? How is the idea relevant to managment and motivation?
3. From a subordinate's perspective, what are the advantages and disadvantages of working for a boss with a high need for achievement versus a high need for affiliation?
4. If you were a manager who had a subordinate who was late for work an average of twice a week, what would you do to resolve the problem?
5. Why might a satisfied worker not be a very productive worker?
6. "Some workers simply cannot be motivated." Do you agree or disagree? Defend your answer.

EXERCISES

1. Read two or three articles where managers give their views on the subject of motivation. Determine the managers' specific views about how to motivate employees. To what extent are the managers' views consistent with any single motivation theory discussed in this chapter? Are the managers' views in opposition to any of the theories discussed in this chapter?
2. Using Maslow's hierarchy as a guide, describe how your various needs have been satisfied on a job you have held. Were any of your needs not met? Why or why not? How could they have been satisfied?
3. Describe two situations from your own experience where you were motivated by a feeling of inequity. What specifically did you do to resolve the inequity? Were any of your actions those indicated in the chapter?
4. Read an article about an organization that has instituted a formal program in either quality circles or job enrichment. What results were evident? What hard data did the organization gather to help them determine whether or not the program was a success?

MANAGEMENT ON LOCATION

CASE 12-1
UNGRATEFUL EMPLOYEES

"I don't believe this!" thought Clayton Miller as he read a letter from the employees' association outlining strong objections to his recently proposed productivity plan. Among the objections in the letter were the following:

1. The employees are sick of working overtime. They want to have their evenings and weekends free to spend with their family and friends.
2. The bonus plan is just a scheme dreamed up by management to get more output from the workers without having to pay them for it. Payments should be related to time spent on the job, not savings achieved.
3. The plan is designed to manipulate the workers into competing with each other. It is divisive and contrary to the team spirit the company brags about.

Miller is president of The Western Note Company, a printer of specialty products such as lottery tickets, bank cheques, and stock and bond certificates. A family-held business, it is the largest of its kind in western Canada, employing 72 hourly paid workers. The plant is equipped with the latest computerized production equipment. The normal workweek is 40 hours, and employees are paid once every two weeks. Hourly wages range from $6.26 to $14.35, the former for press workers, and the latter for master engravers and senior press operators. In terms of annual pay, this works out to approximately $13 000 to $30 000.

During the last six months, demand for the company's products has been very strong. Consequently, most employees have worked six to eight hours of overtime each week. Overtime is paid at the rate of time-and-a-half for the first five hours, and double-time for everything beyond five hours. No work is scheduled on holidays or Sundays. . . .

As part of a continuing effort to achieve efficiency in operations, the cost accounting manager, Anita Yaworski, had developed a productivity incentive plan to be substituted for the overtime payment scheme that is currently being used. It related output per month to cost variance per job on an employee-by-employee basis. She calculated that, assuming the same amount of overtime was worked, the most productive employees could earn about 30 percent over their basic wage for a 48-hour week (this was about 6 percent more than what they could earn under the current overtime scheme). At the same time, the total wage bill for the company would be about 8 percent lower than under the current system. Because of the time required to calculate the bonus earned, employees would not receive their incentive pay until the pay period following the end of each month. This could mean up to a two-week delay in employees receiving their bonus pay.

Miller had sent the proposed incentive plan to the employees' association two weeks ago. Two days later, he outlined the main features of the plan in a speech he gave to the local chapter of the personnel management association. His speech was widely quoted in the local newspaper. ▲

QUESTIONS

1. The proposed incentive plan means that some workers will receive more money than they currently receive, even though they won't have to work any more hours for it. Why does the employees' association oppose a plan like this?
2. What should Miller do to prepare for the upcoming meeting with the employees' association which will take place in 10 days?

CASE 12-2
THE PROBLEM CHEMIST

Martin Stahl was the head of the research and development lab at Beltronics Ltd., a large manufacturing firm involved in the manufacture of plastic products for both consumer and industrial markets. In his role as laboratory head, Stahl supervised 11 chemists, all of whom had Ph.D.s in chemistry. The R & D lab had a dual responsibility: (1) to do pure research on various chemical compounds and how they behaved; and (2) to take any promising results from the pure research output and see how they could be applied in the manufacture of plastic products. The R & D lab had an excellent reputation inside and outside the company. A steady stream of new ideas and compounds had emerged from the lab over the last 10 years, and several patents had been obtained during that period. Most of the members of Stahl's department had also published articles about their work in chemical trade journals. Stahl encouraged this because it gave the company a good reputation and it provided feedback and status for the chemists.

Stahl was on good terms with all but one of the staff chemists. Gary Blaski had been hired four years ago to give some additional expertise in the pure research area. Blaski had gone to school with one of Stahl's group and, on that person's recommendation, Stahl had hired Blaski. However, within about six months of Blaski's hiring, Stahl began to have problems with him. In Stahl's view, although Blaski was a satisfactory chemist, he didn't seem to be motivated to do the kind of work the R & D lab was doing. Blaski showed little enthusiasm for the job, was often absent, and had a very low productivity level as measured by new patents granted, trade journal publications, and research projects completed.

Stahl had several discussions with Blaski about his performance, but Blaski rejected Stahl's position and argued that "research can't be rushed." These discussions were frustrating for Stahl, but he had gradually learned some things about Blaski. For example, he realized that Blaski craved recognition of any sort, no matter how insignificant. Stahl had attempted to use this knowledge to motivate Blaski by suggesting that Blaski get some of his work patented; this would mean considerable recognition. Blaski seemed interested in the idea, but somehow nothing ever came of it.

As time went on, Stahl became more and more unhappy about Blaski's nonchalant attitude and his poor performance. He began putting increasing pressure on Blaski to improve his performance but this just caused their relationship to worsen. Stahl noticed that Blaski seemed to be more and more unhappy; on one occasion Blaski told Stahl that the other chemists didn't seem to like him. He even commented that his former school buddy seemed to be avoiding him. When asked why, Blaski said he didn't know, but that it was unfair that his peers didn't recognize his abilities.

One afternoon Blaski came to Stahl's office and requested permission to take some time off from work (with pay) to attend a meeting of industrial chemists being held in another city. The following conversation took place:

Blaski: I'd like to go to the Industrial Chemists Association meetings. I think it's appropriate that the company pay for my travel and accommodations since I will be improving my work-related expertise by attending this meeting. I know you have reimbursed other people for things like this in the past, and I think I should be treated the same way.

Stahl: I'm sorry, but I can't grant the request. Before laying out money for things like that, I need to see a considerable improvement in your work here.

Blaski: What do you mean?

Stahl: You know exactly what I mean. Your nonchalant attitude has got to change and your productivity must improve.

Blaski: I've told you before, but you just don't listen. You can't rush research.

Stahl: The other chemists don't seem to be having any trouble meeting my productivity standards. I must not be "rushing" them. Why are you the only person who can't seem to do the job?

Blaski: You just don't realize that each person is unique. You're trying to make me fit into a certain mold and that's been weighing on my mind and reducing my productivity. If I were given more freedom to do my own thing, I would be more productive.

Stahl: When you demonstrate some productivity you'll get some freedom.

After Blaski left, Stahl wondered if he had been too harsh with him. However, he was at the end of his rope and had exhausted all the avenues he knew of to motivate Blaski. ▲

QUESTIONS

1. Use each of the motivation theories described in this chapter to analyze this problem. What solutions would each theory suggest?
2. Comment on Blaski's performance problems using the formula:

   performance = motivation × ability
3. What should Stahl do now?

CASE 12-3
THE CAVALIER EMPLOYEE

Frank Russo, the office manager for Motor Freightways, supervised a staff of seven. Russo was well-liked by his staff and pleasant in his dealings with everyone in the firm. He was something of a legend in his local community for his tireless volunteer activity in community service. Reece Snow, Russo's boss, was well aware of Russo's community service and had been very supportive of it because he recognized that it reflected favourably on the company in the local community.

As of late, however, Snow had become increasingly concerned about Russo's long lunch hours. Russo would often leave before noon, and return well after 1 P.M. When Snow checked into Russo's comings and goings, he discovered (to no one's surprise) that Russo was busily involved in taking care of a few community service matters on his lunch hour. As Russo's lunch hours gradually became longer, Snow decided that a serious talk was in order. On January 14, Russo returned from his lunch at 2:15 P.M. Snow called him into his office and the following conversation took place:

Snow: Frank, I'm going to get right to the point. I think you're spending too much time away from the office during your lunch hours. You're modelling bad behaviour for the staff. I think they need you here to direct them.

Russo: Are the staff complaining?

Snow: No, but I feel that your lengthy absences, even if they are for good causes, cannot continue.

Russo: Are the office staff performing below standard?

• • •

Snow: No, but I think their performance would be even better if you were here throughout the day.

Russo: I don't understand. The office staff are very experienced. They certainly wouldn't appreciate my looking over their shoulder all day.

Snow: I'm not suggesting that you look over their shoulder. I am suggesting, however, that this company is paying your salary and that you have the responsibility to give us a full day's work. Now, you've been a productive person for quite a number of years, but I sense that your motivation for this job has declined quite a bit in the last few months. I'd like to see you as motivated to do your work here as you are to get involved in community service.

Russo: I don't think my enthusiasm for community service should be an issue here. If my performance and that of my subordinates is satisfactory, that is all you should be concerned about.

The meeting ended shortly after this. Snow was quite upset, but kept his feelings from Russo for the moment. He tried to reflect calmly on his conversation with Russo, but had difficulty making sense out of his comments. After all, he thought, this guy is being paid by us. Why shouldn't we expect him to adhere to some basic rules? ▲

QUESTIONS

1. Using concepts introduced in the chapter, explain why Russo puts so much effort into unpaid community service and very little effort into his paid job.
2. What factors should Snow consider as he analyzes this problem?
3. Develop a plan of action that Snow can implement that will increase Russo's on-the-job motivation.

CHAPTER 13

LEADERSHIP

LEARNING OBJECTIVES

After reading this chapter, you will be able to:

1. Define leadership and explain how it is different from management.
2. Outline the characteristics of charismatic leaders.
3. Describe the difference between transactional management and transformational management.
4. Explain the concept of leadership style and describe the two basic styles—autocratic and democratic.
5. Describe the difference between universalist and contingency leadership theories, and give examples of each.
6. Understand the three basic approaches to leadership—the trait approach, the leader behaviour approach, and the contingency approach.

MANAGEMENT CHALLENGE

MAKING PARTICIPATIVE LEADERSHIP WORK

In 1987, Robert Frey and a partner bought Cin-Made Corp., a small manufacturer of mailing tubes. The business had generated only marginal profits up to that time, and it had poor union relations and high costs. Frey's initial attempts to increase productivity created worker resistance, and the company became a battleground between workers and management. Before long, it was losing $30 000 a month.

Frey's next step was to cut costs. He did this by cutting wages (by 25 percent), and also cutting vacations and holidays. The workers responded with a strike, which Frey won. As a result, although he had achieved lower costs, he also had an angry work force on his hands.

Finally, Frey decided that something drastic had to be done. In lieu of a wage increase, he offered to give the workers 30 percent of company's profits each year. The workers accepted the deal, but problems remained. Frey pressed on further, announcing that (1) he would not run a company where workers and management were adversaries, and (2) employees would be encouraged to participate in making many decisions that had formerly been made by managers.

After this, the level of hostility seemed to *increase*. Managers, for example, felt that they were paid to be worthy adversaries of the union. They didn't like the idea of worker participation in decision making, and they

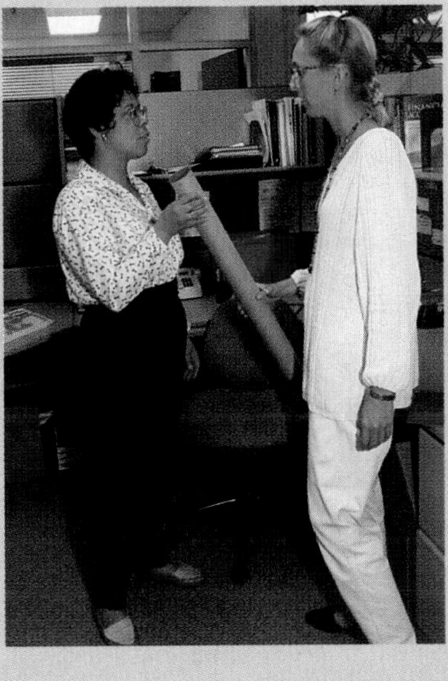

...

thought that profit sharing was a form of communism. In fact, several managers actively obstructed the movement. The workers didn't seem much happier. They had been trained to believe that managers should manage and workers should do what they were told. They wanted generous wages, but they didn't want to take responsibility for anything other than their own jobs. When Frey asked for their advice on various matters, the response was often, "That's not my job."

Frey was determined to continue, however, because he believed that unless workers and managers shared a common interest in the company's success, the company would not succeed. He felt that an attitude change would follow a behavioural change, so he forced a behavioural change. Gradually, managers began sharing more information with subordinates. Information meetings were held where subordinates could ask any questions they liked. Frey also said the company's financial statements were open for the union to look at because without full information about profit, the employees probably wouldn't be motivated by profit sharing.

Slowly, production workers began to take on jobs above and beyond what they had done in the past, and Frey noted that workers sometimes came up with solutions to problems that had stumped the management team. During this period, those managers who couldn't cope with participative management left the company; workers also began to see their jobs in much broader terms. A new plant manager was hired who was strong technically and also had the ability to listen to workers. ▲

Leadership, like motivation, has received much attention during the past few decades. Many managers believe that leadership is *the* determinant of productivity and organizational success, and studies show that leadership is crucial for organizational performance.[1]

The challenge facing leaders is to motivate subordinates to pursue organizational goals, to introduce change, and to manage conflict. Leadership is vital in our society. We frequently hear the claim that effective leadership is necessary if Canada is to remain a strong and unified country.[2] Some writers express the view that a "leadership gap" exists, and that many businesses are adrift in a sea of managerial mediocrity.[3] The Management at Work insert entitled "Leadership in the 1990s" suggests that it may be difficult to find effective leaders in the 1990s.

What does it take to be an effective leader? What is the most effective leadership style? How much does leadership behaviour affect subordinate satisfaction and productivity? These questions have challenged managers throughout history. In this chapter we present what is known about leadership. We begin by defining leadership and comparing it to management. We make the distinction between transactional and transformational management, and look at the issue of charismatic leadership. Next, we analyze the issue of leadership style and its effect on the satisfaction and performance of subordinates. The third section of the chapter describes how thinking about leadership has progressed from the trait approach, to the leader behaviour approach, and finally to the contingency approach. The last section of the chapter contains some reflections on current leadership issues.

WHAT IS LEADERSHIP?

leadership

In practical terms, **leadership** is the ability to influence others to pursue the goals the leader thinks are important and desirable. Leadership also involves many specific activities, such as creating a "vision" which motivates followers to action. The vision is likely to require some major changes in behaviour and attitudes, which in turn may cause conflicts. The leader is therefore a person who institutes the changes that are necessary to achieve the vision, and manages the conflict that inevitably arises along the way.

LEARNING OBJECTIVE 1

Define leadership and explain how it is different from management.

To some people, the word "leadership" has an inspirational connotation, suggesting a leader who inspires followers to achieve great objectives. According to this view, the leader pulls others along by force of personality or vision. Other people

MANAGEMENT AT WORK

Leadership in the 1990s

Finding the right CEO in the 1990s may be a much more difficult task than it was in the 1980s. Increased competition, flatter management pyramids, rapid change, and tougher economic conditions all mean that the job of CEO is becoming more difficult.

There have been several "waves of fashion in CEO appointments" in the past two decades. During the 1970s, marketing experts were in great demand as mass marketing reached its peak. Lee Iacocca's flamboyant rescue of Chrysler is a prime example. After the recession in the early 1980s, finance- and control-oriented executives became prominent as companies were downsized and made "lean and mean." Attempts were made to squeeze as much as possible out of workers and other resources.

There was a similarity between the two decades—each period meant that the person at the top had specialized skills, although the business environment dictated which skills were needed at a given point. While specialists in marketing and finance are still needed, a survey by *Canadian Business* shows that the CEOs who are in highest demand are those who are strong in multiple areas. Whether they are called leaders, renaissance people, or visionaries, leadership in the 1990s will mean inspired general-ship. Companies now view the position of CEO to be too demanding to be filled by individuals with only a narrow functional specialty. No matter how expert a person is in a certain area, this will not compensate for deficiencies in other areas.

The current belief is that real leaders can indeed fill all these needs. Corporate headhunters (recruiters) are being asked to find leaders who can "walk on water." Rapid, revolutionary change has replaced the normal evolutionary change that normally occurs in most companies. When firms hire a new CEO, they want someone who can "hit the ground running." The challenge for CEOs is to deal with a myriad of new situations that constantly arise. Their job, therefore, is not so much to manage a company as it is to transform it.

All this means that recruiting a CEO is now more time-consuming and costly. Companies are no longer content with a candidate who is a "whiz kid" in marketing or finance; instead, they are using more subjective criteria like the ability to look ahead, to motivate subordinates, to make tough, intuitive decisions, and to think internationally. More company officials are involved in the search for a CEO because the cost of making a mistake is higher than it was even five years ago. ▲

see the role of the leader as a supportive one, with the leader assisting followers rather than directing them. The leader, in this view, tends to push people toward goals. In practice, leadership is a combination of these approaches.

Organizations in both the public and private sector benefit from good leadership. Would the British have had the motivation to fight off the Nazi threat during World War II without Winston Churchill's leadership? Would Chrysler Corporation have been able to come back from the brink of bankruptcy without Lee Iacocca's leadership? Would the Toronto Blue Jays have won back-to-back World Series' without Cito Gaston's leadership? Because leaders motivate organizational members to put forth extra effort, they can make a huge difference in organizational performance.

Leaders versus Managers

There is a difference between a "leader" and a "manager."[4] A **manager** performs the functions of planning, organizing, leading, and controlling, and occupies a formal position in an organization. For example, the sales manager is the individual who manages the company's sales force. A **leader**, on the other hand, is anyone who is able to influence others to pursue goals that the leader would like to achieve. For example, a member of a community club who feels that a new hockey arena is needed may be able to spearhead a project designed to achieve this goal. This person is a leader.

manager

leader

One of the most charismatic leaders in recent history was Pierre Elliot Trudeau, who was Prime Minister from 1968–79 and 1980–84. Trudeau was witty, self-confident, and had a strong conviction that the diversity generated by both English- and French-speaking Canadians was necessary to create a strong Canada.

Is a manager also a leader? Not necessarily. The sales manager mentioned above is certainly a manager because of the formal position he or she occupies. Whether the sales manager is also a leader depends on his or her ability to influence the sales staff to pursue certain goals. A good manager is a good leader because he or she will be effective at carrying out all of the functions of management, one of which is influencing (leading) others. A bad manager may be a poor leader, because he or she is not carrying out the leading, or influencing, function.

We can also turn the question around and ask whether a leader is also a manager. Again, the answer must be qualified. A good leader may or may not be a good manager. A leader may be good at motivating people to pursue a certain goal, but if that goal is unwanted by the organization, or if it is harmful to people, then the leader is a poor manager. Adolph Hitler, for example, was able to influence people to pursue his goals, but those goals were destructive to people.

Leaders can be further distinguished from managers if we consider a number of work and personal factors.[5] First, managers pursue goals that are set by top management, while leaders are more active and decide which goals they want to pursue. Second, managers view their work as that of working with people and ideas to achieve goals. On the other hand, leaders view their work as finding new ways of doing things or new ways to resolve long-standing problems. Third, managers see people in terms of the task at hand, while leaders relate to people in intuitive and empathetic ways. Finally, managers view themselves as an integral part of the system in which they work, while leaders see themselves as quite separate from the system.

Many North American organizations have blindly accepted the "managerial mystique," which emphasizes process, structure, and roles, and ignores people, ideas, and emotions.[6] What is needed is a rebirth of creative leadership which will tie leaders and those who are led into a moral, intellectual, and emotional commitment to achieve certain goals.

CHARISMATIC LEADERSHIP

charisma

People with **charisma** have personal abilities and characteristics that allow them to have an unusually strong influence on the behaviour and attitudes of others. While some managers seem to have charisma (for example, Lee Iacocca of Chrysler), we typically think of managers as individuals who methodically plan, organize, and control subordinates. Charismatic leadership is more evident in politics and religion than in the business world. Various political and religious leaders—Gorbachev, Churchill, Hitler, Gandhi, Trudeau—have demonstrated a high degree of charisma.

charismatic leaders

LEARNING OBJECTIVE 2

Outline the characteristics of charismatic leaders.

Charismatic leaders possess three characteristics: self-confidence, dominance, and a strong conviction about the rightness of their beliefs.[7] A charismatic leader models a value system for followers and conveys to them a goal that transcends immediate circumstances. Martin Luther King, Jr., for example, conveyed to followers his conception of what life *could* be like in his famous "I have a dream" speech in the 1960s.

A charismatic leader expects a high level of performance from followers. Winston Churchill's speech about "England's finest hour" during World War II conveyed his expectation that England and her allies could overcome the Nazi threat—even though the situation looked hopeless at the time.

The followers of charismatic leaders have a high degree of motivation because they believe the leader is extraordinarily gifted. The followers are also devoted, loyal, give unquestioned obedience to the leader's commands, and trust the leader implicitly. Thus, the leader is able to bring about dramatic change through the followers' actions. The Ethics in Management insert "The Ethics of Charismatic Leadership" describes some potential problems with charismatic leaders.

ETHICS IN MANAGEMENT

The Ethics of Charismatic Leadership

Charismatic leaders are management heroes. They are able to turn around ailing corporations, revitalize stodgy bureaucracies, and launch exciting new businesses. They are almost always viewed as effective leaders because they communicate a compelling vision to their followers, set high standards, and express great confidence that their followers can achieve the goals they have set.

All of this sounds great. But there is a dark side to charismatic leadership, too. The biggest potential problem lies in the ethical standards of the leader, who may demand blind obedience from followers while in pursuit of dangerous goals. While it is not difficult to find charismatic leaders who have been negatively judged by history—Adolph Hitler, Benito Mussolini, David Koresh, John DeLorean—the risk inherent in charismatic leadership is often not talked about.

In a study by a researcher from The University of Western Ontario, 150 managers in 25 Canadian organizations were asked to identify charismatic leaders. Twenty-five of the charismatics who were identified were later interviewed about their philosophy, values, and attitudes towards followers. The transcripts of these interviews were then analyzed for the presence of themes related to whether the leaders concerned themselves with moral abuses, confronted and resolved dilemmas, encouraged the pursuit of ideals, promoted an ethically responsible culture, and rewarded those who demonstrated moral integrity.

Analysis of the interview data revealed that ethical charismatic leaders (ECLs) and unethical charismatic leaders (UCLs) could be distinguished on six key dimensions:

1. *Power* ECLs used power in socially constructive ways to serve others, while UCLs used power to dominate followers.
2. *Communications* ECLs regularly get follower opinions on critical issues (two-way communication), while UCLs are closed-minded about input from followers (one-way communication).
3. *Feedback* ECLs are willing to take advice and to learn from criticism, while UCLs have an inflated sense of self-importance and reject negative feedback.
4. *Stimulating followers intellectually* ECLs encourage their followers to look at problems from various perspectives, while UCLs demand that their ideas be unconditionally accepted by followers.
5. *Developing followers* ECLs strive to move followers to higher levels of ability, motivation, and morality, while UCLs are insensitive and uncaring about followers' needs and aspirations.
6. *Moral standards* ECLs motivate followers to pursue objectives that are good for both the organization and society, while UCLs use their communication skills to manipulate others into believing that what they are doing is "right."

The end result of all this is that ECLs convert followers into leaders. Because the ECL expresses confidence in followers' abilities and encourages them to think on their own, the followers become more capable of leading themselves. UCLs, on the other hand, produce dependent, obedient, and compliant followers. The self-worth of the followers becomes dependent on their continued support of the leader's opinions. When the UCL swerves into unethical behaviour, the followers are likely to unquestioningly go along. ▲

Transactional and Transformational Managers

LEARNING OBJECTIVE 3
Describe the difference between transactional management and transformational management.

In the past few years, management writers have made a distinction between transactional and transformational management.[8] **Transactional managers** have a traditional view of management functions. They stress planning for the future, setting up a structure to achieve the plans of the organization, and controlling the system so that it performs well. **Transformational managers** stress activities such as revitalizing the organization, communicating the organization's vision and culture to employees, molding employees into effective performers, and encouraging employee commitment to the organization's goals.

transactional managers

transformational managers

Three activities are involved in transformational management:

1. *Creation of a vision* The leader provides the organization's members with a vision of a desired future state.
2. *Mobilization of commitment* The critical mass of people in the organization accept the leader's vision.
3. *Institutionalization of change* New patterns of behaviour are adopted which are consistent with the new vision.[9]

The transformational leader recognizes that people will have mixed emotions about significant changes, and must therefore help move employees from their initial negative reaction to positive ones. Transformational leaders ease the transition by replacing the organization's past glories with a strong vision of future opportunities.

Considerable changes are sweeping through Canadian society, and transactional managers will have to develop transformational skills in order to remain effective. They will need a long-term perspective on problems facing our society, and will increasingly be called upon to make decisions that will benefit not only business firms, but many other types of organizations. Transformational management involves getting·organizations and the people in them to take on new challenges. It is based on the idea that leadership makes a difference in the way organizations cope with change.[10]

Males and Females: Are There Leadership Differences?

As we have seen, more and more women are being promoted into managerial positions. This has led to increased interest in the study of whether men and women differ as they carry out their leadership functions. The systematic study of this issue is important; without solid empirical knowledge about leadership behaviour, certain myths about women in management may be perpetuated. This, in turn, may cause questionable hiring and promotion decisions to be made.

What exactly does the research evidence say? Surveys show that people often stereotype men as task-oriented, aggressive, competitive, and dominant, while women are stereotyped as relationship-oriented, passive, noncompetitive, and compliant.[11] But it is easy to find exceptions to these stereotypes. Former British prime minister Margaret Thatcher was the epitome of the aggressive, forceful leader, while Mohandas Ghandi was the opposite. Research shows that both men and women can be effective in developing motivated and productive subordinates.[12]

Studies do show that the leadership *styles* of men and women differ. Women typically involve subordinates in decisions, share power with subordinates, show concern for subordinates' self-esteem, and rely on charisma to influence subordinates. Men, on the other hand, typically make more decisions on their own, are reluctant to share power with subordinates, use their formal authority to influence people, and use rewards and punishments to shape subordinate behaviour.[13] If we think back to the transactional/transformational distinction made earlier, we see that women tend more toward transformational leadership, while men tend more toward transactional leadership.

leadership style

LEARNING OBJECTIVE 4

Explain the concept of leadership style and describe the two basic styles—autocratic and democratic.

LEADERSHIP STYLES

Leadership style refers to the behaviour the leader exhibits while supervising subordinates. There are as many leadership styles as there are leaders, but two basic styles are generally recognized—autocratic and democratic (participative). The Management at Work insert "The Wrecking Ball Style of Management" describes the leadership style of the CEO of Procter & Gamble.

(Note: The term "management style" is also used by some to describe actions that have nothing to do with how management decisions are made. For example, Wilbert Hopper, former CEO of Petro-Canada was accused of being flamboyant and enjoying a "fat-cat" lifestyle while his company was losing money and his employees were being laid off. He made extensive use of the corporate jet, a limousine, and a personal chef. His successor, James Stanford, has a much more conservative style.[14])

autocratic leader

The **autocratic leader** believes that all decision-making authority must be retained by the leader because employees are either unwilling or unable to make reasonable decisions. Whatever the reasons, the leader gives orders and expects subordinates to follow them. Laurent Beaudoin (Bombardier Inc.) is cited in the business press as being an autocratic leader.[15] Former Prime Minister Brian Mulroney has been seen in the role of an all-powerful PM who cracked the whip to make everybody jump. His leadership style has been described as being like an imperial CEO of the fifties, and as someone who treated most people like dependent children.[16]

Assuming the leader is competent, the autocratic style leads to the efficient, effective accomplishment of tasks. If the leader has developed a good system for doing the work, following the leader's commands may result in positive outcomes (e.g., high pay) for subordinates. But this style often leads to low employee morale, and the

MANAGEMENT AT WORK

THE "WRECKING BALL" STYLE OF MANAGEMENT

Edwin Artzt, chair of Procter & Gamble, has developed a reputation as a "wrecking ball" because of his aggressive management style. Subordinates claim, among other things, that Artzt humiliates them in public meetings (for example, he berated managers for mishandling the Noxema skin care product, and asked them how they could have been so stupid). More than a dozen senior executives have left the company since Artzt took over in 1990, and an executive recruiting firm says it is receiving up to 50 calls a day from P & G managers. Artzt says that managers who left the company did so for reasons that had nothing to do with him. He admits that he can be very feisty, but he says this lets people know where he is coming from.

Artzt may feel that his management style is dictated by market pressures. Makers of generic brands have been undercutting P & G's premium-priced brands, and the company has too many brands that are not performing well (one-quarter of the company's products contribute a total of just 2 percent of sales). Artzt intends to deal with what he sees as massive inefficiencies in the firm by trimming the bureaucracy. Industry analysts predict that about 10 percent of the work force—10 000 jobs—will be cut.

Critics note that Artzt's overbearing management style may undermine his strategy to meet marketplace challenges. Some managers at the firm say that people are so fearful of his disapproval that they are afraid to take the innovative actions that are necessary for the company to be successful in the marketplace. When Artzt hired tennis star Jennifer Capriati as a spokeswoman for Oil of Olay, many managers felt that she did not have enough charisma to appeal to the teen market. But managers were afraid to say this to Artzt. The campaign flopped, and P & G used Capriati only sparingly, in spite of paying her $1 million. More time and money was spent explaining why the campaign failed than had been spent on the actual campaign.

A former manager says that Artzt genuinely wants people to become more effective, but in this manager's view, yelling at subordinates is not the way to do it. This same manager thinks that Artzt wants subordinates who are "running scared" because they will be more motivated.

Sometimes Artzt's intensity yields benefits. When sales of Pert Plus skyrocketed in the U.S., Artzt asked why the product wasn't being sold in Europe and Asia. Managers replied that they didn't have the manufacturing capacity in those areas. Artzt became very angry and told them to set up manufacturing in a tent if necessary. In the end, production was increased faster than it otherwise would have been, and P & G was acclaimed as a leader in global marketing.

Some analysts say that Artzt's harsh management style may be necessary in P & G's current situation. One former manager at the company notes that Artzt has inherited a lot of problems, and perhaps the only way to fix them is to convince everyone in the firm that he means business and will not tolerate relaxed attitudes. ▲

boss may find that workers are maliciously obedient, that is, they follow directions to the letter even when they know the directions are wrong. In one factory, an expensive machine was badly damaged because workers failed to lubricate it properly. When asked by the plant manager why they had not lubricated the machine, they replied that they were carefully following their supervisor's orders not to do anything until he told them to do it.

democratic leader

The **democratic**, or participative, **leader** believes that authority should be delegated to subordinates to make decisions based on their interest and expertise in dealing with certain situations. The Management Challenge described how Robert Frey's belief in participative management was so strong that he actually pressured his managers and workers to participate in important decisions. Democratic leaders assume that employees are both willing and able to make reasonable decisions. The democratic style involves an interplay between boss and subordinate, with both parties having input into decisions. Charles Hantho, the CEO at Dominion Textile, is a democratic leader who readily delegates authority. Bob Hamaberg of Standard Aero Ltd. takes a collegial approach to running his company through a five-person executive committee. Each member of the committee is responsible for one aspect of shop operations.[17] For a more detailed description of how participative management works, see the Management at Work insert "Participative Management at Ciba-Geigy."

Allowing employees to participate in decision making increases both the quality

MANAGEMENT AT WORK

Participative Management at Ciba-Geigy

The traditional management hierarchy has been abandoned at Ciba-Geigy Canada Ltd.'s plant in Cambridge, Ontario. Work teams now develop job descriptions, interview potential employees, set work schedules, and do other duties that used to be reserved for managers. The layers of bureaucracy that smother incentive are gone. When layoffs were unexpectedly required in the middle of the process, workers decided who should be let go and who should remain.

When Gerry Rich joined the company in 1987, he found a plant that was in trouble. Productivity was low, and employees had little interest in taking the lead to improve it. With the help of a management consultant, Rich and the workers developed guiding principles for completely redesigning the work to be done. A design team—composed of managers, production workers, warehouse employees and clerical workers—coordinated the work of various study teams. In turn, these teams made recommendations about how to change jobs to achieve greater productivity.

In the middle of this process, Ciba-Geigy decided to cease producing one of the plant's products; this meant that one-quarter of the staff would have to be laid off. In order to keep the redesign program on track, Rich allowed the workers to decide who would be let go. One of the recommendations for release was the manager of the discontinued product.

Eight months after starting the project, the design team completed its work. The plant was shut down for one week so that all workers could be informed of the changes that would be introduced. At this time additional workers were let go, and those who remained spent the week learning how it would feel to call their own shots.

Under the new system, the emphasis is on participative management. Managers do not give orders; rather, they advise workers, facilitate teamwork, lead training programs, and help with conflict resolution. Supervisors now work alongside those they used to supervise. Some former bosses clung to authority symbols (like suits and ties) even after the change was implemented. Rich, however, provided the proper symbols by not wearing a tie to work.

One year after the system was fully implemented, another major staff cut was announced. Again the participative management mechanisms went into motion, and once more, workers decided who would go and who would stay. When a job opened up a few months later in the warehouse, a work team conducted the interviews and recommended the best candidate.

Rich has discovered that participative management has some sweeping implications—workers may not need as many managers as was formerly thought. In fact, in a recent performance assessment that all workers completed for their colleagues, one gave the opinion that Gerry Rich had done all he could do at the plant, and it was time for him to move on! ▲

of decisions and employee acceptance of them. When head office told Ronald Smith, president of Amdahl Canada, to cut over $1.7 million from his company's operating expenses, Smith did not simply reduce his work force. Rather, he asked his employees to join him in figuring out ways to reduce overhead. The employees succeeded in cutting over $3 million by delaying pay increases, cutting travel, and restructuring the workweek so that overtime could be reduced (this latter decision was one Smith had tried—unsuccessfully—to implement a few years ago).[18]

Proponents of participative management say that it should always be used because it increases subordinate satisfaction and productivity. But the reality is not that simple. One review of the effects of participative management showed that it generally improved employee satisfaction, but not employee productivity.[19] Other reviews show that what is meant by "participation" varies widely across companies, and this makes it difficult to assess its impact on employee satisfaction and performance.[20] Participation is a central feature of the so-called Japanese management system (see the Global Management insert entitled "The Japanese Management System").

Participation can have disadvantages. First, individuals who participate may be pressured by their peers to stop "collaborating" with management. Second, managers may attempt to manipulate the participation process to get the outcomes they want. Third, once employees have been allowed to participate in decision making, they may be unwilling to return to rigidly structured work.[21]

GLOBAL MANAGEMENT

THE JAPANESE MANAGEMENT SYSTEM

Much has been written about Theory Z, or the "Japanese management system," and how it might benefit Canadian firms. At its most basic, the system contains five elements:

1. *Lifetime employment* Employees usually stay at one firm for their entire working career instead of changing jobs as is common in Canada.
2. *Temporary employees* Large Japanese firms have many temporary employees (mostly female). If a downturn occurs, these employees are the first to be laid off. Thus, women act as a buffer to protect men's jobs.
3. *Small satellite firms* These firms, which exist to serve the big Japanese companies, cannot get the licences required to import raw materials necessary for major manufacturing.
4. *Participative decision making* When an important decision is to be made, everyone who will feel its impact is involved in the decision-making process. Often, 60 or 70 people will have an input into the decision. A decision is made only after consensus is reached with the people who will be affected.
5. *Management training* Training for management in Japan is quite different from its counterpart in Canada. The stress on company loyalty underlies much management training in Japan. Employees are often not hired for the specific skills they possess and may not be given a specific job to do until they have been with the company for three to six months. Employees spend the first couple of months becoming familiar with the company. Training is oriented toward groups instead of individuals and is designed to encourage team spirit.

In addition to these general features, the Japanese management system is characterized by the following specific activities:

- daily physical exercise for all employees at the work site
- pep talks by supervisors
- identical uniforms for managers and workers
- no unions
- emphasis on company loyalty
- nonspecific job classifications
- emphasis on quality control
- common dining rooms for managers and workers
- use of just-in-time inventory systems
- company outings for employees and their families

Much of the success of Japanese business firms is attributed to their management system and to the political and economic feature's of Japan. The most commonly held view is that factors such as effective industrial financing, government industrial policy,

• • •

a long-term perspective, labour-management cooperation, lifetime employment, consensus decision making, effective use of technology, and total quality control are responsible for the success of Japanese firms. But a survey of Japanese executives showed that more than half of them attributed Japan's industrial success to cultural factors unique to Japan.

In the 1980s, it was very fashionable to praise the Japanese management system. But in the 1990s, the Japanese are themselves running into problems. During 1992–94, Japan found itself in a major recession, and industrial output declined for 23 consecutive months, the longest decline on record. Consumer confidence is weak, unemployment is rising, GNP is declining, and there are fears that the lifetime employment idea is in danger. The Japanese management system apparently cannot protect Japanese workers from these changes.

Can the Japanese management system be implemented in Canada? Some of its principles will not be acceptable (for example, using women as buffers for men's jobs), while others (for example, participative management) are quite workable.

The number of Japanese-owned and managed manufacturing plants in Canada now exceeds 530. If Japanese-Canadian joint ventures are included, the number is more than 1500. The Japanese have had great success in transplanting their production know-how to Canada, and it is very much in fashion to praise Japanese management techniques in general. But as more manufacturing plants that use these techniques are built in Canada, some problems are beginning to surface.

The greatest publicity has been given to the three major Japanese auto plants built in Canada—Toyota (Cambridge, Ontario), Honda (Alliston, Ontario), and CAMI (Ingersoll, Ontario). It is here that conclusions are being drawn about how well the Japanese management system works in Canada, and what kinds of adjustments will have to be made to suit the Canadian psyche.

Some workers seem to embrace the Japanese system wholeheartedly. They are fascinated by its novelty and efficiency and attracted by the prospect of a secure lifetime job. Others openly dislike wearing a company uniform or working overtime several times a week without advance warning.

Some Japanese managers say that Canadians are more receptive to their management system than Americans are, and some evidence backs up this view. The Toyota plant in Cambridge won the coveted J.D. Power and Associates award for production of the highest quality in North America, and Canadian-made Corollas average fewer problems than those made in Toyota City (Japan) or in Georgetown (Kentucky).

The Japanese system has both a positive and a negative side for Canadian workers. The following benefits are evident:

1. *Job Flexibility* Workers learn all the jobs of their ten-person team and then rotate through these jobs each day.
2. *Company Uniforms* Workers save money on clothing because the company provides the uniforms.
3. *Consensus Decision Making* Many people are involved in making major decisions. Once consensus is reached, it is easier to implement change. Morale is also higher because workers (called associates) are allowed input into the decision.
4. *Pay* The nonunionized workers in Japanese-owned plants receive the same pay as their union counterparts in other plants without having to pay union dues.
5. *Team System* Each worker is part of a team which increases the feeling of belonging.
6. *Job Security* Japanese companies offer the best job security around.

But the following problems have also been noted:

1. *Overtime* Employees are often asked to work overtime, sometimes with little advance notice. Workers who refuse must give management a satisfactory explanation.
2. *Open Office System* Managers and subordinates work side by side in large open offices. Many complain about interruptions that keep them from concentrating on their work.
3. *No Replacement Workers* When one worker is sick, the rest of the work team must keep up production. This policy leads to resentment of workers who do not show up for work, regardless of the reason.
4. *Rigid Rules* Workers complain, for example, that they are not allowed to wear shorts when the weather is hot.
5. *Selective Adoption of Workers' Ideas* Suggestions to improve productivity are immediately adopted whereas suggestions to improve morale may not be.
6. *Attendance Charts* For both office and factory staff, absent days appear as black marks on attendance sheets posted on the wall for all to see.

Interestingly, one of the biggest problems from the Japanese perspective is not Canadian workers but Canadian suppliers. In Japan, companies routinely establish long-term relationships with suppliers based on quality and trust. They will, for example, expect a supplier to gear up for a long production run even without a purchase order. In Canada, however, because banks are unwilling to lend money without a purchase order, suppliers want a formal deal before beginning production. Parts makers are also having difficulty adjusting to the idea that the price they will be paid next year for their parts is likely to be less than they were paid this year. ▲

In the Management Challenge, Robert Frey found that some workers and managers did not like the idea of participative management. Getting workers involved in decision making may have some unexpected consequences. At MacMillan Bloedel, woodland and mill managers have begun sharing detailed financial information with workers, and union representatives have been taken along on sales trips to competing mills to see how fierce competition is. But union leaders worry that this kind of activity dupes union members into making suggestions that will increase company productivity, which in turn will reduce the number of jobs.

Another problem that sometimes arises is that of differing expectations. At the Port Alberni paper mill, workers agreed to get involved in joint union/management committees to search for ways to increase productivity. In return, the company agreed to spend $5 million to extend early retirement benefits. Unfortunately, the hoped-for productivity improvements have not been forthcoming, and management is reducing activity at the mill and has laid off 200 workers. Workers apparently assumed that the agreement meant that the company would upgrade the mill and save jobs. Both management and workers are unhappy.[22]

Autocratic leadership is often found in military organizations. A well-defined hierarchy of authority and sharply defined ranks characterize military organizations. The achievement of battlefield objectives makes it imperative that each person in the hierarchy follows orders.

The autocratic and democratic styles have usually been viewed as the opposite ends of a single continuum. But there are actually two dimensions of leadership style, not one. A leader can be autocratic or democratic when employees *make* decisions, and when employees *carry out* the decisions that have been made.

Therefore there are really four types of leaders:[23]

1. *Directive autocrat* Allows subordinates no discretion in making decisions or in carrying them out.
2. *Permissive autocrat* Allows subordinates no discretion in decision making, but considerable discretion as they carry out decisions.
3. *Directive democrat* Allows subordinates to participate in making decisions, but supervises them closely while they carry out decisions.
4. *Permissive democrat* Allows subordinates great discretion in making decisions and in carrying them out.

LEADERSHIP THEORIES

LEARNING OBJECTIVE 5

Describe the difference between universalist and contingency leadership theories, and give examples of each.

The leadership theories which have been developed during the twentieth century focus on the question, "What is the most effective leadership style?" Effectiveness is usually judged by the criteria of employee performance and employee satisfaction. Although there are many specific leadership theories, there are only two basic types. **Universalist leadership theories** argue that one style of leadership is superior to all others, regardless of the situation in which the leader operates. These theories are based largely on observations of leader traits or behaviours, and they contain statements about how leaders should behave, or what characteristics leaders should possess if they hope to be effective. **Contingency leadership theories** assume that different situations require different leadership styles. These theories emphasize that situational variables must be analyzed to determine which leadership style is best for which situation.

universalist leadership theories

contingency leadership theories

LEARNING OBJECTIVE 6

Understand the three basic approaches to leadership—the trait approach, the leader behaviour approach, and the contingency approach.

In the following paragraphs, we discuss the development of leadership theories. Three major approaches in leadership research can be identified—the trait approach, the leader behaviour approach, and the contingency approach. Generally speaking, the first two approaches resulted in universalist leadership theories, while the third approach led to the development of contingency leadership theories.

THE TRAIT APPROACH

trait approach

The **trait approach** assumes that the leader's personal attributes are the key to leadership success. On the surface, the trait approach seems reasonable and promising. From approximately 1900 to 1945, researchers studied successful leaders in an attempt to identify those traits which were associated with success. If these traits could be identified, employees in the organization could be tested to determine whether or not they possessed them. Those that did could be groomed for positions of leadership.

The research on traits found that leaders had a tendency to be taller, more extroverted, more intelligent, and more self-confident than nonleaders. But many exceptions were found, and only a few of these traits regularly appeared across different studies[24] One review of over 100 trait studies found that only 5 percent of the traits appeared in four or more studies.[25] Thus, the hoped-for benefits of the trait approach never materialized.

The trait approach ran into trouble for the following reasons:

1. People who fail as leaders, as well as people who never become leaders, may have some of the same traits as successful leaders.
2. Many traits are not directly observable, nor are they easily measured; even if they could be measured, it is not known how much of a certain trait is necessary for leadership success.
3. Focussing on leader traits ignores the environment in which the leader works.

If people are asked to list well-known historical leaders, they typically include names like Julius Caesar, Winston Churchill, Adolph Hitler, Abraham Lincoln, Mao Tse Tung, Alexander the Great, Napoleon, Jesus Christ, and John F. Kennedy. If great leaders possessed common traits, we should be able to observe similarities among them. But this is hardly the case. While some similarities exist (e.g., all the leaders were highly motivated to influence others to follow them), obvious differences in both physical traits (e.g., height, weight, body shape) and psychological traits (e.g., intelligence, extroversion, verbal fluency) also emerge. Most people would agree, for example, that both Adolph Hitler and Jesus Christ were able to influence people to follow them; but beyond that they had very little, if anything, in common. Likewise, the physical features of some history's great leaders differ greatly (e.g., Abraham Lincoln was very tall and Napoleon was very short). In spite of these shortcomings, many people continue to believe that the trait approach is a useful way of identifying potential leaders.

Research on traits continues because the idea of identifying a list of traits is so intuitively appealing. The most recent research identifies six traits which seem to give individuals the *potential* to be effective leaders.[26] These traits are:

1. drive (high level of energy; ambition)
2. desire to lead (a desire to influence others)
3. honesty and integrity (developing trust between the leader and the followers)
4. self-confidence (assurance about the rightness of decisions)
5. intelligence (ability to interpret information)
6. job-relevant knowledge (about the company, its industry, and technical matters)

The argument is that individuals who have these traits are more likely to take certain actions (e.g., creating a vision, setting goals) which will make them successful.

A more recent trait-based approach identified managers who failed to get promoted (derailed executives) and then compared them with managers who were promoted (arrivers).[27] In one such study, derailed executives were observed to have many (but not all) of the following traits: insensitivity, arrogance, betrayal of trust, excessive ambition, inability to delegate, inability to think strategically, inability to adapt to a boss with a different style, inability to generate high performance for the business, and overdependence on a mentor. This approach to traits is the mirror image of traditional trait research because it identifies traits that might cause failure rather than looking at traits that are associated with success.

When we think about the tremendous diversity of situations in which leaders operate, it is not surprising that we have had difficulty finding a list of traits that will predict who will be a successful leader. Is it really possible to find a list of traits that would predict leadership success in organizations as diverse as Air Canada, Alcan Aluminum, the Canadian Forces, Canadian Tire, Revenue Canada, Ontario Hydro, Scott Mission, Canada Safeway, the Liberal Party, the Canadian Auto Workers, and the United Way?

THE LEADER BEHAVIOUR APPROACH

Because traits were hard to measure, researchers began to shift their focus to the *behaviour* of leaders, which was easier to observe. The **leader behaviour approach** emphasized observation of managers as they carried out their leadership role. Beginning in the 1940s and continuing through the 1960s, research on leadership shifted to leader behaviour. The largest contributions in the leader behaviour approach came from the Ohio State University studies, the University of Michigan studies, and the managerial grid.

leader behaviour approach

The Ohio State University Studies

Researchers at Ohio State University developed two questionnaires to assess leader behaviour. The Leader Behavior Description Questionnaire (LBDQ) measured subordinates' perceptions of the leader's behaviour, while the Leader Opinion Questionnaire (LOQ) measured the leader's perception of his or her style. Research using these two questionnaires led to the identification of two important leadership behaviours.[28] They were labelled "Initiating Structure" and "Consideration." **Initiating Structure (IS)** refers to the extent to which the leader structures and defines the activities of subordinates so that organizational goals are achieved. It has also been called production-orientation or task-orientation. **Consideration (C)** refers to the extent to which leaders are concerned with developing mutual trust between themselves and subordinates, as well as showing respect for subordinates' ideas and concern for their feelings. It has also been called people-orientation or human relations-orientation.

initiating structure (IS)

consideration (C)

Research in military and blue collar situations indicated that both leader behaviours were important, but that each had different implications. Leaders who scored high on IS generally led high-producing groups and were rated highly by their superiors. However, the subordinates of those leaders tended to have lower morale, higher grievances rates, and higher turnover. Leaders high on C, on the other hand, generally led groups with higher morale, but lower productivity. Thus, each of the specific leader behaviours led to positive and negative outcomes. The extension of these findings by some later writers led to the universalist conclusion that leaders high on both C and IS would simultaneously satisfy their superiors (by achieving high productivity) and their subordinates (by improving their morale).[29]

The University of Michigan Studies

employee-centred managers
production-centred managers

Researchers at the University of Michigan who had studied numerous industrial work situations concluded that two leadership styles (employee-centred and production-centred) influenced employee performance and satisfaction.[30] **Employee-centred managers** were interested in their subordinates as people, showed concern for their well-being, and encouraged worker involvement in goal setting. **Production-centred managers** emphasized the technical aspects of the job, set work standards, and closely supervised workers.

The most well-known study by this group was an experiment in an insurance company which was designed to test the impact of employee-centred and production-centred leadership styles on the output of four divisions in the company.[31] Productivity increased under both leadership styles, but employee satisfaction and turnover were negatively affected by production-centred leadership. The Michigan studies led to the universalist conclusion that employee-centred leadership was always superior to production-centred leadership.

The Managerial Grid

managerial grid

Blake and Mouton designed an organizational development program emphasizing the importance of the two basic leader behaviours originally identified in the Ohio State and Michigan studies.[32] The **managerial grid** shows various ways of combining a concern for people with a concern for production. Each of these two dimensions is measured on a scale from 1 through 9; five basic leadership styles that managers can use are identified (see Table 13-1).

TABLE 13-1 FIVE POSSIBLE LEADERSHIP STYLES.

	Leader Emphasis on	
Style Label	**Production**	**People**
1,1	Low	Low
9,1	High	Low
1,9	Low	High
5,5	Moderate	Moderate
9,9	High	High

The grid is designed to help managers first see their current leadership style and then develop the most desirable style. Blake and Mouton say that the most desirable style is one in which managers show a high concern for both people and production (the "9,9 style"). Blake and Mouton's managerial grid has been criticized by researchers because of their assumption that there is one best leadership style for all situations.[33] It is unlikely that one leadership style will be effective for organizations experiencing different growth rates, different labour relations climates, different degrees of competition, and a host of other differentiating problems.

Table 13-2 summarizes the universalist theories discussed in this section.

The Contingency Approach

The view that there is one best leadership style has been increasingly challenged during the last 20 years. It is now generally accepted that different situations demand different leadership styles. This is true across different companies and across different cultures (see the Global Management insert "Managing Russian Factory Workers"). In this section we look briefly at the most popular contingency leadership theories.

TABLE 13-2 A SUMMARY OF THE UNIVERSALIST LEADERSHIP THEORIES.

Comparison Features	Trait Theory	Ohio State University Studies	University of Michigan Studies	The Managerial Grid
1. Essence of the approach	Effective leaders possess certain traits that are necessary for success. Traits commonly cited include initiative, self-confidence, intelligence, dependability, and sociability.	Two effective leader behaviours are initiating structure (emphasizing task completion) and consideration (emphasizing concern for the people doing the job).	Employee-centred leadership (the leader shows interest in subordinates) is preferred to production-centred leadership (the leader emphasizes the technical aspects of the job).	The most effective leader is one who has a high concern for people and a high concern for production.
2. Assumptions about the leader	Individual qualities (traits) are of overriding importance in determining success of the leader. The leader possessing the right traits will be successful.	Some leaders emphasized both consideration and initiating structure, but most showed a preference for one or the other.	The behaviour of the leader influences the satisfaction and productivity levels of subordinates. The leader who is employee-centred will have satisfied subordinates.	Leaders are able to simultaneously exhibit a high concern for people and a high concern for production.
3. Assumptions about the followers	Subordinates will perform at high levels if led by a person with appropriate traits.	Subordinates generally prefer consideration; initiating structure may generate increased output (but lower morale).	Subordinates have a strong preference for leaders who are employee-centred.	Subordinates will respond to a leader who shows high concern for people and production.
4. Assumed impact of the environment	Low; the leader acts on the environment and uses it to his or her advantage.	Low; leadership effectiveness is achieved by emphasis on initiating structure and consideration.	Low; the effective leader influences the environment by exhibiting certain leader behaviours.	Low; the leader's emphasis on people and production overrides environmental factors.

GLOBAL MANAGEMENT

Managing Russian Factory Workers

Are management theories and techniques which were developed in North America applicable to workers in other cultures? Many of the research studies on which conclusions are based are conducted in the U.S. and Canada, but in those cultures, there is a strong individualistic bias that may not be evident in other countries (e.g., China). Given that fact, perhaps leadership and motivation theories that work here will not work elsewhere.

To test this idea, three popular U.S. management techniques were introduced at the Kalinin Cotton Mill near Moscow in order to observe what effect they had on worker productivity. Three groups of 33 workers each were randomly assigned to one of the three management techniques. In the *extrinsic rewards* condition, products like T-shirts, rock tapes, and peanut butter were given to workers who increased the amount of top-grade fabric they produced. In the *behavioural management* condition, supervisors praised employees who did things like repairing weaving looms, checking looms, and changing rolls of cloth. In the *participative management* condition, meetings were held with workers to get ideas from them about how to improve performance.

Prior to the start of the study, the current levels of factory productivity were measured. One of the three techniques was then introduced for two weeks. At the end of that time, the technique was then withdrawn. Through all of this, the researchers closely observed worker productivity. The key measure of productivity was the amount of high grade fabric the workers produced.

The results were as follows: For the extrinsic reward and behavioural management conditions, worker productivity rose significantly after the application of the techniques, i.e., the amount of top-grade fabric increased. When the techniques were withdrawn, produc-

• • •

tivity again declined (the decline was sharper for the behavioural management technique). In the participative management condition, productivity fluctuated across all three time periods but overall, participation *decreased* the workers' productivity. Interestingly, worker productivity on Saturday shifts was much lower than weekdays for all three management techniques.

Thus, the effectiveness of these three techniques varied. Extrinsic rewards and behavioural management had a positive effect on the productivity of Russian workers, but participative management did not. Discussions with workers suggested that past history caused the poor showing of participative management. Workers had been asked for their ideas in the past, but their bosses rarely implemented any of their suggestions. The workers may therefore have decided that nothing would happen this time either. ▲

The Leader Style Continuum

leader style continuum

The most general contingency approach is Tannenbaum and Schmidt's contingency theory of leadership.[34] In the **leader style continuum**, leadership styles range from an emphasis on the manager's authority to an emphasis on the subordinate's freedom. Seven basic leadership styles are identified (see Figure 13-1).

To decide on an appropriate leadership style, managers must consider three categories of factors:

1. *Characteristics of the manager* Background, experience, knowledge, values, and expectations.
2. *Characteristics of the subordinates* Background, experience, knowledge, values, and expectations.
3. *Characteristics of the situation* The nature of the group being supervised, the nature of the tasks the group is doing, time pressures, external environment factors, the climate of the organization, the impact of technology, and the structure of the organization.

The participative styles of management, which allow subordinates a role in decision making, can be used if subordinates are committed to the goals of the organization, are well educated and experienced, want responsibility for decision making, and expect a participative style of leadership. If subordinates lack these characteristics, a boss-centred style of leadership may be required.

FIGURE 13-1 CONTINUUM OF LEADERSHIP BEHAVIOUR.

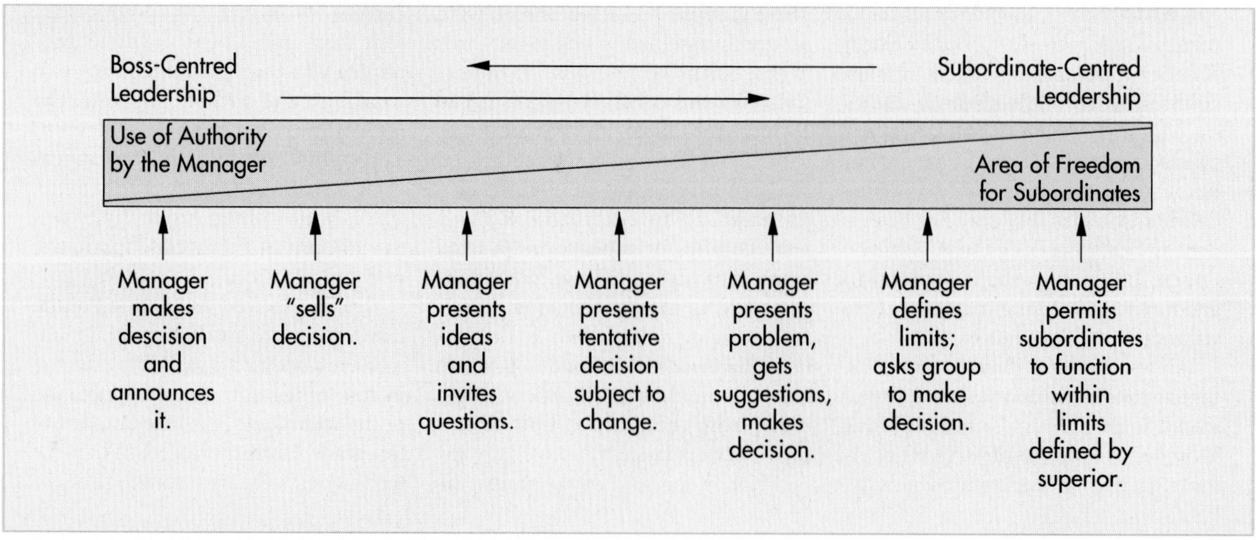

The Situational Leadership Theory

Hersey and Blanchard have developed a contingency theory of leadership based on the Consideration and Initiating Structure dimensions of the Ohio State leadership studies.[35] Slight modifications in terminology are made, with Initiating Structure described as "directive behaviour," and Consideration described as "supportive behaviour." **Directive behaviour** is the extent to which a leader engages in one-way communication, spells out the followers' roles, tells the followers what to do, where to do it, when to do it, and how to do it, and then closely supervises them.[36] **Supportive behaviour** is the extent to which a leader engages in two-way communication, listens, provides support and encouragement, facilitates interaction, and involves the followers in decision making.[37]

directive behaviour

supportive behaviour

The two basic leader behaviours are shown in Figure 13-2. Hersey and Blanchard assume that the two behaviours can occur in various proportions (e.g., a leader can exhibit a lot of directive behaviour and little supportive behaviour, or vice versa). The graph is divided into quadrants, each of which describes one of the four basic leadership styles. As the leader changes styles from S1 to S2, he or she reduces the degree of directive behaviours and gradually increases supportive behaviour. Moving from S2 to S3 means a further reduction in directive behaviour and even more emphasis on supportive behaviour. When proceeding from S3 to S4, the leader reduces both directive and supportive behaviours (an abdicratic type of style).

The model suggests that each of the four styles is effective in certain situations and that the level of development of subordinates is the primary factor in determining which style is most effective. The developmental level of subordinates is measured by two factors: competence (skill and knowledge) and commitment (motivation and confidence). Effective leadership occurs when the subordinate's level of development is matched with the appropriate leadership style. S1 is best for managing an employee with a low level of development (i.e., D1), S2 and S3 for employees with moderate levels of development, and S4 for employees who are highly developed.

FIGURE 13-2 THE SITUATIONAL LEADERSHIP MODEL.

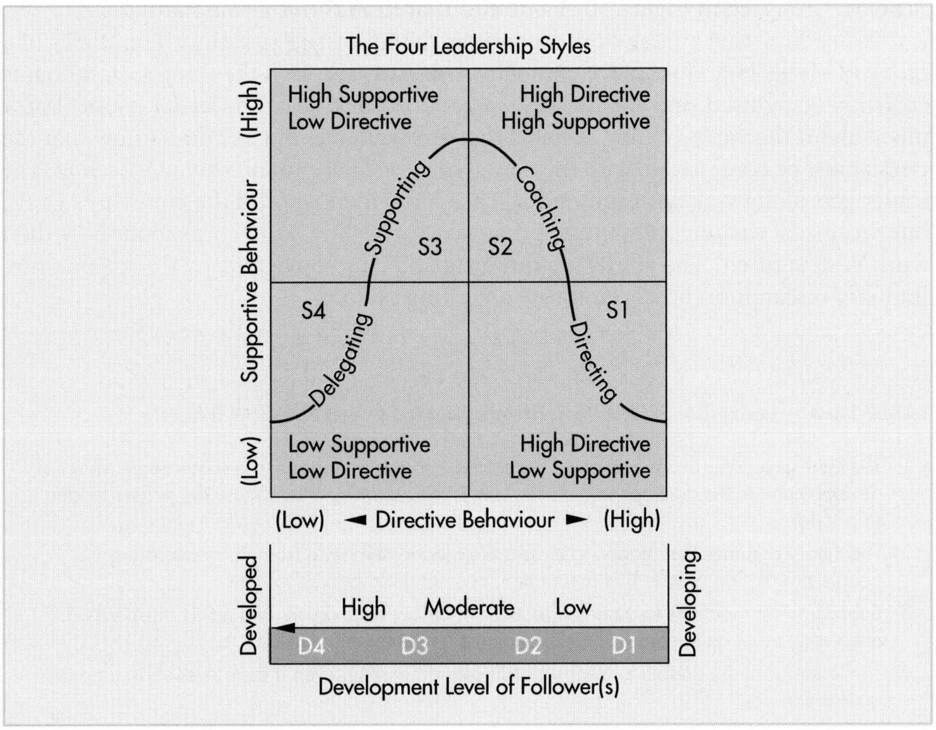

The S1 style is appropriate for individuals who are enthusiastic beginners; they need direction because they don't know what to do. Supportive behaviour is not critical since commitment is already high. The S2 style is suitable when beginners learn how difficult a task might be and are in need of support. Direction is still needed at this stage, but supportive behaviour is important to maintain a subordinate's confidence and motivation. The S3 style is appropriate for subordinates who know how to do a task, but have lost their motivation. They may be bored, have other interests, or be in an emotional state that diminishes their commitment. Here, the model proposes that supportive behaviour from the manager, rather than direction, will rebuild commitment. Finally, the model suggests that employees who are skilled and committed need little direction or support. The S4 style is appropriate under these circumstances.

The situational leadership theory is one of the most popular leadership models, and managers from many organizations have been trained using its ideas. But there are only a few research studies measuring the effectiveness of the model.[38] Table 13-3 summarizes the concerns that have been expressed about the situational leadership theory.

The Normative Leadership Model

normative leadership model

The **normative leadership model** identifies various situational factors which influence the amount of participation subordinates should be allowed when decisions are made.[39] At one extreme, a manager might allow no participation (an autocratic style); at the other extreme, the manager might encourage group problem solving and give subordinates great freedom to make decisions (a participative style).

Five possible leadership styles are shown in Table 13-4. The styles labelled "AI" and "AII" are autocratic, styles "CI" and "CII" are more consultative, and style "G" (group) is the most participative. As we move from AI through G, the degree of subordinate participation increases.

In order to determine which style to use in a given situation, the manager answers eight fundamental questions about the situation. These questions are arranged in a decision tree format (see Figure 13-3). Based on the pattern of answers to the eight questions, the leader chooses the most effective leadership style for the situation. (The decision tree in Figure 13-3 assumes that time is not a constraint.)

To see how this model works, consider the following situation: The leader of a group of clerks in an insurance company is dissatisfied with the filing system that is currently being used, and she wants to introduce a new one. The leader doesn't know much about the various filing systems that are available, but she does know that the clerks must be comfortable with the new system or their productivity will decline. The leader gets along well with the clerks. The clerks identify with the company's goals, but because of the routine nature of their work, they are quite vocal about how their work is structured. The clerks are quite capable, and have already done some preliminary research on how to improve the filing system.

TABLE 13-3 POTENTIAL PROBLEMS WITH THE SITUATIONAL LEADERSHIP THEORY.

1. The theory requires that a leader be perceptive enough to determine a subordinate's level of development. If this assumption is not satisfied, the leader cannot choose the proper leadership style.
2. The theory assumes that leaders can vary their leadership style from task-orientation to people-orientation at will. This assumption has not been proven to date.
3. Subordinates' reactions to a certain leader behaviour may differ. Two newly hired subordinates may react quite differently to a particular leadership style.
4. The leader may be unable to treat subordinates differently, even if their level of development is different.

TABLE 13-4 THE RANGE OF LEADERSHIP STYLES.

AI. You solve the problem or make the decision yourself, using information available to you at the time.

AII. You obtain the necessary information from your subordinates, then decide the solution to the problem yourself. You may or may not tell your subordinates what the problem is in getting the information from them. The role played by your subordinates in making the decision is clearly one of providing the necessary information to you, rather than generating or evaluating alternative solutions.

CI. You share the problem with the relevant subordinates individually, getting their ideas and suggestions without bringing them together as a group. Then *you* make the decision, which may or may not reflect your subordinates' influence.

CII. You share the problem with your subordinates as a group, obtaining their collective ideas and suggestions. Then you make the decision, which may or may not reflect your subordinates' influence.

G. You share the problem with your subordinates as a group. Together you generate and evaluate alternatives and attempt to reach agreement (consensus) on a solution. Your role is much like that of a chairperson. You do not try to influence the group to adopt "your" solution, and you are willing to accept and implement any solution which has the support of the entire group.

FIGURE 13-3 THE NORMATIVE LEADERSHIP MODEL.

QR	Quality Requirement:	How important is the quality of this decision?
CR	Commitment Requirement:	How important is subordinate commitment to the decision?
LI	Leader's Information:	Do you have sufficient information to make a high-quality decision?
ST	Problem Structure:	Is the problem well structured?
CP	Commitment Probability:	If you were to make the decision by yourself, is it reasonably certain that your subordinates would be commited to the decision?
GC	Goal Congruence:	Do subordinates share the organization goals to be attained in solving this problem?
CO	Subordinate Conflict:	Is conflict among subordinates over preferred solutions likely?
SI	Subordinate Information:	Do subordinates have sufficient information to make a high-quality decision?

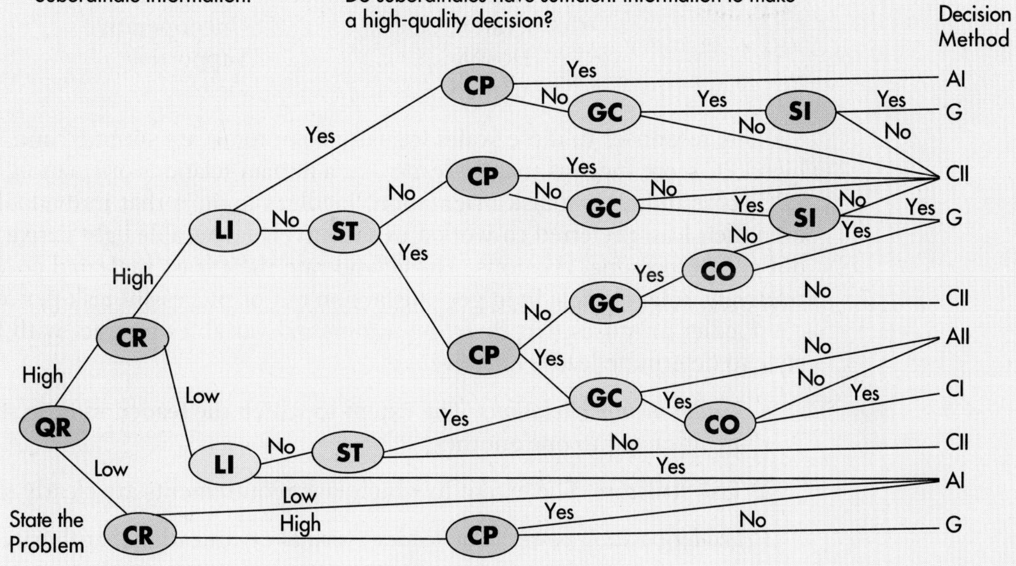

If we consider the questions in Figure 13-3 while using the information in this brief case, we get the following answers:

- QR—High, there is a quality requirement (the system must work).
- CR—High, subordinates are vocal about the operations of the department.
- LI—No, the leader doesn't understand filing systems.
- ST—No, it is not obvious how to go about introducing a new filing system.
- CP—No, it is not likely that subordinates would simply go along with the leader's decision.
- GC—Yes, subordinates share the organization's goals.
- SI—Yes, subordinates have sufficient information.

Given this pattern of answers, the model indicates that the "G" style (full group participation) is most appropriate (note that in this situation, it was not necessary to answer all eight questions). What happens if we change one of the situational features? Suppose the subordinates did not identify with the goals of the organization (question GC). The best leadership style then becomes "CII." The leader should still allow participation, but she must make the final decision because subordinates do not share organizational goals. Allowing them to make a decision in this situation would be unreasonable and an abdication of managerial responsibility.

THE LEADERSHIP CONTINGENCY MODEL

Fiedler's contingency model

Fiedler has developed a contingency model of leadership effectiveness that attempts to explain the fact that both autocratic and democratic leaders can be effective.[40] **Fiedler's contingency model** says that leadership effectiveness is the result of an interaction between the style of the leader and the characteristics of the environment in which the leader works.

The style of the leader is assessed using the "Least Preferred Co-Worker" (LPC) concept. Leaders are asked to think of the person they were least able to work with; they then describe this person with a series of bipolar scales such as those shown below:

Friendly	Unfriendly
Cooperative	Uncooperative
Hostile	Supportive
Guarded	Open

The responses to these scales (usually 16 in total) are summed and averaged. A high LPC score suggests that the leader has a human-relations orientation, while a low LPC score indicates a task orientation. Fiedler's logic is that individuals who rate even their least preferred co-worker in a relatively favourable light derive satisfaction out of interpersonal relations. Those who rate their least preferred co-worker in a relatively unfavourable light get satisfaction out of successful task performance.

Fiedler proposes that three environmental variables interact with the leader's style to determine leader effectiveness:

1. *Leader-member relations* The extent to which the leader and the subordinates are attracted to one another.
2. *Task structure* The extent to which task requirements are clearly stated.
3. *Leader position power* The leader's formal organizational authority.

Each of these variables is divided into "high" and "low" categories after they are measured. This division yields eight possible combinations of the three situational variables (see Table 13-5). On the basis of research in many different leadership situations, Fiedler has reached the following conclusion: in situations that are either extremely favourable or extremely unfavourable (combinations 1, 2, 3, and 8), a task-oriented leader functions best. Under conditions intermediate in favourableness (combinations 4, 5 and 6), a human-relations-oriented leader is best.

Fiedler gives examples to illustrate his theory. He says that it would be inappropriate for the captain of an airliner to ask for the opinions of the crew on how the plane should be landed, since the leader has formal authority, the task is well structured, and the captain has the informal backing of the crew. As another example, the leader of a volunteer committee asked to plan the annual company picnic has no formal authority and faces a relatively unstructured task. Yet this leader may also find that directive leadership is necessary to get the group moving toward its goal. Human-relations-oriented leadership is best in a condition where the leader needs to use the resources of the group (e.g., knowledge about the task) to get the job done. This is typical of newly appointed managers who are less knowledgeable about the task than their subordinates.

One of the practical applications of Fiedler's theory is a training program using the basic ideas of the contingency model. **LEADER MATCH** is a programmed learning system that trains leaders to modify their leadership situation to fit their personality.[41] This contrasts with most training programs that try to change the leader's personality to fit the situation. The LEADER MATCH program has been used to train managers in many different settings.[42]

LEADER MATCH

As with all leadership theories, Fiedler's model has its critics. The objections to his model are as follows:

1. The definitions of the variables are not absolute; a given task may be labelled as "structured" in one study and "unstructured" in another.
2. Studies conducted since Fiedler proposed his model are less supportive of the theory than studies which were conducted to develop the theory.
3. The LPC concept may be an oversimplified way to determine whether a manager is task oriented or relationship oriented.

THE PATH-GOAL MODEL

Robert House has formulated a model of leadership that incorporates concepts from both the leader behaviour approach and from expectancy theory (discussed in Chapter 12).[43] The **path-goal model** suggests that the leader's job is to increase the payoffs to workers for achieving organizational goals. The leader accomplishes this by clarifying

path-goal model

TABLE 13-5 EIGHT LEADERSHIP SITUATIONS.

Combination	Leader-Member Relations	Task Structure	Power Position
1	Good	High	High
2	Good	High	Low
3	Good	Low	High
4	Good	Low	Low
5	Poor	High	High
6	Poor	High	Low
7	Poor	Low	High
8	Poor	Low	Low

FIGURE 13-4 KEY VARIABLES IN THE PATH-GOAL MODEL.

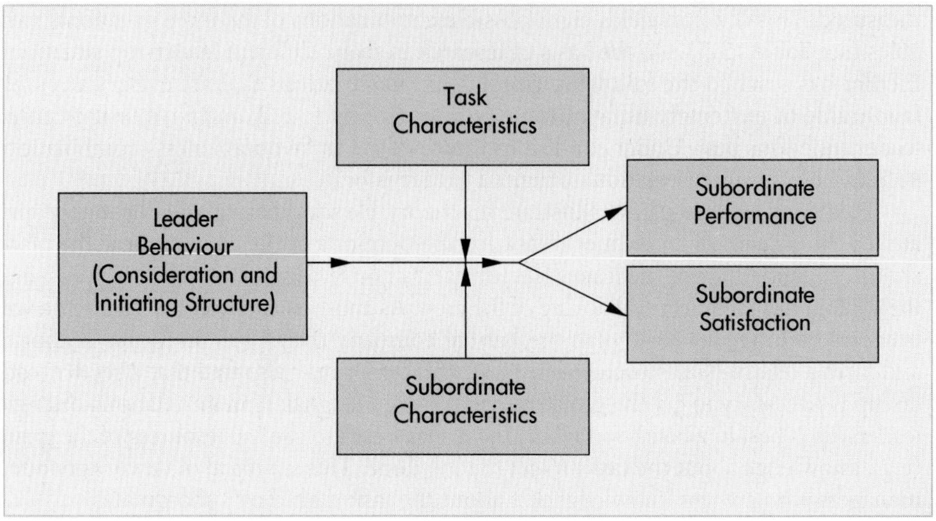

for workers what the path to these goals is, by reducing blockages that prevent workers from reaching their goals, and by behaving in a way that will increase worker satisfaction on the way to achieving the goals.

The path-goal model recognizes that the characteristics of the subordinates and of the task itself moderate the effects of the leader's behaviour (see Figure 13-4). When workers feel that they are capable of accomplishing a task without direction from the boss, or when the task requirements are perfectly clear, directive leadership behaviour becomes unnecessary and causes dissatisfaction if implemented.

A basic assumption in the path-goal model is that high-level jobs are more ambiguous than low-level jobs. High-level employees, therefore, appreciate receiving leader-initiated structure since it clarifies what behaviour is needed to attain their work goals. This reduces their sense of uncertainty. Since this clarification is helpful to high-level employees, the initiation of structure also increases their satisfaction. For routine, low-level jobs, on the other hand, initiating structure is not necessary and subordinates may even interpret it as a lack of trust. In these jobs, initiating structure may cause dissatisfaction. Consideration, on the other hand, may improve job satisfaction for employees who perform routine jobs because it makes their jobs more "human" and therefore more bearable.

The path-goal model is helpful because it deals with specific leader behaviours and how they might influence employee satisfaction and performance. The model differs from others because it recognizes both situational variables and individual differences. But this model, like many others, seems able to predict employee satisfaction better than employee productivity.

Table 13-6 summarizes the contingency leadership theories discussed in this section.

THE EFFECTIVE LEADER

In this chapter, we have looked at many aspects of leadership. Given all these things, what advice can be given to those who want to be effective leaders? If leaders are to be effective, they should (1) have certain values and attitudes about leadership, (2) empower and coach their subordinates, (3) positively influence others in the work place, and (4) use the proper leadership style. Let's look at each of these ideas.

TABLE 13-6 A SUMMARY OF THE CONTINGENCY THEORIES OF LEADERSHIP.

Comparison Features	The Leadership Style Continuum	Situational Leadership Model	The Normative Leadership Model	Leadership Contingency Model	Path-Goal Model
1. Substance of the approach	There are seven leadership styles ranging from very autocratic to very democratic; the most effective leadership style depends on the interaction of the characteristics of (1) the manager, (2) the subordinates, and (3) the situation.	Different leadership styles and behaviour can be effective, depending on the maturity levels of subordinates. Immature subordinates require considerable task direction, while mature subordinates require little supervision.	Different leadership styles are appropriate in different situations. The most appropriate style is determined by considering key factors (for example, the importance of subordinate acceptance of the decision) before making the decision.	One style is not always best. The effectiveness of a leader is determined by the interaction of environmental and personality variables.	Effective leaders are those who increase employee motivation by clarifying for subordinates the paths to effective performance as well as the connection between performance and rewards.
2. Assumption(s) about qualities of the leader	Leaders have the ability to assess themselves, the subordinates, and the situation before deciding on a leadership style. Leaders are able to exhibit different leadership skills.	Leaders can exhibit behaviours that are high or low on task orientation and relationship orientation. Leaders are able to change style as the maturity of subordinates changes.	Leaders are able to determine which key factors are important and which are not. They are also able to use different styles based on their analysis of the key variables.	Leaders are basically autocratic or democratic. The job should be engineered to fit the particular style of the leader. It is difficult to change the style of a leader.	The leader has the interest and ability to increase the effectiveness of his or her area of responsibility by improving the motivation of his subordinates.
3. Assumption(s) about followers	Subordinates prefer different leadership styles in different situations, depending on their commitment to organization goals, their education, experience, and their desire for decision-making responsibility.	Subordinate preferences for a leadership style change as their maturity on the job changes. Immature subordinates prefer a task orientation on the part of the leader, while more mature subordinates prefer a relationships orientation.	Subordinates want to be involved in decision making in some circumstances but do not want to be involved in others.	Subordinates prefer different leadership styles depending on how task structure, leader-member relations, and position power are interrelated.	Certain things (particularly organizational level) influence both the type of supervision that subordinates desire as well as the leader behaviours which are feasible. Differences between subordinates' needs are assumed.
4. Assumed impact of the environment on the leadership process	Moderate; the environment is one of three factors that determines which leadership style will be most effective.	Moderate; the only environmental variable is employee maturity levels.	High; factors such as the quality requirement of the decision, information available on the problem, etc., all govern the leadership decision-making style which is most appropriate.	High; the type of leader behaviour which is most effective depends on the interaction of environmental and leadership style variables.	High; environment variables are task characteristics and subordinate characteristics.

ATTITUDES AND VALUES OF LEADERS

Interviews with over 200 managers in high-performance, high-commitment organizations revealed that they had the following attitudes and values:[44]

1. *Manage by values and vision* Have a clear sense of purpose and direction, and communicate it to followers.
2. *Focus on customers* Employee understanding of customer needs is paramount to the success of the business.
3. *Institutionalize continuous improvement* Create a long-term emphasis on learning among employees.
4. *Treat everyone like a business partner* Have the trust and confidence in employees to do what is good for the business.
5. *Show that work is life* Acknowledge the overlap of work concerns with those of home or community.
6. *Develop people* Accept the fact that employee growth and development will advance the company's interests.
7. *Eliminate barriers to success* Remove impediments that slow the progress of employees.

EMPOWERING AND COACHING SUBORDINATES

empowerment

Effective managers empower their subordinates. **Empowerment** is the process of strengthening subordinates' beliefs in their effectiveness.[45] In the Management Challenge, Robert Frey empowered his workers by giving them the information they needed to make decisions that were important for company survival. Leaders empower themselves by empowering their subordinates.[46] Empowering workers means giving them the right to make important decisions. At GM Canada's Ste. Therese, Quebec, plant workers noticed that coolant was leaking from air conditioners on new Oldsmobile Cieras. They determined the cause (an irregular part), and devised a measuring tool that detected leaks. They also persuaded the parts manufacturer to make adjustments in its production processes.[47]

True empowerment will result in obvious changes in employee discretion. At Camco (part of General Electric), service technicians used to file a report to management every time they made a house call. The paperwork was dealt with slowly, and the customer would not receive a refund until several weeks later. Now, technicians have been given the authority to respond to customer demands on the spot. They can replace defective goods, and can even question customers whose stories seem suspicious.[48]

A study of top-level managers in different industries found that empowering leaders focussed on five activities:[49]

1. *Providing a positive emotional atmosphere* Building confidence among subordinates through the use of inspirational speakers and day-long events which focussed on building confidence.
2. *Rewarding and encouraging* Using personal praise, written letters of commendation, and public ceremonies to recognize accomplishments of employees.
3. *Expressing confidence in subordinates* Spending time each day expressing confidence in subordinates' abilities.
4. *Fostering initiative and responsibility* Giving discretion to subordinates increases their sense of power, which in turn increases their initiative and willingness to take responsibility for their performance.

5. *Build on success* Making changes on a small scale so they are successful, then introduce those changes on a wider scale; success at introducing change empowers subordinates.

Viewing the manager as a coach is an idea that is complementary to the idea of empowerment. **Coaching** refers to the managerial activity of creating, by communication only, the climate, environment, and context that empowers individuals and teams to generate results.[50] The manager who views his or her job as that of a coach will focus on actions that empower subordinates to be highly productive. The traditional view of management stresses the control of subordinates; the coaching perspective stresses cooperation between managers and subordinates.

coaching

In taking on the role of coach, the manager observes "blind spots" in the subordinate, and provides advice and guidance on how to overcome them. Thus, coaching enables subordinates to see something about their performance that they might not be able to see on their own. Coaching makes it possible for a subordinate to make substantial improvements in performance.[51]

Using Influence

A consensus is developing in the field of management that influence (persuading others to do what you want) will replace authority (ordering others to do something).[52] In their day-to-day work, managers must influence bosses, peers, and subordinates. A study of 128 managers in manufacturing and service firms revealed that different influence tactics had different success rates.[53] The three that were generally effective in influencing the task commitment of subordinates, peers, and bosses were: consultation (getting the influence target to participate in planning a strategy), inspirational appeal (appealing to the influence target's values and ideals), and rational persuasion (the use of logical arguments and facts). Three other tactics were generally ineffective: pressure (demanding or threatening), coalition (trying to persuade the influence target to do something because others are doing it also), and legitimating (making reference to organizational rules or policies).

Recent research on leadership suggests that successful leaders possess technical expertise which allows them to understand concerns that subordinates have about technical matters, and to answer technical questions that subordinates may ask. This ski instructor is able to answer detailed technical questions about skiing techniques that these students may have.

Two tactics were effective for influencing subordinates and peers, but not superiors: ingratiation (get the influence target in a good mood) and exchange (offering favours for compliance). Results for most tactics were weaker for upward influence than they were for lateral or downward influence.

When a leader attempts to influence followers, they may react in one of three ways: commitment (enthusiastic pursuit of the leader's goals), compliance (modest pursuit of the leader's goals), or resistance (opposition to the leader's goals).[54] In Chapter 10, we identified seven sources of power (refer back to Table 10-1). Although all of these sources are potential ways to influence subordinates, referent and expert power are the ones most likely to cause subordinate commitment. Legitimate power, information power, and reward power are most likely to lead to compliance, while punishment power is most likely to lead to resistance.[55]

There are basically five practical steps in becoming an influential manager:[56]

1. *Develop a reputation as an expert* Develop expertise in a specific area and build on it.
2. *Balance the time spent on critical relationships* Spend sufficient time with bosses and peers to ensure that influence in the organization is maintained.
3. *Develop a network of resource persons* Seek out resources through carefully planned networks and persistence.
4. *Choose the correct influence tactics* Use a combination of tactics rather than just one.
5. *Implement influence tactics sensitively* Keep the characteristics of the influence target in mind when attempting to use influence.

USING THE PROPER LEADERSHIP STYLE

Leadership situations are complex, and trying to use the same leadership style in every situation is ill-advised. Different styles are required to manage groups as diverse as sales representatives, volunteer workers, Members of Parliament, teachers, automobile workers, research scientists, lawyers, military personnel, church staff, or professional hockey players. The style of leadership that will be most effective depends on the characteristics of the leader, the followers, and the situation. Figure 13-5 shows the relationship among these three factors.

Although we have learned a great deal about leadership during the twentieth century, we still do not know the relative importance of each of these factors in various situations. An example will illustrate this difficulty. Consider the job of coach in the Canadian Football League and compare it with the job of merchandising manager at Eaton's. In the CFL, the leader (coach) has a specific, easy-to-define goal: win the Grey Cup. The followers (players) are highly trained and motivated in specific areas of the game. The situation (the game) provides immediate feedback on the results. At Eaton's, the leader (manager) may or may not have an easy-to-define goal (it may be profit, efficiency, employee satisfaction, customer satisfaction, or some combination of these). The

FIGURE 13-5 DETERMINANTS OF LEADERSHIP STYLE.

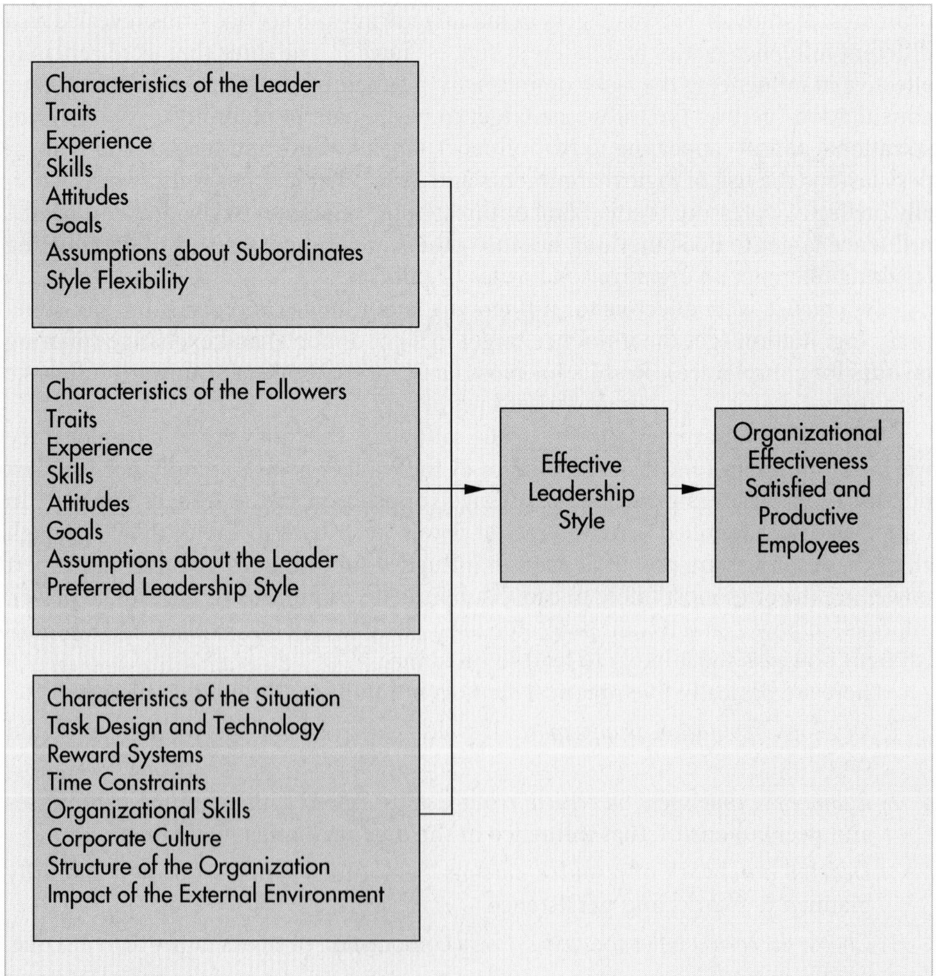

followers (subordinates) may or may not be highly trained in a specific area, and the situation (business operations) may or may not give immediate feedback on the results.

In these two situations, it is easy to see how the three factors might take on differential importance. In one leadership setting, the leader may be the primary element influencing subordinate productivity and satisfaction. In another, the followers or the situation may have the greatest influence. If we consider the thousands of possible leadership situations, each with its own unique characteristics, we can begin to understand why leadership research is proceeding slowly and why clear-cut answers are often impossible.

Not only are we uncertain about the relative importance of the leader, the followers, and the situation, but we may also be making some assumptions about leadership that are incorrect. Three developments during the last decade suggest that this is a possibilty. First, there may be "substitutes" for leadership.[57] For example, if an employee's job requirements are absolutely clear, leadership may not be as critical as it is when job ambiguities exist. When employees have a strong professional orientation (e.g., lawyers, doctors, accountants), leadership may also have little effect. Research in this area is in its infancy, so we cannot make definite statements at this point, but the notion of substitutes for leadership has intuitive appeal.

self-leadership

A second possibility—self-leadership—has also been suggested. **Self-leadership** means that workers motivate themselves to do two kinds of tasks—those that are naturally attractive to them, as well as those that are necessary for the organization, but which may be unattractive.[58] Management must take actions to motivate workers to self-leadership. The most fundamental requirement is to allow the values and attitudes of

MEETING THE CHALLENGE

Making Participative Leadership Work

Over time, the chaos and conflict that had developed as Robert Frey introduced participative leadership began to decline. The union committee took over the functions of allocating overtime, deciding on layoffs, and the hiring and releasing of temporary workers. Hourly workers now are responsible for scheduling operations. A manager may sit in on these discussions, but the workers actually make the decisions. The company and the union jointly administer a merit raise program. Workers now interview all job candidates, including those for managerial positions. No one is hired without the person's future colleagues approving.

Profit sharing has turned the tide at the company, but the first few years were difficult. Three times a year, each worker gets a cheque for his or her equal share of company profits. In year one, this amounted to 58 cents an hour on top of their regular wages. In year two, there was no profit to be shared. In year three, the amount was 41 cents, in year four it was 11 cents, and in year five, $2.82. For the past three years, it has averaged $2.62. These latter numbers have had a major positive impact on employee salaries and motivation.

Absenteeism is down to virtually zero, and productivity is up 30 percent. Grievances have been reduced to only one or two a year. Frey has recently found that he no longer has to push his employees forward; instead, they are pushing him.

Employees have apparently changed their mind about Frey as time has passed. Ocelia Williams, who was the union steward at the plant when Frey bought the company, was very unhappy with his early decisions. Trust was low, and, as the union steward, she had many disagreements with Frey. However, as time passed and he began to share more information with workers, Williams' view of him began to change. (In the year when there were no profits, for example, the employees were given this information ahead of time, and were not surprised when the year-end came.) And more recently, with the sharp increase in take-home pay she has received because of profit-sharing, her attitude toward Frey has improved even more. She notes that he is probably getting rich, but he has more invested in the company than she does. ▲

employees to have some impact in the work place. Proponents of self-leadership argue that if employees are allowed to exercise self-leadership, they are likely to learn productive behaviour, and are more likely to pursue goals that are beneficial to the organization. If these speculations about self-leadership are correct, our traditional view of leadership will have to change to accommodate them.

At Du Pont Canada, self-leadership means that employees become more responsible for their own actions and achievements.[59] Mechanics have been heard to say how motivating it is to have the opportunity to deal with suppliers, and to participate in the development of work schedules. The main role for managers at Du Pont is one of helping employees to establish and achieve their objectives. This philosophy has also led to a reduction in the number of management layers from 11 to 6.

The third development is the idea that leadership may not play the role that most of us have thought.[60] The possibility exists that researchers, managers, students, and the general public have all developed a romanticized (and erroneous) view of what leaders do and how they affect us. This view may have developed because people have difficulty understanding how complex organizations work. This feeling of uncertainty causes people to devise ways of explaining the complex reality, even if these explanations are not accurate. If this hypothesis is correct, it means that leadership research to date has uncovered our subjective perceptions about leadership, rather than what is truly significant about leadership.

SUMMARY

Leadership is the ability to influence others to pursue the goals the leader thinks are important and desirable. Managers perform the managerial functions of planning, organizing, leading, and controlling, while leaders focus on influencing people to pursue certain goals. A good leader may or may not be a good manager, but a good manager will be a good leader.

Charismatic leaders have certain attributes that give them a very strong influence on the behaviour of other people. Charismatic leaders are self-confident, dominant, and have a strong conviction about the rightness of their views.

Transactional managers have a traditional view of the managerial role, and emphasize the management functions of planning, organizing, and controlling. Transformational managers, on the other hand, stress revitalizing the organization and communicating a vision to their followers.

Leaders can exhibit one of two basic leadership styles: autocratic (the leader retains all decision-making power) and democratic (the leader delegates decision-making rights to followers). Universalist leadership theories argue that one style of leadership is best for all situations, while contingency leadership theories argue that the demands of the situation must be assessed before a leadership style is chosen.

The trait approach assumes that the leader's personal attributes are the key to leadership success. Although much research on traits has been conducted, a list of traits that consistently differentiates successful from unsuccessful leaders has been elusive.

The leader behaviour approach stresses observable leader behaviours and tries to relate these to leadership success. Initiating structure (the extent to which the leader structures the tasks of followers) and consideration (the extent to which the leader shows concern for followers) are two leadership behaviours that have been identified as important. Initiating structure is generally associated with high performance, while consideration is generally associated with high morale. The managerial grid of Blake and Mouton is a universalist theory which says that a leader should show high concern for both the task and the people doing the task.

Several contingency leadership theories have been developed to deal with the issue of which leadership style is best. Tannenbaum and Schmidt's leader style continuum indicates how managerial authority and subordinate freedom can have varying emphasis in seven different situations. Hersey and Blanchard suggest that the leader's style is determined by the maturity level of subordinates. Immature workers need a more task-oriented style, while more mature workers benefit from a people-oriented style. In the normative leadership model, the leader decides how much participation subordinates should be allowed after answering several work-related questions. Fiedler's contingency leadership model is based on the idea that the best leadership style depends on several situational factors. The interaction of these factors determines whether a leader should use an autocratic or democratic style. House's path-goal model suggests that the leader's style is influenced by the characteristics of the task as well as the personal characteristics of the subordinates.

The style of leadership which is most effective depends on the leader, the followers, and the situation in which leadership takes place. These three factors take on varying degrees of significance in different leadership situations.

Much remains to be learned about the nature of leadership. It is possible that there are substitutes for leadership in certain jobs, and that leadership is therefore less crucial than has been assumed. People may also be able to lead themselves (self-leadership). A third possibility is that people have a romanticized and subjective perception of what leadership really is. As a result, we may not have learned a lot about the objective aspects of leadership.

KEY TERMS

leadership (p. 396)
manager (p. 397)
leader (p. 397)
charisma (p. 398)
charismatic leaders (p. 398)
transactional managers (p. 399)
transformational managers (p. 399)
leadership style (p. 400)
autocratic leader (p. 401)
democratic leader (p. 402)
universalist leadership theories (p. 405)
contingency leadership theories (p. 405)
trait approach (p. 406)
leader behaviour approach (p. 407)
initiating structure (p. 407)
consideration (p. 407)
employee-centred managers (p. 408)
production-centred managers (p. 408)
managerial grid (p. 408)
leader style continuum (p. 410)
directive behaviour (p. 411)
supportive behaviour (p. 411)
normative leadership model (p. 412)
Fiedler's contingency model (p. 414)
LEADER MATCH (p. 415)
path-goal model (p. 415)
empowerment (p. 418)
coaching (p. 419)
self-leadership (p. 421)

REVIEW QUESTIONS

1. What is meant by the term "leadership"? Why is it necessary for management?
2. Describe the key differences between transactional and transformational managers.
3. What is charismatic leadership? What characteristics do charismatic leaders possess?
4. What is the trait approach to the study of leadership? What are the primary shortcomings of the trait approach?
5. How does the leader behaviour approach differ from the trait approach? How did the leader behaviour approach try to overcome the shortcomings of the trait approach?
6. Describe the main features of the managerial grid. How did it build on the ideas of the leader behaviour approach?
7. What were the Ohio State leadership studies? What dimensions of leader behaviour were identified?
8. How are contingency leadership theories different from universalist leadership theories?
9. What is the key variable affecting leadership effectiveness in the situational leadership theory? How does it affect leader behaviour?
10. What factors are important in leadership effectiveness in the normative leadership model?

11. What are the three environmental factors in Fiedler's leadership model? How do these three factors interact to determine the "favourableness" of the environment for the leader?
12. Describe House's path-goal leadership model. Explain how it is related to the expectancy model discussed in Chapter 12.

DISCUSSION QUESTIONS

1. How are leaders different from managers? Is it possible to be a good leader and a poor manager?
2. How are the autocratic and democratic leadership styles different?
3. What factors should be considered before a manager chooses a style of leadership?
4. Describe one situation where you have encountered transactional leadership, and one where you have encountered transformational leadership. How were they different?
5. Can a leader change his or her style to fit the situation? Defend your answer.
6. What do the contingency leadership theories presented in the chapter have in common? How are they different?
7. "The most effective leaders are those who communicate a vision to their followers." Comment on this statement.

EXERCISES

1. You have four friends who have just been promoted. They will be supervising the following types of workers:
   a. newly hired machine operators
   b. salespeople selling specialized computer software
   c. staff of a large church
   d. research scientists at ICI Canada Ltd.

   Based on the leadership theories discussed in this chapter, what leadership style would you suggest to each one of your friends, given their particular situation?
2. Interview a manager and determine the manager's views on the following issues:
   a. the importance of leadership
   b. how managers differ from leaders
   c. the impact of leadership on employee productivity and satisfaction
   d. whether leaders can change their style from autocratic to democratic (or vice versa) if the situation demands it
3. Read an article about a well-known political, business, or religious leader in a newspaper or magazine. To what extent does the individual possess the characteristics of charismatic leaders as described in this chapter?

MANAGEMENT ON LOCATION

CASE 13-1
ONE OF THE BOYS

Rudie Heinz joined the Talquaat Manufacturing Company as a production worker immediately upon graduation from high school. The company manufactured electric switching equipment that was used in industrial settings.

Rudie got along well with his co-workers, but not with his supervisor. He and his co-workers were united against the supervisor because they felt he was too autocratic and rule-oriented, and because he treated them like children. Consequently, many conflicts arose between the supervisor and the workers. The climate of the work group suffered and worker morale was low (although productivity was satisfactory).

As time passed, it became clear that Rudie had a knack for smoothing over the work-related conflicts that were caused by the supervisor's attitudes. Rudie prided himself on this ability, and he worked at refining it further. He felt that it was critical for management to treat workers with respect and dignity, and he said so to anyone who would listen. His co-workers enthusiastically agreed with his argument that if management treated workers well, they would be happier and more productive.

Two years after Rudie joined Talquaat, the much-despised supervisor was transferred. The plant superintendent approached Rudie and offered him the job. Rudie immediately accepted, and set out to implement his ideas about managing people.

• • •

For the first few weeks, all went well. The workers were very happy to be rid of the old autocratic boss and they told Rudie that it was nice to have "one of the boys" as their boss. For his part, Rudie consciously treated his new subordinates in precisely the way he had always said subordinates should be treated.

As time passed, Rudie began to be concerned about his section because it was obvious that productivity had not increased under his leadership. In fact, a disturbing trend was developing in the opposite direction. Rudie knew how this would be viewed by the plant superintendent, so he started to gently apply pressure for increased output. The workers didn't take this pressure too seriously, and joked that Rudie shouldn't worry so much. This pattern continued for several months and output continued to decline. By now Rudie was deeply concerned and was plagued by doubts about the validity of his leadership ideas.

One day as he was passing the ceramic switch line, he saw four workers looking down at the floor and laughing. As he came closer, he saw several switch boxes (each worth over $700) lying broken on the floor. He asked what had happened and was told in a light-hearted fashion that the production line had been left unattended for a few minutes and the boxes had simply fallen off. Rudie was furious and loudly chewed out the workers who were at fault. He then stormed back into his office. Thirty seconds later, Joe Mankiewicz, one of the four workers, charged into Rudie's office.

Joe: What do you think you're doing Rudie? You can't talk to me like that in front of all our friends!

Rudie: You mean your friends! You guys are not friends of mine anymore. Ever since I took over as supervisor, you've been taking advantage of me and loafing on the job.

Joe: Aw, come on Rudie, don't get so upset. It was only three switch boxes that broke. The company can afford it. We've got to stick together.

Rudie: Don't give me that "we've got to stick together" nonsense! If you guys don't shape up, you won't have a job to come to.

Joe: That sounds like a threat. What happened to all your big talk about treating workers with dignity and respect? Since you got into management, you're a changed person.

Rudie: Go back to work, Joe. I don't want to discuss this now.

Rudie sat in his office pondering his exchange with Joe, and wondered how everything had gotten so fouled up. ▲

QUESTIONS

1. What shortcomings are evident in Rudie's leadership of the production workers?
2. What do the leadership theories presented in this chapter suggest should be done in this situation?
3. What should Rudie Heinz do now?

CASE 13-2
MISSION CHAPEL CHOIR

Mission Chapel is a large, nondenominational church located in the downtown section of a large Canadian city. In addition to the senior pastor, the church has a youth director, an adult education director, and a choir director. The Chapel's choir has 45 volunteers and performs each Sunday at two morning services from September through June.

The choir contains two distinct types of people. Ten choir members are experienced singers with many years of formal music and voice training. The remaining 35 people have little or no musical training, but are in the choir because they like to sing. The experienced singers are expected to help the inexperienced ones; in addition, the experienced singers do solo performances on a regular basis.

The choir director, Carolyn Gonsales, is known throughout the city as an accomplished musician. In addition to directing the choir, she judges various secular musical competitions held in various places across Canada. She is also the producer of a televised local music show. Gonsales is paid a token salary of $8000 per year by Mission Chapel for conducting the choir. Practice is held for two hours each Wednesday evening.

Gonsales runs the choir with a firm hand. She decides which music is to be performed, the date on which it will be performed, who the soloists will be, the nature and timing of special concerts, and the structure of the

Wednesday night practice sessions.

In her opinion, she is effective, since the choir has placed first in all three competitions it has entered in the past 18 months. She is particularly pleased with the choir's first-place showing in a recent Canada-wide competition for church choirs. Morale in the choir is high.

In spite of this obvious success, Gonsales is bothered by three trends. First, absenteeism has been running at about 30 percent at the Wednesday practice sessions (attendance is nearly perfect at the regular Sunday services). She has tried to solve this problem by pointing out to choir members the importance of regular attendance at practice, but this tactic has been ineffective. Second, turnover has been chronically high (also 30 percent) during the past few years. Gonsales is surprised at this, given the success of the choir. Finally, and perhaps the most annoying to Gonsales, certain choir members continually talk and joke during the practice sessions, especially three men in the bass section. These three individuals have a very good time at practice (and they make a real contribution to the choir). Gonsales is particularly irritated when choir members who sit close to these individuals laugh at their antics. On several occasions she has made it clear that she will not tolerate their behaviour, but nothing she says seems to have much effect. Gonsales is reluctant to pursue the matter further because she does not want to lose the singing skills the three men possess.

Given these three problems, Gonsales is wondering if her leadership style is appropriate for the situation, and if she should consider changing it in the hope that doing so will solve the problems currently facing her. ▲

QUESTIONS

1. Use any two contingency leadership theories to analyze Gonsales' situation. Based on these theories, should she change her style?
2. What are some problems that Gonsales might encounter if she decides to change her style?

CASE 13-3
THE IMPORTANT PROJECT

Roberta Peters graduated nine years ago with a Ph.D. in computer science from a prestigious Canadian university. Her first job was with a federal government department where she developed a computer system especially tailored to its needs. The project took 30 months to complete. As a result of the success of this and other projects, Peters found that her reputation was growing. Within two years, her advice was actively being sought by a number of other government departments and agencies who had computer-related projects.

Roberta spent the next eight years on five different projects in the federal government. She found the work to be rewarding and she was provided with substantial financial resources, support personnel, and a great deal of freedom to manage each project as she saw fit. Because she was able to present the results of her work at various meetings of computing science associations and in professional journals, her reputation spread beyond government circles to the private sector.

Last year, a major financial services company approached Peters about an opportunity to head its computer services department. She would report directly to the executive vice-president. Because of changes in government legislation and deregulation of the financial services industry, extensive modifications were to be made to the computer system of the firm. These changes were to be implemented gradually over the next five years. Peters was assured that she would be given substantial support so that the project could be completed in the stipulated time. After hearing this, and after talking at length with several senior managers in the firm, Peters took the job.

Her first three months on the job were spent analyzing the current situation. She determined that some substantial changes would have to be made in the department in order for the project to succeed. She discovered, for example, that a number of the personnel, including some supervisory staff, were not well qualified to work on the new system because they had not kept up with recent computer developments. Peters also thought she detected a distinct reluctance on the part of the staff to update their skills.

• • •

It seemed that the staff were content to simply maintain the system as it was originally configured. She had spoken individually with several people in the department, but whenever the issue of updating came up, the conversation became rather chilly. Any suggestion that staff should take specialized refresher courses in order to improve their knowledge were rather bluntly rejected on the grounds that the department had so much work to do that staff couldn't possibly find the time to take the courses.

Peters felt that in spite of these complaints, the operating budget (which had been set before she joined the firm) was adequate. She learned, however, that additional financial resources were not likely to be available due to "higher priorities for other expenditures."

At the first senior management meeting that Peters attended, most of the discussion focussed on the company's profit performance, particularly as it related to how the firm was doing compared to others in the financial services industry. Peters found this discussion very interesting because her public sector experience had not required her to be concerned about profit. She did not say much during this discussion because she was still trying to "read the signs" about what was important in her new position.

She was disturbed, however, by what she saw as apathy among the executive committee members about the new computer system when that item came up on the agenda. She made some carefully chosen remarks and talked about the importance of the system to the firm, but she got the feeling that the other executives were just being polite while she was speaking. After she finished her remarks, there were a few mildly positive comments about the system. The chair then moved to the next item on the agenda.

The day after the meeting, Peters told the executive vice-president that she was concerned about the somewhat apathetic response her comments had generated. He assured her that the project was indeed essential to the firm. To Peters' surprise, he also said that the project wouldn't just happen, and that she would have to demonstrate considerable leadership with her subordinates and her peers to make sure the project was completed. It was only by doing so, he said, that she could hope to "gain the support needed to bring the project to a successful conclusion."

Later in her office, Peters reflected on this conversation. She believed that she had the leadership skills necessary to make the project a success, but she experienced her first anxiety about having to "sell" a project that her department was responsible for. She also wondered whether the executive vice-president's comments were a subtle hint that she had better start living up to her reputation. ▲

QUESTIONS

1. What factors does Peters need to consider as she attempts to decide how she can show more leadership in her department?
2. What should Peters do to increase the chance that the computer project will be taken seriously by her department members? By the senior management group? Be specific.

CASE 13-4
THE BASEBALL MANAGER

Darrell Porter managed a Triple-A baseball team (Triple-A baseball is the level played immediately below that of major league baseball). During the past season, the team posted a 60-70 won-lost record. During the off-season, Porter contemplated the team's strengths and weaknesses and wondered what he could do to improve its record.

The season had been a difficult one for Porter. On top of the standard problems of low attendance and high turnover of players (the parent club often moved the team's most promising players up to the major leagues), there had been a number of disruptive personality conflicts among the team members. Porter was an easygoing, quiet man who did not involve himself in these disputes unless they occurred in the dugout during the games. Porter had quite a bit of authority over players, including the right to "bench" them if he thought they weren't playing up to their capability, or if he thought that they were disrupting team solidarity, but he tried to avoid being too autocratic.

Although several of the players didn't get along with each other, they

MANAGEMENT ON LOCATION

all got along well with Porter and viewed him as something of a father figure. This was particularly true of the younger players who had just made it to Triple-A ball.

Porter recently had a long talk with the owner of the team about improving the team's performance. The owner, a rather cantankerous and outspoken person, offered Porter the strong opinion that Porter was going to have to be much more aggressive when managing the team. The owner felt that the players would "put out more effort" for a manager who would "show them who's boss" and who would actively direct their energies away from fighting and toward winning games. The owner also noted that since most of the players in Triple-A ball were quite knowledgeable about how to play the game of baseball, that couldn't be the reason they weren't winning more games. Rather, he thought that their committment level might be too low because they weren't being properly motivated by Porter.

Porter knew that some of the most successful major league managers were volatile and aggressive. He recalled watching highlights on "Sports Final Edition" where managers were thrown out of the game after arguing too vigorously about a bad call the umpire had made, or for kicking dirt on the umpire during an argument. The owner thought this kind of behaviour was fine because it showed the players how much the manager cared about winning. Porter was uncomfortable with these ideas, but wondered if changing his leadership style would increase the team's effectiveness. ▲

QUESTIONS

1. Use the leadership theories of Hersey/Blanchard and Fiedler to analyze this situation. What leadership style would each theory suggest that Porter use? Defend your answer by reference to the specifics of each theory.
2. Should Porter change his leadership style? Why or why not?

CHAPTER

14

COMMUNICATION

LEARNING OBJECTIVES

After reading this chapter, you will be able to:

1. Describe the elements in the general communication model.
2. Outline the elements in the superior-subordinate communication model.
3. Understand the difference between downward and upward communication channels.
4. Explain the difference between formal and informal communication channels.
5. Identify and describe the organizational and individual barriers to effective communication.
6. List and describe eight ways to overcome the barriers to communication.

MANAGEMENT CHALLENGE

COMMUNICATION AND SURVIVAL

Honeywell Ltd.'s Scarborough, Ontario, plant produces control devices for heating, cooling, and ventilation equipment. It used to produce 15 different kinds of controls, and most of them were sold in Canada. But in the mid-1980s, it reduced its product line to just three items and won a mandate to export to the U.S. and Europe. In order to stay alive, the plant had to become internationally competitive.

Management realized that it would need a new kind of factory to be successful in the fiercely competitive global market. Its key aspects would have to be just-in-time-inventory systems, total quality management, and self-directed work teams. But when management looked at its work force, it saw some significant problems:

- The average age of production workers was nearly 50.
- Most workers had been at the plant for about 20 years.
- The majority of workers had less than a Grade 12 education.
- For half the workers, English was not their first language.
- Workers did their jobs in isolation, and did not communicate much with their co-workers.

In order to adopt the new system, employees had to become committed to communication, teamwork, understanding company operations, and employee decision making. Management decided to take their existing work force and build in a *new* sense of teamwork.

Management was surprised by the response to its first tentative steps. When they offered 30 spaces in after-work classes in "English as a Second Language," they received 130 applications. Two hundred applications were received for a computer awareness course. When a night-shift worker said

• • •

that she couldn't take one of the courses that was scheduled to begin at 4:15 P.M., the company offered to put on an afternoon session if she could find 20 people who wanted the course at that time. By the next morning, a list with 37 names had been drawn up. Sixty people signed up for a communications course which was designed to increase the workers' ability to work in teams. The course emphasized listening skills, how to deal with stress, and group problem solving.

Communications courses were popular with workers who had difficulties adapting to the new team approach. After considerable conflict in the first month of the new direction, an entire production team signed up for 30 hours of training because they knew they wouldn't be effective without good communication skills.

The company is currently spending about $300 000 per year on training employees. For every hour spent on company time, the average worker spends two more in voluntary, tuition-free classes on their own time. Over half the workers have taken at least one course, and many have taken more. ▲

One of the most overworked clichés is "We have a communication problem." But like most clichés, it contains a lot of truth. Communication is an essential tool which helps managers carry out the functions of planning, organizing, leading, and controlling. Consider the planning function. A well-thought-out plan is useless if communication breaks down and the plan is not effectively communicated to the people who must carry it out. Breakdowns in communication occur frequently in all types of organizations, and they have a negative effect on both interpersonal relationships and on organizational performance.

It is not simply managers who must communicate well. The Management Challenge shows how communication problems caused conflict within work groups at Honeywell. These workers recognized the importance of good communication and signed up for training to improve their skills in this area.

In this chapter, we first look at the general communication process which allows for the transfer of meaning. Second, we examine the formal and informal communication channels in organizations and how information flows through these channels. Then we investigate the research on communication networks and note its implications for organizations. The chapter concludes with descriptions of the biggest barriers to communication and suggestions for overcoming these barriers.

COMMUNICATION AND THE MANAGER

communication

Good communication is essential for effective management.[1] **Communication** is the transfer of meaning and understanding between people through verbal and nonverbal means. In order to get work accomplished through other people, managers must influence their subordinates, peers, and superiors. Communication is a central element in exerting this influence. One of the most significant criticisms that a manager can receive is that he or she cannot communicate well. It is therefore important that aspiring managers understand how good communication skills can enhance their careers and the performance of the organizations for which they work.

Organizational communication has two primary values. First, it provides a means for accomplishing the firm's objectives. The way plans are to be implemented and activities coordinated to achieve these goals must be communicated to the individuals who must reach the goals. Second, communication provides a means by which members of the firm are motivated to carry out organizational plans. Managers have a central role in both these activities.

Studies of managers' communication patterns show that a large amount of time is spent on oral and written communication. An early study by Henry Mintzberg of McGill University showed that CEOs spent 78 percent of their time in oral communication.[2] This took place in situations like scheduled and unscheduled meetings, plant tours, and telephone conversations. A more recent study by other researchers showed that they spent 74 percent of their time in oral communication.[3] In both these studies, executives spent about half of their time with subordinates, and the other half with peers, the board of directors, and people outside the company.

Communication is crucial in each of the three managerial roles identified by Mintzberg (refer back to Chapter 1). Its importance is most obvious when managers gather and disseminate information, that is, in their informational role. Managers act as monitors (analyzing information about the unit's operation), disseminators (giving subordinates information they need to perform their jobs better), and spokespersons (sending information to individuals outside the manager's unit). The other two managerial roles also demand competence in communication. In the interpersonal role, for example, managers interact with subordinates, superiors, peers, and people outside their unit. In the decisional role, managers must exhibit communication skills when they settle conflicts among subordinates, when they negotiate with people outside their unit, and when they communicate how resources have been allocated.

Many modes of communication are available to employees when they deal with associates and customers. Here a salesman checks with a regional sales manager regarding product guarantees prior to a sales call on an important client.

Communication skill is also crucial in carrying out each of the management functions. Planning requires a manager to gather information about threats and opportunities relevant to his or her unit. This information is then conveyed to members of the unit so they can take part in developing plans to deal with these threats and opportunities. Organizing calls for management to tell subordinates where they fit into the total scheme of the firm, what structural changes become necessary, and how work is to be done. Leading involves communicating with subordinates in a way that motivates them to carry out their respective tasks enthusiastically. Controlling requires the manager to gather and interpret data about operations, praise or reprimand subordinates based on their performance, and inform superiors of the level of performance that has been attained.

We saw in Chapter 8 that managers must delegate authority. To do so, they must be able to tell subordinates what is to be done. Some managers perform tasks their subordinates should be doing because they fear that they will be unable to communicate instructions clearly. Poor communication skills can, therefore, cause a marked reduction in organizational effectiveness. Fortunately, communication is a learned skill. People who truly want to improve their ability to communicate can do so.

THE COMMUNICATION PROCESS

communication process

The **communication process** is the series of events that take place to transfer meaning. The basic elements of the communication process are shown in Figure 14-1 and described briefly below. If the communication process is viewed as a chain, it is easy to see why there are so many communication breakdowns. In much the same way that a chain is only as strong as its weakest link, so the communication process is only as strong as the weakest link in the process.

LEARNING OBJECTIVE 1
Describe the elements in the general communication model.

FIGURE 14-1 THE GENERAL COMMUNICATION MODEL.

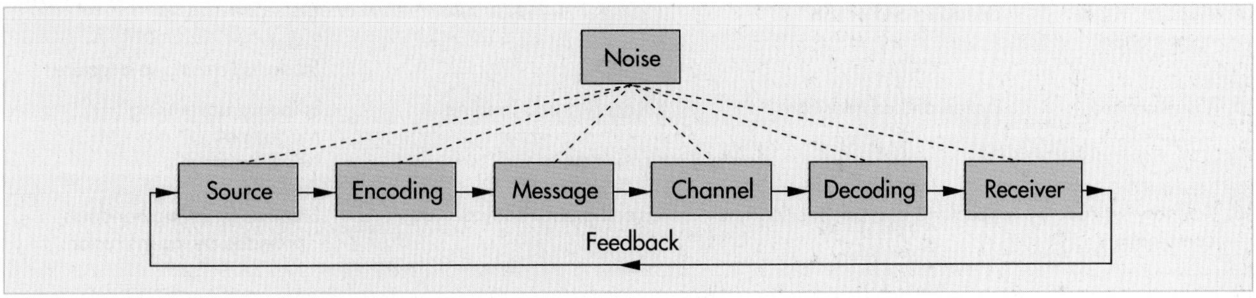

The Source

source

The **source** is the individual or group that develops the message that is to be communicated to another individual or group. The credibility of the source's communication depends, in part, on the characteristics of the source. The source can use a number of tactics to convince the receiver to accept the communication. These include playing on the emotions of the receiver (pathos), using logical arguments (logos), or asking the receiver to accept what is being said because the source is trustworthy (ethos).

A fire engine siren conveys a specific message to listeners. When a manager encodes a message, the message may not be as clear, especially when it concerns an issue that is new or has emotional overtones. Encoding must be done with extreme care.

Research on source credibility indicates that high-credibility sources have more influence on receivers than low-credibility sources.[4] A source can gain credibility by using a high-prestige medium. For example, professors gain credibility by publishing articles in refereed journals (those that use scholars to assess the appropriateness of manuscripts submitted to the journal). A source can also gain credibility by using media that influence large numbers of people. Entertainers gain credibility by using mass media like television and the movies to contact their audiences. Another way of gaining credibility is through authority. In organizations, managers may have credibility simply because they have authority over their receivers (subordinates).

Encoding the Message

encoding

Once the source has decided what message is to be conveyed, the message must be put in a form that the receiver can understand. **Encoding** is the process of converting ideas into symbols that receivers will understand. Words on a page are symbols to readers. The sound of a siren conveys the message that an emergency is in progress and the way needs to be cleared.

The Channel

communication channel

The **communication channel** is the medium by which the message is transmitted to the receiver. Various channels may be used to transmit a message (see Table 14-1).

TABLE 14-1 THE BASIC COMMUNICATION CHANNELS.

Channel	Required Source Activity	Required Receiver Activity	Some Examples
1. Auditory	Speaking Use of mechanical sending device	Listening	Telegraph signals Radio Telephone conversations
2. Visual	Action	Observing	Ship-to-shore visual signals Hand signals
3. Written	Composition	Reading	Reports Company policy manuals Books
4. Auditory-visual combination	Speaking and action	Listening and observing	Television, movies Ballet Students listening to a lecture
5. Visual-written combination	Action and composition	Observing and reading	Billboard advertising Magazines Newspapers Transit advertising
6. Auditory-written combination	Speaking and composition	Listening and reading	Students following handouts provided by the instructor

The spoken word can be carried through such channels as face-to-face communication, telephone, radio, and television. Books, articles, memos, and letters serve as channels for the written word. The senses of sight, sound, touch, smell, and taste also assist in communicating information to the receiver. Senders must select appropriate (and perhaps multiple) channels to avoid problems in either the understanding or the retention of a message. To explain a complex mathematical problem to students, an instructor may use a variety of methods: lecture, graphs, and formulas. Similarly, a manager who wants to increase the chance that a message will be retained by subordinates may follow a verbal instruction with a written memo.

Decoding the Message

decoding

When **decoding**, the receiver converts the encoded symbols into an understandable message. The greater the similarity in the status of the sender and the receiver, the greater the likelihood that the message will be understood as the sender intended. One reason communication between organizational levels is so subject to misinterpretation is that status differences exist among the individuals involved. Thus, a company president may have difficulty communicating with first-line supervisors.

The Receiver

receiver

The **receiver** is the individual or group for whom the message is intended. The receiver may interact face-to-face with the sender (for example, when a salesperson from the Great Canadian Travel Company tells a customer about a tour package to the Caribbean). On the other hand, the sender may not be able to see the receiver (for example, when a Canadian Tire television advertisement is aired across Canada).

Like the sender, the receiver is subject to many influences that can affect his or her understanding of the message. Receivers will interpret a communication in a manner that is consistent with their previous experience. Communications that are inconsistent with past experience are likely be rejected. The message from management that there will be no employee layoffs this year is not likely to be believed if layoffs occurred last year.

Feedback

feedback

Feedback consists of the observable reactions to a message. The sender will observe one of three basic reactions to the message: agreement, disagreement, or apathy. The speed at which feedback occurs varies with each situation. In face-to-face conversations, feedback is practically instantaneous, but in mass advertising, many weeks or months may pass before the source (the advertiser) knows how effective the communication was. Feedback can also take many forms, such as speaking, writing, facial expressions, and purchase patterns.

Noise

noise

At each step in the communication process, both senders and receivers must cope with "noise." **Noise** refers to those physical, personality, perceptual, or attitudinal factors that interfere with the communication process. Examples of noise include machinery noise at a factory, static on a telephone line, poor construction of a message by the sender, and a personality clash between a boss and a subordinate during a performance review. Noise can be powerful enough to completely block communication between senders and receivers.

THE SUPERIOR-SUBORDINATE COMMUNICATION MODEL

LEARNING OBJECTIVE 2

Outline the elements in the superior-subordinate communication model.

The general communication model is an abstract way of explaining how the communication process operates. To get a better insight into how communication operates within organizations, a model focussed on the relationship between bosses and their subordinates is needed. Such a model is shown in Figure 14-2. It is similar to the general communication model in Figure 14-1, but several elements have been added, and some of the terms in the general model have been replaced with terms that are relevant to organizations.

FIGURE 14-2 THE SUPERIOR-SUBORDINATE COMMUNICATION MODEL FOR DOWNWARD COMMUNICATION.

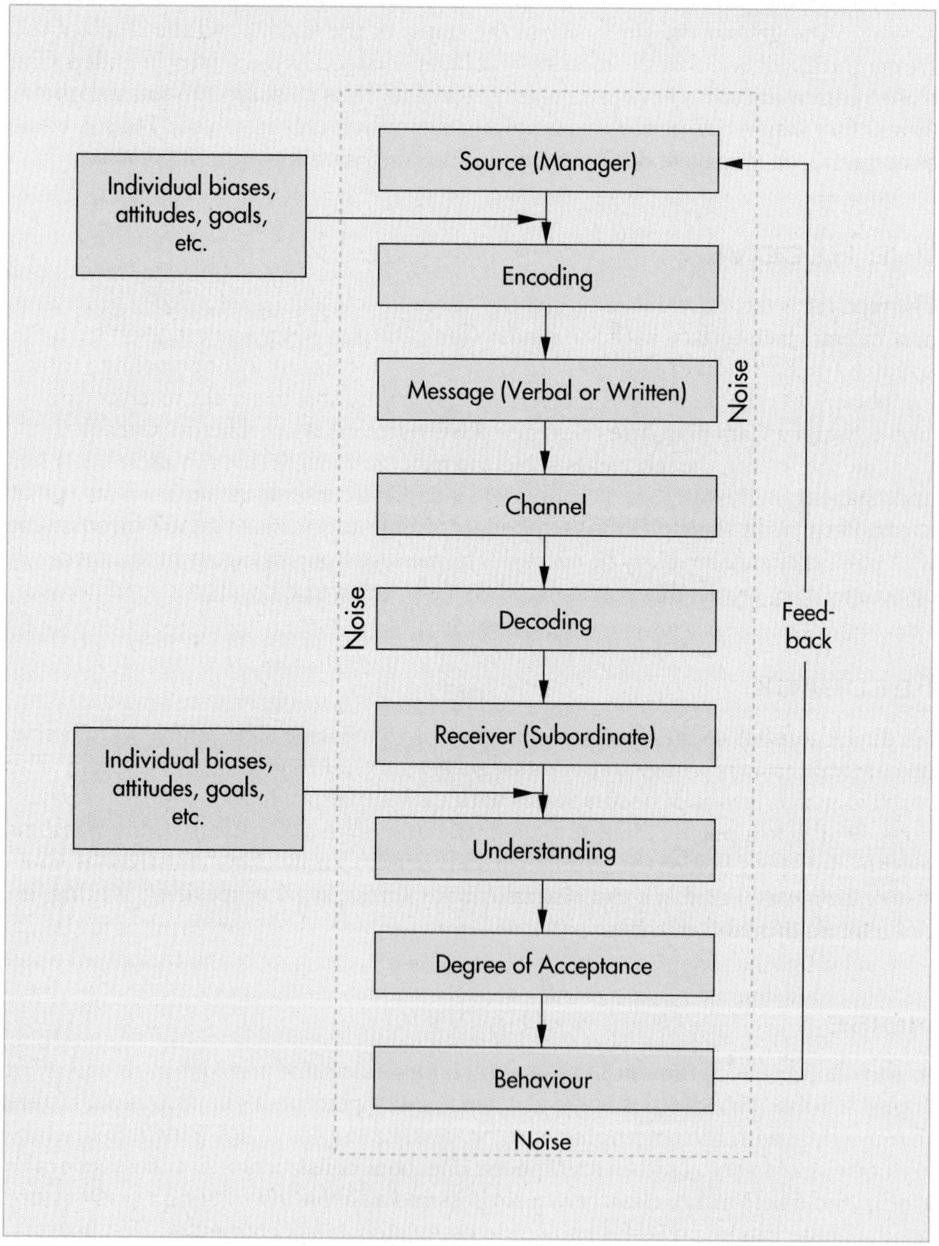

In the normal course of their work, managers (sources) must communicate with subordinates (receivers). When managers are encoding messages, they are influenced by their own individual biases, attitudes, and goals. A manager dealing with a "problem" subordinate will communicate in a certain way, but that same manager will communicate in a much different way with a subordinate who is a strong performer.

The channel through which the message is transmitted may be either verbal or written. If it is verbal, the transmission takes place whenever the manager speaks to subordinates. If it is written, the message is carried by the formal communication system of the organization, which closely parallels the lines of authority indicated on the organization chart.

As the message is decoded, the receiver's individual biases, attitudes, and goals come into play and affect how the message is interpreted. These influence (1) the level of understanding that develops from the communication, (2) the level of acceptance of the communication, and (3) the behaviour that occurs as a result of the communication. Breakdowns in the decoding-understanding-acceptance-behaviour sequence can cause many organizational problems. If a boss encodes a message to subordinates in such a way that they fail to understand it, there is likely to be little acceptance of the message and the behaviour desired by the boss will not occur. The same problems can occur in reverse when subordinates communicate with their boss.

The communication process is completed when the manager observes the employee's behaviour (feedback). On the basis of this feedback, the manager conveys either approval or disapproval of the behaviour to the employee, and the process begins anew.

A subordinate can also initiate this communication process. To describe this situation, we need only reverse the position of manager and subordinate in Figure 14-2. This upward communication gives management some idea of how well employees understand and accept the goals the organization is pursuing.

Superior-Subordinate Communication Methods

Managers and their subordinates may communicate with each other through written, verbal, nonverbal, and electronic means. Each of these has advantages and disadvantages, so managers must be sensitive to when each should be used.

Written Communication

Communicating by written means, such as memos, reports, letters, and company publications, is advantageous when a manager wants to reach several people simultaneously, or when it is important to document what the manager says. Managers tend to think more carefully about their written communications than they do about verbal communication because they are "on the record."

But writing can pose problems. Perhaps the greatest problem is that it is time-consuming. Other shortcomings are that written communications are one-way, impersonal, and open to misinterpretation. Some employees may have literacy problems, other may not be comfortable with English, and the rest may simply be too overburdened with work to read memos carefully.[5]

Oral Communication

Oral communications, such as one-on-one discussions, speeches, and committee meetings, are in some ways the opposite of written communications. Conveying messages orally is beneficial when the boss wants to convey information quickly to another person or group. It provides quick feedback to the manager. The biggest disadvantage of such communication is that the message becomes distorted as it passes from person to person. Because there is no record of the original message to refer to, receivers feel free to add their own interpretation. By the time the message reaches the last person in the chain, it may bear little resemblance to the original comment made by the sender.

Nonverbal Communication

nonverbal communication

Nonverbal communication is that which occurs through human actions and behaviours, rather than words.[6] Much of the communication in organizations falls into this category. Examples include students shuffling papers as the end of the class approaches, grim-looking top executives entering a meeting where downsizing is on the agenda, and an ambulance siren at a busy intersection.

body language

One of the important types of nonverbal communication is **body language**, which involves communicating through facial expressions, tone of voice, body posture, and gestures.[7] For example, crossed arms may suggest that a receiver does not want to accept the message, while leaning forward toward the speaker suggests that the receiver is open to the message. Body language may be intentional or inadvertent. Body language goes hand-in-hand with verbal communication, and has a significant effect on it. One study found that the verbal message accounted for only 7 percent of the impact of the communication on the receiver. The rest came from nonverbal factors such as facial expressions (55 percent) and vocal inflection (38 percent).[8]

The words spoken are not the only source of meaning for the receiver. Body language adds shades of meaning to verbal communication.

Electronic Media

With the advent of microcomputers, fax machines, VCRs, electronic mail systems, voice mail, and many other electronic gadgets, communication opportunities have proliferated (see the Management at Work insert "Communicating through Electronic Media"). These media are technically still written or verbal communication, so all the advantages and disadvantages of written and verbal media apply. But with the interactive capabilities of some types of electronic media, the sender of the message can get much quicker feedback, and this overcomes one of the big disadvantages of traditional written communication.

e-mail

In the past few years, e-mail has been appearing in all kinds of organizations. Electronic mail (**e-mail**) allows people to use their office computer to send letters or memos to other individuals in their own or other organizations. The receiver sees the message on his or her computer screen almost instantaneously, and can respond when it is convenient. E-mail has become very popular because (1) the person sending the message can get quick turnaround time, and (2) it uses computers that are already in place for other work. This should lead to increased productivity. A potential disadvantage is that people may get into nasty disagreements on the e-mail system without ever trying to work out their differences with face-to-face communication.

voice mail

Studies of how electronic media impact organizational communication are now being conducted. **Voice mail**—a computer-based messaging system accessed by telephone—is an illustration. A study of voice mail use among professional, technical, and administrative workers showed that preference for voice mail was high when:[9]

1. The target of the message was physically distant from the sender.
2. The sender was familiar with the voice mail technology.
3. The message being sent was short.
4. The content of the message was simple.
5. The sender expected a positive response from the receiver.
6. Documentation of the message was not needed.

MANAGEMENT AT WORK

COMMUNICATING THROUGH ELECTRONIC MEDIA

The electronics revolution is being put to work helping communication in organizations. Three areas illustrate how electronic media have influenced communication in organizations: executive information systems, faxes, and videos.

Executive information systems In 1987, Montreal-based Teleglobe Canada Inc. installed an executive information system (EIS). Now, when executives want answers to certain questions about financial matters, they can access the information almost immediately on the computer. Touch-screen technology allows retrieval of information by simply touching a menu choice button on a PC.

The EIS terminal looks like any other PC, but there is no keyboard. By pressing the touch-sensitive screen, the executive can choose from various items on the menu (for example, current sales of an important product, or customer satisfaction levels). Information officers in each division of the company prepare the information in a form that can easily be retrieved by the CEO. Top managers are not restricted to historical information; they can also do predictions. The executive can call up the spreadsheet which forecasts next quarter's sales, and then ask several "what if" questions to see how those changes will impact the financial results.

Fax Electronic communication is not limited to communication within a particular organization. Fax machines have changed the way that businesses deal with their customers. Consider the following examples:

1. Customers of TL Travel in Mississauga, Ontario, can access the firm's fax machine at any hour of the day to obtain prices on various vacation packages. They can also obtain an order form, fill it out, and send it back to TL Travel. Each morning, TL agents consult their fax in-tray to see what orders have come in overnight.
2. In northern B.C., students in a long-distance learning program consult their fax log for assignments, send in exams, and receive their grades.
3. Clearwater Lobster uses a fax machine to send out more than 100 price lists to European companies. A one-touch dial sends all the price lists simultaneously from the telephone numbers in the fax's memory bank.

The introduction of the fax machine has created some interesting legal problems. Since material that is faxed is a copy of the original, and since fax copies fade if not photocopied, it is possible that in legal battles over items such as contracts, the court will only have photocopies of faxes as evidence. This evidence may have less weight than originals. Another problem deals with the difficulty of proving where and when a fax was received. Courts have just started to deal with these issues. In one case, the Ontario Court of Appeal ruled that a fax constituted a legal delivery.

Video technology Video is being put to work in a number of ways. General Foods, for example, made a humorous video in an attempt to increase employee morale. Union Carbide produced a video after the disaster in Bhopal, India, to assure company employees that the firm would survive the tragedy.

Canadian Industries Ltd. makes extensive use of video. It has one of the best equipped corporate TV facilities in Canada, comprising $600 000 of equipment and nine full-time camera and production people. The most energetic production to date was a video explaining to all employees the nature of a new corporate culture that the company was introducing. In the video, the CEO explained to employees that the company had to become more competitive and entrepreneurial if it hoped to be successful in the future. Several other senior executives also appeared, each indicating how the new corporate culture would affect each of their areas.

While video technology does give managers some real advantages, it is one-way communication and does not allow managers to listen to employees. This is especially important when change is being introduced, because employees will have all sorts of questions about how the change is going to affect them. ▲

Many firms use electronic media to facilitate communication. The consulting firm of Peat Marwick uses its network of Apple computers to give consultants in one location immediate access to the knowledge, skills, and information that exists in other company locations.[10] This system makes communication between consultants more convenient, and increases employee job satisfaction.

One-Way versus Two-Way Communication

one-way communication

One-way communication takes place when the sender directs a message to the receiver without expecting an immediate, obvious response. When Holiday Inn advertises on national television, the firm expects that there will be some response from consumers, but the response is not immediate or obvious. Likewise, when top management at Cargill Grain develops a new policy statement on a certain issue, it does not expect immediate employee action.

two-way communication

Two-way communication takes place when the sender directs a message to the receiver expecting an immediate, obvious response. When a sales manager calls in a salesperson and demands to know why the salesperson sold a unit at 10 percent below cost, the sales manager expects an immediate response.

Research on one- and two-way communication reveals that one-way communication is faster and more organized than two-way communication, but it conveys the message less accurately. In two-way communication, receivers feel confident they have grasped the point, but the sender may feel somewhat insecure because the receivers sometimes point out ambiguities in the message.[11]

Recall that in Chapter 8 we made the distinction between organic and mechanistic organizations. Research shows that communication patterns are different in these two kinds of organizations. In one study, communication patterns were analyzed in two manufacturing plants, one of which was mechanistic, the other, organic.[12] The mechanistic plant was characterized by one-way communication, competitive interchanges, managerial dominance, subordinates and managers interrupting each other, and statements of nonsupport. The organic plant was characterized by the opposite conditions. Overall, the mechanistic plant exhibited a greater emphasis on one-way communication, the giving of orders by managers, and a high level of disagreement and conflict. The organic plant exhibited a greater emphasis on two-way communication, the giving of advice by managers, and a low level of disagreement and conflict.

ORGANIZATIONAL CHANNELS OF COMMUNICATION

LEARNING OBJECTIVE 3
Understand the difference between downward and upward communication channels.

In organizations, information flows in three basic ways: formal downward channels, formal upward channels, and informal channels (laterally and diagonally). These channels are shown in Figure 14-3 and are discussed below.

Formal Downward Channels

formal downward communication channels

Formal downward communication channels direct communication from bosses to subordinates through the chain of command in the organization. Table 14-2 shows several examples of formal downward channels of communication.

Formal downward channels of communication have received a great deal of attention from both managers and behavioural scientists since they are crucial to organizational functioning. Research has shown that the greater the number of levels in an organization, the smaller the likelihood that employees down the chain of command will have a clear understanding of important issues like corporate objectives. One estimate is that a message loses 80 percent of its meaning as it makes its way down the chain of command—starting with the president and moving through the vice-president, division manager, plant manager, supervisor, and finally the worker.[13] A loss of meaning in downward communication is evident when any one of the following four conditions exist:

FIGURE 14-3 DOWNWARD, UPWARD, LATERAL, AND DIAGONAL COMMUNICATION FLOWS.

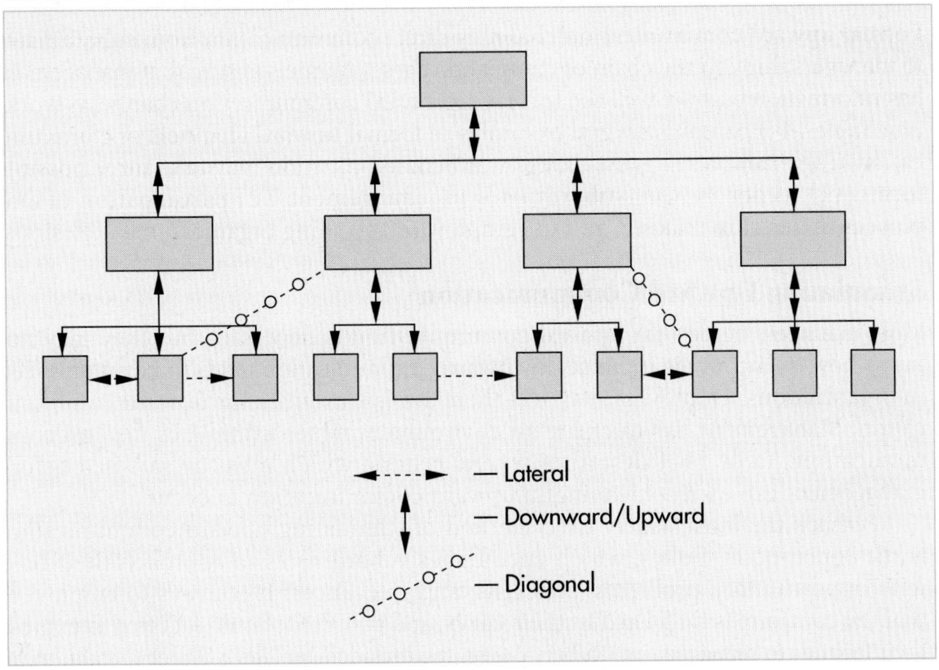

1. A lack of trust exists between boss and subordinate.
2. The communication must pass through many levels.
3. There are clear status and power differences between boss and subordinate.
4. The subordinate has a strong desire for upward mobility.[14]

These difficulties have led some to conclude that the "top-down" communication system should be replaced with some other type (e.g., the "bottom-up" system described below). However, despite its limitations, the top-down system is necessary because much of the information needed to manage an organization originates at the upper levels and must be transmitted to the appropriate lower levels. Employees can misinterpret or disregard what comes down from the top, but they would be worse off if no information were forthcoming.

TABLE 14-2 FORMAL DOWNWARD CHANNELS OF COMMUNICATION.

Channel	Description
1. The chain of command	Written or oral orders are passed down the hierarchy.
2. Policy manuals	Written documents indicating which behaviour is appropriate.
3. Memos	Written instructions from bosses to subordinates and vice versa.
4. Job instructions	Written or verbal instructions about the proper way to do a task.
5. Posters/bulletin boards	Written announcements on various topics that may be of interest to employees.
6. Pay inserts	Written announcements inserted in employee pay envelopes.
7. Loudspeaker system	Oral announcements to employees about issues that need immediate action.

FORMAL UPWARD CHANNELS

formal upward communication channels

Formal upward communication channels direct communication from subordinates to managers through the chain of command. These channels ensure that management has information on how well the formal downward communication channel is working. Table 14-3 contains several examples of formal upward channels of communication. The examples suggest that upward communication may take three possible forms: (1) feedback from subordinates to management, (2) participation of employees in decision making, and (3) employees appealing organizational decisions.

Stimulating Upward Communication

Most managers agree that upward communication is necessary, but they may not know how to encourage it. Since downward communication tends to be emphasized in organizations, employees may feel there are few avenues for upward communication. Management has to create an environment which stimulates upward communication. Table 14-4 describes several criteria which must be satisfied before management can expect meaningful upward communication to occur.

Perhaps the most widely used method of stimulating upward communication is the "open-door" policy, which encourages subordinates to approach their boss with opportunities, problems, concerns, and grievances. It conveys to employees that the company is interested in their views, and that they should feel free to express their feelings to management. Robert Glegg, the president of Glegg Water Conditioning Inc., lunches regularly with small groups of employees to exchange ideas about projects, people, and problems. In one of these sessions, he heard objections from engineers about a proposed open office concept and therefore changed the plans to satisfy their needs.[15]

George Cohon, president of McDonald's Restaurants of Canada, encourages upward communication by casually defining his office space. No doors or walls screen him from visitors. Employees are encouraged to talk to the boss whenever they feel

TABLE 14-3 FORMAL UPWARD CHANNELS OF COMMUNICATION.

Channel	Description
1. The chain of command	Written or oral requests are passed up the hierarchy.
2. Suggestion systems	Written or oral ideas for improvements are formally made known to management.
3. Open-door policy	Written or oral encouragement to employees to talk over any problems with management.
4. Grievance procedure	Written and oral communication allowing employees to formally appeal management decisions.
5. Attitude surveys	Written feedback to management regarding employee feelings on a variety of topics.
6. Special meetings	Oral public communication between management and workers on workplace issues that arise from time to time.
7. Ombudsman	Oral and written communication through an individual assigned to ensure that corporate justice is carried out.
8. Exit interview	Verbal communication designed to discover why an employee is leaving the firm.

TABLE 14-4 CRITERIA FOR EFFECTIVE UPWARD COMMUNICATION.

Criteria	Description
1. Planning	Upward communication must not be left to chance; it must be encouraged by management.
2. Balance	Management must encourage upward communication from many sources, but must not allow upward communication to overwhelm downward communication.
3. Direction	Upward communication must be directed to those who can take action.
4. Listening	Management must listen objectively and sensitively to upward communication.
5. Action	Management must be prepared to take action after hearing upward communication.

the need.[16] Trevor Hayden, president of Ambassador Coffee Services, holds regular meetings with staff to keep them up-to-date on what is happening in the company, particularly during tough economic times.[17]

INFORMAL COMMUNICATION CHANNELS

LEARNING OBJECTIVE 4
Explain the difference between formal and informal communication channels.

Informal communication channels are those which exist outside the formal chain of command in the organization. A *Financial Post* study identified Canadian companies that exhibited excellence in communication.[18] In many of these firms, emphasis was placed on communication outside the formal chain of command. The grapevine (see Chapter 9) is an example of an informal communication channel.

informal communication channels

Whenever communication takes place outside formal channels, an informal communication channel is operating. Hundreds of these informal communication channels exist, but they fall into one of two general categories: lateral or diagonal.

Lateral Channels

lateral communication

Lateral communication takes place between individuals at the same level in the organization. Technically speaking, lateral communication is not recognized by the formal organization. It is, however, very common in organizations because it saves so much time. Without it, the strict vertical chain of command would have to be observed, and workers would have to go through their common superior every time they wanted to solve a problem. Lateral communication can, of course, cause problems because the boss may not know that subordinates have worked out some problems among themselves.

Diagonal Channels

diagonal communication

Diagonal communication takes place between individuals who are not in a superior-subordinate relationship, but are at different levels in the organization. When a salesperson in the marketing area communicates with the manager of marketing research, diagonal communication is taking place because (a) these two individuals are not in the same chain of command, and (b) the manager of marketing research is at a higher level than the salesperson. This type of communication, like lateral communication, often solves problems very efficiently even though the organization does not formally recognize this communication channel.

COMMUNICATION NETWORKS

communication network

In the previous section, we focussed on the upward, downward, diagonal and lateral movement of communication. Within these broad categories there are many specific communication networks. A **communication network** is a path through which messages are transmitted. The many communication networks include the circle, wheel, chain, Y, and all-channel (see Figure 14-4). Many labouratory experiments have been conducted to test the impact and effectiveness of these networks.[19] In these studies, researchers try to determine how the structure of the network influences the speed of communication, the accuracy of communication, and participant satisfaction.

Subjects are usually placed in groups of four to six, randomly assigned to one of the networks, and then asked to perform tasks ranging from simple to complex. While these networks have been examined in the laboratory, they do have real-life counterparts. The *circle* network is analogous to a group working in a physical setting such that group members can communicate with their immediate neighbour but not with others in the group. The *all-channel* network approximates the communication patterns that occur in a task force or functional team employed in a matrix structure (see Chapter 8). In this structure, each person can communicate directly with each other person. The *wheel* arrangement describes a situation in which the subordinates must obtain their information from one source—the boss (e.g., a group of four salespeople reporting to the sales manager). The *chain* describes the downward communication process that is likely to occur in a bureaucracy. Each person receives communications only from the person immediately above his or her position. The Y network is similar to the chain, except at the end of the process two individuals must rely on one person for their information.

FIGURE 14-4 COMMUNICATION NETWORKS.

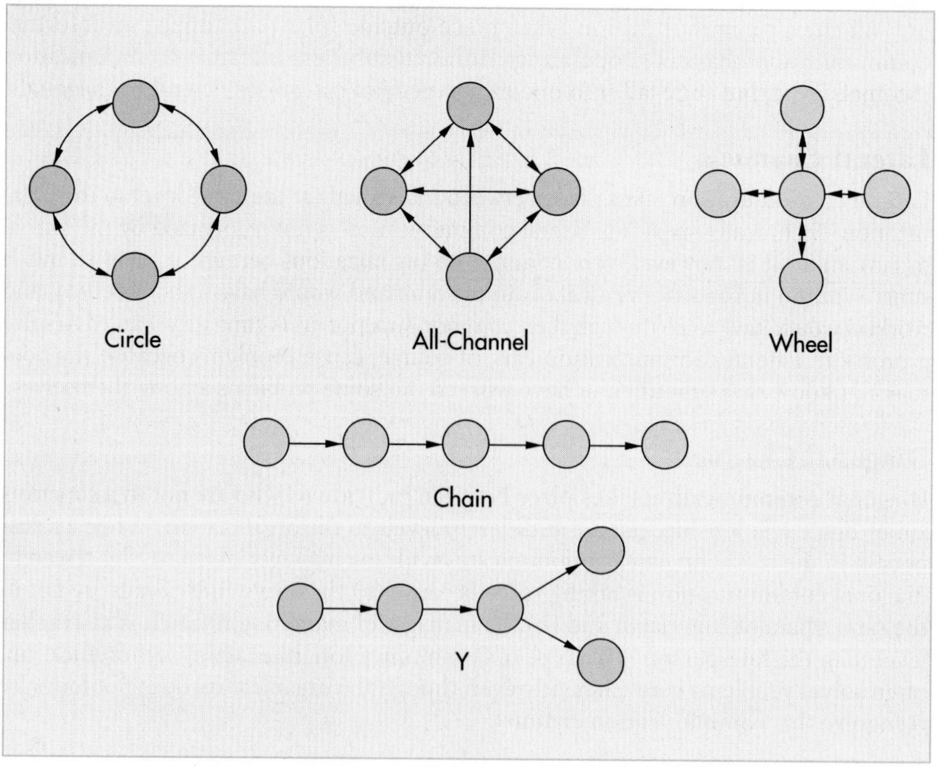

Research on communication networks indicates that each network has a somewhat different impact on the participants.[20] Thus, a manager will want to use the appropriate network for each distinct situation. For simple tasks, speed and accuracy were the highest in the wheel, Y, and all-channel networks, and lowest in the circle and chain networks. For complex tasks, the reverse was generally true. Participants in the circle, Y, and chain networks tended to be quite satisfied regardless of task complexity. Satisfaction was lowest in the wheel network.

The structure of the network is not the only influence on communication effectiveness. For example, establishing a task structure within the group improves performance.[21] Once this structure is in place, the task facing the group is more readily accomplished irrespective of the communication network that is used.

BARRIERS TO EFFECTIVE COMMUNICATION

communication barrier

LEARNING OBJECTIVE 5
Identify and describe the organizational and individual barriers to effective communication.

Communication frequently fails to have the effect intended by the sender because certain "barriers" prevent the transfer of meaning. A **communication barrier** is any physical or psychological factor that inhibits the transfer of meaning from the sender to the receiver.[22] Some barriers are obvious while others are more subtle. If an audience is listening to a speech in a room that is +30°C, it is obvious what needs to be done to make the conditions conducive for communication. On the other hand, if a manager and a subordinate have difficulty understanding each other during a performance appraisal interview, it may not be clear what the cause of the problem is.

Organizations experience two fundamental kinds of communication barriers—organizational and individual. These are summarized in Table 14-5 and discussed in the following sections.

ORGANIZATIONAL BARRIERS TO COMMUNICATION

organizational communication barriers

Organizational communication barriers are those caused by the nature and structure of organizations. Such obstacles include filtering, status differences, conflicting departmental objectives, specialization of labour, information overload, and time pressures.

TABLE 14-5 BARRIERS TO COMMUNICATION.

Organizational Barriers	Individual Barriers
1. Filtering	1. Emotions
2. Status differences	2. Language and cultural differences
3. Differing departmental objectives	3. Differing perceptions
4. Specialization of labour	4. Stereotyping
5. Time pressures	5. Defence mechanisms
6. Information overload	6. The halo effect
	7. Semantics
	8. Lack of trust
	9. Selecting the wrong channels for communication

Filtering

filtering

Filtering refers to the loss of meaning that occurs as information moves upward or downward through the various levels in the management hierarchy. Filtering may be deliberate (e.g., a subordinate may distort information to make himself or herself look good to the boss), or it may be accidental (a subordinate may simply forget to include an important piece of information in a report). In either case, by the time the message reaches its ultimate destination, it may be substantially changed from what the sender intended. As indicated earlier, filtering may cause a message to lose 80 percent of its original meaning as it travels from the president through the various organizational levels to a production worker.[23]

Status Differences

Status differences are obvious in organizations, and lower-level members are often reluctant to communicate honestly with upper-level members. This reluctance is usually caused by fear of the person with higher status, but whatever the reason, the outcome is the same—clear communication fails to occur. Status is a barrier to communication because it may be used to insulate managers from information they don't want to hear.[24]

Differing Departmental Objectives

Teleconferencing is one of many new communication techniques. Northern Telecom's "Teleforum" system uses advanced digital technology to increase the benefits of teleconferencing. Several participants in many locations can be accommodated without loss of audio quality.

Different departments in the same organization have different objectives. Even though the objectives are different, they should all fit together in some coherent pattern so that overall organizational goals are reached. In practice, however, some departments may come to view their objectives as ends in themselves. This attitude leads to the belief that other departments are unimportant. When this view emerges, the quality of communication with other departments declines sharply.

Labour Specialization

Specialization of labour results in each department developing an expertise in a certain narrow area. This specialization, which is so useful in carrying out tasks, may make communication among departments difficult. A classic example of this difficulty is the jargon that develops in the various specialized areas of an organization. The marketing area may, for example, feel befuddled by people in the finance area who use terms like "discounted cash flows." Similarly, people in the finance area may find it hard to understand people in marketing who talk of "focus group interviews."

Time Pressures

In all organizations, managers are confronted with time pressures and deadlines. In this type of environment, communication may be carried out with great haste. Two problems can arise from the need to do things quickly: (1) the formal decision-making network may be side-stepped, causing certain people to become angry because they have been left out, and (2) messages which are transmitted may be poorly thought out.

Information Overload

information overload

While decisions should be based on good information, many managers find themselves in the position of having an excessive amount of information. **Information overload** occurs when someone receives more information than he or she can absorb. This predicament has become common in recent years with the advent of high-speed computer printers and photocopy machines. When information overload occurs, a manager is unable to determine what information is critical to the decision at hand.

Individual Barriers to Communication

Individual communication barriers are caused by the characteristics of the individuals working in an organization. These barriers arise from emotions, cultural differences, perceptions, stereotyping, defence mechanisms, the halo effect, semantics, a lack of trust, and selecting the wrong channels for communication.

individual communication barriers

Emotions

Managers are motivated by both facts and emotions when communicating. **Emotions** are subjective responses to a situation or a person. When senders or receivers experience extreme emotions like love, hate, anger, depression, embarassment, or happiness, communication is likely to be hampered. Such states increase the likelihood that people will exercise bad judgment or make hasty or ill-advised comments.

emotions

Language and Cultural Differences

With the growing internationalization of business, managers are encountering subordinates, superiors, and peers from cultural backgrounds different from their own. These differences can present obstacles to communication because the sender and the receiver may lack a common frame of reference. As a result, they interpret terms and expressions in unexpected ways. Some examples of the complications created by language and culture are described in the Global Management insert entitled "Cultural Differences and Business."

Differing Perceptions

Perception refers to the way that people "see" their environment. Each individual sees the world from a unique perspective because each person's background is unique. In the picture on the left of Figure 14-5, some people see an old woman, while some see a young woman. In the picture on the right, some people see two faces, while others see a vase.

perception

FIGURE 14-5 WHAT DO YOU SEE?

GLOBAL MANAGEMENT

CULTURAL DIFFERENCES AND BUSINESS

Diverse cultures have divergent views on a variety of subjects. Three of these differences have to do with time, body language, and semantics.

Time In North America, time is considered to be a precious commodity. Thus, giving deadlines to people, or expecting them to be on time for meetings is considered perfectly reasonable. In other cultures, however, time may not be regarded in the same way. Consider these examples:

1. In the Middle East, giving someone a deadline is considered rude.
2. In Latin America, business appointments are made for specific times, but people are often kept waiting for 30 minutes or more.
3. In Japan, failure to act on a contract offer for a period of several months does not signal a lack of interest as it does in North America; the delay may simply be a negotiating tactic.

Body language Body language can also vary among cultures, as the following examples indicate:

1. North Americans like to keep about 1.5 to 2.5 metres between themselves and others when talking; Latin Americans prefer a much smaller space.
2. In Canada, winking communicates friendship, but it is considered rude in Australia, Hong Kong, and Malaysia.
3. Raising an eyebrow in Tonga means "I agree," but in Peru it means "pay me."
4. Circling your ear with your finger means "crazy" in most European countries, but in the Netherlands it means "you have a phone call."
5. Waving at someone is a sign of recognition in Canada, but it is considered a severe insult in Nigeria.
6. Nodding your head means "yes" in Canada and the U.S., but it means "no" in Bulgaria and Sri Lanka. In Turkey, people say "no" by shutting their eyes, raising their chin, and throwing their head back.
7. In Canada, giving a person the "thumbs up" signal is a sign that things are going well, but in Bangladesh it is a rude sign.
8. Slapping a person on the back is inappropriate in Japan because touching is viewed as unacceptable.

Semantics The meaning of words from another language can also be misconstrued because of an unfamiliarity with the nuance of the terms. Consider these examples:

1. A company wanted to sell its shirts in Mexico with the following phrase: "When I wore this shirt, I felt good," but it was translated "I felt good until I wore this shirt."
2. General Motors wanted to advertise "Body by Fisher," but it came out "Corpse by Fisher" when translated into Flemish.
3. Pepsi's advertisement "come alive with Pepsi" was translated "come out of the grave with Pepsi" in German; in Asia the phrase was translated "bring your ancestors back from the dead."
4. An advertisement for a battery that was "highly rated" came out as "highly overrated" when translated for use in Venezuela.
5. Parker Pen Company wanted to used the word "bola" (ball) for use in ballpoint pen advertisements in South America. But "bola" can also mean "revolution" or "lie," and it is also used as an obscenity. ▲

Because people view reality from differing perspectives, they will have different reactions to the same situation. Consider the following reactions to an announcement from management that all employees will receive a 5 percent pay increase:

- "It's about time; I've had to wait too long for this."
- "A lousy 5 percent; what a cheap outfit."
- "Joe did way less than I did and he gets the same raise."
- "This company is really concerned about its employees."
- "I don't care much about money."

How can these diverse responses be explained? The differences occur because each person has a unique work history which shapes his or her outlook. Given such diversity, it is hardly surprising that perception has a big impact on communications.

To complicate matters further, people fail to perceive everything in their environment. **Selective perception** involves seeing only what one wants to see. In one study, executives solving a case problem tended to see the problem in terms of their own functional area. Marketing executives saw a marketing problem, while finance executives saw a finance problem.[25] Selective perception impedes interpersonal communication because each person hears only what is consistent with his or her perception of the other person.

selective perception

Stereotyping

Stereotyping means categorizing individuals or groups on the basis of only a few characteristics. In organizations, two frequently found stereotypes are "union members want more money for less work," and "management wants to get the most work out of employees for the least money." Stereotyping frustrates communication because it causes the receiver to hear only those messages that are consistent with the stereotyped images; messages that are inconsistent with the stereotype are ignored, even though they may be factual.

stereotyping

Defence Mechanisms

Defence mechanisms are used by individuals to protect their ego from unpleasant information (e.g., the opinion that they are incompetent). People who have a particular fault often see this same fault in others. One study found that people who scored high on traits such as stinginess, obstinacy, and disorderliness tended to rate others much higher on these traits than did individuals who did not have these traits.[26] The entire communication process is affected by this type of "noise." Defense mechanisms distort the message or prevent receivers from hearing the message at all.

defence mechanism

The Halo Effect

The **halo effect** occurs when we form opinions about one specific characteristic of a person and then generalize that opinion to all other characteristics. For example, if a subordinate has a good attendance record, a manager may conclude that the subordinate is also a high performer, even though the manager may lack objective evidence on the subordinate's performance.

halo effect

Semantics

Semantics is the study of words and what they mean. Since a word may have many shades of meaning, the sender of a communication can never be sure exactly what meaning was received. For example, a manager may tell subordinates that their job goals are easy to reach, but subordinates may soon find that the manager's definition of "easy" is rather different from their own.

semantics

Of the more than half-million words in the English language, the typical adult uses only about 2000 words, and only 500 of those are used with any frequency. One study showed that these 500 words can have over 14 000 meanings.[27] It is no wonder that semantics problems are so common in organizations.

Recognizing that words convey important images, organizations like Disney World, DuPont, McDonald's, and Wal-Mart call employees "associates," "team members," or "cast members." They do this in an attempt to reduce the "we-they" mentality that develops when words like "manager" and "workers" are used.

Lack of Trust

Communication is facilitated when the parties trust each other. An absence of trust causes messages to be scrutinized for hidden meanings. The greater the credibility of the sender, the greater the likelihood that the receiver will believe the information.

Selecting the Wrong Channels for Communication

Managers use both verbal and written channels to communicate with others. They must take care that these channels are appropriate for the particular message. Research on this issue indicates that managers that use appropriate channels are more effective than those who use inappropriate channels (see the Management at Work insert "Using the Right Communication Channels").

OVERCOMING BARRIERS TO COMMUNICATION

LEARNING OBJECTIVE 6
List and describe eight ways to overcome the barriers to communication.

Managers must become competent in two basic areas of communication if they are to be effective: (1) sending clear messages, and (2) actively listening to messages that are sent to them. Techniques which help managers achieve these two goals are listed in Table 14-6 and briefly discussed below the table.

MANAGEMENT AT WORK

Using the Right Communication Channels

The media managers use to communicate with others has an impact on the effectiveness of their communications. Two variables are important in determining communication effectiveness:

1. *Media richness* The extent to which a medium gives multiple information cues, immediate feedback, and a personal focus to the communication; media can range from very rich (face-to-face communication) to very lean (written form letters).
2. *Routineness of the message* The extent to which a message deals with a simple or repetitive problem; messages range from routine to nonroutine; nonroutine messages have greater potential for misinterpretation than routine messages.

Although managers prefer face-to-face communication, research shows that managers should vary the medium, depending on the message they are sending.

In a study of 95 executives, it was found that their preference for face-to-face communication increased as the complexity of the message increased. For routine messages, over two-thirds of the managers used written media, but for the most complex messages, 88 percent of the managers used oral media.

The essential finding in the study was that the most effective managers used "rich" (i.e., oral) media for complicated issues and "lean" (i.e., written) media for routine messages. The researchers determined this by identifying 15 managers who were good at matching the medium with the message, and 15 managers who weren't very good at matching. They then looked at these managers' performance appraisals.

The most "media sensitive" managers were rated as "high performers" in 87 percent of the cases, while the most "media insensitive" managers were rated as high performers in only 47 percent of the cases. ▲

TABLE 14-6 OVERCOMING BARRIERS TO COMMUNICATION.

1. Listen actively.
2. Regulate the flow of information.
3. Encourage feedback from message recipients.
4. Simplify the content of the message.
5. Restrain emotions.
6. Ensure verbal and nonverbal cues are consistent.
7. Use the grapevine.

LISTEN ACTIVELY

Listening takes three basic forms. In **marginal listening**, the receiver spends only part of the time listening to what the sender is saying. Marginal listening is possible because people can understand the spoken word at speeds of 500 words per minute or more, yet most speakers only speak at about 120 words per minute. This type of listening can lead to problems because the receiver's mind wanders as he or she listens to the message.

marginal listening

Evaluative listening involves making a judgment about the reasonableness of what a speaker is saying. This type of listening can also lead to problems because the listener may conclude that the speaker's views are unacceptable. Once this evaluation has been made, the listener hears very little else that is said.

evaluative listening

The type of listening which has the most promise is nonevaluative listening. **Nonevaluative listening** requires the listener to focus all of his or her attention on what is being said without trying to simultaneously evaluate it. If the listener is clear on what is being said, a better decision can be made about its reasonableness.

nonevaluative listening

Carl Rogers and Fritz Roethlisberger argue that ineffective listening is the greatest single barrier to effective communication.[28] They suggest a simple procedure for overcoming it. When two people are having an argument, they should agree that each person can speak only after he or she accurately summarizes the ideas and feelings of the other person. Since one person cannot argue his or her side until the previous statement is properly understood, this forces understanding of the other person's position. This increased understanding reduces the need for the argument.

A related technique—active listening—is also helpful. **Active listening** involves concentrating on the sender's message so that all elements of the message are received. It means listening not only for the content of the message, but also for the underlying feelings, and for nonverbal cues that go with the message. Active listening also requires the receiver to ask questions of clarification to ensure that he or she actually understands what the sender is saying.

active listening

Empathy is an important element in active listening. **Empathy** means putting yourself in the other person's position so that you can sense how the other person is going to react to a communication. Empathy facilitates the encoding process because it helps the sender to construct the message in such a way that the receiver is more likely to accept it.

empathy

Table 14-7 contains a widely cited list of ten rules for effective listening. Note that the first and last rules require the speaker to stop talking.

TABLE 14-7 TEN RULES FOR EFFECTIVE LISTENING.

1. *Stop talking* You cannot listen if you are talking. Polonius (*Hamlet*): "Give every man thine ear, but few thy voice."
2. *Put the talker at ease* Help the speaker feel that he or she is free to talk. This is often called a permissive environment.
3. *Show the speaker that you want to listen* Look and act interested. Do not read your mail while he or she talks. Listen to understand rather than to oppose.
4. *Remove distractions* Don't doodle, tap, or shuffle papers. Will it be quieter if you shut the door?
5. *Empathize with the speaker* Try to put yourself in his or her place so that you can see his or her point of view.
6. *Be patient* Allow plenty of time. Do not interrupt.
7. *Hold your temper* An angry person gets the wrong meaning from words.
8. *Go easy on argument and criticism* This puts the speaker on the defensive. He or she may "clam up" or get angry. Do not argue; even if you win, you lose.
9. *Ask questions* This encourages the speaker and shows you are listening. It helps to develop points further.
10. *Stop talking* This is first and last, because all other commandments depend on it. You just can't do a good listening job while you are talking.

Nature gave man two ears but only one tongue, which is a gentle hint that he should listen more than he talks.

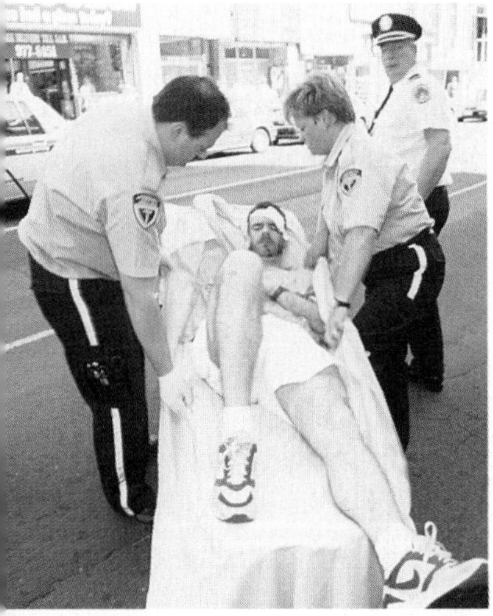

Clear communication between professionals is essential for ensuring human safety. Clear communication between managers and workers helps a business function effectively.

Regulate the Flow of Information

If managers are to avoid information overload, they must regulate the information they receive. One stipulation they can make is that they be informed only when significant deviations occur. An absence of information then means that operations are proceeding normally. This approach is consistent with the exception principle of management (see Chapter 17). The manager might also require brief (less than one page) executive summaries of the work done by subordinates in various areas. This system allows the manager to keep abreast of crucial developments without spending a great deal of time doing so.

Encourage Feedback from Message Recipients

Managers must check to see whether their communications have been understood. Encouraging feedback from subordinates, peers, and superiors will help managers make this determination. This feedback can take the form of either words or actions. After sending out a memo, a manager can check subordinates' reactions to it by talking to several individuals to get their views. Or, the manager can actively encourage subordinates to drop by and talk about any problems that may arise.

Simplify the Content of the Message

Various employees, like engineers, plant managers, secretaries, and janitors usually have varying levels of sophistication with language. Although these employees have much vocabulary in common, the meaning of some words may be clear to an engineer but not to a janitor, and vice versa. Therefore, when communicating, every attempt should be made to use the words that are part of the common vocabulary.

Many people, including managers, have the mistaken notion that their communication will be more impressive if they use large words and complicated phrases. Often these communications simply come across as stilted and pompous. Bureaucratic government communications are the classic example of this kind of problem.

Systems for assessing the appropriateness of reading material have been developed, and these can be used by managers to ensure that they are communicating at the right level of difficulty. The Gunning "fog index" measures how complicated a piece of writing is. When complicated words and phrases are used, a high fog index results, indicating that the writing is difficult to read.[29] The Flesch system measures how interesting a piece of writing is. Both the Flesch and Gunning systems are described in the Management at Work insert entitled "Two Ways to Assess Your Writing."

RESTRAIN EMOTIONS

Emotionally charged situations create communication problems because senders and receivers rely more on feelings than they do on facts. A boss disciplining a subordinate for poor performance may discover that the subordinate responds aggressively. The boss may attempt to resolve this problem by providing the facts on the subordinate's performance, but this tactic will probably have little effect. It would likely be more effective for the boss to empathize with the subordinate and understand the reasons for the emotion. If this approach fails, it may be best to end the discussion until emotions have cooled.

If two individuals are unable to communicate without becoming emotional, a neutral third party (e.g., a common boss of two disputing subordinates, a marriage counsellor, or an arbitrator) may be necessary. The issue of third party interventions in conflict situations is discussed in detail in Chapter 15.

MANAGEMENT AT WORK

TWO WAYS TO ASSESS YOUR WRITING

The "fog index" measures the level at which you write. To compute the fog index, follow these steps:

1. Choose a paragraph of approximately 120 words. Divide the total number of words by the number of sentences. This calculation gives you the average words per sentence.
2. Note each word with three or more syllables (don't count three-syllable words that are made by combining simple words, words that have endings like -ed or -es, or words that start a sentence).
3. Add the word average to the number of polysyllable words and multiply the total by 0.4.

Your score corresponds to your reading comprehension grade level. For example, a score of 9 means that a person who has completed grade nine can understand what you write. A score of 17 or more means that only graduate students can understand what you write.

Another test measures how interesting your writing is. To compute the interest level of your writing, do the following:

1. Take a sample of 100 words and count the personal pronouns—words like I, you, he she, them (but not "it").
2. Count all words that are gender specific (e.g., father, daughter, actress, businessman).
3. Count all collective nouns (e.g., people, folks).
4. Count up the sample's "personal sentences" (i.e., any sentence containing quotation marks, commands, questions, suggestions, and incomplete sentences).
5. Multiply the number of personal words by 3.635. Multiply the number of personal sentences by .314, and add the two products.

The total is your human interest score. A score of 5 indicates that your writing is very dull; a score of 30, interesting; a score of 80, dramatic. ▲

Ensure That Verbal and Nonverbal Cues Are Consistent

When managers communicate with others in the organization, they must ensure that their body language is consistent with their verbal cues. If verbal and nonverbal cues are inconsistent, the receiver may be more influenced by the nonverbal cues than by the verbal cues.[30] If a manager disciplines a subordinate in a firm, no-nonsense tone of voice, and at the same time pounds the table for effect, the subordinate will no doubt get the message that the manager is unhappy. But if a manager tells a subordinate to "come and see me whenever you have any problems," but then conveys by his or her body language that he or she has little patience for sitting and listening to the subordinate's problems, the subordinate will receive mixed signals, and the verbal message will lose credibility.

Use the Grapevine

In Chapter 9, we noted the importance of the grapevine. Managers can plug into the grapevine to find out what kind of information is informally moving around the organization. They can also use it to squelch false rumours and to send out information that they want employees to hear. See the Ethics in Management insert "Ethics and the Grapevine" for a potential problem in this area. Since employees trust the grapevine, it may occasionally be more effective to use this channel of communication than to use the formal organizational channels. The grapevine is particularly important when companies are forced to downsize. A survey of 393 Canadian companies that cut staff in the past five years revealed that workers heard the bad news unoffically in nearly half the cases.[31]

ETHICS IN MANAGEMENT

Ethics and the Grapevine

Managers have varying opinions about the value of the grapevine. Autocratic managers dislike the idea that employees have access to an informal channel of communication that relays information the manager thinks they shouldn't have. These managers regard employees as lower-status individuals who should simply follow orders. Because of their autocratic views, these managers usually try to stamp out the grapevine. But this is really quite unimaginative thinking; the grapevine simply cannot be eliminated. These managers not only waste their time on fruitless activity, they also make their subordinates angry.

A second, and more effective, type of manager is one who recognizes that the grapevine is useful to all members of the organization, not just employees. These managers use the grapevine to gather information about employee views on work-related matters. They can then act on this information and thereby improve their managerial effectiveness. For example, if a manager finds out that employees are very unhappy about a managerial decision, the manager can informally talk with individuals and determine how serious the situation is. The appropriate action can then be taken to resolve the problem.

A third, and more devious, type of manager exists. These managers do not like the grapevine, but they are wise enough to know that attempts to stamp it out will simply infuriate workers. They therefore use the grapevine for their own benefit, even if doing so is harmful.

Suppose that Martin Lane, the vice-president of production, hears through the grapevine that employees are concerned about layoffs. Suppose also that he knows that top management has been having tentative discussions about downsizing as a solution to problems the company is experiencing. Since Lane's workers are in the middle of an important production

• • •

run, however, he is concerned that all this talk about layoffs is distracting the workers' attention from the production effort. So, he starts a rumour that 50 new employees are going to be hired in the next few months (this could also happen if the company gets involved in a new project, but the decision has not yet been made). A few days later, he observes with satisfaction that his rumour is now circulating on the grapevine and is causing employees to discount the earlier rumour about layoffs.

Lane will probably rationalize his behaviour by saying that the new project is a possibility just like layoffs are a possibility—both are rumours, and one has to expect rumours to circulate. In Lane's view, circulating counter-rumours is perfectly acceptable, because the rumours that are already circulating may turn out to be false, and these rumours are harming the company by creating uncertainty for workers.

What do you think of this type of reasoning? Is it ethical to start counter-rumours? Is it ethical to be involved in passing along rumours in the first place? What effect do rumours have on the people who hear them? ▲

MEETING THE CHALLENGE

Communication and Survival

There have been several positive outcomes for both Honeywell and its employees as a result of the company's expenditures on communication and educational activities. The biggest payoff has been the ease with which shop-floor changes have been made. According to company management, although the changes are dramatic, they have been relatively easy to implement, and the increased knowledge that workers have has reduced their fears about the future. The president of the Canadian Auto Workers local in the plant says that management used to be the enemy, but no longer is perceived that way. The enemy now is competitive firms that the company must beat in the marketplace.

Productivity is also up sharply at the Scarborough plant. Employment has declined 50 percent since 1988, yet the plant produces about the same volume it did then. Although jobs have been lost, the president of the local union says that the plant would probably have been closed completely if it had not adopted its new strategy.

Workers also have a keener appreciation for the customer than they formerly did. Every production line has a "customer of the day" program. Each day, a different worker goes to the end of the production line and opens a box of finished goods to see if it meets the specifications demanded by the typical customer. This activity gives the workers a greater appreciation for customer needs as they produce the product.

The communications emphasis of the program has also yielded some unexpected benefits. Eleni Itsou used to speak English very poorly, so she sat back and said nothing even though she had many ideas for improving work processes. Now, she speaks out freely, both on the job and off. She says her own self-esteem has been enhanced by her experience at the company. ▲

SUMMARY

Communication is the transfer of meaning and understanding between people through verbal and nonverbal means. Organizational communication has two purposes—to assist in the accomplishment of organizational goals, and to help managers motivate their subordinates. Communication skill is crucial for managers because it helps them carry out the management functions of planning, organizing, leading, and controlling.

The general communication model shows the series of events that must take place if a transfer of meaning between the sender and the receiver is to occur. The source encodes a message and sends it through a channel so that it can be decoded by the receiver. The sender gets feedback by observing the receiver's actions or attitudes. Noise can inhibit a message that is sent.

Communication between bosses and subordinates can be either one-way or two-way. In the former, the sender does not expect a response from the receiver, while in the latter, the sender expects an immediate response.

Managers can communicate with subordinates through written, verbal, nonverbal, and electronic means. Each of these has advantages and disadvantages that must be taken into account before the manager decides which one to use.

Organizations have three primary communication channels. Formal downward channels direct communication from bosses to subordinates through the formal chain of command. They include company newsletters, bulletin boards, policy manuals, memos, job instructions, pay inserts, and loudspeakers. Formal upward channels direct communication from subordinates to bosses and also follow the formal chain of command. They include suggestion systems, an open-door policy, grievance procedures, attitude surveys, special meetings, an ombudsman, and the exit interview. Informal communication channels are not recognized by the formal organization but are nevertheless very important. There are two types of informal channels: lateral (communication between people at the same level in the organization), and diagonal (communication between individuals at different levels in the organization who are not in a superior-subordinate relationship). The grapevine is a prime example of an informal communication channel.

Within the broad categories of downward, upward, lateral, and diagonal communication, there are specific communication networks. The circle, wheel, chain, Y, and all-channel networks are examples. Research on the impact of communication networks reveals that for simple tasks, the speed and accuracy of communication are highest in the wheel, Y, and all-channel networks, and lowest in the circle and chain networks. For complex tasks the reverse is generally true. Employee satisfaction is highest in the circle, Y, and chain networks, and lowest in the wheel network, regardless of task complexity.

Numerous barriers to communication exist in organizations. Organizational barriers are those caused by the nature and functioning of the organization. They include filtering (the loss of meaning that occurs as a message moves through the management hierarchy), status differences (communication between people with differing status may not be clear), differing departmental objectives (each department thinks that its activity is the most important in the organization), specialization of labour (individuals with different training may have difficulty communicating with each other), time pressures (communication may be hasty or ill-advised), and information overload (managers receive more information than they can process).

Individual barriers to communication include emotions, language and cultural differences, differing perceptions, stereotyping, defence mechanisms, the halo effect, semantics, lack of trust, and selecting the wrong channels for communication.

Several techniques exist to help managers overcome the organizational and individual barriers to communication. These include listening actively, regulating the flow of information to avoid overload, encouraging feedback from message recipients, simplifying the content of messages, restraining emotions, making certain that verbal and nonverbal cues are consistent, and using the grapevine.

KEY TERMS

communication (p. 430)
communication process (p. 431)
source (p. 432)
encoding (p. 432)
communication channel (p. 432)
decoding (p. 433)
receiver (p. 433)
feedback (p. 433)
noise (p. 433)
nonverbal communication (p. 436)
body language (p. 436)
e-mail (p. 436)
voice mail (p. 436)
one-way communication (p. 438)
two-way communication (p. 438)
formal downward communication channels (p. 438)
formal upward communication channels (p. 440)
informal communication channels (p. 441)
lateral communication (p. 441)
diagonal communication (p. 441)
communication network (p. 442)
communication barrier (p. 443)
organizational communication barriers (p. 443)
filtering (p. 444)
information overload (p. 444)
individual communication barriers (p. 445)
emotions (p. 445)
perception (p. 445)
selective perception (p. 447)
stereotyping (p. 447)
defence mechanisms (p. 447)
halo effect (p. 447)
semantics (p. 447)
marginal listening (p. 449)
evaluative listening (p. 449)
nonevaluative listening (p. 449)
active listening (p. 449)
empathy (p. 449)

REVIEW QUESTIONS

1. What are the basic elements in the communication process?
2. What is "noise" in communication terms?
3. How are the general communication model and the superior-subordinate communications model similar? How are they different?
4. What are the advantages and disadvantages of one-way and two-way communication?
5. How are formal downward and formal upward communication channels different? Give examples of each.
6. Describe several criteria which must be satisfied to make upward communication meaningful.
7. What are the two informal communication channels? How do they differ?
8. List and briefly describe the organizational and individual barriers to communication.
9. What is stereotyping? How does it influence the communication process?
10. What is the halo effect? How does it influence the communication process?
11. Describe five techniques for overcoming barriers to communication.
12. Define each of the following terms, and give an example of each one:
    a. marginal listening
    b. evaluative listening
    c. nonevaluative listening
    d. active listening

DISCUSSION QUESTIONS

1. Why is communication so critical ... manager's job?
2. What do... tion n...
3. If you ... use the ... agerial e...
4. You have ... sition of v... porate com... to improve ... nization. W... cific.
5. "Written com... preferable to fa... because in writ... sender can caref... convey the mes... Defend your answ...
6. "Managers should ... open when commu... subordinates." Com...

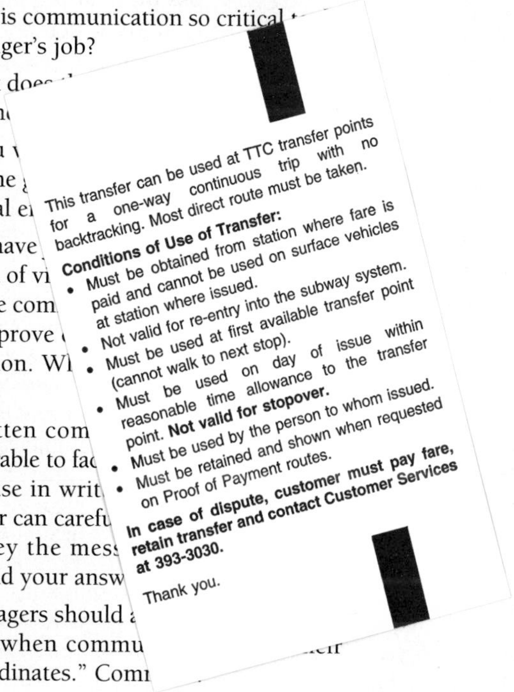

This transfer can be used at TTC transfer points for a one-way continuous trip with no backtracking. Most direct route must be taken.
Conditions of Use of Transfer:
• Must be obtained from station where fare is paid and cannot be used on surface vehicles at station where issued.
• Not valid for re-entry into the subway system.
• Must be used at first available transfer point (cannot walk to next stop).
• Must be used on day of issue within reasonable time allowance to the transfer point. Not valid for stopover.
• Must be used by the person to whom issued.
• Must be retained and shown when requested on Proof of Payment routes.
In case of dispute, customer must pay fare, retain transfer and contact Customer Services at 393-3030.
Thank you.

7. There is often inconsistency between a person's verbal comments and his or her body language. From your own recent experience, describe and analyze such a situation.

EXERCISES

1. Interview a manager from an organization of your choice. Ask the manager to indicate:
   a. the major barriers to communication that he or she regularly experiences
   b. how these barriers are overcome
2. Look out the window and observe what is going on outside the classroom for one minute. Prepare a two-minute talk to be delivered to the class. After two presentations, determine the differences that exist and why they exist.
3. Think back over your previous day's experiences and write down all the barriers to effective communication you can think of, as well as an example which illustrates each barrier. Discuss several of the examples in class.

MANAGEMENT ON LOCATION

CASE 14-1
BE CAREFUL WHO YOU TALK TO!

Jill McMahon took a job with Spantex Corporation upon graduation from community college. Spantex actively recruited in community colleges, and was very happy with the kind of graduates they hired the last few years. Last year the firm hired 27 community college grads across Canada. McMahon was assigned to the Vancouver branch.

Immediately upon her arrival at the branch, McMahon began a training program that was designed to prepare her to be an assistant branch manager at the end of two years. This training had two components. The first was on-the-job training in all phases of the company's operations, including shipping, receiving, inventory control, sales and service, and production. This training was supervised by the branch manager. The second type of training was classroom training which was done at the Toronto head office. During this training, McMahon received additional information about how the company operated. She also met with members of upper management who reviewed her job progress.

Jim Konstanty, the branch manager in Vancouver, was 55 years old and had been with Spantex for 30 years. He had not attended college but had worked his way up through the firm. He was well known in the Vancouver branch for his view that the company's policy of hiring college grads and training them for two years was not a worthwhile way of developing management talent. In his view, people should have to work their way up through the ranks over a period of years just as he had done.

Under Konstanty's direction, McMahon did only some of the activities called for in the management training program. McMahon felt that much of her training was very spur-of-the-moment, and that Konstanty was using her mainly to run errands. As time went on, she became increasingly concerned that she was not receiving adequate training, and that she would not be ready to be an assistant branch manager when her training program was completed.

Nine months after she joined Spantex, McMahon made her third visit to Toronto for the next phase in her classroom training program. During the scheduled discussions with the head office managers who supervised training, McMahon mentioned her concerns about the poor quality of training she was receiving to Dick Donovan, the training director. She did not speak negatively about Konstanty, but focussed on her concerns that she would not be helpful to the company if her training didn't improve. Donovan was very interested and said that he would follow up on her concerns.

On her first day back in Vancouver, McMahon was called in to Konstanty's office and the following conversation took place:

Konstanty (aggressively): Why did you tell Donovan that I'm not doing my job out here? Things are going very well in this branch. Let's get some things straight up front. Most importantly, you work for me, not Donovan. I will not have you undermining my position in this company! I've worked 30 years to get to this position, and I'm not going to have some hot-shot 22-year-old telling me how to run this branch. Do I make myself clear?

McMahon (hesitantly): Mr. Konstanty, I don't want to make any trouble for you. I am honestly trying to do a good job here. But I'm very concerned that I won't be ready to be an assistant branch manager when my training program is over. I feel that I need to know much more about branch operations than I've been exposed to so far.

Konstanty (still aggressive): You *will* learn about this company if you just follow my directions. I have many years of experience that you can benefit from if you will just take the time to listen to what I tell you. Don't be in such a big hurry to get promoted to assistant branch manager.

McMahon (cautious but determined): My concern is that the company training program is not being carried out the way that head office has stipulated. That's going to be very bad for me later on when I'll be expected to know certain things, but I won't know them. That will hurt my career.

Konstanty (exploding): Don't tell me how to run the training program! Those guys in Toronto sit there on the 45th floor dreaming up all sorts of schemes that won't work. Out here in the branches we know what works and what doesn't.

McMahon: What would you like me to do?

Konstanty (calm, but intense): Let me give you a piece of advice. It is unwise to make your boss look bad. People who do that often find that their career takes a definite turn for the worse. Do I make myself clear?

McMahon: Yes.

After the interview, McMahon returned to her office in a very anxious state of mind. She knew that Konstanty had rejected every concern she had raised. She also knew that he expected her to do exactly as he told her, and that if he heard any additional word from head office about the training program, that she would be in big trouble. Yet she knew that the present situation was intolerable and that if she didn't try to alter it, her career would be damaged. ▲

QUESTIONS

1. Should Dick Donovan have told Konstanty about Jill McMahon's concerns about the training she was receiving? Defend your answer.
2. Comment on the state of communications between the Toronto head office and the Vancouver branch.
3. What kind of "noise" is evident in the conversation between Konstanty and McMahon?
4. What should Jill McMahon do now?

CASE 14-2
A CASE OF GOOD INTENTIONS

Treeline Paper Ltd. employed 300 people. Management had always prided itself on the good relations that existed between the company and its employees. A strike had never taken place, and relations with the union were good.

The president of Treeline, Alex Kellner, had formed an executive committee that met every Tuesday morning to discuss specific issues facing management. These meetings also served to improve communications between managers since this was the only time they had the opportunity to meet together. At the most recent meeting, the committee was discussing how valuable the meetings had been and suggested that the company should examine ways of improving communication with the employees as well. One manager related an experience that seemed to sum up the lack of communication with the employees: he had recently been talking with one employee who did not know who the president of the company was.

After considerable discussion, it was agreed that Treeline would embark on a program to improve communications with employees. Several ideas were put forth, and the executive committee eventually decided to start with a simple campaign which would give employees some basic statistics about the company and its operations. The centrepiece of this campaign would be three time series graphs which would summarize company operations. These graphs would show total sales, inventory levels, and total employment. The graphs would be updated weekly.

A memo was sent to all employees indicating that this decision had been made. Employees were encouraged to consult the graphs and to become better informed about the company they worked for.

• • •

After several months, the graphs looked like those below.

About this time, Kellner had a visit from the president of the union. He was very agitated, and said that the union wanted to open up the job security clause of the collective agreement. Several supervisors also reported a noticeable drop in employee morale. One day in the cafeteria, several employees confronted Kellner and demanded to speak to him about the rumour they had heard that the plant would be closing soon. ▲

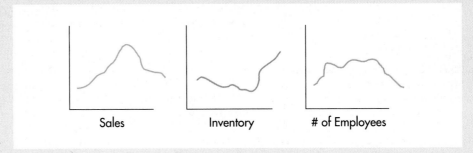

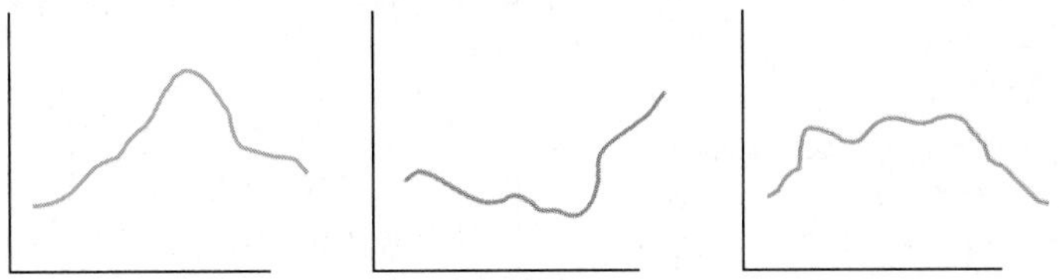

QUESTIONS

1. What has gone wrong here?
2. Using concepts introduced in the chapter, make suggestions about what Kellner should do now.

CASE 14-3
But I Just Need to Complete This Training Course!

Vincent Carletti was a regional sales manager at Electro-Lite Ltd. As part of his regular duties, he monitored the performance of nine salespeople who reported to him. The salespeople had quotas to reach during each six-month period.

Late one afternoon, Carletti's secretary informed him that Randall Lane had arrived for his performance appraisal. Carletti had mixed feelings about Lane. He was pleasant, hard working, and enthusiastic, but his sales performance had been a continual problem since he had been hired two years ago. At the last performance appraisal six months ago, Carletti had informed Lane that if his sales didn't improve, he would have to let him go. Since that meeting, Lane's sales had continued to be below standard, and Carletti had decided to fire him. Carletti therefore had the unpleasant task of informing Lane that he was going to release him as of next month. Carletti found himself getting annoyed as he anticipated his meeting with Lane. Lane was always very calm at these meetings, but Carletti felt that he had trouble accepting reality.

Carletti asked Lane to step into his office, and the following conversation took place:

Carletti: Randy, I'll get right to the point. You've been with us for two years now, and you continue to have difficulty achieving the sales quotas that have been set for you. You know we have a policy that failure to reach your quota for three appraisal periods means that you must be let go. I don't believe that your performance is going to improve much, so I think it's best if you start looking for another position.

Lane (calmly): I admit I've been having trouble lately, but I believe I can increase my sales enough so that you'll want to keep me on.

Carletti: Randy, I just don't think it's going to work out. Your performance simply hasn't been sufficient to warrant keeping you on.

Lane (still calmly): But I know I can fix things. I've been working very hard on the sales training program I'm attending. Once I finish that, my sales will go up. I just know it.

Carletti (getting slightly annoyed): Even if you do complete the training

• • •

MANAGEMENT ON LOCATION

program, it won't make any difference. That program simply sharpens up basic skills that you already have. You don't have those basic skills, so taking a training course will not solve your problem.

Lane (remaining calm): But once I complete the training program, I will have a whole new outlook on my job. That will solve the problem, won't it?

Carletti (getting angry): No, it won't solve the problem! Forget about the training program. You're just kidding yourself. I'm interested in your sales performance, not whether you complete a training program. If you don't perform. I have to let you go. It's as simple as that.

Lane (remaining calm): But once I complete the training program, things will be different. I don't feel that it's reasonable to fire me when I'm so close to completing the training program.

Carletti (totally exasperated): I give up! You can sit there all day pretending everything will be fine after you complete the training program, but that won't change reality. I'm sorry, but I'm going to have to let you go. You can pick up your severance cheque from personnel in a few weeks. ▲

QUESTIONS

1. What mistakes did Vincent Carletti make in communicating with Randall Lane?
2. Why does Lane not understand what Carletti is saying?
3. How should Carletti have dealt with Lane?

CHAPTER

15

CONFLICT, CHANGE, AND STRESS IN ORGANIZATIONS

LEARNING OBJECTIVES

After reading this chapter, you will be able to:

1. Describe four perspectives on conflict.
2. List the three views of conflict.
3. Explain why conflict develops, and identify the various structural and interpersonal means of resolving conflict.
4. Understand the four basic types of change that are introduced in organizations.
5. Describe the manager's role in the change sequence.
6. Outline the reasons people resist change and the ways to reduce the resistance.
7. Define stress, and describe the factors that contribute to it.

MANAGEMENT CHALLENGE

A TALE OF TWO CITIES

Petrocan is a gasoline retailer with outlets across Canada. It recently embarked on a plan to boost sales volume while closing many of its retail outlets. Obviously, this will require a sharp increase in the volume of gasoline sales at the remaining outlets. In Toronto, the effort to introduce this major change is going badly, with store managers claiming that the company is trying to bully them into accepting the change. In Vancouver, on the other hand, the change is proceeding fairly smoothly. Dealers in other centres across Canada are closely watching the unfolding events.

Petrocan is trying to cope with an industry-wide problem: too many retail outlets chasing too few consumer dollars. The corporate plan is to attract new customers by providing them with a "retail shopping experience." This means that customers can not only fill up with gas, they can also buy things like chocolate bars, coffee, soft drinks, and sandwiches. This, in turn, means that employees must learn new merchandising attitudes and skills. Petrocan also intends to shift some costs and risks to individual gas station operators. Head office personnel in Calgary recognize that the proposed changes are dramatic, and that individual dealers may be anxious about the future.

The plan is being resisted in Toronto partly because competition is severe. There are more than 1000 gas stations in the metropolitan area (Petrocan has 240 of these), and dealers cannot see how they are going to meet Petrocan's new volume goals. The company wants to reduce the number of its stations to 150 and increase the average volume per station to 5.5 million litres of gasoline per year (the average Petrocan station currently sells about 3 million).

• • •

But concerns about competition are only part of the problem. Toronto dealers feel that they are being kept in the dark about the strategy that will be used to reach the new volume goals. Station dealers also say they are under pressure of being dropped by the company if they fail to meet the new sales volume goals. They complain that they are being pushed around by company managers and say that there is no empathy for their concerns about the future. They say that when they raise questions at meetings, they are simply told they must "buy into" the new plan.

One sore point in the change is the "performance agent contract." This contract is an attempt by Petrocan to standardize its relations with its retailers, but some see it as an attempt to shift more costs to retailers and limit their margins. Under the contract, lessees would have to pay different rents for things like gas pumps and mechanical service bays. They would also have to pay a fee for the right to sell merchndise and would have to contribute more cash toward funding their inventories. ▲

The Management Challenge demonstrates the close relationship among the three topics that are the focus of this chapter—conflict, change, and stress. Petrocan's attempt to introduce a major change (increasing sales volume and closing retail gas stations) has caused a conflict between the company and its retailers. As a result, the gas station operators are experiencing stress and are anxious about the future. They are resisting the change because they have not been told how it will affect them, and because they feel that their economic livelihood is threatened.

In this chapter, we address these three interrelated concepts. We first define organizational conflict, note the differing views of conflict that exist, and describe several techniques that are available to managers to help them manage conflict. In the second section of the chapter, we discuss organizational change, describe the sequence of events involved in change, note the reasons why people resist change, and offer suggestions on how to reduce resistance to change. The final section of the chapter looks at stress and executive burnout, and includes suggestions on how organizations can help individuals cope with these problems.

ORGANIZATIONAL CONFLICT

conflict

Conflict occurs when (1) individuals or groups have incompatible goals, and (2) these individuals or groups block each other's goal attainment.[1] This blocking may be passive or active. Passive blocking occurs, for example, on a sequential production line where the output of one group is the input for another group. If the first group neglects its job, the second group will be prevented from reaching its targeted level of output. On the other hand, two professional boxers trying to knock each other out demonstrates the concept of active blocking.

TYPES OF CONFLICT

Type I conflict

Three kinds of conflict can be identified, based on the stage at which blocking occurs (see Figure 15-1). **Type I conflict** exists when one party blocks another party's attempts to obtain the resources that the other party needs to achieve its goals (see Figure 15-1a). For example, in the annual budgeting process, the marketing department (unit B) may have a powerful representative on the board of directors who is able to get funds diverted to marketing and away from production (unit A).

Type II conflict

Type II conflict exists when the blocking behaviour occurs at the activity stage instead of the resource-attainment stage. (See Figure 15-1b). For example, a construction crew that pours foundations (unit B) may do its job so poorly that the carpenters (unit A) cannot build on the foundation. This prevents the carpenters from achieving their goals.

FIGURE 15-1 THREE TYPES OF CONFLICT.

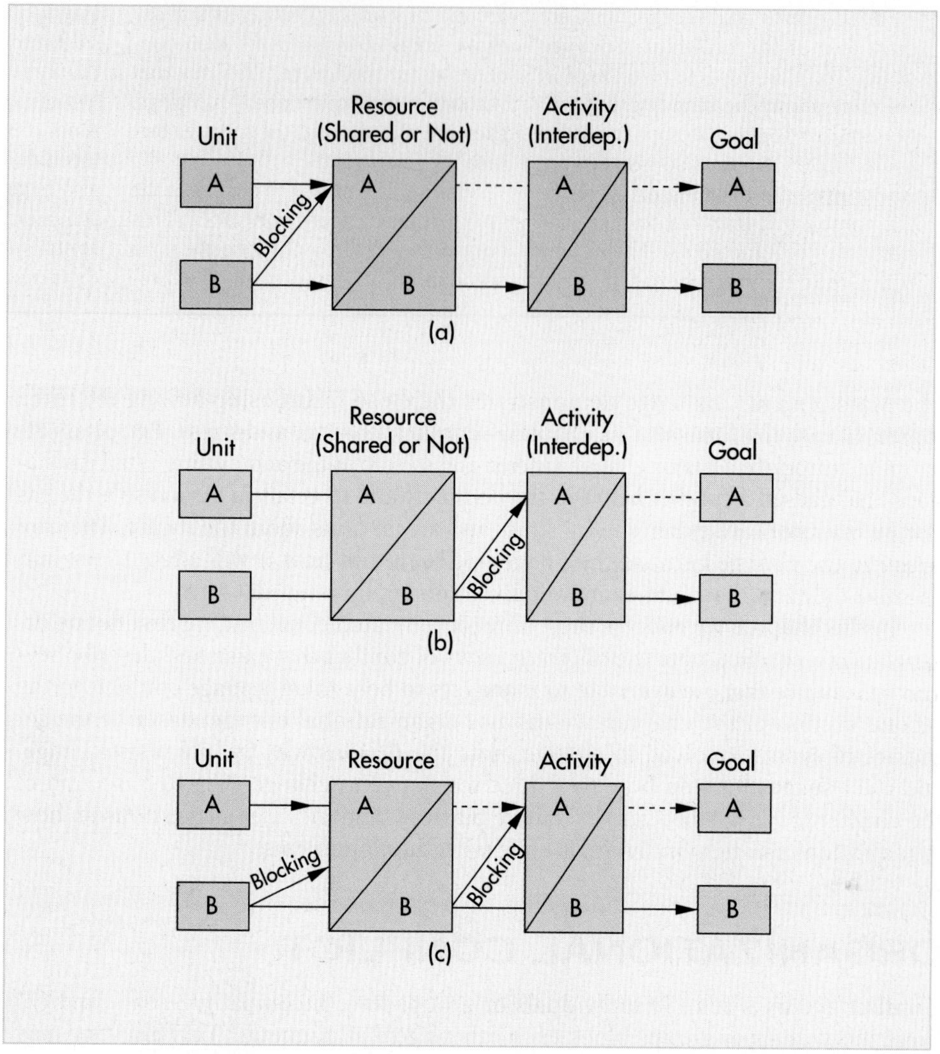

Type III conflict

Type III conflict occurs when interference occurs at both the resource-attainment and activity stages. (See Figure 15-1c). Thus, the marketing department in the example of Type I conflict might also interfere with the production department by demanding that production alter its schedule and activity to accommodate a special order.

LEARNING OBJECTIVE 1
Describe four perspectives on conflict.

PERSPECTIVES IN CONFLICT ANALYSIS

Conflict can be analyzed from various perspectives, ranging from that of the individual to that of the organization.

Intraindividual Conflict

intraindividual conflict

Intraindividual conflict (also called role conflict) is that which occurs within a single person. Someone may experience such a conflict when faced with certain dilemmas at work, for example being required to act in a way he or she feels is immoral, or receiving conflicting demands from two different bosses. We discuss role conflict later in this chapter.

Interpersonal Conflict

Interpersonal conflict refers to conflict between individuals. This type of conflict can arise between co-workers, between bosses and subordinates, or between individuals in different organizations. Research on this type of conflict often focusses on personality differences, and the reasons why individuals try to block each other's goal attainment.

interpersonal conflict

Individual-Group Conflict

Individual-group conflict refers to conflict between a single person and a group of people. It happens basically in two instances: (1) when what an individual wishes to do (e.g., produce a great deal of output) is at odds with what the group norm dictates (e.g., restriction of output); and (2) when what a boss wants (e.g., obedience from subordinates) differs from what a group of subordinates wants (e.g., job freedom). In both cases, the group usually gets its way, because it is more able to block the goal attainment of the individual than vice versa.

individual-group conflict

Intergroup Conflict

Intergroup conflict refers to conflict between two groups of people. Included in this category is interdepartmental conflict within an organization and conflict between organizations. Examples of intergroup conflict include labour-management disputes (see the Management at Work insert "Conflict in the Automotive Industry"), United Nations debates, wars, marketplace conflict by firms trying to outdo each other, elections, and conflicts between departments for an increased share of the organization's budget.

intergroup conflict

MANAGEMENT AT WORK

Conflict in The Automotive Industry

The CAMI Automotive Inc. plant—a 50-50 joint venture between General Motors of Canada and Suzuki Motor Co.—is situated among the farms around Ingersoll, Ontario. CAMI—a Japanese word meaning god or deity—is an attempt to replace the traditional union-management conflict with union-management cooperation. All personnel at the plant wear a name tag and a white shirt and blue slacks (or skirt). Mutual trust between management and labour is emphasized, and there is a formal commitment to excellence. The plant is characterized by worker self-management, simplified job classifications, and streamlined work rules.

Many personnel are positive about the way things are done, but others point to substantial problems at the plant. For example, the plant is suffering the usual start-up difficulties; five months after its inception, it was operating at only 50 percent of capacity. Other, more specific problems are also evident. Production troubles in the paint shop were resolved only after Japanese trainers left in defeat after having failed to get work teams to function as planned. Worker input is often limited, and minor requests can take a long time to be dealt with. For example, a request for picnic tables for summertime breaks took weeks to resolve. There was also a conflict between management and labour regarding the colour of worker sweatshirts for cold weather; labour wanted blue and management wanted white.

The Canadian Auto Workers (CAW) union is on record as opposing such partnerships between workers and management. At its National Council Meeting in Port Elgin, Ontario, in 1989, delegates passed an antipartnership resolution that condemned the "new order of labour relations" and signalled that it intends to revive the militancy and conflict that have characterized labour-management relations for many years.

In the 1980s, the idea of labour-management partnerships took industry by storm. It was believed that the adversarial, top-down approach could be replaced by cooperation and an era of labour peace. The idea gained strength partly because of the arrival of mostly nonunion Japanese automobile operations, offshore competition, and the closure of some Canadian automobile plants. The CAW statement is the first counterattack on this movement.

In spite of the opposition, the union worked with Suzuki to bring the CAMI plant to Ontario. Perhaps the traditional adversarial relationship between union and management can be overcome with the use of Japanese management techniques such as those being applied at CAMI. ▲

Conflict versus Competition

competition

The terms conflict and competition are often mistakenly used interchangeably. **Competition** occurs when individuals or groups have incompatible goals, but do not interfere with each other's efforts at attaining goals. The difference between conflict and competition is easily seen if we compare a track and field race and a boxing match.[2] In a race, the runners have incompatible goals (they both can't win the race), but they do not interfere with each other during the race. In a boxing match, the boxers not only have incompatible goals, but they also try to interfere with each other.

The distinction between conflict and competition is also relevant for managerial activities. Competition occurs, for example, when salespeople get involved in a sales contest where the winner gets a trip to Hawaii. Conflict occurs when different organizations try to convince consumers to buy their product instead of their competitor's product. If we make this distinction, it means that what is normally called "competition" in the business world is really conflict.

Three Views of Conflict

LEARNING OBJECTIVE 2
List the three views of conflict.

Over time, three distinct views about conflict have developed: the traditional view, the human relations view, and the interactionist view.[3]

The Traditional View

traditional view of conflict

The **traditional view of conflict** assumes that conflict is *bad* for organizations and that its existence is proof that there are problems within the organization. This view says that organizational performance declines as the level of conflict increases (see the dotted line in Figure 15-2); it must therefore be avoided at all costs. The sometimes violent confrontations that occurred between labour and management, for example, led many people to conclude that conflict was detrimental and should be avoided.

During the 1988 federal election campaign, Concerned Citizens About Free Trade (CCAFT) carried out a massive educational campaign warning Canadians about the dangers the CCAFT saw in the free-trade agreement. Individual-group and intergroup conflicts occurred when the opposing groups confronted each other.

FIGURE 15-2 TWO VIEWS OF CONFLICT.

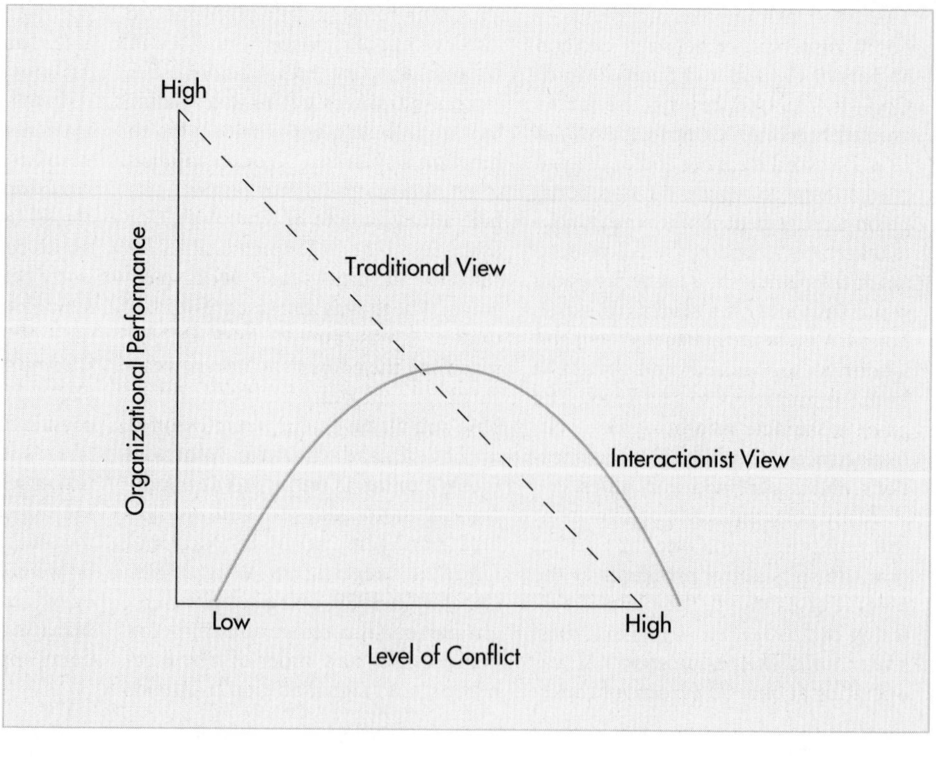

The traditional view of conflict is widely held because the institutions which have a strong influence in our society—home, church, and school—typically support it.[4] In the home, for example, parents suppress conflict between their children by ordering them to stop fighting. In schools, conflict is suppressed by rules governing student behaviour, and by the creation of a climate in which the teacher is presumed to know all the answers and the students are not allowed to argue with the teacher. Most churches stress brotherhood and peace, not conflict.

Because conflict was viewed in a negative light, attention was given to reducing, suppressing, or eliminating it. While tactics like these have sometimes worked, they have not generally been effective because (1) the cause of the conflict is ignored, and (2) some of the positive aspects of conflict fail to emerge.

The Human Relations View

human relations view of conflict

The **human relations view of conflict** assumes that conflict is a *normal* part of organizational life, and it may have either a positive or negative effect (see Table 15-1). If managers accept this perspective, they will expect conflict even if they have carefully defined the work of their employees, and treat their subordinates well. The manager's job is to actively manage any conflicts that arise. The solid line in Figure 15-2 represents this view of conflict.

The Interactionist View

interactionist view of conflict

The **interactionist view of conflict** assumes that conflict is *necessary* if an organization hopes to perform well. Managers who adopt this outlook may actually have to stimulate conflict in certain situations. The solid line in Figure 15-2 is also consistent with this view of conflict.

According to both the human relations and interactionist views, there is an optimal level of conflict which maximizes organizational performance. An organization without conflict has little impetus for innovation and change because employees are too comfortable and unconcerned about improving their performance. One laboratory study demonstrated this point very clearly.[5] The experimental groups had a "planted" member whose job was to challenge the majority view of the group. The control groups had no such member. In all cases, the experimental groups developed better solutions than the control groups. Interestingly, when given the chance to drop a group member, all of the experimental groups wanted to drop the planted member.

TABLE 15-1 POSITIVE AND NEGATIVE FEATURES OF CONFLICT.

Positive Features	Negative Features
1. The energy level of groups or individuals increases with conflict.	1. The increased energy level of groups or individuals may manifest itself in nonproductive ways (e.g., hostility and aggression).
2. Group cohesion increases.	2. Increased group cohesion may cause intense resistance to change.
3. Problems are made known during conflict, and information relevant to the conflict is mobilized.	3. Communication between the conflicting parties declines, so information relevant to the conflict may never be shared between the parties.
4. Conflict motivates groups to clarify the objectives and values they think are important.	4. There is excessive conformity to group demands and views, and no solutions to the conflict may be forthcoming.
5. Conflict forces groups and individuals to adapt to changing environmental conditions.	5. The desire to win may be so intense that no one adapts to changing environmental demands, even if it means that the group's very existence is threatened by failure to adapt.

Conflict Management

conflict management

Since some of the conflict in organizations may be good (because it stimulates people to seek improvements), the management of conflict is a key managerial activity. **Conflict management** involves intervention by managers to increase or decrease the level of conflict that is evident.[6] It encourages constructive conflict and discourages destructive conflict.[7] The most practical criterion for determining whether conflict is good or bad is whether or not organizational goals are attained.[8] Organizations exist to achieve goals, so conflict which facilitates the achievement of goals should be encouraged, and conflict which impedes goal attainment should be discouraged.

Stimulating Conflict

Management can stimulate conflict in five ways.

1. *Accept conflict as desirable on certain occasions*[9] For example, it may be wise to tolerate the sales department's efforts to block the production department's goal of producing a limited number of products because these actions better serve the customer, thus making the firm as a whole better off.
2. *Bring new individuals into an existing situation* Thoughtful questions and comments from newcomers may force long-time members to see new ways of doing things.
3. *Restructure the organization* The new reporting relationships which develop will create some uncertainty, but they will also motivate employees to discover innovative procedures.
4. *Introduce programs which are designed to increase conflict* If an automobile company introduces a sales competition, the various dealers in a given area may come into conflict with each other as they try to reach their goal, but overall sales for the company will probably increase.
5. *Introduce programmed conflict*[10] The "devil's advocate" role (see Chapter 9) and "dialectical inquiry" (see Chapter 6) are both designed to program conflict into the process of managerial decision making and make conflict legitimate.

A Model of Conflict

LEARNING OBJECTIVE 3

Explain why conflict develops, and identify the various structural and interpersonal means of resolving conflict.

Figure 15-3 presents a model of conflict. The model indicates that various sources of conflict lead to goal incompatibility between individuals or groups in an organization. When an individual or group interferes with another individual or group, open conflict develops. Once conflict is out in the open, various interpersonal or structural conflict resolution techniques can be used. Depending on how well the conflict is managed, a functional or dysfunctional resolution occurs.

Sources of Conflict

Conflict can be caused by any one of the following factors:

1. *Limited resources* The demands made upon organizational resources typically exceed the supply of such resources.
2. *Interdependent work activities* Employees must interact to accomplish their work; during this interaction, conflict may develop.
3. *Differentiation of work activities* Each person or group focusses on a specific activity; conflict may develop regarding the relative importance of activities.
4. *Communication problems* People misinterpret what is being said to them and conflict develops.

FIGURE 15-3 THE CONFLICT MODEL.

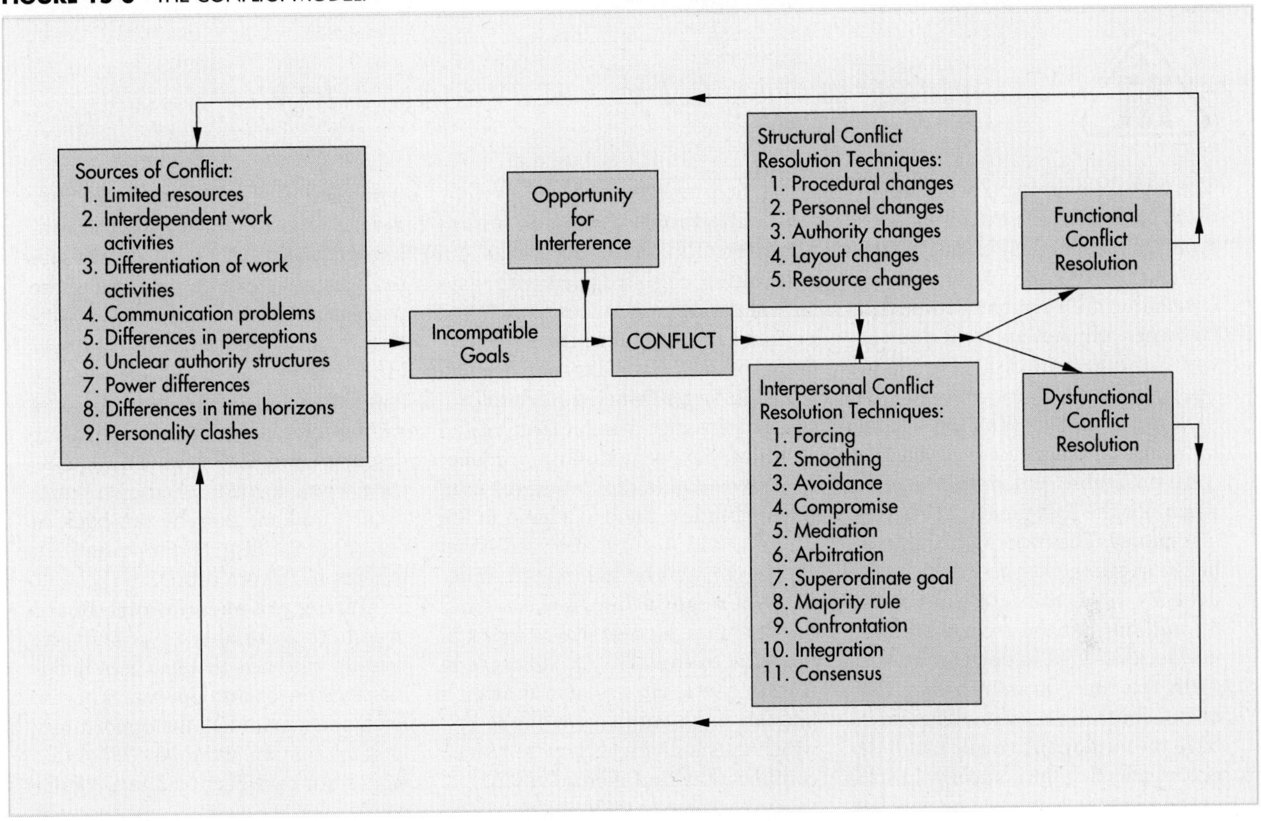

5. *Differences in perceptions* Each person sees the world in a unique way; different views cause conflict.
6. *Unclear authority structures* People don't know how far their authority extends and conflicts develop at the margin.
7. *Power differences* If one group is more powerful than another, this can cause conflict.
8. *Differences in time horizons* Some departments have a long-term view, while others have a short-term view; conflict may develop regarding the importance of each view.
9. *Personality clashes* The fact is that some people simply don't like each other and this may cause conflict.

Conflict

When the sources of conflict lead to incompatible goals, and when there is opportunity for interference, open conflict develops. We saw earlier that three different types of conflict can emerge depending on when blocking behaviour occurs.

Resolution

Once open conflict has developed, managers must decide how it should be resolved. The techniques for resolving conflict may be either interpersonal or structural. The Management at Work insert "Conflict at CTV" describes one interpersonal technique.

MANAGEMENT AT WORK

CONFLICT AT THE CTV TELEVISION NETWORK

The CTV Television Network was set up as a co-op in the early 1960s by a group of independent broadcasters in order to buy U.S. programming. Originally, CTV bought airtime from its owner-affiliates and sold them advertising time. Any cash left over after operating costs were covered went back to the affiliates. This worked fine for nearly 30 years because operations were profitable. But problems arose when, for the first time in 1990, CTV lost money. The owner-affiliates then began haggling over how to share the debt. By 1992, the debt had risen to $5 million, but the owners still had not decided what to do about it.

By this time, the issue had become one of control, i.e., who was going to have the authority to make major decisions affecting the company. In spite of the fact that individual owners had differing numbers of stations, each of the eight owners had one vote, as well as veto power at board meetings. Thus, Newfoundland Broadcasting Company Ltd., with just 1 station, had as much power as Doug Bassett's Baton Broadcasting, which had 11 stations. Bassett felt the network needed a controlling shareholder—him. He made attempts to buy out his partners, but no agreements were reached.

John Cassaday, CEO of CTV, says that there were no serious personality conflicts among the people on the board. Rather, the shareholders (some of whom were independently wealthy) were simply not in awe of anyone. They each had their own ideas about how things should be done.

To help resolve this conflict, CTV first called in Toronto consultant Heather Reisman of Paradigm Consulting. She struggled with ways to heal the wounds for over a year, but couldn't quite achieve the necessary compromises. Cassaday then decided to call in Roger Fisher, a Harvard professor who also runs a firm called Conflict Management Group. Fisher has a worldwide reputation for conflict resolution. He had a hand in the Camp David Accords between Israel and Egypt, and he has trained diplomats in negotiation in the former Soviet Union. He also played a part in the talks to free the U.S. hostages in Iran in 1981. He has also written a popular book entitled *Getting to Yes,* which tells individuals how to reduce conflicts they find themselves in.

Fisher came to CTV as a mediator. All eight owners sat down at the table together and bid against each other to put up equity. Cassaday tried to reduce the tension by putting a baseball cap bearing the words "CTV Ownership Championships" on each chair in the boardroom. Fisher wore a black-and-white striped referee's outfit. The bidding went through three rounds, and at the end only five of the eight owners remained. Western International Communication Ltd., CFCF Inc., and Maclean Hunter Ltd. had each put up $6 million, while Moffatt Communications and Electrohome Ltd. each put up $1 million.

To reach this landmark agreement, CTV's board members had to change the way they went about disputing with each other. The basic plan they agreed to is found in Fisher's well-known book. Fisher essentially says that disputes can be resolved if the parties will consider each other's interests instead of positions. The specific technique used to resolve conflicts is called Alternative Dispute Resolution (ADR). Instead of fighting disputes using lawyers, the disputants themselves negotiate their own settlements, and are thereby put back in control of the dispute. Empowerment is a key buzzword in ADR.

During the negotiations, board members were able to unload the pent-up bitterness that had been building since the boardroom battles began. Each participant had the opportunity to speak frankly, and to say things that would not have been said in a regular courtroom. As well, the process was private, so the company didn't have to air its dirty linen in public. The participants agreed that Fisher had a real knack for keeping the discussions on track, and for moderating a meeting with eight feisty individuals. Although Fisher was highly paid, the participants got a shareholder's agreement and a refinancing agreement within three months of starting negotiations. With its wounds on the mend, CTV can presumably get back to business.

CTV is one of the most visible Canadian firms to use ADR. But many firms in the U.S. have pledged to use ADR before going to court to resolve their disputes. In Canada, there are two government-funded ADR centres, one in B.C. and the other in Quebec. ▲

Structural conflict resolution techniques

structural conflict resolution techniques

Structural conflict resolution techniques focus on the structural features of the organization that may be causing the conflict. These techniques are based on the idea that certain structural aspects of organizations can create conflict even if the individuals behave in a reasonable fashion (see Table 15-2).

TABLE 15-2 STRUCTURAL CONFLICT RESOLUTION TECHNIQUES.

Technique	Description	Example
1. Procedural changes	Work procedures are changed to resolve the conflict.	A sales manager argues that a credit manager is cancelling too many deals for credit reasons. The dispute is resolved by involving the credit manager earlier in the process of selling.
2. Personnel changes	Individuals are transferred into or out of a department in order to resolve personality clashes.	A personality clash between two high-performing workers is disrupting departmental productivity. One of the workers is transferred to another department, and both workers are now able to make a positive contribution to the organization.
3. Authority changes	Authority lines are changed or clarified to reduce conflict.	The head of industrial engineering complains that production managers do not listen to his advice about new high-tech machinery. The head of industrial engineering is given functional authority over the production managers on the issue of new machinery purchases.
4. Layout changes	The work space is rearranged to resolve conflict.	Two work groups harass each other continually. A wall is built between the two groups so they can no longer interact.
5. Resource changes	Resources are expanded so that the disputing parties can each have what they want.	The dean of a business school gets a commitment from the provincial government for funds to hire additional faculty members. This reduces the dispute between department heads because they each get to hire two more faculty members.

Interpersonal Conflict Resolution Techniques

interpersonal conflict resolution techniques

Interpersonal conflict resolution techniques focus on the human interaction in a conflict. These techniques are premised on the idea that conflict is very much influenced by the nature of the people in the conflict. Interpersonal conflict resolution techniques are described in Table 15-3.

Several of the techniques listed in Table 15-3 can be compared by analyzing two key dimensions of a conflict: (1) the extent to which each party tries to satisfy its own desires, and (2) the extent to which each party tries to satisfy its opponent's desires. The conflict management techniques are placed in a 2 × 2 matrix based on the relative emphasis of the above dimensions (see Figure 15-4). Forcing, for example, is characterized by a high desire to satisfy oneself and a low desire to satisfy others.

FIGURE 15-4 CONFLICT MANAGEMENT STRATEGIES.

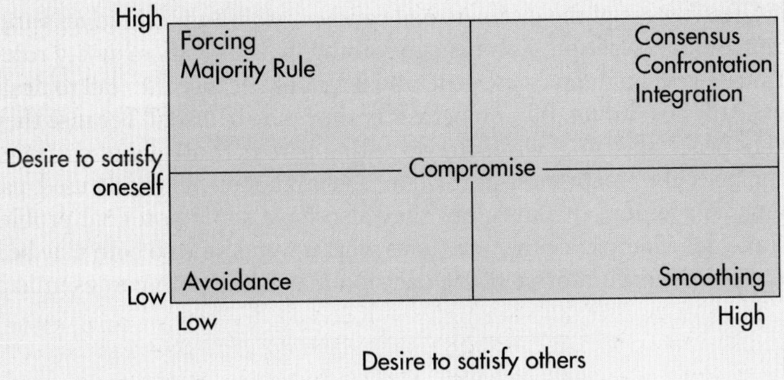

TABLE 15-3 INTERPERSONAL CONFLICT RESOLUTION TECHNIQUES.

Technique	Description	Example
1. Forcing	Managerial authority is used to compel a resolution of the conflict.	A manager orders two disputing subordinates to stop their interpersonal conflict on company time because it is disrupting the work of the department.
2. Smoothing	The manager tries to convince the disputing parties that they really don't have anything to fight about.	A manager tries to calm two disputing subordinates by pointing out all the areas where they are in agreement, and downplaying the one area in which they disagree.
3. Avoidance	The conflicting parties avoid each other.	Two managers who are trying to increase the budget for their respective departments begin avoiding each other because every time they meet they get into an argument.
4. Compromise	Each side gives up some of what it wants in order to resolve the conflict.	During collective bargaining, the union demands a 10 percent increase while management offers only two percent. Eventually they agree on a 6 percent increase.
5. Mediation	A neutral third party tries to help the disputing parties work out a resolution of the conflict.	During a strike, a mediator is called in to help labour and management reach a settlement. The mediator has no authority to force a settlement.
6. Arbitration	A neutral third party imposes a binding resolution on the disputing parties.	An arbitrator imposes a new collective agreement on a company where there has been a major labour-management dispute. The arbitrator's decision is binding on both parties in the dispute.
7. Superordinate goal	An agreed upon goal by the disputing parties is used to override the conflict.	Arab states in the Middle East may not see eye-to-eye on many issues, but they join OPEC to achieve a superordinate goal of high oil prices.
8. Majority rule	The side with the most votes gets its way.	At a committee meeting, a motion to resolve a bitter dispute is passed by a vote of 8-7.
9. Confrontation	The opposing sides openly state their views to each other.	In a marriage counselling session, the husband and wife state how they really feel about each other. Each spouse is likely to hear things they have never heard before.
10. Integration	The disputing parties try to find solutions that generate both their desires so that a "win-win" solution can be developed.	The board of directors of a church resolves a dispute about musical style by having two worship services, one with traditional music, and one with contemporary music.
11. Consensus	The disputing parties must attempt to reach a consensus on what should be done to resolve the conflict.	At a meeting of the new product committee, seven new product ideas are prioritized in order of importance after a three-hour discussion where each person indicates their preferences.

The effectiveness of the interpersonal conflict resolution techniques varies widely, depending on the situation. Forcing, smoothing, withdrawal, majority rule, and the superordinate goal techniques are generally deficient because they fail to deal with the basic cause of the conflict. But, on occasion, they may be useful because they impose a period of peace and quiet while the disputing parties think about their next move.

Techniques like compromise, mediation, and arbitration are widely used, particularly in labour-management disputes, but they also have some potential problems. In a compromise, for example, neither party gets what it wants, and so both may be unhappy. In arbitration, the arbitrator's binding decision may make both parties unhappy.

The interpersonal techniques with the most promise appear to be confrontation, integration, and consensus. Each of these techniques requires the disputing parties to understand the basic causes of the conflict. Once the causes of the conflict are understood, a resolution is more likely.

CONFLICT OUTCOMES

The application of these conflict resolution techniques leads to either functional or dysfunctional outcomes. The two criteria generally used to determine whether an outcome is functional or dysfunctional are (1) the degree of individual or group satisfaction with the outcome, and (2) the organization's performance after the outcome is implemented. An outcome is functional if it satisfies the parties in the conflict and if it leads to increased performance for the organization. An outcome is dysfunctional if it creates dissatisfaction among the disputing parties, makes either one of the parties unhappy, or reduces organizational performance.

Consider a labour-management dispute in which binding arbitration is used to settle the conflict. If the union members are unhappy with the settlement, they may engage in wildcat (unauthorized) strikes, or file more grievances against the company. This will disrupt the smooth functioning of the organization and reduce performance. On the other hand, if both parties are satisfied with the arbitrator's imposed settlement, union members may perform their work without interruption and organizational performance will be high.

ORGANIZATIONAL CHANGE

If there is one term that describes the essence of every manager's job, it is change. Virtually everything a manager does is in some way concerned with implementing change. Hiring a new employee, purchasing a new piece of equipment, and rearranging work stations are just a few of the actions a manager might take. All of these require a knowledge of how to manage change effectively.

Change is a fact of life in any organization, since virtually every time a manager makes a decision some type of change occurs. One study showed that most companies find they must undertake moderate organizational changes at least once a year and major changes every four or five years.[11] The Management Challenge describes a major change being introduced at Petrocan. Marti Smye, president of People Tech Consulting, estimates that 90 percent of Canadian corporations have recently initiated significant changes like a merger, acquisition, restructuring, downsizing, or developing a new corporate strategy.[12]

When change is introduced, some people will be happy and others will be unhappy. When Levi Strauss introduced an "alternative work styles" program in 1990, it embarked on a move away from paying employees on piece rate. Most employees were happy about that, but the top piece-rate producers left the company. GE Canada replaced 22 career levels with 6 career bands for salaried employees. Younger employees like the idea, but some longer-term employees were unhappy about having to step off a structure that provided many levels of status.[13]

The Impetus for Change

The forces that motivate change come from both inside and outside the organization. Some of these forces can be predicted, but others cannot. It is difficult for managers to control the external forces of change, but they can have considerable influence on the internal forces.

External Forces

In Chapter 3, several important factors in the external environment were described (see Figure 3-1). These external forces manifest themselves in hundreds of ways. Consider the following examples:

1. A new product comes on the market unexpectedly and makes a firm's existing product uncompetitive.
2. A negative report in a consumer magazine about the performance of a certain automobile causes sales of that automobile to drop by 30 percent.
3. A sharp decline in the stock market causes investors to leave the market, causing a severe drop in revenue for brokerage firms.
4. The federal government imposes new pollution standards which require a firm to spend money that it simply does not have.
5. A courier service finds the demand for its services declining because more and more organizations are using fax machines.
6. A baby food company finds sales stagnating because of the low birth rate.

These and countless other examples demonstrate how factors in the external environment may threaten an organization. These factors also cause the organization to think about how it can change the way it operates so that it can cope with the threat from the external environment. (See the Management at Work insert "Canada's Changing Work Force.")

Internal Forces

LEARNING OBJECTIVE 4
Understand the four basic types of change that are introduced in organizations.

External forces may motivate the organization to make internal changes. As well, forces inside the organization may cause changes to be introduced. As shown in Figure 15-5, internal changes occur in four areas: structure, technology, people, and products.[14] The arrows in Figure 15-5 indicate that a change in any one of these four areas may have an impact on any of the other areas. For example, a decision to manufacture and sell a new product may mean that a new production technology will have to be adopted. This, in turn, may require training programs to give employees the skills needed for the new technology. The company may also find that a new administrative structure will be needed to manage the new product.

structural change

Structural change focusses on changing the authority structure of the organization. Examples include moving from centralized decision making to decentralized decision making, shifting from a functional structure to a divisional structure, and introducing a new compensation system. In the 1980s, Westinghouse Canada shifted toward a more decentralized structure and away from the centralized structure it formerly used.[15]

technological change

Technological change focusses on changing the way inputs are converted into output. Thus, an organization may change from a mass production system to a small group production system, introduce automation or mechanization, or develop a new information system. For example, Allen-Bradley Canada of Cambridge, Ontario, introduced new technology as a part of its automated warehouse and shipping system.[16]

people change

People change focusses on changing the skills, attitudes, and behaviour of the people in the organization. On-the-job training to improve the performance of operative tasks, management development training to improve the performance of managers,

MANAGEMENT AT WORK

CANADA'S CHANGING WORK FORCE

When managers talk about instituting change in their organization, they are usually referring to changes that the organization wants to introduce and that employees will have to accept. But companies are also going to have to adapt to demographic/labour force changes and attitudinal changes that are occurring in Canada's work force.

DEMOGRAPHIC/LABOUR FORCE CHANGES

Substantial changes have been taking place in these two areas during the last 30 years:

1. The annual rate of population growth is declining (from 3 percent in the 1950s to less than 1 percent in the 1980s).
2. Fertility rates have been declining (the average Canadian woman had four children in 1960 but only 1.7 by the mid-1980s).
3. The population is aging (by 2036, people over the age of 65 will account for 25 percent of the population).
4. The participation rate of women in the work force is increasing (in 1951, less than one-quarter of Canadian women worked outside the home; by 1993, nearly two-thirds will work outside the home).
5. Women increasingly remain in the labour force after getting married or after having children (in 1971, 37 percent of married women were in the labour force; by 1987, the figure had risen to 57 percent).

ATTITUDINAL CHANGES

The way workers view their jobs has also changed significantly in the last few decades. Consider the following:

1. Many women are unwilling or unable to forego their careers for homemaking responsibilities.
2. The "organization man" is being replaced by women and men with new values.
3. Because of insecurity created by "downsizing," employees are shifting their career goals and increasing their emphasis on leisure and family activities.

During 1988 and 1989, the Conference Board of Canada surveyed 1600 organizations and 11 000 public- and private-sector employees to determine how these changes are affecting the work-family relationship. Two-thirds of the surveyed employees indicated that they had some difficulty balancing their responsibilities at home and work.

Conflicting work-family demands show up in absenteeism and turnover rates. Employees who reported difficulties in juggling family and work responsibilities were absent more often than those who experienced no difficulty. More than 10 percent of the employees surveyed said they had quit a job because of work-family conflicts; another 14 percent said they were considering leaving their job for that reason.

Work-family conflicts can also reduce organizational efficiency and performance. Almost 50 percent of the employees surveyed indicated that they had experienced disruption in their work because one or more of their colleagues was absent due to family responsibilities. Over 17 percent said they had turned down a promotion for family reasons, and almost 25 percent had refused a transfer opportunity. ▲

FIGURE 15-5 FOUR TYPES OF ORGANIZATIONAL CHANGE.

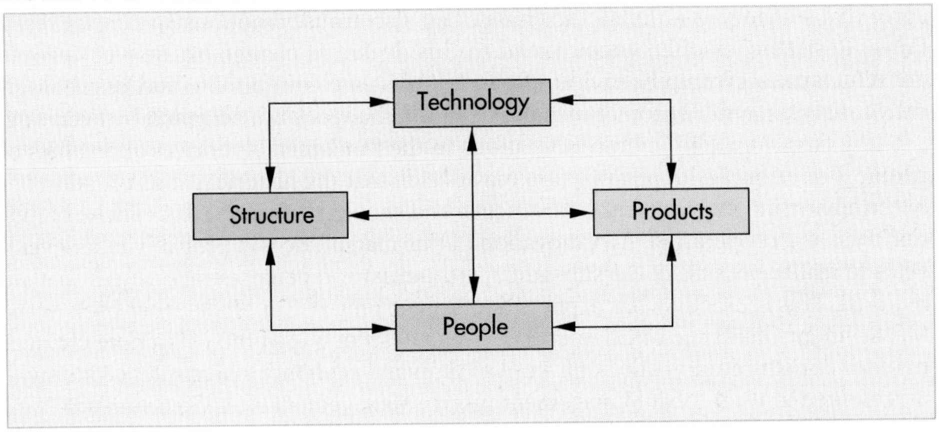

and early retirement programs are ways to create such changes. At IBM Canada, changes were introduced to cope with declining sales. Three hundred employees who used to work in manufacturing went through a 17-week retraining program to learn how to write software. Many other employees were asked to relocate to different branches across Canada, while nearly 1000 others took early retirement.[17] Digital Equipment of Canada Ltd. puts every employee through a two-day "valuing diversity training" course which requires workers to examine their cultural attitudes. The seminar also presents hard facts about topics where misunderstandings often occur. For example, the session debunks myths about immigrants such as "they are unskilled refugees." In fact, fewer than 10 percent of immigrants are refugees, and most have skills that are in high demand.[18]

product changes

Product changes focus on changing the mix of the products or services that the organization produces. Examples include developing a completely new product or service, or making substantial changes to an existing product. When Xerox Corporation realized that profit margins in the photocopying business were much less than those in the document processing business, they launched their new Docutech Publishing Series.[19]

Individual, Group, and Organizational Change

Change can occur at the individual, group, or organizational level. Individual changes include new job assignments, job relocation, or upgrading of task competence. The changes an individual experiences generally have little significance for the overall organization. Changes in groups (e.g., departments, project teams, and informal work groups) include modifications in work flow, job design, social organization, status systems, and communication flows. These alterations have considerably more impact on the total organization than those affecting only individuals. Organizational changes, which typically are implemented over long periods of time, include reorganization's objectives. These have an impact on both groups and individuals in the organization.

Changes requiring only slight behavioural modifications—such as revisions to budgets, work schedules, and communication systems—generally cause only minor changes in patterns of interaction between individuals. Because these shifts tend to be rather mechanical, they create relatively little emotion. Minor changes can therefore be implemented over relatively short periods. For example, if the budget of a department is reduced because fewer funds are available, people may not be very happy, but they will probably go along with the change if they know why it is necessary. In this type of situation, providing adequate information is usually sufficient to successfully implement the change.

Changes requiring moderate behavioural change—for example, the introduction of a training program—create more difficulty for managers. Although people may agree that a change is rational, the change can also arouse emotions and create resistance. Resistance is often encountered to this degree of change because (1) people are reluctant to give up behavioural patterns that are comfortable and psychologically satisfying, and (2) sometimes the need for change is not accepted by everyone.

The largest changes require alterations in the fundamental motives and values of people. For example, an organization may decide that the historical confrontation between labour and management is destructive and should be changed to a climate of mutual trust and cooperation. An innovation of this magnitude will probably take several years to realize because of the substantial attitudinal and behavioural changes that are required. This is exactly what happened to Robert Frey at Cin-Made (refer back to the Management Challenge in Chapter 13). An analysis of one of the wrenching changes in the twentieth century—the shift from a command economy to a market economy—is presented in the Global Management insert "Management after Communism."

GLOBAL MANAGEMENT

Management after Communism: A Big Change

Beginning in 1989, and proceeding rapidly thereafter, Russia and several Eastern European countries dissolved their communist regimes. The pace of change has been extremely fast, and all sorts of problems and opportunities have arisen in the wake of the fall of communism. Two areas where change has been particularly dramatic are (1) the practice of management, and (2) the operation of collective farms.

THE PRACTICE OF MANAGEMENT

Under communism, there was a belief that Marxism provided all the answers, and that management was at best superfluous, and at worst a threat to the system. The job of the manager was to control subordinates so that goals set by the Central Committee would be achieved. Managers themselves were tightly controlled, and were expected to simply carry out orders from above. They felt no need to produce goods and services that satisfied consumers, nor did they put much stress on operating their manufacturing plants efficiently. Rather, they spent their time mechanically carrying out such activities as were needed to get along in the artificially stable environment that was created by a command economy.

All that has changed dramatically. Now, managers must grapple with the reality that simply producing something is no guarantee that anyone will want it. Inflation has become a major problem, with some areas experiencing rates of 3000 percent a year. All this has taken place during an economic recession. Overall, the move to a market economy has meant increased competition, decreased government support, high inflation, a drop in exports, recession, reduction in consumer demand, high inventories, mass layoffs, and increasingly choosy consumers.

These changes have made managers realize that central planning—the antithesis of the market economy—is outdated. Actions taken to adapt to the market economy include drastic reductions in the labour force, a greater market orientation, more consumer responsiveness, improved product quality, competitive pricing, and greater use of advertising.

These major adjustments have now become necessary because of the shortsightedness of the former communist regimes. Under communism, management was intensely disliked, and managers were viewed as a threat. The word "management" did not translate easily into Russian (management was seen as a "capitalist" word) and there was no concept of management as a profession that individuals have as a career. Rather, "bosses" were people with some specific technical training (e.g., technicians, doctors, engineers, lawyers, etc.) who were were put in charge of other people.

There were few management schools in the former U.S.S.R. Those that did exist were famous for their conservatism and their emphasis on communist dogma. While all senior executives were required to do some form of schooling, this was largely indoctrination in what the communist party thought was important. In Czechoslovakia, for example, managers attended the "Evening University of Marxism-Leninism." In this school, Party instructors preached the "class approach" to every problem; failure to complete the course meant a dead end in a person's career. Loyalty to the Communist Party was more important than formal education.

The situation is gradually changing. In prior years, much emphasis was placed on the study of topics like scientific management. Recently, this emphasis has shifted to teaching about the market economy and about behavioural science ideas. But it is unreasonable to expect that the effects of 75 years of communist ideology will disappear overnight. We must also remember that in spite of the ideology of the former U.S.S.R., there was always a need for managers. These managers didn't manage the way we think a twentieth century manager should, but their objectives were different; perhaps they did a reasonable job given the difficult environment they worked in. It is also true that Western managers don't always do a great job, either.

What is needed in the former communist countries is an appreciation that (1) management is an important activity, and (2) it requires training to master. Several Canadian and American schools have sent business professors to various areas of the former U.S.S.R. to teach management concepts, but since they usually stay there for less than a month, their impact may not be significant. What is really needed is the establishment of an educational system which promotes management. Education is needed not only for those who aspire to management, but also for those who are currently practising management without much background or training.

THE OPERATION OF COLLECTIVE FARMS

The collapse of communism in Russia was expected to lead to a sharp increase in agricultural output, but so far very little progress has been made.

The Zaria collective farm is typical. Founded in 1958, it was part of the collective farm system started by Stalin in the 1930s. For decades it filled state orders for corn, wheat, potatoes, and milk. Workers were tightly controlled and living standards were low, but there was a strong sense of security on this and other farms.

When the Soviet Union collapsed, Zaria was divided into six farms and four processing enterprises, each with its own bank account. What happened over the next few months illustrates the problems of shaking off the legacy of communist economic ideology.

In early 1991, Victor Golov was appointed as the new director of Zaria. He intended to increase output by using Western methods of farming and management. But by late 1992, the farm was nearly bankrupt and Golov had been removed as director. What happened?

For one thing, many of the rural areas of Russia are filled with pensioners who want to keep the status quo (including free medical care). For them, free market reforms have little appeal. They are also suspicious of any system which might let a few individuals get rich.

Another problem was Golov himself. Seen as an outsider, he was immediately met with suspicion. Farm workers were disdainful of his ideas and his trips to Canada and the U.S. to observe farming operations. They also disliked the fact that he dramatically raised the rent of some of the tenants and built himself a house that was described by locals as a "mansion" (although it was just a two-bedroom house). Critics said he was acting like a Western capitalist.

Older members of the collective didn't like the new emphasis on individualism. They complained that Golov ignored requests to repair their roofs or to chop wood for them, a favour they had grown accustomed to. They also objected to his selling of collective property in order to get money to reinvest in the farm.

The revolt against Golov was led by Vera Yermakova, a manager in the old socialist system who had come to enjoy certain privileges and whose rent had been raised by Golov from 14 rubles to 140 a month). As distrust of Golov grew, workers decided to ignore his farming experiments. For example, in an attempt to increase milk production and reduce labour costs, Golov built a vast barn which would allow cows to move around more (thus increasing milk production), and which would reduce the number of milkers from 12 to 4. Workers refused to carry out tasks as required because there were fewer jobs and each person had to work harder. In short order, the herd of cows became ill and had to be slaughtered.

The same thing happened at the Ulanova potato farm. When one group of workers were informed what they would have to do, they said the workload was too heavy and refused to work. Other workers were eventually hired, but extra workers could not be organized for the fall harvest so the potatoes rotted in the field. Golov says the workers drank heavily and simply refused to change lazy work habits.

Golov was finally voted out as director at a public meeting where he was accused of taking land from workers and giving them nothing in return. At another meeting a few weeks later, the same people voted to liquidate the private farms and revive Zaria as a collective. When informed that that was illegal, they divided Zaria into 400 private plots and began to run it like a collective. Unfortunately, improvements have been elusive and output remains low.

Golov now runs another farm and vows that on this one he will move more slowly when introducing change. ▲

The Manager as Change Agent

change agent

LEARNING OBJECTIVE 5
Describe the manager's role in the change sequence.

A **change agent** is an individual or group that manages change. All managers are change agents. Top managers are the most visible ones because they provide a vision and a strategy for the entire organization. IBM, which has suffered billion dollar losses and has had to lay off thousands of employees, hired Louis Gerstner as CEO in an attempt to solve the company's problems. Gerstner has a reputation as a "change agent," and had previously helped solve problems at RJR and American Express.[20] When the senior management team at Labatt Breweries met to make decisions about major corporate restructuring, a change agent from People Tech Consulting sat in on the discussions. The change agent helped company executives to play their roles more effectively, and got them to think through the human side of the organization. As a result of the meetings, the company's president did a cross-country tour to talk with employees about what restructuring would mean. People Tech Consulting also arranged workshops on change in each of the company's four divisions.[21]

Middle- and first-line supervisors are also important change agents because they put top management's plans into action. Without middle- and first-line managers, the vision and strategy of the organization could not become reality.

Each manager has a responsibility to be on the alert for new ideas that might improve performance in the manager's area of responsibility. Each manager is also responsible for assessing these ideas to determine which ones should actually be implemented. Failure to be active in both areas means that the manager is committed simply to maintaining the status quo.

THE CHANGE SEQUENCE

The sequence of events needed to bring about change in an organization is shown in Figure 15-6. When either external or internal forces become strong enough, management recognizes a need for change. For example, suppose a production manager becomes aware that production workers are unhappy. Workers are often absent, tardy, create a large amount of waste, and are unproductive. At some point, the production manager will decide that a change is needed to deal with the situation. But the manager must decide what specifically should be altered in order to solve the problem.

FIGURE 15-6 THE CHANGE SEQUENCE.

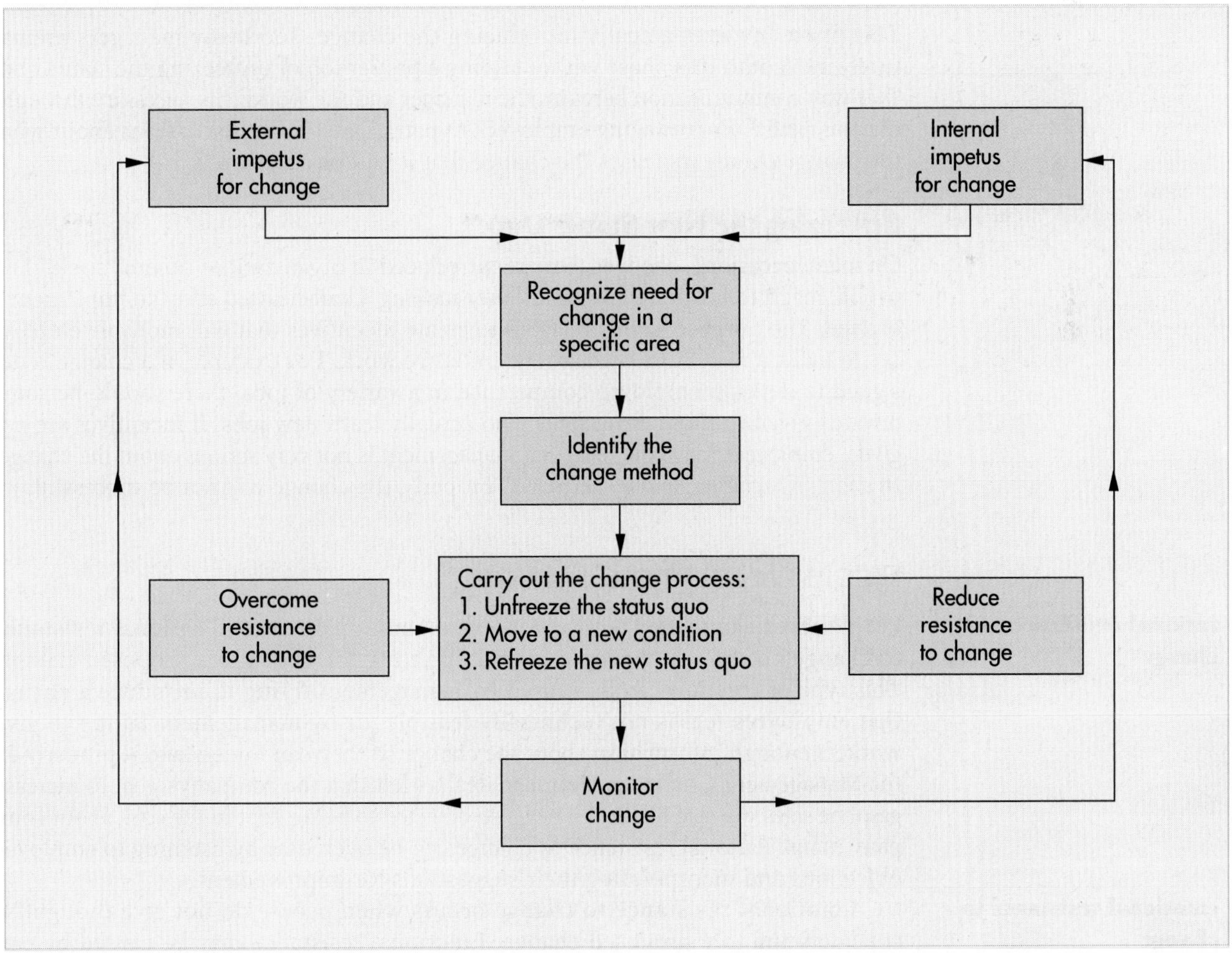

Suppose that after careful analysis, the manager concludes that the problem is caused by the way work is structured. The manager can then look at various alternatives for restructuring the work. From among these alternatives, the manager can pick the specific method of change. The manager might, for example, decide that job enrichment would solve the problem because it would give employees more discretion in their work.

The manager is now ready to work through the change process. This process involves three steps as shown in Figure 15-6.[22] During these three steps, the manager will likely experience some resistance to change, and will therefore have to decide whether to try to overcome the resistance or to reduce it.

Unfreezing the Status Quo

If change is to be successfully implemented, employees must be properly prepared for it. Preparing them involves unfreezing their current attitudes so they can see that the current situation has some shortcomings that must be resolved. Providing information about the change is an important part of this step because it will convey to employees that they can be helpful in implementing the change. Allowing employees to participate in discussions about the change further increases the likelihood that it will be accepted.

Moving to a New Condition

This phase involves actually introducing the change. Too many managers prematurely move into this phase without doing a proper job of unfreezing the status quo. Two-way communication between the manager and the workers is necessary throughout this phase. Encouraging employees to participate in the discussions about what the change entails increases the chance that it will be accepted.

Refreezing the New Status Quo

On many occasions, changes that are introduced in organizations do not "stick," i.e., people revert to former work habits after making a half-hearted effort to implement a change. The purpose of this phase is to create incentives that will motivate employees to make a real effort to make the initiative work. For example, if a change is designed to develop employee competence in a variety of jobs, there should be some rewards given to those employees who actually learn new jobs. If incentives are not given, employees may conclude that management is not very serious about the change. In short, if a change is not "refrozen" properly, the change will not be successful.

RESISTANCE TO CHANGE

rational resistance to change

People resist change for both rational and emotional reasons. **Rational resistance to change** occurs when people have thoughtful objections to a proposed change. This type of reaction can be caused by management trying to introduce a change that employees feel is not technically feasible, or by management failing to give workers enough information about the change so they can understand it properly. In the Management Challenge, Petrocan dealers felt that the company's goal to increase gasoline sales was not realistic. They also objected to being kept in the dark about company plans. Rational resistance to change can be overcome by listening to employee objections and incorporating their suggestions for improvement.

emotional resistance to change

Emotional resistance to change occurs when people do not give thoughtful consideration to a proposed change. Emotional resistance may be caused by employee concerns about how the change will affect established behaviour patterns and friendships. This type of resistance may be very difficult to overcome.

The distinction between rational and emotional resistance may be difficult to make on some occasions. For example, an employee may question a transfer to another city on the grounds that he or she cannot afford the moving costs. When informed that the company will pay all moving costs, the employee may still oppose the change, saying that it will be disruptive to his or her personal life. These situations are very frustrating for managers because they have difficulty determining the real reason for an employee's resistance to change.

The reasons for resistance to change are summarized in Table 15-4 and briefly discussed below. For each of these, it is important to remember that the mere perception of a threat is enough to produce resistance.

LEARNING OBJECTIVE 6
Outline the reasons people resist change and the ways to reduce that resistance.

Fear of Economic Loss

Many people see change as a threat to their economic well-being. Workers at Canada Post, for example, vigorously opposed increased automation because they feared it would mean fewer jobs. Even if the economic effects of a proposed job change are unclear, workers may still resist the change simply because of the possibility of an economic loss. Many Canadian labour unions opposed the Canada-U.S. Free Trade Agreement because of the possibility that jobs would be lost to American workers. In the Management Challenge, Petrocan dealers in Toronto resisted the change because they feared the economic impact on them would be negative.

Concern about Social Disruptions

The social relationships within formal and informal work groups are primary determinants of behaviour. Groups will therefore resist change if it threatens to disrupt well-established social interactions. A study of coal mining groups demonstrated the importance of social interactions on the job.[23] Coal extraction had traditionally been done by small groups of men in which each person was highly dependent on the others for output and safety. In an attempt to improve productivity, management instituted a new production system which stressed specialization of labour and individual work effort. This disrupted well-established social interactions and productivity dropped, even though the new method was technologically superior to the old method.

Fear of a Status Reduction

Any change that threatens the status of a group or an individual will likely be resisted. The introduction of word processing in the 1980s meant that people who were typists suddenly became operators of high-tech equipment. This transformation increased their status, but a secretary who was moved to the word processing pool would probably experience a decrease in status. The change to word processing may also have reduced the status of some managers who did not understand word processing, because they were now dependent on the word processor operator.

TABLE 15-4 REASONS PEOPLE RESIST CHANGE.

1. Fear of economic loss
2. Concern about social disruptions
3. Fear of reduced status
4. Fear of the unknown
5. Threats to skill and competence
6. Lack of trust in management
7. Contrasting interpretations of the change

Fear of the Unknown

People have a need for predictability in their lives, although the level of predictability varies with personality type.[24] The need for this "security blanket" causes people to resist change simply because they fear the unknown. In some companies, white collar workers have been given the choice of either losing their job or taking on a new job that is much different than their old one. At Inco Ltd., for example, about 60 office workers (including 30 women) had to choose between accepting underground mining jobs or losing their jobs. The company has tried to allay their fears about working underground by conducting mine tours, counselling sessions, and fitness training sessions.[25]

Threats to Skill and Competence

Changes that threaten an employee's feeling of competence will be resisted because they deny the employee's ego needs. In the case of the word processing situation noted above, it is quite possible that a typist who is asked to learn word processing will resist, even though status might be increased. The employee may fear that he or she will be unable to master the new technology. Or, the employee may think that any request to learn a new skill implies that the employee's current work is unsatisfactory. This reaction is also seen in relation to computers. People who are not "computer literate" avoid using computers and feel inadequate around those who do.[26]

Lack of Trust in Management

Employees who distrust management are likely to resist change because they will assume that it is designed to benefit the company at the expense of the workers. In this type of environment it is difficult to make many modifications even if they are beneficial to employees.

Contrasting Interpretations of the Change

Managers frequently try to institute changes with the best of intentions, only to be confronted with employee resistance that seems incomprehensible. This resistance arises because employees see the innovation from a different perspective than the manager does, or because employees do not know how the change will benefit them. For example, a manager may decide to introduce flextime in order to give workers more freedom to decide how they will spend their work time. But the concept may be resisted if the manager doesn't tell workers how the concept works and how it will help them.

Analyzing Resistance to Change

force field analysis

If managers are to be effective in introducing change, they must have an understanding of the forces that cause resistance to change, as well as the forces that reduce this resistance. **Force field analysis** analyzes the various forces that operate in social systems to keep the system balanced or unbalanced.[27] Force field analysis proposes that two sets of forces operate in any system: driving forces (those that facilitate change), and resisting forces (those that work against change). If the two sets of forces are equal, the system is in equilibrium.

Figure 15-7 illustrates three possible situations. The length of the arrows for driving forces (D) and resisting forces (R) indicates their relative strength; the numbers along the horizontal axis represent the magnitude of change. Part A shows a system in equilibrium, with the dotted line indicating the system's desired situation. Parts B and C show how the desired situation can be achieved by either increasing the driving forces or decreasing the resisting forces. For example, in (b) driving force #1 has been increased and a new driving force (#5) has been added. Together, these

FIGURE 15-7 FORCE-FIELD ANALYSIS.

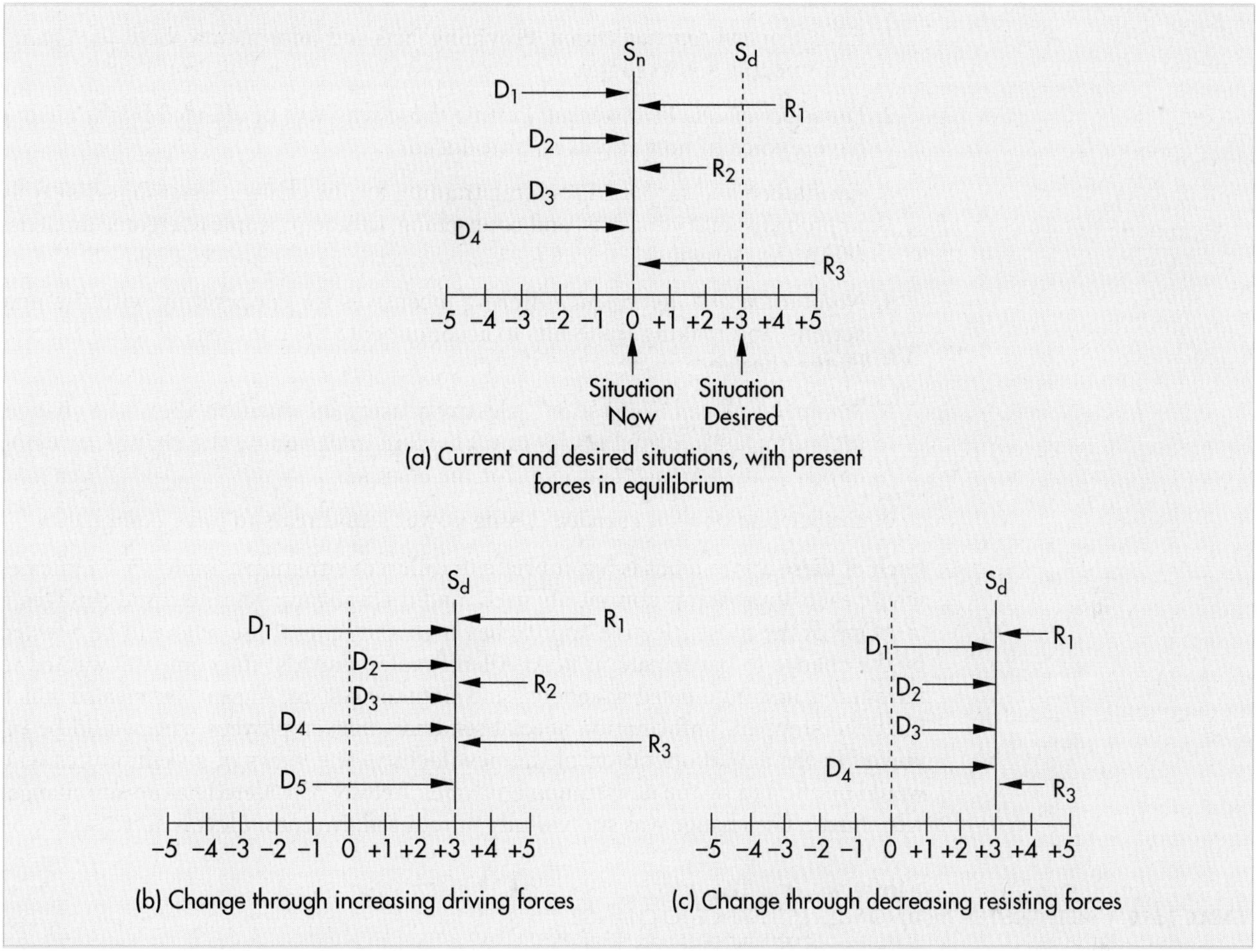

changes move the system to the new equilibrium. In (c), resisting forces #1 and #3 have been reduced, and resisting force #2 has been removed altogether. This is has also led to a new desired equilibrium.

Driving forces and resisting forces are not simply opposites. For example, a driving force for change might be a high cost per unit of output, but the resisting force would not likely be workers' desires to keep cost per unit high. Instead, their resistance would likely come from a fear of losing their jobs because of new technology which is designed to reduce cost.

If managers try to introduce change by simply increasing the driving forces (e.g., trying to force workers to adopt a change in work methods), they will increase tension in the workplace (the "coiled spring" effect).[28] Generally speaking, a more effective approach is to concentrate on reducing the resisting forces (e.g., trying to find out why the workers object to a change in work methods). However, there are occasions when forcing change is the only feasible solution.

Dealing with Resistance to Change

We described the contingency approach to management in Chapter 2. That approach assumes that different solutions to problems are effective in different situations. The contingency idea can be applied to organizational change because the introduction of change is a situational problem.

Six approaches may be used to deal with resistance to change:[29]

1. *Education and communication* Providing facts and information about the change helps people see its logic.
2. *Participation and involvement* Letting those who will be affected by the change have a voice in how it will be introduced.
3. *Facilitation and support* Providing training for the change, listening sensitively to problems and concerns, and counselling, can help people overcome anxieties about the change.
4. *Negotiation and agreement* Offering incentives for cooperating with the new actions, and making trade-offs to accommodate the concerns of those affected by the change.
5. *Manipulation and co-optation* Selectively using information about the change, seconding an informal leader to participate in designing the change, or using covert influence to get support for the change.
6. *Explicit and implicit coercion* Using power and threats to force compliance.

Each of these approaches is appropriate in different situations. Table 15-5 indicates where each approach is commonly used, and their advantages and disadvantages.

One of the most effective approaches is encouraging those who will be affected by the change to participate in it. At Allen-Bradley Canada, the company wanted to introduce a new automated warehouse and shipping system. A team was created which included shippers, information specialists, and other employees who would be involved in the actual operation of the new facility. The views of all employees who would be affected by the new equipment were carefully considered before any changes were made. The change was successfully introduced. Inventory levels decreased by 34

TABLE 15-5 METHODS FOR DEALING WITH RESISTANCE TO CHANGE.

Approach	Commonly Used in Situations	Advantages	Drawbacks
Education and communication	Where there is a lack of information or inaccurate information and analysis.	Once persuaded, people will often help with the implementation of the change.	Can be very time-consuming if lots of people are involved.
Participation and involvement	Where the initiators do not have all the information they need to design the change, and where others have considerable power to resist.	People who participate will be committed to implementing change, and any relevant information they have will be integrated into the change plan.	Can be very time-consuming if participators design an inappropriate change.
Facilitation and support	Where people are resisting because of adjustment problems.	No other approach works as well with adjustment problems	Can be time-consuming, expensive, and still fail.
Negotiation and agreement	Where someone or some group will clearly lose out in a change, and where that group has considerable power to resist.	Sometimes it is a relatively easy way to avoid major resistance.	Can be too expensive in many cases if it alerts others to negotiate for compliance.
Manipulation and co-optation	Where other tactics will not work, or are too expensive.	It can be a relatively quick and inexpensive solution to resistance problems.	Can lead to future problems if people feel manipulated.
Explicit and implicit coercion	Where speed is essential, and the change initiators possess considerable power.	It is speedy, and can overcome any kind of resistance.	Can be risky if it leaves people mad at the initiators.

percent and on-time deliveries to customers improved from 50 percent to 75 percent.[30]

It makes good sense to let those who will be affected by a change be involved in designing it. Yet this often does not happen. In the Management Challenge, Petrocan dealers complained that they were kept in the dark about the company's plans. As another example, Yellow Cab of Dallas, Texas, bought mobile computer terminals for their taxis in order to improve customer service and reduce the number of calls that were "stolen" by rival cab companies who were listening in on Yellow's frequency. But the cab drivers were never consulted about this change. The experienced drivers had learned over the years "where the action was," and they made a lot of money by being in the right place at the right time. They resented having assignments done by computers because it reduced their income. So they sabotaged the new system by sending bad information to dispatchers. As a result, the system failed and had to be dismantled.[31]

STRESS MANAGEMENT

LEARNING OBJECTIVE 7

Define stress and describe the factors that contribute to it.

So far in this chapter we have looked at the issues of organizational conflict and change. As noted earlier, conflict and change can be very disruptive to both the organization and to the individuals working in it. One of the outcomes of conflict and change is stress. **Stress** is the emotional or physiological response a person exhibits in reaction to a demand that might exceed the person's ability to cope with it.[32] Stated more informally, stress occurs when a person is not sure that they can "handle" a situation.

stress

Stress often is evident when major changes are implemented. When Imperial Oil introduced work teams at one of its refineries in an attempt to increase efficiency, workers were required to learn several new jobs. Workers complained of being "stressed out" because they were insecure about how they would fit into the new order. Increased accident rates went along with the increased stress.[33]

In the 1990s, workers have suffered great stress as they worried about whether they would lose their job because of downsizing. But managers also suffer pain and anguish when they have to let people go. In a survey of senior executives in 901 firms across Canada, 71 percent said that the most stressful managerial task is dismissing people. Some managers may actually be in worse shape than the people they are dismissing.[34]

Certain jobs are particularly stressful. Studies of air traffic controllers in Canada and New Zealand, for example, reveal that stress is common in this occupation.[35] Technicians monitoring power generation equipment and steel-making equipment also experience job-related stress,[36] as do telemarketers (the people who call you on the phone during dinner to give you a sales pitch). Telemarketers make one phone call after another in an attempt to sell items like magazines and carpet cleaning services, while supervisors closely monitor their work. Low performers are fired for missing sales targets.[37]

It should not be assumed that all stress is caused by work. A recent study of newly hired workers in a university, an oil-field servicing company, and an electronics manufacturer showed that distress symptoms reported before the people took their new jobs were still evident nine months later. Thus, individuals brought much of their stress with them.[38]

Stress can also come from the interaction of job demands and other responsibilities. A Conference Board of Canada survey of over 11 000 private- and public-sector employees found that almost 80 percent reported some degree of stress while trying to balance the conflicting demands of work and family.[39] Over 25 percent reported moderate to great stress. Employees who experienced substantial stress were absent from work significantly more often than those who reported little or no stress. The Management at Work insert "Balancing Work and Family Relationships" describes how several Canadian companies are trying to help employees balance the conflicting demands of work and family.

MANAGEMENT AT WORK

BALANCING WORK AND FAMILY RELATIONSHIPS

Many Canadian organizations are taking steps to help employees balance the sometimes conflicting demands of work and family. Among these are:

1. *Alberta Children's Hospital (ACH)* The Knob Hill Day Care Centre offers services to employees of the ACH and the surrounding community. The ACH provided a $35 000 start-up loan at 10 percent interest. The daycare centre provides care over a 12-hour period each day, and an out-of-school program for children aged 19 months and older. To date, the ACH has not analyzed the effects of the daycare centre on employee turnover and morale.
2. *Liptons International Ltd.* Liptons is a retail chain with 65 stores and 350 employees across Canada. Most of the executive positions are held by women. To accommodate the family commitment of the employees, Liptons gives "family needs" leave. Full-time employees receive six days per year, and part-time employees receive three days. These days can be used to care for a member of the employee's immediate family. The idea for the program came from the Human Resources Team, which meets regularly to consider innovative approaches in the area of human resources management.
3. *Ontario Hydro* A non-profit daycare centre (Hydrokids) at Ontario Hydro's head office in Toronto has 62 children from birth to five years of age. The centre is operated by a group of volunteers. Hydro provided the space and paid heat, light, and maintenance costs. It also provided $300 000 for capital renovation costs. Fees for daycare range from $530 per month for older children to $660 for infants. The centre gives priority to the children of employees, but children from the community are also taken in when there is space.
4. *Xerox Canada Inc.* Xerox has introduced the Working Parents' Day Care Assurance Plan (WPDCAP), an information, counselling, and referral service available to employees and their spouses. The plan provides employees with counselling which helps them identify the child care factors that are important to them. Child care options (for example, in-home nannies, community daycare centres, leaving a child with a neighbour) are explained to parents and they can then decide which best suits their needs. The company had considered setting up daycare centres, but chose the WPDCAP idea because it seemed to represent the most equitable and practical approach to providing employees with child care support. The WPDCAP is available to all employees as a benefit. It is accessed by simply phoning the local organization.
5. *Canadian Fabricated Products Ltd.* The company contributes two cents per hour per worker to a daycare fund. The money is used to create additional spaces at a daycare centre in Stratford, Ontario. ▲

Sometimes environmental events can cause stress, which in turn, causes health problems. In Brazil, for example, the inflation rate reached 2500 percent in 1993. The number of stroke and heart attack victims was up 20 percent in that year. One hospital director attributed the increase to stress and the lack of money to treat it.[40]

Problems with stress are global. The average Japanese worker is on the job 200 hours more per year than his or her North American and British counterpart, and 500 hours more per year than European workers. This more intense involvement in work has given rise to increased stress and, even more dramatically, *karoshi* (death from overwork).[41]

The study of stress has received increased attention in the last few years, particularly since it has been found to be related to heart disease.[42] Subsequent research has also linked stress to alcoholism, drug abuse, marital breakdown, absenteeism, and child abuse.

eustress

Not all stress is bad. Hans Selye, one of the pioneers of modern stress research, notes that the only people who feel no stress are dead.[43] **Eustress** refers to constructive stress. A student who looks upon final exams as a challenge to be met and mastered experiences eustress. Eustress is often viewed as a motivator; in its absence, the individual does not have the "edge" needed for high performance. Typically, individuals experiencing eustress feel they have control over a situation (e.g., a confident public speaker presenting an important idea).

distress

Distress refers to destructive stress. A student who looks upon a final exam as a crisis experiences distress. Distress is a demotivator; its presence causes physical or emotional suffering and reduces the person's ability to perform. Individuals experiencing distress feel that they have little control over the situation (e.g., a person with a fear of public speaking presenting an idea to a large group).

Sources of Stress

stressors

Stressors are causes of stress The most frequently experienced stressors in organizations are listed in Table 15-6. The first three items—role conflict, role ambiguity, and role overload—have been extensively researched.

Role Conflict

role conflict

Role conflict occurs when an individual receives conflicting expectations from others.[44] Some role conflict is caused when expectations from one source conflict with expectations from another source. If Jim's boss tells him to "crack down" on subordinates in order to increase output, but Jim's subordinates tell him that he will regret doing so, Jim will experience *intersender role conflict.*

Other role conflicts arise when a person is given contradictory orders by another person. If a boss tells Marilyn to get a project completed on time, and then later gives her another project that will prevent her from doing the first one, Marilyn will experience *intrasender role conflict.*

TABLE 15-6 SOURCES OF STRESS IN ORGANIZATIONS.

Source	Description
1. Role conflict	1. Receiving conflicting expectations about how to carry out a task.
2. Role ambiguity	2. Lack of clarity about the authority and responsibility involved in the job that is being performed.
3. Role overload or underload	3. Job demands that exceed (or fall short of) a person's ability to achieve them.
4. Overemphasis on deadlines	4. Continual, unreasonable pressure to finish tasks by certain times.
5. Fear of job loss	5. Concern that poor economic conditions, corporate restructuring, or trouble with one's boss will result in job loss.
6. Corporate politics	6. Competition for promotions, undercutting others with rumours, backstabbing, and jockeying for position.
7. Unsafe working conditions	7. Fear that one may be injured or killed on the job.
8. Sexual harassment	8. Unwanted sexual advances from bosses, co-workers, or subordinates.
9. Performance appraisals	9. Concern that negative feedback and threats will come from the boss during the performance appraisal process.
10. Conflict and change	10. Disputes between individuals and groups about what changes are needed and how they will be introduced.

Still other role conflicts are caused when people are asked to act in a manner they think is wrong. If Caterina's job makes demands that go against her values or beliefs, she will experience *person-role conflict.*

Finally, role conflict can be caused by the multiple roles people play. If Raja is unexpectedly asked by his boss to work overtime (work role), and he promised his son that he would watch him play a crucial soccer game (father role), Raja will experience *interrole conflict.*

Role Ambiguity

role ambiguity

Role ambiguity results when a person has unclear expectations about his or her job responsibilities. Role ambiguity is commonly experienced by new managers, but it can confront anyone in an organization. Role ambiguity is evident if a person cannot clearly answer the following questions:

1. Who is my boss?
2. Who has authority to give me orders?
3. How much authority do I have?
4. What am I responsible for?
5. What constitutes satisfactory performance in my job?
6. What kind of rewards are available for satisfactory performance?
7. What are appropriate job behaviours in my job?

Role Overload and Underload

role overload

One of the most important sources of stress in organizations is role overload. **Role overload** occurs when a person is given more job obligations to fulfill than the person is capable of fulfilling. Role overload may be caused when a person is given (1) work quantity that is too heavy to accomplish, or (2) work which cannot be completed because the person is not properly trained.

Role overload may also be self-imposed. People may create this predicament because they are unable to gauge how much work they can do, because they want to impress others with how much work they are doing, or because they want to avoid some other unpleasant situation (e.g., conflicts at home). The opposite of role overload—role underload—can also cause stress because the job does not require the person to use their full range of skills.

Much of the stress experienced by air traffic controllers is caused by the fear that they will make a decision that will cause someone else to be injured or killed. This contrasts with the stress experienced by industrial workers who usually fear that they will injure themselves on the job.

Effects of Stress

Stress causes problems for individuals and the organizations which employ them. One researcher has identified five areas where the effects of stress are evident.[45] These five areas and some examples of the effects of stress are listed below.

1. *Subjective* Irritability, moodiness, aggression, fatigue.
2. *Behavioural* Drug use, accident proneness, impulsive behaviour, emotional outbursts.
3. *Cognitive* Indecision, forgetfulness, sensitivity to criticism.
4. *Physiological* Increased blood pressure, difficulty in breathing, indigestion.
5. *Organizational* Increased absenteeism, high turnover, job dissatisfaction, low productivity.

The impact of stress on a person's productivity is of great concern to organizations. The general relationship between stress and job performance is shown in Figure 15-8. With low levels of stress, job performance is low because the person lacks any of the excitement or sense of challenge that is necessary for good performance. As stress increases to moderate levels, job performance increases. However, at extremely high levels of stress, job performance declines sharply.

burnout

High stress may lead to burnout. **Burnout** refers to the mental and physical exhaustion that results when a person is subjected to high levels of stress for extended periods.[46] People suffering from burnout feel besieged, display a cynical attitude, are irritable, feel constantly fatigued, and become angry with those making demands on them.[47] Burnout often occurs among high-achievement-oriented managers, perhaps because they set very high standards for themselves.

Managing Stress

Because stress is inherent in every managerial job, individual managers and organizations should have strategies for managing it. If these programs are in place, both the individual and the organization will benefit because an optimal level of stress will exist in the organization. Stress management can be done at both the individual and organizational level.

Individual Stress Management

A variety of tactics are available that individuals can use to cope with stress at work. Probably the most popular current activity is vigorous exercise. Most people who exercise regularly do so for physical reasons. But an added benefit is that people who exercise regularly feel less tension and stress; they are also more confident and optimistic, and are less prone to depression.[48]

FIGURE 15-8 THE RELATIONSHIP BETWEEN STRESS AND PERFORMANCE.

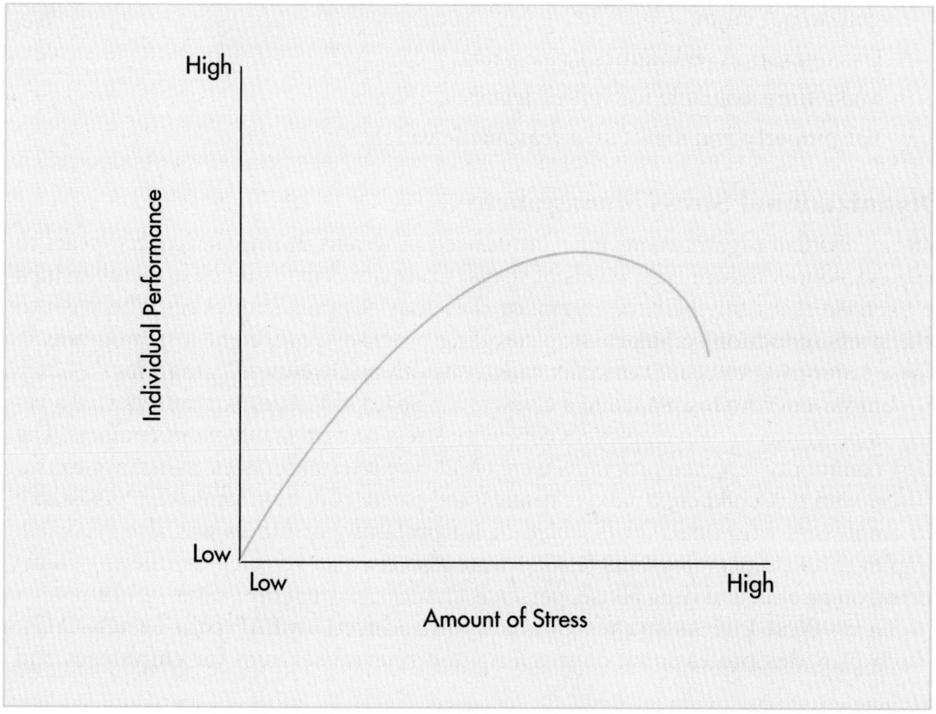

Relaxation techniques are also increasing in popularity. These include taking half-days off from work occasionally, taking extended vacations, and using relaxation techniques like sitting quietly for 10 minutes each afternoon.

time management

Another useful technique in combatting stress is time management. **Time management** involves listing the important goals you want to accomplish, and then prioritizing these goals. A commonly used priority system is the **A-B-C** system. "A" priorities are those which absolutely must be accomplished in the next day or two. "B" priorities are those things which are important, but which do not have to be done immediately. "C" priorities are those which can be postponed indefinitely because they are not central to the person's achievement of important goals.

Once these priorities have been identified, the time management systems involves making "to do" lists each day that are consistent with those priorities. Individuals using time management feel less stress because (1) they have identified those things which are truly important to them, (2) they can see progress toward important goals each day, and (3) they feel more in control of their lives.

support groups

Support groups help people manage stress by providing them with a sympathetic small group setting where people with similar problems can share their concerns. Support groups can be very structured (e.g., Alcoholics Anonymous) or very unstructured (e.g., a group of employees meeting informally to develop methods to cope with an unreasonable boss). Simply being able to talk with people who clearly understand your problem can reduce stress.

Many other specific tactics are used by individuals based on their own personal preferences. For example, the president of Simon Zucker & Associates, has a $5000 stereo system in his office to help him relax. Jackie Young, president of Ink Graphic Design, likes to listen to classical music in the morning and other types of music as the day wears on.[49]

Individuals trying to cope with stress should adhere to the following guidelines.[50]

1. Avoid dependence on caffeine, nicotine, and alcohol.
2. Exercise at least three times per week for 20 minutes each time.
3. Be aware of your values; do not let the values of others induce you to do activities you do not enjoy.
4. Use relaxation techniques twice a day.
5. Make time available for valued leisure activities.
6. Eat properly and maintain a reasonable weight.

Stress can be detrimental to an employee's health and work performance. Making time available for valued leisure activities is just one of the ways individuals can manage stress.

Organizational Stress Management

Many Canadian organizations have introduced programs during the last few years to help employees reduce their levels of stress. Companies may purchase memberships in exercise clubs for their managers, or they may support employees who wish to take stress reduction seminars, stop smoking programs, or weight loss programs.[51] These latter programs are normally called "health and wellness" programs.[52]

Employers who responded to a Conference Board of Canada survey reported a variety of programs to help employees cope with stress or with family-work conflicts. The most commonly reported programs were child care referral services, assistance to employees with sick children, child care centres, and parent education seminars.[53] Assistance for employees who cared for disabled or infirm family members was also reported. Employee assistance programs (EAPs) were also used as vehicles for offering counselling on alcohol and drug abuse, personal finances, marital difficulties, and stress.

Great-West Life Assurance Company introduced an EAP called CONTACT, which provides professional counselling and referral services for employees and their families. It also includes a self-appraisal computer software program. The company feels that if employees receive early assistance with personal problems, their absenteeism will decline and their productivity will increase.[54]

The Bank of Montreal introduced a no-charge stress counselling program for employees who care for elderly family members. Counsellors direct employees toward appropriate community services and answer employees' questions about how to deal with the stress caused by caring for an elderly family member. Other firms offering this type of service include Shell Canada Ltd., Manulife, Crown Life, and Canada Life Insurance.[55]

Some companies use innovative approaches to reduce employee stress levels. The head of Drexis Inc. sent his employees to the Sutherland-Chan massage clinic in Toronto, where they received a half-hour massage. More recently, the firm paid a masseuse to visit corporate offices to give employees shoulder massages. Afterwards, the president met with the employees over hamburgers and hot dogs to discuss company business.[56]

SUMMARY

Conflict occurs when individuals or groups have incompatible goals and an opportunity to block each other's goal attainment. This blocking can take place at the resource-attainment stage or the activity stage. Conflict can occur within an individual, between individuals, between an individual and a group, and between groups. Conflict involves blocking activities, while competition does not.

MEETING THE CHALLENGE

A TALE OF TWO CITIES

The problems of introducing change that have arisen in Petrocan's Toronto territory are caused, in part, by the way the change has been introduced. As noted in the chapter, employee resistance to change is likely to occur when they do not understand the change, when they have fears about the future because of the change, and when they have no part in developing the change. All these factors are present to one degree or another in the Toronto market.

Resistance to change can be dealt with by providing education and information to employees, by getting them involved in implementing the change, and by supporting them as they make the change. Interestingly, this is exactly what has happened in Petrocan's Vancouver territory, and the resistance to the change there is very muted.

In Vancouver, Petrocan managers are meeting with station owners and working with them to cooperatively establish new volume goals, and then to determine how these goals might be reached. Consider one territory of 14 dealers in Vancouver. Sales volume last year exceeded projections by 8 percent. Shirley Dickman, the territory manager, recognized that many operators had a background in auto repair, but not in retailing. So she took them to local malls to generate new merchandising ideas. She also helped them improve their merchandising displays. In one area, she disovered a cappuccino coffeee business that was looking for a retail location with plenty of traffic. A Petrocan station was the perfect place.

Dealers in her territory meet once a month for dinner and shop talk. They reason that a merchandising idea that works for one dealer might also be useful for other dealers. Ms. Dickman has shown a willingness to do things for the dealers and to work with them, rather than simply informing them of what they must do. For example, when operators didn't have enough time to go out and find displays to enhance their stations, she did it for them.

All of these actions have made Vancouver-area gas station owners more open to going along with the change that Petrocan has proposed. Compared to Toronto, in Vancouver far more energy has gone into the development of more effective ways of meeting the new goals; this has meant that far less resistance to change has been evident. ▲

The traditional view of conflict assumes that conflict is bad for organizations, while the human relations approach assumes that conflict is inevitable. The interactionist view is that conflict is necessary for organizational effectiveness. In the human relations and interactionist views, the management of conflict, not its suppression, is what is important. In certain situations, conflict may need to be stimulated rather than reduced.

Conflict can be caused by limited resources, interdependent work activities, differentiation of work activities, communication problems, differences in perceptions, unclear authority structures, power differences, differences in time horizons, and personality differences. Conflict can be resolved by using either interpersonal or structural resolution techniques. Interpersonal resolution techniques include forcing, smoothing, avoidance, compromise, mediation, arbitration, superordinate goals, majority rule, confrontation, integration, or consensus. Structural resolution techniques include procedural changes, personnel changes, authority changes, layout changes, and resource changes.

Change is the essence of a manager's job. Nearly every time a manager makes a decision, some type of change occurs. Managers are thus change agents. There are both external and internal forces for change. Change within an organization takes place in four areas: structure, technology, people, and products, and change can occur at the individual, group, or organizational level.

The change sequence consists of the steps necessary to introduce a change. When external or internal forces become strong enough, management recognizes the need for a change. The specific modifications to make must be decided, and then the process for making the change begins. This process involves unfreezing the status quo, introducing the change, and refreezing the new status quo. It is during this process that resistance to change can arise. People resist change for both rational and emotional reasons. Those reasons include fear of economic loss, concern about social disruptions, fear of a reduction in status, fear of the unknown, threats to skill and competence, lack of trust in management, and contrasting interpretations of the change. Resistance to change can be analyzed using force field analysis, which involves assessing the driving forces (those that facilitate change) and the resisting forces (those that inhibit change).

Six approaches for dealing with resistance to change are education and communication; participation and involvement; facilitation and support; negotiation and agreement; manipulation and co-optation; and explicit and implicit coercion.

Stress is the emotional or physiological response a person exhibits in reaction to a demand that might exceed the person's ability to cope with it. Stress may be good (eustress) or bad (distress). Stressors cause stress. The most frequently encountered stressors in organizations are role conflict, role ambiguity, role overload, overemphasis on deadlines, fear of job loss, corporate politics, unsafe working conditions, sexual harassment, and performance appraisals. Both individual and organizational stress management programs are possible.

KEY TERMS

conflict (p. 461)
Type I conflict (p. 461)
Type II conflict (p. 461)
Type III conflict (p. 462)
intraindividual conflict (p. 462)
interpersonal conflict (p. 463)
individual-group conflict (p. 463)
intergroup conflict (p. 463)
competition (p. 464)
traditional view of conflict (p. 464)
human relations view of conflict (p. 465)
interactionist view of conflict (p. 465)
conflict management (p. 466)
structural conflict resolution techniques (p. 468)
interpersonal conflict resolution techniques (p. 469)
structural change (p. 472)
technological change (p. 472)
people change (p. 472)
product changes (p. 474)
change agent (p.476)
rational resistance to change (p. 478)

emotional resistance to change (p. 478)	eustress (p. 484)	role ambiguity (p. 486)	support groups (p. 488)
force field analysis (p. 480)	distress (p. 485)	role overload (p. 486)	
stress (p. 483)	stressors (p. 485)	burnout (p. 487)	
	role conflict (p. 485)	time management (p. 488)	

REVIEW QUESTIONS

1. What is conflict? What are the three types of conflict, and what does each one involve?
2. Briefly describe the four different perspectives in conflict analysis. Indicate whether conflict is good or bad in each of these situations.
3. What is the fundamental goal of conflict management?
4. Suppose a manager feels that there is not enough conflict in the organization. What can that manager do to stimulate conflict?
5. What are the major sources of conflict in organizations?
6. Describe five structural conflict resolution techniques and eleven interpersonal conflict resolution techniques. How are structural techniques different from interpersonal techniques?
7. Describe the four general areas within organizations where change normally occurs.
8. Describe the steps in the change sequence.
9. What is the difference between rational and emotional resistance to change?
10. What are the principal reasons that people in organizations resist change? Describe the six approaches managers can use to deal with resistance to change.
11. What is stress? What are typical stressors found in organizations?
12. How are stress and burnout related?
13. What are organizations doing to help individuals manage stress?

DISCUSSION QUESTIONS

1. Develop several examples which show how conflict and competition are different.
2. What are the practical implications of the three basic views of conflict presented in the chapter?
3. How can a manager decide whether the level of conflict in his or her department is appropriate?
4. In what way are managers change agents?
5. Using an example from your own experience, describe how force field analysis is helpful in analyzing resistance to change.
6. What fundamental similarity exists in the human relations and interactionist views of conflict?
7. Which of the reasons why people resist change (see Table 15-4) do you think is generally most important? Defend your answer.

EXERCISES

1. Think of a conflict in which you have personally been involved. Use the model in Figure 15-3 to trace through the various stages in the conflict.
2. Think of a significant change in which you have been involved. Use the model in Figure 15-6 to trace through the various stages in the change sequence.
3. From your own experience, describe two change situations, one of which demonstrates rational resistance to change, and one which describes emotional resistance to change.
4. Interview a manager of your choice and get the manager's response to the following questions:
   a. How much stress do you experience in your job?
   b. What kind of stressors exist in the organization?
   c. What do you do to manage stress?

   Once you have these responses (and before you leave the interview), analyze them to determine the extent to which they agree with those mentioned in the chapter. If there are significant differences, ask the manager a few more questions in an attempt to determine why there are differences.

MANAGEMENT ON LOCATION

CASE 15-1
Conflict at Western Gypsum

James Farris was a community college student who, during the summer, worked in the Hamilton plant of Western Gypsum, a manufacturer of drywall material, ready-mix patching compounds, and assorted other home-improvement products for the do-it-yourself market. Farris worked on the second floor and mixed raw materials like diatomaceous earth, dolomite, limestone, and sand together in specified proportions to make the ready-mix compounds. After mixing, the material was gravity-fed to the first floor and bagged. Consumers who purchased these items needed only to add water in the right amount to use the product. Quality control was therefore a key function in the manufacturing process.

Farris hated his job because it was hot and dusty. A typical day was spent frantically running around the second floor gathering the 20- and 40-kg bags of material from storage, carting them to the mixer, slitting them open, and then dumping the contents. Farris wanted desperately to quit, but felt the job was the only way to get the money he needed to pay his way through college. He tried to console himself that school would be starting again in only a few months.

On several occasions Farris had argued with his supervisor about the level of work demanded, but to no avail. One hot July afternoon, the supervisor approached Farris and the following discussion took place:

Supervisor: Farris, you've got to be more careful when mixing those compounds. Walters (the quality-control inspector) tells me that six of the last eight batches you mixed were no good. All that stuff has to be remixed and that's going to cost the company a lot of money. We're paying you to mix those batches right the first time. And another thing, you're not mixing the required 17 batches a day. What's the problem?

Farris: I'm making mistakes because you're too demanding. I'm only doing 14 batches a day because physically I can't do 17. I'm not about to kill myself running around up here in this heat just so I can mix 17 batches a day. Look, I'm the fifth guy to have this job in seven months, right?

Supervisor: So?

Farris: Doesn't that tell you something?

Supervisor: Yeah, it tells me that most young people today aren't willing to do an honest day's work.

Farris: Why don't you look at the job instead of the person doing it? To do this job right, I can only do 11 batches a day. Besides, I'm not so sure all those batches that Walters rejected were actually bad. I've heard that he is very picky when checking quality because it gives him a sense of power over the other workers. I also think he's just trying to cause me trouble because he thinks I nicked his new car in the parking lot two days ago.

Supervisor: Oh, come on! You college guys are all alike. I used to do this job, and I never had any trouble. You're just lazy. And stop blaming Walters. He's been here for 23 years and knows a lot more about ready-mix compounds than you'll ever know. Now get back to work and start pulling your weight around here.

One week later, the supervisor was told by the personnel manager that Farris had quit to take another job. ▲

QUESTIONS

1. Trace the development of this conflict by using the concepts presented in Figure 15-3.
2. Develop a plan for resolving this conflict. Describe specific actions that should be taken, including the use of conflict management techniques.

CASE 15-2
Is Anybody Out There Listening?

Joseph Ginsberg was the newly hired manager of the purchasing department at Western Canada Fixtures Ltd. He had eight years experience as a purchasing agent with another company. He was hired to reorganize the purchasing function in accordance with an overall corporate plan to improve efficiency and reduce costs.

After several weeks on the job, it became clear to Ginsberg that the purchasing department was performing little more than a clerical function. There were no purchasing policies, no central buying, and no control over

•••

who was buying what. The first step he took was to centralize decision making for certain purchases. He decided to start with a dollar amount first, and wrote up a procedure that required all purchase requisitions over $500 to be approved by him before they could be sent to suppliers. He submitted his plan to his manager, who approved it immediately.

Ginsberg then drafted a memo to all other managers in the company (see Figure 15-9). During the next several weeks, Ginsberg received only two completed forms, yet the company appeared to be operating normally. ▲

FIGURE 15-9 JOE GINSBERG'S MEMO.

TO: ALL MANAGEMENT PERSONNEL
FROM: JOE GINSBERG, PURCHASING MANAGER

I'm sure all of you understand the importance of getting the most value for our purchasing dollar. In the past, the company has been very inefficient in its purchasing activities. I am therefore beginning a strategy to improve the purchasing function.

As an initial change, I am creating a new procedure whereby every purchase over $500 must come to the purchasing department for approval. This will provide us with the opportunity to review the purchase and see if we are getting the most for our dollar. Attached is a copy of the new form to be used for this purpose.

I am sure all of you will agree with the wisdom of this approach. I look forward to your cooperation on this matter.

QUESTIONS

1. Comment on Ginsberg's method of implementing this change.
2. Is his new system working? Why or why not?
3. How should the change have been handled?

CASE 15-3
A UNIFORM PROBLEM

ZBK Ltd. was engaged in the delivery of small parcels and letters in a large Canadian city. The company was started by George Zubernik and had grown from a one-man operation into the largest independent delivery service in the city. Zubernik employed 11 full-time drivers, plus several dispatchers who worked in the central office.

The drivers had little in common in terms of their background. Zubernik found that both men and women made good drivers. Age also seemed to make no difference; both older and younger people had worked out well. The main ingredient for success seemed to be a strong dislike for "inside" work and a desire to work on their own. Most of the drivers had been with ZBK for five years or more, and some had been with the company since its beginning.

Zubernik recently engaged a public relations firm to consult with him about the company's image. They had made several recommendations, one of which was that he purchase new uniforms for the drivers. The consultant's study had shown that the public perceived ZBK as a stable organization, but one that lacked flash and innovation. Since competition in the private delivery business was increasing, Zubernik wanted his company to project a new image so that he could retain his share of the market.

The public relations firm presented Zubernik with three alternative designs for the uniforms. Each was quite different from the uniform the drivers were currently wearing. Zubernik intended to be careful about how he broke the news to the employees about the uniforms because he knew that many of them, especially those who had been with the company for a long time, were quite happy with their current uniforms. ▲

QUESTION

1. Using concepts presented in the chapter, develop a plan for implementing this change.

MANAGEMENT ON LOCATION

CASE 15-4
CONFLICT AND CHANGE AT PARALLAX SYSYTEMS

Janet Palica was the assistant to the president of Parallax Systems Ltd. In this staff position, Palica worked on a variety of projects for the president. Recently, she had been asked to draw up plans for renovations to the company's administrative offices. The president stressed how important it was that the renovations proceed efficiently and on time. Palica was looking forward to this project because one of the outcomes would be a new office for her.

Because Palica wanted to make a good impression on the president, she immediately put the project at the top of her priority list. She gave considerable thought to what should be included in the renovations and then contacted a local architect and had him draw up renovation plans. When the blueprints were ready, she circulated a memo to all those who would be affected by the renovations, and invited them to a meeting to announce the changes that would be made.

At the meeting, everything went wrong. Several secretaries who were going to have to move their work stations as a result of the renovation were very upset. After they had received Palica's memo, they had met (on their own time) and drawn up an alternate plan. Palica saw that their plan was better than hers, but she said nothing at the meeting. The secretaries argued that the renovations should be delayed until everyone had a chance to comment on them.

Several other groups were also upset. The drafting department members complained that their proposed new quarters were unacceptable and that no one had consulted them about the specialized type of space they needed. The marketing people complained that there was no area where sales meetings could be held. They reminded Palica that the president had promised that, when renovations were made, a large meeting room would be included. By the end of the meeting, Palica was exhausted. She was concerned that the president would hear about the negative tone of the meeting, and that it would reflect badly on her management skills. She also felt obliged to consult with several of the groups that had been very vocal at the meeting. She realized that she would need more time, and that the renovations project could not possibly be completed by the time the president wanted. Palica thought to herself, "If only I had talked to some of these people before I had the renovation plans drawn up!" ▲

QUESTIONS

1. Why has the problem arisen for Janet?
2. Why did some groups react so vigorously to the proposed changes?
3. What should Janet do now?

CHAPTER 16

ORGANIZATIONAL CULTURE AND DEVELOPMENT

LEARNING OBJECTIVES

After reading this chapter, you will be able to:

1. Define the term "organizational culture."
2. Describe 10 characteristics that identify an organization's culture.
3. Outline how an organization's culture is conveyed to employees and others outside of the organization.
4. Explain the relationship between an organization's culture and its performance.
5. List the steps involved in changing an organization's culture.
6. Define the term "organization development" and outline the key components in the definition.
7. List the prerequisites for a successful organization development program.
8. Describe seven popular organization development programs.
9. Explain why evaluating the effectiveness of organization development programs is difficult.

MANAGEMENT CHALLENGE

The Toronto Experience

Albert Arnot is the president of Fun-Time Ltd. The firm manufactures playground equipment which is sold by major retail outlets across Canada. Most of the firm's 200 employees are production workers; there are 20 managers, including the president and three vice-presidents. Fun-Time is a small firm, and has a rather informal atmosphere. Arnot encourages this atmosphere, and insists that everyone call him by his first name. Some of the managers are not comfortable with this informality, but they go along with it.

A few months ago, Arnot finally decided to attend a management development seminar in Toronto that he had been considering for a long time. After he returned from the three-day experience, he was very enthusiastic about what he had learned. When asked about the details, he had some difficulty saying exactly what had happened, other than that he had "learned more about himself as a person." Several of the managers didn't know quite what to make of this response.

A few weeks later, all managers in the firm received a memo from Arnot summarizing his thoughts about his "Toronto experience." The memo talked in glowing terms about "increasing awareness of one's capabilities" and "gaining insights into one's real being." It also talked about the importance of interpersonal relationships and how improvements in this area could benefit the performance of the organization. The memo concluded by saying that all managers in the firm would profit from such an experience, and that each manager should consult with Arnot to determine when he or she wanted to attend the seminar.

Over the next few days, small groups of executives were seen talking in anxious, animated tones about the president's memo. ▲

The Management Challenge demonstrates the importance of, and the interrelationship between, the two topics that are the focus of this chapter—organizational culture and organization development. We begin by defining organizational culture and noting how it can be identified. We also describe how the culture of an organization is communicated to its employees, the impact of an organization's culture on its performance, and how it can be changed. In the second half of the chapter, we focus on organization development (OD). We define OD, indicate the variety of situations where it is appropriate, list the prerequisites of a successful OD program, and describe several of the popular programs. The chapter concludes with a discussion of the difficulties of evaluating OD programs.

ORGANIZATIONAL CULTURE

Think for a moment about two or three of your close friends. Each of them has certain unique characteristics. The same is true of organizations. Each one is different from all the others. These differences indicate what an organization's culture is (see the Management at Work insert "Culture at Toyota Canada" for an illustration of an organizational culture).

ORGANIZATIONAL CULTURE DEFINED

organizational culture

LEARNING OBJECTIVE 1
Define the term "organizational culture."

Organizational culture is the shared philosophy, ideology, values, assumptions, beliefs, expectations, and attitudes that knit an organization together.[1] The key term in this definition is the word *shared*. There may be many values, assumptions, beliefs, expectations, and attitudes held by individuals in the organization, but only those that are shared and widely held define the true character of the organization. An organization's culture has a very strong influence on the behaviour of employees. While

MANAGEMENT AT WORK

CULTURE AT TOYOTA CANADA

The Toyota Canada plant has a unique culture in which its employees speak their own language of buzzwords (many of them Japanese) and begin their day with a regimen of stretching exercises. They play a Japanese variation of tennis at lunch hour, and they keep the plant clean and tidy. Emphasis is on work teams that function as a unit. Absenteeism and tardiness—serious problems at other automobile manufacturers—are not an issue at Toyota. Employees are at their workstations each day on time so they won't let their team members down.

The Toyota philosophy, transferred from Japan to Canada, has turned the Toyota Corolla into the best Canadian-built vehicle for two years running, according to the Automobile Journalists Association of Canada. The premise is simple—to meld rigour and standards with attention to the workers' desire for comfort and pride in their work.

The method is unique. Every process, every action in the plant is carried out in a specific way. Workers are trained to pick up bolts with a specified hand, insert them in a specific order, and rotate their wrists at a certain angle. With the Japanese process of "kaizen" (constantly searching for improvement), methods have been devised to get the most productivity out of workers with the least amount of effort. When the plant workers who install seats in Corollas developed sore backs due to having to scrunch down to the levels designed for shorter Japanese workers, someone hit upon the idea of lowering the floor. Examples such as this have reduced the "takt time" (time allotted to complete a stage of assembly) from 4.0 minutes to 3.4 minutes. Team members are continually encouraged to trim time and effort off the process, to achieve maximum productivity and minimum stress on the body. ▲

some employees may have a difficult time putting into words exactly what the culture is, they definitely know what behaviours are consistent with it.

At Hewlett-Packard Canada Ltd., the corporate culture stresses equality, open communication, togetherness, high performance, and profit sharing. The president, Malcolm Gissing, wears a name tag like everyone else. The practice of using first names is part of "the H-P way." The H-P way also assumes that people want to do a good job and be creative, and that they will perform well if given the proper environment in which to work. The company emphasizes communication, and encourages employees to talk to each other through its "mandatory coffee break."[2] This is the same kind of culture that was being encouraged by Albert Arnot in the Management Challenge, but with less success.

strong culture

A **strong culture** is one in which the key values of the organization are aggressively held by its present members and explicitly conveyed to new members. Organizations with a strong culture carefully define the way they conduct business, and how they will treat employees, customers, suppliers, and others.[3] Organizations that do not have a strong culture often find that competing subcultures emerge and engage in power struggles which reduce organizational effectiveness.[4]

In 1990, the Toronto affiliate of Montreal-based McMaster Meighen split from its Montreal and Ottawa affiliates because of a clash of corporate cultures.[5] The "slow and easy does it" style of numerous Montreal law firms differs noticeably from the "lean and mean" more aggressive style of many Toronto law firms.

Magna International, a large Canadian producer of auto parts, is a firm with a strong culture.[6] Its founder, Frank Stronach, is well known for his views about employees, working conditions, daycare centres, unions, the free enterprise system, and profit distribution (20 percent to shareholders, 2 percent to charities, 7 percent to R & D, 10 percent to employees, 2 percent to Stronach, and the remainder reinvested in the company). These views have permeated the firm and created a culture that all employees understand.

Four Seasons Hotels and Resorts is another firm with a strong culture.[7] Managers—who are judged by deeds, not words—act as role models, and employees take their cues from them. The culture of the firm motivates employees to "go the extra mile" when providing service to customers. CEO Isadore Sharp says that the firm's first concern is winning customers; if that is done properly, the firm will always beat its competition and gain a large market share.

Some firms have so effectively developed their culture that they have achieved an international reputation. Procter & Gamble is known for having a culture that stresses high-quality products. IBM's culture stresses customer service. Matsushita emphasizes good quality at low prices. 3M's culture stresses product innovation (see the Management at Work insert "Corporate Culture and Innovation"). Because these companies are so successful, many other firms have begun examining their own cultures in an attempt to create effective ones.

The cultures that companies develop may vary even if they belong to the same industry. In the financial services industry, for example, Gordon Capital Corp. and Wood Gundy Ltd. have quite different cultures.[8] Gordon Capital's culture is marked by risk taking, an open-office plan that facilitates quick communication and decision making, warm interpersonal relations between traders, and a profit-sharing plan. Wood Gundy, on the other hand, has a more conservative, traditional culture, with a hierarchical emphasis. In spite of these rather substantial differences, both firms are very successful.

In some firms, the culture results from the vision of one person. Thomas Watson (IBM), Max Ward (Wardair), Frank Stronach (Magna International), Timothy Eaton (Eaton's), Larry Clark (Spar Aerospace), and Jean de Grandpre (BCE) are just a few examples of leaders who have had a strong influence on the culture of their respective organizations.

The corporate culture at Hewlett-Packard Canada Ltd. stresses equality, openness, group cohesiveness, and high performance. Gord McLean, the Senior Vice-President of Finance and Administration, is a part of this culture. Note the name tag, which all employees wear.

MANAGEMENT AT WORK

CORPORATE CULTURE AND INNOVATION

How is it that firms such as Hewlett-Packard, Cray Research, 3M, and Johnson & Johnson are able to continually introduce new products and find new ways of performing? A survey of 500 managers in manufacturing firms revealed that the following norms were evident:

1. *Risk taking* Freedom to experiment and challenge the status quo; assuming that innovation is part of everyone's job and exhibiting positive attitudes about change.
2. *Rewards for change* Top management provides attention and support; there is encouragement of the individual, and a celebration of accomplishments.
3. *Openness* Open communication and broadly based thinking are promoted; adopting the customer's perspective is encouraged, and there is an acceptance of conflict and a willingness to consult others.

Two observations can be made about these norms. First, there was agreement among managers from different industries. Even though the process of innovation differs in the discovery of new drugs, the development of a new oil field, or the manufacture of a new product, the norms remain the same. Second, these norms facilitate the acceptance of new ideas and procedures. Imagine an organization where norms opposite to those listed above were evident.

Having norms that promote innovation is essential, but there must also be norms promoting the implementation of innovations. The managers who were surveyed also revealed a strong consensus on what it takes to put new ideas into practice:

1. *Common goals* Emphasis on consensus, a sense of pride in the organization, sharing a common vision, concern for the whole organization.
2. *Autonomy* Decentralized decision making, belief that the individual can have an impact, flexible decision making, minimization of bureaucracy.
3. *Belief in action* Emphasis on results, eagerness to get things done, quality, meeting commitments. ▲

LEARNING OBJECTIVE 2
Describe 10 characteristics that identify an organization's culture.

ASSESSING AN ORGANIZATION'S CULTURE

Cultural differences across organizations can be assessed by referring to a variety of factors. Ten characteristics which are commonly used to differentiate organizational cultures are shown in Table 16-1.[9] Each of these factors can be viewed as a continuum ranging from low to high. A firm that scored high on most of these factors would have a very different culture from a firm that scored low.

LEARNING OBJECTIVE 3
Outline how an organization's culture is conveyed to employees and others outside of the organization.

CONVEYING CULTURE TO EMPLOYEES AND OTHERS

The most common ways in which the culture of an organization is conveyed to employees and customers are socialization, rites and ceremonies, stories, slogans, and norms.

Socialization

socialization

Socialization is the process by which members of an organization are made aware of the organization's culture. Socialization can be formal (e.g., corporate training programs) or informal (getting direction from co-workers). In either case, the individual is given insights about the values and attitudes desired by the organization and the behaviours that are acceptable. Firms with strong cultures tend to have extensive formal orientations. The largest portion of socialization occurs during the worker's first few months in the organization, but it continues throughout a worker's career.

TABLE 16-1 FACTORS COMMONLY USED TO ASSESS ORGANIZATIONAL CULTURE.

Factor	Situation
1. Individual initiative	Do employees have freedom to pursue new product ideas or are they encouraged to stick with what they know?
2. Risk tolerance	Are managers encouraged to take risks when making decisions, or are they rewarded for being cautious?
3. Direction	Are organizational objectives and performance standards clear, or are employees unsure about them?
4. Integration	Are the various units in the organization encouraged to coordinate their activities, or are they left to "do their own thing?"
5. Management support	Do managers provide support for subordinates, or are subordinates left to fend for themselves?
6. Control	Do rigid rules and regulations dominate the work of employees, or are they encouraged to explore various ways of reaching their goals?
7. Identity	Do employees identify more with their specific work group, or do they identify with the total organization?
8. Reward system	Are rewards like promotions and pay increases based on explicit performance criteria, or are they based on things like seniority?
9. Conflict tolerance	Are employees encouraged to air differences of opinion, or are they encouraged to keep conflict under wraps?
10. Communication patterns	Do communication patterns rigidly follow the formal hierarchy, or are a variety of communication patterns encouraged?

Rites and Ceremonies

rites and ceremonies

Rites and ceremonies are regularly repeated acts that convey the special significance of certain achievements, events, or relationships for the organization. Some of these rites and ceremonies are common to many organizations, for example, the office Christmas party, the company picnic, and the United Way fund drive. But others illustrate the organization's uniqueness. Prior to the bankruptcy of Donald Cormie's Principal Group, the annual Cormie Ranch Field Day brought staff together at the ranch for a cattle show, steak dinner, and Western music.[10] At Mary Kay Cosmetics, a pink Cadillac is given to those individuals who meet certain sales goals. At IBM, salespeople can gain entrance to the 100 percent club (by achieving their sales objectives) or the golden circle (if they are in the top 10 percent of the 100 percent club).[11] These achievements are publicly acknowledged in the company. At McDonald's, a contest is held each year to determine the best hamburger cooking team.[12] This ceremony conveys McDonald's concern about the quality of the food it sells to the public.

Many organizations sponsor company picnics where spouses and children of employees are invited. At these gatherings, employees interact in a less formal setting than the workplace, and their spouses and children get to know at least a little about their work and their co-workers. This activity reinforces the culture the organization is trying to create.

Stories

stories

Stories are narratives that are based on actual incidents, which convey the key values of the organization's culture to employees. At Sony Corporation, for example, a widely circulated story explains why every employee wears a corporate smock. In the early days of the company, not all employees could afford a change of clothes, so the company provided them with smocks to prevent damage to their clothes.[13] This story demonstrates that the firm is concerned about its employees' well-being. At IBM, Thomas Watson, Jr. told a story about taming some wild ducks, and then noted that tame ducks can never become wild again.[14] This story conveyed IBM's desire to encourage innovation and creativity in company employees. At AT&T, one of the firm's first linemen—Angus McDonald—is revered for his commitment to keep telephone wires up during the great blizzard of 1888.

Slogans

slogan

A **slogan** is a phrase or sentence which conveys a value that is important to the organization. At IBM, the story of the wild ducks also became a slogan—"you can make wild ducks tame, but you can't make tame ducks wild."[15] When the former president of Electronic Data Systems, H. Ross Perot said "eagles don't flock," he meant that it was not easy to find good people. Ford Motor's "Quality is job 1" slogan is meant to convey to the public that quality is a priority at the firm. At 3M, the slogan "the 11th commandment is never kill a new product idea" communicates that firm's commitment to product innovation.

Norms

norms

One of the key aspects of an organization's culture is the norms regarding attitudes and behaviour that are instilled and reinforced. **Norms** are created by the dominant forces in the organization and are perpetuated through formal and informal reward systems. For example, a norm of working 60 hours per week may emerge among the vice-presidents if they detect that the president expects it. This expectation may then be transmitted through the organization to other managers and workers.

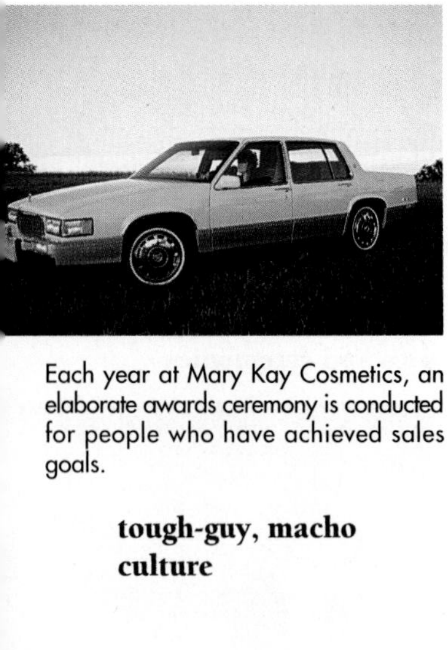

Each year at Mary Kay Cosmetics, an elaborate awards ceremony is conducted for people who have achieved sales goals.

Basic Types of Cultures

Although the culture of each organization is unique, there are several general frameworks that have been developed that allow us to categorize organizations according to their basic culture. One of these frameworks uses two factors to assess cultures: (1) the amount of risk in strategic decisions, and (2) the speed of environmental feedback on strategic decisions. These two factors are combined (see Figure 16-1) to suggest that there are four basic organizational cultures.[16]

tough-guy, macho culture

1. *The tough-guy, macho culture* The **tough-guy, macho culture** exists in organizations that make risky strategic decisions and receive fast feedback on the success of their decisions. Firms in the construction, cosmetics, movie, venture capital, and advertising industries are likely to have this type of culture.

bet-your-company culture

2. *The bet-your-company culture* The **bet-your-company culture** exists in organizations that make risky strategic decisions and receive delayed feedback on the success of their decisions. Companies in the aircraft, oil, mining, biotechnology, and major equipment industries often exhibit this type of culture.

work hard/play hard culture

3. *The work hard/play hard culture* The **work hard/play hard culture** exists in organizations that make low-risk strategic decisions and receive immediate feedback on the success of their decisions. Firms in the fashion, food, and computer industry often display this kind of culture.

process culture

4. *The process culture* The **process culture** exists in organizations that make low-risk strategic decisions and receive delayed feedback about the success of their decisions. Organizations with this type of culture include insurance companies, chartered accounting firms, heavily regulated firms such as electric utilities, and many government organizations.

FIGURE 16-1 FOUR ORGANIZATIONAL STRUCTURES.

Level of risk in strategic decisions	Feedback on effectiveness of strategic decisions: Fast	Feedback on effectiveness of strategic decisions: Slow
High	Tough Guy, Macho Culture Examples: Movie production, Advertising agencies, Major construction projects, Cosmetics, Recording industry	Bet-Your-Company Culture Examples: Oil companies, Aerospace, Mining companies
Low	Work Hard/Play Hard Culture Examples: Electronics, Fashion items, Consumer goods	Process Culture Examples: Many government agencies, Provincial utilities, Financial services organizations

Another framework suggests that there are just two basic organizational cultures: the clan culture and the market culture.[17] Organizations with a **clan culture** emphasize employee commitment to the firm, rather than simply having workers exchange their labour for money. In clan cultures, socialization is a long-term process, and promotion is usually from within. This causes employees to strongly identify with the organization. Tradition is emphasized, and long-time members of the firm serve as mentors and role models for newer members. IBM is an example of a firm with a clan culture.

clan culture

In firms with a **market culture**, employee involvement is simply contractual, i.e., employees exchange their services for money. The organization does not promise job security, and employees are not particularly loyal to the company. The market culture emphasizes individual achievement rather than group performance. If individuals have high performance, they will be rewarded generously. Members do not adhere to any particular norms, and there is no strong sense of company history and identity. Mentoring and role modelling are not as important as in the clan culture. Companies with a market culture may be very successful because the individuals in them are highly motivated by the reward system of the organization. PepsiCo is an example of a firm with many characteristics of a market culture.[18]

market culture

Culture and Organizational Performance

LEARNING OBJECTIVE 4

Explain the relationship between an organization's culture and its performance.

Certain multinational corporations—for example, Hewlett-Packard, 3M, Procter & Gamble, and McDonald's—have attracted a great deal of attention because they seem to be able to sustain consistently high financial performance. Some observers who have looked closely at these companies have attributed their success to their culture.[19] In a now-classic book entitled *In Search of Excellence,* Peters and Waterman analyzed numerous business firms and concluded that the "excellent" ones displayed certain characteristics that resulted in a culture which caused high performance. The eight "excellence characteristics" are shown in Table 16-2. Some culture researchers believe that an organization's culture shows employees "how things are done around here" and that this motivates employees to higher performance.[20]

TABLE 16-2 CHARACTERISTICS OF "EXCELLENT" COMPANIES.

1. A bias for action	The managers in excellent companies do not simply talk about effectiveness; they are action-oriented and continually try out new ideas.
2. Closeness to the customer	Satisfying customer needs is a dominant theme in excellent companies. Managers are encouraged to deal directly with customers to learn what they want.
3. Autonomy and entrepreneurship	Innovation and creativity are encouraged. Product "champions" are encouraged to ensure that a steady stream of new products is ready for the market.
4. Productivity through people	The work force of the firm is considered to be a crucial element in the firm's success. While technical efficiency is important, it is no substitute for good interpersonal relations and an emphasis on people.
5. Hands on, value driven	Employees know exactly what the firm stands for because leaders have provided a vision of what the company is. Top managers get involved in hands-on activity, and are not isolated at company headquarters.
6. Sticking to the knitting	Excellent firms resist the urge to get involved in all sorts of businesses that no one in the firm knows anything about. They stick close to the products and services that they have expertise in producing.
7. Simple form, lean staff	The structure of excellent firms is simple. There is only a small central staff group at headquarters.
8. Simultaneous loose-tight properties	Excellent companies tightly control the core values of the firm, but employees are free to experiment and take risks in other areas.

Some rather sweeping conclusions have resulted from the research on organizational culture. The implication is that a certain "ideal" culture will work for all organizations. For example, the research of Peters and Waterman led them to identify the 10 best-managed companies, based on reference to the characteristics of excellence shown in Table 16-2. This list implied that all firms should strive to have the type of culture exhibited by "the top 10." However, this conclusion must be viewed with caution. A study conducted five years after Peters and Waterman's research showed that 4 of the 10 companies were in serious financial difficulty.[21]

Similar contradictory findings are evident for Canadian companies. In the 1980s, Donald Cormie's Principal Group was identified as a "great workplace."[22] The culture of the company attracted "doers" instead of bureaucrats. It was seen as a friendly place to work, and staff togetherness was encouraged at the annual Cormie Ranch Field Day. As part of its culture, the company placed great emphasis on the achievement of goals by employees. Those who reached sales goals were given gifts such as vacations, records, and champagne. Unfortunately, organizational performance left something to be desired. In 1987, Principal Group declared bankruptcy. Ironically, many employees had no idea the firm was having difficulty. One employee heard about the bankruptcy on the evening news.[23]

Given these difficulties, care must be taken when drawing conclusions about the impact of organizational culture on corporate performance. Before culture can have a positive, sustained impact on organizational performance, three conditions must be met: the culture must be valuable, rare, and difficult to imitate.[24] A culture is *valuable* if it helps the firm achieve goals like high sales which will add financial value to the firm. A culture is *rare* if it has characteristics that are not commonly found in other organizations. A culture is *difficult to imitate* if competing organizations find that they have difficulty duplicating it. If all of these conditions exist, a firm may indeed find that culture will give it a competitive advantage.

Changing an Organization's Culture

The culture of an organization can change when a new CEO takes over or when it merges with another firm. For example, when Michael Cornelissen became CEO of Royal Trust, he imposed a new culture—one that was risk-taking rather than risk-averting. With Cornelissen's departure, the culture is likely to change again.[25]

It is common after a merger for many top managers to leave the company, and this departure can alter an organization's culture.[26] In 1990, the conservative securities firm of Loewen Ondaatje McCutcheon Inc. took over Vancouver's Canarim Investment Corp, a firm known for its speculative stock plays. At the annual shareholders meeting, newly installed president Garrett Herman indicated that the firm would be a blend of entrepreneurial flair and the best traditions of Loewen, and that its culture would be "leaner and meaner" than it was before.[27]

Some organizations have experienced strong external pressures which have forced them to change their internal culture. Ontario Hydro, for example, has long had a cautious "engineering culture," meaning that everything was planned and analyzed down to the last detail before any action was taken. But recent troubles (a $1.6 billion dollar loss in 1993 and a total debt of $34 billion) have forced top management to introduce a more consumer-oriented, risk-taking culture in the company. As part of the new culture, scientists and engineers are being pushed to move ahead with only 80 percent of the information in hand.[28]

Two issues must be considered if an organization wishes to change its culture: (1) what new culture should be adopted, and (2) how to go about adopting it. Many organizations try to change their culture so that it resembles that of the "excellent" companies. The most general approach which can be used to achieve this is to change those factors that convey the organization's culture to employees and others. The organization's socialization processes, norms, stories, slogans, and ceremonies are modified so they will convey the new culture to employees. Of course, changing some of these might be difficult. How does a person change the "wild ducks" story at IBM? Would anyone benefit from changing it?

The Management at Work feature "How to Change an Organization's Culture" suggests several steps organizations can take to introduce cultural change. It also indicates that developments in the firm's external environment can motivate a change in the culture.

LEARNING OBJECTIVE 5

List the steps involved in changing an organization's culture.

MANAGEMENT AT WORK

How to Change an Organization's Culture

1. *Change the reward system* Reward systems establish and reinforce specific behaviours and therefore can help initiate a change in culture. For example, if an organization wants to develop a norm of strong customer service, rewards can be instituted to increase the likelihood of this kind of behaviour.
2. *Add new members to the organization* Adding new members can change an organization's culture, providing that many new members are hired or that they have a great deal of power. Otherwise, they will simply be absorbed into the existing culture.
3. *Implement culture shock* Any event which causes an organization to reexamine its culture can qualify. Events might be a drastic drop in profits, dismissal or death of the company president, or an expensive lawsuit with bad publicity. If such problems can be attributed to the organization's culture, drastic changes can be made.
4. *Change the chief executive officer* The chief executive sets the norms and formal reward systems. Since the chief executive is the personification of the organization's culture, changing the person who occupies the role typically leads to a change in culture. ▲

We noted earlier that a strong culture can be advantageous because it clearly conveys to employees the attitudes and behaviours that are desirable. But a strong culture may be disadvantageous if the external environment suddenly changes. In Canada, deregulation of the trucking, airline, and financial industries has created a much more consumer-oriented, competitive environment. But firms in these industries have been regulated for years, and some of them have developed process cultures which are having difficulty coping with the increased competition in the new environment. These firms may experience some wrenching problems, or even complete failure, as they try to shift to a culture that is consistent with the new environment they are facing.

Whether or not an organization's culture can be changed depends on how deep-seated the culture is, and whether or not multiple cultures exist. The greater the entrenchment of the culture, the more difficult and time-consuming the process of change will be.[29]

ORGANIZATION DEVELOPMENT

As the environment in which organizations operate becomes more complex and dynamic, organizations must develop their human and technical resources so that they can take advantage of opportunities presented by the environment, and cope with threats from the environment. Organization development programs assist businesses in carrying out these two critical tasks. Many firms in Canada have implemented organization development programs, including Honeywell, Hewlett Packard Canada, Procter & Gamble, and 7-Eleven.

ORGANIZATION DEVELOPMENT DEFINED

organization development (OD)

LEARNING OBJECTIVE 6

Define the term "organization development" and outline the key components in the definition.

Organization development (OD) is a long-range effort to improve an organization's problem-solving and renewal processes. This usually takes place through collaborative management of organizational culture—with special emphasis on the culture of formal work teams—with the assistance of a change agent and the use of the theory and technology of applied behavioural science, including action research.[30]

The key concepts in this definition are as follows:

1. *Long-range effort* Improvements in the functioning of an organization cannot occur overnight. A minimum of one year and up to three to five years are required for many OD efforts to show results.
2. *Problem-solving and renewal processes* Problem-solving processes involve making decisions to resolve specific problems facing the organization. Renewal processes are designed to inject "life" into the organization by determining the appropriate mix of personnel, money, and materials for organizational survival.
3. *Collaborative management* In **collaborative management** subordinates share power with managers in making decisions that affect the organization. In contrast to traditional management, where the upper levels of the hierarchy impose decisions, OD stresses collaboration of different levels prior to decision making.

collaborative management

4. *Organizational culture* OD recognizes that the culture of each organization is unique, and that a solution that worked in one organization may not work in another. Solutions consistent with the organization's culture must be developed.
5. *Formal work teams* OD programs emphasize the value of the small group and team development. Certain OD programs do focus on the individual, but attempt to develop each person so that the whole organization improves.

6. *Change agent* The role of the change agent varies across different OD programs. The change agent may take an active decision-making role as data are gathered, interpreted, and fed back to the organization. If the organization is developing a process through which it can solve its own problems, the change agent usually acts as a counsellor or sounding board for ideas.
7. *Action research* **Action research** refers to the process of identifying a specific organization's problems, gathering and analyzing data relevant to the problem, and taking action to resolve the problem. Action research is in sharp contrast to hypothesis testing research, which analyzes problems of interest to organizations in general.

action research

Prerequisites for Effective OD Programs

LEARNING OBJECTIVE 7
List the prerequisites for a successful organization development program.

OD programs will be successful only if several criteria are met (see Table 16-3). Many OD programs have failed because the organization's managers did not ensure that these criteria were satisfied. While satisfying these criteria does not guarantee success, it does provide a favourable environment for the OD program.

Types of Organization Development Programs

LEARNING OBJECTIVE 8
Describe seven popular organization development programs.

Hundreds of OD programs have been used in Canada. However, most of these are variations on a few basic approaches. The most widely used OD approaches are survey feedback, team building, process consultation, sensitivity training, management by objectives, job enrichment, and the managerial grid. Each of these is discussed separately in the paragraphs below, but they are often used in combination.

Survey Feedback

survey feedback

The **survey feedback** method involves systematic collection and measurement of employee attitudes through the use of questionnaires.[31] As shown in Figure 16-2, four basic steps are followed in the survey feedback method.

TABLE 16-3 PREREQUISITES FOR EFFECTIVE USE OF OD PROGRAMS.

1. *The organization must have a specific problem that it wishes to resolve* OD is not a gimmick to be used to "see what happens." Organizations may introduce the latest OD fad even though no specific problem exists, simply because they want to be seen as up-to-date. Development programs must have specific objectives.
2. *Top management must support the OD program* If managers participate in an OD program and then find that their boss will not allow them to implement what they have learned, little has been accomplished. OD programs raise expectations, and when these expectations are not met, frustration results.
3. *Sufficient time must be allowed for the OD program* Organizations which implement OD programs in the hope of a "quick fix" are almost always disappointed. Since an OD program is only one of many variables influencing organizational performance, it is unreasonable to expect that a single OD program will overcome the effects of all other factors in a short period.
4. *The role of outside consultants must be properly conceived* OD programs are designed to help the organization learn to employ their resources more effectively. A consultant who simply prescribes a solution for an organization does not help it develop its own expertise at problem solving. However, if the consultant's efforts are focussed on helping managers work through the problem-solving process, the organization will gain some understanding of how to work through any problem.

FIGURE 16-2 STEPS IN SURVEY FEEDBACK.

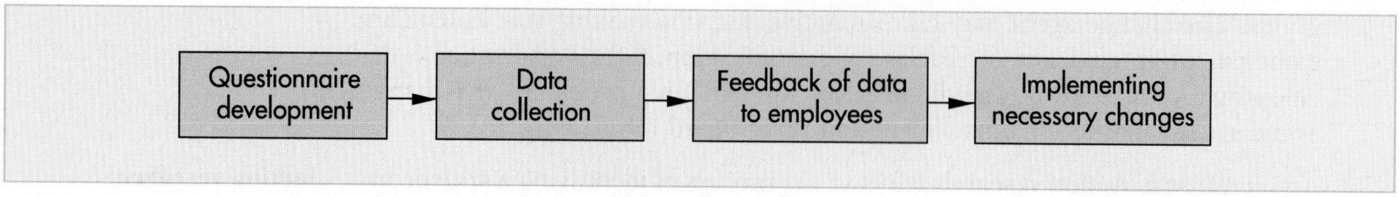

First, a consultant supervises the development of a questionnaire to collect data from employees. The consultant may be from the firm's human resource department or from an outside consulting firm. Employee input in the development of the questionnaire is common. Sample questions that might be asked of employees are shown in Figure 16-3.

Second, data are collected using the questionnaire. Data can be collected on a variety of work-related issues, but management must be careful not to violate employees' rights to privacy. In order to ensure that employees give truthful responses, it is crucial that employee comments be truly anonymous.

FIGURE 16-3 EXAMPLES OF SURVEY FEEDBACK QUESTIONS.

Directions: For each question, place a check mark in the column which reflects how you personally feel about the issue. Remember, there are no right or wrong answers. Do not sign your name on this survey.

	Strongly Agree	Agree	Neutral	Disagree	Strongly Disagree
1. The goals of the unit I work in are very clear.					
2. My boss gives me freedom to use my own discretion when making decisions.					
3. Those who perform well in this organization are more likely to get promoted than those who don't perform well.					
4. This organization encourages new ideas.					
5. I feel free to discuss work-related problems with my boss.					
6. There is a great deal of unresolved conflict in this organization.					
7. My boss trusts me to use good judgment when making decisions.					
8. I am equitably paid for my job.					

Third, the responses to the questionnaires are summarized and presented to the members of the unit that provided the information. Any uncertainties in the data, or any questions about what the data mean can be answered in an open meeting of the unit.

Fourth, decisions are made about what changes need to be instituted. For example, if the questionnaires reveal that employees are satisfied with their level of pay, but feel that the unit lacks a team spirit, a decision might be made to devise a plan to improve team spirit. If the questionnaires reveal that employees aren't very motivated, a scheme to increase the employees' enthusiasm for their jobs might be developed.

Team Building

team building

Team building involves a conscious effort to develop effective work groups in the organization.[32] Team building is designed to improve the functioning of work groups in the areas of structure, decision making, communication, and conflict so that satisfaction and productivity will increase.[33] Quality circles (discussed in Chapter 12) are examples of team building put into practice.

The process of team building involves five steps (see Figure 16-4). The first step is the recognition that team performance has fallen below its potential or that some other specific problem (e.g., excessive absenteeism) exists. Next, data are gathered to discover what the source of the problem might be. To get this data, a manager might meet with subordinates and have an open discussion about the strong and weak points of the department. Once the nature of the dilemma is clear, an action plan can be devised to solve it. When the action plan has been fully developed, it is put into practice. The final step in the process is the evaluation of how well the action plan worked to resolve the problem.

Team building can be used for both temporary and permanent teams. Typically, team members get together in a seminar setting and work through various exercises designed to demonstrate how group cohesiveness and performance can be increased.

At 7-Eleven, for example, team building involves seminars where managers learn about their personalities and how they can interact effectively in the workplace. They also learn how they can help their subordinates reach their full potential.

Process Consultation

process consultation

Process consultation is a set of activities a consultant performs which help the client to perceive, understand, and act upon events which occur in the client's culture.[34] As the definition suggests, this approach to OD begins with the premise that the outside consultant does not merely conduct an analysis of the organization and then suggest a remedy for the problems that are identified. Rather, the consultant and management jointly discuss and diagnose organizational processes and decide what problems need to be resolved.

The steps in process consultation are shown in Table 16-4. Many Canadian companies have used process consultation, including Westinghouse Canada Inc., The Toronto Stock Exchange, and Otis Canada Inc.[35]

FIGURE 16-4 STEPS IN TEAM BUILDING.

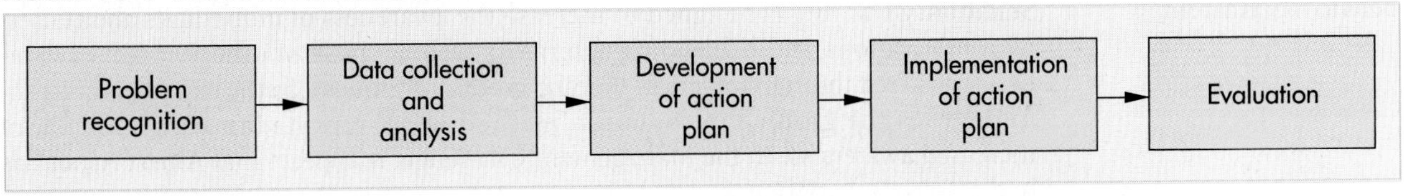

TABLE 16-4 STEPS IN PROCESS CONSULTATION.

Step	Activity
1. Initial contact with the organization	Someone in the organization contacts the process consultant after hearing about the concept and concluding that it may be useful.
2. Defining the formal and psychological contract	The consultant discusses the nature of the problem with the potential client. A formal contract is then drawn up stating the conditions of employment (e.g., the consultant's fee). A psychological contract establishes other expectations that make for a smooth working relationship.
3. Selecting a setting and method of work	The client and the consultant agree on the level of the organization that will serve as the focus for the analysis. The method the consultant will use to gather information is also agreed upon.
4. Data gathering and diagnosis	Informal interviewing and observation are used to generate data which can be analyzed to determine what problems exist. This phase may require several months of work.
5. Intervention	Various interventions are possible, including agenda setting (making the group aware of its internal processes), providing feedback to groups and individuals, counselling groups and individuals, or suggesting structural options (making the client aware of the advantages and disadvantages of various structural alternatives).
6. Reducing involvement	A decision to reduce the consultant's involvement is made after the principal goals of the intervention have been achieved.
7. Termination	When the client and consultant agree that working together productively is no longer possible, the arrangement is terminated.

purchase model

doctor/patient model

Process consultation differs from two other widely used OD models. The **purchase model** assumes that the organization will define its own problems and then hire an outside consultant to make recommendations on how to solve them. This approach is often ineffective, because the organization may incorrectly define its needs or because the consultant is not able to come up with a workable solution. The **doctor/patient model** assumes that the doctor (consultant) will analyze the patient (the organization) and then suggest a cure for the problem. The primary difficulty here is that the unit that is diagnosed may reject the diagnosis. Process consultation overcomes the limitation of these two models since the consultant's main role is not to suggest solutions, but to help management reach its own conclusions about how best to solve the problem. Internally developed solutions are less likely to be resisted by those who must implement them.

Sensitivity Training

sensitivity training

Sensitivity training is designed to increase the awareness of individuals about their own motivations and behaviour patterns as well as those of others.[36] This awareness is fostered through leaderless training groups (T-groups). In the extreme, this technique uses the group confrontation method to achieve its fundamental goal of increased awareness. In the Management Challenge, it appears that Albert Arnot has had a T-group experience.

The T-group operates as follows. Individuals who volunteer for, or are sent to, the T-group meet at a location away from the workplace. These individuals may be complete strangers coming from many different organizations (stranger groups) or they may all come from the same organization (family groups). The groups, usually composed of 10-15 people, meet for approximately 7-10 days. There is no set agenda or required material to cover as there is in a structured seminar. Instead, the members are faced with an unstructured atmosphere in which the decision about what direction to take must be made by the group. The sessions are moderated by a trainer, whose function is to clarify the basic goals of the session and to assist the group in its activity. The trainer usually, but not always, avoids any leadership role.

In such an atmosphere, it is not surprising that high levels of anxiety can build in the group as some members attempt to impose structure on the others. Conflicts of this sort increase members' awareness of their own feelings and behaviours during moments of conflict or attempts to reach a consensus. For example, a group of executives who work together may decide to engage in a T-group session to improve their effectiveness as a team. Each individual might describe how he or she sees the behaviour of others, and the group might suggest possible improvements. Aferward, group members diagnose their own feelings and pursue ways of changing interpersonal relationships.

Sensitivity training is not as widely used as it once was, largely because of three arguments that have been made against it. First, sensitivity training is not so much management training as psychotherapy. Second, people may find themselves under attack during T-group sessions. They may be unable to cope with the experience, and suffer psychological damage. Third, what is learned in the T-group may not be transferable to the workplace. A controversial modern variation on T-groups is described in the Management at Work insert "New Age Training."

MANAGEMENT AT WORK

New Age Training

It is widely accepted by Canadian business managers that employee training is crucial to a firm's survival. But in the last decade or so, a controversy has erupted regarding the type of training some employees are receiving. Specifically, the concern has been expressed that companies may be putting pressure on employees to attend certain types of seminars that the employees do not want to attend.

Seagull Pewter & Silversmiths Ltd. is a successful giftware company operating out of Pugwash, Nova Scotia. The company, which recently gave a series of "new age" motivational training courses to its employees, found that some of them were very unhappy. One employee took eight different courses. She said that some were innocuous, but others caused changes in her behaviour that were significant enough to draw comments from her family and friends. The most dramatic event occurred at a three-day seminar in Halifax, when she became involved in an intense exchange with the seminar leader and ended up crying in front of the assembled group. Other employees have also expressed unhappiness, particularly when one seminar was scheduled during working hours, which meant that partipation was mandatory. Company management says the incident has been blown out of proportion.

The situation at Seagull is not unique. Increasing numbers of Canadian business firms are sending employees to seminars which stress the development of "human potential." The movement had its beginnings in the 1970s, when Werner Erhard developed Erhard Seminars Training (est) to help people take control of their lives. The philosophical descendants of Erhard have now moved into the workplace, promising managers dramatic improvements in employee motivation and productivity through the human potential movement.

Critics say that it's one thing for an individual to try to voluntarily improve his or her own life by deciding to attend a human potential seminar; • • •

it's quite another for a company to require employees to attend such training. Apparently there is a fine line between corporate culture and corporate cults. Cults are very efficient organizations which are able to command extraordinary loyalty to the leader, and it is tempting for business managers to conclude that their firm would benefit if they could extract such loyalty from workers.

Bix Bickson, a successful trainer who used to have ties with Werner Erhard and Associates in Canada, says that he is interested in organizational, not individual transformation. He thinks organizations should be places where traditional hierarchies have been broken down, where there is an environment of cooperation, and where people have the freedom to discuss the problems they are having. He agrees that training sessions can be pretty intense, but "life is intense."

Observers of this type of training aren't sure whether it is simply empty talk or whether it actually produces transformational change in people. Only one thing is certain: demand for the services of human potential consultants is strong enough that many of them are prospering. ▲

Intergroup Development

intergroup development

Intergroup development attempts to change the attitudes and stereotypes that members of opposing groups have of each other. We saw in Chapter 15 that groups often come into conflict with each other. Intergroup development efforts attempt to channel the energy in groups into more productive activity. For example, if two groups are having a conflict, an intergroup development program might first have the two groups meet separately to develop a list of attributes of their own group as well as a list of perceived attributes of the opposing group. Later, the two groups meet to share their lists and begin understanding the actual nature of each other. The process tries to get the two groups to grasp the real causes of the problem that exists between them. Once the problem is understood, progress can be made to resolve it.

Management by Objectives

In Chapter 4, we noted that MBO is a system for encouraging employees to work toward specific organizational goals. An important part of the MBO process is participative goal setting between a boss and subordinate. If we look at MBO in its broadest sense, it is clearly a technique which is designed to improve overall organizational performance.

Job Enrichment

We described job enrichment in Chapter 12. It, too, deals with improving individual motivation, but it focusses on increasing the interest and challenge inherent in the job. Job enrichment becomes a form of OD when most or all of the employees in the organization take on enriched jobs.

The Managerial Grid

The part of the managerial grid program dealing specifically with leadership was described in Chapter 13. In the grid program as a whole, there are six phases (see Table 16-5). The first two phases stress the development of the individual, while the last four emphasize improvements in the overall organization. In total, the phases generally take three to five years to complete.[37]

Organization development programs can focus on individuals, groups, or the whole organization. Sensitivity training, leadership training, and job enrichment usually focus on developing the individual. Process consultation, team building, and intergroup development focus on developing groups. Survey feedback, management by objectives, and the managerial grid focus on development of the total organization.

TABLE 16-5 THE MANAGERIAL GRID PROGRAM FOR ORGANIZATION DEVELOPMENT.

1. *Laboratory training seminar* Problem-solving teams of approximately 12-40 managers are introduced to basic grid concepts. No one is in a group with his or her immediate supervisor.
2. *Team development* Bosses and subordinates begin analyzing their actual management styles and operating methods.
3. *Intergroup development* This phase attempts to change the typical win-lose mentality in intergroup relations to one in which joint problem solving becomes the focus and dilemmas are openly confronted.
4. *Organizational goal setting* Problems requiring a major commitment of time and effort on the part of employees (e.g., cost control, labour relations) are identified.
5. *Goal attainment* The teams formed early in the program are given "task paragraphs" which present a particular problem as well as an organizational goal relevant to the problem. After studying the information, the teams answer true-false questions about the problem and then check their answers against an answer key.
6. *Stabilization* Actions are taken which ensure that changes which have occurred during steps 1-5 will not be lost due to regression to old behaviours.

EVALUATING ORGANIZATION DEVELOPMENT PROGRAMS

LEARNING OBJECTIVE 9

Explain why evaluating the effectiveness of organization development programs is difficult.

Because numerous factors have to be considered before action is taken to remedy a problem, it is difficult to determine whether a specific OD program is effective. The following reasons make such an assessment troublesome:

1. *Measuring the number, nature, and magnitude of confounding variables is problematic* Whenever an OD program is instituted, numerous forces both inside and outside the organization influence its effectiveness. When a change appears in the organization, it is difficult to detect which of the various influences is the primary cause. Suppose that an OD program was started in a business in 1991 and that profits declined by 30 percent during 1992. Did the OD program cause the decline? Not likely. Of far greater importance was the major recession which occurred about that time in Canada.

2. *Measures of behaviour and attitudes are not taken before an intervention is made* The results of many OD interventions are reported as anecdotes. However, in order to judge whether an OD program has been successful, it is necessary to have knowledge of the situation prior to the intervention. It is impossible to state that a leadership training program helped a particular manager unless we can compare that manager's behaviour to his or her previous conduct. Similarly, to claim that an MBO program improved an organization's overall effectiveness, we need to compare specific measures from before and after the program to see if any differences exist.

3. *Those evaluating OD programs often have a vested interest in proving the program is successful* Many OD programs are commercial ventures, with companies paying large sums of money for consultants to come and "develop" the organization. These same consultants then report successes, which in turn, generates more clients. This is not to say that consultants are dishonest, but the situation does create a potential conflict of interest and may result in a biassed evaluation.

MANAGEMENT AT WORK

SOME DIFFICULTIES IN ASSESSING THE EFFECTIVENESS OF OD PROGRAMS

One attempt to analyze the impact of the managerial grid showed that change had taken place in four areas of an organization: (1) profits, (2) productivity, (3) practices and behaviour, and (4) perceptions, attitudes, and values.

Profits The first year after the grid program was implemented, profits rose substantially. Unfortunately, attributing this rise to the grid program was impossible because the firm routinely experienced fluctuating prices for both raw materials and finished goods. These were noncontrollable factors. The firm had also laid off 600 workers during this period.

An analysis of the controllable costs suggested that the grid program could not have accounted for more than 14 percent of the increase in profits. This was calculated as follows: 56 percent of the increase in profits was accounted for by noncontrollable factors. Thus, 44 percent of the increase in profits was accounted for by reductions in controllable costs (costs which the grid program could have reduced). Of the controllable costs savings, 69 percent came from the staff reduction and 31 percent came from improved operations procedures and higher productivity per working hour. Consequently, the maximum grid impact was 14 percent (31 percent of 44 percent).

Productivity The productivity index rose from 103.9 to 131.3 in one year after the grid program was started. It was not clear whether the OD program caused this increase or whether some other factor was at work.

Practices and behaviour The grid program was associated with an increased emphasis on (1) younger line personnel being promoted, (2) more internal transfers, and (3) a greater degree of decentralization in decision making. Whether these changes are improvements would, of course, depend on one's perspective.

Attitudes and values Managers in the program filled out questionnaires indicating their attitudes on work-related issues prior to the start of the program and again, one year later, but both questionnaires were completed at the second point in time, so that managers had to recall what their attitudes were before the program started. The results were very positive, indicating that managers saw improvements in the way they worked with their boss, the way their work group functioned, and the way groups collaborated. The percentage of managers reporting improvements in each of these categories was 49, 55, and 61 percent, respectively. These results seem positive; however, this approach can be criticized because the respondents were required to recall both present and previous attitudes a year after the plan had been put into place. A more appropriate methodology would have been to administer the attitude questionnaire prior to the OD program as well as after it. ▲

4. *Organizational politics makes objective assessment difficult* In Chapter 10, we noted that politics plays a role in all organizations. Consequently, certain programs may be adopted because a powerful person wants them adopted.[38] This was the situation in the Management Challenge. The results of the program may also be presented in a way that generates the most positive public relations. In either case, a purely objective assessment of the OD program is unlikely.

The Management at Work insert "Some Difficulties in Assessing the Effectiveness of OD Programs" indicates what management may encounter when it examines a program, in this case the managerial grid. Generally, OD programs are hard to assess because of a lack of control groups, a focus on short-term changes, and a lack of independent evaluation. As potential users become more critical of poorly designed evaluation studies, there has been a trend toward more scientific approaches to the evaluation of OD programs.[39]

SUMMARY

Organizational culture consists of the shared beliefs and values that knit an organization together. A strong culture is one in which the key values of the organization are aggressively held by existing members and conveyed clearly to new employees.

MEETING THE CHALLENGE

THE TORONTO EXPERIENCE

Albert Arnot, the president of Fun-Time Ltd., is obviously very enthusiastic about creating an organization that is informal, open, and supportive. Unfortunately, several people in the organization do not share Arnot's enthusiasm. In the jargon of organizational culture, there are no "shared values," and the behavioural norms that Arnot is hoping for have not materialized. Although most discussions of organizational culture imply that top management is holding back on the development of an open, participative culture, in this case the reverse is true. This incident demonstrates that if either party is reluctant, the change will fail.

With regard to training, Arnot has let his enthusiasm cloud his judgment. He has neglected to consult with any of his subordinates about their goals. Rather, he has decided that they would all benefit from the same program he took. His subordinates would probably be much more enthusiastic about training if they were allowed to assess their own needs and goals, and then pick an appropriate program to attend. They are obviously dubious about Arnot's "experience," and his decision to make them all attend the same seminar has raised genuine concerns. They feel pressured to attend, yet some of them are clearly uncomfortable about the prospect of doing so.

What is required is an assessment of the kind of training that Arnot's subordinates want. Once that is clear, a decision can be made about which kind of seminar would best suit their needs. Arnot also needs to recognize that managers in this company may be anxious because they perceive that they may be required to change their attitudes and behaviour as a result of the seminar. As we saw in the previous chapter, resistance to change is a common reaction. Arnot can increase the chance that executives will be enthusiastic about training if he follows the change sequence noted in the previous chapter. ▲

An organization's culture can be assessed by reference to various characteristics, including communication patterns, reward systems, tolerance for conflict, emphasis on individual initiative, and tolerance of risk.

The culture of an organization is conveyed to employees in many ways, including socialization (employee orientation), rites and ceremonies (repeated acts that convey the significance of certain achievements), stories (narratives which convey the key values of the organization), slogans (phrases which convey key values in the organization), and norms (standards of acceptable attitudes and behaviours).

Several systems have been developed for categorizing organizational cultures. One system considers the level of risk in strategic decision making and the speed with which the organization receives feedback about its strategic decisions. Four basic organizational cultures are identified in this system: (1) the tough-guy, macho culture, (2) the bet-your-company culture, (3) the work hard/play hard culture, and (4) the process culture. Another system identifies just two basic cultures: the clan culture and the market culture. The clan culture emphasizes the "company-as-family" and long-term employee commitment to the firm, while the market culture emphasizes contractual arrangements between workers and the organization.

Certain organizations have been able to sustain unusually high performance, and some writers argue that their culture is the cause of their high performance. This implies that an ideal culture exists that all organizations should adopt. But firms with widely varying cultures can be effective. In order for an organization's culture to have a positive impact on performance, it must be valuable, rare, and difficult to imitate.

If an organization wishes to change its culture, it must decide which culture to adopt, and how to go about adopting it. An organization can try to change its culture by changing those things which clearly convey to employees what the culture is (i.e., socialization, rites and ceremonies, stories, slogans, and norms). But culture can be difficult to change, particularly if management has been successful in embedding the existing culture.

Organization development is an attempt to improve an organization's problem-solving and renewal processes, usually through collaborative management. Organization development programs can be used to improve communication patterns, the culture of the organization, the structure of the organization, the state of intergroup collaboration, and the motivational levels of employees. If OD programs are to be successful, several prerequisites should be satisfied: management must wish to address a particular problem, top management should support the OD program, sufficient time must be allowed for the program to have an effect, and the role of outside consultants must be clear.

Many OD programs are available to organizations. Survey feedback involves systematic measurement of employee attitudes through the use of questionnaires. Team building involves a conscious effort to develop effective work groups in an organization. Process consultation helps the managers in an organization learn to diagnose and solve problems on their own. Sensitivity training is designed to increase the self-awareness of managers. Intergroup development tries to change the attitudes and stereotypes that members of opposing groups may have about each other. Management by objectives, job enrichment, and the managerial grid are other OD programs that were discussed in previous chapters.

The effectiveness of OD programs is often hard to measure because: (1) there are numerous influences operating on an organization besides the OD program, (2) measures of behaviour are not taken before the OD plan is put into place, (3) those evaluating the OD program may have a vested interest in proving that the program was successful, and (4) organizational politics may impede an objective assessment.

KEY TERMS

organizational culture (p. 496)
strong culture (p. 497)
socialization (p. 498)
rites and ceremonies (p. 499)
stories (p. 499)
slogans (p. 500)
norms (p. 500)
tough-guy, macho culture (p. 500)
bet-your-company culture (p. 500)
work hard/play hard culture (p. 500)
process culture (p. 500)
clan culture (p. 501)
market culture (p. 501)
organization development (OD) (p. 504)
collaborative management (p. 504)
action research (p. 505)
survey feedback (p. 505)
team building (p. 507)
process consultation (p. 507)
purchase model (p. 508)
doctor/patient model (p. 508)
sensitivity training (p. 508)
intergroup development (p. 510)

REVIEW QUESTIONS

1. What is "organizational culture"?
2. Describe five general characteristics of organizational culture.
3. What is the relationship between organizational culture and organizational performance?
4. Define "organization development." What is its goal?
5. What is action research? How does it differ from hypothesis testing research?
6. List and briefly describe four prerequisites for the successful use of organization development programs.
7. Describe the four-step process used in survey feedback.
8. What is the goal of team building? What steps are typically used to achieve this goal?
9. What is sensitivity training? What problems have been identified by critics of sensitivity training?

10. Describe a process that might typically be used in intergroup development.
11. List and briefly describe the six steps in the managerial grid.
12. Which OD programs are oriented toward individual development? Toward group development? Toward overall organization development?
13. Why is it difficult to assess the effectiveness of OD programs?

DISCUSSION QUESTIONS

1. Why is collaborative management such an important part of organization development?
2. Describe three organizational situations that might benefit from the application of an organization development program.
3. How is process consultation different from traditional management consulting?
4. What problems might be encountered when we try to assess the culture of a particular organization?
5. "An organization with a strong corporate culture will almost surely be financially successful." Do you agree or disagree? Defend your answer.
6. "Overall, the clan culture is superior to the market culture." Do you agree or disagree? Defend your answer.

EXERCISES

1. Interview a manager from an organization of your choice. Ask the manager the following questions:
   a. How is the organization's culture conveyed to employees?
   b. What factors are important in determining the organization's culture?

   Analyze the data you have gathered. Do the organizations convey culture to their employees in the ways suggested in the text? How many of the factors that managers mentioned as being important in identifying the organization's culture were mentioned in the text?
2. Read an article about a Canadian firm's corporate culture in *The Financial Post*, *The Globe and Mail*, or *Canadian Business*. Summarize the key points. What kind of culture does the firm have? What impact has the culture had on the firm's financial performance?
3. Have an in-class debate on the following statement:

   "Organization development programs don't work very well because the high turnover in most organizations means that the workers who have been developed leave to work at other firms. Thus, the organization that paid the money for training does not benefit from it."

MANAGEMENT ON LOCATION

CASE 16-1
CREIGHTON LTD.

Creighton Ltd. was established in 1924. It manufactures power and hand tools for the industrial and consumer markets. The company had been very successful for many years, and was the dominant firm in the industry for several decades. However, by the late 1980s, serious problems had emerged. Industry analysts noted that as the firm matured, it had become very conservative and had ceased generating many new products or ideas. The general consensus in the industry was that Creighton was trying to coast along on its past accomplishments.

The company's profits dipped sharply during the recession of the early 1980s, and never really recovered to their former levels. Return on investment, which had been running at nearly 10 percent, dropped below 5 percent for six years. In 1990, the board of directors decided that something significant needed to be done if the firm was to regain its dominant position in the industry.

One of the actions taken to achieve this goal was the hiring of Ferris Lambert as president. Lambert was a hard-driving but personable individual who had a reputation as a "turnaround artist" (a person who could take a company that was in trouble and make it a viable market force again).

Lambert's general view was that North American corporations had no choice but to adopt quite different management strategies from those that had worked in the past. In his many public speeches, Lambert stated his views simply and frankly: to be successful in the new "internationalized" business world, top managers would have to encourage a participative organizational culture, encourage innovation, and stress high-quality products.

Upon his arrival at Creighton, Lambert made several moves to put these general ideas into practice. He made sweeping changes in the executive ranks, instituted a new product development program, and like Lee Iacocca at Chrysler and Victor Kiam at Remington, he began appearing in the company's advertisements.

One of the discoveries Lambert made in his analysis of Creighton was that the firm lacked virtually any management training. He met with the vice-president of personnel and, after informing her of the importance of training for managers, asked her to institute a large-scale training program for all managers in the firm. He indicated that he expected a detailed training plan on his desk in one month. When the vice-president asked Lambert what general direction the training program should take, Lambert told her that she was paid to think for herself. He urged her to use her judgment. ▲

QUESTIONS

1. How is the organizational culture at Creighton going to change as a result of the new president's actions? What will the characteristics of the new culture be?
2. Comment on the president's handling of the training issue.

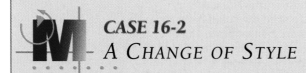

CASE 16-2
A CHANGE OF STYLE

The Sexton Company is a large and successful manufacturer of auto parts located in Ontario. The company has a policy of actively supporting its employees in any self-development program they want to take. This support takes the form of either (1) time off from work to attend seminars, or (2) paying tuition for employees who want to attend evening courses at the local university.

LuAnn Schmidt, an office manager in the company, was known as "a real autocrat" by her subordinates. Stories of her complete refusal to give employees any discretion at all were widely circulated among her subordinates. Schmidt had recently been chosen by her boss to attend a 14-day in-depth seminar entitled "Improving Your Leadership Style." Upon learning of this choice, her subordinates had two reactions: "Of all the people in the company, LuAnn needs this seminar the most," and "Unfortunately, the seminar won't have any effect on her because she thinks she knows everything."

The day after Schmidt returned from the seminar, she called a meeting of her staff and told them in some detail what her experiences had been during the 14 days. After talking for approximately 30 minutes, she concluded by saying, "I know I have been fairly strict in the past, but that is going to change. The program I have just taken convinced me that we will all benefit if I allow much more flexibility in the way you perform your tasks. Are there any questions?"

No one said a word. ▲

QUESTIONS

1. Do you think Schmidt's behaviour will actually change? Why or why not?
2. Assuming that Schmidt actually changes her leadership style, what will be the effect on her subordinates satisfaction and productivity?
3. If Schmidt doesn't change, what will be the effect?

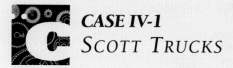

CASE IV-1
SCOTT TRUCKS

"Mr. McGowan will see you now, Mr. Sullivan," said the secretary. "Go right in."

Sullivan looked tired and tense as he opened the door and entered McGowan's office. He had prepared himself for a confrontation and was ready to take a firm approach. McGowan listened as Sullivan spoke of the problems and complaints in his department. He spoke of the department's high personnel turnover and the difficult time he had attracting and keeping engineers. McGowan questioned Sullivan as to the quality of his supervision and direction, emphasizing the need to monitor the work and control the workers.

"You have got to let them know who is boss and keep tabs on them at all times," said McGowan.

"But, Mr. McGowan, that is precisely the point, my engineers resent surveillance tactics. They are well-educated, self-motivated people. They don't want to be treated like soldiers at an army camp."

McGowan's fist hit the table. "Listen, Sullivan, I brought you in here as a department manager reporting to me. I don't need your fancy textbook ideas about leading men. I have 15 years as a navy commander and I have run this plant from its inception. If you can't produce the kind of work I want and control your men, then I will find someone who can. I didn't have complaints and holdups from any other managers. We have systems and procedures to be followed and so they shall, or I will know the reason they aren't.

"But that is just the point," continued Sullivan, "my men do good work and contribute good ideas and in the face of job pressures, perform quite well. They don't need constant supervision and direction and least of all numerous and unnecessary interruptions in their work."

"What do you mean by that?" demand McGowan.

"Well, both Tobin and Michaels have stated openly and candidly that they like their work but find your frequent visits to the department very disconcerting. My engineers need only a minimal amount of control and our department has these controls already established. We have weekly group meetings to discuss project and routine work. This provides the kind of feedback that is meaningful to them. They don't need frequent interruptions and abrasive comments about their work and the need to follow procedures for change."

"This is my plant and I will run it the way I see fit," shouted McGowan. "No department manager or engineer is going to tell me otherwise. Now I suggest, Mr. Sullivan, that you go back to your department, have a meeting with your men, and spell out my expectations."

Sullivan was clearly intimidated by this time and very frustrated. He left the office hastily and visibly upset. McGowan's domineering style had prevailed and the meeting had been quite futile. No amount of pleading or confrontation would change McGowan's attitude.

Sullivan returned to his department and sat at his desk quite disillusioned with the predicament. His frustration was difficult to control and he was plagued with self-doubt. He was astonished at McGowan's intractable position and stubbornness. He posted a notice and agenda for a meeting to be held the next day with his department. He left the plant early that day, worried about the direction he should take, and thought over the events that had led to this situation.

BACKGROUND AT SCOTT TRUCKS

The operation at Scott Trucks is housed in an old aircraft hangar in the Debert Industrial Part, near Truro, Nova Scotia. The government of Nova Scotia sold the building for a modest sum as it no longer had use for the hangar after the armed forces had abandoned it. The facility, together with the financial arrangements organized by McGowan, the president of Scott, made the enterprise feasible. (See the organization chart in Exhibit 1.)

Inside the building, renovations have provided for an office area, a production operation, and an engineering department. The main offices are located at the front of the building, housing sales teams and the office clerks. The sales manager, Mike McDonald, and two assistants make up the sales team at the Debert location of Scott Trucks. Three or four field representatives work in Southern Ontario and the United States. Mike is considered a good salesperson and often assumes a role much broader than sales. Consumer complaints, ordering, and replacement parts also fall into his domain. The production manager frequently makes reference to Mike's ability to talk on two phones at the same time!

Art Thompson has been production manager at Scott Trucks for eight years. The area he manages is behind the sales office and takes up most of the space in the building. The engineering department comprising small offices is located behind the produc- ...

EXHIBIT 1 PARTIAL ORGANIZATION CHART FOR SCOTT TRUCKS.

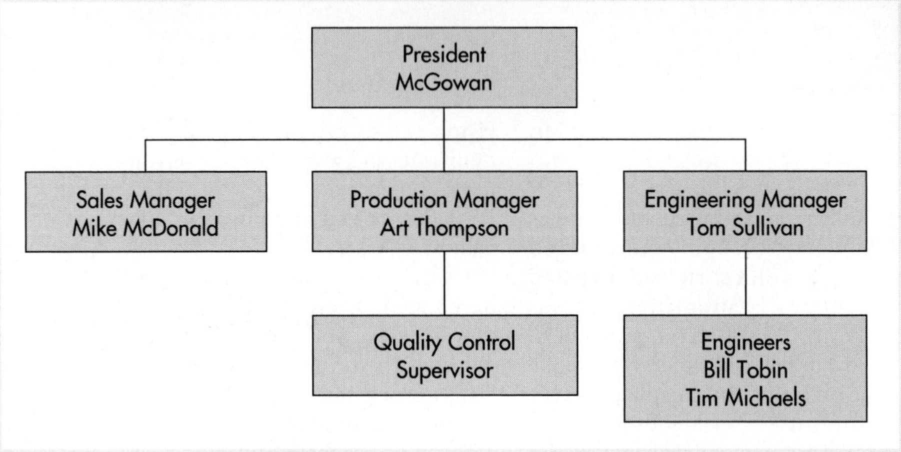

tion department, which is divided into two areas by a long narrow corridor. The shop floor is divided into basic sections of assembly, with a paint, a welding, and a cab section as well as other areas used to assemble the large Scott trucks.

Owing to the limited capacity of the plant only two or three truck units are in production at any one time. Another constraint on capacity is the nature of the system used to produce the trucks. There are no pulleys, belts, or assembly lines used in the system; rather the production takes place in large bays, where sections of the trucks are individually completed in preparation for the final assembly.

The truck units are used for a variety of functions, particularly where a heavy truck requirement is in demand. Fire trucks, highway maintenance trucks, and long-distance hauling trucks are some of the units produced by Scott. To some extent the trucks are custom made as each purchaser will request changes on the basic design. The engineers are also adapting the trucks to meet the various standards and specifications of the Canadian government and of the vigorous and changeable Canadian climates.

Tom Sullivan, who is a recent engineering graduate from Nova Scotia Technical Institute, is the newest of the managers at Scott. He shows good promise as an engineer but, as with his predecessor, Tom Sullivan is having adjustment problems as a manager. Tom also received an M.B.A. from Dalhousie University and majored in management science and organizational behaviour. He completed project work in participative management styles under the direction of a specialist in this area. He tries to practise this approach in his new position and enjoys the ideas and flow of discussion at the department meetings. Tom works in a department with men much his senior and is the youngest of the department managers at Scott Trucks. He works hard and is well liked by his subordinates. Personal satisfaction, though infrequent, comes as a direct result of the open and participative management style he uses.

THE ENGINEERS

The composition of the group of engineers at Scott is unusual. One of the members is not an engineer by qualification but has many years of practical experience. He moved from Detroit to Truro, having worked with Ford Trucks for 15 years. Since his recruitment by McGowan he has worked with Scott for eight years. Retirement for his man is not far off, a fact he frequently makes known to the group. His work is good, and he seems to have many answers to difficult problems, a redeeming factor in the absence of an engineering degree. Don Jones, another member of the group, is a good engineer. His workday is solid; however, most evenings are spent at a local tavern. His wife was killed six months ago, and he does not seem to care any more about anything. The remainder of the group is a combination of senior and junior men who have been with the company for a number of years. Two engineers left the group for better jobs and for a "less confining atmosphere," as they put it. Tom Sullivan's efforts to lead the group are proving to be a difficult task.

THE PRODUCTION WORKERS

Work for the men in the production plant is reasonably stable. A well paying job in production in Truro is dif-

• • •

ficult to find, a situation of which the men are fully aware. Many of them experienced the monotony of unemployment and job hunting before this opening presented itself.

With the exception of a few Francophone Canadian welders, the workers are Maritimers whose experience and skills range from those of a skilled tradesman to those of a casual labourer. The local trade school in Truro has provided the organization with a number of good machinists, welders, and painters that the foreperson hired and began to develop.

The morale on the plant floor has been very good, particularly since the company has improved its sales position. The once frequent layoffs resulting from work shortage have ceased in the presence of higher demand for the trucks. The new field sales group contributes significantly to the situation by their efforts in southern Ontario and the northern United States. The pay scale is above average for the area and there is a good rapport between the production manager and the workers.

ADMINISTRATIVE CONTROL

Administrative control in the plant has been accomplished by two methods; one in terms of quality of the product and the other in terms of its cost. Attention has been paid to the quality control function through a quality control supervisor, whose task it is to examine the end product in a thorough manner using rigorous criteria. The other method of control is that implemented by the accounting office. Through the adoption of a standard cost program, material, labour, and overhead variances are accumulated and presented on data report sheets.

The production manager, Art Thompson, is responsible for collecting cost data and for sending it to the office on a weekly basis. Art is not an easygoing person; he frequently gets upset when problems occur on the shop floor. He is closely watched by McGowan, the president. Consequently, to Art, the monthly meetings of the managers are a real ordeal, since McGowan, as owner, tries to watch the costs very carefully and to make sure the plant is running as efficiently as possible.

McGowan uses three approaches to managing the operation at Scott Trucks: (1) a monthly meeting with the three managers, (2) a series of interdepartmental memos that interpret the results of cost figures presented to him throughout the month, and (3) frequent plant visits and observations.

None of these controls is favourably received by the managers as they feel they are being watched too carefully. Interdepartmental memos may read as follows:

> May 12, 198X
> To: Art Thompson,
> Production Manager
> From: Mr. McGowan, President,
> Scott Trucks
> Re: Materials Quantity Variance
> I noticed a considerable amount of material quantity variance in your production reports last week. The standard cost system has been implemented for six weeks now, and it no longer suffices to say that you are still "working the bugs out of the system." It is time you paid closer attention to the amount of materials going into the production process and to avoiding any spoilage.

Another example of an interdepartmental memo reads as follows:

> May 20, 198X
> To: Art Thompson,
> Production Manager
> From: Mr. McGowan, President,
> Scott Trucks
> Re: Inaccurate Recording of Time and Use of Time Cards
> I noticed last week on your labour cost submissions that a number of employees have been neglecting to punch time cards. Please see that this system is properly followed.

Art Thompson's reaction to these memos has been one of apprehension and concern. It is the practice of the foreperson and himself to try to resolve the problems as quickly as possible and together they have been able to rectify these difficulties quite rapidly, as the men are eager to cooperate.

The plant visits to the production area made by McGowan are frequent and effective. He has been known to come out in shirt sleeves and literally assume the worker's job for a period of time. This is particularly true in the case of a new worker or a young worker, where McGowan will dig in and instruct the individual on how he should be doing his job. On such occasions, McGowan will give specific instructions as to how he wants things done and how things should be done.

It makes McGowan feel right at home when he is involved with the workers. He spent 15 years as a navy commander, and he often used to remark that there was only one way to deal with his subordinates. The reaction of the workers to this approach is mixed. Some of the production people dislike this "peering over the shoulders"; others do not seem to mind and appreciate McGowan's concern for a "job well done." The workers grumble at McGowan's approach but feel most of his criticisms to be constructive.

McGowan's management approach in the monthly meetings with his managers is not considerably different. As

• • •

with the production workers, McGowan assumes a very authoritarian style in dealing with his managers. The monthly meetings are an integrative effort by engineering, sales, and production, with the purpose of ironing out difficulties both on a personality basis and on a work basis. The workload in the engineering department has been growing for the last six months at a considerable rate. This reflects the increase in production and the need for people in the area of engineering and design to provide a high quality of technical expertise.

The number of engineers currently working at Scott is eight. Relations with the engineering department have been less than satisfactory and a good deal of conflict has occurred over a number of issues. For example, the reports from quality control at Scott have been poor from time to time and, increasingly, the problem has been traced to unclear engineering specifications. Upset about these conditions, McGowan has expressed his feelings in his memos to the department.

Lately, the engineers have been bombarded with McGowan's memos, the results of more frequent complaints about the engineering department from the quality-control supervisor and the production manager. Along with other factors, they have provided the ammunition McGowan needed to confront the engineering department. The engineers, however, have resisted, refusing to accept these memos in the same way that the production people have. As a result of these memos, complaints and misunderstandings have risen. The engineers have responded by suggesting that the production people cannot interpret the blueprints and that they never bother to question them when a change is not understood or unclear.

Disturbed by this situation, McGowan has made it a point to visit the engineering department at regular intervals and his tactics have been much the same as with the production people. Unfortunately, the engineering manager, Tom Sullivan, was feeling the pressure and could not seem to keep his department running smoothly. Being new to the job, he did not know how to handle McGowan. Two engineers had quit recently, apparently to leave the "confining atmosphere," going to better jobs elsewhere.

Tom Sullivan had reacted poorly to his new job situation and had been in a somber mood for about two months. His work and his adjustment had not been successful. The veterans in the department, though understanding his frustration, could not help Sullivan, who felt he was better off trying to accommodate McGowan than resisting him. To make matters worse, the two engineers who had recently quit had left a large backlog of work incomplete, and efforts to recruit new engineers had been a strain on Sullivan. The marketplace quickly absorbed all the engineers graduating from Nova Scotia Tech, and Debert had few attractions to enable it to compete with large centres.

Tom did get a big break in his recruiting drive when he discovered, through a contact in Montreal, two engineers who wished to return to the Maritimes. Both men were young and had experience and good training in engineering. In their interview, they discussed their experience and their ability to work independently. Moreover, both were looking for a quiet work atmosphere. Sullivan liked their credentials and hired the two men: Bill Tobin and Tim Michaels.

McGowan had been on vacation at the time and had not met the new engineers until a month after they had been on the job. His first encounter, however, was a cordial meeting with the two engineers and, although the atmosphere in the department was always unpredictable and changing, activities and relations were smooth for a month or two, much to the relief of Sullivan. McGowan maintained his surveillance of the plant, including the engineers. Tim Michaels and Bill Tobin, the new engineers, felt uncomfortable with McGowan around but just proceeded with their work and ignored the long stares and the continued presence of the boss.

One Friday afternoon McGowan walked into the engineering department with a smug look on his face. It was near the end of the month just prior to the monthly meeting. Sullivan looked up immediately as McGowan moved toward Tobin's drafting table. McGowan was irate. He began talking to Tobin in a loud voice. Shaking his fist, he threw down a report on a change proposed by Tobin for the interior of the cabs made at Scott.

"What gives you the right to implement such a change without first going to Sullivan, then to me?" shouted McGowan. "You have only been with this company for two and a half months and already you feel you can ignore the system."

"Well, Mr. McGowan. I thought it was a good idea, and I have seen it work before," responded Tobin, flustered by McGowan's attack.

Sullivan came out from his office to see what the problem was about. McGowan turned to him and asked him why he couldn't control his staff, adding that the changes were totally unauthorized and unnecessary. Sullivan glanced at the blueprint and was taken by surprise as he examined it more carefully. In the meantime, McGowan raved on about Tobin's actions. Sullivan roused himself to reply.

"Oh, um, ah, yes, Mr. McGowan, you're right; this should have been cleared between, uh, you and me before production got it but, ah, I will see that it doesn't happen again."

McGowan stormed out, leaving Tobin and Sullivan standing by the desk. Tobin was upset by "this display

• • •

of rudeness," as he put it. "Tom," he went on, "this was a damn good idea and you know it."

Sullivan shook his head, "Yes, you're right. I don't know how to deal with McGowan; he wears me down sometimes. But you and Bill have to channel your changes through the system."

Tobin turned back to his table and resumed his afternoon's work.

For the next six weeks the plant operated smoothly as production picked up and more people were hired. Work in the engineering department increased correspondingly as people wanted new and better parts on their trucks. New engine and cab designs were arriving and put an increased burden on the engineering department. In fact, it fell well behind in its efforts to change and adapt the truck specifications to meet the Canadian marketplace. The lengthy review process required to implement change put an added burden on the operations at Scott. Moreover, summer was approaching, which meant decreased personnel, owing to the holidays.

McGowan's frequent visits added to the difficult situation in the engineering department. Sullivan had initiated group meetings once a week with the engineers in an attempt to solve engineering problems and personal conflicts. At each meeting, Tobin and Michaels discussed their work with the group and showed signs of real progress and development. They were adjusting well and contributing above expectations. At these meetings, however, they both spoke openly and frankly about McGowan's frequent visits and his abrasive style. A month had passed since they first suggested to Sullivan that he talk to McGowan about the problems he presented to the engineers by his visits to the department. At first the rest of the group agreed passively to the idea that Sullivan confront McGowan on this issue but, by the fourth week, the entire group was very firm with Sullivan on this issue, insisting he have a talk with McGowan.

Tom Sullivan knew the time had come and that he had to face McGowan. Only that morning he had received a call from a local company inquiring about Bill Tobin and the quality of his work. Presumably Tobin had been looking for work elsewhere. This was the last straw. Sullivan had made and kept his appointment with McGowan. ▲

QUESTIONS

1. Contrast in detail the leadership styles of Sullivan and McGowan.
2. Describe the communication process at Scott Trucks. What areas are most effective? What areas are ineffective? What can be done to improve the ineffective areas?
3. What is the most effective leadership style for the engineering manager at Scott Trucks? Support your choice fully.
4. What should Sullivan do now? What limitations exist in the engineering department that might constrain Sullivan's alternatives?

CASE IV-2
The British Columbia Buildings Corporation: A Crowning Achievement

The British Columbia Buildings Corporation (BCBC) was created through a provincial act on June 30, 1976, and began operation April 1, 1978. The mandate of the Canadian Provincial Crown Corporation (government owned) which essentially replaced the former Ministry of Public works, was "to identify the short- and long-term accommodation service requirement of the British Columbia Government, and to satisfy those requirements in a responsive and cost-effective manner." More specifically the corporation saw its own objective as, "The achievement of client satisfaction with proper emphasis on association communication, controls, costs, values and delivery time." The approach reflected a trend in North America towards revenue dependency and accountability in the supply and management of government accommodation. In total, the corporation managed all provincial government property use from ultra modern, multiblock complexes to heritage buildings and highway snow sheds.

STRUCTURE AND ORGANIZATION

By 1987, under the direction of Peter Dolezal (CEO) and his five vice-presidents (see Figure 1 for the organization chart): J. Robinson (Real Estate); B. Wilson (Planning and Client Services); J. Davies (Development); A. Kemp (Property Management), and D. Truss (Administration & C.F.O.), the Corporation was managing a growth of 29 percent with less than 50 percent of the previous staffing levels under the old Ministry. In total this meant close to 1 900 000 metres of property made up 3000 buildings throughout British Columbia overseen by about 900 employees.

During the critical start-up phase, BCBC's management directed its efforts towards a number of major priorities and challenges. The corporation had to establish the basic means for going about its business. The management structure and reporting relationships had to be designed and implemented quickly. Management oversaw the staffing of all positions within the corporation as well as identification, valuation, and acquisition of property.

The start-up complement of permanent staff was 1200 positions. About 200 people came from the private sector with the remainder from the former Ministry of Public Works. Also required was the negotiation of an initial agreement with the B.C. Government Employees' Union. As well, the corporation acquired some 2400 buildings situated on about 1000 pieces of property all of which had to be properly identified and valued. Other transition objectives included improving the relationship with the construction industry since little goodwill prevailed due to previous poor payment practices, the measurement of available space and the acquisition of some 900 leasing agreements representing over 4 million square feet. To compound the challenge the information systems in existence were not at all compatible with the greater fiscal responsibility initiative of BCBC whereby a completely new management information system (MIS) had to be developed within a compressed time frame.

These priorities were the focus of management's attention for the first several months and this was looked upon by BCBC's leaders as a particularly exciting and interesting period in the corporation's history. To quote Dennis Truss:

> For many of us, this was a unique opportunity to not only become involved in a brand new organization and "do it right," but to be able to make and influence many of the key initial decisions.

During and following this period, emphasis was placed on developing a strong, positive working relationship with BCBC's clients, the various government ministries with whom it was very unpopular at the outset. Part of the perception was deserved as initially BCBC's enthusiasm was seen to motivate an aggressive attitude of "one best way" to do things. However, the corporation learned quickly that, in order to succeed, it would have to gain the confidence of ministries and central government agencies. This wasn't easy.

FIGURE 1 ORGANIZATION CHART

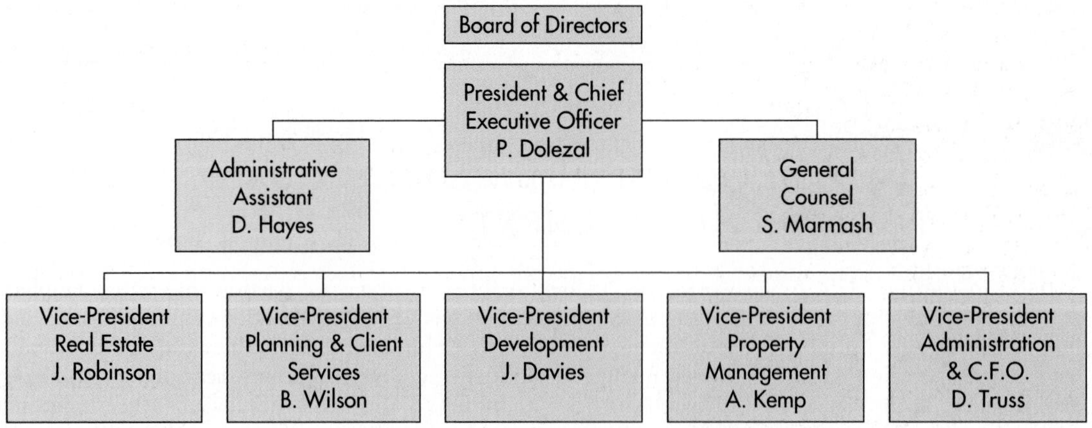

...

The chargeback system introduced was a unique concept and was met with some skepticism by ministries who now had to pay rent for the space they occupied and account for it in their budgets. This was a radical change from the past and the move towards a "private sector philosophy" was felt to be reflective of the so-called "cowboy mentality" of the new management, some of whom had come from the Alberta oil patch. But according to Peter Dolezal:

> By the end of our fourth year of operation, the corporate culture, supported by the reward system for management, was such that it wasn't at all fashionable for supervisors to attempt to build or replace staff—in fact the reverse was true.

An internal imperative concentrated on establishing an environment of trust and security so that employees would have a desire to strive to fulfill the corporation's mandate with efficiency and effectiveness.

Impressively, the transition to a "user-pay" operating basis within government, was achieved with high morale, high productivity and a downsizing initiative which saw not a single person laid off. Signalling this environment were the accepted indicators such as attrition, absenteeism due to sickness, grievance rates, and accident frequencies all of which were carefully monitored by the corporation. For example, in 1986/87 a total of 416 employees (about 44 percent) had a perfect attendance record and grievances amounted to fewer than 1 percent per 100 bargaining unit employees annually.

EXTERNAL AFFAIRS

The secret to much of the success of the corporation was its willingness, as a monopoly, to use free market, private sector standards when reviewing its performance. No fewer than eight such comprehensive external audits (technical/financial and managerial/structural) have been performed in areas as diverse as the effectiveness of leasing negotiation to managerial style. Further, it listened to criticism, and most importantly, it was willing to change.

Certainly, its operation was not "wart free" and when a 1983 external market audit found some "diseconomies of scale leading to inflexibility and bureaucratic inefficiencies," action was taken to attack the problem including decentralization and delegation of authority. Another example of sensitivity of feedback is reflected by a 1986 program called "**Accidents Zero**" which was introduced to respond to a disturbing increase in injuries. The following year accidents had dropped from 21 lost time injuries per million man hours worked to 8.4.

The corporation has introduced Client Feedback Panels whereby prime user representatives participate on committees charged with the responsibility of solving problems and helping with future planning.

INTRAPRENEURSHIP

Intrapreneurship is encouraged with the result being unique and creative low-tech cost-saving ideas invented by employees. For example, Keith Mahler designed a new extension handle which cut wall and ceiling cleaning times in half, and Pauline Byrne developed a new faster way to clean windows with an associated saving of 80 percent. But the cost saving champion was an employee who invented a special scaffolding system for cleaning a spaceframe glass roof on the Vancouver law courts. The reduction on a quarter million dollar estimated cleaning cost was an incredible 99 percent.

Another example of nurturing intrapreneurship was called "**Transition Contracts**" which allowed BCBC employees to leave with a guaranteed dollar volume of corporation business during the first one to three years of operation. As a result of this incentive, former employee Guido Francino now operates a building maintenance company (G.F. Office Maintenance Systems) in Burnaby, B.C. The company has expanded to include cleaning a chain of lumber stores in the lower mainland.

During the early 1980s, the corporation broadened its client base and began leasing to the private sector space which was surplus to ministry needs. In May 1985, Clients Service Manager, Araceli de Ochoa was designated the "seven million dollar woman" in BCBC's internal newsletter, *The Landlord*, in recognition of the annual dollar value of leases to the private sector she arranged.

Employees even developed the corporation's colour scheme when one Property Management Unit decided to paint a truck in nontraditional colours. In the end the new design was adopted by all of BCBC. Such innovative acts are reinforced by CEO Peter Dolezal who contacts each employee personally to offer congratulations.

MANAGEMENT SYSTEMS

Although the corporation uses a number of enlightened management practices such as leaves of absence, work sharing, contract options and comprehensive training, absolutely critical to increased productivity and a decentralized structure has been the development of a sophisticated management information system (MIS) along with the introduction of Management by Results (MBR). The strong information base was the tool with which employees were able to make informed deci-

• • •

sions and was the vital link needed to monitor performances and maintain control. The totally distributed hardware configuration used complemented the geographic dispersion of the organization. Its cost effectiveness is reflected in the elimination of 30 secretarial positions through the introduction of one system alone—electronic mail. Similar to management by objectives (MBO) MBR helped to get everyone pulling in the same direction. The method focussed on measurable results and acted as a management tool to achieve both vertical and horizontal integration. This was facilitated by a two-level approval system and the cascading of the president's own MBR, essentially reflecting the corporation's annual plan. The strategic outlook is five years forward with a definitive emphasis on year one. The commitment to this approach is reinforced since individual performance is evaluated against MBR every quarter and is the foundation of the merit compensation program.

THE CLIENT SERVICES DEPARTMENT

BCBC's organizational design has played a vital role in enhancing client relations. The Client Services Department (see Figure 2) acts as the corporation's interface with the client ministries and it is here where requests and inquiries are processed. Client Services managers and assistants are assigned specific client ministries.

As mentioned, the market audit in 1983 highlighted areas of client concern with BCBC. It was discovered, for instance, that clients appeared to have a lack of understanding of corporate policies. Moreover, they generally felt that Client Services managers and assistants were limited in the amount of time they could devote to ministries and limited as well in their authority and responsibility for resolving prob-

FIGURE 2 PLANNING AND CLIENT SERVICES.

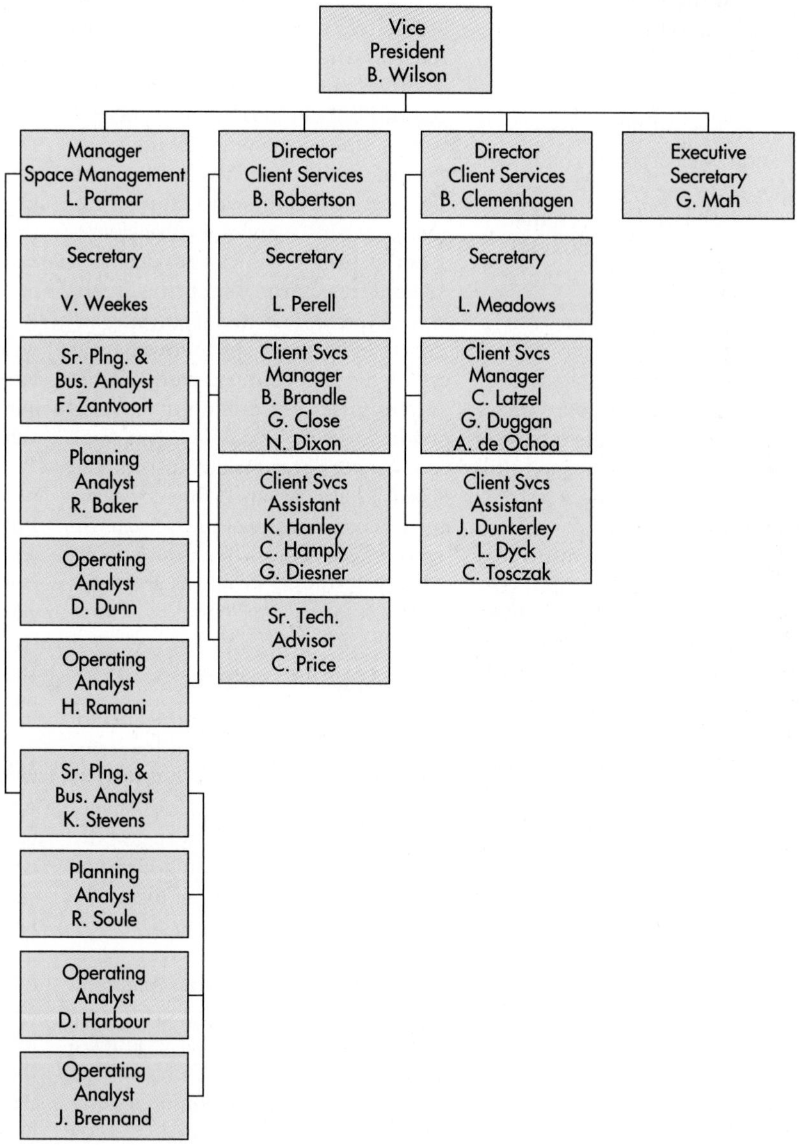

• • •

lems. Furthermore, it was felt that prices were too high and that the corporation could provide better information on the cost of services and their availability.

Some members in the department (Client Services assistants) felt that they were understaffed and that administration did not completely understand their needs. Consequently, they believed that they did not have adequate support staff and felt, moreover, that their job descriptions were too varied, too broadly based, and in a sense, too obscure. Importantly, these concerns did not go beyond themselves as the audit also determined that they were seen as "knowledgeable, hard-working and as having high morale and enthusiasm."

Significantly, because they were dealing with clients outside BCBC, the workflow could not be controlled as in some other departments. In other words, it was difficult to predict, on a day-to-day basis, the number and type of problems that employees might have to handle. Consequently, the "lean and mean" structure at BCBC was felt, in this instance, to be somewhat counterproductive.

In an attempt to assess workloads, a subcommittee was formed and a meeting was set up to determine if it was reasonable for the department, as resourced, to complete the work assigned. Towards that objective a questionnaire called *Client Services Assistance Survey* was devised to collect information about the categories of work (e.g., typing, phone calls, filing, faxing, etc.) undertaken. Initially, the amount of filing required in the job was a major concern. This may have symbolized a retrogressive step in the eyes of the Client Services assistants, many of whom had risen from the clerical ranks, and who had been told their new job would be more challenging than their previous position. Indeed, some felt that the secretaries to the managers should complete the task but they said they didn't have the time either. Hence, the assistants suggested the hiring of a filing clerk as a solution to the problem. Less than a "close to the customer" approach clearly would be antithetical to the "**Priority One**" client orientation pervasively espoused by the corporation. In part to handle this situation, and related to the 1983 client concerns illuminated in the external audit, a manual called *Accommodating You* was redesigned to answer, in simple language, some routine questions, and to give guidance regarding procedural matters to clients. Hence, the corporation challenged itself to be both user-friendly and user-useful.

TOWARDS THE EXCELLENCE-CULTURE

The outcomes of the pursuit of the excellence-culture have been manifold and the movement of BCBC towards a private sector operating system is at 7 on a 10 point scale according to Dennis Truss. To enhance accountability in the public sector he suggests (using BCBC as a model) the following key features as requisite:

1. A board of directors independent except for ministerial linkage.
2. A corporate form of organization structure.
3. An ability to borrow funds in its own name.
4. An ability to buy, sell, lease or build assets in its own name.
5. The right to charge market-based rents.
6. The right to charge market-based overheads.
7. Generally accepted accounting principles to monitor performance.
8. Profitability to be measured in relation to market benchmarks.
9. The payment of dividends using private sector criteria.

In the end the whole BCBC process has drawn the attention of academics and practitioners alike. Whether intrigued by a government agency trying to manage like its private sector counterparts, or simply because of its application of sound business practices, combined with innovative risk taking, the corporation has acted as a role model for others, and when Peter Dolezal won the Lieutenant Governor's Award for commitment to excellence in June 1987, all employees felt a great sense of achievement. ▲

QUESTIONS

1. Describe the corporate culture at BCBC, using Table 16-1 as a checklist. How might the factors in Table 16-1 be in conflict with each other?
2. Based on the information given, which one of the four basic kinds of cultures identified by Deal and Kennedy exists at BCBC?
3. How "strong" is the culture at BCBC? Defend your answer.
4. Use Table 16-2 to determine the extent to which BCBC is adhering to the criteria established by Peters and Waterman for "excellent" companies.

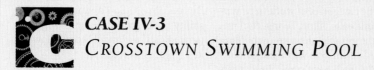

CASE IV-3
CROSSTOWN SWIMMING POOL

CROSSTOWN SWIMMING POOL (A)

Cathy Benson entered the Brocklehurst Town Office eager to start her new job as pool manager of Crosstown Swimming Pool. Cathy was replacing Derek Cooper the temporary pool manager. Martha Weaver, the permanent pool manager, was on an extended maternity leave. Derek had been offered a permanent full-time position in a neighbouring town and quite unexpectedly left the position vacant.

Cathy spent most of her first day with Jennifer Kolb, the recreation supervisor, learning the various procedures associated with the pool (see Exhibit A for the organizational chart). That afternoon, Jennifer took Cathy to the pool and introduced her to the three part-time life guards: Sean Kerr, Joanne Kirby, and Lois Allen as well as the part-time lifeguards who were on duty that afternoon (see Exhibit B for information on the pool employees). It was the responsibility of the head guard on duty to be in charge of the swimming pool in the absence of the pool manager. This individual was accountable for all aspects of the pools operation during that time. Cathy would learn the specific procedures associated with the daily aspects of her new position from the head guards. By the time she went home that day, Cathy was eager to get to know her staff and make her "mark" at the pool.

The First Week

Cathy was quickly thrust into the role of pool manager. During the two-week gap between Derek's departure and Cathy's first day a number of projects had been temporarily put on hold. The pool had been without a volunteer coordinator for almost three weeks, so finding a new coordinator was a priority. Joanne Kirby was leaving her position in another month, so Cathy had to start looking for a new part-time head guard. In addition, the new program brochure had gone to the printer for its first draft without listing any advanced lifesaving courses for the spring. Thus, classes had to be arranged, instructors had to be contacted, and the publicity material sent to Jennifer. It was Cathy's responsibility for the speedy implementation of all the necessary changes.

Day-to-day duties also had to be completed. One session of swimming lessons was ending so Cathy had to process the test sheets, distribute awards, compile statistics and begin to accept registration for a new session of classes. In addition to these tasks, Cathy still found the time to study the staff policy manual, review the personnel files and familiarize herself with the staff.

Spending a little time with the staff Cathy soon realized that the pool was a fun place to work. Everyone seemed to enjoy each other's company and even socialized after work. The atmosphere

EXHIBIT A BROCKELHURST TOWN OFFICE ORGANIZATIONAL CHART.

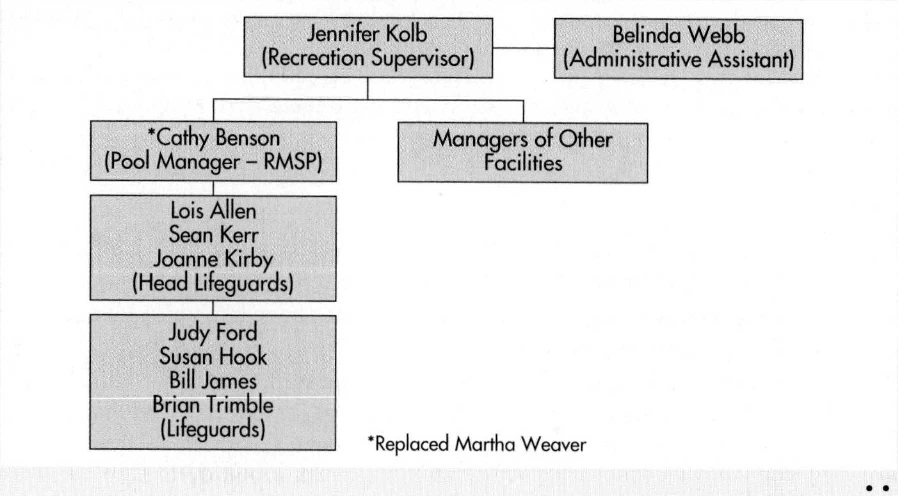

EXHIBIT B POOL EMPLOYEE INFORMATION.

Position	Education	Pool Experience*	Goals
Recreation Supervisor			
Jennifer Kolb (25)	Honours Recreation & Leisure	3 years HLG 2 years LG	More senior administrative position
Pool Manager			
Cathy Benson (22)	Honours B.A.—major in Psychology	2 years HLG 2 years LG	Develop new pool programs, particularly geared to seniors and tots
Head Lifeguards			
Lois Allen (18)	1st yr. B. Comm. student	1-1/2 years HLG 2 years LG	Sports Admin. Older sister worked at pool two years earlier
Sean Kerr (18)	1st yr. Environmental Studies	1 years HLG 2 years LG	Work with Ministry of the Environment
Joanne Kirby (19)	2nd yr. Recreation and Leisure Studies	2 years HLG 2 years LG	Own and manage a summer camp
Lifeguards			
Judy Ford (17)	1st yr. Kinesiology	2 years LG	Occupational therapy
Susan Hook (16)	High School	6 months LG	Not sure
Bill James (16)	High School	1 yr LG	Make money and have fun
Brian Trimble (17)	1st year Bachelor of Arts	10 months LG	Public school teacher

* With the exception of Cathy Benson, the staff have gained all their pool experience from working at Crosstown.

was congenial and people generally seemed to look forward to coming to work.

Late on Thursday evening, while working on a staff schedule for the spring, Cathy suddenly realized that there were flaws in the brochure that was about to be published. Derek had scheduled twelve classes in the pool at the same time—twice the usual number. The whole system had to be redone before the final draft went to the printer on Monday. The next morning when she approached Jennifer with this problem, Cathy was relieved to receive a hearty endorsement for the revised schedule she had drafted.

That night she discussed her first week with her husband. "I'm so excited about all this Joe," she bubbled. "I feel like I have accomplished so much. This job is exactly what I wanted. The staff is terrific. Joanne and Sean and Lois explained all the procedures to me, and most of the kids seemed so helpful. Judy Ford, although not one of the head lifeguards, stayed late to help me write up the test sheets. Surprisingly, she wouldn't even let me pay her for the extra time!"

"Martha Weaver, the permanent pool manager stopped by with her baby this afternoon and we talked a lot about the job. She gave me the name of a woman who would probably be a great volunteer coordinator. Martha provided some helpful insight on the staff. She told me that although they were all dedicated to the pool and the kids, she found Sean and Lois more easygoing than Joanne. She suggested that Joanne could be short-tempered and abrupt with the other staff members, particularly when she was under pressure from exams and deadlines at school. At the end of our conversation Martha told me to give her a call if I run into any trouble, but to feel free to run the pool as I want because I am 'the boss' until September."

"That's what Jennifer kept saying too! As a matter of fact, when I showed her the problem with the lesson schedule, she told me that I was doing a very careful and thorough job so far. Jennifer said that she had heard favourable comments from Martha, and even some parents who were in to register for lessons. In fact, she said that at the rate I'm going, I'll probably be able to get a raise in June, at the time of the annual evaluations."

Cathy and Joe sat up late into the night happily discussing the various aspects of her new job, and the career opportunities it could lead to. Joe was

• • •

really happy to see Cathy feeling so positive about her new job.

The Second Week

The following Monday morning, the beginning of her second week on the job, Cathy entered the Town Office thinking about how much she already felt at home. Shortly after 10:00 A.M., Jennifer poked her head around the corner and asked Cathy to come into her office for a few minutes. Belinda Webb, Jennifer's administrative assistant, looked up a Cathy passed her desk and said teasingly, "Here only a week and you're in trouble already, eh?"

Jennifer appeared a little perturbed as Cathy came in and sat down. "Tell me, how are things going for you so far Cathy," she began. "Are you getting along with the staff?"

Cathy answered a bit apprehensively, "Yes, they are all really good kids. They have all been very friendly and quite helpful."

Jennifer persisted, "What about Joanne and Lois?"

"Well, they seem very capable. Joanne will be leaving in another month and I'll be sorry to lose her. She's been a big help to me so far. And...well, I haven't seen too much of Lois—just Monday when I met her, and then she was in for an hour on Tuesday. She also worked on Saturday, but of course I wasn't there. She seems okay—a nice girl."

"What about a replacement for Joanne. Have you thought about that yet?"

"Yes, I have. Judy Ford spoke to me about the opening. She would like to apply. Judy said that she had sent you a memo to that effect. Martha seemed to think that she would be a good choice. I know that two of the boys, Bill James and Brian Trimble were also applying to be head guards in the summer so I asked them if they'd like to be considered now..."

"Have you spoken to anyone else about the position?"

"No..." she said, looking concerned.

"Has anyone asked you about it?"

"No, not really. One of the guards was chatting with me on Thursday—Susan I think it was. She asked if I knew who would be hired, and I said that so far only Judy had applied."

A look of understanding passed over Jennifer's face. Cathy hesitated, then asked if there was something wrong. Jennifer nodded and said, "Yes, however, now that you've explained a few things to me, I think I know what's going on. I received two memos this morning and I have been trying to figure out how to handle the situation." She picked up two handwritten memos and continued. "These were addressed to me, which makes it awkward, because they are from two members of your staff. I usually prefer to let the pool manager take care of any difficulties that arise until the situation reaches the point where I think that help is needed. I don't like to get involved because sometimes that undermines the authority of the pool manager.

Secondly, I don't want the pool staff running to me behind your back. In fact, one of the policies in the staff manual states that aquatic staff should not approach me unless that individual and the pool manager cannot resolve a situation."

Jennifer paused and placed the memos on her desk. "These are from Joanne and Lois. They say basically the same thing although Joanne's is a much angrier letter. They say that they'd heard you'd promoted Judy to head guard and they feel it's unfair. They believe that you shouldn't have been allowed to make this type of decision by yourself and that you should have asked the present head guards for their input."

Cathy was absolutely shocked. "Are you serious? How could they? Where did they get this information? They didn't even ask me!"

"Frankly, I am as surprised as you are," Jennifer continued. "I've known these girls for three years and I expected much more from them. Their information was wrong. They know it's not up to them to decide who is hired as a head guard. They have an opportunity to voice their concerns regarding the staff after each session when evaluations are done. If they have any complaints about Judy—or anyone else—that is when they should voice them."

"Not only that," Cathy interrupted, "but I wouldn't promote anyone to that position without asking you or Martha for your opinions. Those little sneaks—I still cannot believe that they wrote to you instead of just asking me."

"I'm really sorry that this happened Cathy. It's the first time any of the staff has done something like this. I think it's very important that we handle the situation carefully so that it doesn't get blown out of proportion. As I see it we have two choices—either you handle the situation on your own, or I get directly involved."

"I prefer to talk to them myself, if that is okay with you, Jennifer. I want to hear their side of the story. I will let them know how this makes me feel, and why what they've done is wrong. Hopefully, this will prevent it from happening again."

"All right," conceded Jennifer. "However, because they directed the memos to me, I will write a response. Basically, I will tell them that what they did was wrong, and that I am quite disappointed with them. They should not have come to me without confirming the rumour through you. I'll also make sure that they are aware that at no time are head guards consulted regarding the hiring of other head guards. Lastly, I will instruct them to give you a formal written apology."

"Okay," Cathy agreed. "Both Joanne and Lois work tomorrow evening, so I will talk to them then."

"After you finish talking to them I would like you to give them my response to their memo."

That night Joe listened to Cathy's tirade against the two girls. "Those two-faced witches! They were so sweet and helpful to my face but the moment my back was turned look what they did. I bet Joanne's behind all of this and just dragged Lois in for backup. Martha told me about Joanne. Are they trying to get me fired, or what? I'm just lucky Jennifer thinks I'm doing a good job—what would have happened if she didn't? Who do they think they are doing this to me? Have teenagers changed that much? Wait until I see them tomorrow!"

She didn't know what she was going to do or how to handle it but she was going to make sure that this kind of thing didn't happen again.

CROSSTOWN SWIMMING POOL (B)

The next afternoon, as soon as school was over Lois went directly to the pool, knocked on Cathy's door and barged in. Before Cathy could open her mouth, Lois blurted out, "I've done something really stupid and I wanted you to hear it from me first. I thought you had hired Judy Ford to replace Joanne and I got really upset. I was so angry on Sunday that I called Joanne, told her about it and then I wrote a memo to Jennifer complaining about it. I just found out this morning that you hadn't hired Judy, and that you asked Bill and Brian if they wanted to apply. I really feel badly. I'm terribly sorry and I want to apologize."

Cathy could see how upset Lois was, and her pent-up anger melted away. "As a matter of fact I already know about it. Jennifer discussed it with me yesterday. I had planned to talk to you today anyway. I was really hurt when I found out about it because you didn't even phone me to see if it was true. I was home on Sunday—you could have called."

Lois was miserable. "I know. But we just sat there and complained because we didn't think Judy would be a very good head guard, but you wouldn't know that yet."

"The fact that I don't know the staff yet is not significant. When the time comes to hire a new head guard it won't be just me making the decision. Jennifer will be in on the interviews. I'll be looking at everyone's performance appraisals over the past few years, and Martha will give her opinions too."

"I guess I should have known that, Cathy. I'm really sorry I sent that memo."

Cathy gave Lois the memo Jennifer had written. Lois read it quickly and left the office. A few minutes later she returned with a written apology to Cathy. Now Cathy felt a little guilty for overreacting to the situation. She remembered what it had been like as a teenager—always doing something rash and regretting it later. There were incidents from her own days as a lifeguard that she didn't care to remember.

Feeling satisfied with having cleared the air with Lois, Cathy wanted to do a few things around the pool before looking for Joanne.

CROSSTOWN SWIMMING POOL (C)

A short time later, Cathy was hanging posters in the lobby when she noticed Joanne come in the door. "Could I see you for a few moments, Joanne?" Cathy requested.

"Okay, I'll just put my bag in the change room."

"That can wait. I'd like to see you right away."

Startled, Joanne followed Cathy into the office. "What's up?" Joanne asked nervously.

"Please sit down," Cathy directed. "It's about your memo."

"What memo?" Joanne demanded.

"This memo you sent to Jennifer," Cathy said, as she pulled a copy of the memo from a file.

Joanne flushed. "I didn't send that memo to you—I sent that to Jennifer—it's none of your business," she insisted.

Cathy's calm attitude was infuriating her. "Well it isn't your business and Jennifer had no right to show you my memo. If I had wanted you to see it I would have sent you a copy!"

"Jennifer felt that because the memo was about me and this pool that I should be aware of it. Also, in case you've forgotten, I'd like to remind you that the town has a policy which states that problems are to be discussed with the pool manager before involving the recreation supervisor."

Joanne flushed even more.

"Let's talk about what you wrote." Cathy was still very calm and spoke clearly and slowly. "First of all, I should let you know that no one has yet been hired to take your place. The interviews have been scheduled for next weekend."

Joanne looked at her in surprise. "But I heard...." She suddenly realized that she was wrong and stopped short.

"Yes, you heard?" As she felt herself getting control of the situation, Cathy's voice took on a condescending air.

"Nothing," mumbled Joanne.

"Very well, I will go on. I agree with you and Lois. Since I was hired so recently I shouldn't be making these decisions alone."

• • •

Joanne brightened and sat up a little straighter as Cathy continued. "A decision like this should be made very carefully, taking a lot of things into consideration. Jennifer will sit in on the interviews with me, and I will also speak to Martha before making the final decision. In addition, I have access to everyone's performance appraisals and I feel that will give me enough information to make a good choice."

Joanne digested this information and asked hesitantly, "Are you saying you don't need any help from Sean, Lois and me?"

"That's correct—it's not you who's responsible for the decision—it's me!" snapped Cathy.

Joanne flushed again. "But, but," she stammered, "You don't know the staff. We know what people are really like, and we know how well they get along with the others, and with the public. That's what really matters... and...and..."

"I'm not fooled that easily Joanne, and I don't appreciate you implying that I am."

"What I meant was..."

"I don't care what you meant," Cathy said as she totally lost her patience. "It doesn't matter!"

"What doesn't matter?" demanded Joanne. "Your opinion doesn't matter," stated Cathy.

Joanne was appalled. "Who the hell do you think you are?" she shouted. "Just because you're the manager doesn't mean you can talk to me like that."

Cathy was infuriated. "If you don't like the way I run this pool, you can quit right now. We're getting rid of you in three or four weeks anyway!"

Joanne was speechless with anger and frustration.

Cathy continued. "I would be more than happy to take on your workload for the next month."

"Well, maybe I'll quit!"

"Okay Joanne. Just don't ever expect to get a reference from Brocklehurst."

"You can't do this to me. I put in four goods years here before you came along and I've always had a good reputation."

"If you want to keep it that way you'll finish off your four weeks and keep your nose clean in the meantime."

"If I finish it off it's because I feel I have an obligation to the children I'm teaching, not because of any threats you make. Besides, Jennifer knows that I've always done a good job and she's the one who'll be writing my reference."

"What kind of reference do you think she'll give you after this episode? You might be interested in reading her response to your memo." With that, Cathy tossed the memo to Joanne. Joanne grabbed it and left the office.

A short time later Joanne flung the office door open and shouted, "I'm going to stay for my last few weeks, but you better leave me alone. And you'll rot in hell before you'll get an apology from me!" She slammed the door leaving Cathy alone in her office.

Cathy sat back in her chair and began to review the events that had led to this situation and wondered what she should do next. ▲

QUESTIONS

1. Why might rumours have started that Cathy had promoted someone to head lifeguard?
2. Comment on the strong and weak points of Cathy's leadership in this situation.
3. Use the conflict model in Chapter 15 to trace the development of the conflict between Cathy and Joanne.
4. What should Cathy do now?

PART 5

CONTROLLING

CHAPTER

17

THE CONTROLLING PROCESS

LEARNING OBJECTIVES

After reading this chapter, you will be able to:

1. Give four reasons why control is essential to an organization.
2. Describe the four steps in the control process.
3. Understand the difference between input, process, and output controls, and give an example of each.
4. State 7 reasons why employees often react negatively to controls.
5. Identify the 12 characteristics of an effective control system.

MANAGEMENT CHALLENGE

COST CONTROL AT ONTARIO HYDRO

Ontario Hydro, one of the world's 10 largest utilities, has a long and illustrious history as a major force in Ontario's industrial development. Until recently, its ability to supply cheap, reliable power to business was a major drawing card for the province. But the utility has recently fallen on hard times due to years of overspending, mismanagement, and failed expectations. In 1991, it abruptly postponed a $60 billion planned expansion, saying with some embarrassment that excess capacity already existed. Morale at the utility is at rock bottom.

Ontario Hydro currently has $30 billion of debt, and business customers who use a lot of electricity (chemicals, fertilizers, mining, and abrasives) are getting restless because of large rate increases in recent years. For some businesses, the increases are large enough to drive them out of the province. For example, Nitrochem Inc. recently shut down its ammonia plant in Maitland because its electricity costs had risen by 40 percent in the last five years (to 34 percent of operating costs). Efforts to negotiate a rate reduction with Hydro were unsuccessful, so the company started buying ammonia from the U.S. Forty workers in Maitland lost their jobs as a result. If rate increases continue, power generated by Ontario Hydro may soon cost more than that generated by nearby U.S. utilities.

Hydro is facing four major problems. First, the utility has a long history of building ever-larger power plants (ever-larger fiascos, in the view of critics). These large plants typically have experienced long construction delays and cost overruns. While Hydro does provide reliable service, it may have achieved it through a type of fiscal recklessness which would never be tolerated in the private sector.

Second, the utility's foray into nuclear power has been incredibly expensive. The showpiece of its nuclear strategy is the troubled Darlington plant, which was originally estimated to cost $2.5 billion, but which has so far eaten up $13.8 billion. (If the project had simply been cancelled in

• • •

1983, Hydro would have saved $10 billion dollars—one-third of its current debt load.) High-priced long-term contracts were signed with Denison Mines and Rio Algom in the late 1970s for uranium and natural gas, but prices of those commodities declined sharply over the next 10 years. Soaring interest rates in the early 1980s added to the cost of the Darlington plant, and tougher safety regulations imposed by the Atomic Energy Control Board created further delays.

Third, there are threats about competition from municipalities that are trying to cut utility costs. Both Windsor and Kingston, for example, have put forward plans to build plants which would supply most of their power—at a 10-15 percent saving over what they can get from Ontario Hydro.

Finally, Hydro's costs are astronomical. In 1991, Hydro employed over 28 000 workers whose salaries averaged $54 000. The utility spent $1.3 billion on fuel, $1.1 billion on depreciation charges, and $2.2 billion on financing. When Darlington came on stream in 1993, all these numbers went up even further. ▲

controlling

cybernetic system

noncybernetic system

We saw in Chapter 1 that controlling is one of the basic management functions. As such, it must be performed by all managers. **Controlling** is the process of comparing actual performance with standards, taking corrective action when performance falls short of the standards, and positively reinforcing individuals when they meet or exceed standards. Controlling is concerned with ensuring that results are achieved according to plan. It is therefore intimately related to the planning function of management.

We can see how important the controlling function is by comparing the human body to organizations like Canadian Pacific or the United Way. The human body is a **cybernetic system**, that is, it is self-regulating. When you cut your finger, for example, your body responds immediately and automatically to begin healing the injury. But an organization is a **noncybernetic system**, that is, an artificial system that requires the exercise of human discretion to control operations.The problems facing Ontario Hydro in the Management Challenge shows what can happen in a noncybernetic system if it is not properly controlled.

In this chapter, we first explain why the controlling function is important, and then outline the basic types of control that are available to managers. Second, we describe the steps in the controlling process. Third, we note the necessity of establishing strategic control points, and indicate how the controlling function differs across organizational levels. Fourth, we explain how inputs, processes, and outputs are controlled. Finally, resistance to controls is examined, and several ways to overcome employee resistance to controls are noted.

THE IMPORTANCE OF THE CONTROLLING FUNCTION

Some managers believe that when they have given attention to the functions of planning, organizing, and leading that their managerial responsibilities have been fulfilled. This is not a reasonable view. If controlling is given insufficient attention, all the energy the manager has expended in the planning, organizing, and leading functions may go to waste.

We can see this effect in the problems that many companies experienced after the economic boom of the 1980s ended. Magna, Canada's largest auto parts maker, is typical. Between 1970 and 1988, Magna's sales grew from $5 million to $1.5 billion, but its debt increased from almost nothing to over $1 billion. To make matters worse, the various product groups in the company had become almost totally autonomous and were pursuing a variety of activities that weren't necessarily compatible. Quotes went out on jobs the company didn't even know if it could handle. Finally, changes were finally made to bring the company back from the brink of bankruptcy. Now, no division of Magna can make capital expenditures without approval of the management committee. The firm is also pursuing a goal of no more than 50 cents of debt for each dollar of equity.[1]

The importance of the controlling function can also be seen in a comparison of retail giants Wal-Mart and Kmart. Wal-Mart is the largest retailer in North America with profits per square foot of about $20, while Kmart's are less than $8. Retailing experts say that Kmart is falling behind because it does not have an effective control system. Merchandise is not displayed consistently from store to store, and out-of-stock situations are common. Kmart's selling expenses are 23 cents on the dollar, compared to Wal-Mart's 16 cents. The companies do not differ simply on financial controls. At Wal-Mart, employees are encouraged to offer suggestions about how to improve operations. At Kmart, however, the CEO doesn't like to receive bad news, so few managers are willing to tell him when things are not going right.[2]

Why Controls Are Needed

Controls are needed for four primary reasons:[3]

LEARNING OBJECTIVE 1
Give four reasons why control is essential to an organization.

1. *Unexpected developments may make a plan inoperable* These unexpected developments can affect a society in general or they can affect only one firm. For example, in the summer of 1990, oil was priced at about $16 per barrel. Many Canadian companies made plans based on the assumption that the price of oil would remain stable in the short run. But the Iraqi invasion of Kuwait caused oil to nearly double in price. All firms that had planned on the basis of inexpensive oil had to make adjustments to their plan. In early 1991, oil again dropped sharply in price, and further adjustments had to be made. Appropriate controls help a company determine when changes in plans are necessary.
2. *Employees do not always do what they are supposed to do* Some employees are unwilling to work toward management's plans, while others are simply unable to. In either case, the manager must use some controlling mechanisms to keep workers on track.
3. *Organizations are complex entities, and they require a system for assessing the progress that is being made toward objectives* Until the twentieth century, most organizations were quite small. But with the increasing size of corporations, unions, universities, governments, and volunteer agencies, it has become necessary to establish rigorous control procedures to ensure that what is supposed to happen actually happens, and that customer and client needs are satisfied. The Management at Work insert entitled "The Controlling Process and Customer Satisfaction" shows how the controlling process increases customer satisfaction.
4. *As the delegation of authority increases, more employees acquire the right to make decisions* As we saw in Chapter 7, delegating authority has several advantages. But delegation also increases the chance that employees will make a decision that will hurt the organization. It is therefore essential to have controls for monitoring employee decisions and initiating corrective action if the results are undesirable.

Control in agri-business means ensuring production units (such as beef cattle) are healthy. CIBA-GEIGY has developed the BOVAID insecticide ear tag, which gives cattle protection against disease-carrying flies. The cattle feed better, are healthier, and experience increased weight gain.

Sources of Control in Organizations

Controls originate from four general sources: the stakeholders of the organization, the organization itself, groups within the organization, and individuals.[4] **Stakeholder control** is applied by those who are concerned about how the organization operates. As we saw in Chapter 3, stakeholders include customers, shareholders, financial institutions,

stakeholder control

MANAGEMENT AT WORK

The Controlling Process and Customer Satisfaction

Increased competition and the internationalization of business activity have motivated business firms to more tightly control their production processes so that the goods and services they produce will satisfy customers needs. Truly customer-oriented companies measure their customers' opinions not only when selling goods and services, but also when designing them.

The Conference Board of Canada surveyed 50 Canadian companies to determine their approaches to satisfying customers. Programs at the most successful companies have the following elements:

1. Customer satisfaction is an integral part of the company's strategic plan.
2. Senior management is committed to improving customer satisfaction.
3. Efforts are made to match customer expectations with the company's expertise.

Any firm which is serious about the goal of customer satisfaction must systematically monitor the performance of employees who have contact with customers. To reduce the risk that monitoring may lower employee motivation and morale, performance evaluation must be linked with the rewards that employees receive for good work.

An integral part of the control process involves discovering how customers see the firm's products and services. CP Rail has embarked on a program to uncover discrepancies between what customers want and what the company is actually providing. Service reps are informed about problems with customers before the rep goes to talk to the customer. The customer therefore sees the rep as more informed and professional in approaching problems. Under the Customer Exchange Program, employees of CP go to work for a customer for a day or two. In this way, CP employees get a good idea of what the customer goes through on an average day. CP is also planning to institute a Customer Advisory Panel which will bring CP managers and customers together to discuss customer concerns about service and product development.

In spite of the fact that "getting close to the customer" is a popular phrase, companies may not actively pursue that goal. A Peat Marwick study of the goals of firms in the hotel industry found that profitability and growth ranked first and second, while customer satisfaction ranked fifth. Four Seasons Hotels & Resorts stresses "7 C's of quality" in order to achieve satisfied customers: *comprehension* (accepting the idea that quality is important), *culture* (instilling an attitude of service in employees), *commitment* (no compromises on quality), *credibility* (employees see that management is serious about quality), *control* (monitoring quality standards), *creativity* (thinking up new and useful services for customers), and *continuity* (take the long-term view). ▲

environmental groups, and government agencies. One of the ways that stakeholders exercise control is by putting pressure on an organization to take some specific action. For example, in the Management Challenge, customers of Ontario Hydro were putting pressure on the utility to provide lower power rates. When Hydro wouldn't they began looking around for other sources of power. As another example, McDonald's was under intense pressure from environmentalists in the early 1990s to get rid of its "clamshell" hamburger container. The company finally changed to a paper wrapper.[5]

organizational control

Organizational controls are those which are introduced by management as part of the formal activity of the organization. They include rules, policies, procedures, standards, budgets, management audits, the management hierarchy, quality control, inventory control, financial analysis, profit centres, and break-even analysis. These controls, which are discussed in Chapter 18, tend to be impersonal and may be only grudgingly accepted by employees.

group control

The formal aspects of an organization, however, are not the only means by which employee behaviour is controlled. **Group control** is exercised over individuals by the work groups or friendship groups they belong to. In Chapter 9, we noted that work groups have a powerful influence on individuals. When individuals first join a group, they are socialized to accept the group's "view of the world." The group then rewards individuals who behave "properly" and punishes individuals who do not.

Organizational and group control exercise an external influence on the individual. But individuals may also control their own behaviour internally. Through **individual control**, a person voluntarily behaves in a way that facilitates the goals of the organization. If such individual control is operating, employees do not try to frustrate the organization's performance. They will not, for instance, embezzle money; they will cooperate with other workers, they will come to work on time, and they will put in a fair day's work. This type of control is the least common in organizations because many managers do not trust subordinates to work toward organizational goals. As we saw in Chapter 12, when managers think this way, a self-fulfilling prophecy often develops, that is, subordinates behave in ways that they think management expects.

individual control

These four sources of control usually result in two basic approaches to control in organizations. **Clan control** stresses employee commitment to the organization, group norms, group performance, employee self-control, shared influence, and extensive participation. Levi Strauss is an example of a company that practises clan control. **Bureaucratic control**, on the other hand, emphasizes individual performance, control of employees by the hierarchy, top-down influence, and little employee participation. Many public-sector organizations, such as Revenue Canada, have traditionally used bureaucratic control.

clan control

bureaucratic control

THE CONTROLLING PROCESS

The **controlling process** ensures that planned activities and results actually occur. There are four distinct steps in the controlling process:

controlling process

LEARNING OBJECTIVE 2

Describe the four steps in the controlling process.

1. Setting performance standards.
2. Measuring performance.
3. Comparing actual performance to the standard.
4. Taking corrective action as necessary.

The controlling process is shown in Figure 17-1.

SETTING PERFORMANCE STANDARDS

In order to be effective, both managers and workers must know what is expected of them. Standards convey these expectations. **Standards** are criteria for evaluating the quality and quantity of the products or services produced by employees. Ideally, standards are set and communicated to employees during the planning process. Standards are most helpful in directing employee behaviour when they are stated in quantitative terms. A standard of "20 sales calls per week" guides behaviour much more specifically than a standard of "maximize sales calls each week." Quantitative standards give clear, objective guidance to employees, and allow management to assess performance accurately.[6]

standards

FIGURE 17-1 THE CONTROL PROCESS.

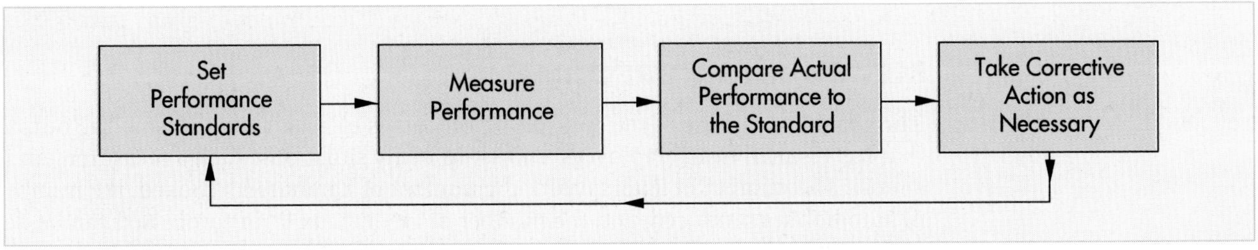

AMP of Canada Ltd. produces electrical interconnection devices. In this highly competitive market, it is imperative that the company find out what customers want and then give it to them. To achieve this, standards of performance have been set for all jobs in marketing.[7] McDonald's is legendary for its adherence to standards. The company's training manual, for example, sets standards on hundreds of activities, ranging from the cooking time for french fries to the cleanliness of the restrooms.

Types of Standards

time standards

Many types of standards are used in organizations.[8] **Time standards** state the length of time it should take to complete a task. At American Express of Canada Inc., customer contact personnel are required to respond to customer inquiries within 24 hours.[9] Time standards are relevant for many other types of workers, including auto mechanics (time standards for tune-ups, engine scope checks, engine rebuilding, and other repairs), airline pilots (time standards for trips between various cities), and production workers (time standards for the work they do, and for the length of time they can spend on coffee break). Setting time standards can result in significant increases in profitability. Hewlett-Packard discovered that when a new product was late getting to the market, it lost 30 percent of the product's profitability over its life. But a 50 percent cost overrun in research and development led to only a 3 percent loss.[10]

output standards

Output standards state the quantity of the product or service that employees should be producing. At a General Motors Canada plant, for example, the overall output standard might be 60 compact cars per hour. At a McDonald's outlet, the standard might be that no more than four people are standing in any line waiting to be served.

cost standards

Cost standards state the maximum cost that should be incurred in the course of producing goods and services. A customer who buys stock from a broker will normally state the maximum price per share he or she is willing to pay. A volunteer organization will state the maximum salary it is willing to pay its executive director. A manufacturing firm will state the maximum price it is willing to pay for raw materials. As we saw in the Management Challenge, Ontario Hydro is having great difficulty staying within its cost standards.

quality standards

Quality standards define the level of quality that is to be maintained in the production of goods and services. McDonald's sets quality standards for the meat it buys. Asics sets quality standards for the material it uses in its "Gel" running shoe. Legal and accounting firms set quality standards for the services they provide to their clients. At American Express of Canada Inc., quality standards are high: customer-contact employees are to provide information that is 100 percent accurate.[11]

behavioural standards

Behavioural standards state the types of behaviour that are acceptable for employees. Most organizations have standards dealing with smoking, employee dress, use of foul language in front of customers, and so forth.

control tolerances

Often, control tolerances are necessary in addition to standards. **Control tolerances** state the degree of deviation from the standard that is permissible. For example, a company may require all employees to be at their workstation by 8:30 A.M. If an employee doesn't arrive until 8:32 A.M., this may be tolerated, but any employee who arrives after 8:35 A.M. will have their pay docked. Both standards and control tolerances should be clearly communicated to workers.

MEASURING PERFORMANCE

The goal of this phase of the controlling process is to accurately measure the output that has resulted from employees' efforts. In many situations, such a measurement is simple. The number of letters typed, the number of hamburgers cooked, the number of automobiles produced, and the number of income tax forms processed can be determined with a high degree of accuracy. But measuring employee output in certain other situations may be problematic. Determining the output level of a psychoanalyst, a university professor, a management consultant, or a researcher in a laboratory may be difficult because of the nature of the work these people are doing. For example, measuring the effect of psychotherapy is difficult because improvements may not be attributable solely to the therapy; other factors, such as the person's home situation, also influence the person's life.

Managers can measure output in various ways. One is through personal observation of the performance of subordinates. At American Express of Canada, for example, supervisors tap into the calls of customer-contact employees 20 times per month to determine if they are dealing properly with customers. Monthly evaluations of customer complaints are also carried out.[12] Personal observation gives the manager firsthand information about surbordinates. However, it is not always practical or advisable for a manager to use this approach since it is very time-consuming. A second approach is to use written reports of employee performance. For example, a manager may require an annual report of activity from an employee. This approach gives the manager a permanent record of employee performance, but has the disadvantage of requiring the employee to do additional work. A third approach is for the manager to require oral reports from subordinates about their performance. This has the advantage of getting the manager and subordinate together for a face-to-face meeting, but problems may develop if the subordinate feels intimidated by the boss. Because each approach has both strong and weak points, it is best to use them in combination.

The importance of time standards is evident in the mass production of automobiles. Each job to be performed is carefully defined and timed by engineers, and each worker is required to carry out a specific set of activities. All of this specific activity translates into a certain number of complete automobiles being produced each hour.

If standards have been clearly stated, the measurement of performance is much easier. However, even if standards are explicitly defined, management cannot simply assume that the reported performance has actually occurred. Employees might have made honest errors when reporting their performance, output might have been at the expense of quality standards, or employees might have deliberately falsified reports of their performance.

Comparing Performance with Standards

In this step, the manager essentially compares "what is" with "what should be." Since the performance of human beings varies, it is necessary for the manager to determine control tolerances. Only if performance is outside the acceptable range does the manager take further action. If the preceding steps in the control process have been carried out properly, the comparison of performance with standards is straightforward. Comparison is also easier if quantitative standards have been set.

Take Corrective Action as Necessary

The final phase in the controlling process requires the manager to decide what corrective action (if any) is required. When making this decision, the manager must ensure that the real cause of the deviation from standard is identified. For example, if the output of a certain product is below standard, it must be determined whether the cause is human failure or machine failure. The corrective action that is necessary will depend on the cause of the deviation.

When comparing performance with the standard, the manager will find that it exceeds, meets, or falls short of the standard. If performance exceeds the standard, the manager must first ensure that the standard is actually reasonable. Once this has been done, the employee should be praised. If performance meets the standard, no further action needs to be taken.

When performance falls short of the standard, the manager must decide whether the shortfall is significant enough to demand corrective action. For example, if instructors in a university or college must achieve at least a 3.0/5 on student evaluations, and an instructor receives a 2.9/5, the department head will have to decide whether this deviation is significant enough to warrant a talk with the instructor. This process is simplified if control tolerances have already been stated.

When performance is not up to standard, managers can choose one of the following actions: (1) take corrective action, (2) change the standard, or (3) do nothing and hope things will improve. If the manager decides to take corrective action, two alternatives are available—immediate and long-term. **Immediate corrective action** solves the problem right now and gets output back to the desired level. If management discovers that a major project is behind schedule and that it is going to hold up other high-priority projects, immediate corrective action is taken. The top priority is getting the project back on schedule, rather than attaching blame for its lateness. Actions such as adding more personnel to the project, authorizing overtime, giving priority in the secretarial pool for project typing needs, and assigning an expediter to speed up the project are all examples of such action.

immediate corrective action

Long-term corrective action determines why deviations occur and what can be done to prevent the problem from happening in the future. Many managers focus too much of their effort on immediate responses and not enough on long-term corrective action. Consider this example: A manager of a department with high turnover finds that she is spending a great deal of his time recruiting new members for the department (immediate corrective action). But the manager never stops to analyze the reasons so many people are leaving the department (long-term corrective action). Unless long-term corrective action is taken, this manager will continually be trying to cope with problems she does not understand. The Global Management insert "How IBM Lost Control" describes IBM's attempts to take corrective action.

long-term corrective action

The second alternative—changing the standard—will occasionally be required due to the installation of newer, more efficient equipment or to new training methods which increase employee productivity. The third alternative—doing nothing—is generally indefensible, but there are exceptions. For example, if during one shift a normally reliable, high-performing worker suddenly has output that is well below standard, and the manager concludes that this is a one-time occurrence, the deviation should probably be ignored.

The Dynamics of Corrective Action

To be effective when taking corrective action, managers must possess a good understanding of why the problem has arisen, and have the necessary interpersonal skills to resolve it. It is best to begin with a positive approach. If a worker's output is below the standard, a manager has to determine why the deviation occurred and attempt to reach an agreement with the worker on how to avoid this type of predicament in the future. It is imperative that the boss praise the work that is being done correctly. The praise improves the worker's self-image and diminishes the chance that corrective action will be resisted. Once a positive environment has been established, it is easier to work toward a resolution of the problem.

This approach will not always work, however. In some cases, workers simply will not accept the fact that their work is not up to par, or that they have violated some fundamental company policy (see Case Study 17-3). In these situations, disciplinary action is necessary. **Disciplinary action** is the process of invoking a penalty against an employee who fails to adhere to some work-related standard. Managers regularly deal with disciplinary actions, but they may deal with them in an unacceptable manner (consider grievances in which arbitrators overrule management discipline decisions).

disciplinary action

GLOBAL MANAGEMENT

How IBM Lost Control

When John Akers took over IBM in 1985, the company looked invincible. Profits in 1984 were $6.6 billion on sales of $46 billion. Antitrust investigations in the U.S. and Europe had been dropped, and the company was predicting that sales would increase to $100 billion by 1990 and $185 billion by 1994. IBM was a company whose managerial and technological strength was admired and feared in the industry.

But how the mighty have fallen. Instead of leading the company to even greater heights, Akers presided over a dramatic decline in the company's fortunes. A chorus of critics began demanding his resignation after 40 000 jobs were cut in 1992 and then another 25 000 in 1993. Crises occurred after the company reported the first loss in its history in 1991, and a loss of nearly $5 billion for 1992, the biggest in U.S. corporate history. The price of the company's shares is now less than one-third of their mid-1980's level. What happened? How did it happen so fast? Does Akers deserve all the blame?

Perhaps the most fundamental problem was IBM's failure to fully capitalize on the personal computer (PC) revolution. IBM had built its reputation on building and selling mainframe computers, a market on which it had a stranglehold. Customers were very loyal to IBM, and since computers built by other companies did not interface with IBM's computers, the company sold high volumes of computers, had little price competition, and made a great deal of money.

With the advent of personal computers that were all made with the same basic parts, the industry was opened up to thousands of new competitors. The result has been ferocious competition, falling prices, soaring demand, and technological advancement at a dizzying rate. IBM is now struggling to find its place in an industry characterized by ruthless price competition.

While IBM did become the world's biggest PC maker, it lost control of the market. Ironically, IBM's entry into the personal computer market helped its competitors because IBM legitimized the PC for thousands of companies that had been wary of them. Its ponderous bureacracy also caused it to lag behind its competitors in the development of new products. And it entirely missed the booming market for PC software. It also failed to see the threat that PCs posed to its mainframe business.

However, Akers cannot be accused of standing idly by while the company's fortunes tumbled. But his actions were limited by the company's size, its complexity, and the complacency of its managers. Akers tried to overhaul IBM's management and operations soon after sales and profits began to falter. Between 1987 and 1991, manufacturing capacity was reduced by 40 percent, management was decentralized, and collaborative agreements were signed with archrivals like Apple, Toshiba, and Siemens. But these actions were insufficient.

The division of the company into 13 autonomous "federations" was a belated recognition that company headquarters could not coordinate a global organization like IBM, especially in an industry with so many smaller and more focussed competitors. Each of the federations is free to pursue its own interests, and each is supposed to deal with the others on an arm's-length basis. This type of structure is very popular in many companies, but observers think IBM's move in this direction is too half-hearted and is taking too long.

Even if the federation idea succeeds, IBM's problems of control may remain: it is the only company in the world that is trying to supply so many market segments in the computer industry. All the other firms have made the difficult decisions about which segment of the market they are going to compete in. ▲

Progressive Discipline

The actions that are taken when employees violate company standards must be appropriate to the offense. **Progressive discipline** means that increasingly severe penalties are applied as evidence of improper behaviour accumulates. Figure 17-2 illustrates the progressive discipline process. This process can be used if an employee's output is substandard, or if an employee violates company policy.

progressive discipline

FIGURE 17-2 PROGRESSIVE DISCIPLINE.

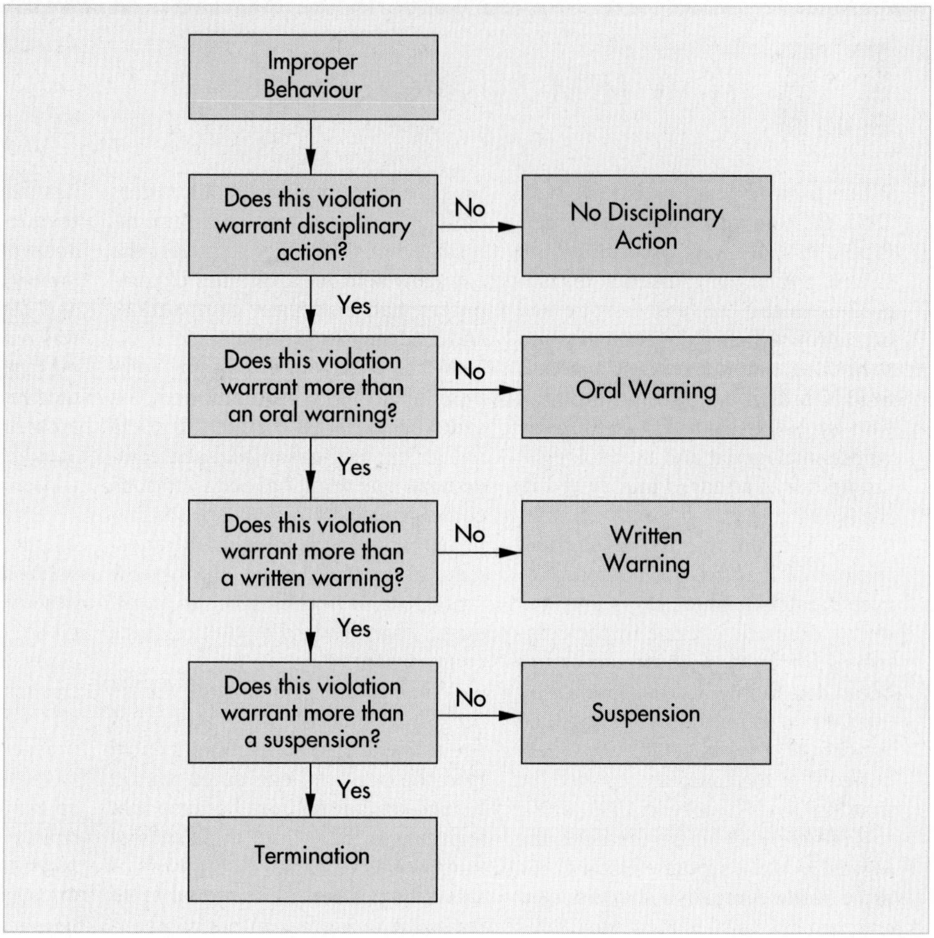

SITUATIONAL FACTORS IN CONTROLLING

The four-stage controlling process described above is applicable in all kinds of organizations. However, it is applied in distinct ways in different organizations. In the application of the general controlling process, managers must take into account two facts:

1. At certain strategic points, control absolutely must be applied.
2. The controlling process requires different managerial behaviours at different levels of the hierarchy.

Each of these issues is discussed below.

Strategic Control Points

strategic control points

All organizations must concern themselves with controlling inputs, processes, and outputs. However, it is costly and time-consuming to try to control every single activity at each phase of operations. Different organizations put different emphases on control at different phases, depending on the kind of work they are doing. **Strategic control**

points are those which an organization finds particularly important to its success; failure to exercise control at these points creates major problems for the organization.

A consumer products company, for example, may feel that since its long-term survival is based on new products, the new product development area is a strategic control point. A management consulting organization might conclude that finding the right people to be consultants is crucial to success, so a strategic control point would be the screening of inputs. An organization in a mature industry with severe competition might feel that high-quality products are crucial to its survival, so a strategic control point would be the actual production process.

A strategic control point has four basic characteristics.[13] First, it should be established to regulate key operations or events. If a problem arises at a strategic control point, the entire input-process-output flow can come to a halt. Second, a strategic control point must identify problems before they become serious. If strategic control points are properly located, they enable problems to be solved before any real harm is done. Third, a strategic control point must be economical, that is, the information it provides must be worth the costs that are incurred to provide it. Finally, a strategic control point must be balanced, that is, it must not overemphasize one element of operations at the expense of another. For example, a credit policy that is too restrictive will result in lost sales; a credit policy that is too loose will result in excessive bad debts.

Control at Different Organizational Levels

When we discussed the planning function in Chapter 4, we noted that planning is carried out at three levels—strategic, tactical, and operational. Since planning and controlling are so closely related, it is not surprising to find that these same three levels are important in the controlling process.

strategic control

Strategic control helps managers assess the effectiveness of strategic plans. It requires the monitoring of external environmental events that can affect the organization. It emphasizes monitoring activities on an annual or semiannual basis. Top managers are responsible for strategic control. **Tactical control** assesses the effectiveness of tactical plans at the middle levels of the organization's hierarchy. It emphasizes the monitoring of activities on a weekly or monthly basis. Middle managers are responsible for tactical control. **Operational control** assesses the effectiveness of plans at the lowest level of the organization. It emphasizes the monitoring of day-to-day results, and is the responsibility of first-line managers. An example of how these three types of control are practised is described in the following paragraphs.

tactical control

operational control

Keith Durham is a front-line supervisor in an assembly plant which produces microcomputers. He plans, organizes, and directs the work of 14 employees who report to him. From Durham's perspective, the matters that need to be controlled are quite specific. He must ensure that each workstation is staffed each day, and that raw materials and inventory are available when needed. He must also deal with any unexpected occurrences, such as machine breakdowns. His focus is generally short-term, and he must quickly deal with any deviations that are discovered. For example, he might decide to recommend replacement of a machine that unexpectedly breaks down.

Janice Belczaka is the plant manager. She coordinates the work of Durham and the four other supervisors in the plant. Belczaka works on a longer time frame than Durham does. She analyzes the information she receives from the supervisors and meets with them once a month to discuss problems and opportunities in the plant. If there are problems in Durham's area, Belczaka will discuss them with him and will determine what action should be taken to resolve them. She is unlikely to make any decisions based on data from only one week or one month. Instead, she will study the overall trends over a longer period of time. For example, if she notices that one of Durham's workers has had difficulty reaching productivity norms for his department, she may ask him to resolve the problem.

Steve Ridzik is the vice-president of manufacturing for the firm. He also performs the controlling function but from a broader perspective than either Durham or Belczaka. Ridzik has three individuals besides Janice reporting to him. He uses control to ensure that the overall objectives of the production function of the firm are achieved. His view is considerably longer-term than that of either Keith or Janice. Steve uses controls to help resolve problems that the various manufacturing departments may be unable to resolve themselves. For example, if the engineering department needs extra funds to develop a new training program on machine maintenance, he might recommend to the president that the funds be allocated. Or, he might coordinate the work of several departments in the firm to market a new product.

CONTROLLING INPUTS, PROCESSES, AND OUTPUTS

LEARNING OBJECTIVE 3
Understand the difference between input, process, and output controls, and give an example of each.

In Chapter 2, we saw that the activity of any organization can be represented by the input-transformation-output model (refer to Figure 2-2). As the discussion of strategic control points indicates, controls can be applied at any stage of the model: before the production process starts (input controls), during the production process (process controls), or after the production process has been completed (output controls). The Management at Work insert shows how input and output are monitored at Four Seasons Hotels.

MANAGEMENT AT WORK

Control at Four Seasons Hotels Inc.

Isadore Sharp is president and CEO of Four Seasons Hotels Inc., the world's largest operator of luxury hotels. Sharp built his first hotel in Toronto thirty years ago; by 1990, the company operated 23 hotels in three countries and was planning to expand into Europe and the Far East. All the hotels in the chain provide luxury service to clients.

The emphasis at Four Seasons is on operating each hotel, not simply owning it. This means a strong emphasis on the control function so that customers get the service they expect. This emphasis is evident even before the construction of a hotel starts. Developers who approach the company must buy land which meets Four Seasons' specifications. The company then puts together a detailed operating plan. Staff are on site up to two years before the hotel opens its doors. Prospective employees go through as many as four screenings and interviews. When hiring, the firm emphasizes character and personality rather than technical skills; it feels it can upgrade employee skills with the right training.

The company pays top wages, and its turnover rate is half the industry average. It was ranked as one of Canada's 100 best companies to work for in a recent *Financial Post* survey. A committee made up of a representative from each department meets monthly with hotel managers to discuss problems or make suggestions for improvements. The "employee-of-the-month" and "employee-of-the-year" programs reward exemplary employees with cash payments and free services. An annual attitude survey is conducted by consultants who talk with every employee and have them fill out a questionnaire regarding their work. The results are checked by Isadore Sharp himself. Data on guest reactions to the hotel are also gathered, and each hotel manager gets a weekly printout of the results. Further controls are evident in the "mystery shopper" reports. An anonymous team of two people is sent out to every hotel once or twice a year. The team scrutinizes every aspect of the hotel's service. ▲

CONTROLLING INPUTS

Managers use input controls primarily as a preventive measure. **Input controls** (also called feedforward or preventive controls) monitor the material, human, and capital resources that come into the organization. Input controls try to ensure that problems will not arise during the production of a good or service, and that resources are used effectively to achieve organizational objectives. Input controls are used with respect to raw materials, people, and capital.

input controls

Materials Controls

Organizations must ensure that the raw materials used in the production process meet the standards desired by the firm. A company producing bicycles needs to inspect the tubular steel that is to be made into the frames of the bicycle to see that it meets quality standards. A printing firm has to check the paper that is to be used to print a magazine. The type of inspection conducted depends on the type of input. In these two cases, only a sample of the incoming product is likely to be inspected. For other products (e.g., parts for commercial airlines or for medical equipment), every single unit may be inspected. The issue of materials controls is discussed in Chapter 18.

An example of materials control is the testing of various products to determine the amount of stress they will take. Research engineer Lars Bach (left) and technologist Leo Regnier of the Alberta Research Council test the safe loading limits for a stress skin panel used in light industrial buildings.

Personnel Selection Controls

Every organization needs to hire new workers as operations expand, or as current employees leave or retire. Establishing controls that help managers choose the right kind of workers is vital. Since this is not an easy task, most firms have human resource departments to assist line managers. This critical area of input controls was described in Chapter 11.

Capital Controls

Organizations must have sufficient capital to achieve their objectives. They must finance equipment and pay their staff. When funds are expended, the organization exchanges today's dollars for the hope of future profits. It must make such an investment in a way that brings the greatest benefit to the organization. Unfortunately, the best way is difficult to determine because the future is uncertain. The net present value technique (discussed in Chapter 18) takes into account the fact that a dollar today is worth more than a dollar a year from now. This helps managers make decisions about capital outlays.

CONTROLLING PROCESSES

Process controls focus on the activities that transform inputs into outputs. **Process controls** (also called steering or concurrent controls) are applied while the product or service is produced. Interaction between bosses and subordinates provides control by keeping both up-to-date on the production of goods or services. Interaction makes both managers and workers aware of problems as they develop; it also suggests actions that might be necessary to get work back on track. For many lower- and middle-level managers, this form of process control takes up a substantial part of their time each day. Other process controls include rules, policies, and procedures (see Chapter 4).

process controls

An example of how process controls can improve organizational performance is described in the Management at Work insert "Controlling Cycle Times."

The greatest opportunity for the discovery and correction of deviations from a standard takes place while the work is in process. Even a little control early in the process can prevent problems. Rather than wait until 50 units of a product is completed and then find out that the entire output is defective, the work could be checked

MANAGEMENT AT WORK

CONTROLLING CYCLE TIMES

Multilin is a Markham, Ontario, firm that makes electronic motor relays. In 1990, the company's sales were expanding rapidly, but its on-time delivery of products had slipped to 55 percent. After replacing the traditional assembly line with flexible work cells of multiskilled employees, the problem was solved. The company's "cycle time"—the time between receipt of an order and its delivery—has dropped from 42 to 4 days. Inventory has been sharply reduced both for Multilin and the customers it sells its components to.

How was this possible? For many years, the company produced its products on a traditional assembly line. In 1989, when it scored a market hit with a new protection relay (a device that signals a motor to shut down when there are problems), the drastically increased demand caused late deliveries, a frustrated sales staff, and a rising defect rate. A consultant who was hired to analyze work processes found that workers did numbingly repetitive work on only isolated parts of a complete product. So, the company designed a new system in which teams of employees assemble complete units.

The new process requires only 29 production steps, compared to the 80-plus that were formerly needed. An on-time delivery rate of 98 percent has also been achieved. Profits are rising, and revenues have risen 30 percent since the changes were implemented. Inventory reduction has also resulted in annual savings of $250 000 in carrying costs. Most of these savings have been redirected into research and development.

Workers say they feel increased responsibility for the relays they turn out because they have more control over how the work is done. Each team member signs a commitment statement which promises customer satisfaction and quality. Colour-coded charts also show the skill level of each team member in each facet of production. Increased coordination is also evident between those who do the work and those who do the design work because designers have been made part of the work teams. The system also allows for more customized manufacturing. Sales reps give requests to the teams and receive immediate responses.

As is usual in these cases of dramatic change, some employees who could not adapt have left the firm. Many were supervisors who could not accept the loss of authority that is inherent in the use of teams. ▲

early and errors rectified before they become costly. The amount of process control that is necessary depends on several factors, including the experience of the person doing the job, the technical complexity of the process, and the extent to which the job is clearly defined. An interesting ethical dilemma can arise when employee work is monitored, as described in the Ethics in Management insert "The Ethics of Monitoring Employees."

Process control is relevant for all sorts of jobs. Consider college students who are taking a course that requires them to read the management literature in a certain area and then write a paper on what they have learned. If the instructor in this situation wanted to exercise process control, he or she could require the student to first develop a written plan of the work that is to be done. The instructor could then make periodic checks to see if the actual work matches what was planned. Students who are not guided by process controls often find to their dismay that their finished paper is not acceptable to the professor.

CONTROLLING OUTPUT

output controls

Managers use output controls to assess the results of the production process. **Output controls** (also called comparison or yes-no controls) are used to determine whether deviations from standards have occurred in a product or service. Examples of output controls include a coach assessing a basketball player's offensive and defensive statistics, a manager surveying users of the firm's products, and a teacher reading

ETHICS IN MANAGEMENT

THE ETHICS OF MONITORING EMPLOYEES

While nearly everyone agrees that organizations have the right to exercise some level of control over their employees, there is great controversy about exactly how much is acceptable. There are three major areas where debate is very intense: drug testing, security testing, and computer monitoring.

Drug and alcohol testing. Drug and alcohol abuse by employees costs organizations money by increasing absenteeism and accident rates, reducing the quality of work, and increasing health care costs. Drug and alcohol abuse also endangers customers; there have been several highly publicized incidents in Canada and the U.S. when train engineers caused serious accidents because they were intoxicated or on drugs.

Testing may be required for persons who wish to become employees, or for those who are already working for the organization. Canadian National Railways, for example, instituted drug testing in 1986 for train, brake, and yard employees; nearly 12 percent of those tested failed. Current employees are usually tested at random. Trucking companies that have carried out random tests have found that nearly one third of drivers who were involved in accidents were on drugs.

Security testing and security agents. Organizations carry out security tests because employees do, on occasion, steal from the company. This includes activities like stealing money or equipment, accepting kickbacks or bribes, vandalism, and arson. One estimate in the U.S. is that employee theft costs companies a total of more than $40 billion. Companies lose about 1-2 percent of their sales to employee theft.

Companies respond to this type of behaviour by carrying out preemployment security tests to determine (a) the prospective employee's past criminal record (if any), and (b) whether the prospective employee is likely to engage in illegal activities. Companies also hire undercover security companies to watch for employee theft. The father of one of the authors of this book was employed by a security firm. He rode city buses all day long, and watched to see if drivers were stealing fare money.

Computer monitoring. Developments in computer technology have made it possible for the boss to monitor employees without them knowing it. Computer software firms even sell programs called "Spy" and "Peek" to facilitate computer monitoring. At General Electric's Answer Center in Kentucky, customer calls are handled by company agents. The agents' bosses monitor their conversations and give the agents feedback on how they are doing. This so-called *silent monitoring* can improve the effectiveness of the agents' telephone work, but it can also increase their stress levels, because they don't know exactly when the boss is listening in on their conversations.

The employer's desire for more information may conflict with the employee's need for privacy. Unions point to studies showing that computer monitoring has a negative effect on employee health. A study of telephone operators showed that those who were monitored had more headaches, back pain, severe fatigue, shoulder soreness, anxiety, and sore wrists than those who were not.

An increasing numbers of lawsuits are being brought against companies by employees who charge that the firm overstepped the bounds of decency when monitoring their work. The most extensive case is the one against Northern Telecom Inc. by the Communication Workers of America. The union claims that Northern Telecom installed telephone bugs and hidden microphones in one of its plants and used them over a period of 13 years to spy on employees.

Are drug and alcohol testing, security testing, and computer monitoring ethical? Where does the company's right to control employee behaviour stop? What criteria should be applied to make sure that employee rights to privacy are properly balanced against a company's right to monitor? ▲

final examination papers. Output controls normally contain guidelines for correcting any deviations and returning the operation to standard.

Output controls can be applied where the product or service is produced, or elsewhere. Output controls for one organization can become input controls for another. For example, the firm which makes tubular steel for bicycle frames may inspect its output before shipping it (output control). When the bicycle firm receives the steel, it inspects the steel before putting it into the production process (input control).

There are some significant differences between process controls and output controls, as shown in Table 17-1. The most common types of output controls are employee performance evaluation, quality and quantity controls, and financial analysis.

TABLE 17-1 DIFFERENCES BETWEEN PROCESS CONTROLS AND OUTPUT CONTROLS.

Process Controls	Output Controls
1. Occur while the work is being done.	1. Occur after the work has been completed.
2. Normally done by the immediate supervisor of the person doing the work.	2. May be done either by the immediate supervisor or by someone else.
3. Involves face-to-face interaction between the boss and subordinate.	3. Is often an impersonal, statistical comparison of output against standards.

Employee Performance Evaluation

An inescapable fact of organizational life is that employees exhibit various degrees of proficiency. However, we saw in Chapter 12 that, regardless of their present performance, employees may improve if they have a clear understanding of their performance level. Output controls play a fundamental role in conveying to employees how well they are doing.

Quality and Quantity Controls

Since the Japanese have developed such a reputation for producing high-quality goods, they have set standards for all competitors. The issue of quality in manufactured goods has become very salient for most Canadians. Anyone who hears a buyer state that he or she got a "lemon" understands that the product was of inferior quality.

But what exactly is meant by the term "quality?" In the past, quality was usually defined as "the degree of conformity to a predetermined standard." Lately, however, quality is more often defined in terms of customer satisfaction. The American Society for Quality Control defines a **quality** product or service as one that has no deficiencies, and which can can meet customer needs.[14] The phrase "delighting the customer" is another way to say this. The issue of quality and quality control is addressed in Chapter 18.

quality

Financial Analysis

The financial statements of organizations provide valuable information about how financial resources are used. An intelligent interpretation of financial data provides an excellent means for controlling a company's financial welfare. Financial ratio analysis (discussed in Chapter 18) provides management with a basis for comparing current and past performance. If the ratios are not in line with what is considered acceptable, the manager is in a position to make corrections.

EMPLOYEE REACTION TO CONTROLS

We saw earlier in the chapter that there are sound reasons for applying controls in organizations. Employees seem generally willing to accept these reasons as a justification for the control of their behaviour, but there are many specific situations where employees object to controls. Why are employees annoyed and offended when a manager wants to assess their work?

Objections to Controls

Perhaps the most basic cause of employees' objections to controls is the desire for independence. When people have their work assessed by someone else, they feel that they have lost some freedom to behave as they see fit. Other reasons why people resist controls, and an example demonstrating each one, are summarized in Table 17-2.

LEARNING OBJECTIVE 4
State seven reasons why employees often react negatively to controls.

Overcoming Objections to Controls

If employees are unhappy about the control system, a manager might simply advise them to accept the system as it is. The manager might say "It's company policy, so we'll all have to live with it." This approach may work on occasion, but a more effective strategy is for the manager to make sure that the control system adheres to certain criteria which will minimize the chance of these concerns arising. Table 17-3 lists 12 characteristics of effective control systems.[15] If these characteristics are evident, negative reactions from employees are minimized.

LEARNING OBJECTIVE 5
Identify the 12 characteristics of an effective control system.

TABLE 17-2 REASONS FOR NEGATIVE REACTIONS TO CONTROLS.

Reason	Examples
1. Employees do not understand the need for controls.	Employees in a manufacturing plant claim that the quality standards on a certain batch of parts are unnecessarily high. Management has failed to tell them that the parts are to be used as components in state-of-the-art medical equipment.
2. Employees lack control over the situation, yet they are held accountable for achieving a certain standard of performance.	A manager is told that his division is to be turned into a profit centre, but he is given no say in employee hiring and compensation decisions.
3. Standards are inappropriate for the needs of the situation.	In an employment agency, interviewers are rated on the number of interviews they conduct with individuals who are looking for work. Interviewers argue that a more appropriate measure of effectiveness is the number of individuals actually placed in a job.
4. Employees do not know what the standards are.	A newly hired professor in a university is told that research is important for promotion and tenure, but no specific guidelines are given which indicate the quantity and quality of research that she is expected to do.
5. Employees feel that standards are unattainable.	A production line supervisor tells a worker that the quality of his work is unacceptable. The worker says he agrees but can't do anything about it because the quantity standards on the job force him to work so fast that he makes errors. The supervisor knows that three previous workers on this job quit after complaining about unreasonable quantity standards.
6. Standards are contradictory.	An office manager in a government agency is told to achieve a certain level of performance while staying within the budget for supplies (e.g., paper, pencils, paper clips, etc.). But attaining the desired level of output is impossible with the supplies budget that is allocated.
7. Standards are used as threats instead of motivators.	Sales personnel at an automobile dealership are told that if they fail to meet their sales targets for three months in a row, they will be let go.

TABLE 17-3 CHARACTERISTICS OF EFFECTIVE CONTROL SYSTEMS.

Characteristics	Explanation
1. Objectivity	The system must be capable of clearly measuring the level of output. If an objective system of measurement is missing, much time is wasted debating how much was produced.
2. Accuracy	The information generated by the system must reflect what actually happened as inputs are converted to outputs, rather than someone's subjective interpretation of what happened. If the system fails to generate accurate information, conflict will arise between management and the workers about what is happening during the production process.
3. Understandability	Those affected by the system must understand how it works, what it is measuring, and the implications the system has for their own work. If the system is not understood, it will likely be resisted.
4. Timeliness	Information should be supplied by the system in time for it to be used to positively influence output. If the control system is not timely, much time and effort will be wasted generating information that will not help to improve performance.
5. Economy	The benefits of the system must exceed the cost. In an uneconomical control system, the value of the information produced is exceeded by the time and money spent getting the information.
6. Instrumentality	The control system must clearly show workers how good performance leads to rewards. If workers are unaware of the connection between performance and rewards, they will hardly be motivated to perform.
7. Reality	The levels of performance that are stated must be attainable by the typical worker who puts forth an honest day's work. If standards are unrealistic, workers will not make a serious effort to achieve them.
8. Flexibility	Unexpected occurrences either inside or outside the organization must be taken into account by the control system. An inflexible control system demotivates workers because it applies standards without regard for extenuating circumstances.
9. Strategic control points	The system must measure the production of goods and services at strategic points. Failure to control the process at strategic points results in high costs when something goes wrong.
10. Acceptability	Those who work under the control system must accept it. When workers do not accept the need for the control system, they continually try to find ways around it.
11. Proactivity	The system should suggest the actions which are necessary to correct deviations. A control system that simply detects deviations does not give workers guidance on how to resolve the problem.
12. Multiple criteria	The system should contain multiple criteria which must be satisfied, especially at higher levels in the organization. If too much emphasis is placed on one criterion (e.g., sales volume), those affected by the control system may place too little emphasis on other important criteria (e.g., after-the-sale service).

MEETING THE CHALLENGE

COST CONTROL AT ONTARIO HYDRO

As problems have mounted at Ontario Hydro, the utility has made some effort to respond to them. As early as 1987, a management consulting firm was hired to make recommendations about how to reduce costs. The consulting firm pointed out many shortcomings, including the fact that there were too many layers of management. They also observed overstaffing in the design and construction branch, inconsistent human resource management, and ineffective cost controls. But apparently nothing was ever done with these suggestions.

In 1991, a reorganization took place that had more success. A layer of senior vice-presidents was eliminated, and "hard" areas (e.g., electricity generation) were separated from "soft" areas (e.g., planning). Hydro cancelled long-term contracts under which it had been paying four times market value for some commodities. An internal task force is also seeking ways to cut an additional \$115 million from operating costs. An external hiring freeze has been imposed, and the utility may cut 2000 jobs from the payroll.

As part of the reorganization, the design and construction division will begin to focus on repairing and maintaining existing generating plants, rather than building new plants. The whole culture of the division will therefore have to change.

But the real cultural change may involve shifting from generation to conservation, and Hydro will have difficulty making this shift, given its history. Some energy conservation programs have been put in place, but critics argue that Hydro has an unrealistic view of consumption patterns. What's worse, Hydro's demand-management programs are not very popular with energy experts; they argue that using incentives to get one set of customers not to consume drives everyone else's rates up.

Other critics of the utility have even more substantial changes to recommend. Jack Gibbons, a senior economic advisor to the Canadian Institute for Environmental Law and Policy, feels that Hydro should not be allowed to build *any* new generating stations. Energy Probe goes even further, arguing that much of Hydro should be privatized, leaving it with only its transmission business and nuclear power generation. ▲

SUMMARY

Controlling is the process of comparing actual performance with standards and taking any corrective action that is necessary. Controls are needed in organizations because (1) unexpected developments may make plans inoperable, (2) employees do not always do what they are supposed to do, (3) organizations are complex entities which require a system for checking progress toward goals, and (4) increased delegation of authority means that lower-level managers may make decisions that are not in the best interest of the organization. The four basic sources of control in organizations are the external environment, formal organizational rules and regulations, the informal work group, and the individual. Together, these help to ensure that what is supposed to happen actually happens.

The controlling process involves four steps: (1) setting performance standards; (2) measuring performance; (3) comparing performance with standards; and (4) taking corrective action as necessary. Disciplinary action may be necessary if employees fail to adhere to some work-related standard. Progressive discipline means that increasingly severe penalties are applied as additional evidence of improper behaviour accumulates.

Strategic control points are those which an organization finds particularly important to its success. Failure to exercise control at these points in the production process results in unusually high costs for the organization. Strategic control points must identify problems before they become serious, must be economical, and should not overemphasize any one element of operations.

Managers at different levels in the organization spend differing proportions of their time on the controlling function. The specific controlling actions they take also differ across organizational levels. Lower-level managers have a shorter time frame for control than upper-level managers do.

Input controls monitor the material, human, and capital resources coming into the organization. Process controls are applied while the product or service is actually being produced. Output controls are used to determine whether deviations from standards have occurred.

Employees frequently object to controls because they do not understand the need for controls or because they have no control over a situation they are held responsible for. Employees are also unhappy with controls when standards are inappropriate, unknown, unattainable, or contradictory. Employee resistance to controls can be overcome if managers ensure that controls are objective, accurate, understandable, timely, economical, realistic, and flexible.

KEY TERMS

controlling (p. 534)
cybernetic system (p. 534)
noncybernetic system (p. 534)
stakeholder control (p. 535)
organizational control (p. 536)
group control (p. 536)
individual control (p. 537)
clan control (p. 537)
bureaucratic control (p. 537)
controlling process (p. 537)
standards (p. 537)
time standards (p. 538)
output standards (p. 538)
cost standards (p. 538)
quality standards (p. 538)
behavioural standards (p. 538)
control tolerances (p. 538)
immediate corrective action (p. 540)
long-term corrective action (p. 540)
disciplinary action (p. 540)
progressive discipline (p. 541)
strategic control points (p. 542)
strategic control (p. 543)
tactical control (p. 543)
operational control (p. 543)
input controls (p. 545)
process controls (p. 545)
output controls (p. 546)
quality (p. 548)

REVIEW QUESTIONS

1. How does the controlling process assist managers in accomplishing their objectives?
2. Briefly describe each phase in the controlling process.
3. Describe five types of standards commonly found in organizations.
4. What are the three basic ways that managers assess the output of subordinates?
5. Explain the two main categories of corrective action. When is each appropriate?
6. What is progressive discipline? Explain by using an example.
7. What is a strategic control point? Give an example from your own work experience.
8. What five characteristics should strategic control points possess?
9. Distinguish input controls, process controls, and output controls. When is each type used?
10. What are the main types of input controls found in organizations?
11. What kind of process controls are normally used by managers?
12. What is the difference between process controls and output controls?
13. Give three examples of output controls.
14. Why do employees resist controls? What can be done to reduce this resistance?
15. What characteristics should an effective control system exhibit?

DISCUSSION QUESTIONS

1. Why are the functions of planning and controlling so closely related?

2. Describe the alternatives that are open to managers when they discover a deviation from a standard. Under what circumstances should each alternative be used?
3. Is the control process for lower-level managers different from that for higher-level managers? Defend your answer.
4. Consider the dynamic day-to-day work environment of managers. What kinds of things can go wrong when managers attempt to follow the steps in the control process?
5. Why is there so much controversy and conflict in organizations about the measurement of employee performance?

EXERCISES

1. Interview a manager of your choice. Determine the manager's responses to the following questions:
   a. What types of controls does the manager use to ensure that performance matches the standard which has been set?
   b. Ask the manager to provide examples of input controls, process controls, and output controls.
   c. How does the manager decide whether or not corrective action is taken if a deviation is noticed?

   After the interview, determine the extent to which the manager's responses are consistent with the ideas presented in the chapter. If there are differences, try to explain them.
2. Think of a major goal that you wish to accomplish. What kinds of controls will you have to apply in order to reach the goal?
3. Identify some strategic control points for the following organizations:
   a. Your college or university
   b. An automobile manufacturing firm
   c. A sporting goods store
   d. A hairdresser

MANAGEMENT ON LOCATION

CASE 17-1
WHAT DO WE DO NOW?

As office manager of the Duncan Life Insurance Company, Robert Costa is responsible for the work of 45 employees (26 stenographers, 13 clerk-typists, and 6 supervisors). Over the past six months, following a recommendation made by the systems and procedures department, the company had introduced new word processing equipment and computer terminals with the objective of increasing efficiency. Under the old system, each stenographer and clerk-typist was assigned work from a certain department. Due to variations in demand among the departments which sent work in, some individuals would be busy, and others would have little to do. The new computer system was designed to systematically assign the work so that each individual had something to do most of the time. Under the new system, each employee now had a workstation which was linked electronically to a central system. When a particular job came to the section for execution, it was recorded at the main control station, and assigned by a computer program to the person who was available and qualified to perform the task.

Under the old system, Costa spent a great deal of time overseeing the allocation of tasks to various individuals in the department. Under the new system, he found that he spent most of his time monitoring how efficiently tasks were performed. He no longer had to circulate through the work areas, but instead could observe what was happening simply by scanning employee performance levels on the terminal in his office. Costa received information on what tasks were assigned to each employee, the nature of the tasks, the time taken to complete each task, and the level of proficiency achieved in comparison with established standards for the task. If Costa noticed a decline in performance, he would leave an electronic message asking the supervisor of the particular employee to investigate the matter and take corrective action.

In accordance with company policies regarding changes in tasks and procedures, last week the personnel department assigned a work team of outside consultants to review job descriptions and revise them in terms of the changes that had taken place due to the introduction of the new work system. The first phase, which involved interviewing all employees about changes in their jobs, was completed in four days. The second phase, which began last Friday, concentrated on making observations of the work done by the employees and recording each detail. Based on the interviews and observations, new job descriptions would be prepared. The third phase would be the reclassification of jobs and pay scales where necessary.

On Monday, Costa noticed that 5 employees were absent. The number increased to 10 on Tuesday. Not only were stenographers and clerk-typists phoning in "sick," but so had 2 supervisors. Wednesday morning started with 12 absences and by noon 3 more had booked off due to "illness." When Costa inquired as to the causes of the absenteeism, he heard almost the identical story—stress and anxiety over potential job changes. One stenographer spoke with him on the phone and told him that she had just seen her physician and he had said she needed to have complete rest for at least a week and should obtain a job transfer if working conditions did not improve.

Just after that conversation ended, the director of human resources dropped in. She indicated that it was impossible for the consultants to complete their assigment because of the lack of cooperation from members of Costa's department. She indicated that unless the situation improved immediately, she had no choice but to call off the assignment and report to the president that the job reclassification could not be carried out. Costa knew that this would be a large blot on his record. He was also concerned that the department's regular work was not being completed because of the high rate of absenteeism. He suddenly felt that he was losing control of his operation. ▲

QUESTIONS

1. What are the problems in this situation, and why have they arisen?
2. What should Robert Costa do to resolve the two problems facing him (i.e., completing the consultant's work, and restoring normal productivity to his department)?

CASE 17-2
THE CASE OF THE FALSIFIED SALES REPORTS

Six months ago, Shirley Reimer assumed her new position as national sales manager for Baxter Pharmaceuticals, a wholesaler of pharmaceutical products. Prior to coming to Baxter, Reimer had been the Ontario District Sales Manager for a leading pharmaceutical manufacturer. She had just completed her first extensive trip through western Canada, where she audited prospective and continuing accounts. She was very disturbed by what she had discovered.

It was company policy that sales reps call on a certain number of prospective and continuing accounts each month. The number of calls to be made was determined by a rather complex formula that had been developed by an operations research consultant two years ago. The formula took into account a variety of factors:

1. The number physicians, hospitals, clinics, and retailers with pharmaceutical departments in a given geographic region.
2. The length of time required per visit by customer classification.
3. The distance between customers in different areas and within the same area.
4. The frequency of calls to be made per month based on customer classification.
5. The size of orders and the length of time the sales rep had served their respective territories.

The consultant's model was presented to the sales reps at a quarterly sales meeting about one year ago. The national sales manager argued persuasively that the consultant's formula was a substantial improvement over current practice, and that the sales reps would benefit from using it. Several reps expressed some doubts about the formula, and others did not seem to understand the formula at all. Nevertheless, after a lengthy discussion, a consensus of sorts emerged, and the model was implemented.

Each week the sales reps complete a detailed report on their calls which are compared with a sales program developed by the marketing department using the model. The results of the comparison form the basis for the monthly bonus paid to the sales reps. Sales reps are paid on a "salary plus bonus" basis, and the bonus can be as much as 30 percent of a rep's monthly salary.

The problem that Reimer had uncovered during her trip was that sales reps were inflating the number of prospecting calls they were making. To her amazement, this falsification was common among all eight of the sales reps, although the magnitude of falsification varied widely. Apparently, the practice had begun soon after the model was implemented. Reimer discovered through the informal grapevine that the regional sales manager was aware that falsification was going on. He rationalized looking the other way because he felt that the model was an infringement on the

• • •

right of sales reps to determine how they could best cover their territory.

When Reimer discovered these facts, she was tempted to summarily dismiss the most flagrant abusers, and withhold bonuses from the others until they started behaving in accordance with company policy. She quickly came to the conclusion, however, that such an action would seriously affect company sales for the next year. With increasing competitive pressure from major pharmaceutical manufacturers to sell directly to end users and bypass wholesalers like Baxter, it would take an all-out effort by the sales force to maintain the firm's competitive position. The sales reps were not likely to be motivated to work hard if they felt that Reimer was harassing them about their reports. On the other hand, Reimer felt that she could not let the fraudulent practice continue. If she didn't act, the sales reps' unethical behaviour would continue to be rewarded, and this would be detrimental to the company. ▲

QUESTIONS

1. What basic principles about introducing organizational change were violated when the computer model was first introduced? (Review the material on organizational change in Chapter 15 before answering this question.)
2. What should be done with regard to the sales reps falsifying their reports?
3. What steps should Shirley Reimer take to ensure that problems like this do not recur in the future?

CASE 17-3
A QUESTION OF STANDARDS

Steven Dowling was a regional sales manager for McGavin-Shane Ltd., a firm that manufactured hydraulic and pumping equipment for industrial uses. Dowling supervised seven salespeople in southern Ontario. To ensure good performance from the salespeople, Dowling met with each one twice a year to set sales goals for the salesperson's territory. At the end of each month, he received sales reports from each salesperson. Every three months, he met with each salesperson and discussed the reports, then set goals for the next six-month period. Whenever a salesperson fell short of a six-month goal, Dowling tried to be positive and to encourage the person to do better during the next period.

Recently, Dowling has become quite concerned about Mike Litvin's performance. Litvin had worked for another firm in the same business for two years, but he had been with McGavin-Shane for only seven months, and Dowling didn't yet know him very well. For the last three months, Litvin had failed to reach his targeted sales; worse, the shortfall in each succeeding month had increased. A trend was clearly developing that had to be investigated.

At the regular three-month meeting with Litvin, Dowling raised the issue of the shortfall.

Dowling: I'm concerned about your sales volume during the last few months, Mike. You haven't been up to standard for three months now, and I'm worried about that.

Litvin: I've been meaning to speak to you about my sales territory and some of the things that are going on there. You know, you're very fortunate that I'm in that territory and have some experience in this business. There has been a big drop in demand for our equipment, but I'm doing a good job at getting the sales that are available.

Dowling: I'm very surprised to hear you say that. The other salespeople aren't reporting any problems.

Litvin: Well, maybe they just don't want to worry you. I've never experienced so much difficulty in getting sales as I have during the last three months.

Dowling: But Mike, the sales figures for the other people are right up to standard. Yours aren't.

Litvin: Steve, if anybody else was in my territory, they wouldn't have sold nearly as much as I have.

Dowling: Mike, aren't you missing the point? Your performance has fallen below standard.

Litvin: That's one way of looking at it. Another way is to say that my performance is very good given the tough sales conditions in my territory.

At this point, Dowling terminated the interview. He was astonished that Litvin would not even admit the obvious fact that his sales were not up to standard. He was concerned that if Litvin would not even admit this fact, that it was going to be very difficult to motivate Litvin to resolve the problem. ▲

QUESTIONS

1. What is Litvin really saying about the sales standard that has been set for him?
2. What should Dowling do to resolve this problem?

CASE 17-4
CAN-MARK MANUFACTURING

Henry Friesen was a supervisor at Can-Mark Manufacturing, a company which produced a variety of consumer goods. Recently, Friesen had been put in charge of a group of nine people who were to produce the company's latest addition to its product line. The production process for the new product required state-of-the-art equipment, and the company's industrial engineers had just completed a lengthy series of tests to determine reasonable production standards for the new machines.

The production line experienced trouble right from the start. The workers had difficulty getting the machines to work and rejects were running substantially above the level that was considered acceptable. One afternoon, as Friesen was sitting in his office wondering how to resolve this problem, the plant superintendent, Peter Jansen, appeared at his door. Friesen invited him in and the following conversation took place:

Jansen: Henry, what's the problem with our new line? You know this product is high profile, and I'm already getting pressure from the vice-president. He says the new product is crucial to our company, and he wants these production flaws corrected immediately. There's a lot of demand out there for this product, and we've got to get production volume up.

Friesen: After talking to the workers, I'm convinced the production standards are out of line. My people are very motivated and experienced, but they can't meet the standards the engineering people have set.

Jansen: But our engineers have a very good reputation for setting realistic job standards.

Friesen: I know that, but this time they've made a mistake. This state-of-the-art equipment we're using is more difficult to work with than they could have imagined.

Jansen: We've got to get output on this line up to standard or we'll both be in trouble with top management.

At this point, one of Friesen's workers entered his office and told him of yet another problem with the new equipment, so Friesen had to cut the meeting short. For the rest of the day his discussion with Jansen weighed heavily on his mind. ▲

QUESTIONS

1. What is the problem here? What is causing the problem?
2. Why are the workers objecting to the standards?
3. What can be done to reduce employee objections? Be specific.

CHAPTER

18

CONTROL TECHNIQUES

LEARNING OBJECTIVES

After reading this chapter, you will be able to:

1. List and describe nine nonfinancial and six financial control techniques.
2. Outline the main features of quality control.
3. List the main features of inventory control.
4. State the key elements in the just-in-time inventory system.
5. List and describe six financial control techniques.
6. Describe how budgets are used to facilitate the control function.
7. Perform a break-even analysis.
8. Explain how ratio analysis helps managers determine how effective their organization is.
9. Compare financial audits and management audits.
10. Describe the manager's responsibility in choosing appropriate control techniques.

MANAGEMENT CHALLENGE

BANKRUPTCY AT O & Y

Olympia & York Developments Ltd. is a real estate and natural resources conglomerate that sought bankruptcy protection under the *Companies' Creditors Arrangement Act* in May, 1992. O & Y had been hailed in the mid-1980s as a pioneer in new financial techniques when it issued short-term debt (commercial paper) to finance some of its office buildings. The firm believed it could issue short-term debt during the double-digit inflation of the early 1980s and replace it with lower cost long-term debt later.

In adopting this strategy, O & Y departed from the industry's traditional practice of paying for skyscrapers with 20- or 30-year mortgages. By 1990, O & Y had borrowed more than $1 billion in short-term financial instruments such as commercial paper as well as an additional $1 billion in five- and ten-year bonds. O & Y's major mistake, according to investment bankers, was to finance long-term assets with short-term debt.

When the recession caused a steep decline in real estate prices in 1991, investors began to back away from buying further commercial paper from O & Y. The company was left short of cash to pay the interest on other loans it had taken out from nearly 100 banks worldwide. In turn, investors threatened to seize O & Y's assets for nonpayment of interest. Eventually, the cracks in the O & Y empire became so great that the firm had to file for

...

protection under bankruptcy laws. Had O & Y used long-term bonds to finance its real estate activities, it might have averted many of its difficulties.

A brief summary of the events leading to O & Y's bankruptcy is presented below.

February, 1992
- Dominion Bond Rating Service downgrades its rating on O & Y's bonds.
- Bank stocks decline as investors worry about bank exposure to O & Y loans.
- CIBC and Royal Bank each have more than $500 million in outstanding loans to O & Y.
- Rumours begin to circulate that O & Y is in danger of collapse. The $7 billion Canary Wharf project in London, England, is seen as the big drain on the company.

March 6, 1992
- O & Y retreats further from the commercial paper market.
- O & Y denies it is headed for bankruptcy.
- O & Y sells its interest in Interprovincial Pipeline Inc. for $665 million and begins retiring $500 million in commercial paper.

March 25, 1992
- Thomas Johnson replaces Paul Reichmann as president of O & Y; he is hired to work out restructuring on debt of $14.3 billion.
- O & Y discusses the possibility of loan guarantees from the federal government.

March 28, 1992
- Albert Reichmann personally buys O & Y's interest in Damdev Corp. (the former Campeau Corp.).
- Company executives meet with bankers to begin discussions on restructuring; lenders asked to extend deadlines on debt falling due.

April 23, 1992
- O & Y states that it has no intention of applying for bankruptcy protection in Britain, the U.S., or Canada.

May, 1992
- O & Y has a difficult series of meetings with bankers. They finally agree to lend enough money to keep the Canary Wharf project going for just one month.

May 14, 1992
- U.S. court rules that O & Y must pay Morgan Stanley International $231 million for its building at Canary Wharf; if O & Y does not make the payment, Morgan Stanley can seize the asset.
- Investors threaten to seize O & Y's First Canadian Place in Toronto unless the company pays $17 million in interest due.

May 15, 1992
- O & Y files for bankruptcy protection in Canada and the U.S. as it continues to try to restructure $14.9 billion in debt; investors increasingly threaten to seize O & Y's assets because the firm failed to make interest payments on loans.
- Documents show the company's assets equal its liabilities; under bankruptcy, O & Y must develop a plan for restructuring and talk with investors about its plan. ▲

Olympia & York is a dramatic example of what can happen when management does not exercise the proper control over its internal operations. Because of this failure, the firm's stakeholders began making demands on the company that eventually forced it into bankruptcy. In this chapter, we describe several control techniques which can help management better control operations. Proper use of these techniques will help managers avoid many kinds of problems, including those faced by Olympia & York.

nonfinancial control techniques

financial control techniques

To simplify the discussion, we divide the control techniques into two main categories: financial and nonfinancial. **Nonfinancial control techniques** are used to monitor employee behaviour without reference to corporate financial data. **Financial control techniques** are used to monitor employee behaviour when financial data like costs, profit, or sales revenue are available. Neither category is more important than the other; rather, they complement each other. In total, these techniques allow managers to perform the controlling function effectively.

NONFINANCIAL CONTROL TECHNIQUES

LEARNING OBJECTIVE 1
List and describe nine nonfinancial control techniques.

The most widely used systems of nonfinancial control are: (1) rewards and punishments, (2) selection procedures, (3) socialization and training, (4) the management hierarchy, (5) management audits, (6) management by exception, (7) quality control, (8) inventory control, and (9) network models. Most of these are used in all areas of the firm, but the latter three tend to dominate in the production area.

Rewards and Punishments

Every organization has some system for rewarding behaviour that is desirable and punishing behaviour that is undesirable. The effectiveness of rewards and punishments as control devices depends greatly on how they are administered by particular managers. The manager must identify what employees find rewarding and punishing, measure employee performance accurately, and apply rewards and punishments. If any of these steps are bypassed, managers may have trouble controlling employee behaviour.

In one company, management thought that they were doing workers a favour by not making them work overtime, but they later discovered that workers wanted to work overtime to earn extra money. Thus, management was punishing workers instead of rewarding them. The reverse situation existed in a prison where disruptive inmates were sent to solitary confinement and fed only bread and water as a form of punishment. When prison officials realized that a diet of bread and water was actually a status symbol, the diet in solitary confinement was changed to baby food. Inmate behaviour improved noticeably after this change. The role of rewards and punishments in motivation was discussed in Chapter 12.

Selection Procedures

Organizations also control employees by controlling the type of people that are hired in the first place. When the personnel department recruits people for various jobs in the organization, it stipulates certain characteristics that applicants must have. In this way, it controls the types of people that come into the organization. If a company is hiring electrical engineers, for example, it will likely require applicants to have a degree in electrical engineering. The company knows that it can count on these people to have certain levels of skill. It may also find that their behaviour is controlled by the formal and informal groups they join when they are hired.

This kind of control can, of course, be detrimental to a company. Eventually, employees who start with a similar perspective may narrow their views even further. Without the infusion of new perspectives, they may come to dominate the firm, stifling innovation and creativity. If this type of stagnation develops, the company may find itself unable to respond to changes in its markets. Thus, the firm may experience difficulties precisely because it is so efficient in controlling the type of people it hires.

Socialization and Training

When a new employee comes into a company, he or she is given information about both the formal and informal activities of the firm. One of the subtle, but powerful, forms of control is **socialization**, the gradual change of attitudes and behaviour of individuals as they are assimilated into the organization.[1]

socialization

Socialization occurs in all organizations. In grade school and high school, students learn not only about math and grammar, but they also develop views on fundamental issues like race relations, economic systems, conflict, status, and so forth. Graduates often don't realize that their conception of the world has been strongly shaped by their years in the school system.

A similar process of socialization happens in the workplace. Each organization has certain attitudes and behaviours it wants employees to accept, and over time, these attitudes and behaviours are communicated to employees and reinforced as "good" or "right." Those employees who cannot accept these values leave the firm. A person who wishes to be a nurse, but who does not have a caring attitude toward patients, will probably resist socialization attempts by other nurses and hospital administrators. This person will likely leave the organization because of difficulties in socialization. Overall, socialization is a very powerful form of control.

Training is also used to mold employee attitudes and behaviour so that they are in line with the aims of the organization. For instance, if a company rates quality as one of its most important objectives, it may require all production-line employees to take a course in quality control. If a company is a leader in technological innovation, it may systematically train its employees in creative thinking. Whatever the strategic goal, a company may use training to control the outlook and behaviour of employees so they suit the firm's goals. Employees who resist training will be unable to keep up with the performance of peers who have been trained; they are also likely to find that their career progress is retarded because they are seen as uncooperative.

THE MANAGEMENT HIERARCHY

Employees in all organizations know that they are responsible to the manager above them in the chain of command. That manager, in turn, knows that he or she is responsible to the next manager up the line, and so forth. The hierarchy is a control device because each person must account for their behaviour to the next person up the line. Rules, policies, procedures, and objectives are examples of control techniques embedded in the management hierarchy (see Chapter 4). All of these hierarchical controls allow management to more accurately predict how employees will behave, and how they might be motivated to improve.

THE MANAGEMENT AUDIT

management audit

A **management audit** systematically analyzes the strengths and weaknesses of the managerial talent in an organization. It is a control device because it measures how successful the managers have been in getting the company to perform up to the desired level. The goal of the management audit is to improve the organization by making sure that weaknesses in management are identified and corrected. Some areas of the firm that might be subject to a management audit are economic performance, the level of research and development, production efficiency, sales effectiveness, and growth in earnings. All these areas reflect how well top management has been doing its job of strategic planning, organizing, leading, and controlling the activities of the organization.

The management audit is usually conducted by an outside consulting firm because the areas to be asessed are ones that managers are sensitive about. They may also be hard to measure objectively, so an organization without a vested interest in the results should be used.

MANAGEMENT BY EXCEPTION

management by exception (MBE)

Management by exception (MBE) means that a manager becomes involved in the detailed supervision of subordinates only when there is an obvious deviation from standard levels of performance. Management by exception is a control technique because it requires the manager to watch overall trends and take action when certain aspects of the operation become exceptional.

exception principle

The **exception principle**—which states that employees should handle routine matters and the supervisor should handle exceptional matters—is the basis for MBE. For example, in a manufacturing firm, a manager might require that employees inform him or her when product quality is below standard for more than 2 percent of the units of output. Otherwise, employees retain the right to continue production without consulting the supervisor. In a service organization, a manager might want to know about customer complaints only when they exceed a certain percentage of customers handled, or when they deal with certain issues.

MBE frees the manager's time for other important duties and encourages workers to exercise judgment and develop their skills. They need not continually consult with the manager to see if their work is acceptable. As long as they are within the guidelines that have been established, they can continue to work as they see fit.

Quality and Quality Control

We saw in the last chapter that quality products and services are those that satisfy customer needs. But quality products don't just happen. **Quality control** refers to the activities that are carried out by managers and workers to ensure that quality levels are appropriate for customer needs.

quality control

LEARNING OBJECTIVE 2

Outline the main features of quality control.

Quality standards vary across firms. Extremely high standards may be applied for products like computers, pharmaceuticals, and nuclear power, while less rigid standards are normally used for products like garbage cans, nails, and sand. Quality standards may also vary across products within a single firm. A manufacturer of canned foods is likely to exercise greater care to ensure the highest quality for products it sells under its own brand. For those it sells as unbranded or generic products, however, it may be content to simply meet the minimum government standards for quality. This practice is followed for many products. Kitchenaid, for example, sets higher standards for its top-of-the-line dishwasher than for its bottom-of-the-line model.

The Hubble Space Telescope demonstrates the practical importance of quality control. After the telescope was launched in 1990, it was discovered that a flaw existed in its primary mirror, and this flaw produced blurred images. Since the telescope had been designed to observe distant stars, this was a major problem. Had more exacting quality control been applied, these problems could have been solved *before* the telescope was launched into space. Because proper controls had not been applied, it was necessary for astronauts to go up and fix the telescope. Needless to say, the expense of doing the repairs was very high.

Dofasco sales and technical representatives evaluate the performance of the company's high-strength steel which is used by car manufacturers to reduce the weight of automobiles. They are comparing performance with standards.

The Development of Thinking about Quality

In the years following World War II, a U.S. consultant named W. Edwards Deming tried to convince U.S. firms of the value of high-quality products. He was not successful in the U.S., but he did convince the Japanese. His work there transformed the phrase "Made in Japan" from a synonym for shoddy merchandise into a hallmark of reliability and quality. Now, Japan's highest award for industrial achievement is the Deming Award for Quality.

Deming developed 14 points on how to improve quality, including:[2]

1. Make a long-term commitment to improving quality.
2. Reduce dependence on inspection after the product is produced; instead, build quality into the product.
3. Minimize total cost by constantly improving the production system.
4. Be concerned about quality.
5. If you are a leader, you should help workers do a better job.

Deming's ideas gained prominence in Canada and the U.S. during the economic troubles of the 1970s and 1980s, and emphasis on quality manufacturing in the U.S.

and Canada still continues to increase. In the U.S., the Malcolm Baldridge Quality Award signifies the highest level of quality processes in manufacturing. In Canada, the Awards for Business Excellence acknowledge those businesses which increase Canada's competitiveness in international business. The Gold Plant Quality Award was given to the workers of Toyota's Cambridge, Ontario, plant in 1991. This award honours the plant as the top-quality producer of automobiles in North America. The award is proof of Toyota's emphasis on *kaizen* (continual search for improvement) and *jidoka* (defect detection).

However, a word of caution is in order here. Jumping on the quality "bandwagon," or winning one of the quality prizes mentioned above, is no guarantee that a company will be successful. The introduction of quality improvement programs can cause serious disruptions in the way a firm operates. There have been firms that have won a prestigious quality prize one year and then found themselves in serious financial difficulty the next. As usual, sound management of *all* aspects of operations is the only guarantee of company success.

Total Quality Management

total quality management (TQM)

The **total quality management** (TQM) concept is based on the idea that no defects are tolerable, and that employees are responsible for maintaining quality standards.[3] Traditionally, organizations formed separate departments (quality control) and set up specific jobs (quality-control inspector) to monitor quality levels. The workers' responsibility was to make the product, and the quality-control department's responsibility was to check the work. TQM does away with this distinction and makes each worker responsible for achieving high-quality standards. For example:

- At Toyota's Cambridge, Ontario, plant, workers can push a button or pull a rope to stop the production line when something is not up to standard.[4]
- Motorola has achieved a level of "six-sigma quality," which translates into just over three defects per million parts produced.
- When Levi Strauss introduced an "alternative work styles" program, it required workers to inspect their own output. Since the program began, there has been a 50 percent decline in defective pieces.[5]

TQM ideas were introduced in Japan in the 1950s and were so powerful that Japan is still the world leader in quality products. The U.S. and Canada trail Japan, but are still more quality-conscious than countries like Great Britain, France, and Germany. In Canada, the move to TQM is strongest in the automotive, photocopying, and computer industries.[6]

The new emphasis on quality can be seen in slogans that companies use to try to sell their products. Consider these:[7]

- "Where quality is Job 1" (Ford)
- "Quality, service, cleanliness, value" (McDonald's of Canada)
- "Quality means the world to us" (Motorola Cellular Canada)
- "Leadership through quality" (Xerox Canada Inc.)

These are not simply empty slogans. Many Canadian companies are actively involved in TQM projects. At Hymac Ltee., a Laval, Quebec firm that makes pulp processing machinery, employees take a large amount of the responsibility for dealing with customers. Committees are set up to examine and improve the company's procedures and to get customer input. The process has improved quality by ensuring that customers get products that meet their needs.[8]

Hewlett-Packard introduced TQM in 1979. By 1989, the company had reduced defects by a factor of ten, saved $600 million in warranty costs, reduced accounts receivable by $200 million, and cut work-in-process inventory by $500 million.[9]

Moldcraft Plastics is another organization which typifies this new approach.[10] The company provides custom molding services for companies like IBM, Northern Telecom, and Mitel. It must ensure degrees of reliability that were unheard of only a few years ago. A 2 percent rejection rate used to be acceptable in the industry, but even that is no longer good enough. Now, almost any rejection rate is unacceptable. When an order is received, a sheet listing the specifications of the mold is posted so that all workers can see what needs to be done. As the job progresses, both workers and management keep track of how well the specifications are being met. This system has created an increase in paperwork, but a very low rejection rate.

Quality control also plays a crucial role at McDonald's Restaurants.[11] In the Canadian franchise operation, quality control is vital because consistency must be maintained at over 400 outlets across the country. McDonald's, for instance, specifies the quality of meat that it wants from independent suppliers, and the suppliers must make sure that quality control at the meat plant meets McDonald's standards. People from McDonald's purchasing department regularly visit these plants to ensure that the quality standards are adhered to.

The emphasis on quality is not limited to private-sector, profit-oriented firms. Not-for-profit organizations are also focussing on the quality of the services they are delivering to customers. The Student Federation at the University of Ottawa, for example, collected student opinions about a campus retail outlet by putting a computer with an on-screen questionnaire in a high-traffic area.[12] The data provided by students helped the federation decide what changes to make in the store's operation. As another example, the Carleton County Law Assocation started its TQM initiative with a survey designed to educate Ottawa-area lawyers about its services.[13]

TQM is even being used by companies that normally give others advice on how to do business—management consulting firms. Andersen Consulting, for example, introduced a TQM program which included a client report card indicating how well the consulting firm was doing in meeting client needs.[14] The company also established the position of Chief Quality Officer to convey to employees the importance of TQM.

The introduction of a TQM program is no guarantee that a company will be successful, because an emphasis on quality is just one component. It must be combined with allowing employees to try new ideas and a recognition system that rewards them when they are successful. Some managers have difficulty adapting to TQM because they deal with workers using a "leave your brains at home and do what I say" management philosophy. Workers may also resist the move to TQM because they fear it will lead to a reduction in the number of jobs. When TQM is introduced, companies typically find that about 5-10 percent of the employees are enthusiastic, 5-10 percent are totally opposed, and the rest are somewhere in between.[15] For a description of one company's experience, see the Management at Work insert "TQM at Standard Aero Ltd."

In spite of the increased emphasis that many companies are putting on quality, there is still a gap between the level of quality that customers see and the level companies think they are delivering. A survey of 51 top executives of discount and department stores showed that they felt the quality of service in their stores had improved markedly in the previous year. But a survey of 1000 customers showed that they felt the quality of the service hadn't changed at all.[16]

Quality control is typically conducted by the firm making the product, but is sometimes done by independent organizations. Here, a researcher in the Electronics Test Centre division of the Alberta Research Council retrieves electronic gear which is being evaluated for its performance under sub-zero conditions. In 1989, the Centre worked on over 300 projects for more than 150 companies.

MANAGEMENT AT WORK

TQM AT STANDARD AERO LTD.

In 1991, the U.S. Air Force visited Standard Aero in Winnipeg, Manitoba. Standard had submitted a bid to overhaul aircraft that undercut its competitors by more than 50 percent, and the Air Force wanted to see the firm's factory before it signed the contract. They must have liked what they saw, because Standard got the contract. What the Air Force didn't know was that the impetus for the bid came not from Standard's managers (who were concerned about the size of the contract), but from shop floor employees.

Standard Aero has made TQM work where other companies have failed because it is dedicated to an often overlooked tenet of TQM: the only definition of quality that really counts is "what the customer wants." Standard employees talk to customers to find out exactly what they expect from the firm's work. Top management is also committed to TQM, has spent $13 million on the program to date and has fired several top managers who would not commit to the program.

TQM became popular in the late 1980s, but has lately been greeted with increasing skepticism, with many companies being disappointed with the lack of fast results. Bob Hamaberg, CEO, says that there is nothing wrong with TQM; it has simply been applied badly in many companies.

The TQM process began at Aero in 1990 with the election of a "change council" consisting of Hamaberg and five senior managers. This council ensured that the TQM process received the money, equipment, and support necessary for success. A full-time "change manager" was appointed from within the company to make sure that the process didn't pull other managers from their regular duties.

Next, a nine-person task force was formed that consisted of employees who had done the full range of jobs on one of Standard's major overhaul contracts. Their first task was to find out what the customer wanted. To do this, the team designed a questionnaire and then visited customer plants around the world to gather information. Even though the cost of this part of the process was about $100 000, much new information was gathered and many old beliefs about customers were shattered. For example, Standard found that in spite of free trade some U.S. firms were reluctant to deal with them because of complex cross-border paperwork. So Standard now does the paperwork for the customer. As a result of these actions, the task force picked up $7 million in new business.

The task force also worked within Standard to determine exactly how the company did its aircraft overhaul work. After weeks of analysis, the team was able to reduce the flow and complexity of work dramatically. For example, one gearbox had previously required 213 steps as it moved through the plant; the task force reduced the distance travelled by 80 percent, and cut the number of times the component changed hands by 84 percent. Also, by reducing paperwork involved in tracking the item they saved the company $150 000 per year.

Training is a major feature of the TQM program. Workers receive training in technical areas like statistics and machine operation, as well as in team building. The price tag at Standard has been about $1.5 million per year. Getting workers to be enthusiastic about TQM was not easy at first. Hamaberg's pep talks were crucial in getting workers to try it.

Hamaberg says that implementing TQM has been very hard, but that the results have been impressive. The task force members worked 12 to 14 hours per day, and he was concerned that they would burn out. He also notes that you can't do TQM all at once; it must be implemented step by step because people can't handle large amounts of immediate change. ▲

Quality Improvement Methods

There are several popular methods that are currently being used by Canadian firms to increase quality levels. These include statistical quality control, control charts, benchmarking, cause-and-effect diagrams, and ISO 9000. The importance of quality can be seen in the Global Management insert "The Impact of Quality on Exports."

Statistical quality control Even if a company inspected 100 percent of all the items it produced, some defects would go undetected because of human error. In many cases, it is impossible to test all the items because such testing would destroy the product. If the standard for the life of a light bulb was 200 hours, every bulb under such a system would have to be burned for this number of hours to determine if it met standards. Unfortunately, doing so would leave the company without any product to sell. Likewise,

GLOBAL MANAGEMENT

THE IMPACT OF QUALITY ON EXPORTS

For the past decade or so, we have heard a lot about how the Japanese are driving North American car manufacturers crazy with their high-quality automobiles. But the balance of power is about to shift. Within the next five years, almost a million Canadian- and American-made cars and trucks will be exported each year to Europe, Asia, and Latin America. That is a dramatic increase from 1986, when the number was only 48 000. These increased exports will require the equivalent of two assembly plants employing about 5000 workers, plus an additional 50 000 jobs in companies supplying the automakers. A strong indication of the commitment to export markets is seen in structural reorganizations. Ford, for example, is opening three dealerships in China and has moved its Mideast sales office from Dearborn, Michigan, to Dubai.

What is behind this turnaround? Part of the answer lies in the weaker dollar in both Canada and the U.S. This means that our exports are cheaper and therefore more competitive. Even foreign car manufacturers recognize this, and are planning to produce more cars in the U.S. and then export them.

The intense competition in the industry also explains what is happening. Put simply, North American car plants have become among the most productive in the world. Ford, for example, uses half as much labour to build a car as it did in the 1970s. European automakers, on the other hand, are struggling to become more productive. Currently, they are 50 percent less efficient than Ford's best plant in the U.S.

A third answer is quality. During the 1980s, Japanese cars had a definite edge, but North American automakers have recently made an amazing comeback—quality levels in Japan and North America are now about equal. Toyota continues to lead in quality surveys, but Ford ranks higher than BMW, Mitsubishi, Mazda, and Audi. In fact, North American automakers may actually have the advantage because of the "price-quality" relationship. While Japanese cars continue to have high quality, they are also very high priced. Since roughly equal quality can be obtained from Canadian and American cars at a significantly lower price, consumers are making the switch.

These changes have occurred very rapidly. In 1992, for the first time in years, the big three (Chrysler, General Motors, and Ford) became net exporters of cars. All through the 1980s they complained about Japanese imports and unfair trade practices, even though they sold up to 400 000 Japanese cars each year under their own nameplates. Japanese sales in North America have dropped sharply, from 4.1 million in 1986 to 2.3 million in 1992. In spite of this, politicians and automobile and union executives continue to claim that the Japanese are threatening jobs in North America. The shifts in quality and the exchange rate have come so quickly that the political discussion of the issue has been left behind by actual developments. ▲

if a tire manufacturers placed each tire on a machine to see if it would run the number of kilometres designated as the standard, no tires would be left to sell. For some products, 100 percent testing is not done because the cost of testing is prohibitive. Inspecting every nail in a keg would put the cost of nails beyond their worth.

statistical quality control

A technique is available for overcoming many of the problems associated with testing. **Statistical quality control** involves testing just a portion of the total output of a product and then drawing probability-based inferences about the quality of the remaining items which have not been tested. For example, 10 items might be tested out of a total of 200 that are produced. Based on the characteristics of the 10 items, a conclusion is then reached about the quality of the remaining 190 items. Of course, when this approach is used, some error is possible. If the 10 items that are chosen for inspection happen to be the only defective ones in the batch of 200, it will be wrongly concluded that the whole batch is bad. Conversely, if there are only 10 good items in the batch, and these are the 10 items that are tested, it will be wrongly concluded that the entire batch is good. However, both these situations are extremely unlikely. It is much more likely that a random sampling of some of the items in the batch will give an accurate picture of the quality of the whole batch.

Toronto Plastics Ltd. decided to implement statistical process control to achieve more consistent quality; machine operators must now continually assess the performance of their equipment. To facilitate this, the company trained 75 machine operators in statistics and mathematics.[17]

variable sampling

attribute sampling

When statistical quality control is used, one of two basic sampling approaches is used: variable sampling or attribute sampling. In **variable sampling**, a product is assessed to determine how closely it adheres to quality standards. For example, an automobile axle may be acceptable if it is within 0.08 mm either side of the standard. Thus, the axle can exhibit varying degrees of "goodness." **Attribute sampling** classifies products as either completely acceptable or completely unacceptable. For example, a batch of home repair compound made by National Gypsum will either be acceptable or unacceptable. If it is found to be unacceptable, it will have to be completely remixed. In attribute sampling, no degrees of "goodness" are allowed.

control chart

The Control Chart When tracking the quality level of products, it is helpful to represent pictorially what production quality looks like. A **control chart** shows how closely the product or service being produced adheres to the quality standards that have been set. The control chart also shows the upper and lower limits of product tolerance (see Figure 18-1).

benchmarking

Benchmarking An organization which uses **benchmarking** compares the quality of its output with the quality of the industry leaders. If differences are noted, the firm can figure out how the leaders are achieving their quality levels and then pursue the same strategy. Benchmarking can also be used to compare different departments or divisions in the same organization.

cause-and-effect diagram

Cause-and-effect diagrams A **cause-and-effect diagram** summarizes the four possible causes of quality problems—materials, manpower, methods, and machines. For example, if car bodies are being produced with rippled paint, the problem might be thin paint (materials), poor training (manpower), a defective sprayer (machines), or a layer of paint that is too thick (methods). The cause-and-effect diagram is used to identify the source(s) of the problem. Once the source is identified, actions can be taken to resolve the problem.

FIGURE 18-1 A CONTROL CHART.

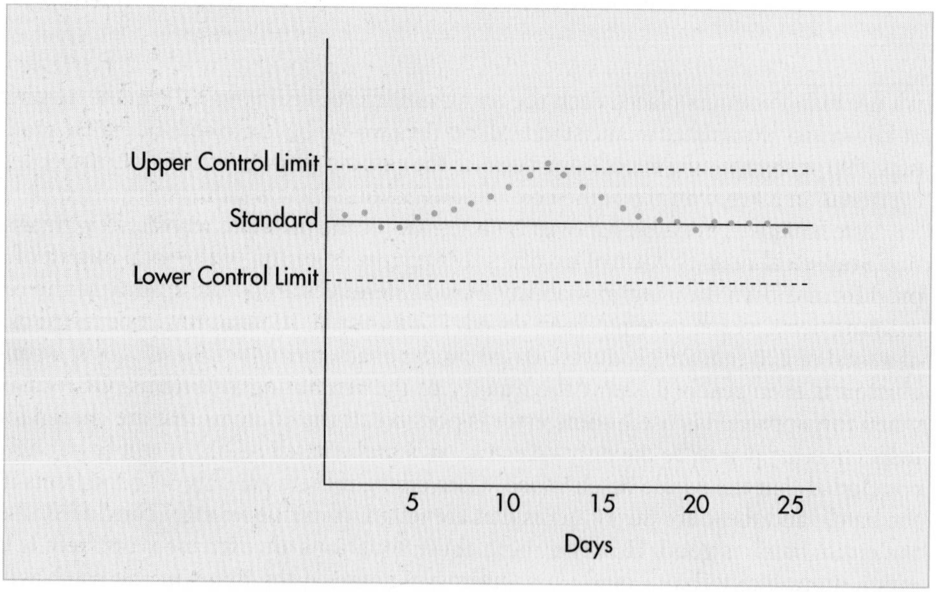

ISO 9000 ISO 9000 is a quality "scorecard" developed in Europe. It is fast becoming a prerequisite for selling to the European Community. Whereas TQM embraces the entire firm, the aim of ISO 9000 is to find the cause of product defects at the production-line level. Toronto Plastics, with annual sales of about $15 million, was awarded the ISO 9000 designation after it conducted a detailed audit of its factory operations; it is one of almost 200 Canadian sites to receive the designation. After receiving the designation, defects fell to 15 000 parts per million, down from 150 000 parts per million. The company's goal is to achieve 1000 parts per million.[18] Note that this is still far short of Motorola's achievement of 3-4 defective parts per million.

INVENTORY CONTROL

inventory
raw materials inventory

Inventory refers to the items an organization keeps on hand either for use in the production process or as a result of the production process. **Raw materials inventory** consists of the basic inputs into the production process. At McDonald's, raw materials include potatoes, meat, milk, and hamburger buns. At Northern Paint, raw materials include petroleum distillate, linseed oil, and pigment. **Goods-in-process inventory** includes those items which are part way through the production process. At Chrysler Canada, goods-in-process inventory includes engine blocks, tires, transmissions, and dashboards. At Wendy's, goods-in-process includes hamburgers cooking on the grill and baked potatoes in the microwave. **Finished goods inventory** includes those items that have passed through the entire production process and are ready to be sold to customers. New Buicks in an automobile dealer's showroom, french fries sitting under a heat lamp at Burger King, running shoes at Athlete's Wear, and computers on the counter at Computerland are finished goods inventory.

goods-in-process inventory

finished goods inventory

The fact that there are 70 000 members in an organization called the American Production and Inventory Control Society (APICS) shows the importance of effective management of inventory. APICS is an international, not-for-profit educational society for manufacturing professionals. It provides a number of educational services to members, including workshops, a monthly magazine, a professional library, discounts on reference material, and a certification program in production and inventory management (CPIM). The Canadian Association of Production and Inventory Control (CAPIC) is part of APICS. It has chapters in most major cities in Canada.

Inventory is also necessary in service operations. Magicuts Inc. introduced computers to record customer arrival and departure times, keep track of inventory, and record how demand for hairstyling services ebbs and flows over the course of a day. This helps the company to serve customers better by maintaining proper inventory, knowing a given customer's history at the shop, and matching available stylists with customer traffic patterns so that customers don't have to wait for service.[19]

LEARNING OBJECTIVE 3
List the main features of inventory control.

Until recently, many organizations carried large amounts of inventory. Assembly line operations in particular stressed carrying inventory so their operations would not be disrupted if a supplier experienced a strike or failed to deliver inventory on time. Increasingly, however, managers have come to the conclusion that inventory should be minimized, and cite several reasons for this decision. First, inventories require an investment of money. If a company can avoid this investment, it will be more efficient and will make a greater profit. Second, inventories take up space. Space costs money, so a company that is able to carry less inventory will be more efficient. Third, inventory may deteriorate, be stolen or be damaged, again costing money. Finally, inventory may become obsolete and hence unusable.

A variety of techniques have been developed to manage inventory. These include the ABC inventory method, economic order quantity, materials requirement planning, and just-in-time inventory systems.

The ABC Inventory Method

ABC inventory system

If an organization has thousands of different items in inventory, it may be very costly to keep track of all of them. In this case, it may be useful to categorize items in inventory based on how closely they need to be controlled. The **ABC inventory system** classifies inventory items into one of three categories based on the rate of their use and their cost. The categories and their definitions are as follows:

1. *A priority* Those items which are few in number, but which have high unit costs (e.g., custom machinery).
2. *B priority* Those items which are moderate in number and cost (e.g., personal computers).
3. *C priority* Those items which are high in number, but which have low unit cost (e.g., paper clips).

Once the items have been identified, the manager can set up a monitoring system that recognizes the value of inventory in the various categories. So, for "A" priority items, the system will be more sophisticated than for "B" priority items, which in turn will be more sophisticated than the system for "C" priority items. In fact, some "C" priority items may not be monitored at all because the cost of monitoring exceeds the value of the items.

Economic Order Quantity

economic order quantity (EOQ)

The **economic order quantity (EOQ)** system is a procedure for minimizing total inventory costs by balancing ordering costs and carrying costs. *Ordering costs* are incurred when inventory is ordered (e.g., postage, telephone bills, inspection costs, and receiving costs). *Carrying costs* are incurred when inventory is stored (e.g., taxes, interest on invested capital, and storage). The manager's job is to purchase inventory in a way that minimizes total costs. If the manager orders inventory frequently, carrying costs will go down, but ordering costs will go up. Conversely, if inventory is ordered infrequently, carrying costs will go up and ordering costs will go down.

In order to use the EOQ model, the manager must be able to state carrying costs and ordering costs. Suppose a company uses a glass container as part of a product it is making. After analyzing its records, management discovers that annual demand is 700 units, ordering costs are $16, and annual carrying costs are $7. Putting this information into the EOQ formula yields the following:

$$\sqrt{\frac{2 \times \text{Ordering Costs} \times \text{Annual Demand}}{\text{Carrying Costs}}} = \sqrt{\frac{2\,(16)\,(700)}{7}}$$

This equation tells the manager that the optimum quantity to order is 56.56, or 57 units.

The manager can also determine when to send the order by using the following formula (assume that it takes four days for the firm to receive the order once they have placed it):

$$\text{Reorder Point} = \frac{\text{Annual Demand (Lead Time)}}{365} = \frac{700(4)}{365} = 7.64$$

This formula tells management that 7 units of the product should be in inventory when the order is placed. When inventory reaches the level of 7 units, an order should be placed for 57 units.

Materials Requirement Planning (MRP)

The EOQ formula works well when the various products the company is ordering are not dependent on one another. For example, in a retail auto parts store like Bumper-to-Bumper, the demand for carburetors is independent of the demand for fan belts. In these cases, the economic order quantity can be calculated for each separate inventory item. But in many other situations, inventory items are highly interrelated. For example, if General Electric Canada plans to make 50 000 air conditioners, it will need 50 000 compressors, 100 000 litres of Freon, 500 000 screws, and so forth. The demand for all these items is dependent on the demand for air conditioners. **Materials requirement planning system (MRP)** helps management cope with demand-dependent inventory. A materials requirement planning system shows all the parts that are needed in a finished product and then calculates when these parts should be ordered. Because detailed calculations are necessary, the MRP system is typically computerized.

materials requirement planning system (MRP)

The MRP system is particularly valuable for firms using mass production methods, where thousands of parts may routinely be used. The MRP system allows management to tightly control inventory and thereby reduce costs. Managers at Delco Electronics reported a $12 million reduction in inventory when the MRP system was installed there.[20] As well, additional money was saved because extra floor space was freed up when less inventory was needed.

The Just-In-Time Inventory System

In the **just-in-time (JIT) inventory system**, inventory is scheduled to arrive just in time to be used in the production process. This system, which was pioneered by Toyota, is based on the idea that very little inventory is actually necessary if it is scheduled to arrive at precisely the time it is needed. Properly managed, the JIT system saves the company considerable money because inventory levels can be drastically reduced. In addition, all the risks normally associated with inventory—obsolescence, theft, deterioration, or damage—can be avoided. One expert suggests that the JIT system can result in zero inventory.[21]

just-in-time (JIT) inventory system

LEARNING OBJECTIVE 4

State the key elements in the just-in-time inventory system.

In the JIT system, production at one work station is triggered by demand for its output by the next work station. In an automobile manufacturing plant, for example, as the chassis moves down the production line, a signal goes out for the door subassembly unit to send doors to the assembly line. The doors would have been scheduled to be completed just as they were needed in the main assembly line. What number and type of door to send at this time has been determined in Japanese automobile plants by the *kanban* system. The ***kanban* system** specifies how many and what kind of items are to be produced. The JIT and *kanban* systems work in conjunction with each other.

***kanban* system**

JIT is also useful in the service sector. For example, when a pair of jeans is sold in a retail outlet, the bar code on the jeans is read by the cash register. This information can then be transmitted directly to the manufacturer to let them know that another pair of jeans is needed.

Omark Canada Ltd., a manufacturer of chain saw bars and sprockets, began using JIT in the 1980s. Prior to that time, its suppliers took three or four days to make deliveries, and loads were often overweight or underweight. The company solved both these problems by leasing a truck and hiring their own driver. Under the new JIT system, the driver picks up the steel needed to make the saw bars and sprockets and delivers it the next day. The driver times his arrival with the time the load is required at the plant. The new method has meant savings of $30 000 per year.[22]

The introduction of JIT at 3M also meant considerable savings. Its manufacturing facilities report reductions in space requirements for storing inventory (25 to 60 percent), reductions in work-in-process (75 to 95 percent), and reductions in the

The CN Tower and Skydome are two of Canada's most well known structures. PERT and CPM are important managerial control techniques in the construction of skyscrapers, stadiums, and hydroelectric dams.

distance material has to travel (80 to 95 percent). A tape-converting operation, for example, reduced order cycle time from 10 days to 2 days and processing flow time from 250 hours to 3 hours.[23]

The JIT system influences company operations in ways that go beyond inventory. Changes may also be needed in the way the firm deals with other firms. The JIT system requires suppliers to time deliveries with much greater precision than formerly. Achieving this precision requires a very close working relationship between suppliers and manufacturers. At Chrysler Canada's Windsor, Ontario, plant over 300 truckloads of raw materials are delivered each day, so care must be taken to ensure that shipments arrive on schedule. Thus, when one shipment arrived 12 hours ahead of schedule because the truck driver hadn't stopped to sleep, the driver had to wait 12 hours to unload.[24]

One way to achieve precision in deliveries is for manufacturers to purchase a given raw material from only one supplier. This arrangement motivates the supplier to be more careful when scheduling deliveries because it knows how much business is at stake. In the past, many manufacturers purchased a given part from several different suppliers. This practice fostered competition among suppliers, but since the business available to a given supplier was small, that company might be less careful about its shipments. JIT has also changed labour-management relations in supplier plants. Now, there is an attitude on both sides that there must not be a strike.[25]

Network Models

Complex construction projects like the CN Tower and Sky Dome in Toronto, the Ataturk Dam in Turkey, or the hydroelectric generating stations on the LaGrande River in Quebec require coordination of thousands of diverse tasks. Many people cannot understand how all these tasks are coordinated to ensure completion of the project. The two control techniques which are used to facilitate completion of large, complex projects like these are the Program Evaluation and Review Technique (PERT) and the Critical Path Method (CPM).

Program Evaluation and Review Technique (PERT)

PERT

PERT is a planning and control technique which is used to display the various activities and events that are needed to complete a project. PERT was originally developed in the 1950s to facilitate the development of the Polaris missile project in the U.S. To use PERT, a manager must be able to:

1. Identify all the essential tasks that need to be completed.
2. State the sequence in which these tasks are to be performed, and determine whether any tasks can be performed simultaneously.
3. Determine how much time will be required for the completion of each task.

Once this information is complete, the manager can draw a PERT chart.

Figure 18-2 shows a PERT chart for construction of a domed stadium. It shows the weighted average time estimate for each activity. This weighted average is composed of three possible times—the optimistic time (the time required if everything goes well), the most likely time (the realistic time that will be required to complete the activities), and the pessimistic time (the time that will be required if troubles are encountered).

event

activity

An **event** is the beginning or end of a step on the way to completion of the project. It does not consume time or resources, and it is represented by a circle on the chart. Thus, "begin laying foundation" and "foundation laid" are events. An **activity** consumes time and resources as work is done on the way to completion of the project. It is represented by an arrow on the chart. Thus, "lay foundation" is an activity.

FIGURE 18-2 PERT CHART FOR CONSTRUCTION OF A DOMED STADIUM.

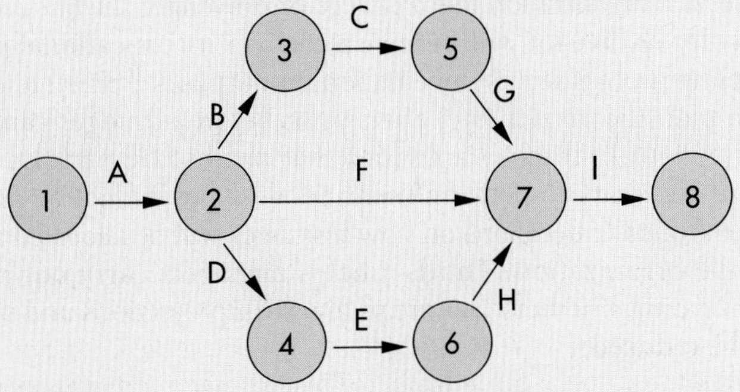

Key

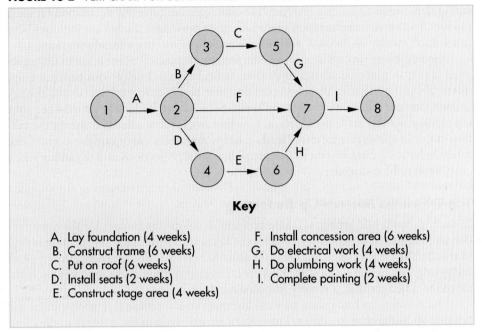

A. Lay foundation (4 weeks)
B. Construct frame (6 weeks)
C. Put on roof (6 weeks)
D. Install seats (2 weeks)
E. Construct stage area (4 weeks)
F. Install concession area (6 weeks)
G. Do electrical work (4 weeks)
H. Do plumbing work (4 weeks)
I. Complete painting (2 weeks)

critical path

slack time

The **critical path** is the series of activities which takes the longest time to complete. In Figure 18-2, the critical path is activity sequence A-B-C-G-I (total time equals 22 weeks). **Slack time** may occur during a project. Slack time is the difference between the total time estimate for a certain path and the total time estimate for the critical path. For example, slack time on path A-F-I is 10 weeks (22 − 12 = 10). There is, of course, no slack time on the critical path. Any delay on the critical path will hold up the project. Delays on the noncritical paths may or may not hold up the project, depending on how long they are.

Critical Path Method (CPM)

critical path method (CPM)

Critical path method (CPM) is much like PERT except that each project activity is assigned a specific time estimate rather than a range of optimistic, realistic, and pessimistic estimates. CPM was developed at about the same time as PERT by researchers at DuPont and Remington Rand who used the technique to assist in the construction of chemical plants.

FINANCIAL CONTROL TECHNIQUES

LEARNING OBJECTIVE 5
List and describe six financial control techniques.

In addition to the nonfinancial control techniques described so far, many financial control techniques are available to managers. The most widely used financial control are (1) budgets, (2) break-even analysis, (3) net present value, (4) profit centres, (5) financial statements and ratio analysis, and (6) accounting audits.

BUDGETS

budget

The most prevalent planning and control technique in organizations is the budget. A **budget** is a statement, in dollars and cents, of the expenditures that an organization plans to make during the next year. In a manufacturing firm organized along functional lines, the budget will state how much money each of the functional areas (marketing, finance, and production) are to receive for the next year. In a manufacturing firm organized along product lines, budgets are typically developed for each product. In a service organization like a college or university, the budget indicates how much each faculty or division will receive to deliver its educational programs.

LEARNING OBJECTIVE 6
Describe how budgets are used to facilitate the control function.

The budgeting process serves three important purposes.[26] First, it forces managers at all levels to plan the activities of their unit; before a budget can be drawn up, managers must identify the key activities that need to be performed and the resources that are necessary to perform them. Second, the budgeting process requires top management to make decisions on how resources will be allocated among the various units in the organization. Third, it helps managers carry out the controlling function by indicating whether costs are in line with projections and signalling when costs need to be reduced.

Top-Down vs. Bottom-Up Budgeting

top-down budgeting

In the **top-down budgeting**, top management develops the budget for the organization and imposes it on lower-level managers. Because top management has a great deal of information about the organization and its external environment, this type of budgeting can be very efficient. However, lower-level managers may not be committed to a budget that is simply imposed on them.

bottom-up budgeting

The bottom-up budgeting process attempts to overcome this problem. In the **bottom-up budgeting** lower-level managers are involved in the process of deciding how resources will be allocated to the various units in the organization. Individual managers suggest to their boss what the budget for their area should be. This process is repeated at each step in the hierarchy until the top of the organization is reached. Top management then develops a budget based on the suggestions of many managers in the organization. This system motivates managers to support the budget, but it may be very time-consuming. It may also lead to unrealistic budget proposals from certain managers who cannot take an overall perspective and who think only of the welfare of their own unit.

Regardless of the budgeting process that is used, much political activity may arise as each unit tries to get a larger share of the budget than it received last year. Since the total amount of money available is finite, when one unit receives more money, another unit receives less. This predicament can lead to great conflict over what proportion of the total budget each unit should receive (see Chapter 15). It can also lead to budgeting gamesmanship (see the Ethics in Management insert "Budgeting Gamesmanship").

Types of Budgets

Budgets can be developed for virtually any area of an organization's operations. The types of budgets that are most commonly found in organizations are listed and described in Table 18-1.

Approaches to Budgeting

incremental budgeting

Three fundamental approaches can be followed in setting budgets: the incremental approach, zero-based budgeting, and program budgeting. The most common approach is the incremental approach. In **incremental budgeting** the relative proportion of the total budget given to each unit in the organization changes very little from year to year. In most organizations, each department's budget is largely determined by what its budget was last year, plus an amount for inflation or any special projects that it might have planned.

The principal shortcoming of incremental budgeting is that little analysis takes place before allocating funds to the units. Such scant study is insufficient because it may overlook changes occurring in the firm's external environment that demand alterations in budget allocations. Top management should know when external changes

ETHICS IN MANAGEMENT

BUDGETING GAMESMANSHIP

Budgeting gamesmanship—the deliberate and premeditated manipulation of sales, cost, and profit data by product managers—was studied by conducting in-depth interviews with product managers in eight large firms. Budgeting gamesmanship was discovered in six of these eight firms, but managers never referred to what they were doing in those terms. Rather, they used terms like "hedge," "war chest," "slush fund," "cookie jar," and "secret reserve" to describe their budget activities.

TYPES OF BUDGETING GAMES

The most common types of budgeting games played were:

1. Understating volume estimates (48 percent of respondents).
2. Overstating advertising expenses (48 percent).
3. Overstating consumer promotion expenses (45 percent).
4. Understating price increases (39 percent).
5. Understating cost reduction programs (36 percent).

These responses showed that managers had opportunities to play budgeting games whenever they were asked to make cost estimates of their plans.

SIZE OF BUDGETING GAMES

The cushions that product managers had built into their budgets were sizable. The average amount over the six firms was $364 million dollars; this represented about 1.5 percent of corporate sales.

FACTORS AFFECTING BUDGETING GAMES

Product managers noted that certain situations encouraged budgeting games. These included the size of the budget (the bigger the budget the greater the opportunity for games), product history (new products generally allowed greater cushions than existing products), time constraints (top managers didn't have time to check all figures submitted by product managers), and the experience level of top managers (the less experience they had, the easier it was to pad budgets).

WHY DO PRODUCT MANAGERS PLAY BUDGETING GAMES?

Many managers assumed that their budget requests would be cut by top management, so they felt compelled to ask for more than they actually needed. Other managers were motivated by their wish to achieve profit targets (which, in turn, led to a bonus for achieving their target). Still other managers played budgeting games in order to have their targets set at a level they could achieve so that when performance appraisal time came around, they would look good.

IS TOP MANAGEMENT AWARE THAT BUDGETING GAMES ARE BEING PLAYED?

Top management in these firms was aware that budgeting games were being played. The problem was dealt with in two ways. In some firms, top management openly discouraged budgeting gamesmanship at the product level, and argued that top management would decide what "cushion" should be built into budgets. At other firms, top management took a more relaxed approach to budgeting games, and felt that it was beneficial for lower-level managers to have some flexibility. Interestingly, in those firms where top management actively discouraged budgeting gamesmanship, there was actually more of it than in the firms that tolerated it. ▲

TABLE 18-1 TYPES OF BUDGETS.

Type of budget	Explanation
1. Operating budget	Indicates the revenues and expenses the organization expects as a result of next year's activity.
2. Labour budget	States the number of individuals and the dollars allocated to each job category in the organization. A manufacturing firm, for example, would include categories like engineers, production workers, secretaries, and market researchers.
3. Cash budget	States the cash receipts and disbursements the organization predicts will occur during the next year.
4. Capital budget	Lists planned expenditures for major capital acquisitions (for example, a new manufacturing plant or new state-of-the-art machinery).
5. Research and development budget	Indicates planned expenditures for items like new product development.
6. Materials budget	States the expected purchases of various categories of raw materials and semifinished goods.

are becoming severe enough to threaten the organization and necessitate increases in the budget of some units and decreases in the budgets of others. But such a decision would cause much conflict within the organization, and the human tendency is to avoid such unpleasantness.

zero-based budgeting (ZBB)

Zero-based budgeting is an attempt to overcome the most serious problem in incremental budgeting. **Zero-based budgeting (ZBB)** requires managers in each budget unit to rationalize their allocations "from the ground up" each year, rather than simply assuming that next year's budget will be similar to last year's budget.

Stated more bluntly, managers in each unit must show why their unit should receive any money at all.[27] Each expenditure must be justified. ZBB was developed by the Department of Agriculture in the U.S. in the early 1960s, and then adopted by a variety of private sector U.S. firms shortly after that. In Canada, it became popular in the 1970s, but mostly in public-sector firms. The procedure for using ZBB involves three steps:

1. The activities of the various departments in the organization are divided into "decision packages." These provide information which allows top management to compare the costs and benefits of each activity of the department.
2. Each decision package is evaluated and then ranked against all other decision packages based on priorities for activities that have been established by top management.
3. Resources are allocated to the various units in the organization based on the rankings of the decision packages.

ZBB takes up a great deal of a manager's time and generates a large amount of paperwork. Although the goal of avoiding the problems of incremental budgeting is admirable, it appears that the effort required to achieve the goal is more than most organizations are willing to expend.[28] It may, however, be effective when an organization is experiencing declining resources and has to make tough decisions about where to make budget cuts.[29]

planning-programming budgeting system (PPBS)

The **planning-programming budgeting system (PPBS)** focusses on allocating budget money to programs instead of departments. It emphasizes the identification and elimination of programs that duplicate other programs, and it provides for an analysis of the benefits and costs of each organizational program. PPBS was originally developed for the U.S. Air Force by the Rand Corporation. During the 1960s and 1970s, it was adopted by many public-sector organizations in Canada and the U.S.

The PPBS process is as follows:

1. The objectives of each significant program in the organization are specified.
2. The output of each program is compared to the objectives of the program.
3. The total annual costs of the program are determined for a period of several years.
4. The most effective way to achieve program objectives is determined.
5. The program is systematically monitored to see if program objectives are being met.

Overall, PPBS combines MBO with the budgeting process. By doing so, it attempts to focus managerial attention on achieving certain desirable objectives within the constraints imposed by a budget. Like ZBB, the paperwork and time needed to make the PPBS process work seems to be too excessive to be worthwhile to most organizations.

Advantages and Disadvantages of Budgets

Budgets are necessary for organizations, and on balance, they are advantageous. However, budgets can give rise to several potential problems that must be taken into account during the budgeting process. Table 18-2 summarizes the advantages and potential disadvantages of budgets.

TABLE 18-2 ADVANTAGES AND POTENTIAL DISADVANTAGES OF BUDGETS.

Advantages	Potential Disadvantages
1. Provides a standard against which both employees and management can judge their performance.	1. If the amount budgeted is inadequate to do the job, frustration will result. If the amount budgeted is excessive, the unit may still spend all the money for fear that its budget will be cut next year if it doesn't. In either case, the budget causes scarce resources to be used unwisely.
2. Communicates a clear message about the activities top management views as important.	2. If employees are not involved in the budget process, they may become unmotivated. Disagreements with the allocations may result in political infighting and interdepartmental conflict.
3. Motivates managers and workers to behave in an effective way by giving them a monetary structure to work within.	3. Workers and managers may feel constrained by the budget rather than motivated by it. If budget categories are too rigid, the budget may simply reduce the discretion and creativity of those who must work within it.
4. Helps top management coordinate the activities of the different departments in the organization.	4. Lower-level managers and workers may not view the budget as a coordination device, but as a tool to evaluate their performance (i.e., those who stay within the budget are viewed as good performers, while those who don't are viewed as bad performers).
5. Helps managers at all levels to recognize problems (e.g., overexpenditures) as they develop.	5. Management may cut off funds before analyzing why a certain unit is overspending. A proper analysis might reveal that the unit is doing work that should be encouraged with a larger budget.

BREAK-EVEN ANALYSIS

As part of the controlling process, managers must know how increases or decreases in product sales will affect profit. **Break-even analysis** compares product revenues and costs at different sales volumes to show how profit is affected. The break-even point shows where total costs equal total revenues. Sales volume beyond the break-even point generates profit for the firm.

break-even analysis

In order to do a break-even analysis, the manager must know the fixed and variable costs of the product as well as the price at which the product will be sold. **Fixed costs** are those which do not vary as the quantity produced increases or decreases. Fixed costs include such items as management salaries, rent, property taxes, and fire insurance. **Variable costs** increase or decrease, depending on the level of production. Variable costs include things like raw materials, labour, and electricity.

fixed costs

variable costs

The formula for computing the break-even point is:

LEARNING OBJECTIVE 7

Perform a break-even analysis.

$$\text{Break-Even Point} = \frac{\text{Total Fixed Costs}}{\text{Price} - \text{Variable Costs}}$$

To demonstrate how break-even analysis works, consider the following example. Suppose a company is selling a product for \$25 a unit. It has determined that variable cost is \$18 per unit and total fixed costs are \$40 000. Using the formula above, the break-even point is:

$$\frac{\$40\ 000}{\$25 - \$18} = \frac{\$40\ 000}{\$7} = 5715 \text{ units}$$

The relationship between revenue and costs can also be shown graphically (see Figure 18-3). Costs and revenues are shown on the vertical axis, while units of output are shown on the horizontal axis. The graph shows that the company does not

FIGURE 18-3 BREAK-EVEN ANALYSIS.

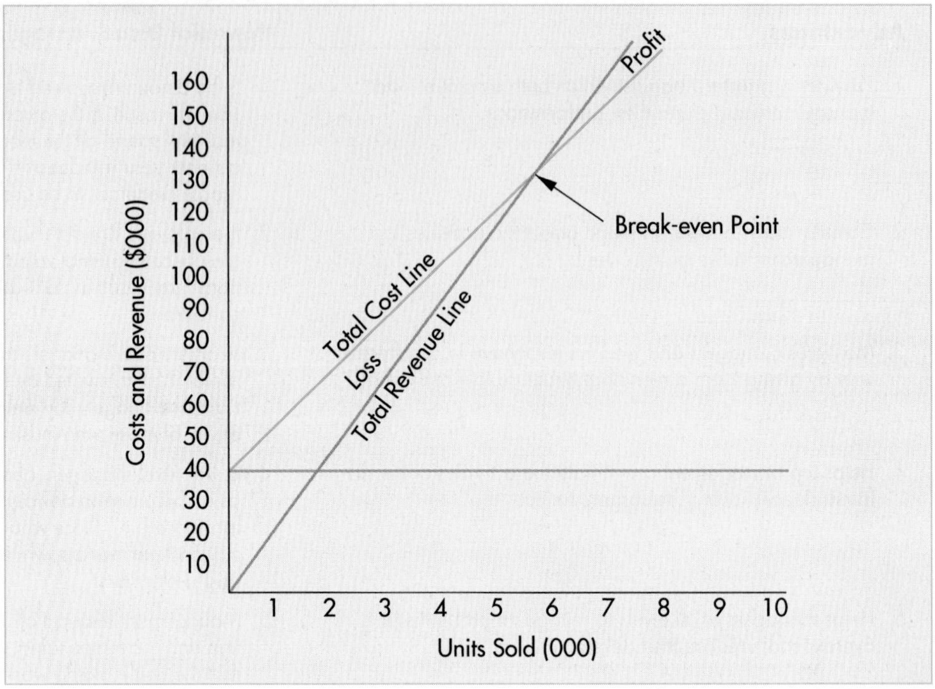

begin making a profit on this product until it sells at least 5715 units. For each unit produced and sold beyond this point, the firm makes $7 more profit ($25 selling price minus $18 variable cost).

Break-even analysis is helpful in managerial decision making. For example, if a manager is trying to decide whether to purchase a new machine, break-even analysis can show how the new machine might change the production cost structure (fixed costs), and how it might contribute to increased revenues by allowing the firm to make more units of the product. (Another technique for analyzing costs is described in the Management at Work insert "Controlling Costs with Activity-Based Costing.")

NET PRESENT VALUE

If you were given the opportunity to get a dollar today or a dollar one year from now, which would you prefer? Since you can earn interest on a dollar if it is given to you today, you should prefer to receive the dollar now rather than later. This principle of the time value of money is behind the net present value concept.

net present value

The **net present value** approach recognizes that a dollar received today is worth more than a dollar received at some point in the future. The net present value approach helps managers make investment decisions. Suppose that the vice-president of manufacturing is trying to decide which of two machines to purchase for the factory. Machine A costs $500 000 and will provide a saving of $200 000 per year for the next five years. Machine B costs $1 100 000 and will generate savings of $600 000 for the next three years. What should the vice-president do (assuming an interest rate of 15 percent per year)?

Net present value can be used to solve this problem (see Table 18-3). The vice-president should purchase Machine B because the net discounted cash flow (using the net present value idea) would be $270 400 for Machine B and only $170 600 for Machine A.

As a control technique, net present value is important to managers because large amounts of money are often involved in equipment purchases, and because the time value of money can have a large influence on the alternatives facing management.

MANAGEMENT AT WORK

CONTROLLING COSTS WITH ACTIVITY-BASED COSTING

Toronto-based Indal Ltd. has 28 subsidiaries and 8000 employees in Canada and the U.S.A cost management consultant at the company was searching for ways to figure out which subsidiaries were winners and which were losers, when he came upon a technique called "activity-based costing" (ABC). ABC helps managers figure out how much it costs to do specific activities that are necessary when making a product or delivering a service. For example, consider a company selling a high-volume and a low-volume product. Managers intuitively know that it takes more time and money to service low-volume accounts. But traditional accounting spreads overhead costs over everything a company produces; ABC breaks down cost items and attaches them to specific products. Companies using ABC can better understand things like set-up times and thereby better understand the cost structure for various products. This will allow them to decide which orders are most profitable.

Consider how the technique was applied at Brampton Foundries, one of Indal's subsidiaries. Brampton takes carefully designed and tooled shapes and makes aluminum copies of them. To do this, it must first make a mold of the shape. One of the methods it uses to make molds is called "sand casting," which involves creating a mold of the shape by packing damp sand around it, then pouring molten metal into the mold. In the old days, craftspeople checked the dampness of the sand by running their fingers through it. If they were wrong in their guessing, the mold was not acceptable and the aluminum had to be melted down and the process tried again. Now, computer probes measure the dampness of the sand; if it is not correct, the computer will not try to make the mold until the sand reaches the proper level of dampness.

Thom Santos, the president of Brampton Foundries, thought his company was a good money-maker until he starting analyzing his mold-making costs with the new ABC system. The computer model showed that the molds were wearing out very quickly and therefore needed a lot of maintenance. Santos told the machine operator that this was happening, reasoning that the operator would figure out a way to resolve the problem. The test of the system came when a Japanese buyer gave Brampton a worn-out die and a couple of castings to replicate. When the completed material was returned, the potential buyer found that the quality of Brampton's output was higher than that of a Japanese company they had been using.

But quality is not the only issue in competitive business. Price is also important. Once again, ABC helped by showing how much it would cost the foundry to make a certain casting. The ABC system also allowed Brampton to test "what if" questions like "What if we use process A to make this product?" versus "What if we use process B?" So far, the ABC system has been instrumental in the generation of about $1.5 million in new business. Managers at Brampton say that the ABC system helps their company "lose the bad jobs and keep the good ones." It is also better for Brampton if their competition is wasting time doing the bad jobs. ▲

TABLE 18-3 AN EXAMPLE OF NET PRESENT VALUE.

	Savings Per Year				
Year	**Machine A**	**Machine B**	**Present Value of $1**	**Machine A**	**Machine B**
1	200 000	600 000	0.870	$174 000	$522 000
2	200 000	600 000	0.756	151 200	453 600
3	200 000	600 000	0.658	131 600	394 800
4	200 000		0.572	114 400	
5	200 000		0.497	99 400	
				$670 600	$1 370 400
	Less cost of equipment			500 000	1 100 000
	Net discounted cash flow			$170 600	$270 400
	Difference in cash flow			$99 800	

PROFIT CENTRES

profit centre

A **profit centre** exists when a department or division in an organization is given the responsibility of making a profit, i.e., of making sure that its revenues exceed its costs. Designating an area as a profit centre is both a motivational and a control technique. It is motivational because the people in the unit know that their unit's profitability, or lack of it, can be identified. They will therefore work to ensure that revenues exceed costs. It is also a control device because, at the end of the fiscal year, both top management and the unit in question can tell whether the established objectives have been achieved.

Top management must ensure that the profit centre concept makes sense before they implement it. For example, in a functional organization (refer back to Figure 7-5), a profit centre would cause great difficulty because none of the functional areas makes a profit by itself. Rather, they must coordinate their efforts so that the total company makes a profit.

A profit centre would, however, be very appropriate for a company with a divisional structure (refer back to Figure 7-6). Each of the divisions can be held accountable for its profit because each is operating as a separate entity. Each has the resources it needs to conduct business independently.

FINANCIAL STATEMENTS AND RATIO ANALYSIS

LEARNING OBJECTIVE 8

Explain how ratio analysis helps managers determine how effective their organization is.

ratio analysis

balance sheet

income statement

When a company wants to assess how effective its financial performance has been, it may use ratio analysis. **Ratio analysis** involves taking two figures from the company's balance sheet or income statement and dividing one figure by the other. The resulting ratio is then reviewed to see if it is indicative of good management. Since the figures used for ratio analysis come largely from the firm's income statement and balance sheet, these two documents are briefly described below.

The **balance sheet** describes the company's financial position with respect to assets, liabilities, and owners' (shareholders') equity at one point in time. It is a snapshot of the company's financial position. The balance sheet is normally divided into three main sections (see Figure 18-4).

The first section contains information about the company's assets. These are subdivided into current assets (cash, inventory, and accounts receivable), and fixed assets (plant and equipment). The second section shows the company's liabilities, or debts. These are divided into short- and long-term liabilities. The former must be paid within one year, while the latter do not come due for at least one year. The third section is shareholders' equity, which is the residual value of the corporation after liabilities have been subtracted from assets.

The **income statement** shows the company's financial performance over a period of time (usually one year). Income statements contain two parts—a revenue section and a cost section (see Figure 18-5). Although income statements can be very complex for large organizations, they basically show the organization's revenues and the expenses which were incurred to obtain those revenues. The difference between revenues and expenses is profit.

The balance sheet and income statement provide information about how effectively the company is utilizing its financial resources. Intelligent interpretation of financial data provides an excellent way for management to control its financial welfare. Current performance can be compared not only to past performance within the company, but also to other firms in the industry. If the ratios are not in line with what is considered acceptable, management can make corrections.

Four general categories of ratios are computed. **Liquidity ratios** measure a firm's ability to meet its financial obligations as they come due. **Leverage ratios** measure how well an organization has used outside financing in the operation of the business. These ratios focus on the percentage of total funds that have been contributed by creditors, and how interest payments are affecting the firm. **Profitability ratios** measure the firm's overall efficiency and profitability. These ratios assess net income in relation to several important factors such as sales, total assets, and shareholder equity. **Activity ratios** measure how efficient a firm is in utilizing its resources.

liquidity ratios

leverage ratios

profitability ratios

activity ratios

The meaning of these ratios and the procedures for calculating them are shown in Table 18-4. A new (and controversial) ratio is described in the Management at Work insert "Financial Analysis at PWA Corp."

FIGURE 18-4 A BALANCE SHEET.

NORCAN LTD.

Balance Sheet as of December 31, 199X

Current Assets:		*Current Liabilities:*	
Cash	$ 60 000	Account Payable	$100 000
Accounts Receivable	180 000	Accrued Expenses Payable	10 000
Inventory	100 000	Estimated Tax Liability	70 000
Prepaid Expenses	20 000		
Total Current Assets	$360 000	Total Current Liabilities	$180 000
Fixed Assets:		*Long-Term Liabilities:*	
Land	$ 40 000	Bonds Payable	$100 000
Building	80 000		
Less Depreciation	40 000	*Shareholder's Equity:*	
		Common Stock (25 000 shares)	250 000
Other Assets:		Retained Earnings	10 000
Goodwill	100 000		
Total Assets	$540 000	Total Liabilities and Equity	$540 000

FIGURE 18-5 AN INCOME STATEMENT.

NORCAN LTD.

Income Statement

Year Ending December 31, 199X

Sales		$2 670 000
Less Cost of Goods Sold		1 520 000
Gross Profit		1 150 000
Less Expenses:		
Wages Paid	$682 000	
Administrative Expenses	380 000	
Interest Expenses	15 000	
Operating Profit		$1 077 000
Net Profit before Taxes		$ 73 000
Taxes		20 000
Net Profit after Taxes		$ 53 000
Less Dividends		40 000
Added to Retained Earnings		$ 13 000

TABLE 18-4 SUMMARY OF FINANCIAL RATIO ANALYSIS.

Type of Ratio	Name of Ratio	Formula for Calculation	Meaning and Definition of Ratio
Liquidity	Current ratio	current assets / current liabilities	Measures ability to meet debts when due—short-term liquidity
	Quick ratio	(current assets − inventory) / current liabilities	Measures ability to meet debts when due—very short-term liquidity
Leverage	Debt to total assets	total debt / total assets	Measures percentage of total funds that have been provided by creditors (debt = total assets − equity)
	Times interest earned	(profit before tax + interest charges) / interest charges	Measures the extent to which interest charges are covered by gross income
Profitability	Return on sales (net profit margin)	net income / sales revenue	Measures percent of profit earned on each dollar of sales
	Return on total assets	net income (after tax) / total assets	Measures the return on total investment of a firm
	Return on equity	net income (after tax) / shareholder equity	Measures rate of return on shareholder's investment
	Earnings per share	net income (after tax) / number of common shares outstanding	Measures profit earned for each share of common stock
Activity	Total asset turnover	revenues / total assets	Measures effectiveness of assets in generating revenues
	Collection period	receivables / revenues per day	Measures amount of credit extended to customers
	Inventory turnover	sales / inventory	Measure number of times inventory is used to generate sales

ACCOUNTING AUDITS

accounting audit

LEARNING OBJECTIVE 9

Compare financial audits and management audits.

An **accounting audit** is an independent analysis of the financial statements of a business organization. Corporations in Canada are required by law to conduct an audit each year. Auditing is done by chartered accountants (CAs) and in some provinces by certified general accountants (CGAs). These experts analyze a corporation's financial statements and give an opinion on whether or not it has followed generally accepted practices in developing its financial statements. CAs and CGAs do not develop a firm's financial statements; rather, they assess them after they have been prepared by the corporation's internal accounting staff.

The accounting audit is one of the best-known control techniques used by organizations. Even though it looks back on the financial transactions over the past year, it influences day-to-day operations because managers know that "the books" will be examined. This knowledge acts as a deterrent against fraud. The audit is also a good control device for investors and the general public. They can examine the company's audited statements in order to make decisions about where to invest their money.

MANAGEMENT AT WORK

FINANCIAL ANALYSIS AT PWA CORP.

In November, 1992, when PWA Corp. announced that it was no longer able to make payments on its leases and debts, Ross Healy was not surprised. Healy had concluded three years prior to that time that PWA was going to have financial trouble. How did he come to that conclusion?

Healy, an M.B.A. and a chartered financial analyst, has developed a method of analyzing corporate balance sheets that is a dramatic departure from traditional practice. Using formulas developed by maverick economist Verne Atrill, Healy argues that traditional debt/equity ratios are not much good in predicting a company's ability to keep paying its bills. A better way of expressing the relationship between what a company owes and what it owns is the operational activity ratio (the op ratio).

To calculate this ratio, Healy divides operational assets (total assets plus accumulated depreciation, minus net plant and equipment, minus inventories) by the company's total debt. Healy claims this figure is more meaningful than the traditional debt/equity figure.

Because the op ratio captures all the inputs and outputs that make up the activity of a company, it is an indicator of financial stress. If the op ratio falls too low, it is virtually impossible to restore financial health to a company without it selling assets. The ideal ratio occurs when a company owes no more than twice its operating assets.

Several break points are identified along the curve. One is at .499 (the point at which a company's debts equal about twice its operating assets). If the ratio is lower than this, even small increases in debt cause costs to rise uncontrollably, regardless of what management does. Another break point is .289, which is the borderline between what Healy calls first- and second-order insolvency. A company with a ratio below .289 is virtually dead.

Most companies never cross even the first line (.499) because their bankers won't let them. But Healy observes that governments do cross the line, and that both the Canadian and U.S. governments are somewhere between first- and second-order insolvency. If they were private companies, he says, they would have gone broke long ago.

Some observers view Healy's ideas as mumbo-jumbo, and a misguided attempt to relate the fields of physics and financial management (two fields in which the aforementioned Atrill worked). In physics, for example, a ratio of .499 is the first radiation constant—the point at which atoms at a given temperature emit most of their radiation. A ratio of .289 corresponds to Wien's Constant—a number that relates atomic wavelengths to absolute temperature. ▲

USING THE FORMS OF CONTROL

The control techniques discussed in this chapter are widely used by Canadian companies. Since managers are always looking for ways to simplify their options, they may be tempted to ask which of these methods of control is best.

This question lacks a simple answer because no single technique can solve the multitude of control problems that managers face. Rather, each of the forms of control is useful for a different purpose. For example, designating profit centres helps to identify costs and revenues for a division, while ratio analysis shows how well the organization as a whole is performing. Both of these types of control focus on financial data, but neither is sufficient by itself to fulfill the demands of the controlling function. Likewise, rewards and punishments motivate employees to perform in certain ways, while selection helps recruit certain types of individuals. Both of these nonfinancial controls are necessary, but management cannot choose only one of them and hope to do an adequate job of controlling behaviour.

LEARNING OBJECTIVE 10
Describe the manager's responsibility in choosing appropriate control techniques.

The biggest task for management is to decide which control technique is appropriate for which job. When making this decision, managers must balance the need for control against the potential for employee resistance to controls. Controls should not convey to employees that they are not trusted. Rather, they should indicate that certain fundamental checks will be done so that the organization can continue to function and provide employment opportunities.

In order to make rational choices about which form of control to use, managers must understand what each can and cannot do. Unfortunately, controls are often misunderstood. Consider corporate financial statements. When profit figures are reported in the newspaper, some critics immediately charge that "windfall profits" are being made. This expression implies that the company made an "excessive" amount of profit. But what is "excessive" profit? The profit figures reported on the company's income statement are arrived at only after many judgments have been made about which costs are associated with the revenues the company generated. The amount of profit reported therefore depends to a considerable degree on the assumptions that are made when the income statement is prepared.

The problem of misunderstanding control techniques is not restricted to financial statements. Take budgets, for example. Some managers assume that once the budget is set, everything is under control. But they fail to realize that people may go over their budget, even though safeguards are supposed to prevent this from happening. Once an overexpenditure has occurred, what should be done? Since the money has probably already left the company, little can be done except to ensure that it doesn't happen again.

Even if spending is kept within the budget, it can still be done unwisely. In many public- and private-sector organizations in Canada, budget money is spent just before the end of the fiscal year. These last-minute expenditures may do little to help the organization reach its goals. Similar problems are evident with control techniques like policies, rules, and procedures. These are frequently violated in organizations, yet some managers assume that because these controls exist, all the potential problems have been dealt with. Managers must recognize that simply having controls in place does not guarantee that everyone will abide by them.

Managers must also deal with objections to controls on the part of employees. As we noted in the previous chapter, employees resist controls for a variety of reasons. The manager must therefore spend some time thinking about which controls are necessary, and then explain these controls to employees. If the manager and the employees can come to a consensus about what kinds of controls are required for the work they are doing, resistance to controls can be minimized. The specific kinds of controls that are necessary at the Canadian Mint are different from those needed at Hy's, yet controls are necessary in both organizations.

SUMMARY

Nonfinancial control techniques are used to monitor the behaviour of employees without reference to corporate financial data. Many such techniques are used in organizations. Rewards and punishments are designed to encourage employees to behave in ways that are desirable to the organization. Selection procedures control employees by controlling the type of employee hired in the first place. Socialization and training are control techniques because they convey to employees what behaviour and attitudes are acceptable. The management hierarchy, or chain of command, is a control device because each person must account for their behaviour to the person above them. Rules, policies, procedures, and objectives are control techniques embedded in the management hierarchy. Management audits systematically analyze the strengths and weaknesses of the managers in an organization. These audits are a control device because they measure how well the managers in a firm have been able to get the company to perform at the desired level. Management by exception is another fundamental control technique; it stipulates that a manager becomes involved in detailed supervision of subordinates only when there is an obvious deviation from standard performance levels.

MEETING THE CHALLENGE

OLYMPIA & YORK

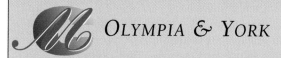

When Olympia & York announced its "liquidity crisis" in March, 1992, world financial markets reacted in fear. Thousands of investors had gambled more than $14 billion on the Reichmann mystique and it seemed that if O & Y was in trouble, we all were. At first, things appeared to be very bad. Upon release of the news, the Canadian dollar declined, the commercial paper market seized up, and Canadian bank stocks nosedived.

However, one year later, the situation didn't look nearly as bad. O & Y was being slowly liquidated by creditors, and Canadian banks were still standing. Now, financial markets are in an overall process of building immunities to corporate disasters like the one at O & Y.

While the financial system seems sound, many small investors have had to pay the price for investing in a company that failed to exercise effective management control over its activities. Shareholders in Canadian banks have lost nearly $2 billion in pretax profits as a result of bank loans to O & Y; millions of dollars have also been erased from the value of bank stocks. And thousands of small business owners are feeling the effects of tighter lending rules as a result of the fiasco. Finally, many O & Y employees in London, New York, and Toronto lost their jobs as a result.

But some companies and individuals have benefited from O & Y's problems. Observers note that there will be a huge amount of work for accountants and lawyers as they carve up the O & Y empire. There have already been many battles among creditors for the rights to company assets. Investors in stocks also see opportunities. So-called "vulture funds" have sprung up in recent years to invest in companies that have had financial problems. These investors believe that the company's stock price is currently undervalued and will increase once the financial problems are ironed out. Prospects have also improved for the massive Canary Wharf project in London, England. Bankers recently authorized an additional $500 million to help finance a subway line and office construction.

During the 1980s, the view emerged that some companies were just too big to fail. The result was that the government had to bail them out. The O & Y bankruptcy disabused us of this idea because when O & Y tried to get a bailout, it was unsuccessful. The firm's tangled financial situation simply worried government officials too much. ▲

A product or service exhibits high quality if it satisfies customer needs. Quality control refers to the set of activities that are carried out by managers to ensure that quality levels are appropriate for customer needs. An emphasis on quality products has been a hallmark of Japanese firms since the 1960s, but North American manufacturers have only recently accepted the idea of a great emphasis on quality.

The total quality management concept assumes that no defects are tolerable, and that employees are responsible for maintaining quality standards. In some cases, quality standards can be maintained by 100 percent inspection of output, while in others it makes more sense to sample only a portion of total output. Quality improvement methods include statistical quality control, the control chart, benchmarking, cause-and-effect diagrams, and ISO 9000.

Inventory refers to the items an organization keeps on hand either for use in the production process or as a result of the production process. The control of raw materials inventory, goods-in-process inventory, and finished goods inventory is important for organizational efficiency. Various systems have been developed to help managers control inventory. These include the ABC inventory method (the degree of monitoring varies according to the usage rate and cost of the inventory item), economic order quantity (balances carrying costs and ordering costs of inventory), materials requirements planning (shows the parts that are needed to make a product and indicates when these parts should be ordered), and just-in-time inventory (schedules inventory to arrive at precisely the moment it is needed in the production process).

Network models like PERT and CPM identify the various activities and events that must occur in order for complex projects to be completed on time. Network models function as both planning and control techniques.

Financial control techniques are used to monitor employee behaviour when financial data like costs, profit, or sales revenue are available. The most widely used financial control technique is the budget, which lists the expenditures the organization plans to make during the next fiscal year. Incremental budgeting means that the relative proportion of the total budget that each unit in the organization receives does not change much from year to year. Zero-based budgeting requires managers to rationalize their budget allocation "from the ground up" each year. Program budgeting focusses on allocating budgets to programs rather than departments.

Break-even analysis compares product revenues and costs at different sales volumes to show how profit is affected. To compute the break-even point, managers must be able to state the selling price of the product, fixed costs (those which do not vary as production volume varies), and variable costs (those which vary with production volume). The break-even point is computed by dividing total fixed costs by price minus variable costs.

The net present value approach is based on the fact that a dollar gained today is worth more than a dollar gained sometime in the future. This approach helps managers make capital investment decisions.

A profit centre exists when a department or division in an organization is given the responsibility of making a profit, i.e., of making sure that its revenues exceed its costs. Before setting up a profit centre, management must ensure that the unit in question can actually identify its costs and revenues.

Ratio analysis involves taking two figures from a company's balance sheet or income statement and then dividing one figure by the other. Liquidity ratios measure a firm's ability to meet its financial obligations as they occur. Leverage ratios measure how well an organization has used outside financing. Profitability ratios measure the firm's overall profitability. Activity ratios measure how efficient a firm is in using its resources.

An accounting audit is an independent analysis of the financial statements of an organization. Although the audit looks at financial transactions for the last year, it influences day-to-day activity because managers know that the audit will take place. This reduces the likelihood of fraud.

No single control technique will solve all of management's problems. Rather, each technique is useful for different purposes. Managers have the responsibility of understanding control techniques well enough to determine when each should be applied, and then explaining clearly to subordinates why a particular control technique is to be used.

KEY TERMS

nonfinancial control techniques (p. 558)
financial control techniques (p. 558)
socialization (p. 559)
management audit (p. 560)
management by exception (MBE) (p. 560)
exception principle (p. 560)
quality control (p. 561)
total quality management (TQM) (p. 562)
statistical quality control (p. 565)
variable sampling (p. 566)
attribute sampling (p. 566)
control chart (p. 566)
benchmarking (p. 566)
cause-and-effect diagram (p. 566)
inventory (p. 567)
raw materials inventory (p. 567)
goods-in-process inventory (p. 567)
finished goods inventory (p. 567)
ABC inventory system (p. 568)
economic order quantity (EOQ) (p. 568)
materials requirement planning system (MRP) (p. 569)
just-in-time inventory system (p. 569)
kanban system (p. 569)
PERT (p. 570)
event (p. 570)

activity (p. 570) critical path (p. 571) slack time (p. 571) critical path method (CPM) (p. 571) budget (p. 571) top-down budgeting (p. 572)	bottom-up budgeting (p. 572) incremental budgeting (p. 572) zero-based budgeting (p. 574)	planning-programming budgeting system (PPBS) (p. 574) break-even analysis (p. 575) fixed costs (p. 575) variable costs (p. 575) net present value (p. 576) profit centre (p. 578)	ratio analysis (p. 578) balance sheet (p. 578) income statement (p. 578) liquidity ratios (p. 579) leverage ratios (p. 579) profitability ratios (p. 579) activity ratios (p. 579) accounting audit (p. 580)

REVIEW QUESTIONS

1. What is the difference between financial and nonfinancial control techniques?
2. What are the benefits and costs of personnel selection procedures as a control device?
3. How is a management audit different from an accounting audit?
4. Explain the concept of management by exception as a control technique.
5. What is statistical quality control?
6. What is the purpose of a control chart?
7. What are the advantages and disadvantages of (a) the traditional Canadian inventory system, and (b) the Japanese just-in-time inventory system?
8. What is the EOQ procedure used for?
9. In what circumstances is the ABC inventory method appropriate?
10. What is the difference between PERT and CPM?
11. What kind of businesses use PERT or CPM network controls?
12. What are the benefits and limitations of budgets?
13. What problem may arise in using break-even analysis?
14. In what situations are profit centres appropriate? In what situations are they inappropriate?
15. Describe what each of the basic types of ratios—liquidity, leverage, activity, and profitability—are designed to measure. Give an example of each.

DISCUSSION QUESTIONS

1. Explain how the traditional Canadian inventory system differs from the Japanese just-in-time inventory system.
2. What factors determine how effective rewards and punishments will be in controlling employee behaviour? (Use the material on organizational behaviour modification from Chapter 12 to help in answering this question.)
3. Why are socialization and training considered to be control techniques?
4. How does the management hierarchy act as a control device? What other controlling devices are part of the management hierarchy?
5. Give three examples of statistical quality control and explain why a 100 percent inspection could not be conducted instead.
6. What is management's responsibility when choosing controlling techniques?

EXERCISES

1. Obtain the annual reports of an automobile manufacturing firm, a retail chain, and a computer firm. Compute at least one profitability, leverage, activity, and liquidity ratio for each of these firms. What similarities and differences are evident in these ratios across the three firms? What causes these similarities and differences?
2. Interview a chartered accountant and determine the uncertainties that exist in an accounting audit. How much confidence can investors put in the opinions of chartered accountants?
3. Have a panel discussion with three other students in front of the class on the following question: What specific control techniques would be most obvious in:
   a. a community college
   b. an insurance company
   c. a computer manufacturer
   d. a gas station

MANAGEMENT ON LOCATION

CASE 18-1
SECOND CUP LTD.

With 177 retail outlets, Second Cup Ltd. is Canada's largest retailer of speciality coffee. Specialty retailing is a competitive business, and Second Cup has its share of competitors: A.L. Van Houtte Ltd. (Montreal), Timothy's Coffees of the World Inc. (Toronto), and Starbucks Coffee Co. (Seattle). With about 40 percent of its sales coming from specialty coffee, the company actively seeks out contracts with suppliers of high-quality beans to attract customers.

Almost all of Second Cup's retail outlets are franchised. The average transaction is only $1.84, and this means that customer loyalty is extremely important. If a franchisee loses a customer, it is not just a $2.00 sale that is being lost. It could mean $2 per day for 10 years, or almost $5000.

New franchisees must attend Coffee College, which includes sessions on how to recognize high-quality coffee. A company consultant taste-tests every sample of beans purchased by the company. In fact, each batch of product is tested at least 70 times before it is sent out to the retail outlets. One weekend, two head office employees went to a mall to conduct a taste-test between a Second Cup blend and a supermarket coffee. Consumers overwhelmingly selected the Second Cup offering.

It can cost franchisees as much as $225 000 to open a store (including a $20 000 franchising fee). The average Second Cup franchise had revenue of over $300 000 in 1992; a typical franchisee keeps about 20 percent of that as profit. Franchisees are expected to be absolutely dedicated to the business. Applicants are screened closely and interviewed at least three different times. The company receives over 100 franchise applications each year, but accepts only about one quarter of them.

Second Cup demands that its franchisees work full-time in their store and have no other business on the side. They must also agree to run their franchise *exactly* as Second Cup stipulates, including passing the course at Coffee College. And, they must *love* to drink coffee. The company feels that franchisees will not be truly dedicated unless they love the product. Franchisees are also exhorted to apply high standards when hiring employees. Second Cup tells them to hire employees with four qualities: a happy face, good grooming, a high energy level, and a love for coffee.

To check up on how franchisees are operating, head office sends out "mystery shoppers" to test staff members and rate the store's appearance. Field consultants from head office also visit the various retail outlets to assess how things are going. Some franchisees object to both these tactics, arguing that it is too authoritarian and restricts their freedom. Other franchisees say that while they may be a bit upset when a visit occurs, they recognize that their store will be more profitable if they stick to the company plan. ▲

QUESTIONS

1. Discuss the various control techniques that are being employed by the head office of Second Cup.
2. At what stage in the controlling process are each of these control techniques being used? (Refer back to Chapter 17).

CASE 18-2
TOTAL QUALITY MANAGEMENT AT NATIONAL SEA PRODUCTS

National Sea Products is Canada's largest fish processor. Its High Liner brand is particularly popular. In 1988, the vice-president of quality at National Sea started talking about eliminating quality inspections in the firm's plants. His reasoning? It was costing too much money to "inspect quality into products" rather than "having quality control built into everyone's job." Eventually, he was able to convince other executives to allow him to measure the cost of quality and the firm's Total Quality Management (TQM) program was begun.

...

Although other top executives were interested in the idea, nothing much happened initially, and the firm continued to limp along with significant operating problems. At this point, a fortuitous event occurred: the Conference Board of Canada asked the company if it wanted to send a representative on an international study tour to see how other firms achieved high quality. Kelly Nelson, the executive vice-president of finance and administration, was chosen to represent the company.

From the beginning of the tour of foreign firms, it dawned on Nelson that National Sea had a long way to go in quality improvement. His major conclusion was that senior management had to support TQM absolutely or it would not work. Since the management team at National Sea was concerned about where the firm was heading (it had lost $30 million the year before), they were highly motivated to implement TQM.

In an attempt to return to profitability, National Sea had just completed some major restructuring. It had reduced the number of its plants from 13 to 7, the number of vessels from 58 to 48, and the number of employees from 7000 to 4500. Top management recognized that the next step would be to motivate employees to make the many small changes necessary to improve product quality. The vice-president of quality was initially assigned to oversee the shift to TQM, but the company soon realized that this would not work—the president and the entire top management team had to support the idea actively.

Management came to understand that they had to walk, talk, and breathe TQM if employees were going to get excited about it. Nelson's experiences on the tour were discussed at length in management meetings, and then a TQM plan was implemented. An outside consultant was hired to teach basic TQM skills, first to top management and then to succeeding levels of management in the firm.

TQM issues are now discussed for the first two hours of the weekly meeting of top managers of the firm. This keeps the issue uppermost in their minds. These discussions deal with issues such as human resource policy changes, reviewing the progress of new TQM initiatives (e.g., employee surveys and the firm's new suggestion system), and dealing with communication issues.

Top management must be receptive to change because employees who are given the chance to make suggestions capitalize on it. One team of employees asked to solve a logistical problem decided that the firm's structure would have to be changed. Since the firm had made a major structural change just three years earlier, top management was a bit reluctant. Nevertheless, after carefully analyzing the suggested change, they became convinced of its merit. The results are already noticeable.

The company also found it hard sometimes to practise what top management preached. For example, the firm recently implemented a new employee performance evaluation system more consistent with TQM principles. After several months, top management received a report stating that some people were not doing timely performance appraisals. Who were these people? Top management.

Some managers have found it difficult to change their behaviour to bring it in line with TQM principles. Most middle-level managers are promoted because of their technical skills rather than their people skills, and they sometimes have a tendency to engage in too much "doing" and not enough "leading." ▲

QUESTIONS

1. Why is quality so important? What is the relationship between quality and productivity?
2. What limiting factors might be present in a typical company that would reduce the positive impact of a TQM program?
3. What practices has National Sea Products adopted to motivate employees to be quality conscious?
4. How do quality circles fit into TQM?
5. Read an article about another firm that has implemented TQM. What similarities and differences in approach are evident when comparing that company to National Sea Products?

MANAGEMENT ON LOCATION

CASE 18-3
A NEW PRODUCT DECISION

Carolyn Loewen is the vice-president of marketing for Novelties Ltd., a small firm that manufactures and sells promotional material such as buttons, decals, and book covers. She recently came up with the idea of producing miniature Canadian flag decals that could be sold to companies for conventions or sales meetings.

Loewen is familiar with break-even analysis, so she develops some cost figures for producing the flags. She estimates that the fixed costs for the project will be $5000; the variable costs will be 70 cents per flag, and the company should be able to sell them for $2 apiece. ▲

QUESTIONS

1. How many flags must Novelties Ltd. sell in order to break even?
2. How many flags must the company sell to make a profit of $2000?
3. If Carolyn Loewen thinks that the maximum number of flags the company can sell is 5000, do you think that Novelties Ltd. should get involved in this project?
4. What uncertainties exist in this situation?

CASE 18-4
RATIO ANALYSIS AT NORCAN LTD.

Norcan Ltd. is a Saskatoon-based manufacturing firm that produces oil field equipment. At the last meeting of the board of directors, one of the outside board members expressed some concern about the company's financial condition. Several long-standing board members were surprised and said that they believed the company was doing very well. The outside member persisted in his questions, however, and a lengthy discussion took place regarding the company's activities over the last year.

After approximately 45 minutes of listening to various opinions and very few facts, the chairperson appointed a subcommittee to analyze Norcan's financial statements and report back to the board regarding the firm's financial condition. As part of its responsibility, the subcommittee was asked to do a thorough ratio analysis. ▲

QUESTIONS

1. Assume that you are the chairperson of the subcommittee. Use the balance sheet and income statement shown in Figures 18-4 and 18-5 to compute the liquidity, leverage, profitability, and activity ratios for Norcan. (Refer to Table 18-4 for ratios; for the collection period ratio, assume revenues are collected 365 days a year.)
2. Based on this ratio analysis, what can you say about the company's financial condition?
3. What additional information do you need to make an overall judgment of the financial condition of the company?

CHAPTER

19

INFORMATION MANAGEMENT

LEARNING OBJECTIVES

After reading this chapter, you will be able to:

1. Explain what a management information system is.
2. Contrast the terms "data" and "information."
3. Explain how information needs differ for top-, middle-, and lower-level managers.
4. Describe the four stages in the development of a management information system.
5. Understand how to properly implement a management information system.
6. Understand the role of computers in management information systems, and how computers impact management.

MANAGEMENT CHALLENGE

FLIMFLAM OR FACT?

National Research Group Inc. dominates consumer research in the motion picture business. It is the exclusive research firm for Paramount Communications, Metro-Goldwyn-Mayer, Twentieth Century-Fox, Columbia, TriStar, and Walt Disney. NRG gathers data on the effectiveness of certain advertisements, which movies people plan to see, and their reactions to advance screenings of soon-to-be-released films.

Most major films are shown to test audiences that have been recruited by NRG personnel; NRG then analyzes audience reactions through the use of questionnaires. Summary information about audience reaction to the film is conveyed to the movie studio prior to release of the film. On the basis of the audience data, scenes may be altered or the movie's ending may be changed. For example, the movie "The Bodyguard" was reworked after young males in the test audience said that Kevin Costner was not involved in enough action scenes.

Since NRG's research findings help determine how much hype a movie gets, its audience reaction data are very important. The relationship between NRG and the studios is therefore delicate and ambiguous. After movie screenings, studio executives look to NRG to determine what the public thinks about its latest offering. But NRG has tried to maintain a very low profile, partly because movie producers still like to think of their output as art rather than a tube of toothpaste that needs to be sold.

Recently, some disturbing claims about NRG have been made by about two dozen former employees of the company. Put bluntly, they claim that audience reactions about soon-to-be-released movies are sometimes falsified.

...

Some of these individuals say that the head of NRG, Joseph Farrell, admitted doctoring data; others say they actually saw him fabricating or manipulating data at the request of studio officials. Still others claim that "focus group" data is questionable. (Before a film begins, a small group of viewers are asked to remain afterward to discuss it. These individuals are supposed to be picked randomly, but ex-employees claim that NRG officials culled out those who didn't like the film.)

NRG also does extensive phone surveys of moviegoers, and former employees claim that data-doctoring was also evident in this part of the business. One former employee said she routinely saw phone-room personnel completing unfinished questionnaires. She claimed these practices had been standard operating procedure at the company for many years. When she reported these practices to her boss, the boss seemed genuinely concerned and promised to do something, but nothing ever happened.

Another former employee said he and others made up results in connection with the movie "Dick Tracy" when they couldn't find enough people willing to fill out questionnaires. And another said that NRG sent him and others to movie screenings masquerading as regular audience members. They were told to fill out the questionnaires indicating that they liked the film. Finally, one ex-employee said he received compliments from his boss on his ability to fill out questionnaires in different handwriting styles.

Joseph Farrell denies that the company has ever falsified questionnaire data. ▲

All kinds of organizations, business and otherwise, gather data about their activities and how well they are performing in satisfying customers or clients. As we saw in Chapter 6, managers depend on this data to make managerial decisions. If managers can rapidly and accurately gather and analyze information from the external and internal environment of the organization, they are better able to carry out the controlling function. This, in turn, makes it more likely that the organization will be successful. In the Management Challenge, studio executives were receiving data from NRG very quickly, but there were serious questions raised about the accuracy of it.

In this chapter, we address the important issue of information gathering and information analysis. We first describe what a "management information system" (MIS) is, and why all organizations need one. Next, we look at how organizations develop and implement an MIS, using a human resource management MIS as an illustration. We then describe the role of computers in an MIS, and the impact of computers on management. The chapter concludes with a discussion of recent trends in computing and information analysis that impact management.

MANAGEMENT INFORMATION SYSTEMS

In this chapter, we have focussed on managerial decision making. In several places, we stressed the importance of managers having good information on which to base decisions. Management information systems help managers by providing needed information.

MIS Defined

LEARNING OBJECTIVE 1
Explain what a management information system is.

management information system (MIS)

All organizations have some system—either simple or sophisticated—for gathering the information they need to make decisions. A **management information system (MIS)** collects, analyzes, organizes, and disseminates information from both internal and external sources so that managers can make decisions that are beneficial to the organization (see the Management at Work insert "MIS and EDI"). A good MIS gives managers information on past and present organization activities and makes some projections about future activities. An effective MIS also provides managers with information that is timely, accurate, and useful. In doing so, the MIS helps managers perform the four basic functions of management—planning, organizing, leading, and controlling.

Looking back to the Management Challenge in Chapter 7, we see that Rama Chakalas was really trying to convince Pat McGlothin that there was not enough information about truck maintenance costs to make a rational decision. A good MIS would have provided the information necessary to help these two managers find out exactly what the problem was with truck maintenance. This, in turn, would have helped them carry out the controlling function.

Although an MIS need not utilize a computer, most organizations are using computers because they can analyze large amounts of data quickly. We discuss the role of computers in MIS later; for now, keep in mind that even when a computer is used, it is only one part of the MIS.

LEARNING OBJECTIVE 2
Contrast the terms "data" and "information."

data
information

An important distinction in discussions of MIS is the difference between data and information. **Data** are unanalyzed facts about an organization's operations. Data become information only when they are useful for some sort of analysis. **Information** is anything which is useful and relevant for managers, including analyzed data. Information is most valuable when it is of high quality (accurate), when it is relevant (helpful to the manager), and when it is timely (available before the decision needs to be made). A good MIS takes data and converts them to information managers can use to help make decisions.

MANAGEMENT AT WORK

MIS AND EDI

When a four-slice Black & Decker toaster slides across the counter at Price Club's Mississauga store, the checkout clerk taps out a code and the toaster is deducted from the store's inventory. But that's not all. The transaction sets off a chain reaction ensuring that the toaster's replacement will be manufactured and shipped. The sale of the toaster is recorded in a central computer at Price Club's Montreal office. When supplies get down to a predetermined level, the computer automatically issues a purchase order to an electronic mailbox in Columbus, Ohio. A customer service agent checks the mailbox several times a week and downloads the order to a personal computer. Then a message is left for Price Club confirming the order has been received. The order is first transmitted to Black & Decker in Baltimore, Maryland, then on to Brockville, Ontario. From there the toasters are shipped to Price Club at Mississauga. Black & Decker also sends an electronic bill for the goods. In all of this activity, no paper is exchanged, just electronic signals.

Welcome to the world of electronic data interchange (EDI). The system eliminates the flow of paper between suppliers and their customers and results in faster delivery, reduced inventories, fewer human errors, and lower costs. Over 4000 Canadian companies now use it. Price Club estimates that it will save an amount equal to 1 percent of its annual sales (which were $1.7 billion in 1991).

Some suppliers are not enthusiastic about EDI because they feel the major benefits accrue to the retail outlets like Price Club and Sears. But suppliers may not have alternatives if they drag their feet. Price Club conducted a series of seminars in Montreal to tell suppliers to start using EDI or Price Club would find another supplier that would.

But companies like Black & Decker (which got on EDI with Sears recently) are positive about the system because it gets information back and forth quickly and allows everyone to carry less inventory.

There are costs associated with the system. Black & Decker has had to hire three programmers at an annual cost of about $200 000; there are also hardware and software costs that are incurred. The system is not yet profitable, but the company is confident it will be once the system becomes more widely used. ▲

THE NEED FOR AN MIS

Managers in all the functional areas of an organization need information to make decisions. Production managers need information on how much of the plant's capacity is being used in order to determine whether plant expansion will be necessary if demand increases. They also need regular information on such items as production costs, labour costs, order backlogs, and machine breakdowns.

Marketing managers need information on sales trends so that they can coordinate their activities with those of the production people. They also need information on new product development, new product sales trends, selling costs, marketing research, and sales territories (see the Management at Work insert "Information Systems in the Toy Industry").

Personnel managers need information on work force turnover and absenteeism, employee skill levels, labour markets, and wage levels in order to decide how to mobilize the firm's human resources in the most effective way.

Finance managers need information on corporate profitability, the efficiency of resource utilization, the firm's stock and bond prices, trends in interest rates, the cost of capital, internal and external sources of funds, and other information which will help in making wise decisions about how to finance the activities of the firm.

MANAGEMENT AT WORK

INFORMATION SYSTEMS IN THE TOY INDUSTRY

In August, 1993, a Target Stores employee noticed unusual sales activity on his computer screen for a toy called Mighty Morphin Power Rangers. He conferred with some co-workers to determine if this new toy might compare with other recent toy hits like Teenage Mutant Ninja Turtles. The computer data suggested that Power Rangers would be a big seller, but the TV program which was going to feature them hadn't even aired yet. So, Target waited to see what would develop.

The wait was costly. By the time Target placed an order in early October, the toy was hard to get (most other retailers had also placed their orders late). Only 600 000 Power Rangers had been shipped by Christmas, even though the estimated demand was 12 million. This level of demand was unexpected, because the idea for the Power Rangers TV show had been ridiculed by network executives for eight years.

This incident illustrates unexpected problems that have developed as retailers introduce sophisticated management information systems in an attempt to increase their profitability and reduce the risks associated with carrying inventory. For years, retailers have been trying to take the guesswork out of predicting which toys will be winners. In the last few years, a new strategy has emerged—retailers order small initial amounts of various toys, and then track sales very closely with computers and cash register scanners. If a certain toy sells well, they place an additional order.

So far so good. But if a toy sells well, retailers begin placing large orders and the toy manufacturer is simply unable to keep up with the demand. It is really a "just-in-time" system applied to retailing, and it is used by retail giants like Wal-Mart and Toys "R" Us.

Retailers who use this system have created problems not only for manufacturers, but also for themselves. Because toy sales are faddish and concentrated around the Christmas season, retailers run the risk of losing many transactions because they are not able to get "hot" toys into inventory fast enough. In the case of Power Rangers, for example, stores were unable to get inventory in time; as a result, the toy's first year revenue was only around $15 million. This compares poorly with first year sales of Cabbage Patch dolls ($67 million), Transformers ($114 million), and Teddy Ruxpin ($93 million). These items sold well because orders were placed by retailers well before Christmas and the manufacturers had time to adapt.

In spite of the problems, retailers seem committed to the new system of gathering information about consumer preferences because it reduces their risks. Although they might lose sales, they also avoid the high risks associated with inventory that might or might not sell. Coupled with the failure of some large toy retailers in recent years, this new system gives remaining retailers even more clout. They expect to be able to put additional pressure on manufacturers to deliver on short notice. ▲

Managers at different levels in the organization—top, middle, and lower—need different kinds of information, at different periods of time. Top management uses the MIS to set overall corporate policies and strategy to ensure the organization's growth and survival. Because these kinds of decisions have a long-term impact, this information is generally only needed quarterly, and perhaps only yearly. The most useful information for top management deals with whether the general direction of the organization is appropriate and whether changes will increase the chance that goals will be reached.

LEARNING OBJECTIVE 3

Explain how information needs differ for top-, middle-, and lower-level managers.

Middle managers put into operation the overall plans and strategies that top management has developed. They use the MIS to set up control procedures and to allocate resources. Because this information is more specific, middle managers need information on a weekly or monthly basis. The information most useful to middle managers indicates whether the operational system can reach top management's overall objectives.

Lower-level managers ensure that the goods or services offered by the organization are actually produced. They use the MIS to determine what raw materials they need, to develop work schedules, and to make sure that materials and people are in the right place at the right time so that production activities are not held up. Because these activities are very detailed, lower-level managers need information on an hourly or daily basis. The information most useful at this level centres on whether goods and services have been produced on schedule and whether customers are getting the products they want when they want them.

Table 19-1 summarizes these and other ideas regarding the different information needs at different management levels.

Developing an MIS

An MIS may be developed for a particular department in an organization or for the total organization. When an organization decides to develop a company-wide MIS, it must realize that it will probably take many months before the new system is fully operational. Determining the information needs of an organization is not a simple matter, so time must be allocated to the developmental process. As well, top management must give its wholehearted support to the developmental process. Without it, the MIS will probably not generate the information that the organization truly needs, nor will it be used by those who are supposed to benefit from it. The design and introduction of an MIS is itself a complex decision-making process.[1]

LEARNING OBJECTIVE 4

Describe the four stages in the development of a management information system.

The development of an MIS generally involves four stages.[2] In the first stage, an MIS task force is selected to determine the information needs of the company. The task force studies the internal and external environment of the firm to see what information is needed to plan and operate effectively. The information needs of all the

TABLE 19-1 INFORMATION REQUIREMENTS AT DIFFERENT MANAGEMENT LEVELS.

	Management Level	
Characteristics of Information	**Operational**	**Strategic**
Source	Largely internal	External
Scope	Well defined, narrow	Very wide
Level of aggregation	Detailed	Aggregate
Time horizon	Historical	Future
Currency	Highly current	Quite old
Required accuracy	High	Low
Frequency of use	Very frequent	Infrequent

primary areas of the firm are identified, and any possible constraints on the development of the system are noted.

In the second stage, the task force proposes various MIS designs. The kind of output that the organization will need from the MIS must be identified at this stage. Managers and workers in the organization are asked for their input. Kenneth Copeland, president of Digital Equipment Canada, says that users must be consulted at this stage or they will view the proposed changes as a threat, rather than an improvement.[3] Once alternative MIS designs are assessed, a specific design is proposed.

In the third stage, the proposed MIS is tested to see whether it will generate the needed information. Based on feedback from managers in the firm, necessary revisions to the system are made.

In the final stage, many detailed preparations for the actual operation of the MIS are made. For example, forms for data collection are designed, training programs are written, computer software is developed (if a computer is part of the system), and files are developed. This stage concludes with a final test of the new system.

Implementing an MIS

LEARNING OBJECTIVE 5
Understand how to properly implement a management information system.

The implementation of an MIS constitutes a major change in an organization.[4] Great care must be taken to ensure that the change will be accepted by the people who must work with the new system. Whenever an organization decides to install an MIS, it runs the risk of making many costly mistakes. Some common mistaken assumptions that are made during the implementation process are shown in Table 19-2.

TABLE 19-2 MISTAKEN ASSUMPTIONS ABOUT MIS.

Assumption	Fact
1. More information is better.	1. An MIS is often introduced on the assumption that that managers suffer from a shortage of information. While managers sometimes do lack the information they should have, it is more likely that they have a lot of irrelevant information. They may therefore be spending excessive amounts of time analyzing information that is not very helpful. If an MIS simply generates more irrelevant information, it is not serving its purpose.
2. Managers actually need all the information they request.	2. Managers often ask for a great deal of information, particularly on issues which they do not know very much about. They do this because they think that more information may help them find a solution. If the designer of the MIS gives managers all the information they request, the MIS may simply worsen information overload.
3. If managers are given all the information they need, they will make better decisions.	3. Just having information on which to base a decision does not guarantee managers will use it to make a good decision. If managers cannot use information effectively, they will not make good decisions no matter how much information is provided.
4. More information communication means better performance.	4. In most cases, an MIS can provide more current information about what the various parts of a firm are doing. Some people assume that this alone will allow managers in different areas of the firm to coordinate their activities and that this coordination will increase organizational performance. This is certainly possible, but information dissemination alone does not constitute either communication or coordination.
5. Managers do not have to understand how the MIS works in order to use it.	5. MIS designers try to make the system as easy as possible to use, but usually they do not stress that managers understand it. As a result, managers may be unable to evaluate the system properly and may end up being controlled by the MIS instead of the other way around.

Any one of these mistaken assumptions can reduce the effectiveness of an MIS. Fortunately, many lessons have been learned in the past 20 years.[5] First and foremost is that managers/users must be involved in the MIS developmental process. One study which examined 15 cases involving the introduction of computer-based information systems found that if users were involved during the early phases of the project, the system was more effective than when they were not involved.[6]

Second, timing and the cost of establishing the system must be carefully assessed. During the early stages of MIS design, all concerned parties must have a reasonable estimate of what the MIS will cost and when it will be operational. It is frustrating for users to be told repeatedly that the system "isn't quite ready yet." Top management is displeased when its new system is not only behind schedule, but also costlier than originally planned.

Third, human problems need attention. The introduction of an MIS can lead to significant changes in the way people relate to one another and to the amount of information they have about each other. Suppose a company institutes a computerized MIS and finds that the most effective approach is to combine the purchasing and inventory functions. The people in these two areas may be unhappy that the distinctive nature of their work has disappeared. They may also be required to work with new people. Productivity may decrease as people retaliate against the system that imposed an uncomfortable working environment on them.

Fourth, the performance goals of the MIS must be stated at the outset. Both designers and users must understand just exactly what the MIS is supposed to achieve once it is operational. In many instances, managers are surprised to learn that the MIS will not do something they assumed it would do.

Finally, understandable training and directions for users must be provided, especially when a computer is part of the MIS system. Many managers are fearful of computers, so systems analysts must provide easy-to-understand directions and training manuals. If this is not done, few people will use the system. Training and documentation must be geared to managers, not technical experts.

Computers are an integral part of the MIS in most firms. The emergence of end-user computing—the use of computers by people who are not computer experts—means that managers can access the information in the MIS.

An Example of an MIS

We have noted that an MIS can be developed for any functional area of an organization, or for the entire organization. Consider how an MIS might work in the human resources management area of an organization. The goal of human resources management is to ensure that appropriate human resources are available when the organization needs them. (The human resources function is described in detail in Chapter 11.)

In order to be effective, human resource managers need information about several aspects of the work force (see Figure 19-1):

1. Information about potential employees and their characteristics.
2. Finanical data about payroll and budgets.
3. Job data regarding the number and types of jobs that need to be filled.

These three factors constitute the inputs to the MIS. The information developed through these three input areas is combined into *databases*. These databases can be manipulated to provide outputs, such as wage and salary programs, promotion plans, and fringe benefits reports. The entire system of inputs, transformation, and outputs makes up the MIS. It allows human resource managers to make sound decisions regarding the use of the firm's human capital.

Databases are useful not only for a company's internal activity, but also for assessing its customers. At Edmonton's Eaton Centre Mall, the concept of the "frequent

FIGURE 19-1 AN EXAMPLE OF AN MIS.

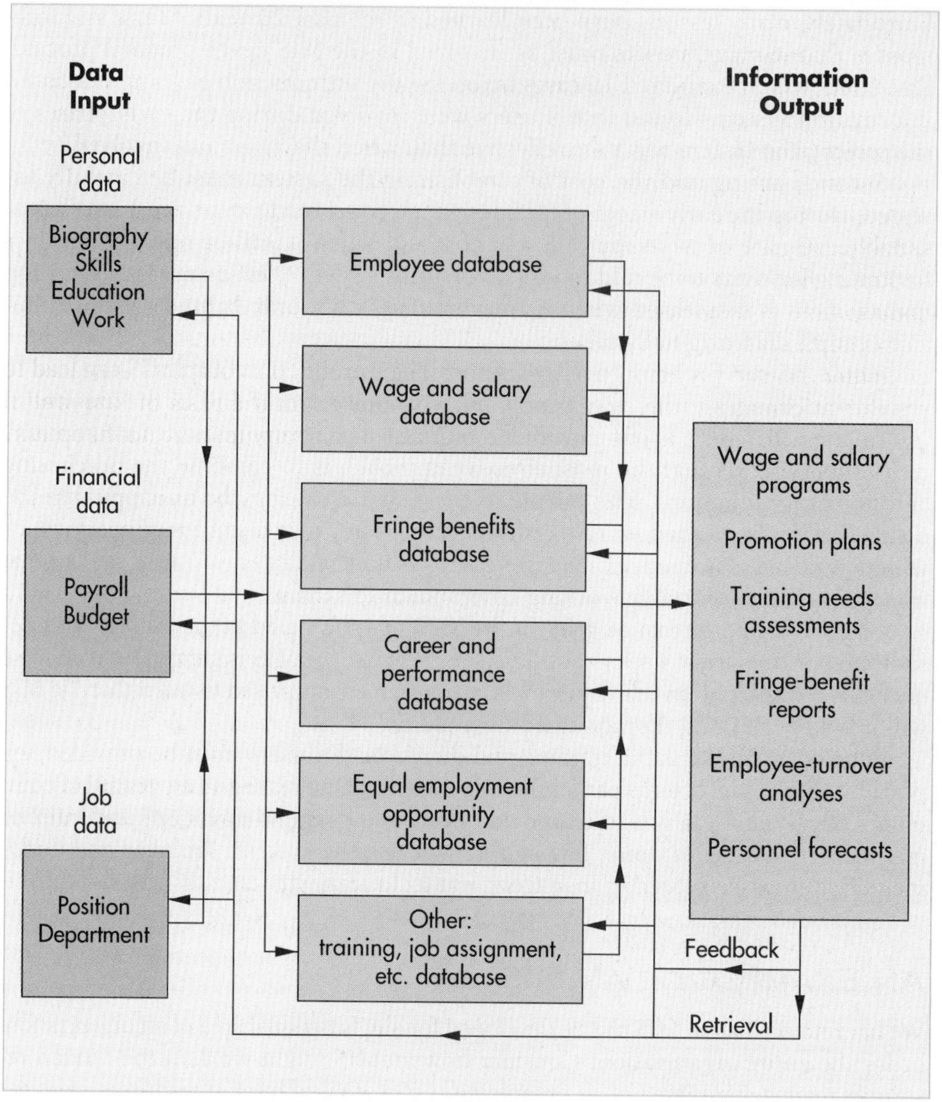

shopper" card has been introduced. Modelled partly on the frequent flyer programs of airlines, the card offers points to shoppers for every dollar they spend in the mall. They can then select items from a Dream Book catalogue when they get enough points. The system allows retailers to find out who their customers are, what they buy, and how much they spend. An analysis of customers showed that 3.1 percent of cardholders generated 25 percent of member sales, and 10.7 percent accounted for 50 percent of member sales.[7]

COMPUTERS AND MIS

LEARNING OBJECTIVE 6
Understand the role of computers in management information systems, and how computers impact management.

Because an MIS is likely to include a computer, managers/users have to be computer literate. This does not mean that managers must become data-processing experts, but they need to know something about what computers can and cannot do. Computers were first used by business firms in the early 1950s. Their use was restricted to extremely mechanical, high-volume work like processing employee paycheques. As computer technology improved, the use of computers expanded. During the 1960s and 1970s, computer programs were developed to deal with frequently recurring routine decisions such as ordering inventory. Now, computers are used to control sophisticated networks of company activity.

Changes in computer technology are occurring with such tremendous speed that we cannot foresee the uses that may eventually develop. At Shell Canada's new lubricants plant in Brockville, Ontario, a network of five integrated computer systems ties together the marketing, production, warehousing, and delivery activity that is needed to produce the plant's 240 different lubricant products. In the blending process, for example, a computer stores recipes for the different lubricant blends and tells operators how to mix them. The operator then manually connects and disconnects the proper hoses that carry the ingredients to their destination.[8]

Computers make fine tools for an MIS, but too many firms purchase or lease a computer and then attempt to design their MIS around it. If a computer is needed to provide information, the computer should be chosen on the basis of how well it converts raw data into useful information. Choosing a computer may not be an easy task, since a wide variety of computers are available.

Computers fall into three generally accepted categories—microcomputers, minicomputers, and mainframe computers—although the distinction between these three categories has become somewhat blurred in recent years. The **microcomputer**, or personal computer, is the smallest kind of computer. It allows the operator to enter, store, and manipulate data in a self-contained unit. Microcomputers were adopted by all kinds of organizations in the 1980s. Many individuals and smaller firms have purchased their own computers because of their convenient size and relatively low price (as low as $1000). But microcomputers are not used just by small businesses and individuals. Large corporations also use microcomputers extensively.

microcomputer

The **minicomputer** has capacities that are intermediate between micros and mainframes. Minis are faster and more powerful than micros and have a larger memory capacity. Minicomputers may cost up to $50 000.

minicomputer

Mainframe computers are able to handle vast amounts of data and do millions of computations each second. They are used mainly by large organizations with massive information processing needs. A mainframe computer may cost hundreds of thousands of dollars.

mainframe computer

THE IMPACT OF COMPUTERS ON MANAGEMENT

Rapid developments in computer technology are having an enormous impact on managerial decision making. New developments in information technology allow managers easy access to information that is important in their deliberations. These include, but are not limited to, electronic mail, voice messaging, computer conferencing, video conferencing, and electronic bulletin boards.[9]

The office of the future is also expected to change dramatically because of the computer. Specialized workstations are being created for professionals and managers that provide managers access to information with the touch of a button.[10] Word processing and office automation are already well established. **Word processing** uses a computer to do text-editing by enabling the user to manipulate words, tables, and figures. WordPerfect and WordStar are two of the most popular word processing systems now in use and can be used on most microcomputers. **Office automation** refers to the combination of word processing, electronic spreadsheets, and communication networks.

word processing

office automation

Some computer equipment can be carried in a briefcase, permitting a manager to work almost anywhere. **Telecommuting** involves computer hookups from office to home. Employees can work at home and still be in contact with important technical aspects of their work. The Management at Work insert "The New Wave: Telecommuting" gives additional information on this trend.

telecommuting

end-user computing

In recent years, there has been a dramatic increase in end-user computing. **End-user computing** refers to the use of computers by people who are not computer experts. Two specific examples of end-user computing are decision support systems and expert systems (part of the field called artificial intelligence).

Decision Support Systems

decision support system (DSS)

A **decision support system (DSS)** allows managers to interact conversationally with the computer to solve unstructured problems.[11] The emphasis in DSS is on user accessibility to data for the purpose of making decisions. During the last decade, many DSS applications have been developed, but their effectiveness is not yet clear.[12] The Global Management insert "Decision Support Systems and Retail Food Sales" describes recent developments in this area.

To understand how a DSS works, consider a manager who wants to know what would happen if a new salary structure were instituted, or a certain warehouse were closed, or a new corporate strategy were adopted. The manager could interact with the computer and

MANAGEMENT AT WORK

THE NEW WAVE: TELECOMMUTING

In his book *The Third Wave,* Alvin Toffler predicted that many workers would no longer need to go to a central workplace. Rather, they would "telecommute" with the office. Although Toffler's predictions have been slow to come true, the declining cost of communication and the increasing cost of real estate have combined to make telecommuting look like an idea whose time has arrived.

At IBM Canada, a pilot project took 29 salespeople out of IBM's Ottawa office and saved the company millions of dollars a year on lowered real estate requirements. Salespeople do their work at home or in their customers' offices. While travelling, they carry "electronic briefcases" equipped with radio-linked PCs.

British Columbia Telephone Co. has discovered another advantage to telecommuting: reduced travel time for employees. It also has a pilot project which has taken 15 employees out of the downtown Vancouver and Burnaby offices and relocated them in a satellite office in Langley (the suburb where they all live). Employees save the hour-plus drive into and out of Vancouver each day. Reducing commuting stress has increased the motivation levels of the employees in Langley. When they arrive at the office, they are ready to work, instead of tired from a long commute.

Telecommuting may be the trend of the '90s, as more and more people stay away from crowded city centres. If it is, there will be fewer traditional problems that cities will have to cope with, such as upgrading roads. Increasing numbers of companies (e.g., the Royal Bank of Canada, the Treasury Board, and the federal Department of Communication) have adopted policies that give employees the right to work at home at least a few days each week.

But telecommuting is not quite that simple, and has been resisted by some managers who feel they have to keep employees under surveillence. Interestingly, research consistently shows that telecommuting increases employee productivity, partly because employees feel they have more control over their work. Telecommuting experts argue that the technique forces managers to do what they should have always been doing: setting clear goals for their subordinates and then giving them the freedom to pursue those goals.

A bigger problem with telecommuting is the isolation that individual workers feel. A lot of work gets done in organizations when people interact with each other. With telecommuting, these benefits are lost. To overcome these problems, companies require employees to attend one or two meetings a month where everyone can share ideas and catch up on company happenings.

Another concern is security. When employees are allowed access to sensitive company information, they must agree to abide by the company's security checks and procedures. Employees must devise a system of passwords to gain access to computer files, and they must buy electronic scramblers for sending data over phone lines.

A final concern is employee suitability for telecommuting. Some people draw a sharp line between work and home, and for these people telecommuting may not be a good idea. The Royal Bank gives employees a set of questions to answer which helps them decide whether telecommuting is for them. The success of telecommuting seems to depend less on the job than it does on the character of the employee. ▲

GLOBAL MANAGEMENT

DECISION SUPPORT SYSTEMS AND RETAIL FOOD SALES

When sales of Frito-Lay's Tostitos tortilla chips suddenly began declining in one region of Texas, company managers turned on their computers and began analyzing local sales data. They quickly isolated the problem: a small regional competitor had introduced a product called El Galindo, a white corn tortilla chip, which was getting good word of mouth and more supermarket shelf space at the expense of Tostitos. Within three months, Frito-Lay began producing a white corn version of Tostitos that helped it regain its market share.

This rapid response was possible because Frito-Lay has a sophisticated decision support system which generates data on supermarket sales of the company's products. The system gathers information daily from supermarkets using checkout scanners to collect the data. Although scanners have been in use for quite some time, it was not until recently that computer software existed that would allow marketing executives to effectively use scanner-based data.

The new software programs break down brand performance by region, show how competing brands are performing, indicate which in-store displays are attracting customers, and show which promotions are the most effective. They also generate summary reports and graphs which highlight unusual product performance.

Around the country, 10 000 Frito-Lay workers use hand-held terminals to update—on a daily basis—the movement of the company's products. Information is available on 100 different Frito-Lay product lines in 400 000 different stores. This data appears on company computer screens in an easy-to-read format—red indicates a sales drop, yellow a slowdown, and green an upsurge.

In addition to giving managers instant information about product sales, the decision support system allows managers at Frito-Lay to coordinate their work with that of managers at parent company PepsiCo. It allows them, for example, to coordinate promotions, discount, and coupon campaigns on complementary products like soft drinks and chips.

These decision support systems will likely give food manufacturers more clout with supermarkets. Kraft Foods, for example, uses data from its system to advise supermarkets on how to most effectively use shelf space. The system will also make it easier for large companies to compete regionally by giving them rapid feedback about local sales.

There are concerns on the horizon, however. Some marketing consultants fear that decision support systems could end up hurting both retailers and manufacturers. They fear that these new systems will cause an overemphasis on short-run sales at the expense of building long-term brand loyalty. And, they argue, even if sales data are only one day old, using that data for planning is like driving a car by looking in the rear view mirror. ▲

use the data stored there to get some idea of the possible impact of these changes. The accuracy of these predictions is, of course, determined by the quality of information that is put into the computer in the first place. Lotus 1-2-3 is an example of DSS software because it recalculates outcome values each time the manager changes a basic assumption.

There are two basic differences between DSS and MIS: First, a DSS places more emphasis on the user's ability to manipulate data, while an MIS stresses data storage and retrieval.[13] Second, a DSS is typically used for unstructured problems, while an MIS is used for routine, recurring problems.[14]

Artificial Intelligence and Expert Systems

artificial intelligence (AI)

expert systems

Artificial intelligence (AI) is the field of study which tries to simulate intelligent human thought with the computer. The application of AI that is most relevant to management is expert systems. **Expert systems** duplicate the thinking process of an expert in a particular area by using decision rules that are built into the expert system.[15] Stated another way, expert systems allow managers to get advice from the computer that is much like the advice they would get from an expert. The Global Management insert "Developing an Expert System at Campbell's Soup" describes an interesting example of the development of an expert system.

In both DSS and MIS, the manager makes the decision and is supported by the computer. With expert systems, the computer makes the decision and is supported

GLOBAL MANAGEMENT

Developing an Expert System at Campbell's Soup

The outlook was bleak at Campbell's Soup as the company faced the impending retirement of Aldo Cimino, a production engineer who had been with the firm for 44 years. Cimino knew more about the intricacies of soup making than anyone, and he had intimate knowledge of just how to cope with the company's tempermental soup kettles. To ensure that his expertise remained after his departure, Campbell's invested time and money to create an "expert system" to replace Cimino with a computer. The program would embody Cimino's knowledge and experience about the finicky soup cauldrons, an expertise that took Cimino over four decades to perfect.

A trained computer programmer called a "knowledge engineer" picked Cimino's brain in order to devise a system that would mimic Cimino's decision-making processes. At the start, Cimino estimated that it would take about an hour to convey what he knew to the programmer. After seven months of close cooperation between Cimino and the programmer, the project was completed. Because the job of the programmer was to map out the unknown terrain of the expert's knowledge, the process included extensive interviews as well as long periods of time where the programmer would simply observe Cimino at his work. Sometimes the process even included videotaping in order to pick up any nonverbal cues that might be an important part of the work process. Good communication was vital, since misunderstandings could lead to months of work in the wrong direction.

More and more firms are creating expert systems to retain the expertise of valued employees after they leave. Using this process, a business can permanently retain the knowledge and experience of many highly skilled professionals from different fields—from doctors and financial advisors to geologists and craftspeople.

The development of an expert system is not a simple process. Complications arise because experts are often unaware of how extensive their knowledge is, or exactly what it is that makes them an expert. As well, experts may not do what they say they do. They may, for example, give long explanations about why they do something, but these explanations are simply rationalizations to cover up the fact that hunches are often the basis of their work. Experts may not be sure why they do what they do; they simply know it "feels" right.

In spite of these potential problems, the procedure at Campbell's Soup had a happy ending. The programmer succeeded in precisely detailing every step of the soup making process, as well as all of Cimino's thought processes as he did his job. Cimino's knowledge was transferred into a computer program of 151 "if-then" statements, making Cimino an eternal part of the process. ▲

by the manager. In DSS and MIS, the manager asks questions of the computer, but with expert systems, the computer asks questions of the manager.[16] Some people predict that expert systems will replace many kinds of decision support systems.[17]

Managerial Concerns about Computers

In spite of the positive aspects of computers, some middle- and lower-level managers are worried. While it is true that they will be able to monitor their subordinates more effectively, they know that they in turn will be monitored more closely by their bosses. This monitoring could create anxiety and unhappiness, especially for managers who may be insecure in their positions. Some managers may dislike the fact that they must supply information to MIS specialists rather than directly to their boss. Such managers may feel a loss of control. Another potential problem for middle- and lower-level managers is that the MIS allows top management to centralize decision making; some middle- and lower-level managers may feel that they have lost some discretion. They also fear that a computerized MIS will actually do away with some managerial positions.

Top management generally does not share these concerns because it is benefiting from the MIS. The managers at the top of the firm with an effective MIS will be getting timely, accurate information and therefore feel in control. As a result, they are usually favourably impressed by an MIS. However, top management should make itself aware of the concerns of other managers and try to allay those fears.

When top management turns to outside companies to manage the firm's information systems, this is called **outsourcing**. In 1990 Andersen Consulting began providing a service which allows clients to modify, enhance and maintain their existing MIS. Organizations are beginning to use outsourcing because they lack the in-house technical expertise to deal with rapid changes in computer technology.[18] More and more organizations are deciding to outsource their data processing needs, including both the Nova Scotia government and the Maritime Telegraph and Telephone Co. who decided to outsource to SHL Systemhouse Inc. the work required to process thousands of vehicle registrations, medical claims, phone bills, and paycheques. With Systemhouse's expertise and economies of scale, it can do the job better and cheaper. Government officials estimate the deal will save taxpayers $20 million over the next seven years.[19]

outsourcing

SUMMARY

A management information system (MIS) collects, analyzes, organizes, and disseminates information from both internal and external sources so that managers can make decisions that are beneficial to the organization. Data are unanalzyed facts about an organization's operations, while information is anything which is useful and relevant for managers. A good MIS converts data into information.

Top managers use an MIS to set overall corporate policies and strategy. Middle managers use an MIS to set up control procedures and to allocate resources. Lower-level managers use an MIS to determine what raw materials they need, to develop work schedules, and to make sure that materials and people are in the right place at the right

MEETING THE CHALLENGE

FLIMFLAM OR FACT?

When Joseph Farrell founded NRG in 1978, movie research was in its infancy. Although moviemakers had for decades previewed new movies to test audience reactions, research on the subject had remained primitive. Due in part to Farrell's intense efforts and hard work, movie research has become an indispensable part of Hollywood.

Charges that NRG is making up or manipulating data are very serious. What would motivate a company like NRG to give movie studios misleading or doctored survey data about customer reactions to their movies? Former employees claim there are three reasons: (1) NRG top executives did not want to be the "bearer of bad tidings" to movie studios, so they inflated the ratings of some movies, (2) changing audience data rationalized changes in the movie that studio moguls wanted to see implemented, and (3) NRG's corporate culture put intense pressure on workers to generate numbers quickly, so they felt obliged to fudge numbers rather than tell clients (studio bosses) that the data wouldn't be ready by a certain time.

The head of NRG, Joseph Farrell, dismisses these claims as ridiculous, and says that it would be impossible to manipulate audience survey data. He notes that there is only a one-half hour time span from the time a test screening ends until the time preliminary summaries of audience reactions are conveyed to studio heads. It would therefore be very difficult to alter the data. As well, studio representatives are almost always in the "counting room" when the questionnaires are being analyzed. More generally, Farrell says that NRG maintains elaborate safeguards so doctoring is not possible. He also notes that because so much of NRG's data are interrelated, it would be difficult to pull off such a deception.

Farrell notes that if data were being falsified, the firm would be much less accurate in its predictions than it is. Its forecast of opening weekend box office receipts are within 10 percent of those actually collected about 80 percent of the time.

Farrell attributes the claims of former employees to "sour grapes" because they were fired for violating company policies. Several of those interviewed by reporters had, in fact, been fired in 1991 during a bitter union-organizing drive. Top studio officials who were interviewed in the case also expressed surprise at the allegations, mostly because they thought it would be suicidal for Farrell. For his part, Farrell says he has never been asked by a studio executive to doctor data. ▲

time. The MIS is important for managers in the functional areas of marketing, human resource management, production, and finance.

The four steps in the development process of an MIS are: (1) formation of an MIS task force to determine the information needs of the company, (2) proposal of various MIS designs and the choice of one of these designs, (3) testing of the new MIS system to see whether it will generate the needed information, and (4) making detailed preparations for the actual operation of the MIS (for example, the development of forms for data collection).

When implementing an MIS, care must be taken to avoid making some common mistaken assumptions such as "more information is better," "managers actually need all the information they request," "managers will make better decisions if they are given all the information they need," and "managers don't need to understand how the MIS works in order to use it." When implementing the MIS, it is important to involve managers in the development of the system, determine the cost of the system early in the process, give attention to human concerns about the system, establish the performance goals of the system, and introduce training for users of the system.

Computers are almost always a key part of an MIS. There are three basic kinds of computers: (1) microcomputers (the smallest kind of computer), (2) minicomputers (faster, more powerful, and more costly than micros), and (3) mainframe computers (able to handle vast amounts of data and do millions of computations per second).

Computers impact the practice of management by making large amounts of data available to managers during the decision-making process. Decision support systems allow managers to interact with computers to solve unstructured problems. Artificial intelligence is the field of study which tries to simulate intelligent human thought with the computer. The computer has also changed the nature of clerical work by facilitating word processing, office automation, and telecommuting.

The computer has many positive aspects, but many middle- and lower-level managers are worried that their work will be unusually closely monitored by their bosses, and that decision making will become more centralized at the upper levels of the organizational hierarchy. Top management does not generally share these concerns because it benefits from the MIS.

KEY TERMS

management information system (MIS) (p. 590)
data (p. 591)
information (p. 591)
microcomputer (p. 597)
minicomputer (p. 597)
mainframe computer (p. 597)
word processing (p. 597)
office automation (p. 597)
telecommuting (p. 597)
end-user computing (p. 598)
decision support system (DSS) (p. 598)
artificial intelligence (AI) (p. 599)
expert systems (p. 599)
outsourcing (p. 601)

REVIEW QUESTIONS

1. Explain how a management information system helps managers perform their functions.
2. What is the difference between "data" and "information?"
3. Why do all organizations need a management information system? Defend your answer by using an example from one of the functional areas (marketing, production, finance).
4. Contrast the information needs of managers at the strategic and operational levels of an organization.
5. What are the four steps necessary in the development of an MIS?
6. List and briefly describe five mistaken assumptions that people make about MIS.
7. What are the three basic classes of computers?
8. What is artificial intelligence? How do expert systems help managers?

DISCUSSION QUESTIONS

1. What role do computers play in management information systems?
2. Explain how developments like word processing, office automation, telecommuting, and e-mail have impacted management activities.
3. How is the development of end-user computing likely to change the relationship between managers in computer experts?
4. Why are middle- and lower- level managers worried about computer developments?
5. Why might computer experts in a given company be worried about outsourcing?
6. "Artificial intelligence and expert systems will make the job of the manager obsolete within 20 years." Do you agree or disagree? Give reasons for your position.

EXERCISES

1. Visit a company and interview an individual who is knowledgeable about the firm's management information system. Determine what problems and opportunities exist because of the system.
2. Have an in-class debate on the following issue: That management information systems violate employees' rights to privacy.
3. Get together with two other people and develop a list of ways in which your day-to-day activities are affected by management information systems.
4. Interview a person in the central administration of your college or university who can tell you in some detail how the school's management information system works. What problems are evident in the system? To what extent is it oriented toward student satisfaction (as opposed to administrative ease of operation)?

MANAGEMENT ON LOCATION

CASE 19-1

PRIMO FOODS LTD.

Primo Foods Ltd. is a manufacturer and distributor of Italian food products based in Woodbridge, Ontario. Started in 1954 by Primo Poloniato, in 1986 the company was sold to Pet Inc. for $107 million. At first, very few changes were made by the new owner, but before long it became clear that there was not nearly enough information available about company operations to allow managers to control costs properly. Management consultants who were brought in to suggest improvements concluded that there was a need for basic management controls in the areas of understanding costs and setting budgets. Now, everything at Primo Foods Ltd. is counted, measured, and analyzed so that excessive costs can be pinpointed and fixed.

The vice-president of manufacturing says that the crucial activity is to get information to the operative employees so they can make adjustments that will solve (or prevent) problems. At the Woodbridge plant, work teams have analyzed fundamental problems in the areas of process control and maintenance management and have been able to generate large savings for the company. In the manufacturing plant, this type of analysis resulted in savings of over $1 million; in the warehousing and distribution area, savings of $2 million.

Changes in the distribution system are illustrative. The company once had the view that keeping delivery trucks on the road for many years was a sign of good management and wise use of funds. But the management consultant showed them that maintenance costs on old trucks were so high that it was better to buy new trucks more frequently. The annual cost of fleet maintenance has now been cut from nearly $700 000 per year to just $157 000. The decision to purchase new trucks also meant that different kinds of trucks could be purchased. The company moved away from reliance on "straight trucks" (where the cab and box are one unit) to tractor-trailers. This allows for more flexibility in distribution, because the right trailer can be chosen for the territory or load.

As another example, Primo trucks used to make regular deliveries to major grocery chains. But the search for data uncovered the fact that many of those chain-owned trucks were returning home empty after making their own deliveries to stores. So, Primo now pays them to stop and pick up the next regular shipment. Primo saves on its trucking costs, and the chains reduce their "deadhead" trips.

Fabian Venier, the vice-president of distribution, logistics, and purchasing for the company, says that the most important thing in controlling costs is data. The process of gathering data increases the manager's understanding of the business. Once an understanding is achieved, many cost-saving ideas can be introduced using common sense. ▲

QUESTIONS

1. What benefits are evident at Primo Foods as a result of information management?
2. What assumptions are being made about workers with respect to the new information that is being made available?
3. What potential problems are evident as a result of the increased availability of information?

CASE 19-2
THE PURCHASING AGENT

Petra Alexander is a purchasing agent for a medium-sized firm that has outlets throughout Metro Toronto. Until two years ago, Alexander drove around the city on a rotation schedule to collect the purchasing requirements from each outlet. Then, she'd compile master lists of items, decide where they ought to be purchased, and pass them along to order clerks. A popular person, Alexander is cheerful and sympathetic. Outlet managers have for years found her an easy person to talk to—to air complaints, to make suggestions, to discuss new products or procedures that might benefit other outlets. Alexander would tell what she'd heard to the appropriate managers in the central office. She is considered to be an above average employee, cooperative and efficient.

Two years ago, Alexander's boss sent her on courses to train her to use computers. Soon, all the firm's outlets were on-line, linked to the central office through telephone hookups. Petra was enthusiastic about the computer and spent many hours learning beyond the courses. She worked closely with the programmer who designed her purchasing programs and made useful suggestions to streamline procedures. Under the new system, the computer compiles the master lists and Alexander spends her time making money-saving purchasing decisions. Her efficiency remains high, and her boss congratulates himself that, at least in this department, the move to high tech has been negotiated successfully.

Alexander's boss is shocked, therefore, when Petra tells him she wants to quit. She explains that she's tried the new system for two years and she's very unhappy with it. She admits that the retraining was challenging and exciting. But, she says, the work itself is repetitive and boring. Typing at the keyboard all day makes her feel like a clerk; she feels tied to her terminal and misses the contact she used to have with the outlet managers. Alexander's boss is dismayed that he's about to lose one of his most productive employees. Thinking it over later, he realizes that the flow of valuable information Petra used to bring from the outlet managers has also disappeared. ▲

QUESTIONS

1. What changed about Petra Alexander's job to prompt her to resign? Can you suggest anything her boss might say or do to persuade her not to quit?
2. What steps might the firm take to prevent other employees from leaving?
3. Can the benefits of the informal organization be gained in the context of a highly computerized operation?

COMPREHENSIVE CASES
PART V

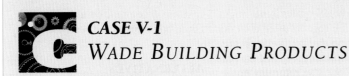

CASE V-1
WADE BUILDING PRODUCTS

Jack Clark, purchasing manager of Wade Building Products of Windsor, felt frustrated. By April, 1985, Wade's inventory control system was causing him headaches. He couldn't predict how much product to order, and did not know what current stocks were in the four retail operations for which he was responsible. Last month, the accountant had indicated that inventory levels had risen 3 percent. Jack couldn't pinpoint who had the inventory, but he could guess.

THE COMPANY

Wade was a privately owned three-store company in the home construction and repair market. Sales for 1985 were expected to be approximately $30 million. Cost of sales was about 75 percent. Stores were large self-serve operations which catered to builders and do-it-your-selfers. Recently Wade had added a You Do Building Supply Centre franchise. Economic conditions in Ontario had greatly stimulated the "home" market and Wade's business was booming.

THE INVENTORY CONTROL SYSTEM

The current system operated through automatic reorder when shelf or bin quantities were low, or stock cards. The card-controlled items (Exhibit 1) were supposed to be counted every two weeks and reordered when low. In practice, counts were made every one to three weeks. An early count could produce overstock and a late count could produce a stock out by the time fresh quantities arrived.

EXHIBIT 1 TYPICAL ENTRIES FROM THE OLD STOCK CARD SYSTEM.

Product PINE SHUTTERS E
Branch DOWNTOWN
Supplier EXPO
Address 205 LIMESTON CR. DOWNSVIEW

PAGE 1

ARTICLE	MAX. STOCK	MIN. STOCK	Feb. 25		Mar. 25		Apr. 23		May 26		June 21		July 12		July 27		Aug. 23		Sept. 24		Oct. 25		Nov. 22		Dec. 21	
			Stock	Order	Stock	Order	Stock	Order	Stock	Order	Stock	Order	Stock	Order	Stock	Order	Stock	Order	Stock	Order	Stock	Order	Stock	Order	Stock	Order
2 × 4 Clear Ceiling Panel	GEN12C		14	25	17	25	7	50	38	25	36	25	44/100	0	18	—	52	25	45	25	32	50	87/25	—	40	50
2 × 4 White Ceiling Panel	GEN12B		16	30	34	25	31	25	36	25	58	—	30/0	50	21	—	42	25	64	—	60	—	47	25	53	—
2 × 4 Eggcrate	GP2×4		25	30	30/32	—	30/15	15	21	30	29	30	34/0	30	22	15	14	30	23	15	19	15	15	15	12	15
2 × 4 Ceiling Panel Grid	GC036		40	0	7	40	38	—	33	—	30	—	25/0	0	25	—	23	—	19	—	15	20	12/20	—	39	—
7 × 16			—								—	—	0	0					4				0	4	4	—
7 × 20			16	—	9	6	15	—	13	—	—	16	11	0	4	8	19	—	18	—	15	—	17	—	13	—
7 × 24			3	6	9	—	9	—	9	—	—	3	9	0	9	3	9	—	9	—	9	—	9	—	9	—
7 × 28			5	—	5	—	5	6	4	6	—	5	4	12	7	5	16	—	16	—	16	—	3	8	0	8
7 × 32			4	6	5	6	6	6	6	6	—	4	12	0	12	—	8	6	10	—	10	—	9	—	9	—
7 × 36			18	—	6	6	4	40/10	8	6	—	18	16	0	18	—	12	—	10	—	10	—	10	—	10	—
8 × 16							8					18	0/−22	0	0	—	8	—	2	6	2	—	2	6	2	6
8 × 20			12	—	4	12	16	—	17	—	—	12	0/−8	0	13	—	12	—	13	—	12	—	2	8	8	—
8 × 24			13	—	13	—	8	6	2	12	—	13	13	36	1	—	14	—	5	—	28	—	28	—	16	—
8 × 28			11	—	11	—	11	—	11	—	—	11	11	24	0	—	15	—	16	—	24	—	29	—	24	—
8 × 32			6	—	6	6	4	12	14	—	—	6	6	12	4	—	7	8	12	—	3	6	5	3	8	—
8 × 36			8	—	4	6	4	12	12	—	—	8	10	0	7	6	7	4	7	4	3	6	3/6	—	—	6
P.O. NUMBER																										

• • •

However, it seemed the system would be good enough if only the clerks would do the counts on time.

Some stock came with control cards put on by the vendor. These cards gave the date an item came into inventory. If the clerks put the new stock behind the old, Jack could determine how long inventory sat before it was sold. Often though, the new stock was put at the front of the display.

A board was set up at the back of each store to inform salespersons if items ran out of stock. With 18 000 items in stock (SKU), and inventory turns running at 3.4 per year, something was always running out. Often this was not known until after it was sold.

Customers with large orders would buy in the store. They would take copies of the handwritten form to the adjacent warehouse to be filled. If there was not enough stock of an item, customers would receive what was available and have the rest crossed off their forms. One copy was sent to the store as a reminder to adjust the customer's account. Cash customers, having paid in the store, had to return to sales for a refund. Once or twice a day an angry customer confronted the clerks for a refund.

The order revised at the warehouse and returned to the store's office also indicated that more of an item needed to be ordered. This information was sent by the morning or afternoon courier to head office. With a day to process it, an item requested on Monday would be back in stock by Thursday morning, unless a "rush" was put on.

If an order beyond the capacity of a single store was received, the salesperson had to phone the other locations. Often the other stores promised inventory when they didn't have it, or denied having what they did have. Either was a problem.

There was occasionally a concern with sales advertised in flyers. Customers who bought sales items might be charged the regular price if clerks didn't remember that item being on sale. This was a particular problem if the customer found out after returning home, and had to return to the store.

Jack had the feeling store managers were hoarding safety stock against stock outs. Jack couldn't prove where it was going and the managers denied hiding it away.

POOR INVENTORY INFORMATION

Every month Jack received an analysis of sales and inventories from the company computer. The computer, purchased in 1979 at the recommendation of Bill Black (Vice-President Finance), had software developed specifically for Wade's reporting needs by the company programmer.

Unfortunately, most SKUs were lumped in general categories. Jack would not establish the volume cycles for most products—and these varied from store to store. An item could be tracked if it were given a special code, and if you could get the clerks to write the code on the sales order form.

The lack of information led to inventory speculation. Sometimes Mr. Wade would buy a great amount of pressed wood pieces, betting against a rising market. These buys could represent months of inventory. Often the speculation saved money when the wood market rose.

The alternative was to buy as needed with poorer price breaks on smaller volume discounts. Wade might buy 1 million board feet at the best rate in the winter. By early summer it would be clear that another 1 million board feet were needed at the regular price since mill capacity was pressed at that time. If another 0.5 million board feet were needed, it was purchased at spot market prices. Jack felt if he could predict historical demand on a product, he could buy more at the best price.

ALTERNATIVES

Jack wished there was a better way. He expected he could get the programmer to write better programs but it would mean expanding the memory of the mainframe. Then perhaps the clerks could be trained to always put product codes on the order forms. Although it was no longer possible to buy monitors or printers for the old system, Jack liked the programmer and was somewhat comfortable with the old system.

Bill Black had suggested that he, Jack and Sandy (Vice-President Operations) meet as a committee to recommend getting a whole new computer reporting system. Bill was such a computer enthusiast. Now he was enthraled by a system in use at the You Do Centre. It was a point-of-purchase inventory system that recorded every sale against stock. It could keep track of minimums and signal when to buy and up to what maximum (Exhibit 2).

To apply the system to all of Wade's stores would cost $250 000 just for the basics. Probably, he would be swamped with inventory information and would not be able to look at it all. Clerks would have to learn the system and so would managers. What would they do with the old computer and programmer—or if the new system went down? Besides, Sandy said the old system would work fine once the boom ended, as it had in 1982.

The new committee—Jack, Bill and Sandy—would meet tomorrow to discuss things. Jack wondered what he should recommend. Perhaps the old system would do. But, the information provided at the You Do Centre would solve many of his problems (Exhibit 2). Any decision that expensive would have to be approved by Mr. Wade himself. ▲

• • •

EXHIBIT 2 TYPICAL ENTRIES FROM THE YOU DO CENTRE STOCK STATUS REPORT.

Order # / WH	Item Code / Units Sold MTD	YTD	Description / Date Last Sale	Quantity On Hand	On Res.	U/M GGSS / On B.O.	No. Open Po.s / On P.O.	Last PO Date / Min Qty	Max Qty	Exp Del Date / Avg Unit Cost	Inv Value	C TRN L	S Pe T
287	1400M	1×4	Common Pine			LF 704		00/00/00		00/00/00			
1	556	3536	04/21/89	1017	197			500	3000	.248	252.22	4.2 1	214
2	1021	3354	04/24/89	8247	132			1000	4000	.248	2045.26	1.8 1	83
3	719	2052	04/22/89	215	40			500	2000	.238	53.32	1.5 1	81
	2296	8942		9479	369			2000	9000		2350.80	2.2	
288	1600M	1×6	Common Pine			LF 704		03/14/89		03/31/89			
1	880	5139	04/22/89	3232	101			1000	3000	.370	1195.84	30.2 1	970
2	706	2710	04/24/89	4073	90			2000	5000	.398	1621.05	1.4 1	52
3	1191	3452	04/24/89	4004	42			500	3000	.397	1589.89	7.9 1	261
	2777	11301		11309	233			3500	11000		4406.48	4.4	
289	1800M	1×8	Common Pine			LF 704	1	04/24/89		04/24/89			
1	424	2819	04/22/89	1058	64			500	2000	.495	523.71	12.6 1	542
2	500	1416	04/24/89	453			3000	500	3000	.497	225.14	2.9 1	125
3	360	1540	04/22/89	169	48			500	2000	.497	83.99	5.2 1	234
	1284	5775		1680	112		3000	1500	7000		832.84	5.7	
290	11000M	1×10	Common Pine			LF 704		03/14/89		03/31/89			
1	502	1270	04/21/89	1505	20			500	2000	.700	1053.50	4.4 1	163
2	123	572	04/24/89	1047				500	2000	.730	764.31	1.4 1	39
3	225	1201	04/21/89	1189	600			500	2000		870.35	3.7 1	141
	850	3043		3741	620			1500	6000		2688.16	3.0	
291	11200M	1×12	Common Pine			LF 704		03/14/89		03/31/89			
1	136	799	04/20/89	1889				500	2000	.906	1711.43	6.5 1	280
2	15	571	04/20/89	1883				500	3000	.930	1751.19	1.8 1	65
3	484	1258	04/21/89	1158				500	2000	.930	1076.94	7.2 1	295
	635	2628		4930				1500	7000		4539.56	4.2	
							Section				14817.84	3.4	
							Group 7				14817.84	3.4	

• • •

COMPREHENSIVE CASES
PART V

QUESTIONS

1. Briefly describe the controlling process at Wade. How well is it working?
2. What are the strategic control points in the inventory area?
3. How are input and output controls relevant?
4. Why might there be resistance to change as far as a new computer system is concerned?
5. Suppose a decision is made to change to a new computer. Develop a plan for doing so.

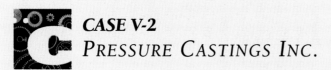

CASE V-2
PRESSURE CASTINGS INC.

Returning to his office from a meeting with the planning group and the production supervisors, Jan Fenwick wondered about which problems he should tackle first.

Jan had recently been appointed to his new job as plant manager at the Pressure Castings powdered metal parts plant in Pickering, Ontario. The former manager had been relieved of his job because of serious complaints from their largest customer about lack of service, inconsistent quality and poor delivery. The customer had become so upset with the plant's performance that they had threatened to award the contract to a competitor. An investigation reported by the divisional engineering staff into the problems earlier this year led to the change in management.

Jan had been fully aware of both the report and the directive from the division president to get the plant back on track and keep the customer. During his first week he had listened to a recital of ongoing problems. Most of the customer complaints had been based on poor production performance. To learn more about the production problems he had sat in on a number of the daily scheduling meetings with the planning manager and his production supervisors.

The comments from the production supervisors had only added to the problems and made a priority listing even more difficult:

"Why did QC wait until the last operation to reject those parts especially when the first stage inspection passed them?"

"The presses were running fine on the second shift but all the third-shift production was rejected this morning."

"The dies for that new part were removed because the parts were running out of tolerance. Maintenance can't do anything until engineering makes the design changes but the designer said he won't be able to do anything until next week because he was assigned to work on a quotation for head office engineering."

"The customer seems to be changing the specifications. That shipment returned this week is the same as the previous shipment which they accepted and used."

"That number 3 press is really in bad shape and causes all kinds of trouble in production. I've complained to maintenance for the last two years but they say their budget requests for rebuild work on presses is always being turned down."

THE PROCESS

The powdered metal part (P/M) was produced by pressing an iron powder mixture of iron, nickel, copper and other alloys with some wax for lubrication in a die made to the exact finished shape of the part required. This process called "briquetting" used large hydraulic presses of up to 675 tonnes capacity, depending on the size and desired strength of the finished part. After briquetting the parts were passed through an atmospheric furnace at 1148°C in a process called "sintering" which metallurgically bound the powdered mixture into a high-strength solid part. Additional operations were usually required to achieve the finished parts dimensions. As the total labour content was about 50 percent less than with conventional machining of steel bars or castings, powdered metal parts could be produced at less cost providing there was sufficient volume to recover the initial development and tooling costs. The minimum break-even quantity varied from 10 000 to ...

25 000 units depending on the part's size and complexity. The volume of a particular part required for a typical automotive contract generally ranged from 200 000 to 2 000 000 units for a model year.

Most of the sales came from direct substitution of P/M for parts already designed for conventional processes. However the lower weight of P/M parts encouraged designers to search out additional uses for this technology in their efforts to reduce weight in the new car designs. This demand had been a mixed blessing. The smaller sizes produced a need for much tighter tolerances on the finished part, and when coupled with a drive to upgrade the quality of all auto components, it forced suppliers such as the Pickering plant to considerably improve their process control with an increased emphasis on statistical quality control.

THE INDUSTRY

There were about 150 P/M manufacturers in North America, with the largest 30 controlling about 80 percent of the market. The 6 largest manufacturers, which primarily served the automotive industry, comprised the single largest market segment. The second most important market segment was the smaller producer who depended less on the automotive industry, but nevertheless posed a continuing threat to the larger P/M manufacturers. Pressure Castings Inc. was North America's largest producer with 90 percent of its production going to the automotive P/M industry.

Large and smaller P/M manufacturers alike faced increasing demands for improved quality and shorter delivery times. The conventional use of P/M technology was well established. In the past, the automotive customers sourced their parts based on price. As a result, there was a very large supplier base, poor quality standards and little cooperation between the suppliers and the users. Competitive advantage was gained only if a manufacturer either produced a product that the others couldn't, or produced at the lowest possible cost.

The three automotive users had changed their buying strategy over the past five years. All three had set up value ratings for their suppliers. Ford, for example, had a special weighted average it used to balance off the price, quality and delivery of its suppliers.

High-quality parts were vitally important for the automotive companies. Ford had its Q-1 program, GM had its spear program (in 1989 it was being changed again), and Chrysler had a similar rating program. The quality-control programs were based on rigorous statistical process control (SPC) concepts to ensure high-quality parts. It was not only a distinct competitive advantage to be certified under these programs, but necessary for the firm's survival if it hoped to supply the automotive industry.

JIT was also becoming increasingly important to the automotive companies. Although production requirements should be known for a few months in advance, the auto firms often changed their production schedules, and suddenly had different parts requirements. This meant the suppliers would have to either carry inventory of the more standard parts, or respond faster to the changing needs of the users.

In conjunction with these changes, the auto firms were reducing their number of suppliers. Ford had reduced its P/M suppliers from over 20 to just 5. Similar cuts were expected at GM and Chrysler. With the reduced supplier base there would be increased cooperation between the suppliers and the users.

To add to the suppliers' woes the Japanese were producing top-quality P/M parts, delivering on time and at lower prices.

THE COMPANY

The Pickering plant was part of Pressure Castings Inc., a U.S.-based corporation with head offices in Detroit, Michigan. The corporation reported sales from all operations of $620 million and a net profit of $8.2 million in 1988. The company designed and manufactured a broad line of industrial products for transportation equipment and fluid power systems. The Pickering plant was the largest in the Powdered Metal Division contributing $47 million sales out of a total division sales of $63 million. Seventy-five percent of their sales went to General Motors and Ford.

The Pickering plant had been profitable, although gross margins which had been relatively stable over the past three years were budgeted to decline by 6% for 1989 (Exhibit 1). Selling prices and sales volume were controlled by Divisional Sales operating out of Cleveland. The Pickering plant manager could, however, influence gross profit margin by controlling material costs, labour efficiency, scrap and overhead expenses.

The plant was built 25 years ago with powdered metal parts introduced a few years later. As powdered technology improved and demand increased, the other product lines were phased out and the plant concentrated on powdered metal parts. In 1981 the parent company was sold to a management group in the U.S. who, with outside financial support, formed the present company.

Management at Pickering continued relatively unchanged during this transition and reported to a divisional management group for Powdered Metal Parts at the sister plant in Cleveland, Ohio. The divisional management in

• • •

EXHIBIT 1

PRESSURE CASTINGS INC.
POWDERED METAL DIVISION
PROFIT AND LOSS STATEMENT

Year	1983		1984		1985		1986 Bud.	
	$	%	$	%	$	%	$	%
Sales	38 171		40 240		47 683		47 345	
Cost of Sales								
Material	7 252	17	7 243	18	8 106	17	8 048	17
Labour	2 672	8	3 219	8	3 815	8	3 788	8
Overhead	12 978	34	14 486	36	17 643	37	19 885	42
Scrap	1 145	4	1207	3	1 430	3	1 420	3
Total	24 047	63	26 155	65	30 994	65	33 141	70
Gross Margin	14 124	37	14 085	35	16 689	35	14 204	30
Variances	1 908	5	3 220	8	3 815	8	2 367	5
C.O.G.S.	25 955	68	29 375	73	34 809	73	35 508	75
Gross Profit	12 216	32	10 865	27	12 874	27	11 837	25
Admin. Exp.	763	2	805	2	954	2	947	2
Marketing Exp.	380	1	410	1	479	1	474	1
Engrg. Exp.	780	2	830	2	960	2	940	3
Corp. & Div.	2 290	6	1 625	4	1 430	3	1 894	4
Total Exp.	4 213	11	3 670	9	3 823	8	4 255	10
Pretax Income	$ 8 003	21	$ 7 195	18	$ 9 051	19	$ 7 582	15

turn reported to the head office corporate management in Detroit, Michigan.

ORGANIZATION

The divisional organization structure is shown in Exhibit 2. Pressure Castings divisional management was located in the Cleveland plant and the divisional president reported to the corporate group in Detroit. The company used a functional organization with all the functions represented in Cleveland. The plant managers each had responsibility for manufacturing materials and human resources in their respective plants. The controller and quality-control manager in the Pickering plant reported to their divisional counterpart with a dotted line relationship to Jan Fenwick, the plant manager. When questioned on how he thought the reporting relationship affected his ability to manage the plant Jan felt he had received full cooperation from everyone involved and did not think it made any practical difference whether they reported directly to Cleveland or to him.

QUALITY CONTROL

The quality-control (QC) personnel in the plant reported directly to the divisional office. This reporting relationship did not create any hardship for Jan Fenwick since he had had a good working relationship with the divisional quality-control manager. He felt the quality personnel were reasonable in letting the production go through without having interferred too much with his operations.

PRODUCTION PLANNING AND SCHEDULING

The manager of Planning, Julie Olsen, described the role of her group. Sales supplied a tentative master schedule for each car model year beginning in July. A more detailed schedule would be issued three months ahead of actual delivery. Whenever the auto customers revised their schedules the information would be provided either directly by the customer or through

• • •

EXHIBIT 2 POWDERED METAL DIVISIONAL ORGANIZATION CHART.

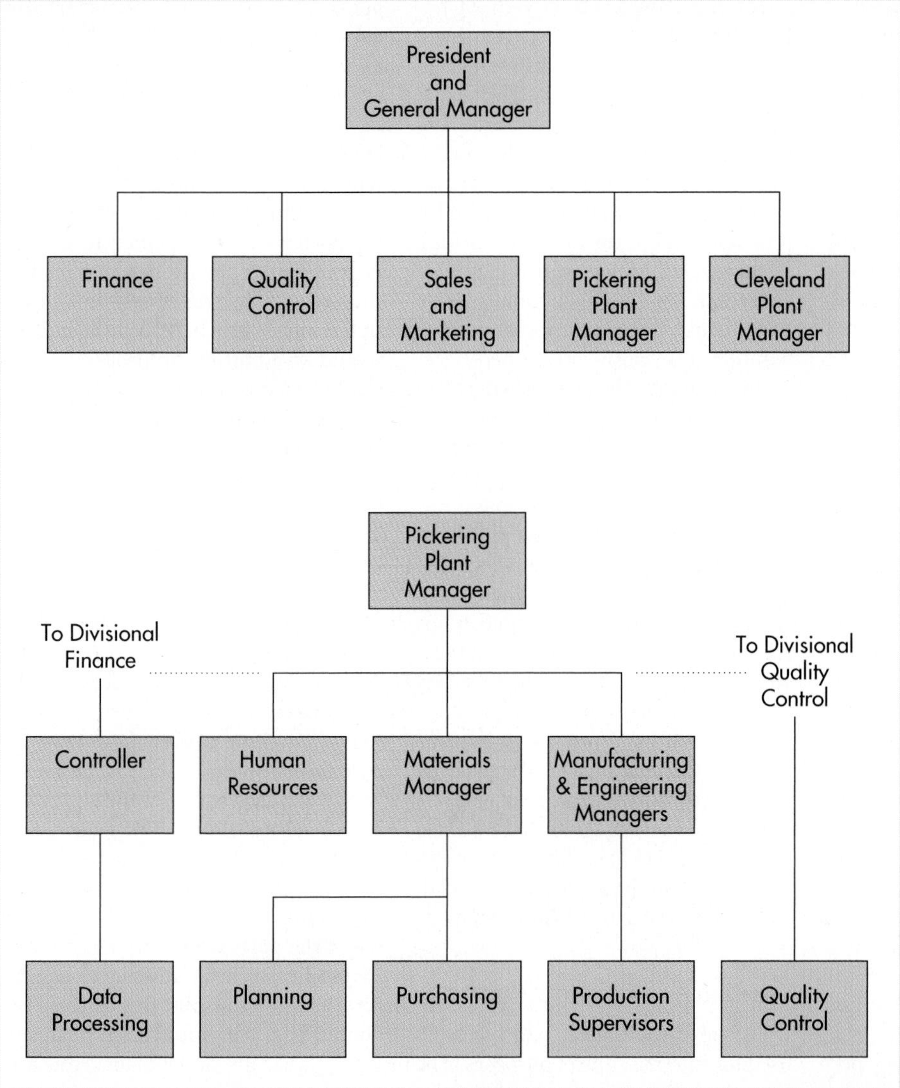

divisional marketing. Final daily shipment schedules for each part number were transmitted directly from the customer by phone or computer link.

The plant was scheduled for three shifts per day. Scheduling, in turn, had to balance the dies available with the press capability, as each die could only be run on a limited number of presses. The furnaces further complicated the scheduling, since settings varied across parts. Scheduling's responsibility was to find a balance between the 27 presses and 8 furnaces. A daily scheduling meeting was held with the production supervisors to discuss problems, set shipping priorities, monitor parts ready for shipment and make any necessary schedule changes.

The new quality standards demanded by the automotive customers had caused Pressure Castings serious scheduling problems. Often the first parts at the start of a production run would be accepted by QC, but later the parts were out of tolerance and rejected. The correction required anywhere from

• • •

a few minutes to several hours depending on whether it needed a few adjustments of the press or the removal and replacement of the die. Some of the quality problems were undoubtedly caused by the poor maintenance of the presses over the last several years. Consequently, the presses required a major rebuilding program. It was also felt there must be problems with the furnace temperature control as the quality of parts after sintering were consequently inconsistent.

EVALUATION OF THE PLANT MANAGER

The Pickering Plant was treated as a profit centre, and Jan Fenwick was paid an annual bonus for exceeding the plant's budgeted gross margin.

The plant had surpassed the budget in each of the last four years so there was no reason for Jan to believe he could not easily have earned his bonus. Determining the gross margin had been a fairly simple process. The divisional office gave the plant manager the forecasted sales for the coming year by customer, part number, and quantity to be produced. The sales forecasts were fully discussed with the plant until a finalized forecast was agreed upon. Jan Fenwick then had to produce a budget to meet both the agreed upon production levels, and the minimum corporate guidelines of 26.8 percent gross margin and 7 percent labour productivity improvement.

With these parameters established, the financial controller, by looking at last year's costs and making appropriate adjustments, put together an operating budget that would meet the guidelines. In this first year of Jan Fenwick's role as plant manager, it was fairly easy to meet the minimum gross margin, consequently, accounts such as maintenance and manufacturing engineering were padded so the corporate guidelines would just be met.

This budget was then submitted for final approval to the division. As long as the overall budget was met and/or exceeded, Jan Fenwick would receive his bonus. The variance accounts would not be closely examined,

In addition to the financial target, Jan Fenwick was also expected to meet some less quantifiable goals. These included improving customer relations, improving on delivery times, implementing SPC and becoming a world-class producer. There were no direct measures to evaluate these subjective goals. There was a scrap figure and a cost of quality inspection that could be used as a measure of quality, but these had already been accounted for in the budget.

The plant had initiated and implemented Improshare, a labour productivity program which allowed the labour productivity gains to be shared with the workers. The 7 percent labour productivity gain included in the budget was part of Improshare.

CONTROLLING OPERATIONS

Up to now, the budget had not been used for internal control purposes. The financial controller made all the allocations, and the departments went about their activities.

In an effort to reduce costs, Jan Fenwick planned to have the financial controller present the finalized budget to each of the line managers. By explaining the amounts that had been allocated to each of their functional areas, he hoped the managers would be more aware of both the kinds of expenses that they were incurring, and where savings could be made. Next year, if time permitted, these people would have been expected to get involved in preparing the budget for their particular area of responsibility. In the longer run, he hoped the budget would be a bottom-up process rather than the current top-down process.

More recently, Jan Fenwick had been required to produce a three-month projection of operating costs and sales based on current revised forecasts. These were reviewed with the division each month, and updated monthly.

To help Jan Fenwick keep abreast of activities in the plant, he had asked all the line managers to produce a common monthly activity report. The information forced the line managers to communicate with each other to assure their operations were in line with those of the other departments. Information included how many units of what product would be going through their department, what the problems were expected to be, and when the parts would be ready, etc.

Jan Fenwick sat down at his desk, and thought about the action he should take. He would soon be meeting with the divisional manager again, and knew that some concrete plans were needed. Not knowing where to start, he even wondered whether he was being encouraged to work in the best interest of the plant. ▲

QUESTIONS

1. What problems are evident in the control system currently used at the Pickering plant?
2. Develop a list of suggested changes that should be implemented so the control system will be more effective.

PART 6

SPECIAL ISSUES IN CONTEMPORARY MANAGEMENT

CHAPTER 20

MANAGING SMALL BUSINESS

LEARNING OBJECTIVES

After reading this chapter, you will be able to:

1. Identify the role of small business in the Canadian economy.
2. Define a small business.
3. Describe an entrepreneur and explain why some people start their own businesses.
4. Identify trends in small business.
5. Describe the ways in which someone can become a small businessperson.
6. List some of the challenges to starting a small business.
7. Explain and assess planning in small business enterprises.
8. Identify and explain the growth stages and transitions.
9. List reasons for small business failure.
10. Describe entrepreneurship in large organizations.

MANAGEMENT CHALLENGE

THE FUTURE OF RELCON INC.

Relcon Inc., in Brampton, Ontario, is a Canadian leader in the field of producing electronic drives that precisely control the speed of electric motors, thus improving the performance of motors as well as conserving energy. The company specializes in "AC drives" for motors that operate on alternating current.

Relcon, originally named Rumble Equipment, was founded by George Rumble in the 1940s as a welding equipment distributor. When Rumble died in the early 1960s, the company was bought by its employees who changed the name. The company served as the Canadian distributor for varible speed controls for motors and gradually in got into the manufacturing of these motors.

In the 1980s, an opportunity emerged for Relcon. The demand for AC drives (used for a variety of purposes in industries such as pulp and paper and ventilation systems manufacturing) could not be filled. Even though other companies sold drives, their products were not designed for Canadian voltages and were too expensive to modify. As Relcon had experience in the technology, it was able to enter into a technology licensing agreement with its U.S. supplier to adapt their equipment.

By the late 1980s, Relcon managers recognized that techological developments were threatening their business. Foreign competitors had developed technology that could link drives together which allowed them to be controlled centrally in a network. The challenge confronting Relcon was how it would respond to this threat to its market and to the need for additional funds for R & D and other expenditures associated with expansion. ▲

Every year, thousands of individuals, who want to be their own boss and to earn a better income launch a new business venture. These individuals, often called entrepreneurs, are essential to the growth and vitality of the Canadian economic system. Entrepreneurs develop or recognize new products or business opportunities, secure the necessary capital, and organize and operate businesses. Most people who start their own business get a great deal of satisfaction from owning and managing their own firm. The entrepreneurial spirit is alive and well in Canada, but despite the enthusiasm of entrepreneurs and encouragement from numerous government agencies, many challenges face those who wish to start and operate a small business, and the failure rate is high.

This chapter examines the crucial role that small business plays in the Canadian economy and the management of these enterprises. The alternative approaches to becoming a small business owner are identified. We then outline the challenges an entrepreneur encounters in the start-up and operation of a small business. A final section discusses the application of small business management approaches to large business organizations.

If you are aware of the challenges you might encounter as an entrepreneur, you are more likely to avoid the classic problems small business owners face. It is easy to start a business, but to operate one at a profit over a period of years requires the knowledge and application of the fundamentals of management. This chapter is designed to give you realistic expectations about small business management.

SMALL BUSINESS IN CANADA

LEARNING OBJECTIVE 1

Identify the role of small business in the Canadian economy.

The Canadian media pays considerable attention to the activities of large business enterprises and often neglects the fact that small businesses are thriving and are making a significant contribution to the economic well-being of Canada. A small business may be a corporation, sole proprietorship, or a partnership. Small businesses include those operated by professionals, such as doctors, lawyers, and accountants, and self-employed owners, such as mechanics, television technicians, and restauranteurs. They are found in virtually every industry and are particularly prominent in the retail trade. In terms of numbers, small business is the dominant type of business in Canada. According to Statistics Canada, small business enterprises account for about 98 percent of 900 000 enterprises in Canada and account for about 19 percent of total business revenue.

The value of small business to Canada's economy has been recognized by the federal and provincial governments with the establishment of Small Business departments and lending institutions catering to these enterprises. Government agencies sponsor awards to recognize entrepreneurs or enterprises that have performed in an outstanding manner. An example of one such award is the Canada Awards for Business Excellence. Started in 1984 by the federal government and now administered by the National Quality Institute, these awards were created to acknowledge exceptional business achievements which contribute to Canada's competitiveness in national and international business. The awards are given each year to honour extraordinary performance in various categories of business activity including entrepreneurship and small business. Several of the Management at Work inserts in this chapter will highlight winners of this award, beginning with the Management at Work feature entitled Sajjad Ebrahim.

MANAGEMENT AT WORK

SAJJAD EBRAHIM

When Sajjad Ebrahim left Karachi, Pakistan, to emigrate to Canada, he had a young family, an M.B.A. from Columbia University and a dream he wanted to pursue. That dream was to establish a profitable business in an open and competitive environment. In 1977, Ebrahim invested most of his life savings, approximately $100 000, to buy PAR-PAK, a manufacturer of semi-rigid plastic containers. He persuaded relatives to invest another $100 000, and spent a first difficult year, struggling to learn the industry and working extremely long hours. Ebrahim has maintained his own individual commitment to PAR-PAK, with 90 percent of his personal assets invested in the business. This personal risk-taking, combined with innovative products and excellent customer service, has enabled Ebrahim to transform PAR-PAK from a local firm located in Brampton, Ontario, into a viable global competitor with sales of over $16 million in 1992. For these achievements, Sajjad Ebrahim has been awarded winner status in the 1993 Canada Awards for Business Excellence Entrepreneurship category.

PAR-PAK sells the vast majority of its clear and coloured plastic containers to the food industry, especially fast food companies and supermarkets. Clients include Loblaws, Safeway, Weston Bakeries, McDonald's Restaurants and other major fast food and supermarket chains.

From the firm's beginnings, Ebrahim has emphasized total dedication to customer service. PAR-PAK specializes in custom design, developing individual containers for particular customer needs. The company's idea for a line of "invisible packaging," for example, resulted in 400 percent increases in sales for supermarket baked goods. Replacing the old concept of bulk bins and brown bags, these clear containers give the buyer a full view of the product in its own safe environment. PAR-PAK has 500 custom and proprietary designs, plus other innovative features like tab and button locks so that containers with lids can be closed securely.

About 1986, Sajjad Ebrahim began aggressively pursuing the export market. He decided that the only way to succeed in the United States was to ensure a "trouble-free" service by quoting prices in U.S. dollars and paying any duty incurred in shipping goods. So successful was this approach that in 1991 Mr. Ebrahim opened a plant in Houston, Texas. He offers the same service to European customers; in 1992, 38 percent of his sales came from exports.

Ebrahim believes in specializing in what PAR-PAK does best. He reinvests all profits after taxes into the company, so as to obtain the finest equipment available. The company's entire growth has been financed in this way, based on his principle of operating independently of outside lenders. Ebrahim also ensures that PAR-PAK takes a leading role in environmental management. The company avoids overpackaging and recycles 100 percent of process scrap. All these elements of his entrepreneurial philosophy have contributed to Ebrahim's outstanding success. ▲

THE INCREASE IN SMALL BUSINESSES

Since the 1970s, small business has been a "growth industry" in Canada and there are several reasons for this trend:

1. Big businesses offer less job security, since layoffs are more likely. Growing numbers of employees are also dissatisfied with working for large organizations which are impersonal and where efforts of employees often go unrecognized.
2. Many large companies and government departments are being reduced in size creating opportunities for subcontracting work and consulting services. Former employees often leave their employment and start businesses to provide these services.
3. For most of the past 15 years, it has been easier to start a small business than previously. The economy has grown, especially the service industries that require less investment to enter.
4. Persons who are self-employed earn almost 50 percent more, on the average, than persons who are employees. Thus, small business is financially attractive.[1]

SMALL BUSINESS DEFINITIONS

small business

There are almost as many definitions of small business as there are books on the topic. Two approaches will be used here to define a small business: one based on characteristics and the other based on size. A **small business** is one that is independently owned and operated and is not dominant in its field of operations. It possesses most of the following characteristics:

LEARNING OBJECTIVE 2

Define a small business.

1. Management of the firm is independent. Usually the managers are also the owners.
2. Capital is supplied and the ownership is held by an individual or a small group.
3. The area of operations is usually local, and the workers and owners live in the same community. However, the markets are not always local.
4. The enterprise is smaller than others in the industry. This measure can be in terms of sales volume, number of employees, or other criteria. It is free of legal or financial ties to large business enterprises.
5. The enterprise qualifies for the small business income tax rate under the Canada Income Tax Act.

Even this small operation is a business enterprise. Such enterprises are usually sole proprietorships and often part-time. This entrepreneur experiences the same challenges and rewards as other small business owners.

The size of a small business and how the size should be measured are matters of debate. Two common measures are sales, or revenues, and the number of employees. The Canadian Government's Small Business Office in conjunction with Statistics Canada defines a small business as having less than $2 million in annual sales. But Statistics Canada's publication, *Small Business in Canada: A Statistical Profile 1984-1986,*[2] profiles businesses with less than $5 million in gross annual revenue as small businesses. Various government agencies also use the number of employees to define small business. However, this number differs widely among each government agency: the Federal Ministry of State for Small Business stipulates 50 or less, Federal Business Development Bank says 75 or less, Statistics Canada uses numbers ranging from 100 to 1500 for manufacturing industries, and 50 for service industries.

As these figures may indicate, how big or small a small business is said to be depends upon the government agency or program and the reason it collects the statistics. These discrepancies in the definition can result in differences in statistics. For example, statistics on the percentage of employment provided by small business can vary greatly according to the number of employees used as a criterion for a small business.

For our purposes, a small business can be considered one that is independent and smaller than the main enterprises in an industry, generally employing 1 to 1500 people.

entrepreneurs
entrepreneurship

Persons who start and operate small businesses are called **entrepreneurs.** Another term used in conjunction with small business is **entrepreneurship**, which can be defined as an individual's willingness to take advantage of business opportunities and to assume the risk of establishing and operating a business. Insights into entrepreneurs and entrepreneurship can be gained by examining their motivation.

LEARNING OBJECTIVE 3

Describe an entrepreneur and outline why some people start their own business.

Dozens of studies have identified common traits and motivations among entrepreneurs. A researcher at The University of Western Ontario compiled a list of many of the characteristics identified by these studies, including assertiveness, challenge seeking, charismatic, coping, creative, improvising, opportunistic, persevering, risk taking, self-confident, tenacious, venturesome, and oriented toward achievement and action.[3] The motivations of entrepreneurs both in starting a business and in striving for success have been summarized in the Ontario Government's report *The State of Small Business.* The report lists motivations identified by other studies in addition to its own. The main reasons for starting a business were found to include:

1. The need to achieve, or the sense of accomplishment. Entrepreneurs believed that they could make a direct contribution to the success of the enterprise.
2. The need to be their own boss and to control their time.
3. The perceived opportunity in the marketplace to provide a product or service.
4. The wish to act in their own way or have the freedom to adapt their own approach to work.
5. The desire to experience the adventure of independence and a variety of challenges.
6. The desire to make money.
7. The need to make a living.[4]

The motivations of successful entrepreneurs have also been studied. These motivations include:

1. Having fun.
2. Building an organization.
3. Making money.
4. Winning in business.
5. Earning recognition.
6. Realizing a sense of accomplishment.[5]

Entrepreneurship has both benefits and costs. On the positive side, entrepreneurs get a tremendous sense of satisfaction from being their own boss. They also derive satisfaction from successfully bringing together the factors of production (land, labour, and capital) to make a profit. Perhaps the greatest benefit, however, is the fact that entrepreneurs can make a fortune if they have carefully planned what the business will do and how it will operate.

On the negative side, entrepreneurs can go bankrupt if their business fails. Customers can demand all sorts of services or inventory that small businesses cannot profitably supply. Entrepreneurs must work long hours and often get little in return in the first few years of operation. An entrepreneur may find that he or she is very good at one particular aspect of the business—for example, marketing—but knows little about managing the overall business. This imbalance can cause serious problems; in fact, poor management is the main reason businesses fail.

Some Trends in Small Business and Entrepreneurship

LEARNING OBJECTIVE 4
Identify trends in small business.

The growth in small business has resulted in many implications for the Canadian economy. About 4 of every 10 Canadians employed in the private sector work for small business and it is claimed that these businesses are responsible for a large portion of the increase in employment. According to Statistics Canada, the private sector created 70 000 paid worker jobs in 1993, self-employed unincorporated employment increased 86 000, and family, non-salary jobs increased 10 000. Employment with governments declined 23 000.[6] The trend to more private-sector jobs in small enterprises has implications for employees as entrepreneurs are quite different to work for than a large corporation or government.

An increasing number of women are becoming entrepreneurs.[7] Eleven percent of men are self-employed, compared to 4.5 percent of women. But women now account for one-half of the increase in entrepreneurs, represent one quarter of all entrepreneurs, and own 22 percent of all businesses with paid employees. They have shown more conservative expectations of business performance by investing less capital than men on average. Women prefer to test ideas and thus their failure rate is lower than their male counterparts. However, on average they earn less from a business enterprise.[8]

Younger people are increasingly turning to small business for employment, often as an entrepreneur, and departing from the traditional career paths. Many young people are now considering self-employment as a viable option, especially since other jobs are simply not available. More college and university students are identifying themselves as campus capitalists and are involved in educational efforts to increase their enterpreneurial ability.

Large organizations are attempting to become enterpreneurial, that is, they are trying to organize themselves in ways that will allow them to obtain the advantages of a small enterprise. This phenomenon will be discussed later in the chapter.

The trend to small business and entrepreneurship is occurring on an international scale. Europe, including the former communist countries, and most of the Pacific Rim countries are experiencing this first stage in capitalism.

BECOMING A SMALL BUSINESS OWNER

LEARNING OBJECTIVE 5
Describe the ways in which someone can become a small businessperson.

Most people become involved in a small business in one of four ways: (1) taking over a family business, (2) buying out an existing firm, (3) starting their own firm, (4) acquiring a "spun off" business, or (5) purchasing a franchise. There are pros and cons to each.

TAKING OVER A FAMILY BUSINESS

Taking over and operating a family business owned by one's family poses many challenges. There may be disagreement over which family member assumes control. If the parent sells his or her interest in the business, the price paid may be an issue. Typical of the matters that make managing such an organization difficult are expectations of family members. Some may consider a job, promotion, and impressive title their birthright, regardless of their talent or training. Selecting an appropriate successor and insuring that he or she receives adequate training, and disagreements among family members about the future of the business are two problem areas. Sometimes the interests of the family and those of the enterprise are in conflict, and thus family enterprises often fail to respond to changing market conditions (see the Management at Work insert entitled "Family Disagreement at Birks"). The challenges faced in running such an organization are summarized in Figure 20-1.

A family business also has some strengths. It can provide otherwise unobtainable financial and management resources because of the personal sacrifices of family members; family businesses often have a valuable reputation or goodwill resulting in important community and business relationships; employee loyalty is often high; and an interested, unified family management and shareholders group may emerge.

BUYING AN EXISTING ENTERPRISE

Because a family-run business and other established firms are already operating, they have certain advantages for the purchaser: the clientele is established, financing might be easier since past performance and existing assets can be evaluated, experienced employers may already be in place, and lines of credit and supply have been

FIGURE 20-1 FAMILY-OWNED BUSINESS LEADER'S KEY CHALLENGES.

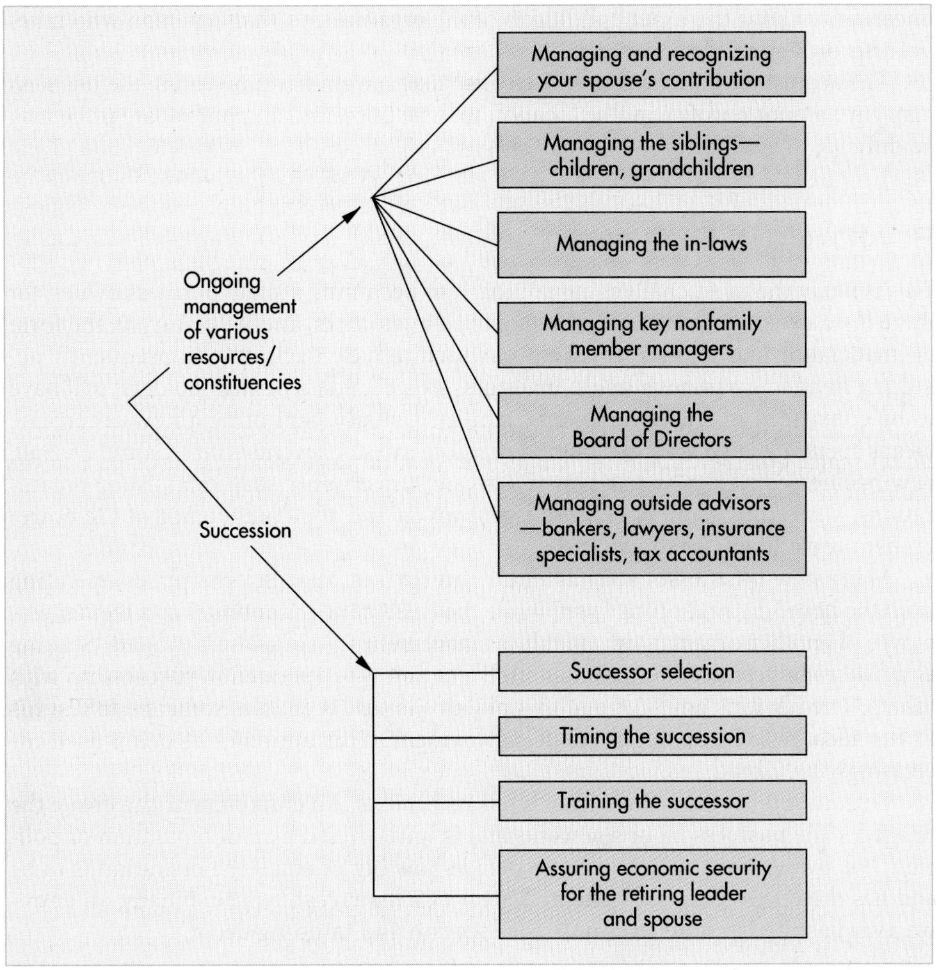

MANAGEMENT AT WORK

FAMILY DISAGREEMENT AT BIRKS

Henry Birks & Sons, Ltd. was established in 1879 by Henry Birks who was a descendant of a long line of silversmiths. One hundred years later, the enterprise was operated by the fifth generation of Birks, three brothers, Jonathan, Thomas, and Barrie, all in their forties.

According to newspaper accounts, the brothers were "bright, highly motivated, ambitious" and all were vying for control of the company. The manoeuvring eventually lead to an agreement in January 1990 that saw Jonathan buy out his brothers. Jonathan acquired 100 percent of the voting stock and about 70 percent of the company's equity with the remainder being held by a small group of employees, the Birks Family Foundation, the pension plan, and a family trust.

This was not the first Birks family feud and such conflicts are common in small family businesses that become very large (along with the family). Jonathan Birk was then in charge of the company and was free to select the strategy he believed was most appropriate for Birks.

However, the strategy failed as the company was deep in debt from the leveraged buyout of the brothers and expansion into the U.S., and the recession also hit sales. In January 1993, Birks filed for bankruptcy protection and shut down about one-half of its stores. In April 1993, the remaining stores were sold to Borgosesia SpA, an Italian giftware maker. After 114 years, family ownership ended at Henry Birks & Sons Ltd. ▲

established. An entrepreneur who buys someone else's business, however, faces more uncertainty about the exact conditions of the organization than a person who takes over his or her family's operation.

The acquisition of an existing enterprise may have other drawbacks: the business may have a poor reputation, the location may be poor, and an appropriate price may be difficult to ascertain.

Starting a Business

This is likely the most challenging approach to becoming a small business owner, for there is no existing operation, no established customers, and no history in the form of financial or marketing records upon which to base decisions. Consequently acquiring financing can be difficult; investors, either lenders or shareholders, will have to be convinced of the enterprise's viability. Usually beginning a new enterprise means spending large amounts of money before sales or revenues materialize. Overall, new businesses pose a higher risk and greater uncertainty than established organizations, since the business venture is unproven and the competence of the entrepreneur most likely unknown.

microenterprises

Many new businesses start as **microenterprises**, that is, enterprises operating from the home on a part-time basis, while the entrepreneur continues as a regular employee of another organization (see the Management at Work insert entitled "Starting as a "Microenterprise"). Sometimes such a business is operated in partnership with others. The obvious advantage of this practice is that it enables someone to test his or her idea before quitting regular employment. This approach is being used increasingly by Canadians.

Beginning a business from scratch has its benefits. An entrepreneur can create the image for the business he or she wants and is unrestricted by past reputation or policies. The owner has the flexibility to decide how big or small the operation is to be and has the chance to start small and grow at a manageable pace. Finally, an entrepreneur has the freedom to choose the location and building decor.

Acquiring a "Spun off" Business

Many larger businesses and government departments are ridding themselves of activities that they performed for themselves. In effect, they "spin off" the activities as a separate unit which can operate commerically on its own or call for bids from outside businesses to perform the activities. A buyer is sometimes sought for the new small business and often someone previously associated with the unit acquires it. Managers or employees are the usual purchasers, but a saleperson who serviced the account, for example, is another possible purchaser or it could be someone in the same business. In other situations, the activites are simply put out on a bid.

Regardless of the approach, opportunities are made available for entrepreneurs to acquire the business. An example is provided by printing services in universities. The University of Alberta decided that it would have the private sector perform all the printing it required. Richard McCallum, president of Quality Color Press won the contract. McCallum had been in the printing business for sometime and convinced the university that his company could perform the service most efficiently.[9]

The advantages and disadvantages to this approach are similar to those for buying an existing enterprise and starting a business. The type of "spin off" will determine the particular advantages or disadvantages involved.

MANAGEMENT AT WORK

Starting as a Microenterprise

Studies of entrepreneurship estimate that up to 50 percent of small businesses start as "microenterprises." Two categories of persons start businesses with this approach: people with full-time employment outside the home who operate the business on off-hours; and homemakers starting on a small scale to supplement a spouse's or partner's income. By the year 2000, it is estimated that 40 percent of the work force will operate full-time from their homes, either by operating microenterprises or telecommuting.

A key source of micro-business opportunities is the increased use of outside services by business and government. Even small- and medium-size businesses are hiring consultants to provide some services thus avoiding the obligations of hiring full-time employees. Microenterprises have also grown because of the overall growth in the service industry, and the computerization and increased affordability of office equipment.

The principal benefits of microenterprises are that their start-up and operating costs are low; little financial risk is encountered if the business fails; the work environment is casual; family responsibilities can be accommodated; and the hours of operation can be tailored to an individual's schedule. But, such businesses also have disadvantages: the owners may feel isolated, having little, if any, social interaction with others; distractions and disruptions may be caused by family and friends; a productive working environment may not be available; and self-discipline is required to keep working and not be distracted.

Home Inc: The Canadian Home-Based Business Guide was written on the subject of microenterprises and the Canadian Federation of Independent Business has studied the trend because it encourages entrepreneurship. The National Home Business Association has a database of over 10 000 home-based entrepreneurs from all over Canada. This association provides a package of services to members that includes group rates on health insurance, educational seminars, a referral service to promote members' services, and discounts from stationery and equipment suppliers.

An example of a micro- or home-office business is Lori M Consulting in Toronto. It was formed by Lori Molmar, an executive with the Federation of Women Teachers' Association of Ontario. She left that job to set up a business as an interior designer and environmental gerontologist in her home. The cost of operating from her home was lower and she even built an addition to accommodate the business. ▲

Purchasing a Franchise

One of the fastest ways to establish a business is to purchase a franchise. Franchising became popular during the 1960s and has continued to increase in economic importance. **Franchising** involves drafting a contract between a manufacturer and a dealer that stipulates how the manufacturer's or supplier's product or service will be sold. The dealer, called a **franchisee**, agrees to sell the product or service of the manufacturer, called the **franchisor**, in return for royalties. Franchising organizations that are well-known in Canada include Holiday Inn, McDonald's, College Pro Painters, Weight Watchers, Kentucky Fried Chicken, Midas Muffler, and Canadian Tire.

franchising

franchisee

franchisor

The franchising arrangement can be beneficial to both the franchisee and the franchisor. The franchisee enjoys the following benefits:

1. *Recognition* The franchise name gives the franchisee instant recognition with the public.
2. *Standardized appearance of the franchise* Customers know that consistency exists from one outlet to another.
3. *Management assistance* The franchisee can obtain advice on how to run the franchise effectively.

Midas Canada Inc. is one of Canada's better known franchisers. It has operated for 30 years and has over 2000 shops across North America, servicing automobile brake, exhaust, steering, and suspension systems. Planning more outlets, these "Top Guns" call themselves the "under car specialists."

4. *Economies of scale in buying* The head office of the franchise buys in large volume and resells to the franchisee at lower prices than she or he could get if buying personally.
5. *Promotional assistance* The head office of the franchise provides the franchisee with prepared advertising and other promotional material.

The franchisee is not the only party who gains in franchising. The following benefits are available to the franchisor:

1. *Recognition* The franchisor is able to expand its area of operation by signing agreements with dealers in widely dispersed places.
2. *Promotion savings* The various franchisees can decide on local advertising efforts; this arrangement saves the franchisor money on wasted coverage in areas where it does not have a franchise.
3. *Franchisee payments* The franchisees pay the franchisor for the right to operate their franchises.
4. *Attention to detail* Since franchisees own their franchises, they are motivated to do a good job and to sell the franchisor's product or service aggressively.

Franchising has facilitated the growth of small business in Canada. The financial and management assistance franchisees can receive from the franchisor removes many of the risks that typically face small business owners. In fact, whereas about 80 percent of all small businesses fail within five years, less than 20 percent of franchises fail in the same period.

Franchising, however, does have its shortcomings. Not all the franchises on the market are as successful as McDonald's. Many entrepreneurs are uninterested in becoming franchisees because their behaviour will be too closely regulated by the franchiser. They would rather start their own business and take whatever risks are necessary in return for freedom to do what they want.

After reading this section, it should be clear that there is no one best way to becoming a small business owner. In fact, starting the business is only the first of many challenges confronting the entrepreneur.

CHALLENGES FOR THE ENTREPRENEUR

LEARNING OBJECTIVE 6
List some of the challenges to starting a small business.

Starting and operating a business enterprise is challenging: financing must be obtained, the small enterprise must be carefully managed, and planned, and assistance must often be found. In fact, running a small business may not be all that it is claimed to be.

Financing the Small Enterprise

Securing the funds necessary to start and obtain a small business usually presents a challenge to entrepreneurs. An Ontario government report stated that the average investment needed to start a new enterprise in the mid-eighties was about $58 300, and that more than one-half of all start-ups have less than $15 000 invested.[10]

The amount of capital needed to start a small business prevents some people from becoming entrepreneurs. However, sources of funding are available and a list is given in Table 20-1. It should be noted that some sources are more likely to provide money. Lenders also may or may not lend money to entrepreneurs depending upon whether the enterprise is beginning or ongoing.

TABLE 20-1 PRINCIPAL SOURCES OF FUNDS FOR SMALL BUSINESS ENTERPRISES.

Debt Source

These are funds borrowed by the enterprise. They may come from:

- The entrepreneur who may loan money to the enterprise
- Private lenders, that is, individuals or corporations
- Financial institutions such as banks, credit unions, trust companies, and finance companies. Sometimes such borrowing may be by the enterprise but guaranteed by the entrepreneur, or secured against other nonbusiness assets of the entrepreneur
- Trade credit, that is, the delayed payment terms offered by suppliers
- Government agencies, for example, the Federal Business Development Bank
- The selling of bonds or debentures (usually only done when enterprise is larger)

Equity Sources

This money is invested in the enterprise and represents an ownership interest. It comes from:

- The entrepreneur's personal funds
- Partners, either individuals or corporations
- Family and friends
- Venture capitalists
- Governments
- The selling of shares to the public (usually only done when enterprise is larger)
- Employees who may participate in a stock purchase plan or simply investment in the enterprise.

Retained Earnings

Profits, that is, funds generated from the operation of the business, can be either paid to the owners in dividends or reinvested in the enterprise. If retained or reinvested, profits are a source of funds.

Funds for Starting a Business

The most likely sources of financing are the personal funds of individuals, in particular, the entrepreneurs themselves. Some government agencies may provide assistance funds for start-up and so might chartered banks if they think that the proposed business has promise.

Funds for an Ongoing Business

After the enterprise has operated for some time, other services are more likely to be utilized if a good financial reputation has been established. Trade credit (that is, the delayed payment terms offered by suppliers), chartered banks, trust companies, and venture capitalists are examples of lending institutions. Another source of funds is profits from the business. Entrepreneurs seldom pay themselves all the profits generated by the enterprise. Some profits are reinvested in the enterprise, and are referred to as **retained earnings.**

retained earnings

Managing Funds

You will note in Table 20-1 that each source is identified as debt or equity. **Debt** refers to borrowed funds that require interest payments and must be repaid. **Equity** refers to the money, or capital, invested in the enterprise by individuals or companies who become owners, and to profits reinvested. In the case of small enterprises, the

debt
equity

entrepreneur is often the sole owner. The challenge for entrepreneurs is to keep the amounts of funds borrowed and invested in ownership in balance. If debt is relied upon too heavily, interest payments might become burdensome and could lead to the failure of the enterprise.

Through their equity investment, these investors obtain ownership and have some influence on the firm's operations. If investors owned 51 percent or more of the firm's equity, they could control the enterprise. As enterprises require funds to grow, this diminishing of control frequently cannot be avoided.

PLANNING IN SMALL BUSINESS

LEARNING OBJECTIVE 7
Explain and assess planning in small business enterprises.

Small business owners must be familiar with many of the concepts, theories, and practices discussed under the four management functions: planning and decision making; organizing; leading; and controlling. Although all four functions are important, planning in particular is critical to small enterprise survival at the start-up stage and as the business grows. The following sections discuss the approaches to planning from these two perspectives.

PLANNING AT THE BEGINNING

As a business begins, the suppliers of any funds will require a business plan as outlined in Table 20-2. Indeed, any entrepreneur should prepare such a plan to clarify the new enterprise's purpose and to assess its feasibility. The components of the business plan would also be appropriate for ongoing enterprises. Business plans are not without problems and it is recommended that entrepreneurs consider using a strategic management approach to planning.

PROBLEMS WITH BUSINESS PLANS

Business plans sound good but in practice they are rarely followed or used appropriately. The preparation of the plan is usually done to facilitate a start-up period or to support additional financing, and then it is neglected. Entrepreneurs view them as a hurdle to overcome, and bankers and accountants have a tendency to view them as being carved in stone. In reality, a small enterprise operates in very dynamic circumstances and must be flexible, adaptive and responsive to its changing environment.

There are several other weaknesses to business plans. They often are dominated by numbers required by financial institutions, and fail to establish the company's mission, objectives, and basic strategies. The measurement of results is seldom outlined and alternatives are not identified if a strategy fails. Entrepreneurs are not prepared to use plans in a dynamic way and instead consider them to be rigid restrictions on their creativity and activities.

Plans should be fluid and evolve over time, but they cannot accommodate entrepreneurs who chase new opportunities indiscriminately or prefer to operate "by the seat of their pants," adapt a short-term focus, or rarely step back and review and analyze progress. Preparing a plan only to satisfy a banker or government funding agency is not enough motivation. The owner-entrepreneur must have firm commitment to a planning process and the use of a strategic management is one approach.[11]

TABLE 20-2 A BUSINESS PLAN.

The contents of a business plan vary depending upon the information required by the financial institutions or government agencies. Some entrepreneurs develop plans as a personal guide and way to check on where they are or want to be. The following are the components that might be included in such a plan:

Cover Page
Contains the enterprise's name, address, telephone numbers, and key contacts.

Table of Contents

Executive Summary
A brief statement, usually about one page long, summarizing the plan's contents.

Background/History of the Enterprise
A concise outline of when and how the enterprise got started, the goods or services it sells, and its major suppliers and customers.

Management
Background information on the entrepreneur and other employees, especially other managers (if there are any).

Marketing Assessment
Might include descriptions of the products or a service profile, the results of any market research, a market description and analysis, an identification of competition, and an account of the marketing strategy.

Production Assessment
A brief description of the production process, the technological process employed, quality requirements, location and physical plant, and details of machinery and equipment.

Financial Assessment
A review of the capital structure and the money needed to finance the business. Usually including a projected balance sheet, profit and loss statement, and a cash flow forecast. Lenders might also require details of loan collateral and a repayment proposal.

Research and Development (R&D)
For many enterprises, R & D is important and a statement of what is planned would be included. There might also be an assessment of the risks anticipated with any new products or ventures.

Basic Data
Data on the enterprise's bankers, accountants, lawyers, shareholders (if any), and details of incorporation (if applicable).

Appendices
The following might be attached to a plan: detailed management biographies, product literature, evaluation of assets, detailed financial statements and cash flow forecast, and list of major contracts.

STRATEGIC MANAGEMENT IN SMALL BUSINESSES

Strategic management can assist entrepreneurs as their enterprises face the same problems and challenges as other businesses. The strategic management process can be abbreviated to satisfy the needs of small business and does not have to be as elaborate as it is for large corporations. Indeed, the entrepreneur can think through the process and need not prepare detailed written plans.

Each of the eight strategic components discussed in Chapter 5 has some applicability to small enterprises. The entrepreneur has the enterprise's mission in mind and has general goals associated with that mission. He or she should be aware of the general situation in the country and the changes to the industry environment. A realistic assessment should be made of resources so that the enterprise's capabilities are obvious. Objectives can be established, an area in which entrepreneurs are weak. Strategic options are identified and a strategy selected, which is often based upon serving a market niche or providing a service based upon some technology. How the strategy will be carried out, or implemented, should be thought through. Lastly, the strategy should be monitored and reviewed, another weak area for entrepreneurs.

Strategic management becomes more important, and may be even critical, as the company grows. Researchers found that the plans developed from the strategic management process are important for three reasons: the process forces managers to think critically about what they are doing, the plans assist in communicating corporate direction inside and outside the corporation, and a control mechanism is created for course correction. Companies use the plans not only to guide corporate operations and measure performance, but also to establish incentives for managers, to obtain funds for growth, and to assist in attracting major customers. It was also concluded that there is a significant association between strategic planning and profitability.[12]

Raytel Equipment Ltd. of Calgary experienced declining profits in the late 1980s and used the strategic management process to ascertain reasons for the decline and to decide how the company should reposition itself. As a consequence, the manufacturing aspect of the business was discontinued and U.S.-made equipment was distributed instead because of the company's excellent rapport with truck and van customers in the Calgary area. President Janet Marshall attributes the company's survival to the strategic management process.[13]

If strategic management is so important and leads to better performance, why don't more entrepreneurs engage in the process? Part of the reason is the personality of entrepreneurs. They are creative individuals with a personal vision and have little patience for documenting it. They want to personally control everything and often there is a lack of trust and openness towards others who will be involved in the process. They lack knowledge of and expertise in the process and claim not to have the time necessary.

MANAGING GROWTH AND TRANSITIONS

LEARNING OBJECTIVE 8
Identify and explain the growth stages and transitions.

After the start-up and initial operating stages of the new enterprise, the entrepreneur must be concerned about planning for changes and the transitions necessary in management practices. (Business growth sometimes results in failure and this is discussed later.) Expansion of the business can occur by simply increasing sales of the same products or services. This growth often occurs in markets outside Canada as illustrated in the Global Management insert "Innovator Manufacturing Inc."

Sometimes an entrepreneur will merge with another company, or simply sell the business. There is also the possibility that the entrepreneur will acquire other enterprises. No matter how the enterprise grows, there will be challenges to be faced.

MODELS OF BUSINESS GROWTH

Models of small business growth have been developed that help explain these changes in management.[14] Table 20-3, while not comprehensive, gives examples of the shift in management approaches necessary as the small enterprise develops.

The launch stage covers the preparatory activities as well as the actual start-up, while the survival stage is the initial period of operation (up to five years) in which many enterprises fail. During expansion, the organization passes the break-even point, and success appears to be more likely. Finally, the maturity stage involves slowed or slight growth and might be referred to as a "comfort" stage where success is assured.

GLOBAL MANAGEMENT

INNOVATOR MANUFACTURING INC.

In 1989, Innovator Manufacturing Inc., located in Brampton, Ontario, was a five-year-old company making marginal profits by manufacturing material handling equipment for the agricultural industry. By three years later, the company's revenues had soared to $4.4 million, through the manufacture and sale of an innovative line of products for grinding wood and organic waste. Innovator's extraordinary business success is due to the company's readiness to enter a brand-new industry despite having only limited capital, and its commitment to making products superior in every way to its competitors'. Today, Innovator's exports account for 92 percent of total sales, and its equipment is operating in the United States, Australia, Belgium, the United Kingdom and Japan. For these achievements, Innovator Manufacturing Inc. was awarded winner status in the 1993 Canada Awards for Business Excellence Small Business category.

It was in late 1989 that a client in the agricultural industry asked the company about the possibility of manufacturing a machine to grind waste wood. Innovator's management recognized immediately that this was the industry and the product that could fuel the company's growth. Because capital for R&D was very limited, Innovator obtained a 50 percent deposit from the customer, in exchange for the company's guarantee of satisfactory operation. Innovator then had only seven employees, but in just seven weeks, they designed, manufactured and delivered a Tub Grinder to the customer's yard. This machine can grind up pallets, construction and demolition waste wood, brush, stumps, leaves and grass clippings. The resulting ground-up product is used for landscape mulch, particle board, fire logs and fuel for power plants.

In 1991, in response to the industry's demand for a machine with a much greater capacity, Innovator designed its Tumbler Grinder, which has revolutionized the method for processing organic waste. Not only can it deal effectively with large, bulky material, but it also screens out dirt, sand and other abrasive material. In addition, the operating costs of Innovator's patented Tumbler Grinder are 5 to 10 times less than competitors' machines. Because it has dramatically reduced the cost of processing wood and organic waste, the Tumbler Grinder currently accounts for 50 percent of Innovator's sales revenues.

Currently, Innovator has a 5.3 percent market share in North America and an estimated 50 percent share in Canada. Its customers include Los Angeles County Sanitation, major municipalities, contractors and recycling plants. Innovator expects its U.S. and global market share to improve as it continues to expand its dealer network and line of products. ▲

Maturity is not necessarily the end of growth for the business. Expansion opportunities are still sought and diversification is considered, sometimes through the takeover of or merging with other enterprises.

During these stages, the firm changes from an entrepreneurial one to a professionally managed one usually once it employs between 50 to 100 people. Then the entrepreneurial approach to management where one individual, the owner, dominates, shifts to a professional management style with several top, middle, and supervisory managers necessary to operate the enterprise.

MANAGING TRANSITIONS BETWEEN GROWTH STAGES

Researchers associated with Laurentian University in Sudbury, Ontario, have pointed out that understanding the stages of growth model is not sufficient to explain what actually occurs as an enterprise grows. The challenge to entrepreneurs is in managing the transitions between the stages. The researchers propose that there are five phases of small business development:

TABLE 20-3 GROWTH MODEL FOR SMALL ENTERPRISES.

Characteristics	Launch	Survival	Expansion	Maturity
Key Issues	Development of business Raising funds Obtaining customers	Generating revenues Breaking even	Managing and funding growth Obtaining resources Maintaining control	Expense control Productivity Consideration of diversification and other expansion
Management Style	Entrepreneurial, individualistic, direct supervision	Entrepreneurial, individualistic, direct supervision Entrepreneurial, allows others to administer but supervises closely	Delegation, coordinative, but still entrepreneurial	Decentralization, reliance on others Monitoring
Organizational Structure	Unstructured	Simple	Functional, centralized	Decentralized functional/product
Product/Market	Single-line and market	Single-line and market but increasing	Wider product range and more markets	Several product lines, multimarket and channels
Main Sources of Funds	Owners, friends and relatives	Owners, suppliers (trade credit), banks	Banks, new partners, retained earnings, secured long-term debt	Retained earnings, long-term debt, maybe public shareholders

1. *The owner-operated organization.* The enterprise is small, depends on the skills of the entrepreneur and revolves around one product or market niche. The entrepreneur concentrates on such things as operating details, selling activities, order processing, and the organization of facilities, credit lines and equipment.

2. *Transition to an owner-managed organization.* As sales increase, services formerly performed by outsiders on a demand basis become part of the operations of the enterprise. Quite often, the bookkeeping function is performed by an employee and a person is hired as a sales representative. Permanent positions are created in accounting and marketing, and perhaps in personnel, finance, operations, and control as well. The entrepreneur must recognize the need for professional managers and must exercise management skills in the supervision of these employees. Entrepreneurs often find this a difficult thing to do and resist the transition.

3. *The owner-managed organization.* In this phase, the entrepreneur does recruit and hire support management and exercises managerial skills. Also, industry contacts are developed and the supplier and customer networks are expanded. The owner is less dominant, there is a more deliberate approach to decision making, and a tendency to shared authority. The entrepreneur is less "hands on" and leaves operating details to others.

4. *Transition to emergent functional management.* Even though a middle management emerged in Phase 3, all the management authority and responsibility have been in the owner's hands. If the functional or departmental managers are to operate effectively, the enterprise will have to change how it operates—for example, the owner will have to seek consensus among functional managers, and appropriate information systems will have to been created.

5. *Emergent functional management.* This phase is characterized by the presence of a general manager and a management team made up of functional area managers. Three management practices are now important: the sharing of authority and responsibilities from the top; an effective exchange of information up and down the organization; and the fostering of consistent action. All these organizational aspects must be considered if the larger enterprise is to continue to operate effectively.

It is critical for entrepreneurs to recognize the shift to managing operations rather than actually doing tasks as was possible when the enterprise was smaller. More managing and communication are involved as the business grows. The transition phases identify what the entrepreneur needs to do to be successful in the next phase. Navigating the transitions is the key to managing growth successfully.[15] The Management at Work insert "Recruiting a Manager and a Partner" discusses how one entrepreneur handled growth and transition.

Unfortunately, not all enterprises grow, and many fail. This is the topic of the next section.

THE SURVIVAL OF SMALL BUSINESS

LEARNING OBJECTIVE 9
List reasons for small business failures.

Numerous statistics on the survival rate of small businesses have been compiled. The following data are representative:

1. About 13-15 percent of all business enterprises disappear each year.
2. One-half of new businesses fail in the first three years, and after that, the failure rate levels off.
3. After 10 years, only 25 percent of businesses are still in existence.
4. The average life span of small enterprises is 7.25 years.
5. Female entrepreneurs have a survival rate about twice as good as that of males.[16]

MANAGEMENT AT WORK

RECRUITING A MANAGER AND A PARTNER

Compustep Products Corp. of Peterborough, Ontario, manufacturers large-scale, computer-controlled drilling machines for industry and has sales of about $3 million. It was founded by David Piggott, an engineer who has been an entrepreneur since the mid-1960s.

In the 1970s, Piggott found a way to turn recycled and scrap polyethylene into garbage bags and set up POLY Converters Ltd. which became known as PCL Industries. After this business was successful, he sold his stake and set about looking for another opportunity.

Piggott set up a machine shop in Mississauga to produce drilling machines. As machine operators were paid high salaries, he decided to automate the equipment. Customers liked the idea and the business grew. But with growth came many challenges. There was the need to constantly improve the company's products because competition was intense. Supervision of plant operations was time-consuming as was dealing with customers. Piggott concluded that he needed help.

Management consultants were hired to search for a chief executive who would also be willing to invest in the company. After a six-month search, a suitable candidiate was found, Joseph Lipsett, aged 53. Lipsett had experience as a computer industry manager, had an M.B.A., and had run his own small computer systems company. An agreement was negotiated where Lipsett became a minority shareholder, but would become an equal partner over time.

Lipsett is now president and Piggott vice-president, manufacturing. Each is doing what they are best at: Piggott can spend time developing innovative products and supervising production while Lipsett looks over the front office and deals with customers. ▲

One indication of small business failure is the empty store with the for sale or for lease sign. Economic downturns result in many business failures especially in small businesses which are vulnerable when consumer spending declines.

The low rate of survival need not be viewed as a serious problem. Some enterprises are absorbed by others, and others cease operation when the owner retires. It is common for some people to fail two or three times before achieving success, and each failure is included in the statistics. Finally, failures are natural in a competitive economic system. In some cases, enterprises are poorly managed and are replaced by more efficient and innovative entrepreneurs. In recent years, more enterprises have started than have failed indicating the resiliency of small business and entrepreneurs.

Many small business enterprises collapse for a number of reasons. The reasons for the failure of new business may differ from those for the failure of an enterprise that has been operating for some time. One reason an established business may fail is that it shows an inadequate response to change. For example, the entrepreneur may not anticipate competitive actions or respond sufficiently to them. A change in the environment, including changes in society's preferences and in technology, may go unaddressed.

Some of the causes of the failure of businesses listed in Table 20-4 are ones over which the entrepreneur may have no control and cannot influence, for example, the death of a key employee or the extensive damage from a flood. However, most items on the list can be influenced and this is the main reason an entrepreneur must learn as much as possible about management.

ASSISTANCE FOR ENTREPRENEURS AND SMALL BUSINESS

There are many initiatives designed to encourage entrepreneurial activity in Canada and to help small enterprises survive. Assistance is available both from governments and various organizations in the private sector. This assistance is summarized in Table 20-5.

TABLE 20-4 CAUSE OF SMALL BUSINESS FAILURE.

Poor management skills
poor delegation and organizational ability
lack of depth in management team
entrepreneurial incompetence, such as a poor understanding of finances and business markets
lack of experience

Inadequate marketing capabilities
difficulty in marketing product
market too small, nonexistent, or declines
too much competition
problems with distribution systems

Inadequate financial capabilities
weak skills in accounting and finance
lack of budgetary control
inadequate cash flow forecasts
inadequate costing systems
incorrect valuation of assets
inability to obtain financial backing

Inadequate production capabilities
poorly designed production systems
old and inefficient production facilities and equipment
inadequate control over quality
problems with inventory control and condition

Personal reasons
lost interest in business
accident, illness
death
family problems

Disasters
fire
weather
strikes

Fraud
by entrepreneur or others

Other
mishandling of large project
excessive standard of living
lack of time to devote to business with full-time employment
difficulties with associates or partners
government policies change

TABLE 20-5 SUMMARY OF ASSISTANCE FOR SMALL BUSINESS.

Government Assistance

- Industry Canada is the department in the federal government responsible for small business and has many programs to promote entrepreneurship. Provincial governments also have numerous programs.
- The National Entrepreneurship Development Institute was established as a non-profit organization to serve as a clearing house for information about enterepreneurship.
- Taxation policy allows small business to pay lower levels of taxes than other enterprises.
- The Federal Business Development Bank (FBDB) administers the Counselling Assistance for Small Enterprises (CASE) program which offers one-on-one counselling by experienced people to thousands of entrepreneurs each year.
- The Small Business Loans Act (SBLA) encourages the provision of term loan financing to small enterprises by private-sector institutions by guaranteeing the loans.
- The Program for Export Market Development shares the cost of efforts by business to develop export markets.
- Incubators and techology centres operate across Canada. Incubators are centres where entrepreneurs can start their business with the assistance of counselling services. Federal government funds support technology centres that evaulate innovations under research and development.
- Schools for entrepreneurs funded by government but operated by the private sector prepare prospective entrepreneurs by training them in all aspects of small business. An example is the Regina Business and Technology Centre.

Private Sector

- The Canada Opportunities Investment Network (COIN) is a computerized national investment match-making service operated through Chambers of Commerce. This service brings potential entreprenuers together with people who might be willing to supply them with capital.
- Banks and other financial institutions not only lend money but also provide advice to entrepreneurs.
- Venture capitalists finance high-risk enterprises to which others are unwilling to lend money. "Business angels" are a special category of private venture capitalists who invest in new, high-risk enterprises that they feel should be supported even though no one else will.
- Consultants and numerous publications exist to answer questions.
- The Canadian Federation of Independent Business (CFIB) is the largest of the organizations formed to protect the interests of small business. It is a non-profit, nonpartisan group, or lobby, which represents the interests of about 75 000 small- and medium-size enterprises.

ENTREPRENEURSHIP AND LARGE BUSINESS

LEARNING OBJECTIVE 10
Describe entrepreneurship in large organizations.

Large business organizations will continue to exist even with the success of small businesses. This section discusses three aspects of the relationship between large and small business enterprises, challenging some of the claims of small business accomplishments, showing how bigger organizations can perform better in some industries, and discussing how attempts are being made to make large organizations more entrepreneurial.

DEMYSTIFYING SMALL BUSINESS

Canadians are enthusiastic about small business and governments are infatuated with it. Few people have questioned the desirability of entrepreneurship until recently. Now it is admitted that not everyone can, or should, be an entrepreneur. Some people are simply not suited to be entrepreneurs. They prefer to be employees and are more productive in that role. While self-employment certainly has its attractions, starting one's own enterprise is not necessarily the ultimate business experience.

Whether entrepreneurship facilitates the independence and initiative commonly assumed it does, may be in doubt, as expressed here by Grant McCracken, in his article, "Not So Lean Means Not So Mean," appearing in *The Globe and Mail:*

> When Ottawa tries to create young entrepreneurs, what does it do? It spoon feeds them with government programs and government money. It's not the sort of lesson that will stand them in good stead for the real world.[17]

McCracken goes on to wonder why, while the rest of the world is trying to get government out of the market place, the Canadian government is introducing program after program to assist entrepreneurs, and give the impression that everything is "free." McCracken questions whether this is the way to build resourceful, independent, and determined young entrepreneurs and doubts whether there is any hope for these young entrepreneurs if they have to be persuaded to entrepreneurship with government sponsorship.

Bigger Is Better—Sometimes!

Despite the desirability of small enterprise, there are some industries in which size is necessary and essential for succsss. Smallness is not a solution to all organizational difficulties. The following are examples of industries where bigness is still important.

1. *Mass production, resource industries* Large production units are necessary so that economies of scale can be achieved. This is the case in many Canadian resource industries, for example, pulp and paper with large companies such as Noranda Forest Inc., MacMillan Bloedel Ltd., and Abitibi-Price Inc. Other examples would be chemical and oil refining industries.
2. *Marketing/distribution-intensive companies* These companies make products that cost little to produce but that require large marketing and distribution efforts which create barriers to small new entrants. Examples are Coca-Cola in the soft drink industry and Nike in athletic footwear.
3. *High-volume purchasers* Some firms operate activities that require high volumes of purchased materials which will lead to lower unit costs. In retailing, Wal-Mart Stores and Toys "R" Us are examples. This would also be the case in automobile manufacturing in which large amounts of components and parts are necessary.
4. *Technology-intensive business* In these businesses, large-scale operations can help to fund risky R & D and to recover investments in products with a short life. Pharmaceuticals is such an industry with Merck Frosst Canada Inc. being an example of a technology-intensive business.[18]

Small is beautiful much of the time, but there is still need for large corporations. This being the case, many managers in large organizations are attempting to make themselves more entrepreneurial.

The Entrepreneurial Corporation

Large business corporations are often described as bureaucracies making top-down decisions, being risk adverse, rewarding political gamesmanship, and missing opportunities. Now attempts are being made to unleash the spirit of enterprise in these organzations. Managers want to recapture the allegiance and commitment of employees and to develop the symbiotic relationship between inspired employees and corporate performance.

This is being attempted in many ways. Parts of corporations are spun off as small enterprises partly or wholly owned by the parent. Partnerships are being formed with smaller enterprises that can supply more efficiently something the large corporation needs. For example, Canadian Airlines is in partnership with Air Atlantic who services the less populated parts of Atlantic Canada. Sometimes large organizations can acquire technology this way, or enter niche markets.

Large corporations are also trying to make themselves more attractive to work for by creating smaller units. Small management teams operate highly decentralized units which maintain the flexibility of small business and allow new products to be introduced more quickly and customers to be serviced better. Sometimes managers in these small units are motivated by stock options or other incentives.

Companies such as IBM, General Motors, and Sears are attempting to become more entreprenerial. Asea Brown Boveri, a Swiss holding company with revenues of $32 billion, has reorganized itself into 5000 decentralized profit centres some of which are in Canada. This decentralization allows the huge company to capitalize on local differences. All these corporations are attempting to combine the advantages of bigness—that is, access to capital, research capabilities, and global marketing—with the human scale, sharp focus, and fervent entrepreneurship of small businesses.

According to a *Business Week* article, five attributes of small business are found in entrepreneurial corporations:

1. Managers in entrepreneurial corporations have become opportunity seekers in the same way entrepreneurs find and exploit markets that others have overlooked or that new technologies create.
2. In a small business, the entrepreneur is the owner, and thus reaps the benefits of success and suffers the consequences of failure. Although it is very difficult to duplicate these circumstances in a large corporation, there are incentive systems and profit-sharing schemes in some of them that have encouraged enterepreneurial behaviour.
3. Because small enterprise owners or managers are flexible, they are able to move quickly into initiatives and to abandon them if appropriate. Managers in entrepreneurial corporations are likewise able to think and act on their own because of less hierachical organization and because strategic planning is performed by line managers instead of staff departments.
4. The culture of many large companies often discourages teamwork and commitment. Employees of smaller enterprises are often willing to put in extra effort to meet deadlines. Employees of enterpreneurial companies are encouraged to learn and develop skills, and are less preoccupied with status-reflecting perks. In small companies, status comes from performance and faithfulness to the company's culture and values.
5. Entrepreneurs are sensitive to controlling resources instead of owning them. For example, contracting out is used instead of building a plant. The same type of thinking is important in large companies who have in the past spent lavishly on resources without thinking where such resources could be more effectively secured.[19]

MEETING THE CHALLENGE

THE FUTURE OF RELCON INC.

In 1992, Relcon was acquired by Siemens AG, a very large German electronics company with sales of $60 billion and 400 000 employees. Relcon was absorbed into Siemans' Canadian operations, a common event when small enterprises face pressures from competition and finances.

The ownership change meant a cultural change for managers and employees. The independence and entrepreneurial energy of a small enterprise were gone. A manager arrived from Germany, and the loose collaborative management style was replaced with rigid structures and job descriptions. There was more pressure to meet deadlines, and Relcon had to follow Siemans' systems and procedures. Relcon will operate more as a high-volume manufacturing plant instead as a custom workshop. The performance of employees is measured more accurately as productivity is emphasized.

But, there were advantages to the acquisition. Relcon could enter the export market, especially into the U.S., through Siemans' worldwide operations. The company, now actually a division within Siemens' Canadian operations, has product mandates for AC drives that will be sold in the United States, Canada, South Africa, Australia, and the Pacific Rim. Relcon expects to achieve $100 million in sales by the year 2000 compared to less than $50 million when it was taken over.

Although no longer a Canadian small enterprise, the Relcon operations are a success story, the plant will survive, and jobs are being provided to Canadians. A small business started by George Rumble 50 years ago has grown, changed focus, and has new owners. This is a natural evolution for a successful business enterprise. ▲

SUMMARY

The Canadian economy relies upon a business enterprise system to provide the goods and services needed by consumers. In turn, the business enterprise system relies upon entrepreneurs, persons who start and operate small businesses. New business start-ups provide new products for consumers, provide competition for established enterprises, increase employment opportunities for Canadians, and might even become large companies if they are successful. The business system is continuously evolving, and small businesses are the source, or beginning, of that system.

Throughout the 1980s, the small business sector grew substantially and received recognition for its role in the business system. Governments increased their efforts in assisting small businesses as did banking and educational institutions. As a result, we know much more about the challenges facing entrepreneurs who want to start a business, and the difficulties of operating a business. We have also learned about the traits or characteristics of persons who are entrepreneurs. There have been several developments in the small business areas that were identified—for example, the employment being generated, the enthusiasm of young people for entrepreneurship, the role played by women, and the application of the entrepreneurial concept in large organizations.

A person could become involved in a small business by taking over a family business, buying an existing enterprise, starting a business from scratch, acquiring a "spun off" business, or purchasing a franchise. Each of these has advantages and disadvantages. In addition, there are several challenges for the businessperson regardless of the way they become entrepreneurs. It is also difficult to identify the appropriate sources of funds and then the acquisition of the financing necessary to start and continue a business.

Entrepreneurs face many challenges in starting and operating business enterprises. Financing is always a hurdle as is how to plan for a small business. Business plans are usually requested by financial backers, but they are often ignored by entrepreneurs in the operation of the business. This is unfortunate, but is consistent with the characteristics of an enterpreneur. Managing growth is a major challenge that many enterpreneurs do not handle well, and this sometimes leads to failure. Managing the growth of the enterprise through the transitions to get from one stage to another is difficult. The survival of small business is considered important to the economy and there are numerous sources of assistance from the public and private sectors.

Large corrporations are now attempting to make their businesses more entrepreneurial. It is recognized that "small" has its advantages and many businesses are restructuring to instill an entrepreneurial spirit. It is of interest to note how Relcon, the company described in the Management Challenge, started as a small business and over the years grew, eventually becoming a part of a large corporation. Now that company is concerned about the problems of being part of a big organization, and it and its parent corporation, will have to make efforts of preserve an entrepreneurial spirit.

Not all small businesses survive. The failure rate is high and there are numerous reasons for this. Efforts are being made by governments and others institutions to improve the chances of success by supplying funds, lowering taxation rates, and providing advice on all aspects of operation including the management of people and technology. However, small business should not be coddled so much that it cannot fail. Failure is a characteristic of the business system and will occur when businesses do not supply the goods and services wanted by consumers.

KEY TERMS

small business (p. 618)	microenterprises (p. 622)	franchisor (p. 623)	equity (p. 625)
entrepreneurs (p. 618)	franchising (p. 623)	retained earnings (p. 625)	
entrepreneurship (p. 618)	franchisee (p. 623)	debt (p. 625)	

REVIEW QUESTIONS

1. Why have the numbers of small businesses in Canada increased?
2. What are the characteristics of a small business?
3. Why do Canadians become entrepreneurs?
4. What are the main trends in small business and entrepreneurship?
5. What is a "microenterprise"?
6. What are the drawbacks to the business plan?
7. Why should entrepreneurs consider using strategic management?
8. What are the sources of funding for a small business?
9. What are the stages of growth that a small business goes through?
10. What are the causes of small business failure?
11. In what types of industries will large businesses be necessary?
12. What are the attributes of an entrepreneurial corporation?

DISCUSSION QUESTIONS

1. Why are small businesses important to the Canadian economy?
2. Why are the reasons for starting a business somewhat different from the ones that motivate successful entrepreneurs?
3. Why would a person want to become involved in a "microenterprise" instead of going into business full time?
4. Why would an entrepreneur use several sources of funds to start and operate a small business?
5. Why do entrepreneurs ignore the business plans they have prepared? Why is strategic management not more commonly used by entrepreneurs?
6. Why do small businesses fail despite all the assistance available? Should we be concerned about these failures?
7. How can a large corporation benefit from entrepreneurial thinking?

EXERCISES

1. Write the Canadian Federation of Independent Business for information on small business. The head office address is 4141 Yonge Street, Suite 401, Willowdale, ON M2P 2A6. Check for a branch in your community.
2. Interview a person who is involved in a family business to identify the management challenge he/she faces. Check your findings against the key challenges identified in Figure 20.1. Write the Canadian Association of Family Enterprises for more information at 1 Ava Rd., Suite #102, Etobicoke, Ontario, M9C 4Z5.
3. Invite the owner/manager of a local franchised fast food chain to speak to your class on the operation of a franchise operation.
4. Research a business that you are interested in and prepare a plan for starting that business utilizing the contents of a business plan as listed in Table 20-2.
5. Interview the manager of a local bank to ascertain the assistance it provides to small business. The manager could also be invited to speak to the class.
6. Visit three successful small businesses in your local area. Discuss with the owner/manager of each business the reasons for their success. Ask them if they would advise a person to start up his or her own small business.

MANAGEMENT ON LOCATION

CASE 20-1
GeoVision Systems Fails

GeoVision Systems Inc. of Ottawa is a pioneer in a type of computer software called geographical information systems (GIS), an automated map-making program that turns maps into "spatial databases." The company was formed by Douglas Seaborn in 1984 when it was spun off from SHL Systemshouse Inc., a corporation which Seaborn had helped to found. When Systemshouse experienced financial problems in 1984, GeoVision was formed with about 20 employees.

Competition from large American companies was very intense. An R&D program assisted by federal tax credits was undertaken to explore new applications allowing GeoVision to be competitive. The company was successful in developing new products, many of which were sold to municipal governments and utility companies. Sales grew from $2 million in 1984 to more than $20 million in 1991. The GIS appeared to be a growing market.

The company decided to increase its presence in the U.S. through a major sales and marketing effort. However, problems arose when managers and salespeople were hired who were not familiar with GIS and GeoVision's technology which was among the most complicated in the industry. The U.S. business grew but some customers were dissatisfied with the service they were receiving. Other problems arose, including the departure of the U.S. manager and the termination of a partnership with IBM because that company was in financial difficulty. GeoVision expanded by purchasing a company in Wisconsin for the primary purpose of forging the links with IBM.

Customers began to worry about GeoVision's financial viability and whether it would survive. In mid-1993, GeoVision went into receivership in both the U.S. and Canada. The technology and assets of GeoVision were taken over by Systemhouse in October 1993. ▲

QUESTIONS

1. GeoVision provides an example of which approach to starting a business?
2. In your view, what went wrong at GeoVision?
3. Could the problems have been anticipated?

CASE 20-2
Dynamic Software Inc.

Mike Green and John Barclay graduated from Engineering School in the same year and remained friends even though they went to work for different computer software companies. Four years later they happened to meet in the Lester B. Pearson Airport in Toronto while waiting for flights. The conversation focussed on their work, as they were involved in similar activities. Before departing, they agreed to meet the following week to discuss the possibility of going into business for themselves.

The meeting lead to the establishment of Dynamic Software Inc. in Oshawa, Ontario. Each partner invested $25 000 in the business which developed software for dispatching, scheduling, and monitoring the location of vehicles in large fleets such as rental cars, taxis, and delivery vans. They began by designing and selling small operator programs that could be used on personal computers avoiding the need for clients to make large capital investments.

The business was successful and profitable enough to pay Mike and John good salaries and provide funds for investing in office facilities, computers, and the development of new software programs. The software projects were getting more complex as the company was designing software for clients with larger fleets and more complicated situations. For example, Dynamic was developing programs for a national trucking firm and a large urban transit system, each with several hundred vehicles.

The development of these new programs required a lot of money. Mike and John concluded that they would have to either invest more money themselves or get it from other sources. They had very little money to invest as both were raising young families, and in fact, John's father was asking for the $15 000 he had loaned him initially. Tom Pardy, a business administration graduate who had joined the company the previous year, wanted to invest in the business. The success of the company had not gone unnoticed, and a venture capital company was willing to invest money.

• • •

Mike and John even looked at the idea of selling shares to the public and allowing employees to purchase stock. Dynamic had no long-term debt, so several financial institutions would most likely be willing to lend to the company. The federal and Ontario governments had financial assistance programs of loans and grants for which Dynamic was eligible because they were in a high-technology business.

The business needed money to grow and Mike and John would have to make up their minds soon. ▲

QUESTIONS

1. Identify the sources of funds available to Dynamic Software.
2. What are the advantages and disadvantages of each source?
3. What recommendation would you make to Mike and John?

CASE 20-3
PAUL'S PIZZA PALACE LTD.

Paul, a graduate of a business administration course, decided to start a business of his own. Paul had entertained friends on numerous occasions by preparing pizzas. Everyone loved his pizza and he was asked many times why he did not open his own pizzeria.

Paul began to give the possibility of establishing a business some thought and decided to establish a pizzeria named Paul's Pizza Palace. He found a suitable building and purchased the equipment and other materials with $15 000 he had saved.

Paul needed more funds to finance the business, so he approached others to invest in the company. The idea of opening a pizzeria was enthusiastically endorsed by Paul's wife, Joan, and several friends. As a result, the group agreed to incorporate and operate a company under the name, Paul's Pizza Palace, Ltd. There were to be six shareholders and the shares were to be held in the following proportions: Paul 40 percent; Joan 20 percent; and four friends with 10 percent each. Paul was the president of the company and manager of the pizzeria. He received a modest salary as did Joan, who helped in the shop and also looked after the books.

The company was incorporated under the Companies Act of the province. A lawyer was hired to facilitate the incorporation procedure and charged a fee of several hundred dollars. It took three weeks to complete the incorporation.

The pizzeria was an instant success. Sales increased and the business was very profitable. The shareholders were somewhat disappointed to discover that not only were the profits of the company taxed, but also that the dividends they paid themselves were taxed as personal income. Paul enjoyed operating the pizzeria and received little interference from the other shareholders.

The company soon expanded by opening a pizzeria across town which also proved to be very successful. Within two years, the company had opened a chain of 10 pizzerias throughout the province. As the company grew, two problems emerged for Paul. It seemed as if dozens of government departments wanted forms completed and confirmation that various regulations were being followed. Secondly, Paul found that he no longer had time to work in the pizzeria and missed greeting and chatting with customers. Paul's time was now occupied with paper work in his office and training and supervising managers, which he found very difficult. Paul felt that he was spending all his time settling disagreements between employees and listening to complaints from managers.

About this time, Paul was also having personal problems. His wife divorced him and soon afterwards teamed up with the other shareholders to fire him. Paul maintained his 40 percent share in the company and received dividends but another person, a recent food technology graduate, was hired as president. Paul was offered a job as a manager of one of the pizzerias but he declined and went to work as the produce manager with a local supermarket. ▲

QUESTIONS

1. Why did Paul lose control of this business?
2. How did Paul fail to make the necessary transition in management as the company grew?
3. What can Paul do now?

CHAPTER 21

MANAGING INTERNATIONALLY

LEARNING OBJECTIVES

After reading this chapter, you will be able to:

1. Realize the importance of thinking internationally for Canadian managers.
2. Define trade and describe its importance in the Canadian economy.
3. Understand that trade takes place in services as well as goods.
4. Describe the involvement of governments in trade.
5. List the approaches a company can use to manage internationally.
6. Identify and describe the challenges in world markets for Canadian business.
7. Describe the main forms of organization used by corporations operating internationally.
8. Discuss the trend towards large corporate organizations, and define the borderless corporation.
9. Relate the task of managing internationally to the management functions of planning, organizing, leading and controlling.

MANAGEMENT CHALLENGE

ALEX GRAY AND FREE TRADE

Alex Gray wondered about the impact of the Canadian-U.S. Free Trade Agreement on his firm after January 1, 1989, when the agreement took effect. Gray operated Gray Tool of Brampton, Ontario, a privately owned, third-generation family business. The firm manufactured socket wrenches, screwdrivers, and other hand tools for automobile and maintenance mechanics. Besides the head office in Brampton, Gray Tool had two plants in Welland and employed about 250 people.

During the eighties, Gray had attempted to export his tools in the U.S. and by 1988 exported about 25 percent of production. Nonetheless, the Free Trade Agreement created some uncertainly for Gray.

Gray's competitors in the U.S. were much larger and engaged in aggressive business practices. No doubt they would seize the opportunity to export their products into Canada, threatening Gray's home market. Gray knew that his company would need to work harder and smarter to survive in the competitive market for hand tools. The question was whether or not Gray Tool could survive under the new competitive environment created by the Free Trade Agreement. He knew he could view the development as a disaster or as an opportunity, and he believed that he could influence what would happen to the business that had been established by his grandfather and that he hoped would be operated by his children. ▲

Alex Gray's experience illustrates just one of the many predicaments facing enterprises conducting business outside of Canada. But in spite of the obvious and not-so-obvious problems, more enterprises are getting involved in international business.

LEARNING OBJECTIVE 1

Realize the importance of thinking internationally for Canadian managers.

Many people believe that international business activities have the potential for distributing goods and services more equitably and for improving standards of living for all people. Enterprises subject to market forces and managed by private rather than government employees are felt to be more efficient at supplying the goods and services needed by citizens in any country. A dissenting view is that such business leads to the exploitation of developing countries and benefits only the companies themselves. The one certain result is that international trade has caused the countries of the world to become more closely interrelated; people in all countries are increasingly aware of what is happening in other parts of the world.

In this chapter we examine the phenomenon of international business and the challenges of managing in what is referred to as a global economy. After demonstrating the importance of international trade, we describe the ways that business becomes involved in trade. A third section identifies the challenges in the world market as the trend to globalization of business activity continues. Several forms of corporate organizations operating in the global market are described, and a final section relates managing global business to the planning, organizing, leading, and controlling functions.

THE ROLE OF TRADE IN THE CANADIAN ECONOMY

trade

Trade involves the exporting or importing of goods to and from other countries. Principal goods exported are automobiles and parts, machinery and equipment, forest products, metals and minerals, energy products, and wheat and other grains. The volume of exports is about 35 percent of the total Canadian production which indicates their importance to the Canadian economy. The Canadian government believes that exports are critical to the economy and recognizes firms that do well in exporting goods. Exporting is performed by very large companies, such as Canadian Pacific, Inco, and Alcan Aluminium, and by small companies across Canada.

LEARNING OBJECTIVE 2

Define trade and describe its importance in the Canadian economy.

While many enterprises export goods, others import goods for sale to Canadians. The principal goods imported are machinery and equipment, automobiles and parts, chemicals, energy products, and goods such as fruit and vegetables.

TRADE IN SERVICES

LEARNING OBJECTIVE 3

Understand that trade takes place in services as well as goods.

Until recently, little emphasis was placed on the fact that an increasing portion of the trade between nations is in services, as opposed to goods. A report published in 1989 by the General Agreement on Tariffs and Trade (GATT) stated that service industries were largely responsible for a period of unprecedented growth in international trade during the late 1980s. The report estimates that the total trade in services in 1988 was $560 billion (U.S.), which was equal to all trade in food and energy.[1] The industries involved included telecommunications, transportation, banking, hotels, advertising, computer software, management consulting, and accounting. One reason for the activities in these areas is the advent of global industries, that is, business activities are performed on a worldwide scale.

Imports of services are those that are purchased from residents of another country, while exports of services are those that are sold to residents of another country.

Table 21-1 provides examples of such trade. Business persons must not limit themselves to thinking that trade only involves manufactured goods or commodities. Opportunities exist for enterprises that import or export services. However, the same types of challenges that exist in goods trade also exist in the services trade, for example, protectionism which prevents trade in services. The airlines industry has been protected from foreign competition which has resulted in higher fares being paid by Canadians. Nontariff barriers exist for services as they do for trade in goods. For example, some nations restrict the flow of data across borders.

The Global Management insert, "Knowledge-based Exports," illustrates the trade in consultancy services by Canadian firms.

TABLE 21-1 EXAMPLES OF TRADE IN SERVICES.

Exports of Services
An advertising agency in Toronto develops T.V. commercials for an American client.
A taxi delivers a foreign person or tourist from the airport to the hotel.
A television show produced in Canada is broadcast abroad, e.g. *Anne of Green Gables.*
An accountant is hired to prepare financial statements for a foreign corporation.
A Canadian engineer designs a bridge to be built in another country.
Import of Services
Vacations taken by Canadians in a foreign country.
The purchase of a ticket to see a performance by a foreign entertainer.
The accessing and extracting of information from a foreign database.
The repair of a Canadian tourist's camera in Europe.
The purchase of securities on a foreign stock exchange by Canadians.

GLOBAL MANAGEMENT

Knowledge-based Exports

Exporting of goods receives most of the attention in Canada's trade. Goods have been the traditional form of trade, but now knowledge-based skills are also being exported, including the skill of how to construct pulp and paper mills, something Canadian consulting firms know a lot about.

Indonesia is building several large pulp and paper mills to exploit its plantations of hardwoods which produce harvestable trees in as little as 7 years (compared to 40 to 70 years in Canada). The wood costs are lower, as are labour and transportation costs, allowing the Indonesians to produce paper at a lower cost than possible in Canada or the U.S.

Many Canadian consulting firms have extensive experience in the construction of large projects like pulp and paper plants. Several such firms in British Columbia are selling their expertise in this area to the developers of the Indonesian mills.

H.A. Simons Inc., Vancouver, has set up an office in Indonesia and is assisting in the construction of an $800-million project. It has prepared technical studies for the project and is the consortium manager for the new plant in Kalimantan (Indonesian Borneo). As the manager, Simons coordinates the design, construction, and equipment purchases for the plant. It is in charge of engineering design and assures lenders that the project incorporates proven, state-of-the-art technology that will produce a marketable product.

Commonwealth Construction Co. of Burnaby, B.C., was selected by Simons to perform about $100-million worth of construction work, and Hatfield Consultants Ltd. of North Vancouver is involved in a joint venture consultancy relating to environmental assessment work.

A Simons' competitor, Sandwell Inc. of Vancouver, is also involved in an Indonesian pulp mill project. It has performed engineering design and tendered documents for a world-scale mill proposed for South Sumatra. ▲

Trade and the Challenges for Canadian Managers

There are many challenges confronting managers as their companies become involved in international trade and business. A company seeking to do business in another country is confronted by legal, political, cultural, and financial barriers. For example, exports from Canada have to overcome various forms of protection imposed by governments for the benefit of their own business firms. The most common form is the imposition of a tariff, that is, a levy on the value of the export that increases its price. Also, some countries erect nontariff barriers such as requirements that Canadian goods meet specific standards or quality levels.

For Canadian companies establishing operations in a foreign country, there are other challenges. Some foreign governments impose ownership restrictions on companies. Some governments require Canadian firms to find local partners, and managers often have difficulty finding suitable partners. The political situation in some countries is unstable and Canadian corporations have lost investments when governments change. Understanding the social customs and culture is necessary when doing business in most foreign countries. The business practices and approaches used in Canada may not be acceptable to other countries. The financing of international business is often difficult. Smaller businesses have problems financing exports since there are usually long delays before payments are received for shipments. Corporations establishing operations in foreign countries sometimes cannot find sufficient capital to finance the undertaking and even if financed, the transfer of profits from the country may be restricted. Once involved in international trade or business activities, the fluctuations of currency exchanges can play havoc with anticipated prices and profits.

Forest products are a leading Canadian export. Softwood lumber is exported to over 70 countries and was valued at $5.3 billion in 1990. Lumber exports depend upon economic conditions in other countries making the market cyclical and causing prices to fluctuate. Canada is also facing competition in the lumber market from countries like Sweden, the United States, Brazil and New Zealand.

The Canadian government recognizes the challenges to trade and attempts to encourage it. Table 21-2 provides a selected list of assistance and services that are offered by the government to Canadian business. Some provinces have trade offices similar to the federal government's trade services or have premiers visit foreign countries to promote trade. While the government provides assistance in one way, it restricts international business in another. The government levies tariffs on imports and introduces nontariff barriers such as quotas and strict testing requirements to protect Canadian industry from foreign competitors. Canadian businesses wishing to import goods and services sometimes must pay duties and other charges that increase the price Canadians must pay for these products. In some cases, imports are

LEARNING OBJECTIVE 4

Describe the involvement of governments in trade.

TABLE 21-2 GOVERNMENT ASSISTANCE FOR EXPORTS.

The following are four examples of the assistance programs and services available from the federal government to promote exports by Canadian business.

The Program for Export Market Development (PEMD)
Assists in export promotion activities
Shares financial risks of entering new foreign markets

The Technology Inflow Program (TIP)
Facilitates the flow of foreign technology into Canada
Assists Canadian scientists to gain technological knowledge

Trade Commissioner Service
Promotes export trade and represents and protects Canadian interests abroad

Export Development Corporation
A Crown corporation that facilitates and develops Canada's export trade through provision of insurance, guarantees, loans and related services

prevented from entering the country so that potential sales for businesses relying on foreign suppliers are reduced.

Despite the challenges, Canadian business is extensively involved in international trade and business. The following section discusses the various approaches, or dimensions, of this involvement.

MANAGING INTERNATIONAL CORPORATIONS

international corporation

A large portion of business enterprises are, in some form, involved with trade in goods and services. In other words, many Canadian enterprises are considered to be an **international corporation** of some sort. Such a corporation is defined as one that engages in any combination of activities from the exporting or importing of goods and services to full-scale operations in foreign countries.

EXPORTING GOODS AND SERVICES

LEARNING OBJECTIVE 5
List the approaches a company can use to manage internationally.

This is the most commonly thought of dimension of global business. Canadian business enterprises sell goods and services to other enterprises and governments in hundreds of countries. Large enterprises are involved in exporting as illustrated by MacMillan-Bloedel and Abitibi-Price who sell newsprint and other forest products around the world. But, many small enterprises are also involved in trade. For example, Seagull Pewter & Silversmiths Ltd. of Pugwash, Nova Scotia, sells pewter giftware in the U.S. and Europe, and I.P. Constructors Ltd. of Calgary designs and manufacturers a complete range of oil- and gas-processing equipment 97.2 percent of which is exported. This involvement in international trade is supervised from Canadian-based operations. Companies have a sales force to contact customers or use representatives overseas to market their products.

Exports are another way that a Canadian business can grow. With exporting, increases in sales volume generate a flow of funds that can lead to profits. Exporting also reduces the unit cost of production because of the increased volume, allows for greater use of plant capacity, lessens the dependence on a single traditional market, offers some protection against a downturn in Canadian sales, and provides an opportunity to gain a knowledge of and experience with other products and potential markets. But there are also disadvantages to exporting, such as the additional travel, time, and expense required to develop export markets, the modifications to products necessary to meet government regulations, the acquisition of further financing, and the obligation to learn about the customs, culture, language, local standards, and government regulations of the new customers.

Stable beer sales in Canada mean that Canadian breweries such as Labatt must look for markets outside the country. About 24 percent of Labatt's beer sales are outside of Canada, mainly to the U.S. But the competition is intense in the American market and Labatt will have to seek profitable beer markets elsewhere, such as Europe.

IMPORTING GOODS AND SERVICES

While many enterprises sell Canadian goods and services abroad, many are also involved in purchasing goods and services in foreign countries for resale to Canadians. For example, Gendis Inc., a large Winnipeg-based corporation, distributes Sony electronic products throughout Canada. On a local level, most large shopping malls (for example, the Wicker Emporium in the Rideau Centre, Ottawa) contain a retail outlet selling wicker goods, brass objects, carpeting, and similar products imported from India and various Far Eastern countries. Canadian importing businesses employ buyers who travel around the world seeking out goods that could be sold in this country. Foreign suppliers might have salespersons or representatives based in Canada to market these products.

Licensing Agreements

licensing agreements

Licensing agreements exist where the owner of a product or process allows an enterprise to produce, distribute, or market the product or process for a fee or royalty. Such agreements can involve a Canadian enterprise licensing another enterprise in a foreign country to produce, distribute, or market its products in that area. But the agreement could work the other way, whereby enterprises in foreign countries allow Canadian enterprises to produce, distribute, and market their products in Canada. Some examples of these agreements are mentioned in the Global Management insert entitled "Managing Internationally at Can-Eng Manufacturing." Note that Can-Eng is involved in both types of licensing agreements.

This approach is used when the company does not wish to establish a plant or marketing network in another country. Licensing arrangements avoid the need to manage operations in foreign countries, and allow the owner of the product or process to concentrate on further technological research and development financed, in part, from the royalties received.

Establishment of Subsidiaries

If the volume of business to be conducted is large and will be continuing for some time, Canadian enterprises may choose to establish subsidiary or branch operations in foreign countries through which they can market goods and services. Other reasons for establishing a subsidiary are that it may be required by a foreign government and may increase sales because locally operated branches can respond more quickly to delivery and service requests. Sometimes these branches are established from scratch, that is, by forming an operation where none previously existed. Another

GLOBAL MANAGEMENT

Managing Internationally at Can-Eng Manufacturing Inc.

Can-Eng is a Niagara Falls, Ontario-based company that specializes in the manufacture of industrial furnaces. The company employs about 50 people and has sales of about $10 million.

The company is Canada's largest supplier of industrial furnaces which heat materials to different temperatures to enhance properties such as toughness and hardness. The furnaces are used mainly for heating metals, but they are also used for ceramics, carbon fibres, and glass. Can-Eng works with its clients to design furnaces to meet particular needs and is constantly updating technology.

Can-Eng involvement in international markets includes the following:

1. In 1979, the company purchased the North American rights to British patents for fluidized bed furnace technology.
2. The company owns furnace manufacturing facilities in the U.S.
3. Its industrial furnaces have been exported under license agreements to Japan, Brazil, the United Kingdom, Germany, Korea, Taiwan and Mexico.
4. The Canada-U.S. Free Trade Agreement is expected to increase sales to the U.S. Can-Eng already exports 40 to 50 percent of their product to the U.S. The company has 13 representatives in the U.S. marketing its products.
5. In 1987, Can-Eng obtained a license for unique mesh belt carburizing furnaces technology from a Japanese company and will build and market this technology in the U.S. and Canada.
6. In 1990, Can-Eng reached a cooperative agreement (or joint venture) with a company in the Netherlands to market its technology in Europe and the Soviet Union. In turn, Can-Eng will represent the Dutch company in the U.S. market. ▲

approach is to become established by acquisition of an operating enterprise in the foreign country. Of course, this process works both ways with foreign enterprises doing the same in Canada. The establishment of subsidiaries can lead to the sensitive issue of foreign ownership and the analysis of its benefits and drawbacks.

This dimension of international business requires changes in corporate structures, information systems, and staffing. Usually the company will have an international division to oversee such operations. Companies must design information systems to keep employees in other countries informed and to monitor these overseas operations. Staffing is more complex as existing employees must be adequately prepared to serve in foreign countries, or local workers trained in a manner suitable for the home office. Managing this form of international involvement complicates the management tasks for Canadians accustomed to supervising employees and operations within Canada.

Merger

Closely related to the establishment of subsidiaries is the situation in which a Canadian enterprise merges with an enterprise in a foreign country. The new enterprise is jointly owned by the previous owner and now is multinational in the sense that it operates in at least two countries. As with any merger, a new organization is formed which usually requires adjustments to planning, information, and human resource systems and to authority relationships. One of the merged firms will perform the role of a head office.

Product Mandating

When a business enterprise operates branches, plants or subsidiaries in several countries, it may assign to one plant or subsidiary the responsibility for researching, developing, manufacturing, and marketing one product or line of products. This approach allows the enterprise to achieve optimum levels of efficiency due to the fact that economies of scale are possible through specialization, which is not possible when a company provides a full range of products. The assignment of a product responsibility to a particular branch is known as **world product mandating**.

world product mandating

About 100 Canadian-based subsidiaries are now involved in some form of world product mandates. Some examples are:

1. Pratt & Whitney Canada (subsidiary of United Technologies) produces small gas turbine engines.
2. Black and Decker Canada makes orbital sanders, the "Workmate" work bench, the "Workwheel" power stripper, and the "Workhorse" scaffold.
3. Westinghouse Canada is mandated to produce steam and gas turbines, airport lighting, and digital-video converters and displays.

Canadian enterprises operating in other countries might also use this approach.

Strategic Alliances

strategic alliances

Strategic alliances refers to a variety of relationships that involve two or more enterprises cooperating in the research, development, manufacture, or marketing of a product. The relationship is more subtle than the usual supplier-customer relations yet less formal than the rights of ownership. These relationships, which have become more popular in the last decade, take many forms and are referred to as cooperative strategies, joint venturing, strategic networking, and strategic partnering. In all cases, some form of collaborative arrangement exists between enterprises that involves a willingness to share or split managerial control over a particular undertaking. There are various reasons for entering into a strategic alliance, such as gaining access to new markets or customers, acquiring advanced or new technology, sharing the costs and risks of new ventures, obtaining financing to supplement a firm's debt capacity, and sharing production facilities to avoid wasteful duplication. Figure 21-1 provides some examples of alliances formed by Northern Telecom. The Global Management insert, "Barely Speaking at Home: Partners Abroad," explains why two companies are participating in a joint venture in England.

While strategic alliances between firms can be advantageous to both parties, the management of such alliances or partnerships presents challenges. It is not easy to know whether or not a partner will be compatible. There must be a clear vision of what the alliance is to achieve and the benefits to both parties. The appropriate structure for ownership and control must be designed so that the partners will achieve their objectives and are involved in decisions. Such alliances are considered satisfactory by the partners about 40 percent to 60 percent of the time.[2]

Although these dimensions are listed separately, one enterprise could be involved in two or more dimensions at any one time. This is especially true of larger companies. The involvement of a Canadian enterprise in the world market place is not without its challenges as discussed in the following section.

CHALLENGES IN WORLD TRADE FOR CANADIAN BUSINESS

LEARNING OBJECTIVE 6
Identify and describe the challenges in world markets for Canadian business.

World trade is very dynamic and the changes occurring must be constantly monitored by Canadian managers. The following sections briefly discuss some of the challenges of world trade in the 1990s for Canadian business.

FIGURE 21-1 DIMENSIONS OF MANAGING GLOBALLY AT NORTHERN TELECOM.

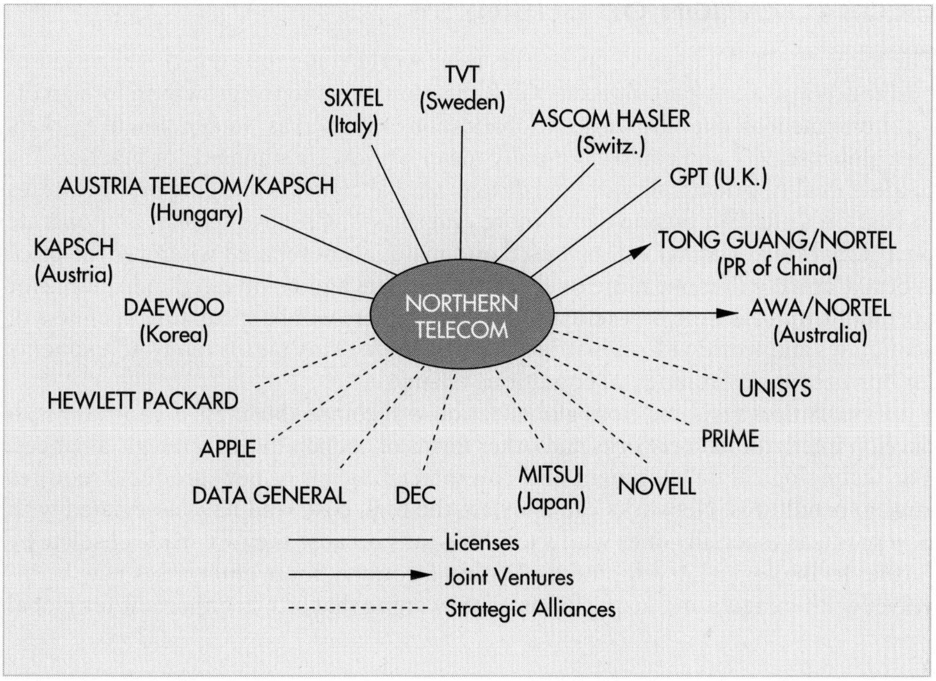

GLOBAL MANAGEMENT

Barely Speaking at Home: Partners Abroad!

The technologies used by the cable television and telephone industries are advancing, making possible the convergence of cable television, telephones, and computers to provide consumers with a variety of interactive services such as home banking and shopping, and entertainment features.

As most of Canada is wired for both cable and telephone, cable television companies want to provide interactive services to Canadians, and telephone companies want to expand into the cable television business in order to do the same.

There are two companies barely talking to each other here in Canada because of this very problem. They are Le Groupe Videotron Ltee. which supplies cable television to most of Quebec, and BCE Inc., the parent company of Bell Canada, which supplies telephone services in the same region. They both want to provide interactive services to homes in Quebec and the only reason that they are not is that government regulation prevents it. The government is examining the issue and a decision is forthcoming. Meanwhile, the companies keep their distance!

At the same time, ironically, Videotron and BCE are partners in a British venture, Videotron Southampton and Eastleigh Ltd. (VS&E), which has a franchise to operate in London and Southampton where their potential market in the fledgling cable TV industry is 1.1 million households. As the cables for the new franchise were being installed, a separate set were also installed in the same ductwork which would allow VS&E to provide telephone and other services. VS&E now offers subscribers not only cable television and local telephone services but also interactive entertainment. The interactive service, called Videoway, provides video games, information services, and requests for instant replays during live sports broadcasts. The company now has 72 000 cable television subscribers and 30 000 residential telephone customers.

Why are two Canadian companies that barely talk to each other cooperating in an English joint venture? England provides a good location in which to learn about being a complete provider as a separate cable television system does not exist. Both companies are learning from the partnership and will quite likely apply the knowledge in Canada when government regulations change. ▲

Globalization of Business

globalization

The focus in this chapter so far has been on world trade, but the globalization of business is also an important issue. **Globalization** refers to the growth in foreign direct investment all over the world. Globalization is defined as "integration of markets on a global scale"[3] and could eventually mean worldwide standards or practices for product quality, pricing, service, and design. Globalization is bringing new pressures to bear on Canadian business and more enterprises will have to plan and operate on a global scale. Capital will be raised and materials purchased wherever the price is best. Capital will move more freely across borders and be invested in locations or operations that offer the best returns. In general, there will be increasing openness of economies and worldwide industrial rationalization. This means many adjustments for business as environmental conditions change.

The changes resulting from globalization will compel business organizations to develop international networks and other forms of cooperative or strategic alliances. The technological development and commercialization of new products requires large expenditures. Networks can alleviate the high costs and risks associated with new products especially ones with short life spans because they are made obsolete by further technological developments. Within a country, more enterprises may be involved with mergers and acquisitions as they argue that size is important for global competition. Such consolidations enable companies to better position themselves to survive in a world market.

According to Investment Canada, there are some lessons for Canadian business from globalization:

1. With global markets emerging, Canadian business is under pressure to forge international links as there will be less distinction between domestic and foreign firms. For Canadians and their governments, ownership and control of business will be less important than performance and value added (the increase in value of the product to customers added at various stages in the production and distribution systems).
2. Canada, and Canadian business, has no choice but to meet the challenges of global industrial restructuring in a wide range of areas such as R & D, education and training, competition policy, cost of capital, transportation and communication services, industrial and regional development policies, and interprovincial barriers to trade.
3. Canada must attract more investment in plants that further process our natural resources. Such investment will lead to productivity growth, increased competitiveness, and greater employment opportunities.
4. Canadian direct investment abroad is a critical element in globalization. Businesspeople must be willing to invest money in operations outside of Canada.
5. Federal and provincial governments must "think globally" when developing programs and policies. Governments must also be aware of the trend to globalization and encourage business to react appropriately.
6. New geographical dimensions of trade and investment are emerging that have to be recognized. Events and trends around the world cannot be ignored.[4]

FREER TRADE WITHIN NORTH AMERICA

Canada and the United States have long been major trading partners. This relationship was further enhanced with the signing of the Canada-U.S. Free Trade Agreement (FTA) which took effect January 1, 1989. The FTA eliminates tariffs on manufactured goods by 1998. As Canadian industry is generally at a disadvantage, these tariff reductions are being phased in over ten years to allow Canadian producers to adjust.

The FTA was replaced on January 1, 1994, when the North American Free Trade Agreement (NAFTA) came into effect. The implementation of NAFTA changes many aspects of Canadian business dealings with the United States and Mexico and improves some aspects of the FTA. Some of highlights of the NAFTA which will impact Canadian business are outlined in Table 21-3.

While all elements of the FTA remain intact, the NAFTA preserves, expands and strengthens the gains Canada made in that agreement. Some of the key improvements include: clearer and more precise rules of origin which will narrow the scope in disputes; expanded access to the U.S. market for textiles and apparel; and the addition of intellectual property rights to protect work and inventions of Canadian creators, inventors and researchers. The Global Management insert, "Hyd-Mech Saws Ltd.," illustrates one Canadian businessperson's attitude to NAFTA and the benefits it provides.

TABLE 21-3 THE NORTH AMERICAN FREE TRADE AGREEMENT (NAFTA).

Some highlights of the many ways in which the NAFTA will impact Canadian business are:

Tariff Reductions
There are thousands of tariffs affected by the NAFTA, and exporters are advised to consult the Tariff Schedules for specific guidance. Among the Mexican tariffs eliminated as of January 1, 1994: aircraft parts, radar and navigational equipment; most fresh and frozen fish, and most dried and smoked fish and many shellfish, including crabs; sulphur, aluminum oxide and hydroxide, carboxylic acids, nitrogen function compounds, sulphates. Tariffs on passenger cars and light trucks are reduced by 50 percent immediately.

Government Procurement
For the first time, government procured services in the U.S. and Mexico will be open to Canadian suppliers. In the U.S. alone, the services market is approximately U.S.$30 billion per year. Among new opportunities created by this provision is access to construction contracts procured by the U.S. Army Corps of Engineers. In Mexico, NAFTA opens access to, among other things, contracts procured by PEMEX, the state-owned oil company, and CFE, the state-owned electricity company.

Investment
All investors from the NAFTA countries are to be treated equally; investment restrictions in Mexico will be reduced in numerous sectors, including autos, mining, agriculture, fishing, financial services, transportation and most manufacturing.

Transportation Services
Opening up the trucking of cargo between the United States and Mexico (over a six-year period) will ease shipment of goods by land across borders throughout North America. Canadian truckers will be able to pick up loads in the U.S., ship them into Mexico, and return bearing goods for both U.S. and Canadian destinations.

Telecommunications
Mexican trade barriers to the provision of enhanced services (e.g., advanced data processing) are eliminated. NAFTA guarantees access to contracts offered by government-operated telecommunications services in Mexico, in a market expected to grow by 42 percent before the end of the decade.

Financial Services
Access to Mexico's financial markets, previously closed, will be opened over time to Canadian and U.S. financial institutions. Firms will be able to open wholly owned subsidiaries in Mexico; while these will initially be subject to market-share limitations, these will disappear by the year 2000.

Temporary Entry
Business people will find it easier to gain temporary entry to any NAFTA country.

THE GENERAL AGREEMENT ON TARIFFS AND TRADE (GATT)

The General Agreement on Tariffs and Trade (GATT) is a multinational treaty subscribed to by over 90 countries, which together account for more than four-fifths of world trade. GATT delineates rules for international trade and its primary objective is to liberalize world trade so that economic growth and development is encouraged.

After seven years of negotiations another version of the treaty was agreed to in December 1993. Such a treaty has many implications for Canadian businesses involved in international trade, and managers must keep themselves informed of changes.

GLOBAL MANAGEMENT

HYD-MECH SAWS LTD.

"It's another culture down there," says Ian Tatham of Mexico. "You do business differently in the southern United States—Georgia or Tennessee—than you do in Chicago, and Mexico is that much more different again."

Tatham is President of Hyd-Mech Saws Ltd., a medium-sized business in Woodstock, near London, Ontario. The company, whose claims to fame include having cut the roof of the Skydome, was founded as a family business by Stan Jasinski in 1977, operating out of garages. It has grown to occupy 100 000 square feet of manufacturing space with about 75 workers. Overall sales are now in the $7 million ballpark, and Tatham estimates that "about 80%" of sales are exports.

The product is a band saw whose applications make it valuable in the aerospace and automotive industries. "There's lots of competition, but we make a heavy duty product at a good price; it's easy to run; it's adaptable, which is a big part of how we happened to get the Skydome contract; and it's easy to get parts—our customers can get parts anywhere, not only from us."

Hyd-Mech sold its first saws in the United States in 1983. "We distribute in the U.S. through a group of about 100 machine-tool dealers, and our sales in the States went from $4 million to $6 million in 1992."

"We manufacture in large runs, which allows us the economies of scale. We don't sell a high-price product: our profits are driven by volume."

Hyd-Mech is a relatively recent entrant to the Mexican market. After trade shows in 1992 in Monterrey, they had sales of about $150 000. Tatham engaged a Mexican sales representative, Juan Cardenas, whom he had met previously in Canada. Cardenas, an engineering graduate from a Louisiana university, had worked here in the machine tool industry before returning to Mexico to establish a company to help Canadian businesses in Mexico.

"The first trade show I went to was the Canada Expo. That's what really got things started. Juan had been kind of interested in us, but non-committal, until he saw the response to the product at that show, and he immediately signed on to our team."

Hyd-Mech is well-placed to move into Mexico. "We have a plant in Houston that is basically a service depot and spare parts arm—we felt we should have an identity in the community we serve, and the vast majority of our sales are in the States. It will help us produce and distribute more easily for the Mexican market." ▲

The effects of the new GATT are far reaching, but some of the main influences are:

- Agricultural Industries—Import barriers, such as bans and quotas, are to be gradually replaced by tariffs, and subsidies to farmers and exporters reduced.
- Manufacturing Industries—Subsidies to boost exports will not be allowed, but subsidies will be allowed that help poor regions or promote research.
- Textiles and Apparel Industries—Quotas on clothing imports are to be phased out over ten years.
- Intellectual Property Protection—Computer programs, songs, films, books and industrial designs will be better protected with patents, trademarks, and copyrights for 20 years.

Canadian exports, for example, pulp and paper and wood products, will face lower tariffs in many markets. On the other hand, Canadian producers will face greater competition from imports as Canada's trade barriers are reduced. For Canadian managers, the GATT represents challenges in the form of opportunities for some and threats for others.

European Union

The European Community 1992 (EC 1992) symbolized the goal of the economic integration of 12 nations: Belgium, Denmark, France, West Germany, Greece, Ireland, Italy, Luxembourg, the Netherlands, Portugal, Spain, and the United Kingdom. The EC 1992 comprises 320 million people, compared to the U.S.'s 250 million and Japan's 120 million, and thus has become a strong trading block.

EC 1992 is based on the following:

1. The removal of barriers through about 300 legislative actions to create one internal market allowing for the free movement of goods, services, people, and capital.
2. The standardization and harmonization of national laws and regulations so that they no longer interfere with the free trade of goods and services within the community.
3. The opening of government purchases to all companies within the community.
4. Companies free to develop cooperative arrangements with companies in other member states allowing industry to organize on a large scale.
5. An attempt to harmonize consumer sales and excise tax rates.[5]

In 1994, the EC gained new members and became known as the European Union (EU). Sweden Finland, and Austria have agreed to join and negotiations are underway with Norway. With 16 members, the EU would have a population of 375 million which would be larger than the number representing the North American Free Trade Agreement linking Canada, Mexico and the United States.

Although this EU forms one market, cultural distinctions will continue, nine languages will be spoken, a common currency is unlikely, and different taxation policies will remain. National identities and national preferences or tastes will not be obliterated. For example, British consumers will still prefer front-loading washing machines while French consumers will continue to like top-loading machines.

Many challenges for Canadian business emerge from this new trade block. The business enterprises within the EU that survive will be more efficient, more aggressive and more likely to compete around the world, including in Canada. It has become more difficult for Canadian enterprises to export to the EU unless they are already established in Europe, as there is protection for EU enterprises from "outsiders."

Canadian enterprises that do export to the EU or have plants or branches there must learn about the different markets within the EU and understand the new dynamics of EU, particularly the competitive situation. Competing in the EU has become different from doing business in North America. Moreover, differing competitive environments between some member countries remain. Canadians need to use a variety of approaches to market in the EU, from exports to licensing agreements to types of strategic alliances depending upon which part of the EU is involved.

The Asian Countries

This trading block is comprised of four units: (1) Japan as a major industrialized nation; (2) the newly industrialized countries (NICs) Hong Kong, South Korea, Singapore, and Taiwan; (3) the emerging NICs of Indonesia, Malaysia, Thailand, and the Philippines; and (4) mainland China.

Much has been written about Japanese business and how it operates.[6] Japanese enterprises have been very successful at exporting manufactured goods around the world, and have made huge inroads into Canadian markets. Japanese businesses have major investments in Canadian business including such direct investment as ownership of pulp and paper mills in Alberta and automobile plants in Ontario.

Japanese portfolio investment, which includes holdings of federal and provincial bonds, and corporate bonds and stocks, was estimated to be about $40 billion in 1988[7] and has increased every year since.

Canadian business enterprises have been most successful at selling Japan commodity goods such as pulp and paper, coal, and iron ore. Little progress has been made at selling manufactured and high-technology goods. Part of the problem is Japan's protectionist policies towards its domestic market, but others suggest that Canadian businesspeople fail in their business dealings because they don't understand cultural practices. The Global Management insert "Advice about the Conducting of Business and Behaviour in Japan" illustrates how important cultural practices of another country can be when conducting business internationally.

The newly emerging industrialized nations present another challenge for Canadian business. Enterprises in these nations are producing consumer goods, such as clothing and electronics, at much lower costs than can be done in Canada. Some Canadian companies have products produced in these countries and then sent to Canada for assembly.

Mainland China is a huge market that is experiencing change. Formerly, Canada sold large amounts of grain to China but recently this market has been lost to other grain producers. With the unstable political situation in China, Canadian businesspeople are not sure how involved they should become in this market.

DEVELOPING COUNTRIES

Canadian business cannot ignore developing countries, or less developed countries (LDCs), as future markets. Approximately 77 percent of the world's population lives in such countries; about 142 of them exist, principally in South America, Africa, and Asia. These countries are buyers, suppliers, competitors and capital users and are

GLOBAL MANAGEMENT

ADVICE ABOUT THE CONDUCTING OF BUSINESS AND BEHAVIOUR IN JAPAN

A manager's knowledge of culture and practice when negotiating business in other countries might be critical to success. The following advice might be useful to a Canadian businessperson visiting Japan:

1. Many Japanese find it difficult to say no, but instead indicate that "your request might be hard to fulfill." If a definite answer is not received, the matter should be dropped. Do not be aggressive in making a point or pressing for an answer. A hint of aggression would most likely kill the deal. Have patience!
2. Be alert to hesitation and allow for silence as it indicates productive thought. Use apologies liberally and remember that body language is as important as words.
3. Canadian managers are often taught to make eye contact. The Japanese consider it offensive to maintain a high degree of eye contact. Looking down occasionally is a sign of humility.
4. When meeting to discuss business, it is sometimes appropriate to bring a gift. Present gifts (and business cards) formally, with two hands. Scotch whisky is considered an excellent and respected gift as it is very expensive in Japan. Note also that it is considered rude not to wrap gifts. Other appropriate gifts are items with company logos and products relating to Canada (e.g., Canadian wines).
5. If staying at a Japanese *ryokan*, or traditional inn, certain etiquette is followed: when having tea or dining, men sit cross-legged on the floor, while women kneel and sit on their heels; do not wear toilet slippers outside the toilet; blowing your nose at the table is taboo as you are expected to leave the dining area (appropriate anywhere in Japan); and tipping is not customary in Japan. ▲

TVX Gold Inc. of Toronto is a large producer of precious metals in Brazil and Chile. In 1989, the company produced 79 000 ounces and has increased production since. Canadians have acquired expertise in mining and use this expertise to exploit mineral deposits in developing countries.

becoming increasingly important players in international business, accounting for about 25 percent of the world's imports and 28 percent of exports. Doing business in these Third World nations presents some special challenges for Canadian businesspeople, including:

1. Many of these countries conduct business in diverse ways. Different practices may be followed in government relations, competitive analysis, employee training and retention, organizational structures, marketing, production technology management, and financial strategies.
2. Environmental factors—economic, political, cultural, and demographic—must be viewed in the context of the native country, rather than that of Canada.
3. Relations between business and government are a key, and governments and bureaucrats must be approached with local practices and customs in mind. In some countries, political corruption may exist, making dealings with government more sensitive.
4. A country may experience inflation, currency devaluation, and a shortage of capital, and managers of operations in such countries must plan for these possibilities even though they are largely beyond their control.
5. Managers have to learn to cope with difficulties associated with technology transfer, technology choice and adaptation, and shortages of materials and skilled workers. Local conditions may prevent the effective use of some technology. For example, unreliable electricity supplies hamper the use of some electronic equipment.
6. Cross-cultural understanding is essential as it affects everything, including marketing research and interpersonal exchanges. For example, questions on market surveys must be worded differently in other countries than in Canada as English translations are not always suitable. In some cultures, eye contact is avoided, something quite different than Canadian practice.[8]

THE FORMER COMMUNIST COUNTRIES

With the emergence of more market-based economic systems in many Eastern European countries and the republics emerging from the Soviet Union, Canadian business may have opportunities to conduct more trade with, or to invest in, business enterprises in these areas. One of the first Canadian enterprises to operate a business in the Soviet Union was McDonald's of Canada, which operates a fast food outlet in Moscow.

Glasnost and *perestroika* have led to the demise of the "socialist planned economy" of the Soviet Union. The progress, and the form, of the economic liberalization in that region are not clear, and many pros and cons face the Canadian enterprise that wishes to do business there.[9] Canadian companies may still encounter bureaucratic red tape and political instability.

Doing business in Eastern Europe is also a challenge.[10] Not all the communist systems are changing at the same rate. East Germany is now integrated with West Germany, and Poland and Hungary are introducing market mechanisms, but other countries are not as progressive.

The globalization of business presents many challenges for Canadian enterprises, no matter where in the world they are doing business. The globalization of business has put a focus on "competitiveness." This concept was discussed in Chapter 3, but is mentioned here to reinforce its importance to Canadian business as it attempts to respond to the challenges of world markets.

CANADIAN COMPETITIVENESS IN WORLD MARKETS

Politicians, ambassadors, financial writers, and trade associations, to name a few, have pointed out Canada's weaknesses in international management.

A decline in Canada's share of world trade indicates that our products are not obtaining the markets they should. The lack of R & D by enterprises reduces the availability of innovative products, and high-technology imports surpass exports, meaning that we rely on others for technological innovation. Canadian labour costs are rising more quickly than elsewhere and Canadian companies do not commit sufficient resources to job training and education. Governments are not much help either. Barriers to trade between provinces exist, and patent issuance takes too long. Some critics even claim that Canada lacks a competitive culture, that is, the attitudes and beliefs necessary in a market system where business faces many other sellers and managers are motivated by the possibility of achieving profits. It is important to note that Canadian businesspeople cannot directly influence all the weaknesses, but they do contribute to the weakened position of Canadian business as it confronts world competition.

In addition to the measures of Canadian competitiveness discussed in Chapter 3, we should also consider the competitiveness of nations assessed in Michael Porter of the Harvard Business School in his book *The Competitive Advantage of Nations.* He identified the following four elements of competitive advantage that reinforce each other:

1. *Firm Strategy, Structure, and Rivalry* The conditions under which companies are created, organized, and arranged, the number of companies in an industry, the intensity of competition, and the extent of public versus private ownership.
2. *Factor Conditions* The nation's position in factors of production such as skilled labour, natural resources, education, and wage rates.
3. *Demand Conditions* The nature of home-market demand for the industry's product or service, and the sophistication of consumers and the media exposure of products.
4. *Related and Supporting Industries* The presence or absence of supplier industries and other related industries that are internationally competitive.[11]

The four elements and their interrelatedness are shown in Figure 21-2. Porter did not study Canada's competitiveness although he has since been hired by the Canadian government to carry out such an assessment. The report, "Canada at the Crossroads: The Reality of a New Competitive Environment" was released in October 1991. It is difficult to summarize the report but brief mention will be made of Porter's assessment of Canadian competitiveness according to his four determinants.

With regard to "Firm Strategy, Structure and Rivalry," the report stated that surveys of Canadian attitudes toward competition and risk reflect a greater emphasis on security, and that static, cost-based strategies are used in many industries because of factor (resource) abundance. Strategies in many industries were inward-looking with 70 percent of Canadian manufacturers not serving export markets. This insular orientation could be traced to a number of characteristics of the Canadian market: traditionally high tariffs that sheltered Canadian firms; weak domestic rivalry; high levels of corporate concentration, historically weak competition laws, and interprovincial trade barriers.

Canada ranked quite well in basic factors such as natural resources, climate and unskilled and semiskilled labour. In particular, Canada's physical resources are a significant source of international competitive advantage. Advanced factors which are developed through sustained and sophisticated investment in both human and physical capital are much weaker. There are problems with Canada's educational system,

FIGURE 21-2 THE DETERMINANTS OF NATIONAL COMPETITIVE ADVANTAGE.

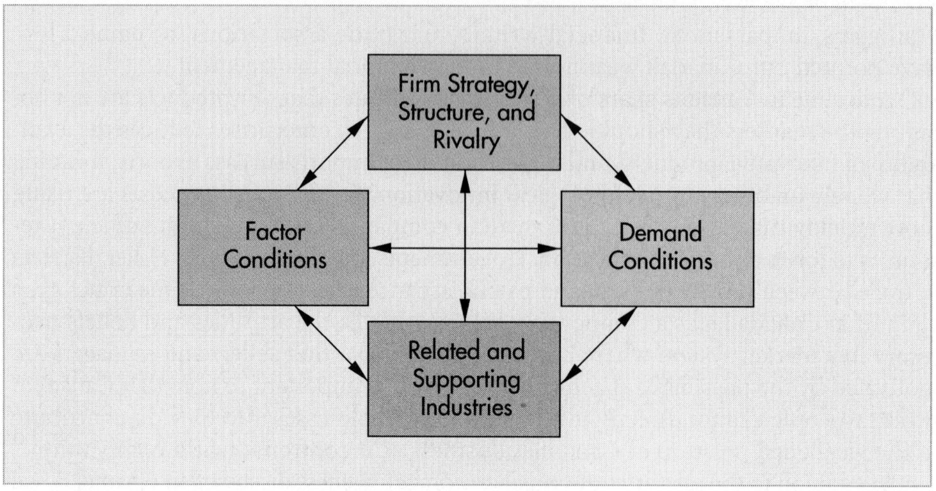

shortages of skilled labour in some occupations, and declining enrolment in the science and engineering disciplines. Canada's capital market and financial system are adequate but the cost of capital has been a problem.

In his studies of competitive advantage in various countries, Porter found that if companies are to gain competitive advantage it is important to have demanding buyers for their products or sources in the domestic market. In Canada, he found that demand conditions have not put strong pressure on companies to innovate, upgrade or anticipate international needs. Apparently Canadian consumers are rarely at the leading edge in demanding innovative consumer goods and are reluctant to voice complaints or to utilize advocacy agencies to pressure companies to improve.

Lastly, Canada's industry clusters are usually narrow and shallow reflecting a very limited presence of indigenous related and supporting industries. Such key inputs as machinery and equipment are purchased from foreign suppliers. The reasons for this include: the tendency for foreign-owned firms to source firms abroad; a high degree of internal integration and to obtain their own supply capabilities; government policies that spread industrial development across the country rather than concentrating it; and underdeveloped linkages among the other determinants of competitive advantage.

Porter concluded that Canadian business was ill-equipped for the future, that the comfortable insularity of the old order would have to change, systemic barriers to change must be removed, and a new vision for the Canadian economy is needed.[12]

Overall, globalization of world business means that Canadians will not find managing in this environment easy (see the Global Management insert entitled "Canadian Retailers Fail in the U.S. Markets").

CORPORATE ORGANIZATION IN THE GLOBAL MARKET

LEARNING OBJECTIVE 7

Describe the main forms of organization used by corporations operating internationally.

In the previous section, the dimensions of managing globally or becoming an "international" business enterprise were outlined. Few businesses start out as "international" enterprises; instead they begin as suppliers of goods or services within a local area. Table 21-4 provides an explanation of how an enterprise becomes international by progressing through four degrees or stages. Enterprises at the first degree of internationalization are passively involved in foreign markets by filling orders but not

GLOBAL MANAGEMENT

CANADIAN RETAILERS FAIL IN THE U.S. MARKET

Some very successful Canadian retailers have had a difficult time being as successful in the U.S. One explanation for the failure of Canadians to do well in the U.S. has been that Canadian retailers did not understand the intensity of competition in the U.S. market.

IMASCO LTD.

Imasco, owner of the successful Shoppers Drug Mart chain, has been unsuccessful in the drug store market in the U.S. In 1984, it purchased Peoples Drug Stores Inc. for $400 million and spent more money expanding it from a group of 575 stores to a chain of more than 800 stores in 13 states. The chain was not performing well and in 1987 a turnaround plan was initiated. Peoples lost $22.5 million in 1987, and $8.3 million in 1988, but made a profit of $8 million in 1989. This performance was not good enough for Imasco, and over 300 stores were sold in 1988-1989, and the remaining 400 stores sold in 1990.

CANADIAN TIRE CORPORATION LIMITED

In 1981, Canadian Tire acquired White Stores Inc. in Texas in an attempt to expand internationally. The stores were converted to the "Canadian Tire" format but many difficulties were experienced. The stores didn't perform well and adversely affected the financial results of the parent company. During 1985 and 1986, the White's operations were disposed of after Canadian Tire had experienced losses of $250 000 000. The company is still seeking to expand to the U.S. but is now being very cautious.

DYLEX LIMITED

Dylex operates several well known men's and women's wear and family stores in Canada, including: Tip Top, Harry Rosen, Big Steel Man, Fairweather, Braemar, Susy Shier, Bi-Way, and Thrifty's. In 1989, Dylex stores in the U.S. had sales of almost $400 million from Foxmoor Specialty Stores (junior women's clothing), Wet Seal (young women's fashion chain), NBO Stores (low priced men's apparel), and Club International (men's wear chain). In 1987, Dylex wrote off its $118 042 000 investment in Brooks Fashion Stores (a 721 store U.S. chain selling medium-range clothing to young women). It has closed a U.S. manufacturing subsidy and sold its interest in another. In 1989, Dylex announced that 225 Foxmoor stores had been sold and in January 1990, Foxmoor filed for protection under the U.S. bankruptcy code. ▲

TABLE 21-4 FOUR DEGREES OF INTERNATIONALIZATION.

	First-Degree Internationalization	Second-Degree Internationalization	Third-Degree Internationalization	Fourth-Degree Internationalization
Nature of contact with foreign markets	Indirect, passive	Direct, active	Direct, active	Direct, active
Locus of international operations	Domestic	Domestic	Domestic and international	Domestic and international
Orientation of company	Domestic	Domestic	Partially domestic	Multinational (domestic operations viewed as part of the whole)
Type of international activity	Foreign trade of goods and services	Foreign trade of goods and services	Foreign trade, foreign assistance contracts, foreign direct investment	Foreign trade, foreign assistance contracts, foreign direct investment
Organizational structure	Traditional domestic	International department	International division	Global structure

aggressively selling abroad. More direct contact with foreign customers takes place in the second degree of internationalization. Managers travel abroad but no employees are based in foreign countries. An international department is usually established at home office to handle imports or exports. In the third degree, foreign business activity is actively pursued with an international division and operations established abroad. The fourth degree of internationalization is the focus of discussion in this section. An enterprise in this category is now referred to as a multinational, or having a global structure and are all very large in size. In addition to these multinational corporations, this section will discuss "*Keiretsu*," the organization utilized by the Japanese so successfully; and the trend to borderless or transnational business organizations.

The Largest Global Enterprises

LEARNING OBJECTIVE 8

Discuss the trend towards large corporate organizations, and define the borderless corporation.

Large businesses operating internationally are becoming an increasing influence on the world economy. According to *Fortune* magazine,[13] 167 of the 500 world's largest corporations in 1990 were from the United States, 111 from Japan, 43 from Britain, and 32 from West Germany. Only 13 were from Canada. Table 21-5 lists the world's 10 largest and Canada's 10 largest corporations from the *Fortune* 500 listing. Canadian Pacific, the largest Canadian corporation, ranks 134th with sales of $9306.3 million compared with General Motors, the world's largest company, with sales of $126 974.3 million. Much the same situation exists with commercial banks. The largest commercial bank is Dailihi Kangyo Bank of Japan with assets of $413 214.4 million while the largest Canadian bank, The Royal Bank of Canada, ranks 46th with assets of $97 657.4 million. Only a few of these 500 world-class corporations are Canadian (2.5 percent) and the Canadian corporations are relatively small. Many argue that this fact does not position Canada very well in a global market.

Multinational Corporations

multinational corporation (MNC)

The most commonly used term for enterprises in the fourth degree of internationalization is the **multinational corporation** (MNC). It is defined as a business enterprise that controls assets, factories, mines, sales offices and the like operated either as branch offices or affiliates in two or more foreign countries. MNCs are extremely large organizations with sales in the billions of dollars. Six hundred MNCs accounted for about one-quarter of the activity in the world's market economies. These enterprises are in the forefront of economic trends and technological development and are able to adapt quickly to new conditions.

The headquarters of these enterprises are primarily located in developed countries, referred to as the "home" country. More than half of the MNCs are headquartered in the United States, and most of the others in countries such as the United Kingdom, France, Germany, Holland, and Japan. The "host" countries, that is, countries where the MNC's branches and affiliates are located, are other developed and developing countries.

Table 21-5 compares the size of Canada's largest corporations to the world's. Canadian MNCs are relatively small and must compete with very large corporations from other countries. Other well-known Canadian MNCs include: Moore Corporation, a manufacturer of business forms and related products; Bata Shoe Co., a footwear manufacturer operating in almost 100 countries; and McCain Foods Ltd., a food processor operating around the world. The Global Management "Profile of a Canadian MNC" describes the activities of one Canadian company.

TABLE 21-5 THE WORLD'S AND CANADA'S TEN LARGEST CORPORATIONS, 1993.

World Rank	World's Largest Corporations	Market Value* U.S. ($ millions)	World Rank	Canada's Largest Corporations	Market Value* U.S. ($ millions)
1.	Nippon Telegraph & Telephone (Japan)	140 521	172	Seagram	10 795
2.	American Telephone & Telegraph (U.S.)	82 400	177	BCE (Bell Canada Enterprises)	10 682
3.	Royal Dutch/Shell Group (Neth./Britain)	81 351	234	Northern Telecom	8 960
4.	Exxon (U.S.)	81 351	294	Imperial Oil	7 217
5.	General Electric (U.S.)	79 341	305	Royal Bank of Canada	7 036
6.	Mitsubishi Bank (Japan)	73 564	308	Thomson	6 991
7.	Sumitomo Bank (Japan)	65 970	337	American Barrick Resources	6 557
8.	Wal-Mart Stores (U.S.)	64 065	423	Canadian Pacific	5 298
9.	Industrial Bank of Japan (Japan)	63 215	448	Bank of Montreal	5 060
10.	Sanwa Bank (Japan)	61 189	461	Canadian Imperial Bank of Commerce	4 929

*Market value: Share price on May 31, 1993, multiplied by latest available number of shares outstanding translated into U.S. dollars.
Note: Changes in currency exchange rates might alter the size of the corporations listed.

GLOBAL MANAGEMENT

PROFILE OF A CANADIAN MNC

Bombardier Inc., Montreal, operates in four areas of activity: transportation equipment; aerospace and defence; motorized consumer products; and financial and real estate services. It has production facilities in Canada, United States, Mexico, Austria, Belgium, Finland, France, and United Kingdom and has 34 000 employees. It markets products on five continents, with a high concentration in North America and Europe, and nearly 90 percent of its $4 448 000 000 sales are made in markets outside Canada.

Bombardier's mission is to be a leader in the countries where it operates and to be recognized internationally as a world-class designer, manufacturer and distributor of transportation equipment and other products and services related to its technology.

Examples of Bombardier's activities outside of Canada include:

United States

- transportation equipment such as subway cars, light rail vehicles, and shuttle train cars for the English Channel tunnel.
- line of Learjet business aircraft
- dealer inventory financing in a broad range of industries; aircraft and industrial equipment financing.

Mexico

- subway cars, light rail vehicles, freight train cars

Belgium

- passenger rail cars, locomotives and freight cars, subway cars, light rail vehicles.

France

- subway cars, bilevel self-propelled commuter cars, turbotrains.

United Kingdom

- body structures for mainline and underground locomotives and for rail coaches; road tankers, railway wagons.
- military trainer and transport aircraft.

Austria

- engines for snowmobiles, watercraft, and motorcycles, ultra-light aircraft.

Finland

- snowmobiles and all-purpose tracked vehicles. ▲

Bata Ltd., headquartered in Toronto, is a Canadian multinational corporation considered to be the world's preeminent shoe manufacturer and retailer. Bata manufactures almost one million pairs of shoes daily in plants in 65 countries, owns more that 6000 retail shoe stores in 70 countries, and has 70 000 employees worldwide.

ADVANTAGES OF THE MULTINATIONAL CORPORATION

MNCs have encouraged economic growth in many areas of the world by providing financing, technological expertise, and the managerial know-how to operate industry. Sometimes financing is not available locally and the MNCs provide funds from other sectors of their operations. MNCs bring technological expertise to less developed areas. The management capabilities of MNCs are also utilized to organize and operate business enterprises in parts of the world other than the corporation's home country.

Since MNCs operate in many parts of the world, they have access to different markets and can arrange for the distribution of goods produced in one country through their branches or affiliates in other countries. By facilitating international trade, the transfer of capital, technology, and managerial know how, MNCs further international economic development and cooperation.

A multinational organization allows managers to focus corporate activities by geographical area. Units of the MNC are established in several countries and perform production and marketing activities that contribute to the performance of the parent company. Such an arrangement allows managers to transfer technology to units that require it. Funds generated by profitable units can be used to finance newly established units or to subsidize necessary unprofitable units. This type of organization enables managers to delegate authority for operations to units enabling them to respond to local conditions while at the same time maintaining accountability and enabling unit activities to be coordinated.

CHALLENGES OF MANAGING THE MULTINATIONAL CORPORATION

Managers of multinational corporations face many challenges, but the greatest is the need to respond to criticisms made of MNCs. These criticisms include the MNC's alleged nonallegiance to the host country, transferring profits from the host country, failing to promote research and development activities, exporting jobs by not producing finished products, and not hiring local personnel. The managers in the head office find it difficult to control and coordinate the activities of the branches located in foreign countries. The managers sent to the foreign country must cope with different cultural, social, and economic environments and may be restricted in many ways, for example, by local laws and religious practices.

The criticisms of MNCs have not gone unnoticed. The United Nations has developed a code of conduct and the Organization for Economic Cooperation and Development (OECD) has formulated guidelines to influence the behaviour of MNCs. The contents of these codes are listed in Table 21-6 and provide guidelines for MNCs and their managers as they supervise operations in foreign countries.

The negative attitudes towards MNCs may be changing. A 1988 United Nations Centre on Transnational Corporations report found that more countries were welcoming MNCs as a source of economic development and growth. The report stated, "There is a growing awareness, in countries at all levels of development and in both market and centrally planned economies, that many public goals can best be achieved in a decentralized fashion, through the operation of market forces."[14] It is not clear how long this view toward MNCs will last.

The ethics associated with international business are of considerable concern to managers. In some countries, bribes are expected and common practice, and determining what is right in these situations is rarely simple. Many corporations have codes of conduct or ethics of their own that provide some guide to managers. It is important that top executives clearly support these codes so as not to send the wrong message to employees. Apparently corruption is widespread in many parts of the world and some businespersons claim that it is necessary to pay bribes in order to obtain contracts and conduct business. As such practice is not common in Canada, Canadian managers operating in other parts of the world find the ethics of international business challenging.[15]

TABLE 21-6 CONTENTS OF CODES OF CONDUCT FOR MULTINATIONAL CORPORATIONS.

The topics covered by the United Nations Code of Conduct on Transnational Corporations and the OECD Guidelines for Multinational Enterprise include:

Political Factors

MNCs must respect the national sovereignty and observance of domestic laws, regulations and administrative practices. Also, enterprises will not interfere (illegally) in the internal affairs of the countries in which they operate, or with intergovernmental relations.

Sociocultural Objectives and Values

MNCs should respect the social and cultural objectives, values, and traditions of the countries in which they operate.

Disclosure of Information

Information about operations should be available, but not to the extent that business confidentiality is violated.

Competition

Activities should not be undertaken that adversely affect competition by abusing a dominant position of market power.

Financing

Enterprise financing should be arranged to consider national balance of payments and credit policies, and cooperate in the collection of taxes.

Employment and Industrial Relations

Enterprises should respect the right of their employees to join trade unions, observe standards of employment and industrial relations, train persons from the local labour force, and be sensitive to layoffs and closures. MNCs should respect human rights and fundamental freedoms of the citizens.

Science and Technology

MNCs must cooperate with the scientific and technological policies of countries in which they operate and grant licenses for the use of industrial property rights under reasonable terms.

Corrupt Practices

MNCs shall refrain from offering, promising or giving of any payment, gift or other advantage to the benefit of a public official.

Environmental Protection

MNCs shall carry out their activities in accordance with national laws, regulations, administrative practices and policies relating to the preservation of the environment of the countries in which they operate and with due regard to relevant international standards.

Japan's Keiretsu Companies

keiretsu

Canadian business enterprises face a formidable challenge when competing with the ***keiretsu*** companies of Japan.[16] These are loosely affiliated groups of companies in industry and banking and can encompass hundreds of companies. Of the 1612 companies in the Tokyo stock exchange, 1100 belong to a *keiretsu* and the six major *keiretsu* companies account for 78 percent of the total capitalization of the exchange. The Mitsubishi *keiretsu* alone accounts for 11 percent of the capitalization. The main features of a *keiretsu* are:

1. The existence of cross-shareholdings, that is, countries owning shares in each other, but without any company dominating ownership.
2. The formation of a president's club in which top executives meet regularly to exchange information.
3. Joint investment among member companies.
4. Financing arrangements are provided by *keiretsu* member banks to member companies.
5. Extensive buying and selling relationships exist among member companies.

Sometimes *keiretsu* companies are referred to as cartels, that is, a group of companies behaving as a monopoly. They are hostile to outsiders, especially to foreign enterprises. They are very demanding of new recruits, they extract special deals or cheap loans, and demand obedience from all members. Their philosophy towards business differs from that of Western companies. Western multinationals emphasize profits and shareholders are the most powerful stakeholders. With *keiretsu* companies, profits and the interests of shareholders are subordinated to long-range goals.

It is important to appreciate the impact this form of corporate capitalism has over Canadian enterprises that usually operate as individual corporations. The existence of *keiretsu* companies makes it difficult for a Canadian enterprise to enter the Japanese market. They are also strong competitors for other markets. *Keiretsu* companies have focussed on trade and foreign investment in recent years and have advantages in doing so, including the stronger yen, weakened Western companies, and numerous alliances around the world. A *keiretsu* such as Mitsubishi with its familiar three diamond symbol can enter dozens of markets usually financed by *keiretsu* member financial institutions.

The single Canadian enterprise is hard pressed to compete against this type of organizational structure.

The "Borderless" Corporation

borderless corporation

Corporations that operate globally are now being referred to as "borderless," "stateless," and "transnational" corporations rather than as multinational corporations. The **borderless corporation** functions globally with little recognition of national boundaries. According to *Business Week,* examples of "stateless" manufacturing corporations would be: Nestle (Switzerland), Philips (Netherlands), Volvo (Sweden), Coca-Cola (U.S.), Seimans (Germany), and Nissan (Japan).[17] The only Canadian example of such a corporation is Northern Telecom. Stateless corporations are also coming into existence in service industries, for example: Reuters (Britain), McDonald's (U.S.) and American Express (U.S.). The characteristics of the borderless or stateless corporation are listed in Table 21-7.

TABLE 21-7 CHARACTERISTICS OF THE STATELESS CORPORATION.

1. Global company with no clear nationality.
2. International ownership and international management.
3. International operations: specializes in global products.
4. Very mobile across international borders.
5. Headquarters of convenience.
6. No allegiance to a country or region.
7. Principal allegiance is to shareholders and to senior management.
8. Will locate anywhere where profits can be maximized.
9. Seeks most favourable monetary and fiscal zones.
10. Seeks areas with minimum environmental legislation.
11. Seeks areas with minimum social legislation.
12. Overall behaviour is amoral (neither moral nor immoral).

There are several reasons for this increase in borderless corporations.

1. *Lowering of Trade Barriers* Freer trade is now more likely as tariffs are being reduced and other barriers removed, and corporations are taking advantage of this. In fact, some argue that national trade figures may become obsolete as economies become increasingly interlinked. Governments and national boundaries will become invisible and consumers will be able to make their own choices as tariff and other barriers to trade are reduced.

2. *Trend towards an Interlinked Economy* The economies of the U.S., Europe and Japan are now extensively interlinked. This will grow to include Eastern Europe, the industrialized Asian economies, and parts of North and South America. The ultimate objective of interlinking the economies is the free flow of information, money, goods and services, and people.

3. *International Executives* Today many MNCs are headed by executives who are not citizens of the MNC's home country. It is claimed that executives of the "borderless" corporations will be loyal to the country in which they are located. Personnel systems will be country neutral as they seek the best managers from anywhere in the world.

4. *Global, but with Local Orientation* The borderless corporation will not operate as a federation of overseas subsidiaries, but instead as a portfolio of national companies each responding to its own operating environment. Operations will not be appendages for producing products designed and engineered in the home country. Business activities in other countries will take into consideration local markets but in reality all activities are being orchestrated by the corporation from a global perspective. The concept of headquarters with overseas branches will be banished.

5. *Rethinking Products and Markets* Companies no longer think of products as having a nationality. Instead, the objective will be to develop products that customers will value sufficiently to purchase, not to focus on creating barriers to competitors by seeking government protection. Global product managers will have power over country or regional managers as "borderless" corporations attempt to market worldwide.

6. *Use of Strategic Alliances* There will be less "going it alone" and more sharing of control among corporations who will form some type of alliance. This "co-operative," or "partnership" attitude is quite different from outlooks of the past, especially for North American MNCs. Corporations will search for more partnerships or alliances in the future.

The borderless corporation must have the multinational's flexibility to respond to local market needs, be aware of global competitiveness to capture efficiencies of scale, and have the ability to understand the social and political circumstances in many countries. This will lead to more innovative approaches to doing business. It is not clear how rapidly "borderless" corporations will form and many questions are being raised including: Does it make any difference what a company's nationality is as long as it provides jobs? What national controls will there be over technology? What obligation will there be to adhere to the rules of any country?

The trend to the borderless corporation will challenge much of the conventional thinking about the management functions discussed in this book. New ways of planning will evolve as will new structural forms. The approaches to leading and to controlling operations will have to change. These changes are not clear, but some possibilities are discussed in the following section.

MANAGING INTERNATIONALLY AND THE MANAGEMENT FUNCTIONS

LEARNING OBJECTIVE 9
Relate the task of managing internationally to the management functions of planning, organizing, leading, and controlling.

Managing in the global environment is even more challenging than managing a business enterprise in Canada. The following is a discussion of some of the dynamics confronting managers.

PLANNING

Strategic management is even more important for the international corporation as the scope of operations is broader and the risks are different and most likely greater. Instead of operating in one environment, the enterprise has multiple environments making the assessment of the environment more complex.

Objectives must be set for the international operations generally and for the individual units abroad. Managers will have to design planning systems appropriate for the various units and will have to assist local managers with the planning process.

In general, the planning process becomes more difficult as uncertainty increases as political situations change, cultural practices in different countries are considered, and world currency and commodity markets fluctuate. This situation means the managers must be able to scan and assess the environment even more carefully before they make plans, and they must be able to adjust their plans, and planning processes, in light of changes in a dynamic environment.

ORGANIZING

Many factors will change the approach to departmentation and other structural arrangements in the enterprise as indicated in Table 21-4. But, there are many other aspects of organizing that must be considered including:

1. How much authority should be delegated to the various operations abroad?
2. What are the politics and power struggles that exist, or might exist among the units in various countries?
3. How are the activities of the units coordinated?
4. To what extent will strategic alliances or partnerships be used and how are they set up?
5. How are cultural preferences in various countries incorporated into how an enterprise is organized at different locations?

Another area of challenge is staffing, and is illustrated by the following job advertisement:

> WANTED: Future managers with a global vision, but also sensitive to local Canadian markets. Fluency in two or more languages is essential, and the ability to quickly learn other languages as necessary is an asset. Must be willing to travel often and relocate frequently. High salary, excellent benefits and incentives package available. Apply to any Canadian company with international operations.

Enterprises involved in global operation will be seeking particular managers and will have to make employment attractive. Some individuals like the adventure of living in foreign countries (see the Global Management insert "The Well-Travelled Executive") while others are reluctant to move across town. It may be difficult to find suitable employees in foreign locations as working practices and expectations differ from those in Canada. The selection and training of local employees may be challenging.

LEADING

Most research on motivation, group dynamics, leadership, and communication has been done in North America and may not be applicable in the cultural and social environment of foreign countries. Managers assigned to locations abroad will most likely have to rethink their approach to managing, a change that may not be easy for some.

GLOBAL MANAGEMENT

THE WELL-TRAVELLED EXECUTIVE

John Akitt believes in management by walking around, but as the globetrotting president of Exxon Chemical International he has a longer way to walk than most.

Based in Brussels for the past four years, the former president of Esso Chemical Canada, a division of Imperial, travels 75 percent of the time. He has just come back from 10 days in Singapore and Bangkok and is about to go to New York. He figures that in the previous month he spent exactly one afternoon in his European office. He also has an office in Connecticut. "The travel is demanding," he says. "But you can't run a business completely by remote control, even in the nineties."

But Akitt admits to enjoying his globetrotting life. "How many people can live in the capital of Europe, travel all over the world, deal with a multitude of cultures and run a very successful business?" he asks. "The diversity of people, business and geography is pretty hard to beat. It's a super job, extremely challenging and stimulating."

Akitt says he was lucky that his job came along when it did, when his four children were grown: "I wouldn't do it with young kids. I wouldn't do it if my wife couldn't travel a lot with me. And I couldn't do it if I weren't in good health."

Despite being constantly on the move, Akitt still thinks of Toronto as home, where he moved from Winnipeg as a student. He joined Imperial in 1956 and 20 years later was appointed executive vice-president of Esso Chemical. This is his second posting to Brussels. He has also been posted to New York twice.

He says the benefits of international assignments and travel are superb for everybody in a family. "Usually it is the parents who are the fearful ones; the kids seem to handle it just fine. They receive an education that is better than it ever could be if they stayed in one place."

John and Anne Akitt's children are now far-flung themselves, launching their own careers. One daughter recently completed an M.B.A. in Switzerland and is working in Barcelona; another teaches English in Rome. One son is working in London, Ont., as a medical representative for a German chemical company; the other is a student at the University of Ottawa.

But one inviolable family tradition is an annual Christmas holiday. In recent years the Akitts have gathered in Singapore, Florida, Brussels, and London.

Akitt says his children have a different perspective on the world as a result of their international exposure and education. "They don't just read, for example, about current events in Europe, they feel the dynamic." ▲

For example, in Canada much emphasis is placed upon individualism, achievement, competition, advancement, and material rewards. These attitudes may not be appropriate for viewing employees in other countries where a more collective view and concern for the community or group is highly valued. Canadians assigned abroad will have to be very sensitive to the leadership styles needed to manage in other cultural and social settings.

CONTROLLING

The controlling process is also difficult to implement in global operations, but its implementation is most likely more important than it is for domestic operations. Less direct control is possible and the various control techniques discussed in Chapter 18 are even more crucial. The variety and number of location of operations makes it increasingly difficult to establish standards applicable to all units, and even with modern technology, the distances involved make observation and data collection formidable.

Operating globally adds another dimension to the management of the business enterprise. The knowledge of planning, organizing, leading, and controlling gained in Parts II, III, IV and V of this textbook are still applicable, but must be adapted to the environment of the particular global operations.

SUMMARY

Managing internationally encompasses the efforts of small businesses selling their products in foreign markets through to the direction of the huge borderless corporations. All Canadians should understand how imperative international trade is in the Canadian economy. Without trade, our standard of living would be lower and many Canadians would not be employed. Canadians are also involved internationally through borderless corporations either as managers or employees.

The first section establishes the importance of trade to Canadians and emphasizes that both goods and services are included in international trade. As soon as a business either starts to sell its products in foreign countries or to purchase products

MEETING THE CHALLENGE

ALEX GRAY AND FREE TRADE

Gray gained some benefits from the Free Trade Agreement, which reduced the tariffs on the round-bar steel that he had to purchase from U.S. mills. As round-bar was a major component of hand tools, this resulted in considerable savings although fluctuations in the dollar sometimes reduced the benefit.

In terms of marketing in the U.S., the American tariffs on Gray's tools were reduced and would disappear by 1995 enabling him to price more competitively. The agreement also allowed Gray easier access to trade shows in the U.S., a key to selling in that market.

However, Gray's American competitors gained easier access to the Canadian market. Fierce competition and the lower demand for tools during the recession kept prices down. Gray countered by providing better service to customers and by introducting labour-saving technology such as computer-assisted design and robotics.

The result is that 40 percent of Gray Tool's production is exported to the U.S. The increased sales in the U.S. have offset declining Canadian sales due to the recession. Gray met the challenge of global competition by deciding that he had to manage internationally if his company was to survive. ▲

from outside Canada, the managers have increased the scope of their activities to an international or global perspective. The section on the dimensions of managing internationally identifies the variety of ways Canadian businesses become involved in international business.

Doing business in a global or world market is not without challenges. Canadian managers must prepare themselves to compete against businesses operating in areas of the world that have formed trading blocks. How effectively and efficiently Canadian managers operate their businesses is critical to determining the competitiveness of our country in world markets.

The global focus in international business has resulted in large business enterprises being established. The most commonly known form is the multinational corporation. Other forms of international business organizations are emerging including Japan's *keiretsu* companies and the borderless corporation, an enterprise that behaves in a global manner without attention to national boundaries.

Canadian managers will be extending what they have learned about the management functions of planning, organizing, leading and controlling to their efforts at managing internationally. Given the importance of trade and the emergence of the global perspective, the future well-being of the Canadian economy will depend to a great degree on the ability of managers to apply their skills to managing internationally.

KEY TERMS

trade (p. 641)
international corporation (p. 644)
licensing agreements (p. 645)
world product mandating (p. 646)
strategic alliances (p. 646)
globalization (p. 648)
multinational corporation (MNC) (p. 658)
keiretsu (p. 662)
borderless corporation (p. 662)

REVIEW QUESTIONS

1. Why is the exporting and importing of goods and services important to Canada and Canadian business?
2. How is trade in services different from trade in goods?
3. How is the government involved in the exporting and importing of goods and services?
4. What are the possible ways that Canadian businesses could be involved in managing from a global perspective?
5. What is product mandating?
6. What is a strategic alliance?
7. What is meant by the globalization of business?
8. What are the major trading blocks emerging in the world?
9. What are the four degrees of internationalization of a business enterprise?
10. What are the advantages and disadvantages of the multinational corporation?
11. What are the reasons for the emergence of the borderless corporation?
12. Are the management functions of planning, organizing, leading and controlling important to managing globally?

DISCUSSION QUESTIONS

1. What can be concluded about Canada's principal exports and imports?
2. Why does the Canadian government sponsor the Canada Export Awards?
3. Why should managers be concerned about the competitiveness of Canada in world markets?

4. Would there be any difference between managing in a European country such as France versus a developing country in Africa?
5. Should we be concerned about the small size of Canada's largest corporations compared to the largest corporations in the world?
6. Is it possible to control multinational corporations or the borderless corporations that some of them are becoming?

EXERCISES

1. List examples of imported services you or your family have used in the past year.
2. If you were a manager responsible for selecting personnel to be sent on international assignments in your company, what qualities, experience, and competencies would you look for in prospective personnel?
3. Assume that you have agreed to accept a two-year assignment in Helsinki, Finland. You are married, and have a six-year-old daughter. What would you do to prepare yourself and your family for this assignment?
4. Obtain a copy of the OECD's or United Nations' codes of conduct for multinational corporations (a reference source is provided in Table 21-6). Outline how the contents of these codes would influence the managers of multinational corporations.
5. Review two current articles on the borderless corporation. (Some references are provided in the endnotes). Identify how multinationals are becoming borderless and prepare a list of such corporations.

MANAGEMENT ON LOCATION

CASE 21-1
TRADE AND TWO CANADIAN CORPORATIONS

The headline, "Trade tribunal supports cuts in textile tariffs," in *The Globe and Mail* on March 24, 1990, was bad news for textile manufacturers but good news for apparel manufacturers. The Canadian International Trade Tribunal (CITT) had decided that tariffs on textiles were too high and recommended a reduction of 26 percent over nine years starting in 1991. The CITT is a federal government agency that decides whether or not foreign goods are being sold in Canada below the cost of production (referred to as dumping) and on the appropriate level of tariffs (duties or charges) on foreign goods imposed by the government. This decision meant that Canadian textile manufacturers would face greater competition from foreign producers, and that Canadian apparel manufacturers would have access to lower-priced textiles with which to produce their clothing. Fabric Creators Inc., a textile manufacturer, and Everyday Clothing Limited, an apparel manufacturer, both of which are located in Cornwall, Ontario are affected by the decision.

Fabric Creators Inc.

Jim Rowland, the president of Fabric Creators, was greatly disturbed by the decision as he would now have to compete with textiles from low-cost countries. He already had to compete with U.S. producers as a result of the Free Trade Agreement which eliminated tariffs on textiles. Rowland was proud of the business that his grandfather had established in 1920. Today, it sold textile products to about 25 clothing manufacturers in the Cornwall, Montreal, and Toronto areas. The CITT decision would most likely lead to a loss of sales and would mean that he would have to lay off some of his 60 employees. Fabric Creators would also have to be more innovative in fabric designs and marketing in order to survive. Located next door to Fabric Creators in the Riverside Industrial Park was Everyday Clothing Limited, a company that viewed CITT's decision quite differently.

Everyday Clothing Limited

Elizabeth Smithers is the owner and general manager of Everyday Clothing which manufactures children's garments for discount retailers across Canada. CITT's decision was good news because Everyday would have access to lower-priced textiles, and the company would be in a better position to compete with U.S. apparel manufacturers across the river in New York state. Although located next door, ...

Everyday Clothing did not purchase any textiles from Fabric Creators as they were too expensive. Instead, Smithers purchased her textiles from firms in Quebec and the Far East. She now felt that she could increase her business as the prices of textiles from foreign sources would be lower. Apparel manufacturing was very labour intensive and Everyday employed 120 people year round. As the cost of labour was rising, Smithers needed to reduce other costs including raw materials.

Smithers and Rowland both belonged to the Cornwall Chamber of Commerce and the local Rotary Club, but had very different feelings about CITT's decision. ▲

QUESTIONS

1. Why did the change in trade policy impact so differently on the two businesses?
2. What can Jim Rowland do now?
3. Could either of the companies have planned for this change in trade policy?

CASE 21-2
INTERNATIONAL EXPANSION

James Cartwright is the marketing manager for communications products for National Systems Limited, a Canadian company based in Halifax with sales in all 10 provinces. Sales revenues are in the area of $210 million annually. National Systems had indicated its intention to expand its marketing efforts to countries other than Canada.

In Canada, the communications products division had a 28 percent market share. Its product competes against products imported from other countries. It is regarded as having one of the better products for the Canadian market.

Issues that Cartwright is considering, in determining whether to enter international markets and how to enter them, include the product he offers, what markets he should attempt to sell, what personnel he can utilize to develop these market opportunities, and what arrangements if any he should make with organizations in potential foreign markets.

Regarding the product, Cartwright knew that the National Systems product competed well in Canada. He wondered whether the same product features and characteristics would be equally well accepted in various foreign markets. He also wondered whether it was necessary to develop new products for each foreign market or whether he should follow an approach of testing and proving his products in Canada and not offering them for sale in other countries until they were proven successful in Canada.

Regarding the market, Cartwright was concerned whether he should attempt to penetrate the United States market right away, or focus on developing the market for his product in developing countries. His major concern about the United States was that competition was fierce. Offsetting this concern was the fact that this very large market was geographically and culturally the most similar to the Canadian market, with which he was most familiar. Regarding markets in developing countries, he felt that the Canadian reputation and the quality of his products were particularly strong points. He would be able to use products that had been tried, tested, and proven in the Canadian market, some of them for a number of years. Cartwright had reports indicating certain cultural and market development problems associated with the sophistication of product use in many of the developing countries.

Another issue was the personnel he had available to develop these markets. He had what he considered to be five key senior marketing people in Canada, along with 15 other people at the level immediately below them. They were all fully engaged in their present jobs and none had any international marketing experience. Cartwright himself had no international marketing expertise other than a two-week seminar he attended on international marketing. One option was to recruit a new graduate from a university program in business administration. His concern in this instance was that the individual would not have sufficient experience to be able to handle the area. Another option was to recruit someone from a major consulting firm which specialized in international marketing. However, this approach would not lead to long-run development of an international marketing team.

Another issue was to decide how to enter different foreign markets. Should they export from plants in Canada? Should they license people to manufacture the product in foreign markets? Should they enter into a joint venture agreement to market the product in these other countries?

There was also the general issue, raised by board of directors of National Systems Limited, of whether or not expansion from the Canadian market was wise. On the one hand, international expansion would mean increases in sales and potential for profit, and the chance to learn about business in other countries. (Many of their domestic competitors were from other countries, and international experience would make it easier for National Systems to compete in the Canadian market.) On the other hand, some of the disadvantages to international expansion were the investment that would be required to develop these markets, the fact that other companies had a considerable lead on National System in the international market, and the fact that they were already doing well and were profitable in serving only the Canadian market. ▲

QUESTIONS

1. Are there other considerations that James Cartwright should take into account in formulating his recommendation about whether to advise National Systems to go into foreign markets?
2. Are there other issues that are important to Cartwright if the company does decide to enter foreign markets?
3. Considering the issues he faces regarding products, markets, personnel, and business arrangements, what are the options available and what are the pros and cons of each option? Where can Cartwright look for information that will be useful to him in addressing these issues?

CHAPTER 22

SOCIAL RESPONSIBILITY AND ETHICS

LEARNING OBJECTIVES

After reading this chapter, you will be able to:

1. State the concerns being expressed by society about the role of business.
2. List the various stakeholders of business and their expectations.
3. Define social responsibility.
4. Name the ways in which corporate social responsibility can be measured.
5. Define business ethics.
6. Identify the sources of ethics among businesses and the influences on management behaviour.
7. List the initiatives that might be taken by business to reinforce ethical behaviour.
8. State how businesses are managing the environmental issue.
9. Describe socially responsible investment.
10. Relate business social responsibility and ethics to the management functions.

MANAGEMENT CHALLENGE

COSMOS BEAUTY PRODUCTS INC.

Rick Boswell is the 45-year-old CEO and chairperson of Cosmos Beauty Products, a cosmetics marketing firm based in Toronto. The company's headquarters are located on the 33rd floor of a Bay Street office building and Cosmos has one plant in King City just north of Toronto. The company focusses on marketing a full range of beauty products for women under the name "Lady Beautiful." The line includes lipsticks, makeup, shampoos, body powders, skin creams, hair dyes, and perfumes. Most of the company's products were produced by subcontractors in Canada and overseas.

Cosmos has sales of over $20 million divided evenly between small booths or stands operated in aisles of shopping centres and office shopping arcades across Canada, and as a supplier of private brand-name cosmetics to drug store chains. Plans included the development of cosmetic boutiques and a line of cosmetics for men.

Bosswell is a B. Comm. graduate who started Cosmos 15 years ago after working for a large cosmetics company. Five years ago shares were sold to the public and the stock was listed on the Toronto Stock Exchange. Cosmos' success is based on the fact that fewer women were purchasing cosmetics from companies that sold door to door such as Avon. Boswell felt that many women still wanted to purchase cosmetics as conveniently as possible, thus Cosmos' location in malls and arcades.

Despite the success of the company, Boswell and his senior managers were meeting to discuss several matters that were affecting sales. In the past year, Cosmos had been confronted with the following incidents:

1. Animal rights groups protested Cosmos' use of animals in product testing.
2. A low ranking had been given to its product in a test of shampoos by an independent consumer group.

...

3. About 5 percent of Cosmos' skin creams were being returned with customers complaining about rashes.
4. Competition had increased, especially from companies promoting natural products like the The Body Shop.
5. Environmentalists objected to what they considered Cosmos' use of excessive and wasteful packaging.
6. An investment firm has recommended to its clients that they sell Cosmos stock, and an ethical mutual fund announced that Cosmos stock did not qualify.
7. The franchise operators of the booths and stands were complaining that Cosmos had not carried out promises and some conditions of their agreement.
8. A salesperson had been charged with attempts to bribe a purchasing agent with a large drug store chain.

Somehow the emergence of these issues had occurred without management being aware of them. Boswell and his managers admitted that they knew very little about social responsibility and the new focus on business ethics. As sales had declined in the past year, and profits were the lowest in 10 years, Cosmos was being threatened by changes in the environment that it did not fully understand. There was silence after Boswell asked his managers "What do we do now?" ▲

The Management Challenge demonstrates what is perhaps the fundamental dilemma facing the management of Canadian businesses today: should they pursue profit only, (i.e., economic objectives), or should they consider what society perceives as social objectives? This question has no easy answers, as we shall see in this chapter. Social objectives are concerned with social responsibility and business ethics. Managers often have to agonize over which course of action is best from other than an economic view. In many situations, managers find themselves doing a juggling act as they try to adhere to government regulations, to pursue their profit objectives, and to meet the competing demands of many stakeholders.

You will note that a distinction is being made between social responsibility and ethics. In this chapter, social responsibility represents the broadest relationship between business and society. Business ethics, on the other hand, is a subcategory of social responsibility focussing on the moral principles involved. A business demonstrates social responsibility when it makes donations to charities, an activity that neither follows nor breaks a moral rule. It is merely a response to a social cause. However, offering kickbacks to a purchasing agent is unethical and illegal. It breaks a moral (and legal) precept.

It is difficult to define business ethics since it has different meanings for different managers. A definition is given, and there is a discussion of its main components, which provides a basis for understanding the concept. Lastly, a distinction should be made between social responsibility and business ethics. Social responsibility is the broader term describing business' commitment to, or relationship with, society, and includes ethics. Business social responses do not always involve morality. For example, several large corporations in Montreal supported the Montreal Job Creation Initiative, a project to assist young entrepreneurs plan and establish small businesses. The corporations were being socially responsive, not morally right or wrong.

Because there are no easy resolutions to many social and ethical issues, the purpose of this chapter is to sharpen your awareness of the issues so you will be better prepared to deal with them. The chapter is divided into four main parts. The first part describes some of the expectations society has of business. The second defines social responsibility and examines the arguments for and against it. The third part presents a definition of ethics and describes some ethical dilemmas facing managers. There is a discussion of business' response to society in three areas: corporate giving, the environment, and socially responsible investment. Finally, a connection is made between social responsibility and the management functions. Overall, this chapter demonstrates some of the difficult decisions that managers must make in their day-to-day work. The fact that straightforward formulas for handling such matters are unavailable underlines the dynamic nature of the manager's job.

SOCIETY'S EXPECTATIONS OF BUSINESS

Most Canadians consider the business enterprise system to be the legitimate mechanism for providing the goods and services they require. But events do occur that upset or annoy consumers which cause antibusiness attitudes.

LEARNING OBJECTIVE 1
State the concerns being expressed by society about the role of business.

CRITICISMS OF BUSINESS

Business has been confronted with criticisms from the business community, civil servants and politicians, consumer activists and environmentalists, trade union leadership, colleges and universities, and the media. It has been accused of plundering our natural resources and of polluting the environment, of associating too closely with governments thereby acquiring inordinate power to serve its own interests, of treating employees unequally and exposing some to health and safety hazards, and of marketing unnecessary and sometimes unsafe products to consumers. The fear is expressed that business (e.g., corporations), has become so large and powerful that it is not as responsible or accountable as it should be. Business, some believe, has become an "elite," a capitalist ruling class, which dominates economic decision making in society.[1]

LEARNING OBJECTIVE 2
List the various stakeholders of business and their expectations.

Since society is dissatisfied with the behaviour of business enterprises, one may ask what society expects from business. One way of identifying these expectations is to look at what various stakeholders of an enterprise expect. For example, shareholders expect to receive a return on their investment, employees assume they will receive adequate compensation and be treated fairly, consumers want to receive quality goods and services at reasonable prices, competitors expect to receive fair treatment according to the norms established by society and business for competitive conduct, interest groups want to be recognized and listened to by managers, and society-at-large expects business enterprises to behave in a manner consistent with the morals of society.

The criticisms levelled at business show that these expectations are not always met. To satisfy its various stakeholders, a business must concern itself with economic and social expectations, although these matters are sometimes disappointed. The managers of a business enterprise must not only respond to an economic need, such as dividends to a shareholder, but they must also be sensitive to social needs, like those addressed by charities.

Some stakeholders expect social concerns to be addressed by the enterprise. For example, interest groups that represent the environment or the poor, and society-at-large are preoccupied with social matters. For managers, it is often difficult to distinguish between responses to economic concerns and responses to social issues. For example, Petro-Canada sponsored the Olympic torch relay across Canada in 1988. It is not clear whether this sponsorship was to benefit Canadians by creating a national spirit, which it appeared to do, or to increase gasoline sales which it also did. This blending of economic and social concerns complicates the manager's task. Social response is often considered to involve only responses to interest groups, but this is not the case. A further complication arises from the fact that many stakeholders make economic and social demands on the enterprise, often in contradiction of each other. For example, shareholders may demand high dividends as investors, but as theatre-goers want the enterprise to increase support for the arts.

social contract

One concept that shows the relationship between economic and social objectives is the **social contract**. A social contract is the understanding between society and its institutions. It is written partly in legislation, but is also found in custom, precedent, and articulated societal approval or disapproval.[2] In a business context, the social contract is that business functions with stakeholder consent to meet the needs of society. Business acquires legitimacy through the consent of the stakeholders.

Corporations respond to social issues in many ways. Seagram, a producer of alcoholic beverages, warns its customers not to drink and drive. Seagram was prompted to sponsor such messages when concerns were raised about the deaths and injuries caused by drunk driving.

Corporations are given the right to pursue their economic objectives in return for accountability to society, which requires some degree of responsibility for, or contribution to, social needs. The social contract is a dynamic one that changes as the relationship between business and its stakeholders evolves. Today, business is much more accountable to society than it was 50 years ago.

CORPORATE SOCIAL RESPONSIBILITY

TRADITIONAL VIEW

Originally society felt that a business enterprise had fulfilled its social responsibility by surviving and realizing the maximum profit possible. By making a profit, business enterprises would be contributing to a growing, healthy economic system that would provide employment and adequate incomes for all. In other words, a corporation's social responsibility was to operate profitably; a corporation could not survive without profits, much less play a social role. The resources of society could be used by the business to make profits as long as the enterprise complied with the few rules imposed by governments to check abusive practices. The market system would provide the regulation necessary to police the system, and profits would provide incentive and insure efficiency. A work ethic and self-interest were to be the guiding principles of the system.

CONTEMPORARY VIEW

The contemporary view of business is that business exists for more than making profits, and the public expects more from business than economic benefits. As a result, the original concept of social responsibility as synonymous with the maximization of profits has been modified. Social responsibility is no longer seen in purely economic terms. While making profits is still considered a legitimate pursuit, companies are now expected to respond to issues in society when there is no economic reward. For example, a corporate donation to a literacy program may be expected, even though it does not result in increase profits (see the Management at Work insert called "The Body Shop *Is* Social Responsibility").

What is socially responsible cannot be easily determined. As an illustration, consider the following questions: How can corporate performance in society be judged apart from traditional economic standards? Are there goals and measures which individuals inside and outside the corporation can use to gauge the social responsibility of a company? To what extent should the corporation involve itself in social concerns? How do corporations typically respond to opportunities for social involvement? Is there a management technique or approach which will enhance the understanding of the corporation's social role?

SOCIAL RESPONSIBILITY DEFINED

social responsibility

LEARNING OBJECTIVE 3
Define social responsibility.

The concept of **social responsibility** has evolved over the past 10–15 years. Today it may be defined as the notion that business enterprises have an obligation to stakeholders in society to examine the impact of their self-interest actions and, if necessary, modify a business decision beyond that prescribed by law, regulation, custom, or competition.

There are two critical facets to this definition. First, the self-interested actions of business, such as the pursuit of profit growth and market share, may not be in the best interest of all stakeholders, and there may be a conflict between this self-interest and the

MANAGEMENT AT WORK

THE BODY SHOP IS SOCIAL RESPONSIBILITY

Anita Roddick founded The Body Shop in 1976 in England. Today the company retails soap and hair care products through more than 850 shops in 41 countries. The first Canadian shop was opened in 1979 by Margot Franssen and her sister, Betty-Ann. Margot, the president, has developed a chain of over 100 franchise and company-owned stores across Canada, and in seven northeastern U.S. states. Sales in Canada are almost $100 million.

As a retailer of cosmetics, the company wanted to avoid the existing image of that industry. It was an industry thought to exploit women, torture animals during product development and testing, pollute the environment, and use misleading advertising. Instead, The Body Shop has sought to promote sustainable development, enhance social justice, and work towards a balanced environment. It is involved in helping developing economies, and is promoting trade, not aid.

The philosophy of the company is expressed in the following two quotations by Franssen:

> We believe that retailers should do more than simply sell products. At The Body Shop we get involved with our customers and social issues, environmental concerns and community projects.

> Business should do more than make money; we believe that companies should actually help solve major social problems and be a driving force for change.

Its efforts are well known and it is a leading example of a business enterprise with humanitarian and environmental ideals. It has been recognized many times for its efforts, including: recipient of a *Financial Post* Environmental Award in the Green Product Category for its commitment to operating in an environmentally responsible manner. It has been named one of the "100 Best Companies to Work for in Canada" because of its high level of personal development, job satisfaction, promotion potential and working atmosphere.

Social responsibility is reflected in everything the Body Shop does. The following are some examples:

- The Body Shop's cosmetics are all natural and are not tested on animals.
- The containers are recyclable and refundable.
- The company is attempting to have products made in the Third World and high-unemployment areas.
- The Body Shop features window displays that are given to "causes," for example, Friends of the Earth or the Wildlife Federation.
- Each store is involved in a community project to which staff must devote an aggregate of four paid hours a week.

The Body Shop is an excellent example of how practising social responsibility can be good business. ▲

social concerns of various stakeholders. Secondly, it assumes that the obligation to stakeholders is voluntarily accepted. This obligation is a broad one that extends beyond the traditional duty to shareholders to encompass all stakeholders that are influenced by a company's actions. Businesses may make decisions to take actions that are beyond what they are normally required to do; that is, they may become involved in social activities outside their normal sphere of activities. Most managers have accepted accountability to stakeholders other than shareholders, but not necessarily to all stakeholders.

LEVELS AND STAGES OF CORPORATE SOCIAL RESPONSIBILITY

The definition of social responsibility can be enlarged to identify levels, or categories, of social responsibility. The Royal Commission on Corporate Concentration[3] grouped social responsibility into three categories: (1) the regular activity of a corporation such as providing for health and safety, and quality of working; (2) activities that are slightly outside the regular business activities, sometimes referred to as externalities, such as pollution, product safety, plant closings, and layoffs; and (3) activities that are clearly external to the corporation, such as social problems, urban decay, poverty, and regional disparities.

Another categorization of social responsibility was provided by MacTaggart[4] in a study performed for the Royal Commission on Corporate Concentration. It suggested responsibility had three stages: (1) an awareness among corporate management that the firm is a social and political institution, as well as an economic one, and a recognition of the specific impacts of corporate activity on society; (2) an analysis and planning by management as a result of action, or policy change, general awareness, and specific impacts; and (3) a direct response, including changes in internal policies and organization structures as well as modifications to external behaviour. MacTaggart's stages point out that action, or a response is required in addition to awareness. An example of a corporation's response to an awareness of social responsibility is presented in the Management at Work insert entitled "Social Responsibility at Québec-Téléphone."

Social Responsibility in Practice

Acting with social responsibility presents a dilemma for business. How can a business enterprise reconcile the social demands made upon it and still keep in mind its economic objectives and its own well-being? Business enterprises must make a profit to

MANAGEMENT AT WORK

Social Responsibility at Québec-Téléphone

Québec-Téléphone sees it as its duty to financially support various projects which foster a better quality of life within its territory.

RESEARCH

In the field of research, Québec-Téléphone sponsors a chair in optical communications at Laval University whereby new engineers can further their education in leading edge technologies to the Master's and Ph.D. levels. The company also contributes to a Laval project on the use of solar energy to power fibre optic transmission systems in remote areas.

The company entrusted CEFRIO *(Centre francophone de recherche en informatisation des organisations)* with the mandate of analyzing information management methods within Québec-Téléphone.

ARTS AND CULTURE

Québec-Téléphone's support of the arts took on a new dimension in 1992 with contributions towards the cultural infrastructure. The company invested in the complete renovation of the *Musée régional de Rimouski*, the opening of a *Maison de la culture* in Saint-Joseph-de-Beauce and the installation of special sound systems for the hearing impaired in the Baie-Comeau and Sept-Îles concert halls.

Along with these various contributions, the company sponsored the prize for the best feature film at the *Carrousel international du film pour enfants*, the Arthur-Buies literary prize and also sponsored classical concert series.

HEALTH

Québec-Téléphone's involvement in the public health sector took the form of a $350 000 donation for the establishment of a hostel to provide lodging for out-of-town patients undergoing radiotherapy treatments in Rimouski. The company also participated in a campaign to support victims of domestic violence by distributing the list of emergency numbers for thirteen shelters to all its customers.

ENVIRONMENT AND TOURISM

In taking part in the campaign promoting Restigouche, Pointe-au-Père and Forillon, the three high points in the territory's marine history, Québec-Téléphone maintained its tourism development support to the Canadian Parks Service.

Québec-Téléphone's concern for environmental issues led to the production of completely recyclable telephone directories printed with vegetable-based inks and bound with water-soluble glue. This initiative is in keeping with the company's general paper recycling policy.

OLYMPIC ACHIEVEMENT

The company's sponsorship of Guillaume Leblanc's athletic career gave this employee the chance to fulfil his quest for excellence. Guillaume's silver medal in the 20-km racewalk event of the Barcelona Olympic Games provided international recognition to his courage and determination. His brilliant performance encourages his colleagues to do their best every day for customer satisfaction. ▲

survive, and they cannot possibly satisfy every minority interest. Realistically, business can be asked to sacrifice only a portion of profitability for social aims.

This dilemma can be expressed another way. Why should the business enterprise go beyond its legal requirements, or industry standards, to act in a socially responsible manner? This is an especially difficult question when only one, or just a few enterprises respond to social demands while those that do not will have some competitive advantage as a result. Nevertheless, business must respond to social issues to some extent, but the level of response may ultimately be determined by profits.

It is generally accepted that the blind pursuit of maximum profits is socially irresponsible. It is also believed that most enterprises have multiple objectives, some of which are social in nature. If these statements are accurate, it is interesting to speculate about the relationship between the extent of socially responsible actions of an enterprise and its level of profitability:

1. Expenditures on social objectives reduce profits especially in the short term.
2. Expenditures on social objectives contribute to long-term profits.
3. The benefits from expenditures on social objectives may diminish after some point.

The conclusion from studies made on this topic is that the relationship between social responsibility and profits is not a very clear one. However, there is some agreement that the relationship might look something like that shown in Figure 22-1. Up to some point, increased expenditures in social responsibility are associated with higher profits, but further increases are associated with lower profit levels.[5]

MEASURING CORPORATE SOCIAL PERFORMANCE

The following are brief explanations of some approaches to measuring corporate performance from a social perspective.

FIGURE 22–1 SOCIAL RESPONSIBILITY AND PROFITS.

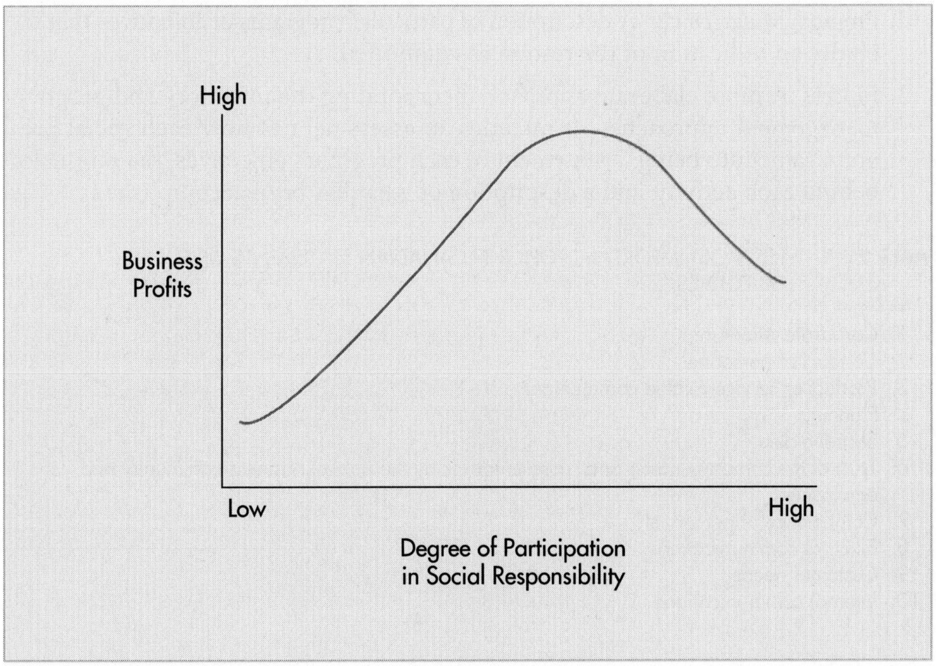

Measuring Social Objectives of Canadian Business

LEARNING OBJECTIVE 4

Name the ways in which corporate social responsibility can be measured.

A comprehensive study of the social performance of Canadian business was undertaken by Brooks. His study found that the 10 most common topics in the social objective statements of Canadian business enterprises were those listed in Table 22–1. This study was completed in the mid-1980s; this timing explains why topics such as business ethics and concern for the environment were not included. Brooks' main findings and conclusions are as follows:

1. Effects of corporate decisions on the quality of life should be included in the social performance scale and, as more Canadian executives pursue corporate social performance, an integration of economic and social objectives will occur.
2. The management of corporate social performance will be increasingly formalized through such practices as the preparation of statements of corporate social objectives and programs to raise the social awareness of employees.
3. Social Performance Guidelines (SPG) should be developed by industry to provide a basis for the comparison of enterprise performance, and management should emphasize managing and disclosing corporate social performance.
4. Canadian society will continue to expect higher levels of social performance and accountability from business enterprises.[6]

The Social Audit

social audit

One measure of social performance is the **social audit**, a systematic assessment that identifies, measures, evaluates, reports, and monitors the effects an enterprise is having on society that are not covered in the traditional financial reports. The purpose of a social audit is to provide information to management and to various stakeholders about the impact of the enterprise on society, and to provide a basis for an accountability of the social consequences of corporate activities. Such audits can be used to assess existing performance, to evaluate the performance of managers in relation to social objectives, to provide an information base for planning, and to serve as a measure for assessing future performance. Social audits take many forms including:

1. *Inventory* A listing of social activities without an evaluation.
2. *Program Management* A description of particular programs or initiatives that includes an indication of the resources committed.
3. *Process* A more elaborate approach incorporating the inventory and program management approaches. It includes an assessment of how each social program came into being, a statement of each program's objectives, the rationales behind each activity, and a description of what has been accomplished.

TABLE 22–1 TEN MOST IMPORTANT TOPICS IN CANADIAN STATEMENTS OF SOCIAL OBJECTIVES.

1. Corporate citizenship
2. Conduct of personnel
3. Product or service-related commentary
4. Planning
5. Shareholders
6. Trust of the company name and representatives by the public, business community and employees
7. Competence of personnel
8. External communications
9. Customer needs
10. Internal communications

4. *Cost or Outlay* A socioeconomic operating statement that tabulates the expenditures an enterprise makes on social objectives less the negative costs for social objectives not addressed. The approach is to measure the total social impact, positive and negative.
5. *Social Responsibility Accounting* A system of accounting that tabulates estimates of social costs and benefits with the objective of getting the best social return for the social investment made.
6. *Social Indicators* An audit of the community is conducted using social indicators to provide data on the needs which are the most pressing. Corporate social performances would be compared or related to the community or social indicators.

TVX Gold Inc. of Toronto, a producer of precious metals in South America, supports the Cruzada Do Menor, an Independent charitable organization providing assistance to children between 5 and 15 years old. The company funded the construction of a house in Rio de Janeiro and helps raise donations from other corporations to further Cruzada Do Menor's activities.

Although often referred to, there are few examples of social audits that can be identified in Canadian business. It is not an easy process since the list of all social activities may be lengthy, there are problems with standards and measurements, and it is of limited value if not made public.

Social Impact Monitoring

Enterprises are more likely to monitor the environment for social issues than conduct a social audit. In large organizations, departments may be established to do this and operate under a variety of titles including corporate or public affairs. The executive heading such a unit might be referred to as public affairs director, community relations officer, manager of social and environmental affairs, or vice-president of corporate affairs.

The purpose of this type of department would be to monitor or scan the environment for social or public issues that might affect the organization. This information would be forwarded to top management with an interpretation and perhaps some recommendations for possible action. This process is sometimes referred to as issues management.[7]

This section reviewed corporate social responsibility. The following section gives an in-depth discussion of business ethics which is an aspect of social responsibility.

BUSINESS ETHICS

LEARNING OBJECTIVE 5
Define business ethics.

Ethics have always been a concern for society and its various institutions. Business corporations, and their management, are also concerned with ethics despite the view held by many that business persons are somehow less ethical than others. To some extent, this view has been a product of the traditional view of the free enterprise system which alleged that profits were the only motivating force for business, that business activity required and rewarded deception, that business evaded the law, that businesspersons and managers manipulated others, and that business activity lead to materialism. During the 1980s, and especially in the latter half of the decade, business ethics became a primary concern in society and with managers. This section will examine the business ethics "fad," define business ethics, identify sources of ethics, and list initiatives taken by management to enforce ethical behaviour.

Business Ethics—An "In" Issue

Few Canadians can avoid the discussion of business ethics. Several books have been written on the topic in addition to hundreds of newspaper and magazine articles. Many academic journals contain articles on business ethics and one, the *Journal of Business Ethics*, is completely devoted to the topic.

The National Film Board has produced many films on social issues related to business. Two that address business ethics are: *A Choice of Two,* a portrayal of unethical and illegal practices that occurred because of one executive's greed; and *After the Axe,* a film about the firing of a senior executive after years of service. Ethical issues in business organizations is also the basis for movie plots. Recent examples include: *Barbarians at the Gate, The Firm, The Fugitive, Glengary Glenross,* and *Pretty Woman.* Several organizations have been established to monitor the ethical behaviour of Canadian business. Business ethics courses are now being taught at colleges and universities.

Since the 1980s, business ethics has become the "in" topic or fad (although it was considered prior to the 1980s). The task now is to define the term, identify the sources of ethics, and list ways business enterprises are enforcing ethical behaviour.

Ethics Defined

business ethics

Many definitions of **business ethics** exist. The definitions include terms such as moral principles, morality of human actions, standards of conduct, rights and wrongs, truth, honesty and fairness, values, customs, the Golden Rule, and philosophy. One researcher has developed a definition that synthesizes what he found to be the four most often mentioned concepts that appear in existing definitions:

> Business ethics is rules, standards, codes or principles which provide guidelines for morally right behaviour and truthfulness in specific situations.[8]

This definition indicates that moral guidelines, such as rules or codes, exist to prevent unethical behaviour. An example of this are the rules governing the behaviour of chartered accountants established by the Canadian Institute of Chartered Accountants. "Morally right behaviour" consists of the actions of businesspersons that conform to principles of justice, the law, or another standard whereby integrity is maintained. Thus, a clause in the Association of Canadian Franchisers Code of Ethics states that "all advertisements shall comply, in letter and spirit, with all applicable rules, regulations, directions, guides and laws of any governmental body or agency having jurisdiction."[9]

"Truthfulness" in the definition of business ethics suggests that statements and actions will at least have the appearance of truth. For example, Canadian Pacific's Code of Business Conduct includes a clause that requires employees to maintain the company's books and records in an accurate manner, and it forbids undisclosed or unrecorded funds or assets. Finally, occasions of personal moral dilemma that call for ethical decisions are the "specific situations." For example, codes of conduct will specify behaviour for dealing with the media, suppliers, labour unions, and so on.

Sources of Ethics

LEARNING OBJECTIVE 6
Identify the sources of ethics among businesses and the influences on management's behaviour.

Guidelines for ethical behaviour are taken from many sources. Some of the fundamental sources for all managers are:

1. *Individual morals* Managers often make ethical decisions based upon the morals they acquire while growing up. The family or home environment is a major influence in this regard. Thus the personal convictions of individual managers are a source of ethical standards.

2. *Government legislation and the law* Government legislation also influences ethical decisions. For example, the Competition Act makes some questionable market practices illegal and thus discourages some managers from becoming involved in such practices. Certain government and industry regulations require the disclosure of certain information to protect the interests of stakeholders, especially

shareholders. When selling shares to the public, a corporation must clearly state certain information about its finances and operations. The law makes some behaviour illegal and most managers are sensitive to maintaining behaviour that is within the law.

3. *Religion* An individual's religious upbringing and his or her contact with religious organizations as an adult provides guidance for some managers when confronted with ethical decisions.

4. *Colleagues and peers* The moral standards set by other businesspersons may become the basis upon which the individual manager might consider ethical issues.

5. *Education* A person's education helps shape his or her moral outlook. Ethical matters in general are examined in schools and some managers may even have postsecondary education in ethics or philosophy.

In addition to these fundamental sources of ethical standards, other aspects of society and the business system may influence the ethical behaviour of management, such as the following:

1. *Media* The possibility of exposure influences decisions. In fact, one test of ethical behaviour is whether or not the manager could defend the decision if it became public knowledge.

2. *Corporate missions, objectives, and culture* These topics have been discussed in various chapters. A mission statement usually involves the identification of the values held by the organization, and these values are reflected in the culture. Objectives that are socially oriented often emphasize moral considerations.

3. *Union contracts* Union contracts often specify the type of action that can or cannot be taken by managers. For example, when a layoff occurs, managers cannot retain their favourite employees but must release workers according to seniority.

4. *Competitive behaviour* The behaviour of others in the same industry affects a manager. For example, if one soft drink manufacturer decides to mount an advertising campaign attacking the competitor's product rather than emphasizing the qualities of its own product, it is likely that the attacked soft drink manufacturer will respond with a similar campaign.

5. *Activist or advocacy groups* The numerous activist or advocacy groups existing in society can have an impact on business decisions. An example was provided by the task force on the Churches and Corporate Responsibility. They were instrumental in getting some Canadian corporations to withdraw from South Africa.

6. *Business and industry organizations* Many business or industry organizations encourage members to act ethically. For example, the Better Business Bureau (BBB) is comprised of "businesses, organizations and individuals who believe that it is in the interests of good business to be honest and fair to their customers and clients."[10] BBB services are designed to promote and ensure ethical business practices.

7. *Professional associations* Business employs professionals such as lawyers, architects, engineers, and doctors. Ethical codes or guidelines have been developed by the professional associations and must be adhered to by their members.

These fundamental sources and other influences affect the decisions of managers and how ethical they are. None of these sources or influences can guarantee proper behaviour. The management of many businesses is now taking initiatives that it anticipates will reinforce ethical behaviour among staff.

Management Initiatives to Reinforce Ethical Behaviour

LEARNING OBJECTIVE 7

List the initiatives that might be taken by business to reinforce ethical behaviour.

Business organizations have made various attempts to institutionalize ethics, that is, tried to implement policies or programs for raising an awareness of ethics. Some of these initiatives are discussed below.

Statement of Values or Philosophy

Some businesses prepare statements of their "core values" or "philosophy" that will serve as a guide for ethical decision making and indicate what the corporation's beliefs are. An example of one corporation's values is provided in the Ethics in Management insert "Corporate Values of Nova Corporation." This topic was also discussed in Chapter 5 in conjunction with mission statements. A statement of values also becomes the basis for a code of ethics.

Codes of Ethics

code of ethics

A **code of ethics** or conduct is a statement of ethical principles and acceptable behaviour or rules and policies that describe the general value system within which a corporation attempts to operate in a given environment. Many business enterprises, business associations, and professional organizations have established codes of ethics; it is the most common approach to institutionalizing ethical behaviour. Codes of ethics are developed for several reasons:

1. They can improve customer confidence in the quality of a product or level of service and help ensure the ethical and fair treatment of customers.
2. Codes simplify the detection of unethical behaviour in competitors and employees by standardizing norms of behaviour.
3. The reputation of the business enterprise or organization that develops codes is improved and attracts high-calibre employees and customers.
4. Codes provide for self-regulation, which is preferable to external control.
5. Since codes increase awareness, they discourage ethical apathy, facilitate ethical decision making, and make it easier to refuse an unethical request.

Components of codes The common components that comprise a typical code of ethics include:

1. General statement of ethics, values or philosophies.
2. Responsibility for employees, including items such as health and safety, nondiscrimination, and privacy.
3. Conflict of interests, their identification, and how to handle them.
4. Protection of enterprise assets, including accurate accounting, security of property, and insider information.
5. Appropriate business practices, including honesty, fairness and obeying the law.
6. Appropriate relationships with customers, suppliers, competitors, creditors, and government.
7. Responsibilities to society at large, including contributions to political parties, responses to media, treatment of communities, and concern for environmental protection.
8. Implementation procedures including familiarity with the code, reporting of violations, refusing unethical requests, and seeking help on ethical matters.

ETHICS IN MANAGEMENT

CORPORATE VALUES OF NOVA CORPORATION

NOVA values its international scope of operations and its ability to compete worldwide from its Canadian base. Corporate values create the base for long-term prosperity and growth.

HUMAN RESOURCES

The NOVA workforce is highly trained and productive. Employees share and support an entrepreneurial business style that values leadership, innovation, planning and hard work.

NOVA practices non-discriminatory hiring, compensation and employee development policies that reinforce performance as the key to career development.

Reflecting these values, an innovative employee compensation program was implemented in January 1990 to provide a competitive package that rewards performance. It includes a savings and profit sharing plan and flexible benefits package that allows employees to tailor compensation programs.

HEALTH, SAFETY AND ENVIRONMENT

NOVA is committed to the operation of its businesses at a standard that will establish the Corporation as an industry leader.

All employees practise and encourage safe work habits and environmental responsibility as integral conditions of work. Through policies and routine audits, NOVA ensures that operating units aim to meet or exceed all applicable laws and standards, while continuing to work in a productive manner. NOVA supports the environmental codes of practice as established by groups such as the Canadian Chemical Producers Association, the Canadian Petroleum Association and the Chemical Manufacturers Association in the United States.

In 1989, NOVA had capital expenditures of $30 million and operating expenditures of $21 million related to pollution abatement and control measures. In addition, NOVA expends substantial efforts in the areas of occupational health, product and process toxicology, industrial hygiene and safety, to protect NOVA's employees and the public.

RESEARCH AND TECHNOLOGY

NOVA's business objectives are supported by a commitment to applied research and technology development.

Reaserch allows development of value-added products that meet specific customer needs. This is an essential component of NOVA's ability to achieve and maintain its position as a preferred supplier of goods and services. Unified activities are conducted at three major research facilities in Canada and the United States to provide a comprehensive approach to specific research projects for all NOVA operations. The research group employs about 400 scientists, engineers and technical support staff.

In 1989, NOVA spent approximately $48 million on research and development activities and an additional $17 million on product support research activities related to the improvements of existing products, services and processes.

CORPORATE CONTRIBUTIONS

NOVA supports non-profit activities designed to support the quality of life in the communities in which it operates.

Contributions support national organizations and reflect NOVA's international business activities. Emphasis is directed to health and welfare, education, the environment, arts and culture and recreation.

In 1989, major initiatives included a program to match employee contributions to charities such as the United Way, support for litter clean-up campaigns and donations to universities. ▲

The content and format of codes of ethics vary substantially among enterprises. Often codes are organized in a format where ethical matters are discussed in relation to each stakeholder. Although the existence of codes is widespread, especially in large corporations, they have some drawbacks.

Drawbacks to codes Some critics claim that codes of ethics or conduct are at best a minimal but enforceable standard and at worst a hollow pretense. An implication of this claim is that most enterprises and professionals operate at an ethical level above that specified in the codes. It is only for the less scrupulous that the codes are intended, but the guidelines may not be very effective with this group. Most codes are characterized by voluntary compliance. It is, therefore, difficult to enforce the codes and, even if they are enforced, the penalties may be insignificant. Those following the code may also be placed in a disadvantageous position because those who don't adhere to the code are not restricted in their actions. As a result, convincing everyone to comply is not easy. In business enterprises, codes are sometimes pointed to with pride but ignored in practice. Frequently, the codes are idealistic, or written in meaningless generalities.

Sometimes codes of ethics are developed merely to control competitive conduct among business enterprises or individuals. They specify conduct that is considered unprofessional such as advertising by lawyers and certain pricing practices in some industries. The code of conduct, in these cases, is really designed to reduce competition, and this kind of self-regulation is sometimes a stopgap measure of questionable intent designed merely to prevent government legislation and serve as a response to public criticism.

Ethics Training

Ethics training involves teaching employees about the values and policies on ethics they should follow in decision making. The teaching sessions involve an orientation on values or ethics and related policies. A code of ethics or statement of values might be used in this orientation process in addition to handbooks or policy statements. Such teaching can be done by line managers or outside consultants and may be addressed to all levels of employees or more likely, to management levels. The reasons for establishing such training are to develop employee awareness of ethics in business and to draw attention to ethical issues to which an employee may be exposed.[11] Ethics training at Imperial Oil is discussed in the Ethics in Management insert "Ethics at Imperial Oil Limited."

Ethics Audits

ethics audit

An **ethics audit** is a systematic effort to discover actual or potential unethical behaviour in an organization. These audits are similar to the social audits discussed previously but focus on morals or values. They are not only designed to uncover

ETHICS IN MANAGEMENT

Ethics at Imperial Oil Limited

Ethics, or the moral factor, is a consideration in how Imperial Oil Limited operates. The company has a 20-page ethics statement entitled "Our Corporate Ethics," which covers the ethical attitudes of Imperial in all aspects of its operations. Some of the items covered are: the fair treatment of employees; relationships with customers, suppliers, and the community at large; the giving or accepting of gifts and entertainment; and descriptions of what constitutes conflict of interest, insider trading, and restrictive trade practices.

But, consideration of ethical questions does not stop with the ethics statement. The statement has become the basis for seminars and workshops that examine ethic concerns or issues. Employees throughout Canada attend sessions where they discuss and apply Imperial's code of ethics in case exercises often based on actual incidents at Imperial. The purpose of these sessions is to put ethics in practice and to develop a sensitivity among employees to the ethical dimension of all business decisions and relationships.

Imperial's efforts at promoting ethical behaviour have been documented in a 14-page case written at the School of Business Administration of The University of Western Ontario and used in the classroom. Jeffrey Gantz, a Western professor concluded that "It (Imperial Oil) wants to be more than just barely ethical; it wants to be deeply ethical. And it wants to be seen as ethical." ▲

unethical behaviour, but also to identify the opportunities for unethical behaviour that might exist. They have a preventive as well as a remedial purpose. Audits are particularly useful when used in conjunction with a code of ethics, since the code can serve as a measure of how well or poorly the organization is doing. Regular audits foster ethical practices.

Ethics Consultants

Consultants knowledgeable in ethics advise management on how to put "integrity" into an enterprise's culture. Ethics audits, or surveys, might be conducted by consultants to determine ethical standards, and they could be involved in training and code development. The consultants are people from outside the organization.

Ethics Ombudsman or Ethics Advocate

This is an independent executive reporting to the CEO who reviews complaints or information from anyone in the organization or any stakeholder, studies the situation, and recommends action if necessary. Toll-free telephone numbers are sometimes provided for employees in large enterprises to report ethical problems. This approach provides a "release" mechanism for disenchanted or concerned employees. The advocate must be independent of the corporation to ensure the trust of stakeholders. Such a person could alert the organization to ethical problems or issues before they become public knowledge, allowing it time to prepare a defence or take remedial actions. This approach is seldom used and there are no known Canadian examples.

Ethics Committees (or Business Conduct Committees)

Ethics committees are usually formed at the board of directors level to monitor ethical standards and behaviour. The formation of such a committee injects ethics at the highest level in the organization and is a symbol to all stakeholders of a commitment to ethical practice This type of committee would be involved in developing a code of ethics and might monitor management and employee behaviour for ethical consideration. The report of an ethics committee is presented in the Ethics in Management insert "Report of the Business Conduct Review Committee—Royal LePage Limited."

Ethics committees can also exist within the organization itself and be comprised of management, employees, and outside stakeholders. The present practice appears to be that ethics committees are upper-management focussed. They are also called corporate ethics and responsibility committees, or advisory boards or councils and are usually comprised of a variety of stakeholders.[12]

Executive Speeches

As business ethics became popular, many chief executives used it as a topic of their public speeches. The speeches were made to inform certain stakeholders that the business enterprise and its management are concerned about ethics and are responding to society's interest in the matter. It is not always clear to which stakeholders the speeches were addressed but most likely society at large, activist and advocacy groups, employees, and possibly some shareholders. The influence that these speeches have is even less clear.

Teaching Ethics in Business Schools

Colleges and universities are being pressured to teach ethics in business and management programs. In addition, short courses in ethics are being offered at management development training centres. But it is not clear that ethics can be taught at this level in the education system or to adults.

ETHICS IN MANAGEMENT

REPORT OF THE BUSINESS CONDUCT REVIEW COMMITTEE—ROYAL LEPAGE LIMITED

The most effective system for dealing with conflict of interest situations is a combination of strict but workable regulatory framework and appropriate self-governance mechanisms.

At Royal LePage, corporate self-governance responsibilities are honoured by adhering to certain business principles. Included are:

- a major commitment to the quality, timeliness and accuracy of board and committee reporting;
- a significant number of independent directors on the board;
- a policy which invites substantial public investment, reflected in a public shareholding of 48 percent in Royal LePage;
- substantial equity participation by senior management; and
- a high level of accountability to a major shareholder.

The Business Conduct Review Committee was constituted on October 25, 1985 and subsequently approved by shareholders. The committee is composed of four directors of Royal LePage who are unaffiliated in any way with a major shareholder of Royal LePage.

The committee has established a Code of Business Conduct for Royal LePage which includes policies regarding business ethics and conflicts of interests applicable to employees, directors and shareholders. It must approve all significant investments, loans or other business activities of Royal LePage, which may involve a material conflict of interest.

The committee is provided with ready access to senior management and Royal LePage's auditors and it can, as it deems necessary, retain independent legal counsel to advise on matters which come before it. Members of the committee are Samuel T. Paton, Lorne K. Lodge, Susan C. Bassett-Klauber and Roy MacLaren.

During the year, the committee reviewed and approved all significant transactions and policies under its mandate. It is of the opinion that during its sixth year of existence, it continues to comply with both the spirit and the substance of its mandate.

On behalf of the Committee
Samuel T. Paton Chairman,
January 18, 1990 ▲

Some academics argue that it is critical to sensitize students to ethical issues. Ethics courses can provide students with some tools or techniques of analysis or a conceptual framework for analyzing ethical issues. The essential tools of moral recovery, deliberation and justification can be taught and would be helpful to future business persons in explaining corporate behaviour. Counter-arguments are that ethics are not a major problem in Canadian business, instructors are unlikely to influence the ethical behaviour of students, and there are few instructors who are qualified to teach the subject. The debate will continue until the current preoccupation with business ethics fades. Watch for discussions of ethics in your business courses.

BUSINESS RESPONDS TO SOCIETY

Throughout this chapter, examples have been given of how business enterprises have responded to society's needs. In particular, the Management at Work inserts have been selected to provide a range of examples. A long list of responses by business enterprises to various stakeholders could be prepared. Consider the following examples:

1. The Distillers of Canada have sponsored a responsible drinking campaign.
2. "Share the Light" is an energy assistance program sponsored by Newfoundland Power Limited and administered by the Salvation Army designed to help families in need to pay their energy bills.

3. The Royal Bank Award gives $100 000 to a Canadian, or Canadians, whose outstanding accomplishments have made an important contribution to the human welfare and common good.
4. McDonald's Restaurants of Canada sponsors Ronald McDonald houses where the parents of seriously ill youngsters can stay while their children are treated in hospital.
5. Hook Outdoor Advertising, Calgary, supported an outdoor gallery of contemporary Albertan art.
6. The Canadian Business Task Force on Literacy was formed by 32 corporations to combat literacy.
7. Alexanian & Sons, a small, family-owned carpet business, pledged almost $75 000 to Opera Hamilton, has sponsored Theatre Aquarius, and supported the Hamilton Philharmonic Orchestra.

Corporate giving takes different forms with different companies. The Executive Vice-President of Marketing and Public Affairs for 3M Canada Inc. and the Minister of State for Fitness and Amateur Sport hold a news conference announcing the company's support for coaching development through the National Coaching Certificate Program.

Even this short list suggests that the social needs supported by business vary. Rather than attempt to develop an exhaustive list of business social achievements, three of the more common and current responses will be discussed in more detail: corporate giving or philanthropy; action on the environment; and socially responsible or ethical investing.

CORPORATE GIVING

Canadian business enterprises donate to a variety of causes and organizations, including health and welfare agencies, educational institutions, community services, service clubs, civic projects, arts and culture groups, athletic organizations, and environmental groups. Some enterprises spread contributions across a variety of causes while others are focussed in their giving. In addition to the donation of money, corporate giving, or philanthropy, can involve the donation of goods and services.

Figure 22–2 provides data on charitable donations by Canadian corporations. Note that even though profits have fallen, the level of corporate donations remained about the same in the last three years.

Society expects business to direct some of its profits to social causes and organizations. In 1986, a Decimal Research survey found that 8 out of 10 Canadians believed corporations have a responsibility to provide support to charities and nonprofit organizations.[13] This section will provide the arguments for and against corporate giving, examine how the decision to donate is made, and indicate some trends in corporate giving.

The following are the main arguments in support of giving by business:

1. Corporate giving is one way to express social responsibility to the community and to show that business is not just concerned with society as a market.
2. It promotes an image of good citizenship and creates goodwill which is critical if business is to be accepted by society.
3. Most businesspersons recognize that the volunteer sector provides some very important services and that even business enterprises benefit from these services (e.g., employees benefiting from Alcoholics Anonymous).
4. There are direct benefits to the enterprise from corporate giving, like promotion or advertising, tax breaks, and public recognition for good deeds.

FIGURE 22-2 STATISTICS ON CORPORATE GIVING IN CANADA.

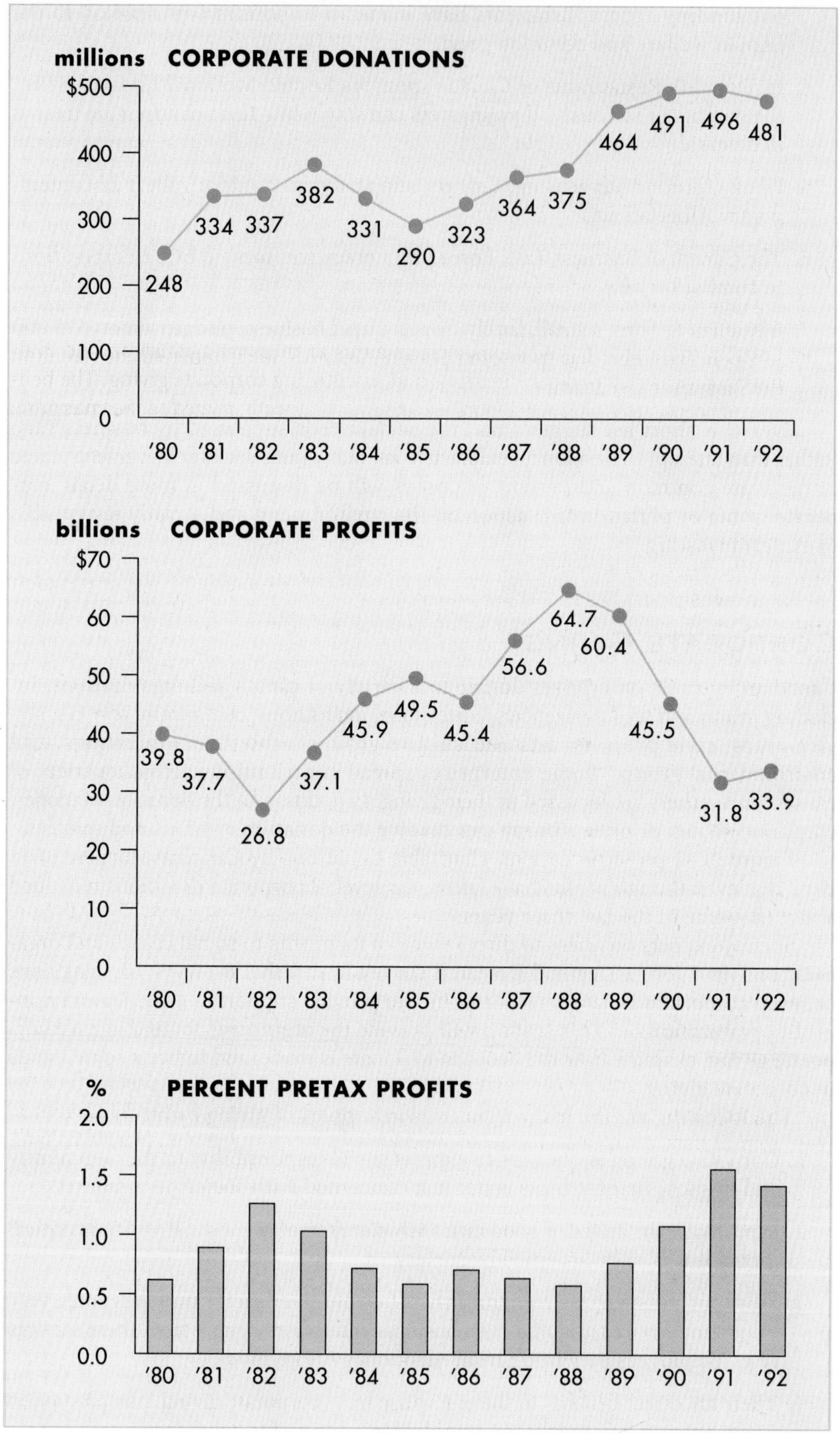

The following summarizes the arguments against corporate giving:

1. The funds given actually belong to shareholders, and it is presumptuous for management to make the decision to give the funds in the first place, and then to choose particular recipients.

2. Business enterprises should not become involved with social welfare, since that is the job of government. If business did support causes, it could give business more power in society when many feel that it already has too much power.

3. By supporting any cause or organization, the enterprise might become accountable for the actions taken by the charity, or adverse publicity might even damage the enterprise's image or reputation.

4. Usually, there are no guidelines, no standards to measure against, and no evaluation process for making decisions and monitoring corporate giving. The benefits of corporate giving are seldom measurable or directly related to the enterprise.

Making Corporate Giving Decisions

In the past, corporate giving decisions were made by individual executives, often by members of the family owners such as the Eatons, Woodwards, Burtons, Molsons, and Labatts. Today, this individual dominance has, in many cases, yielded to a committee consensus and the process is now more complicated. In the more formalized processes, decisions on corporate giving are made in head offices by chief executives and the board of directors with assistance from a committee. The first decision they make is on the donations budget. According to Martin, budgets are set as a percentage of expected pretax profit, increased an arbitrary amount from the previous year, set in relation to industry norms or in comparison to peers, or determined by a formula based upon the number of employees.[14]

Corporate giving to charitable non-profit organizations by Canadian business is about one-half that of American business. The Canadian Centre for Philanthropy, a non-profit organization has initiated the IMAGINE program, a bilingual Canada-wide awareness program, to promote increased corporate and individual giving.

Some corporations carefully establish the objectives for giving so that some guidelines are available to ascertain how much money is given and to whom. Criteria for evaluating requests are formulated and used by in-house staff or consultants in making decisions. Grants given in one year are evaluated prior to another grant being made. Some corporate givers, such as Imperial Oil Ltd. and John Labatts Ltd., have managers of contributions to supervise the process. Despite the formalization suggested above, the single most important influence in the decision-making process is still the chairperson of the board or the CEO.

Some families and corporations have chosen to establish foundations to support charities. These foundations are established by wealthy individuals or families and support a wide variety of social activities or causes. The largest private foundation in Canada is the J.W. McConnell Foundation with assets of over $325 million (McConnell was a former publisher of the *Montreal Star*). In his will, Harold Ballard, owner of the Toronto Maple Leafs, directed that a large part of his estate be used to endow a foundation in his name.[15]

Either through formal or case-by-case processes, decisions are made not only to fund, but also to reject requests. There are several reasons for rejecting a request, including corporate policies that exclude a particular type of project or charity; insufficient funds; a donation had already been made to an organization with parallel services; the organization was located outside of the corporation's community; there was no Revenue Canada registration number; there were inadequate financial statements; no new approaches were being accepted; the size of the request was too large; and the corporation received too many requests.[16]

Trends in Corporate Giving

Some trends in corporate giving have developed. Requests from universities and hospitals for large donations over several years have resulted in a higher portion of a donation budget being committed to contributions. This leaves few funds for new causes or groups. Donations have become tied to sales, or marketing efforts. For example when a customer designates his or her account as "green," Canada Trust donates $5 to the nonprofit Friends of the Environment Foundation that finances environmentally friendly projects. These "green" accounts automatically contribute 1 cent per $1 interest each month to the foundation. Some corporations are turning away from traditional giving and towards a more "market" driven, bottom-line approach to philanthropy. Giving is tied to sales and the benefits are clearly measurable by the corporation and the recipient.

Corporate sponsorship, the funding of an organization sometimes in exchange for publicity, is increasing because television and other forms of advertising have become less appealing as rates increase and audiences decrease. Such sponsorship links the corporation's product to a leisure pursuit and to a marketing strategy. In other words, it is merely another way of advertising. Sponsorship is undertaken when it will raise awareness of a brand or company in a particular target market; for example, a running shoe manufacturer may sponsor a marathon race.

More than 500 major sporting events each year in Canada are funded by breweries, while banks and distillers tend to be associated with arts events. For such sponsorship to be successful, there should be some relationship between the corporation and the event, and the purpose of the event must be clearly spelled out. A well-defined plan is needed so the donating corporation receives exposure for its products and the event receives financial assistance. It is important for the sponsorship to fit a company's marketing scheme.

Corporate giving, in total, appears to be stable. New tax incentives might increase the level of giving, or charities may have to do a better job at convincing corporations that their money will be spent effectively. The impact of the IMAGINE program, an initiative of the Canadian Centre for Philanthropy, is not yet known. The objective of this program is to increase corporate charitable donations to an amount equal to 1 percent of average pretax profits. Business enterprises in Canada are supporting a wide variety of charities in Canada, and this support has become much more crucial as government grants have declined. By those corporations that donate on a regular basis, philanthropy is seen as a responsibility, a part of the cost of doing business. For other corporations, it is a frill or option. It appears that some enterprises are willing to give, but are becoming more selective and will have to be convinced to part with their money.

Action on the Environment

LEARNING OBJECTIVE 8

State how businesses are managing the environmental issue.

"Environment" and "green" have become popular words as Canadians have grown more concerned about their physical surroundings.[17] The environment has also become a prominent concern among businesses. The environmental issues that have received attention include the depletion of the ozone layer, the greenhouse effect, acid rain, deforestation and land loss, pollution of all types, energy conservation, and waste management.

Managing the Environmental Issue

Managers can take a positive stance on environmental questions and attempt to respond to them. The following are some of the initiatives that have been taken:

Environmental Management A business that adopts this approach is committed to all forms of environmental protection programs. It considers a concern for the environment to be a priority, as important as a business function. Top management is involved in overseeing funding for environmental projects which is unrestricted. One or more corporate objectives relate to the environment, and formalized internal and external reporting mechanisms exist to ensure that environmental programs are carried out.[18]

Many businesses are involved in recycling programs like the Blue Box program pictured above. Such recycling is good for the environment, but is not always good for business. Some materials are collected in greater quantities than can be processed and resold, and as more paper is recycled, the demand for virgin paper declines reducing the sales of Canadian pulp and paper products.

An Environment Manager Progressive enterprises are hiring senior managers to focus on environmental matters. These head office positions bear such titles as environmental director, vice-president of the environment, corporate manager of environmental affairs, and environmental coordinator. It is still not clear what impact these managers have within the enterprise.[19] Even the cartoon "Back Bench" questioned the role of these managers when a strip contained three definitions for such managers:

- Environment Director: You get to water some of the plants.
- Senior Environment Director: You get to water all of the plants.
- Environment Specialist: You get to talk to the plants.

Monitoring Environmental Groups Dozens of environmental groups exist in Canada, such as Greenpeace Canada, Pollution Probe, Earth Day, and the Canadian Coalition on Acid Rain. The activities, policies, and initiatives of these groups are often monitored to ascertain their potential impact upon the enterprise. This monitoring function may be performed by the environmental departments, the managers mentioned above or by consultants.

Environmental Consultants Business enterprises can also hire environmental experts as consultants. The most well known consultant is Colin Isaacs, formerly with Pollution Probe.

Environmental Reporting Many business enterprises are reporting on the effect of their operations on the environment and the initiatives undertaken to reduce adverse effects. The environment is a popular topic in annual reports, and enterprises and industry associations advertise the actions they are taking to protect the environment. In November 1989, McDonald's placed full-page advertisements in major Canadian newspapers elaborating on "Our Commitment to the Environment." A brochure on the topic was available from their restaurants.

Executive Speeches The environment has become a topic of many speeches made by top management. Roy Aitken, executive vice-president of Inco Ltd., has spoken widely about his company's efforts to address environmental problems. Ray Smith, chairperson of MacMillan Bloedel Inc. has addressed the impact of tree harvesting on the environment.

Environmental Codes Many enterprises have prepared environmental policy statements or codes. One such code is reproduced in the Management at Work insert entitled "Petro-Canada's Environmental Protection Policy." The purpose of environmental codes is much the same as it is for codes of ethics: to increase awareness of the issue throughout the organization and to signal to other stakeholders that the enterprise is active in this area.

Environmental Audits and Assessments

Governments have passed legislation such as the federal government's Canadian Environmental Protection Act and Ontario's Environment Assessment Act, to protect the environment. It is not uncommon for the legislation to require an **environmental audit** be undertaken by enterprises or governments involved in environmentally

environmental audit

MANAGEMENT AT WORK

PETRO-CANADA'S ENVIRONMENTAL PROTECTION POLICY

The code below is one developed by a Canadian enterprise as a response to the concern for the environment.

The Corporation regards environmental protection as a high priority in the conduct of its operations. This applies to all activities under the Corporation's control. The Corporation will be exemplary in environmental protection by expecting a standard of excellence in the stewardship of this policy. This commitment will be incorporated into business strategies through the following guiding principles. The Corporation will:

1. Evaluate the operations of the Corporation to ensure compliance with Corporate policy, government legislation and the industry standards concerning the protection of the environment.
2. Determine, evaluate and act to mitigate the environmental effects of project implementation, operations, decommissioning, and waste management.
3. Respond to emergencies in a prompt and efficient manner, and correct any environmental damage caused by the Corporation's activities.
4. Ensure that its employees are informed of the need to protect the environment while carrying out their duties.

Vice-Presidents are responsible for creating specific operational procedures which are consistent with this general policy. These procedures are subject to sign-off by the Corporate Environmental Affairs department. All employees are responsible for ensuring the achievement of these commitments in their work activities.

Accountability for the maintenance and interpretation of this policy rests with the Vice-President, Corporate Services. ▲

sensitive projects. The acts often stipulate that an environmental assessment document, or report, be submitted to Environment Canada for review, and approval. The report usually has to contain a description of the project, a list of reasons for the project, alternatives to the project, an outline of how the project and its alternatives will affect the environment directly or indirectly, an identification of the actions necessary to prevent those effects, and an evaluation of the advantages and disadvantages of the project to the environment, and alternative ways to carry it out. The report is submitted for evaluation to an environmental assessment agency and is often followed by public hearings. Organizations are now familiar with the environmental process and incorporate it into their decision making.

Green Marketing

Green seems to be the most popular colour with business today, since it expresses society's concern for the environment. Take, for example, the following headlines: "Going for the Green—Marketers Target Environment"; "Ignoring Green Revolution Means Disaster, Companies Warned"; "Marketers Must Plan for Green Future"; and "Greening the Profits." Green marketing involves selling environmentally friendly goods to consumers. As the headlines suggest, doing so may be necessary if enterprises are to survive and provides a new opportunity to make money.

Dozens of friendly so-called "green" products are on the market: liquid soap products that offer plastic refill pouches to reduce packaging waste; coffee filters made without bleach, which can contain dioxin; recyclable or degradable trash bags; dishwasher detergent that is phosphate free; and foam plates and cups without chlorofluorocarbons.[20]

The federal government has initiated an "Environment Choice" Program which certifies products to be environmentally friendly, the first three of which are re-refined oil, insulation material from recycled paper, and six types of household and office products made from recycled plastic.

Green or environmentally friendly products and the whole green marketing approach has been questioned. To many, it is not clear whether or not "green marketing" is as friendly to the environment as it appears. Some of the questions being posed are:

1. Will the promotion of green products provide an opportunity for marketers to inflate prices?
2. Will products labelled "green" or "environmentally friendly" in advertising actually be so, or will they mislead consumers?
3. Are adequate methods of assessment available to evaluate the claims of particular products regarding their "greenness?"
4. Will the participation in the "Environment Choice" program benefit manufacturers more than consumers?
5. How long will the environment phenomenon last with business and consumers?

Pollution Reduction

All Canadians pollute the environment, and the volume of garbage is growing faster than the population. But despite the fact that pollution is so widespread, there are still problems defining it. Some possible definitions are (1) anything that degrades the quality of the environment, (2) anything that detrimentally changes ecosystems, and (3) the deliberate discharge of particular or effluent matter that is harmful to the natural environment and to people.

No matter how it is defined, pollution comes from many sources, including aerosols, hydrocarbons, lead in gasoline, untreated sewage, and pesticides. Even packaging is a form of pollution. Convenience goods pollute as they are usually packaged in throwaway containers. Often pollution is attributed to large business enterprises that dump wastes into the water, air, or land fills. But consumers create pollution also.

Waste Management and Recycling

waste management

Waste management is the handling and disposal of unwanted materials left after industrial production or individual consumption. The traditional method of getting rid of our garbage has been to bury it in landfills. These are easy to operate and are relatively inexpensive. But the problem exists now of finding locations for new landfill sites because no one wants to live anywhere near a "dump." As a result, many governments and businesses are developing various methods to utilize or manage waste. The method discussed here will be referred to as **recycling**, the retrieval for reuse of suitable waste materials, such as paper, bottles, and cans.

recycling

The diagram in Figure 22–3 serves as a basis for discussion of the involvement of business in recycling. Raw materials are used in the manufacture of goods at the beginning of the production process. Today, R & D and design take into account the impact of particular materials on the environment. Waste from the manufacturing process may even be recycled as an input in the production of another product.

Once a good has been used by the consumer, it can be disposed of as waste in a landfill or it could become a recyclable product. As a recyclable product, two alternative means of disposal exist: incineration or reuse. Incineration can be used to generate energy, which in turn can be utilized by consumers or manufacturers. Of course, there would be some discharge of pollution to the environment.

Reuse involves collecting and sorting items and this is often performed by business enterprises. New technology for the processing of recycled materials, and the availability of markets for recycled materials, are making recycling businesses more viable. But, problems still exist. The public has been so enthusiastic about recycling materials that the capacity of recycling facilities has been overtaxed. In some cases,

FIGURE 22-3 THE RECYCLING PROCESS.

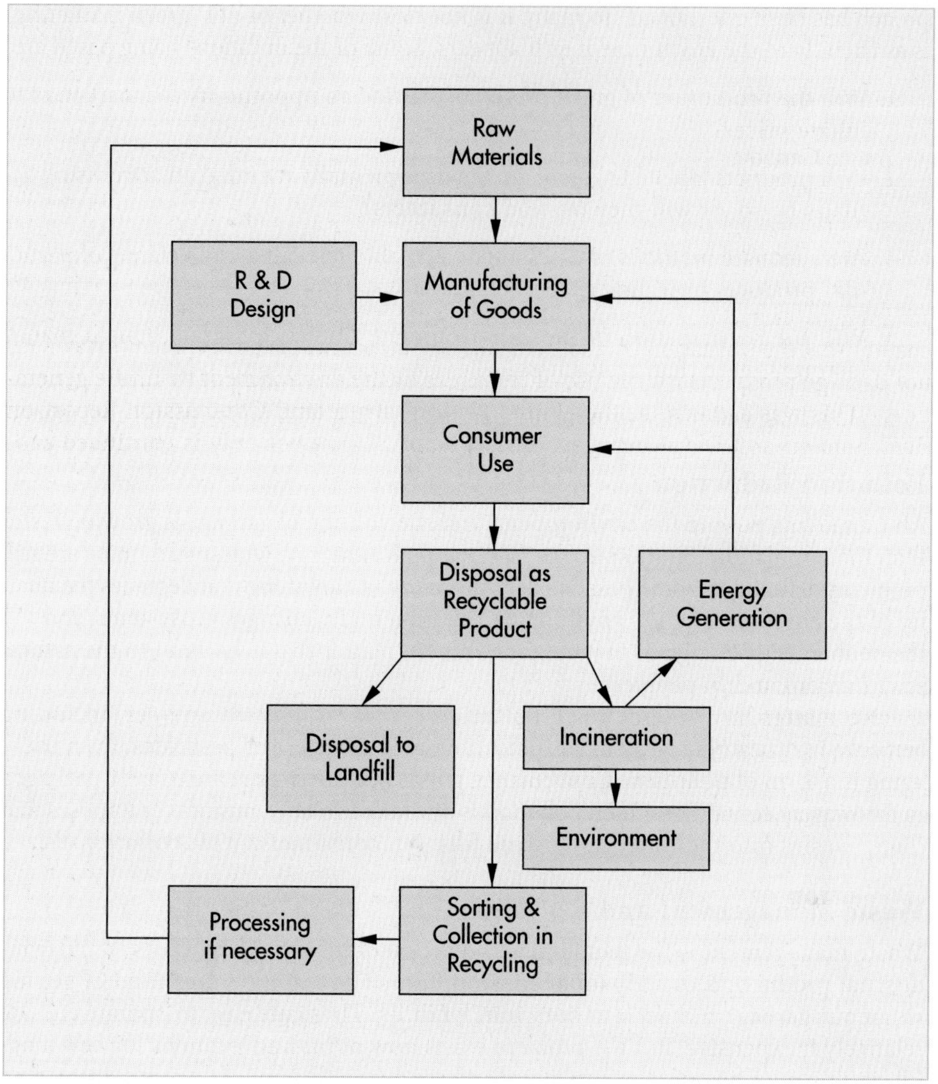

markets for recycled materials have not grown fast enough to keep pace with the collection of recyclable materials. Once processing of the materials has occurred, they are recycled as raw materials in the manufacturing process.

Although business may often provide the goods that create the waste, a growing number of organizations are participating in waste management, especially recycling.

Energy Conservation

Canadians are great users and abusers of energy, and growth in energy consumption has been steady. As consumption rises, additional sources of energy must be found placing demands on the environment, as hydro and petroleum exploration sites must be established. Furthermore, preserving the environment adds costs to energy that consumers may not be aware of.

Business is taking many actions to conserve energy. Companies are reducing their consumption in the various aspects of producing and marketing goods and services as well as in the construction of more energy efficient buildings. Also, enterprises are introducing products which will enable consumers to conserve energy.

The Environmental Ethic

environmental ethic

The **environmental ethic** is evolving from this focus on ecology. It is a set of values or principles about practices relating to the environment. Society and many businesspersons now have some sense of obligation or moral responsibility to the environment which is expressed in different ways.

Some Canadians are committed to the three "Rs" of environmental protection—reducing, reusing, and recycling. Sometimes two more "Rs" are promoted, refuse and reject; they suggest that society should refuse to use products or engage in activities harmful to the ecology and reject the products that do not respect the environment.

sustainable development

The concept of "sustainable economic development" has received attention from some business quarters. **Sustainable development** is defined as development which ensures that the utilization of resources and the impact on the environment today does not damage prospects for the use of resources or the environment by future generations. This was a theme in the United Nation's Bruntland Commission Report on Environment and Development which concluded that not only is continued economic growth possible but necessary to reduce poverty. This concept has been endorsed by many businesspersons as an approach that allows environmental and economic concerns to coincide and makes economic progress possible.

SOCIALLY RESPONSIBLE INVESTMENT

socially responsible investment (SRI)

Socially responsible investment (SRI) refers to the screening of investments in the corporate sector for their social, as well as economic or financial, benefits. The investments are usually securities of publicly traded enterprises. The practice is also referred to as "ethical investment," "socially conscious investment," and in the context of the environment "green investment."

Promotion of Social Objectives

LEARNING OBJECTIVE 9
Describe socially responsible investment.

An awareness of the possibilities of achieving acceptable rates of return and promoting social objectives at the same time is growing. While individual investors have been conscious of this possibility for a while, awareness in the business world was most likely prompted by investment decisions made by organizations, trade unions, women's organizations, cooperative systems, the environmental movement, universities and colleges, and pension funds. The Canadian financial community has quickly responded to the growing demand for socially responsive investments. Several mutual funds have been established that have socially responsible objectives: Ethical Growth Fund established by Vancouver City Savings Credit Union; Environmental Investment Canadian Fund and Environmental Investment International Fund sponsored by Energy Probe of Toronto; Crown Commitment Fund managed by Crown Life Insurance of Toronto; and The Summa Fund managed by Investors Group Inc. of Winnipeg. These funds, plus a few others have assets of $500 million (out of a $72 billion Canadian mutual fund market) and this figure is growing (see the Ethics in Management insert "Social Responsibility at the Ethical Growth Fund").

The existence of these funds has sensitized managers to the fact that at least some investors make investment decisions based upon how socially responsible the enterprise is. But it is not possible to measure the effect of this trend on business in any definitive manner.

It is interesting to consider the motives of the financial community. Do they really believe in socially responsible investing or is it simply a response to a market demand? Are the funds merely a trendy marketing concept? The motives of investors can also be questioned. How long would they continue to invest in a socially responsible fund that lost money?

ETHICS IN MANAGEMENT

Social Responsibility at the Ethical Growth Fund

THE FUND

Ethical Growth Fund (the "Fund") was established under the laws of the Province of British Columbia by a trust declaration dated as of January 6, 1986, (the "Trust Declaration") of Vancouver City Savings Credit Union (the "Trustee") which trust declaration was amended July 15, 1986 to assign VanCity Investment Services Ltd. (the "Fund Administrator"), the management and administrative function of the Fund. The head office and principal place of business of the Fund is at the head office of the Fund Administrator and the Trustee at 515 West 10th Avenue, Vancouver, British Columbia, V5Z 4A8. The Trustee took the initiative in founding the Fund and accordingly, under applicable securities legislation, is the promoter of the Fund. Under applicable securities legislation the Trustee and Fund Administrator are both considered managers of the Fund.

INVESTMENT OBJECTIVE

Mutual funds have different objectives and policies. The Fund will be prudently managed by the Fund Administrator primarily as a common share equity fund in order to maximize capital return on the funds invested, all within the framework of the investment policies. The assets of the Fund may from time to time, however, be placed in different classes of assets such as short-term investments, bonds, debentures and equities (common or preferred shares). The proportions of these classes of assets will be varied as appropriate in accordance with the assessment by the Fund Administrator of trends in the capital markets and the needs of the Fund.

INVESTMENT POLICIES

In addition to the fundamental investment objective of the Fund, the Trust Declaration provides certain investment policies. The Fund will be socially responsible (meaning, the Fund will use specified ethical and moral standards in making investments) and the monies of the Fund will only be invested in securities of Canadian corporations which meet the criteria established from time to time by the board of directors of the Trustee. For these purposes the following criteria must be met on any investment in a Canadian corporation:

1. The corporation must have either its registered or head office located in Canada and its shares must be either traded or about to be traded on a stock exchange in Canada.
2. The corporation should encourage progressive industrial relations with all members of its staff or employees. Initially in order to determine the corporations within this criteria, a review of current publications relating to employment practices is conducted and a specific analysis is made of any corporations on any published "hot lists." From time to time thereafter published reports are followed (particularly at the time of any labour strife) to determine if there is any pattern of significant deterioration whereby a corporation should be considered for removal from the Fund's investment portfolio.
3. The corporation should regularly conduct business in, or with, a country or countries that provide racial equality within its or their political boundaries.
4. The normal business of the corporation should be the provision of products or services for civilians (nonmilitary).
5. If the corporation is an energy corporation or utility, its major source of revenue should be from nonnuclear forms of energy.
6. The corporation should consistently strive to comply with environmental regulations established by governments and government agencies, and be committed to implementing environmentally conscious practices.
7. The corporation should not derive a significant portion of its income from tobacco. ▲

The Investment Criteria

The criteria used in making socially responsible investments varies by fund. The activities or characteristics of a company that might be considered socially irresponsible or unethical include:

1. Poor employee or labour relations.
2. Failure to promote racial and sexual equality and affirmative action programs.
3. The manufacture of weapons.

4. Any involvement in the nuclear industry.
5. The manufacture of "sin" products such as alcohol or tobacco.
6. Conducting business in oppressive regimes that violate human rights, such as China.
7. Enterprises that are not environmentally sensitive, for example, those that pollute.
8. The manufacture of, or provision of, unsafe goods and services, such as asbestos products.
9. Enterprises involved with questionable marketing practices (for example, misleading advertising) and especially exploitative marketing in Third World countries.
10. Enterprises that use animals to test products.
11. Involvement in gambling and pornography.

It should be noted that not all funds apply all of the above criteria. In fact most are very selective (see the Ethics in Management insert about the Ethical Growth Fund which lists the seven criteria used by the Fund).

The Difficulty of Remaining Socially Responsible

What is a socially responsible investment? Ideally, it should be investment that does not violate any of the criteria in the above list. If this list were used as criteria, it is quite likely that no investments would be made. Making socially responsible investments is hardly simple, as the following situations suggest:

1. What should be done if the company experiences a violent strike after several years of good labour relations?
2. How does a fund distinguish between good and bad? For example, does military production include trucks and jeeps? Do airlines pollute the environment?
3. What should be done if society's standards change? For example, fast food firms may fall from favour. What does the fund do if it has substantial holdings in those firms?

Ethical Growth Fund discovered the difficulty of acting socially responsible when it was questioned about the ownership of Imasco Ltd. shares, the parent company of Imperial Tobacco. When the fund was originally established, this type of investment was considered acceptable.

The Performance of Socially Responsible Investment

The performance of socially responsible investment funds has been mixed.[21] Consider the results to January 31, 1994, as an example. Equity mutual funds gained an average of 38.9 percent for the year. The gains for some socially responsible funds were: Ethical Growth Fund, 31.7 percent; Clean Environment Equity Fund, 43.5 percent; Fonds Desjardins Environnement; 30.0 percent; and Summa Fund, 25.7 percent. It is unclear whether or not mixing profits and principles actually pays investors. Despite the problems of, and mixed returns from, socially responsible investing, the attempt is an example of business responsiveness to society's needs.

This chapter has attempted to provide an overview of social responsibility and business ethics as it affects Canadian business. Many challenges confront managers as they guide the economic and social activities of business enterprises and attempt to satisfy what are sometimes conflicting demands being placed on the enterprise by a variety of stakeholders.

SOCIAL RESPONSIBILITY AND ETHICS AND THE MANAGEMENT FUNCTIONS

LEARNING OBJECTIVE 10

Relate business social responsibility and ethics to the management functions.

A manager's responsibility to consider a social and ethical perspective in the functioning of any organization has been the main purpose of this chapter. Social responsibility and business ethics issues must be treated mutually with the functions of management. In fact, the planning, organizing, leading, and controlling functions all relate to this topic with examples provided below.

PLANNING

In the planning process, managers will survey the environment to become familiar with social issues and the stakeholders involved. Some statements of objectives will be social in nature such as reducing air pollution or supporting charities. Mission and values statements also reflect the social concerns of society. Social issues will be integrated into the strategic management planning process.

ORGANIZING

The Body Shop's Margot Fransson is a well-known Canadian businesswoman who advocates socially responsible behaviour. In addition, being socially responsible can result in a very successful business.

Various organizational arrangements are made to institutionalize social responsibility and ethics in the corporation. Some of the arrangements mentioned in this chapter include the appointment of an ethics ombudsman or advocate, the formation of ethics committees, and the appointment of environment managers. Various departments are responsible for interacting with stakeholders. Large corporations have investor relations departments, public relations offices deal with the media, and government relations are handled by the legal department or by a separate department specifically designed for that purpose.

LEADING

Corporations must try to make all persons in the organization aware of social responsibility and business ethics. In the simplest forms, managers' attention to social concerns signals their importance to all employees. Codes of ethics, training, and executive speechmaking make organization stakeholders more knowledgeable of social issues. Corporate giving, in particular sponsorship, influences consumers and interest groups. Top managers influence lower-level managers and other employees by setting a good example of socially responsible and ethical behaviour.

CONTROLLING

Businesses can monitor themselves to ascertain whether or not social issues are being addressed. Social responsibility and ethics are being assessed by social, ethics, and environmental audits. A code of ethics also serves as a control mechanism as does a statement of values and environmental reporting. Managers retain control by responding to social concerns, because if they don't, other stakeholders, especially government, might take control.

A variety of approaches are used by managers to plan, organize, lead, and control for the organization's consideration of and responses to social responsibility and ethics.

MEETING THE CHALLENGE

COSMOS BEAUTY PRODUCTS INC.

While Cosmos' management was preoccupied with economic objectives—sales, market shares, and profits, social objectives appear to have been neglected. To illustrate this point, look at each of the following incidents and determine what aspect of social responsibility and ethics and also which stakeholders were involved.

Animal Rights Protest Public interest groups are concerned about the treatment of animals. This is clearly a social responsibility and an ethical example.

Low-Ranking in Consumer Test Product testing is one way consumer organizations influence corporations. This may not be a social responsibility matter, but management should have been monitoring these groups.

Product Returns Consumers are affected by what could be hazardous products and an economic objective—sales or profits—will be affected as a result. But, corporations have a social responsibility to ensure that these products are safe.

Increase in Competition Some competitors have gained an advantage over Cosmos by developing and marketing natural products. If Cosmos had been monitoring the social environment, they also would have introduced such products.

Excessive Packaging With society's increased awareness of environmental problems, management should have redesigned their packaging.

Ethical Mutual Fund Owners are affected by Cosmos' inability to cope with social concerns. In particular, the ineligibility for selection by an ethical mutual fund is a signal of Cosmos' inadequate response to social responsibility and ethics.

Franchise Complaints The franchises are crucial in Cosmos' marketing channel and should be treated fairly. The interpretation of the agreement might be thought of as a legal matter, but this is not important if they are unhappy and consider themselves to have been treated unfairly.

Bribery An ethical issue is involved here, and of course, a legal one.

Contemporary managers should not have to pose the question: "What do we do now?" They should have been monitoring the organization's activities from a social responsibility and ethics perspective. There is more to managing than sales, marketing, and profits. Most of the incidents could have been prepared for, or at least anticipated, if Cosmos had also been managed from a social perspective. Boswell and his managers should at least read this chapter to familiarize themselves with social responsibility and business ethics. ▲

SUMMARY

Canadian managers must pursue social objectives as well as economic ones if society is to accept business. Society has expectations of business, but it is also critical of many aspects of business activities. Both economic and social expectations are sometimes not fulfilled and this presents a challenge for managers. Business' obligation to society and its accountability for social objectives is referred to as social responsibility. Today, most businesspeople accept the concept of social responsibility as a part of managing a business enterprise.

A social audit is one way in which the accomplishments of social objectives is measured. Progressive managers constantly monitor and interpret the environment for social concerns. They try to understand and respond to these concerns; if they fail to do so, society may reject business' role or influence governments to regulate the activities of business. An audit allows managers to measure the social performance of their business to ascertain if social objectives have been accomplished.

Business ethics is a subcategory of social responsibility that involves morally right behaviour and truthfulness on the part of businesspeople and managers. Sources of ethics for all individuals are such things as their moral upbringing, religious education, behaviour of peers, and the law. Moral behaviour in business organizations is influenced by the media, corporate mission statements, the nature of competitive behaviour, the activities of activist or advocacy groups, and the standards developed by business and professional organizations. Codes of ethics have been established by many business enterprises as guides to acceptable moral behaviour. Other initiatives undertaken by business to influence ethics include training, audits, committees, hiring of advocates, and speechmaking.

The chapter examined three responses to society by business: corporate giving, managing the environment, and socially responsible investing. These responses illustrate the scope of social concerns and the various ways business could react. The response by business to social responsibility and ethics is now incorporated into the management process and is implemented through the planning, organizing, leading and controlling functions.

KEY TERMS

social contract (p. 673)
social responsibility (p. 674)
social audit (p. 678)
business ethics (p. 680)
code of ethics (p. 682)
ethics audits (p. 684)
environmental audit (p. 691)
waste management (p. 693)
recycling (p. 693)
environmental ethic (p. 695)
sustainable development (p. 695)
socially responsible investment (SRI) (p. 695)

REVIEW QUESTIONS

1. What are society's criticisms of business?
2. Define social responsibility.
3. What is a social audit?
4. Define business ethics.
5. What are the sources of ethics in any person?
6. What influences ethical standards in business?
7. What initiatives can managers take to reinforce ethical behaviour in their business?
8. What are arguments for and against corporate giving?
9. What trends are occurring in corporate giving?
10. How are business enterprises responding to the environmental issue?
11. What are the criteria for socially responsible investing?
12. How do the topics of social responsibility and ethics relate to the management functions?

DISCUSSION QUESTIONS

1. State what you believe could be some clauses or items in a social contract between business and society.
2. What is the relationship between social responsibility and profits?
3. Why is there such a concern over business ethics?
4. Should ethics be taught in college or university business programs?
5. Why is corporate giving by Canadian business much lower that than for American business?
6. Why is the concept of sustainable economic development supported by business people?

EXERCISES

1. Visit two local companies that have formal codes of ethics. Evaluate the code of ethics, keeping in mind our discussion of ethics in this chapter.
2. Interview a manager about an ethical dilemma that he or she has faced. How did the manager resolve it?
3. Read the children's story, *The Lorax* by Dr. Seuss (A.S. Geisel, Random House, 1971). Identify the social responsibility issues mentioned. What conclusions are reached in the book?
4. Select what you consider to be a local social or ecological problem—such as water or air pollution. Make a list of the stakeholders within the community that are concerned with the problem. Analyze the impact of the problem of the various stakeholders. Develop a proposal for solving the problem, giving consideration to the benefits and costs of your solution.
5. Select a portfolio of stock that meet the criteria for a socially responsible investment.

MANAGEMENT ON LOCATION

CASE 22–1
FOOD ADVERTISING ON TELEVISION

A group of University of Western Ontario researchers found that the foods advertised on television were mostly of low nutritional value. If the foods advertised were consumed as a steady diet, it is possible that the risks of obesity, heart disease, and some cancers would increase.

The study analyzed all food and drink advertising on five stations received in the London, Ontario, area: MuchMusic (the music video channel), CBC, CTV, CBC-French, and a local independent channel. The time period was one week between 7 p.m. and 11 p.m., plus Saturday morning. The results from MuchMusic caused the most concern, and were significant because it is a channel targeted at youth with 20 percent of the station's viewers between 12 and 17 years of age and 55 percent between 18 and 34.

Some findings from the MuchMusic channel were:

- Alcohol products accounted for nearly 20 percent of all food and food-product advertising (not including beer-company sponsorship of some features and the frequent appearance of brewery logos).
- The channel had the highest percentage of pop commercials (41 percent of all food advertising) mostly for brands containing sugar, and sweets and candies.
- Fruits and vegetables, and meats and alternatives were not advertised at all.

Saturday morning advertising was of concern because of the large audience of young children. CBC English and French channels do not air commercials aimed at children. On CTV, 53 percent of the food and drink commercials promoted low-nutrient foods, fast-foods, and high-sugar cereals. The figure for the independent channel was even higher at 69 percent.

Overall, after analyzing all the advertised food products, the researchers found that the average nutritional content of all the products failed to meet any of the federal Health Department's guidelines for protein, carbohydrates, fat, and alcohol. No fresh vegetables were advertised on any of the stations and fresh apples were the only fruit promoted. ▲

QUESTIONS

1. Are the food manufacturers and TV stations behaving in a socially responsible and ethical manner?
2. What, if anything, should be done about this situation? If nothing, indicate why. If something, indicate what and by whom.

MANAGEMENT ON LOCATION

CASE 22–2
THE EXPRESS PETROLEUM COMPANY

Barbara Shortall was the owner and operator of the Express Petroleum Company, an independent chain of 25 gasoline stations and convenience stores. Barbara had made a name for herself as a successful entrepreneur since she had leased a small independent gas bar 10 years ago. Now at the age of 33, Shortall had expanded to cover the whole metropolitan area. Her business strategy was to sell gasoline at the lowest prices in town through quick service gasoline bars with convenience stores stocked with only high-volume items. The operations were supported by extensive and innovative advertising often featuring herself.

Shortall was proud of her accomplishments and supported various community activities as she felt that it was important to return to the community some of the profits she made from the business. The list of community activities supported was long. Shortall's stations were used by groups as pickup or dropoff locations for various charity campaigns. She sold holly in December for the Lion's Club fundraiser at no cost to the club and allowed local food banks to use her stations as locations for pickup boxes. She permitted groups to have car washes and set up stalls in the stores to sell crafts and baked goods. Shortall was active in many charitable and service organizations. For her variety of community-oriented activities, Barbara was last year's recipient of the "Citizen of the Year" award.

Shortall didn't deny that her community activities helped her business, and viewed her relationship with the community as a partnership where both she and the local community benefited. She encountered only positive reaction from the community in any of the various activities she participated in and considered her business to be socially responsible.

About six months ago Shortall became aware of the public's concern for the environment. She also noted that large competitors were involved in various environmental projects. For example, Shell was funding projects to clean up the environment and Petro-Canada was selling merchandise with proceeds going to wildlife organizations. Barbara came up with the idea of asking customers to suggest ways to protect the environment. The 10 best ideas each month would be awarded $25 certificates that could be used to purchase gasoline or merchandise at any of her stations.

The contest went well for the first two weeks and then some problems surfaced. A coalition of local environmental groups held a media conference to denounce the contest. They claimed that it encouraged the increased consumption of petroleum, a resource that was limited and, worse still, was one of the biggest pollutants. The groups pointed out the irony of a gasoline dealer protecting the environment when it contributed so much to its destruction. Letters to the editor of the local daily newspaper suggested a boycott of her gasoline stations.

Shortall was surprised by the reaction and didn't know what to do. Something would have to be done as the local media was calling for a response and two television stations wanted to film her comments at one of her stations. ▲

QUESTIONS

1. Was Barbara Shortall a socially responsible businessperson?
2. What should Barbara do now?
3. What should Barbara have done when developing the environment contest?

CASE 23–3
DILEMMA AT CAN-ROC LTD.

Sandi Bentley is the chairperson of the board of Can-Roc Ltd., a manufacturing firm with headquarters in a large Canadian city. During the past few years the company has been under considerable but polite pressure from the business school at the local university to contribute to a scholarship fund for promising students. The dean of the business school argues that, since business firm like Can-Roc are one of the prime beneficiaries of university business schools, they should help with the cost of training students.

The university is not the only organization applying pressure for funds. The symphony and the ballet are also asking for charitable donations so that ...

they can continue to contribute to the cultural richness of the city. Their representatives suggest that business firms like Can-Roc should contribute to the arts—like patrons in past eras—because they have a responsibility for the cultural development of the city where they carry on business activities.

After several years of this pressure, the board of directors agreed to establish a $10 000 university scholarship and to contribute $5000 each to the ballet and the symphony on a one-year trial basis. The board hoped that these donations would demonstrate the firm's good citizenship. Bentley has pointed out that Can-Roc would get considerable free publicity from these philanthropic actions.

At the annual meeting at the close of the fiscal year, these contributions were mentioned by Bentley. At that point, Peter Illych stood up and, noting that he represented a group of 40 shareholders, said that they were unhappy with the donations. Illych claimed that the board had no right to give $20 000 to scholarships and cultural activities; he argued that the board was supposed to run the business well and see that it made a good profit. By giving to charity, the board was taking money out of the shareholders' pockets because less money could be distributed as dividends. Illych stated that shareholders had bought Can-Roc shares to get good dividend payments; with this kind of behaviour, the board was preventing them from achieving their financial goals. Illych also questioned the board's competence to make decisions on charitable donations.

At the conclusion of this negative speech, several other shareholders stood up to say that they disagreed with the sentiments Illych expressed. While they agreed that the board's action meant a slight reduction in dividends, they felt that the decisions were reasonable. These shareholders agreed with the university and the arts groups that Can-Roc could not ignore important organizations in the city that were in real need of funds and that the corporation had a responsibility to consider requests for charitable donations.

The meeting ended with a promise by Bentley that the board would examine the issue of corporate charity and would report to the shareholders at the next annual meeting. ▲

QUESTIONS

1. What kinds of arguments can you pose in favour of and opposed to corporate charitable donations?
2. What should the board of directors do about this issue? How should they defend their decision to shareholders represented by Illych and to the shareholders not opposed to charitable donations?

COMPREHENSIVE CASES
PART VI

CASE VI-1
PALLISER FURNITURE CORPORATION IN TAIWAN (A)

INTRODUCTION

Palliser Furniture President Art DeFehr felt the evening had been going quite well up till that point. He had been enjoying dinner with a prospective supplier discussing Palliser's intention to expand dealings into Taiwan. He now felt uneasy. Two attractive Taiwanese women had just quietly sat down at their table and now looked expectantly toward them. Their host's subtle nodding smile to the two women as they had sat down seemed to indicate that the womens' visit was not unexpected. As a native Canadian, Art was aware that foreign business dealings were often accompanied by the unwritten "extras." Were these women one of the extras in doing business in Taiwan?

The Canadian manager had often heard that platitude "When in Rome, do as the Romans do" and now wondered if Palliser's dealings in Taiwan meant accepting those dealings being accompanied by what one company salesman had crassly summarized as "booze, broads, and bribes." Was accepting these offers a necessary part of doing business in Taiwan? He also wondered whether he had any right as a foreigner to challenge national custom? He wondered further whether this *was* in fact the custom? He contemplated further what effect his response would have on future business dealings. A precedent was about to be set. It was a warm Taipei evening in March 1986.

PALLISER FURNITURE CORPORATION: COMPANY HISTORY

Palliser Furniture Corporation began in 1933 in the Winnipeg suburb of North Kildonan where Albert A. DeFehr started a woodworking company in the basement of his home. Building step-stools, planters, ironing boards, and clothes racks, Mr. DeFehr's new company, A.A. DeFehr Manufacturing, began with the very modest output level of three pieces per day. Now, over 40 years later, the company had become the largest furniture manufacturer in Canada.

COMPANY OWNERSHIP AND MANAGEMENT

By the time Palliser was planning its venture into Taiwan, Albert DeFehr was no longer directly involved in the day-to-day running of the business. While still involved as Chairman of the Board, Mr. DeFehr's three sons, Frank, Art and Dave, essentially ran the business. The eldest, Frank, served as executive vice-president of manufacturing and was also involved in plant layout and set-up operations, as well as management of the two upholstery plants. Art was more involved in the public side of the business, serving as company president. In addition, he also maintained a keen interest in the marketing and product design areas. Dave, the youngest of the three sons, managed the single largest plant, the DeFehr Division, which employed over 600 of Palliser's 1600 employees. Irene (nee DeFehr) Loewen, the only daughter, and five years Dave's younger, served on Palliser's board, and was actively involved in the administration of the DeFehr Foundation.

While the company had begun exclusively as a family enterprise, the circle of ownership had in recent years been expanded to include senior employees in a stock-ownership plan, and all employees in a profit-sharing bonus plan. The effort to inspire excellence in efficiency, quality, and productivity had generally been quite effective as evidenced by the company's ascendancy to the position of Canadian industry leader.

COMPANY STRATEGY

Palliser Furniture Corporation's strategy was essentially to become one of the leading manufacturers/suppliers of medium-priced upholstered furniture and case goods in the North American furniture industry. With manufacturing plants in Winnipeg, Calgary, and Fargo (North Dakota) and showroom/distribution centres in Vancouver, Winnipeg, Toronto and Montreal, the company was poised to realize this objective.

THE NORTH AMERICAN FURNITURE INDUSTRY

The industry Palliser competed in had become increasingly segmented, with segmentation occurring on the multiple bases of price, construction, material (i.e., wood/nonwood), case goods/upholstered products, and design style. As a medium-priced, wood-based manufacturer of traditional and contemporary case goods and upholstered furniture, Palliser was effectively left to compete for only about 50 percent of the furniture dollar.

As a manufacturer of wood furniture, Palliser missed out on the glass, metal, and plastic markets, which accounted for about 20 percent of the total furniture market. On the basis of price, Palliser was outpriced by about 15 to 20 percent of high-end wood furniture manufacturers (such as Gibbard and Sterling), and likewise underpriced by another 15 to 20 percent of • • •

the low-end wood furniture manufacturers (such as South Shore and Citation House). Finally, about one-fifth of the products sold in the North American market were manufactured outside Canada and the U.S. either because of uniqueness in design, uniqueness in construction materials, or simply on the basis of manufacturing cost.

PALLISER WORLD TRADE CENTRE: GROWTH THROUGH PRODUCT DIVERSIFICATION

Given the trends towards industry segmentation, the company had in recent years increasingly recognized its needs for an expanded product line. To this end it began in the early 1980s to import leather recliner chairs and marble end tables from selected Italian manufacturers. The company had also begun importing selected component parts which it incorporated into its manufacturing operations. These included unfinished chair parts, and bulk brass and glass from Yugoslavia and Czechoslovakia.

It therefore came as no surprise when a new division, Palliser World Trade was formed in 1985 and given the explicit mandate of locating, purchasing and distributing such products and parts. The criteria in product and country selection were four-fold:

1. Fashionability: any and all assembled/semi-assembled products chosen for import were to be compatible with Palliser's existing lines under manufacture in Canada and the U.S.
2. Quality: any and all products chosen were expected to satisfy the same quality standards as those required of existing lines under manufacture in Canada and the U.S. because all imported products would be covered by the same Palliser warranty as North American manufactured pieces.
3. Profitability: any and all products chosen were expected to generate gross operating profits of not less than 15 percent.
4. Stability: any and all countries chosen to trade with were to have low-inflation currencies and stable governments.

MANAGER PROFILE: ARTHUR DEFEHR

Having been significantly influenced by his Christian home and church upbringing, Palliser President Art DeFehr had deliberately made it a priority to integrate volunteer service involvements into his business career. During the 1970s Art had worked under the auspices of the Mennonite Central Committee on two separate assignments in Bangladesh in 1975, and later in Thailand, in 1980. These two involvements had introduced him to Asia, not only as a place of need, but also as a place of opportunity. A Harvard M.B.A., Art sensed the strategic opportunity emerging from the countries of the Pacific Rim. One such country was the Republic of China, or as it was more commonly known, Taiwan.

COUNTRY PROFILE: TAIWAN

Taiwan, the Republic of China was situated in the far western Pacific at the crossroads of Northeast and Southeast Asia.[1] Bisected by the Tropic of Cancer, the island had an area of 13 900 square miles inhabited by almost 20 million people. The national language was Mandarin, but English was one of the more commonly spoken foreign languages. The climate was described as subtropical with an average annual temperature of between 21.7 and 24.1 degrees Celsius, for the northern and southern parts of the island, respectively.[2]

INDUSTRY PROFILE: TAIWAN'S FURNITURE MANUFACTURING INDUSTRY

There were over 200 furniture manufacturers in Taiwan. These were concentrated along the country's southwest coast. Some of these companies manufactured unfinished component parts, while others manufactured completely finished "showroom-ready" furniture.

OPPORTUNITY CREATION THROUGH PARADIGM SHIFT

During a visit to Taiwan on one of his Asian services tours, Art had recognized the emergence of the Taiwanese furniture manufacturing industry. Eager to learn, the Taiwanese manufacturers were developing quickly to a position of parity with their North American counterparts. However, what he had also observed was that the mindset of most of the North American buyers was not evolving proportional to the growth of the Taiwanese manufacturers' expertise.

In the early stages of the industry's evolution in Taiwan the price and quality of the Taiwanese furniture products vis-à-vis North American products had been inexpensive and of low quality. This quality differential had implicitly fostered a condescending attitude on the part of the North American buyers toward their Taiwanese suppliers. This condescension manifested itself in the North American's low trust level of the Taiwanese. Loyalty, the North American too often assumed, was to price, not to person.

[1] Travel in Taiwan, 4, No. 6, January 1990, p.38.

[2] Ibid.

These communication difficulties had created an opportunity for a group of people who could essentially be described as "managers of fortune." These free-lance North Americans would typically be hired by individual Taiwanese manufacturers to work as manufacturer's agents in representing their company's product line to foreign buyers. However, from the vantage point of the Taiwanese, the arrangement was far from perfect as the agents often manipulated the situation for their own interests, playing manufacturer off against manufacturer in a strategy of maximizing their own short-term sales commissions. Clearly, from the viewpoint of the Taiwanese manufacturer, the arrangement gave too much power to the man in the middle.

Art had picked this signal up from several discussions with Taiwanese furniture manufacturers. The Taiwanese furniture manufacturers had evolved not only in terms of their abilities in product design and manufacturing quality, but also in their general abilities as businesspeople. The Taiwanese therefore felt increasingly frustrated by the condescending attitudes displayed by many of their North American buyers. During one discussion with a North American agent Art had even heard the agent speak derogatively about the reliability of a particular Taiwanese supplier all the while standing within earshot of the particular supplier. It was just one more example of colonialism's lagging hold on the mindset of the colonizer.

Art concluded a slightly different opportunity now existed than had historically. It was an opportunity based not simply on the obvious dimensions of price or product features, but on capitalizing on the Taiwanese's businessperson's desire to be treated as an equal and competent trading partner rather than as a "second-class business citizen." Those North Americans who clung to old assumptions of Asian inferiority would in the long term stand to lose.

Many North Americans lacking his Asian service experience had viewed the Taiwanese as untrustworthy and disloyal, eager only to make the "fast buck." Art's perspective was quite different. Treated as equals he had found the Asian business person to be reliable, committed and quality conscious. In short, the Japanese economic miracle was not to be limited to Japan alone. A long-term opportunity existed for those North American buyers who were prepared to extend relational parity to their Taiwanese suppliers.

THE TAIWANESE OPPORTUNITY EXPLORED FURTHER

In early spring 1986 the DeFehr brothers together with key Palliser World Trade personnel had visited Taiwan to explore the country's potential as a supplier of complementary furniture products and accessories. Visits to about 20 Taiwanese furniture manufacturing plants during a whirlwind tour of the country had quickly convinced the brothers of Taiwan's potential as a supplier of complementary products. The country's exchange rate of $0.25 (U.S.) only served to sweeten the opportunity even more.

DETERMINING THE SUPPLIER POOL

It was decided by the DeFehr brothers after their initial visit that the Palliser World Trade venture would start cautiously, beginning dealings with only about six dealers. Gradually, it hoped, the suppliers would grow to about a dozen. Likely inclusions in the initial supplier pool were Yeh Brothers of Kaohsiung, Sanyu Manufacturers of Pingtung (east of Kaohsiung), and Hwaung Manufacturers of Hsinchu. Products initially targeted for export to Canada included unpainted wood designs for assembly in dining room china cabinet fronts, and fully finished black lacquer end tables. Operations were targeted to begin in late 1986.

AN EVENING OUT IN TAIWAN

McGill professor Henry Mintzberg, in his popular article, "The Manager's Job: Folklore and Fact" had observed that one of the key roles senior management played was that of liaison. Explained most simply, this meant that the executive was responsible to build and maintain a network of relationships with the external environment that were necessary to ensure the effective functioning of the organization. One such contact was Yan Kee Suppliers of Taiwan Inc. On one of his last evenings in the country, Art had set aside time for dinner and socializing with the company president. The evening had been intended to be an evening of network development and thus far had gone very smoothly.

THE SITUATION

He now felt uneasy. Two attractive Taiwanese women had just quietly sat down at their restaurant table and now waited expectantly across from them. Their host's subtle nodding smile to the two women as they sat down seemed to indicate that the women's visit was not unexpected. Their Taiwanese host commented on their arrival. "I thought you, like some of your American counterparts, might enjoy some ... 'companionship' shall we say, for the evening." Their smiling host waited for his guests' response.

THE OPTIONS: TO AVOID, ACCOMMODATE, OR ACCOST?

The DeFehr family had always prided themselves on integrating their religious convictions into the daily dealings of Palliser Furniture. But now Art wondered whether growth into Taiwan

• • •

could result in the company's compromising of its ethnical ideals. He had often heard of "palms being greased" in one way or another and knew such practices were not uncommon. If a lot of Palliser's competitors were involved in such dealings as their host inferred was it just a part of doing business in Taiwan? He also wondered if he could be offending his host by turning down his offer. His mind quickly jumped ahead to a possible future situation where one of his employees would be confronted with the same decision. Ought he to leave each Palliser employee to decide for themselves what their response to such offers would be or was it his responsibility to provide a company directive on what was and wasn't acceptable in business dealings? He thought further. Were the traditional conservative Christian convictions that Palliser had been built on simply outmoded in the global marketplace? A scene from the musical "Fiddler on The Roof" came to mind as he contemplated the situation. The scene involved the story's central character Tevye, who discovers that some of his age-old Jewish traditions are no longer sustainable in an ever-changing world. Were Palliser's ethics no longer sustainable as well? ▲

QUESTIONS

1. Four degrees of internationalization are discussed in Chapter 21. In which degree is Palliser? How is this relevant to the situation described?
2. There are several sources of ethical behaviour. Which of these sources is influencing Art DeFehr?
3. What should Art DeFehr do?
4. What should Palliser Furniture do to prepare other employees who will be visiting Taiwan?

CASE VI-2
FOOTWEAR INTERNATIONAL

John Carlson frowned as he studied the translation of the front page story of the afternoon's edition of the *Meillat*, a fundamentalist newspaper with close ties to an opposition political party. The story, titled "Footwear's Unpardonable Audacity," suggested that the company was knowingly insulting Islam by including the name of Allah in a design used on the insoles of sandals it was manufacturing. To compound the problem, the paper had run a photograph of one of the offending sandals on the front page. As a result student groups were calling for public demonstrations against Footwear the next day. As Managing Director of Footwear Bangladesh, Carlson knew he would have to act quickly to defuse a potentially explosive situation.

FOOTWEAR INTERNATIONAL

Footwear International is a multinational manufacturer and marketer of footwear. Operations span the globe and include more than 83 companies in 70 countries. These include shoe factories, tanneries, engineering plants producing shoe machinery and moulds, product development studios, hosiery factories, quality control labouratories and approximately 6300 retail stores and 50 000 independent retailers.

Footwear employs more than 67 000 people and produces and sells in excess of 270 000 000 pairs of shoes every year. Head office acts as a service centre and is staffed with specialists drawn from all over the world. These specialists, in areas such as marketing, retailing, product development, communications, store design, electronic data processing and business administration, travel for much of the year to share their expertise with the various companies. Training and technical education, offered through company run colleges and the training facility at headquarters, provide the latest skills to employees from around the world.

Although Footwear requires standardization in technology and the design of facilities, it also encourages a high degree of decentralization and

• • •

autonomy in its operations. The companies are virtually self-governing, which means their allegiance belongs to the countries in which they operate. Each is answerable to a board of directors which includes representatives from the local business community. The concept of "partnership" at the local level has made the company welcome internationally and has allowed it to operate successfully in countries where other multinationals have been unable to survive.

BANGLADESH

With a population approaching 110 000 000 in an area of 143 998 square kilometres (Exhibit 1), Bangladesh is the most densely populated country in the world. It is also among the most impoverished with a 1987 per capital Gross National Product of $160 U.S. and a high reliance on foreign aid. Over 40 percent of the Gross Domestic Product is generated by agriculture and more than 60 percent of its economically active population works in the agriculture sector. Although the land in Bangladesh is fertile, the country has a tropical monsoon climate and suffers from the ravages of periodic cyclones. In 1988 the country experienced the worse floods in recorded history.

The population of Bangladesh is 85 percent Moslem, and Islam was made the official state religion in 1988. Approximately 95 percent of the population speaks Bengali with most of the remainder speaking tribal dialects.

Bangladesh has had a turbulent history in the twentieth century. Most of the country was part of the British ruled East Bengal until 1947. In that year it joined with Assam to become East Pakistan, a province of the newly created country of Pakistan. East Pakistan was separated from the four provinces of West Pakistan by 1600 kilometres of Indian territory and, although the East was more populus, the national capital was established in West Pakistan. Over the following years widespread discontent built in the East whose people felt that they received a disproportionately small amount of development funding and were under-represented in government.

Following a period of unrest starting in 1969 the Awami League, the leading political party in East Pakistan, won an overwhelming victory in local elections held in 1970. The victory promised to give the league, which was pro independence, control in the National Assembly. To prevent that happening the national government suspended the convening of the Assembly indefinitely. On March 26th, 1971, the Awami League proclaimed the independence of the People's

EXHIBIT 1 BANGLADESH.

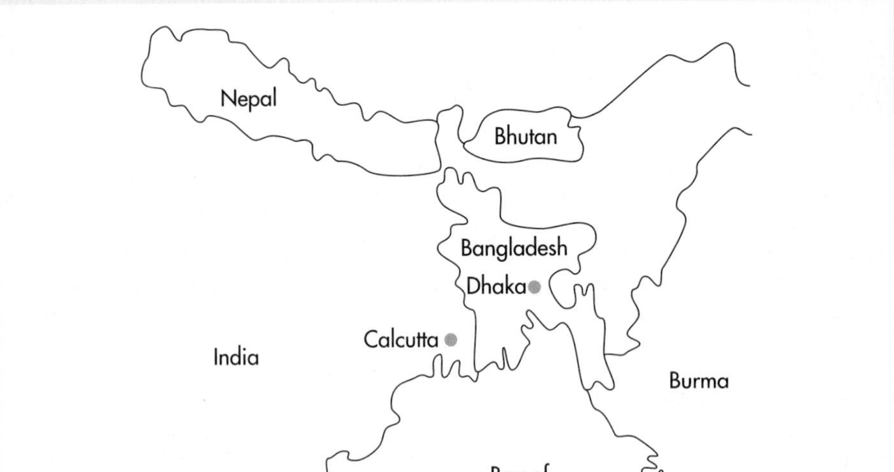

• • •

Republic of Bangladesh and civil war quickly followed. In the ensuing conflict hundreds of thousands of refugees fled to safety across the border to India. In December, India, which supported the independence of Bangladesh, declared war and twelve days later Pakistan surrendered. Bangladesh had won its independence and the capital of the new country was established at Dhaka. In the years immediately following independence industrial output declined in major industries as the result of the departure of many of the largely non-Bengali financier and managerial class.

Throughout the subsequent years, political stability proved elusive for Bangladesh. Although elections were held, stability was threatened by the terrorist tactics resorted to by opposition groups from both political extremes. Coups and counter-coups, assassinations and suspension of civil liberties became regular occurrences.

Since 1983 Bangladesh had been ruled by the self-proclaimed President General H.M. Ershad. Despite demonstrations in 1987 that led to a state of emergency being declared, Ershad managed to retain power in elections held the following year. The country remains politically volatile, however. Dozens of political parties continually manoeuvre for position and alliances and coalitions are the order of the day. The principal opposition party is the Awami League, an alliance of eight political parties. Many of the parties are closely linked with so called "opposition newspapers" which promote their political positions. Strikes and demonstrations are frequent and often result from cooperation among opposition political parties, student groups and unions.

FOOTWEAR BANGLADESH

Footwear became active in what was then East Bengal in the 1930s. In 1962 the first major investment took place with the construction of a footwear manufacturing facility at Tongi, an industrial town located 30 kilometres north of Dhaka. During the following years, the company expanded its presence in both conventional and unconventional ways. In 1971 the then managing director became a freedom fighter while continuing to oversee operations. He subsequently became the only foreigner to be decorated by the government with the "Bir Protik" in recognition of both his and the company's contribution to the independence of Bangladesh.

In 1985 Footwear Bangladesh went public and two years later spearheaded the largest private-sector foreign investment in the country, a tannery and footwear factory at Dhamrai. The new tannery produced leather for local Footwear needs and the export market while the factory produced a variety of footwear for the local market.

By 1988 Footwear Bangladesh employed 1800 employees and sold through 81 stores and 54 agencies. The company introduced approximately 300 new products a year to the market using their in-house design and development capability. Footwear managers were particularly proud of the capability of the personnel in these departments, all of whom were Bangladeshi.

Annual sales in excess of 10 000 000 pairs of footwear gave the company 14 percent of the national market in 1988. Revenues exceeded $30 million U.S. and after-tax profit was approximately $1 million. Financially, the company was considered a medium contributor within the Footwear organization. With a population approaching 110 000 000, and per capita consumption of one pair of shoes every two years, Bangladesh was perceived as offering Footwear enormous potential for growth both through consumer education and competitive pressure.

The managing director of Footwear Bangladesh was John Carlson, one of only four foreigners working for the company. The others were the managers of production, marketing and sales. All had extensive and varied experience within the Footwear organization.

THE INCIDENT

On Thursday, June 22, 1989, John Carlson was shown a copy of that day's *Meillat,* a well-known opposition newspaper with pro-Libyan leanings. Under the headline "Footwear's Unpardonable Audacity," the writer suggested that the design on the insole of one model of sandal produced by the company included the Arabic spelling of the word "Allah" (Exhibit 2). The story went on to suggest that Footwear was under Jewish ownership and to link the alleged offence with the gunning down of many people in Palestine by Jews. The story highlighted the fact that the design was on the insole of the sandal and, therefore, next to the foot, a sign of great disrespect to Moslems.

Carlson immediately contacted the supervisor of the design department and asked for any information he could provide on the design on the sandals. He already knew that they were from a medium-priced line of women's footwear known as "Chappels" which had the design on the insole changed often as a marketing feature. Following his investigation the supervisor reported that the design had been based on a set of Chinese temple bells that the designer had purchased in the local market. Pleased by the appearance of the bells she had used them as the basis for a stylized design which she submitted to her supervisor for consideration and approval (Exhibit 3).

• • •

EXHIBIT 2 TRANSLATION OF THE *MEILLAT* STORY.

In Bangladesh a Sandal with Allah as Footwear trade mark in Arabic designed in calligraphy has been marketed although last year Islam was made the State Religion in Bangladesh. The Sandal in black and white contains Allah in black. Prima facie it appears it has been designed and the Alif "the first letter in Arabic" has been jointly written. Excluding Alif it reads LILLAH. In Bangladesh after the Satan Rushdies[2] Satanic Verses which has brought unprecedented demonstration and innumerable strikes (Hartels). This International shoe manufacturing organization under Jewish ownership with the design of Allah has made religious offence. Where for sanctity of Islam one million people of Afghanistan have sacrificed their lives and where in occupied Palestine many people have been gunned down by Jews for sanctity of Islam in this country the word Allah under this guise has been put under feet.

Last night a group of students from Dhaka university came to *Meillat* office with a couple of pairs of Sandal. The management staff of Footwear was not available over telephone. This sandal has got two straps made of foam.

[1] The translation is identical to that which Carlson was given to work with.

[2] Salman Rushdie was the author of the controversial book, "The Satanic Verses." The author has been sentenced to death, in absentia, by Ayatollah Khomeini, the leader of Iran, for crimes against Islam.

FIGURE 3 THE TEMPLE BELLS AND THE DESIGN USED ON THE SANDAL.

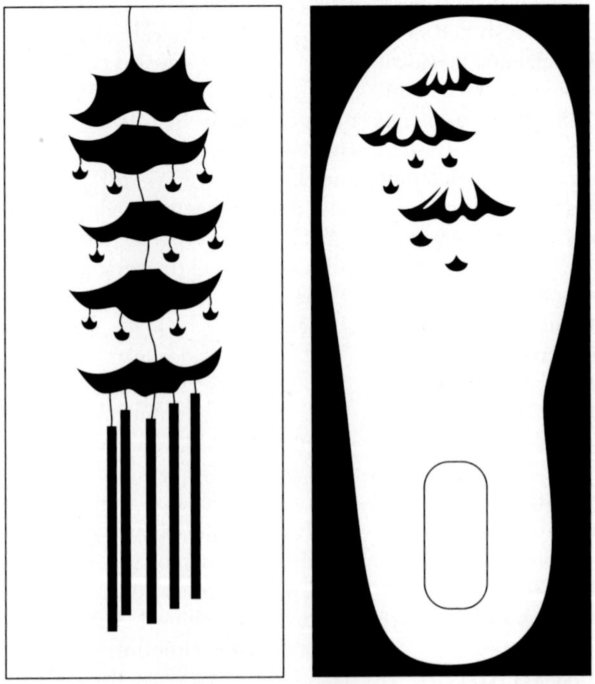

[1] The images in Figure 3 were redrawn from a copy of a facsimile sent to headquarters by John Carlson.

All of the employees in the development and marketing department were Moslems. The supervisor reported that the woman who had produced the offending design was a devout Bengali Moslem who spoke and read no Arabic.

The same was true of almost all of the employees in the department. The supervisor confirmed to Carlson that numerous people in the department had seen the new design prior to its approval and no one had seen any problem or raised any objection to it. Following the conversation Carlson compared the design to the word Allah which he had arranged to have written in Arabic (Exhibit 4).

Carlson was perplexed by the article and its timing. The sandals in question were not new to the market and had not been subject to prior complaints. As he reread the translation of the *Meillat* article he wondered why the Jewish reference had been made when the family that owned Footwear International were Christian. He also wondered if the fact that students from the university had taken the sandals to the paper was significant.

As the day progressed the situation got worse. Carlson was shown a translation of a proclamation that had been circulated by two youth groups calling for demonstrations against Footwear to be held the next day (Exhibit 5). The proclamation linked Footwear, Salman Rushdie and the Jewish community, and ominously stated that "even at the cost of our lives we have to protest against this conspiracy."

More bad news followed. Calls had been made for charges to be laid against Carlson and four others under a section of the criminal code that forbade "deliberate and malicious acts intended to outrage feelings of any class by insulting its religion or religious believers" (Exhibit 6). A short time later Carlson received a copy of a statement that had been filed by a local lawyer, although no warrants were immediately forthcoming (Exhibit 7).

While he was reviewing the situation Carlson was interrupted by his secretary. In an excited voice she informed him that the prime minister was being quoted as calling the sandal incident an "unforgivable crime." The seriousness of the incident seemed to be escalating rapidly and Carlson wondered what he should do to try to minimize the damage. ▲

EXHIBIT 4 THE ARABIC SPELLING OF ALLAH.

[1] The figure in Exhibit 4 was redrawn from a copy of a facsimile sent to headquarters by John Carlson.

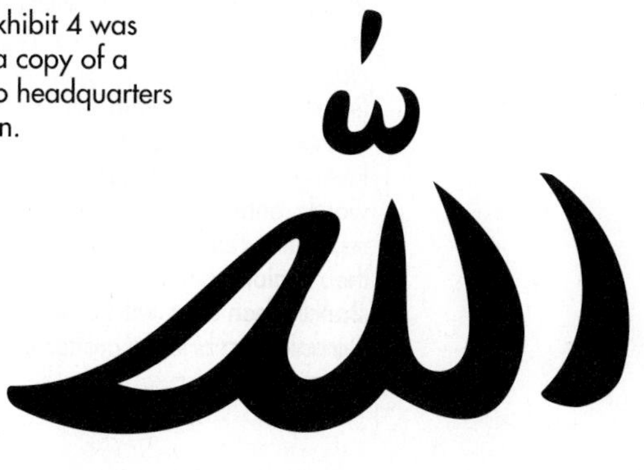

EXHIBIT 5 TRANSLATION OF THE STUDENT GROUPS PROCLAMATION.[1]

The audacity through the use of the name "Allah" in a sandal.

Let Rushdies Jewish Footwear Company be prohibited in Bangladesh.

Dear People who believe in one God It is announced in the holy Quran Allahs name is above everything but shoe manufacturing Jewish Footwear Shoe Company has used the name Allah and shown disrespect of unprecedented nature and also unpardonable audacity. After the failure of Rushies efforts to destroy the beliefs of Moslems in the Quran, Islam and the prophet (SM) who is the writer of Satanic verses the Jewish people have started offending the Moslems. This time it is a fight again Allah. In fact Daud Haider, Salam Rushdie Viking Penguin and Footwear Shoe Company all are supported and financed by Jewish community.

Therefore no compromise with them. Even at the cost of our lives we have to protest against this conspiracy. For this procession and demonstration will be held on 23rd. June Friday after Jumma prayer from Baitul Mukarram Mosque south gate. Please join this procession and announce we will not pardon Footwear Shoe Company audacity. Footwear Shoe Company has to be prohibited, don't buy Jewish products and Footwear shoes. Be aware Rushies partner.

Issued by Bangladesh Islamie Jubashibir (Youth Student Forum) and Bangladesh Islamic Satrashbir (Student Forum)

[1] The translation is identical to that which Carlson was given to work with.

EXHIBIT 6 SECTION 295 OF THE CRIMINAL CODE.

295-A. *Deliberate and malicious acts intended to outrage religious feelings of any class by insulting its religion or religious believers.* Whoever, with deliberate and malicious intention of outraging the religious feelings of any class [of citizens...], by words, either spoken or written, or by visible representations insults or attempts to insult the religion or religious beliefs of that class, shall be punished with imprisonment....
...In order to bring a matter under S. 295-A it is not the mere matter of discourse or the written expression but also the manner of it which has to be looked to. In other words the expressions should be such as are bound to be regarded by any reasonable man as grossly offensive and provocative and maliciously and deliberately intended to outrage the feelings of any class of citizens....If the injurious act was done voluntarily without a lawful excuse, malice may be presumed.

EXHIBIT 7 THE STATEMENT OF THE PLAINTIFF.

The plaintiff most respectfully states that:

1) The plaintiff is a lawyer, and a Bangladeshi Citizen and his religion is Islam. He is basically a devout Moslem. According to Islamic tradition he regularly performs his daily work.
2) The first accused of this...is the Managing Director of Footwear Shoe Company, the second accused is the Production Manager of the said company, the third accused is the Marketing Manager, the fourth accused is the Calligrapher of the said company and the last accused is the Sales Manager of the said company. The said company is an international organization having shoe business in different countries.
3) The accused persons deliberately wanted to outrage the religion of Muslims by engraving the calligraphy of "Allah" in Arabic on a sandal thereby to offend the Religion of majority this Muslim country. By marketing this sandal with the calligraphy of "Allah" they have offended the religious duty and responsibility of every devout Muslim to protect the sanctity of "Allah." The plaintiff first saw the sandal with this calligraphy on 22nd June 1989 at Elephant road shop.

The accused persons collectively and deliberately wanted this calligraphy under the feet thereby to offend the religion of mine and many other Muslims and have committed a crime under provisions of section 295A of the Penal Code. At the time of hearing the evidence will be provided.

Therefore under the provisions of section 295A of the Penal Code the accused persons be issued with warrant of arrest and be brought to court for justice.

The names of the Witnesses

1)

2)

3)

QUESTIONS

1. What is the issue confronting the management of Footwear International?
2. What explanation is there for the escalation of the incident to such a serious situation?
3. Can the incident be attributed to some aspect of Footwear International's and Footwear Bangladesh's organizational arrangements or structure?
4. How could this incident have been prevented?
5. What should Carlson do "to try and minimize the damage?"

CASE VI-3
LONGHURST PULP AND PAPER INC.

Arthur Smith, General Manager of Longhurst pulp and paper mill in Westborough, Nova Scotia, sat pensively in his office. It was February, 1990, and he had just been informed that new regulations would be introduced in the spring to limit pollution from pulp and paper mill effluents. According to the federal government, these requirements would be phased in "according to a schedule which recognizes the time required for mills to modify their processes." "I'm afraid this decision will have a terrible impact on both the mill and the community of Westborough," warned Mr. Smith. "Last year we spent $10 million to bring us in line with existing regulations and we simply cannot afford a comparable expenditure this year. This is an old mill and it doesn't take a genius to figure out that full compliance will force layoffs through downsizing or possibly even closure. That's hardly the right tonic for a one industry town."

A BRIEF HISTORY OF THE MILL

Overview

In 1905, the Nova Scotia Development (NSD) company began construction on the mill and the town of Westborough itself with $5 million in capital and 1000 workers. Westborough was the perfect site for a pulp and paper mill as there was a railway, a nearby deep-water port at Anspach, Nova Scotia, a huge supply of softwood trees and a large river which could be used to generate power and to transport pulpwood. In 1909, the first roll of newsprint was produced at the mill.

Westborough was truly a company town—NSD built houses, schools and roads and originally operated the town's only grocery and dry goods store. It was not until 1960 that Westborough finally became incorporated as a municipality.

For many years the mill prospered. Even during the Great Depression it experienced very little downtime. Workers became accustomed to a high standard of living derived from the success of the NSD facility. This success, however, did not carry over to labour relations. Union-management discord had been a reality at the mill for much of its history and had been manifested by several bitter labour disputes and work stoppages over the years.

Currently, the town of Westborough has a total of 4000 residents and the majority of its working population is employed by the mill which is owned and operated by Longhurst, Inc., a large Canadian firm which owns approximately 25 paper mills. The Westborough mill has a thermochemical facility that produces pulp which is later transformed into newsprint on two paper machines. About 60 percent of its power requirements is generated by three hydro facilities owned by Longhurst. Workers are represented by six unions, five of which are locals of the Canadian Paperworkers Union and the other is a local of the International Brotherhood of Electrical Workers Union. The mill now employs only about 1250 workers, down from 1500 in January, due to the recent shutdown of its third paper machine.

Environment Record

Until recently, concern for the environment was not a high priority for mill management. In fact, prior to 1989, there had been no steps taken to reduce water or air pollution caused by the facility. "I don't deny that there has been some environmental negligence over the years, but one must remember that only mills built after 1971 were required to comply with pollution control regulations" said Mr. Smith. "By avoiding environmental expenditures, old mills were able to keep costs down and this helped them compete with the newer, more efficient facilities. And you have to realize that prior to the green movement, managers could not justify environmental expenditures to shareholders who were simply interested in the bottom line. I'm not making excuses—I'm simply pointing out a few basic facts."

In 1989, mill management announced a $10 million treatment program to meet old guidelines for pollution control. To cut sulphur emissions, circulating fluidized bed boilers were installed to burn low-grade coal and fuel oil more efficiently. Also a number of initiatives were undertaken to help reduce dioxin discharges responsible for polluting nearby rivers and streams. "We realize that the long-term success of the mill will depend on how effectively we respond to the environment issue" declared Mr. Smith. "This expenditure not only makes us more socially responsible, it also serves a strategic purpose."

STRATEGIC PRIORITIES

For much of the mill's history, management considered low cost leadership to be the mill's dominant strategic objective. However, some recent changes in the external environment have prompted a reassessment of the mill's strategic focus.

The Market

The Westborough pulp and paper mill relies almost exclusively on export trade to countries in Europe, Central America
• • •

and South America (see Exhibit 1). There is intense competition within these markets as many mills worldwide vie for market share. Since the mid-1990s, factors such as the relatively high value of the Canadian dollar and the comparatively low wages paid to mill workers in countries such as Mexico have forced changes in strategic emphases for Canadian pulp and paper manufacturers away from low-cost leadership. For many mills, including the Westborough facility, these changes have been manifested in a new strategic focus: the improvement of product quality.

A New Strategy

In 1986, given the considerable demand for premium quality paper, particularly in the European market, management at the Westborough mill adopted a product differentiation strategy as a hedge against unfavourable export conditions. Machines were modernized, processes were rationalized and financial gains were realized over time (see Exhibit 2). The largest single project undertaken to support the new strategy was the construction of a chlorine-based chemical pulping plant in 1987. The high-quality pulp produced by this facility considerably improved the quality of the finished paper and contributed to higher sales for the mill's products, particularly in Europe (see Exhibit 1).

In November, 1988, Mr. Smith commented on the success of the new pulping facility: "It has enabled us to penetrate new markets overseas. We've signed more new contracts for paper in the past six months than we had signed in the previous two years! We now have a reputation abroad as a manufacturer of superior quality paper and, believe me, there's just no substitute for quality."

Recently, the mill's third paper machine was shut down with the loss of approximately 250 jobs, because it was inefficient and incapable of producing a high-quality sheet. According to Mr. Smith, "It's unfortunate, but we could no longer afford to compromise our strategic objectives by leaving the machine in operation."

EXHIBIT 1 DELIVERIES PER COUNTRY (IN TONS).

Country	1989	1988	1987
Belgium and Luxembourg	7 906	6 562	5 613
Denmark	15 097	12 531	10 719
France	22 352	18 552	15 870
Germany, Federal Republic of	47 060	39 059	33 412
Ireland	3 621	3 005	2 570
Netherlands	13 629	11 312	9 674
United Kingdom	104 835	87 195	74 543
Europe	214 500	178 216	152 401
Argentina	19 547	20 321	18 218
Brazil	47 775	49 647	44 581
Chile	3 689	3 834	3 440
El Salvador	587	610	539
Mexico	17 453	18 139	16 254
Peru	2 328	2 419	2 184
Venezuela	24 869	25 846	23 200
Latin America	116 248	120 816	108 416
Export Deliveries	330 748	299 032	260 817
Canada	21 781	21 529	17 996
Total Deliveries	352 529	320 561	278 813

• • •

EXHIBIT 2 INCOME SUMMARY (IN THOUSANDS).

	1989	1988	1987
Sales	$272 116	$228 406	$204 623
Less: Expenses			
C.O.G.S.	171 820	143 658	128 912
Salaries	48 043	47 216	46 942
Rents	3 043	2 896	2 741
Other	20 149	8 216	7 294
Operation Margin	29 061	26 420	18 734
Depreciation and amortization			
Machinery and equipment	3 866	3 458	3 261
Other fixed assets	407	386	372
Net earnings (operations)	24 788	22 576	15 101
Other income			
Interest received	2 062	1 246	1 092
Net income	26 850	23 822	16 193
Less:			
Interest expenses	916	784	521
Taxes	8 055	7 147	4 858
Gain for the period	$17 879	$15 891	$10 814

RECENT DEVELOPMENTS

Government Regulations

In February, 1990, Environment Canada advised Canadian pulp and paper manufacturers that strict pollution control regulations would be introduced in the spring. The regulations, under the Canadian Environmental Protection Act, will require virtual elimination of dioxin and furan discharges from pulp and paper mills and will restrict the sales and use of some defoamers which contribute to dioxin formation. Amendments to the Fisheries Act will set new limits on chlorine discharges in bleach plant effluents. This will be the first time the federal government has issued regulations applicable to all pulp and paper facilities in Canada. Previously, only mills built after 1971 were required to adhere to federal environment standards.

The pressure to introduce tough, uniform regulations primarily came from environmentalist groups, such as Greenpeace. Many of these groups contend that dioxin, a by-product of bleached chemical pulp, is an extremely deadly toxin and maintain that there are no safe levels of the substance—no matter how small. However, a recent study of 104 pulp and paper mills in the United States indicated that the small amounts of dioxin typically produced in the pulping process pose a negligible environmental risk.

Public Opinion Survey

As a means to determine opinions on a diversity of issues, a survey of Westborough residents was conducted in September of 1989. Designed by Phil Simms, a statistician employed in the mills' marketing department, the questionnaire was intended to elicit the attitudes of approximately 350 local residents on a variety of topics of relevance to the mill, one of which was the issue of compliance with environmental regulations (see Exhibit 3 for survey design considerations and statistical significance of results).

When asked "Should the mill comply fully if federal environment regulations are extended to apply to mills built prior to 1972?", 94 percent of respondents replied "yes". For those who responded affirmatively, a follow-up question was posed. "If the result of full compliance was a streamlining of operations with consequent layoffs, would you still favour full compliance?" Respondents could select one of the following answers:

...

EXHIBIT 3 PUBLIC OPINION SURVEY.

Methodology and Design

Target Population:	Adults, over the age of 17 Permanent residents of Westborough
The Frame:	Total number of households in Westborough
Sample Design:	Simple random sample of 350 people One from each selected household 26 nonrespondents
Method of Measurement:	Mailed questionnaire
Measurement Instrument:	Questions ordered and phrased so as to minimize nonresponse and incorrect response bias.
The Pretest:	Conducted with subsample of 40 adults

Statistical significance of results

Findings accurate (within + or −5%) 19 times out of 20

Note: Sample size required to estimate a population proportion p with a bound on the error of estimation of B = 0.05:

$$n = M\, pq/(N-1)\, D + pq$$

where: N = population value

q = 1 − P

D = B 2/4

For this survey, n = 312

A) NO

B) YES, only if consequence was fewer than 10 layoffs.

C) YES, only if consequence was fewer than 50 layoffs.

D) YES

The results were as follows:

18 percent chose A
22 percent chose B
34 percent chose C, and
26 percent chose D

Mr. Smith thought that the results were predictable but not very useful. "Sure the public wants a clean environment and I do as well," he said. "But last September there had been no layoffs. I'm sure the responses would change considerably if the questions were asked today, given what happened last month."

Not everyone agreed with Smith's assessment of the poll's results, nor was there unanimous approval for his overall position on the environment issue. Union officials, in particular, were not convinced by the General Manager's arguments.

A CONVERSATION BETWEEN ART SMITH AND JIM PETERS

After receiving the news about the impending pollution regulations, Mr. Smith was visited by Jim Peters, head of local 63 of the Canadian Paperworkers Union, and a spirited conversation ensued.

Art: This is bad news Jim, I just hope that it isn't the coup de grâce for the mill.

Jim: Art, you know where I stand, I favour full compliance and I don't see the necessity of laying off anyone to achieve it.

Art: Be realistic Jim! The pulping plant alone employs 120 workers. With the new regulations, we'll probably have to shut it down since it is a chlorine-based chemical facility. But its closure would mean more than 120 lost jobs—it would significantly reduce the quality of our sheet and who knows how many lost customers that would mean.

Jim: Art, you only see things in black and white. Surely there are alternatives to closing down the plant. I was just talking with Frank in production and he has read about a chlorine substitution process which could virtually eliminate chlorine demand in the bleach plant. And what's more, apparently our plant could be modified in this way.

Art: But Jim we simply cannot afford any major modifications this year. You know we just spent $10 million for environmental improvement last year. And what about the bonus severance package for the workers laid off last

• • •

month—that's a multimillion dollar commitment. Eventually, there comes a point when the well runs dry you know.

Jim: Well you can only blame yourself for that. If drastic measures have to be taken, it's because of poor planning rather than the imposition of stiff regulations. Art, for the past 20 years the mill hasn't had to comply with any regulations. If contributions to an environmental program had been started back then, we'd have no problems meeting requirements today. And another thing, to build a chlorine-based pulping plant three years ago was clearly improvident—I didn't understand it then and I still don't now.

Art: Well I didn't see you complain about the 120 jobs it created. Anyway it accomplishes nothing to point fingers. What we need is a constructive plan for the future.

Jim: I don't think there's a lot of room to manoeuvre. The feds have made their minds up and we're going to have to comply fully. After all, that's what the community wants—just look at last year's survey. And there's another thing, I don't want the health of any of my workers to be endangered by the presence of dioxins or any other harmful substances in the work environment.

Art: I think I can explain the position you've taken on this issue. You favour full compliance because you're not fearful of the potential consequences. Even if there are layoffs, you know that there'll be a more than generous severance package for the employees. Furthermore, the success of the mill over its 80 year history has fostered a sense of complacency among union members and community residents. Nobody thinks that the bubble will ever burst. Well let me tell you something, if it does then the town will close down along with the mill.

I think the key to this whole issue is the compliance schedule. If the government gives us adequate time, then maybe we can conform with the rules. Otherwise, I would hope that they would consider the potential loss of a community to be more important than the marginal benefits of improved pollution control."

DIRECTION FOR THE FUTURE

Art Smith did not like the idea of being at the mercy of government officials. Clearly it was impossible for him to fully control the situation, but he felt he could make decisions which would lessen the negative impact of the imminent regulations. "I want to be proactive rather than reactive" he thought, "but, at the moment, I'm just not sure where to start. There are so many factors to consider." ▲

QUESTIONS

1. What stakeholders, that is, individuals or groups, will influence, or will be influenced by, Smith's decision relating to the new regulations limiting pollution?
2. Which of the stakeholders identified in Question 1 will favour compliance with the new regulations and which will favour some degree of noncompliance?
3. What is the socially responsible thing for Smith, and the company, to do?
4. What courses of action are available to Longhurst and which is the company most likely to take? Why?

GLOSSARY

A

ABC inventory method Classifies inventory items into one of three categories based on the rate of their use and cost (p. 568).

ability A person's competence at a certain task (p. 363).

accountability Making people answerable for the results of the work assigned to them (p. 235).

accounting audit An independent analysis of the financial statements of a business organization (p. 580).

achieved status That which a person attains through personal choice, such as education, job skills, or marital status (p. 281).

action plans Detail the specific tasks that are to be done in order to fulfill the objectives that have been set (p. 107).

action research The process of identifying a specific organization's problems, gathering and analyzing data relevant to the problem, and taking action to resolve the problem (p. 505).

active listening Concentrating on the sender's message so that all elements of the message are received (p. 449).

activity Consumes time and resources as work is done on the way to completion of a project (p. 570).

activity ratios Measure how efficient a firm is in utilizing its resources (p. 579).

adjourning Last stage of group development; group activity is terminated (p. 267).

advisory staff Advise line managers in areas where the staff has particular expertise (p. 242).

artificial intelligence (AI) The field of study which tries to simulate human thought with a computer (p. 599).

ascribed status That which a person possesses because of certain unchangeable characteristics such as age, sex, and ethnic background (p. 281).

assessment centre A series of exercises in which management candidates perform realistic management tasks under the watchful eyes of expert appraisers (p. 326).

attribute sampling Classifies products as either completely acceptable or completely unacceptable (p. 566).

authority The right given to managers to take certain actions themselves or to require their subordinates to take certain actions (p. 231).

autocratic leader Believes that all decision-making authority must be retained by the leader (p. 401).

B

balance sheet A financial document that describes a company's financial position with respect to assets, liabilities, and owner's equity (p. 578).

behavioural approach Stresses the importance of people in attaining organizational productivity (p. 37).

behavioural standards States the types of behaviour that are acceptable for employees (p. 538).

benchmarking Comparative analysis of competitor's strategies and objectives to establish reference points, or benchmarks, that assist in the formulation of organizational objectives (p. 566).

benefits What a firm offers its workers other than wages and salaries in return for their labour (p. 332).

bet-your-company culture Exists in organizations that make risky strategic decisions and receive only delayed feedback on the success of their decisions (p. 500).

board of directors Group that is given the power to govern the corporation's affairs and to make general policy (p. 13).

body language Communicating through facial expressions, tone of voice, body posture, and gestures (p. 436).

bona fide occupational requirement Means that an employer may choose one person over another based on overriding characteristics of the job in question (p. 319).

borderless corporations Those that operate globally; also called "stateless" or "transnational" corporations (p. 662).

bottom-up budgeting Lower-level managers are involved in the process of deciding how resources will be allocated to the various units in the organization (p. 572).

boundary spanners Facilitate coordination between two departments that have an ongoing need to coordinate their work (p. 222).

bounded rationality model Makes the assumption that managers do not have perfect information about problems, and that they do not always use rational decision processes when they make decision (p. 162).

brainstorming A technique which is designed to encourage creativity by having group members present freewheeling solutions to problems in a nonjudgmental setting (p. 167).

break-even analysis Compares product revenues and costs at different sales volumes to show how profit is affected (pp. 140, 575).

budget A statement in dollar-and-cents terms of the expenditures that an organization plans to make during the next year (p. 571).

bureaucracy Emphasizes rules and regulations, clearly defined authority and responsibility, and rational, impersonal decision making to increase organizational effectiveness (p 34).

bureaucratic control Emphasizes individual performance, control of employees by the hierarchy, top-down influence, and little employee participation in decision making (p. 537).

burnout The mental and physical exhaustion that results when a person is subjected to high levels of stress for extended periods (p. 487).

business competitiveness Ability to design, produce and market goods and services, produce and market goods and services, the price and nonprice qualities of which form a more attractive package of benefits than those of competitors (p. 60).

business ethics Rules, standards, codes, or principles which provide guidelines for morally right behaviour and truthfulness in specific situations (p. 680).

business firm An entity that seeks to make a profit providing products or services that satisfy consumer demand (p. 10).

C

cafeteria benefits A flexible approach to providing benefits in which employees are allocated a certain sum to cover benefits and can "spend" this allocation on the specific benefits they prefer (p. 333).

Canadian Human Rights Act of 1977 Prohibits a wide variety of practices in the recruitment, selection, promotion, and dismissal of personnel, including discrimination on the basis of age, gender, nationality, religious preference, and marital status (p. 319).

cause-and-effect diagram Summarizes the four possible causes of quality problems (materials, manpower, methods, and machines) (p. 566).

centralization Occurs when top management retains the right to make most of the decisions that need to be made (p. 202).

certainty Exists when the manager knows exactly how many alternatives are available, what each alternative involves, the payoffs for each alternative, and the probability that chance events will occur (p. 156).

change agent An individual or group that manages the change sequence (p. 476).

changing environment One where major shifts occur in products, in customers, and in the technology which an organization uses (p. 248).

charisma Possessed by people who have an unusually strong influence on the behaviour and attitudes of others (p. 398).

charismatic leaders Possess self-confidence, dominance, and a strong conviction about the rightness of their beliefs (p. 398).

chief information officer (CIO) Responsible for determining the organization's overall information needs, and for controlling the information that is contained in the organization's databases (p. 253).

clan control Stresses employee commitment to the organization, group norms, group performance, employee self-control, shared influence, and extensive participation by employees in decision making (p. 537).

clan culture A culture which emphasizes employee commitment to the organization, rather than simply having workers exchange their labour for money (p. 501).

classical management approach Tried to provide a rational and scientific basis for the practice of management (p. 33).

closed promotion system An internal promotion system in which managers choose the workers who will be considered for a promotion (p. 324).

coaching The managerial activity of creating, by communication only, the climate, environment, and context that empowers individuals and teams to generate results (p. 419).

coacting groups The work of individual group members is independent (p. 264).

code of ethics A statement of ethical principles and acceptable behaviour or rules and policies that describe the general value system within which a corporation attempts to operate in a given environment (p. 682).

collaborative management Subordinates share the power with managers in making decisions that affect the organization (p. 504).

common stock Confers ownership and voting rights in a corporation (p. 13).

communication The transfer of meaning and understanding between people through verbal and nonverbal means (p. 430).

communication barrier Any physical or psychological factor that inhibits the transfer of meaning from the sender to the receiver (p. 443).

communication channel The medium by which the message is transmitted to the receiver (p. 432).

communication network A path through which messages are transmitted (p. 442).

communication process The series of events that take place to transfer meaning (p. 431).

comparable worth A legal idea that aims to pay equal wages for work of equal value (p. 332).

compensation system What a firm offers its employees in return for their labour (p. 328).

competition Occurs when individuals or groups have incompatible goals, but do not interfere with each other's efforts to attain goals (p. 464).

complexity The number of distinctly different job titles and departments in an organization (p. 203).

compressed workweek A work design system in which the number of days that employees work is decreased, but the number of hours worked each day is increased (p. 386).

concentration The degree to which the economy is dominated by a few large firms (p. 59).

concentric diversification Adding new, but related, products or services to the existing business (p. 138).

conceptual skills Help a manager see the organization as a complete unit, and to integrate and give direction to its diverse activities so that organizational objectives are achieved (p. 23).

conflict Occurs when individuals or groups have incompatible goals and these individuals or groups block each other's goal attainment (p. 461).

conflict management Involves intervention by managers to increase or decrease the level of conflict that is evident. (p. 466).

conglomerate diversification Addition of unrelated products or services to the existing business (p. 138).

consideration The extent to which leaders are concerned with developing mutual trust between themselves and subordinates, as well as showing respect for subordinates' ideas and concern for their feelings (p. 407).

consumer goods Tangible products that people buy for their own consumption (p. 42).

consumer services Intangible items that people buy for their own enjoyment (p. 42).

contact chart Identifies the informal connections that an individual has with other members of the organization (p. 275).

content analysis Examination of the contents of publications for reference to specific items of interest (p. 103).

content theories Try to identify the specific needs that motivate people (p. 365).

contingency planning Identifying possible future outcomes and then developing a plan for coping with them (p. 103).

contingency situational theories Assume that different individuals and situations require different managerial practices (p. 43).

contingency leadership theories Assume that different situations require different leadership styles (p. 405).

continuous reinforcement schedule A reward or a punishment follows each time the behaviour of interest occurs (p. 376).

controlling The process of comparing actual performance with standards and taking corrective action when performance falls short of the standard (p. 17).

controlling process Ensures that planned activities and results actually occur (p. 537).

control chart Shows how closely the product or service being produced adheres to the quality standards that have been set (p. 566).

control staff Responsible for controlling some aspect of the organization (e.g., quality control) (p. 242).

control tolerances State the degree of deviation from the standard that is permissible (p. 538).

cooperative strategies May take the form of joint ventures, alliances, networks, strategic partnering, and strategic networks (p. 138).

corporate culture The complex set of values, beliefs, assumptions, and symbols, that define the way in which an organization conducts its business (p. 125).

corporation An artificial being, invisible, intangible, and existing only in contemplation of law (p. 12).

corporation bylaws The rules by which the corporation operates (p. 14).

correlation Making a prediction about one outcome based on knowledge of other outcomes (p. 102).

cost/benefit analysis Attempts to put a monetary value on all the costs and benefits of a strategic option (p. 141).

cost standards State the maximum cost that should be incurred in the course of producing goods and services (p. 538).

counteracting groups Groups that interact with each other to reconcile differences between them (p. 264).

creativity The discovery of new and useful ideas (p. 171).

crisis decisions Made when major disruptive events occur that require immediate action (p. 154).

critical path The series of activities that take the longest time to complete (p. 571).

critical path method Much like PERT except that each project activity is assigned a specific time estimate rather than a range of optimistic, realistic, and pessimistic estimates (p. 571).

critical success factors (CSF) Identifies a limited number of variables in which high performance is crucial to the success of a strategy (p. 139).

customer departmentation Used when an organization wants to focus on the needs of specific types of customers (p. 212).

cybernetic system A self-regulating system (e.g., the human body) (p. 534).

D

data Unanalyzed facts about an organization's operations (p. 591).

debt Borrowed funds that require interest payments and must be repaid (p. 625).

decentralization Occurs when the right to make decisions is pushed down to the middle and lower levels of the management hierarchy (p. 236).

decisional role Requires the manager to use information to make major decisions about the unit's direction and how resources should be committed to reach the unit's objectives (p. 19).

decision making The process of choosing between alternative courses of action to deal with a crisis, solve a problem, or take advantage of an opportunity (p. 153).

decision-making phase (of decision making) The decision maker develops a solution to the problem or opportunity that has been defined (p. 160).

decision matrix Helps decision makers systematically develop and weight the criteria that are to be used in making a decision (p. 165).

decision support systems (DSS) Allows managers who are not computer experts to interact conversationally with the computer to solve unstructured problems (p. 598).

decision trees Pictorial representations of problems or opportunities, showing the alternatives, chance events, and payoffs in a way that allows management to compare the desirability of each alternative (p. 140).

decoding The receiver converts the encoded symbols into an understandable message (p. 433).

defence mechanisms Used by individuals to protect their ego from unpleasant information (p. 447).

delegation The assignment of specific tasks to subordinates along with the authority to carry out those assignments (p. 232).

Delphi technique A procedure for getting consensus among experts through the use of questionnaires and feedback of results (p. 168).

democratic leader Believes that authority should be delegated to subordinates to make decisions based on their interest and expertise in dealing with situations they face (p. 402).

departmentation Grouping functions or major work activities into coherent units (p. 210).

deregulation A reduction in the number of laws affecting business activity and of the powers of government enforcement agencies as well as other forms of governmental control or intervention (p. 66).

development Application of research findings, or other scientific knowledge, for the creation of new or significantly improved products or processes (p. 69).

deviates Group members who violate group norms and who are excluded from normal group functions (p. 269).

diagonal communication Takes place between individuals who are not in a superior-subordinate relationship, but are at different levels in the organization (p. 441).

dialectical inquiry An approach to group decision making that deliberately introduces conflict into decision making so that conflicting assumptions and solutions will be seriously considered (p. 169).

differentiation The differences that exist across departments in an organization (p. 220).

direct (foreign) investment The commitment of capital to take over an existing Canadian corporation, or to establish a wholly owned corporation in Canada (p. 58).

direct owners Canadians who own shares in corporations as investors, but also as entrepreneurs, managers, employees, customers, and producers (p. 54).

directive behaviour The extent to which a leader engages in one-way communication, spells out the followers' roles and tells the followers what to do, where to do it, when to do it, and how to do it, and then closely supervises them (p. 411).

disciplinary action The process of invoking a penalty against an employee who fails to adhere to some work-related standard (p. 540).

distinctive competence Function that the organization performs particularly well and generally better that its competitors (p. 133).

distress Destructive stress (p. 485).

divisional structure Divides the organization into several divisions, each of which operates as a semiautonomous unit and profit centre (p. 218).

doctor-patient model Assumes that the consultant (the doctor) will analyze the patient (the organization) and then suggest a cure for the problem (p. 508).

downsizing The planned reduction in the scope of an organization's operations, usually by cutting large numbers of employees (p. 207).

E

economic order quantity (EOQ) A procedure for minimizing total inventory costs by balancing ordering costs and carrying costs (p. 568).

effectiveness Achieving the organizational goals that have been set (p. 5).

efficiency Achieving the greatest possible output with a given amount of input (p. 5).

effort-performance expectancy Reflects a person's belief that effort expenditure will lead to good performance (p. 373).

electronic brainstorming Group members type ideas into a computer; these ideas then show up simultaneously on the computer screens of other group members (p. 168).

e-mail System which allows people to use their office computers to send letters or memos to other individuals in their own or other organizations (p. 436).

emotional resistance to change Occurs when people resist a change, but give no thoughtful consideration as to why they are resisting (p. 478).

emotions Subjective responses to a situation or a person (p. 445).

empathy Putting yourself in the other person's position so that you can sense how the other person is going to react to a communication (p. 449).

employee-centred managers Those who are interested in their subordinates as people, who show concern for their well-being, and encourage worker involvement in goal setting (p. 408).

Employment Equity Act of 1986 Addresses the issue of discrimination in employment by designating four groups as employment disadvantaged—women, visible minorities, Aboriginal people, and people with disabilities (p. 320).

empowerment The process of strengthening subordinates' beliefs in their effectiveness (p. 418).

encoding The process of converting ideas into symbols that receivers will understand (p. 432).

end-user computing The use of computers by people who are not computer experts (p. 598).

entrepreneurs Persons who start and operate small businesses (p. 618).

entrepreneurship An individual's willingness to take advantage of business opportunities and to assume the risk of establishing and operating a business (p. 618).

environmental audit An environmental assessment document which must be submitted to Environment Canada for review and approval if an enterprise or a government undertakes an environmentally sensitive project (p. 691).

environmental ethic A set of values or principles about practices relating to the environment (p. 695).

equity Refers to the money, or capital, invested in the enterprise by individuals or companies who become owners, and to profits reinvested in the firm (p. 625).

equity theory States that a worker compares his or her inputs and his or her outputs with those of other workers doing the same or similar jobs; the person tries to maintain a balance between what he or she puts into a job and what he or she gets out of it (p. 371).

ERG theory Existence, relatedness, and growth needs are three needs that motivate people (p. 368).

escalation of commitment Refers to a situation where a manager becomes increasingly committed to a previously chosen course of action even though that course of action has been shown to be ineffective. (p. 163)

ethics audit A systematic effort to discover actual or potential unethical behaviour in an organization (p. 684).

eustress Constructive stress (p. 484).

evaluative listening Involves concentrating on the sender's message so that all elements of the message are received (p. 449).

event The beginning or end of a step on the way to completion of a project (p. 570).

exception principle States that employees should handle routine matters and the supervisor should handle exceptional matters (p. 560).

expectancy theory Says that the effort a person puts into a job is determined by the outcomes the person sees as desirable, and the person's belief that these desired outcomes can be attained (p. 372).

expected value Calculated by multiplying the probability of an outcome by the dollar return that would result from that outcome (p. 167).

experience curve Organized framework for analyzing the production cost and selling price of a product over a period (p. 134).

expert power The power a person with expert knowledge has over another who needs the knowledge (p. 291).

expert systems Duplicates the thinking process of an expert in a particular area by using decision rules that are built into the expert system (p. 599).

extrapolation The projection of past and present circumstances into the future (p. 102).

extrinsic motivation Person works hard at a task because of the promise that some obvious reward will be given if the job is done well (p. 361).

extrinsic rewards Rewards that are separate from the task performed and are controlled by other people (p. 361).

F

feedback Observable reactions to a message (p. 433).

Fiedler's contingency model Says that leadership effectiveness is the result of an interaction between the style of the leader and the characteristics of the environment in which the leader works (p. 414).

filtering The loss of meaning that occurs as information moves upward or downward through the various levels in the management hierarchy (p. 444).

financial control techniques Used to monitor employee behaviour when financial data like costs, profit, or sales revenue are available (p. 558).

finished goods inventory Those items that have passed through the entire production process and are ready to be sold to customers (p. 567).

first-line managers Supervise operative workers and are directly responsible for the production of goods and services (p. 20).

fixed costs Those which do not vary as the quantity produced increases or decreases (p. 575).

fixed interval schedule A reinforcement is applied after a certain time period has passed, regardless of the number of responses that have occurred (p. 376).

fixed ratio schedule A reinforcement is applied after a fixed number of desired behavioural responses have occurred, regardless of the time that has passed (p. 377).

flextime A system which allows workers increased discretion in deciding when they will be at their place of work (p. 386).

force field analysis Describes and analyzes the various forces that operate in a social system to keep the system balanced or unbalanced (p. 480).

forecasting Predicting future events which will have a positive or negative effect on the organization (p. 101).

formal downward communication channels Direct communication from bosses to subordinates through the chain of command in the organization (p. 438).

formal group Established to achieve certain organization goals; are part of the formal structure of the organization (p. 263).

formal upward communication channels Direct communication from subordinates to managers through the chain of command (p. 440).

formalization The amount of written job descriptions, rules, policies, and procedures that guide employee behaviour (p. 202).

forming First stage of group development; group members get acquainted with each other and with the roles they are expected to carry out (p. 267).

franchisee Sells the product or service of the manufacturer (the franchisor) (p. 623).

franchising Drafting a contract between a manufacturer and a dealer that stipulates how the manufacturer's or supplier's product or service will be sold (p. 623).

franchisor The manufacturer who provides the product or service to the seller (the franchisee) (p. 623).

free-lancers Individuals with special skills who supplement the organization's core group of full-time employees (p. 387).

functional authority The authority that staff experts have over line managers in the staff person's area of expertise (p. 242).

functional departmentation Units are formed on the basis of the functions that must be carried out to reach organizational goals (p. 211).

functional managers Oversee the activities of a specific function like marketing, production, finance, or personnel (p. 22).

functional status Derives from an individual's function within an organization (p. 281).

functional structure Units in the organization are formed on the basis of the functions that must be carried out to reach the key organizational goals (p. 215).

G

gain-sharing plan An incentive program in which employees receive a bonus if the firm's costs are reduced because of greater worker efficiency and/or productivity (p. 330)

gap analysis The gap is the difference between the performance potential of each strategic option (p. 140).

garbage can model Assumes that decisions get made only when several factors happen to come together at the right time (p. 164).

general managers Oversee the activities of an entire division or organization (p. 23).

globalization The growth of foreign direct investment and the integration of markets on a global scale (p. 648).

goal distortion Occurs when a reasonable goal is interpreted in such a way that it causes unreasonable behaviour, or when an unimportant goal is given too much emphasis (p. 98).

goods-in-process inventory Those items which are partially through the production process (p. 567).

grapevine The informal system used to transmit information to members of an organization (p. 278).

group A collection of two or more interdependent individuals who must coordinate their activity in order to achieve goals (p. 263).

group cohesiveness The degree of attraction a group has for its members (p. 269).

group control Exercised over individuals by the work or friendship group they belong to (p. 536).

groupthink Occurs when members of a group voluntarily suspend their critical thinking abilities and suppress any conflict and disagreement that could challenge group solidarity (p. 272).

H

halo effect Forming opinions about one specific characteristic of a person and then generalizing that opinion to all other characteristics (p. 447).

Hawthorne effect The tendency of work groups to show improved productivity if management pays special attention to them (p. 37).

Hawthorne studies Found that social factors in the workplace were at least as important as physical factors in determining employee productivity (p. 37).

hierarchy of objectives Links objectives at all levels in the organization in a consistent pattern (p. 97).

horizontal differentiation Differences among departments at the same level in the organizational hierarchy (p. 220).

horizontal integration A company purchases, or increases control over, another enterprise in the same business (p. 138).

human relations movement Examines how managers and subordinates interact; advocates that management make the gratification of workers' social and psychological needs a primary concern (p. 37).

human relations view of conflict Assumes that conflict is a normal part of organizational life, and that it may have either positive or negative outcomes (p. 465).

human resource management Developing, administering, and evaluating programs to acquire and enhance the quality and performance of people in a business (p. 314).

hygienes Factors that are concerned with the environment in which work is performed; their absence causes workers to be dissatisfied (p. 368).

I

immediate corrective action Solves a problem "right now" and gets output back to the desired level (p. 540).

implementation phase (of decision making) The process of putting into practice the solution that has been chosen (p. 161).

impression management Projecting a certain image or identity to the boss in the hope that you will obtain rewards such as promotion and increased pay (p. 300).

incentive program Any program in which a company offers its workers additional pay over and above the normal wage or salary level in order to motivate them to perform at higher-than-normal levels (p. 330).

income statement Shows the company's financial performance over a period of time (usually one year) (p. 578).

incremental budgeting The relative proportion of the total budget given to each unit in the organization changes very little from year to year (p. 572).

indirect (foreign) investment Purchase of corporate stocks and bonds (p. 58).

indirect owners Canadians who contribute to mutual and pension funds which in turn make investments in business (p. 55).

individual characteristics (in motivation) Include the needs of people, their attitudes about work, their value system, and their feelings about different kinds of jobs (p. 360).

individual control A person voluntarily behaves in a way that facilitates the goals of the organization (p. 537).

individual communication barriers Caused by characteristics of the individuals working in an organization (p. 445).

individual-group conflict Conflict between a person and a group (p. 463).

industrial goods Tangible products purchased by businesses and other institutions to use in producing other goods or services (p. 42).

industrial services Intangible items purchased by businesses and other institutions to use in producing other goods and services (p. 42).

informal communication channels Those which exist outside the formal chain of command in the organization (p. 441).

informal group Are set up to meet people's social needs; are not part of the formal structure of an organization (p. 263).

informal group leader That person who best satisfies the needs of the group (p. 269).

informal organization The pattern of social behaviour and influence that arises spontaneously whenever people work together within the formal structure (p. 273).

information Anything which is useful and relevant for managers, including analyzed data (p. 591).

information centre Help users deal effectively with computer departments (p. 253).

information management Manipulating, withholding, or filtering information, or communicating only positive information about performance to the boss (p. 300).

information power Person A has information that convinces Person B to pursue a course of action desired by Person A (p. 291).

informational roles Put the manager in a central position for sending and receiving information (p. 18).

information overload Occurs when someone receives more information than he or she can absorb (p. 444).

informed judgment Expert opinion on an issue (p. 102).

initiating structure The extent to which the leader structures and defines the activities of subordinates so that organizational goals are achieved (p. 407).

innovation Taking a creative idea and actually putting it into use (p. 171).

input controls Monitor the material, human, and capital resources that come into an organization (p. 545).

integrated work teams Are assigned certain tasks by management; team members then decide how they will divide up the work (p. 264).

integration The state of collaboration that exists among the various departments in an organization (p. 221).

integrator Person who is assigned responsibility for coordinating the ongoing work of several departments whose work is highly interdependent (p. 224).

intensive technology Used to create a change in a specific object (p. 251).

interacting groups The work of each group member is dependent upon that of the others in the group (p. 264).

interactionist view of conflict Assumes that conflict is necessary if an organization hopes to perform well (p. 465).

intergroup conflict Conflict between two or more groups of people (p. 463).

intergroup development Attempts to change attitudes and stereotypes members of opposing groups have of each other (p. 510).

intermittent reinforcement schedule Desired behavior is reinforced only some of the time. As a result, this behavior is more enduring (p. 376).

international corporation One that engages in any combination of activities from the exporting or importing of goods and services to full-scale operations in foreign countries (p. 644).

interpersonal roles Involve the manager in relationships with other individuals both inside and outside the firm (p. 18).

interpersonal conflict Conflict between individuals (p. 463).

interpersonal conflict resolution techniques Focus on the human interaction in a conflict (p. 469).

intraindividual conflict Conflict which occurs within one person (p. 462).

intrapreneurship Entrepreneurship within larger business enterprises (p. 124).

intrinsic motivation Exists if a person performs a task in the absence of any obvious reward for doing so (p. 361).

intrinsic rewards Are an integral part of the task and are administered by the individual doing the task (p. 361).

intuition Judgment by an individual or group based on limited information (p. 102).

inventory The items an organization keeps on hand, either for use in the production process or as a result of the production process (p. 567).

iron cage of bureaucracy Describes the trapped feeling individuals experience in a culture which is cold, depersonalized, and lacking in moral purpose due to overemphasis on rationality (p. 35).

isolate A group member who is psychologically, socially, and possibly physically isolated from the group for failure to conform to group norms (p. 269).

J

job analysis A detailed study of the specific duties in a particular job and the human qualities required for that job (p. 316).

job characteristics (in motivation) Those attributes that are evident in the job the employee is performing (p. 360).

job design The process of altering the nature and structure of jobs for the purpose of increasing productivity (p. 383).

job description A document describing the objectives, responsibilities, and key tasks of a job (p. 316).

job enlargement Requires the worker to learn several different jobs involving somewhat different skill levels (p. 383).

job enrichment Increases the level of responsibility in a work role (p. 383).

job-relatedness The principle that all personnel decisions, policies, and programs should be based on the requirements of a position (p. 314).

job rotation A worker is rotated through a series of similar jobs (p. 383).

job satisfaction Employees' overall attitudes toward their jobs (p. 362).

job sharing Two or more workers collectively take responsibility for doing a traditional, full-time job (p. 387).

job specification The specific skills, education, and experience needed to perform a job (p. 316).

joint ventures An enterprise created by two or more sponsoring firms which combine resources and skills for a new venture. Also known as strategic partnership or alliance. (p. 57).

just-in-time inventory system Inventory is scheduled to arrive just in time to be used in the production process (p. 569).

K

***kanban* system** Specifies how many and what kind of items are to be produced (p. 569).

***keiretsu* companies** Loosely affiliated groups of industrial and banking companies that dominate the Tokyo Stock Exchange (p. 662).

L

lateral communication Takes place between individuals at the same level in an organization (p. 441).

lateral relationships Develop between organizational members who do not interact through formal lines of authority on the organization chart (p. 222).

law of reciprocity The belief that people should be compensated for what they do (p. 292).

leader Anyone who is able to influence others to pursue goals that the leader would like to achieve (p. 397).

leader behaviour approach Emphasized observation of managers as they carried out their leadership role (p. 407).

LEADER MATCH A programmed learning system that trains leaders to modify their leadership situation to fit their personality (p. 415).

leader style continuum Leadership styles range from an emphasis on the manager's authority to an emphasis on the subordinate's freedom (p. 410).

leadership The ability to influence others to pursue the goals the leader thinks are important and desirable (p. 396).

leadership style The behaviour the leader exhibits while supervising subordinates (p. 400).

leading Process of motivating and communicating with the organization's human resources to ensure that they pursue the organization's objectives (p. 16).

legitimate power The power a person has over another who believes that person has the "right" to give orders (p. 291).

leverage ratios Measure how well an organization has used outside financing in the operation of the business (p. 579).

licensing agreements The owner of a product or process allows an enterprise to produce, distribute, or market the product or process for a fee or royalty (p. 645).

line managers Managers in the regular chain of command of the organization (p. 240).

line organization All the positions are line positions and there is a direct line of authority from the top of the firm to the bottom (p. 240).

line-staff organization Has both line managers and staff experts (p. 241).

liquidity ratios Measure a firm's ability to meet its financial obligations as they come due (p. 579).

long-range plans Forecasts based on current and past performance (p. 118).

long-term corrective action Determines why deviations occur and what can be done to prevent the problem from happening in the future (p. 540).

M

mainframe computer Able to handle vast amounts of data and do millions of computations each second (p. 597).

management The process of planning, organizing, leading, and controlling other people so that organizational objectives are reached (p. 4).

management audit Used to systematically analyze the strengths and weaknesses of the managerial talent in an organization (p. 560).

management by exception A manager becomes involved in the detailed supervision of subordinates only when there is an obvious deviation from standard levels of performance (p. 560).

management by objectives (MBO) A system in which managers and subordinates set mutually agreed upon goals; these goals motivate subordinates and encourage them to exercise self-control over their performance (p. 104).

management development programs Development programs in which current and prospective managers learn new conceptual, analytical, and problem-solving skills (p. 326).

management information system Collects, analyzes, organizes, and disseminates information from both internal and external sources so that managers can make decisions that are beneficial to the organization (p. 590).

management science approach Emphasizes the use of mathematics and statistics to solve management problems in the areas of production, marketing, and finance (p. 39).

manager Performs the functions of planning, organizing, leading and controlling, and occupies a formal position in an organization (p. 4), (p. 397).

managerial grid Shows various ways of combining a concern for people with a concern for production (p. 408).

marginal listening The receiver spends only part of the time listening to what the sender is saying (p. 449).

market culture Employee involvement in an organization is simply contractual, i.e., employees exchange their labour for money (p. 501).

Maslow's hierarchy of needs Those needs which are lower in the hierarchy must be largely satisfied before needs further up the hierarchy will emerge to motivate behaviour (p. 366).

mass production The manufacture of large volumes of identical products for sale to the mass market (p. 250).

materials requirement planning system (MRP) Shows all the parts that are needed in a finished product and then calculates how these parts should be ordered (p. 569).

mechanistic organization Those which stress highly structured work, clearly stated authority relations, centralized authority, and vertical communications (p. 248).

mediating technology Brings buyers and sellers together (p. 251).

megaprojects Large-scale construction and development undertakings (p. 53).

mentoring Occurs when the experienced manager helps the aspiring manager by giving advice, conveying important informal rules of behavior, and generally acting as a sounding board for the aspiring manager's ideas and behavior (p. 301).

microcomputer The smallest kind of computer (p. 597).

microenterprises Enterprises operating from the home on a part-time basis while the entrepreneur continues as a regular employee in another organization (p. 622).

middle managers Work in the middle of the management hierarchy; they supervise first-line managers and have wider areas of responsibility than first-line managers (p. 20).

minicomputer Has capacity that is intermediate between microcomputers and mainframe computers (p. 597).

mission First step in the strategic management process (p. 127).

motivation The result of factors, either internal or external to the individual, that initially cause behaviour, channel it in certain directions, and maintain it over time (p. 360).

motivators Factors that are concerned with the work itself; they alone can cause a worker to be satisfied (p. 368).

multinational corporation (MNC) A business enterprise that controls assets, factories, mines, sales offices, etc. in two or more foreign countries (p. 658).

N

need for achievement The need to achieve goals (p. 370).

need for affiliation The need to be liked by others (p. 370).

need for power The need to control others (p. 370).

negative reinforcement Occurs when an unpleasant stimulus is withheld from a person (p. 375).

net present value Recognizes that a dollar received today is worth more than a dollar received at some point in the future; used to help managers make investment decisions (p. 576).

network corporation structure The organization is a small central processing unit connected electronically to other organizations that perform functions like production, sales, and engineering (p. 253).

noise Those personality, perceptual, and attitudinal differences in individuals that reduce their ability to communicate effectively (p. 433).

nominal grouping A decision-making technique emphasizing the equal contribution of group members through the mechanism of voting (p. 169).

noncybernetic system An artificial system that requires the exercise of human judgment to function (e.g., an organization) (p. 534).

nonevaluative listening Requires the listener to focus all of his or her attention on what is being said without trying to simultaneously evaluate it (p. 449).

nonfinancial control techniques Used to monitor employee behaviour without reference to corporate financial data (p. 558).

nonprogrammed decisions One-time decisions for which no routine or standard procedures have been established (p. 154).

nonverbal communication That which occurs through human actions and behaviours, rather than words (p. 436).

normative leadership model Identifies various situational factors which influence the amount of participation subordinates should be allowed when decisions are made (p. 412).

norming Third stage of group development; characterized by cooperation and understanding of what is acceptable behaviour for group members (p. 267).

norms Standards of behaviour resulting from the interaction of individuals in a group (p. 500).

not-for-profit organization Stresses service objectives instead of profit (p. 15).

O

objective probabilities Based on quantifiable facts (p. 157).

objectives The results that the organization wants to achieve (p. 95).

office automation The combination of word processing, electronic spreadsheets, and communication networks (p. 597).

off-the-job training Development programs in which employees learn new skills at a location away from the work site (p. 325).

omission Occurs when a pleasant stimulus is withheld from a person (p. 376).

one-way communication Takes place when the sender directs a message to the receiver without expecting an immediate, obvious response (p. 438).

on-the-job training Development programs in which employees gain new skills while performing them at work (p. 325).

open promotion system An internal promotion system in which all employees are advised of open positions and may apply for those positions if they wish (p. 324).

open system One that interacts with its environment (p. 40).

operational control Used to help managers assess the effectiveness of plans at the lowest level in the organization (p. 543).

operational plans Specify the activities that are necessary to implement the strategic plans (p. 100).

opportunity Favourable circumstances or conditions that represent a good chance or prospect for the organization (p. 130).

opportunity decisions Involve taking new initiatives or doing a current activity more effectively even if no problem exists (p. 154).

organic organization Those which deemphasize hierarchical authority, and which encourage managers and subordinates to work together as a team to solve problems (p. 248).

organization Exists when two or more people decide to cooperatively work toward the achievement of some goal (p. 5)

organization chart A pictorial representation of formal authority relationships in an organization at one point in time (p. 204).

organization development A process for improving the company as a whole by letting the employees themselves analyze problems and suggest solutions (p. 504).

organizational behaviour modification (OBM) The application of Skinner's reinforcement theory to the behaviour of people in organizations (p. 378).

organizational characteristics (in motivation) The reward system, rules, policies, procedures, and managerial practices that are evident in the organization (p. 360).

organizational communication barriers Barriers caused by the nature and structure of organizations including filtering, status differences, conflicting departmental objectives, specialization of labour, information overload, and time pressures (p. 443).

organizational control Those which are introduced by management as part of the formal activity of the organization (p. 536).

organizational culture The shared philosophy, ideology, values, assumptions, beliefs, expectations, and attitudes that knit an organization together (p. 496).

organizational design The process of structuring or restructuring an organization in the most appropriate way, given the organization's external environment, technology, and size (p. 247).

organizational life cycle The series of events that takes place from the time an organization is formed until the time it ceases to exist (p. 254).

organizational politics The activities individuals pursue in organizations to develop and exercise power to achieve their own desired outcomes (p. 295).

organizational strength Resource or capability that assists the organization in carrying out its activities (p. 133).

organizational structure The pattern of formal relationships that exists between groups and individuals in an organization (p. 201).

organizational weakness Inadequacy that prevents the organization from doing what it wants (p. 133).

organizing The process of deciding which specific functions must be performed, and how these functions should be coordinated so that organizational goals are reached (p. 16).

orientation The initial acquainting of new employees with the company's policies and programs, personnel with whom they will interact, and the nature of the job (p. 325).

output controls Used to determine whether deviations from standards have occurred in a product or service (p. 546).

output standards State the quantity of the product or service that employees should be producing (p. 538).

outsourcing Turning to outside firms instead of the firm's own employees to do some of the work that is necessary for organizational performance (p. 601).

P

path-goal model Suggests that the leader's job is to increase the payoffs to workers for achieving organizational goals (p. 415).

partnership Comes into being when two or more individuals combine their financial, managerial, and technical abilities for the purpose of operating a company for a profit (p. 11).

people change Focusses on changing the skills, attitudes, and behaviour of the people in the organization (p. 472).

people skills The ability to lead, motivate, and communicate with both groups and individuals (p. 23).

perception The way that people "see" their environment (p. 445).

performance appraisal A formal program for comparing employees' actual performance with expected performance (p. 328).

performance-outcome expectancy Reflects a person's belief about the connection between performance and rewards (p. 373).

performing Fourth stage of group development; group reaches a productive maturity where members spend most of their time working on the group's central task (p. 267).

personal staff Assist specific line managers, but generally lack the authority to act for them in their absence (p. 242).

persuasive power Person A is able to convince Person B to take a certain course of action by making logical arguments (p. 291).

PERT A planning and control technique which is used to display the various activities and events that are needed to complete a project (p. 570).

planning The process of deciding what objectives to pursue and choosing strategies that will help the organization reach those objectives (p. 16).

plan Focus on the activities that must be performed in order to achieve objectives (p. 99).

policy A guide to action which suggests in general terms what managers should do in various decision situations (p. 100).

policy manual Contains an organization's policies, procedures, and rules, and may also contain the organization's code of ethics and its views about social responsibility (p. 101).

political model of decision making Assumes that organizational decisions are made on the basis of whether or not they will increase the status, power, or economic well-being of the decision maker (p. 164).

political model of organizations Views organizations as places where there is much competition for resources, and where people with different values and biases are often in conflict with each other (pp. 276, 293).

pooled interdependence Exists when the various departments in an organization can each work independently to make their contribution to overall organizational effectiveness (p. 251).

portfolio analysis Classification of the present and future position of businesses, products, or SBUs according to the attractiveness of the market and the ability to compete within the market (p. 134).

PPBS Focusses on allocating budget money to programs instead of departments (p. 574).

positive reinforcement Occurs when a pleasant stimulus is presented to a person (p. 375).

power The ability to get another person to do what you want them to do, even if they do not want to do it (p. 289).

preferred stock Shows ownership in a corporation; preferred shareholders usually do not have the right to vote (p. 13).

privatization The transfer of functions or activities from the government to the private sector (p. 66).

problem analysis phase (of decision making) The decision maker's goal is to come to a clear understanding of what the problem is (p. 157).

problem decisions Necessary when results are different from those that were planned (p. 154).

problem solving Refers to those managerial actions that are necessary to determine what the problem is and why it occurred (p. 153).

procedure A step-by-step description of how certain activities should be carried out (p. 100).

process consultation Activities the consultant performs which help the client organization to perceive, understand, and act upon events which occur in the client's organization (p. 507).

process controls Applied while the product or service is being produced (p. 545).

process culture Exists in organizations that make low-risk strategic decisions and receive delayed feedback about the success of their decisions (p. 500).

process production The manufacture of standardized products that are sold by weight or volume (p. 250).

process theories Focus not on individual needs, but on the processes that motivate people (p. 365).

product change Focusses on changing the mix of products or services an organization produces (p. 474).

product departmentation Used when it is important to focus on the products or services the organization sells (p. 211).

production-centred managers Emphasize the technical aspects of the job, set work standards and closely supervise workers (p. 408).

production norm The range of acceptable production behaviour among group members (p. 268).

productivity The ratio of physical output to physical input (p. 61).

profit The difference between the cost of inputs and the revenue from output (p. 11).

profitability ratios Measure the firm's overall efficiency and profitability (p. 579).

profit centre Exists when a department or division in an organization is given the responsibility of making a profit (p. 578).

profit-sharing plan An incentive program in which employees receive a bonus depending on the firm's profits (p. 330).

programmed decisions Recurring decisions on routine matters which are made using established procedures (p. 154).

progressive discipline Increasingly severe penalties are applied as evidence of improper behaviour accumulates (p. 541).

project departmentation Used when the work of an organization consists of a series of projects with a specific starting and ending point (p. 213).

project management The process of planning, organizing, leading, and controlling the work of employees, and all available resources, to complete projects on schedule and within budget (p. 53).

project manager The person who is responsible for completing the project on time and within budget (p. 244).

project organization A team of specialists from different functional areas of the organization work on a specific project (p. 243).

punishment Occurs when an unpleasant stimulus is presented to a person (p. 376).

punishment power The power a person has to determine the punishment that another person receives (p. 291).

purchase model Assumes that the organization will define its own problems and then hire an outside consultant to make recommendations on how to solve them (p. 508).

Q

qualitative forecasting Making predictions based on subjective managerial judgments and intuition (p. 102).

quality The degree of conformity to a predetermined standard (p. 63).

quality circles Consist of periodic meetings of groups of five to fifteen employees who discuss ways to improve the quality and quantity of work (p. 384).

quality control Refers to the activities that are carried out by managers and workers to ensure that quality levels are appropriate to customer needs (p. 561).

quality standards Define the level of quality that is to be maintained in the production of goods and services (p. 538).

quantitative forecasting Making predictions based on trends and patterns found in statistical data (p. 102).

R

rational model of decision making Assumes that decision makers proceed through a series of well-defined steps before making a decision (p. 157).

rational model of organization Views organizations as places where resources are rationally and efficiently used to pursue organizational objectives (pp. 276, 293).

rational resistance to change Occurs when people have thoughtful objections to a proposed change (p. 478).

raw materials inventory The basic inputs into the production process (p. 567).

receiver The individual or group for whom the message is intended (p. 433).

reciprocal interdependence Exists when individuals and departments must deal with work continually flowing back and forth until the job is completed (p. 252).

recruitment The phase in the staffing of a company in which the firm seeks to develop a pool of interested, qualified applicants for a position (p. 318).

recycling The retrieval for reuse of suitable waste materials, such as paper, bottles, and cans (p. 693).

referent power The power a person has over another who admires him or her (p. 291).

regular group members Individuals whose behaviour remains in the zone of acceptance of group norms (p. 269).

reinforcement Any event that increases or decreases the likelihood of a future response (p. 375).

reinforcement theory Views internal needs as unimportant, and says that a person's motivation can be explained through knowledge of their past experience (p. 375).

research Original investigation undertaken on a systematic basis to gain knowledge (p. 69).

resource audit Systematic examination and verification of the capabilities available to the organization (p. 134).

restructuring Changing an organization's structure so that it can more effectively cope with changes in its customers, markets, and products (p. 201).

responsibility The obligation of a subordinate to carry out a job in a timely fashion (p. 234).

retained earnings Profits which are reinvested in a business (p. 625).

reward power The power a person has to control the rewards another person receives (p. 291).

rites and ceremonies Regularly repeated acts that convey the special significance of certain achievements, events, or relationships for the organization (p. 499).

risk Exists when the manager is able to define the problem clearly, can list many (but not all) alternatives, and can estimate the probability of the payoffs for each alternative (p. 156).

role The pattern of behaviour that is expected of a person in a certain job (p. 17).

role ambiguity Results when a person has unclear expectations about his or her job responsibilities (p. 486).

role conflict Occurs when an individual receives conflicting expectations from others (p. 485).

role overload Occurs when a person is given more job obligations to fulfill than the person is capable of fulfilling (p. 486).

rumours An unsubstantiated statement about what is happening in an organization (p. 278).

rule Requires employees to behave in a specific way (p. 101).

S

salary Dollars paid at regular intervals in return for doing a job, regardless of the amount of time or output involved (p. 330).

satisficing Choosing an alternative which is acceptable, but which is not ideal (p. 162).

scalar principle A clear, unbroken line of authority should run from the top of the organization to the bottom (p. 206).

scalar status A person's level in the formal hierarchy (p. 281).

scenarios Statements of how future events might unfold (p. 102).

scientific management Attempts to discover the one best way to do a job, and to scientifically select and train workers to do that job (p. 33).

selection The process of sorting through a pool of candidates to choose the best one for a job (p. 321).

selective perception Seeing only what one wants to see (p. 447).

self-control Occurs when we set goals and then reward ourselves for achieving those goals (p. 380).

self-efficacy Refers to a person's beliefs about his or her ability to perform certain tasks (p. 380).

self-fulfilling prophecy A prediction which comes true because people do things to make it come true (p. 365).

self-managed teams Groups which have great discretion in how they do their work; they usually decide which tasks they are going to do, order the supplies necessary to do their work, hire new team members, and set their own quality standards (p. 264).

self-leadership Workers motivate themselves to do two kinds of tasks—those that are naturally attractive to them, as well as those that are necessary for the organization (p. 421).

semantics The study of words and what they mean (p. 447).

sensitivity analysis Techniques for incorporating the assessment of risk into the selection of a strategy (p. 140).

sensitivity training Designed to increase the awareness of individuals about their own motivations and behaviour patterns as well as those of others (p. 508).

sequential interdependence Exists when work must be completed in a specific way, and when the output of one individual or department becomes the input for another individual or department (p. 251).

service staff Provide a specific service to line managers (p. 242).

shareholders Persons who own shares in a corporation (p. 12).

simulation Developing a model of an actual situation and working through the simulation to see what kind of outcome results (p. 102).

single-industry communities A community of between 25 000-35 000 where at least 75 percent of the working population is employed by a single industry (p. 52).

single-use plans Those which are developed for a specific purpose and which will not be used again (p. 100).

skunkworks Informal groups of people that develop new ideas and innovations that are outside the normal structure of the organization (p. 173).

slack time The difference between the total time estimate for a certain path and the total time estimate for the critical path (p. 571).

slogans Phrase or sentence that conveys a value which is important to the organization (p. 500).

small business One that is independently owned and operated, and is not dominant in its field of operations (p. 618).

social audit A systematic assessment that identifies, measures, evaluates, reports, and monitors the effects an enterprise is having on society that are not covered in the traditional financial reports (p. 678).

social contract The understanding between society and its institutions (p. 673).

socialization The process by which members of an organization are made aware of the organization's culture (p. 498).

social learning theory Says that human motivation results from the interaction of both external and internal factors (p. 380).

social loafing The tendency of individuals to put forth less effort in a group than they do when they work individually (p. 171).

socially responsible investment (SRI) The screening of investments in the corporate sector for their social, as well as economic, benefits (p. 695).

social responsibility The notion that business enterprises have an obligation to stakeholders in society to examine the impact of their self-interested actions and, if necessary, modify a business decision beyond that prescribed by law, regulation, custom, or competition (p. 674).

sociogram Illustrates how the members of a work group interact with each other (p. 276).

sole proprietorship A business owned and managed by one person (p. 11).

source The individual or group that develops the message that is to be communicated to another individual or group (p. 432).

span of control The number of direct subordinates that report to a manager (p. 207).

specialization Breaking a complex task into simple parts so that the individual or group performing the task can focus on specific parts of it (p. 203).

stable environment One in which there are only minor changes in the type of customers, in the products customers demand, and in the technology used to convert inputs into output (p. 247).

staff experts People who have specialized training in technical areas like law, market research, industrial safety, and accounting (p. 240).

stakeholder Individual or group who can influence, or is influenced by, the operations or activities of an organization (p. 126).

stakeholder analysis Identifies the criteria by which the organization will be judged by stakeholders and how well the organization is performing against these criteria (p. 128).

stakeholder control Control which is applied by those who are concerned about how an organization operates (e.g., the shareholders) (p. 535).

standard operating procedures Step-by-step activity performed over and over in the normal course of organizational operations (p. 100).

standards Criteria for evaluating the quality and quantity of the products or services produced by employees (p. 537).

standing committees Meet on a regular basis and are a relatively permanent feature of an organization's structure (p. 223).

standing plans Those which will be used over and over in the course of normal organizational functioning (p. 100).

statistical quality control Involves testing just a portion of the total output of a product and then drawing inferences about the quality of the remaining items which have not been tested (p. 565).

status The relative position of an individual in a group (p. 280).

status symbol A tangible sign of a person's social position (p. 281).

stepladder technique Reduces the chance that problems associated with group decision making will appear by structuring the entry of group members into a core group in a systematic fashion (p. 171).

stereotyping Categorizing individuals or groups on the basis of only a few characteristics (p. 447).

stories Narratives that are based on actual incidents, and which convey the key values of the organization's culture to employees (p. 499).

storming Second stage of group development; conflict appears within the group regarding who will have control over the group (p. 267).

strategic alliances A relationship that involves two or more enterprises cooperating in the research, development, manufacture, or marketing of a product (p. 646).

strategic audit All components in the strategic management process are systematically examined to ascertain or verify whether or not appropriate strategic decisions have been made (p. 144).

strategic business unit Smallest operating division of an enterprise that is given authority to make its own strategic decisions within corporate guidelines (p. 124).

strategic control Used to help managers assess the effectiveness of strategic plans (p. 543).

strategic control points Those which an organization finds particularly important to its success (p. 542).

strategic funds programming Budget and control system that provides management with the decision-making information needed to implement strategy (p. 143).

strategic group Enterprises with similar competitive approaches and positions in the industry (p. 132).

strategic issues Issues that are crucial to the success of an organization (p. 140).

strategic leadership People who have overall responsibility for an organization—their characteristics, what they do, and how they do it (p. 124).

strategic management Establishes an organization's mission and objectives, analyzes the environment and resource capabilities in order to formulate a strategy, creates the organizational systems and processes needed to implement the strategy, and devises mechanisms for monitoring and reviewing the organization's performance that results from the strategy chosen (p. 117).

strategic plans Deal with the activities that are necessary to achieve the organization's overall objectives (p. 99).

strategic planning Planning that is based on future opportunities to succeed rather than past practice. It includes emphasis on environmental analysis, markets, competition and strategic alternatives (p. 119).

strategic report card Strategists review the components of strategic management regularly to make sure that the strategy remains appropriate and that implementation is proceeding as intended (p. 144).

strategist Someone responsible for the success or failure of an organization through the initiation, formulation, implementation, and review of a strategic management process (p. 122).

strategy The unified, comprehensive, and integrated plan that applies the resources of the firm to the challenges of the environment and ensures that the mission and objectives of the organization are achieved (p. 117).

stress The emotional or physiological response a person exhibits in reaction to a demand that might exceed the person's ability to cope with it (p. 483).

stressors Those things which cause stress (p. 485).

strong culture One in which the key values of the organization are aggressively held by its present members and explicitly conveyed to new members (p. 497).

structural change Focusses on changing the authority structure of the organization (p. 472).

structural conflict resolution techniques Focus on the structural features of the organization that may be causing the conflict (p. 468).

subjective probabilities Based on management intuition, values, preferences, and experience with similar situations (p. 157).

supportive behaviour The extent to which a leader engages in two-way communication, listens, provides support, and encouragement, facilitates interaction, and involves the followers in decision making (p. 411).

survey feedback A systematic collection and measurement of employee attitudes through the use of questionnaires (p. 505).

sustainable development Development which insures that the utilization of resources and the impact on the environment today does not damage prospects for the use of resources or the environment by future generations (p. 695).

systems approach Views an organization as a complex set of interrelated factors that must be integrated in order for the organization to reach its goals (p. 40).

T

tactical control Used to help managers assess the effectiveness of tactical plans at the middle level of the management hierarchy (p. 543).

tactical plans Specify the activities that departments within an organization must carry out if overall strategic objectives are to be reached (p. 100).

task force Temporary team of specialists who are organized to solve a problem involving two or more departments (p. 223).

team building A conscious effort to develop effective work groups in the organization (p. 507).

technical skills Allow a person to apply certain procedures or techniques that are relevant to a specific field of work (p. 23).

technological change Focusses on changing the way inputs are converted into output (p. 472).

technological interdependence The amount of coordination that is necessary to successfully complete tasks (p. 251).

technology The application of knowledge about how to use people, work methods, and materials to convert inputs to output (p. 250).

telecommuting Computer hookups from home to office (p. 597).

territorial departmentation Used when an organization carries on its activities over large geographic areas (p. 212).

Theory X managers Assume that it is necessary to coerce, control, or threaten employees in order to motivate them (p. 364).

Theory Y managers Assume that employees are mature and responsible, and do not require coercion or excessive control in order to perform effectively (p. 364).

threats Arise from the possibility of an adverse or harmful trend or event (p. 130).

time and motion studies Using a movie camera and stopwatch to do a detailed analysis of how a worker is doing a job (p. 33).

time standards State the length of time it should take to complete a task (p. 538).

top-down budgeting Top management develops the budget for the organization and imposes it on lower-level managers (p. 572).

top managers Are responsible for the overall operation of the organization (p. 20).

total quality management (TQM) A set of principles, tools, and procedures providing guidance to the creation of an environment that will enable employees to do a good job, allow good ideas to work, involves suppliers, and focusses on the satisfaction of the customer or consumer (pp. 63, 562).

tough-guy, macho culture Exists in organizations that make risky strategic decisions and receive fast feedback on the success of their decisions (p. 500).

trade Involves the exporting or importing of goods to and from other countries (p. 641).

traditional view of conflict Assumes that conflict is bad for organizations, and that its existence is proof that something is wrong (p. 464).

trait approach Assumes that the leader's personal attributes are the key to leadership success (p. 406).

transactional managers Have a traditional view of the management functions of planning, organizing, leading, and controlling (p. 399).

transformational managers Stress activities such as revitalizing the organization, communicating the organization's vision and culture to employees, molding employees into effective performers, and getting employee commitment to the organization's goals (p. 399).

two-way communication Takes place when the sender directs a message to the receiver with the expectation of an immediate, obvious response (p. 438).

Type I conflict Exists when one party blocks another party's attempts to obtain the resources that the other party needs to achieve its goals (p. 461).

Type II conflict Exists when the blocking behaviour occurs at the activity stage instead of the resource-attainment stage of conflict (p. 461).

Type III conflict Occurs when one party interferes with another party at both the resource-attainment and activity stages (p. 462).

U

uncertainty Exists when managers cannot assign even subjective probabilities to the possible outcomes that might occur for each of the alternatives they are considering (p. 157).

unit production The manufacture of small quantities of custom products for specific customers (p. 250).

unity of command principle Each person in an organization should report to only one boss (p. 206).

universalist theories Propose that there is "one best way" to manage organizations and people (p. 42).

universalist leadership theories Assume that one style of leadership is superior to all others, regardless of the situation in which the leader operates (p. 405).

V

valence The desirability of an outcome as subjectively seen by a person (p. 373).

value chain Diagnostic process for pinpointing and analyzing the activities of an organization that add value to a product or service (p. 135).

values audit Systematic effort to discover the beliefs or attitudes held by all members in an organization (p. 129).

variable costs Costs which increase or decrease, depending on the level of production (p. 575).

variable interval schedule A reinforcement is applied after a varying amount of time has passed, regardless of the number of desired responses that have occurred (p. 376).

variable ratio schedule Behaviours are reinforced after a varying number of responses have occurred; sometimes a reinforcement occurs after three responses, sometimes after ten, sometimes after fifty, and so on (p. 377).

variable sampling A product is assessed to determine how closely it adheres to quality standards (p. 566).

venture capital The provision of equity (common stock) or equity-related funds to any business entity where there is risk of loss of capital and when such financing cannot be obtained from conventional sources upon reasonable terms (p. 56).

venture capitalist Individual or company that provides such financing (p. 56).

vertical differentiation Differences among departments at different levels in the organizational hierarchy (p. 220).

vertical information systems Sends information up and down the hierarchy so that more informed decisions can be made (p. 221).

vertical integration The corporation can seek ownership or control of a supplier, or over a firm's distribution or retailers (p. 138).

vicarious learning Learning which occurs as we observe others (p. 380).

visioning Process of establishing a vision for an organization which guides those choices that determine the nature and direction of an organization (p. 129).

voice mail A computer-based messaging system accessed by telephone (p. 436).

vulnerability analysis Process that forces strategists to question the strategy or plan (p. 144).

W

wages Dollars paid based on the number of hours worked or the number of units produced (p. 330).

waste management The handling and disposal of unwanted materials left over from industrial production or individual consumption (p. 693).

word processing Uses a computer to do text editing by allowing for the manipulation of words, tables, and figures (p. 597).

work hard/play hard culture Exists in organizations that make low-risk strategic decisions and receive immediate feedback on the success of their decisions (p. 500).

work teams Formal work groups established by an organization to achieve a specific goal (p. 264).

world product mandating The assignment to one subsidiary the responsibility for researching, developing, manufacturing, and marketing a product or a line of related products (p. 646).

Z

zero-based budgeting Requires managers in each budget unit to rationalize their allocations from the ground up each year rather than simply assuming that next year's budget will be similar to last year's budget (p. 574).

zone of acceptance Denotes what workers are willing to do without questioning a manager's authority (p. 39).

ENDNOTES

CHAPTER 1

1. Mary Parker Follett, *The New State*. Gloucester, Massachusetts: Peter Smith, 1918.
2. Merle MacIsaac, "Born-Again Basket Case," *Canadian Business*, May 1993, pp. 38–44.
3. Neal Templin, "Ford Giving Every Worker a Purpose," *The Globe and Mail*, December 28, 1992, p. B6.
4. Peter Drucker, *Managing for Results*. New York: Harper and Row, 1964.
5. *The Canadian Business Failure Record*. Dun and Bradstreet Canada Ltd., 1985, p. 4.
6. John Ivancevich, James Donnelley, and James Gibson, *Management*. Homewood, Illinois: BPI Irwin, 1989, p. 4.
7. Stephen Robbins and Robin Stuart-Kotze, *Management*. Scarborough, Ontario: Prentice-Hall Canada Inc., 1990, p. 35.
8. L.E. Boone, D.L. Kurtz, and C.P. Fleenor, "CEO's: Early Signs of a Business Career," *Business Horizons*, September-October 1988, p. 21.
9. David Leidl, "Follow Me Team," *Manitoba Business*, April 1990, p. 13.
10. Henry Mintzberg. *The Nature of Managerial Work*. New York: Harper and Row, 1973.
11. See, for example, Colin P. Hales, "What Do Managers Do? A Critical Review of the Evidence," *Journal of Management Studies*, 23, 1986, pp. 88–115; also Lance B. Kurke and Howard E. Aldrich, "Mintzberg Was Right! A Replication and Extension of *The Nature of Managerial Work*, *Management Science*, 29, 1983, pp. 975–984.
12. Margot Gibb-Clark, "Taxing on Staff," *The Globe and Mail*, August 27, 1990.
13. L. Gomez-Mejia, J.E. McCann, and R.C. Page, "The Structure of Managerial Behaviors and Rewards," *Industrial Relations*, 24, 1985, pp. 147–154.
14. Allen Kraut and Patricia Pedigo, "The Role of the Manager: What's Really Important in Different Management Jobs?," *Academy of Management Executive*, November 1989, pp. 286–293.
15. Harry S. Jonas, Ronald E. Fry, and Suresh Srivastva, "The Office of the CEO: Understanding the Executive Experience," *Academy of Management Executive*, August 1990, pp. 36–48.
16. Kraut and Pedigo, pp. 289–290.

CHAPTER 2

1. Nicolo Machiavelli. *The Prince*. (Translated by Luigi Ricci). New York: New American Library, 1952.
2. Frederick W. Taylor, *Principles of Scientific Management*. New York: Harper, 1911, pp. 41–47.
3. C.D. Wrege and A.G. Perroni, "Taylor's Pig-Tale: A Historical Analysis of Frederick Taylor's Pig-Iron Experiments," *Academy of Management Journal*, 17, 1974, pp. 6–27; also C. D. Wrege and A. M. Stotka, "Cooke Creates A Classic: The Story Behind F. W. Taylor's Principles of Scientific Management," *Academy of Management Review*, 3, 1978, pp. 736–749.
4. Peter Drucker, "The Coming Rediscovery of Scientific Management," *The Conference Board Record*, 13, 1976, pp. 23–27.
5. Edwin A. Locke, "The Ideas of Frederick W. Taylor: An Evaluation," *Academy of Management Review*, 7, 1982, pp. 14–24.
6. Claude S. George. *The History of Management Thought*. Englewood Cliffs, New Jersey: Prentice-Hall, 1968.
7. Ibid.
8. Max Weber. *The Theory of Social and Economic Organizations*. (Translated by A.M. Henderson and Talcott Parsons.) New York: Oxford University Press, 1947. Recently, there has been some debate about exactly what Weber was saying about bureaucracy: see R. M. Weiss, "Weber on Bureaucracy: Management Consultant or Political Theorist?", *Academy of Management Review*, 8, 1983, pp. 242–248.
9. G. Morgan, *Images of Organizations*. Beverly Hills, California: Sage, 1986, pp. 25–38.
10. John Godard, *Industrial Relations: The Economy and Society*, The Canadian Variant. Toronto: McGraw-Hill Ryerson, 1993.
11. Henri Fayol, *Industrial and General Administration*. (Translated by J. A. Coubrough.) Geneva: International Management Institute, 1930.
12. F. Roethlisberger and W. J. Dickson, *Management and the Worker*. Cambridge, Massachussets: Harvard University Press, 1935.
13. R.G. Greenwood and C. D. Wrege, "The Hawthorne Studies," In D. A. Wren and J. A. Pearce II (eds.), *Papers Dedicated to the Development of Modern Management*. Starkville, Mississippi: Mississippi State University, Academy of Management, 1986, pp. 24–35.

14. Mary Parker Follett, *The New State. Gloucester, Massachusetts: Peter Smith, 1918.*

15. Chester Barnard, *The Functions of the Executive.* Cambridge, Massachussets: Harvard University Press, 1938.

16. J. R. Miller and H. Feldman, "Management Science—Theory, Relevance, and Practice in the 1980's," *Interfaces,* 13, 1983, pp. 56–60.

17. Ludwig von Bertalanffy, Carl G. Hempel, Robert E. Bass, and Hans Jonas, "General Systems Theory: A New Approach to Unity of Science," I–VI *Human Biology,* 23, 1951, pp. 302–361.

18. Fred Luthans, "The Contingency Theory of Management: A Path Out of the Jungle," *Business Horizons,* 16, 1973, pp. 62–72; also Fred Luthans and Todd I. Stewart, "A General Contingency Theory of Management," *Academy of Management Review,* 2, 1977, pp. 181–195.

19. Gordon Allan, "Management Flexibility," *The Canadian Personnel and Industrial Relations Journal,* May 1971, pp. 13–21.

CHAPTER 3

1. Data from Bell Canada Information Form for year ended December 31, 1991, and Financial Statements for 1991 as provided by Micomedia Limited.

2. *Employee Share Ownership at Canada's Public Corporations.* Toronto: The Toronto Stock Exchange, 1987.

3. Project management techniques are discussed in Chapter 8.

4. *Canadian Shareowners: Their Profile and Attitudes.* Toronto: The Toronto Stock Exchange, 1989. p. 6.

5. Lisa Grogan, "Trading of a Different Kind," *The Financial Post,* October 1, 1990, p. 18 and Kenneth Kidd, "North West Selling Stores," *The Globe and Mail,* January 26, 1991, p. B3. It is interesting to note that in 1990, North West sold shares in the business to the public.

6. *Canadian Shareowners: Their Profile and Attitudes.* Toronto: The Toronto Stock Exchange, 1989. p.6.

7. Gail Lem, "Sherritt Gordon Holders Dump Board of Directors," September 20, 1990, p. B1 and "Delaney to Lead Sherritt's Board," September 21, 1990, p. B9 both in *The Globe and Mail.*

8. "Foreign Ownership Up Slightly," *The Globe and Mail,* May 22, 1992, p. B12.

9. "Top 500 Rankings," *The Financial Post,* May 1993, pp. 92–95.

10. Ken Romain, "Teamwork at Toyota raises Corolla output," *The Globe and Mail,* February 22, 1990, pp. B1, B4.

11. *World Competitiveness Report,* Geneva: The World Economic Forum and Lausanne: International Institute for Management Development. 1990, and Margot Gibb-Clark, "Canada's competitiveness slips", *The Globe and Mail,* June 20, 1990, B3.

12. Catherine Harris, "New Ways to Measure Productivity Growth Developed by Stat Can," *The Financial Post,* June 25, 1990, p. 10.

13. Bruce Little, "Productivity growth returns," *The Globe and Mail,* May 18, 1993, page B1.

14. Madeline Drohan, "Internationals lead unions on government holdings," *The Globe and Mail,* September 1989, p. B6.

15. This definition is used by Revenue Canada and Statistics Canada.

16. "B.C. mill fined $200,000 for polluting," *The Globe and Mail,* January 11, 1991, p. B3.

17. "Women at the Top: A Progress Report," *Report on Business Magazine,* October 1990, pp. 56–69.

CHAPTER 4

1. Deidre McMurdy, "Bovar Changing its Focus to Waste Management," *The Globe and Mail,* May 15, 1990, p. B7.

2. Henry Mintzberg, "The Manager's Job: Folklore and Fact," *Harvard Business Review,* 53, No. 4, 1975, pp. 49–61.

3. Ibid., p. 51.

4. Charles B. Shrader, Lew Taylor, and Dan R. Dalton, "Strategic Planning and Organizational Performance: A Critical Appraisal," *Journal of Management,* 1984, p. 52; also Gordon E. Greenley, "Does Strategic Planning Improve Company Performance?," *Long Range Planning,* April 1986, pp. 101–109; also Duane L. Wood and Robert L. LaForage, "The Impact of Comprehensive Planning on Financial Performance," *Academy of Management Journal,* 22, 1979, pp. 516–526.

5. V. Ramanujam and N. Venkatraman, "Excellence, Planning, and Performance," *Interfaces,* May–June 1988, pp. 23–31; also B.K. Boyd, "Strategic Planning and Financial Performance: A Meta-Analytic Review," *Journal of Management Studies,* July 1991, pp. 353–374.

6. Ernest A. Kallman and H. Jack Shapiro, "The Motor Freight Industry: A Case Against Planning," *Long Range Planning,* February 1978, pp. 81–86; also Milton Leontiades and A. Tezel, "Planning Perceptions and Planning Results," *Strategic Management Journal,* January–March 1980, pp. 65–75.

7. John Raymond, "For The Long Haul," *The Globe and Mail,* May 17, 1990, p. B2.

8. Peter Drucker, *The Practice of Management.* New York: Harper, 1954, pp. 62–87; also Peter Drucker, *Management: Tasks, Responsibilities, Practices.* New York: Harper, 1974, pp. 100–117.

9. Lawrence Surtees, "Unitel Must Sell Itself: Survey," *The Globe and Mail,* October 22, 1990, p. B10.

10. Geoffrey Rowan, "Xerox Launches Document Processing Products," *The Globe and Mail,* October 3, 1990, p. B7.

11. Andre Picard, "Turn Green or Wilt, Business Told," *The Globe and Mail,* October 13, 1990, p. B6.

12. Merle MacIsaac, "Born Again Basket Case," *Canadian Business,* May 1993, pp. 38–44.

13. A.G. Bedeian, *Management.* Fort Worth, Texas: The Dryden Press, 1993, pp. 134–135.

14. G.P. Latham and Gary Yukl, "A Review of Research on the Application of Goal Setting in Organizations," *Academy of Management Journal,* 1975, pp. 824–845; also G.P. Latham and E.A. Locke, "Goal Setting—A Theory That Works," *Organizational Dynamics,* 8, 1979, pp. 68–80; also A.J. Mento, R. P. Steel, and R. J. Karren, "A Meta-Analytic Study of the Effects of Goal Setting on Task Performance," *Organizational Behavior and Human Decision Processes,* 39, 1987, pp. 52–83.

15. K.G. Smith and Edwin Locke, "Goal Setting, Planning, and Organizational Performance: An Experimental Simulation," *Organizational Behavior and Human Decision Processes,* 46, 1990, pp. 118–134.

16. F.A. Starke, R. W. Mondy, A. Sharplin, and E. Flippo, *Management Concepts and Canadian Practice.* Toronto: Allyn and Bacon, 1988, p. 103.

17. Rowan, "Xerox Launches Document Processing Products."

18. Karen Howlett, "What Went Wrong at Central Capital," *The Globe and Mail,* June 13, 1992, p. B4.

19. Rona Maynard, "The Pain Threshold," *Canadian Business,* February 1993, p. 24.

20. John Lorinc, "Power Failure," *Canadian Business,* November 1992, pp. 50–58.

21. Barrie McKenna, "How a Megaproject Became a Millstone," *The Globe and Mail,* December 22, 1992, p. B18.

22. D.M. Georgoff and R.G. Murdick, "Manager's Guide to Forecasting," *Harvard Business Review,* January–February 1986, pp. 110–122.

23. Christopher Cerf and Victor S. Navarsky, *The Experts Speak.* New York: Pantheon, 1984.

24. K. Romain, "Killer Computer Is Making Pilots Sweat," *The Globe and Mail,* September 27, 1985, p. B12.

25. Martin Cash, "MTS Locks in Clients in Face of Deregulation," *Winnipeg Free Press,* November 20, 1990, p. 17.

26. Margot Gibb-Clark, "Part-Time Solution," *The Globe and Mail,* August 16, 1990, p. B5.

27. Peter F. Drucker, *The Practice of Management.* New York: Harper, 1954.

28. Peter F. Drucker, *Management Tasks, Responsibilities, Practices.* New York: Harper, 1974.

29. M.C. McConkie, "A Clarification of the Goal Setting and Appraisal Processes in MBO," *Academy of Management Review,* 4, 1979, pp. 369–380.

30. W.C. Giegold, *Volume III: Performance Appraisal and the MBO Process.* New York: McGraw-Hill, 1978.

31. Jack N. Kondrasuk, "Studies in MBO Effectiveness," *Academy of Management Review,* 1981, pp. 419–430.

32. Robert C. Ford, Frank S. McLaughlin, and James Nixdorf, "Ten Questions About MBO," *California Management Review,* Winter 1980, p. 92.

33. Kondrasuk, "Studies in MBO Effectiveness."

34. S. Kerr, "Some Modifications in MBO as an OD Strategy," *Academy of Management Proceedings,* 1972.

CHAPTER 5

1. This definition is based on one proposed by Lawrence R. Jauch and William F. Glueck, *Strategic Management and Business Policy.* Third Edition. New York: McGraw-Hill, 1988, p. 11.

2. For history of strategic management concept, refer to Jeffrey Bracker, "The Historical Development of the Strategic Management Concept," *Academy of Management Review,* 1980, 5, No. 2, pp. 219–224; also "From Strategic Planning to Strategic Management" in William D. Guth, editor, *Handbook of Business Strategy 1986/87 Handbook,* pp. 1–7 to 1–9; also Donald H. Thain, "Strategic Management: The State of the Art," *Business Quarterly,* Autumn 1990, pp. 95–102.

3. These factors follow closely those listed in William D. Guth, editor, *Handbook of Business Strategy 1986/1987 Yearbook,* Boston: Warren, Gorham & Lamont. 1987. pp. 15–3 to 15–6.

4. As listed in Guth, p. 15–4 (refer to note 3).

5. *Annual Review and Report 1989,* Renaissance Energy Ltd., p. 1.

6. John A. Pearce and Richard A. Robinson Jr., *Formulation and Implementation of Competitive Strategy.* Third Edition. Homewood, Illinois: Irwin, 1988, p. 278 and Alan J. Rowe, Richard O. Mason, Karl E. Dickel, and Neil H. Snyder. *Strategic Management: A Methodological Approach.* Third Edition. Reading, Massachusetts: Addison-Wesley Publishing, 1989, p. 69.

7. Examples of intrapreneurship in Canadian enterprises are given in Jerry S. White, *Intrapreneuring: The Secrets of Corporate Success in Canada.* Markham, Ontario: Viking, 1989 and Erik G. Rule and Donald W. Irwin, "Fostering Entrepreneurship: The New Competitive Edge," *The Journal of Business Strategy,* May/June 1988, pp. 44–47.

8. Donald C. Hambrick, "Putting Top Managers Back in the Strategic Picture," *Strategic Management Journal,* 10 1989, Special Issue, p. 6.

9. A good discussion of the role of values in strategic management is in a paper by R. Edward Freeman, Daniel R. Gilbert, Jr., and Edwin Hartman, "Values and the Foundations of Strategic Management," *Journal of Business,* 7, 1988, pp. 821–834.

10. Jay Barney, "Organizational Culture: Can It Be a Source of Sustained Competitive Advantage," *Academy of Management Review,* II, No. 3, 1986, pp. 656–665.

11. Y. Allaire and M. Firsirota, "How to Implement Radical Strategies in Large Organizations," *Sloan Management Review,* 26, No. 3, Spring 1985, p. 19.

12. There is an extensive literature about corporate culture, but the following are references relating culture to strategic management: Colin Camerer, and Ari Vepsalainen, "The Economic Efficiency of Corporate Culture," *Strategic Management Journal,* 9, 1988, pp. 115–126; Rohit Deshpandé, and A. Parasuraman, "Linking Corporate Culture to Strategic Planning," *Business Horizons,* May–June 1988, pages 28–37; Jay W. Lorsch, "Managing Culture: The Invisible Barrier to Strategic Change," *California Management Review,* XXVII, No. 2, Winter 1986, pp. 95–109; Edgar Schein, "Coming to a New Awareness of Organizational Culture," *Sloan Management Review,* Winter 1984, pp. 3–16; Christian Scholz, "Corporate Culture and Strategy—The Problem of Strategic Fit," *Long Range Planning,* 20, No. 4, 1987, pp. 78–87; and Paul Shrivastava, "Integrating Strategy Formulation with Organizational Culture," *Journal of Business Strategy,* 5, No. 3, Winter 1985, pp. 103–111.

13. Adapted from R. Edward Freeman, *Strategic Management: A Stakeholder Approach.* Boston: Pitman. 1984, p. 53.

14. Fred R. David, "How Companies Define Their Mission," *Long Range Planning,* 22, No. 1, 1989, p. 90.

15. W. R. King, and D.I. Cleland, *Strategic Planning and Policy.* New York: Van Nostrand Reinhold. 1979, p. 124.

16. David, p. 91 (refer to endnote 14).

17. John M. Bryson, *Strategic Planning for Public and Nonprofit Organizations: A Guide to Strengthening and Sustaining Organizational Achievement.* San Francisco: Jossey-Bass Publishers. 1988, p. 99.

18. Freeman, pp. 53–73 (refer to endnote 9).

19. Center for Business Ethics, "Are Corporations Institutionalizing Ethics?", *Journal of Business Ethics.* 5, No. 2, April 1980, p. 88.

20. Benjamin B. Tregoe, John W. Zimmerman, Ronald A. Smith, and Peter M. Tobia. *Vision in Action: Putting A Winning Strategy To Work.* New York: Simon and Schuster, 1989, p. 33.

21. Andrew Campbell, "How to Translate a Corporate Vision Into Reality," *The Globe and Mail,* April 24, 1989, p. A7.

22. Jauch and Glueck, pp. 137–140 (refer to note 1).

23. Harold Klein, and William Newman, "How to Use SPIRE: A Systematic Procedure for Identifying Relevant Environments for Strategic Planning," *The Journal of Business Strategy,* 1, No. 1, Summer 1988, pp. 32–45.

24. Burt Nanus, "QUEST—Quick Environmental Scanning Technique," *Long Range Planning,* 15, No. 2, 1982, 39–45.

25. Don Lebell, and D.J. Krasner, "Selecting Environmental Forecasting Techniques from Business Planning Requirements," *The Academy of Management Review,* 2, No. 3, July 1977, pp. 373–383.

26. Richard D. Michman, "Why Forecast for the Long Term?," *The Journal of Business Strategy,* September/October 1989, pp. 36–41.

27. Michael E. Porter, *Competitive Strategy: Techniques for Analyzing Industries and Competitors.* New York: The Free Press. 1980.

28. Summarized from Strategic Planning Institute brochures.

29. David A. Aaker, "Managing Assets and Skills: The Key to a Substainable Competitive Advantage," *California Management Review,* Winter 1989, pp. 95–106.

30. Jorge, Vasconcellor e Sá, "The Impact of Key Success Factors on Company Performance," *Long Range Planning,* 21, No. 6, 1988, pp. 56–64.

31. Jauch and Glueck, Chapter 5 (refer to endnote 1).

32. Fred R. David, *Concepts of Strategic Management,* Second Edition, Columbus: Merrill Publishing, 1989, Chapter 5. This chapter contains a good check list for audits.

33. Pankaj Ghemawat, "Building Strategy on the Experience Curve," *Harvard Business Review,* 63, No. 2, 1985, pp. 143–149.

34. Guth, Chapter 6 (refer to endnote 2).

35. Michael E. Porter, *Competitive Advantage: Creating and Sustaining Superior Performance.* New York: The Free Press, 1985.

36. G.S. Odiorne, *Management by Objectives.* New York: Pitman, 1985.

37. L.J. Mennon, and D.W. Landers, *Advanced Techniques for Strategic Analysis,* Chicago: The Dryden Press, 1987.

38. Porter, 1980, Chapter 2 (refer to endnote 27).

39. Gerry Johnson, Kevan Scholes, and Robert W. Sexty, *Exploring Strategic Management,* Scarborough, Ontario: Prentice-Hall Canada, 1989.

40. There are descriptions of this technique in most strategic management textbooks, but the source frequently referred to is Heinz Weihrich, "The TOWS Matrix—A Tool for Situational Analysis," *Long Range Planning,* 15, No. 2, 1982, pp. 54–66.

41. Andrew C. Boynton, and Robert W. Zmud, "An Assessment of Critical Success Factors," *Sloan Management Review,* Summer 1984, pp. 17–27; Joel K. Leidecker, and Albert V. Bruno, "Identifying and Using Critical Success Factors," *Long Range Planning,* 17, No. 1, 1984, pp. 23–32.

42. Bryson (refer to endnote 17).

43. H. Igor Ansoff, *Corporate Strategy,* New York: McGraw-Hill Book Company, 1965.

44. Michel Godet, *Scenarios and Strategic Management.* London: Butterworths, 1987; William R. Huss, and Edward J. Honton, "Scenario Planning—What Style Should You Use?" *Long Range Planning,* 20, No. 4, 1987, pp. 21–29; and Steven P. Schnaars, "How to Develop and Use Scenarios," *Long Range Planning,* 20, No. 1, 1987, pp. 105–114.

45. Johnson et al., pp. 252–54 (refer to endnote 39).

46. A good discussion of using this methodology to evaluate strategic alternatives is in Rowe et al., pp. 248–250 (refer to endnote 6)

47. Recent articles emphasizing this point include Donald C. Hambrick, and Albert A. Cannella, Jr., "Strategy Implementation as Substance and Selling," *The Academy of Management EXECUTIVE,* III, No. 4, 1989, pp. 278–285, and David M. Reid, "Operationalizing Strategic Planning," *Strategic Management Journal,* 10, 1989, pp. 553–567.

48. Hambrick and Cannella (refer to endnote 47).

49. Robert H.J. Waterman Jr., "The Seven Elements of Strategic Fit," *The Journal of Business Strategy,* 7, No. 3, 1982, pp. 69–73.

50. Rowe et al., p. 194 (refer to endnote 6).

51. Paul J. Stonich, "How to Use Strategic Funds Programming, *The Journal of Business Strategy,* 1, No. 2, 1980, 35–40, and Rowe et al., pp. 194–198 (refer to endnote 6).

52. Michael Goold, and John J. Quinn, "The Paradox of Strategic Controls," *Strategic Management Journal,* II, No. 1, January 1990, pp. 43–57.

53. Georg Schreyögg, and Horst Steinman, "Strategic Control: A New Perspective," *Academy of Management Review,* 12, No. 1, 1987, pp. 91–103.

54. Rowe et al., pp. 90, 95–97 (refer to endnote 6).

55. One such report card was proposed by Donald K. Yee, "Pass or Fail? How to Grade Strategic Progress," *The Journal of Business Strategy,* May/June 1990, pp. 10–14.

CHAPTER 6

1. H.A. Mintzberg, D. Raisingham, and A. Theoret, "The Structure of "Unstructured" Decision Processes," *Administrative Science Quarterly,* 21, 1976, pp. 246–275.

2. W.E. Pounds, "The Process of Problem Finding," *Industrial Management Review,* 1969, pp. 1–19.

3. L. Thorson, "Tanker Insurance Rates Soar After Iraq's Latest Attack Claims," *Bryan-College Station Eagle,* May 26, 1984, p. 13.

4. This model of the decision-making process is a composite of numerous models that have appeared during the last several decades.

5. The most comprehensive analysis of this phase of the process appears in C. Kepner and B. Tregoe, *The Rational Manager.* Princeton: Kepner-Tregoe, Inc., 1976.

6. N.R.F. Maier, "Assets and Liabilities in Group Problem Solving: The Need For An Integrative Function," *Psychological Review,* 74, 1967, pp. 239–249.

7. R. Lipshitz, "Either a Medal or a Corporal: The Effects of Success and Failure on the Evaluation of Decision Making and Decision Makers," *Organizational Behavior and Human Decision Processes* 44, 1989, pp. 380–395.

8. J.A. March and H.A. Simon. Organizations. New York: Wiley, 1958.

9. Jerry Ross and Barry Staw, "Expo '86: An Escalation Prototype," *Administrative Science Quarterly,* 1986, Vol. 31, pp. 274–297.

10. Barry Staw and Jerry Ross, "Behavior in Escalation Situation: Antecedents, Prototypes, and Situations. In L.L. Cummings and B.M. Staw, *Research in Organizational Behavior,* 1987, Vol. 9, pp. 39–78. For an alternate explanation for this behaviour, see P. Harrison and A. Harrell, "Impact of Adverse Selection on Managers' Project Evaluation Decisions," *Academy of Management Journal,* 1993, Vol. 36, pp. 635–643.

11. D. Conlon and H. Garland, "The Role of Project Completion Information in Resource Allocation Decisions," *Academy of Management Journal,* 1993, Vol. 36, pp. 402–413.

12. Ross and Staw, "Expo '86: An Escalation Prototype."

13. Jerry Ross and Barry Staw, "Organizational Escalation and Exit: Lessons from the Shoreham Nuclear Power Plant," *Academy of Management Journal,* 1993, Vol. 36, pp. 701–732.

14. J. Schaubroeck and S. Williams, "Type A Behavior Pattern and Escalating Commitment," *Journal of Applied Psychology,* 1993, Vol. 78, pp. 862–867.

15. Ross and Staw, "Expo '86: An Escalation Prototype."

16. I. Simonson and B. Staw, "Deescalation Strategies: A Comparison of Techniques for Reducing Commitment to Losing Courses of Action," *Journal of Applied Psychology,* August 1992, Vol. 77, pp. 419–426.

17. Barry Staw and Jerry Ross, "Knowing When to Pull the Plug," *Harvard Business Review,* March–April 1987, pp. 68–74.

18. M.D. Cohen, J.G. March, and J.P. Olsen, "A Garbage Can Model of Organizational Choice," *Administrative Science Quarterly,* 17, 1972, pp. 1–25.

19. F. Magee, "Decision Trees for Decision Analysis," *Harvard Business Review,* July–August 1964.

20. A.F. Osborn. *Applied Imagination.* New York: Scribner, 1957.

21. R. Kerwin, "Brainstorming as a Flexible Management Tool," *Personnel Journal,* 62, 1983, p. 414.

22. D. Taylor, C. Block, and P. Berry, "Does Group Participation When Using Brainstorming Facilitate or Inhibit Creative Thinking?" *Administrative Science Quarterly,* 3, 1958, pp. 23–47; also T.J. Bouchard, "Personality, Problem-Solving Procedure, and Performance in Small Groups," *Journal of Applied Psychology Monograph,* 53, 1969, 1, part 2; also T.J.

Bouchard, "Training, Motivation, and Personality as Determinants of the Effectiveness of Brainstorming Groups and Individuals," *Journal of Applied Psychology*, 59, 1974, pp. 226–227; also P.C. Dillion, V.K. Graham, and A. Aidells, "Brainstorming on a Hot Problem," *Journal of Applied Psychology*, 56, 1972, pp. 487–490.

23. R. Gallupe, L. Bastianutti, and W. Cooper, "Unblocking Brainstorms," *Journal of Applied Psychology*, February 1991, Vol. 76, pp. 137–142.
24. Gallupe, Bastianutti, and Cooper, "Unblocking Brainstorms."
25. A. Dennis and J. Valacich, "Computer Brainstorms: More Heads are Better than One," *Journal of Applied Psychology*, 1993, Vol. 78, pp. 531–537.
26. Gerry Blackwell, "You, Too, Can Be An Einstein," *Canadian Business*, May 1993, pp. 66–69; also William M. Bulkeley, "Computerizing Dull Meetings Is Touted As an Antidote to the Mouth That Bored," *Wall Street Journal*, January 28, 1992, p. B1.
27. N. Delkey, *The Delphi Method: An Experimental Study of Group Opinion*. Santa Monica, California: Rand Corporation, 1969.
28. A.L. Delbecq, A.H. van de Ven, and D.H. Gustafson. *Group Techniques for Program Planning: A Guide to Nominal and Delphi Processes*. Glenview, Illinois: Scott Foresman and Company, 1975.
29. G.D. Burton, D.S. Pathak, and R.M. Zigli, "Using Group Size to Improve the Decision Making Ability of Nominal Groups," *Proceedings of the 37th Annual Meeting of the Academy of Management*, 1977, pp. 53–56; also T.B. Green and P.H. Pietri, "Using Nominal Grouping to Improve Upward Communication," *MSU Business Topics*, Autumn, 1974 pp. 37–43; also W.M. Colley, "Size and Performance of Nominal Groups As Related to Problem Identification in a Management Environment," *Dissertation Abstracts International*, 38, 1978, p. 4251A.
30. S.E. White, J.E. Dittrich, and J.R. Lang, "The Effects of Group Decision Making Process and Problem-Situation Complexity on Implementation Attempts," *Administrative Science Quarterly*, 25, 1980, pp. 428–440.
31. R.O. Mason, "A Dialectical Approach to Strategic Planning," *Management Science*, 15, 1969, pp. B402–B414.
32. An example of the four phases of dialectical inquiry in making a strategic decision about marketing a new product is contained in R.O. Mason, I.I. Mitroff, and V.P. Barabba," Creating the Manager's Plan Book: A New Route to Effective Planning." In A.J. Rowe, R.O. Mason, and K.E. Dickel (eds.), *Strategic Management and Business Policy: A Methodological Approach*. Reading, Massachussets: Addison-Wesley, 1982, pp. 82–86.
33. D.M. Schweiger, W.R. Sandberg, and J.W. Ragan, "Group Approaches for Improving Strategic Decision Making: A Comparative Analysis of Dialectical Inquiry, Devil's Advocacy, and Consensus," *Academy of Management Journal*, 29, 1986, pp. 51–71; also D.M. Schweiger, W.R. Sandberg, and P.L. Rechner, "Experiential Effects of Dialectical Inquiry, Devil's Advocacy, and Consensus Approaches to Strategic Decision Making," *Academy of Management Journal*, 32, 1989, pp. 745–772.
34. P.C. Nutt, "Hybrid Planning Methods," *Academy of Management Review*, 7, 1982, pp. 442–454.
35. Margaret Philp, "Campeau Executives Offered a Carrot," *The Globe and Mail*, June 27, 1990, p. B9.
36. Harvey Enchin, "Consensus Management? Not For Bombardier's CEO," *The Globe and Mail*, April 16, 1990, p. B1.
37. Fred Moody, "No Ordinary Ambassador," *Canadian Transportation*, August 1990, p. 13.
38. Peter Larson, "Winning Strategies," *Canadian Business Review*, Summer 1989, p. 41.
39. C.R. Holloman and H.W. Hendrick, "Adequacy of Group Decisions as a Function of the Decision-Making Process," *Academy of Management Journal*, 15, 1972, pp. 175–184; also H.H. Kelley and J.W. Thibaut, "Group Problem Solving," *The Handbook of Social Psychology*, G. Lindzey and E. Aronson (eds.), Reading, Massachussets: Addison-Wesley, 1969, Ch. 29.
40. E.A. Locke, D.M. Schweiger, and G.P. Latham, "Participation in Decision Making: When Should It Be Used?," *Organizational Dynamics*, 1986, pp. 65–79.
41. For a review of this problem, see I.D. Steiner. *Group Process and Productivity*. New York: Academic Press, 1971; also J. Rohrbaugh, "Improving the Quality of Group Judgment: Social Judgment Analysis and the Delphi Technique," *Organizational Behavior and Human Performance*, 24, 1979, pp. 73–92.
42. B. Latane, K. Williams, and S. Harkins, "Many Hands Make Light The Work: The Causes and Consequences of Social Loafing," *Journal of Personality and Social Psychology*, Vol. 37, 1979, pp. 822–832.
43. J. George, "Extrinsic and Intrinsic Origins of Perceived Social Loafing in Organizations," *Academy of Management Journal*, Vol. 35, 1992, pp. 191–202.
44. I.L. Janis. *Victims of Groupthink*. Boston: Houghton-Mifflin, 1972.
45. S. Rogelbert, J. Barnes-Farrell, and C. Lowe, "The Stepladder Technique: An Alternative Group Structure Facilitating Effective Group Decision Making," *Journal of Applied Psychology*, October 1992, Vol. 77, pp. 730–737.
46. L.B. Mohr, "Determinants of Innovation in Organizations," *American Political Science Review*, 63, 1969.
47. A. Oxenfeldt, D. Miller, and R. Dickinson, *A Basic Approach to Executive Decision Making*. New York: Amacon, 1978.
48. D.W. MacKinnon, "The Nature and Nurture of Creative Talent," In H.J. Leavitt (ed.), *Readings in Managerial*

Psychology. Chicago: University of Chicago Press, 1965; also G. Vessels, "The Creative Process: An Open Systems Conceptualization," *Journal of Creative Behavior*, 16, 1982, pp. 185–196.

49. G.A. Steiner, *The Creative Organization*. Chicago: University of Chicago Press, 1965; also G. Zaltman, R. Duncan, and J. Holbek, *Innovations and Organizations*. New York: Wiley, 1973; also J.D. Femina and C. Sopkin, *From Those Wonderful Folks Who Brought You Pearl Harbor*. New York: Simon and Schuster, 1970; also N.R. Baker, E. Winofsky, L. Langmeyer, and D.J. Sweeney, *Idea Generation*. Cincinnati: University of Cincinnati, 1976.
50. T. Peters and N. Austin, *A Passion for Excellence: The Leadership Difference*. New York: Random House, 1985.
51. Christopher K. Bart, "New Venture Units: Use Them Wisely to Manage Innovation," *Sloan Management Review*, Vol. 29, Summer 1988, pp. 35–43.

CHAPTER 7

1. Danny Miller, "The Genesis of Configuration," *Academy of Management Review*, 1987, 691–692.
2. Saul Gellerman, "In Organizations, as in Architecture, Form Follows Function," *Organizational Dynamics*, Winter 1990, pp. 57–68.
3. Richard S. Blackburn, "Dimensions of Structure: A Review and Reappraisal," *Academy of Management Review*, 1982, pp. 59–66.
4. Eric J. Walton, "The Comparison of Measures of Organization Structure," *Academy of Management Review*, 1981, pp. 155–160.
5. Adam Smith, *Wealth of Nations*, New York: Modern Library, 1937.
6. J.A.F. Stoner and R.E. Freeman, *Management*, Englewood Cliffs, New Jersey: Prentice-Hall, 1989.
7. Harold Stieglitz, "What's Not On An Organization Chart," *Conference Board Record*, 1, 1964, pp. 7–10.
8. See, for example, David Van Fleet and Arthur G. Bedeian, "A History of the Span of Management," *Academy of Management Review*, 3, 1977, pp. 356–372; also David Van Fleet, "Empirically Testing Span of Management Hypotheses," *International Journal of Management*, 2, 1984, pp. 5–10; also J. Stieglitz, "Optimizing the Span of Control," *Management Record*, 24, 1962, pp. 25–29; also M. Keren and D. Levhari, "The Optimum Span of Control in a Pure Hierarchy," *Management Science*, 25, 1979, pp. 1162–1172.
9. Barrie McKenna, "Abitibi in Sweeping Reorganization," *The Globe and Mail*, October 6, 1993, p. B1; also Gail Lem, "Bell to Slash 5,000 Jobs," *The Globe and Mail*, September 29, 1993, p. B1; also Lawrence Surtees, "NorTel Starts Swinging the Axe," *The Globe and Mail*, September 2, 1993, p. B1; also "Royal Bank Cuts 4,100 Jobs," *The Winnipeg Free Press*, November 25, 1993, p. A4; also "Coca-Cola Spares City in Cuts," *The Winnipeg Free Press*, November 25, 1993, p. A4; also Larry Johnsrude, "Klein Warns of Layoffs Unless Salary Cuts OK'd," *The Winnipeg Free Press*, November 25, 1993, p. A4.
10. Harvey Enchin, "Corporate Productivity Drive Swells Unemployment Ranks," *The Globe and Mail*, January 11, 1993, pp. B1–B2.
11. John Lorinc, "Managing When There's No Middle," *Canadian Business*, June 1991, pp. 86–94.
12. Michael Crawford, "After the Fall," *Canadian Business*, December 1992, pp. 46–54.
13. J.B. White, "Toyota Wants More Managers Out on the Line," *The Wall Street Journal*, August 2, 1989, p. A10; also Y. Ono and M. Brauchli, "Japan Cuts the Middle-Management Fat," *The Wall Street Journal*, August 8, 1989, p. B1.
14. T. O'Boyle, "From Pyramid to Pancake," *The Wall Street Journal*, June 4, 1990, pp. R37ff.
15. Enchin, "Corporate Productivity Drive Swells Unemployment Ranks."
16. J.S. McClenahen, "Managing More People in the '90s," *Industry Week*, March 20, 1989, p. 30.
17. Randall Litchfield, "Trouble Is My Business," *Canadian Business*, February 1993, pp. 31–32.
18. W. Cascio, "Downsizing: What Do We Know? What Have We Learned?", *Academy of Management Executive*, Vol. 7, 1993, pp. 95–104.
19. "Can GM Solve Its Identity Crisis?" *Business Week*, January 23, 1984, pp. 32–33.
20. Mathew Horsman, "CP Changing Tracks," *The Financial Post*, October 11, 1986, pp. 1–2.
21. Marie Day, "Organizational Integration," *Canadian Manager*, Summer 1990, pp. 16–18.
22. Margot Gibb-Clark, "High-Voltage Pain at Hydro," *The Globe and Mail*, July 14, 1993, pp. B1, B12.
23. Christopher Donville, "Alberta Tel Reorganized," *The Globe and Mail*, July 28, 1990, p. B5.
24. Paul Lawrence and Jay Lorsch, *Organization and Environment: Managing Differentiation and Integration*. Boston: Harvard Business School, 1967.
25. J.R. Galbraith, "Organization Design: An Information Processing View," *Interfaces*, 4, 1974, pp. 28–36; also M.L. Tushman and D.A. Nadler, "Information Processing as an Integrating Concept in Organizational Design," *Academy of Management Review*, 3, 1978, pp. 613–624.
26. W.J. Altier, "Task Forces—An Effective Management Tool," *Sloan Management Review*, 27, 1986, pp. 69–76.

CHAPTER 8

1. "Who's the Boss? Don't Ask Harvard," *The Globe and Mail*, January 12, 1993, p. B1.
2. Based on an idea contained in R.W. Mondy, A. Sharplin, R.E. Holmes, and E. Flippo, *Management Concepts and Canadian Practice*. Boston: Allyn and Bacon, 1985, p. 187.
3. F. Starke, R.W. Mondy, A. Sharplin, and E.B. Flippo, *Management Concepts and Canadian Practice*. Toronto: Allyn and Bacon, 1988, p. 263.
4. Jacquie McNish, "A Chairman with Worries Lots of Others Would Like," *The Globe and Mail*, April 14, 1990, p. B6.
5. Ann Gibbon, "CN's New Boss Takes Hard Line," *The Globe and Mail*, February 8, 1993, pp. B1–B2.
6. Peter Larson, "Winning Strategies," *Canadian Business Review*, Summer 1989, p. 41.
7. Ian Allaby, "The Search for Quality," *Canadian Business*, May 1990, p. 31–42.
8. "Can Japan's Giants Cut the Apron Strings?" *Business Week*, May 14, 1990, pp. 105–106.
9. Leonard W. Johnson and A.L. Frohman, "Identifying and Closing the Gap in the Middle of Organizations," *Academy of Management Executive*, May 1989, pp. 107–114.
10. R.W. Keidel, "Triangular Design: A New Organizational Geometry," *Academy of Management Executive*, November 1990, pp. 21–37.
11. G.G. Fisch, "Line-Staff Is Obsolete," *Harvard Business Review*, 1961, pp. 67–69.
12. Galbraith, J. "Matrix Organization Designs: How To Combine Functional and Project Forms," *Business Horizons*, 1971, pp. 29–40; also H.F. Kolodny, "Evolution to a Matrix Organization," *Academy of Management Review*, 4, 1979, pp. 543–553.
13. Lawton R. Burns, "Matrix Management in Hospitals: Testing Theories of Matrix Structure and Development," *Administrative Science Quarterly*, 34, 1989, pp. 349–368.
14. J.M. Stewart, "Less is More," *Canadian Business Review*, Summer 1989, pp. 48–50.
15. H. Kerzner, "Matrix Implementation: Obstacles, Problems, Questions, and Answers," in D.I. Cleland (ed.), *Matrix Management Systems*, New York: Van Nostrand Reinhold, 1984, pp. 307–329.
16. Some of the material in Table 8-1 is from J. McCann, and J.R. Galbraith, "Interdepartmental Relations." In P.C. Nystrom and W.H. Starbuck (eds.), *Handbook of Organizational Design*, 2. New York: Oxford University Press, 1981, p. 61; also H. Kerzner, "Matrix Implementation."
17. T.J. Peters, and R.H. Waterman, *In Search of Excellence*. New York: Harper & Row, 1982; also R.A. Pitts, and J.D. Daniels, "Aftermath of Matrix Mania," *Columbia Journal of World Business*, 19, 1984, pp. 48–54.
18. E.W. Larson, and D.H. Gobeli, "Matrix Management: Contradictions and Insights," *California Management Review*, 1987, pp. 126–138.
19. T. Burns, and G.M. Stalker, *The Management of Innovation*. London: Tavistock, 1961.
20. Christian Allard, "The Entrepreneur: Loyalties—Running from the Family," *Canadian Business*, July 1989, p. 16.
21. J.A. Courtright, G.T. Fairhurst, and L.E. Rogers, "Interaction Patterns in Organic and Mechanistic Systems," *Academy of Management Journal*, 32, 1989, pp. 773–802.
22. P.R. Lawrence, and J.W. Lorsch, *Organization and Environment*. Homewood, Illinois: Richard D. Irwin, 1967.
23. J.J. Morse, and J.W. Lorsch, "Beyond Theory Y," *Harvard Business Review*, 48, 1970, pp. 61–68.
24. Tom Peters, "Restoring American Competitiveness: Looking for New Models of Organization," *Academy of Management Executive*, May 1988, pp. 103–109; see also Warren Bennis, "The Coming Death of Bureaucracy," *THINK*, 32, November–December 1966, pp. 32–33.
25. William Innes, "The Challenge for Canadian Managers Today and Tomorrow," *Canadian Manager*, Summer 1990, p. 7.
26. R.L. Daft, *Management*. Chicago: The Dryden Press, 1988, p. 256.
27. J.D. Thompson, *Organizations in Action*. New York: McGraw-Hill, 1967.
28. J. Woodward, *Industrial Organization*. London: Oxford University Press, 1965.
29. D.J. Hickson, D.S. Pugh, and D.C. Pheysey, "Operations Technology and Organizational Structure: A Critical Reappraisal," *Administrative Science Quarterly*, 14, 1969, pp. 378–397.
30. Martin Cash, "Unitel Chief Spreads Gospel of Competition," *The Winnipeg Free Press*, November 17, 1990, p. 34.
31. J.P. Murray, "How an Information Center Improved Productivity," *Management Accounting*, March 1984, pp. 38–44.
32. P. M. Blau, and R. A. Schoenherr, *The Structure of Organizations*. New York: Basic Books, 1971; also D.S. Pugh, "The Aston Program of Research: Retrospect and Prospect," In A.H. Van de Ven and W.F. Joyce (eds.), *Perspectives on Organization Design and Behavior*. New York: John Wiley, 1981, pp. 135–166.
33. J. Child, "Predicting and Understanding Organization Structure," *Administrative Science Quarterly*, 1973, p. 171.
34. S.P. Robbins, and R. Stuart-Kotze, *Management*. Scarborough, Ontario: Prentice-Hall Canada Inc., 1990, p. 245.
35. J.R. Kimberly, R.H. Miles, et al., *The Organizational LIfe Cycle*. San Francisco: Jossey-Bass, 1980.

CHAPTER 9

1. S. Robbins, *Management.* Englewood Cliffs, N.J.: Prentice-Hall, 1993, pp. 442–443.
2. Fred E. Fiedler, *A Theory of Leadership Effectiveness.* New York: McGraw-Hill, 1967.
3. B. Dumaine, "Who Needs a Boss?," *Fortune,* May 7, 1990, pp. 52–60; also P. Galagan, "Work Teams That Work," *Training and Development Journal,* November 1986, pp. 33–35; also "The Payoff From Teamwork," *Business Week,* July 10, 1989, pp. 56–62.
4. Merle MacIsaac, "Born-Again Basket Case," *Canadian Business,* May 1993, pp. 38–44.
5. Anne Kingston, "Power to the People," *Canadian Business,* July 1992, pp. 15–22.
6. S. Robbins, *Management.* Englewood Cliffs, N.J.: Prentice-Hall, 1993, pp. 453–454.
7. B. Tuckman and M. Jensen, "Stages of Small Group Development Revisited," *Group and Organization Studies,* 1977, Vol. 2, pp. 419–427; see also D. Davies and B. Kuypers, "Group Development and Interpersonal Feedback, *Group and Organization Studies,* 1985, pp. 184–208.
8. D.C. Feldman, "The Development and Enforcement of Group Norms," *Academy of Management Review,* 1984, pp. 47–53.
9. MacIsaac, "Born-Again Basket Case"
10. R.R. Bales, *Personality and Interpersonal Behavior.* New York: Holt, Rinehart, and Winston, 1970.
11. The conclusions listed are taken from a variety of studies, including: S. Adams, "Status Congruency as a Variable in Small Group Performance," *Social Forces,* 1953, pp. 16–22; also H. Lasswell and A. Kaplan, *Power and Society: A Framework for Political Inquiry.* New Haven: Yale University Press, 1950; also L. Festinger and J. Thibault, "Interpersonal Communication in Small Groups," *Journal of Abnormal and Social Psychology,* 1951, pp. 92–99; also B. Lott, "Group Cohesiveness: A Learning Phenomenon," *Journal of Social Psychology,* 1961, pp. 275–286; also L. Festiner, "Laboratory Experiments: The Role of Group Belongingness," In *Experiments in Social Processes,* edited by J. Miller. New York: McGraw-Hill, 1950, pp. 31–46; also J. Litterer, *The Analysis of Organizations.* New York: John Wiley and Sons, 1973, p. 222; also R. Blake and J. Mouton, "Reactions to Intergroup Competition Under Win-Lose Conditions," *Management Science,* 1961.
12. The conclusions listed are taken from a variety of sources, including: S. Seashore, *Group Cohesiveness in the Industrial Work Group.* Ann Arbor: Survey Research Center, University of Michigan, 1954; also J. Litterer, *The Analysis of Organizations.* New York: John Wiley and Sons, 1973, p. 213; also R.H. Van Zelst, "Sociometrically Selected Work Teams Increase Productivity," *Personnel Psychology,* 1952, pp. 175–185; also S. Schacter. "An Experimental Study of Cohesiveness and Productivity," *Human Relations,* 1951, pp. 229–239; also F. Luthans, *Organizational Behavior.* New York: McGraw-Hill, 1973, p. 448.
13. Adapted from Dorothy Lipovenko, "One Way To Cut Mangement Flab," *The Globe and Mail,* January 1, 1987, pp. B1–B2.
14. I. Janis, *Victims of Groupthink.* Boston: Houghton-Mifflin, 1972; for an alternate view of decision-making problems in groups, see Glen Whyte, "Group-think Reconsidered," *Academy of Management Review,* 14, 1989, pp. 40–56.
15. Example provided by Professor Olga L. Crocker, Faculty of Business Administration, University of Windsor.

CHAPTER 10

1. G.R. Salancik and J. Pfeffer, "Who Gets Power—And How They Hold On To It: A Strategic Contingency Model of Power," *Organizational Dynamics,* 5, 1977, p. 3.
2. J. Pfeffer, *Power in Organizations.* Boston: Pitman, 1980, p. 7.
3. J.P. French and B. Raven, "The Bases of Social Power," in D. Cartwright (ed.), *Studies in Social Power.* Ann Arbor: University of Michigan Institute for Social Research, 1959, pp. 150–167.
4. G. Yukl and C. Falbe, "Importance of Different Power Sources in Downward and Lateral Relations," *Journal of Applied Psychology,* June 1991, Vol. 76, pp. 416–423.
5. R.W. Mondy, A. Sharplin, R.E. Holmes, and E.B. Flippo, *Management Concepts and Practices.* Boston: Allyn and Bacon, 1986, p. 232.
6. D.C. McClelland and D.H. Burnham, "Power Is The Great Motivator," *Harvard Business Review,* 54, March/April 1976, p. 102.
7. A.R. Cohen and D.L. Bradford, "Influence Without Authority: The Use of Alliances, Reciprocity, and Exchanges to Accomplish Work," *Organizational Dynamics,* Winter 1989, p. 11.
8. Ibid., pp. 10–14.
9. J. Pfeffer and G. Salancik, "Organization Design: The Case for a Coalitional Model of Organizations," *Organizational Dynamics,* Autumn 1977, pp. 15–29.
10. F.H. Goldner, "Success vs. Failure: Prior Managerial Perspective," *Industrial Relations,* October 1970, pp. 457–474.
11. George Strauss, "Tactics of Lateral Relationship: The Purchasing Agent," *Administrative Science Quarterly,* 7, 1962, pp. 161–186.
12. D. Izraeli, "The Middle Manager and the Tactics of Power Expansion," *Sloan Management Review,* 1975, pp. 57–70.

13. M. Granovetter. *Getting a Job: A Study of Contacts and Careers*. Cambridge, Massachusetts: Harvard University Press, 1974.

14. Fred Luthans, "Successful vs. Effective Real Managers," *Academy of Management Executive*, May 1988, pp. 127–132.

15. P.M. Fandt and G.R. Ferris, "The Management of Information and Impressions When Employees Behave Opportunistically," *Organizational Behavior and Human Decision Processes*, 45, 1990, pp. 140–158; also R. Allen, D. Madison, L. Porter, P. Renwick, and B. Mayes, "Effective Organizational Communication," *California Management Review*, 22, 1979, pp. 77–83.

16. Ibid.

17. David Leidl, "Baby Boomers Lament," *Manitoba Business*, April 1990, p. 15.

18. S.J. Wayne and G.R. Ferris, "Influence Tactics, Affect, and Exchange Quality in Supervisor-Subordinate Interactions: A Laboratory Experiment and Field Study," *Journal of Applied Psychology*, 75, 1990, pp. 487–499.

19. J. Pfeffer. *Power in Organizations*. Boston: Pitman, 1981.

20. Margot Gibb-Clark, "Making Mentors," *The Globe and Mail*, July 3, 1990, p. B4.

21. John Lorinc, "The Mentor Gap," *Canadian Business*, September 1990, p. 94

22. M. Crozier, *The Bureaucratic Phenomenon*. Chicago: University of Chicago Press, 1964.

23. C.R. Hinings, D.J. Hickson, J.M. Pennings, and R.E. Schneck, "Structural Conditions of Intraorganizational Power," *Administrative Science Quarterly*, 18, 1974, pp. 22–44.

24. C.S. Sanders and R. Scamell, "Intraorganizational Distributions of Power: Replication Research," *Academy of Management Journal*, 25, 1982, pp. 192–200.

25. Cathy Enz, "The Role of Value Congruity in Intraorganizational Power," *Administrative Science Quarterly*, 33, 1988, pp. 284–304.

26. J. Pfeffer and G. Salancik, "Organizational Decision Making as a Political Process: The Case of a University Budget," *Administrative Science Quarterly*, 19, 1974, pp. 135–151.

27. J. Pfeffer and W.L. Moore, "Power in University Budgeting: A Replication and Extension," *Administrative Science Quarterly*, 25, 1980, pp. 637–653; also F. Hills and T. Mahoney, "University Budgets and Organizational Decision Making," *Administrative Science Quarterly*, 23, 1978, pp. 454–465.

28. J. Pfeffer and A. Leong, "Resource Allocations in United Funds: Examination of Power and Dependence," *Social Forces*, 55, 1977, pp. 775–790.

29. K. Provan, J. Beyer, and C. Kruytbosch, "Environmental Linkages and Power in Resource Dependent Relations Between Organizations," *Administrative Science Quarterly*, 25, 1980, pp. 200–225.

30. J.V. Gandz and V.V. Murray, "The Experience of Workplace Politics," *Academy of Management Journal*, 23, 1980, 237–251.

31. Allen, et al., "Effective Organizational Communication," (refer to note 15).

32. Jacquie McNish, "A Chairman With Worries Lots of Others Would Like," *The Globe and Mail*, April 14, 1990, p. B1.

33. G.R. Salancik and J. Pfeffer, "Who Gets Power—And How They Hold On To It: A Strategic Contingency Model of Power," *Organizational Dynamics*, 5, 1977, p. 3.

CHAPTER 11

1. For a recent review of the entire field of human resources management, see C.D. Fisher, L. Schoenfeldt, and B. Shaw, *Personnel/Human Resources Management*. Boston: Houghton Mifflin, 1990.

2. Margot Gibb-Clark, "Keeping staff begins at hiring stage," *Globe and Mail*, March 25, 1991, p. B4.

3. "More Firms Use Personality Tests for Entry-Level Blue Collar Jobs," *Wall Street Journal*, January 16, 1986, p. 25.

4. Bruce McDougall, "The Thinking Man's Assembly Line," *Canadian Business*, November 1991, p. 40.

5. "Testing for Drug Use: Handle With Care," *Business Week*, March 28, 1988, p. 65.

6. Jacquie McNish, "Akers Out As IBM CEO," *The Globe and Mail*, January 27, 1993, pp. B1–B2.

7. Tiimothy Pritchard, "GM Reinvents the Factory," *The Globe and Mail*, June 16, 1992, p. B28.

8. Jane Allan, "Literacy at Work," *Canadian Business*, February 1991, pp. 70–73.

9. Harvey Enchin, "Employee training a must," *The Globe and Mail*, May 15, 1991, p. B6.

10. I.L. Goldstein, *Training in Organizations: Needs Assessment, Development, and Evaluation*, 2nd ed. Monterey, CA: Brooks/Cole, 1986.

11. Jerry Zeidenberg, "Extra-Curricular," *Canadian Business*, February 1991, pp. 66–69.

12. Charles Davies, "Strategy Session 1990," *Canadian Business*, January 1990, p. 50.

13. Scott Feschuk, "Phi Betta Cuppa," *The Globe and Mail*, March 6, 1993, pp. B1, B4.

14. John Southerst, "Kenworth's Gray Revolution," *Canadian Business*, September 1992, p. 74.

15. Margot Gibb-Clark, "Managers Learn Fine Art of Cooperation at Swiss School," *The Globe and Mail*, March 26, 1990, p. B6.

16. "Well-Paid Workers, Low-Paid Bosses?" *Canadian Business*, December 1992, p. 17.

17. R. Kopelman, "Linking Pay to Performance is a Proven Management Tool," *Personnel Administrator,* October 1983, pp. 60–61.

18. See Fisher, Schoenfeldt, and Shaw (note 1) for a review.

19. "Women's Job Status Fails to Improve, Reports Show," *Winnipeg Free Press,* December 24, 1988, p. 11.

20. Gordon Pitts, "Equal Pay Issue: Business Uneasy," *Financial Post,* August 31, 1985, pp. 1–2.

21. "Ouch! The Squeeze on Your Health Benefits," *Business Week,* November 20, 1989, pp. 110–116.

22. McDougall, "The Thinking Man's Assembly Line," (refer to note 4).

23. Ted Kennedy, "Beware of Health and Safety Law: It Could Bite You," *Canadian Business,* December 1990, p. 19.

24. Moira Farr, "Work That Wounds and How to Cure It," *Canadian Business,* December 1991, p. 90; also "Industrial Workers Learn to Stretch and Save," *Canadian Business,* October 1991. p. 15.

25. Christian Allard, "Hanging in at Eighty Something," *Canadian Business,* October 1990, pp. 46–50.

26. Margot Gibb-Clark, "Harrassment cases can also hurt employees," *Globe and Mail,* September 16, 1991, p. B4.

27. Vivian Smith, "Breaking Down the Barriers," *The Globe and Mail,* November 17, 1992, p. B24.

28. Thomas Claridge, "Fired Jumbo Boss Awarded $226,000," *The Globe and Mail,* May 31, 1993, p. B5.

CHAPTER 12

1. Dale Feuer, "Brave New Managers," *Training,* June 1986, pp. 42–47.

2. Summarized from M. Stern, "The Brass Ring Has A Hollow Sound," *The Globe and Mail,* September 15, 1990, p. B4; also D. Marty, "Fast Tracking Heretics," *Canadian Business,* August 1990, p. 9.

3. The exceptions are generally in those jobs where employee input is minimal, e.g., assembly line jobs or other tasks in which performance is determined by external factors such as technology. In these jobs motivation has no outlet—and in some cases may be a detriment because employees become frustrated.

4. For some interesting views on how Japanese managers view North American workers, see "At Sanyo's Arkansas Plant The Magic Isn't Working," *Business Week,* July 14, 1986, pp. 51–52.

5. Ronald Morrison, "Living in the New Real World," *The Globe and Mail,* July 28, 1990, p. B4.

6. Rob Carrick, "Car Makers Target Absenteeism in Talks," *The Globe and Mail,* August 1, 1990, p. B3.

7. L.W. Porter and R.E. Miles, "Motivation and Management." In J. McGuire (ed.), *Contemporary Management: Issues and Viewpoints.* Englewood Cliffs, New Jersey: Prentice-Hall, 1974, p. 547.

8. Barrie Whittaker, "Increasing Market Share Through Marketing Excellence," *Canadian Business Review,* Spring 1990, pp. 35–37.

9. E. L. Deci. "The Effects of Externally Mediated Rewards on Intrinsic Motivation," *Journal of Personality and Social Psychology,* 22, 1972, pp. 113–120.

10. W.E. Scott, J.H. Farh, and P.M. Podsakoff, "The Effects of Intrinsic and Extrinsic Reinforcement Contingencies on Task Behavior," *Organizational Behavior and Human Decision Processes,* 41, 1988, pp. 405–425.

11. Margot Gibb-Clark, "Canadian Workers Need Some Respect," *The Globe and Mail,* September 4, 1991, pp. B1, B6.

12. Margot Gibb-Clark, "Frustrated Workers Seek Goals," *The Globe and Mail,* May 2, 1991, p. B7.

13. Margot Gibb-Clark, "Family Ties Limit Workers," *The Globe and Mail,* January 22, 1991, pp. B1–B2.

14. A.H. Brayfield and W.H. Crockett, "Employee Attitudes and Performance," *Psychological Bulletin,* 52, 1955, pp. 396–428.

15. Cheri Ostroff, "The Relationship Between Satisfaction, Attitudes, and Performance: An Organizational Level Analysis," *Journal of Applied Psychology,* 77, 1992, pp. 963–974.

16. Marty York, "Expos Prefer Their Theory of Motivation," *The Globe and Mail,* June 23, 1990, p. A16.

17. Douglas McGregor, *The Human Side of Enterprise.* New York: McGraw-Hill, 1960.

18. Chris Argyris, *Personality and Organization.* New York: Harper, 1957.

19. R. Rosenthal and L. Jacobson. *Pygmalion in the Classroom: Teacher Expectation and Pupils' Intellectual Development.* New York: Holt, Rinehart, and Winston, 1968. For a study demonstrating the self-fulfilling prophecy in the military, see D. Eden and A.B. Shani, "Pygmalion Goes to Boot Camp: Expectancy, Leadership, and Trainee Performance," *Journal of Applied Psychology,* 67, 1982, pp. 194–199.

20. J.L. Single, "The Power of Expectations: Productivity and the Self-Fulfilling Prophecy," *Management World,* 19, 1980, pp. 19, 37–38.

21. J.A.F. Stoner and R.E. Freeman, *Management.* Englewood Cliffs, New Jersey: Prentice-Hall, 1989, pp. 429–430.

22. Abraham Maslow, "A Theory of Human Motivation," *Psychological Review,* 50, 1943, pp. 370–396.

23. D.T. Hall and K.E. Nougaim, "An Examination of Maslow's Need Hierarchy in an Organization Setting," *Organizational Behavior and Human Performance,* 3, 1968, pp. 12–35.

24. E.E. Lawler and J.L. Suttle, "A Causal Correlational Test of the Need Hierarchy Concept," *Organizational Behavior and Human Performance,* 7, 1972, pp. 265–287.

25. J. Rauschenberger, N. Schmitt, and J.E. Hunter, "A Test of the Need Hierarchy Concept by a Markov Model of Change in Need Strength," *Administrative Science Quarterly,* 1980, pp. 654–670.

26. A.H. Maslow, "Deficiency Motivation and Growth Motivation." In M.R. Jones (ed.), *Nebraska Symposium on Motivation.* Lincoln, Nebraska: University of Nebraska Press, 1955.

27. D. Hellriegel and J.W. Slocum, *Management.* Reading, Massachusetts: Addison-Wesley, 1989, pp. 433–434.

28. C.P. Alderfer, *Existence, Relatedness, and Growth.* New York: Free Press, 1972.

29. F. Herzberg, B. Mausner, and B. Snyderman, *The Motivation to Work.* New York: Wiley, 1959.

30. R. House and L. Wigdor, "Herzberg's Dual-Factor Theory of Job Satisfaction and Motivation," *Personnel Psychology,* 20, 1967, 369–389.

31. V. Vroom, *Work and Motivation.* New York: Wiley, 1964; see also R. Bobbitt and O. Behling, "Defense Mechanisms as an Alternate Explanation of Herzberg's Motivator-Hygiene Results," *Journal of Applied Psychology,* 56, 1972, pp. 24–27.

32. D.C. McClelland et al., *The Achievement Motive.* New York: Appleton-Century-Crofts, 1953.

33. R.M. Steers, *Introduction to Organizational Behavior.* Santa Monica, California: Goodyear Publishing Company, 1981.

M.J. Stahl, "Achievement, Power, and Managerial Motivation: Selecting Managerial Talent with the Job Choice Exercise," *Personnel Psychology,* 36, 1983, pp. 775–789.

34. J.S. Adams, "Toward an Understanding of Inequity," *Journal of Abnormal and Social Psychology,* 67, 1963, p. 425.

35. For a review of much of the early research evidence, see P.S. Goodman and A. Friedman, "An Examination of Adams' Theory of Inequity," *Administrative Science Quarterly,* 16, 1971, pp. 271–286; for a more recent summary, see R.T. Mowday, "Equity Theory Predictions of Behavior in Organizations," In R. M. Steers and L.W. Porter (eds.), *Motivation and Work Behavior.* New York: McGraw-Hill Book Co., 1987, pp. 89–110; also J. Greenberg, "Approaching Equity and Avoiding Inequity in Groups and Organizations," in J. Greenberg and R. L. Cohen (eds.), *Equity and Justice in Social Behavior,* New York: Academic Press, 1982, pp. 389–435.

36. J. Greenberg, "Equity and Workplace Status: A Field Experiment," *Journal of Applied Psychology,* 73, 1988, pp. 606–613.

37. J. Greenberg, "Cognitive Reevaluation of Outcomes in Response to Underpayment Inequity," *Academy of Management Journal,* 32, 1989, pp. 174–184.

38. J. Greenberg, "Employee Theft as a Reaction to Underpayment Inequity: The Hidden Cost of Pay Cuts," *Journal of Applied Psychology,* 75, 1990, pp. 561–568.

39. V. Vroom, *Work and Motivation.* New York: Wiley, 1964; also B. Staw, "Organizational Behavior: A Review and Reformulation of the Field's Outcome Variables," *Annual Review of Psychology,* 35, 1984, pp. 627–666.

40. See, for example, H.J. Arnold, "A Test of the Multiplicative Hypothesis of Expectancy-Valence Theories of Work Motivation," *Academy of Management Journal,* March 1981, pp. 128–141.

41. For a review of this literature, see G.P. Latham and G.A. Yukl, "A Review of Research on the Application of Goal Setting in Organizations," *Academy of Management Journal,* 1975, pp. 824–845; also J.B. Miner, *Theories of Organizational Behavior.* Hinsdale, Illinois: Dryden Press, 1980, pp. 168–200.

42. For an analysis of the laboratory evidence see E.A. Locke, "Toward a Theory of Task Motivation and Incentives," *Organizational Behavior and Human Performance,* 1968, pp. 157–189.

43. W.W. Ronan, G.P. Latham, and S.B. Kinne, "Effects of Goal Setting and Supervision on Worker Behavior in an Industrial Setting," *Journal of Applied Psychology,* 58, 1973, pp. 302–307.

44. Ibid.

45. G.P. Latham and E.A. Locke, "Goal Setting—Motivational Technique that Works," *Organizational Dynamics,* 8, 1979, pp. 68–80; also J.A. Riedel, D.M. Nebeker, and B.L. Cooper, "The Influence of Monetary Incentives and Goal Choice, Goal Committment, and Task Performance," *Organizational Behavior and Human Decision Processes,* 42, 1988, pp. 155–180; also A. J. Mento, R.P. Steel, and R.J. Karren, "A Meta-Analytic Study of the Effects of Goal Setting on Task Performance," *Organizational Behavior and Human Decision Processes,* 39, 1987, pp. 52–83.

46. Wendy Trueman, "Alternate Visions," *Canadian Business,* March 1991, pp. 29–33.

47. E.A. Locke and G.P. Latham, *Goal Setting: A Motivational Technique that Works!* Englewood Cliffs, N.J.: Prentice-Hall, 1984.

48. B.F. Skinner, *Beyond Freedom and Dignity,* New York: Knopf, 1971.

49. Ed Pedalino and Victor U. Gamboa, "Behavior Modification and Absenteeism," *Journal of Applied Psychology,* 59, 1974, pp. 694–698.

50. W. Clay Hamner and Ellen P. Hamner, "Behavior Modification and the Bottom Line," *Organizational Dynamics,* 4, 1976, p. 12.

51. "At Emery Air Freight: Positive Reinforcement Boosts Performance," *Organizational Dynamics,* 1, 1973, pp. 41–50.

52. R.S. Haynes, R.C. Pine, and H.G. Fitch, "Reducing Accident Rates with Organizational Behavior Modification," *Academy of Management Journal,* 25, 1982, pp. 407–416.

53. E.J. Feeney, J.R. Staelin, R.M. O'Brien, and A.M. Dickinson, "Increasing Sales Performance Among Airline Reservation Personnel," in O'Brien, Dickinson, and Rosow, *Industrial Behavior Modification,* pp. 141–158.

54. Albert Bandura, *Social Learning Theory.* Englewood Cliffs, N.J.: Prentice-Hall, 1977.

55. J. Barling and R. Beattie, "Self-Efficacy Beliefs and Sales Performance," *Journal of Organizational Behavior Management,* 5, 1983, pp. 41–51.

56. For an in-depth review of much of this literature, see E.E. Lawler, *Pay and Organizational Effectiveness.* New York: McGraw-Hill, 1971.

57. Ian Allaby, "The Search for Quality," *Canadian Business,* May 1990, pp. 31–42.

58. J.R. Hackman and G.R. Oldham, *Work Redesign.* Reading, Massachusetts: Addison-Wesley, 1980.

59. J. Mansell, R. Wilkinson, and A. Musgrave, *An Inventory of Innovative Work Arrangements in Ontario.* Research Branch, Ontario Ministry of Labour, 1978, p. 23.

60. Ibid., p. 66.

61. Ibid., p. 37.

62. "The New Industrial Revolution," *Business Week,* May 11, 1981, pp. 85–89.

63. See J.P. Elvins, "Communication in Quality Circles: Members' Perceptions of Their Participation and Its Effect on Related Organizational Communication Variables," *Group and Organizational Studies,* 10, 1985, pp. 479–507; also Anat Rafaeli, "Quality Circles and Employee Attitudes," *Personnel Psychology,* 38, 1985, pp. 603–615.

64. Merle O'Donnell and R. J. O'Donnell, "Quality Circles: The Latest Fad or a Real Winner?," *Business Horizons,* May–June 1984, pp. 48–52.

65. Mansell et al., pp. 67 and 96.

66. Wilfred List, "Employers Find Rewards in Employment Equity," *Canadian Business Review,* Spring 1989, pp. 35–38.

67. J. McBride-King and H. Paris, "Balancing Work and Family Responsibilities," *Canadian Business Review,* Autumn 1989, p. 21.

68. R.T. Golembiewski and C.W. Proehl, "A Survey of the Empirical Literature on Flexible Workhours: Character and Consequences of a Major Innovation," *Academy of Management Review,* October 1978, 837–853; also S.D. Nollen, "Does Flextime Improve Productivity?" *Harvard Business Review,* September–October 1979, pp. 12, 16–18, 22.

69. J.S. Kim and A.F. Campagna, "Effects of Flextime on Employee Attendance and Performance: A Field Experiment," *Academy of Management Journal,* December 1981, pp. 729–741.

70. Margot Gibb-Clark, "Middle Managers Resist Flexible Schedules, Survey Finds," *The Globe and Mail,* May 15, 1990, p. B15.

71. Robert White, "Changing Needs of Work and Family: A Union Response," *Canadian Business Review,* Autumn 1989, pp. 31–33.

72. J.L. Pierce and R.B. Dunham, "The 12-Hour Work Day: A 48-Hour, Eight Day Week," *The Academy of Management Journal,* 35, 1992, pp. 1086–1098.

73. R. B. Dunham, J.L. Pierce, and M.B. Castaneda, "Alternative Work Schedules: Two Field Quasi-Experiments," *Personnel Psychology,* Summer 1987, pp. 215–242; also D. Olson and A.P. Brief, "The Impact of Alternative Workweeks," *Personnel,* January–February 1978, p. 73.

CHAPTER 13

1. A.B. Thomas, "Does Leadership Make a Difference to Organizational Performance?," *Administrative Science Quarterly,* 33, 1988, pp. 388–400; also S. Lieberson and J.F. O'Connor, "Leadership and Organizational Performance: A Study of Large Corporations," *American Sociological Review,* 37, 1972, pp. 117–130.

2. W.A. Wilson, "A Lack of National Leadership," *Winnipeg Free Press,* March 12, 1990, p. 6.

3. A. Zaleznik, "The Leadership Gap," *Academy of Management Executive,* 4, February 1990, pp. 7–22.

4. Ibid.

5. A. Zaleznik, "Managers and Leaders: Are They Different?" *Harvard Business Review,* May 1977, pp. 67–68.

6. Zaleznik, "The Leadership Gap."

7. R.J. House, "A 1976 Theory of Charismatic Leadership," in J.G. Hunt and L.L. Larson (eds.), *Leadership: The Cutting Edge.* Carbondale, Illinois: Southern Illinois University Press, 1976, pp. 189–207.

8. N.M. Tichy and D.O. Ulrich, "The Leadership Challenge—A Call for the Transformational Leader," *Sloan Management Review,* Fall 1984, pp. 59–68; also B.M. Bass, "From Transactional to Transformational Leadership: Learning to Share the Vision," *Organizational Dynamics,* Winter 1990, pp. 19–31.

9. Tichy and Ulrich, "The Leadership Challenge."

10. G. Kozmetzky, *Transformational Management.* Cambridge, Massachusetts: Ballinger Publishing, 1985.

11. B.M. Bass, J. Krusell1, and R.A. Alexander, "Male Managers' Attitudes Toward Working Women," *American Behavioral Scientist,* 15, 1971, pp. 221–236; also B. Rosen and T.H. Jerdee, "Perceived Sex Differences in Managerially Relevant Characteristics," *Sex Roles,* 4, 1978, pp. 837–843.

12. K.M. Bartol and D.C. Martin, "Women and Men in Task Groups," in R.D. Ashmore and F.K. Del Boca (eds.), *The Social Psychology of Female-Male Relations,* Orlando, Florida: Academic, 1986, pp. 259–310; also G.H. Dobbins and S.J. Platz, "Sex Differences in Leadership: How Real Are They?," *Academy of Management Review,* 11, 1986, pp. 118–127.

13. See, for example, A.H. Eagly, S.J. Karau, and B.T. Johnson, "Gender and Leadership Style Among School Principals: A Meta-Analysis," *Educational Administration Quarterly,* February 1992, pp. 76–102; also "Debate: Ways Men and Women Lead," *Harvard Business Review,* January–February 1991, pp. 150–160; also J.B. Rosener, "Ways Women Lead," *Harvard Business Review,* November–December 1990, pp. 119–125; also S. Helgesen, *The Female Advantage: Women's Ways of Leadership.* New York: Doubleday, 1990.

14. Cathryn Motherwell, "Petrocan to Change Management Style," *The Globe and Mail,* February 6, 1993.

15. Harvey Enchin, "Consensus Management? Not for Bombardier's CEO," *The Globe and Mail,* April 16, 1990, p. B1; also Margaret Philp, "Campeau Executives Offered a Carrot," *The Globe and Mail,* June 27, 1990, p. B9.

16. Michael Stern, "New Tory Chief Must Motivate by Leading," *The Globe and Mail,* March 29, 1993, p. B4.

17. M. Love, "Let's Forget Tradition," *Winnipeg Business People,* August/September 1990, p. 11.

18. Anne Kingston, "Power to the People," *Canadian Business,* July 1992, pp. 15–22.

19. E. Locke and D.M. Schweiger, "Participation in Decision Making: One More Look," in B.M. Staw (ed.), *Research in Organizational Behavior,* 1, Greenwich, Connecticut: A1 Press, 1978, pp. 265–339.

20. For a debate on this issue, see J.L. Cotton, D.A. Vollrath, K.L. Froggatt, M.L. Lengnick-Hall, and K.R. Jennings, "Employee Participation: Diverse Forms and Different Outcomes," *Academy of Management Review,* 13, 1988, pp. 8–22; also C.R. Leana, E.A. Locke, and D.M. Schweiger, "Fact and Fiction in Analyzing Research on Participative Decision Making: A Critique of Cotton, Vollrath, Froggatt, Lengnick-Hall, and Jennings," *Academy of Management Review,* 15, January 1990, pp. 137–146; also J.L. Cotton, D.A. Vollrath, M.L. Lengnick-Hall, and K.L. Froggatt, "Fact: The Form of Participation Does Matter—A Rebuttal to Leana, Locke, and Schweiger," *Academy of Management Review,* 15, January 1990, pp. 147–153.

21. N. Baloff and E.M. Doherty, "Potential Pitfalls in Employee Participation," *Organizational Dynamics,* 17, Winter 1989, pp. 51–62.

22. Mark Stevenson, "Being Nice For A Change," *Canadian Business,* November 1993, pp. 81–85.

23. J.P. Muczyk and B.C. Reimann, "The Case for Directive Leadership," *Academy of Management Executive,* 1, November 1987, pp. 301–311.

24. For example, see R. Stogdill, "Personal Factors Associated with Leadership: A Survey of the Literature," *Journal of Psychology,* 25, 1948, 35–72; also C. Gibb, "Leadership," *Handbook of Social Psychology,* G. Lindzey (ed.), Reading, Massachusetts: Addison-Wesley, 1954. For a comprehensive analysis of leadership traits, see R. Stogdill, *Handbook of Leadership,* New York: The Free Press, 1974, especially Chapters 5 and 6.

25. R. Stogdill, *Handbook of Leadership.* New York: Free Press, 1974, pp. 35–71.

26. S.A. Kirkpatrick and E.A. Locke, "Leadership: Do Traits Really Matter?" *Academy of Management Executive,* May 1991, pp. 48–60.

27. M.W. McCall and M.M. Lombardo, "What Makes a Top Executive?" *Psychology Today,* February 1983, pp. 26–31.

28. A. W. Halpin and B.J. Winer, "A Factorial Study of the Leader Behavior Descriptions," in R.M. Stogdill and A.E. Coons (eds.), *Leader Behavior: Its Description and Measurement.* Columbus, Ohio: Ohio State University, Bureau of Business Research, 1957.

29. The value of this assumption has been questioned in L. Larson, J. Hunt, and R. Osborn, "The Great Hi-Hi Leader Behavior Myth," *Academy of Management Journal,* 19, 1976, pp. 628–641; also P. Nystrom, "Managers and the Hi-Hi Leader Myth," *Academy of Management Journal,* 21, 1978, pp. 325–331. At a more fundamental level, the whole idea that the two key dimensions of leadership are "task" and "human" is questioned in B. Karmel, "Leadership: A Challenge to Traditional Research Methods and Assumptions," *Academy of Management Review,* 3, 1978, pp. 475–482.

30. R. Kahn and D. Katz, "Leadership Practices in Relation to Productivity and Morale," in D. Cartwright and A. Zander (eds.), *Group Dynamics,* Evanston, Illinois: Row Petersen and Company, 1960.

31. N. C. Morse and E. Reimer, "The Experimental Change of a Major Organizational Variable," *Journal of Abnormal Social Psychology,* 51, 1956, pp. 120–129.

32. R. Blake and J. Mouton, *The Managerial Grid.* Houston, Texas: Gulf, 1964.

33. H.J. Bernardin and K. Alvares, "The Managerial Grid As A Predictor of Conflict Resolution and Managerial Effectiveness," *Administrative Science Quarterly,* 21, 1976, p. 84.

34. R. Tannenbaum and W.H. Schmidt, "How To Choose A Leadership Pattern," *Harvard Business Review,* May/June 1973, pp. 162–180.

35. P. Hersey and K. Blanchard, *Management of Organizational Behavior.* Englewood Cliffs, New Jersey: Prentice-Hall, 1982.

36. Since the origins of this theory, Hersey and Blanchard have developed individual variations of the model that have resulted in different terminologies for the variables. In this

discussion, we are using the terms developed by Ken Blanchard in "Situational Leadership II," Blanchard Training & Development, Escondido, California, 1985.

37. See note 36.

38. J.E. Stinson and T. W. Johnnson, " The Path-Goal Theory of Leadership: A Partial Test and Suggested Refinement," *Academy of Management Journal,* 18, 1975, pp. 242–252; also Arriso L. Angelini, Paul Hersey, and Sofia Caracushansky, "The Situational Leadership Theory Applied to Teaching: A Research on Learning Effectiveness," an unpublished paper cited by Hersey and Blanchard: also Raymond A. Gumpert and Ronald K. Hambleton, "Situational Leadership: How Xerox Managers Fine-Tune Managerial Styles to Employee Maturity and Task Needs," *Management Review,* 1979, pp. 8–12.

39. V. Vroom and P. Yetton, *Leadership and Decision Making,* Pittsburgh: University of Pittsburgh, 1973.

40. F. Fiedler, *A Theory of Leadership Effectiveness.* New York: McGraw-Hill Book Co., 1967.

41. F.E. Fiedler, M.M. Chemers, and L. Mahar, *Improving Leadership Effectiveness: The LEADER MATCH Concept.* New York: Wiley, 1976.

42. Several of these studies are discussed in F.E. Fiedler, and L. Mahar, "The Effectiveness of Contingency Model Training: A Review of the Validation of LEADER MATCH," *Personnel Psychology,* 32, 1979, pp. 45–62; also F.E. Fiedler and L. Mahar, "A Field Experiment Validating Contingency Model Leadership Training," *Journal of Applied Psychology,* 55, 1971, pp. 196–201.

43. R. House, "A Path-Goal Model of Leader Effectiveness," *Administrative Science Quarterly,* 16, 1971, pp. 321–338.

44. K. K. Fisher, "Managing in the High Commitment Workplace," *Organizational Dynamics,* 17, Winter 1989, pp. 31–50.

45. Jay Conger, "Leadership: The Art of Empowering Others," *Academy of Management Executive,* 3, 1989, pp. 17–24.

46. W. Bennis and B. Nanus, *Leaders: The Strategies for Taking Charge,* 1985, New York: Harper and Row.

47. A.R. Cohen and D.L. Bradford, "Influence Without Authority: The Use of Alliances, Reciprocity, and Exchanges to Accomplish Work," *Organizational Dynamics,* Winter 1989, p. 11.

48. Kingston, "Power to the People," (refer to endnote 18).

49. Jay Conger, "Leadership: The Art of Empowering Others."

50. R.D. Evered and J.C. Selman, "Coaching and the Art of Management," *Organizational Dynamics,* 18, Autumn 1989, pp. 16–32.

51. Ibid.

52. A.R. Cohen and D. L. Bradford. *Influence Without Authority.* New York: John Wiley, 1990.

53. G. Yukl and J. Tracey, "Consequences of Influence Tactics Used With Subordinates, Peers, and the Boss," *Journal of Applied Psychology,* 77, 1992, pp. 525–535.

54. G.A. Yukl, *Leadership in Organizations.* Englewood Cliffs, N.J.: Prentice-Hall, 1989, 2nd edition, p. 44.

55. Ibid.

56. B. Keys and T. Case, "How to Become an Influential Leader," *Academy of Management Executive,* 4, November 1990, pp. 38–51.

57. S. Kerr, "Substitutes for Leadership: Some Implications for Organization Design," *Organization and Administrative Sciences,* 8, 1977, pp. 135–150; also S. Kerr and J. Jermier, "Substitutes for Leadership: Their Meaning and Measurement," *Organization Behavior and Human Performance,* 22, 1978, pp. 350–403; also J.P. Howell and P. Dorfman, "Substitutes for Leadership: Test of a Construct," *Academy of Management Journal,* 24, 1981, pp. 714–728.

58. C.C. Manz and H.P. Sims, "Leading Workers to Lead Themselves: The External Leadership of Self-Managing Work Teams," *Administrative Science Quarterly,* 1987, 32, pp. 106–107.

59. J.M. Stewart, "Less is More," *Canadian Business Review,* Summer 1989, pp. 48–49.

60. J.R. Meindle, S.B. Ehrlich, and J.M. Dukerich, "The Romance of Leadership," *Administrative Science Quarterly,* 30, 1985, pp. 78–102.

CHAPTER 14

1. Fred Luthans and Janet K. Larsen, "How Managers Really Communicate," *Human Relations,* 39, 1986, pp. 161–178; also Larry E. Penley and Brian Hawkins, "Studying Interpersonal Communication in Organizations: A Leadership Application," *Academy of Management Journal,* 28, 1985, pp. 309–326.

2. H. Mintzberg, *The Nature of Managerial Work.* New York: Harper & Row, 1973.

3. L.B. Kurke and H. Aldrich, "Mintzberg was Right!: A Replication and Extension of *The Nature of Managerial Work,*" *Management Science,* 29, 1983, p. 979.

4. An early summary of this research is found in P.F. Secord and C.W. Backman, *Social Psychology,* New York: McGraw-Hill, 1964, pp. 130–131.

5. Margot Gibb-Clark, "Communication Breakdown," *The Globe and Mail,* June 22, 1990, p. B4.

6. I. Thomas Shephard,"Silent Signals," *Supervisory Management,* March 1986, pp. 31–33.

7. Ibid.

8. Albert Mehrabian, *Silent Messages.* Belmont, California: Wadsworth, 1971.

9. N.L. Reinsch and R.W. Beswick, "Voice Mail Versus Conventional Channels: A Cost Minimization Analysis of Individuals' Preferences," *Academy of Management Journal,* 33, 1990, pp. 801–816.

10. Tom Kelly, "Networks Mean Good Business," *Office Equipment and Methods,* May 1989, p. 56.

11. Harold Leavitt and Ronald Mueller, "Some Effects of Feedback on Communicating," *Human Relations,* 4, 1951, pp. 401–410.

12. J.A. Courtright, G.T. Fairhurst, and L.E. Rogers, "Interaction Patterns in Organic and Mechanistic Systems," *Academy of Management Journal,* 32, 1989, pp. 773–802.

13. E. Scannell, *Communication for Leadership.* New York: McGraw-Hill, 1970, p. 5.

14. L.W. Porter and K.H. Roberts, "Communication in Organizations," in M.D. Dunnette, (ed.), *Handbook of Industrial and Occupational Psychology,* 2nd ed. New York: Wiley, 1983, pp. 1553–1589.

15. Ian Allaby, "The Search For Quality," *Canadian Business,* May 1990, pp. 31–42.

16. Patrick Conlon, "Open for Business," *Report on Business,* June 1990, p. 75.

17. Murray McNeill, "Slump Called Opportunity to Trim Fat," *Winnipeg Free Press,* September 21, 1990, p. 68.

18. Eva Innes, Robert L. Perry, and Jim Lyon, *The Financial Post Selects the 100 Best Companies to Work For in Canada.* Toronto: Collins, 1986.

19. See, for example, H.J. Levitt, "Some Effects of Certain Communication Patterns on Group Performance," *Journal of Abnormal Social Psychology,* 46, 1951, pp. 38–50; also M.E. Shaw, "Some Effects of Problem Solution Efficiency in Different Communication Nets," *Journal of Experimental Psychology,* 48, 1954, pp. 211–217; also A. Bavelas, "Communication Patterns in Task-Oriented Groups," *Journal of the Acoustical Society of America,* 22, 1950, pp. 725–730; also H. Guetzkow and H.A. Simon, "The Impact of Certain Communication Nets Upon Organization and Performance in Task-Oriented Groups," in A.H. Rubentstein and C.J. Haberstroh, (eds.), *Some Theories of Organization.* Homewood, Illinois: Dorsey Press, 1960, pp. 259–277; also A. Bavelas and D. Barrett, "An Experimental Approach to Organization Communication," *Personnel,* 27, 1951, pp. 366–371.

20. R.L. Burgess, "Communication Networks: An Experimental Reevaluation,"*Journal of Experimental Social Psychology,* 4, 1968, p. 235.

21. H. Guetzkow and H.A. Simon, "The Impact of Certain Communication Nets."

22. C. Glenn Pierce, Ross Figgins, and Steven P. Golen, *Principles of Business Communication: Theory, Application, and Technology.* New York: John Wiley, 1984, p. 516.

23. E. Scannell, *Communication for Leadership.* New York: McGraw-Hill, 1970.

24. Don Hellriegel and John W. Slocum, *Management.* Reading, Massachussets: Addison-Wesley, 1989, p. 523.

25. Dewitt C. Dearborn and Herbert A. Simon, "Selective Perception," *Sociometry,* 21, 1958, pp. 140–143.

26. R.R. Sears, "Experimental Studies in Perception, I. Attribution of Traits," *Journal of Social Psychology,* 7, 1936, pp. 151–163.

27. K. Griffin and R. Patton, *Fundamentals of Interpersonal Communication.* New York: Harper & Row, 1971, p. 111.

28. Carl F. Rogers and F.J. Roethlisberger, "Barriers and Gateways to Communication," *Harvard Business Review,* 30, 1952, pp. 44–49.

29. "Measure Your Fog Index," *Business Week,* July 6, 1981.

30. John Keltner, *Interpersonal Speech—Communication.* Belmont, California: Wadsworth, 1970.

31. Margot Gibb-Clark, "Most Job Losers Find out Second-Hand," *The Globe and Mail,* April 14, 1993, pp. B1, B4.

CHAPTER 15

1. S. Schmidt and T. Kochan, "Conflict: Toward Conceptual Clarity," *Administrative Science Quarterly,* 17, 1972, pp. 359–370.

2. E. Ross, *Principles of Sociology.* New York: Century, 1930.

3. S. Robbins, *Organizational Behavior.* Englewood Cliffs, New Jersey: Prentice-Hall, 1979, p. 289.

4. S. Robbins, *Managing Organizational Conflict: A Nontraditional Approach.* Englewood Cliffs, New Jersey: Prentice-Hall, 1974, pp. 11–14.

5. E. Boulding, "Further Reflections on Conflict Management," In R. Kahn and E. Boulding (eds.), *Power and Conflict in Organizations.* New York: Basic Books, 1964, pp. 146–150.

6. L.D. Brown, *Managing Conflict at Organizational Interfaces.* Reading, Massachusetts: Addison-Wesley, 1983.

7. M. Afzalur Rahim, "A Strategy for Managing Conflict in Complex Organizations," *Human Relations,* 38, 1985, pp. 81–89.

8. This criterion is of little comfort to those who may be involved in an unpleasant conflict.

9. The techniques discussed here are based on those described in S. Robbins, *Managing Organizational Conflict.* Englewood Cliffs, New Jersey: Prentice-Hall, 1974, Ch. 9.

10. R.A. Coser and C.R. Schwenk, "Agreement and Thinking Alike: Ingredients for Poor Decisions," *Academy of Management Executive,* 4, February 1990, pp. 69–74.

11. Stephen A. Allen, "Organizational Choice and General Influence Networks for Diversified Companies," *Academy of Management Journal,* 1978, p. 341.

12. Shona McKay, "The Challenge in Change," *The Financial Post Magazine,* April 1992, pp. 43–44.

13. Anne Kingston, "Power to the People," *Canadian Business,* July 1992, pp. 15–22.

14. Harold J. Leavitt, "Applied Organizational Change in Industry: Structural, Technical, and Human Approaches," in W.W. Cooper, H. J. Leavitt, and M.W. Shelly (eds.) *New Perspectives in Organization Research,* New York: Wiley, 1964, pp. 55–74.

15. Margot Gibb-Clark, "Managing Change: A Long, Tough Road But a Key to Survival, Executive Warns," *The Globe and Mail,* April 30, 1987, p. B8.

16. Peter Larson, "Winning Strategies," *Canadian Business Review,* Summer 1989, pp. 41–42.

17. Karen Howlett, "IBM Canada Realigns: Staff to Go Back to School," *The Globe and Mail,* March 17, 1987, pp. B1–B2.

18. Michael Crawford, "The New Office Etiquette," *Canadian Business,* May 1993, pp. 22–31.

19. Geoffrey Rowan, "Xerox Launches Document Processing Products," *The Globe and Mail,* October 3, 1990, p. B7.

20. Jacquie McNish, "It's Official: Gerstner Wins Top IBM Job," *The Globe and Mail,* March 27, 1993, p. B1.

21. Mc Kay, "The Challenge in Change."

22. Kurt Lewin, *Field Theory and Social Science.* New York: Harper, 1964, Chapters 9 and 10.

23. E.L. Trist and K.W. Bamforth, "Some Social and Psychological Consequences of the Longwall Method of Coal-Getting," *Human Relations,* 4, 1951, pp. 1–38.

24. See, for example, T.W. Adorno, E. Frenkel-Brunswik, D.J. Levinson, and R.N. Sanford, *The Authoritarian Personality.* New York: Harper and Row, 1950.

25. "30 Women Opt to Become Miners," *The Globe and Mail,* February 24, 1993, p. B1.

26. Computer experts are famous for the intimidating techniques they use with novices.

27. Kurt Lewin, "Frontiers in Group Dynamics," *Human Relations,* 1, 1947, pp. 5–42.

28. Theodore T. Herbert, *Dimensions of Organizational Behavior.* New York: The MacMillan Company, 1976, p. 345.

29. J.P. Kotter and L.A. Schlesinger, "Choosing Strategies for Change," *Harvard Business Review,* 1979, pp. 102–121.

30. Larson, "Winning Strategies," p. 50.

31. K.T. Fougere, "The Future Role of the Systems Analyst as a Change Agent," *The Journal of Systems Management,* November 1991, pp. 6–9.

32. Joseph E. McGrath, "Stress and Behavior in Organizations," in Marvin D. Dunnette (ed.), *Handbook of Industrial and Organizational Psychology.* New York: Wiley, 1983, p. 1352.

33. Merle MacIsaac, "Born-Again Basket Case," *Canadian Business,* May 1993, pp. 38–44.

34. Miriam Cu-Uy-Gam, "CEOs Say Letting Employees Go Their Biggest Source of Stress," *The Financial Post,* May 8, 1993, p. 21.

35. L.A. McBride and S. Freeman, "The Psychosocial Impacts of a Labour Dispute," *Occupational Psychology,* 54, 1981, pp. 125–134; also G. Shouksmith and S. Burrough, "Job Stress Factors for New Zealand and Canadian Air Traffic Controllers," *Applied Psychology: An International Review,* 37, 1988, pp. 263–270.

36. G. Johansson and P.O. Sanden, "Mental Load and Job Satisfaction of Control Room Operators," Reports from the Department of Psychology, University of Stockholm, 1982.

37. Dana Milbank, "Telemarketers Get No Respect," *The Globe and Mail,* September 11, 1993, pp. B1, B3.

38. D.L. Nelson, and C. Sutton, "Chronic Work Stress and Coping: A Longitudinal Study and Suggested New Directions," *Academy of Management Journal,* 33, 1990, pp. 859–869.

39. Judith McBride-King and Helen Paris, "Balancing Work and Family Responsibilities," *Canadian Business Review,* Autumn 1989, pp. 17–21.

40. Katherine Ellison, "Heart Attacks Price of Brazil's Chaotic Economy," *The Winnipeg Free Press,* January 17, 1994, p. C8.

41. David Leidl, "Relaxation 101," *BC Business,* October 1990, p. 13.

42. R.H. Rosenman et al., "A Predictive Study of Coronary Heart Disease," *Journal of the American Medical Association,* 1964, pp. 15–22.

43. Hans Selye, *The Stress of Life.* New York: McGraw-Hill, 1956.

44. Daniel Katz and Robert L. Kahn, *The Social Psychology of Organizations.* New York: Wiley, 1978.

45. T. Cox, *Stress.* Baltimore: University Park Press, 1978.

46. Jeannie Gaines and John M. Jermier, "Emotional Exhaustion in a High Stress Organization," *Academy of Management Journal,* 26, 1983, pp. 567–586.

47. Harry Levinson, "When Executives Burn Out," *Harvard Business Review,* 1981, p. 76.

48. C. Folkins, "Effects of Physical Training on Mood," *Journal of Clinical Psychology,* April 1976, pp. 385–390.

49. Tim Falconer, "Ways and Means," *Canadian Business,* June 1990, p. 173.

50. R.S. Eliot and D.L. Breo, *Is It Worth Dying For?* Bantam Books, Inc., 1984.

51. C.R. Stoner and F.L. Fry, "Developing a Corporate Policy for Managing Stress," *Personnel,* 1983, pp. 66–76.

52. J. Aberth, "Worksite Wellness Programs: An Evaluation," *Management Review,* 1986, pp. 51–53.

53. McBride-King and Paris, "Balancing Work and Family Responsibilities."

54. Paul Samyn, "Healthy Workplace Promoted," *Winnipeg Free Press*, September 23, 1990, p. 7.

55. Margot Gibb-Clark, "Stress Counselling," *The Globe and Mail*, August 27, 1990, p. B3.

56. Bruce McDougall, "Perks With Pizzazz," *Canadian Business*, June 1990, p. 79.

CHAPTER 16

1. Ralph Kilmann, Mary J. Saxton, and Roy Serpa, "Issues in Understanding and Changing Culture," *California Management Review*, 28, 1986, p. 88.

2. Daniel Stoffman, "Great Workplaces and How They Got That Way," *Canadian Business*, September 1984, pp. 30–33, 34, 36, 38.

3. Jay B. Barney, "Organizational Culture: Can It Be A Source Of Sustained Competitive Advantage?" *Academy of Management Review*, 11, 1986, pp. 656–665.

4. R. Lucas, "Political-Cultural Analysis of Organizations," *Academy of Management Review*, 12, 1987, pp. 144–156.

5. Marina Strauss, "Cultural Differences Cited in Law Firm Splitting," *The Globe and Mail*, June 13, 1990, p. B1.

6. Ric Dolphin, "Magna Force," *Canadian Business*, May 1988.

7. Isadore Sharp, "Quality for All Seasons," *Canadian Business Review*, Spring 1990, pp. 21–23.

8. Alexander Ross and Mike Macbeth, "Bay Street's One-Night Stand," *Canadian Business*, August 1986, pp. 19–23, 74.

9. Stephen P. Robbins and Robin Stuart-Kotze, *Management*. Toronto: Prentice-Hall Canada, 1990, p. 85.

10. Daniel Stoffman, "Great Workplaces and How They Got That Way,"; also "Principal Failures Shock Salesman," *Winnipeg Free Press*, November 13, 1987, p. 17.

11. Francis G. Rodgers with Robert L. Shook, *The IBM Way*. New York: Harper & Row, 1986.

12. Thomas J. Peters and Robert H. Waterman, Jr., *In Search of Excellence*. New York: Harper & Row, 1982.

13. William Burpeau, Theresa McMurray, and Mike Clifford, "Sonyvision: A Report on the Sony Corporation," Unpublished manuscript, Texas A & M University, 1985.

14. T. E. Deal and A. A. Kennedy, *Corporate Cultures: The Rites and Rituals of Corporate Power*. Reading, Massachusetts: Addison-Wesley, 1982, pp. 87–88.

15. Richard L. Daft, *Organization Theory and Design*. St. Paul, Minnesota: West, 1986.

16. Deal and Kenney, *Corporate Cultures*.

17. J. Kerr and J.W. Slocum, "Managing Corporate Culture Through Reward Systems," *Academy of Management Executive*, 1987, 1, pp. 98–108.

18. B. Dumaine, "Those High Flying PepsiCo Managers," *Fortune*, April 10, 1989, pp. 78–86; also P. Sellers, "Pepsi Keeps on Going After No. 1," *Fortune*, March 11, 1991, pp. 61–70.

19. Peters and Waterman, *In Search of Excellence*.

20. Deal and Kennedy, *Corporate Cultures*.

21. Daniel T. Carroll, "A Disappointing Search for Excellence," *Harvard Business Review*, November/December 1983, pp. 78, 79, 83, 84, and 88.

22. Stoffman, "Great Workplaces and How They Got That Way."

23. "Principal Failures Shock Salesman," *Winnipeg Free Press*, November 13, 1987, p. 17.

24. Barney, "Organizational Culture."

25. Patricia Best, "Royal Bust," *Canadian Business*, November 1992, pp. 36–47.

26. Margot Gibb-Clark, "Staying on Top," *The Globe and Mail*, July 31, 1990, p. B5.

27. John Saunders, "Loewen's New Personality Leaner and Meaner," *The Globe and Mail*, June 22, 1990, p. B18.

28. John Lorinc, "Power Failure," *Canadian Business*, November 1992, pp. 50–58.

29. Kilmann, Saxton, and Serpa, "Issues in Understanding and Changing Culture."

30. W.H. French and C.H. Bell, "A Definition and History of Organizational Development," *Academy of Management Proceedings*, 1971, p. 146.

31. R. Wayne Mondy, Arthur Sharplin, Robert E. Holmes, and Edwin Flippo, *Management Concepts and Practices*. Boston: Allyn and Bacon, 1986, p. 386.

32. Edgar F. Huse, *Organization Development and Change*. St. Paul, Minnesota: West, 1975, p. 230.

33. W. G. Dyer, *Team Building: Issues and Alternatives*. Reading, Massachusetts: Addison-Wesley, 1987.

34. Edgar Schein, *Process Consultation: Its Role in Organization Development*. Reading, Massachusetts: Addison-Wesley, 1969, p. 9.

35. Christian Allard, "The Entrepreneur: Loyalties—Running from the Family," *Canadian Business*, July 1989, p. 14.

36. For a detailed review of 100 research studies on sensitivity training, see P.B. Smith, "Control Studies on the Outcome of Sensitivity Training," *Psychological Bulletin*, 1975, pp. 597–622.

37. R.R. Blake and J.S. Mouton, *The Managerial Grid*. Houston: Gulf, 1964.

38. N. Margulies and A.P. Raia, "The Politics of Organization Development," *Training and Development Journal*, 38, 1984, pp. 20–23.

39. William Vicars and Darrell D. Hartke, "Evaluating OD Evaluations: A Status Report," *Group and Organizational*

Studies, 9, June 1984, pp. 177–188; also J.M. Nicholas and M. Katz, "Research Methods and Reporting Practices in Organization Development: A Review and Some Guidelines," *Academy of Management Review,* 10, 1985, pp. 737–749; also J.M. Nicholas, "The Comparative Impact of Organizational Development Interventions on Hard Criteria Measures," *Academy of Management Review,* 7, 1982, pp. 531–542; also D.E. Terpstra, "The Organization Development Evaluation Process: Some Problems and Proposals," *Human Resource Management,* 20, 1981, pp. 24–29.

CHAPTER 17

1. Kenneth Kidd, "Magna's Next Hurrah," *Canadian Business,* June 1992, p. 41.
2. F. Rice, "Why Kmart Has Stalled," *Fortune,* October 9, 1989, pp. 79–80; also B. Saporito, "Is Wal-Mart Unstoppable?," *Fortune,* May 6, 1991, pp. 50–59; also R.F. Lusch, "Retail Control Systems for the 1990s," *Arthur Andersen Retailing Issues Letter,* January 1990.
3. Peter Lorange, Michael S. S. Morton, and Sumantra, *Strategic Control.* St. Paul, Minneapolis: West, 1986.
4. G. W. Dalton, "Motivation and Control in Organizations," In G.W. Dalton and P.R. Lawrence (eds.), *Motivation and Control in Organizations.* Homewood, Illinois: Richard D. Irwin, 1971, pp. 1–35.
5. Jeb Blount, "The Battle of the Clamshell," *Report on Business Magazine,* April 1991, pp. 40–47.
6. S.M. Klein and R.R. Ritti, *Understanding Organizational Behavior.* Boston: Kent Publishing, 1984, p. 509.
7. Barrie Whittaker, "Increasing Market Share Through Marketing Excellence," *Canadian Business Review,* Spring 1990, pp. 35–37.
8. R. Wayne Mondy, Arthur Sharplin, Robert E. Holmes, and Edwin Flippo, *Management Concepts and Practice.* Boston: Allyn and Bacon, 1986, p. 416.
9. Eva Kiess-Moser, "Customer Satisfaction," *Canadian Business Review,* Summer 1989, pp. 44–45.
10. John Gilks, "Total Quality: A Strategy for Organizational Transformation," *Canadian Manager,* Summer 1990, pp. 19–21.
11. Kiess-Moser, "Customer Satisfaction," p. 44.
12. Ibid.
13. Mondy et al., *Management Concepts and Canadian Practice,* pp. 425–428.
14. Karen Bemowski, comp., "The Quality Glossary," *Quality Progress,* February 1992, pp. 20–29.
15. Based on a variety of sources, including William H. Newman, *Constructive Control.* Englewood Cliffs, New Jersey: Prentice-Hall, Inc., 1975; also William H. Sihler, "Toward Better Management Control Systems," *California Management Review,* Winter 1971, pp. 33–39; also K.A. Merchant, *Control in Business Organizations.* Boston, Massachusetts: Pitman, 1985.

CHAPTER 18

1. J. Van Maanen and E.H. Schein, "Towards a Theory of Organizational Socialization," in B.M. Staw (ed.), *Research in Organizational Behavior.* 1, Greenwich, Connecticut: JAI Press, 1979, pp. 209–264.
2. W. Edwards Deming, *Out of the Crisis.* Cambridge, Mass.: Center for Advanced Engineering Study, 1986.
3. Richard J. Schonberger, "Production Workers Bear Major Quality Responsibility in Japanese Industry," *Industrial Engineering,* December 1982, pp. 34–40.
4. Bruce McDougall, "The Thinking Man's Assembly Line," *Canadian Business,* November 1991, p. 40.
5. Chris Argyris, *Personality and Organization.* New York: Harper, 1957.
6. Carey French, "Breaking the Information Barrier," *The Globe and Mail,* October 26, 1993, p. B25.
7. "Quality is the Magic Word for Corporate Slogans," *The Globe and Mail,* October 26, 1993, p. B26.
8. Ian Allaby, "The Search for Quality," *Canadian Business,* May 1990, pp. 31–42.
9. John Gilks, "Total Quality: A Strategy for Organizational Transformation," *Canadian Manager,* Spring 1990, pp. 23–25.
10. Judith Nancekivell, "The Pursuit of Excellence," *Canadian Plastics,* June 1984, pp. 24–25.
11. Dean Walker, "Conversation with George Cohon of McDonald's," *Canadian Business,* June 1983, pp. 32–36; Don Champion, "Quality—A Way of Life at B.C. Tel," *Canadian Business Review,* Spring 1990, pp. 32–34; John Gilks, "Total Quality: Wave of the Future," *Canadian Business Review,* Spring 1990, pp. 17–20.
12. Greg Topolski, "Surveys Help Not-For-Profit Groups," *The Globe and Mail,* October 26, 1993, p. B28.
13. Ibid.
14. Carlie Oreskovitch, "How the Experts Tend Their Own Shop," *The Globe and Mail,* October 26, 1993, p. B27.
15. Carey French, "A Question of Survival," *The Globe and Mail,* October 26, 1993, p. B27.
16. Carey French, "Satisfaction Can Prove Elusive," *The Globe and Mail,* October 26, 1993, p. B28.
17. Gordon Pitts, "Stepping on the Quality Ladder," *The Globe and Mail,* June 30, 1992, p. B20.

18. Ibid.

19. Carolyn Leitch, "The Hair-Cutting Edge," *The Globe and Mail,* April 27, 1993, p. B22.

20. "MRP Drives AS/RS—Cuts Inventory $12 Million," *Modern Materials Handling,* August 5, 1983, pp. 38–41.

21. William E. Dollar, "The Zero Inventory Concept," *Purchasing,* September 29, 1983, p. 433.

22. Shelley Boyes and Michelle Ramsay, "Just-In-Time—The New Eastern Philosophy," *Canadian Transportation & Distribution Management,* June 1984, p. 33.

23. John Tracy, "Corporate Strategy and Artificial Intelligence," *Canadian Transportation,* November 1989, p. 87.

24. Boyes and Ramsey, "Just-In-Time—The New Eastern Philosophy."

25. Timothy Pritchard, "Peace Breaks Out on the Shop Floor," *The Globe and Mail,* July 6, 1993, p. B18.

26. D. Hellriegel and J. Slocum, *Management.* Reading, Massachusetts: Addison-Wesley, 1989, p. 648.

27. P.A. Pyhrr, *Zero-Base Budgeting: A Practical Management Tool For Evaluating Expense.* New York: John Wiley, 1973.

28. Stanton C. Lindquist and K. Bryant Mills, "Whatever Happened to Zero-Based Budgeting?", *Managerial Planning,* January/February 1981, pp. 31–35.

29. "Zero-Base Budgeting—A Technique for Planned Organizational Decline," *Long Range Planning,* June 1981, pp. 68–76.

CHAPTER 19

1. J.A. Algera, P.L. Keepman, and H.P.J. Vijlbrief, "Management Strategies in Introducing Computer-Based Information Systems," *Applied Psychology: An Interna-tional Review,* 38, 1989, pp. 87–103.

2. Robert G. Murdick, "MIS Development Procedures," *Journal of Systems Management,* 21, December 1970, pp. 22–26.

3. Tom Kelly, "Opinion: No Room for Zoo-Keepers," *Office Equipment and Methods,* April 1989, p. 5.

4. A.L. Lederer and R. Nath, "Making Strategic Information Systems Happen," *Academy of Management Executive,* 4, August 1990, pp. 76–83.

5. C. Brod, "Managing Technostress: Optimizing the Use of Computer Technology," *Personnel Journal,* October 1982, p. 754.

6. Algera et al., "Management Strategies in Introducing Computer-Based Information Systems."

7. John Southerst, "The Reinvention of Retail," *Canadian Business,* August 1992, pp. 26–31.

8. Bruce Little, "How to Make a Small, Smart Factory," *The Globe and Mail,* February 2, 1993, p. B24.

9. R.L. Daft, *Management.* Chicago: The Dryden Press, 1988, p. 606.

10. "Will the Boss Go Electronics, Too?" *Business Week,* May 11, 1981, p. 106.

11. E.D. Carlson, "Decision Support Systems: Personal Computing Services for Managers," *Management Review,* January 1977, pp. 5–11.

12. F.C. Sainfort, D.H. Gustafson, K. Bosworth, and R.P. Hawkins, "Decision Support Systems Effectiveness: Conceptual Framework and Empirical Evaluation," *Organizational Behavior and Human Decision Processes,* 45, 1990, pp. 232–252.

13. "Fourth-Generation Languages Make DSS Feasible for All Managers," *Management Review,* April 1984, pp. 4–5.

14. A.T. Masland, "Integrators and Decision Support System Success in Higher Education," *Research in Higher Education,* 20, 1984, pp. 211–233; also H.J. Watson and M.M. Hill, "Decision Support Systems or What Didn't Happen with MIS," *Interfaces,* October 1983, pp. 81–88.

15. T.J. O'Leary and B.K. Williams, *Computers and Information Processing.* Menlo Park, California: Benjamin Cummings, 1985.

16. Daft, *Management,* p. 606.

17. "What's Happening With DSS?" *EDP Analyzer,* July 1984, pp. 1–6.

18. Geoffrey Rowan, "Consulting Service Plans to Open Centre Offering Computer Services," *The Globe and Mail,* April 10, 1990, p. B11.

19. Anderew Safer, "Revenge of the Nerds," *Canadian Business,* October 1992, p. 137.

CHAPTER 20

1. *The State of Small Business 1989, Annual Report on Small Business in Ontario.* Toronto: Ministry of Industry, Trade and Technology, 1990, pp. 3–4.

2. Canada, Statistics Canada. Ottawa: Supply and Services Canada, April 1989. Cat. No. 61–231.

3. Alan M. Cohen, "Entrepreneur and Entrepreneurship: The Definition Dilemma," Working Paper Series No. NC89–08, National Centre for Management Research and Development, The University of Western Ontario, London, February 1989.

4. *The State of Small Business,* pp. 24–27 (refer to endnote 1).

5. Ibid., p. 29.

6. Terence Corcoran, "Guess Who's Creating Jobs, and Who's Not," *The Globe and Mail,* January 12, 1994, p. B2.

7. This phenomenon has been extensively studied. Two Canadian studies are Monica Belcourt, "A Family Portrait of

Canada's Most Successful Female Entrepreneurs," *Journal of Business Ethics*, 9, pp. 435–438, and H. Lee-Gosselin & J. Grisé. "Are Women Owner-Managers Challenging Our Definitions of Entrepreneurship? An In-Depth Survey," *Journal of Business Ethics*, 9, pp. 423–433.

8. *Small Business in Canada: Growing To Meet Tomorrow*. Ottawa: Supply and Services Canada. Cat. No. C28–1/2, 1989E, p. 12; also *The State of Small Business*, p. 8 (refer to endnote 1).
9. Ted Byfield, Good Service Is Key to Success For Small Printer," *The Financial Post*, November 20, 1993, p. S3.
10. *The State of Small Business*, p. 70 (refer to endnote 1).
11. Jerry White, "Why Business Plans Rarely Work," *The Evening Telegram*, May 27, 1993, p. 27.
12. William H. Baker, H. Lon Addams and Brian Davis, "Business Planning in Successful Small Firms," *Long Range Planning*, 1993, Vol. 26, No. 6, pp. 82–88.
13. Jerry Zeidenberg, "Entrepreneurs Learn From Strategic Planning," *The Globe and Mail*, June 8, 1992, p. B4
14. Many models of organizational growth have been developed. One that is often described in management books in Larry E. Greiner, "Evolution and Revolution as Organizations Grow," *Harvard Business Review*, 50, No. 4, July–August 1972, pp. 37–46. One example of growth model developed for small business is: Mel Scott and Richard Bruce, "Five Stages of Growth in Small Business," *Long Range Planning*, 20, No. 3, 1987, pp. 45–52.
15. Joan Mount, J. Terence Zinger, and George R. Forsyth, "Organizing for Development in Small Business," *Long Range Planning*, 1993, Vol. 26, No. 5, pp. 111–120.
16. The statistics in this section are from *Small Business in Canada;* also *The State of Small Business* (refer to endnote 1)
17. Grant McCracken, "Not So Lean Means Not So Mean," *The Globe and Mail*, July 2, 1990, p. A18.
18. "When Bigger is Better," *Business Week/Entreprise*, 1993, p. 201.
19. Mark Maremont, "Summing Up," *Business Week/Enterprise* 1993, pp. 248–257.

CHAPTER 21

1. Edward Greenspon, "Service Industries Driving Growth, GATT Report Says," *The Globe and Mail*, September 15, 1989, pp. B1, B4.
2. Barry Critchley, "Wanted: A Partner," *The Financial Post 500* Summer 1990, pp. 46–53.
3. Alan Nymark, Executive Vice-President, Investment Canada, *Investing in Canada*, 4, No. 1, Spring 1990, p. 4.
4. Ibid.
5. Herman Daems, "The Strategic Implications of Europe 1992," *Long Range Planning*, 23, No. 3, 1990, pp. 41–48.
6. For example: James C. Abegglen and George Stalk, Jr., *Kaisha: The Japanese Corporation*, New York: Basic Books. 1986.
7. Tim Richardson, "Reaping The Yen," *Canadian Business*, August 1990, pp. 49–57.
8. James E. Austin, *Managing in Developing Countries: Strategic Analysis and Operating Techniques*. New York: The Free Press. 1990.
9. For a discussion of doing business in the Soviet Union refer to Carl H. McMillan, "Eastward Ho! Tackling the Last Frontier," *Canadian Business Review*, Summer 1990, pp. 17–26.
10. For a discussion of practical ideas and useful information in surviving and succeeding in Eastern Europe refer to Tarif Korabi, and David G. Grieve, "Doing Business in Eastern Europe: A Survival Guide," *Canadian Business Review*, Summer 1990, pp. 22–25.
11. Michael E. Porter, "The Competitive Advantage of Nations: *Harvard Business Review*, March–April 1990, pp. 73–93.
12. Michael Porter, *Canada At the Crossroads: The Reality of a Competitive Environment*. Ottawa: Business Council on National Issues and Minister of Supply and Services, 1991.
13. *Fortune*. July 30, 1990, pp. 264–298.
14. Quoted in Martin Mittelstraedt, "World Learns to Love Multinationals; *The Globe and Mail*, October 20, 1988, p. B32.
15. Madelaine Drohan, "To Bribe or Not to Bribe," *The Globe and Mail*, February 14, 1994, p. B7.
16. Edith Terry wrote an excellent series on the *keiretsu* for *The Globe and Mail:* "The Land of the Rising Cartels," September 22, 1990, pp. B1–2; also "The Ties That Bind," September 24, 1990, pp. B1, B4; also "Looking in From the Outside," September 25, 1990, p. B1–2. A story of the Mitsubishi *keiretsu* was featured in *Business Week*, September 24, 1990, pp. 98–107.
17. "The Stateless Corporation: Forget Multinationals—Today's Giants are Are Really Leaping Boundaries," *Business Week*. May 14, 1990, pp. 98–105, 166.

CHAPTER 22

1. This topic has been written about extensively. Refer to Wallace Clement, *The Canadian Corporate State: An Analysis of Economic Power*. Toronto: McClelland and Stewart, 1975; also Peter C. Newman; *The Canadian Establishment*, Toronto: McClelland and Stewart, 1975; and Jorge Niosi, *Canadian Capitalism: A Study of Power in the Canadian Business Establishment*. Toronto: James Lorimer, 1981.
2. George A. Steiner and John F. Steiner. *Business, Government, and Society: A Managerial Perspective*. New York: McGraw-Hill, Inc. 1991, p. 16.

3. Canada. Report of the Royal Commission on Corporate Concentration. Ottawa: Supply and Services Canada. Cat. No. Z1–1975/1, 1978, p. 377.

4. R. Terrence MacTaggart et al., *Corporate Social Performance in Canada.* Royal Commission on Corporate Concentration. Study No. 21. Ottawa: Supply and Services Canada. Cat. No. Z1–1957/1–41. 1977.

5. E.H. Bowman and W. Haire, "A Strategic Posture Toward Corporate Social Responsibility," *California Management Review*, 18, 1975, pp. 49–58, and Leonard J. Brooks, Jr. *Canadian Corporate Social Performance*, Hamilton: The Society of Management Accountants of Canada, 1986, pp. 10–14.

6. Brooks, 1986, pp. 263–7 (refer to endnote 5).

7. Peter F. Bartha, "Managing Corporate External Issues: An Analytical Framework," *Business Quarterly*, Autumn 1982, pp. 78–80, and Steven L. Wartick and Robert E. Rude, "Issues Management: Corporate Fact or Corporate Function?", *California Management Review*, XXIX, No. 1, 1986, pp. 124–139.

8. Phillip V. Lewis, "Defining 'Business Ethics': Like Nailing Jello to a Wall," *Journal of Business Ethics*, 4, 1985, p. 381.

9. Special Advertising Feature, *Financial Times of Canada*, February 23, 1987, p. 42.

10. Better Business Bureau materials.

11. Center for Business Ethics, "Are Corporations Institutionalizing Ethics?" *Journal of Business Ethics*, 5, 1986, p. 88.

12. Richard Finlay, "Social Behavior Now on Business Agenda," *The Financial Post*, March 16, 1987, p. 8.

13. Susan Montague, Letter to the Editor, *The Globe and Mail*, September 9, 1989, p. D7.

14. Samuel A. Martin, *An Essential Grace: Funding Canada's Health Care, Education, Welfare, Religion and Culture.* Toronto: McClelland and Stewart. 1985, p. 240.

15. Donn Downey, "Ballard's Generosity Surpasses That of Several Billionaires," *The Globe and Mail*, April 28, 1990, p. A1.

16. Martin, p. 240 (refer to endnote 14).

17. The topic of business and the environment has received considerable attention. It is not feasible to identify one source of further reading but the following may be helpful to readers: "Report on Environmental Protection," *The Globe and Mail* Section C, February 27, 1990; also "Focus: A Special Report," *The Globe and Mail* Section D, April 15, 1989; also "Special Report: The Environment Business," *The Financial Post*, Section 4, June 4, 1990; also "Special Report: The Environment," *The Financial Post*, Section 4, June 29, 1989; also Robert Collison, "The Greening of the Boardroom," *Report on Business Magazine*, July 1989, pp. 41f; "The Environment & The Economy," several articles in the Summer 1989 issue of *Canadian Business Review*; and two issues of *The Financial Post Moneywise Magazine*, June 1989 and April 1990.

18. Christopher B. Hunt and Ellen R. Auster "Proactive Environmental Management: Avoiding the Topic Trap," *Sloan Management Review*, Winter 1990, pp. 7–18.

19. Patricia Lush, "Firms Giving Environmental Bosses Stature, If Not Clout," *The Globe and Mail*, April 3, 1990, pp. B1, B4.

20. For a review of such products refer to *The Canadian Green Consumer Guide*, Toronto: McClelland and Stewart, 1989; also Helen Kohl, "Are They Nature's Choice? 'Green' Products Claim to be the Answer, But If They Aren't What Is?", *The Financial Post Moneywise Magazine*, April 1990, pp. 16–29; and *Canadian Consumer*, No. 7 & 8, 1990.

21. There are many articles on the pros and cons of socially responsible investing, but a good one was provided by Jeannine Mitchell, "The Green Investor: Cleaning Up Their Acts," and "The Green Investor: A Shareholder's Environmental Audit," *The Financial Post Moneywise Magazine*, April 1990, pp. 48–63. Although the articles focussed on the environment, they provided a good example of the challenges of this type of investment and ranked five enterprises on their performance (Alcan, Imperial Oil, INCO, MacMillan Bloedel, and Northern Telecom).

SOURCE NOTES

CHAPTER 1

Global Management Adapted from J.A. Wall, "Managers in the People's Republic of China," *Academy of Management Executive,* May 1990, pp. 19–32. **Global Management** Summarized from John Southerst, "There Goes the Future," *Canadian Business,* October 1992, pp. 98–105. **Table 1-1** Summarized from S.P. Robbins and R. Stuart-Kotze, *Management.* Scarborough, Ontario: Prentice-Hall Canada Inc., 1990, pp. 4–11. **Global Management** Summarized from Madelaine Drohan, "Lloyd's Ends Tradition of Unlimited Liability," *The Globe and Mail,* April 30, 1993, pp. B1, B8. **Management at Work** Summarized from J. Heinzl, "People's Ex-Directors Face Suit," *The Globe and Mail,* September 22, 1993, pp. B1–B2; also John Pawling, "Accountability is Directors' New Watchword," *The Globe and Mail,* September 9, 1991, p. B4; also James Gillies, "The New Improved Board Game," *Canadian Business,* April 1992, pp. 74–77; also Patricia Lush, "Being a Director Means Being a Worker," *The Globe and Mail,* March 16, 1987, pp. B1, B8; also Drew Fagan, "Despite Recent Gains, Women Still a Rare Breed on Company Boards," *The Globe and Mail,* May 2, 1990, p. B7; also Gail Lem, "Sherritt Gordon Dispute Heats Up," *The Globe and Mail,* September 11, 1990, p. B13. **Table 1-3** Summarized from H. Mintzberg, *The Nature of Work.* New York: Harper and Row, 1973. **Figure 1-4** Drawn from data contained in L. Gomez-Mejia, J.E. McCann, and R.C. Page, "The Structure of Managerial Behavior and Rewards," *Industrial Relations,* 1985, 24, pp. 147–154. **Management at Work** Summarized from Sandy Fife, "CEO Switch Hitters," *The Financial Post Magazine,* November 1992, pp. 76–86; also Ann Gibbon, "CN's New Boss Takes Hard Line," *The Globe and Mail,* February 8, 1993, pp. B1–B2; also Marina Strauss, "Veteran Businessman Gets Chance to Make a Legal Firm Businesslike," *The Globe and Mail,* January 22, 1987, p. B6. **Case 1-1** Summarized from David Napier, "Beeston Plays Hardball," *The Financial Post Magazine,* September 1992, pp. 28–32. **Case 1-3** Summarized from Karen Howlett, "A Question of Governance," *The Globe and Mail,* July 19, 1993, pp. B1, B3.

CHAPTER 2

Management Challenge and **Meeting the Challenge** Summarized from K. Labich, "Big Changes at Big Brown," *Fortune,* May 22, 1989, pp. 56–64; also Resa King, "UPS Isn't About To Be Left Holding the Parcel," *Business Week,* February 13, 1989, p. 69; also T. Vogel and C. Hawkins, "Can UPS Deliver the Goods in a New World?," *Business Week,* June 4, 1990, pp. 80–82; also W. Keenan, "America's Best Sales Forces," *Business Week,* September 1992; also L. Wilson, "Stand and Deliver," *Information Week,* November 23, 1992; also C. Hawkins and P. Oster, "After a U-Turn, UPS Really Delivers," *Business Week,* May 31, 1993; also J. Alden, Speech given to the Association of Corporate Growth, February 17, 1992. **Table 2-2** Summarized from Max Weber, *The Theory of Social and Economic Organizations.* New York: Free Press, 1947, pp. 328–337. **Figure 2-1** Richard H. Franke and J.D. Kaul, "The Hawthorne Experiments: First Statistical Interpretation," *American Sociological Review,* October 1978, p. 626. Used with permission. **Table 2-4** Lee Krajewski and Larry P. Ritzman, *Operations Management: Strategy and Analysis.* Reading, Mass.: Addison Wesley Publishing Co. Inc., 1987, Table 1.1 on p. 4. Reprinted with permission. **Case 2-1** Written by John Mundie, Professor of Business Policy, University of Manitoba. Used with permission. **Case 2-2** Summarized from D. Machalaba, "Up to Speed: United Parcel Service Gets Deliveries Done by Driving its Drivers," *The Wall Street Journal,* April 22, 1986, pp. 1, 23.

CHAPTER 3

Ethics in Management Robert Williamson, "And death shall have no dominion," *The Globe and Mail,* September 4, 1992, p. A5; also Deborah Wilson, "Closing leaves residents nothing," *The Globe and Mail,* August 3, 1992, pp. A1, A3. **Figure 3-2** Based on data in issues of *Bank of Canada Review,* "General Economic Statistics Section," Cat. No. FB12–1. **Management at Work** Adam Corelli, "Joining forces for fun, profit—and survival," *Financial Times of Canada,* January 2, 1990, p. 8; also Oliver Bertin, "Joint ventures to help Prairie pools expand operations," *The Globe and Mail,* April 4, 1989, p. B3; also Gordon Pitts, "Why foreign joint ventures end in divorce," *The Financial Post,* November 13, 1989, p. 7; also Kimberly Noble, "Drug makers find common cause," *The Globe and Mail,* November 9, 1993, p. B20; and Carolyn Leitch, "Delta to operate 5 hotels in Asia," *The Globe and Mail,* December 3, 1993, B3. **Management at Work** Prepared by Robert W. Sexty and based, in part, on John Ralston Saul, "The Secret Life of the Branch Plant Executive," *Report on Business Magazine,* January 1988, pp. 81–86. **Table 3-1** Statistics Canada. *Corporations and Labour Unions Returns Act Annual Report. Part I—Corporations.* Ottawa: Supply and Services Canada. Cat. No. 61–210. 1991. p. 85. **Table 3-2** Prepared from Harvey Enchin. *The Globe and Mail,* June 22, 1992, pp. B1, B2. **Figure 3-4** *au courant,* Economic Council of Canada, vol. 13, No. 1, 1992, p. 5. **Management at Work** Kenneth W. Harrigan, "Ensuring Quality is Job 1 at Ford," *Business Quarterly,* 54, No. 2, Autumn 1989, pp. 33–37 (Supplement); also Bruce White, "How Quality Became Job #1 at Ford," *Canadian Business Review,* Spring 1990, pp. 24–27, and "1993 Canada Awards for Business Excellence," *The Globe and Mail,* November 12, 1993, page

C9. **Figure 3-5** Statistics Canada, *Canada Year Book,* various years. **Management at Work** Jonathan N. Goodrich, "Telecommunicating in America," *Business Horizons,* July—August 1990, pp. 31–37; also Cathryn Motherwell, "No Office Grind, No Office Laughs," *The Globe and Mail,* April 27, 1987, p. B1; also "Ottawa Eyes Letting Public Servants 'Telecommute'," *The Globe and Mail,* November 10, 1987, p. B17 **Global Management** *The 1993 Canada Export Awards*, a supplement prepared by External Affairs and International Trade Canada; pp. 2–3. **Management at Work** Amy Willard Cross, "Why Docs' rise is no mean feat," *The Globe and Mail,* December 15, 1993, p. A11; and Harvey Enchin, "High-tech heart, lots of sole," *The Globe and Mail,* July 14, 1992, B24. **Case 3-1** David Roberts, "The brew crew takes over," *The Globe and Mail,* December 21, 1993, p. A20; also Janet Fielding, "Big beer's war on the microbreweries," *Financial Times of Canada,* December 11, 1993, p. 3.

Comprehensive Cases Part I

Case I-1 was prepared by Professor Ravi Tangri, Saint Mary's University, as a basis for classroom discussion, and is not meant to illustrate either effective or ineffective management. Copyright © 1993, the Atlantic Entrepreneurial Institue, an Atlantic Canada Opportunities Agency funded organization. Printed by permission. **Case I-2** was prepared by Professor Peter McGrady.

Chapter 4

Management Challenge Summarized from Geoffrey Rowan, "JAL Bows out of Link With Canadian," *The Globe and Mail,* January 15, 1993, pp. B1, B12; also Drew Fagan, "Showdown for Canadian," *The Globe and Mail,* February 2, 1993, pp. B1, B6; also Geoffrey Rowan, "Judge Scolds Air Canada, Gives AMR Hefty Award," *The Globe and Mail,* February 13, 1993, p. B5; also "The PWA Videotape," *The Financial Post,* April 1, 1991, p. 7; also Donald Campobell, "Airlines Holding Pattern," *Winnipeg Free Press,* November 14, 1992, p. 1; also John Douglas, "Tories Raise Ante in Airline Bailout," *Winnipeg Free Press,* November 20, 1991, p. 1; also Alex Binkley, "Key Advice in Transport Study Spurned," *Winnipeg Free Press,* November 20, 1992, p. A8; also John Douglas, "Number of Flights to be Cut," *Winnipeg Free Press,* November 24, 1992, p. 1; also Brad Oswald, "Air Deal Approval Stirs Joy, Anxiety," *The Winnipeg Free Press,* May 28, 1993, p. 1; also, J. Douglas and Bonnie Bridge, "Ruling May Kill Gemini," *Winnipeg Free Press,* November 25, 1993, p. 1 **Management at Work** Adapted from Randall Litchfield, "The 90s Way to Tackle the Recession," *Canadian Business,* November 1990, pp. 80–88. **Management at Work** Adapted from Charles Davies, "The Crash at Leigh," *Canadian Business,* July 1990, pp. 28–34. **Management at Work** Adapted from Jeannette Logan, "The Road to Success—Putting Prevention First," *Occupational Health and Safety Canada,* 6, pp. 55–60. **Table 4-5** Christopher Cerf and Victor Navasky, *The Experts Speak.* New York: Pantheon Books, 1984. Reprinted with permission of Pantheon Books, a division of Random House, Inc. **Global Management** Adapted from Roland Huntford. *The Last Place on Earth.* New York: Atheneum, 1985. **Management at Work** Based on interviews with Sterling McLeod and Wayne Walker, vice-presidents of sales at Investors Group. **Table 4-6** Jack N. Kondrasuk, "Studies in MBO Effectiveness," *Academy of Management Review,* 6, 1981, p. 425. Reprinted with permission. **Table 4-7** R.C. Ford, F.S. McLaughlin, and J. Nixdorf, "Ten Questions About MBO," *California Management Review,* 23, Winter 1980, p. 92. Copyright 1980 by the Regents of the University of California. By permission of the Regents. **Case 4-1** Summarized from Shona McKay, "High Spirits," *Report on Business Magazine,* October 1992, pp. 92–99. **Case 4-2** Based on a case in R. Mondy, R. Holmes, and E. Flippo, *Management: Concepts and Practices.* Boston: Allyn and Bacon, 1983.

Chapter 5

Management Challenge/Meeting the Challenge Information for the "Management Challenge" and "Meeting the Challenge" was obtained from Johanna Powell, "Taste shift hits Schneider," *The Financial Post,* February 4, 1991, p. 15; also Oliver Bertin, "A slaughter-house on the cutting edge," *The Globe and Mail,* August 11, 1992, p. B20; also D.B. Scott, "Lean Machine," *Report on Business Magazine,* November 1992, pp. 90–98; also "Fat trimming helps Schneider to build a leaner organization," *The Financial Post,* August 6, 1993, p. 14; also Douglas W. Dodds, "Making It Better ... and Better," *CMA Magazine,* February 1992, pp. 16–21. **Management at Work** Mark's Work Wearhouse Ltd., *Annual Report—January 30, 1993.* **Ethics in Management** *Saskoil 1993 Annual Report,* inside front cover. **Global Management** Kevin Dougherty, "The rebuilding of Domtex," *The Financial Post,* September 12, 1991, p. 17; also Kenneth Kidd, "The Denim Kings." *Report on Business Magazine,* September 1993, pp. 21–29; also Barrie McKenna, "Denim revival gives Domtex new style," *The Globe and Mail,* October 26, 1993, pp. Bi, B5. **Table 5-3** Jorge Vasconcellos e Sá, "The Impact of Key Success Factors on Company Performance," *Long Range Planning,* 21, 1988, No. 6, pp. 56–64. **Figure 5-4** This portfolio analysis matrix is based on the one developed by the Boston Consulting Group. **Table 5-4** *Annual 1992 Report,* Cameco Corporation, inside front cover **Table 5-5** This example builds on similar classifications provided in Mark C. Baetz and Paul W. Beamish, *Strategic Management: Text, Readings and Canadian Cases,* Second Edition, Homewood, IL.: Irwin, 1990, Chapter 6; also John R. Montanari, Cyril P. Morgan and Jeffrey S. Bracker, *Strategic Management: A Choice Approach,* Chicago: The Dryden Press, 1990, Chapter 4. **Management at Work** John Geddes, " 'Good Book' Good Business for Paper Makers," *The*

Financial Post, January 8, 1989, pp. 1, 4. **Management at Work** Interprovincial Pipe Line System Inc., *1992 Annual Report*, pp. 4–6. **Figure 5-6** Robert H. Waterman, Jr., "The Seven Elements of Strategic Fit," *The Journal of Business Strategy*, 2, No. 3, 1982, pp. 69–73. Reprinted from the *Journal of Business Strategy* (New York: Warren, Gorham & Lamont) © 1982 Warren, Gorham & Lamont Inc. Used with permission. **Management at Work** Harvey Enchin, "Conducting Business," *The Globe and Mail*, May 25, 1993, p. B20; and "A Vision for the Future," *Newfoundland Churchman*, September 1992, pp. 12–13; and "A Vision for the 21st Century: Strategic Plan 1993–1998," Canadian Museum of Civilization Corporation, Ottawa, June 1993. **Case 5-1** Gina Mallet, "The Greatest Romance on Earth," *Canadian Business*, August 1993, pp. 19–23; also Christopher Harris, *The Globe and Mail*, April 8, 1993, p. B1.

Chapter 6

Management at Work Information provided by Garry Veak of the Southern Alberta Institute of Technology. **Management at Work** Summarized from John Heinzl, "Supply and Command," *The Globe and Mail*, December 15, 1992, p. B20. **Table 6-1** G.A. Gorry and M.S. Morton, "A Framework for Management Information Systems," *Sloan Management Review*, Fall 1971, p. 59. Copyright 1992 by the Sloan Management Review Association. All rights reserved. **Table 6-2** Summarized from R. Ackhoff, "Management Misinformation Systems," *Management Science*, December 1967, pp. 147–156. **Figure 6-6** L.J. Gitman and C. McDaniel Jr., *Business World*. New York: Wiley, 1983, p. 182. Reprinted with permission. **Global Management** Summarized from Emily Smith, "Turning an Expert's Skills into Computer Software," *Business Week*, October 7, 1985, pp. 104–107.

Comprehensive Cases Part II

Case II-1 Prepared by Raymond Klapstein, Dalhousie University, as a basis for classroom discussion, and is not meant to illustrate either effective or ineffective management. © 1992, the Atlantic Entrepreneurial Institute, an Atlantic Canada Opportunities Agency funded organization. Reprinted by permission. **Case II-2** was written by John William Pullen. Source of information is Minister of Supply SC93–214–1990 E. ISBN 0–662–17713–4. Reproduced with permission. **Case II-3** This case was prepared by Professor Niels A. Nielsen, formerly at University of Prince Edward Island now at Mount Allison University for the Atlantic Entrepreneurial Institute. Copyright © 1990, the Atlantic Entrepreneurial Institute. Reproduction of this case is allowed without permission for educational purposes, but all such reproductions must acknowledge the copyright. This permission does not include publication. Reprinted with permission.

Chapter 7

Global Management Summarized from S. Gellerman, "In Organizations, as in Architecture, Form Follows Function," *Organizational Dynamics*, Winter 1990, pp. 57–68. **Management at Work** F. Starke, R. Mondy, A. Sharplin, and E. Flippo, *Management Concepts and Canadian Practice*. Toronto: Allyn and Bacon, 1988, p. 232. **Management at Work** R.W. Griffin, R.J. Ebert, and F. Starke, *Business*. Scarborough, Ontario: Prentice-Hall Canada Inc., p. 118. **Figure 7-5** Consumers Distributing, *Annual Report*, 1986. **Figure 7-7** Federal Industries, *Annual Report*, 1988. **Figure 7-8** Montreal Trust, *Annual Report*, 1989. **Global Management** Summarized from Robert Collison, "How Bata Rules the World," *Canadian Business*, September 1990, pp. 28–34. **Figure 7-10** Montreal Trust, *Annual Report*, 1989. **Figure 7-11** Federal Industries, *Annual Report*, 1988; also Falconbridge Ltd., *Annual Report*, 1992; also Algoma Central Railway, *Annual Report*, 1992. **Case 7-1** Summarized from Harvey Enchin, "Conducting Business," *The Globe and Mail*, May 25, 1993, p. B20. **Case 7-3** Written by Dr. John Mundie, Professor of Business Policy, the University of Manitoba. Used with permission.

Chapter 8

Management Challenge Summarized from Greg Boyd, "Big Oil Starts Thinking Small," *Canadian Business*, January 1992, pp. 24–29. **Management at Work** Summarized from R. Ackhoff, "The Circular Organization: An Update," *Academy of Management Executive*, February 1989, pp. 11–16; also R. Ackhoff, *Creating the Corporate Future*. New York: Wiley, 1981, Chapter 7. **Management at Work** Summarized from Alexander Ross, "The Long View of Leadership," *Canadian Business*, May 1992, pp. 46–51; also E.E. Lawler, "Substitutes for Hierarchy," *Organizational Dynamics*, Summer 1988, pp. 5–15. **Management at Work** Interview with Tom Ward, Operations Manager for Genstar Shipyards Ltd.

Chapter 9

Management Challenge Gordon Pitts, "The Cheese Plant Nobody Wanted," *The Globe and Mail*, February 16, 1993, p. B24. **Management at Work** Summarized from Gordon Brockhouse, "Can This Marriage Succeed?" *Canadian Business*, October 1992, pp. 128–135. **Global Management** Summarized from Gordon Pitts, "How Good Jobs Can Come to a Bad End," *The Globe and Mail*, June 1, 1993, p. B16. **Management at Work** Bruce Little, "How to Make a Small, Smart Factory," *The Globe and Mail*, February 2, 1993, p. B24. **Table 9-1** Summarized from I. Janis, *Victims of Groupthink*. Boston: Houghton-Mifflin, 1973. **Table 9-2** Summarized from I. Janis, *Victims of Groupthink*. Boston: Houghton-Mifflin, 1973. **Management at Work** Summarized from Jerry Amernic, "The Perks of Power," *The Financial Post Magazine*, November 1, 1982, p. 78; also J. Gray and F. Starke, *Organizational Behavior*. Columbus, Ohio: Merrill, 1984. p. 419.

CHAPTER 10

Management at Work Adapted from Barrie McKenna, "Family Feud Reveals Kruger Secrets," *The Globe and Mail,* April 10, 1993, pp. B1, B3; also Anne Beirne, "Kruger vs. Kruger," *Canadian Business,* January 1986, pp. 61–66; also "Arbitrator Named in McCain Dispute," *The Globe and Mail,* October 28, 1993, p. B3; also Karen Howlett, "McCains Fade From Spotlight as Succession Talks Continue," *The Globe and Mail,* September 25, 1993, p. B4; also Karen Howlett, "McCains Try to Patch Up in Private," *The Globe and Mail,* September 24, 1993, pp. B1, B4; also Chris Morris, "Those Battlin' McCains: Wallace Shoots Back," *The Globe and Mail,* September 18, 1993, p. B2; also Kevin Cox, "McCain Filings Warn of Paralysis, "*The Globe and Mail,* September 15, 1993, pp. B1, B4; also Paul Waldie, "McCain Feud Scary for Company Village," *The Financial Post,* August 28, 1993, p. 5. **Table 10-4** Summarized from G. Strauss, "Tactics of Lateral Relationship: The Purchasing Agent," *Administrative Science Quarterly,* 7, 1962, pp. 161–186. **Figure 10-1** D. Izraeli, "The Middle Manager and the Tactics of Power Expansion," *Sloan Management Review,* 1975, pp. 57–70. Copyright 1992 by the Sloan Management Review Association. All rights reserved. **Management at Work** Summarized from C.O. Longenecker, H.P. Sims, and D.A. Gioia, "Behind the Mask: The Politics of Employee Appraisal," *Academy of Management Executive,* 1, 1987, pp. 183–193. **Ethics in Management** Summarized from Ian Brown, "Trouble in Tireland," *Canadian Business,* November 1989, pp. 95–111. **Case 10-1** Written by Dr. John Mundie, Professor of Business Policy, the University of Manitoba. Used with permission.

COMPREHENSIVE CASES PART III

Case III-1 This case was prepared by Peter McGrady. **Case III-2** This case was prepared by Peter McGrady and Dennis Humphreys. **Case III-3** Prepared by Bill House, Small Business Centre, Central Newfoundland Community College, as a basis for classroom discussion, and is not meant to illustrate either effective or ineffective management. © 1992, the Atlantic Entrepreneurial Institute, an Atlantic Canada Opportunities Agency funded organization. Reprinted by permission.

CHAPTER 11

Management Challenge Summarized from Marie Tellier, "Equity on Track," *Canadian Business Review,* Summer 1991, pp. 28–29; also R. Franklin, "Promoting Equity at Hydro," *Canadian Business Review,* Summer 1991, pp. 26–27; also Prem Benimadhu and Ruth Wright, "Impact of the Legislation," *Canadian Business Review,* Summer 1991, pp. 22–24. **Management at Work** Summarized from Bruce Little, "Employment Sweepstakes Requires Flexible Ticket," *The Globe and Mail,* January 13, 1993, pp. B1, B6. **Global Management** Summarized from David Sanger, "No Fast Track for Japanese Women," *The Globe and Mail,* December 18, 1992, p. B7; also Michael Clugston, "The Oriental Dilemma," *Maclean's,* November 30, 1987, pp. 26ff; also "Japanese Women: A World Apart," *The Economist,* May 14, 1988, pp. 19ff; also Urban Lehner and Kathryn Graven, "Japanese Women Rise in Their Workplaces, Challenging Tradition," *Wall Street Journal,* September 6, 1989, pp. A1ff; also Lee Smith, "Divisive Forces in an Inbred National," *Fortune,* March 30, 1987, pp. 24ff; also Steven Weisman, "Sex Harassment: Glare of Light on a Man's World," *New York Times,* November 13, 1989, p. A4. **Management at Work** Summarized from Rose Fisher, "Screen Test," *Canadian Business,* May 1992, pp. 62–64. **Ethics in Management** Summarized from John Saunders, "What Executives Earn," *The Globe and Mail,* April 3, 1993, pp. B1, B4; also Lawrence Surtees, "Stern Farewell to Cost NorTel $3 Million," *The Globe and Mail,* April 3, 1993, pp. B1, B4; also Alexander Ross, "Sixty-Five and Ouch," *Canadian Business,* July 1992, p. 44; also Susan Noakes, "CEO Pay-Packets Come Under Greater Scrutiny," *The Financial Post,* May 8, 1993, p. 24; also J. Castro, "How's Your Pay?," *Time,* April 15, 1991; pp. 40–41; also A. Byrne, "The Flap Over Executive Pay," *Business Week,* May 6, 1991, pp. 90–96; also T. McCarroll, "Motown's Fat Cats," *Time,* January 20, 1992, pp. 34–35; also Frances Misutka, "The Biggest Headache Money Can Buy," *Canadian Business,* July 1992, pp. 50–54; also Kimberley Noble Stone, "Executive Pay Highest in Canada," *The Globe and Mail,* May 5, 1990, p. B1; also John Partridge, "How Top Pay Matches Performance," *The Globe and Mail,* May 12, 1987, pp. B1–B2; also Frances Russell, "Tycoons Set Own Salaries and Keep Them Secret," *The Winnipeg Free Press,* November 21, 1990. **Management at Work** Summarized from Diane Forrest, "Guess Who You Can't Fire?," *Canadian Business,* November 1991, pp. 97–100; also Margot Gibb-Clark, "Campeau Faces Hurdles in Lawsuit," *The Globe and Mail,* July 13, 1991, p. B1. **Case 11-1** Summarized from John Southerst, "What Price Fairness?," *Canadian Business,* December 1991, pp. 67–74. **Case 11-2** Summarized from "Bias or Safety?," *Time,* October 16, 1989, p. 61; also "Danger in the Clean Room," *Time,* January 26, 1987, p. 48; also "Job Rights for Mothers-to-be," *Good Housekeeping,* November 1989, p. 272; also "Moms-to-be Banned from 'Chip Room'," *Science News,* January 21, 1987, p. 73; also Mark Pinsky, "VDT Radiation," *The Nation,* January 9–16, 1989, p. 41.

CHAPTER 12

Management at Work Summarized from Wendy Cuthbert, "Corporate Life After Downsizing," *The Financial Post,* March 20, 1993, p. 8; also Joanne Sisto, "Onward and ... Oops!," *Canadian Business,* July 1990, pp. 70–71. **Table 12-1** Based on Douglas McGregor, *The Human Side of Enterprise,* New York: McGraw-Hill, 1960. **Figure 12-3** The "Hierarchy of Needs" by Abraham Maslow, *Motivation and Personality,* 2nd edition, New York: Harper and Row, Inc., 1970. Reprinted by permission. **Global Management** Summarized from

M.A. Hauenstein and R.G. Lord, "The Effects of Final-Offer Arbitration on the Performance of Major League Baseball Players: A Test of Equity Theory," *Human Performance,* 2, 1989, pp. 147–165; also R.D. Bretz and S.L. Thomas, "Perceived Equity, Motivation, and Final-Offer Arbitration in Major League Baseball," *Journal of Applied Psychology,* 77, 1992, pp. 280–287; also J.W. Harder, "Equity Theory Versus Expectancy Theory: The Case of Major League Baseball Free Agents," *Journal of Applied Psychology,* 77, 1991, pp. 458–464; also R.G. Lord and J.A. Hohenfeld, "Longitudinal Field Assessment of Equity Effects on the Performance of Major League Baseball Players," *Journal of Applied Psychology,* 64, 1979, pp. 19–26; also D. Duchon and A.G. Jago, "Equity and the Performance of Major League Baseball Players: An Extension of Lord and Hohenfeld," *Journal of Applied Psychology,* 66, 1981, pp. 728–732. **Table 12-4** From Fred Luthans and Robert Kreitner, *Organizational Behavior Modification,* Scott, Foresman and Company, 1975. Reprinted with permission. **Management at Work** Interview with Carol Postnieks, Manager of Training and Development, Burroughs Memorex Inc. **Management at Work** Adapted from Bruce McDougall, "Perks With Pizzazz," *Canadian Business,* June 1990, pp. 78–79; also Don Champion, "Quality—A Way of Life at BC Tel," *Canadian Business Review,* Spring 1990, p. 33; also Margot Gibb-Clark, "Companies Find Merit in Using Pay as a Carrot," *The Globe and Mail,* May 9, 1990, p. B1; also Margot Gibb-Clark, "The Right Reward," *The Globe and Mail,* August 10, 1990, p. B5; also Peter Matthews, "Just Rewards—The Lure of Pay for Performance," *Canadian Business,* February 1990, pp. 78–79; also Bud Jorgensen, "Do Bonuses Unscrupulous Brokers Make?," *The Globe and Mail,* May 28, 1990, p. B5; also David Evans, "The Myth of Customer Service," *Canadian Business,* March 1991, pp. 34–39; also Ian Allaby, "Just Rewards," *Canadian Business,* May 1990, p. 39; also Wayne Gooding, "Ownership is the Best Motivator," *Canadian Business,* March 1990, p. 6; also Neal Templin, "Ford Giving Every Worker A Purpose," The Globe and Mail, December 28, 1992, p. B6. **Management at Work** Summarized from Peter Lawson, "Winning Strategies," *Canadian Business Review,* Summer 1989, p. 41; also Don Champion, "Quality—A Way of Life at BC Tel," *Canadian Business Review,* Spring 1990, p. 33; also, an interview with Carole Postnieks, Manager of Training and Development, Burroughs Memorex Inc. **Ethics in Management** Summarized from Robert Williamson, "Tradition Gives Way to World of Free-lancers," *The Globe and Mail,* January 15, 1993, pp. B1, B4; also Sally Ritchie, "Rent-A-Manager," *The Globe and Mail,* August 17, 1993, p. B22.

CHAPTER 13

Management Challenge Summarized from "Bullied into Believing," an excerpt of an interview with Robert Frey, author of *Empowerment or Else,* reprinted in *The Globe and Mail,* October 12, 1993, p. B16. **Management at Work** summarized from Randall Litchfield, "They Walk on Water," *Canadian Business,* September 1990, pp. 46–49. **Ethics in Management** Summarized from J.M. Howell and B.J. Avolio, "The Ethics of Charismatic Leadership: Submission or Liberation?," *Academy of Management Executive,* 6, 1992, pp. 43–54. **Management at Work** Summarized from Carol Hymowitz and Gabriella Stern, "P & G's Wrecking Ball Swinging Freely," *The Globe and Mail,* May 15, 1993, pp. B1, B4. **Management at Work** Summarized from John Southerst, "First, We Dump the Boss," *Canadian Business,* April 1992, pp. 46–51. **Global Management** R. Griffin, R. Ebert, and F. Starke, *Business.* Toronto: Prentice-Hall Canada, pp. 232–233. **Global Management** Summarized from D.H.B. Welsh, F. Luthans, and S.M. Sommer, "Managing Russian Factory Workers: The Impact of U.S.-Based Behavioral and Participative Techniques," *Academy of Management Journal,* 36, 1993, pp. 58–79. For a brief summary of this research project, see L. Mainiero, "Participation? Nyet: Rewards and Praise? Da!," *Academy of Management Executive,* 7, 1993, pp. 86–88. **Figure 13-1** R. Tannenbaum and W.H. Schmidt, "How to Choose a Leadership Pattern," *Harvard Business Review,* May/June 1973. Copyright 1973 by the President and Fellows of Harvard College. Reprinted with permission. **Figure 13-2** P. Hersey and K.H. Blanchard. The Situational Leadership Model (SLII) as illustrated in *The Color Model,* Blanchard Training and Development Inc. Reprinted with permission. **Table 13-4** Reprinted from V. Vroom and P.W. Yetton, *Leadership and Decision Making.* Pittsburgh: University of Pittsburgh Press, 1973, p. 13. Reprinted with permission of the University of Pittsburgh Press. **Figure 13-3** V. Vroom and P. Yetton, *Leadership and Decision Making.* Pittsburgh: University of Pittsburgh Press, 1973. Used with permission of the University of Pittsburgh Press.

CHAPTER 14

Management Challenge Summarized from Bruce Little, "A Factory Learns to Survive," *The Globe and Mail,* May 18, 1993, p. B22. **Management at Work** Summarized from Derek Coomber, "Fax-Finding Entrepreneurs," *Financial Times of Canada,* October 22, 1990, p. A6; also Howard Druckman, "Infotech: Helping Hands," *Canadian Business,* July 1989, pp. 57–59; also James Rusk, "Fax of the Matter," *The Globe and Mail,* June 20, 1990, p. B4; also Tony Leighton, Sure He's Good Looking, But Can He Act?," *Canadian Business,* May 1985, pp. 54–63. **Table 14-4** Summarized from E.G. Planty and W. Machaver, "Stimulating Upward Communication," *Effective Communication on the Job.* American Management Association, 1956. **Global Management** Summarized from J. Lieblich, "If You Want a Big New Market," *Fortune,* November 21, 1988, pp. 181–188; also Hugh A. Mulligan, "Ordinary Gestures Can Shock Foreign Visitors," *Baton Rouge Sunday Advocate,* August 5, 1990, p. 6E; also M.J. Trimby, "What Do You Really Mean?," *Management World,* 17, 1988, pp. 12–13; also F.A. Starke, R.M. Monday, A. Sharplin, and E.B. Flippo, *Management Concepts and Canadian Practice.* Toronto: Allyn and Bacon, 1988, p. 488; also R.E. Axtell (ed.)

and the Parker Pen Company (producer), *Do's and Taboos Around the World.* Elmsford, New York: The Benjamin Company, 1985; also D. Ricks and V. Mahajan, "Blunders in International Marketing: Fact or Fiction?," *Long Range Planning,* 17, 1984, pp. 78–82; also D. Ricks, *Big Business Blunders: Mistakes in Multinational Marketing.* Homewood, Illinois: Richard D. Irwin, 1983, pp. 74–95. **Management at Work** Summarized from R.H. Lengel and R.L. Daft, "The Selection of Communication Media As An Executive Skill," *Academy of Management Executive,* 2, 1988, pp. 225–232. **Table 14-7** Keith Davis, *Human Behavior at Work.* New York: McGraw-Hill, 1972, p. 396. Reprinted with permission. **Management at Work** Summarized from "Measure Your Fog Index," *Business Week,* July 6, 1981, p. 110.

CHAPTER 15

Management Challenge Summarized from Cathryn Motherwell, "Full-Service Furor," *The Globe and Mail,* June 22, 1991, p. B22. **Figure 15-1** S. Schmidt and T. Kochan, "Conflict: Toward Conceptual Clarity," *Administrative Science Quarterly,* 17, 1972, pp. 364–365. Copyright 1972 by Cornell University. Used by permission. **Management at Work** Summarized from "The CAMI Experience: Paradise Postponed," *Canadian Business,* January 1990, p. 65; also Jeb Blount, "Behind the Lines," *Canadian Business,* January 1990, p. 63. **Management at Work** Summarized from John Greenwood, "Masters of Compromise," *The Financial Post,* April 1992, pp. 35–38. **Figure 15–4** Based on K.W. Thomas, "Conflict and Conflict Management," in M.D. Dunnette (ed.), *Handbook of Industrial and Organizational Psychology.* Chicago: Rand McNally, 1976, p. 900. **Management at Work** Summarized from McBride-King and H. Paris, "Balancing Work and Family Responsibilities," *Canadian Business Review,* Autumn 1989, pp. 17–21. **Figure 15-5** H.J. Leavitt, "Applied Organizational Change in Industry: Structural, Technical and Human Appraoches," in W.W. Cooper, H.J. Leavitt, and M.W. Shelley (eds.), *New Perspectives in Organization Research.* New York: Wiley, 1964, pp. 55–74. **Global Management** Summarized from Laurie Hays, "Animal Farm 1992," *The Globe and Mail,* November 28, 1992, p. B4; also Michal Cakrt, "Management Education in Eastern Europe: Toward Mutual Understanding," *Academy of Management Executive,* 7, November 1993, pp. 63–68; also Nancy McNulty, "Management Education in Eastern Europe: 'Fore and After," *Academy of Management Executive,* November 1992, pp. 78–87; also Avraham Shama, "Management Under Fire: The Transformation of Managers in the Soviet Union and Eastern Europe," *Academy of Management Executive,* 7, February 1993, pp. 22–35. **Figure 15-7** Kurt Lewin, "Frontiers in Group Dynamics," *Human Relations,* 1, 1947, Plenum Publishing Corporation. Used with permission. **Table 15-5** Reprinted by permission of the *Harvard Business Review.* An exhibit from "Choosing Strategies for Change," by Kotter and Schlesinger, March/April 1979. Copyright 1979 by the President and Fellows of Harvard College. All rights reserved. **Management at Work** Summarized from "Case Studies: Canadian Organizations and Their Family-Related Programs," *Canadian Business Review,* Autumn 1989, pp. 22–25; also Robert White, "Changing Needs of Work and Family: A Union Response," *Canadian Business Review,* Autumn 1989, pp. 31–33.

CHAPTER 16

Management at Work Summarized from Rona Maynard, "The Next Labor Crisis," *Report on Business Magazine,* June 1990, pp. 41–48. **Management at Work** Summarized from Charles O'Reilly, "Corporations, Culture, and Commitment: Motivation and Social Control in Organizations," *California Management Review,* Summer 1989, pp. 9–25. **Table 16-1** Summarized from S. Robbins and R. Stuart-Kotze, *Management.* Toronto: Prentice-Hall Canada Inc., 1990, p. 85. **Figure 16-1** Based on ideas presented in T.E. Deal and A.A. Kennedy, *Corporate Cultures: The Rites and Rituals of Corporate Life.* Reading, Mass.: Addison-Wesley, 1982, pp. 107–108. **Table 16-2** Summarized from T.J. Peters and R.H. Waterman, *In Search of Excellence.* New York: Harper and Row, 1982. **Management at Work** Summarized from Arthur Johnson, "Mind Cults Invade the Boardroom," *Canadian Business,* January 1992, pp. 38–42. **Management at Work** Summarized in part from R. Blake et al., "Breakthrough in Organization Development," *Harvard Business Review,* 42, 1964, pp. 131–155.

COMPREHENSIVE CASES PART IV

Case IV-1 was prepared by Peter McGrady, Administrative and Policy Studies, Trent University, Peterborough, Ontario. **Case IV-2** was prepared by Professor Rick Roskin of Memorial University of Newfoundland. **Case IV-3** was written by Mary Byrne under the direction of G. Deszca and T. Cawsey. Copyright © 1991 by Wilfrid Laurier University. No part of this publication may be reproduced, stored in a retrieval system, or transmitted in any form or by any means—electronic, mechanical, photocopying, recording, or otherwise—without the permission of the School of Business and Economics, Wilfrid Laurier University. Distributed through the LAURIER INSTITUTE, School of Business and Economics, Wilfrid Laurier University, Waterloo, Ontario, Canada N2L 3C5.

CHAPTER 17

Management Challenge Summarized from John Lorinc, "Power Failure," *Canadian Business,* November 1992, pp. 50–58. **Management at Work** Summarized from Eva Kiess-Moser, "Customer Satisfaction," *Canadian Business*

Review, Summer 1989, pp. 44–45; also Isadore Sharp, "Quality for All Seasons," *Canadian Business Review,* Spring 1990, pp. 21–23. **Global Management** Summarized from "How Big Blue Lost Control," *The Globe and Mail,* January 23, 1993, p. B4. **Figure 17-2** R. Wayne Mondy and M. Noe, III. *Personnel: The Management of Human Resources.* Boston: Allyn and Bacon, 1981, p. 493. **Management at Work** Summarized from Paul King, "Building a Team the Sharp Way," *Canadian Business,* November 1990, pp. 96–102. **Management at Work** Summarized from Sally Ritchie, "Life in the Fast Lane," *The Globe and Mail,* June 8, 1993, p. B24. **Ethics in Management** Summarized from J. Southerst, "In Pursuit of Drugs," *Canadian Transportation,* November 1989, pp. 58–65; also "Preventing Crime on the Job," *Nation's Business,* July 1990, pp. 36–37; also N. Snyder and K. Blair, "Dealing with Employee Theft," *Business Horizons,* May–June 1989, pp. 27–34; also G. Bylinsky, "How Companies Spy on Employees," *Fortune,* November 4, 1991, pp. 131–140. **Case 17-2** written by Dr. John Mundie, Professor of Business Policy, University of Manitoba. Used with permission.

CHAPTER 18

Management Challenge Summarized from Jacquie McNish and Margaret Philp, "O & Y Backs Away from Commercial Paper," *The Globe and Mail,* March 6, 1992, pp. B1, B7; also Brian Milner, Margaret Philp, Alan Freedman, Drew Fagan, and John Saunders, "Reichmann's Call in Cavalry: U.S. Banker to Head O & Y," *The Globe and Mail,* March 25, 1992, pp. B1, B4; also Brian Milner and Margaret Philp, "Reichmann Shuffle Gives Camdev Stake to Albert," *The Globe and Mail,* March 28, 1992, pp. B1, B8; also J. McNish, M. Philp, and B. Milner, "O & Y's Hard Times Stem from Shift to Short-Term Debt," *The Globe and Mail,* April 4, 1992, pp. B1, B8; also M. Drohan, "O & Y Has No Plans for Bankruptcy Filing," *The Globe and Mail,* April 23, 1992, pp. B1, B6; also M. Drohan and J. McNish, "O & Y Reported on Verge of Bankruptcy Protection," *The Globe and Mail,* May 15, 1992, pp. B1, B5; also B. Milner and M. Philp, "O & Y Puts On Brave Face to Mask Predicament," *The Globe and Mail,* May 16, 1992, pp. B1, B4; also J. McNish, "The Lessons of Olympia & York," *The Globe and Mail,* March 23, 1992, pp. B1, B3. **Management at Work** Summarized from Ted Wakefield, "No Pain, No Gain," *Canadian Business,* January 1993, pp. 50–54. **Global Management** Summarized from D. Lavin and A. Choi, "North America Unveils Latest Trade Weapon: Quality Exports," *The Globe and Mail,* October 19, 1993, p. B9. **Ethics in Management** Summarized from Christopher Bart, "Budgeting Gamesmanship," *Academy of Management Executive,* 2, 1988, pp. 285–294. **Management at Work** Summarized from Bruce Little, "A Foundry Finds Its Way," *The Globe and Mail,* October 5, 1993, p. B28. **Management at Work** Summarized from Alexander Ross, "A Litmus Test for Corporate Lemons," *Canadian Business,* February 1993, pp. 54–58.

CHAPTER 19

Management Challenge Summarized from R. Turner and J.R. Emshwiller, "FlimFlam? Movie Research Czar Is Said By Some to Sell Manipulated Findings," *The Wall Street Journal,* December 17, 1993, pp. A1, A7. **Management at Work** Summarized from John Heinzl, "Supply and Command," *The Globe and Mail,* December 15, 1992, p. B20. **Management at Work** Summarized from Joseph Pereira, "Tough Game: Toy Industry Finds It's Harder and Harder to Pick the Winners," *The Wall Street Journal,* December 21, 1993, pp. A1, A5. **Table 19-1** G.A. Gorry and M.S. Morton, "A Framework for Management Information Systems," *Sloan Management Review,* Fall 1971, p. 59. Copyright 1992 by the Sloan Management Review Association. All rights reserved. **Table 19-2** Summarized from R. Ackhoff, "Management Misinformation Systems," *Management Science,* December 1967, pp. 147–156. **Figure 19-6** L.J. Gitman and C. McDaniel Jr., *Business World.* New York: Wiley, 1983, p. 182. Reprinted with permission. **Management at Work** Summarized from Frances Misutka, "The Workplace Takes Wing," *Canadian Business,* May 1992, pp. 73–77. **Global Management** Summarized from J. Rothfeder, J. Bartimo, L. Therrien, and R. Brandt, "Software is Making Sales a Piece of Cake," *Business Week,* July 2, 1990, pp. 54–55. **Global Management** Summarized from Emily Smith, "Turning an Expert's Skills into Computer Software," *Business Week,* October 7, 1985, pp. 104–107. **Case 19-1** Summarized from Bruce Little, "Savings by the Truckload," *The Globe and Mail,* August 3, 1993, p. B18.

COMPREHENSIVE CASES PART V

Case V-1 Neil Abramson prepared this case during the 1989 Case Writing Workshop with funding by the Purchasing Management Association of Canada. Copyright © 1989. The Purchasing Management Association of Canada. School of Business Administration, The University of Western Ontario. **Case V-2** written by Prof. Neil Hill. Copyright © 1989 by the Laurier Institute. No part of this publication may be reproduced, stored in a retrieval system, or transmitted in any form or by any means—electronic, mechanical, photocopying, recording, or otherwise—without the permission of the The Laurier Institute for Business and Economic Studies, Wilfrid Laurier University, Waterloo, Ontario, Canada N2L 3C5.

CHAPTER 20

Management Challenge/Meeting the Challenge Hugh McBride, "How to Lose Freedom and Gain the World," *The Globe and Mail,* January 25, 1994, p. B22. **Management at Work** Sajjad Ebrahim, Canada Awards for Business Excellence, *Profiles of Excellence 1993,* National Quality Institute, Ottawa, 1993, p. 9. **Figure 20-1** From: Allan J.

Magrath, "The Thorny Management Issues in Family-Owned Business," *Business Quarterly*, Spring 1988, p. 73. Reprinted with permission of *Business Quarterly*, published by the Western Business School, The University of Western Ontario, London, Ontario, Canada. **Management at Work** Barrie McKenna, "Family Era Ends for Birks," *The Globe and Mail*, April 22, 1993; also Bertrand Marotte, "The Bustup at Birks & Sons," *Financial Times of Canada*, January 22, 1990, pp. 8, 9, Rod McQueen, "Brawl in the Family," *Canadian Business*, March 1984, pp. 62–68. **Management at Work** Kara Kuryllowicz, "Designer at Home in Her Office," *The Financial Post*, October 7, 1993, p. 25; also "The Home Office," *The Financial Post*, October 7, 1993, pp. 17–26; Al Emid, "Trend to Micro-Enterprises Helps Neophytes," *The Globe and Mail*, March 13, 1990, p. C5; Laura Fowlie, "How to Feel at Home in Your Home Office," *The Financial Post*, June 25, 1990, p. 34; also Douglas and Diana Lynn Gray, *Home Inc.: The Canadian Home-Based Business Guide*, Toronto: McGraw-Hill Ryerson, 1990. **Global Management** Canada Awards for Business Excellence, *Profiles of Excellence 1993,* National Quality Institute, Ottawa, 1993, p. 20. **Table 20-3** Adapted from Mel Scott and Richard Bruce, "Five Stages of Growth in Small Business," *Long Range Planning*, 20, 1987, p. 48. **Management at Work** Carolyn Leitch, "Impatient Owner Gets Hard-nosed Manager," *The Globe and Mail*, January 31, 1994, p. B6. **Case 20-1** Drew Fagan, "Software Pioneer Falls Off the Map," *The Globe and Mail*, Novemger 2, 1993, p. B26.

CHAPTER 21

Management Challenge/Meeting the Challenge Shawn McCarthy, "Why One Family-owned Toolmaker is Singing the Praises of Free Trade Deal," *The Toronto Star,* Janaury 1, 1994, p. D4. **Global Management** Robert Williamson, "Canadians Key Players in Indonesian Pulp Mill," *The Globe and Mail,* October 26, 1993, p. B19. **Global Management** "In Hot Pursuit of International Markets," *Innovation,* Summer 1990, pp. 11–13. **Figure 21-1** "Strategic Alliances," *Investing in Canada,* 3, No. 4 Spring 1990, p. 1. (Northern Telecom, A. Ahmad). **Global Management** Gerry Blackwell, "Battle Royal," *enRoute,* February 1994, pp. 17–19. **Table 21-3** "Access," Supplement to CANADEXPORT Foreign Affairs and International Trade Canada, Ottawa, January 1994, p. 1. Articles may be reprinted with credit to CANADEXPORT. **Global Management** "Access," Supplement to CANADEXPORT, External Affairs and International Trade Canada, Ottawa, November 1993, p. III. Articles may be reprinted with credit to CANADEXPORT. **Global Management** Marina Strauss, "Imasco Sells Stores," *The Globe and Mail,* June 26, 1990, pp. B1–2; also Karen Howlett, "Once Bitten in U.S. Market, Canadian Tire Not Shy About Re-Entering," *The Globe and Mail,* May 6, 1988, p. B3; also Kenneth Kidd, "Success Breeds Prudence as Canadian Tire Peers Over 49th Parallel, *The Globe and Mail,* January 31, 1990, p. 36; also Frances Phillips, "Canadian Tire Finds Texas Trail a Bit Bumpy," *The Financial Post,* March 26, 1983, p. 18; also Jean Matthews and Greg Boyd, "Can Lionel Robbins Rescue Dylex?" *Canadian Business,* November 1990, pp. 106–114; also Beppi Crosariol, "What Makes the U.S. So Tough," *Financial Times of Canada,* October 8, 1990, p. 14; and *The Financial Post* Information Service, History Sections on Canadian Tire Corporation Limited and Dylex Limited. **Figure 21-3** Christopher M. Korth, *International Business: Environment and Management,* 2nd ed., p. 7. Copyright 1985. Reprinted by permission of Prentice Hall, Inc., Englewood Cliffs, New Jersey. **Table 21-4** "A Topsy-Turvy Year for Giants," *Business Week,* July 12, 1993, pp. 52–108. **Global Management** *Annual Report,* Bombardier Inc., year ended January 31, 1993. pp. 2–3. **Table 21-5** *The OECD Guidelines for Multinational Enterprises.* Paris: Organization for Economic Co-operation and Development. 1986; and *The United Nations Code of Conduct in Transnational Corporations.* New York: United Nations. 1986. **Table 21-6** Kimon Valaskakis, "A prescription for Canada Inc.," *The Globe and Mail,* October 31, 1992, p. B4. **Global Management** Jane Finlayson, "Exotic Assignments," *Imperial Oil Review,* Summer, 1990, 74, No. 397, p. 30.

CHAPTER 22

Management at Work Margot Franssen, "Beyond Profits," *Business Quarterly*, Autumn 1993, pp. 15–20; Raymond Cote et al., eds., *Business Meets the Environmental Challenge: Essays with Profiles of N.S. Companies.* Hantsport, N.S.: Lancelot Press, 1993, pp. 177. A book is available on The Body Shop: Anita Roddick, *Body and Soul*, London: Ebury Press, 1992. **Management at Work** *Annual report 1992*, Québec Téléphone, pp. 10–11. **Table 22-1** Leonard J. Brooks, Jr., *Canadian Corporate Social Performance*, Hamilton: The Society of Management Accountants of Canada, 1986, Chapter 6. **Ethics in Management** Nova Corporation of Alberta, *Annual Report*, 1989, p. 17. **Ethics in Management** Kenneth Bagnell, "Ethics at the Centre," *The Review* (published by Imperial Oil Limited), Summer 1988, pp. 21–25. **Ethics in Management** Royal LePage Limited, *Annual Report*, 1990, p. 1. **Figure 22-2** Corporate donation figures are supplied by Revenue Canada/Statistics Canada. Copyright The Canadian Centre for Philanthropy. Used with permission. **Management at Work** Christian Allard, "Coming Up Fast: 1990's Successors," *Canadian Business*, September 1990, pp. 55–56. Reprinted by permission of *Canadian Business Magazine*. **Management at Work** Brochure No. 841–90, Petro-Canada. Used with permission. **Figure 22-3** Adapted from a student assignment by Gary G. Bradshaw, Winter 1989, Memorial University of Newfoundland. **Ethics in Management** Simplified Prospectus Offering Units of Ethical Growth Fund dated April 20, 1990, VanCity Investment Services Ltd. **Case 22-1** Truls Ostbye et al., "Food and Nutrition in Canadian 'Prime Time' Television," *Canadian Journal of Public Health*, November–December 1993, pp. 370–374; also Rod Mickleburgh, "TV Food Makes Poor Eating," *The Globe and Mail*, January 1, 1994, pp. A1, A3.

Comprehensive Cases Part VI

Case VI-1 was written by Reg Litz for the University of Manitoba's Bachelor of Commerce Program. The financial assistance provided by the Department of Business Administration and the Center for International Business Studies, both at the Faculty of Management of the University of Manitoba in Winnipeg, is gratefully acknowledged. Copyright © 1990 Reg Litz. **Case VI-2** was written by R. William Blake, Faculty of Business Administration, Memorial University. © 1990 by R. William Blake. **Case VI-3** was written by Gary Black under the direction of Professor Robert W. Sexty. Copyright © 1991. Faculty of Business Administration, Memorial University of Newfoundland. **References:** Cootes, J.F., "Ottawa releases draft reforms on pollution control," *Pulp and Paper Journal*, May 1990, p. 11; DeKing, N., "Taking the high ground on the environment." *Pulp and Paper*, April 1990, p. 7; Klien, R.E., "Simpson Tacoma Kraft Co. mill starts up new bleach plant," *Pulp and Paper*, October 1990, pp. 889–92; McGrath, R. "Discoveries about dioxin formation have changed some mill operations." *Pulp and Paper*, April 1990, pp. 133–136.

NAME AND COMPANY INDEX

SUBJECT INDEX

J

K

L

M

N

O

P

Q

R

S

PHOTO CREDITS

Dave Starrett, p. 3; Izaak Walton Killam Children's Hospital, p 6; Canada Safeway Limited, p. 14; Katherine Lash, p. 31; Marko Shark, p. 42; Katherine Lash, p. 49; Hibernia Management and Development Company Ltd., p. 51; Alcan Aluminum Limited, p. 55; Wascana Energy Inc., p. 69; Terminal 3, p. 89; Wascana Energy Inc., p. 91; Alberta Research Council, p. 99; Imperial Oil, p. 104; Schneider, p. 116; Athletic Information Bureau, p. 119; TransCanada Pipelines, p. 123; IBM Canada, p. 123; Fairweather, Division of Dylex Limited, p. 123; Leons Furniture Limited, Toronto, p. 123; The Jim Pattison Group, p. 123; CANCOM, p. 123; Alcan Aluminum Limited, p. 139; CanadaWide, p. 152; Wascana Energy Inc., p. 154; Sobey's Store, p. 155; Prentice Hall Canada, p. 169; Prentice Hall Canada, p. 199; Molson Indy Library, p. 203; Dave Starrett, p. 210; Imasco Limited, p. 219; Petro Canada, p. 230; TransCanada Pipelines Limited/Communications Dept., p. 243; Banff Springs Hotel, p. 250; Dofasco, Inc., p. 251; Marko Shark, p. 262; Dave Starrett, p. 268; CanadaWide, p. 272; PH Archives (Sharon Houston), p. 278; MTCVA, p. 288; Geoff Tupling, p. 301; DGPA, p. 313; PH Archives (Jeremy Jones), p. 318; Dave Starrett, p. 333; Dave Starrett, p. 334; Dave Starrett, p. 357; Stephen Mooney/Camdec Real Estate, p. 361; Prentice Hall Canada Inc., p. 375; Athlete Information Bureau, photo: Eileen Langsley, p. 373; Alberta Research Council, p. 378; Katherine Lash, p. 395; Public Archives of Canada/PA111214, p. 398; DGPA, p. 405; Canadian Ski Instructor's Alliance, p. 419; Katherine Lash, p. 429; Angelika Baur, p. 431; City of Toronto Fire Department Information Section, p. 432; Photo courtesy of Telecom Canada, p. 436; Photo courtesy of Telecom Canada, p. 444; Marko Shark, p. 450; Petro Canada, p. 460; Citizens Concerned About Free Trade, photo: Keith Starks, p. 464; John McNeill, p. 486; John McNeill, p. 488; Marko Shark, p. 495; Hewlett-Packard Canada Ltd., p. 497; Ken Stewart, p. 499; Mary Kay Cosmetics, Limited, p. 500; Darlington Nuclear Plant, p. 533; CIBA-GEIGY Canada Ltd., p. 535; Japanese Consulate, p. 539; Alberta Research Council, p. 545; Sygma Photo News, p. 557; Dofasco Inc., p. 561; Alberta Research Council 563; Mediacom, p. 570; CanadaWide, p. 589; MTCVA, p. 615; Manca Food Services, p. 618; Midas Canada, Inc., p. 624; Kim Kirk, p. 632; Roy Taylor, p. 640; Ports Canada, p. 643; Labatt, p. 644; TVX Mining Corporation, p. 654; Bata Limited, p. 660; Dick Hemingway, p. 671; Seagrams of Canada, p. 674; TVX Mining Corporation, p. 679; 3M Canada Inc., p. 687; Canadian Centre for Philanthropy, p. 689; DOMTAR Inc., p. 691; The Body Shop, p. 698.